The Gallup Poll

Public Opinion 2008

Other Gallup Publications Available from SR Books:

The Gallup Poll Cumulative Index: Public Opinion, 1935–1997
ISBN 0-8420-2587-1 (1999)

The Gallup Poll: Public Opinion Annual Series

2007 (ISBN 0-7425-6239-5)   *1991* (ISBN 0-8420-2397-6)
2006 (ISBN 0-7425-5876-2)   *1990* (ISBN 0-8420-2368-2)
2005 (ISBN 0-7425-5258-6)   *1989* (ISBN 0-8420-2344-5)
2004 (ISBN 0-7425-5138-5)   *1988* (ISBN 0-8420-2330-5)
2003 (ISBN 0-8420-5003-5)   *1987* (ISBN 0-8420-2292-9)
2002 (ISBN 0-8420-5002-7)   *1986* (ISBN 0-8420-2275-0)
2001 (ISBN 0-8420-5001-9)   *1985* (ISBN 0-8420-2249-X)
2000 (ISBN 0-8420-5000-0)   *1984* (ISBN 0-8420-2234-1)
1999 (ISBN 0-8420-2699-1)   *1983* (ISBN 0-8420-2220-1)
1998 (ISBN 0-8420-2698-3)   *1982* (ISBN 0-8420-2214-7)
1997 (ISBN 0-8420-2697-9)   *1981* (ISBN 0-8420-2200-7)
1996 (ISBN 0-8420-2696-0)   *1980* (ISBN 0-8420-2181-7)
1995 (ISBN 0-8420-2695-2)   *1979* (ISBN 0-8420-2170-1)
1994 (ISBN 0-8420-2560-X)   *1978* (ISBN 0-8420-2159-0)
1993 (ISBN 0-8420-2483-2)   *1972–77* (ISBN 0-8420-2129-9, 2 vols.)
1992 (ISBN 0-8420-2463-8)   *1935–71* (ISBN 0-394-47270-5, 3 vols.)

International Polls

The International Gallup Polls: Public Opinion, 1979
ISBN 0-8420-2180-9 (1981)

The International Gallup Polls: Public Opinion, 1978
ISBN 0-8420-2162-0-9 (1980)

The Gallup International Opinion Polls: France, 1939, 1944–1975
2 volumes ISBN 0-394-40998-1 (1976)

The Gallup International Opinion Polls: Great Britain, 1937–1975
2 volumes ISBN 0-394-40992-2 (1976)

The Gallup Poll

Public Opinion 2008

EDITED BY
ALEC M. GALLUP AND FRANK NEWPORT

ROWMAN & LITTLEFIELD PUBLISHERS, INC.
Lanham • Boulder • New York • Toronto • Oxford

ACKNOWLEDGEMENTS

The Gallup Poll is a result of the efforts of a number of talented and dedicated individuals. We wish to express our gratitude to James Clifton, Chairman and CEO of Gallup; the Poll staff, including Jeffrey Jones, Managing Editor; Lydia Saad, Senior Editor; Lymari Morales, News Director for Gallup.com; and Maura Strausberg, Data Librarian. Judith Keneman, Executive Assistant to the Editor in Chief, managed the assembly of materials and the publication process. Special appreciation for this volume goes to Tracey Sugar for her invaluable assistance in creating the chronology and editing the text and graphics. Professor Fred Israel, City University of New York, and George Gallup, Jr., deserve special credit for their contributions to the first twenty-six volumes in this series.

ROWMAN & LITTLEFIELD PUBLISHERS, INC.

Published in the United States of America
by Rowman & Littlefield Publishers, Inc.
A wholly owned subsidiary of The Rowman & Littlefield Publishing Group, Inc.
4501 Forbes Boulevard, Suite 200, Lanham, Maryland 20706
www.rowmanlittlefield.com

PO Box 317
Oxford
OX2 9RU, UK

ISSN 0195-962X

Cloth ISBN-13: 978-1-4422-0105-7
eISBN: 978-1-4422-0107-1

Printed in the United States of America

♾™ The paper used in this publication meets the minimum requirements of American National Standard for Information Sciences—Permanence of Paper for Printed Library Materials, ANSI/NISO Z39.48-1992.

For Alec Gallup

Alec Gallup, the co-editor of the *Gallup Poll* series, passed away on June 22, 2009, just as this volume was going to press. Alec worked with the Gallup Poll for over 50 years, first with his father, Dr. George Gallup, who founded the Poll, and then with new associates after Dr. Gallup's death in 1984. Alec was one of the world's most knowledgeable pollsters and had a lifelong commitment to the value of measuring public opinion scientifically and releasing the results publicly for all to use. He will be truly missed.

It is my privilege to dedicate *The Gallup Poll Public Opinion 2008* to Alec Gallup.

Jim Clifton
Chairman and CEO
Gallup, Inc.

CONTENTS

INTRODUCTION

The Gallup Poll: Public Opinion 2008 contains the findings of the more than 1,000 daily Gallup Poll reports released to the American public during the year 2008. The latest volume reveals the attitudes and opinions of individuals and key groups within the American population concerning national and international issues and events of the year.

The 2008 volume is the most recent addition to the 35-volume Gallup collection, *Public Opinion, 1935-2008*, the largest compilation of public opinion findings ever published and one of the largest reference works produced on any subject. The Gallup collection documents the attitudes and opinions of Americans (and where appropriate, citizens of other countries) on national and international issues and events from Franklin D. Roosevelt's second term to the present. In 2007 a new index volume was published, so that with the previous index volumes, readers can search for topics all the way back to 1935.

Shown in detail are results of the more than 65,000 questions that the Gallup Poll—the world's oldest and most respected public opinion poll—has asked of the public over the last seven decades. Results of the survey questions appear in the nearly 12,000 Gallup Poll reports, reproduced in the 35 volumes. These reports, the first of which was released on October 20, 1935, have been provided on a continuous basis since that time, most recently as daily updates on Gallup's website, gallup.com.

The 35-volume collection documents public opinion from 1935 to the present in the following five separate and distinct areas:

1. *Recording the Public's Response to Major News Events.* Gallup has recorded the public's attitudes and opinions in response to every major news event of the last seven decades. Examples include Adolf Hitler's invasion of the Soviet Union, the bombing of Pearl Harbor, the dropping of the atomic bomb on Hiroshima, the assassination of President John F. Kennedy, the moon landing, the taking of U.S. hostages in Iran, the O.J. Simpson trial verdict, the impeachment of President Bill Clinton, the 9/11/01 terrorist attacks, the Iraq War, Hurricane Katrina and its aftermath.

2. *Measuring the Strength of Support for the President, Political Candidates, and Political Parties.* For over seventy years, Gallup has measured, on a continuous basis, the strength of support for the president, for the congressional opposition, and for various political candidates and parties in national elections. This is the role most closely associated with Gallup in the public's mind.

3. *Monitoring the Economy.* An important Gallup Poll objective has been monitoring the U.S. economy in all of its permutations from the prospective of the American consumer. Gallup now assesses American's views on economic conditions, the job market, and personal financial concerns on a daily basis—providing a continuous record of this vital component of the U.S. economy.

4. *Revealing American Lifestyle Trends.* Another ongoing Gallup polling activity has been to document American lifestyles, including periodic measurements of participation in a wide range of leisure activities and other pursuits. Additional examples include frequent series describing the public's tastes and favorites in various areas, and their knowledge level as revealed by national "quizzes" in geography, history, science, politics and the like.

5. *Gauging and Charting the Public's Mood.* From its earliest days the Gallup Poll has sought to determine, on an ongoing basis, Americans' satisfaction or dissatisfaction with the direction in which the nation appeared to be headed and with the way they thought that their personal lives were progressing. This process also has involved regular assessments of the people's mood regarding the state of the nation's economy as well as the status of

their personal finances, their jobs, and other aspects of their lives.

Two of the most frequently asked questions concerning the Gallup Poll are: Who pays for or provides financial support to the Poll? And who determines which topics are covered by the Poll or, more specifically, who decides which questions are asked on Gallup surveys? Since its founding in 1935 the Gallup Poll has been underwritten by Gallup itself, in the public interest, and by the nation's media. In recent years, funding has come from the national daily newspaper *USA Today.* The Gallup Poll also receives financial support from subscriptions to the Gallup Brain, sales of the monthly magazine, and this annual volume.

Suggestions for poll questions come from a wide variety of sources, including *USA Today,* other print and broadcast media, and from institutions as well as from individuals, including members of Congress and other public officials, university professors, and foundation executives. In addition, the public themselves are regularly questioned about the problems and issues facing the nation as they perceive them. Their answers establish priorities and provide an up-to-the-minute list of topic areas to explore through the Poll.

The Gallup Poll, as it is known today, began life on October 20, 1935, as a nationally syndicated newspaper feature titled "America Speaks—The National Weekly Column of Public Opinion." For brevity's sake, the media quickly came to refer to the column as The Gallup Poll, after its founder and editor-in-chief, Dr. George H. Gallup. Although Dr. Gallup had experimented during the 1934 congressional and 1932 presidential election campaigns to develop more accurate techniques for measuring public opinion, including scientific sampling, the first Gallup survey results to appear in print were those reported in the initial October 20, 1935, column.

Although the new scientific opinion polls enjoyed almost immediate popular success, their initial efforts were met with skepticism from many quarters. Critics questioned, for example, how it was possible to determine the opinions of the entire American populace based on only 1,000 interviews or less, or how one know whether people were telling the truth. The credibility of the polls as well as their commercial viability was enhanced significantly, however, when Gallup correctly predicted that Roosevelt would win the 1936 presidential election in a landslide, directly contradicting the forecast of the Literary Digest Poll, the poll of record at that time. The Digest Poll, which was not based on scientific sampling procedures, claimed that FDR's Republican challenger, Alfred M. Landon, would easily win the election.

Over the subsequent seven decades scientifically based opinion polls have gained a level of acceptance to where they are used today to investigate virtually every aspect of human experience in most nations of the world. To a large extent, this acceptance is due to the record of accuracy achieved by the polls in pre-election surveys. For example, in the eighteen presidential elections since 1936, the average deviation between Gallup's final pre-election survey figures and the actual election results is 2.0 percentage points and, since 1960, only 1.5 points. Correspondingly, in the thirteen midterm congressional elections measured since 1950, the deviation between Gallup's final election survey figures and the actual election results is 1.4 percentage points. These tests of candidate strength or "trial heats," which were introduced by Gallup in the 1930s (along with the presidential "approval" ratings), demonstrate that scientific survey techniques can accurately quantify public sentiment.

Alec M. Gallup and Frank Newport

THE SAMPLE

Most Gallup Poll findings are based on telephone surveys. The majority of the findings reported in Gallup Poll surveys are based on samples consisting of a minimum of 1,000 interviews.

Design of the Sample for Telephone Surveys

The findings from the telephone surveys are based on Gallup's standard national telephone samples, consisting of directory-assisted random-digit telephone samples utilizing a proportionate, stratified sampling design. The random-digit aspect of the sample is used to avoid "listing" bias. Numerous studies have shown that households with unlisted telephone numbers are different from listed households. "Unlistedness" is due to household mobility or to customer requests to prevent publication of the telephone number. To avoid this source of bias, a random-digit procedure designed to provide representation of both listed and unlisted (including not-yet-listed) numbers is used.

Beginning in 2008, Gallup began including cell phone telephone numbers in its national samples to account for the growing proportion of Americans who are "cell-phone only."

Telephone numbers for the continental United States are stratified into four regions of the country. The sample of telephone numbers produced by the described method is representative of all telephone households within the continental United States.

Only working banks of telephone numbers are selected. Eliminating nonworking banks from the sample increases the likelihood that any sampled telephone number will be associated with a residence.

Within each contacted household, an interview is sought with the adult 18 years of age or older living in the household who has had the most recent birthday (this is a method commonly employed to make a random selection within households without having to ask the respondent to provide a complete roster of adults living in the household). In the event that the sample becomes disproportionately female (due to higher co-operation rates typically observed for female respondents), the household selection criteria are adjusted to select only the male in the household who has had the most recent birthday (except in households where the adults are exclusively female). Calls made on cell phones do not use the same respondent selection procedure since cell phones are typically associated with a single individual than shared among several members of a household.

A minimum of three calls (and up to six calls) is attempted to each selected telephone number to complete an interview. Time of day and the day of the week for callbacks are varied to maximize the chances of finding a respondent at home. All interviews are conducted on weekends or weekday evenings in order to contact potential respondents among the working population.

The final sample is weighted so that the distribution of the sample matches current estimates derived from the U.S. Census Bureau's Current Population Survey (CPS) for the adult population living in households with a landline or cellular telephone in the continental United States.

Weighting Procedures

After the survey data have been collected and processed, each respondent is assigned a weight so that the demographic characteristics of the total weighted sample of respondents match the latest estimates of the demographic characteristics of the adult population available from the U.S. Census Bureau. Gallup weights data to census estimates for gender, race, age, educational attainment, and region. Telephone surveys are weighted to match the characteristics of the adult population living in households with access to a telephone.

The procedures described above are designed to produce samples approximating the adult civilian population (18 and older) living in private households.

Survey percentages may be applied to census estimates of the size of these populations to project percentages into numbers of people. The manner in which the sample is drawn also produces a sample that approximates the distribution of private households in the United States. Therefore, survey results also can be projected to numbers of households.

Sampling Tolerances

In interpreting survey results, it should be borne in mind that all sample surveys are subject to sampling error—that is, the extent to which the results may differ from what would be obtained if the whole population surveyed had been interviewed. The size of such sampling errors depends largely on the number of interviews.

The following tables may be used in estimating the sampling error of any percentage. The computed allowances have taken into account the effect of the sample design upon sampling error. They may be interpreted as indicating the range (plus or minus the figure shown) within which the results of repeated samplings in the same time period could be expected to vary, 95 percent of the time, assuming the same sampling procedure, the same interviewers, and the same questionnaire.

Table A shows how much allowance should be made for the sampling error of a percentage. Let us say a reported percentage is 33 for a group that includes 1,000 respondents. First, we go to the row headed "Percentages near 30" and then go across to the column headed "1,000." The number here is 3, which means that the 33 percent obtained in the sample is subject to a sampling error of plus or minus 3 points. Another way of saying it is that very probably (95 chances out of 100) the average of repeated samplings would be somewhere between 29 and 37, with the most likely figure being the 33 obtained.

In comparing survey results in two samples, such as for men and women, the question arises as to how large must a difference between them be before one can be reasonably sure that it reflects a real difference. In Tables B and C, the number of points that must be allowed for in such comparisons is indicated. Table B is for percentages near 20 or 80, and Table C is for percentages near 50. For percentages in between, the error to be allowed for is between those shown in the two tables.

Here is an example of how the tables would be used: Let us say that 50 percent of men respond a certain way and 40 percent of women also respond that way, for a difference of 10 percentage points between them. Can we say with any assurance that the 10-point difference reflects a real difference between men and women on the question? The sample contains approximately 500 men and 500 women.

Since the percentages are near 50, we consult Table C, and since the two samples are about 600 persons each, we look for the number in the column headed "500" that is also in the row designated "500". We find the number 7 here. This means that the allowance for error should be 7 points, and that in concluding that the percentage among men is somewhere between 3 and 17 points higher than the percentage among women, we should be wrong only about 5 percent of the time. In other words, we can conclude with considerable confidence that a difference exists in the direction observed and that it amounts to at least 3 percentage points.

If, in another case, men's responses amount to 22 percent and women's 24 percent, we consult Table B because these percentages are near 20. We look for the number in the column headed "500" that is also in the row designated "500" and see that the number is 5. Obviously, then, the 2-point difference is inconclusive.

TABLE A
Recommended Allowance for Sampling Error of a Percentage

In Percentage Points
(at 95 in 100 confidence level)*
Sample Size

	1,000	750	500	250	100
Percentages near 10	2	2	3	4	6
Percentages near 20	3	3	4	5	9
Percentages near 30	3	4	4	6	10
Percentages near 40	3	4	5	7	10
Percentages near 50	3	4	5	7	11
Percentages near 60	3	4	5	7	10
Percentages near 70	3	4	4	6	10
Percentages near 80	3	3	4	5	9
Percentages near 90	2	2	3	4	6

*The chances are 95 in 100 that the sampling error is not larger than the figures shown.

TABLE B
Recommended Allowance for Sampling Error of the Difference

In Percentage Points
(at 95 in 100 confidence level)*
Percentages near 20 or Percentages near 80

	750	500	250
Size of sample			
750	4		
500	5	5	
250	6	7	8

*The chances are 95 in 100 that the sampling error is not larger than the figures shown.

TABLE C
Recommended Allowance for Sampling Error of the Difference

In Percentage Points
(at 95 in 100 confidence level)*
Percentages near 50

	750	500	250
Size of sample			
750	6		
500	6	7	
250	8	8	10

*The chances are 95 in 100 that the sampling error is not larger than the figures shown.

Gallup Poll Accuracy Record
Presidential Elections

	Candidates	*Final Gallup Survey*	*Election Result*	*Gallup Deviation*
2008	Obama	55	53	2
	McCain	44	46	-2
	Other	1	1	0
2004	Bush	49	51	-2
	Kerry	49	48	1
	Other	2	1	1
2000	Gore	46	48.4	-2.4
	Bush	48	47.9	0.1
	Nader	4	2.7	1.3
	Buchanan	1	0.4	0.6
	Other	1	0.6	0.4
1996	Clinton	52	49.2	2.8
	Dole	41	40.9	0.1
	Perot	7	8.5	-1.5
1992	Clinton	49	43	6
	Bush	37	37.5	-0.5
	Perot	14	18.9	-4.9
1988	Bush	56	53.4	2.6
	Dukakis	44	45.7	-1.7
1984	Reagan	59	58.8	0.2
	Mondale	41	40.6	0.4
1980	Reagan	47	50.8	-3.8
	Carter	44	41	3
	Anderson	8	6.6	1.4
	Other	1	1.6	-0.6
1976	Carter	48	50.1	-2.1
	Ford	49	48	1
	McCarthy	2	0.9	1.1
	Other	1	0.9	0.1
1972	Nixon	62	60.7	1.3
	McGovern	38	37.6	0.4
1968	Nixon	43	43.4	-0.4
	Humphrey	42	42.7	-0.7
	Wallace	15	13.5	1.5

2008 Chronology

December 2007

December 6 The Senate and House intelligence committees vote to ban severe methods of interrogation prohibiting water boarding and other harsh techniques that have been used by the CIA.

December 6 The Senate votes to approve tax relief for the middle class to prevent millions of Americans from having to pay the alternative minimum tax.

December 13 Former US Senator George Mitchell, after an extensive investigation, accuses 89 current and former Major League Baseball players of using illegal performance-enhancing drugs.

December 27 Benazir Bhutto dies in suicide attack at a campaign rally in Rawalpindi. President Pervez Musharraf blames al-Qaeda for the attack on the former prime minister.

January 2008

January 3 Presidential Primaries begin.

January 6 Mikheil Saakashvili is reelected as President of Georgia despite massive protests by demonstrators who accused him of abusing power and stifling dissent.

January 28 President Bush delivers his last State of the Union address.

January 29 The House votes in favor of President Bush's proposed stimulus package.

January 30 John Edwards and Rudy Giuliani both fail to win a primary or caucus. Both drop out of presidential race.

February 2008

February 1 A report by the Bureau of Labor Statistics, states that 17,000 jobs were eliminated in January stirring fears of imminent recession.

February 5 John McCain emerges as the clear Republican front runner during the primaries and caucuses that were held in 24 states. Democrat Hillary Clinton wins big states, but Barak Obama takes more states.

February 7 Senate passes a $168 billion stimulus package that gives rebates of $300-$600 for individuals earning up to $75,000 and to couples with incomes up to $150,000.

February 14 A gunman opens fire on a classroom at Northern Illinois University killing six students and then himself and wounds 15 more. The gunman was a former graduate student at the university.

February 17 Kosovo declares independence from Serbia after months of negotiations with the European Union, Russia and Washington. Serbian Prime Minister Vojislav Kostunica says he would never recognize the "false state".

February 19 Fidel Castro resigns as president of Cuba after 49 years in power.

February 24   Raul Castro succeeds his brother, Fidel Castro, as president of Cuba, though he will consult Fidel when making important decisions.

March 2008

March 2   Dmitri A. Medvedev, former aide to Vladimir Putin, wins the Russian presidential election in a landslide. Putin will remain in a position of power, serving as prime minister.

March 4   John McCain secures Republican presidential nomination after primary wins in Texas, Ohio, Rhode Island and Vermont. Mike Huckabee bows out of race.

March 10   New York governor, Eliot Spitzer, admits involvement in a prostitution ring.

March 11   Federal Reserve intervenes to avert a financial crisis with a $200 billion loan program that lets the country's biggest banks borrow Treasury securities at discount rates.

March 12   Eliot Sptizer announces his resignation as governor of New York. Lt. Gov. David A. Patterson will replace him.

March 16   The Federal Reserve approves a $30 billion loan to JB Morgan Chase so it can take over Bear Stearns which is on the verge of collapse.

March 18   Senator Barak Obama gives a significant speech denouncing provocative remarks on race made by his former pastor, Rev. Jeremiah Wright, Jr.

March 19   The fifth anniversary of the US led warn in Iraq. President Bush acknowledges the toll the war has taken on US financial deficit and loss of life.

March 23   US suffers 4,000[th] death in Iraq after a roadside bomb kills four US soldiers.

March 24   Detroit mayor, Kwame Kilpatrick, is indicted on eight felony charges. The charges stem from a past affair with his former chief of staff, Christine Beatty.

April 2008

April 15   In his first visit to the US, Pope Benedict XVI denounces pedophile priests.

April 15   Vladimir Putin is chosen as chairman of the United Russia party and agrees to become prime minister when Dmitri Medvedev assumes the presidency in May.

April 17   Benedict XVI celebrates a mass before 46,000 people at Washington National stadium. Later he holds a surprise meeting with several victims of sexual abuse by priests in the Boston archdiocese.

April 23   President Bush nominates Gen. David Patraeus, the four-star general, to succeed Adm. William Fallon, who recently retired as head of Central Command.

May 2008

May 1   Dmitri Medvedev is sworn in as the new president of Russia.

May 8   Parliament elects Vladimir Putin, head of the United Russia party as prime minister.

May 15   The state of California's highest court says that same-sex couples have a constitutional right to marry.

May 20   Senator Edward Kennedy, long time Democrat from Massachusetts, is diagnosed with malignant brain cancer.

May 31   Democratic National Committee officials reach a compromise to seat all of the delegates from Florida and Michigan but allot them only half vote each at the Democratic National Convention. The two states were stripped of their delegates because they held primaries earlier than the DNC permitted.

June 2008

June 1

The US military announced that fatalities in Iraq dropped in may to the lowest level since the war began in 2003.

June 3

Senator Barak Obama secures 2,154 delegates and becomes the presumptive Democratic presidential nominee. Hillary Clinton does not withdraw from race.

June 5

Suspects in the September 11, 2001 attacks are arraigned and face a tribunal for the first time at Guantanamo Bay, Cuba.

June 5

An inquiry by the Senate Select committee on Intelligence states that President Bush exaggerated evidence that Saddam Hussein possessed "weapons of mass destruction" and misled the public about ties between Iraq and al-Qaeda.

June 6

The US Department of Labor states the jobless rate increases from 5% to 5.5% which represents the biggest monthly increase in 22 years.

June 7

Hillary Clinton suspends her campaign and endorses Barak Obama for the presidency.

June 16.

California begins performing same-sex marriages. California is the second state, behind Massachusetts, to legalize same-sex marriage

June 19

Presumptive Democratic Presidential nominee Barak Obama opts out of public funding for the general election.

June 19

In a agreement intended to quell the violence in the Gaza strip, Egypt brokers a cease-fire deal between Israel and Hamas.

July 2008

July 1

Violence is on the upswing in Afghanistan with June 2008 being the deadliest month for US and coalition troops since the American-led invasion began in 2001.

July 8

Members of the Group of 8 (US, Japan, Germany, Britain, France, Italy, Canada and Russia) set goals to cut the amount of greenhouse gasses that are emitted into the environment in half by 2050. Critics believe shorter-term goals should also be set.

July 9

Senate approves legislation to expand the Foreign Intelligence Surveillance Act giving legal immunity to telephone companies that participated in the National Security Agency secret wiretapping program after the September 11, 2001 terrorist attacks.

July 13

A rescue plan is proposed by the Treasury Department to pump billions of dollars into Fannie Mae and Freddie Mac. An unsteady stock market is diminishing the confidence in these two companies that either own or guarantee half of the mortgages in the US.

July 14

President Bush, in a series of executive orders, lifts a ban that placed a moratorium on drilling for gall and oil 3 to 200 miles off the US coastline. The first President Bush signed an executive order in 1990 prohibiting such drilling.

July 19

Representatives from the US, France, Britain, Germany, Russia and China meet with Iran's chief negotiator to discuss a proposal that calls on Iran to freeze its nuclear program in exchange for a freeze on further sanctions with Iran.

July 23	The House votes in legislation that gives the Treasury Department authority to rescue Fannie May and Freddie Mac if it becomes necessary. This rescue plan is to help homeowners avoid foreclosure by allowing them to refinance their mortgages.
July 29	A microbiologist, Bruce Ivins, who worked in the bio-defense research center in Frederick, MD, commits suicide from an overdose after he was informed that he was being indicted on charges of murder in the string of mail-based anthrax attacks in September and October of 2001.
July 30	Israeli Prime Minister, Ehud Olmert, announces he will step down once a new party leader is selected in September. Olmert is under investigation for fraud, bribery and breach of trust.

August 2008

August 7	The Pakistani government says it will "immediately initiate impeachment proceedings" against President Pervez Musharraf on charges of violating the constitution and misconduct.
August 8	The Summer Olympic games opened with a spectacular ceremony in Beijing, China.
August 8	Former Democratic senator and presidential candidate, John Edwards, admitted to having an extra-marital affair in 2006 with Rielle Hunter, a campaign aide. He denies being the father of her child.
August 8	Russia enters the entanglement with Georgia by directing troops and tanks into South Ossetia to support the region.
August 13	France brokers a deal between Russia and Georgia that calls both sides to end the fighting and use of force and withdraw troops.

August 17	Michael Phelps, swimmer from the US, wins his eighth gold medal breaking Mark Spitz's world record of seven gold medals in the 1972 games. This also sets the record for the most gold medals in a single Olympics.
August 18	Pakistani president, Pervez Musharraf, resigns.
August 18	The Taliban launches a major attack in Afghanistan with as many as 15 suicide bombers in the eastern province of Khost. Fighting between US troops and the Taliban rages overnight, though no US casualties occur.
August 22	US and Iraq agree on a timeframe to withdraw troops from Iraqi cities by June 2009.
August 23	Delivered via text message to his supporters, Democratic Presidential candidate Barak Obama announces that he has selected Delaware senator Joe Biden as his pick for vice president.
August 25	The Democratic National Committee opens in Denver, CO. Michelle Obama, the wife of Sen. Barack Obama, and Sen. Ted Kennedy deliver well-received speeches.
August 26	Hillary Clinton delivers her speech at the Democratic National Convention in an attempt to unify the Democratic party and calling for her supporters to rally behind Barack Obama.
August 27	Senator Barack Obama is formally elected the Democratic presidential nominee. Former President Bill Clinton addresses the convention and strongly endorses Obama's candidacy for president.
August 28	Senator Barack Obama accepts the Democratic Presidential nomination and addresses the convention with an im-

passioned speech that that attacks John McCain on many fronts. The speech is delivered to a huge crowd of 83,000 at Invesco Field in Denver.

August 29   Diplomatic ties between Russia and Georgia are severed, marking the first time in history that Russia has cut off formal relations with one of its former republics.

September 2008

September 1   The opening day of the Republican National Convention in New Orleans, LA, is affected by the impending arrival of Hurricane Gustav. Party officials scale back the first day making it a business-only affair without the celebratory mood and speeches. Hurricane Katrina devastated New Orleans back in 2005.

September 1   Yasuo Fukuda, the Japanese Prime Minister, resigns his position after being in office barely one year. His party, the Liberal Democrats, will select his successor. Fukuda was censored by the upper house of Parliament for mismanagement of domestic issues. The lower house supported him in a vote of confidence.

September 1   The US transfers control of the Anbar Province in Iraq to the Iraqi military and police. This province until recently was the center of Sunni insurgency and more than 1,000 members of the US military have been killed here.

September 2   President George Bush delivers a speech via video saying that John McCain is the man most fit to become president during these difficult and dangerous times.

September 3   Sarah Palin, Governor of Alaska, makes her debut at the Republican National Convention by delivering a widely praised speech. Shortly after

Palin's speech, the delegates select Sen. John McCain as the Republican presidential nominee.

September 4   Sen. John McCain delivers his acceptance speech calling for change from the status quo and indicates that he will not always tow the party line.

September 5   In its most recent report, the Bureau of Labor Statistics indicates that the jobless rate in the US hit 6.1%, the highest point since 2003. Eighty-four thousand jobs were lost in the month of August.

September 6   Benazir Bhutto's widower and the leader of the Pakistan People's Party, Asif Ali Zardari, is elected the President of Pakistan. With his election, Zardari faces the monumental task of rooting out members of al Qaeda and the Taliban, who control much of the country's tribal areas.

September 7   The US government places Fannie Mae and Freddie Mac, who together hold more than half of the country's mortgages, under government conservatorship which is similar to bankruptcy reorganization. US treasury secretary Henry M. Paulson, Jr. says this move is crucial to avoid turmoil in the national and international economies.

September 14   Merrill Lynch agrees to be acquired by Bank of America for $50 billion and Lehman Brothers prepares to declare bankruptcy when it fails t find a buyer.

September 15   The Dow Jones Industrial average plunges more than 500 points fueling concerns about a financial crisis. This represents the worst one-day loss since the September 11, 2001 terrorist attacks.

September 16   The Federal Reserve proceeds with an $85 billion rescue of American International Group (AIG) which is one of the largest insurance companies that covers financial institutions.

September 16 US Military command in Iraq changes hands. Gen. David Patraeus will become commander of the US Central Command that covers all of the Middle East. His replacement on the ground in Iraq is US Gen. Ray Odierno.

September 20 The Bush administration asks Congress to allow the Treasury Department to buy up to $700 billion in bad mortgage assets from private investment companies. If this happens, it will be the largest bailout in US history.

September 21 Israeli Prime Minister, Ehud Olmert, steps down during an investigation for corruption. He will be replaced by Foreign Minister Tzipi Livni who was recently elected the head of Olmert's party, Kadima.

September 26 In the first Presidential debate, Barack Obama and John McCain face off at the end of a tumultuous week in which the country's financial system teetered on the brink of disaster. Both candidates agree that the government needs to intervene but that conditions and safeguards must be included in any bailout package.

September 28 A $700 billion bailout plan is agreed upon by Congressional negotiators and Treasury secretary Henry Paulson. The bailout plan gives the Treasury unprecedented authority to buy a wide range of troubled financial assets, limits executive pay, etc.

September 29 The House shocks the financial world by rejecting the $700 billion bailout plan. The Dow Jones Industrial average plummets 778 points, its biggest point decline ever.

October 2008

October 1 Two days after the House rejected a similar deal, the Senate passes a "sweetened" bailout plan. In addition to the provisions in the $700 billion, the Senate plan increases from $100,000 to $250,000 the amount of bank deposits covered by the FDIC and extends $150 billion in tax breaks to individuals and companies.

October 2 The vice presidential candidates, Democrat Joe Biden and Republican Sarah Palin, meet for a debate. The two face off on issues relating to the war in Iraq, tax policy, oil and the environment, and the financial crises gripping the country.

October 3 President Bush signs the bailout package into law.

October 3 The economy suffers significant job losses in September. The Labor Department reports that 159,000 jobs were lost in September, the most in five years.

October 6 The first day of trading after the approval of the bailout experiences the steepest declines in the American, European and Asian markets in two decades.

October 7 In the second presidential debate between Democratic candidate Barack Obama and Republican candidate John McCain, the economic crisis is the front and center issue.

October 9 The Dow closes below 9,000 for the first time in five years. The New York Stock Exchange experiences the most active day in its history with investors selling off stocks in a panic.

October 11 Finance ministers from the Group of 7 industrialized nations meet in Washington to develop a coordinated plan to stem the escalating global financial crisis.

October 11 The US State Department removes North Korea from its list of state sponsors of terrorism. In exchange, North Korea agrees to give international inspectors access to its nuclear plant and to continue disabling its plutonium-processing facility.

October 15 In the third and last presidential debate, Republican candidate John McCain and Democratic candidate Barack Obama meet for their most contentious debate yet.

October 17 The US and Iraq complete a draft agreement that calls for all US troops to be withdrawn from Iraq by the end of 2011, depending on the conditions in Iraq. This agreement was outlined in the media though not formally released to the public.

October 19 Former secretary of state, and Republican, Colin Powell endorses Barack Obama for president.

October 27 Three months after Georgia's war with Russia that demolished Georgia's infrastructure, the president of Georgia, Mikhail Saaksahvili replaces the countries Prime Minister.

October 30 The economy shrinks for the first time in years as the gross domestic product drops 0.3%. It's the first decrease in the GDP in 17 years.

October 31 Gen. David Petraeus takes over as Head of Central Command operations in Iraq, Afghanistan, Pakistan, Syria, Iran, and other countries.

November 2008

November 4 Democrat Barack Obama is elected President of the United States, taking 338 electoral votes to John McCain's 161.

November 7 The economy continues to tumble as the Labor Department reports 240,000 jobs lost in October. This brings the unemployment rate up to 6.5% which is the highest since 1994.

November 12 In a shift in course in the bailout package, the Treasury Department says it will instead use part of the $700 billion authorized by Congress to help banks lend to consumers. This is in contrast to earlier plans for the government to buy troubled mortgage assets from banks and financial institution.

November 15 Officials from the Group of 20 (wealthy countries and those with emerging economies) met in Washington and agree to tighten supervision on banks and credit-rating companies and consider controls on executive pay.

November 19 The Dow Jones continues to tumble 5.1% to hit 7,997.28. The Consumer Price Index fell by one percentage point in October, the steepest one-month drop since the index began in 1947.

November 20 The big three US auto makers (Ford, GM, and Chrysler) make pleas for government bailouts. Democratic lawmakers say that after two days of deliberations, the leaders of the big three failed to put forth a strategy that would salvage their flagging businesses.

November 23 Newly elected President Barack Obama starts to the process of assembling his administration. Timothy F. Geithner, the president of the Federal Reserve Bank in New York, is nominated as treasury secretary.

November 23 The US Treasury and the FDIC will back up to $306 billion in potential losses incurred by Citigroup from high-risk loans and securities and will also inject $20 billion in cash into the troubled company.

November 25 The US government announces further plans to help boost the economy. The Federal Reserve and the Treasury

Department will finance $800 billion in lending programs — $600 billion to buy debt guaranteed by Fannie Mae and Freddie Mac; the remaining $200 billion will help consumers secure student loans, car loans, small-business loans, etc.

December 2008

December 1 President-elect Barack Obama announces National Security Team and other Cabinet members. Most notably Obama introduces Hillary Clinton, his rival in the Democratic presidential primary, as his pick for Secretary of State.

December 9 Illinois Governor Rod Blagojevich is accused of selling now former Senator Barack Obama's senate seat. Several phone conversations with advisers were recorded by the FBI since the Nov. 4, 2008 election where they discovered that the Governor plotted ways to benefit financially from his duty to fill Chicago's senate seat which was vacated by Obama.

December 10 Congress votes in favor of a $14 billion rescue package that provides emergency loans to Chrysler and General Motors. This assistance is critical considering that these two companies have said they cannot survive until the end of 2008.

December 11 Despite the Bush administrations persistence, the Senate fails to deliver enough support to vote on the bailout package for the automakers, thus killing it.

December 11 Well-known investment manager, Bernard Madoff, is charged with defrauding hundreds of clients of as much $50 billion is a huge Ponzi scheme. This could be one of the largest swindles in Wall Street history.

December 14 A reporter for Al Baghdadia, a Cairo-based satellite television network, hurls his shoes at President Bush and calls him a "dog" at a news conference in Baghdad.

December 15 The Illinois state legislature begins impeachment proceedings against Governor Rod Blagojevich.

December 19 Out-going President George Bush hands the fate of the automakers to president-elect Barack Obama as he announces plans to lend GM and Chrysler $17.4 billion to survive the next three months.

December 28 Hamas begins launching rocket attacks into Israel just days after the cease-fire expired. Israel retaliates with airstrikes that killed more than 300 people.

December 30 Rod Blagojevich names Roland Burris as former Senator Barack Obama's successor. The move is criticized by state legislators.

If Hillary Clinton loses the Iowa Democratic caucus, would you view that as -- a temporary setback for her campaign, (or as) a sign that her campaign is in serious trouble?

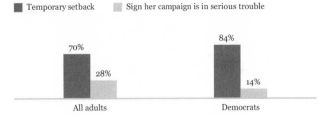

■ Temporary setback   ■ Sign her campaign is in serious trouble

70%   28%   84%   14%

All adults   Democrats

Dec. 10-13, 2007

January 02, 2008

AMERICANS SPECULATE ABOUT IOWA'S IMPACT

Predict opportunity for Obama; trouble in sight for Giuliani

by Lydia Saad, Gallup Poll Senior Editor

The Jan. 3 Iowa caucuses are positioned to transform the dynamics, if not the outcome, of the major parties' presidential nomination races, particularly if the results defy expectations. An upset win by a candidate in this first contest of the season could sway New Hampshire primary voters on Jan. 8, and from there it's anybody's guess what happens.

Gallup recently asked Americans to adopt the role of political pundit and speculate about how various possible outcomes in Iowa and New Hampshire might affect the candidacies of the winners and losers.

According to the Dec. 10-13, 2007, Gallup Panel survey, Americans tend to play up the significance of Barack Obama possibly winning in Iowa, as well as the significance of hypothetical back-to-back defeats for Rudy Giuliani in Iowa and New Hampshire. Americans play down the significance of a John Edwards win in Iowa, and also of Hillary Clinton potentially winning in both Iowa and New Hampshire. Americans have mixed views about what winning Iowa would mean for the campaigns of Mitt Romney and Mike Huckabee.

Speculation on the Democratic Race

Most polls of likely Iowa Democratic caucus-goers show a highly competitive race among Clinton, Obama, and Edwards, making it appear that any of the three could win Iowa. That's a much different position for Clinton than is the case in the national polls, where she leads Obama by a considerable margin, and where Edwards is in a distant third place.

What effect do Americans think losing Iowa would have on Clinton's shot at the nomination? Seven in 10 Americans, including 84% of Democrats, would consider losing Iowa to be "a temporary setback" for Clinton's campaign. Fewer than one-third would see it as "a sign that her campaign is in serious trouble."

At the same time, and somewhat contrary to their views of a Clinton loss in Iowa, most Americans—including nearly three in four Democrats—believe an Obama win in Iowa would be "a sign that he will seriously challenge Hillary Clinton for the nomination," and not just a "temporary victory" for him.

Thus, the impact of a potential Obama victory in Iowa on the psychology of the race is a bit unclear. Americans say it would make him a force to be reckoned with; at the same time, they don't seem to believe it would seriously derail the "Clinton Express."

The public is less likely to consider a potential Edwards victory in Iowa to be significant than they are to see an Obama win as significant. Four in 10 Americans (including 47% of Democrats) say

If Barack Obama wins the Iowa Democratic caucus, would you view that as -- a temporary victory for his campaign, (or as) a sign that he will seriously challenge Hillary Clinton for the nomination?

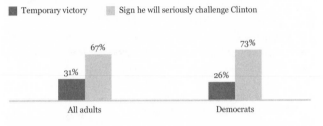

■ Temporary victory   ■ Sign he will seriously challenge Clinton

31%   67%   26%   73%

All adults   Democrats

Dec. 10-13, 2007

Edwards winning Iowa would be a sign that he will seriously challenge Clinton for the nomination. However, the majority tends to believe this would be only a temporary victory for Edwards.

If John Edwards wins the Iowa Democratic caucus, would you view that as -- a temporary victory for his campaign, (or as) a sign that he will seriously challenge Hillary Clinton for the nomination?

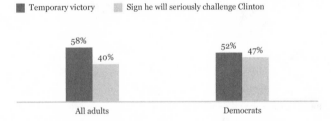

■ Temporary victory   ■ Sign he will seriously challenge Clinton

58%   40%   52%   47%

All adults   Democrats

Dec. 10-13, 2007

While Clinton has a lot to lose in Iowa, particularly from an Obama victory, winning in both Iowa and New Hampshire doesn't guarantee her candidacy a sense of inevitability with the public. Fifty-six percent of Americans, and the same percentage of Democrats, say that if Clinton wins both the Iowa caucuses and New Hampshire primary, another candidate could still win the Democratic nomination; only 43% to 44% say the nomination would be essentially decided.

Republican-Based Prognostications

With Giuliani essentially ceding Iowa to his competitors, the race to win the Republican caucuses in Iowa is down to Romney, Huckabee, and—to a lesser extent—John McCain and Fred Thompson. Most polls now show Huckabee and Romney with a significant lead over

If Hillary Clinton wins both the Iowa caucus and the New Hampshire primary, which would come closer to your view -- the Democratic presidential nomination will essentially be decided, (or) another candidate could still come back to win?

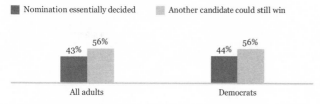

Dec. 10-13, 2007

the other candidates in Iowa, and recent national Republican polls show Romney and Huckabee challenging Giuliani's front-runner position. Thus, for both Huckabee and Romney, winning Iowa has major significance for their positions nationally, not just in the early primary states.

Americans are divided almost evenly over whether winning the Iowa caucuses would be a temporary victory for Romney (51%) or a sign that he is a serious challenger to win the Republican nomination (46%). Republicans tend to take a Romney win a bit more seriously, as the slight majority (53%) say winning Iowa would be a significant sign of Romney's strength as a challenger.

If Mitt Romney wins the Iowa caucus, do you think that would be -- a temporary victory for his campaign, (or do you think it would be) a sign that he is a serious challenger to win the Republican nomination?

Dec. 10-13, 2007

Americans on the whole are also closely divided over the meaning of a Huckabee win in Iowa: 51% say it would be a temporary victory for him while 46% say it would be a sign that he is a serious challenger for the GOP nomination. Republicans are no more likely than the public as a whole to believe that a Huckabee win in Iowa would be significant.

If Mike Huckabee wins the Iowa caucus, do you think that would be -- a temporary victory for his campaign, (or do you think it would be) a sign that he is a serious challenger to win the Republican nomination?

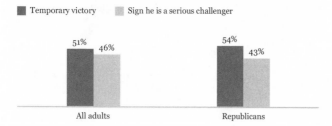

Thus, the possible impact of either a Huckabee or a Romney victory in Iowa is mixed. Republicans—the constituency that counts in the short term—are slightly more likely to consider a potential Romney victory in the Hawkeye state as significant than would be the case for a Huckabee victory, but views are split in both situations.

Giuliani has explained that he is running minimal campaigns in Iowa and New Hampshire in an effort to focus on the voting that will take place on Feb. 5, when 22 states, including delegate-rich California and New York, will hold their contests. However, given Giuliani's recent decline in the national polls, this would appear to be a risky strategy, and one voters won't buy into should he lose Iowa and New Hampshire, as is expected.

Only 28% of Americans believe that losing both contests would be a temporary setback for Giuliani; 71% say it would be a sign his campaign is in serious trouble. Republicans are not much more forgiving: 38% say that it would be a temporary setback while 61% say it would be a sign of serious trouble.

If Rudy Giuliani loses both the Iowa caucus and the New Hampshire primary in the Republican campaign for president, would you view that as -- a temporary setback for his campaign, (or as) a sign that his campaign is in serious trouble?

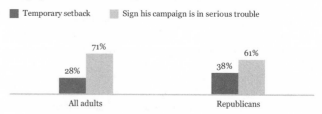

Dec. 10-13, 2007

Bottom Line

The real fallout from the Iowa caucuses will depend on the precise results, media coverage and spin, and the way the candidates handle their lot in the days following the vote.

Still, the attitudes reported here offer some clues as to how Americans might react. On the Democratic side, the potential impact of a Clinton loss in Iowa appears to be mixed: Democrats say losing Iowa would be only a temporary setback for her campaign. At the same time, Democrats say an Obama win would be a sign that he was seriously challenging Clinton's front-runner position.

On the Republican side, the data suggest that the situation for Giuliani is more grave than his campaign would like to acknowledge. As much as he is trying to manage expectations around the early contests, a majority of Republicans say that back-to-back losses for Giuliani in Iowa and New Hampshire spell serious trouble for his campaign.

Survey Methods

Results for this panel study are based on telephone interviews with 1,008 national adults, aged 18 and older, conducted Dec. 10-13, 2007. Respondents were randomly drawn from Gallup's nationally representative household panel, which was originally recruited through random selection methods. The final sample is weighted so it is representative of U.S. adults nationwide.

For results based on the total sample of national adults, one can say with 95% confidence that the maximum margin of sampling error is ±4 percentage points.

For results based on the sample of 344 Republicans, the maximum margin of sampling error is ±7 percentage points.

For results based on the sample of 331 Democrats, the maximum margin of sampling error is ±7 percentage points.

In addition to sampling error, question wording and practical difficulties in conducting surveys can introduce error or bias into the findings of public opinion polls.

January 02, 2008
TIME PRESSURES, STRESS COMMON FOR AMERICANS
Nearly half do not have enough spare time, 40% are frequently stressed

by Joseph Carroll, Gallup Poll Assistant Editor

Gallup's annual Lifestyle poll finds Americans about equally likely to say they do not have enough time to do what they want these days as to say they do. Most Americans sometimes experience stress in the daily lives, including 4 in 10 who say they encounter it frequently. Parents of younger children, working Americans, and younger Americans are most likely to report enduring time pressures and stress.

Time and Stress Management

The Dec. 6-9, 2007 poll finds 53% of Americans saying they generally have enough time to do what they want to do these days, while 47% say they do not. Gallup first asked this question in 1990, and has asked it annually since 2001. The current results are right in line with what Gallup has found most years. In the 2004 survey, Americans were somewhat more optimistic about their spare time, with 56% saying they had enough time and 44% saying they did not.

Generally speaking, do you have enough time to do what you want to do these days, or not?

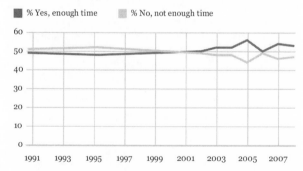

Most Americans also say they experience stress in their daily life—40% deal with stress frequently and 36% sometimes do. The percentage of Americans who experience stress in their life has been relatively stable. So has the percentage who frequently experience stress, which, apart from an abnormally low 33% reading in 2003, has been consistently around 40%.

Lack of time and stress go hand in hand, as evidenced by the data: 54% of Americans who do not have enough spare time these days say they frequently experience stress. This is twice the percentage of those who have sufficient time to attend to their matters.

In general, how often do you experience stress in your daily life -- never, rarely, sometimes, or frequently?

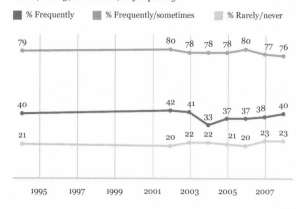

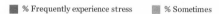

Spare Time Versus Stress Frequency

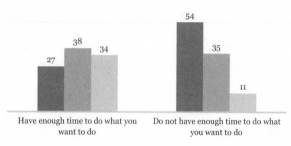

(Dec 6-9, 2007)

Who's Feeling the Pressure?

Some groups of Americans experience more time strains and stress than other groups do. These groups include parents of young children, working adults, and younger Americans.

Only 38% of parents with younger children say they have enough time to do what they want to do these days, while 62% do not have enough time. These results are the opposite for those without young children—62% have enough time to do what they want and 38% do not. Nearly half of parents, 49%, frequently encounter stress in their lives, while only 34% of non-parents feel stress often.

Only 40% of working Americans say they have enough time in their daily lives, compared with an overwhelming 72% of non-working Americans. Employed adults are also more likely to experience stress frequently than those who are not employed, by a 45% to 32% margin.

Time pressures may ease as people get older, which could be because many older Americans are retired. The vast majority of adults aged 55 and older (72%) say they have enough time to do what they want, and only 27% frequently endure stress in their life. By comparison, roughly 4 in 10 Americans who are younger than age 55 say they have enough spare time, and just less than half frequently experience stress.

Men and women tend to agree about their time and stress problems—a slim majority of men and women say they have enough time to do what they want to do these days, and roughly 4 in 10 say they frequently encounter stress in their daily lives.

Time and Stress

By Parental Status

December 2006-December 2007 Aggregate

	Parents of children younger than age 18	Not parents of children younger than age 18
	%	%
Have enough time to do what you want to do these days?		
Yes	38	62
No	62	38
Experience stress in your daily life?		
Frequently	49	34
Sometimes	37	38
Rarely/Never	15	28

Time and Stress

By Employment Status

December 2006-December 2007 Aggregate

	Employed	Not employed
	%	%
Have enough time to do what you want to do these days?		
Yes	40	72
No	60	28
Experience stress in your daily life?		
Frequently	45	32
Sometimes	40	34
Rarely/Never	15	34

Time and Stress

By Age

December 2006-December 2007 Aggregate

	18- to 34-year-olds	35- to 54-year-olds	55 and older
	%	%	%
Have enough time to do what you want to do these days?			
Yes	45	42	72
No	55	58	28
Experience stress in your daily life?			
Frequently	45	46	27
Sometimes	37	39	37
Rarely/Never	18	15	35

Survey Methods

Results are based on telephone interviews with 1,027 national adults, aged 18 and older, conducted Dec. 6-9, 2007. For results based on the total sample of national adults, one can say with 95% confidence that the margin of sampling error is ±3 percentage points.

Time and Stress

By Gender

December 2006-December 2007 Aggregate

	Men	Women
	%	%
Have enough time to do what you want to do these days?		
Yes	54	52
No	45	47
Experience stress in your daily life?		
Frequently	38	41
Sometimes	37	38
Rarely/Never	26	21

In addition to sampling error, question wording and practical difficulties in conducting surveys can introduce error or bias into the findings of public opinion polls.

January 04, 2008
AMERICANS TAKING FRONT-LOADED PRIMARIES IN STRIDE
Few are troubled that the contests start in January

by Lydia Saad, Gallup Poll Senior Editor

Americans are taking the acceleration of the primary process around the 2008 presidential election fairly well in stride. Although the first nominating elections are in January, and the identity of the 2008 nominees will likely be known by early February, these aren't vexing developments to most Americans. In fact, for the plurality, these are good things.

At worst, most Americans are neutral about the front-loaded nature of the 2008 primaries. About half (49%) say that having the caucuses and primaries begin in January is a good thing and another 27% say it is neither good nor bad, leaving less than one-quarter calling it bad.

Americans are slightly more negative about having the races essentially decided by early February, with 36% calling this a bad thing. However, more (45%) consider it a good thing.

Perceptions of Aspects of 2008 Presidential Nomination Process

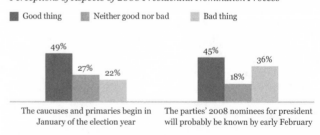

Dec. 10-13, 2007

Of course, the flip side of knowing early on in the process who the nominees will be is that the states that go to the polls later in the primary season have little to no impact on choosing the nominees.

Despite their relatively positive reactions to getting the nominations decided early, most Americans consider the limited influence of states with later primaries and caucuses a bad thing.

What Americans Think About Nominees Being Determined Before Many States Have Held Their Contests

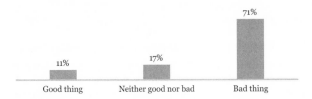

Dec. 10-13, 2007

Americans are generally ambivalent about Iowa's and New Hampshire's position as the states that traditionally kick off the presidential primary season. Nearly as many Americans consider the two states' initiation of the primary season good as call it bad, while most say it is neither.

What Americans Think About Iowa and New Hampshire Always Being the First Contests

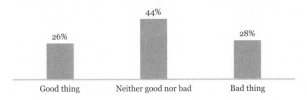

Dec. 10-13, 2007

More generally, most Americans like choosing the party nominees for president through a system of state primaries and caucuses.

What Americans Think About Nominations Being Decided by a Series of State Primaries and Caucuses

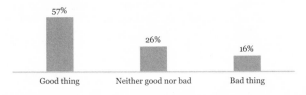

Dec. 10-13, 2007

Survey Methods

Results for this panel study are based on telephone interviews with 1,008 national adults, aged 18 and older, conducted Dec. 10-13, 2007. Respondents were randomly drawn from Gallup's nationally representative household panel, which was originally recruited through random selection methods. The final sample is weighted so it is representative of U.S. adults nationwide.

For results based on the total sample of national adults, one can say with 95% confidence that the maximum margin of sampling error is ±4 percentage points.

In addition to sampling error, question wording and practical difficulties in conducting surveys can introduce error or bias into the findings of public opinion polls.

January 07, 2008
OBAMA, MCCAIN LEAD AMONG NEW HAMPSHIRE LIKELY VOTERS
Obama riding crest of great enthusiasm on Democratic side

by Frank Newport, Gallup Poll Editor in Chief

Sen. Barack Obama has taken a substantial lead over Sen. Hillary Clinton among Democratic likely voters in New Hampshire, and Sen. John McCain now has a modest lead among likely Republican voters. Obama does particularly well among independents who say they will vote in the Democratic primary, and Democratic voters' choice of Obama as the Democratic candidate best able to win next November has surged since mid-December. Despite his highly publicized victory in last Thursday's Iowa caucuses, former Arkansas Gov. Mike Huckabee only marginally improved his status among Republicans compared to Gallup's mid-December poll, and is in third place—significantly behind McCain and Mitt Romney.

These results are from a USA Today/Gallup poll of likely voters in New Hampshire, conducted Jan. 4-6. Full details on the methodology of the poll are at the end of this story.

The New Hampshire Democratic Primary

Sens. Obama and Clinton were essentially tied among both registered voters and likely voters in New Hampshire in the Dec. 17-19 *USA Today*/Gallup poll. By this past weekend, after the Iowa caucuses, Obama had moved slightly ahead of Clinton among registered voters, but jumped more significantly ahead among likely voters. Obama now has a substantial 13-point, 41% to 28% lead over Clinton among likely voters, with Sen. John Edwards following in third place, with 19% of the vote. This marks a dramatic shift from just 2 1/2 weeks ago.

Suppose the Democratic primary for president were being held today. If you had to choose among the following candidates, which candidate would you vote for --

	Likely voters, Jan 4-6	Likely voters, Dec 17-19	Registered voters, Jan 4-6	Registered voters, Dec 17-19
	%	%	%	%
Barack Obama	41	32	39	32
Hillary Clinton	28	32	34	35
John Edwards	19	18	17	16
Bill Richardson	6	8	4	6
Dennis Kucinich	3	3	3	3
Mike Gravel	*	--	*	--
Joe Biden	n/a	4	n/a	3
Chris Dodd	n/a	1	n/a	1
Other	1	*	1	*
No opinion	2	2	2	3

* Less than 0.5%
n/a = Not asked

All in all, Obama's share of the vote among likely voters went up by nine points between the two polls, Clinton's dropped by four points,

Edwards' share went up by one point, Gov. Bill Richardson's dropped by two points, and Rep. Dennis Kucinich's share stayed the same. The "no opinion" or "other" percentage went from 2% to 3% between the two polls. (The mid-December *USA Today*/Gallup poll included the names of Sens. Joseph Biden and Christopher Dodd—both of whom dropped out of the race after last Thursday's Iowa caucuses. Those two candidates had 5% support between them in the December poll.)

The *USA Today*/Gallup polls in New Hampshire included a question that asked Democratic voters to indicate which candidate best fits each of a list of "characteristics" or descriptions.

The percentage of Democratic likely voters selecting Obama went up at least a little for each of the six descriptions.

The largest shift came in Democratic voters' views of the candidate who "has the best chance of beating the Republican in November." Obama jumped by 19 points on this dimension between the two polls, while Clinton fell by 13 points. The result? Whereas Clinton led Obama on this dimension by 21 points in mid-December, Obama now leads Clinton by 11 points after Iowa.

These data underscore the conclusion that one significant effect of Obama's Iowa win was the apparent transformation of the first-term Illinois senator's image from that of a new kid on the block competing against Clinton's vast experience, to a candidate who has the best chance of winning against the Republican nominee in November.

The New Hampshire Republican Primary

A key question since Huckabee's dramatic win in Iowa has been its potential impact on New Hampshire Republican primary voters. Iowa—with a significant proportion of evangelical Christians—was fertile ground for the former Baptist minister's campaign, but it has been unclear whether more secular New Hampshire would be as receptive to his appeal.

There are indications that Huckabee has moved up sharply among Republicans nationally since the Iowa vote. But the weekend poll in New Hampshire shows little sign that Huckabee has been able to transform his Iowa victory into anything approaching the type of surge seen for Obama among New Hampshire Democrats. Huckabee had 9% of the vote in mid-December and 13% in the weekend, post-Iowa poll, a gain of just four percentage points.

Suppose the Republican primary for president were being held today. If you had to choose among the following candidates, which candidate would you vote for --

	Likely voters, Jan 4-6	Likely voters, Dec 17-19	Registered voters, Jan 4-6	Registered voters, Dec 17-19
	%	%	%	%
John McCain	34	27	33	26
Mitt Romney	30	34	29	34
Mike Huckabee	13	9	14	9
Ron Paul	8	9	9	10
Rudy Giuliani	8	11	8	13
Fred Thompson	3	4	3	3
Duncan Hunter	1	1	1	1
Alan Keyes	*	--	*	*
Tom Tancredo	n/a	*	n/a	*
Other	1	--	1	*
No opinion	2	5	2	4

* Less than 0.5%
n/a = Not asked

The more significant change that occurred between the two polls was in the relative positioning of the two front-runners in the Republican field—Romney and McCain. Whereas Romney led McCain

among likely New Hampshire primary voters by seven points in mid-December, McCain now leads Romney by four points. The four-point McCain lead is not statistically significant, but suggests he has a real chance of coming away from New Hampshire with a victory, as he did in 2000. Rudy Giuliani's share of the New Hampshire vote dropped by three points, and he is tied with Ron Paul for fourth place in the poll. Fred Thompson, who tied McCain for third in Iowa, looks to be an afterthought in New Hampshire.

There has been some movement in the percentage of Republican voters in New Hampshire selecting various candidates as best fitting each of the six descriptive phrases included in the survey.

As was the case on the Democratic side, the biggest change here involved perceptions as to who is the candidate best able to win in November. McCain gained, while former New York City Mayor Rudy Giuliani, who did not compete in Iowa, and Mitt Romney both fell on this dimension.

Composition of the Turnout

The success of both front-runners—Obama and McCain—in New Hampshire will depend on the impact of independents voting in the respective primaries. Both of these candidates do better among "undeclared" voters than among registered voters of the Democratic or Republican Parties; Clinton and Romney do better among their respective parties' more hard-core faithful.

While Obama leads Clinton among registered voters, it is significantly smaller than among all Democratic voters. McCain and Romney tie among registered Republicans.

Bottom Line

Obama has followed his dramatic victory in Iowa last Thursday with a jump to front-runner status among likely Democratic voters in Tuesday's New Hampshire primary. Obama—tied with Clinton in mid-December—is now ahead of her by 13 points.

Obama has gained significant leverage within the group of New Hampshire voters that Gallup deems most likely to actually turn out and vote in the Democratic primary. (He has only a small lead over Clinton among all registered Democratic voters in New Hampshire.) Obama enjoys relative strength among independents who lean toward the Democratic Party.

Obama's victory in Iowa apparently helped convince large numbers of New Hampshire Democratic likely voters that he can win in November if he is the Democratic nominee. He trailed Clinton in mid-December by 21 points as the candidate perceived to have "the best chance of beating the Republican in November," but now leads her on this dimension by 11 points.

The post-Iowa change on the Republican side has not been quite as dramatic. Romney led McCain by seven points in December; McCain now leads Romney by four points. Of note is the fact that the Iowa winner, Huckabee, appears unlikely to duplicate his feat in New Hampshire. He gained only four points in the post-Iowa poll in New Hampshire, and is in third place, far behind the two GOP front-runners.

The relatively close nature of the GOP race is reflected in the fact that McCain and Romney are now essentially tied as the candidate Republican voters in New Hampshire see as most likely to be able to win in November. A big change here was the decline of Giuliani, who has dropped significantly on this dimension since December.

Survey Methods

The results for Republicans in this report are based on interviews conducted Jan. 4-6, 2008, with 776 New Hampshire residents deemed most likely to vote in the Republican primary. For this sample, the maximum margin of error attributable to sampling is ±4 percentage points.

The likely voter model assumes a turnout rate of 60% of those who say they plan to vote in the Republican presidential primary, approximately 25% of New Hampshire adults. The likely voter results are weighted to match this assumption (weighted sample size is 732).

All results reported here are based on likely voters.

	Plan to vote in Republican primary	Likely voters	Margin of error, likely voter sample
	(number of interviews)	(number of interviews)	pct. pts.
2008 Jan 4-6	1,217	776	±4
2007 Dec 17-19	768	477	±5

The results for Democrats in this report are based on interviews conducted Jan. 4-6, 2008, with 778 New Hampshire residents deemed most likely to vote in the Democratic primary. For this sample, the maximum margin of error attributable to sampling is ±4 percentage points.

The likely voter model assumes a turnout rate of 60% of those who say they plan to vote in the Democratic presidential primary, approximately 25% of New Hampshire adults. The likely voter results are weighted to match this assumption (weighted sample size is 722).

All results reported here are based on likely voters.

	Plan to vote in Democratic primary	Likely voters	Margin of error, likely voter sample
	(number of interviews)	(number of interviews)	pct. pts.
2008 Jan 4-6	1,224	778	±4
2007 Dec 17-19	768	510	±5

In addition to sampling error, question wording and practical difficulties in conducting surveys can introduce error or bias into the findings of public opinion polls.

January 08, 2008
IN N.H., OBAMA TOPS ON MOST CHARACTER DIMENSIONS
Leads on all dimensions except "can get things done in Washington"

by Jeffrey M. Jones, Gallup Poll Managing Editor

The *USA Today*/Gallup New Hampshire primary election poll shows Sen. Barack Obama strongly positioned to win Tuesday's contest. The poll also provides important insights into the dimensions of Obama's rise to front-runner status in New Hampshire. Perhaps most importantly, he has overtaken Sen. Hillary Clinton as the candidate

perceived as having the best chance of beating the Republican in November. He has also gained substantially in Democratic voter perceptions of which candidate would bring new ideas to bear on the country's problems.

The Republican contest is shaping up as a tight battle between Sen. John McCain and former Massachusetts Gov. Mitt Romney, with McCain holding a slight edge in the *USA Today*/Gallup poll. Republican voters are equally likely to perceive McCain and Romney as having the best chance of beating the Democrat in November. They perceive Romney as the "new ideas" candidate, but view McCain as the candidate who is most able to get things done in Washington, who stands up for what he believes in, and who is in touch with average Americans.

Views of the Democratic Candidates' Character

In the Jan. 4-6 survey, likely New Hampshire Democratic primary voters were asked which of the candidates most embodied six personal characteristics.

Perceptions of Democratic Presidential Candidates on Personal Characteristics
Results based on likely Democratic New Hampshire primary voters

	Obama	Clinton	Edwards
	%	%	%
In touch with the average American	39	17	32
Has best chance of beating Republican	45	34	13
Stands up for what he/she believes in	36	24	23
Shares your values	35	26	24
Has new ideas to help solve the country's problems	51	19	18
Can get things done in Washington	25	49	13

Jan. 4-6, 2008

In a year when "change" has become the word candidates most want to be associated with, Obama appears to have convinced New Hampshire voters that he is the candidate most likely to possess new ideas to help solve the country's problems. Fifty-one percent of likely New Hampshire Democratic primary voters say this about Obama, compared with 19% who associate this characteristic with Clinton and 18% who believe it best describes former Sen. John Edwards. That is the largest advantage for any candidate on any of the six character dimensions tested in the poll. It also represents an improvement for Obama from the December *USA Today*/Gallup poll of New Hampshire likely voters, when these voters still viewed him as the change candidate, but by a 42% to 20% margin over Edwards.

Obama also holds substantial leads over Clinton and Edwards on four of the remaining five items tested in the poll. His only disadvantage comes in terms of getting things done in Washington, where Clinton is the clear leader, 49% to 25%. In an election in which "change" has become the dominant theme, a candidate's experience in Washington may be as much a liability as an asset.

Perhaps the most dramatic change in New Hampshire voter perceptions is that Obama is the candidate most likely to defeat the Republican in the general election. In the latest poll, 45% believe Obama has the best chance, while 34% believe Clinton does. In December, Clinton led on this dimension, 47% to 26%, even though Obama and Clinton were tied in likely voters' candidate preferences. This represents a gain of 19 points for Obama and a decline of 13 for Clinton in perceived electability after Obama's win in the Iowa caucuses.

Obama also bests Clinton and Edwards in terms of "standing up for what he believes in" and sharing voters' values. He edges out

Edwards when it comes to being in touch with the average American, 39% to 32%, Edwards' highest rating.

Views of the Republican Candidates' Character

McCain and Romney are the dominant front-runners among New Hampshire Republicans in the contest for the party's presidential nomination, ranking well ahead of third-place Mike Huckabee, with all other candidates in single digits.

Not surprisingly, then, McCain and Romney tend to fare best in the eyes of New Hampshire GOP voters on the various dimensions of character tested in the poll.

Perceptions of Republican Presidential Candidates on Personal Characteristics
Results based on likely Republican New Hampshire primary voters

	McCain	Romney	Huckabee	Giuliani	Paul
	%	%	%	%	%
In touch with the average American	29	17	21	11	8
Has best chance of beating Democrat	32	34	10	12	2
Stands up for what he believes in	43	18	12	9	9
Shares your values	30	27	18	7	8
Has new ideas to help solve the country's problems	18	31	15	10	12
Can get things done in Washington	39	28	6	13	4

Jan. 4-6, 2008

McCain has a significant advantage on three items—standing up for what he believes in (his best showing on any dimension, at 43%), being in touch with the average American, and getting things done in Washington.

Romney has an advantage on just one, but it is the one that most closely gets at the theme of change. Thirty-one percent of New Hampshire GOP voters say Romney is the candidate with new ideas to help solve the country's problems, compared with 18% for McCain, 15% for Huckabee, 12% for Rep. Ron Paul, and 10% for former New York City Mayor Rudy Giuliani.

McCain and Romney are evenly matched on the remaining two characteristics—sharing voters' values and having the best chance of beating the Democratic candidate in November. Romney's 34% on the electability dimension is his highest on any of the six tested in the poll.

Compared with the December results of this question, the most notable change has been in the perceptions of who can beat the Democrat in the general election. Romney fell from 40% on this measure in December to 34% in the latest poll. But the more substantial changes were a sharp drop in the percentage believing that Giuliani is best able to win in November (from 27% to 12%), and a sharp increase in the percentage who think McCain can win (from 12% to 32%).

Survey Methods

These results are based on telephone interviews with a randomly selected sample of 778 likely Democratic New Hampshire primary voters and 776 likely Republican New Hampshire primary voters, conducted Jan. 4-6, 2008. For results based on these samples, one can say with 95% confidence that the maximum error attributable to sampling and other random effects is ±4 percentage points.

In addition to sampling error, question wording and practical difficulties in conducting surveys can introduce error or bias into the findings of public opinion polls.

January 08, 2008
OBAMA, HUCKABEE SURGE IN LATEST NATIONAL POLL
Obama ties Clinton; Huckabee has slight edge over Giuliani, McCain

by Lydia Saad, Gallup Poll Senior Editor and Jeffrey M. Jones, Managing Editor

The political jolt created by the Jan. 3 Iowa caucuses is being felt well beyond the nation's heartland, causing a sea change in voter preferences in the New Hampshire Democratic primary, significant changes in the New Hampshire Republican primary, and transforming the national race as well.

The latest *USA Today*/Gallup poll of national adults was conducted in the days immediately following the Iowa caucuses, from Jan. 4-6. According to that survey, both winners out of Iowa—Republican Mike Huckabee and Democrat Barack Obama—now have pulled even or slightly ahead in their respective primary races among voters nationwide. Prior to Iowa, Obama was mired in second position behind Hillary Clinton and Huckabee was tied for second place with several Republicans behind then-front-runner Rudy Giuliani.

Obama Rising

The survey finds Obama tied with Clinton for first place, his best showing in months. Both candidates are now chosen by 33% of Democrats and Democratic-leaning independents nationwide as the preferred candidate for the nomination. This is a major shift from mid-December, when Clinton led Obama by 18 points, 45% to 27%.

Much of the shift toward Obama is because of a 12-point decline in support for Clinton over that period. But not all of those voters have gone directly to Obama; some have shifted to John Edwards. Support for Obama has grown by 6 points since mid-December, while Edwards has picked up 5 points over the same period, going from 15% to 20%. This represents the highest level of support for Edwards in any Gallup election poll over the past year.

Democratic Trial Heat, National USA Today/Gallup Poll
Among Democrats and Democratic leaners

	Clinton	Obama	Edwards	Kucinich	Richardson	Gravel	Biden	Other	None/No opinion
	%	%	%	%	%	%	%	%	%
2008 Jan 4-6	33	33	20	3	1	--	n/a	1	8
2007 Dec 14-16	45	27	15	2	2	3	3	1	4

n/a = Not asked

Jan. 4-6, 2008

Obama's post-Iowa public image includes the important perception that he is the man to beat for the nomination. Forty-six percent of all Americans, including 42% of Democrats, believe Obama is the candidate most likely to win the Democratic nomination for president. Slightly fewer—35% of Democrats—pick Clinton, while only 14% pick Edwards.

This finding is no doubt because of the extraordinarily high publicity given to the events in Iowa over the past week, resulting in more than three-quarters of Americans, and 81% of Democrats, being

Just your best guess, which candidate do you think will win the Democratic nomination for president this year -- [ROTATED: Hillary Clinton, John Edwards, (or) Barack Obama], or another Democratic candidate?

Jan. 4-6, 2008

	Democrats
	%
Barack Obama	42
Hillary Clinton	35
John Edwards	14
No opinion	9

able to correctly name Obama as the winner of the Iowa Democratic caucuses. When asked if they happen to know who won, most of those who don't name Obama say they don't know; only a small fraction (1% each) incorrectly name Clinton or Edwards.

The Republican Picture

Following Huckabee's Iowa win, 25% of Republicans nationwide now rate him as their top choice for the 2008 Republican presidential nomination, up from 16% in mid-December. Sen. John McCain also saw his support increase during that time, from 14% to 19%. After losing the expectations game in Iowa by coming in second, Romney is now suffering a decline in national support, putting him well out of range for the lead. His current 9% of the vote is his worst showing in the race since early October.

Support for Giuliani, who chose not to compete in Iowa and has been shut out of the media spotlight, has also dropped, from 27% to 20%. Fred Thompson and Ron Paul are essentially holding steady at 12% and 4%, respectively.

Huckabee's five-point advantage over Giuliani and six-point edge over McCain still fall within the poll's margin of error, so from a strict statistical perspective, the three are essentially tied.

National Republicans' Preference for 2008 Republican Presidential Nominee, November 2007 to January 2008

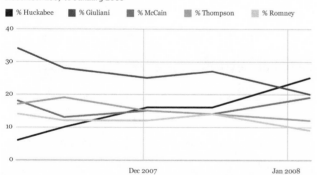

The Jan. 4-6 poll marks the first time in nearly a year that Giuliani has not held a significant lead on the national ballot, though he clearly had been losing ground, slipping below the 30% mark in November and December. In late 2006 and early 2007, McCain and Giuliani were essentially running even. Then Giuliani surged into the lead in February, and had remained in first position ever since. The 20% support for him in the current poll also marks his low point since Gallup began tracking the national numbers in November 2006.

While Giuliani has reached his low point, Huckabee is now enjoying his highest level of national support since the campaign

began. Huckabee's rise is reminiscent of other dark-horse candidates who rose from low single digits in the national polls during the early stages in the campaign to become real factors—if not winners—in previous nomination campaigns. Some of these candidates include Jimmy Carter in 1976, George H.W. Bush in 1980, Gary Hart in 1984, Michael Dukakis in 1988, and Bill Clinton in 1992. Carter, Dukakis, and Clinton all went on to win their party's nomination, while Bush and Hart seriously challenged their party's front-runners although both eventually lost the nomination. Huckabee was in the low single digits in the national polls throughout much of 2007. He did not reach double digits until mid-November.

Huckabee's current front-runner status is bolstered by the poll finding that 33% of Americans, including 36% of Republicans, think he will win the Republican nomination for president. Eighteen percent each believe McCain or Giuliani will prevail, while 14% believe Romney will emerge as the Republican nominee.

Which Candidate Do You Think Will Win the 2008 Republican Nomination?

	National adults	Republicans	Independents	Democrats
Huckabee	33	36	32	32
McCain	18	16	18	20
Giuliani	18	18	18	18
Romney	14	16	14	13
Thompson	2	3	2	1
No opinion	14	8	16	17

Jan. 4-6, 2008

The public's attention was not captured by Huckabee's Iowa win to the same degree it was by Obama's victory. Sixty percent of Americans correctly name Huckabee as the winner of the Iowa caucuses. Republicans (68%) are more likely to mention Huckabee as the winner than are independents (61%) or Democrats (54%).

Survey Methods

These results are based on telephone interviews with a randomly selected national sample of 1,023 national adults, aged 18 and older, conducted Jan. 4-6, 2008. For results based on this sample, one can say with 95% confidence that the maximum error attributable to sampling and other random effects is ±3 percentage points.

For results based on the sample of 499 Democrats and independents who lean to the Democratic Party, the maximum margin of sampling error is ±5 percentage points.

For results based on the sample of 423 Republicans and independents who lean to the Republican Party, the maximum margin of sampling error is ±5 percentage points.

Interviews are conducted with respondents on land-line telephones (for respondents with a land-line telephone) and cellular phones (for respondents who are cell-phone only).

In addition to sampling error, question wording and practical difficulties in conducting surveys can introduce error or bias into the findings of public opinion polls.

January 10, 2008

ECONOMIC ISSUES GAINING IMPORTANCE POLITICALLY

Gallup's economic data suggest the consumer credit crunch is getting worse

by Dennis Jacobe, Gallup Chief Economist

New Hampshire exit polls show that economic conditions were a major issue for voters in the Democratic and Republican primaries. Goldman Sachs' new assertion/projection that the U.S. economy is slipping into recession suggests that voter concerns about the economy are likely to increase significantly during the months ahead. Gallup's economic data also reflect this and suggest that the consumer credit crunch is slowly intensifying.

More Consumers Know People Turned Down for Credit

In December 2007, more than one in five consumers (21%) said they know someone close to them who has been turned down for credit he or she applied for during the past three months. This is up 3 percentage points from November and up 4 percentage points from October/September.

Do you know anyone close to you who has been turned down for credit they applied for during the past three months?

Yes

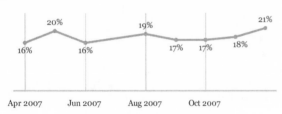

Lower-Income Consumers Know More People Not Approved for Credit

About one in four consumers (26%) making less than $40,000 a year said they know someone who has been turned down for credit he or she applied for during the past three months. This compares with one in five consumers (20%) making $75,000 or more annually and a similar percentage (18%) of those making $40,000 but less than $75,000 a year.

Do you know anyone close to you who has been turned down for credit they applied for during the past three months?

By income

Yes

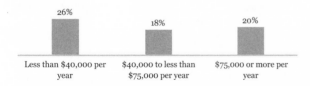

Recognition of Consumer Credit Crunch Takes Time

Most individuals associated with consumer finance recognize that underwriting standards have tightened during recent months. When major financial companies are reporting enormous losses, no lender wants its investors or regulators to see it as adding to its credit risk exposure. While well-run banking institutions have the competitive advantage of being able to portfolio good consumer loans, still, they will only want to do so if they are sure that these are top-quality credits.

Unlike a consumer credit squeeze resulting from increasing interest rates, the process of tightening consumer lending underwriting standards takes time to work its way through the banking and consumer finance system. It also takes time for consumers to recognize what is happening and for "word" of these tighter standards to spread. Consumers can also temporarily mitigate the impact of the credit crunch on themselves by turning to higher-cost sources of credit such as credit cards.

Still, Gallup's economic data suggest that consumers are beginning to recognize that the consumer credit crunch is intensifying. On the other hand, it also seems clear that they have yet to fully recognize or appreciate the consumer credit crunch. For example, in December 13% of consumers said that they know someone who has filed for bankruptcy or had a foreclosure during the past three months. This percentage has been essentially unchanged since October.

As the U.S. economy continues to slow, the consumer credit crunch intensifies, unemployment increases, and gas/food prices continue to surge, we can expect a plethora of new proposals to "fix" the economy from the president, Congress, and presidential candidates. The fact that we see increasing signs of voter concern about the condition of the U.S. economy suggests that many in the political arena—just like many at the Fed—need to give these data greater attention.

Survey Methods

Results for the survey are based on telephone interviews with 1,043 adults, aged 18 and older, conducted Dec. 3-9, 2007. For results based on the total sample, one can say with 95% confidence that the margin of sampling error is ±3 percentage points.

January 10, 2008

NO IMPROVEMENT IN JOB SCORES FOR BUSH OR CONGRESS

Approval ratings hold steady at previous levels from December

by Lydia Saad, Gallup Poll Senior Editor

Public approval ratings of President George W. Bush and the United States Congress haven't budged from their most recent December readings. Both figures continue to be extraordinarily weak, approaching historical low points in Gallup trends. While President Bush at least enjoys majority support from members of his own Republican Party, disapproval of Congress is a bipartisan affair. The Democratic-controlled Congress is rated no better by Democrats than it is by Republicans.

Gallup's latest national poll, conducted Jan. 4-6, finds 32% of Americans approving of the job Bush is doing as president and a mere 23% approving of the job Congress is doing. The previous figures were 32% and 22%, respectively.

More generally, Bush's approval rating has bobbed between 31% and 34% for almost the entire period from May 2007 through today, averaging 33%. It fell outside this range only three times: 29% in July (the lowest reading of Bush's presidency), 36% in September, and 37% in early December. It averaged a slightly higher 35% in the first few months of 2007.

Bush Job Approval, January 2007 to January 2008

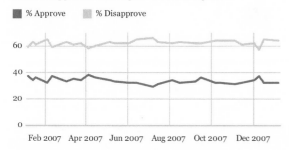

Over the same period, Congress' approval has varied between 18% (tied for the lowest congressional approval in Gallup records) and 29%, although it has consistently been on the low end of that range since November.

Congressional Job Approval, January 2007 to January 2008

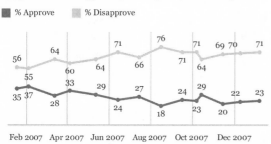

Republicans Back Bush

Three-quarters of Republicans (76%) currently approve of Bush's job performance, compared with 20% of independents and 7% of Democrats.

Support for Bush among Republicans today is comparable to what it was a year ago, when Bush's overall approval rating averaged 36%: 75% of Republicans approved of the job he was doing in January 2007 and 76% approve today. His minimal support among Democrats also hasn't changed. However, among independents, Bush's approval is lower today than it was a year ago: now 20%, down from 29%.

Bush Approval by Party ID -- One Year Ago vs. Today

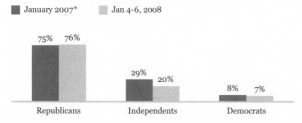

* Note: January 2007 figures are based on an average of three surveys.

Republican approval of Bush dipped below 70% in two surveys in July 2007—possibly a symptom of Republican disagreement with Bush's support for the comprehensive immigration reform bill that died in Congress in late June.

He has clearly recovered from that period, but is still less well rated by members of his party than he was for much of the period from the beginning of his presidency in 2001 through about 2005.

Democrats Not Boosting Congress' Ratings

Despite the Democratic majority in Congress, rank-and-file Democrats are not nearly as supportive of the job Congress is doing as Republicans are of the job the Republican president is doing. Only 27% of Democrats currently approve of the job Congress is doing, nearly identical to the percentage of Republicans saying the same. A smaller number of independents approve (16%).

Congress enjoyed a slight boost in approval from Democrats in the first few months after taking control of Congress last year. From about February through July 2007, more Democrats than Republicans approved of the job Congress was doing. However, since August, ratings of Congress by members of the two parties have generally been similar.

Congressional Approval, by Party ID

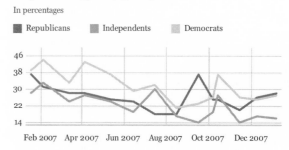

Bush Approval and Congressional Approval, Among Major Groups
Jan. 4-6, 2008

	Bush approval	Congressional approval
	%	%
National adults	32	23
Men	36	22
Women	29	24
18- to 29-year-olds	24	36
30- to 49-year-olds	34	26
50- to 64-year-olds	37	15
65 years old or older	32	16
East	24	25
Midwest	38	21
South	39	23
West	26	24
Republicans	76	28
Independents	20	16
Democrats	7	27
$75,000 and over	41	22
$30,000 to $74,999	31	22
Less than $30,000	24	29

Bush receives a higher approval rating than Congress from most major societal groups. The notable exceptions are young adults (aged 18 to 29) and groups that tend to be more Democratic in party affiliation, including residents of the East, West, and low-income households.

Survey Methods

Results are based on telephone interviews with 1,023 national adults, aged 18 and older, conducted Jan. 4-6, 2008. For results based on the total sample of national adults, one can say with 95% confidence that the maximum margin of sampling error is ±3 percentage points.

For results based on the sample of 423 Republicans or Republican leaners, the maximum margin of sampling error is ±5 percentage points.

For results based on the sample of 499 Democrats or Democratic leaners, the maximum margin of sampling error is ±5 percentage points.

In addition to sampling error, question wording and practical difficulties in conducting surveys can introduce error or bias into the findings of public opinion polls.

January 10, 2008

RELATIVES OF MILITARY SERVICE MEMBERS DIVIDED ON IRAQ WAR

About half say it was a mistake to send troops to Iraq

by Joseph Carroll, Gallup Poll Assistant Editor

An analysis of recent *USA Today*/Gallup polls shows that Americans with close family members who have served in the military since the Sept. 11 terrorist attacks—including those who have served in Afghanistan or Iraq—are divided in their overall views of the war. About half of this group says it was a mistake to send troops to Iraq. Most Americans who do not have a close relative who has served in the military since 9/11 also say the war was a mistake.

This finding is based on aggregated results of four polls conducted between September and early December 2007. Poll respondents were asked if they "have a close relative who has served in the U.S. military in any capacity since the Sept. 11th terrorist attacks," including a parent, child, sibling, spouse, son-in-law, or daughter-in-law. Fourteen percent of Americans fit this description.

Respondents who said they had a close relative in the military were asked if any of those relatives "served in either Afghanistan or Iraq since the Sept. 11th terrorist attacks." Roughly half of those with a close relative in the U.S. military since 9/11 have had a close family member serve in Iraq or Afghanistan since 9/11. That translates to 7% of all U.S. adults.

Of the 7% of Americans who report having a close family member who has served in Iraq or Afghanistan since 9/11, 51% say it was a mistake to send troops to Iraq, while 47% say it was not a mistake. That compares with 58% of those without a close relative serving in Iraq or Afghanistan who say entering Iraq was a mistake.

The pattern of results is essentially the same for the larger group of Americans with a close relative who has served in the U.S. military since 9/11—either in Iraq or Afghanistan, or in some other capacity. Forty-nine percent of these respondents say it was a mis-

Iraq War Support, by Close Relatives' Military Service in Afghanistan or Iraq Since 9/11

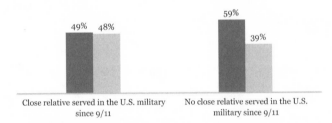

September-December 2007 aggregated results

take to send troops to Iraq and 48% say it was not a mistake. By comparison, 59% of those without a close relative serving in the U.S. military over this period of time say it was a mistake to send troops, and only 39% say it was not a mistake.

Iraq War Support, by Close Relatives' U.S. Military Service Since 9/11

September-December 2007 aggregated results

The accompanying table shows the incidence among the U.S. population of family members serving in the military or in Iraq since 9/11.

September-December 2007 Aggregated Sample,
by Service of Family Members in U.S. Military and
Afghanistan/Iraq Since 9/11

	%
Close relative served in Afghanistan or Iraq since 9/11^	7
• Spouse	1
• Father	1
• Mother	*
• Brother	1
• Sister	--
• Son	*
• Daughter	*
• Grandson	*
• Granddaughter	--
• Son-in-law	*
• Daughter-in-law	--
• Brother-in-law	1
• Sister-in-law	--
Did not serve in Afghanistan or Iraq but served in some capacity	5
No family member served in Afghanistan or Iraq since 9/11	87

^ Total combined percentages of specific family members (such as father, son, son-in-law) may not equal the total percentage of close relatives serving in Afghanistan or Iraq, or in the U.S. military more generally, due to rounding.
* Less than 0.5%

September-December 2007 Aggregated Sample,
by Service of Family Members in U.S. Military and
Afghanistan/Iraq Since 9/11

	%
Close relative served in U.S. military since 9/11 ^	14
• Spouse	2
• Father	1
• Mother	*
• Brother	5
• Sister	1
• Son	3
• Daughter	1
• Grandson	2
• Granddaughter	*
• Son-in-law	1
• Daughter-in-law	*
• Brother-in-law	3
• Sister-in-law	*
Extended family member served in military since 9/11	19
No family member served in military since 9/11	67

Close relative served in Afghanistan or Iraq since 9/11 ^	7
• Spouse	1
• Father	1
• Mother	*
• Brother	1
• Sister	--
• Son	*
• Daughter	*
• Grandson	*
• Granddaughter	--
• Son-in-law	*
• Daughter-in-law	--
• Brother-in-law	1
• Sister-in-law	--
Did not serve in Afghanistan or Iraq but served in some capacity	5
No family member served in Afghanistan or Iraq since 9/11	87

^ Total combined percentages of specific family members (such as father, son, son-in-law) may not equal the total percentage of close relatives serving in Afghanistan or Iraq, or in the U.S. military more generally, due to rounding.

* Less than 0.5%

Survey Methods

Results are based on telephone interviews with 4,067 national adults, aged 18 and older, conducted across four polls from September 2007 through early December 2007. For results based on the total sample of national adults, one can say with 95% confidence that the maximum margin of sampling error is ±2 percentage points.

For results based on the sample of 548 adults who have a close relative who has served in the U.S. military in any capacity since the Sept. 11 terrorist attacks, the maximum margin of sampling error is ±4 percentage points.

For results based on the sample of 301 adults who have a close relative who has served in the U.S. military in Afghanistan or Iraq since the Sept. 11 terrorist attacks, the maximum margin of sampling error is ±6 percentage points.

In addition to sampling error, question wording and practical difficulties in conducting surveys can introduce error or bias into the findings of public opinion polls.

January 11, 2008
AMERICANS: ECONOMIC ISSUES COUNTRY'S TOP PROBLEM TODAY
Iraq receives second-highest percentage of mentions

by Frank Newport, Gallup Poll Editor in Chief

Americans' satisfaction with the way things are going in the United States remains quite low, at 24%, essentially unchanged over the past nine months. Americans are most likely to mention aspects of the economy as the country's most important problem, followed by the war in Iraq. Top-of-mind concern about the economy has risen slightly this month, and is now as high as it has been in about a year and a half.

Satisfaction

Only about a quarter of Americans are satisfied "with the way things are going in the United States at this time," a percentage that has held remarkably constant every month since May of this year.

In general, are you satisfied or dissatisfied with the way things are going in the United States at this time?

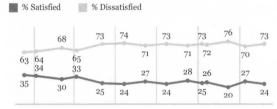

The average satisfaction level across all of 2007 was 28%. Satisfaction was slightly higher in the first four months of last year, but fell in May and, with some month-to-month changes, has remained at an average of 25% since that time. In short, there has been little lasting change in Americans' attitudes about the state of affairs in this country over the past nine months.

By point of reference, the lowest reading on this satisfaction measure since Gallup began using it in 1979 has been 12% in July of that year, followed by 14% in June 1992. The low point for George W. Bush's administration was 20%, recorded in November of last year. The highest satisfaction level Gallup has recorded since 1979 was 71% in February 1999.

There continue to be big differences in this satisfaction measure according to political party: Republicans remain significantly more satisfied than Democrats.

Half of Republicans are satisfied, but only small percentages of independents and Democrats agree.

Most Important Problem

What's behind these low levels of satisfaction?

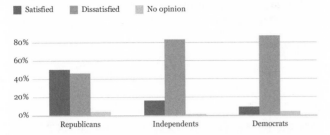

One possible answer is to look at the responses to Gallup's January reading of the question: "What do you think is the most important problem facing this country today?"

What do you think is the most important problem facing this country today?
[OPEN-ENDED]
Selected trend

	Jan 4-6, '08	Dec 6-9, '07	Nov 11-14, '07	Oct 4-7, '07	Sep 14-16, '07	Aug 13-16, '07	Jul 12-15, '07
	%	%	%	%	%	%	%
ECONOMIC PROBLEMS (NET)	38	31	31	22	25	24	16
Economy in general	18	13	14	9	11	8	6
Fuel/Oil prices	6	5	7	2	3	4	4
Unemployment/Jobs	5	3	4	5	4	4	3
NON-ECONOMIC PROBLEMS (NET)	75	74	77	81	83	82	86
Situation in Iraq/War	25	29	24	33	30	32	35
Poor healthcare/ hospitals; high cost of healthcare	13	9	12	13	12	13	14
Immigration/ Illegal aliens	11	11	7	9	9	12	11
Dissatisfaction with gov't./ Congress/ politicians; poor leadership; corruption; abuse of power	8	8	11	8	10	9	8

Almost 4 out of 10 Americans now mention some aspect of the economy as the most important problem, the highest since May 2006. The most frequently occurring response in this broad category is simply "the economy" or some general variant thereof, followed by smaller percentages of respondents who mention fuel prices, unemployment/jobs, and other economic issues.

Still, the percentage mentioning the economy is relatively low by historical standards. As recently as May 2003, over half—52%—of Americans said that some aspect of the economy was the most important problem. Going back further in time, in March 1991, 73% of Americans said some aspect of the economy was the nation's top problem.

The most frequently cited non-economic problem is Iraq, with 25% of Americans mentioning it in January. Roughly the same percentage mentioned Iraq in December and November, but in general, these percentages are slightly lower than readings earlier in 2007.

More generally, the percentage of Americans who have viewed Iraq as the nation's top problem since the war began in March 2003 has ranged from 5% in August 2003 to 38% in February of last year. By way of comparison, however, the percentage mentioning the Vietnam War was as high as 55% in January 1967.

Other problems Americans mention include:

- Healthcare, mentioned by 13%
- Immigration (11%)
- Dissatisfaction with government (8%)

Other than the broad trends mentioned above relating to the economy and Iraq, there have not been any sharp changes over the last several months in the problems Americans think are the nation's toughest. Interestingly, despite the rising price of gas, the subprime mortgage and housing crisis, and the drop in the stock market, there has been no sharp increase in the percentage of Americans mentioning any of these specifically as the country's top problem.

Survey Methods

These results are based on telephone interviews with a randomly selected sample of 1,023 national adults, aged 18 and older, conducted Jan. 4-6, 2008. For results based on the total sample of national adults, one can say with 95% confidence that the maximum margin of sampling error is ±3 percentage points.

In addition to sampling error, question wording and practical difficulties in conducting surveys can introduce error or bias into the findings of public opinion polls.

January 14, 2008
CLINTON AND MCCAIN ON TOP FOLLOWING NEW HAMPSHIRE
Both hold moderate-sized leads

by Lydia Saad, Gallup Poll Senior Editor

A new *USA Today*/Gallup poll documents the net effect of the mixed results from the Jan. 3 Iowa caucuses and Jan. 8 New Hampshire primary on national preferences for the Republican and Democratic presidential nominations.

On the Republican side, John McCain and Rudy Giuliani have essentially swapped positions since a mid-December *USA Today*/Gallup poll. According to the weekend survey, conducted Jan. 10-13, McCain now leads the GOP field with 33% of the vote of Republicans or Republican-leaning independents. Giuliani has traded his front-runner position for third place (although he is just two points ahead of Mitt Romney), with 13% now supporting him for the nomination, down from 27% in the Dec. 14-16 poll. Mike Huckabee is in second place with 19%—similar to where he was before the real voting started. He was tied for second place with 16% in mid-December, though he briefly rose to first place with 25% support immediately after his strong win in Iowa.

Romney is hanging on to his second-tier position with 11%. Support for Fred Thompson, at 9% in the new poll, has faded from the 14% recorded in December, and is his worst showing since he entered the race last spring.

Ron Paul, Duncan Hunter, and Alan Keyes share the support of 6% of Republican voters among them, the same as in mid-December.

Clinton On Top

On the Democratic side, Hillary Clinton leads Barack Obama by a 12-point margin—45% vs. 33%—among Democrats and Democratic-leaning independents. This is slightly narrower than her 18-point lead in mid-December.

That narrowing is entirely because of an increase in support for Obama since December, from 27% to 33%. At 45%, Clinton's support is exactly the same today as it was in December. An interim

Recent Trend in National Republican Preferences

Based on Republicans/Republican leaners

	Pre-primaries (Dec. 14-16, 2007)	Post-Iowa (Jan. 4-6, 2008)	Post-New Hampshire (Jan. 10-13, 2008)
	%	%	%
McCain	14	19	33
Huckabee	16	25	19
Giuliani	27	20	13
Romney	14	9	11
Thompson	14	12	9

Gallup Poll, conducted immediately after the Iowa caucuses in early January, showed Clinton and Obama tied at 33%. However, that bounce for Obama—coming off his big win in Iowa—was largely, though not entirely, erased by his unexpected second-place showing in New Hampshire.

After jumping up to 20% immediately after Iowa, John Edwards' support is back to its December level, in the low double digits. Since December, Bill Richardson, Joe Biden, and Christopher Dodd have all dropped out of the race, and at least by the overall numbers, it appears that their support has mostly gone to Obama. The only remaining lower-ranked candidates still in the race are Dennis Kucinich and Mike Gravel, both with 1%.

Recent Trend in National Democratic Preferences

Based on Democrats/Democratic leaners

	Pre-primaries (Dec. 14-16, 2007)	Post-Iowa (Jan. 4-6, 2008)	Post-New Hampshire (Jan. 10-13, 2008)
	%	%	%
Clinton	45	33	45
Obama	27	33	33
Edwards	15	20	13

Survey Methods

Results are based on telephone interviews with 2,010 national adults, aged 18 and older, conducted Jan. 10-13, 2008. For results based on the total sample of national adults, one can say with 95% confidence that the maximum margin of sampling error is ±2 percentage points.

For results based on the sample of 831 Republicans or Republican leaners, the maximum margin of sampling error is ±4 percentage points.

For results based on the sample of 1,021 Democrats or Democratic leaners, the maximum margin of sampling error is ±3 percentage points.

Interviews are conducted with respondents on land-line telephones (for respondents with a land-line telephone) and cellular phones (for respondents who are cell-phone only).

In addition to sampling error, question wording and practical difficulties in conducting surveys can introduce error or bias into the findings of public opinion polls.

January 14, 2008
GOP IDENTIFICATION IN 2007 LOWEST IN LAST TWO DECADES
Rise in independent identification in 2007

by Jeffrey M. Jones, Gallup Poll Managing Editor

The percentage of Americans who identified as Republicans in 2007 is the lowest of any of the 20 calendar years since 1988 that Gallup has conducted its interviewing primarily by telephone. An average of 27.7% of Americans identified as Republicans, based on more than 26,000 Gallup interviews in 2007. The previous low in Republican identification was 28.1% in 1999.

Meanwhile, 32.5% of Americans identified as Democrats and 38.6% as political independents last year. The latter percentage is on the high end of what Gallup has measured in the last two decades, surpassed by only the 39.1% independent identification average from 1995. The high point for Democratic identification came in 1988, when 35.6% said they were Democrats.

Yearly Averages of Partisan Identification, Gallup Polls, 1988-2007

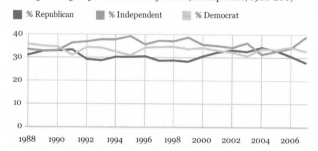

Republican identification has dropped by roughly two percentage points in each of the last three years, and is now nearly seven points below the 20-year high of 34.2% in 2004. Democratic identification also dropped by about two percentage points in 2007—from 34.3% in 2006—while the proportion of independents rose significantly, from 33.9% in 2006 to 38.6% last year.

The current inflation in the number of political independents is consistent with a cyclical pattern to party identification that corresponds with the political calendar. Gallup typically observes a rise in the percentage of independents during the year between national elections. Conversely, Gallup has seen a dip in independents in the third quarter of years right before national elections (such as in 1992, 1996, 1998, 2000, 2004, and 2006). At that stage, people are presumably more tuned in to political matters, the major parties are holding their conventions, and voters are staking out their sides in the election.

The net effect of the recent changes is that Democrats now have a nearly five-point advantage in party identification, up from roughly four points in 2006, when the Democrats prevailed in the midterm elections. In 2004 and 2005, roughly equal proportions of Americans identified as Republicans and Democrats.

The Democratic advantage is even greater when taking into account the partisan leanings of independents. In addition to the 32.5% of Americans who initially identified as Democrats in 2007, another 18.1% initially said they were independents but expressed a Democratic leaning, for a total of 50.6% Democrats and Democratic leaners. A total of 39.6% of Americans identified with, or leaned to, the Republican Party.

Democratic Advantage in Yearly Partisan Identification, Gallup Polls, 1988-2007

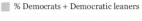

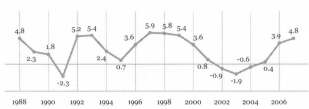

That 11-point gap in partisan leaning is the largest Gallup has observed since it began regularly measuring partisan leanings in 1991, topping the previous high gap of 10.2 points from last year.

Yearly Percentage of Partisans and Leaners, Gallup Polls, 1991-2007

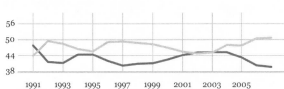

Implications

The Democrats not only maintained but increased their partisanship advantage over the Republicans in 2007, at a time when the ranks of independents were also swelling in the mid-phase of the two-year party ID cycle. As a result, the Democrats are heading into the presidential election year in a position of strength relative to the Republican Party.

History suggests that the percentage of Americans identifying as independents will dip later this year, most likely over the summer. The question is by how much, and whether either party will grow proportionally larger as a result.

Survey Methods

These results are based on combined data from 26,282 telephone interviews with randomly selected national samples of approximately 1,000 adults, aged 18 and older, conducted in 2007. The yearly average is computed by averaging the four quarterly averages from 2007.

For results based on this sample, one can say with 95% confidence that the maximum error attributable to sampling and other random effects is ±1 percentage point.

In addition to sampling error, question wording and practical difficulties in conducting surveys can introduce error or bias into the findings of public opinion polls.

January 14, 2008
MOST CONSUMERS SAY ECONOMY GETTING WORSE
Fed's actions under Bernanke continue to trail consumer psychology

by Dennis Jacobe, Gallup Chief Economist

Last week, Federal Reserve Board Chairman Ben Bernanke signaled a willingness to act in response to deteriorating economic conditions. New Gallup Poll economic data suggest that this avowed willingness to lower interest rates at the next Federal Open Market Committee (FOMC) meeting is not only warranted but actually overdue.

Consumer Expectations Back Near Historic Lows

New Gallup Poll data, from a Jan. 4-6 poll, show only 15% of U.S. consumers saying current economic conditions are getting better while 77% say they are getting worse. Consumer expectations have thus returned to the historic low they hit two months ago, when only 13% said economic conditions were getting better and 78% said they were getting worse.

Consumer pessimism about the future of the economy is now more widespread than it was in March 2003—just prior to the beginning of the war with Iraq—when 23% of consumers said the economy was getting better and 67% said it was getting worse. Similarly, consumers are more widely pessimistic now than they were in September 2001—just prior to 9/11—when 19% said economic conditions were getting better and 70% said they were getting worse.

Right now, do you think that economic conditions in the country as a whole are getting better or getting worse?

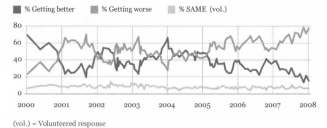

(vol.) = Volunteered response

Can the Fed Change the Current Consumer Psychology?

In the past, a change in Fed policy has generally had a significant impact on consumer psychology, but it is not clear that a cut in interest rates can cure the current downturn in U.S. consumer psychology. Lower rates may stimulate an increase in mortgage refinancing applications as well as all other consumer loan applications. The problem is that the current consumer credit crunch is not the result of high interest rates but of tighter underwriting standards. As a result, it is not clear that lower interest rates will help the housing market and/or the auto market.

On the other hand, lower rates could also increase the downward pressure on the U.S. dollar. As a result, lower rates might actually end up exacerbating the surge in food and energy prices, rather than quelling it.

Given the downward momentum of the economy, declining business/consumer optimism, the relatively reduced impact of monetary policy in the current economic environment, and the fact that the Fed is already late to act, it is going to take a lot to change the current consumer psychology. In this regard, even a 1/2-point cut in rates at the next FOMC may not be enough. If the Fed wants to significantly affect U.S. consumer expectations at this point, it probably needs to cut rates by 1/2 point immediately—or by a full point if it waits for the FOMC meeting at the end of this month.

Survey Methods

Results are based on telephone interviews with 1,023 national adults, aged 18 and older, conducted Jan. 4-6, 2008. For results based on the total sample of national adults, one can say with 95% confidence that the maximum margin of sampling error is ±3 percentage points.

In addition to sampling error, question wording and practical difficulties in conducting surveys can introduce error or bias into the findings of public opinion polls.

January 15, 2008

BLACK DEMOCRATS MOVE INTO OBAMA'S COLUMN

Majority now prefer Obama rather than Clinton for the nomination

by Lydia Saad, Gallup Poll Senior Editor

After running for the Democratic presidential nomination for nearly a year, Barack Obama has finally won the support of a majority of black Democrats nationwide. Only a month ago, more blacks still said they preferred Hillary Clinton for the nomination—as they did throughout 2007. Since then, Obama broke an important barrier to his perceived viability with his victory in the Jan. 3 Iowa caucuses, and Clinton came under fire for minimizing Martin Luther King Jr.'s role in the passage of landmark civil rights legislation.

Clinton now trails Obama among blacks by a 25-point margin, whereas in late November and early December, she led Obama among blacks by 14 points. The latest results come from a Jan. 10-13, 2008, *USA Today*/Gallup poll, including interviews with more than 2,000 national adults, and more than 140 black Democrats and independents who lean Democratic.

Preference for the 2008 Democratic Presidential Nomination

Based on black Democrats/Democratic leaners

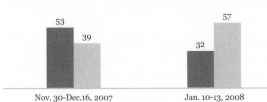

This reversal spans a period when national Democratic preferences for the nomination changed relatively little. This is evident in the fact that over the same period, Clinton had a consistent 17- to 18-point lead among whites.

As noted, black Democrats consistently favored Clinton over Obama for the nomination during 2007, although by a much bigger margin in August than at other points during the year. This makes the current reversal all the more significant.

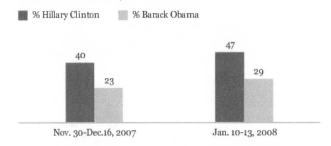

Preference for the 2008 Democratic Presidential Nomination

Based on white Democrats/Democratic leaners

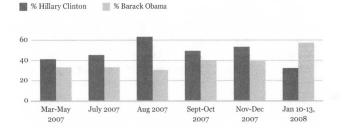

Trend in Black Preferences for the 2008 Democratic Presidential Nomination

Implications

According to the new poll, 82% of black Democrats say they have a favorable view of Hillary Clinton, down slightly from an average 90% favorable rating in November and December. Her unfavorables increased from 9% to 15%. Thus, while Clinton's King remarks may have cost her some support in the black community, they do not appear to have scarred her image too deeply, at least during the time the new poll was conducted.

Over the same period, Obama's favorable rating rose from an average 78% in November/December to 86% today. However, there has been no change in his unfavorable score; rather, the percentage of black Democrats saying they have no opinion of him dropped from 12% in November/December to 4% today. In short, blacks have been getting more familiar with Obama since the primaries began, and in the process have grown to view him more positively.

This is the first time Obama has been on par with Clinton in terms of blacks' familiarity with the two as public personalities.

Black Democrats' Opinions of Hillary Clinton and Barack Obama

	Nov. 30-Dec. 16, 2007	Jan. 10-13, 2008
	%	%
CLINTON:		
Favorable	90	82
Unfavorable	9	15
No opinion/Never heard of	1	3
	100%	100%
OBAMA:		
Favorable	78	86
Unfavorable	10	10
No opinion/Never heard of	12	4
	100%	100%

Additionally, blacks who believe Obama would win the general election in November if he leads the Democratic ticket are supporting him in big numbers for the nomination. Two-thirds of those who think he would win if nominated say they favor him in the primaries, while a majority of those who think he wouldn't win favor Clinton.

Black Preferences for the Democratic Nomination
Based on perceptions of Obama's ability to win the fall election if nominated

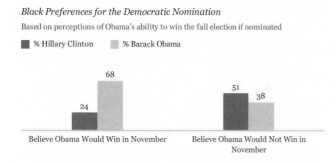

Most black Democrats (63%) think that, if nominated, Obama would win the election in November—not as many as say this about Clinton (77%), but still a substantial number. Essentially, the "Obama Could Be the First Black President" genie appears to be out of the bottle, and if Obama is able to sustain that perception through the next few states, it could be a potent factor in keeping black Democrats in his column through the primaries.

Survey Methods

The latest results are based on telephone interviews with 2,010 national adults, aged 18 and older, conducted Jan.10-13, 2008. For results based on the total sample of national adults, one can say with 95% confidence that the maximum margin of sampling error is ±2 percentage points.

For results based on the sample of 141 black Democrats and black Democratic leaders, the maximum margin of sampling error is ±9 percentage points.

For results based on the sample of 746 white Democrats and white Democratic leaders, the maximum margin of sampling error is ±4 percentage points.

Interviews are conducted with respondents on land-line telephones (for respondents with a land-line telephone) and cellular phones (for respondents who are cell-phone only).

In addition to sampling error, question wording and practical difficulties in conducting surveys can introduce error or bias into the findings of public opinion polls.

January 15, 2008
HUCKABEE, MCCAIN LEAD AMONG HIGHLY RELIGIOUS REPUBLICANS
Giuliani, Thompson fade

by Frank Newport, Gallup Poll Editor in Chief

Highly religious Republicans continue to support former Arkansas Gov. Mike Huckabee more than any other GOP candidate, but just barely. In the wake of his win in last week's New Hampshire primary, Arizona Sen. John McCain's support has risen among religious Republicans to the point where he is just below Huckabee. Religious Republicans' support for former front-runner Rudy Giuliani has fallen precipitously, while support for former Massachusetts Gov. Mitt Romney has remained constant at a relatively weak level.

About 36% of Republicans nationwide report attending church every week, an important indicator of their overall religiosity. The presidential preferences of a group this large can be significant in the political process, and GOP candidates have, to varying degrees, attempted to win their allegiance as the 2008 campaign has progressed.

This year's Republican nomination contest has an unusual variety of religions represented among the major candidates, including a Mormon (Mitt Romney), a Catholic (Rudy Giuliani), and an ordained Baptist minister and former seminarian (Mike Huckabee).

Perhaps not surprisingly, Huckabee in recent months has gained the strongest allegiance from highly religious Republicans (operationalized for purposes of analysis as those who report attending church on a weekly basis). Among this group, Huckabee has been the top choice for the GOP nomination in each of four Gallup surveys conducted since late November.

Republican Candidate Preference Among the Highly Religious
Based on Republicans/Republican leaners who attend church every week

	Jan 10-13 2008	Jan 4-6 2008	Dec 14-16 2007	Nov 30 - Dec 2 2007
	%	%	%	%
Mike Huckabee	30	33	24	27
John McCain	26	16	11	11
Rudy Giuliani	5	10	21	14
Mitt Romney	12	10	14	10
Fred Thompson	10	10	13	23

Despite his religious background, however, Huckabee by no means has a lock on the support of highly religious Republicans.

In Gallup's November/early December 2007 survey, Huckabee was just four percentage points ahead of former Tennessee Sen. Fred Thompson among this group. In December, he was just three points ahead of Rudy Giuliani, and in the current Jan. 10-13 survey, he is only four points ahead of John McCain. Only in the Jan. 4-6 survey—conducted in the immediate aftermath of Huckabee's dramatic victory in the Iowa caucuses—did he enjoy a sizable lead over every GOP contender.

The pattern of religious support for the other GOP contenders follows their overall national popularity at any given time.

- John McCain's support from religious Republicans has risen in January, particularly in the latest survey conducted after his win in New Hampshire.
- Rudy Giuliani has seen his support erode among religious Republicans, concomitant with his loss of support nationwide, which in turn reflects his strategic decision not to focus on winning the Iowa or New Hampshire contests.
- Mitt Romney's support has been basically flat over the past two months.
- Fred Thompson was, as noted above, at one point close to the lead among Republicans. Along with his downward drift among all Republicans, his support among religious Republicans has dropped to the 10% level in both of Gallup's January surveys.

Bottom Line

The short-term impact of the vote of highly religious Republicans varies from state to state as the primary season unfolds. Huckabee did well in Iowa, which has a strong cadre of evangelical Republican voters, but did relatively poorly in New Hampshire, where the rate of church attendance is one of the lowest of any state in the union. It can be predicted that Huckabee will do better in states that have a more religious population—including South Carolina, which has one of the highest churchgoing percentages in the nation—and in selected southern states on Feb. 5.

John McCain has generated significant support among the highly religious Republican group coming off his victory in New Hampshire. Whether he can maintain this support remains to be seen, and the upcoming primary contests in Michigan, Nevada, and South Carolina will be important tests of his ability to sustain this momentum among highly religious Republicans. Rudy Giuliani and Mitt Romney perform relatively less well among religious Republicans at this point. Although, history shows that Giuliani has done well among this group in the past, and therefore presumably has the potential to gain among them in the future.

Survey Methods

These results are based on telephone interviews with a randomly selected national sample of 2,010 adults, aged 18 and older, conducted Jan. 10-13, 2008. For results based on this sample, one can say with 95% confidence that the maximum error attributable to sampling and other random effects is ±2 percentage points.

For results based on the sample of 1,598 likely voters, the maximum margin of sampling error is ±3 percentage points.

Interviews are conducted with respondents on land-line telephones (for respondents with a land-line telephone) and cellular phones (for respondents who are cell-phone only).

In addition to sampling error, question wording and practical difficulties in conducting surveys can introduce error or bias into the findings of public opinion polls.

January 15, 2008
MCCAIN, CLINTON ESSENTIALLY TIED IN HEAD-TO-HEAD MATCHUP
McCain leads Obama, Huckabee trails both Clinton and Obama

by Jeffrey M. Jones, Gallup Poll Managing Editor

The latest *USA Today*/Gallup poll finds a close race between the current Republican and Democratic front-runners in a trial heat matchup for the 2008 presidential general election. The Jan. 10-13 poll of 1,598 likely voters nationwide shows that 50% prefer Republican John McCain to Democrat Hillary Clinton, while 47% prefer Clinton. McCain's advantage over second-place Democrat Barack Obama is 50% to 45% in their head-to-head matchup, which is a statistically significant lead for McCain. At this point, Mike Huckabee, the second-place GOP candidate, would appear to be the weakest of the four leading national contenders, as he trails both Clinton (by 51% to 45%) and Obama (by 53% to 43%) in these early general-election trial heats.

This is the first poll in the presidential election cycle in which Gallup has examined the preferences of likely voters. So far, the likely voter results are quite similar to those for the broader sample of all registered voters.

Based on registered voter trends from earlier Gallup Polls, McCain has now moved ahead of both Clinton and Obama in the general election trial heats after mostly running behind them—albeit in close contests—in polls conducted last year.

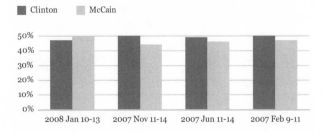

General Election Trial Heats

Based on registered voters, Gallup Polls

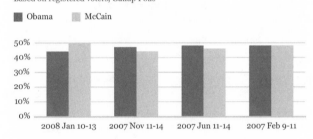

General Election Trial Heats

Based on registered voters, Gallup Polls

The Likability Factor

McCain's victory in the New Hampshire primary no doubt has helped to reinvigorate his candidacy. He now is the clear leader in national GOP nomination preferences, and his current 59% favorable rating among national adults is the highest it has been during the current campaign. As recently as August, when his campaign was facing financial difficulties and his support for a compromise immigration bill seemed to hurt his standing among Republicans, his favorable rating was just 41% and he had about as many negative reviews (42%) as positive ones.

McCain's all-time best favorable rating of 67% came in February 2000, immediately after he won that year's New Hampshire Republican presidential primary

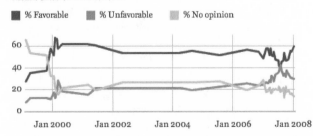

Favorability of John McCain, Gallup Polls

Results based on all Americans

Obama matches McCain's 59% favorable rating, which is Obama's highest to date. Clinton (50%) and John Edwards (48%) have somewhat lower favorable ratings, although Clinton has much higher negatives than Edwards. Views of both Huckabee and Rudy

Giuliani are about equally positive and negative. Mitt Romney is the only one of the leading candidates whom Americans view significantly more negatively than positively.

Favorability of Leading Presidential Candidates,
Jan. 10-13 USA Today/Gallup Poll

Results based on all Americans

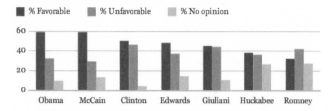

Giuliani's declining image is notable; for much of the campaign, he was the candidate with the highest favorable ratings. His ratings have declined at least somewhat in each of the last four polls, falling from 55% in November to 45% in the latest poll.

Favorable Ratings for Rudy Giuliani, 2006-2008 Gallup Polls

Results based on all Americans

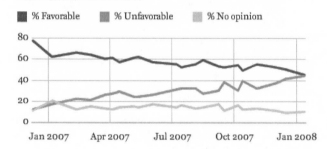

Giuliani's poor performance in the early states—because of his decision to concentrate his efforts on the bigger states that come later in the campaign—has likely hurt his standing nationally as other candidates now receive the lion's share of media attention. The decline in ratings of Giuliani since early November is broad-based, evident in most major subgroups.

Likewise, McCain's resurgence is broad-based. For example, his favorable rating has improved by 20 percentage points among Republicans, 17 points among independents, and 19 points among Democrats since the Aug. 3-5 poll, when his favorable rating bottomed out at 41%.

Both McCain (64%) and Obama (61%) exceed the 60% likability threshold among likely voters. Clinton's favorable rating is the same among likely voters as among national adults (50%).

Implications

McCain's victory in New Hampshire has not only propelled him to the front of the GOP field but makes him look like a formidable candidate should he reach the general election phase of the campaign, at least based on these early trial heat and likability data. Americans apparently love a winner and are hard on the losers, as evidenced by Giuliani's and McCain's shifting fortunes over the course of the campaign.

In terms of basic party attitudes, the Republicans begin 2008 in a position of weakness versus the Democrats. Americans view the

Democratic Party much more favorably than the Republican Party and Democrats continue to hold a sizable advantage in party leanings (see "GOP Identification in 2007 Lowest in Two Decades" on page 15). But the latest results suggest Republicans may be able to offset much of that advantage by nominating a popular candidate such as McCain who can hold the party's base but who also exhibits a strong appeal to independents.

Survey Methods

These results are based on telephone interviews with a randomly selected national sample of 2,010 adults, aged 18 and older, conducted Jan. 10-13, 2008. For results based on this sample, one can say with 95% confidence that the maximum error attributable to sampling and other random effects is ±2 percentage points.

For results based on the sample of 1,598 likely voters, the maximum margin of sampling error is ±3 percentage points.

Interviews are conducted with respondents on land-line telephones (for respondents with a land-line telephone) and cellular phones (for respondents who are cell-phone only).

In addition to sampling error, question wording and practical difficulties in conducting surveys can introduce error or bias into the findings of public opinion polls.

January 15, 2008
UPDATING THE NOMINATIONS AFTER NEW HAMPSHIRE
McCain emerges as the big winner; Clinton reasserts her lead

by Lydia Saad, Gallup Poll Senior Editor

A new *USA Today*/Gallup poll finds the winners of the New Hampshire primaries leading their respective fields for the Republican and Democratic nominations, in some cases erasing candidate gains coming off of Iowa. More broadly, the Democratic race is similar to where it was before the real voting began this month, while the Republican race has been transformed.

According to the new survey, conducted Jan. 10-13, John McCain now leads the GOP field with 33% of the vote of Republicans and Republican-leaning independents. Mike Huckabee is in second place with 19%, and Rudy Giuliani about ties Mitt Romney for third, with both men in the low double digits (13% and 11%, respectively). Fred Thompson lags slightly behind with 9%.

McCain is now the favorite among men and women; middle-aged and older Republicans; lower-, middle-, and upper-income Republicans; Republican identifiers; and, separately, independents who lean Republican. He leads Huckabee 47% to 12% among self-described "moderate" Republicans, but the two are about tied among "conservatives" (26% for McCain vs. 24% for Huckabee). More generally, conservative preferences in the race are highly dispersed across the five top-ranked candidates, while close to half of moderates choose McCain.

A 51% majority of Republicans and Republican leaners name McCain as either their first or second choice for the nomination—potentially important for him when lesser-ranked candidates start to

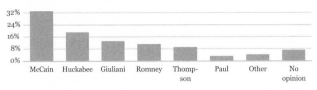

Candidate Preferred for the Republican Presidential Nomination

Based on Republicans/Republican leaners

Jan. 10-13, 2008

drop out. The next-closest candidate in total support is Huckabee, with 36%, followed by Giuliani with 34%.

The Democrats Post-New Hampshire

On the Democratic side, Hillary Clinton leads Barack Obama among Democrats and Democratic-leaning independents by a 12-point margin: 45% vs. 33%. John Edwards trails in third place with 13%.

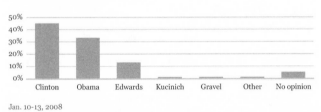

Candidate Preferred for the Democratic Presidential Nomination

Based on Democrats/Democratic leaners

Jan. 10-13, 2008

Clinton leads Obama by substantial margins among whites, women, middle-aged adults, seniors, people who identify themselves as Democrats, and among self-described conservatives, moderates, and liberals. Obama leads, and leads big, among young adults and blacks. The two are closely matched among men and independents who lean Democratic.

Factoring in second choices, Clinton and Obama are nearly evenly matched in total support among Democrats—70% for Clinton and 64% for Obama—suggesting just how nip and tuck this race could be if they keep swapping wins in the early primary states.

McCain's Big Comeback

Stepping back and comparing the Republican race today to where it was in Gallup's last poll prior to the Iowa caucuses—conducted Dec. 14-16, 2007—the big winner is McCain, whose support has more than doubled in less than a month. His unexceptional fourth-place showing in Iowa made little impression on national voters, according to a Jan. 4-6 Gallup Poll; but his big win in New Hampshire has now catapulted him into first place.

Recent Trend in National Republican Preferences

Based on Republicans/Republican leaners

	Pre-primaries (Dec. 14-16, 2007)	Post-Iowa (Jan. 4-6, 2008)	Post-New Hampshire (Jan. 10-13, 2008)
	%	%	%
McCain	14	19	33
Huckabee	16	25	19
Giuliani	27	20	13
Romney	14	9	11
Thompson	14	12	9

The clear losers—at least for now—appear to be Giuliani and Thompson, both of whom have seen their support shrink since December. Giuliani's tenuous front-runner position in December rapidly disintegrated through the early election period that he chose not to contest. At 9% in the new poll, support for Thompson has faded from the 14% recorded in December, and is his worst showing since he entered the race last spring.

Romney reportedly hoped to gain more from the initial rounds of state voting; so to the extent he didn't, that could be perceived as a loss. However, in terms of straight numbers, his current support registers about what it was prior to Iowa—in the low double digits. Support for Huckabee surged nationally following his Iowa victory, putting him briefly in first place, but his support has since fallen back to about where it was in mid-December.

Ron Paul, Duncan Hunter, and Alan Keyes share the support of 6% of Republican voters among them, the same as in mid-December.

Clinton Back On Top

The millions of dollars spent in pursuit of the Democratic presidential nomination, along with back-to-back dramatic election nights in Iowa and New Hampshire, have resulted in little net change in the Democratic race, nationally, since December.

At 45%, Clinton's support is exactly the same today as it was in mid-December. The interim Gallup Poll, conducted immediately after the Iowa caucuses in early January, showed Clinton and Obama tied at 33%. Edwards, who edged out Clinton for second place in Iowa, rose to 20% in that same poll. However, following Clinton's unexpected win in New Hampshire, her national support has rebounded and that of Edwards has receded—also to December's level. Obama's support level is the same as it was post-Iowa.

Recent Trend in National Democratic Preferences

Based on Democrats/Democratic leaners

	Pre-primaries (Dec. 14-16, 2007)	Post-Iowa (Jan. 4-6, 2008)	Post-New Hampshire (Jan. 10-13, 2008)
	%	%	%
Clinton	45	33	45
Obama	27	33	33
Edwards	15	20	13

Since December, Bill Richardson, Joe Biden, and Christopher Dodd have all dropped out of the race, and, at least by the overall numbers, it appears their support has mostly gone to Obama. The only remaining lower-ranked candidates still in the race are Dennis Kucinich and Mike Gravel, both with 1%.

Bottom Line

Politically speaking, McCain is back, and Huckabee, Clinton, and Obama all survived the grueling Iowa and New Hampshire contests, but Giuliani and Thompson are on life support. The near-term fates of Romney and Edwards seem most uncertain following their Iowa and New Hampshire losses, depending in part on what expectations are set for their candidacies in the coming primaries.

But one shouldn't look back, or perhaps even take too much stock in the present. The upcoming contests in Michigan, Nevada, South Carolina, and Florida offer fresh opportunities for more drama and turmoil in what is developing into a most interesting set of races.

Survey Methods

Results are based on telephone interviews with 2,010 national adults, aged 18 and older, conducted Jan. 10-13, 2008. For results based on the total sample of national adults, one can say with 95% confidence that the maximum margin of sampling error is ±2 percentage points.

For results based on the sample of 831 Republicans or Republican leaners, the maximum margin of sampling error is ±4 percentage points.

For results based on the sample of 1,021 Democrats or Democratic leaners, the maximum margin of sampling error is ±3 percentage points.

Interviews are conducted with respondents on land-line telephones (for respondents with a land-line telephone) and cellular phones (for respondents who are cell-phone only).

In addition to sampling error, question wording and practical difficulties in conducting surveys can introduce error or bias into the findings of public opinion polls.

January 17, 2008
AMERICANS SEE QUALITY JOBS AS HARDER TO FIND
Economic stimulus should address potential for rising unemployment

by Dennis Jacobe, Gallup Chief Economist

Federal Reserve Board Chairman Ben Bernanke testified before the House Budget Committee Thursday morning about the U.S. economic outlook and repeated the Fed's willingness to ease interest rates, which he signaled in a speech last week. He also supported the idea of an immediate short-term fiscal stimulus.

New federal stimulus efforts are likely to focus on increasing consumer spending this year in hopes of mitigating the impact of the current economic slowdown. Still, as the president and Congress design a fiscal stimulus plan, they should be mindful of last month's increase in the unemployment rate. Additional increases in the ranks of the unemployed seem likely given the results of a recent Gallup Poll showing that the percentage of Americans who say now is a bad time to find a quality new job is at a two-year high.

Americans' Views on Finding a Quality New Job

A Gallup Poll conducted Jan. 4-6, 2008, found 6 in 10 Americans saying now is a "bad time to find a quality job." This is up 13 percentage points from January 2007 and is the highest percentage since early December 2005, when 60% of Americans also held this view of the job market. Even so, it is well below the 81% who said it was a bad time to find a good job back in March and August 2003, during the buildup to and early stages of the war in Iraq.

Assessing the Fed's Potential for Impact

Fed policy is likely to be less effective in boosting the economy in the current low-interest-rate, consumer-credit-crunch environment than in many past economic downturns. Further, the Fed's actions tend to take considerable time to have any significant impact on the overall level of economic activity. Despite Bernanke's willingness to lower rates, monetary policy really can't stimulate consumer

Thinking about the job situation in America today, would you say that it is now a good time or a bad time to find a quality job?

Among national adults

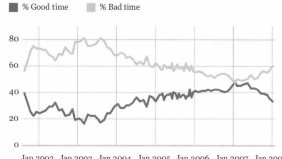

spending or prevent an increase in the unemployment rate as the economy slows in the months ahead.

Understanding this and the political pressure to take action during this presidential election year, it is not surprising that the Fed chairman supports the idea of a "well designed" federal fiscal stimulus plan. Nor should it be surprising that policymakers favor the idea of repeating the 2001 fiscal stimulus plan that involved sending checks directly to consumers—not a bad idea politically in an election year. Lawmakers might be wise to also consider including something to help those who are at risk of joining the ranks of the unemployed.

While a short-term economic stimulus plan will not do much to address the many factors that have created the current economic slowdown, it will help mitigate the situation until after the election. At that point, perhaps a new post-election consensus can be reached to begin addressing some of the major factors affecting the U.S. consumer and the economy as a whole.

Survey Methods

Results are based on telephone interviews with 1,023 national adults, aged 18 and older, conducted Jan. 4-6, 2008. For results based on the total sample of national adults, one can say with 95% confidence that the margin of sampling error is ±3 percentage points.

In addition to sampling error, question wording and practical difficulties in conducting surveys can introduce error or bias into the findings of public opinion polls.

January 17, 2008
AMERICANS TUNED IN TO THE ELECTION THIS YEAR
More have given it "quite a lot" of thought than in recent election years

by Frank Newport, Gallup Poll Editor in Chief

Almost two-thirds of Americans already report giving "quite a lot" of thought to the presidential election this year, the highest such number Gallup has recorded in January of an election year, including 2004, 2000, and 1992.

Some of this enthusiasm for the election this year may be a result of the early start of the caucuses and primaries.

First, we have some questions about the election for president, which will be held in November; that is, in November 2008. First, how much thought have you given to the upcoming election for president -- quite a lot, or only a little?

	Quite a lot	SOME (vol.)	Only a little	None	No opinion
	%	%	%	%	%
2008 Jan 10-13	64	5	27	3	1
2007 Aug 3-5	55	5	37	3	*
2007 Mar 2-4	48	3	46	2	*

TRENDS FOR COMPARISON: January of Previous Election Years

	Quite a lot	SOME (vol.)	Only a little	None	No opinion
	%	%	%	%	%
2004 Jan 29-Feb 1	58	5	32	4	1
2004 Jan 9-11	48	4	44	4	*
2004 Jan 2-5	45	2	48	4	1
2000 Jan 17-19	33	9	52	6	--
2000 Jan 13-16	32	7	54	6	1
2000 Jan 7-10	32	8	54	6	*
1992 Jan 6-9	30	6	55	8	1

* Less than 0.5%
(vol.) = Volunteered response

In 2004, for example, only 45% of Americans said they had given quite a lot of thought to the election in early January, but by the end of that month—when the primary season was getting under way in earnest—the percentage giving quite a lot of thought to the election had jumped to 58%, not too far behind where it is today.

In 2000, the year in which Bill Clinton was leaving office, the percentage giving quite a lot of thought remained low throughout the month. It picked up only a little in early February (to 39%) following the Iowa caucuses and New Hampshire primary that year, perhaps because Vice President Al Gore was largely a shoo-in for the Democratic nomination, and Texas Gov. George W. Bush was a strong front-runner on the Republican side.

There are only slight differences by party in this "thought given" measure this year.

Percentage Giving "Quite a Lot" of Thought to the Election

Jan. 10-13, 2008

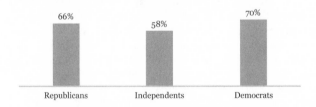

Independents, predictably, are slightly less likely to say they have given quite a lot of thought to the election than are Republicans and Democrats.

There are a number of plausible hypotheses about why Americans are paying more attention to the election this year, in addition to the early start. This year is the first election since 1928 in which neither a sitting president nor a sitting vice president is seeking his party's presidential nomination, leaving true "open" contests within both major parties. There is also the fact that the cast of characters this year is widely varied and interesting, including the first major runs of a woman and a black candidate for their party's nomination, and the first-ever candidacy of a former president's spouse.

Survey Methods

These results are based on telephone interviews with a randomly selected national sample of 2,010 adults, aged 18 and older, conducted Jan. 10-13, 2008. For results based on this sample, one can say with 95% confidence that the maximum error attributable to sampling and other random effects is ±2 percentage points.

Interviews are conducted with respondents on land-line telephones (for respondents with a land-line telephone) and cellular phones (for respondents who are cell-phone only).

In addition to sampling error, question wording and practical difficulties in conducting surveys can introduce error or bias into the findings of public opinion polls.

January 17, 2008
JUST WHAT TYPES OF CHANGE DO AMERICANS WANT?
Fixing problems is major focus

by Frank Newport, Gallup Poll Editor in Chief

One of the most frequently heard mantras on the presidential campaign trail this year has been the call for "change." Several of the leading presidential candidates have adopted "change" as a campaign theme and have rushed to claim that they themselves are the candidates for change. Barack Obama has made change the central motif of his campaign from the beginning, saying he is for "real change in Washington." Former President Bill Clinton responded to Obama's claim to own the "change" theme by saying Obama is the "establishment" candidate and would engender only the "feeling of change." Republican Mitt Romney put out a press release entitled, "Governor Mitt Romney Calls for Change." A recent news story about John McCain carried the title: "McCain Also Calls Himself 'Agent of Change,'" quoting McCain as saying, "I've made the greatest change."

Given Americans' low levels of satisfaction with the way things are going in the United States, their very low ratings of government, Congress, and the president, and their low satisfaction level with the way the government system works, the desire for change is not surprising.

It's abundantly clear that Americans want a change from the presidency of George W. Bush, at a time when Bush's job approval rating has been stuck in the 30% to 35% range for many months. A question included in the Jan. 10-13 *USA Today*/Gallup poll found that almost 8 out of 10 Americans express the desire for the next president to change direction from Bush's policies.

But exactly what form that "change" should take has been a little murky. Change is such a broad concept that—like a Rorschach inkblot test—an individual can read into it what he or she wants. One can seek a change from the way in which the Bush administration (and/or Congress) operates, a change in specific policy decisions, or perhaps just a more general change in the type of inspirational leadership the country has.

To help understand the "change" situation a little better, the Jan. 10-13 *USA Today*/Gallup poll included this open-ended question: "As you may know, a common theme in this year's presidential election has been a desire for change in this country. What type of change

(Asked of a half sample) Would you like to see the next president generally continue with George W. Bush's policies, or would you rather see the next president change direction from Bush's policies?

Based on 1,021 national adults in Form B

would you, personally, most like to see the next president bring about?"

The responses are in the accompanying table.

As you may know, a common theme in this year's presidential election has been a desire for change in this country. What type of change would you, personally, most like to see the next president bring about? (OPEN-ENDED)

	2008 Jan 10-13
End the war in Iraq/Bring troops home	26
Healthcare reform	19
Fix the economy/Create more jobs	18
Secure the country's borders/Address illegal immigration issue	10
Change tax laws	7
Change U.S. foreign policy/Improve the U.S. role in the world	6
Better honesty/ethics in government	6
More domestic spending, less international spending	6
Balance the budget/Better fiscal discipline	5
Improve the schools	5
Lower gas prices/Less dependence on foreign oil	4
Change in leadership from Bush/New direction	4
Increased morality/religion/spirituality/values	3
Fix the Social Security system	2
More help for the poor/Address poverty issue	2
World peace	2
Address environmental problems/global warming	2
Less government intrusion/interference in personal lives	1
More help for the middle class	1
Overturn Roe v. Wade/End abortions/Fewer abortions	1
Less corporate influence	1
More/Better care for the elderly	1
Other	5
Nothing/No change (vol.)	2
Change everything (vol.)	1
No opinion	6

(vol.) = Volunteered response

Note: Percentages add to more than 100% due to multiple responses.

First and foremost, it is clear from these results that when Americans look ahead to the "change" the next president could bring about, they think very topically and specifically about problems and concerns, not about more general changes in the structure or systems of government.

In fact, these results to a significant degree mirror those found when Gallup asks Americans each month to name the most important problem facing the nation. The top four problems Americans mention in our January "most important problem" update are Iraq, the economy, healthcare, and immigration—matching the top four specific areas in which Americans want to see "change" take place from the Jan. 10-13 poll. This finding is significant. It suggests that

when Americans say they want the next president to bring about change, they mainly are thinking about solving what they perceive to be the nation's significant problems. There is very little discussion in these open-ends of a desire to bring about more fundamental changes in the way Washington operates, in the process of governing, and so forth.

It is possible, of course, that Americans see these more fundamental changes in the process to be necessary to solve problems. A Jan. 4-6 survey tracked Americans' satisfaction with "our system of government and how well it works" and found that the latest results continue a trend of declining satisfaction in recent years.

Next, I'm going to read some aspects of life in America today. For each one, please say whether you are -- very satisfied, somewhat satisfied, somewhat dissatisfied, or very dissatisfied. How about -- [ITEM A READ, THEN ITEMS B-G ROTATED]?

B. Our system of government and how well it works

	Very satisfied	Some-what satisfied	Some-what dis-satisfied	Very dis-satisfied	No opinion	Total satisfied	Total dis-satisfied
	%	%	%	%	%	%	%
2008 Jan 4-6	14	39	27	20	1	53	47
2007 Jan 15-18	17	39	25	18	1	56	43
2006 Jan 9-12	18	41	25	16	1	59	41
2005 Jan 3-5	18	42	24	15	1	60	39
2004 Jan 12-15	17	44	26	13	*	61	39
2003 Jan 13-16	19	45	25	10	1	64	35
2002 Jan 7-9	25	51	16	7	1	76	23
2001 Jan 10-14	16	52	21	9	2	68	30

* Less than 0.5%.

Back in 2001, before the 9/11 terrorist attacks, satisfaction with the government was at 68%. That rose in January 2002 to 76% but has been declining ever since, to the current 53%.

So the responses to the open-ended question about change do not in and of themselves preclude changes that are more fundamental to the government system. This question asked Americans what they wanted the next president to change, and the responses might have been different had the question asked about desired changes in Washington, or in government more generally. But the results reviewed here do suggest that the first reaction of the American people, when they hear discussion of the "changes" a new president could bring about, is to focus on change that very specifically involves solving the nation's problems.

Survey Methods

These results are based on telephone interviews with a randomly selected national sample of 2,010 adults, aged 18 and older, conducted Jan. 10-13, 2008. For results based on this sample, one can say with 95% confidence that the maximum error attributable to sampling and other random effects is ±2 percentage points.

For results based on the sample of 1,023 national adults, aged 18 and older, conducted Jan. 4-6, 2008, the maximum margin of sampling error is ±3 percentage points.

Interviews are conducted with respondents on land-line telephones (for respondents with a land-line telephone) and cellular phones (for respondents who are cell-phone only).

In addition to sampling error, question wording and practical difficulties in conducting surveys can introduce error or bias into the findings of public opinion polls.

January 18, 2008
BUSH'S YEARLY APPROVAL AVERAGE FOURTH WORST SINCE 1945
Averaged 33.3% job approval for his seventh year in office

by Jeffrey M. Jones, Gallup Poll Managing Editor

For his seventh full year in office, beginning Jan. 20, 2007, and ending Jan. 19, 2008, George W. Bush averaged a 33.3% job approval rating. That is down from a 37.3% average for his sixth year in office, and is the lowest of his presidency. It is also one of the lowest for a president since Gallup regularly began tracking presidential job approval in 1945.

After receiving very strong approval ratings for his first two years in office, fueled by strong public support following the Sept. 11 terrorist attacks, Bush's approval ratings have shown consistent decline. His yearly approval average has now fallen in each of the last five years of his presidency, and has dropped a total of 38 points from where it was during his second year in office.

George W. Bush's Yearly Job Approval Averages

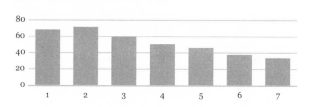

Only Richard Nixon (January to August 1974, when he resigned because of the Watergate scandal) and Harry Truman (January 1951 to January 1952, and January 1952 to January 1953) had lower approval rating averages for a year in office than Bush's most recent year.

Only four other presidents have served a seventh year in office since World War II. Truman, like Bush, had very low approval ratings during his seventh year. In contrast, Dwight Eisenhower and Bill Clinton were quite popular, with approval ratings above 60%. Ronald Reagan fell in between the two extremes.

Bush's most recent quarterly average, for the time between Oct. 20 and Jan. 19, is 33.1%, essentially the same as in the prior quarter's 33.2%. His worst quarter to date was the quarter before that, when he averaged 31.8% approval. Bush's five most recent quarters rank in the bottom 10% of all quarters for which Gallup has data, going back to the Truman administration.

In the most recent *USA Today*/Gallup poll, 34% of Americans approve and 60% disapprove of the job Bush is doing as president. Bush has not had a job approval rating above 40% since September 2006, and has not had a rating above 50% since very early in his second term (March 2005).

Lowest Yearly Job Approval Averages, Gallup Polls, 1945 to present

President	Dates	Year in presidency	Approval average
Nixon	Jan 20-Aug 9,1974	6	25.4
Truman	Jan 20, 1951-Jan 19, 1952	7	26.5
Truman	Jan 20, 1952-Jan 19, 1953	8	29.7
George W. Bush	Jan 20, 2007-Jan 19, 2008	7	33.3
George W. Bush	Jan 20, 2006-Jan 19, 2007	6	37.3
Carter	Jan 20, 1979-Jan 19, 1980	3	37.4
Carter	Jan 20, 1980-Jan 19, 1981	4	37.6
Truman	Jan 20, 1950-Jan 19, 1951	6	38.6
Nixon	Jan 20, 1973-Jan 19, 1974	5	41.1
George H.W. Bush	Jan 20, 1992-Jan 19, 1993	4	41.3

Yearly Job Approval Averages for Presidents in Seventh Year in Office, Gallup Polls

President	Dates	Approval average
Truman	Jan 20, 1951-Jan 19, 1952	26.5
Eisenhower	Jan 20, 1959-Jan 19, 1960	63.9
Reagan	Jan 20, 1987-Jan 19, 1988	48.2
Clinton	Jan 20, 1999-Jan 19, 2000	60.5
George W. Bush	Jan 20, 2007-Jan 19, 2008	33.3

Quarterly Job Approval Averages for George W. Bush, Gallup Polls

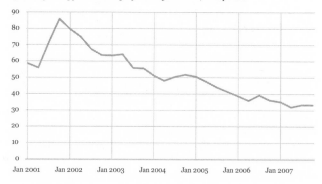

Bush averaged 62.2% approval for his first four years in office, one of the better term averages since World War II. His average approval rating in his second term so far is 38.8%, which would be one of the worst.

Survey Methods

The current results are based on telephone interviews with a randomly selected national sample of 2,010 national adults, aged 18 and older, conducted Jan. 10-13, 2008. For results based on this sample, one can say with 95% confidence that the maximum error attributable to sampling and other random effects is ±3 percentage points.

Interviews are conducted with respondents on land-line telephones (for respondents with a land-line telephone) and cellular phones (for respondents who are cell-phone only).

In addition to sampling error, question wording and practical difficulties in conducting surveys can introduce error or bias into the findings of public opinion polls.

Optimism About Presidential Candidates Being Able to Bring About Change in Washington

	All Americans		Democrats/ Democratic leaners		Republicans/ Republican leaners	
	Optimistic	Pessimistic	Optimistic	Pessimistic	Optimistic	Pessimistic
	%	%	%	%	%	%
Obama	61	34	75	22	47	49
McCain	59	37	53	44	68	28
Clinton	57	40	79	20	31	67
Huckabee	46	47	37	56	57	36

Jan. 10-13, 2008

January 18, 2008
OBAMA, CLINTON CLOSELY MATCHED AS "CHANGE" CANDIDATE
Most Democrats believe they are committed to change and can bring it about

by Jeffrey M. Jones, Gallup Poll Managing Editor

The most recent *USA Today*/Gallup poll finds that Democrats are equally likely to believe that Sens. Barack Obama and Hillary Clinton are committed to changing Washington, and are optimistic that both could bring change about if elected president.

According to the Jan. 10-13 poll, 56% of Democrats (including Democratic-leaning independents) believe Obama is "very committed" to "bringing about real change in Washington," and an additional 32% believe he is "somewhat committed." But Obama has no stranglehold on the change issue, at least among Democrats. Fifty-four percent of Democrats say Clinton is very committed to bringing about real change, and 35% say she is somewhat committed.

The Clinton campaign has tried to make the argument that the desire for change and the ability to bring it about are two different things, implying that Obama would fall short on the latter count. But Democrats do not agree that the less experienced Obama is incapable of delivering the change he is espousing on the campaign trail, as 75% express optimism that he could change Washington, including 23% who are very optimistic. Clinton fares only slightly better, as 79% of Democrats are optimistic that she can bring about change in Washington if elected, including 24% who say they are very optimistic.

Gallup asked this optimism/pessimism question not only of Democrats but of the full sample of Americans. In addition to rating Obama and Clinton, the public was asked to rate Republicans John McCain and Mike Huckabee on this dimension.

Overall, 61% of all Americans (regardless of party affiliation) are optimistic that Obama can change Washington and 57% are optimistic that Clinton can. McCain's numbers fall in between the two, at 59%. Notably, a slim majority of Democrats, 53%, are optimistic that McCain can change Washington.

Of the four leading candidates, Americans are least optimistic about Huckabee's ability to change Washington, with as many saying they are pessimistic (47%) as optimistic (46%) that the former Arkansas governor could change Washington.

Implications

Obama and Clinton—not to mention third-place John Edwards—are competing fiercely to be considered the candidate of "change." While in some early exit polls Obama has been faring best among voters

who are most interested in change, these data suggest that most Democrats believe Clinton is as committed to changing Washington as Obama, and that Obama is as capable of delivering change as Clinton.

But Americans—including a slim majority of Democrats—believe Republican John McCain could change Washington as well.

Survey Methods

These results are based on telephone interviews with a randomly selected national sample of 2,010 adults, aged 18 and older, conducted Jan. 10-13, 2008. For results based on this sample, one can say with 95% confidence that the maximum error attributable to sampling and other random effects is ±2 percentage points.

For results based on the sample of 1,021 Democrats and Democratic-leaning independents, the maximum margin of sampling error is ±3 percentage points.

Interviews are conducted with respondents on land-line telephones (for respondents with a land-line telephone) and cellular phones (for respondents who are cell-phone only).

In addition to sampling error, question wording and practical difficulties in conducting surveys can introduce error or bias into the findings of public opinion polls.

January 21, 2008
ON KING HOLIDAY, A SPLIT REVIEW OF CIVIL RIGHTS PROGRESS
Only 4 in 10 say all or most of the civil rights movement's goals have been achieved

by Lydia Saad, Gallup Poll Senior Editor

On this 23rd celebration of the Martin Luther King Jr. holiday, new Gallup polling finds most Americans hesitant to say the goals of King and the 1960s civil rights movement, more broadly, have been achieved. Just 43% say all or most of the goals have been achieved while 54% say only some of the goals have been achieved; another 3% say almost none have.

Still, perceptions of progress on civil rights are more positive today than they were a decade ago. In January 1997, only 26% of Americans were generally upbeat, saying all or most of the goals of King and the 1960s civil rights movement had been met, while 70% were more cautious.

In the current poll, conducted Jan. 17-19, 2008, whites are much more positive than blacks about the success of the movement. Whites

Thinking about the goals of Martin Luther King and the 1960s civil rights movement, do you think that all of their goals have been achieved, most have been achieved, only some have been achieved, or almost none of their goals have been achieved?

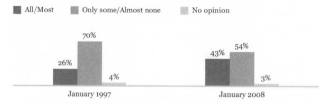

are about evenly divided between those saying all or most of the goals have been achieved (46%) and those saying only some or almost none of the goals have been achieved (52%). By contrast, only 29% of blacks say all or most of the goals have been achieved, while 70% say only some or almost none have.

Thinking about the goals of Martin Luther King and the 1960s civil rights movement, do you think that all of their goals have been achieved, most have been achieved, only some have been achieved, or almost none of their goals have been achieved?

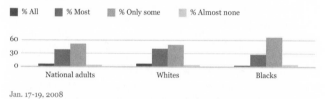

Jan. 17-19, 2008

From other Gallup data, it appears Americans want to see continued progress on the goals of King and his 1960s civil rights compatriots. Public attitudes about the civil rights movement have been mostly positive in recent years. In April 2000, Gallup found nearly half of Americans (49%) saying they "strongly agree" with the goals of the civil rights movement, and another 37% saying they "somewhat agree." Only 12% disagreed to any degree.

A December 1999 Gallup Poll of U.S. national adults found King to be tied with John F. Kennedy and Albert Einstein as one of the most admired people to have lived in the 20th century, second only to Mother Teresa. Two-thirds of Americans said King was the person they "most admired" or admired from that century, while another 22% said they somewhat admired him. Only 10% said they did not admire him.

King edged out such world leaders as Franklin Delano Roosevelt, Pope John Paul II, and Winston Churchill in the 1999 ratings, and far outranked two other pacifist icons: Nelson Mandela and Mahatma Gandhi.

As evidenced by these findings, public respect for King's life and work is so prevalent in the United States today that Americans' rejection of King and his political methods some 50 years ago may be hard to conceive of, especially for modern-day schoolchildren enjoying a day off in his honor.

In August 1963, Gallup found considerable public opposition to the now-famous civil rights march on Washington in which King delivered his "I Have a Dream" speech. The poll was conducted about two weeks before the march, at which time 71% were familiar with "the proposed mass civil rights rally to be held in Washington, D.C., on Aug. 28." Of those who were familiar, only 23% said they had a favorable view of "the rally"; 42% had an unfavorable

view of it (including 7% who predicted violence would occur) and 18% said it wouldn't accomplish anything.

In May 1964, Gallup asked, "Do you think mass demonstrations by Negroes are more likely to help or more likely to hurt the Negro's cause for racial equality?" In response, only 16% of Americans—including just 10% of whites but 55% of nonwhites—said such mass demonstrations would help the cause.

Gallup Polls chronicling public attitudes toward King, personally, start with a May 1963 survey, conducted one month after King penned his open "Letter From Birmingham Jail," in which he argued that "one has a moral responsibility to disobey unjust laws." In that survey, Gallup found nearly as many Americans holding an unfavorable view of King (37%) as held a favorable view (41%).

In August 1964, a year after King's "I Have a Dream" speech at the March on Washington for Jobs and Freedom, and a month after President Lyndon Johnson signed the 1964 Civil Rights Act into law, the picture was not much different: 44% of Americans had a favorable view of King and 38% an unfavorable view.

Between August 1964 and Gallup's next favorability measure on King, in May 1965, King won the Nobel Peace Prize for his nonviolent efforts to end segregation and racial discrimination. However, in that May 1965 poll, public opinion of King was even more negative than it had previously been: 45% of Americans had a favorable view of him and 46% an unfavorable view.

In 1965, King began to speak out against the Vietnam War, and in 1966, he and his family moved from the South to the slums of Chicago, where he joined other black leaders in agitating for an end to housing and employment discrimination, among other reforms. An August 1966 poll found public attitudes toward King the most negative to date: 33% favorable, 63% unfavorable.

King was assassinated on April 4, 1968, standing on the balcony outside his room at the Lorraine Motel in Memphis, Tenn. On Jan. 20, 1986, the United States observed the first Martin Luther King Jr. holiday.

About a year later, an April 1987 Gallup Poll found three-quarters of Americans expressing a "very favorable" or "mostly favorable" view of King; only 20% said they had a mostly unfavorable or very unfavorable view of him.

Survey Methods

The latest results are based on telephone interviews with 3,082 national adults, aged 18 and older, conducted Jan. 17-19, 2008. For results based on the total sample of national adults, one can say with 95% confidence that the maximum margin of sampling error is ±2 percentage points. Results based on the sample of 2,628 whites have a maximum margin of sampling error of ±2 percentage points. Results based on the sample of 204 blacks have a maximum margin of sampling error of ±8 percentage points.

In addition to sampling error, question wording and practical difficulties in conducting surveys can introduce error or bias into the findings of public opinion polls.

January 22, 2008

CONSUMER CONFIDENCE TAKES A TUMBLE IN MID-JANUARY

Early January preliminary index of consumer sentiment already out of date

by Dennis Jacobe, Gallup Chief Economist

Investors were pleasantly surprised last Friday when it was reported that the Reuters/University of Michigan preliminary index of consumer sentiment increased to 80.5 in January from December's 75.5. To many economic observers, this finding seemed highly counterintuitive given all of the economic pressures on the average consumer—including high energy prices, the housing debacle, a consumer credit crunch, and, most recently, a plunging stock market.

Unfortunately, Gallup polling conducted over the last several weeks does not show any sustained post-holiday uptick in consumer optimism. In fact, Gallup measures show that consumer confidence has declined even in the weeks since the new year began. Any positive consumer reaction to proposed interest-rate cuts and fiscal stimulus plans prior to Tuesday's Federal Reserve Board rate cut is not yet measurable.

Consumer Expectations Back Near Historical Lows

Right now, 30% of U.S. consumers rate current economic conditions as "poor," according to Gallup Poll measurements involving more than 2,000 interviews conducted on Jan. 19-20, 2008. This is up from 25% in a Jan. 4-6 Gallup Poll and is the highest percentage providing this rating since Oct. 24-26, 2003, when 30% held a similar view of the U.S. economy during the first year of the war in Iraq.

Even more significantly, in the most recent poll, only 12% of U.S. consumers say current economic conditions are getting better while 82% think they are getting worse. This marks a drop from the 15% who said conditions were getting better and 77% who said they were getting worse earlier this month. It also brings consumer expectations below the historical low point they hit two months ago, when 13% said conditions were getting better and 78% said they were getting worse. Gallup began measuring consumer expectations with this question in July 1991.

Right now, do you think that economic conditions in the country as a whole are getting better or getting worse?

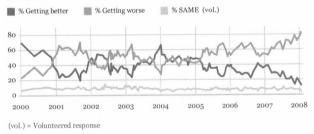

(vol.) = Volunteered response

Will Fiscal Stimulus Change Expectations?

During recent weeks, Fed Chairman Ben Bernanke has made it clear that monetary policy-makers will continue to lower interest rates; many observers assume the Fed will do so even after the 1/2-point reduction Tuesday. Late last week, Bernanke also endorsed a new fiscal stimulus plan, and the president—along with key members of Congress—put forth their ideas about how such an immediate effort might be structured. Still, the stock market continues to tumble and

current consumer expectations remain below those that existed just prior to Sept. 11, 2001, when 19% of consumers said economic conditions were getting better and 70% said they were getting worse.

Obviously, the acknowledgment by the Fed and the president that the current economic situation demands immediate action on their part is something of a "two-edged sword" in terms of consumer and investor psychology. On the one hand, the willingness of public policy-makers to respond immediately to deteriorating economic conditions should bolster consumer confidence. On the other, the acknowledgment that action is urgently needed to bolster the economy confirms the fears of many that the economy is entering a significant recession if one hasn't already begun.

So far, the polls and the markets suggest that consumer and investor fears are winning out. Of course, the impact of Tuesday's interest-rate cut on consumers is yet to be measured and it is possible that the beneficial impact of an immediate fiscal stimulus plan on current consumer psychology has yet to be reflected in Gallup's polling conducted as of Sunday night. However, the fear of a significant recession may more than offset the psychological benefits on consumers of both the Fed's action and the proposed fiscal stimulus—at least until federal checks begin appearing in consumer mailboxes.

Survey Methods

These results are based on telephone interviews with 2,053 national adults, aged 18 and older, conducted Jan. 19-20, 2008. For results based on this sample, one can say with 95% confidence that the maximum margin of sampling error is ±2 percentage points. Other results are based on telephone interviews with 1,023 national adults, aged 18 and older, conducted Jan. 4-6, 2008. For results based on this sample, the maximum margin of sampling error is ±3 percentage points.

In addition to sampling error, question wording and practical difficulties in conducting surveys can introduce error or bias into the findings of public opinion polls.

January 22, 2008

DEMOCRATS TOP REPUBLICANS ON ELECTION ENTHUSIASM

Nearly three in four Democrats are "more enthusiastic about voting than usual"

by Jeffrey M. Jones, Gallup Poll Managing Editor

According to the most recent *USA Today*/Gallup poll, Democrats are highly enthused about the 2008 presidential election, while Republicans lag behind at a level more consistent with January in prior election years.

The Jan. 10-13 poll included two questions tapping Americans' interest in the election—one asking them to rate how enthusiastic they are about voting in this year's election, and another asking them to assess whether they are more enthusiastic or less enthusiastic about voting than in prior elections.

Overall, 58% of Americans say they are either "extremely" or "very" enthusiastic about voting for president this year. That is a slight increase from what Gallup found last April (53%), though not as high as what Gallup found in the final weeks leading up to the

2004 election. Typically, measures of interest in an election show increases over the course of a campaign.

Enthusiasm About Voting in the Presidential Election
Based on all Americans

	Extremely/Very enthusiastic	Somewhat enthusiastic	Not too/ Not at all enthusiastic
	%	%	%
2008 Jan 10-13	58	25	17
2007 Apr 13-15	53	27	18
2004 Oct 14-16	69	17	13
2004 Sep 3-5	60	24	16
2004 Aug 23-25	59	23	17
2004 Jul 30-Aug 1	62	24	14
2004 Jul 19-21	56	22	21
2003 Oct 24-26	50	32	17

Meanwhile, 60% of Americans say they are "more enthusiastic about voting than usual," while 29% report being less enthusiastic. Gallup has asked this question in January of the last two presidential election years, and the current figure surpasses the results from 2000 and 2004.

Enthusiasm About Voting Compared With Previous Elections
Based on all Americans

■ More enthusiastic   ▨ Less enthusiastic

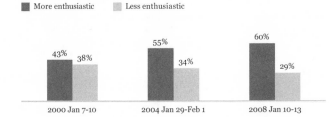

2000 Jan 7-10	2004 Jan 29-Feb 1	2008 Jan 10-13
43% / 38%	55% / 34%	60% / 29%

Both enthusiasm questions show a significant Democratic advantage. Sixty-four percent of Democrats (including Democratic-leaning independents) say they are extremely or very enthusiastic about voting, compared with 52% of Republicans (including Republican-leaning independents). At no point during the 2004 presidential election campaign did Democrats report a significantly higher level of enthusiasm than Republicans.

Enthusiasm About Voting in the Presidential Election, by Party Affiliation
Percentage "extremely" or "very" enthusiastic

	All Americans	Democrats/ Democratic leaners	Republicans/ Republican leaners
	%	%	%
2008 Jan 10-13	58	64	52
2007 Apr 13-15	53	59	50
2004 Oct 14-16	69	65	77
2004 Sep 3-5	60	57	70
2004 Aug 23-25	59	63	60
2004 Jul 30-Aug 1	62	65	63
2004 Jul 19-21	56	57	60
2003 Oct 24-26	50	48	58

The partisan gap is even wider on the comparative enthusiasm measure. Seventy-four percent of Democrats say they are more

enthusiastic about voting than usual, but only 49% of Republicans do. That 25-point gap is the largest party difference Gallup has ever measured in a presidential election year.

Enthusiasm About Voting Compared With Previous Elections,
by Party Affiliation
Percentage "more enthusiastic than usual"

	All Americans	Democrats/ Democratic leaners	Republicans/ Republican leaners
	%	%	%
2008 Jan 10-13	60	74	49
2004 Oct 14-16	65	67	68
2004 Sep 3-5	64	62	69
2004 Aug 23-25	57	60	60
2004 Jul 30-Aug 1	67	73	62
2004 Jul 19-21	59	68	51
2004 Mar 26-28	51	51	52
2004 Jan 29-Feb 1	55	59	53
2000 Mar 10-12	37	33	45
2000 Jan 7-10	43	39	51

The higher levels of enthusiasm among the general public this January are essentially because Democrats are more fired up about the 2008 election than they were in January of prior election years. Republican enthusiasm levels are more typical. For example, the 49% of Republicans who say they are more enthusiastic about voting than usual is basically equivalent to what Gallup measured in January 2004 (53%) and January 2000 (51%).

Implications

While Gallup has not been able to establish a statistical link between heightened enthusiasm and greater turnout among a party's supporters in past presidential and midterm election years, in general, the party that has the advantage in enthusiasm has tended to fare better in the elections. The fact that enthusiasm is higher among Democrats than Republicans is yet another indicator pointing to a political environment that is currently favorable for the Democrats.

Survey Methods

These results are based on telephone interviews with a randomly selected national sample of 2,010 adults, aged 18 and older, conducted Jan. 10-13, 2008. For results based on this sample, one can say with 95% confidence that the maximum error attributable to sampling and other random effects is ±2 percentage points.

For results based on the 989 national adults in the Form A half sample and the 1,021 national adults in the Form B half sample, the maximum margins of sampling error are ±3 percentage points.

For results based on the sample of 515 Democrats and Democratic leaners in the Form A half-sample and 506 Democrats and Democratic leaners in the Form B half-sample, the maximum margins of sampling error are ±5 percentage points.

For results based on the sample of 397 Republicans and Republican leaners in the Form A half-sample and 434 Republicans and Republican leaners in the Form B half-sample, the maximum margins of sampling error are ±5 percentage points.

Interviews are conducted with respondents on land-line telephones (for respondents with a land-line telephone) and cellular phones (for respondents who are cell-phone only).

In addition to sampling error, question wording and practical difficulties in conducting surveys can introduce error or bias into the findings of public opinion polls.

January 22, 2008
VOTERS NOT CLAMORING FOR THIRD-PARTY CANDIDACY THIS YEAR
Americans seem satisfied with current crop of presidential candidates

by Frank Newport, Gallup Poll Editor in Chief

New York City Mayor Michael Bloomberg continues to mull over the possibility of running for president as an independent candidate, much as fellow billionaire Ross Perot did in 1992. Last week, Bloomberg said, "I am not a candidate." But speculation that he might jump into the presidential race continues unabated, in part because his personal wealth would make it easy for him to begin a campaign without the usual rounds of fund raising, and in part because he refuses to rule out the possibility and expresses obvious interest in running.

There has been much discussion this year about the American public's desire for "change," at a time when the significant majority of Americans indicate that they are dissatisfied with the way things are going in the United States today, and when there is growing concern about the economy. At the same time, change after this year's election is inevitable, given that the incumbent president and vice president are not running for re-election.

Additionally, recent Gallup polling has assessed some of the public's attitudes that could be related to the ultimate success of an independent or third-party candidate running against the two major-party candidates this year. The data show that Americans are quite positive about the candidates running for president so far, and believe they have suggested good solutions to the nation's problems, marking a sharp contrast with what these same measures showed in early 1992. Thus, while dissatisfaction in general is high, the American public does not appear to believe it is important or necessary for an independent candidate outside of the traditional two major parties to step into the race in order to save the nation.

Is There a Candidate Running Who Will Make a Good President?

One key finding comes from an analysis of the responses to the question, "Is there any candidate running this year that you think would make a good president, or not?"

The most interesting comparison here is between the responses to this question in 1992 and this year's responses. More than twice as many Americans this year say there is a candidate they think would make a good president as said so in January 1992.

In terms of the political environment, there are, of course, a number of differences between the two years to explain the large gap. In early January 1992, an incumbent Republican president with low job approval ratings (George H.W. Bush) was seeking re-election, while no nationally known candidate was running on the Democratic side. Bill Clinton emerged as the front-runner and eventual nominee once the primary season began, which it had not at the time of the

Next we have some questions about the 2008 presidential campaign. Please try to answer each question based on what you may have heard or read so far about the campaign and the candidates. [RANDOM ORDER]

B. Is there any candidate running this year that you think would make a good president, or not?

	Yes	No	No opinion
	%	%	%
2008 Jan 10-13	84	11	5
2007 Dec 14-16	83	14	4
2000 Mar 10-12	71	24	5
2000 Jan 7-10	75	16	9
1996 May 9-12	57	39	4
1992 Oct 23-25	68	26	6
1992 Sep 11-15	61	32	7
1992 Apr 20-22	47	44	9
1992 Jan 6-9	40	41	19

Jan. 6-9, 1992, poll. This year, there is an open race in both major parties, high-profile and well-liked candidates are running in each party, there has been active campaigning for over a year, and the primary season began particularly early.

Still, whatever the reasons, voters are much more enthusiastic about the "cast of characters" running this year than was the case in January 1992, which suggests that voters' desire for a third-party candidate to enter the race is considerably weaker now than it was 16 years ago.

Talking About Issues You Care About?

Another question in Gallup's Jan. 10-13 poll asked Americans whether the presidential candidates are talking about issues they really care about.

D. Are the presidential candidates talking about issues you really care about, or not?

	Yes	No	No opinion
	%	%	%
2008 Jan 10-13	72	24	4
2000 Oct 13-15 ^	77	20	3
2000 Mar 10-12	60	35	5
2000 Jan 7-10	54	37	9
1996 May 9-12	57	40	3
1992 Oct 23-25	76	22	2
1992 Sep 11-15	66	30	4
1992 Apr 20-22	53	43	4
1992 Feb 28-Mar 1	53	42	5
1992 Jan 6-9	60	30	10

^ Based on registered voters

The 72% who say "yes" is higher than the figures at comparable points in 2000 (54%) and 1992 (60%). In fact, the percentage saying "yes" this year is almost as high as it has been in October of previous election years—a time when positive responses to these types of questions usually rise.

Have Candidates Come Up With Good Ideas for Solving the Country's Problems?

Almost 6 out of 10 Americans say the presidential candidates have come up with good ideas for solving the country's problems.

E. Do you feel that any of the presidential candidates have come up with good ideas for solving the country's problems, or not?

	Yes	No	No opinion
	%	%	%
2008 Jan 10-13	58	36	6
1996 May 9-12	44	52	4
1992 Oct 23-25	65	30	5
1992 Sep 11-15	50	44	6
1992 Apr 20-22	35	58	7
1992 Mar 20-22	32	57	11
1992 Jan 6-9	29	61	10

Jan. 17-19, 2008

On a comparative basis, again, this is twice as high as the comparable measure taken in January 1992, and one of the highest Gallup has ever measured at any point during an election year.

Bottom Line

There is no way of judging precisely at this point the impact or potential success of a third-party or independent candidate, were he or she to jump into the race. Much will depend on how the remainder of the primary campaign plays out, who the eventual major-party nominees are, and what the state of the nation is by later this spring or into the summer.

When Perot jumped into the campaign in the spring of 1992, he moved to the top of the national horse-race polls, pulling in more potential voters than either President Bush or Clinton. Perot later left the race and then re-entered it, creating a highly unusual set of campaign dynamics, but ended up gaining 19% of the 1992 popular presidential vote.

The data reviewed above suggest that the environment would not be nearly as propitious this year as it was for Perot that year. It is true that Americans are broadly dissatisfied this year with both the state of the nation and the economy, as they were in 1992. But Americans at this juncture seem much more willing to say that the current crop of candidates running in the major parties have discussed good solutions to the nation's problems and, as a result, there is a high level of satisfaction with those currently running. Thus, were Bloomberg to jump into the race, his first job would be to convince voters that he would bring to the table something that the major party candidates have not.

Survey Methods

These results are based on telephone interviews with a randomly selected national sample of 2,010 adults, aged 18 and older, conducted Jan. 10-13, 2008. For results based on this sample, one can say with 95% confidence that the maximum error attributable to sampling and other random effects is ±2 percentage points.

Interviews are conducted with respondents on land-line telephones (for respondents with a land-line telephone) and cellular phones (for respondents who are cell-phone only).

In addition to sampling error, question wording and practical difficulties in conducting surveys can introduce error or bias into the findings of public opinion polls.

January 23, 2008

AN INEXPLICABLE JUMP IN AMERICANS' LONG-TERM OPTIMISM
Two-thirds expect conditions in the U.S. five years from now to be positive

by Lydia Saad, Gallup Poll Senior Editor

Gallup's annual Mood of the Nation survey, conducted Jan. 4-6, 2008, finds a striking increase since January 2007 in Americans' belief that the country will be better off five years from now than it is today. Americans are typically upbeat on this measure, but today's level of optimism is the highest in four years.

The finding comes from a set of three questions that ask respondents to use an 11-point scale—from 0 to 10—to indicate 1) where they think the nation stands at the present time, 2) where it stood five years ago, and 3) where it will stand five years from now.

Nearly-two thirds of Americans (65%) today predict that conditions in the country five years from now will be on the positive end of the scale (from 6 to 10). That's up from 52% last January. Perceptions about where the country stood five years ago have improved slightly (from 71% to 77%) and, as a result, Americans remain more positive about the past than they do about the future. At the same time, there has been no change in perceptions about where the country stands at present. Half of Americans give present conditions a positive rating.

Positive Ratings of U.S. Conditions: Present, Past, and Future

Percentage rating the United States 6-10 on each time frame

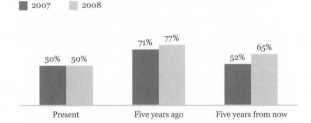

These findings stand in contrast to much more negative attitudes about the country found in recent Gallup polling. For instance, the January Mood poll finds only 24% of Americans saying they are "satisfied" with the way things are going in the country today, and 73% dissatisfied. Also, according to Gallup's latest economic polling (see "Consumer Confidence Takes a Tumble in Mid-January"), the percentage of Americans rating economic conditions as either "excellent" or "good" is a dismal 24%, and only 12% of consumers think the economy is getting better.

Americans appear to be willing to express attitudes that are more positive about national conditions on the 11-point scale, in which finer gradations of positive and negative views can be conveyed.

Detailed ratings, 0-to-10 scale

	Present	Five years ago	Five years from now
	%	%	%
8-10	13	43	38
6-7	37	34	27
5	21	11	13
3-4	22	8	11
0-2	5	3	7
No opinion	2	2	5
Summary:			
Total 6-10	50	77	65
5	21	11	13
Total 0-4	27	11	18

Jan. 4-6, 2008

Gallup has asked this "striving scale" set of questions each January since 2001. The 2001 poll turns out to have been the recent high point for public contentment with national conditions (73%). The percentage rating current conditions anywhere from 6 to 10 fell to 64% in 2002 and to 50% in 2003. (Older Gallup trends show much lower percentages of Americans giving the country positive ratings on the 0-to-10 scale at several points in the 1970s, including the lowest point of 33% in April 1974.)

While positive perceptions of current national conditions have remained flat at about the 50% level since 2003, Americans' forecast for where the country would be "five years from now" continued to decline, from 78% in 2002 to 53% in 2006. It held about steady in 2007 (at 52%) before increasing this year to 65%.

Recent Trends in Positive Ratings of the United States

Percentages rating U.S. 6 to 10 on each time frame

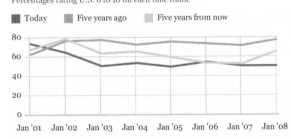

The recent boost in optimism about the future is seen about equally among Republicans and Democrats, suggesting it is not explained simply by Democrats looking forward to a new administration in Washington.

Percentage Predicting Positive Conditions in U.S. Five Years From Now,
by Party ID

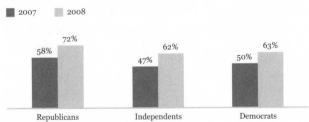

Whether Americans perceive that changes for the better are on the horizon, or believe current conditions are so bad they can only improve, isn't clear.

Survey Methods

Results are based on telephone interviews with 1,023 national adults, aged 18 and older, conducted Jan. 4-6, 2008. For results based on the total sample of national adults, one can say with 95% confidence that the maximum margin of sampling error is ±3 percentage points.

For results based on the sample of 423 Republicans or Republican leaders, the maximum margin of sampling error is ±5 percentage points.

For results based on the sample of 499 Democrats or Democratic leaders, the maximum margin of sampling error is ±5 percentage points.

For results based on the sample of 2,053 national adults, aged 18 and older, conducted Jan. 19-20, 2008, the maximum margin of sampling error is ±2 percentage points.

In addition to sampling error, question wording and practical difficulties in conducting surveys can introduce error or bias into the findings of public opinion polls.

January 24, 2008
GAUGING AMERICANS' LEVEL OF FINANCIAL WORRY
Concerns about money and jobs exist across all income levels

by Dennis Jacobe, Gallup Chief Economist

According to a series of Gallup Polls conducted Jan. 17-20, 2008, about one in three Americans (34%) say they worried about money "yesterday," with 10% saying they were "very worried" and 24% saying they were "somewhat worried." Lower-income consumers are more likely to worry about money than their higher income counterparts are, but even among higher income Americans, there are many who say they worry about money.

Forty-five percent of those making less than $24,000 annually report being worried about money recently, while 26% of those making $90,000 or more a year also report having such worries. Thirty-four percent of those making $24,000 but less than $60,000 a year say they worry, and 28% of those making $60,000 but less than $90,000 annually say the same.

Did you worry about money yesterday?

National adults, by income

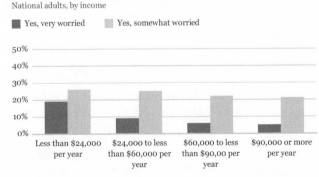

Based on polls conducted January 16-20, 2008

Worries About Jobs

About 8% of Americans say they worried yesterday about losing their job. While this may not seem high given the talk of recession and the 5% unemployment rate, people's concerns about losing their jobs tend to lag as the economy slows down and the unemployment rate increases. Thirteen percent of those making less than $24,000 a year say they worry about losing their jobs, compared to just 4% of those making $90,000 or more who say the same. Of those making $24,000 but less than $60,000 a year, 8% say they similarly worry, as do 6% of those making $60,000 but less than $90,000 annually.

Did you worry yesterday that you might lose your job?

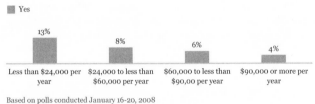

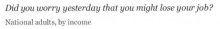

Based on polls conducted January 16-20, 2008

Will Emergency Government Action Reduce Money Worries?

In the past, economic slowdowns were often the result of high interest rates reducing the demand for credit and consumer spending. Given such an economic scenario, the Fed's emergency cut in the federal funds rates earlier this week would represent strong anti-recessionary medicine, as would the tax-rebate package the Bush administration and congressional Democrats are now considering.

Survey Methods

Results are based on 5,123 telephone interviews with national adults, aged 18 and older, conducted January 16-20, 2008. For results based on the total sample of national adults, one can say with 95% confidence that the margin of sampling error is ±2 percentage points.

January 24, 2008
STATE OF THE UNION: BOTH GOOD AND BAD
Americans mostly satisfied with 9 areas; dissatisfied with 14

by Lydia Saad, Gallup Poll Senior Editor

The national mood in advance of President George W. Bush's upcoming State of the Union address is not positive. Given scant public approval for how the nation's elected leaders are doing their jobs, and even lower consumer optimism about the nation's economy, Americans are highly discontent with the direction of the country. Public attitudes have been trending down on these indicators for the past several years, and are now, collectively, at their worst levels of Bush's presidency.

That's the broad picture. Focusing on some specifics, however, the public's take on the state of the nation is not all bad. According to Gallup's annual Mood of the Nation poll, Americans are satisfied

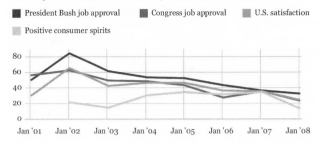

January Trends on Basic Indicators of U.S. Mood, 2001-2008

with some important aspects of life and public policy in the United States. They just happen to be dissatisfied with a greater number of things at the moment.

What's Working, and What Isn't?

Out of 28 aspects of the country rated in the Jan. 4-6, 2008, survey, a majority of Americans are satisfied with 9, and Americans are about equally divided on another 5. (That leaves majority dissatisfaction with 14 of the aspects tested.)

The most positive ratings are for the overall quality of life, the position of women in the nation, and the opportunity for a person to get ahead by working hard. A majority of Americans are satisfied with an additional six items. Taken together, the results suggest Americans feel the American Dream is at least viable, if not thriving.

Issues With Which Majority of Americans Are Satisfied

Listed by net satisfied

	Satisfied	Dissatisfied	Net satisfied
	%	%	Pct. pts.
The overall quality of life	82	17	65
The position of women in the nation	72	26	46
The opportunity for a person to get ahead by working hard	68	31	37
The nation's military strength and preparedness	66	30	36
The position of blacks and other racial minorities in the nation	58	34	24
The nation's security from terrorism	58	37	21
The influence of organized religion	56	39	17
The state of race relations	51	40	11
Our system of government and how well it works	53	47	6

Jan. 4-6, 2008

Guns laws, crime policies, abortion policies, the quality of the environment, and the quality of medical care all get roughly split reviews from the public.

Issues With Which Similar Proportions Are Satisfied vs. Dissatisfied

Listed by net satisfied

	Satisfied	Dissatisfied	Net satisfied
	%	%	Pct. pts.
The nation's laws or policies on guns	48	44	4
The nation's policies to reduce or control crime	48	48	0
The nation's policies regarding the abortion issue	43	43	0
The quality of the environment in the nation	47	49	-2
The quality of medical care in the nation	45	53	-8

Jan. 4-6, 2008

The most negative ratings are seen for 14 varied cultural, economic, and foreign and domestic policy issues. No more than 4 in 10 Americans are satisfied with current conditions in any of these areas, with the least satisfaction shown for the level of immigration into the country and the availability of affordable healthcare. Americans are also substantially more dissatisfied than satisfied with government policies on poverty, Social Security and Medicare, energy, and taxes.

Issues With Which Majority of Americans Are Dissatisfied
Listed by net satsified

	Satisfied	Dissatisfied	Net satisfied
	%	%	Pct. pts.
The acceptance of homosexuality in the nation	38	52	-14
The quality of public education in the nation	42	57	-15
The size and power of the federal government	41	57	-16
The role the U.S. plays in world affairs	40	56	-16
The moral and ethical climate	39	59	-20
The nation's campaign finance laws	26	50	-24
The state of the nation's economy	36	61	-25
The size and influence of major corporations	35	61	-26
The amount Americans pay in federal taxes	34	62	-28
The nation's energy policies	31	59	-28
The Social Security and Medicare systems	31	64	-33
The nation's efforts to deal with poverty and homelessness	26	69	-43
The availability of affordable healthcare	25	72	-47
The level of immigration into the country today	23	72	-49

Jan. 4-6, 2008

National Security Elicits Most Satisfaction, on Average

The 28 individual issues rated in the January Mood survey can be grouped into five distinct categories: national security, economic security, domestic issues, cultural flashpoints (such as abortion, homosexuality, and religion), and the American landscape (including the overall quality of life, the U.S. system of government, and corporate power, among others).

On this basis, Americans appear to be most satisfied with national security, followed by cultural flashpoints and the American landscape. They are least satisfied with economic security and domestic issues.

More specifically, public satisfaction with the nation's security from terrorism and the nation's military strength and preparedness

Average Satisfaction Scores by Category

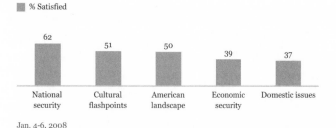

Jan. 4-6, 2008

averages 62%, with a majority of Americans satisfied with conditions in both areas.

U.S. Public Satisfaction by Category -- National Security

	% Satisfied
Nation's military strength and preparedness	66%
Nation's security from terrorism	58%
Average	62%

Jan. 4-6, 2008

A majority of Americans are also content with the seven cultural flashpoint issues rated, averaging 51% satisfied. However, satisfaction on these items varies widely, and ranges from 72% for the position of women to only 38% for the acceptance of homosexuality.

U.S. Public Satisfaction by Category -- Cultural Flashpoints

	% Satisfied
Position of women	72%
Position of blacks and other racial minorities	58%
Influence of organized religion	56%
State of race relations	51%
Nation's policies regarding abortion	43%
Moral and ethical climate	39%
Acceptance of homosexuality	38%
Average	51%

Jan. 4-6, 2008

Satisfaction with the five aspects of the American landscape averages 50%, ranging from 82% for the quality of life and 53% for the U.S. system of government, down to only 35% for the size and influence of major corporations.

U.S. Public Satisfaction by Category -- American Landscape

	% Satisfied
Overall quality of life	82%
Our system of government and how it works	53%
Size and power of the federal government	41%
The role the U.S. plays in world affairs	40%
Size and influence of major corporations	35%
Average	50%

Jan. 4-6, 2008

Satisfaction with economic security averages only 39%, with Americans negative about four of the five specific economic issues. Still, most are satisfied with the ability of Americans to get ahead by working hard.

Less than half of Americans are satisfied with any of the nine non-economic issues that comprise the "domestic issues" category, resulting in a 37% average satisfaction score.

Bottom Line

In his State of the Union address next week, President Bush will likely address what is most troubling Americans about the country at the start of 2008. According to Gallup's 2008 Mood survey, this

U.S. Public Satisfaction by Category -- Economic Security

	% Satisfied
Opportunity to get ahead by working hard	68%
State of the nation's economy	36%
Amount Americans pay in federal taxes	34%
Social Security and Medicare systems	31%
Nation's efforts to deal with poverty	26%
Average	39%

Jan. 4-6, 2008

U.S. Public Satisfaction by Category -- Domestic Issues

	% Satisfied
Nation's policies to reduce or control crime	48%
Nation's laws or policies on guns	48%
Quality of the environment	47%
Quality of medical care	45%
Quality of public education	42%
Nation's energy policies	31%
Nation's campaign finance laws	26%
Availability of affordable healthcare	25%
Level of immigration	23%
Average	37%

Jan. 4-6, 2008

includes such domestic issues as the economy, immigration, healthcare, campaign finance, poverty, energy policy, and education. (The war in Iraq will also be an important subject for Bush, but is not addressed directly in the annual Mood of the Nation's list of enduring topics.)

State of the Union speeches are traditionally also used to amplify all that is going well in the country. Based on the data reviewed here, most Americans would agree with Bush were he to tout the overall quality of life in the country, the nation's military strength, safety from terrorism, and the freedom and opportunity Americans have to achieve the American Dream.

Survey Methods

Results are based on telephone interviews with 1,023 national adults, aged 18 and older, conducted Jan. 4-6, 2008. For results based on the total sample of national adults, one can say with 95% confidence that the maximum margin of sampling error is ±3 percentage points.

In addition to sampling error, question wording and practical difficulties in conducting surveys can introduce error or bias into the findings of public opinion polls.

January 25, 2008
MIKE HUCKABEE'S CHALLENGE
Former Arkansas governor dependent on religious vote

by Frank Newport, Gallup Poll Editor in Chief

What's ahead for former Arkansas Gov. Mike Huckabee? Huckabee—an ordained Southern Baptist minister—dominated national news coverage after his win in the Iowa Republican caucuses on Jan. 3, but he lost in New Hampshire, Nevada, Michigan, and South Carolina, and has since slipped from the forefront of national news coverage.

Gallup polling conducted this week shows that Huckabee is still in second place among Republicans nationally—roughly tied with Mitt Romney, but behind John McCain by about 10 points. Huckabee's long-shot chance to win the GOP nomination of course depends on his being able to chalk up more wins soon. But Gallup analysis suggests that Huckabee's ability to do well in a state's GOP primary is highly related to how religious that state is. Based on this criterion, Huckabee's chances of doing well in Florida are not particularly strong, and while on Super Tuesday his chances look good in certain Southern states, he will be challenged to do well in the big-prize states of California, New York, Arizona, and New Jersey.

Huckabee's Religious Base

Huckabee's support is strongly related to church attendance, at both the state and national level. His win in Iowa—as widely noted—was based to a large degree on his ability to attract the strong support of more religious Iowa Republican caucus-goers. In contrast, his lackluster third-place showing in New Hampshire was related to the fact that there simply weren't enough highly religious Republicans in that state to vote for him.

For example, Gallup surveys conducted before the New Hampshire primary showed that while weekly church attenders constitute 39% of national Republicans (according to Gallup's Jan. 4-6 poll), they constitute only 24% of New Hampshire Republicans.

In fact, for Huckabee, New Hampshire was probably the worst state in which to try to continue his momentum after his win in Iowa. A 2006 Gallup analysis of more than 68,000 nationwide interviews showed that New Hampshire, along with its neighboring state of Vermont, had the lowest level of self-reported church attendance of any state measured. The average in the United States was 42% weekly or almost every week church attendance. Only 24% of New Hampshire residents said they attended weekly or almost every week. (Iowa was above the average, at 46%.)

Indeed, New Hampshire exit polls showed that while Huckabee had some strength among Republicans who were frequent church attenders, he had very little among anyone else. Huckabee got 34% of the vote among those who said they attended more than once a week, winning among that group. He received 21% among those who attended once a week—somewhat behind McCain and Romney. Huckabee received only 6% among the rest.

South Carolina was a different story, with the highest estimated church attendance of any state in the union. Sure enough, Huckabee last week came in a strong second in that state, three points behind McCain. The Edison-Mitofsky exit poll conducted after South Carolina voting last Saturday showed that among weekly church attenders, Huckabee beat McCain by a 43% to 27% margin. Still, Huckabee's margin among this religious group of Republicans was not high enough to offset McCain's performance among those who were less religious, resulting in Huckabee's 3-point loss.

Nevada has one of the lowest rates of average church attendance in the United States, and Huckabee tied for fourth in that state's caucuses, with 8% of the vote, although he did not actively campaign there.

Florida's church attendance is slightly below average at 39%, so Huckabee—everything else being equal—wouldn't be predicted to do particularly well there. (Maine, with one of the lowest church attendance averages in the country, has caucuses Feb. 1. Huckabee certainly will not do well in that state.)

Five of the Super Tuesday states—Alabama, Arkansas, Georgia, Tennessee, and Utah—have average church attendance levels above 50%, well ahead of the national average. Except for Utah, which should belong to Mitt Romney given the Mormon connection, these states could be fertile territory for the Huckabee campaign.

Even if Huckabee does well in the Southern states on Feb. 5, however, the results will most likely be overwhelmed by the attention given to the delegate-rich states of California, New York, Arizona, Illinois, and New Jersey. Of these five, Illinois ties the national average on church attendance, while the other four are all well below average. And, of course, Arizona is home to McCain, further diminishing Huckabee's chances in that state.

Implications

Highly religious Republicans comprise Huckabee's main source of voting strength. He is an ordained Baptist minister who went to a Baptist college in Arkansas and attended Southwestern Baptist Theological Seminary in Fort Worth, Texas. He has been able to parlay that background into a strong appeal to religious Republicans around the country, which worked well in the more religious state of Iowa. But that candidate positioning works less well in states that have below-average levels of religiosity.

Huckabee and his advisers are no doubt aware of these realities, and have tried to expand his appeal beyond moral and values issues—talking instead about taxes and emphasizing a more general populist message compatible with his working-class background. At the same time, Huckabee's ability to win continues to depend on his ability to activate religious voters, something he was not able to do at a sufficiently high level in South Carolina to gain a victory.

A Gallup analysis of church attendance levels in forthcoming primary states suggests that—everything else being equal—Huckabee will have a hard time doing well in Florida, and that he will be deeply challenged in the big Super Tuesday states like New York, California, Arizona, and New Jersey, all of which have below-average church attendance levels.

Survey Methods

The results discussed in this article are based on Gallup Poll interviewing conducted in January in New Hampshire and at the national level, as well as on exit polls conducted by Edison Media Research and Mitofsky International for a consortium of media outlets. State church attendance estimates are based on an aggregate of Gallup Poll interviewing conducted in 2004 through 2006.

January 25, 2008

STATE OF THE UNION: COMPARING SATISFACTION 2001 TO 2008

Steepest decline in satisfaction in regard to state of the economy

by Jeffrey M. Jones, Gallup Poll Managing Editor

As George W. Bush prepares to address the nation Monday for the 2008 State of the Union address, he will find an American public that is less satisfied with the state of nation in many specific areas than it was just before he took office in 2001. The greatest drops in national satisfaction over the past seven years concern the state of the economy and the United States' role in world affairs. Americans are also less satisfied with the way government works than they were just before Bush was inaugurated as president. But there are some areas in which satisfaction has increased over the course of the Bush presidency, including taxes, gun laws, and the strength of the military.

These results are based on a comparison of data from Gallup's annual Mood of the Nation survey, conducted each January since 2001. Each year, Gallup measures public satisfaction in each of 28 specific areas of U.S. society or policy (an item on security from terrorism was added in 2002). This year's poll was conducted Jan. 4-6, 2008. For a complete discussion of this year's results, please see "State of the Union: Both Good and Bad."

It would be reasonable to expect a decline in satisfaction in most areas, since just 24% of Americans are satisfied with the way things are going in the United States at this time, compared with 56% in mid-January 2001. But there have been significant decreases in reported satisfaction in only about half (13) of the 27 issue areas measured in both surveys.

Items on Which Americans' Satisfaction Ratings Have Declined, 2001 to 2008

	January 2001	January 2008	Change
	%	%	Pct. pts.
Availability of affordable healthcare	29	25	-4
Nation's efforts to deal with poverty	30	26	-4
Social Security and Medicare systems	38	31	-7
Overall quality of life	89	82	-7
Influence of organized religion	64	56	-8
Opportunity to get ahead by working hard	76	68	-8
Quality of the environment	56	47	-9
Level of immigration	32	23	-9
Size and power of the federal government	50	41	-9
Size and influence of major corporations	48	35	-13
Our system of government and how it works	68	53	-15
The role the U.S. plays in world affairs	61	40	-21
State of the nation's economy	68	36	-32

The steepest decline in satisfaction has occurred with the state of the nation's economy, which has dropped from 68% in 2001 to 36% today. That 2001 figure is the highest level of satisfaction Gallup has measured during the eight-year history of the Mood of the Nation poll, and the current number is one of the lowest. It's conceivable that economic satisfaction could have dropped even further since the poll was conducted, given the intense focus on the nation's economic problems in the past two weeks.

Americans are also considerably less satisfied with the role the United States plays in world affairs—just 40% are satisfied today, compared with 61% in 2001. Much of that decline could be attributed to United States' war with Iraq. Evidence of declining satisfaction on this measure was first apparent in early 2003, during the run-up to the war, and it has further eroded since that time.

Satisfaction with the government has declined, in terms of both how the system works (down 15 points) and the size and power of the government (down 9 points). The other item showing a double-digit decline in satisfaction is "the size and influence of major corporations," down 13 points since 2001.

Immigration has been a major public issue in the last several years. The public was not overly satisfied with the level of immigration back in 2001 (32%), but is less satisfied today (23%).

There are six areas in which public satisfaction is significantly higher now than in 2001. The biggest change in any single area is for the nation's gun laws, with which 48% are now satisfied compared with 38% seven years ago. While Americans have always been somewhat reluctant to express satisfaction with the amount they pay in federal taxes, they are more likely to do so today than they were in 2001. Bush has pushed through two major tax cuts during his presidency (the poll was conducted before the administration's recent proposals to provide tax relief to stimulate the economy). Americans also show increased satisfaction with U.S. military strength, race relations, and the standing of women and minorities.

Items on Which Americans' Satisfaction Ratings Have Increased, 2001 to 2008

	January 2001	January 2008	Change
	%	%	Pct. pts.
Nation's laws or policies on guns	38	48	+10
Amount Americans pay in federal taxes	26	34	+8
State of race relations	44	51	+7
Nation's military strength and preparedness	61	66	+5
Position of blacks and other racial minorities	53	58	+5
Position of women	67	72	+5

In the remaining eight areas, Americans are about as satisfied now as they were in 2001. Some have shown a very slight increase, including the moral climate, acceptance of homosexuality, campaign finance, crime, and education. The quality of medical care and energy policy are down just slightly from where they were seven years ago.

The fact that there has been little change in satisfaction in some of the areas could be considered a disappointment from the standpoint that major legislative initiatives in education and energy were passed during Bush's tenure. One could argue, however, that satisfaction levels could potentially be lower (rather than stagnant) if this legislation had not been passed.

Items on Which Americans' Satisfaction Ratings Have Stayed Relatively Constant, 2001 to 2008

	January 2001	January 2008	Change
	%	%	Pct. pts.
Moral and ethical climate	36	39	+3
Acceptance of homosexuality	35	38	+3
Nation's campaign finance laws	23	26	+3
Nation's policies to reduce or control crime	45	48	+3
Quality of public education	40	42	+2
Nation's policies regarding abortion	43	43	0
Nation's energy policies	32	31	-1
Quality of medical care	48	45	-3

Implications

Considering the overall drop in national satisfaction since 2001—not to mention Bush's low approval ratings—the fact that Americans are

not currently more dissatisfied across all policy or societal areas is notable. However, it should be pointed out that most items reported here saw increased satisfaction ratings between 2001 and 2002, following the rally in government support post-9/11. Thus, the 2001 to 2008 comparison may indicate a slightly lower degree of change over the course of the Bush presidency than a 2002 to 2008 comparison would suggest.

Survey Methods

These results are based on telephone interviews with a randomly selected national sample of 1,023 adults, aged 18 and older, conducted Jan. 4-6, 2008. For results based on this sample, one can say with 95% confidence that the maximum error attributable to sampling and other random effects is ±3 percentage points.

Interviews are conducted with respondents on land-line telephones (for respondents with a land-line telephone) and cellular phones (for respondents who are cell-phone only).

In addition to sampling error, question wording and practical difficulties in conducting surveys can introduce error or bias into the findings of public opinion polls.

January 31, 2008
RACE, ETHNICITY SPLIT DEMOCRATIC VOTE PATTERNS
Clinton does well among Hispanics, Obama among blacks

by Frank Newport, Gallup Poll Editor in Chief

A review of candidate support patterns from Gallup Poll Daily tracking interviews conducted over the month of January underscores the significant racial and ethnic divide in the Democratic Party's nominating process this year. Barack Obama is now beating Hillary Clinton by a 2-to-1 margin among black Democrats nationally. Clinton, on the other hand, is beating Obama by almost 30 points among Hispanic Democrats.

Black Democrats

There is a major divide in the Democratic race for president between black Democrats and white Democrats. Blacks throughout the month of January have consistently supported Obama over Clinton by roughly a 2-to-1 margin. In an aggregate of black Democratic voters based on interviewing conducted Jan. 23-29, Obama received 60% of the black vote compared to Hillary Clinton's 29%.

Support for Democratic Candidates, Among Black Democrats

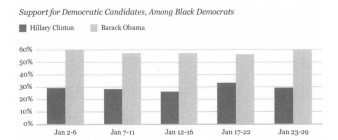

Hispanic Democrats

Clinton has enjoyed a strong positioning in support from Hispanic Democrats. In the recent Jan. 23-29 aggregate, 57% of Hispanics supported Clinton compared to 29% who supported Obama. Gallup's definition of "Hispanics" used in this analysis is the group of respondents who answered "yes" to the question: "Are you, yourself, of Hispanic origin or descent, such as Mexican, Puerto Rican, Cuban, or other Spanish background?"

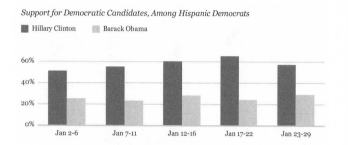

Support for Democratic Candidates, Among Hispanic Democrats

Implications

This race is the first in U.S. history in which a black candidate is a leader in the race for his party's nomination this deep into the process. Although both Bill and Hillary Clinton have enjoyed strong support in the black community over the years, these data demonstrate conclusively that Obama has been able to gain the allegiance of a clear majority of black Democratic voters throughout this month. The level of that support has varied some from week to week, but Obama has a 2-to-1 margin over Clinton among black Democrats in the latest Gallup aggregate of interviews, conducted from Jan. 23 to Jan. 29.

Obama's strong support was evident in his overwhelming victory in South Carolina, where exit polls showed him receiving up to 80% of the black vote. The vote of black Democrats promises to be significant in many states—and congressional districts within states—in next Tuesday's crucial Super Tuesday primaries.

At the same time, Clinton has strong support from Hispanic Democrats across the country. In the Jan. 23-29 aggregate, Clinton has almost a 30-point margin over Obama among Hispanics. The Hispanic vote—as is the case for the black vote—will be crucially important in some states voting on Tuesday and in some districts within states with high percentages of Hispanic voters.

It should be noted, of course, that the candidates' relative positioning this year has been subject to substantial change over time. In the broad analysis, daily Gallup tracking shows that Obama is catching up with Clinton after his victory in South Carolina last Saturday and after high-profile endorsements of members of the Kennedy family. It is possible, therefore, that Obama's support among blacks could climb even higher between now and next Tuesday, and that Clinton's support among Hispanics could weaken.

Survey Methods

These results are based on telephone interviews with randomly selected samples of 1,081 Hispanic Democratic voters and 1,520 black Democratic voters interviewed between Jan. 2 and Jan. 29, 2008. These interviews are part of the Gallup Poll Daily tracking project, involving independent random samples of the U.S. adult population conducted on a daily basis. For results based on each aggregate of Hispanic and black voters, one can say with 95% confidence that the maximum error attributable to sampling and other random effects is ±6 percentage points.

Interviews are conducted with respondents on land-line telephones (for respondents with a land-line telephone) and cellular phones (for respondents who are cell-phone only).

In addition to sampling error, question wording and practical difficulties in conducting surveys can introduce error or bias into the findings of public opinion polls.

February 01, 2008

HILLARY CLINTON'S GENDER ADVANTAGE OVER OBAMA NARROWS

Clinton's lead over Obama declines disproportionately among women

by Frank Newport, Gallup Poll Editor in Chief and Jeffrey M. Jones, Managing Editor

Sen. Hillary Clinton, the first woman to become a front-runner for her party's presidential nomination, has enjoyed disproportionately strong support from female voters. For example, an analysis of 11,794 interviews conducted with Democratic voters since Jan. 2 of this year shows that Clinton receives the vote of 48% of women, compared to 38% of men.

But in recent days, the overall gap between Clinton and her only remaining serious competitor, Sen. Barack Obama, has been closing, and an analysis of the patterns of vote choice by gender shows that Obama's gains over the last 10 days have come disproportionately among women. Clinton has been losing more support from women than from men, in essence moving closer to a point where the "gender playing field" has been leveled.

The accompanying table displays the trend in vote choice between Clinton and Obama by gender for the three-day rolling averages of polls conducted over the last 10 days. Comparing the three-day average of polls conducted Jan. 18-20 to the three-day average of polls conducted Jan. 28-30 shows that while Clinton's level of support among men has essentially stayed the same, she has lost 8 points among women. At the same time, Obama has gained 6 points among men, but has gained even more—13 points—among women.

Support for Clinton and Obama Among Democratic Voters, by Gender
Based on Gallup Poll Daily tracking data

	Clinton, men	Obama, men	Clinton, women	Obama, women
	%	%	%	%
Jan 28-30	40	40	46	37
Jan 27-29	36	37	47	36
Jan 26-28	36	39	50	30
Jan 25-27	35	38	50	29
Jan 24-26	40	36	48	30
Jan 23-25	44	32	49	32
Jan 22-24	43	33	51	28
Jan 20, 22-23	42	34	53	28
Jan 19-20, 22	36	36	53	25
Jan 18-20	41	34	54	24

Whereas there was a 13-point difference between female and male support for Clinton in the Jan. 18-20 interviewing, there is now just a 6-point gap. And whereas Obama was operating with a 10-point deficit among women compared to his support among men roughly 10 days ago, that gender gap in support for Obama is now just 3 points. In general, the patterns of support for the two candidates by gender are much closer to one another than they were just 10 days ago. Gender now appears to make less of a difference.

Support for Clinton Minus Support for Obama, by Gender
Three-day rolling averages
Differences in percentage points

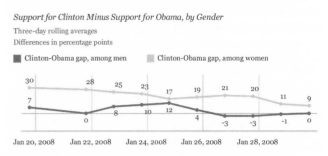

The narrowing of the race by gender is apparent in most key subgroups of women, including by age, race, education, and marital status.

Implications

The major trend evident in the Gallup Poll Daily tracking data over the last 10 days has been the narrowing of the race for the Democratic nomination. Obama has been gradually chipping away at Clinton's lead, to the point where he trails her by just a few points.

A detailed analysis of the patterns evident in the trend data over the last 10 days shows that Clinton's loss of support has occurred disproportionately among Democratic women. While Clinton is still supported by a higher percentage of Democratic women than Democratic men, the difference in that gender gap has shrunk from 13 points in interviews conducted Jan. 18-20 to just 6 points in Jan. 28-30 polling. Most of the change is because of a drop in support for Clinton among women (8 points), rather than an increase in support among men.

Clinton is the first female to become a major party's front-running candidate for the presidential nomination, and her particular appeal to female voters has long been considered one of her political strengths. If Obama continues to increase his appeal to women to the point where Clinton's gender gap is neutralized, she will have lost one of her most reliable bases of support going into next week's all-important Super Tuesday vote.

Survey Methods

These results are based on combined three-day rolling averages of Democratic voters. Each rolling average consists of data from interviews with approximately 1,200 national Democratic voters, 18 and older. For results based on these samples, one can say with 95% confidence that the maximum error attributable to sampling and other random effects is ±3 percentage points.

Each daily rolling average consists of interviews with approximately 600 male Democratic voters and 600 female Democratic voters. For results based on these samples, the maximum margin of sampling error is ±4 percentage points.

Interviews are conducted with respondents on land-line telephones (for respondents with a land-line telephone) and cellular phones (for respondents who are cell-phone only).

In addition to sampling error, question wording and practical difficulties in conducting surveys can introduce error or bias into the findings of public opinion polls.

February 01, 2008

ONE IN SIX AMERICANS GAMBLE ON SPORTS

State lotteries are most common form of gambling

by Jeffrey M. Jones, Gallup Poll Managing Editor

The Super Bowl is set to kick off this Sunday. Super Bowl Sunday is not only a big day for football fans, but also for TV watchers, partygoers, and, of course, gamblers. According to Gallup's annual Lifestyle Poll, 17% of Americans report gambling on professional sports in the past 12 months—either by betting on the outcome of a specific game or by participating in an office pool around a sporting event.

Analysis of the data from the Dec. 6-9 poll finds that four demographic characteristics are related to one's propensity to gamble on professional sports: gender, age, income, and education.

Men (22%) are nearly twice as likely as women (13%) to gamble on professional sports, probably not surprising since men in general are more likely to be sports fans.

Younger Americans are much more likely to gamble on sports than older Americans—26% of 18- to 34-year-olds do so, compared with 18% of 35- to 54-year-olds and just 11% of those aged 55 and older.

Just 6% of those living in lower-income households (those with annual incomes of $30,000 or less) gamble on sports, compared with 17% of those residing in middle-income households (incomes between $30,000 and $75,000), but 28% of those in households whose income is $75,000 or greater.

College graduates (24%) are significantly more likely than non-graduates (14%) to gamble on sports.

Gambling on sports in both formats has declined over the past 15 years. In 1992, 12% of Americans said they had bet on a professional sports event in the past year, compared with just 7% today. The percentage who say they have participated in an office pool has dropped from 22% in 1992 to 14% today.

Most Common Forms of Gambling

Based on all Americans

	Yes	No
	%	%
Bought a state lottery ticket	46	54
Visited a casino	24	76
Participated in an office pool on the World Series, Super Bowl, or other game	14	86
Played a video poker machine	12	88
Done any other kind of gambling not mentioned here	9	91
Bet on a professional sports event such as baseball, basketball, or football	7	93
Played bingo for money	7	93
Bet on a horse race	5	95
Bet on a college sports event such as basketball or football	4	96
Bet on a boxing match	3	97
Gambled for money on the Internet	2	98

Dec. 6-9, 2007

Sports gambling is not the most common game of chance for Americans—that distinction belongs to playing state lotteries. Close to half of Americans say they have bought a state lottery ticket in the last year, nearly double the percentage who have participated in the next-most-common gambling activity, visiting a casino.

Participation in Sports Gambling, by Type

Based on all Americans

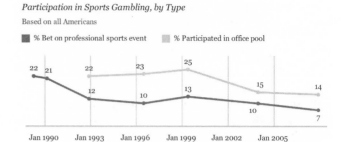

All told, 65% of Americans report that they participated in one or more forms of the 11 types of gambling tested in the poll.

Patterns of gambling in general do not necessarily follow those found for sports gambling. For example, men and women are about equally likely to participate in any form of gambling, 67% versus 63%. There are only modest differences by age, with older Americans (59%) somewhat less likely to gamble than younger (66%) or middle-aged (69%) adults. And there are no differences in gambling behavior between college graduates and non-graduates.

But general gambling behavior is significantly related to household income, with gambling activity much more common among higher-income (72%) than lower-income (55%) Americans. Middle-income Americans, at 66%, are closer to higher-income Americans in their gambling activity.

Survey Methods

These results are based on telephone interviews with a randomly selected national sample of 1,027 adults, aged 18 and older, conducted Dec. 6-9, 2007. For results based on this sample, one can say with 95% confidence that the maximum error attributable to sampling and other random effects is ±3 percentage points.

Interviews are conducted with respondents on land-line telephones (for respondents with a land-line telephone) and cellular phones (for respondents who are cell-phone only).

In addition to sampling error, question wording and practical difficulties in conducting surveys can introduce error or bias into the findings of public opinion polls.

February 03, 2008

CLINTON AND OBAMA TIED: BOTH ARE SATISFYING TO DEMOCRATS

Majority of Democrats would enthusiastically vote for either in the fall

by Lydia Saad, Gallup Poll Senior Editor

A new *USA Today*/Gallup poll, conducted Jan. 30-Feb. 2, finds Hillary Clinton and Barack Obama in a statistical tie for the Democratic presidential nomination, with Clinton preferred by 45% of Democrats nationally and Obama by 44%. In the Republican contest, John McCain leads Mitt Romney by 42% to 24%, and Mike Huckabee is in third place with 18%.

Given the current state of both races, this week's Super Tuesday elections have tremendous potential for solidifying McCain's position as the probable Republican nominee and for clarifying who is likely to win the Democratic prize. The new poll indicates that whatever the outcome, Democrats nationwide will be equally satisfied with their nominee. They show equal levels of enthusiasm for the prospects of Clinton and Obama each being on the ballot in November. In addition, they are no more likely to believe one of the candidates is more electable in the fall than the other.

Specifically:

- Fifty-five percent of Democrats (including independents who lean to the Democratic Party) say they would vote for Obama "enthusiastically" in November were he the Democratic nominee; 53% say the same of Clinton.

Impact on November 2008 Vote if [Hillary Clinton/Barack Obama] Wins the Democratic Nomination for President

Based on Democrats/independents who lean Democratic

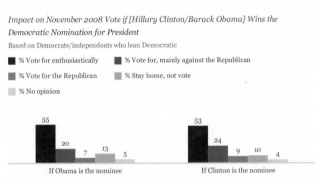

USA Today/Gallup, Jan. 30-Feb. 2, 2008

- Forty-five percent of Democrats think Clinton has the better chance of beating the Republican candidate for president in November; 43% choose Obama.

By contrast, Gallup finds more lopsided attitudes among Republicans—working strongly in McCain's favor. Republicans are less enthusiastic about voting for each of the leading potential nominees than the Democrats are about theirs; however, McCain is the clear leader on this score over Romney. McCain also beats Romney handily in perceptions of which of the two has the better chance of winning in November.

- Just under half of Republicans (including independents who lean to the Republican Party) say they would vote enthusiastically for McCain in the fall, compared with only 35% who are enthusiastic about potentially voting for Romney.

Impact on November 2008 Vote if [John McCain/Mitt Romney] Wins the Republican Nomination for President

Based on Republicans/independents who lean Republican

■ % Vote for enthusiastically   ■ % Vote for, mainly against the Democrat
■ % Vote for the Democrat   ■ % Stay home, not vote
■ % No opinion

47	35						
		6	8	5	35	42	
							7 9 7

If McCain is the nominee   If Romney is the nominee

USA Today/Gallup, Jan. 30-Feb. 2, 2008

- Republicans choose McCain by nearly 3 to 1—68% vs. 24%—as the Republican more likely to beat the Democrat in November.

February 05, 2008
AMERICANS DISPLAY RECORD LEVEL OF INTEREST IN THE ELECTION
More than 7 in 10 are already giving election quite a lot of thought

by Frank Newport, Gallup Poll Editor in Chief

Americans are unusually focused on this year's election, more so than for any recent election at this time in the election-year cycle. Democrats and Republicans appear equally interested in the election, although Democrats are more enthusiastic about their particular set of candidates running this year. The overall high level of voter engagement in the election most probably reflects several factors, including the early start of the primaries and caucuses, but interest at this point is higher than interest at any point throughout the winter and spring of the 2000 and 2004 elections. Other factors that may be producing high interest in the election include the fact that this is a truly open election with no incumbent president or vice president running, and perhaps the presence of a unique set of candidates who have captured the imagination of the American public.

Gallup monitors interest in presidential elections by asking: "How much thought have you given to the upcoming election for president—quite a lot, or only a little?"

The early start of campaigning for Election 2008 is reflected in the fact that Gallup began asking this "thought" question last March, a year and a half before the election. Even at that point, almost half of Americans said they were giving the election quite a lot of thought. That percentage has risen steadily in the three times Gallup has asked this question since then. In the latest *USA Today*/Gallup poll, conducted Jan. 30-Feb. 2, 71% of Americans say they are giving the upcoming election for president quite a lot of thought.

How much thought have you given to the upcoming election for president -- quite a lot, or only a little?

	Quite a lot	SOME (vol.)	Only a little	None	No opinion
2008 Jan 30-Feb 2	71	3	24	2	*
2008 Jan 10-13	64	5	27	3	1
2007 Aug 3-5	55	5	37	3	*
2007 Mar 2-4	48	3	46	2	*

* Less than 0.5%

(vol.) = Volunteered response

The 71% "quite a lot of thought" figure is extraordinarily high for this time in the election cycle. In a late January/early February 2004 poll—conducted immediately after the New Hampshire primary and 10 days after the Iowa caucuses—only 58% of Americans were giving the election quite a lot of thought. And over a month later, in polling conducted after the March 2, 2004, Super Tuesday primaries, still only 62% of Americans had given quite a lot of thought to the election. In fact, in 2004, not until late July and early August did Gallup measure 70% or more of Americans giving quite a lot of thought to the election.

In mid-January 2000—a week before the Iowa caucuses and two weeks before the New Hampshire primary—only 33% of Americans were giving quite a lot of thought to the election. However, this increased to only 39% in polling after the Feb. 1 New Hampshire primary, and to 50% in mid-March, after Super Tuesday. In 2000, among registered voters (a group that would be expected to pay more

How much thought have you given to the upcoming election for president --
quite a lot, or only a little?

Trends for comparison: January of previous election years

	Quite a lot	SOME (vol.)	Only a little	None	No opinion
	%	%	%	%	%
2004 Jan 29-Feb 1	58	5	32	4	1
2004 Jan 9-11	48	4	44	4	*
2004 Jan 2-5	45	2	48	4	1
2000 Jan 17-19	33	9	52	6	--
2000 Jan 13-16	32	7	54	6	1
2000 Jan 7-10	32	8	54	6	*
1992 Jan 6-9	30	6	55	8	1

* Less than 0.5%
(vol.) = Volunteered response

attention than all adults), the 70% level wasn't reached until mid-October.

The early attention Americans are giving to this election probably has as its cause several unique factors that have come together this year. First, no incumbents are running for re-election—the nominations are up for grabs within both parties, which in turn generates interest in the election across the political spectrum. Second, this year's "cast of characters" has unique characteristics and appeal. This election marks the first time in U.S. history that major-party front-runners this deep into the process have included a woman, a black, a Mormon, and a Baptist minister. Third, the primary and caucus season occur much earlier; Iowa's caucuses kicked off actual voting just three days after the beginning of the new year. Fourth, the races themselves got underway much earlier than usual, with full-scale announcements and campaigns initiated a year ago or more.

Gallup research has shown that Democrats are in general more enthusiastic about their candidates this year than are Republicans. But there is little difference in the thought given to the election between those who identify with each of the two major parties. Seventy-six percent of Republicans and 78% of Democrats are giving the election quite a lot of thought (predictably, only 61% of independents, who are usually less engaged in the political process, are giving it quite a lot of thought).

Additionally:

- There has been persistent talk about young people being engaged in this election (in part because of Barack Obama's appeal to young people). The results of this latest poll show that 60% of those aged 18 to 29 are giving the election quite a lot of thought, which is high on an absolute basis, but still significantly lower than the thought given by those who are 30 and older.
- Interest in the election is positively correlated with both education and income. For example, 83% of Americans with post-graduate degrees are giving the election a lot of thought, compared to 60% of those with high school education or less.
- Unmarried men are paying less attention to the election than are married men, and either unmarried or married women.

Survey Methods

These results are based on telephone interviews with a randomly selected national sample of 2,020 adults, aged 18 and older, conducted Jan. 30-Feb. 2, 2008. For results based on this sample, one can say with 95% confidence that the maximum error attributable to sampling and other random effects is ±2 percentage points.

Interviews are conducted with respondents on land-line telephones (for respondents with a land-line telephone) and cellular phones (for respondents who are cell-phone only).

In addition to sampling error, question wording and practical difficulties in conducting surveys can introduce error or bias into the findings of public opinion polls.

February 06, 2008
AMERICANS GIVE BIPARTISAN SUPPORT TO STIMULUS PACKAGE
Income-capped tax rebates are widely favored

by Lydia Saad, Gallup Poll Senior Editor

Somewhere between the $161 billion economic stimulus package the House of Representatives passed a week ago, and the $204 billion alternative now being pushed by Senate Democrats, is a combination of tax rebates and incentives that Washington's leaders hope will boost the nation's economy.

According to a new *USA Today*/Gallup poll, the American public is hoping the same thing. While there is some public opposition to the idea, nearly three-quarters of Americans (73%) are in favor of federal legislation aimed at stimulating economic growth.

Do you favor or oppose the federal government passing a bill that
would attempt to stimulate growth in the economy?

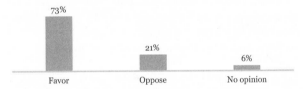

USA Today/Gallup, Jan. 30-Feb. 2, 2008

The reason for this broad support is clear. Ongoing Gallup polling of consumer confidence finds two-thirds of Americans holding negative views of economic conditions—saying the economy is less than good and either staying that way or getting worse. The new *USA Today*/Gallup survey, conducted Jan. 30-Feb. 2, finds relatively few Americans saying the economy is "in a depression," but 33% believe it is in a recession and another 46% say it is slowing down.

Widespread Support by Party,
Ideology, and Income

Just as the federal effort to pass a stimulus package has been largely bipartisan—the House bill passed on a vote of 385 to 35—Republicans and Democrats nationwide are equally likely to favor the proposal.

There is also broad support at all household income levels, ranging from 67% among those earning less than $20,000 per year to 81% among those earning $50,000 to less than $75,000.

The greatest variation in support for an economic stimulus package is seen by political ideology. Those at opposite ends of the ideological spectrum—calling themselves "very conservative" or "very

Reaction to Economic Stimulus Bill, by Party ID

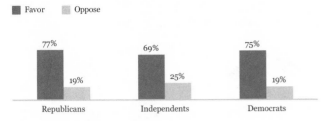

■ Favor ▨ Oppose

USA Today/Gallup, Jan. 30-Feb. 2, 2008

liberal"—are most likely to say they oppose it; however, the majority of all ideological groups are in favor.

Reaction to Economic Stimulus Bill, by Political Ideology

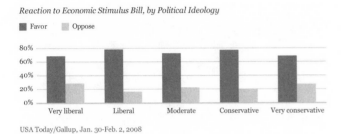

■ Favor ▨ Oppose

USA Today/Gallup, Jan. 30-Feb. 2, 2008

Income-Capped Tax Relief a Crowd Pleaser

The centerpiece of both the House and Senate stimulus plans is direct cash payments to Americans, aimed at spurring consumer spending. The House plan calls for roughly $100 billion in income tax rebates, ranging from $600 per person making less than $75,000 per year to $1,200 per married couple earning less than $150,000, plus an additional $300 per child. It includes payments of $300 per person and $600 per couple for those making too little to pay federal income taxes.

This focus on tax relief for lower- and middle-income Americans is right in line with public opinion. More than four in five Americans say they favor proposals either lowering the federal income tax rate for Americans in these income brackets (87%) or giving them tax rebates (84%).

Other broadly popular stimulus proposals—some included in the House plan, others not—are increasing spending on U.S. infrastructure such as roads and bridges, giving tax breaks and tax incentives to businesses that invest in new equipment and technologies, and lowering the federal income tax rates for all Americans. At least two-thirds of Americans support each of these. More than half also support extending unemployment benefits and providing citizens with certain protections against home foreclosures (the details of which match those proposed by Hillary Clinton in January).

Only one proposal tested in the new survey is opposed by a majority of Americans: giving tax rebates to Americans regardless of income.

A large majority of Americans across the ideological spectrum—ranging from very conservative to very liberal—are in favor of lowering tax rates for low- and middle-income families, for giving tax rebates to these two groups, and for increasing government spending on infrastructure. At least two-thirds of Americans of all ideologies favor each of these.

Liberals show less support than conservatives for giving federal tax breaks to businesses and for lowering federal income tax rates

Regardless of whether you think an economic stimulus package should be passed, do you favor or oppose each of the following proposals?

	Favor	Oppose
	%	%
Lowering federal income tax rates for low- and middle-income families	87	12
Giving tax rebates to low- and middle-income Americans	84	16
Increasing government spending on U.S. infrastructure such as roads and bridges	78	20
Giving federal tax breaks and tax incentives to businesses that invest in new equipment and technologies	73	24
Lowering federal income tax rates for all Americans	67	32
Extending unemployment benefits	64	35
Instituting a 90-day moratorium on home foreclosures and freezing adjustable mortgage rates for five years	63	30
Giving tax rebates to almost every American regardless of income	40	59

USA Today/Gallup, Jan. 30-Feb. 2, 2008

for all Americans. Very few liberals favor giving tax rebates to almost all Americans regardless of income. In fact, the only group to show majority support for this is those calling themselves very conservative.

Conservatives show less support than liberals for extending unemployment benefits, and for instituting protections against home foreclosures.

Support for Specific Stimulus Proposals, by Political Ideology

	Very liberal	Liberal	Moderate	Conservative	Very conservative
	%	%	%	%	%
Lowering tax rates for low-/middle-income families	92	89	88	87	82
Giving tax rebates to low-/middle-income Americans	77	85	85	81	84
Increasing government spending on U.S. infrastructure	86	77	83	75	69
Giving federal tax breaks and tax incentives to businesses that invest in new equipment/technologies	67	64	72	78	80
Lowering federal income tax rates for all Americans	52	52	64	77	80
Extending unemployment benefits	67	71	65	60	60
Instituting a 90-day moratorium on home foreclosures and freezing adjustable mortgage rates	65	78	67	58	49
Giving tax rebates to almost every American regardless of income	33	38	37	43	51

USA Today/Gallup, Jan. 30-Feb. 2, 2008

Survey Methods

These results are based on telephone interviews with 2,020 national adults, aged 18 and older, conducted Jan. 30-Feb. 2, 2008. For results based on the total sample of national adults, one can say with 95% confidence that the maximum margin of sampling error is ±2 percentage points.

For results based on the sample of 867 Republicans or Republican leaners, the maximum margin of sampling error is ±4 percentage points.

For results based on the sample of 985 Democrats or Democratic leaners, the maximum margin of sampling error is ±3 percentage points.

For results based on the sample of 867 Republicans and Republican-leaning independents, the maximum margin of sampling error is ±4 percentage points.

Interviews are conducted with respondents on land-line telephones (for respondents with a land-line telephone) and cellular phones (for respondents who are cell-phone only).

In addition to sampling error, question wording and practical difficulties in conducting surveys can introduce error or bias into the findings of public opinion polls.

February 06, 2008
MAJORITY CONTINUES TO CONSIDER IRAQ WAR A MISTAKE
No change in attitudes in past two months

by Jeffrey M. Jones, Gallup Poll Managing Editor

The latest *USA Today*/Gallup poll finds that a majority of Americans continue to express opposition to the war in Iraq, attitudes that are unchanged in the last two months. According to the Jan. 30-Feb. 2 poll, 57% of Americans say it was a mistake for the United States to send troops to Iraq, while 41% say it was not a mistake. Those numbers are identical to what Gallup measured in late November/early December.

This broad measure of the correctness of the U.S. decision to go to war in Iraq has not changed much, even with more positive assessments of U.S. progress in Iraq in the last three months.

About a year ago, shortly after the U.S. troop surge was announced, a Feb. 9-11 *USA Today*/Gallup poll showed that 56% of Americans thought the United States had made a mistake—nearly identical to the current figure. There has been minor variation on this measure since that time, but in general, a majority of the U.S. public has expressed opposition to the war in all but a few Gallup Polls conducted since August 2005.

Do You Think the United States Made a Mistake in Sending Troops to Iraq?

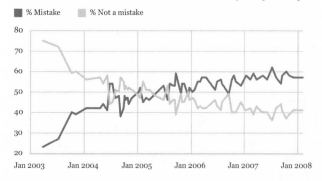

It has been well-established that opinions about the war are strongly related to party affiliation and ideological orientation. But ideology and party interact, such that support increases as one moves from the left to the right of the ideological spectrum. Liberal Democrats are almost universally opposed to the war, while the vast majority of conservative Republicans support it.

Even though war support is strongly related to one's party affiliation, there is still enough variation within each party to assess how views of the war are related to candidate preference in the 2008 presidential primaries. The poll was conducted before the Feb. 5 Super

Do You Think the United States Made a Mistake in Sending Troops to Iraq?
Results by party affiliation (with leaners included) and ideology

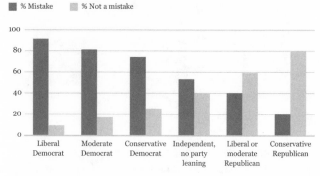

Jan. 30-Feb. 2 USA Today/Gallup Poll

Tuesday primaries, so the following analysis is based on "pre-Super Tuesday" attitudes, which could change if candidate support patterns shift in the coming days.

As of last weekend, Democrats who opposed the war were about equally likely to support Hillary Clinton and Barack Obama as the party's 2008 presidential nominee. This is in spite of the fact that Obama has continually stressed that Clinton voted to authorize the use of force in Iraq while he publicly opposed the war from the beginning. Democrats who support the war showed greater support for Clinton.

Preference for 2008 Democratic Presidential Nominee, by Iraq War Position
Based on Democrats and Democratic-leaning independents

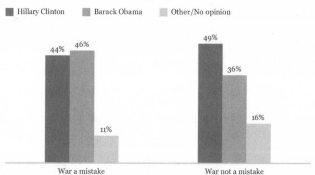

Jan. 30-Feb. 2 USA Today/Gallup Poll

John McCain was the leading candidate among both Republican war supporters and opponents, in part because he had a sizable overall lead of nearly 20 points in the most recent poll. McCain is perhaps the staunchest supporter of the war in Congress, but his support was as high (or higher) among Republican war opponents as it was among war supporters in that poll. The only Republican presidential candidate who opposes the war—Ron Paul—had much greater support among war opponents (12%) than among war supporters (2%). Notably, 88% of Republican war supporters favored one of the three leading (all pro-war) GOP candidates, but only 70% of Republican war opponents did.

Implications

Americans' opinions about U.S. involvement in Iraq are well-formed at this point, and even the more positive news out of Iraq in recent

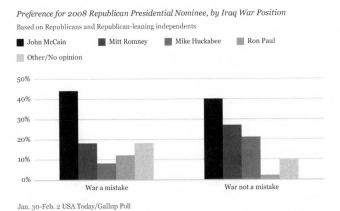

Preference for 2008 Republican Presidential Nominee, by Iraq War Position

Based on Republicans and Republican-leaning independents

■ John McCain ■ Mitt Romney ■ Mike Huckabee ■ Ron Paul
■ Other/No opinion

Jan. 30-Feb. 2 USA Today/Gallup Poll

months has done nothing to lessen public opposition to the war. Attitudes about the war are strongly related to one's political point of view, ranging from 91% opposition among liberal Democrats to 80% support among conservative Republicans. Thus, while the war will be a major issue during the fall presidential campaign, its impact is less clear, since war supporters (largely Republicans) will most likely support the GOP candidate and war opponents (largely Democrats) will probably back the Democrat.

Survey Methods

These results are based on telephone interviews with a randomly selected national sample of 2,020 adults, aged 18 and older, conducted Jan. 30-Feb. 2, 2008. For results based on this sample, one can say with 95% confidence that the maximum error attributable to sampling and other random effects is ±2 percentage points.

Interviews are conducted with respondents on land-line telephones (for respondents with a land-line telephone) and cellular phones (for respondents who are cell-phone only).

In addition to sampling error, question wording and practical difficulties in conducting surveys can introduce error or bias into the findings of public opinion polls.

February 07, 2008
FORTY-FIVE PERCENT SEE U.S. IN RECESSION OR DEPRESSION
One in four low-income Americans say the economy is in an "economic depression"

by Dennis Jacobe, Gallup Chief Economist

While much of the nation was focused on the Super Tuesday elections earlier this week, and Americans were telling pollsters that the condition of the economy was one of their top concerns, the Institute for Supply Management issued a stunning report. Its January index of business activity—activity outside of the manufacturing sector—took its biggest plunge in its more than 10-year history. This important measure of current economic activity also turned negative for the first time since March 2003—the month the war with Iraq began. Given that the backdrop for this news was the Commerce Department's report last week that the U.S. economy actually lost jobs in January, it should not be surprising that Wall Street took a plunge.

Nor should it shock anyone that 8 in 10 Americans now believe the U.S. economy is experiencing either a slowdown or a recession. However, it may be surprising how many lower-income Americans think the country is not only in a recession but in an economic depression.

Assessing the Current Economy

In a new *USA Today*/Gallup poll, conducted Jan. 30-Feb. 2, 45% of Americans describe the U.S. economy as already being in a recession (33%) or a depression (12%). Another 46% say the economy is currently experiencing an economic slowdown; only 7% say the economy continues to grow.

Right now, do you think the U.S. economy is growing, slowing down, in a recession, or in an economic depression?

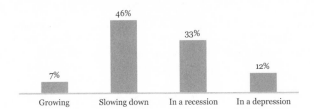

More Lower-Income Consumers See Recession/Depression

As might be expected, a higher percentage of lower-income than upper-income consumers describe the current economy as being in a recession or a depression. Nearly 6 in 10 consumers making less than $20,000 a year think the U.S. economy is experiencing a recession or a depression, with more than one in four (27%) saying the economy is in a depression. While still a high percentage, only 31% of those making at least $75,000 think the economy is already in a recession and only 8% say it is experiencing a depression.

Right now, do you think the U.S. economy is growing, slowing down, in a recession, or in an economic depression?

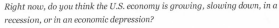

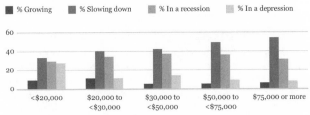

Defining Recession and Depression

An old saying defines the difference between a recession and an economic depression: A recession takes place when *you* are unemployed, while a depression takes place when *I'm* unemployed. Given the relatively good employment levels during recent years and the technical definition of a recession, usually described as two consecutive quarters of negative economic growth, many economists argue that the U.S. economy is not really in a recession—let alone anything resembling an economic depression.

On the other hand, to many economists, the application of the terms "recession" and "depression" has a much more psychological and emotional connotation. The fact that the U.S. economy has not experienced anything resembling a severe recession in about a quarter century tends to set the bar pretty low as far as economic hardship is concerned. Clearly, many Americans associated with the housing, auto, and manufacturing industries have good reason to think of the economy as in a depression, as do the unemployed and underemployed.

Regardless, the fact that so many Americans feel the country is already in a recession or a depression does not spell good things for consumer spending, business activity, or the future direction of the U.S. economy. Still, even with all the current doom and gloom, many Americans of all income groups remain optimistic about the economy just a year from now: 44% of all Americans, including 45% of those with lower incomes, say they expect the economy to be growing at that time. This suggests that while many Americans seem to feel the current economic downturn could be severe, they also believe it will be mercifully brief.

Survey Methods

Results are based on telephone interviews with 2,020 national adults, aged 18 and older, conducted Jan. 30-Feb. 2, 2008. For results based on the total sample of national adults, one can say with 95% confidence that the maximum margin of sampling error is ±2 percentage points.

Interviews are conducted with respondents on land-line telephones (for respondents with a land-line telephone) and cellular phones (for respondents who are cell-phone only).

In addition to sampling error, question wording and practical difficulties in conducting surveys can introduce error or bias into the findings of public opinion polls.

February 08, 2008
CONSUMER CREDIT CRUNCH INTENSIFIES
Nearly one in four know someone turned down for credit in past three months

by Dennis Jacobe, Gallup Chief Economist

Early this week, the Federal Reserve Board reported that according to its January 2008 Senior Loan Officer Opinion Survey on Bank Lending Practices, financial institutions tightened their lending standards over the past three months. Although it usually takes some time for the average American to feel this kind of credit crunch, recent Gallup polling suggests that consumers are already getting the message.

More Consumers Know People
Turned Down for Credit

According to a new *USA Today*/Gallup poll, conducted Jan. 30 to Feb. 2, nearly one in four consumers (23%) say they know someone close to them who has been turned down for credit over the past three months. This is technically the highest percentage that has been recorded on this measure since Gallup began tracking it in April of last year. It is up slightly from the 21% who said the same thing in December, and significantly from the 18% of November and the low point of 16% seen in April and June 2007. Gallup does not have a reading on this measure from previous years, when credit policies were looser and, presumably, the percentage who knew someone

who was turned down would have been still lower than the lowest reading from 2007.

Do you know anyone close to you who -- [RANDOM ORDER]?

A. Has been turned down for credit they applied for during the past three months

▨ % Yes, know someone

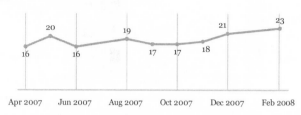

Middle-, Lower-Income Consumers More
Likely to Know People Turned Down for Credit

One in four consumers (25%) making less than $30,000 a year, and 28% of those making between $30,000 and $74,999, said they know someone close to them who has been turned down for credit they applied for during the previous three months. This compares with about one in five consumers (19%) making $75,000 or more annually.

Do you know anyone close to you who has been turned down for credit they applied for during the past three months?

By annual household income

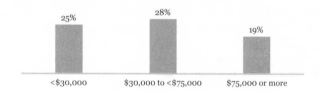

Is the Fed "Pushing on a String"?

Over the past few weeks, the financial markets have demanded lower short-term interest rates, and the Fed has complied. While some have argued that lower interest rates are essential to cushion the current economic downturn, the steadily expanding consumer credit crunch shows that the Fed's ability to expand consumer credit availability in the current economic environment is highly limited. The Fed can make money cheaper and readily available to the nation's financial institutions but it can't make them lend—essentially this is like pushing on a string from a Fed policy perspective.

Lower interest rates can help financial services firms' earnings, but they shouldn't and won't undo the need to go back to the more reasonable loan underwriting standards that prevailed prior to the creation of the so-called "subprime" debacle. And this tightening of lending standards seems to be having a significant impact already, according to Thursday's Fed report, which showed consumer debt expanded at the slowest pace in eight months during December.

Gallup's polling also indicates that the consumer credit crunch is spreading; it appears to be having the greatest proportional effect on middle-income rather than on lower-income households. Of course, the former tend to be bigger users of consumer credit than their lower-income counterparts. In turn, this suggests a growing impact on consumer spending, particularly as far as larger purchases are concerned.

Significantly, the Fed's Loan Officer Survey shows that financial institutions are tightening their lending standards for small businesses and larger companies as well. This suggests that the current consumer credit crunch is expanding to ensnare the nation's businesses.

In sum, the Fed's lowering of interest rates is a lot more like pushing on a string than it has been in past recessions. The Fed's actions may help the consumer and business psychology, but the Fed's ability to significantly moderate the current economic downturn is extremely limited right now.

Survey Methods

Results are based on 995 telephone interviews with national adults, aged 18 and older, conducted Jan. 30-Feb. 2, 2008. For results based on the total sample of national adults, one can say with 95% confidence that the maximum margin of sampling error is ±3 percentage points.

Interviews are conducted with respondents on land-line telephones (for respondents with a land-line telephone) and cellular phones (for respondents who are cell-phone only).

In addition to sampling error, question wording and practical difficulties in conducting surveys can introduce error or bias into the findings of public opinion polls.

February 09, 2008
EDUCATION AND GENDER HELP PREDICT DEMOCRATIC PREFERENCES
College education a major differentiator in choosing Clinton vs. Obama

by Frank Newport, Gallup Poll Editor in Chief and Lydia Saad, Senior Editor

Gender and education are both strong predictors of Democrats' preferences for their party's presidential nominee. Generally speaking, the more education a Democrat has, the less likely he or she is to support Hillary Clinton, and the more likely to support Barack Obama. Additionally, women are more likely than men to support Clinton, while men are more likely than women to support Obama.

An aggregate of Gallup Poll Daily election tracking interviews with Democrats, conducted from Feb. 1 through Feb. 7, shows that these two variables combine to become a powerful predictor of a Democrat's vote. Among the most highly educated Democrats—those with postgraduate educations—both men and women are more likely to support Obama than Clinton. Among the least educated—those with no college experience—both men and women are more likely to support Clinton than Obama.

The range of support for the candidates according to education and gender is as follows:

- Obama beats Clinton by a 2-to-1 margin, 62% to 31%, among men with postgraduate-level educations. Although the margin is much smaller (49% vs. 42%), Obama also beats Clinton among women with postgraduate degrees. In other words, the strength of Obama's appeal to highly educated Democrats seems to be stronger than the pull of gender (i.e., Clinton's appeal to women).

Democratic Presidential Preferences, by Gender and Education: Postgraduates

Based on Democrats and independents who lean Democratic

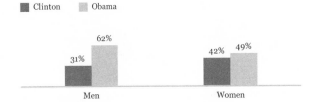

Gallup Poll Daily: Feb. 1-7, 2008

- Among those with college degrees but no postgraduate education, Obama wins over Clinton among men, but women in this group tilt slightly toward Clinton, by a 47% to 43% margin.

Democratic Presidential Preferences, by Gender and Education: College Graduates

Based on Democrats and independents who lean Democratic

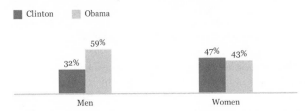

Gallup Poll Daily: Feb. 1-7, 2008

- Among those with some college education (but not a four-year degree), Obama still wins among men (50% vs. 39%), while women show a slight preference for Clinton (49% vs. 44%).

Democratic Presidential Preferences, by Gender and Education: Those With Some College Education

Based on Democrats and independents who lean Democratic

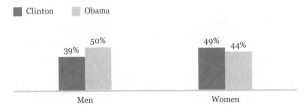

Gallup Poll Daily: Feb. 1-7, 2008

- Finally, in the group of Democrats with high-school diplomas or less, the impact of education is strong. Clinton beats Obama overwhelmingly among both men and women in this education group.

In short, education is a highly significant predictor of Democrats' vote choices, particularly among the two groups at the extreme ends of formal education—those with postgraduate degrees and those with high school educations or less. Gender, too, is a predictor, but is essentially overwhelmed by the impact of education in the two extreme groups, such that both men and women who have postgraduate educations prefer Obama, and both men and women who have no formal education beyond high school fairly strongly support Clinton.

Democratic Presidential Preferences, by Gender and Education:
High School Graduates or Less

Based on Democrats and independents who lean Democratic

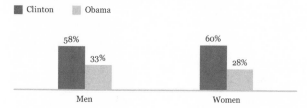

Gallup Poll Daily: Feb. 1-7, 2008

Survey Methods

These results are based on an aggregate of Gallup Poll Daily tracking interviews conducted Feb. 1-7, 2008. Each night, approximately 1,000 national adults, aged 18 and older, are interviewed by telephone. Interviews are conducted with respondents on land-line telephones (for respondents with a land-line telephone) and cellular phones (for respondents who are cell-phone only).

The aggregate of the Democratic nomination trial heats includes telephone interviews with 2,871 Democrats and Democratic leaners. One can say with 95% confidence that the maximum margin of sampling error for these results is ±2 percentage points.

Results based on the aggregates of Democratic men, Democratic women, and various subsets of these groups according to level of formal education are associated with higher margins of maximum sampling error.

In addition to sampling error, question wording and practical difficulties in conducting surveys can introduce error or bias into the findings of public opinion polls.

February 11, 2008
BLACK MEN, WOMEN EQUALLY LIKELY TO SUPPORT OBAMA
Gender gap evident among whites and Hispanics

by Frank Newport, Gallup Poll Editor in Chief and Lydia Saad, Senior Editor

The gender gap in Democratic preferences for Hillary Clinton versus Barack Obama—with a greater share of women than men supporting Clinton—is evident among whites and Hispanics, but not blacks. Blacks' overwhelming support for Obama to be the 2008 Democratic presidential nominee is just as strong among women as it is among men.

In Gallup Poll Daily tracking interviews conducted Feb. 1-9, only a quarter of black men (25%) and black women (23%) say they support Clinton for the nomination, while about two-thirds of each group favors Obama. This is based on blacks who are Democrats or are independents who lean to the Democratic Party.

Across the same period, Gallup finds white Democrats of both sexes more likely to favor Clinton than Obama. However, among white Democratic women, the margin in favor of Clinton is 28 points, 59% vs. 31%, compared with a 10-point margin (50% vs. 40%) among white Democratic men. In short, the gender gap is significant among this group.

Candidate Preference for Democratic Nomination, Among Blacks

Based on Democrats and independents who lean Democratic

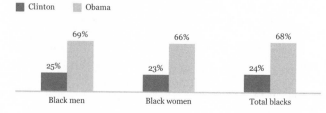

Gallup Poll Daily -- Feb. 1-9, 2008

Candidate Preference for Democratic Nomination, Among Whites

Based on Democrats and independents who lean Democratic

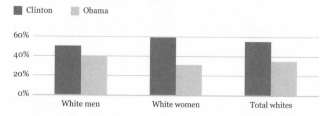

Gallup Poll Daily -- Feb. 1-9, 2008

A gender gap of similar scope is seen among Hispanic Democrats, who, overall, have been supporting Clinton to an even higher degree than have whites. Hispanic women favor Clinton by a 37-point margin, compared with the 17-point margin seen among Hispanic men.

Candidate Preference for Democratic Nomination, Among Hispanics

Based on Democrats and independents who lean Democratic

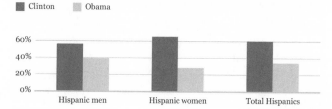

Gallup Poll Daily -- Feb. 1-9, 2008

Blacks as Favorable Toward Clinton as Obama

The Gallup Poll Daily tracking survey does not measure favorability toward the candidates, but according to two *USA Today*/Gallup polls from January through early February, blacks' preference for Obama is not necessarily a rejection of Clinton. Her favorability scores among black Democrats are about as high as Obama's.

Thus, it appears that blacks' uniformly high support for Obama is not because of any major contrast in perceptions of Obama versus Clinton, but because of the greater appeal of his candidacy (perhaps because he could become the first black president in U.S. history).

Similarly, white Democratic women's support for Clinton is not necessarily a rejection of Obama. In fact, Clinton's favorability score among white Democratic women in these recent polls is only slightly higher than Obama's (78% vs. 71%).

Favorable Ratings of Clinton and Obama, Among Black Democrats

Based on Democrats and independents who lean Democratic

■ Favorable toward Clinton   □ Favorable toward Obama

81% 83%   84% 84%

Black men   Black women

No. of interviews: 98   152
USA Today/Gallup -- Jan. 10-Feb. 2, 2008

Favorable Ratings of Clinton and Obama, Among White Democrats

Based on Democrats and independents who lean Democratic

■ Favorable toward Clinton   □ Favorable toward Obama

67% 73%   78% 71%

White men   White women

USA Today/Gallup -- Jan. 10-Feb. 2, 2008

Bottom Line/Implications

There are major differences in Democrats' support for Clinton versus Obama based on race, ethnicity, and gender. Blacks overwhelmingly support Obama. Hispanics and women disproportionately support Clinton. It can be hypothesized that the cross-voting pressures of gender and race on voters could be particularly strong on black women. The tug of supporting a woman for president could draw them to Clinton, while the tug of supporting a black could draw them toward Obama.

This analysis shows that a bias for supporting the female candidate may be in play with white and Hispanic Democratic women. However, whatever desire black women may have to vote for someone who could become the first woman president in U.S. history is muted by their apparently stronger desire to support Obama—who could become the first black president in U.S. history.

Survey Methods

The Democratic trial-heat results reported here are based on an aggregate of Gallup Poll Daily tracking interviews conducted Feb. 1-9, 2008. Each night, approximately 1,000 national adults, aged 18 and older, are interviewed by telephone. Interviews are conducted with respondents on land-line telephones (for respondents with a land-line telephone) and cellular phones (for respondents who are cell-phone only).

The aggregate of the Democratic nomination trial heats includes telephone interviews with 3,820 Democrats and Democratic leaners who say they are "extremely," "very," or "somewhat" likely to vote in the 2008 Democratic primary or caucus in their state. One can say with 95% confidence that the maximum margin of sampling error for these results is ±2 percentage points.

Sample sizes for the race/gender and Hispanic/gender groups reported here, and the associated margins of error for sampling error alone, are as follows:

- 197 Democratic black men: ±8 percentage points.
- 289 Democratic black women: ±6 percentage points.

- 1,161 Democratic white men: ±3 percentage points
- 1,600 Democratic white women: ±3 percentage points
- 136 Democratic Hispanic men: ±9 percentage points
- 141 Democratic Hispanic women: ±9 percentage points

The candidate favorability ratings reported here are based on an aggregate of the Jan. 10-13, 2008, and Jan. 30-Feb. 2, 2008, *USA Today*/Gallup national surveys, including 4,031 national adults.

Sample sizes for the race/gender groups reported here, and the associated margins of error for sampling error alone, are as follows:

- 98 Democratic black men: ±10 percentage points
- 152 Democratic black women: ±8 percentage points
- 663 Democratic white men: ±4 percentage points
- 807 Democratic white women: ±4 percentage points

In addition to sampling error, question wording and practical difficulties in conducting surveys can introduce error or bias into the findings of public opinion polls.

February 11, 2008
PESSIMISM CLOUDS HOUSING MARKET
Most Americans no longer assume local housing prices will increase

by Dennis Jacobe, Gallup Chief Economist

Late last week, the National Association of Realtors reported that its December 2007 Pending Home Sales Index was down 24.2% from December 2006. New Gallup polling results suggest that such reports—reflecting a virtual depression in much of the nation's residential real estate markets—are likely to continue. Americans no longer simply assume that housing prices will increase in their local areas or that they can put their houses on the market and sell them quickly.

Far Fewer Americans See Housing Price Increases

Not quite three years ago, in May 2005, 7 in 10 Americans believed that over the coming year, the average price of houses in their areas would increase; only 1 in 20 expected them to decrease. In April 2006, only 60% expected an increase in home values and 11%—double the 2005 reading—expected a decrease. By April 2007, 52% of consumers expected house prices to increase and 18%—nearly another doubling—expected them to decline.

Ten months later, barely half of the April 2007 percentage expect home prices to rise. In a new *USA Today*/Gallup poll, conducted Jan. 30-Feb. 2, only 29% of Americans expect home prices in their local areas to increase over the year ahead. At the same time, the percentage of consumers expecting home prices to decrease has doubled from the 2007 reading and now stands at 35%. More Americans now expect housing values to decrease in their local residential real estate markets than expect them to increase.

Consumers Are Having Difficulty Selling Their Homes

Three in 10 consumers say they know someone close to them who currently has their house on the market but has been unable to sell it for 12 months or longer. The same percentage (30%) say they know someone who has taken their house off the market in the past three months because it did not sell. Further, 14% of Americans say they

Over the next year, do you think that the average price of houses in your area will increase, stay the same, or decrease?

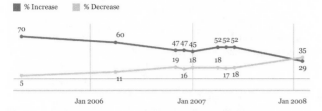

know someone close to them who has filed for bankruptcy or had a foreclosure during the past three months.

Do you know anyone close to you who --

B. Has filed for bankruptcy or had a foreclosure during the past three months?

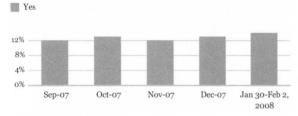

Based on 995 national adults in Form B

Deteriorating Housing Market Psychology

In the past, most national housing-market recessions have been characterized by surging interest rates that significantly reduced housing affordability. In such housing environments, many sellers simply took their homes off the market while some builders eliminated their inventories and others went out of business; when the Fed acted to reduce interest rates, home buyers and home sellers returned to the market. Although the housing cycle took some time, and was often complicated by rising unemployment associated with a recession, housing values were largely maintained, and it wasn't too long after lower interest rates took effect before the housing sector began to recover.

Gallup's polling reflects the highly different nature of the current housing recession/depression. Right now, buyers are fearful of making a housing purchase because the value of the homes they buy might actually decline. The usual assumption by everyone in the housing marketplace that prices will simply increase every year has proven untrue: According to the S&P/Case-Shiller home-price index, home prices in 20 U.S. metropolitan areas have fallen for 11 straight months. At the same time, many home sellers are not willing to accept the lower prices being dictated by conditions in today's residential real estate markets. They leave their homes on the market and after an extended period, they often take them off the market to wait for a better time to sell. Since selling an existing home is essential before a person moves up to a better home, this tends to further slow an already struggling real estate market.

Turning the current housing market psychology around will not be easy. Lower mortgage rates can help. So will an increase in the Fannie Mae, Freddie Mac, and FHA loan limits. However, the real key to a housing recovery is increased consumer confidence that housing prices have bottomed out and that it is once again "safe" to buy. This is not likely to happen in the immediate term as under-

writing standards continue to tighten, an economic slowdown or recession unfolds, and new job growth disappears or unemployment rates increase. Don't be surprised if all kinds of inventive new "solutions" are proposed to revive the housing sector, as it becomes clear that it is the housing market psychology—not just mortgage finance—that needs to be fixed if there is to be a significant housing recovery anytime soon.

Survey Methods

Results are based on 2,020 telephone interviews with national adults, aged 18 and older, conducted Jan. 30-Feb. 2, 2008. For results based on the total sample of national adults, one can say with 95% confidence that the maximum margin of sampling error is ±2 percentage points. For results based on the Form B sample of 995 adults, the maximum margin of sampling error is ±3 percentage points.

In addition to sampling error, question wording and practical difficulties in conducting surveys can introduce error or bias into the findings of public opinion polls.

February 12, 2008
DEMOCRATS MUCH MORE ENTHUSED ABOUT THEIR CANDIDATES
Six in 10 Democrats believe Clinton, Obama better than most prior candidates

by Jeffrey M. Jones, Gallup Poll Managing Editor

Clearly the 2008 presidential election will be remembered for the historic Democratic nomination battle between a female candidate and a black candidate. But beyond those distinctions, Democrats currently view the election as historic in terms of the quality of their leading candidates—6 in 10 say both Obama and Clinton are better than most presidential candidates who have run during their lifetimes. In contrast, most Republicans view John McCain as neither better nor worse than prior candidates, and barely half of the party's supporters say they would be satisfied if he won the party's presidential nomination. It is unclear how this gap in candidate enthusiasm may play out in the general election, given that McCain is closely matched with both Democrats in Gallup's latest trial heats.

The Feb. 8-10 *USA Today*/Gallup poll asked Americans to size up the leading presidential contenders against "all the people who have run for president during your lifetime." The results show a substantial difference by party affiliation. Most Democrats say Clinton (62%) and Obama (60%) are better than most presidential candidates who have run during their lifetimes, including 12% who rate each as the "best presidential candidate." In stark contrast, only about half as many Republicans (34%) rate McCain as better than most candidates. The majority of Republicans, 52%, believe McCain is not much different from prior candidates.

Because independents and Republicans rate Obama more positively on this measure than they rate Clinton, he is rated the best overall, in that he scores highest among all Americans. Republicans' disdain for Clinton is clear—nearly three in four rate Clinton as worse than most (34%) if not *the* worst (40%) presidential candidate in their lifetimes. But it is important to point out that Democrats—despite the positive momentum now swirling around Obama's

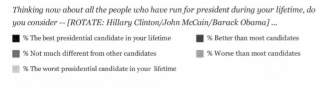

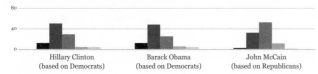

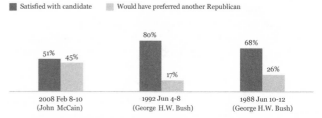

- ■ % The best presidential candidate in your lifetime
- ■ % Not much different from other candidates
- ■ % The worst presidential candidate in your lifetime
- ■ % Better than most candidates
- ■ % Worse than most candidates

USA Today/Gallup, Feb. 8-10, 2008

Republicans' Reaction to the Likely or Emergent Republican Presidential Nominee
Based on Republicans and independents who lean Republican

- ■ Satisfied with candidate
- ■ Would have preferred another Republican

candidacy—are as likely to give Clinton as Obama a positive historical review.

McCain's ratings on this measure are not all that different by party—the majority of independents, Democrats, and (as noted) Republicans see him as a "run-of-the-mill" candidate.

Ratings of 2008 Presidential Candidates Compared With Other Candidates Who Have Run in Your Lifetime

	Best in lifetime	Better than most	Not much different	Worse than most	Worst in lifetime
BARACK OBAMA	%	%	%	%	%
All Americans	7	36	32	12	8
Democrats	12	48	25	5	4
Independents	5	35	37	9	5
Republicans	1	20	33	25	15
HILLARY CLINTON					
All Americans	5	28	28	18	18
Democrats	12	50	29	4	4
Independents	2	24	33	20	17
Republicans	0	5	20	34	40
JOHN McCAIN					
All Americans	1	26	53	12	3
Democrats	*	18	57	13	5
Independents	1	29	52	11	2
Republicans	2	32	52	11	1

USA Today/Gallup, Feb. 8-10, 2008
*Less than 0.5%

The poll provides further evidence of Republican unease with McCain as the GOP presidential nominee with an update of a Gallup trend question asked in the 1988 and 1992 elections. Barely half of Republicans and Republican-leaning independents (51%) say they would be satisfied if McCain ends up the winner in the Republican race; 45% say they would have preferred to see one of the other Republican candidates win.

In 1988 and 1992, Republicans were much more enthusiastic about George H.W. Bush as the party's standard-bearer. In 1988, 68% said they were satisfied that Bush was the Republican winner, and in 1992, 80% were.

The question was also asked of Democrats in 1988 and 1992—Republicans' ratings of McCain are a little worse than what Democrats (and Democratic-leaning independents) said in June 1992 about Bill Clinton's nomination (58% were satisfied at that point in the campaign) and in June 1988 about Michael Dukakis' nomination (62%).

McCain does, however, fare about as well on a basic likability test within his party as do the Democrats in theirs. Seventy-one percent of Republicans have a favorable opinion of McCain—essentially the same as Obama's 72% favorable rating among Democrats. Clinton is rated slightly higher by her party's supporters, with a 78% favorable rating.

Favorable Ratings of 2008 Presidential Candidates

	Favorable	Unfavorable	No opinion
BARACK OBAMA	%	%	%
All Americans	58	34	8
Democrats	72	20	8
Independents	62	30	8
Republicans	33	59	7
HILLARY CLINTON			
All Americans	48	49	4
Democrats	78	19	3
Independents	44	50	5
Republicans	12	86	3
JOHN McCAIN			
All Americans	54	36	9
Democrats	39	48	13
Independents	57	35	9
Republicans	71	24	6

USA Today/Gallup, Feb. 8-10, 2008

Perhaps most importantly, at this point, McCain is basically even with both Clinton and Obama in likely voters' general-election preferences. That is in part because of his appeal to independents, but also because he currently does as well (if not better) at holding his own party's base as do Clinton and Obama.

General Election Trial Heats, by Party Affiliation
Based on likely voters

	Democrats	Independents	Republicans
Obama vs. McCain	%	%	%
Obama	79	54	12
McCain	16	44	85
Clinton vs. McCain			
Clinton	87	41	6
McCain	10	52	92

USA Today/Gallup, Feb. 8-10, 2008

Implications

Clearly, the Democratic race has attracted a lot of attention from the media and the public, as these two historic candidates continue to be locked in a tight battle for the party's presidential nomination. The

Republican nomination is all but decided, but Republicans apparently are not overly thrilled with the outcome. It is unclear at this point if another Republican candidate would have generated any more enthusiasm among the party than McCain currently does. But more importantly, it is also unclear whether the apparent lack of GOP enthusiasm will sink the party's chances of winning in November.

Survey Methods

These results are based on telephone interviews with a randomly selected national sample of 1,016 adults, aged 18 and older, conducted Feb. 8-10, 2008. For results based on this sample, one can say with 95% confidence that the maximum error attributable to sampling and other random effects is ±3 percentage points.

For results based on the sample of 353 Democrats, the maximum margin of sampling error is ±6 percentage points.

For results based on the sample of 305 Republicans, the maximum margin of sampling error is ±6 percentage points.

For results based on the sample of 351 independents, the maximum margin of sampling error is ±6 percentage points.

For results based on the sample of 424 Republicans and Republican-leaning independents, the maximum margin of sampling error is ±5 percentage points.

Interviews are conducted with respondents on land-line telephones (for respondents with a land-line telephone) and cellular phones (for respondents who are cell-phone only).

In addition to sampling error, question wording and practical difficulties in conducting surveys can introduce error or bias into the findings of public opinion polls.

February 12, 2008

MCCAIN HOLDS HIS OWN AGAINST OBAMA, CLINTON

November election would be close if held today

by Frank Newport, Gallup Poll Editor in Chief

John McCain essentially holds his own when pitted against either of the two leading Democratic candidates for president in hypothetical general-election trial heats. This is despite the fact that Democrats have a decided advantage on several non-election measures of party strength and positioning.

The new *USA Today*/Gallup poll, conducted Feb. 8-10, shows that McCain leads Hillary Clinton by one point, 49% to 48%, in a hypothetical general-election matchup among likely voters. He trails Barack Obama by four points, 46% to 50%. Both of these differences are within the poll's margin of error, and suggest that if the election were held today, it would be a close race if McCain were the Republican nominee and either Obama or Clinton were the Democratic nominee. The results also suggest that despite vigorous discussions of whether Clinton or Obama would be most electable in November, Obama has at best a slight advantage over Clinton on that dimension.

At the same time, a number of recent measures included in the Gallup Poll and other polls show that the Democrats in theory have some strong structural political advantages at this point. In terms of the parties' favorable images, Democrats have double-digit leads over Republicans in recent Gallup Polls. Within the current sample,

54% of those interviewed either identify with or lean toward the Democratic Party, compared to just 39% who identify with or lean toward the Republican Party. And on generic presidential election questions, in which respondents are asked which party's candidate they would like to win the presidency next fall (without naming names), the Democrats have typically been winning by double-digit margins.

In short, there appears to be a significant advantage for the Democrats over the Republicans on several general measures of party image and strength. McCain thus outperforms what would be predicted in the general-election trial heats, everything else being equal.

Bottom Line

Many things can and will change between now and Election Day next Nov. 4. For the moment, several indicators in recent polls point to a propitious political environment for the Democrats. Despite that, the front-running GOP nominee, McCain, tests quite well against the two leading Democratic candidates—beating Clinton by one point and losing to Obama by four points, both of which are gaps within the margin of error. If these types of numbers were to hold through the fall, the coming election could be a close one, regardless of voters' apparently negative attitudes toward the Republican Party.

Suppose the election were being held today, who would you vote for: Hillary Clinton, the Democrat or John McCain, the Republican?

(Asked of those who are undecided) As of today, do you lean more toward : Clinton, the Democrat or McCain, the Republican?

	Clinton	McCain	OTHER (vol.)	NEITHER (vol.)	No opinion
LIKELY VOTERS	%	%	%	%	%
2008 Feb 8-10	48	49	1	2	1
2008 Jan 10-13	47	50	1	2	1
REGISTERED VOTERS					
2008 Feb 8-10	48	48	1	3	1
2008 Jan 10-13	47	50	1	2	1
2007 Nov 11-14	50	44	*	3	2
2007 Jun 11-14	49	46	*	3	2
2007 Feb 9-11	50	47	*	1	1
2005 Oct 21-23	43	53	1	2	1
2005 Jul 25-28	45	50	--	2	3
NATIONAL ADULTS					
2008 Feb 8-10	47	48	1	3	1
2008 Jan 10-13	48	48	1	2	1
2007 Nov 11-14	50	42	*	4	3
2007 Jun 11-14	50	45	*	3	2
2007 Feb 9-11	52	46	*	1	1
2005 Oct 21-23	43	53	1	2	1
2005 Jul 25-28	45	50	--	2	3

* Less than 0.5%

Survey Methods

Results are based on telephone interviews with 1,016 national adults, aged 18 and older, conducted Feb. 8-10, 2008. For results based on the total sample of national adults, one can say with 95% confidence that the maximum margin of sampling error is ±3 percentage points.

For results based on the sample of 926 registered voters, the maximum margin of sampling error is ±4 percentage points.

Results for likely voters are based on the subsample of 706 survey respondents deemed most likely to vote in the November 2008 general election, according to a series of questions measuring current voting intentions and past voting behavior. For results based on

8. Suppose the election were being held today. If Barack Obama were the Democratic Party's candidate and John McCain were the Republican Party's candidate, who would you be more likely to vote for -- [ROTATED: Barack Obama, the Democrat (or) John McCain, the Republican]?

8A. (Asked of those who are undecided) As of today, do you lean more toward -- [ROTATED: Obama, the Democrat (or) McCain, the Republican]?

	Obama	McCain	OTHER (vol.)	NEITHER (vol.)	No opinion
LIKELY VOTERS	%	%	%	%	%
2008 Feb 8-10	50	46	*	2	1
2008 Jan 10-13	45	50	1	2	2
REGISTERED VOTERS					
2008 Feb 8-10	49	46	1	3	2
2008 Jan 10-13	44	50	*	2	3
2007 Nov 11-14	47	44	*	6	4
2007 Jun 11-14	48	46	*	3	2
2007 Feb 9-11	48	48	*	2	2
NATIONAL ADULTS					
2008 Feb 8-10	49	45	1	3	2
2008 Jan 10-13	46	48	*	3	2
2007 Nov 11-14	47	42	*	7	5
2007 Jun 11-14	48	45	*	4	3
2007 Feb 9-11	47	48	*	2	3

* Less than 0.5%
(vol.) = Volunteered response

the total sample of likely voters, one can say with 95% confidence that the maximum margin of sampling error is ±4 percentage points. The "likely voter" model assumes a turnout of 60% of national adults. The likely voter sample is weighted to match this assumption, so the weighted sample size is 606.

In addition to sampling error, question wording and practical difficulties in conducting surveys can introduce error or bias into the findings of public opinion polls.

February 13, 2008
IRAQ AND THE ECONOMY ARE TOP ISSUES TO VOTERS
Republicans focused more on terrorism, moral values

by Lydia Saad, Gallup Poll Senior Editor

More than 40 candidate debates and forums have been held in the 2008 presidential election cycle thus far—with at least 20 for each party. Factoring in the speeches, interviews, and position papers coming out of the campaigns, there has already been a tremendous flow of information on national issues, and the general election campaign hasn't started.

This may be fortunate, because new Gallup data suggest that Americans are interested in having a lot of material covered as they make their voting decisions. According to the latest *USA Today*/Gallup poll, most Americans rate candidates' positions on 14 issues—*all* of the issues listed in the Feb. 8-10 poll—as either "extremely" or "very" important in their decision-making in choosing a new president. Although none of the issues is considered extremely important by a majority of Americans (the situation in Iraq registers the highest level, with 43%), all of them are rated as either extremely or very important by at least 60%.

The situation in Iraq and the economy tie as the issues Americans say are most important to their vote; the environment and illegal immigration tie for the least important.

Importance of Candidates' Positions on Each Issue in Influencing Americans' Vote for President

Ranked by extremely/very important

	Extremely/ Very important	Extremely important
	%	%
The economy	89	41
The situation in Iraq	87	43
Education	81	35
Corruption in government	79	40
Healthcare	79	37
Energy, including gas prices	79	36
Terrorism	77	40
Social Security	73	30
The federal budget deficit	73	30
Moral values	69	33
Medicare	69	29
Taxes	69	27
The environment, including global warming	62	27
Illegal immigration	60	26

USA Today/Gallup, Feb. 8-10, 2008

Positions on Terrorism Most Important to Republican Voters

With Hillary Clinton and Barack Obama still battling for the Democratic nomination, and John McCain yet to officially wrap up the Republican nomination, the current discussion of issues in the election remains focused on how the candidates' positions compare with what voters in their respective parties are looking for.

Some of the strongest distinctions among issues within each party group are seen at the "extremely" important level. On this basis, the top issue for Republicans is clear: terrorism. Fully half of Republicans say the candidates' positions on terrorism are extremely important to their vote, suggesting a possible reason why McCain, with his military background and tough anti-terrorist positions, has been successful in recent weeks at filling the void created when Rudy Giuliani's campaign deflated early in the primary season.

At least a third of Republicans rate an assortment of other issues as extremely important, led by moral values with 39%. The relatively high ranking of this issue can help explain why Mike Huckabee has continued to present a challenge to McCain in some states, and why he has pledged to stay in the race even if it is only to give voters a clearly conservative pro-life alternative to McCain.

Numerous Issues Influential to Democrats

For Democrats, the top issue of importance to their vote is a tie between the situation in Iraq and healthcare—Iraq being an issue that Obama and Clinton are highly competitive on, and the latter one that most Democrats perceive is a strength of Hillary Clinton.

However, the economy, education, government corruption, and energy all follow closely behind these two in perceived importance, and at least a third of Democrats rate an additional five issues as extremely important. Of interest are the relatively low positioning of terrorism and moral values on this issues list among Democrats, a sharp contrast to their high rankings among Republicans.

Importance of Issues in Influencing Republicans' Vote for President

	% Extremely important
Terrorism	50
Moral values	39
Corruption in government	37
The economy	35
The situation in Iraq	35
Illegal immigration	34
Taxes	31
Energy, including gas prices	26
Healthcare	25
Education	24
Social Security	21
The federal budget deficit	18
Medicare	18
The environment, including global warming	12

USA Today/Gallup, Feb. 8-10, 2008

Importance of Issues in Influencing Democrats' Vote for President

	% Extremely/ Very important
The situation in Iraq	50
Healthcare	48
The economy	45
Education	44
Corruption in government	43
Energy, including gas prices	43
Social Security	39
The federal budget deficit	39
Medicare	39
The environment, including global warming	38
Terrorism	36
Moral values	29
Taxes	29
Illegal immigration	22

USA Today/Gallup, Feb. 8-10, 2008

Economy and the War Loom Large for Independents

Come the fall, both nominees will be striving to attract independent swing voters. Right now, the most highly rated issues for independents are the economy, the situation in Iraq, and government corruption—all issues that rank fairly high among Democrats as well. However, the more Republican-oriented terrorism issue ranks a close fourth.

Bottom Line

In general, most Americans are reluctant to say that any of the issues tested in the new survey are less than very important to their vote for president this year. However, on a relative basis, the economy and Iraq are likely to be most influential. These are top-rated by Democrats as well as independents, and are fairly important to Republicans.

Republicans' particular focus on terrorism was widely considered to be one of the factors that helped George W. Bush activate his "base" in 2004 and win re-election—and is likely to be important again this fall in energizing Republicans around their party's nominee. No other issue so unites Republicans. Democrats express high interest in the candidates' positions on numerous issues, but as with

Importance of Issues in Influencing Independents' Vote for President

	% Extremely/ Very important
The economy	42
The situation in Iraq	41
Corruption in government	41
Terrorism	38
Energy, including gas prices	36
Healthcare	35
Education	34
Moral values	33
The federal budget deficit	31
The environment, including global warming	29
Social Security	28
Medicare	28
Illegal immigration	24
Taxes	22

USA Today/Gallup, Feb. 8-10, 2008

Republicans, these are issues likely to further attach Democrats to their own party.

The key to how the issues play out in the election could be whether political independents are more likely to favor the Republican or the Democratic candidate's approach to their key issues, which at the moment appear to be the economy, Iraq, and government corruption, with terrorism not far behind.

Survey Methods

These results are based on telephone interviews with 1,016 national adults, aged 18 and older, conducted Feb. 8-10, 2008. For results based on the total sample of national adults, one can say with 95% confidence that the maximum margin of sampling error is ±3 percentage points.

For results based on the sample of 305 Republicans or Republican leaners, the maximum margin of sampling error is ±6 percentage points.

For results based on the sample of 353 Democrats or Democratic leaners, the maximum margin of sampling error is ±6 percentage points.

For results based on the sample of 351 Democrats or Democratic leaners, the maximum margin of sampling error is ±6 percentage points.

Interviews are conducted with respondents on land-line telephones (for respondents with a land-line telephone) and cellular phones (for respondents who are cell-phone only).

In addition to sampling error, question wording and practical difficulties in conducting surveys can introduce error or bias into the findings of public opinion polls.

February 14, 2008

CONSUMER CONFIDENCE DOWN IN FEBRUARY

Gallup's daily polling provides new insights into consumer perceptions

by Dennis Jacobe, Gallup Chief Economist

Gallup Poll Daily tracking shows that consumer confidence for the first part of February is down from the same period in January—particularly among middle-income consumers. Daily tracking of consumer perceptions provides much more detailed information than the traditional month-to-month comparisons of consumer confidence. Gallup data not only show a more detailed picture of consumer confidence by income but also allow tracking of changes in consumer perceptions within the month.

For example, Gallup Daily tracking shows that consumer confidence actually began to deteriorate slightly in the first two weeks of January, reaching its most negative level in the period between Jan. 16 and Jan. 27—right around the time of the Fed's emergency rate cut. There was a slight recovery in late January, but consumer perceptions of the U.S. economy remain more negative now than they were when the year began, and show no signs—at least so far—of responding to the Fed's interest-rate cuts or the newly passed economic stimulus package.

Consumer Ratings of the Current Economy Fell Significantly in Early February

During Gallup's most recent week of surveying, Feb. 6-12, one in three consumers rated current economic conditions as "poor"—up significantly from the 27% who provided this rating during Jan. 6-12 polling (and 24% who said the economy was poor as the year began). This early February reading of consumer perceptions represents the highest percentage of consumers rating the U.S. economy as "poor" since February 2003 (just before the war with Iraq began), when 34% of consumers reported a similar view.

How would you rate economic conditions in this country today -- as excellent, good, only fair, or poor?

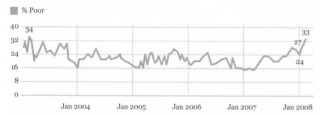

Comparing the Feb. 6-12 data to the Jan. 6-12 data, the largest decline in consumer ratings of the current economy took place among middle-income consumers. During early January, 39% of lower-income consumers (those making less than $24,000 a year) rated current economic conditions as "poor," compared to 27% of middle-income consumers (those with annual incomes of $24,000 to less than $60,000). By early February, the percentage of lower-income consumers saying the economy was poor had increased by 2 percentage points to 41%, while the percentage of middle-income consumers saying "poor" had surged by 10 points to 37%.

Consumer Expectations for the Economy Deteriorated in February

In early February, only 14% of U.S. consumers said current economic conditions were "getting better" while 79% thought they were

Percentage of Consumers Rating the Current Economy as "Poor," by Annual Income

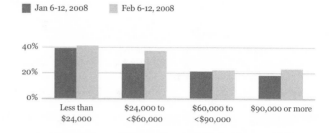

"getting worse." This represents a slight deterioration in consumer expectations from Jan. 6-12 polling (17% getting better, 77% getting worse), and more of a deterioration from the first few days of January (20% getting better, 73% getting worse). More importantly, it means current consumer economic expectations remain below their prewar (March 2003—23% better, 67% worse) and pre-9/11 (September 2001—19% better, 70% worse) levels.

Right now, do you think that economic conditions in the country as a whole are getting better or getting worse?

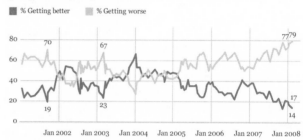

From early January to early February, the economic outlook of consumers making less than $90,000 a year grew more pessimistic. In contrast, among those with annual incomes of at least $90,000, the percentage saying conditions were getting worse actually declined by four percentage points (from 77% to 73%) in early February.

Percentage of Consumers Saying Economic Conditions in the Country Are "Getting Worse," by Annual Income

Middle-Income Consumer Confidence Deteriorating

Gallup's new daily polling shows that consumer confidence—in terms of both how consumers rate the current economy and their expectations for the economy's direction—deteriorated in early February compared in particular to early January. These findings comport with those of Bloomberg's survey of economists that show them expecting the Reuters/University of Michigan preliminary index of consumer sentiment for February 2008 (to be reported Friday) declining from its final January rating of 78.4 to 76 in early February.

The large number of consumer interviews that Gallup's daily polling provides—more than 6,000 so far in February—offers added reliability to estimates that consumer perceptions of the economy are deteriorating. It also allows a more in-depth look at consumer perceptions and gives evidence that the greatest deterioration in consumer confidence is taking place among middle-income consumers. In turn, this implies that the financial squeeze that has played such havoc with lower-income consumers in recent years is now spreading to middle-income consumers. Daily tracking of consumer perceptions also allows for monitoring of consumers' immediate reactions to the Fed's lowering of interest rates and the announcement of a new fiscal stimulus plan—both of which appear to have had little, if not a slightly negative, effect on consumer perceptions during recent weeks.

Of course, none of this is good news for the nation's retailers or for the outlook for the U.S. economy in the months ahead.

Survey Methods

Results are based on telephone interviews with 5,448 national adults, aged 18 and older, conducted Jan. 6-12, 2008, and 2,624 interviews conducted Feb. 6-12, 2008. For results based on these samples of national adults, one can say with 95% confidence that the maximum margin of sampling error is ±2 percentage points.

Interviews are conducted with respondents on land-line telephones (for respondents with a land-line telephone) and cellular phones (for respondents who are cell-phone only).

In addition to sampling error, question wording and practical difficulties in conducting surveys can introduce error or bias into the findings of public opinion polls.

February 14, 2008
HOW DOES MCCAIN'S SUPPORT COMPARE HISTORICALLY?
His 51% is at low end of historical spectrum

by Frank Newport, Gallup Poll Editor in Chief

Most observers now say that with Sen. John McCain's victories in Virginia, Maryland, and the District of Columbia on Tuesday, he is all but certain to be the Republican nominee this year, based on mathematical calculations of the number of GOP delegates necessary to gain the nomination.

But Mike Huckabee continues to campaign vigorously against McCain, and the news media spend a substantial amount of time highlighting the alleged rifts within the Republican Party in terms of conservative unwillingness to support McCain as their party's nominee.

Gallup Poll Daily election tracking makes it possible to place McCain's current status as his party's presumptive nominee in historical perspective by providing the basis for a comparison to the support other front-runners have enjoyed in previous elections.

At some point in every election, once a party's nominee is essentially known and agreed upon, Gallup has quit asking members of that party about the nomination process and has moved to asking about the general election. So the "final" nomination survey each election year serves as an interesting indicator of the overall support level that nominee was receiving among members of his party at the

time he was deemed (by Gallup editors at any rate) to have the nomination sewn up.

McCain is not quite yet at that point. But the analysis of where previous front-runners were when they were assumed to have the nomination in hand provides a framework to use in calibrating just how "wounded" a nominee McCain may be. At this point, it can be said that while McCain's current 51% support for his presumptive candidacy is not overwhelming based on Gallup's historical record, it is not unprecedentedly low either. And there is still room for McCain to improve his standing in the days ahead.

Here are some year-by-year examples of where things stood in previous elections:

2004

Gallup's last 2004 primary-nomination survey in which the Democratic candidates were pitted against one another was conducted Feb. 16-17. In that survey, John Kerry (who at that point was the presumptive nominee) received 64% of the vote, to John Edwards' 18%. Incumbent President George W. Bush was unchallenged for the GOP nomination.

2000

Gallup's last primary-nomination survey for both parties in 2000 was conducted Feb. 25-27. Al Gore, who as incumbent vice president was all but assured of getting the nomination but who had some primary opposition, ended up in that final survey with 65% of the vote to Bill Bradley's 28%. On the Republican side, despite having been the leading Republican to get his party's nomination extending well back into 1999, George W. Bush was receiving a relatively modest 57% of Republican support. Who was in second place? None other than McCain, who at 34% actually had a slightly higher level of Republican support than Huckabee does now.

1996

Bob Dole, the eventual GOP nominee in 1996, had 58% of the Republican vote in Gallup's last primary survey of that year, conducted March 8-10. Pat Buchanan and Steve Forbes trailed, both with 15% of the GOP vote. Bill Clinton was the incumbent Democratic president seeking re-election.

1992

Clinton had 71% of the Democratic vote in Gallup's final primary survey of 1992, conducted March 20-22; Jerry Brown received 25%. On the Republican side, incumbent President George H.W. Bush received 86%, with Buchanan behind at 11% (the final GOP nomination survey in 1992 was conducted March 11-12).

1988

Michael Dukakis was at 69% of the vote in Gallup's final primary Democratic primary poll in 1988, conducted May 13-15, with Jesse Jackson second at 21%. On the Republican side, George H.W. Bush was in the lead by a virtually identical margin, 69% to 22% over Dole at the time of Gallup's last Republican primary poll, March 10-12.

1984

Gallup's last primary survey in 1984 was conducted May 18-21—even later than the final survey of 1988—and showed that Walter

Mondale (who won the nomination) was ahead of Gary Hart by a relatively small margin, 46% to 34%, with Jackson at 10%. (Mondale's 46% was the lowest margin by any nominee in the final Gallup survey from 1980 through 2004.) Ronald Reagan was the incumbent president running for re-election on the GOP side and was not seriously challenged.

1980

Gallup's final primary nomination survey of 1980 was conducted Feb. 29-March 3. Reagan received 55% of the vote in that survey, followed by George H.W. Bush (the man who became his vice president) with 25%. Jimmy Carter was the Democratic incumbent seeking re-election.

Implications

These data show that at 51%, McCain's current support level is relatively low compared with the support that presumptive nominees in either party have enjoyed since 1980 at the time Gallup finished its primary polling. In fact, only Mondale in 1984 had a lower level of support in the final Gallup survey.

Surveying over the next several days will show whether McCain's support picks up after news of his three wins on Tuesday—or whether it drops, given the news that Huckabee did well in Virginia among religious, conservative Republicans. If McCain's support climbs to at least 55%, then he will at least be able to say that his support is where Ronald Reagan's was in 1980 at the point when he was assumed to have won his party's nomination.

Survey Methods

The results showing John McCain's current standing are based on combined data from Feb. 10-12, 2008, including interviews with 1,002 Republican and Republican-leaning voters. For results based on this sample, the maximum margin of sampling error is ±3 percentage points.

The results for the various primary nominations from 1980 through 2004 discussed in this article are based on Gallup Polls conducted in each of those years on the dates indicated in the text. The sample sizes and sampling error associated with each vary from poll to poll.

In addition to sampling error, question wording and practical difficulties in conducting surveys can introduce error or bias into the findings of public opinion polls.

February 14, 2008
MARITAL STATUS AND PARTY PREFERENCE OFTEN RELATED
GOP fares better among married Americans

by Jeffrey M. Jones, Gallup Poll Managing Editor

It's not clear whether love and politics go together, but a special Valentine's Day review of Americans' party affiliation shows there is a strong relationship between marital status and party affiliation. Unmarried Americans are more likely to identify as Democrats than as independents or in particular Republicans, while married Ameri-

cans tilt toward the GOP. Among all Americans who identify as Republicans, the married vastly outnumber the unmarried. Since both marriage and gender are related to party identification, their effects build on each other, such that married men are the most likely to identify with the Republican Party and unmarried women are the most likely to identify with the Democratic Party.

These results are based on an analysis of data from Gallup Poll Daily tracking, conducted Feb. 1-12, 2008, including interviews with more than 12,000 Americans aged 18 and older.

The majority of U.S. adults—57% according to the tracking results—are currently married. Among this group, slightly more identify as Republicans (35%) than as independents (32%) or Democrats (32%). But among Americans who are not currently married—including those who have never married, or are divorced, widowed, separated, or living with a partner— 41% consider themselves Democrats, 38% independents, and just 19% Republicans.

Party Identification, by Marital Status

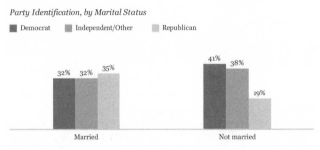

Gallup Poll Daily Tracking data, Feb. 1-12, 2008

The net result is that married Republicans outnumber unmarried Republicans by better than a 2-to-1 ratio. There are more married than unmarried independents and Democrats, but only by a slight margin in each group.

Percentage of Partisans Who Are Married and Who Are Not Married

Gallup Poll Daily Tracking data, Feb. 1-12, 2008

The gender gap in politics is well-documented, and the recent tracking results confirm this as a fact of American political life. Among women, 41% currently identify as Democrats, 32% as independents, and just 25% as Republicans. Men are more evenly divided between the two parties (32% Republican, 31% Democratic), during a time when the political mood strongly favors the Democratic Party. Thirty-seven percent of men do not affiliate with either party at the moment.

Thus, as one would expect, the variation in party preference is even more pronounced when taking into account both Americans' gender and their marital status. Married men show a 10-point gap in favor of the Republican Party, and are currently the only one of the four marriage-by-gender groups that favors the GOP. The Democratic advantage among married women is 6 points, but is much larger among unmarried men (13 points) and in particular unmarried women (29 points).

Party Identification, by Gender and Marital Status

	Married men	Unmarried men	Married women	Unmarried women
Democrat	28%	35%	37%	46%
Independent/Other	33%	41%	30%	35%
Republican	38%	22%	31%	17%

Gallup Poll Daily Tracking data, Feb. 1-12, 2008

Implications

Clearly, married Americans (especially married men) form a large part of the Republican base. The marriage gap has been evident in voting preferences for president since 1996 (as far back as Gallup has data), and the data analyzed here indicate that it will continue in the 2008 election.

Survey Methods

Results are based on telephone interviews with 12,181 national adults, aged 18 and older, conducted Feb. 1-12, 2008, as part of Gallup Poll Daily tracking. For results based on the total sample of national adults, one can say with 95% confidence that the maximum margin of sampling error is ±1 percentage point.

For results based on the samples of 6,896 married Americans and 5,205 unmarried Americans, the maximum margin of sampling error is ±1 percentage point.

For results based on the samples of 6,066 men and 6,115 women, the maximum margin of sampling error is ±1 percentage point.

For results based on the samples of 3,891 married men, 2,129 unmarried men, 3,005 married women, and 3,076 unmarried women, the maximum margin of sampling error is ±2 percentage points.

Interviews are conducted with respondents on land-line telephones (for respondents with a land-line telephone) and cellular phones (for respondents who are cell-phone only).

In addition to sampling error, question wording and practical difficulties in conducting surveys can introduce error or bias into the findings of public opinion polls.

February 15, 2008
DEMOCRATS' HOLD ON HOUSE LOOKS SECURE, FOR NOW
Current advantage is greater than that seen in last two elections

by Lydia Saad, Gallup Poll Senior Editor

The Republican Party last carried a majority of seats in the U.S. House of Representatives in 2004, and Gallup polling conducted in the days preceding the election that year found 47% of likely voters planning to vote for the Republican candidate in their district. In 2006, with their final pre-election support at 44% of likely voters, the Republicans lost control of Congress. Today, even fewer likely voters say they will vote Republican.

According to the latest *USA Today*/Gallup poll, conducted Feb. 8-10, 2008, only 41% of adults likely to vote this November say they would support the Republican candidate running in their congressional district. Fifty-five percent say they would vote for the Democratic candidate.

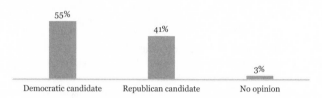

Based on likely voters

Democratic candidate 55% Republican candidate 41% No opinion 3%

USA Today/Gallup, Feb. 8-10, 2008

The current 14-point margin in favor of the Democrats among likely voters is one of the highest Gallup has seen in recent years, along with two others late in the 2006 campaign.

Preference in Vote for Congress -- Recent Trend
Based on likely voters

	Democratic candidate	Republican candidate	Advantage
	%	%	Pct. pts.
2008 Feb 8-10	55	41	+14 Dem
2006 Nov 2-5	51	44	+ 7 Dem
2006 Oct 20-22	54	41	+13 Dem
2006 Oct 6-8	59	36	+23 Dem
2006 Sep 15-17	48	48	0
2004 Oct 29-31	48	47	+1 Dem
2004 Oct 22-24	47	50	+3 Rep
2004 Sep 3-5	46	48	+2 Rep
2004 Jul 30-Aug 1	47	47	0
2004 Jan 2-5	45	50	+ 5 Rep
2002 Oct 31-Nov 3	45	51	+ 6 Rep
2002 Oct 21-22	49	46	+ 3 Dem
2002 Oct 3-6	48	47	+ 1 Dem
2002 Sep 20-22	50	46	+4 Dem

If the same result were found right before this year's Nov. 4 elections, it would almost certainly portend an increase in the Democrats' share of seats in the U.S. House of Representatives. However, as Gallup's long-term "generic ballot" trend shows, preferences on this question can shift substantially in the course of an election year, so it is far too soon to be making those kinds of predictions.

Implications

Voters' overall preference for Democratic congressional candidates mirrors the underlying Democratic advantage in Americans' current party identification. As Gallup has noted in recent months, the percentage of Americans identifying themselves as Democrats or as leaning to the Democratic Party far outpaces those identifying as or leaning Republican: 51% vs. 40% in 2007.

This deficit does not appear to be an insurmountable problem for the Republican Party in the presidential election—Gallup finds the likely Republican nominee, John McCain, running about even with both Hillary Clinton and Barack Obama in general-election trial heats. However, party identification is typically much more closely related to national generic congressional-ballot preferences. The question is whether a popular Republican presidential candidate would cause Republican party identification to rebound enough to blunt Democratic gains in Congress, or even roll them back.

Survey Methods

Results are based on telephone interviews with 1,016 national adults, aged 18 and older, conducted Feb. 8-10, 2008. For results based on the total sample of national adults, one can say with 95% confidence that the maximum margin of sampling error is ±3 percentage points.

Results for likely voters are based on the subsample of 706 survey respondents deemed most likely to vote in the November 2008 general election, according to a series of questions measuring current voting intentions and past voting behavior. For results based on the total sample of likely voters, one can say with 95% confidence that the maximum margin of sampling error is ±4 percentage points. The "likely voter" model assumes a turnout of 60% of national adults. The "likely voter" sample is weighted to match this assumption, so the weighted sample size is 606.

In addition to sampling error, question wording and practical difficulties in conducting surveys can introduce error or bias into the findings of public opinion polls.

February 18, 2008

JFK AND RONALD REAGAN WIN GALLUP PRESIDENTS DAY POLL

Clinton ranks highest among living ex-presidents

by Lydia Saad, Gallup Poll Senior Editor

Being "a man for his times" is among the highest praise a president could want or need. But two past presidents, both long out of office, are widely seen as the right man for today.

John F. Kennedy and Ronald Reagan are each chosen by about a quarter of Americans as the former president they would most like to bring back as the next president of the United States if they could. That is not to say Americans would choose Kennedy or Reagan over all of the current candidates for president. Rather, if they could select from the presidents whose images now hang at the National Portrait Gallery, these would be their top choices.

Bill Clinton and Abraham Lincoln are roughly tied for third (chosen by 13% and 10% of Americans, respectively), with Franklin Roosevelt trailing closely behind. No other president is named by more than 5% of Americans, but a number are mentioned by at least 1%.

Bring Back Reagan

Republicans are unambiguous about whom they would restore to office if they could. Reagan wins an outright majority (51%) of their votes.

Two of Republicans' top five choices are Democrats: Kennedy, at 12% (roughly tied with Abraham Lincoln for second place), and Franklin Roosevelt, in fifth place with 4%.

Suppose you could bring back any of the U.S. presidents, living or dead, to be the next president of the United States. Who would you most want to be the next president?

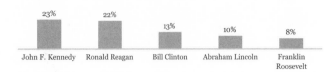

Feb. 11-14, 2008

The other name in the Republicans' top five is George Washington, in fourth place with 6%.

Besides Reagan and Kennedy, no other modern-day president—most notably Republicans George H.W. Bush, Gerald Ford, and Richard Nixon—is mentioned by more than a handful of Republicans.

Republicans' Top Five Ex-Presidents to Serve as Next U.S. President

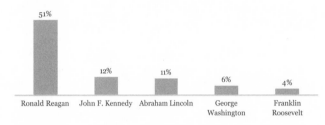

Feb. 11-14, 2008

Clinton or Camelot?

Democrats are less settled on one particular president as their hypothetical choice to return to the Oval Office. The most popular ex-president for the job is Kennedy, mentioned by 34%. However, Clinton ranks a fairly close second, with 24%. Roosevelt is favored for the position by 12% of Democrats.

Seven percent of Democrats would bring back the symbolic father of the Republican Party—Lincoln—as president, while 4% would restore Democratic Party founder Thomas Jefferson.

Democrats' Top Five Ex-Presidents to Serve as Next U.S. President

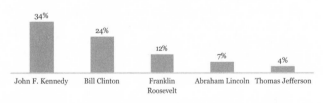

Feb. 11-14, 2008

Independents' views are a hybrid of Republican and Democratic opinions; their top choices are Reagan (with 21%) and Kennedy (with 19%). These are followed by Lincoln, Clinton, and Roosevelt.

Boomers vs. Generation X

Nostalgia appears to play a modest role in Americans' choice of past president to serve the country today. The most popular choice of

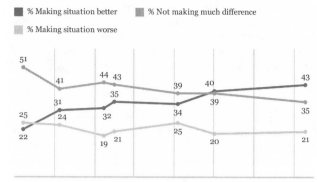

Feb. 11-14, 2008

Feb. 8-10 USA Today/Gallup Poll

Baby Boomers, now aged about 50 to 64, is the man who was president of their youth: Kennedy. The top choice of those 30 to 49 years of age (broadly speaking, Generation X) is the president who served during their childhood or young adult years: Reagan.

Seniors are more likely than any other group to choose Roosevelt. Younger adults—those 18 to 29 and 30 to 49—are the most likely to choose Clinton.

Top Five Ex-Presidents Named to Serve as Next U.S. President, by Respondent Age

	18 to 29 years	30 to 49 years	50 to 64 years	65 years and older
	%	%	%	%
John F. Kennedy	22	18	32	21
Ronald Reagan	8	30	19	20
Bill Clinton	19	14	9	10
Abraham Lincoln	17	9	8	7
Franklin Roosevelt	8	7	7	14

Feb. 11-14, 2008

Survey Methods

Results are based on telephone interviews with 1,007 national adults, aged 18 and older, conducted Feb. 11-14, 2008. For results based on the total sample of national adults, one can say with 95% confidence that the maximum margin of sampling error is ±3 percentage points.

Results based on 276 Republicans have a maximum margin of sampling error of ±6 percentage points. Results based on 389 Democrats have a maximum margin of sampling error of ±5 percentage points. Results based on 331 independents have a maximum margin of sampling error of ±6 percentage points.

In addition to sampling error, question wording and practical difficulties in conducting surveys can introduce error or bias into the findings of public opinion polls.

February 18, 2008
MAJORITY STILL FAVORS TIMETABLE FOR TROOP WITHDRAWAL
Yet views of the surge's progress are becoming more positive

by Jeffrey M. Jones, Gallup Poll Managing Editor

Roughly one year after the United States began increasing the number of troops it has in Iraq, Americans give the "surge" their most positive assessment to date.

Nevertheless, basic attitudes about the war are largely unchanged, including views about setting a timetable for U.S. troop withdrawal. The majority of Americans continue to favor a timetable for withdrawal, though relatively few favor a rapid withdrawal, similar to what Democratic presidential candidate Barack Obama is advocating. Six in 10 express opposition to the war effort more generally.

The Feb. 8-10 *USA Today*/Gallup poll was conducted just before Secretary of Defense Robert Gates announced his probable support for a "pause" in U.S. troop withdrawals this summer after several brigades are removed as planned, which would result in the United States at least temporarily maintaining a troop force larger than pre-surge levels. Gates argues that a pause may be needed to evaluate whether the security gains made in Iraq can be maintained with smaller forces.

According to the poll, 43% of Americans say the surge of U.S. troops in Iraq is making the situation there better, a slight increase from 40% in late November, but up more substantially from 34% in early November. This is the most positive review of the surge Gallup has measured since it began. Thirty-five percent now say the surge is not making much difference, and just 21% say it is making things worse.

Republicans, Democrats, and independents have divergent views of the surge. Seventy-five percent of Republicans say it is making things better in Iraq, compared with 40% of independents and 21% of Democrats. Democrats are most likely to believe the surge is "not making much difference."

Perceived Effect of Increased U.S. Troop Presence on Situation in Iraq
Results by party affiliation

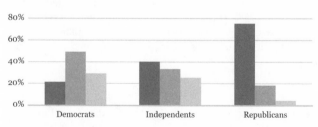

Feb. 8-10 USA Today/Gallup Poll

But perceptions of progress brought by the surge have done little to move Americans' well-entrenched views of the war. The majority, 56%, still favors setting a timetable for removing U.S. troops from Iraq and sticking to that timetable "regardless of what is going on in Iraq at the time." That is little different from the 59% and 60% readings Gallup obtained last May through November, when views of the surge were not as optimistic as they are today. Currently, 39% of Americans oppose a timetable.

Views of What to Do About U.S. Troops in Iraq

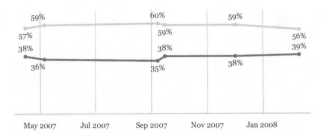

Those who favor a timetable are more than twice as likely to favor a schedule of gradual troop withdrawal (67%) as they are to prefer a more immediate removal of troops (32%). All told, 18% of Americans favor removing troops from Iraq as rapidly as possible.

Both Democratic presidential candidates, Obama and Hillary Clinton, favor a timetable, while the GOP's likely nominee, John McCain, strongly opposes one. Obama is advocating a fairly rapid withdrawal of U.S. troops from Iraq, which would have all troops out within 16 months of his taking office. Clinton favors a slower withdrawal, which would be complete by 2013. Thus, no candidate's position really represents the views of most Americans, but the poll suggests that currently McCain's and Clinton's positions are closest to the largest number of Americans. This is not to suggest that Americans would necessarily oppose any of the candidates' Iraq policies should they be elected president.

Americans who do not assess the surge positively overwhelmingly advocate a timetable, including 76% of those who see the surge as not making much difference, and 86% of those who think it is making things worse. Meanwhile, Americans who believe the surge is working are solidly against (70%) a timetable.

In the current poll, 60% oppose the decision to go to war: they call the decision to send troops a mistake, one of the highest readings to date. A majority has called the war a mistake in all but a few Gallup measurements since the summer of 2005, and since January 2007, the percentage has been closer to 60% than to 50%.

Do You Think the United States Made a Mistake in Sending Troops to Iraq?

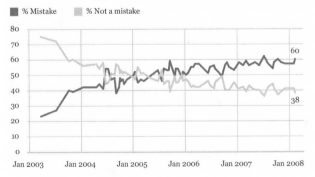

Implications

Even with mostly positive reports out of Iraq in recent months, Americans' expressed desire for a timetable for troop withdrawal has largely remained unchanged. Defense Secretary Gates' recent announcement appears to be at odds with that sentiment. Gates is arguing that the military needs time to evaluate whether the United States can maintain the security gains it has made in Iraq with a smaller force. It is unclear at this point whether Americans would support temporarily halting troop withdrawal to allow for a period of evaluation after an initial drawdown.

Survey Methods

Results are based on telephone interviews with 1,016 national adults, aged 18 and older, conducted Feb. 8-10, 2008. For results based on the total sample of national adults, one can say with 95% confidence that the maximum margin of sampling error is ±3 percentage points.

Interviews are conducted with respondents on land-line telephones (for respondents with a land-line telephone) and cellular phones (for respondents who are cell-phone only).

In addition to sampling error, question wording and practical difficulties in conducting surveys can introduce error or bias into the findings of public opinion polls.

February 19, 2008

JOBS OUTLOOK WORST IN FOUR YEARS

More middle- and upper-income Americans say now is a "bad time" to get a quality job

by Dennis Jacobe, Gallup Chief Economist

Surging pessimism about the job market suggests the Federal Reserve should rethink its economic outlook.

Thinking about the job situation in America today, would you say that it is now a good time or a bad time to find a quality job?

Among national adults

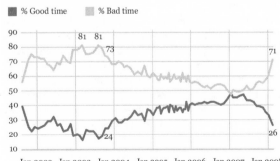

Gallup's Job Measure Plunges

Federal Reserve Chairman Ben Bernanke testified last week before the Senate, stating that "Payroll employment, after increasing about 95,000 per month on average in the fourth quarter, declined by an estimated 17,000 jobs in January." He went on to note that there remain downside risks to the Fed's baseline economic outlook, including that "the labor market may deteriorate to an extent beyond that currently anticipated." A new Gallup Poll, conducted Feb. 11-14, 2008, suggests such a deterioration of conditions in the job market may already be underway.

The percentage of Americans saying now is a "bad time" to find a quality job surged from 60% in January to 71% in February. This represents the largest monthly increase in the percentage holding this view since Gallup began asking this question on a regular basis in August 2001, with the sole exception of a 15-point increase following 9/11. The latest increase puts the percentage holding this negative view of the jobs market at its highest level since November 2003, when 73% said it was a bad time to find a quality job. The all-time high is 81%, reached twice during 2003.

Of course, this sharp deterioration in job-market perceptions is taking place in conjunction with a similar sharp drop in consumer confidence, as Gallup has been reporting. As a result, today's negative labor-market perceptions may not only reflect current trends in jobs and hiring, but also, as Bernanke mentioned in his testimony, they "seem likely to weigh on consumer spending in the near term."

More Upper-Income Americans Say This Is a "Bad Time" to Get a Quality Job

As might be expected, in January, a higher percentage of lower-income Americans than of those with higher incomes said it was a bad time to get a quality job. However, the February surge in those holding this view comes disproportionately from those in middle- and higher-income households.

Thinking about the job situation in America today, would you say that it is now a good time or a bad time to find a quality job?

Percentage saying "bad time," by annual household income

■ Less than $30,000   ■ $30,000 to <$75,000   ■ $75,000 or more

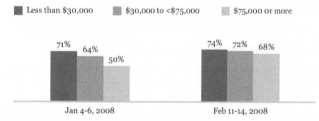

The percentage of lower-income families (those making less than $30,000 a year) who are pessimistic on this measure increased by just 3 percentage points, from 71% in January to 74% in February. In sharp contrast, among higher-income households (those making more than $75,000 annually), the percentage holding this same view increased by 18 points, from 50% to 68%. The percentage of middle-income households (those making $30,000 but less than $75,000 a year) with this view increased by 8 points, from 64% to 72%.

Americans Are Worried About Losing Their Jobs

Nearly one in four Americans say they are worried that they or their spouse will lose their job in the next 12 months. This is similar to the percentage having such worries in January 2004 (21%) and December 2002 (24%), but remains below the roughly one-third of Americans who said they were worried during late 1991 and early 1992, when consumer confidence was as low as it is today.

Please tell me whether you are worried or not worried about each of the following happening. How about that -- [RANDOM ORDER]?

A. You or your spouse will lose a job within the next 12 months

Jan. 30-Feb. 2, 2008

The Fed May Have to Rethink Its Baseline Outlook

Many observers referred to the nation's last economic recovery as a so-called "jobless recovery." As the economy expanded, job growth was anemic, at best, by historical standards. Some of this may have been related to increased productivity, globalization, and even the growth of the underground economy. Similarly, it may be that as the economy has slowed, these same factors have mitigated the impact of the slowdown on the U.S. job market. Regardless, it is the continued strength in the jobs market during the past several months that many economists point to as a reason for optimism that the U.S. economy will avoid a recession.

Gallup's new polling data suggest that soon, the jobs outlook may more fully reflect the economic slowdown, with another decline in jobs and an increase in the unemployment rate in the months ahead. This suggests that Bernanke's 2008 baseline outlook of "sluggish growth, followed by a somewhat stronger pace of growth starting later this year" may already be out of date. Bernanke concluded his testimony last week by alluding to a possible further drop in interest rates: "The FOMC (Federal Open Market Committee) will be carefully evaluating incoming information bearing on the economic outlook and will act in a timely manner as needed to support growth and to provide adequate insurance against downside risks." He is likely to find the markets ready to take him up on this implied promise.

Survey Methods

For results based on telephone interviews with 1,023 national adults, aged 18 and older, conducted Jan. 4-6, 2008, and on 1,007 interviews conducted Feb. 11-14, 2008, one can say with 95% confidence that the maximum margin of sampling error is ±3 percentage points. For results based on telephone interviews with 2,020 national adults, conducted Jan. 30-Feb. 2, 2008, the maximum margin of sampling error is ±2 percentage points.

Interviews are conducted with respondents on land-line telephones (for respondents with a land-line telephone) and cellular phones (for respondents who are cell-phone only).

In addition to sampling error, question wording and practical difficulties in conducting surveys can introduce error or bias into the findings of public opinion polls.

February 19, 2008

OBAMA GAINING AMONG MIDDLE-AGED, WOMEN, HISPANICS

Also running even with Clinton among core Democrats

by Jeffrey M. Jones, Gallup Poll Managing Editor

The momentum in the Democratic nomination race has clearly swung toward Barack Obama. Not only has he won all of the post-Super Tuesday contests, but he has steadily gained in Gallup Poll Daily tracking to the point where he has overtaken Clinton as the national leader for the first time, holding a statistically significant lead in each of the last three tracking poll results.

Gallup Daily Election Polling Results for the Democratic Presidential Nomination: Recent Trend (since Jan. 26-28, 2008)

Based on national Democratic and Democratic-leaning voters

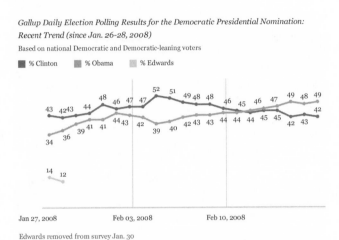

Edwards removed from survey Jan. 30

Obama's standing has improved among most Democratic subgroups over the past several days. But one of the more substantial shifts has been the changing preferences of middle-aged Democratic voters, who have moved away from Clinton and toward Obama in the past week. Obama has also made gains among three other groups that have favored Clinton throughout much of the campaign—women, Hispanics, and self-identified Democrats. Obama and Clinton are now running even among these three key groups in the most recent Gallup tracking data.

These findings are based on a comparison of Democratic voters' nomination preferences in Feb. 5-9 polling with those in Feb. 13-17 polling. Each of these five-day tracking periods consists of interviews with roughly 2,000 Democratic voters nationwide. Overall, in the Feb. 5-9 data, Clinton led Obama by an average of 49% to 42%. In the most recent five days (Feb. 13-17), the candidates' standings have basically flipped, with Obama leading Clinton by an average of 49% to 43%.

The Age Effect

Throughout the campaign, exit polls have shown that Obama has appealed to younger voters, and Clinton to older voters. Even as the momentum has swung in Obama's favor, those basic relationships at opposite ends of the age spectrum still hold. The change in recent days has been in middle-aged Democratic voters' preferences. In the Feb. 5-9 period, Clinton led among Democratic voters aged 35 to 54 by a 49% to 42% margin. Now, Obama is the leader among this group by 51% to 42%.

This suggests that middle-aged voters will be a key swing group to monitor in the remaining Democratic primaries and caucuses. For the moment, Obama has captured their allegiance.

Democratic Nomination Preference, by Voter Age Group

Based on Democratic voters

	Clinton, Feb 5-9	Obama, Feb 5-9	Clinton, Feb 13-17	Obama, Feb 13-17
18 to 34 years old	37%	57%	34%	61%
35 to 54 years old	49%	42%	42%	51%
55 years and older	58%	32%	51%	37%

The Gender Gap

Clinton's primary victories to date have been fueled in large part by support from female voters. The former first lady and current New York senator has always demonstrated a particular appeal to women.

When Obama has closed the gap with Clinton nationally—as he did in the days leading up to Super Tuesday—he has usually been able to do so by reducing her lead among women.

In the days immediately after Super Tuesday, Clinton rebuilt her lead among women, enjoying a 53% to 38% lead in the Feb. 5-9 polling. But her gender advantage has once again dissipated, and in the latest data, female Democratic voters are about as likely to say they prefer Obama (45%) as Clinton (46%).

Democratic Nomination Preference, by Gender

Based on Democratic voters

	Clinton, Feb 5-9	Obama, Feb 5-9	Clinton, Feb 13-17	Obama, Feb 13-17
Men	44%	48%	39%	54%
Women	53%	38%	46%	45%

Hispanics

Many credited Clinton's strong appeal to Hispanics for helping her win the important Feb. 5 California primary, and her support among this key group gives the campaign hope for a comeback victory in the March 4 Texas primary. But the tracking data suggest her support advantage among Hispanics may be eroding, at least on a national level. In the Feb. 5-9 data, Clinton led Obama by nearly 2-to-1, 63%-32%, among Hispanic Democratic voters. In the most recent polling, the two are essentially tied among this constituency, with 50% preferring Obama and 46% Clinton.

Democratic Nomination Preference, by Hispanic Ethnicity

Based on Democratic voters

	Clinton, Feb 5-9	Obama, Feb 5-9	Clinton, Feb 13-17	Obama, Feb 13-17
Hispanic	63%	32%	46%	50%
Non-Hispanic	47%	44%	42%	49%

Party ID

Clinton looked like a solid bet for the nomination early in the campaign process not only because of her consistent lead, but also because she was typically the preferred choice among core Democrats (those who identify as Democrats when asked to give their party affiliation). Meanwhile, Obama tended to fare better among those who initially identify as independents but then say they "lean" to the Democratic Party.

In the Feb. 5-9 data, Clinton continued to lead Obama, 51% to 41%, among Democratic identifiers, while trailing slightly (48% to 42%) among independents. In the most recent results, Obama has expanded his lead among independents (58% to 36%) while achieving parity with Clinton among core Democrats (46% Obama, 45% Clinton).

Democratic Nomination Preference, by Party Affiliation
Based on Democratic voters

	Clinton, Feb 5-9	Obama, Feb 5-9	Clinton, Feb 13-17	Obama, Feb 13-17
Democrat	51%	41%	45%	46%
Independent/Lean Democratic	42%	48%	36%	58%

Other Democratic Voter Groups

The following table shows how the race has shifted among other Democratic voter groups of note.

Democratic Nomination Preference, by Voter Subgroup
Based on Democratic voters

	Clinton, Feb 5-9	Obama, Feb 5-9	Clinton, Feb 13-17	Obama, Feb 13-17
White	54%	36%	50%	40%
Black	24%	68%	20%	77%
High school or less	60%	30%	53%	38%
Some college	44%	48%	35%	57%
College graduate	40%	53%	37%	56%
Married	51%	40%	43%	49%
Not married	47%	45%	43%	49%
Northeast	53%	39%	47%	45%
Midwest	42%	48%	40%	50%
South	49%	42%	45%	48%
West	52%	42%	39%	54%

Among the highlights:
- Obama has further expanded his dominant positioning among black Democrats.
- Both candidates have maintained their leads among their core supporters by education—Clinton among those with less formal education and Obama among college graduates. The middle group of those who attended college but did not graduate shows movement toward Obama in the latest polling.
- Married Democratic voters have shifted from a Clinton-leaning to an Obama-leaning group.
- Clinton's leads among Democrats in the Northeast and West have dissipated.

Survey Methods

Results are based on telephone interviews with 2,072 national Democratic voters, aged 18 and older, conducted Feb. 5-9, 2008, and 2,022 national Democratic voters, aged 18 and older, conducted Feb. 13-17, 2008, as part of Gallup Poll Daily tracking. For results based on these samples, one can say with 95% confidence that the maximum margin of sampling error is ±2 percentage points.

Margins of error for subgroups of Democratic voters will be larger.

Interviews are conducted with respondents on land-line telephones (for respondents with a land-line telephone) and cellular phones (for respondents who are cell-phone only).

Interviews are conducted in Spanish for respondents who request a Spanish-language interview.

In addition to sampling error, question wording and practical difficulties in conducting surveys can introduce error or bias into the findings of public opinion polls.

February 20, 2008
DISAPPROVAL OF BUSH SPANS THE ISSUES
Across seven categories, more disapproval than approval

by Lydia Saad, Gallup Poll Senior Editor

President George W. Bush is starting his last year in office with the American public feeling more negative than positive about his leadership, on multiple fronts.

President Bush's Net Job Approval Ratings -- Feb. 11-14, 2008
Percentage approve minus percentage disapprove

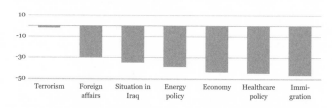

More Americans disapprove than approve of Bush's job performance on all seven national issues included in a new Feb. 11-14 Gallup Poll. He is rated least negatively for the way he is handling terrorism: 47% of Americans approve and 49% disapprove, yielding a net -2 job performance score. With only 22% approving and 69% disapproving, his ratings are the most negative for immigration. However, his ratings on healthcare and the economy are nearly as bad.

The net result is an overall job approval rating that's more than 2-to-1 negative: 65% of Americans disapprove of how Bush is doing overall, and only 31% approve. Bush's approval rating has consistently fallen below 40% for more than a year—since September 2006.

George W. Bush Overall Job Approval -- Trend Since January 2006

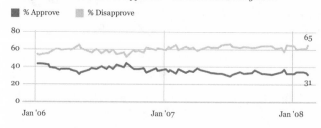

Ratings on Economy Plummet

Compared with a year ago, public approval of Bush has held fairly constant on terrorism, foreign affairs, healthcare, immigration, and energy policy, albeit at low levels. His approval score on Iraq is up slightly, from 26% to 31%. However, it is down substantially on the economy, from 41% approving in February 2007 (and 35% in August 2007) to 27% today.

Public Approval of Bush on Issues -- Today vs. a Year Ago

Percentage saying "approve" on each issue

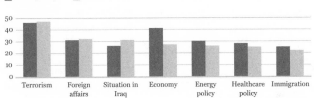

Bush has not scored majority approval for any of these issues since August 2006, when 55% still approved of the job he was doing on terrorism. This fell to 46% two months later, and has since remained below 50%.

A majority of Americans have not approved of Bush on foreign affairs since February 2005, on Iraq since March 2004, on the economy since January 2004, on energy policy since January 2003, and on healthcare policy since March 2002. At no time since Gallup began measuring public attitudes about Bush's handling of immigration in January 2005 has a majority approved.

Bush continues to enjoy majority approval from Republicans nationwide on terrorism, foreign affairs, Iraq, the economy, and healthcare. Extremely small percentages of Democrats approve of Bush on most of the issues, except for terrorism (24% approve).

Percentage Approving of Bush on Issues, by Party ID

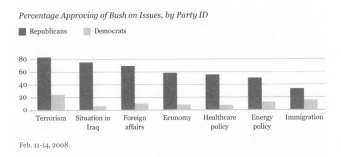

Feb. 11-14, 2008

The increase in approval of Bush on the Iraq war over the past year is because of enhanced ratings from Republicans (from 64% in February 2007 to 75% today) and independents (from 19% to 28%). Most of the decrease in approval of Bush on the economy is because of Republicans (from 83% in February 2007 to 58% today).

Survey Methods

Results are based on telephone interviews with 1,007 national adults, aged 18 and older, conducted Feb. 11-14, 2008. For results based on the total sample of national adults, one can say with 95% confidence that the maximum margin of sampling error is ±3 percentage points.

Results based on 276 Republicans have a maximum margin of sampling error of ±6 percentage points. Results based on 389 Democrats have a maximum margin of sampling error of ±5 percentage points.

Interviews are conducted with respondents on land-line telephones (for respondents with a land-line telephone) and cellular phones (for respondents who are cell-phone only).

In addition to sampling error, question wording and practical difficulties in conducting surveys can introduce error or bias into the findings of public opinion polls.

February 20, 2008

ECONOMY SURPASSES IRAQ AS MOST IMPORTANT PROBLEM
First time in four years Iraq is not No. 1

by Jeffrey M. Jones, Gallup Poll Managing Editor

The percentage of Americans mentioning "the economy" as the most important problem facing the country has sharply increased since early January. Now, for the first time since March 2004, the Iraq war is not the No. 1 problem.

Most Important Problem Facing the Country, 2004-2008 Gallup Polls

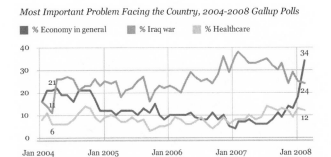

The latest Gallup Poll, conducted Feb. 11-14, finds 34% of Americans mentioning "the economy" in general terms as the most important problem facing the country. That is nearly double the 18% who said this in January, and is the highest Gallup has measured since another 34% reading in February 2003. The last time a higher percentage of Americans gave this response was at the tail end of the first Bush presidency in December 1992 and January 1993.

In addition to these general mentions of the economy, Americans cite more specific economic problems such as unemployment or jobs (7%), gas prices (3%), and the federal budget deficit (3%). All told, 49% of Americans bring up an economic issue of one sort or another in their answer, compared with 38% in January, and the highest since May 2003 (52%).

The surge in economic concern this month did not come at the expense of the Iraq war, however. Twenty-four percent of Americans mention the war, virtually unchanged from last month (25%). However, mentions of Iraq are lower today than in 2007, when an average of 33% named it as the nation's No. 1 problem.

Beyond Iraq and the economy, healthcare (12%) and immigration (9%) also figure prominently in Americans' minds. The following table shows the list of all problems mentioned by 1% or more of Americans.

Top-of-mind mentions of the economy as the nation's most important problem do not vary much by subgroup. There is some variation by income level, but not in the expected direction. Upper- and middle-income respondents are more likely to mention the economy in general terms than are lower-income respondents, who would presumably be more affected by the struggling economy. But lower-income respondents are significantly more likely to mention unemployment and jobs than are middle- and upper-income respondents.

Survey Methods

Results are based on telephone interviews with 1,007 national adults, aged 18 and older, conducted Feb. 11-14, 2008. For results based on the total sample of national adults, one can say with 95% confidence that the maximum margin of sampling error is ±3 percentage points.

Most Important Problem Facing the Country, Feb. 11-14, 2008, Gallup Poll

Category	% Mentioning
Economy in general	34
Situation in Iraq/War	24
Poor healthcare/hospitals; high cost of healthcare	12
Immigration/Illegal aliens	9
Unemployment/Jobs	7
Dissatisfaction with government/Congress/politicians; poor leadership; corruption; abuse of power	6
Terrorism	4
Ethical/Moral/Religious decline; dishonesty; lack of integrity	4
Federal budget deficit/Federal debt	3
Fuel/Oil prices	3
Education/Poor education/Access to education	3
Foreign aid/Focus overseas	3
Lack of money	2
High cost of living/Inflation	2
Poverty/Hunger/Homelessness	2
National security	2
Lack of respect for each other	2
Recession	1
Taxes	1
Corporate corruption	1
Election year/Presidential choices/Election reform	1
Judicial system/Courts/Laws	1
Lack of energy sources; the energy crisis	1
Abortion	1
Social Security	1
Environment/Pollution	1
International issues/problems	1
Care for the elderly	1

Mentions of Economy and Unemployment as Most Important Problem, by Annual Household Income Level

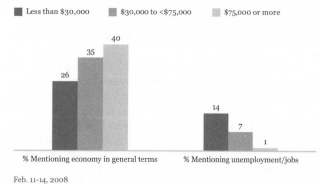

Feb. 11-14, 2008

Interviews are conducted with respondents on land-line telephones (for respondents with a land-line telephone) and cellular phones (for respondents who are cell-phone only).

In addition to sampling error, question wording and practical difficulties in conducting surveys can introduce error or bias into the findings of public opinion polls.

February 21, 2008
AMERICANS SEE CHINA CROWDING OUT U.S. AS ECONOMIC LEADER
China's rapid growth, U.S. economic slowdown may explain misconception

by Lydia Saad, Gallup Poll Senior Editor

In a sharp turnaround from eight years ago, Americans no longer believe the United States is the world's leading economic power. They are now more likely to bestow that mantle on China.

Country or Group of Countries Perceived as the Leading Economic Power in the World "Today"

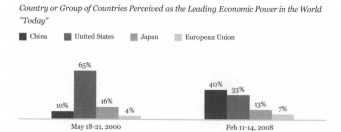

(India and Russia mentioned by 2% or fewer respondents in both time periods)

According to Gallup's annual World Affairs survey, updated Feb. 11-14, 2008, 4 in 10 Americans consider China to be the world's leading economic power; only 33% choose the United States. By contrast, in May 2000, the United States dominated public perceptions on this question, with 65% saying it was No.1.

Nearly all of the movement away from the United States as the perceived leading economic power has gone toward China. The percentages today choosing Japan, the European Union, and India are about what they were in 2000.

The United States' drop on this measure is nearly as sharp as the decline in U.S. consumer confidence over the same period. In a May 2000 Gallup Poll, when the country was still riding the dot-com boom, 66% of Americans rated economic conditions in the country as "excellent" or "good." Today, with the country poised on the edge of recession, only 23% are positive about the economy.

The Future Looks the Same

Eight years ago, most Americans (55%) were confident the United States would retain its No. 1 economic positioning for at least the next two decades. Few believed China, Japan, or the EU would overtake the United States. Now, when asked to look ahead 20 years, more Americans predict China, rather than the United States, will be the world's leading economic power.

Country or Group of Countries Expected to Be the Leading Economic Power in 20 Years

(India and Russia mentioned by 4% or fewer respondents in both time periods)

Notably, not many more Americans think China will advance to the economic superpower position in 20 years (44%) than think it is already there (40%). About a third believe the United States will be the top economic power, similar to the percentage naming it as the leading economic power today. Relatively few Americans expect Japan, the EU, India, or Russia to emerge as the top economic superpower.

Facts of the Matter

When considered against the backdrop of China's enormous population, the story of China's explosive economic growth over the last few decades (averaging 9.6% annual growth in GDP since 1978) can seem formidable. According to a recent *Newsweek* article, "In 2007 China contributed more to global growth than the United States, the first time another country had done so since at least the 1930s."

Still, according to the most recent World Bank figures, the United States leads the world in economic output (as measured by GDP), and by a substantial margin over second-ranked Japan. China has been making impressive strides in climbing the rank order of national economies, rising from sixth in the world in 2000 to fourth in 2006, but still falls below the United States, Germany, and Japan.

Americans' misperceptions about the economic rank order of nations also overlook Japan's stature on the economic playing field, ranking second worldwide. Also, although few Americans mention the EU as an economic powerhouse, 5 of the EU's 27 member countries, including third-place Germany, rank in the top 10 of the world's largest economies.

Total GDP for 2006

Source: World Bank

Ranking	Economy	Millions of U.S. dollars
1	United States	13,201,819
2	Japan	4,340,133
3	Germany	2,906,681
4	China	2,668,071
5	United Kingdom	2,345,015
6	France	2,230,721
7	Italy	1,844,749
8	Canada	1,251,463
9	Spain	1,223,988
10	Brazil	1,067,962

Bottom Line

Americans are in an economic funk at a time when China's extraordinary economic growth is getting considerable attention. The contrast is evidently sharp enough to be causing Americans to assume the economic tables have turned.

Survey Methods

Results are based on telephone interviews with 1,007 national adults, aged 18 and older, conducted Feb. 11-14, 2008. For results based on the total sample of national adults, one can say with 95% confidence that the maximum margin of sampling error is ±3 percentage points.

Interviews are conducted with respondents on land-line telephones (for respondents with a land-line telephone) and cellular phones (for respondents who are cell-phone only).

In addition to sampling error, question wording and practical difficulties in conducting surveys can introduce error or bias into the findings of public opinion polls.

February 22, 2008

AMERICANS WORRIED ABOUT THEIR STANDARD OF LIVING

Rising costs and concerns about jobs among reasons for financial stress

by Dennis Jacobe, Gallup Chief Economist

A higher percentage of Americans are currently worried about maintaining their standard of living than were worried during the 1991-1992 recession.

Please tell me whether you are worried or not worried about each of the following happening. How about that --

B. You will not be able to maintain your standard of living

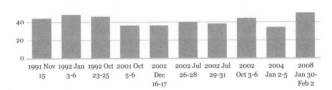

Family Finances Squeezed in Many Ways

Americans cite many reasons for their financial stress. Eighty-six percent of Americans say their families' financial situations have been very (57%) or somewhat (29%) negatively affected by the rise in gasoline and home heating prices. Three in four consumers point to the rise in food prices and healthcare costs as creating financial stress for their families. Around 6 in 10 consumers feel their financial situations are being negatively affected by the recent decline in the stock market (61%), by more people losing their jobs (58%), and by the rise in the cost of a college education (57%). Other sources of financial stress include the outsourcing of jobs overseas (53%) and problems in the housing market (47%).

Next, we'd like to know how various problems with the U.S. economy are affecting your family's financial situation. For each of the following economic problems, please say whether it has had a very negative effect, somewhat negative effect, no effect, or a positive effect on your family's financial situation. How about -- [RANDOM ORDER]?

It's clear most consumers are being squeezed by higher prices for food, energy, healthcare, and a college education. At the same time, significant percentages believe that people losing their jobs, declines in the stock market, and all the problems associated with the housing market have negatively affected their families' financial situations. None of this suggests a recovery in consumer spending anytime soon.

Survey Methods

Results are based on telephone interviews with 2,020 national adults, aged 18 and older, conducted Jan. 30-Feb. 2, 2008. For results based on the total sample of national adults, one can say with 95% confidence that the maximum margin of sampling error is ±2 percentage points.

For results based on the 995 national adults in the Form B half-sample, the maximum margin of sampling error is ±3 percentage points.

Interviews are conducted with respondents on land-line telephones (for respondents with a land-line telephone) and cellular phones (for respondents who are cell-phone only).

In addition to sampling error, question wording and practical difficulties in conducting surveys can introduce error or bias into the findings of public opinion polls.

February 22, 2008
CLINTON HAS EDGE AMONG HIGHLY RELIGIOUS WHITE DEMOCRATS
Relationship persists within age, gender groups

by Frank Newport, Gallup Poll Editor in Chief

Hillary Clinton enjoys a significant edge in support over Barack Obama among white Democrats who are highly religious.

White Democrats' Support for Clinton and Obama, by Church Attendance
Feb. 15-20, 2008

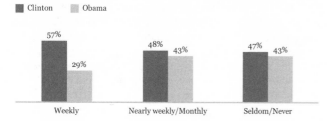

All in all, in interviews conducted Feb. 15-20 as part of Gallup Poll Daily election tracking, 57% of white, non-Hispanic Democratic voters who attend church support Clinton, while only 29% support Obama. Among those who attend church less frequently or never, Clinton's support drops while Obama's climbs.

This analysis is based on white Democrats. There is less of a relationship between candidate support and religion among black Democrats, who are both highly religious and highly likely to support Obama.

Much of the attention to the relationship between religion and the election this year has been focused on the Republican primaries. Baptist preacher Mike Huckabee has consistently performed disproportionately well among highly religious Republicans in polls and primary voting, and, prior to his leaving the race, Mitt Romney faced questions about his Mormon faith and how well his candidacy would play among evangelical Christians.

But the data reviewed here show that religion makes a difference on the Democratic side of the election as well. Underlying demographic patterns help account for this relationship.

Church attendance is related to gender, and women are more likely than men to support Clinton. (In this sample of white Democrats, 44% of men support Clinton, compared with 54% of women.) An analysis of the support patterns for Clinton and Obama by reli-

gion and gender, however, shows that it is not just the gender factor that accounts for the overall relationship. Men who attend church weekly are more likely to support Clinton and less likely to support Obama than are men who attend less frequently or not at all. Women who attend church weekly are also somewhat more likely to support Clinton over Obama than women who attend less frequently or never, although the difference is not as pronounced.

Support for Clinton and Obama Among White Democratic Men, by Church Attendance
Feb. 15-20, 2008

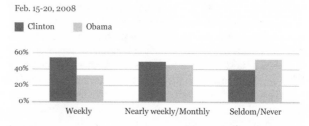

Support for Clinton and Obama Among White Democratic Women, by Church Attendance
Feb. 15-20, 2008

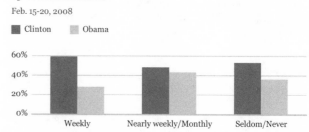

Another underlying demographic factor that helps account for the relationship is age. Church attendance is positively correlated with age. (In this sample of white Democratic voters, for example, the percentage attending church weekly more than doubles, from 16% to 34%, in a comparison of those who are 18 to 34 and those who are 55 and older.) In addition, older Democrats are more likely than younger Democrats to support Clinton.

There are too few 18- to 34-year-olds who attend church weekly in this sample to provide the basis for meaningful analysis. But the relationship between religiosity and support for Clinton does hold among 35- to 54-year-old white Democrats. Among those in this age group who attend church weekly, 56% support Clinton compared with 32% who support Obama. Among those who attend less frequently, the gap is narrower.

Even among the 55-and-older group of white Democrats, who tend to strongly support Clinton, there is a modest relationship between religiosity and candidate choice. The Clinton over Obama gap among weekly church attenders 55 and older is 37 points, 61% to 24%, while it is a somewhat smaller 24 points (56% to 32%) among those in this age group who seldom or never attend.

Implications

Gaining the allegiance of highly religious voters can be a significant plus in an election. Religious voters are strongly attached to their positions, motivated, easy to reach based on targeted media and through church contact, and can form an important core of a winning election strategy.

Support for Clinton and Obama Among 35- to 54-Year-Old Democrats, by Church Attendance

Feb. 15-20, 2008

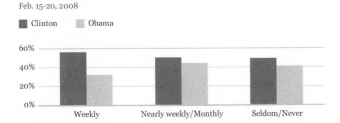

Support for Clinton and Obama Among Democrats 55 and Older, by Church Attendance

Feb. 15-20, 2008

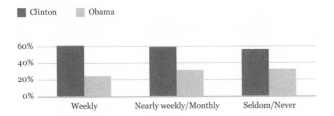

Most of the attention in past elections has been focused on the Republicans' ability to mobilize this group in support of their candidate, based in part on specific values issues.

Clinton, as seen in this analysis, at this point in the campaign has been able to disproportionately gain the support of religious white Democrats. Whether this national pattern can bolster her efforts to prevail over Obama as the Democratic nominee is less clear. For one thing, the percentage of the white Democratic electorate that is highly religious is smaller than is the case among Republicans. In the sample used for this analysis, 25% of white Democrats attend church weekly, while 57% say they seldom or never attend church. Thus, the allegiance of highly religious white Democrats has limited impact in that they constitute a minority of white Democratic voters. Still, in a close election, small voter segments can make a difference. Additionally, of course, the current targets for Clinton are the March 4 Texas and Ohio primaries, and it is unclear to what degree the national patterns are replicated in these two states.

In general, one does not typically associate Clinton with conservative positions on the values positions that the typical religious voter cares about: abortion, gay marriage, and stem-cell research. But Democratic voters in the remaining primary states may have other concerns that she can tap into, and if the Clinton campaign is able to devise a strategy for nurturing her connection to religious voters, it could make a difference.

Survey Methods

Results are based on telephone interviews with 1,795 Democrats and Democratic-leaning independent non-Hispanic white voters aged 18 and older, conducted Feb. 15-20, 2008. For results based on these total samples of national adults, one can say with 95% confidence that the maximum margin of sampling error is ±2 percentage points. The margin of sampling error is larger for specific subsamples.

Interviews are conducted with respondents on land-line telephones (for respondents with a land-line telephone) and cellular phones (for respondents who are cell-phone only).

In addition to sampling error, question wording and practical difficulties in conducting surveys can introduce error or bias into the findings of public opinion polls.

February 25, 2008
MCCAIN COMPETITIVE WITH DEMOCRATS IN LATEST TRIAL HEATS
McCain 48%, Obama 47% among likely voters

by Jeffrey M. Jones, Gallup Poll Managing Editor

Democratic front-runner Barack Obama and likely Republican nominee John McCain are essentially tied in likely voters' preferences for president if the general election were held today.

General Election Preference for President: John McCain vs. Barack Obama
Based on likely voters

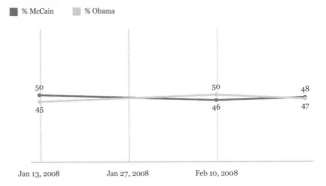

Forty-eight percent of likely voters say they prefer McCain for president, and 47% Obama, according to a new *USA Today*/Gallup poll, conducted Feb. 21-24. The two have been closely matched each of the three times the question has been asked of likely voters this year.

The contest would be about as tight if Hillary Clinton were the Democratic nominee. In that test ballot, 50% of likely voters choose McCain and 46% Clinton.

General Election Preference for President: John McCain vs. Hillary Clinton
Based on likely voters

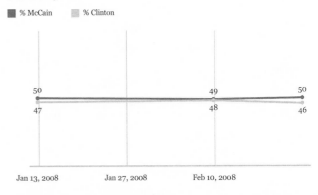

The Democratic candidates do slightly better among all registered voters, but the two hypothetical races are still a statistical tie among this larger group of voters.

General Election Preference for President

Based on registered voters

	McCain	Democratic candidate
	%	%
McCain vs. Obama	45	49
McCain vs. Clinton	49	47

Feb. 21-24 USA Today/Gallup poll

These close contests come in a political environment that is currently quite favorable to the Democratic Party: Democrats have a significant edge in terms of current party identification; the Democratic Party has much higher favorable ratings than the Republican Party; and when various polling organizations ask the "generic ballot," Americans decisively say that in theory they would prefer a Democrat to a Republican in office.

Thus, it appears McCain is doing better than what might be expected of the Republican nominee in general. One reason for this is that McCain is able to attract support beyond just Republican Party loyalists. McCain currently attracts more support among likely voters who identify as Democrats than either Democratic candidate attracts among Republicans who are likely to vote. Also, McCain is competitive with Obama among politically independent likely voters and leads Clinton by 10 percentage points among this group.

General Election Preference for President, by Party Affiliation

Based on likely voters

■ % Obama   ▨ % McCain

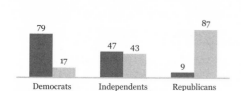

Feb. 21-24 USA Today/Gallup poll

General Election Preference for President, by Party Affiliation

Based on likely voters

■ % Clinton   ▨ % McCain

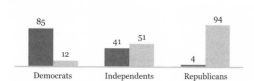

Feb. 21-24 USA Today/Gallup poll

Implications

Gallup polling on the general presidential election thus far has suggested the contest may be quite close, and the outcome could be similar to what occurred in the prior two presidential elections. This is in spite of the fact that everything else being equal, the Democratic candidate this year should be leading the Republican candidate. As these data show, McCain is able to transcend party to some degree, because he has more crossover appeal than either Democrat. Also, the general election campaign is just getting started. Over the next eight months, Democrats will attempt to link McCain to an unpopular incumbent president, and to hold the Republican Party responsible for a faltering economy and general discontent with the way things are going in the country. If they are successful in doing so—assuming Americans' attitudes do not improve considerably between now and November—then the Democratic candidates may run stronger in future general election trial heats. At the same time, of course, Republicans will be attacking the Democratic nominee—all to suggest that a lot can change between now and next Nov. 4.

Survey Methods

Results are based on telephone interviews with 1,653 likely voters, aged 18 and older, conducted Feb. 21-24, 2008. For results based on the total sample of national adults, one can say with 95% confidence that the maximum margin of sampling error is ±3 percentage points.

Interviews are conducted with respondents on land-line telephones (for respondents with a land-line telephone) and cellular phones (for respondents who are cell-phone only).

In addition to sampling error, question wording and practical difficulties in conducting surveys can introduce error or bias into the findings of public opinion polls.

February 25, 2008

PUBLIC VIEWS OBAMA, MCCAIN AS UNIFYING CANDIDATES
More believe Clinton would divide than unite country as president

by Jeffrey M. Jones, Gallup Poll Managing Editor

Most Americans think Barack Obama and John McCain would unite rather than divide the country as president, but view Hillary Clinton as a potentially more divisive chief executive.

Do you think each of the following candidates would do more to unite or more to divide the country as president?

■ More to unite   ▨ More to divide

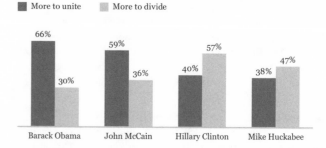

Feb. 8-10 USA Today/Gallup

These results are based on a Feb. 8-10 *USA Today*/Gallup poll, which asked Americans if they think the four leading presidential candidates "would do more to unite or more to divide the country as president."

The public is most likely to view Obama as a unifying force, with 66% believing he would do more to unite the country and 30% saying he would do more to divide it if he were elected. McCain is a close second, with Americans viewing him as more of a "uniter" rather than a "divider" by a 59% to 36% margin.

On the other hand, Americans believe Clinton and Mike Huckabee are more likely to divide Americans than bring them together. Forty percent say Clinton would unite Americans as president, but the majority, 57%, say she would do more to divide them. One of the reasons Clinton may be seen as more of a divider is her long history as a partisan politician in the public eye.

Huckabee's attempts to rise above negative campaigning have not necessarily enhanced his image as a unifying candidate—38% believe he would do more to unite Americans, but 47% believe he would do more to divide them.

Generally speaking, party identifiers are more likely to rate their party's candidates as uniters rather than dividers. But a closer examination of the results by party affiliation suggests that these ratings are more than just knee-jerk partisan reactions. For example,

- Democrats are significantly more likely to view Obama (79%) than Clinton (65%) as a unifying candidate.
- Likewise, more Republicans think McCain (79%) would unite the country than think Huckabee (57%) would.
- By better than 2-to-1 margins, independents think both Obama and McCain would tend to bring Americans together. But independents think Clinton would maintain or create divisions by nearly the same 2-to-1 margin, 62% to 35%.
- Republicans are far more critical of Clinton than Obama on this measure. In fact, those who identify with the GOP are more than six times as likely to believe Clinton would tend to divide the country (85%) as to unite it (13%). Meanwhile, Republicans are just as likely to say Obama would bring the country together as to say he would keep it apart.

Do you think each of the following candidates would do more to unite or more to divide the country as president?

Results by party affiliation

	Democrats	Independents	Republicans
Barack Obama			
Unite	79%	67%	48%
Divide	18%	30%	48%
Hillary Clinton			
Unite	65%	35%	13%
Divide	32%	62%	85%
John McCain			
Unite	41%	63%	79%
Divide	54%	31%	18%
Mike Huckabee			
Unite	21%	42%	57%
Divide	59%	46%	33%

Feb. 8-10 USA Today/Gallup

Implications

In 2000, many Americans were looking to heal the partisan divisions of the prior eight years. George W. Bush promised to be more of a

uniter than a divider, but even if he did have the best intentions, his policies and governing style may in the end leave the country more divided than it was when he took office. A public yearning to move past party divisions may help explain the success of Obama and McCain in their respective parties' nomination campaigns to date, and may set up a general election between what the public perceives to be two unifying candidates.

However, the realities of the general election phase of the presidential campaign may work against the candidates' desires to unite the country. Obama's and McCain's "unifying" images could be put to a strong test if they wind up on the giving or receiving end of the partisan attacks so common in a tightly contested campaign. Thus, the challenge for both would be to maintain the perception that they would bring the country together for the duration of the campaign.

Survey Methods

Results are based on telephone interviews with 510 national adults, aged 18 and older, conducted Feb. 8-10, 2008. For results based on the total sample of national adults, one can say with 95% confidence that the maximum margin of sampling error is ±5 percentage points.

Interviews are conducted with respondents on land-line telephones (for respondents with a land-line telephone) and cellular phones (for respondents who are cell-phone only).

In addition to sampling error, question wording and practical difficulties in conducting surveys can introduce error or bias into the findings of public opinion polls.

February 26, 2008
DEMOCRATS, REPUBLICANS: OBAMA LIKELY TO WIN NOMINATION
Americans also say Obama would be harder for McCain to beat

by Frank Newport, Gallup Poll Editor in Chief

Both Republicans and Democrats appear convinced at this point that Barack Obama is going to win the Democratic presidential nomination.

Who Do You Think Will Win the Democratic Nomination for President?
Feb. 21-24, 2008

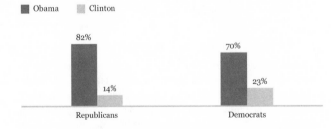

Not only does Obama enjoy this perceptual aura of inevitability, but he also is widely seen as the candidate who would provide the stiffer challenge for John McCain in November. Republicans say he would be tougher for McCain to beat, and Democrats say he would have the best chance of beating McCain come November.

The latest *USA Today*/Gallup poll asked Americans which candidate "will win the Democratic nomination this year," Hillary Clinton or Obama. There's little question about Americans' feelings on this issue. Almost three-quarters say Obama will win his party's nomination, compared with only 20% who say Clinton will win. That perception of inevitability is present among both Republicans and Democrats: 82% of Republicans and 70% of Democrats say Obama will win. Only 23% of Democrats believe Clinton will win their party's nomination—despite the fact that in this sample, about 4 out of 10 Democrats say they personally support Clinton. In fact, only half of Democrats who support the former first lady believe she will win the nomination; 43% believe she will not. Only 5% of Democrats who support Obama think Clinton will be the nominee; 91% think "their" candidate, Obama, will win.

Gallup first asked Americans in early January who they thought would win the Democratic nomination. At that point, just after the Iowa caucuses that Obama had swept, the American public was much less certain that Obama would win his party's nomination. Democrats in particular were almost as likely to say Clinton (36%) would win as to say Obama (41%) would win.

Not only do the significant majority of Americans see Obama's capture of the Democratic Party's nomination as inevitable, both Republicans and Democrats perceive him as the candidate who would present the more formidable challenge to presumptive Republican nominee McCain.

Who Has the Best Chance of Beating the Republican in November?

Asked of Democrats and Democratic leaners

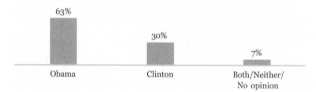

Feb. 21-24, 2008

Whom Would John McCain Have a Better Chance of Beating?

Asked of Republicans and Republican leaners

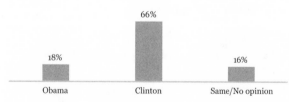

Feb. 21-24, 2008

Democrats by more than a 2-to-1 margin (63% to 30%) say Obama—rather than Clinton—"has the best chance of beating the Republican in November." Democrats no doubt would be pleased to find out that Republicans are much more fearful of Obama than Clinton. A separate question asked of Republicans found them saying by an overwhelming 66% to 18% margin that McCain would have an easier time of beating Clinton than Obama.

Bottom Line

It appears the substantial majority of Americans have concluded that Obama is going to be the Democratic Party's nominee this year—even before he has won the required number of delegates and before

voting takes place in the crucial March 4 primary states of Texas and Ohio. Importantly, close to half of Democrats who say they support Clinton concede that Obama is going to win their party's nomination. Another sign of Obama's strength is the perception of Democrats and Republicans alike that Obama would be the more difficult opponent for McCain to beat in November.

These perceptions can change, but the data show that Obama currently has the strong edge in both perceptions and momentum. This puts even more pressure on Clinton not only to do well in the March 4 primaries, but to win impressively.

Survey Methods

Results are based on telephone interviews with 2,021 adults, aged 18 and older, conducted Feb. 21-24, 2008. For results based on the total sample of national adults, one can say with 95% confidence that the maximum margin of sampling error is ±2 percentage points. The margin of sampling error is larger for specific subsamples.

Interviews are conducted with respondents on land-line telephones (for respondents with a land-line telephone) and cellular phones (for respondents who are cell-phone only).

In addition to sampling error, question wording and practical difficulties in conducting surveys can introduce error or bias into the findings of public opinion polls.

February 27, 2008
FEW DEMOCRATS SAY "EXPERIENCE" IS CRITICAL TO THEIR VOTE
Barack Obama's "vision" and electability seem attractive to Democrats

by Lydia Saad, Gallup Poll Senior Editor

According to a new *USA Today*/Gallup poll, conducted Feb. 21-24, more than four in five Democrats (including independents who lean Democratic) believe Hillary Clinton has "the experience necessary to be a good president." Only about three in five Democrats say the same of Barack Obama.

Does Each Have the Experience Necessary to Be a Good President?

Based on Democrats and independents who lean Democratic

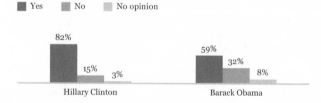

USA Today/Gallup, Feb. 21-24, 2008

Given this, Clinton seems to have won the argument in the Democratic Party over whether she or Obama has the better résumé to be president, but that is just one of many flanks in their nomination battle, and not one on which Democrats put a tremendous amount of weight.

Democrats also believe Clinton is more apt than Obama to "get things done," to offer "a clear plan for solving the country's problems," and to be a "strong and decisive leader."

Does Each Quality Apply More to Hillary Clinton or More to Barack Obama?
Clinton Strengths

Based on Democrats and independents who lean Democratic

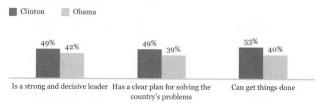

USA Today/Gallup, Feb. 21-24, 2008

At the same time, Obama beats Clinton among Democrats in perceptions that he cares about the needs of people like themselves, shares their values, has a vision for the country's future, is honest and trustworthy, and has the best chance of beating the Republican candidate for president in November.

Obama's better than 2-to-1 lead over Clinton in electability is the strongest advantage seen for either candidate on any issue or dimension measured in the survey.

Does Each Quality Apply More to Hillary Clinton or More to Barack Obama?
Obama Strengths

Based on Democrats and independents who lean Democratic

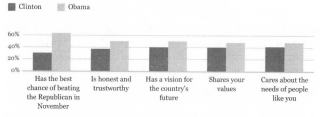

USA Today/Gallup, Feb. 21-24, 2008

The two are closely matched (Obama 47%; Clinton 43%) in ratings of who better "understands the problems Americans face in their daily lives."

What Matters Most?

In the new poll, Democratic voters were asked to say which of three qualities—leadership skills and vision, positions on the issues, or experience—is most important to their vote for president. Of these, experience is last by a significant margin.

If you had to choose, which of the following candidate characteristics will be most important to your vote for president ...

Based on Democrats and independents who lean Democratic

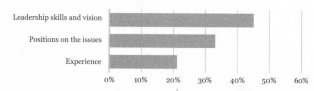

USA Today/Gallup, Feb. 21-24, 2008

The top-ranked quality is leadership skills and vision. Both candidates have perceptual strengths with voters that speak to different aspects of this.

- As noted, Clinton has the higher marks for such leadership qualities as being able to "get things done," offering a clear plan to solve the country's problems, and being a "strong and decisive leader."
- Obama beats Clinton by 10 points on having a vision for the country's future.

Regarding "positions on the issues," which Democrats rank second in importance, the two candidates are nearly at a draw in Democratic perceptions of who is better on each of seven national issues.

- Clinton and Obama are quite close when Democrats are asked to say which of the two would better handle five specific issues: energy, Iraq, the economy, the environment, and terrorism.

Regardless of which presidential candidate you support, please tell me if you think Hillary Clinton or Barack Obama would better handle each of the following issues.

Based on Democrats and independents who lean Democratic

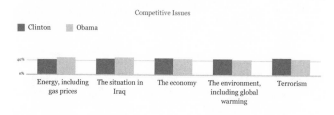

USA Today/Gallup, Feb. 21-24, 2008

- Obama has a strong advantage on handling corruption in government (leading Clinton by 24 points), but this is matched by Clinton's strong advantage on her signature issue, healthcare (leading Obama by 21 points).

Regardless of which presidential candidate you support, please tell me if you think Hillary Clinton or Barack Obama would better handle each of the following issues.

Based on Democrats and independents who lean Democratic

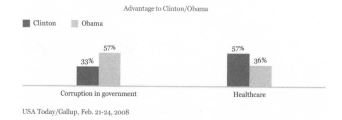

USA Today/Gallup, Feb. 21-24, 2008

Putting this all in context, Democrats attach much more importance to the economy—an issue on which the two are about tied—than to healthcare.

Bottom Line

Clinton beats Obama in Democrats' perceptions of the two candidates' experience and leadership skills. Obama has solid advantages in Democrats' perceptions about his vision, values, and honesty, and enjoys a big advantage on electability. He and Clinton are about evenly matched in voter perceptions of their handling of major issues, though Obama captures the outsider image as the one who can better clean up government corruption, while Clinton has a big advantage on healthcare.

If you had to choose, which of the following issues will be most important to your vote for president ...

Based on Democrats and independents who lean Democratic

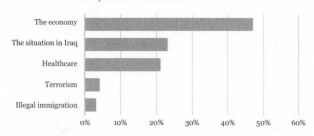

USA Today/Gallup, Feb. 21-24, 2008

Although it is not entirely clear how much Obama's perceptual deficits on "experience" and healthcare hurt him with Democrats, or how much his perceived strengths on vision, anti-government corruption, and electability help him, it all seems to balance out in his favor. The same poll producing these findings shows Obama favored for the nomination by a 12 percentage-point margin over Clinton, 51% to 39%.

Survey Methods

Results are based on telephone interviews with 2,021 national adults, aged 18 and older, conducted Feb. 21-24, 2008. For results based on the total sample of national adults, one can say with 95% confidence that the maximum margin of sampling error is ±2 percentage points.

For results based on the sample of 1,009 Democrats or Democratic leaners, the maximum margin of sampling error is ±3 percentage points.

Interviews are conducted with respondents on land-line telephones (for respondents with a land-line telephone) and cellular phones (for respondents who are cell-phone only).

In addition to sampling error, question wording and practical difficulties in conducting surveys can introduce error or bias into the findings of public opinion polls.

February 28, 2008
MCCAIN'S AGE SEEN AS LESS PROBLEMATIC THAN DOLE'S IN 1996
Twenty percent say Arizona senator is too old to be president

by Frank Newport, Gallup Poll Editor in Chief

More Americans said Bob Dole was too old to be president when he ran in 1996 than say John McCain is too old this year.

Twenty-seven percent of American adults in February 1996 said Dole was too old to be president. Twenty percent this year say McCain is too old.

In fact, Dole was slightly older during his run for the presidency than McCain is this year. Dole was born in July 1923, making him 72 and 73 during the course of the 1996 campaign year. McCain was born in August 1936, making him 71 now and 72 in the fall. (McCain would be the oldest president to be elected for the first time if he were to win in November.)

Of some comfort to McCain is the fact that Americans on average perceive him to be slightly younger than his real age. When the

1996 and 2008 Comparison: Is John McCain/Bob Dole Too Old to Be President?

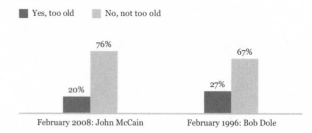

public is asked to guess McCain's age, the average of all guesses puts McCain at 67. The majority of Americans—57%—guess that he is 70 or younger, including 35% who say he is 65 or younger. A small 4% say he is 76 or older.

How Old Is John McCain?

Average: 67

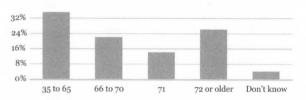

USA Today/Gallup, Feb. 21-24, 2008

There is a partisan difference in perceptions of the impact of McCain's age. Twenty-eight percent of Democrats say McCain is too old to be president, compared with 11% of Republicans.

Counterbalancing McCain's older age on the Republican side is Barack Obama's relative youth on the Democratic side. Obama was born in August 1961, making him 46 now and 47 next fall. Obama would not be the youngest president were he to win in November; John Kennedy was 43 when he was inaugurated in January 1961 and Theodore Roosevelt was 42 when he ascended to the presidency upon the death of William McKinley in 1901.

Only 13% of Americans say Obama is too young to be president. Republicans are only slightly more likely than Democrats to say Obama is too young.

Is Barack Obama Too Young to Be President?

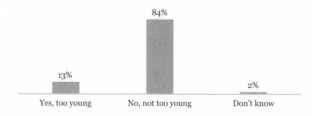

USA Today/Gallup, Feb. 21-24, 2008

Americans are quite accurate in their estimates of Obama's age. The average guess is his actual age, 46. Seventeen percent of Americans guess that Obama is 40 or younger, while 15% say he is 51 or older.

Hillary Clinton is between McCain and Obama in terms of age. She was born in October 1947, making her 60 now and 61 before

How Old Is Barack Obama?

Average: 46

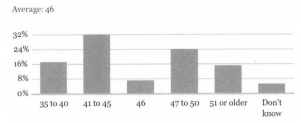

USA Today/Gallup, Feb. 21-24, 2008

Vote Preference for 2008 Presidential Election, by Gender

Based on likely voters

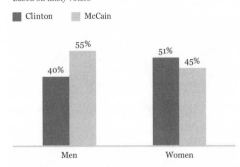

Feb. 21-24 USA Today/Gallup poll

Inauguration Day for the next president in January 2009. The recent Gallup Poll did not ask Americans whether Clinton was too young or too old to be president, but did ask them to guess her age. There's presumed good news for Sen. Clinton in the results. The average guess is a youthful 56, and 66% of Americans guess that she is under 60, including about 4 in 10 who believe she is 55 or younger. Only 12% of Americans say she is 61 or older.

How Old Is Hillary Clinton?

Average: 56

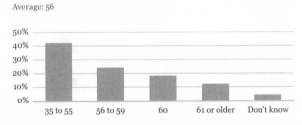

USA Today/Gallup, Feb. 21-24, 2008

Survey Methods

Results are based on telephone interviews with 2,021 national adults, aged 18 and older, conducted Feb. 21-24, 2008. For results based on the total sample of national adults, one can say with 95% confidence that the maximum margin of sampling error is ±2 percentage points.

For results based on the 1,010 national adults in the Form A half-sample and 1,011 national adults in the Form B half-sample, the maximum margins of sampling error are ±3 percentage points.

Interviews are conducted with respondents on land-line telephones (for respondents with a land-line telephone) and cellular phones (for respondents who are cell-phone only).

In addition to sampling error, question wording and practical difficulties in conducting surveys can introduce error or bias into the findings of public opinion polls.

February 28, 2008
THE GENDER GAP AND OTHER DIVIDES IN THE 2008 ELECTION
Vote by groups may differ depending on whom Democrats nominate

by Jeffrey M. Jones, Gallup Poll Managing Editor

The gender gap in voting for president may be significantly larger if Hillary Clinton rather than Barack Obama is the Democratic nominee.

Vote Preference for 2008 Presidential Election, by Gender

Based on likely voters

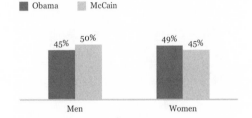

Feb. 21-24 USA Today/Gallup poll

But this is not because Clinton would perform significantly better among female voters than Obama would. Rather, it is because male voters are much more likely to prefer the Republican John McCain in a matchup with Clinton than they would be in an Obama-McCain contest.

That is just one example of several possible differences in how various demographic groups might vote in the 2008 presidential election under the two possible scenarios: Clinton vs. McCain or Obama vs. McCain.

These results are based on the latest *USA Today/*Gallup poll, which interviewed a large sample of 1,653 Americans who are considered likely voters. This larger sample allows for an in-depth look at current candidate preference by subgroup.

A contest pitting the 71-year-old McCain against the 46-year-old Obama would surely offer a stark contrast by age. But regardless of whether the Democrats nominate Obama or Clinton to face McCain, initial indications are that voting by young and old will likely differ this November, with younger voters more likely to support the Democrat and older voters McCain. But the generational divide would be much wider if Obama is the Democratic candidate instead of Clinton.

For example, McCain's advantage over the Democratic candidate among senior citizens would be 10 percentage points if he were running against Clinton but 20 points versus Obama. At the other end of the age spectrum, Obama's advantage over McCain among the youngest voters is 39 points, compared with a 15-point Clinton edge in this group.

Obama owes many of his Democratic primary and caucus wins thus far to the support of college-educated voters. According to the current poll, Obama's appeal to college-educated voters may continue in the general election phase of the campaign.

Vote Preference for 2008 Presidential Election, by Age

Based on likely voters

■ Clinton   ▨ McCain

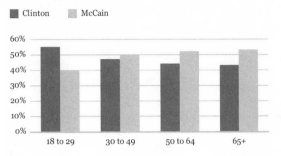

Feb. 21-24 USA Today/Gallup poll

Vote Preference for 2008 Presidential Election, by Age

Based on likely voters

■ Obama   ▨ McCain

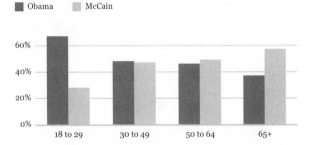

Feb. 21-24 USA Today/Gallup poll

In an Obama-McCain matchup, voters who attended college prefer Obama while those who did not attend prefer McCain. The poll suggests that there would be essentially no educational differences in a Clinton-McCain matchup.

Vote Preference for 2008 Presidential Election, by Education

Based on likely voters

■ Clinton   ▨ McCain

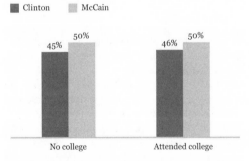

Feb. 21-24 USA Today/Gallup poll

The poll also asked voters which of the following characteristics would be most important to their vote—experience, candidate issue positions, or the candidate's perceived leadership skills and vision.

In a Clinton-McCain contest, the candidates would essentially tie among both "experience" and "leadership" voters, but McCain would have an edge among "issues" voters.

Vote Preference for 2008 Presidential Election, by Education

Based on likely voters

■ Obama   ▨ McCain

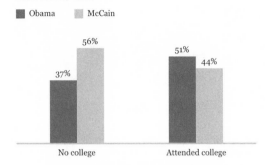

Feb. 21-24 USA Today/Gallup poll

Vote Preference for 2008 Presidential Election, by Most Important Candidate Characteristic to Vote

Based on likely voters

■ Clinton   ▨ McCain

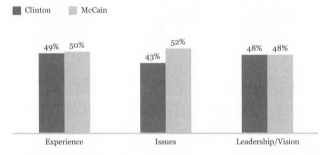

Feb. 21-24 USA Today/Gallup poll

A McCain-Obama matchup would present voters with a clear choice on the experience and leadership dimensions, with those valuing experience overwhelmingly preferring McCain for president, and those preferring leadership firmly in Obama's camp. Whereas McCain has an advantage over Clinton with issues voters, he and Obama essentially tie among this group.

Vote Preference for 2008 Presidential Election, by Most Important Candidate Characteristic to Vote

Based on likely voters

■ Obama   ▨ McCain

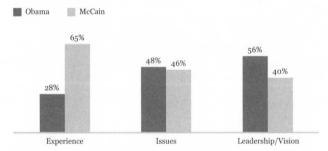

Feb. 21-24 USA Today/Gallup poll

These are a few examples in which support patterns may differ significantly in the fall. But many other key subgroups would probably vote for the same party's candidate regardless of whether the Democrats nominate Clinton or Obama, including subgroups of race, ideology, religiosity, marital status, and veteran status.

Also, as discussed previously, a McCain-Clinton contest would likely be more of a partisan fight than a McCain-Obama contest, in which many party-aligned voters may choose to vote for the candidate of the other party.

Survey Methods

Results are based on telephone interviews with 1,653 likely voters, aged 18 and older, conducted Feb. 21-24, 2008. For results based on the total sample of national adults, one can say with 95% confidence that the maximum margin of sampling error is ±3 percentage points.

Margins of error for subgroups will be larger than the margin of error for the entire sample of likely voters.

Interviews are conducted with respondents on land-line telephones (for respondents with a land-line telephone) and cellular phones (for respondents who are cell-phone only).

In addition to sampling error, question wording and practical difficulties in conducting surveys can introduce error or bias into the findings of public opinion polls.

Countries With Positive Image Ratings from Americans

Net favorable: percent favorable minus percent unfavorable

	Favorable	Unfavorable	Net favorable
	%	%	Pct. pts.
Canada	92	6	+86
Great Britain	89	7	+82
Germany	82	13	+69
Japan	80	15	+65
Israel	71	25	+46
India	69	22	+47
France	69	27	+42
Egypt	62	26	+36
South Korea	60	31	+29
Mexico	58	40	+18

Feb. 11-14, 2008

Countries With Highly Mixed Image Ratings From Americans

	Favorable	Unfavorable	No opinion
	%	%	%
Russia	48	46	5
Kenya	42	38	21

Feb. 11-14, 2008

Countries With Negative Image Ratings From Americans

Net favorable: percent favorable minus percent unfavorable

	Favorable	Unfavorable	Net favorable
	%	%	Pct. pts.
China	42	55	-13
Venezuela	37	50	-13
Saudi Arabia	31	61	-30
Cuba	27	67	-40
Pakistan	22	72	-50
Afghanistan	21	73	-52
Iraq	20	77	-57
The Palestinian Authority	14	75	-61
North Korea	12	82	-70
Iran	8	88	-80

Feb. 11-14, 2008

- Israel, Saudi Arabia, Afghanistan, Pakistan, and Iraq are all viewed more favorably by Republicans than by Democrats.
- France, Mexico, China, Venezuela, and Cuba are all viewed more favorably by Democrats than by Republicans.
- Two of the starkest demographic distinctions in survey ratings are age differences in perceptions of Russia and China. About 6 in 10 young adults (those aged 18 to 34) have a favorable view of these countries, compared with no more than half of middle-aged adults and only about a third of those 55 and older.
- Younger adults are also more likely than those 55 and older to have favorable views of France, Egypt, Mexico, Kenya, Venezuela, Cuba, the Palestinian Authority, North Korea, and Iran.

Survey Methods

Results are based on telephone interviews with 1,007 national adults, aged 18 and older, conducted Feb. 11-14, 2008. For results based on the total sample of national adults, one can say with 95% confidence that the maximum margin of sampling error is ±3 percentage points.

March 03, 2008
AMERICANS' MOST AND LEAST FAVORED NATIONS
Canada and Great Britain remain the most popular allies

by Lydia Saad, Gallup Poll Senior Editor

Of 22 countries rated in Gallup's 2008 World Affairs survey, Canada, Great Britain, Germany, and Japan win favor with at least 80% of Americans, while Iraq, the Palestinian Authority, North Korea, and Iran are viewed favorably by no more than 20%.

Most and Least Favored Nations

Percentage of U.S. adults with a very or mostly favorable view of each country

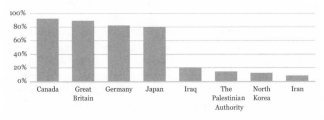

Feb. 11-14, 2008

Canada and Great Britain have topped Gallup's country rankings each of the 12 times since 1989 that both countries have been measured, although in most cases Canada has led Great Britain by a few percentage points. The only other country to approach 90% favorability over the years has been Australia. On each of the three occasions it was included in Gallup's country list, including last year, it ranked just as high as Great Britain.

Altogether, 10 countries rated in the Feb. 11-14, 2008, poll are viewed favorably by a majority of Americans. Following the top four, Israel receives a 71% favorable rating, similar to the 69% for both India and France. About 6 in 10 Americans have a favorable view of Egypt, South Korea, and Mexico.

Americans are about equally divided in their views of Russia and Kenya, with a fairly large percentage (21%) having no opinion of Kenya.

Ten countries are viewed unfavorably by at least half of Americans. Of these, Iran, North Korea, the Palestinian Authority, Iraq, Afghanistan, Pakistan, and Cuba are viewed more negatively than positively by a greater than 2-to-1 margin. Saudi Arabia, Venezuela, and China have somewhat more moderately negative images.

Notable Differences

Gallup finds some significant generational and partisan gaps in favorability toward some countries.

	18 to 34 years	35 to 54 years	55+ years	Republican	Democrat
	%	%	%	%	%
Afghanistan	18	24	22	29	16
China	60	38	34	34	46
Cuba	37	27	20	16	29
Egypt	69	61	59	64	60
France	74	69	64	53	78
Iran	12	8	5	10	10
Iraq	16	24	18	30	12
Israel	65	74	72	84	64
Kenya	53	44	30	42	40
Mexico	63	56	54	49	64
North Korea	17	11	9	13	12
Pakistan	23	21	21	28	16
Palestinian Authority	20	12	12	15	16
Russia	62	50	36	46	50
Saudi Arabia	29	34	28	38	25
Venezuela	49	39	26	29	42

Feb. 11-14, 2008

Interviews are conducted with respondents on land-line telephones (for respondents with a land-line telephone) and cellular phones (for respondents who are cell-phone only).

In addition to sampling error, question wording and practical difficulties in conducting surveys can introduce error or bias into the findings of public opinion polls.

March 04, 2008
ECONOMIC PESSIMISM CLIMBING THE INCOME SCALE
Weekly ratings are bad news for mid-tier retailers

by Dennis Jacobe, Gallup Chief Economist

The gap between the percentage of Americans rating the economy "poor" and the percentage rating it "excellent or good" was at its highest level of 2008 as March began.

How would you rate economic conditions in this country today -- as excellent, good, only fair, or poor?

■ % Excellent   ■ % Good   ■ % Only fair   ■ % Poor

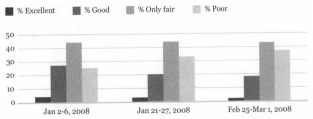

Jan 2-6, 2008   Jan 21-27, 2008   Feb 25-Mar 1, 2008

Consumer Ratings Show Declining Weekly Trend

Last Friday, Reuters and the University of Michigan reported that its Index of Consumer Sentiment decreased from 78.4 in January to 70.8

in February. This follows the preliminary Index reading of 69.6 for February and places consumer sentiment at its lowest level since February 1992.

Gallup's daily tracking of Americans' economic perceptions provides significant new insights into what has actually happened to consumer confidence over the first nine weeks of 2008. During the first week of January, more consumers rated current economic conditions "excellent" or "good" (31%) than rated them "poor" (25%), for a gap of +6 percentage points. By the fourth week of the month (Jan. 21-27), these percentages had reversed, with about one in four consumers rating the economy as excellent or good (23%) while one in three rated it as poor (33%), for a gap of -10 points. After improving slightly in early February, consumer ratings continued deteriorating: during the week of Feb. 25-March 1, only 20% gave the economy an excellent or good rating and 37% gave it a poor rating, for a gap of -17 points.

Ratings Gap Is Climbing the Income Distribution Scale

As might be expected, lower-income consumers were consistently more likely to be pessimistic about current economic conditions than was true for higher-income consumers over the first nine weeks of 2008. What might not be expected or understood is the way consumer pessimism is spreading across consumer income groups.

During the first week of January, 22% of those making less than $24,000 a year rated current economic conditions as excellent or good while 36% rated them as poor, for a gap of -14 percentage points. At that time, the comparable gap among those making $24,000 to less than $60,000 a year was 0. In sharp contrast, the gap among those making $60,000 to less than $90,000 was +24 and among those making at least $90,000, it was +23.

Over the past nine weeks, economic ratings have deteriorated across all income groups. By the week of Feb. 25-March 1, the gap among those making less than $24,000 had increased to -36; the early January gap of 0 among those making $24,000 to less than $60,000 had become -20; and among those making $60,000 to less than $90,000 annually, January's +24 gap had become +2. The early January gap of +23 among those making $90,000 or more a year was now 0.

More Bad News for Mid-Tier Retailers

In another Friday report, the Commerce Department reported that January consumer spending was essentially flat on an after-inflation basis for the second consecutive month. At the same time, mid-tier retailer Target reported that it has lowered its sales expectations for the first half of 2008. These trends seem consistent with the steady decline in consumer economic perceptions—particularly because such pessimism has increased among consumers who usually make their purchases at retailers like Target.

More importantly, the continued deterioration in consumer ratings across ever-higher income groups during recent weeks suggests that these trends are not only continuing but intensifying. In turn, this indicates that real consumer spending will probably continue to decline in March. While the "move-down" of middle-income consumers to retailers serving lower-income consumers (such as Wal-Mart) may benefit these retailers, this is not good news for retailers serving middle-income consumers or for the overall U.S. economy over the months ahead.

The results reported here are based on combined data of approximately 3,500 interviews conducted each week during 2008. For results based on these samples, the maximum margin of sampling error is ±2 percentage points.

In addition to sampling error, question wording and practical difficulties in conducting surveys can introduce error or bias into the findings of public opinion polls.

March 04, 2008

PUBLIC DIVIDED ON WHETHER OBAMA HAS NECESSARY EXPERIENCE

Roughly two-thirds of Americans believe McCain, Clinton do

by Jeffrey M. Jones, Gallup Poll Managing Editor

The most recent *USA Today*/Gallup poll finds 46% of Americans saying Barack Obama has the experience necessary to be president, and 46% saying he does not.

Has the Experience Necessary to Be President

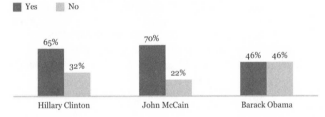

USA Today/Gallup, Feb. 21-24, 2008

The Feb. 21-24 poll finds a sharp contrast between these attitudes about the three-year senator from Illinois and views of his rivals for the presidency—Washington veterans John McCain and Hillary Clinton. Seventy percent of Americans believe McCain has the necessary experience to be president, slightly more than say this about Clinton (65%).

When Americans are asked to choose among the three candidates the one most ready to be president based on his or her experience, McCain wins more decisively, with Obama a distant third.

Who Do You Think Is Most Ready to Be President Based on His or Her Experience?

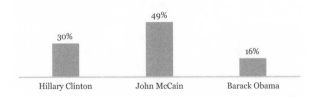

USA Today/Gallup, Feb. 21-24, 2008

McCain's advantage on this dimension is not entirely because Clinton and Obama "split" the Democratic vote, so to speak. McCain dominates among Republicans as expected, but he also leads by a

wide margin among independents. A majority of Democrats say Clinton is most ready to be president, with Obama and McCain closely matched for second.

Who Do You Think Is Most Ready to Be President Based on His or Her Experience?
Results by party affiliation

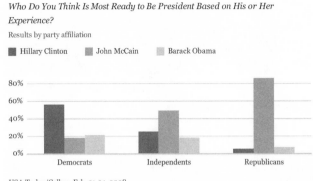

USA Today/Gallup, Feb. 21-24, 2008

The expected party differences occur when Americans are asked to rate each candidate individually on having the necessary experience to be president. The party gaps are most evident for Clinton, with 85% of Democrats saying she has the necessary experience but only 33% of Republicans agreeing. A majority of all three major party groups think McCain has sufficient experience. Democrats are about as likely to say Obama has the necessary experience as to say this about McCain.

Has the Experience Necessary to Be President
Results by party affiliation

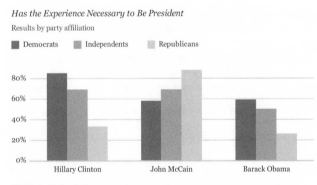

USA Today/Gallup, Feb. 21-24, 2008

While experience is often an important entry on a candidate's résumé, it may not be what voters are most looking for this year. When asked which of three candidate characteristics is most important to their 2008 vote, only 22% of Americans say experience. Thirty-four percent say the candidate's issue positions, and the most, 42%, say the candidate's leadership skills and vision.

These importance ratings show mild variation by party. Democrats choose leadership skills and vision by a wide margin over both issue positions and experience, something clearly working in Obama's favor. Independents choose leadership by a slim margin over issue positions, and Republicans' preferences are almost evenly divided between issue positions and leadership.

Implications

Obama's relative lack of experience has been an issue in the presidential campaign to date, and it could become a bigger issue if he were McCain's Democratic opponent in the general election. As many Americans believe Obama, the three-year U.S. senator, lacks

Which Candidate Characteristic Will Be Most Important to Your Vote for President?

Results by party affiliation

■ Leadership skills/Vision   ■ Issue positions   ■ Experience

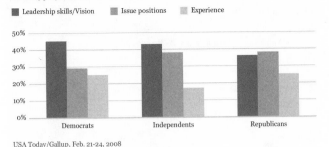

USA Today/Gallup, Feb. 21-24, 2008

Which candidate are you most likely to support?

Based on Democratic voters

■ Hillary Clinton   ■ Barack Obama   ■ Other/Don't know/Refused

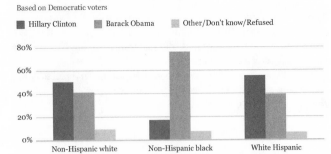

Feb. 25-March 2, 2008

the experience needed to be president as believe he possesses it. However, experience does not seem to be very high on Americans' list of qualifications for the next president, so this apparent weakness for Obama may not be fatal. Americans are more likely to be looking for a candidate with leadership skills and vision, characteristics on which Obama has obvious strengths.

Survey Methods

Results are based on telephone interviews with 2,021 national adults, aged 18 and older, conducted Feb. 21-24, 2008. For results based on the total sample of national adults, one can say with 95% confidence that the maximum margin of sampling error is ±2 percentage points.

For results based on the sample of 1,010 national adults in Form A and the 1,011 national adults in Form B, the maximum margins of sampling error are ±3 percentage points.

Interviews are conducted with respondents on land-line telephones (for respondents with a land-line telephone) and cellular phones (for respondents who are cell-phone only).

In addition to sampling error, question wording and practical difficulties in conducting surveys can introduce error or bias into the findings of public opinion polls.

March 04, 2008
WHITE, HISPANIC DEMOCRATIC VOTERS STILL FAVOR CLINTON
Obama wins overwhelmingly among black Democratic voters

by Frank Newport, Gallup Poll Editor in Chief

Barack Obama's extremely strong support among black Democratic voters offsets Hillary Clinton's advantages among whites and Hispanics.

An analysis of almost 3,000 interviews conducted over the last week with national Democratic voters highlights the degree to which Obama has been able to secure the support of black Democrats, while Clinton, his major opponent, has held on to her edge among white and Hispanic Democratic voters.

The interviews were conducted as part of Gallup Poll Daily election tracking between Feb. 25 and March 2. During this period, Obama had an overall 48% to 43% lead over Clinton among all Democratic voters nationwide (in the latest three-day average of interviews conducted March 1-3, the candidates are tied at 45%). But the detailed analysis shows much wider differences in support for the two leading Democratic candidates within major racial and ethnic subgroups.

Obama had a substantial lead among non-Hispanic black Democratic voters—76% to 17%—in the Feb. 25- March 2 sample. Blacks comprise about 19% of the Democratic voters surveyed across this period.

At the same time, Clinton had a 50% to 41% lead among non-Hispanic whites in the sample. Whites—about two-thirds of the Democratic voters in the sample—comprise by far the largest racial or ethnic segment of the Democratic electorate.

Over this seven-day period, Clinton also had a substantial lead among white Hispanic voters, 55% to 39%. An analysis of Clinton's support among Hispanic Democratic voters this year shows that while there have been week-to-week fluctuations, she has generally led each week. (White Hispanics comprise about 6% of the national Democratic vote, based on the data from Feb. 25-March 2.)

In addition to non-Hispanic whites, non-Hispanic blacks, and Hispanic whites, there is a small group of Democratic voters that falls into other racial classifications. These include those who identify their race as Asian, those who claim a racial classification other than white, black, or Asian, and those who do not identify their race or ethnic origin. Obama leads among this group.

Implications

It may not be surprising to find that Obama—the first black to be his party's front-runner at this point in the campaign—dominates the vote preferences of black Democratic voters. The current analysis suggests that Obama's powerful strength among this group has propelled him—during the week of Feb. 25-March 2 at any rate—to his overall modest lead in support among Democrats nationwide. His major opponent, Clinton, leads among the majority of Democratic voters who are non-Hispanic white and Hispanic white, but that lead has not been large enough to offset Obama's overwhelming strength among blacks.

These are national data, and do not necessarily represent the voting patterns in specific states—particularly the key Tuesday primary states of Texas and Ohio. Still, should Obama win the Democratic nomination, these data provide some basis for looking ahead to the general election. Obama's ability to generate the support of black voters in the general election would not be much different from that of Democratic candidates who have come before him, given historical voting patterns. But Obama's particularly strong appeal to blacks could potentially aid his campaign if he is able to mobilize black voters to higher turnout levels than has been traditionally the case—particularly in key states.

In addition, of course, Obama's chances of winning the general election—should he win the Democratic nomination—would hinge on his ability to convince key segments of the white and Hispanic population in swing states to support him. And among Democrats to this point, these groups have not been Obama's strength.

Results are based on telephone interviews with 2,901 national Democratic voters, aged 18 and older, conducted Feb. 25-March 2, 2008. For results based on the total sample of national adults, one can say with 95% confidence that the maximum margin of sampling error is ±2 percentage points. The margin of sampling error is larger for subgroups used in this analysis.

Interviews are conducted with respondents on land-line telephones (for respondents with a land-line telephone) and cellular phones (for respondents who are cell-phone only).

In addition to sampling error, question wording and practical difficulties in conducting surveys can introduce error or bias into the findings of public opinion polls.

March 05, 2008

DISCONTENT WITH U.S. GLOBAL POSITION HITS RECORD HIGH

Steady increase evident since commencement of Iraq war

by Lydia Saad, Gallup Poll Senior Editor

Americans' view of the United States' position in the world has undergone a complete reversal over the course of the Bush administration. Since February 2001, Americans' dissatisfaction with the country's position in the world has more than doubled.

On the whole, would you say that you are satisfied or dissatisfied with the position of the United States in the world today?
Recent trend

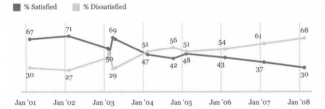

Public dissatisfaction with the United States' global position was 27% in February 2002, shortly after the 9/11 terrorist attacks. It rose to 50% during the pre-Iraq war period in 2003 when the United States was actively lobbying its allies and other countries at the United Nations to support military action against Iraq. It then quickly dipped to 29% at the very beginning of the war in Iraq in March 2003, but has risen steadily since.

Today's 68% dissatisfaction rating is the highest Gallup has recorded on this question, including during the Vietnam War era. At three different points in the 1960s, the public was consistently divided in its responses, with about 44% satisfied and 46% dissatisfied.

Diminished Perceptions of U.S. Global Image

A separate indicator of Americans' confidence in the United States' global image—public perceptions of how the rest of the world views the United States—follows the same path.

The percentage of Americans saying the United States rates favorably in the eyes of the world has declined from 75% in February 2001 to 43% today. Gallup trends document a steady decline in this positive sentiment from the post-9/11 period onward, broken only temporarily by a slight rebound shortly after U.S. forces invaded Baghdad near the start of the Iraq war.

In general, how do you think the United States rates in the eyes of the world -- very favorably, somewhat favorably, somewhat unfavorably, or very unfavorably?

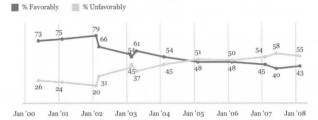

Current attitudes about the United States' global position are highly partisan, with a majority of Republicans (60%) saying they are satisfied with the country's position in the world, and the vast majority of Democrats (85%) saying they are dissatisfied. The ratings of political independents tend to be closer to Democrats' ratings than to those of Republicans.

Although the question is implicitly an evaluation of the nation's leadership, Gallup did not find a similarly strong partisan breach at the end of President Bill Clinton's second term. In May 2000, 78% of Democrats were satisfied with the United States' position in the world, along with 57% of Republicans.

The majority of Democrats were satisfied with the U.S. global position in the first two measures of Bush's presidency—69% in February 2001 and 61% in February 2002. However, their satisfaction plunged to 30% by February 2003, rebounded to 50% during the start of the Iraq war, and, beginning in 2004, has not registered more than 26%.

Satisfaction With U.S. Position in the World -- by Party ID
Percent "satisfied"

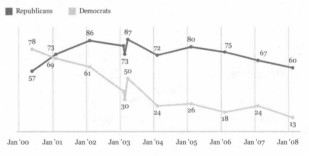

The percentage of Democrats currently satisfied on this measure (13%) is similar to what it was two years ago (18%). At the same time, satisfaction among Republicans has dropped by 15 percentage points, from 75% to 60%.

Survey Methods

Results are based on telephone interviews with 1,007 national adults, aged 18 and older, conducted Feb. 11-14, 2008. For results based on the total sample of national adults, one can say with 95% confidence that the maximum margin of sampling error is ±3 percentage points.

Interviews are conducted with respondents on land-line telephones (for respondents with a land-line telephone) and cellular phones (for respondents who are cell-phone only).

In addition to sampling error, question wording and practical difficulties in conducting surveys can introduce error or bias into the findings of public opinion polls.

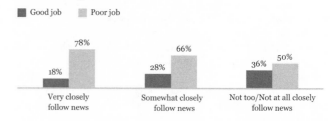

United Nations' Job Performance According to How Closely Follow News About World Affairs

Feb. 11-14, 2008

March 06, 2008

AMERICANS' OPINION OF U.N. AT RECORD LOW

Ratings soured at start of 2003 Iraq war, but continue to slump

by Lydia Saad, Gallup Poll Senior Editor

Americans' rating of the United Nations has gone from bad to worse in recent years, and now the percentage saying the organization is doing a "good job" in its role has reached a record low 27%.

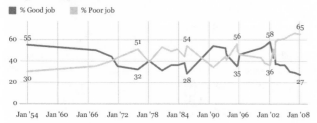

Do you think the United Nations is doing a good job or a poor job in trying to solve the problems it has had to face?

Gallup's annual World Affairs survey, updated Feb. 11-14, finds 65% of the public saying the United Nations is doing a poor job. Last year's ratings, from February 2007, were similar to this year's, with 29% saying "good job" and 66% "poor job."

The last time Gallup found a majority of Americans saying the United Nations was doing a good job was in February 2002, when the figure was 58%. In fact, from May 2000 to February 2002, both before and after 9/11, the United Nations received some of its best ratings from the American people—with a majority of Americans consistently applauding its efforts.

Americans' views of the United Nations turned sharply negative in 2003 when the organization rebuffed the United States' request for authorization of the use of military force in Iraq. Its "good" rating fell from 50% in January 2003 to 37% in March 2003, and—with ongoing bad publicity surrounding U.N. mismanagement of the Iraqi Oil for Food program, sexual abuse charges against U.N. peacekeepers in Africa, and various financial corruption scandals—this view has continued to sink.

The closer Americans say they follow news about world affairs, the less likely they are to praise the job the United Nations is doing. Only 18% of those who follow the news very closely say the United Nations is doing a good job, compared with 28% of those following it somewhat closely, and 36% not following it closely.

Most Still Want an Active United Nations

Despite its significant image problems, the United Nations continues to earn Americans' support for continuing as a major policy-making body.

Given three options for what kind of role the United Nations should play in world affairs, the plurality of Americans (42%) say it should play a major policy-making role, but where individual countries can still act separately when they disagree with it. An additional 26% say the United Nations should play the leading role where all countries are required to follow its policies.

Only 27% of Americans say it should play a minor role, serving primarily as a forum for communication among nations with no policy-making role. Two percent volunteer that they believe the United Nations should not exist.

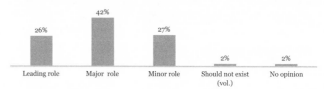

Which of the following roles would you like to see the United Nations play in world affairs today -- a leading role where all countries are required to follow U.N. policies, a major role, where the U.N. establishes policies, but where individual countries still act separately when they disagree with the U.N., (or) a minor role, with the U.N. serving mostly as a forum for communication between nations, but with no policy making role?

Feb. 11-14, 2008

Except for a dip in February 2007 in the percentage wanting to minimize the United Nation's role, attitudes on this question have varied little over the past five years. Americans were slightly less likely to favor a leading role for the United Nations when Gallup first asked the question in 2001 than they are this year (19% vs. 26%).

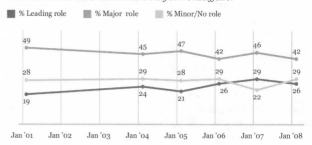

What Role Should the United Nations Play in World Affairs?

U.N. Attitudes Not Highly Partisan

Republicans are more negative than Democrats are in their views of the United Nations, but the differences are relatively modest. A majority of both partisan groups say the United Nations is doing a poor job this year, but the percentage saying it is doing a good job is about twice as high among Democrats as among Republicans, 38% vs. 18%.

Whereas the plurality of Democrats (44%) favor a major policy-making role for the United Nations, Republicans are divided between assigning it a major role (37%) versus a minor or no role (40%).

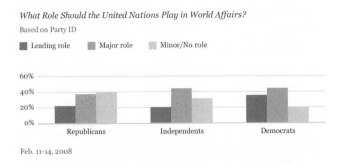

What Role Should the United Nations Play in World Affairs?
Based on Party ID

Feb. 11-14, 2008

Survey Methods

Results are based on telephone interviews with 1,007 national adults, aged 18 and older, conducted Feb. 11-14, 2008. For results based on the total sample of national adults, one can say with 95% confidence that the maximum margin of sampling error is ±3 percentage points.

Interviews are conducted with respondents on land-line telephones (for respondents with a land-line telephone) and cellular phones (for respondents who are cell-phone only).

In addition to sampling error, question wording and practical difficulties in conducting surveys can introduce error or bias into the findings of public opinion polls.

March 06, 2008
NET NEW HIRING ACTIVITY DECLINES IN FEBRUARY
Gallup daily surveys show biggest February declines occurring in Midwest and East

by Dennis Jacobe, Gallup Chief Economist

An analysis of daily Gallup polling shows a drop of 2.1 percentage points in net new hiring activity in the U.S. economy from January to February 2008.

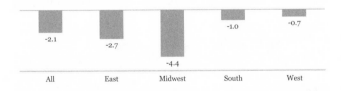

Change in Net New Hiring Activity From January to February 2008, by Region
In percentage points

Survey Data Suggest Weak Job Growth

On Wednesday, an employment report from ADP Employer Services showed that private companies in the United States reduced their payrolls in February. While the ADP employer survey has not always

been an accurate predictor of future job growth, Gallup's new jobs data lead to a similar conclusion: job growth probably declined at least slightly in February.

Gallup's net new hiring activity measure fell 2.1 percentage points in February. The measure is based on employees' perceptions of hiring and firing activity at their places of employment. It shows that employees were slightly more likely to see their employers reducing their net hiring activity in February than was the case in January. The biggest drops were in the Midwest, where perceptions of employment activity fell 4.4 points, and in the East, where net new hiring fell 2.7 points. Smaller net new hiring declines took place in the South (-1.0 points) and the West (-0.7 points).

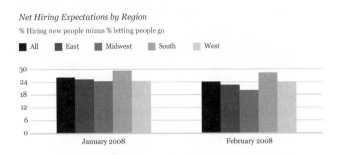

Net Hiring Expectations by Region
% Hiring new people minus % letting people go

New Hiring Activity Declines and Layoffs Increase

Gallup has been tracking net new hiring activity on a daily basis since the beginning of January 2008. In order to calculate this measure, Gallup asks employees whether their employers are hiring new people and expanding the size of their workforces, not changing the size of their workforces, or letting people go and reducing the size of their workforces. Net new hiring activity is computed by subtracting the percentage of employers letting people go from the percentage hiring new employees.

The percentage of employees saying their employers are hiring new people declined slightly from 39.8% in January to 38.5% in February. These calculations are based on more than 15,000 interviews conducted in January and more than 8,000 interviews conducted in February. This Gallup measure is new, and shows a net positive reading even in the current negative economic climate and even as overall U.S. employment declines. Companies are continuously hiring, and employees often find it difficult to differentiate hiring for new jobs from hiring to replace employee turnover.

At the same time, the percentage of employees saying their employers are letting people go increased from 13.7% in January to 14.5% in February. Again, this reading could be influenced by downsizing within some part of a company while the company overall is actually increasing the size of its workforce.

Of course, the importance of measuring these two areas despite some of their limitations involves trending and regional comparisons. By subtracting the percentage of employers letting people go from the percentage hiring, a measure of net new hiring activity is derived that can be analyzed and monitored over time. As a result, less emphasis is placed on the overall absolute levels of "hiring" or "letting people go," or the net of these two measures, and more emphasis is given to the change in net new hiring activity over time and across regions over time. Therefore, while net new hiring activity equaled 26.1% in January and 24.0% in February, the important finding involves the drop of 2.1 points in this overall activity level.

Is the U.S. Economy Creating New Jobs?

On Friday morning, the Bureau of Labor Statistics (BLS) will issue a new jobs report. Of course, there has been a lot of bad economic news recently with all of the factors buffeting the U.S. economy, including surging oil and food prices, the credit crunch, the decline in the value of the U.S. dollar, falling housing prices, and signs consumers are pulling back on their non-essential purchases. Given such an economic backdrop, Friday's report takes on added significance because it could confirm or deny the recessionary nature of the current economic downturn, not to mention the need for the Fed to continue driving down interest rates.

As noted, Gallup's net new hiring activity estimates are based on large sample sizes involving more than 15,000 employees in January and more than 8,000 in February. The government's unemployment rate and the new job growth numbers reported by the BLS tend to be volatile and subject to substantial revisions over time. Given those facts, however, Gallup's daily monitoring of the U.S. jobs situation suggests that the unemployment rate has a reasonable probability of ticking up slightly in February while the number of new jobs created may have declined somewhat. Of course, given the brief history of Gallup's daily tracking of the employment outlook, its relationship to the government figures and other economic indicators is still being determined. Over time, the accuracy of Gallup's tracking data for predictive purposes should improve.

Survey Methods

Gallup is interviewing no fewer than 1,000 U.S. adults nationwide each day during 2008. The economic questions analyzed in this report are asked of a random half-sample of respondents each day. The results reported here are based on combined data of more than 15,000 interviews conducted in January and more than 8,000 interviews in February. For results based on these samples, the maximum margin of sampling error is ±1 percentage point.

In addition to sampling error, question wording and practical difficulties in conducting surveys can introduce error or bias into the findings of public opinion polls.

March 07, 2008
ALMOST HALF OF AMERICANS SAY MILITARY IS NOT STRONG ENOUGH
But 44% say too much is being spent on military and national defense

by Frank Newport, Gallup Poll Editor in Chief

A record proportion of Americans—47%—say the United States' national defense is not strong enough. Another 41% say the country's defense is about right, while 10% say it is stronger than it needs to be.

Gallup has asked this question consistently every February since 2001 as part of its Gallup Poll Social Series on World Affairs. In February 2001—before the 9/11 terrorist attacks—44% of Americans said the nation's defense was not strong enough. In February 2002, the number was virtually the same. But in February 2003 and 2004, the "not strong enough" number dropped to 34%. It has risen slightly each year since, to the current 47%, the highest in Gallup's history.

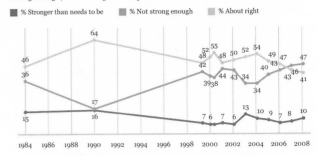

Do you, yourself, feel that our national defense is stronger now than it needs to be, not strong enough, or about right at the present time?

Gallup asked this question on an infrequent basis several times before 2001. The low point for the "not strong enough" sentiment was 17% in January 1990, at which time almost two-thirds of Americans said that the national defense was about right.

There are modest, but certainly not dramatic, differences in views on the country's national defense by partisan orientation.

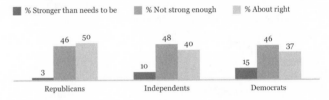

Is U.S. National Defense Stronger Than It Needs to Be, Not Strong Enough, or About Right?

Feb. 11-14, 2008

Democrats are slightly more likely than Republicans to believe that the nation's defense is stronger than it needs to be, but both partisan groups are about equal in terms of views that the national defense is not strong enough.

Despite the fact that almost half of Americans say the national defense is not as strong as it should be, there is an increasing feeling on the part of Americans that the government in Washington spends too much for national defense and military purposes.

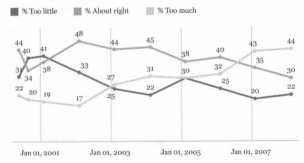

Do you think we are spending too little, about the right amount, or too much on national defense and the military?

In February 2001, just as President Bush took over the presidency from President Clinton, 38% of Americans said the amount being spent on defense and the military was about right, 41% said too little was being spent, and only 19% said "too much." Despite or perhaps because of the 9/11 terrorist attacks and the wars in Afghanistan and Iraq, the percentage of Americans saying too much is being spent on the military and defense has increased over the past seven years.

Now, in the February 2008 survey, 44% of Americans say the United States is spending too much on the military and on defense, while just 22% say the country is spending too little.

There have been widely varying views on this military spending issue over the years prior to 2001.

The all-time high point of sentiment that too much was being spent on the military came in November 1969, in the middle of the Vietnam War (the first time Gallup asked the question using this wording), when 52% said this.

In January 1981, just as President Ronald Reagan was taking office, a little more than half of Americans said the United States was spending too little on defense, perhaps as a reaction to Reagan's presidential campaign positions that the military needed strengthening. By 1987, in the middle of Reagan's second term, only 14% said the United States was spending too little.

There is a major disjuncture in current attitudes on this issue of military spending by partisan orientation. Democrats are more than three times as likely as Republicans to say the government is spending too much on national defense and the military, while Republicans are much more likely to say the government is spending about the right amount or too little.

Is U.S. Spending Too Little, About the Right Amount, or Too Much for National Defense and the Military?

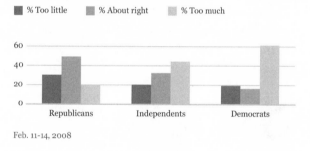

Feb. 11-14, 2008

Survey Methods

Results are based on telephone interviews with 1,007 national adults, aged 18 and older, conducted Feb. 11-14, 2008. For results based on the total sample of national adults, one can say with 95% confidence that the maximum margin of sampling error is ±3 percentage points.

Interviews are conducted with respondents on land-line telephones (for respondents with a land-line telephone) and cellular phones (for respondents who are cell-phone only).

In addition to sampling error, question wording and practical difficulties in conducting surveys can introduce error or bias into the findings of public opinion polls.

March 10, 2008
CLINTON SUPPORTERS FAVOR QUICK CREATION OF "DREAM TICKET"
But most Democrats say continuing campaign neutral or good for party

by Frank Newport, Gallup Poll Editor in Chief

Fifty-nine percent of Hillary Clinton supporters favor a quick decision to form a "dream ticket" with both Clinton and Barack Obama, while a majority of Obama supporters oppose the idea and would rather the campaign for the nomination continue.

Which would you, personally, favor -- Hillary Clinton and Barack Obama getting together immediately to settle on a joint ticket where one is the presidential nominee and the other the vice presidential nominee (or) Hillary Clinton and Barack Obama continuing to campaign against each other for the Democratic presidential nomination?

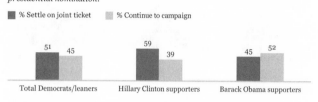

March 6-9, 2008

Putting the sentiments of the two candidates' supporters together (and adding in a few undecideds), the overall results from the latest Gallup Poll, conducted March 6-9, show 51% of Democrats favoring an immediate settlement on a joint ticket between the two candidates, while 45% of Democrats think the candidates should soldier on. (Four percent have no opinion on the issue.)

One possible reason Clinton supporters are more likely than Obama supporters to favor negotiating a joint ticket now is that Clinton supporters may be more worried that she will lose if the campaigning continues. (Obama is currently ahead in numbers of pledged delegates, and most experts believe Clinton will have difficulty erasing that lead if the primaries and caucuses remain close contests.)

But a poll question asking who is thought most likely to win the nomination shows that both candidates' supporters believe their candidate will win, although there is slightly more optimism among Obama supporters. Seventy-one percent of Clinton supporters say they believe she will win the nomination, compared to a just slightly higher 83% of Obama supporters who say he will prevail. (More generally, 51% of all Democrats and leaners believe Obama will win, while 42% think Clinton will. But this marks a downtick in perceptions that Obama will emerge the victor; prior to Clinton's wins in the crucial Ohio and Texas primaries last week, 70% of Democrats thought Obama would win.)

The battle for the Democratic nomination—if not stopped by some means—could last at least as long as the Pennsylvania primary scheduled for April 22, and conceivably could continue into the summer and even up to and including the Denver convention at the end of August.

Some argue that this would be good for the Democrats because it keeps their race in the media spotlight and would therefore result in less coverage of the Republican nominee, John McCain. Others argue that the continuing campaign, with both Obama and Clinton focusing on the other candidate's negatives and faults, could end up hurting the eventual nominee, while at the same time allowing

McCain to sail above the fray, raise funds, and, in general, focus on the November election.

National Democrats clearly have mixed feelings on this issue of the pluses and minuses of the continuing Democratic campaign. A plurality of 46% of Democrats say that the fact that the Democrats are continuing to campaign while the Republicans have decided on their nominee doesn't make much difference. While 23% say it is bad for the party, another 29% say it is good for the party. There is little significant difference between Clinton and Obama supporters in responses to this question.

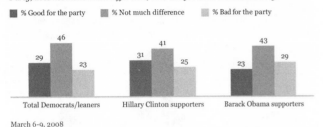

Do you think the fact that the Democratic candidates are continuing to campaign while the Republican nomination is already settled is good for the Democratic Party, does not make much difference, or is bad for the Democratic Party?

March 6-9, 2008

Survey Methods

Results are based on telephone interviews with 1,012 national adults, aged 18 and older, conducted March 6-9, 2008. For results based on the total sample of national adults, one can say with 95% confidence that the maximum margin of sampling error is ±3 percentage points. For results based on the sample of 528 Democrats or Democratic leaners, the maximum margin of sampling error is ±5 percentage points.

In addition to sampling error, question wording and practical difficulties in conducting surveys can introduce error or bias into the findings of public opinion polls.

March 10, 2008
MOST SMALL-BUSINESS OWNERS DON'T PLAN TO "FULLY" RETIRE
Many prospective retirees will delay retirement because of the current financial squeeze

by Dennis Jacobe, Gallup Chief Economist

Only 11% of small-business owners say they plan to retire and stop working in their businesses in the long run, according to the Wells Fargo/Gallup Small Business Index survey.

Declining and Delaying Retirement

Nine in 10 small-business owners say they are satisfied with being small-business owners—21% are extremely satisfied, 37% very satisfied, and 31% somewhat satisfied. Perhaps most indicative of their contentment, 83% say they would do it again and become small-business owners instead of doing something else. In other words, small-business owners overwhelmingly like what they do.

Because small-business owners like their work and have the option to continue working past retirement, it may not be surprising

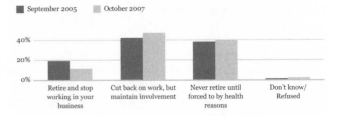

In the long run, which do you expect to do -- 1) retire and stop working in your business, 2) cut back on work, but always maintain some involvement in your business, or 3) never retire until forced to stop working for health reasons?

that 40% say they will continue to work as long as their health allows them to do so—essentially the same as the 38% who felt this way in 2005. Another 47% say they eventually plan to cut back on the work they do but maintain their involvement in their businesses—up from 42% in 2005. The percentage of small-business owners actually planning to retire and stop working in their businesses fell from 19% in 2005 to 11% in the most recent survey.

Thirty-eight percent of small-business owners say they will retire or cut back on their work at a different time than they had originally planned. Six in 10 of these owners say they will retire later than planned and many of those delaying retirement will do so for financial reasons. Sixty-two percent of small-business owners say they expect their small businesses to keep going after they stop working, while one in three feel their businesses will stop—essentially the same as in 2005.

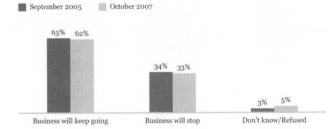

When you are no longer working at your business, do you expect that 1) your business will keep going, or your business will stop when you stop working?

A Good Time to Have Retirement Flexibility

An April 2007 Gallup Poll showed that only 53% of Americans thought they would have enough money to live comfortably when they retire. Obviously, current economic conditions are even less conducive to retirement than they were last year, given declining housing prices, a weak stock market, low interest rates on most safe forms of savings and investment, and surging food and energy prices. As a result, it is not surprising that earlier this year, 45% of Americans said they were worried that they would have to retire at a later age than they had originally planned.

In the Wells Fargo/Gallup Small Business Index survey of last October, a much higher 79% of small-business owners said they thought they would have enough money to live comfortably in retirement. In part, this may be because small-business owners tend to have higher incomes than the average American. More importantly, however, small-business owners also have more flexibility than the average American in deciding whether and when they will retire.

This ability to time one's retirement may be of even more importance in the months ahead. Last Friday's Bureau of Labor Statistics report showing another drop in U.S. jobs makes it obvious that the

U.S. economy is now experiencing a recession. During such an economic downturn, many companies lay off employees and encourage early retirement as their business slows. As a result, many Americans may soon be more worried—not that they will have to work to a later age than they had hoped, but that they will have to retire earlier than they desire and with far fewer resources than they had hoped.

Survey Methods

Results for the total dataset are based on telephone interviews with 600 small-business owners, conducted Oct. 4-14, 2007. For results based on the total sample of small-business owners, one can say with 95% confidence that the maximum margin of sampling error is ± 4 percentage points. The margins of error for subgroups will be slightly larger.

Other results are based on telephone interviews with 1,008 national adults, conducted April 2-5, 2007. For results based on this sample, the maximum margin of sampling error is ±3 percentage points.

In addition to sampling error, question wording and practical difficulties in conducting surveys can introduce error or bias into the findings of public opinion polls.

March 11, 2008
DEMOCRATS DIVIDED OVER HOW SUPER-DELEGATES SHOULD VOTE
Clinton, Obama supporters diverge

by Jeffrey M. Jones, Gallup Poll Managing Editor

The Democratic rank-and-file is fairly evenly divided between those saying super-delegates should vote for the candidate with the most delegates after all the primaries and caucuses are run, and those saying super-delegates should vote for the candidate they believe would make the better president. Clinton and Obama supporters take opposing views on the matter.

Opinion of How Superdelegates Should Vote, by Candidate Preference
Based on Democrats and Democratic-leaning independents

■ Vote for candidate who has won more delegates in primaries and caucuses

░ Vote for candidate superdelegate thinks would be a better president

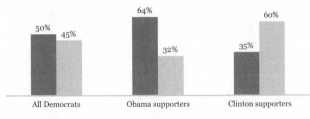

March 6-9 Gallup Poll

There is a real possibility the Democratic Party super-delegates—party activists, officeholders, and elders who are free to support any candidate they choose—will ultimately decide who the nominee is.

That is because it is unlikely that either Barack Obama or Hillary Clinton will amass enough pledged delegates in the state primaries and caucuses to clinch the nomination.

A new Gallup Poll, conducted March 6-9, asked Democrats how super-delegates should vote if one candidate has more delegates at the time of the convention but they believe the other candidate would be a better president. Fifty percent believe super-delegates should side with the voters and choose the leader in the delegate count, while 45% believe super-delegates should vote their consciences and cast their ballots for the candidate they think would be the better president.

Odds are Obama will have more delegates at the time of the convention, and the data suggest that Democrats are aware of this, and respond accordingly. By a 2-to-1 margin (64% to 32%), Democrats who support Obama believe super-delegates should vote for the candidate with more pledged delegates. Meanwhile, Clinton supporters take the opposing view and say by nearly the same margin, 60% to 35%, that super-delegates should vote for the candidate they think would be the better president.

Implications

Clinton's wins in the Ohio and Texas primaries eliminated the possibility of an early conclusion to the Democratic campaign, and increased the possibility of the nomination being decided at the convention in late August.

In one sense, the split over how super-delegates should vote is not surprising given that Democrats have been fairly evenly divided in their preferences between Clinton and Obama as the party's nominee for most of this year. Many Democrats are apparently tuned in to the issues and understand the implications of one outcome or another for each candidate, and thus tend to favor an approach that works in their preferred candidate's best interests.

Survey Methods

These results are based on telephone interviews with a randomly selected national sample of 528 Democrats and Democratic leaning independents, aged 18 and older, conducted March 6-9, 2008. For results based on this sample, one can say with 95% confidence that the maximum error attributable to sampling and other random effects is ±5 percentage points.

Interviews are conducted with respondents on land-line telephones (for respondents with a land-line telephone) and cellular phones (for respondents who are cell-phone only).

In addition to sampling error, question wording and practical difficulties in conducting surveys can introduce error or bias into the findings of public opinion polls.

March 12, 2008
BEFORE SPITZER SCANDAL, MIXED ETHICS REVIEWS FOR GOVERNORS
Ranked 14th out of 23 professions rated for honesty and ethics

by Lydia Saad, Gallup Poll Senior Editor

Despite New Yorkers' apparent shock over their corruption-slaying governor's involvement with a prostitution ring, Americans may not be surprised to see another governor in ethical trouble. As of

December 2006, just 22% of Americans held state governors in high esteem for their moral character, saying their honesty and ethics were generally high or very high.

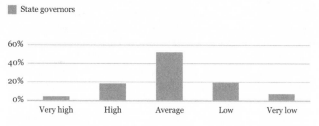

Honesty and Ethics Ratings of Professions

■ State governors

Dec. 8-10, 2006

Still, only 26% of Americans said the honesty and ethics of these leaders was generally low—most said they were average—meaning scandals like the one now befalling New York Gov. Eliot Spitzer could risk lowering the reputation of governors even further.

Gallup conducts an annual rating of the perceived honesty and ethical standards of people serving in various professions, but does not include all professions on the list every year. State governors were last included in December 2006, at which time nurses were the most well-regarded profession, with 84% rating them highly, and car salesmen the least respected, with 7%.

Honesty and Ethics Ratings -- Best and Worst

■ Total high ■ Average ■ Total low

Dec. 8-10, 2006

Governors were positioned in the bottom half of the 2006 list, ranking No. 14 out of 23 professions rated, based on the percentage giving them a high ethics rating.

However, relative to other types of politicians, state governors are among the most well regarded. In 2006, they were viewed as more ethical than "senators" (ranked 18ᵗʰ) and "congressmen" (19ᵗʰ). The contrast was especially sharp in terms of the percentage saying each group has low ethics: 26% for state governors, compared with 35% for senators and 40% for congressmen.

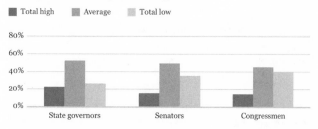

Honesty and Ethics Ratings -- Elected Officials

■ Total high ■ Average ■ Total low

Dec. 8-10, 2006

Gallup's 2007 "honesty and ethics" list included "state office-holders," at which time this broad category (which could include governors along with other state officials) was rated highly by only 12% of Americans. On the few occasions that Gallup included both state governors and state officeholders in the same survey, state governors received the higher scores. For example, in 1999, 24% of Americans rated the ethics of state governors high or very high, compared with 16% for state officeholders.

Gallup trends show generally little change in the ratings of state governors since they were first included on Gallup's honesty and ethics of professions survey in 1999. Positive ethics ratings for governors were higher in November 2000 (30%), but have otherwise been in the 22% to 26% range.

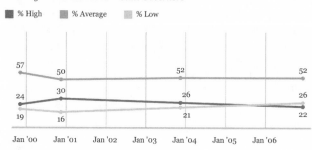

Honesty and Ethics Trend -- State Governors

■ % High ■ % Average ■ % Low

Survey Methods

Results are based on telephone interviews with 1,009 national adults, aged 18 and older, conducted Dec. 8-10, 2006. For results based on the total sample of national adults, one can say with 95% confidence that the maximum margin of sampling error is ±3 percentage points.

In addition to sampling error, question wording and practical difficulties in conducting surveys can introduce error or bias into the findings of public opinion polls.

March 12, 2008
POLLUTED DRINKING WATER WAS NO. 1 CONCERN BEFORE AP REPORT
Global warming way down the list

by Jeffrey M. Jones, Gallup Poll Managing Editor

When Americans are asked to rate their level of worry about each of 12 environmental concerns, their top four concerns relate to water quality, with pollution of drinking water the top overall concern.

Gallup's annual Environment survey was conducted March 6-9, just before a widely publicized Associated Press investigation reported that drinking water is not necessarily as pure as people think. While it is safe to drink, the report stated that drinking water in a number of major U.S. cities has been found to contain trace elements of pharmaceutical drugs. Thus, the report was released at a time when concern about drinking water was already at a relatively high level.

Prior to the release of the AP story, Gallup found no notable increase over the past 12 months in concern on any of the water-related items. In fact, for all 10 of the environmental items asked in

I'm going to read you a list of environmental problems. As I read each one, please tell me if you personally worry about this problem a great deal, a fair amount, only a little, or not at all.

 % Great deal

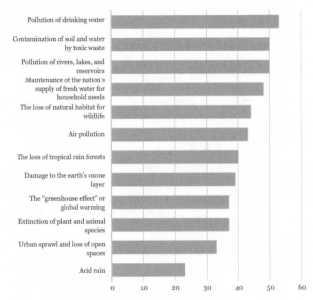

March 6-9, 2008, Gallup Poll

both 2007 and 2008, the percentage who report worrying "a great deal" about the problem is lower now. Ironically, the largest decline in reported worry was with respect to the safety of drinking water.

I'm going to read you a list of environmental problems. As I read each one, please tell me if you personally worry about this problem a great deal, a fair amount, only a little, or not at all.

	% Great deal, 2007	% Great deal, 2008	Change (pct. pts.)
Pollution of drinking water	58	53	-5
Pollution of rivers, lakes, and reservoirs	53	50	-3
Contamination of soil and water by toxic waste	52	50	-2
Maintenance of the nation's supply of fresh water for household needs	51	48	-3
Air pollution	46	43	-3
The loss of tropical rain forests	43	40	-3
Damage to the earth's ozone layer	43	39	-4
Extinction of plant and animal species	39	37	-2
The "greenhouse effect" or global warming	41	37	-4
Acid rain	25	23	-2

March 6-9, 2008, Gallup Poll

The rank-ordering of the items, with water-related issues including polluted drinking water, polluted bodies of water, maintenance of the nation's water supply, and contamination of water and soil, is typical of what Gallup has found since 1989, when it first measured concern about various environmental problems. The list includes global warming—arguably the most discussed environmental issue these days. Water quality is probably a more immediate concern to Americans, while global warming may seem like a somewhat more remote issue.

The accompanying table shows the top overall concern each time Gallup has asked Americans to rate their level of worry about environmental threats. Polluted drinking water has topped the list every time it has been included. When it hasn't been asked, as in May 1989, another concern about water safety finished first.

Top Environmental Concern, 1989-2008 Gallup Polls

	Top concern	% Worried a great deal
2008 Mar 6-9	Pollution of drinking water	53
2007 Mar 11-14	Pollution of drinking water	58
2006 Mar 13-16	Pollution of drinking water	54
2004 Mar 8-11	Pollution of drinking water	53
2003 Mar 3-5	Pollution of drinking water	54
2002 Mar 4-7	Pollution of drinking water	57
2001 Mar 5-7	Pollution of drinking water	64
2000 Apr 3-9	Pollution of drinking water	72
1999 Apr 13-14	Pollution of drinking water	68
1991 Apr 11-14	Pollution of drinking water / Pollution of rivers, lakes and reservoirs	67
1990 Apr 5-8	Pollution of drinking water	65
1989 May 4-7	Pollution of rivers, lakes, and reservoirs	72

Even so, concerns about water safety are generally reduced now compared to what they were in the late 1980s and 1990s, and down from where they were in 2000, the first year of Gallup's annual Environment poll. The one exception to that general pattern is maintaining the nation's supply of fresh water for household needs, concern about which increased in 2002 and has been steady since then.

Percentage Worried a Great Deal About Water-Related Environmental Concerns, 1989-2008 Gallup Polls

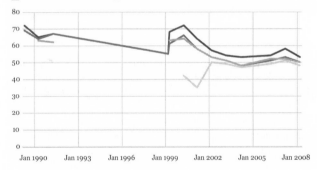

■ Pollution of drinking water
■ Pollution of rivers, lakes, and reservoirs
■ Contamination of soil and water by toxic waste
■ Maintenance of the nation's supply of fresh water for household needs

Implications

Over the years, Americans have shown greater concern about environmental problems that touch on water than on any other environmental issue. The attention the AP report has generated makes sense in this light. It is unclear at this early stage whether Americans' concerns will increase following this report, and whether that might lead to public pressure to try to make drinking water purer.

Survey Methods

Results are based on telephone interviews with 1,012 national adults, aged 18 and older, conducted March 6-9, 2008. For results based on the total sample of national adults, one can say with 95% confidence that the maximum margin of sampling error is ±3 percentage points.

Interviews are conducted with respondents on land-line telephones (for respondents with a land-line telephone) and cellular phones (for respondents who are cell-phone only).

In addition to sampling error, question wording and practical difficulties in conducting surveys can introduce error or bias into the findings of public opinion polls.

March 13, 2008
AMERICANS ON IRAQ: SHOULD THE U.S. STAY OR GO?
Most Americans favor an exit timetable, but disagree about timing

by Lydia Saad, Gallup Poll Senior Editor

Americans are as divided today as they have been since last September about the United States' troop presence in Iraq: 41% favor setting a timetable for gradually pulling out of Iraq while 35% want to maintain troops there until the situation improves. Only 18% of Americans favor an immediate withdrawal of all U.S. troops.

Preference for U.S. Troop Presence in Iraq

■ % Set timetable for gradual withdrawal

■ % Keep troops in Iraq until situation gets better

■ % Withdraw troops on timetable as soon as possible

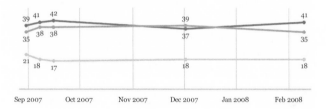

Looking at the same data differently, 60% of Americans want the United States to set a timetable for removing troops from Iraq rather than maintain an indefinite military commitment. But there is no national consensus on how soon the United States should start pulling out: 18% of Americans favor immediate withdrawal on a timetable, 41% favor gradual withdrawal on a timetable, and 35% favor no withdrawal. (An additional 1% favor a timetable, but have no opinion about whether withdrawal should be immediate or gradual.)

Regardless of what they may personally want to happen, a slight majority of Americans—52%—believe the United States will continue to have a significant number of troops in Iraq for at least another four years. Only 39% predict the major U.S. troop deployment will end within the next three years.

Predicted Number of Years the United States Will Maintain a Significant Number of Troops in Iraq

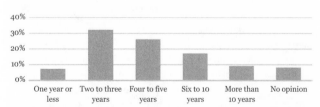

USA Today/Gallup poll, Feb. 21-24, 2008

One reason most Americans object to maintaining troop levels indefinitely may be that, to many, it is unclear the troops are achieving their goals. While 40% of Americans perceive that the 2007 U.S. troop surge in Iraq is having a positive effect on the situation there, nearly as many (38%) say the surge is not making much difference, and 20% say it is making things worse.

This is a much more positive balance of opinion about the U.S. troop surge than Gallup found in July 2007, when as many Americans thought it was making matters worse as said it was improving things. Positive attitudes about the surge grew last summer and fall—rising from 22% in July to 40% in late November/early December—but have failed to expand any further.

Effect of U.S. Troop Surge on the Situation in Iraq

■ % Making it better ■ % Making it worse ■ % Not making much difference

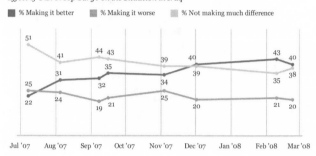

Survey Methods

Results are based on telephone interviews with 2,021 national adults, aged 18 and older, conducted Feb. 21-24, 2008. For results based on the total sample of national adults, one can say with 95% confidence that the maximum margin of sampling error is ±2 percentage points.

Interviews are conducted with respondents on land-line telephones (for respondents with a land-line telephone) and cellular phones (for respondents who are cell-phone only).

In addition to sampling error, question wording and practical difficulties in conducting surveys can introduce error or bias into the findings of public opinion polls.

March 13, 2008
ECONOMY WIDELY VIEWED AS MOST IMPORTANT PROBLEM
55% of Americans point to some aspect of the economy as the most important problem

by Dennis Jacobe, Gallup Chief Economist

In March, the percentage of Americans mentioning the economy as the most important problem facing the country almost doubled the January mentions.

Consumer Is Being Squeezed

Increasing food and energy prices, falling housing prices, declining job growth, and financial market chaos have created an extremely negative consumer psychology. As a result, it is not surprising that in Gallup's March 6-9 poll, 35% of Americans, when asked (without prompting) to name the most important problem facing the nation, simply said "the

What do you think is the most important problem facing this country today?

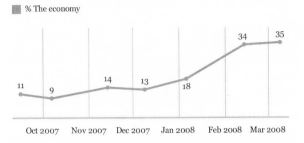

■ % The economy

economy"—matching the high level of February (34%) but nearly double the January level. Nor is it surprising that, all told, 55% of Americans—up from 49% in February—now mention some aspect of the economy, such as fuel and oil prices, unemployment, and the high cost of living. As recently as last October, only 22% of Americans mentioned some aspect of the economy as the most important problem.

Instead, the surprise may be that an even higher percentage of Americans aren't pointing to the economy right now. Indeed, a review of Gallup's historical records shows that as recently as 1993, two-thirds of Americans mentioned some aspect of the economy as the nation's top problem. Gallup's daily economic measures now show 86% of Americans saying current economic conditions are getting worse, with 40% rating the economy as poor—both of these are historically high numbers. Similarly, Thursday morning's consumer spending report showed a sharper drop in consumer purchases last month than was generally expected. Thus, it is possible that mentions of the economy as the nation's top problem will increase even further.

Non-Economic Problems

As mentions of some aspect of the economy as the most important problem have increased, the percentage pointing to non-economic issues has declined. For example, the percentage of Americans saying poor healthcare is the most important problem fell to 8% in March from 12% in February and 13% in January. Similarly, the percentage pointing to illegal immigration fell to 6% in March from 9% in February and 11% in January.

While the percentage of Americans pointing to the Iraq war as the most important problem has also declined, the decline has been proportionally more modest than in other areas: mentions were at 25% in January and 24% in February before declining to 21% in March.

Most Important Problem Facing the Country, 2004-2008 Gallup Polls

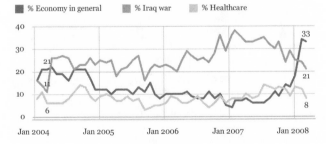

■ % Economy in general ■ % Iraq war ■ % Healthcare

Financial Turmoil

While Gallup's polling reflects the latest in consumer economic perceptions, the current economic turmoil in the financial markets has

most likely not been fully reflected in recent poll results. The Federal Reserve's action earlier this week to make liquidity more available to financial institutions and, in particular, to investment banks was initially cheered as the stock market rallied, but that initial enthusiasm has quickly dissipated.

Now, the most notable financial issues are probably the historically low level of the U.S. dollar, surging oil and commodity prices, and the turmoil in the financial markets. The full impact of these somewhat complex financial issues on the average American may take some time to be fully realized. At the same time, the ability of monetary authorities and the Treasury to ameliorate their impact on the average consumer is essentially unknown. Gallup's daily polling in the days and weeks ahead will allow for the measurement, monitoring, and reporting of this fallout on the consumer as it unfolds.

Most Important Problem Facing the Country, March 6-9, 2008, Gallup Poll

Category	% Mentioning
Economy in general	35
Situation in Iraq/War	21
Poor healthcare/hospitals; high cost of healthcare	8
Fuel/Oil prices	8
Immigration/Illegal aliens	6
Unemployment/Jobs	5
Dissatisfaction with government/Congress/politicians; poor leadership; corruption; abuse of power	5
Ethical/Moral/Religious decline; dishonesty; lack of integrity	4
Education/Poor education/Access to education	4
High cost of living/Inflation	4
Poverty/Hunger/Homelessness	3
National security	3
Terrorism	2
Federal budget deficit/Federal debt	2
Foreign aid/Focus overseas	2
Lack of money	2
Recession	2
Lack of energy sources; the energy crisis	2
International issues/problems	2
Lack of respect for each other	1
Taxes	1
Judicial system/Courts/Laws	1
Social Security	1
Environment/Pollution	1
Wage issues	1
Crime/Violence	1
Guns/Gun control	1

Survey Methods

Results are based on telephone interviews with 1,012 national adults, aged 18 and older, conducted March 6-9, 2008. For results based on the total sample of national adults, one can say with 95% confidence that the maximum margin of sampling error is ±3 percentage points.

Interviews are conducted with respondents on land-line telephones (for respondents with a land-line telephone) and cellular phones (for respondents who are cell-phone only).

In addition to sampling error, question wording and practical difficulties in conducting surveys can introduce error or bias into the findings of public opinion polls.

March 14, 2008

AMERICANS CONCERNED ABOUT IMPACT OF LEAVING IRAQ

Majority think Iraqi civilian deaths would increase

by Frank Newport, Gallup Poll Editor in Chief

Most Americans think the United States has an obligation to remain in Iraq until a reasonable level of stability and security has been reached.

Do you think the United States has an obligation to establish a reasonable level of stability and security in Iraq before withdrawing all of its troops?

■ Feb 21-24, 2008

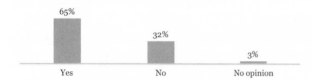

Although about 60% of Americans perceive that the United States' initial involvement in the Iraq war was a mistake, fewer than 20% say the United States should initiate an immediate withdrawal of troops. (See "Americans on Iraq: Should the U.S. Stay or Go?")

Why is this the case? A review of the responses to several questions on Iraq in a recent *USA Today*/Gallup poll provides some indication of the reasons an apparently conflicted American population is hesitant to recommend immediate withdrawal despite its basic feeling that U.S. involvement there has been a mistake.

As the accompanying graph indicates, almost two-thirds of Americans believe the United States has an obligation to establish a reasonable level of stability in Iraq before withdrawing all troops.

The poll did not ask Americans directly if they felt that such a "reasonable level of stability" had yet been reached. But a recent CBS News/*New York Times* poll found that a majority of Americans believe things are going badly for the "U.S. in its efforts to bring stability and order to Iraq." This suggests that Americans don't feel stability is yet the norm in Iraq, and thus—based on the attitudes measured in the Gallup Poll question—that it is necessary for troops to remain in Iraq until such a stable state is reached.

Additionally, more than 60% of Americans feel al Qaeda would be more likely to use Iraq as a base for its terrorist operations if the United States withdraws its troops than if it keeps its troops there, mirroring one of the Bush administration's (and presidential candidate John McCain's) most frequently used arguments against an immediate withdrawal of troops from Iraq.

A majority of Americans also believe more Iraqis would die from violence in that country if the United States withdraws its troops than would be the case if the United States keeps its troops there.

Half of Americans say the likelihood of a broader Middle East war would increase if the United States withdraws its troops from Iraq, while just 35% say that prospect is more likely if the United States keeps its troops in Iraq.

Americans are not convinced, however, that the possibility of terrorist attacks against the United States would increase if the country withdraws its troops from Iraq—about as many say such attacks

Do you think Al-Qaeda would be more likely to use Iraq as a base for its terrorist operations if the U.S. keeps its troops in Iraq or if the U.S. withdraws its troops from Iraq?

■ Feb 21-24, 2008

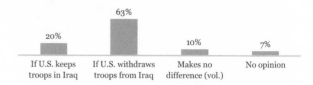

Do you think a greater number of Iraqis would die from violence in that country if the U.S. keeps its troops in Iraq or if the U.S. withdraws its troops from Iraq?

■ Feb 21-24, 2008

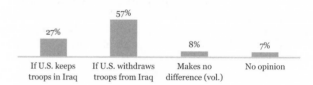

Do you think a broader war involving several Middle East nations would be more likely to occur if the U.S. keeps its troops in Iraq or if the U.S. withdraws its troops from Iraq?

■ Feb 21-24, 2008

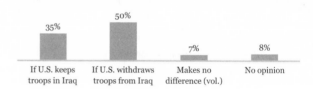

are more likely if the United States keeps troops in Iraq as say they are more likely if the United States withdraws its troops.

Do you think the United States would be more likely to be attacked by terrorists if the U.S. keeps its troops in Iraq or if the U.S. withdraws its troops from Iraq?

■ Feb 21-24, 2008

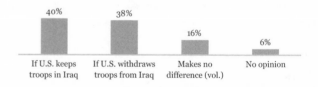

Implications

Americans have—perhaps inevitably, given the complex nature of the war in Iraq—a set of somewhat ambivalent attitudes about the situation there. In Gallup's latest poll, 59% of Americans say U.S. involvement in the war in Iraq was a mistake. One might think, therefore, that a similar majority would favor an immediate withdrawal of troops from that country. But that's not the case. Less than 20%, in fact, say the United States should withdraw troops immediately. The rest say either that troops should stay in Iraq as long as necessary, with no timetable for withdrawal, or that there should be a gradual timetable for withdrawal.

The data reviewed here suggest that there are reasons Americans hesitate to recommend an immediate withdrawal of troops. A majority of Americans believe that withdrawing troops from Iraq would lead to a greater possibility of al Qaeda using Iraq as a base for terrorist operations, a greater number of Iraqi deaths from violence, and a greater likelihood of a broader Middle East war.

Additionally, Americans believe the United States has an obligation to remain in Iraq until that country is stable, and recent poll results suggest that a majority of Americans do not believe a level of stability has yet been reached.

(Americans are not inclined to believe there would be an increased chance of terrorist attacks against the United States if its troops were withdrawn.)

The next U.S. president will face this confused landscape. Americans obviously are negative about the entire Iraqi enterprise (a recent Gallup Poll question shows a majority saying history will judge the U.S. involvement in Iraq to have been a failure), but—perhaps realistically—they believe the attempt to extricate the U.S. military from that country is not going to be a simple or straightforward matter.

Survey Methods

Results are based on telephone interviews with 2,021 national adults, aged 18 and older, conducted Feb. 21-24, 2008. For results based on the total sample of national adults, one can say with 95% confidence that the maximum margin of sampling error is ±2 percentage points.

Interviews are conducted with respondents on land-line telephones (for respondents with a land-line telephone) and cellular phones (for respondents who are cell-phone only).

In addition to sampling error, question wording and practical difficulties in conducting surveys can introduce error or bias into the findings of public opinion polls.

2008 Job Approval Ratings

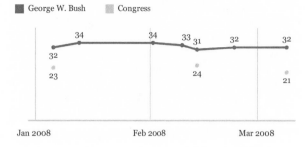

■ George W. Bush   ▪ Congress

2007. Congress' approval rating has been below 30% since May 2007.

Despite Bush's low overall ratings, nearly three in four Republicans, 72%, still think he is doing a good job. Only 23% of independents and 9% of Democrats agree. Congress' ratings are low among all three party groups—24% among Republicans, 18% among independents, and 21% among Democrats. The Democratic Party controls both houses of Congress, but that apparently does not endear Democrats to Congress very much.

Survey Methods

Results are based on telephone interviews with 1,012 national adults, aged 18 and older, conducted March 6-9, 2008. For results based on the total sample of national adults, one can say with 95% confidence that the maximum margin of sampling error is ±3 percentage points.

Interviews are conducted with respondents on land-line telephones (for respondents with a land-line telephone) and cellular phones (for respondents who are cell-phone only).

In addition to sampling error, question wording and practical difficulties in conducting surveys can introduce error or bias into the findings of public opinion polls.

March 14, 2008
PUBLIC SHOWS LITTLE LOVE FOR BUSH, CONGRESS
Thirty-two percent approve of Bush, 21% of Congress

by Jeffrey M. Jones, Gallup Poll Managing Editor

The public's job approval ratings of President Bush and Congress continue to be very low from a historical perspective, with Bush's ratings in the low 30% range and Congress' in the low 20% range this year.

The latest Gallup Poll, conducted March 6-9, finds 32% of Americans approving of Bush and 21% approving of Congress.

Bush's job approval rating has been stable in recent months, ranging narrowly from 31% to 34% so far this year. His approval rating has been below 40% for 18 months, since September 2006. It has not been at the 50% level since May 2005, shortly after his second term in office began. Bush's low point in office was a 29% approval rating in July 2007. The all-time low for any president is a 22% approval rating for Harry Truman in a February 1952 Gallup Poll.

Congress' current approval rating is just 3 percentage points above the all-time low—18% readings from March 1992 and August

March 17, 2008
CRISIS OF CONFIDENCE INCLUDES CONSUMERS
More upper-income Americans are becoming worried, making the situation worse

by Dennis Jacobe, Gallup Chief Economist

More Americans are rating the economy "poor" and fewer are rating it "excellent" or "good" as every week passes in 2008.

Consumer Ratings Declining Weekly

Over the weekend, the Federal Reserve bailed out Bear Stearns as the latter experienced what might be called an old-fashioned "run on the bank." The Fed also lowered the discount rate and, more importantly, allowed most securities firms access to the discount window to provide them with ready availability to emergency liquidity. The Fed is acting to stabilize the financial sector during a chaotic situation in the global financial markets.

When the Federal Open Market Committee (FOMC) meets on Tuesday, it will focus on its responsibility to maintain financial stability. However, Gallup's daily tracking of Americans' economic perceptions suggests it should also keep consumer confidence in

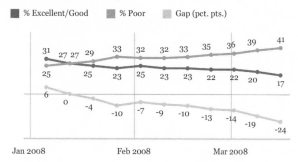

How would you rate economic conditions in this country today -- as excellent, good, only fair, or poor?

Combined weekly data, among national adults

■ % Excellent/Good   ■ % Poor   ▪ Gap (pct. pts.)

dence. In fact, to the degree that these actions are seen as signs that the current financial situation is worse than previously anticipated, the Fed's actions may actually have the opposite effect—and reduce consumer confidence.

The reality is that it may take direct and dramatic action by the president and the U.S. Treasury to significantly and positively affect consumer confidence. In this regard, the statements by Treasury Secretary Paulson over the weekend concerning the Bear Stearns bailout and the U.S. dollar, as well as those of the president Monday reassuring Americans that the U.S. economy is sound, might be seen as something of a disappointment by the markets. Of course, the situation may change in the days and weeks ahead—particularly if Gallup's daily polling shows consumer confidence continuing to deteriorate.

Survey Methods

Gallup is interviewing no fewer than 1,000 U.S. adults nationwide each day during 2008. The economic questions analyzed in this report are asked of a random half-sample of respondents. The results reported here are based on combined data of approximately 3,500 interviews conducted per week. For results based on this sample, the maximum margin of sampling error is ±2 percentage points.

In addition to sampling error, question wording and practical difficulties in conducting surveys can introduce error or bias into the findings of public opinion polls.

mind. The Fed needs to act to bolster consumer perceptions, not just confidence in the financial markets.

During the first week of January, more consumers rated current economic conditions "excellent" or "good" (31%) than rated them "poor" (25%), for a difference of +6 percentage points. By the fourth week of the month (Jan. 21-27), these percentages had reversed, with about one in four consumers rating the economy as excellent or good (23%) while one in three rated it as poor (33%), for a difference of -10 points. After improving slightly in early February, consumer ratings continued deteriorating, so that by the last week of February, the difference was -14 points—a difference that increased to -24 points for the most recent week of data (March 10-16).

Ratings Gap Is Climbing the Income Distribution Scale

During the first week of January, 22% of those making less than $24,000 a year rated current economic conditions as excellent or good while 36% rated them as poor, for a difference of -14 points. At that time, the comparable gap among those making $24,000 to less than $60,000 a year was 0. In sharp contrast, the gap among those making $60,000 to less than $90,000 was +24 and among those making at least $90,000, it was +23.

Over the past 11 weeks, economic ratings have deteriorated across all income groups. During the week of March 10-16, the gap among those making less than $24,000 a year has increased to -36 points, while the gap among those making $24,000 to less than $60,000 is -26. Among those making $60,000 to less than $90,000, January's +24 gap has become -13. The January gap of +23 among those making $90,000 or more a year is now -10.

Will Consumer Confidence Get Worse Before It Gets Better?

The FOMC is expected to lower interest rates significantly at its Tuesday meeting—anywhere from 1/2 point to 1 full percentage point. While such a drop may have only a limited benefit in terms of consumer and investor confidence, it will lower the cost of money to the nation's financial institutions and, thus, help them to weather the financial storm.

The problem is that the average American consumer is not really suffering from the current level of interest he or she is paying to borrow money. Instead, consumers are being buffeted by surging energy and food prices, declining housing prices, job cuts, and worries about the safety of their financial investments, not to mention the lower interest rates available to them on federally insured deposits.

At this point, it is not clear that the Fed can do what is necessary to stabilize the financial markets and build consumer/investor confi-

March 17, 2008
U.S. SATISFACTION DIPS TO 19%
Lowest score since August 1992

by Lydia Saad, Gallup Poll Senior Editor

A March 6-9, 2008, Gallup Poll finds only 19% of Americans satisfied with the way things are going in the United States today. This is similar to the 20% found in early February and in November 2007, but is technically the lowest Gallup has recorded since August 1992.

In general, are you satisfied or dissatisfied with the way things are going in the United States at this time?

■ % Satisfied   ■ % Dissatisfied

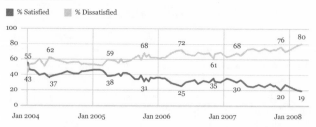

Recent Trend: January 2004 to March 2008

Gallup initiated the U.S. satisfaction measure in 1979 and has been tracking it monthly since October 2000. The low point came in July 1979, when only 12% of Americans were satisfied with the state of the country. Americans' mood sank to nearly this level in 1992, when the percentage satisfied registered 14% in June of that election year and 17% in August.

The high points of satisfaction—70% and 71%—came in January and February 1999 (under a booming economy), and in the post-9/11 period in December 2001 (when Americans were rallying in support of the country).

The last time a majority of Americans were satisfied with the direction of the country was in January 2004. After some volatility in 2004 and early 2005, satisfaction has essentially been in decline continuously since September 2005.

U.S. Satisfaction, Full Trend

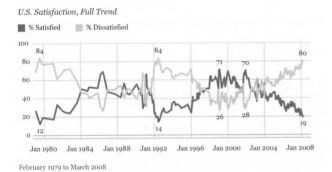

February 1979 to March 2008

Since January 2007, U.S. satisfaction has dropped by nearly half, from 35% to 19%. However, it has dropped much more among Republicans (from 60% to 33%) than among Democrats (from 16% to 7%).

The 33% of Republicans satisfied with the country today is the lowest Gallup has found for members of President Bush's party since he took office in 2001.

U.S. Satisfaction by Party ID -- January 2007 to March 2008

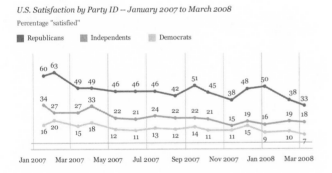

Survey Methods

Results are based on telephone interviews with 1,012 national adults, aged 18 and older, conducted March 6-9, 2008. For results based on the total sample of national adults, one can say with 95% confidence that the maximum margin of sampling error is ±3 percentage points.

Interviews are conducted with respondents on land-line telephones (for respondents with a land-line telephone) and cellular phones (for respondents who are cell-phone only).

In addition to sampling error, question wording and practical difficulties in conducting surveys can introduce error or bias into the findings of public opinion polls.

March 18, 2008

MCCAIN'S 67% FAVORABLE RATING HIS HIGHEST IN EIGHT YEARS

Obama has a 62% favorable rating, while Clinton's is 53%

by Frank Newport, Gallup Poll Editor in Chief

John McCain's 67% favorable rating is the highest of any of the three major candidates running for president, and ties for his highest in Gallup polling history.

Do you have a favorable or unfavorable opinion of Hillary Clinton, John McCain or Barack Obama?

Mar 14-16, 2008

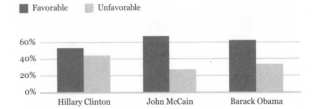

McCain's favorable rating matches the 67% he received in February 2000, when he was in the middle of his first run for president. But since that point, McCain's image in the eyes of Americans has undergone significant shifts. The Arizona senator had favorable ratings in the 57% range as he began his presidential campaign last winter, but as his campaign floundered this past summer, his favorable rating dropped as low as 41%. At that point, many observers had written off the former POW's campaign. But McCain came roaring back, winning the New Hampshire primary and then clinching the Republican nomination. His current favorable rating represents a gain of 26 points since last summer, including an 11-point increase since he won enough delegates to ensure his nomination on March 4.

Do you have a favorable or unfavorable opinion of John McCain?

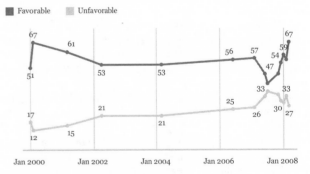

Illinois Sen. Barack Obama's favorable rating is now at 62%, by one point the highest Gallup has recorded for Obama since the first reading in December 2006 (at which point almost half of Americans did not know enough about him to give him a rating). Obama's ratings have been fairly stable in recent months, ranging between only 58% and 61% across five Gallup Polls conducted since January.

Hillary Clinton's favorable rating, 53%, is significantly lower than those of the other two candidates, in part no doubt because of her long history in the public eye, including eight years as first lady

Do you have a favorable or unfavorable opinion of Barack Obama?

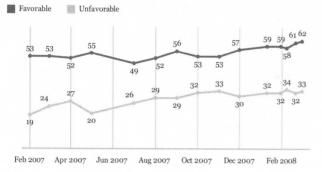

■ Favorable ☐ Unfavorable

dence that the maximum margin of sampling error is ±3 percentage points.

Interviews are conducted with respondents on land-line telephones (for respondents with a land-line telephone) and cellular phones (for respondents who are cell-phone only).

In addition to sampling error, question wording and practical difficulties in conducting surveys can introduce error or bias into the findings of public opinion polls.

in her husband's administration. Still, this is Clinton's highest favorable rating since October of last year.

Do you have a favorable or unfavorable opinion of Hillary Clinton?

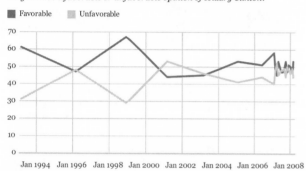

■ Favorable ☐ Unfavorable

Clinton over the years has seen a number of ups and downs in her image. Her highest favorable rating of 67% came in December 1998, just as her husband was being impeached for charges relating to his involvement with a White House intern. Since then, however, her rating has fallen as low as 44% in March 2001, and 45% as recently as April of last year. Her current rating represents an increase of five points since late February (prior to her wins in the crucial Ohio and Texas primaries).

Both Obama and Clinton have slightly higher favorable ratings among Democrats now than they had in February, suggesting that the negative infighting that has characterized the Democratic campaign in recent weeks is not damaging either candidate's image in the eyes of the party faithful.

One reason for the higher favorable ratings McCain and Obama enjoy is their cross-appeal to Americans who identify with the "other" party.

McCain gets an extraordinarily high 52% favorable rating from Democrats and independents who lean Democratic, while Obama gets a 39% favorable rating from Republicans and Republican leaners. Clinton, on the other hand, receives only a 20% favorable rating from Republicans and Republican leaners.

McCain is also helped by the fact that he receives an 87% favorable rating from Republicans, higher than the 80% and 79% that Clinton and Obama, respectively, currently receive from Democrats.

Survey Methods

Results are based on telephone interviews with 1,025 national adults, aged 18 and older, conducted March 14-16, 2008. For results based on the total sample of national adults, one can say with 95% confi-

March 18, 2008
OBAMA SEEKS TO BRIDGE RACIAL DIVIDE AMONG DEMOCRATS
Fifty-three percent of Non-Hispanic whites support Clinton, while 38% prefer Obama

by Frank Newport, Gallup Poll Editor in Chief

Barack Obama's major speech on race in Philadelphia Tuesday is a reminder of the continuing, and highly charged, impact of race in American society and in this presidential campaign.

Gallup Daily Election Polling Results for the Democratic Presidential Nomination, by Race/Ethnicity

Based on national Democratic and Democratic-leaning voters

■ Barack Obama ☐ Hillary Clinton

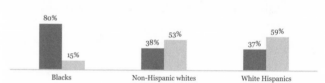

March 1-16, 2008

Obama, confronted with the continuing controversy over statements made by his former minister, Rev. Jeremiah Wright, tried to limit the damage by discussing what he called "a misunderstanding that exists between the races." Obama's speech presumably had the objective of shoring up as much white support for his presidential candidacy as possible among Democratic voters, particularly in the large state of Pennsylvania, the location for his speech and a state that holds its Democratic primary on April 22.

There is a large racial divide in the Democratic presidential campaign at this point. In Gallup Poll Daily election tracking, race is the single issue that divides the Democratic electorate more than any other. In an aggregate of 6,721 interviews Gallup has conducted between March 1 and March 16, 80% of black Democrats support Obama while only 15% support Hillary Clinton. Non-Hispanic whites split 53% for Clinton and 38% for Obama, while white Hispanics are even stronger for Clinton, 59% to 37%.

While Obama's focus at this point is largely on his attempt to win the Democratic nomination, his viability in the general election (should he win the nomination) will also be affected by white voters' views of his candidacy. At this time, however, there is very little racial divide between Obama and Clinton in Gallup's general election matchups. Blacks overwhelmingly support either Democratic candidate over John McCain, as would be expected given historical voting patterns. There is little significant difference in black or white support for the Democratic candidate against McCain, whether that candidate is Obama or Clinton.

Survey Methods

Gallup is interviewing no fewer than 1,000 U.S. adults nationwide each day during 2008.

The Democratic nomination results are based on combined data from March 1-16, 2008. For results based on this sample of 6,721 Democratic and Democratic-leaning voters, the maximum margin of sampling error is ±2 percentage points.

In addition to sampling error, question wording and practical difficulties in conducting surveys can introduce error or bias into the findings of public opinion polls.

March 18, 2008
PERCEIVED HONESTY GAP FOR CLINTON VERSUS OBAMA, MCCAIN
McCain most likely to be viewed as a strong leader

by Jeffrey M. Jones, Gallup Poll Managing Editor

Hillary Clinton is rated as "honest and trustworthy" by 44% of Americans, far fewer than say this about John McCain (67%) and Barack Obama (63%).

Ratings of Presidential Candidates as Honest and Trustworthy

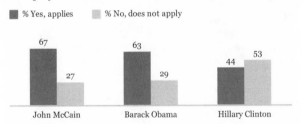

■ % Yes, applies   ■ % No, does not apply

USA Today/Gallup, March 14-16, 2008

The latest *USA Today*/Gallup poll, conducted March 14-16, asked Americans to rate the presidential candidates on honesty and nine other character dimensions. The 23-point gap separating Clinton and McCain on honesty is the largest between any two candidates for any dimension tested in the poll. The accompanying table shows how Americans rate the candidates on each dimension.

In addition to his strong showing on honesty, McCain also fares well on leadership. Sixty-nine percent of Americans describe the Arizona senator as "a strong and decisive leader," giving him an advantage over both Clinton (61%) and Obama (56%) in this regard.

Obama's strengths lie in his perceived empathy—two in three Americans say he "understands the problems Americans face in their daily lives" and "cares about the needs of people like you." Clinton and McCain are in the 50% range on both of these dimensions.

Obama (51%) also edges McCain (46%) and Clinton (45%) on "shares your values."

Clinton is the leader on what proves to be a weakness for both McCain and Obama—having a clear plan for solving the country's

Ratings of Presidential Candidates on Character and Quality Dimensions

	McCain	Obama	Clinton
	%	%	%
Cares about the needs of people like you	54	66	54
Is a strong and decisive leader	69	56	61
Is honest and trustworthy	67	63	44
Shares your values	46	51	45
Has a clear plan for solving the country's problems	42	41	49
Has a vision for the country's future	65	67	68
Can manage the government effectively	60	48	51
Understands the problems Americans face in their daily lives	55	67	58
Would work well with both parties in Washington to get things done	61	62	49
Is someone you would be proud to have as president	55	57	47

Figures are percentages saying each characteristic applies to the candidate
USA Today/Gallup, March 14-16, 2008

problems. Forty-nine percent say Clinton does, compared with 41% for Obama and 42% for McCain. Clinton has tried to emphasize this theme in her campaign in order to draw a distinction between her and Obama, and it rates as Obama's (and McCain's) lowest score.

Clinton has perhaps been less successful in convincing voters that she can better navigate her way through the Washington policy process than the other candidates. McCain (60%) leads both Clinton (51%) and Obama (48%) in terms of being able to manage the government effectively. Also, Obama (62%) and McCain (61%) finish well ahead of Clinton in terms of being able to "work well with both parties in Washington to get things done."

All three candidates are rated well with respect to having a vision for the country's future—68% say this about Clinton, 67% about Obama, and 65% about McCain.

One final dimension underscores another potential vulnerability for Clinton—47% of Americans say she is someone they would be proud to have as president (51% say they would not be proud to have Clinton). Obama (57%) and McCain (55%) both score above the majority level on this measure, which highlights that both tend to fare better on basic likability measures than Clinton.

Implications

It is clear that voters are able to distinguish among the three major presidential candidates and rate some areas as strengths and some areas as weaknesses for each. Clinton would appear to have more weaknesses in the public's eyes than McCain or Obama, though that might reflect the fact that she is a better-known figure (and has lower favorable ratings). Currently, she holds a significant lead over Obama on only 2 of the 10 character dimensions evaluated here (strong and decisive leader, and having a clear plan for solving the country's problems) and McCain on one (clear plan). Despite this, she remains competitive with McCain in general-election matchups and she has held off Obama's attempts to wrap up the Democratic nomination.

Survey Methods

Results are based on telephone interviews with 1,025 national adults, aged 18 and older, conducted March 14-16, 2008. For results based on the total sample of national adults, one can say with 95% confidence that the maximum margin of sampling error is ±3 percentage points.

Interviews are conducted with respondents on land-line telephones (for respondents with a land-line telephone) and cellular phones (for respondents who are cell-phone only).

In addition to sampling error, question wording and practical difficulties in conducting surveys can introduce error or bias into the findings of public opinion polls.

March 19, 2008

MOST AMERICANS SAY U.S. IS NOW IN ECONOMIC RECESSION

Almost half worry "a great deal" about a possible economic depression

by Frank Newport, Gallup Poll Editor in Chief

More than three-quarters of Americans say the U.S. economy is now in a recession, more than twice the number who felt that way five months ago.

Do you think the economy is now in a recession, or not?

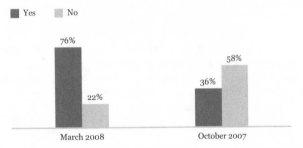

Gallup's wide-ranging measures of the American public's economic perceptions have documented Americans' increased worry about economic conditions over the last several months, and the degree to which they say the economy is in bad shape. However people may define a recession—whether by the classic definition of two successive quarters of negative economic growth, some other definition, or more generally just a bad economy—most Americans believe the country is in one.

The current 76% affirmative response when asked about a recession is not unprecedented. In three polls Gallup conducted in 1991 and 1992, between 79% and 84% of Americans said the economy was in a recession. In other words, on the issue of the United States being in a recession, the public is now about where it was some 16 years ago.

Do you think the economy is now in a recession, or not?

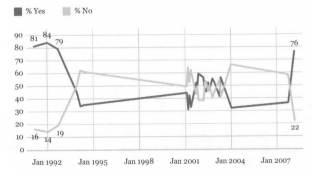

Democrats and independents are significantly more likely than Republicans to say the country is in a recession.

Do you think the economy is now in a recession, or not?

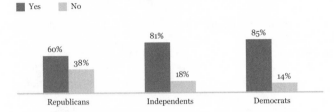

USA Today/Gallup, March 14-16, 2008

This pattern is not unusual. Those who identify with the party in the White House are typically more positive than others about the state of affairs in the country. But in the current environment, it is apparently difficult for even Republicans to muster a great deal of positive thinking about the economy; a clear majority agree that the country is now in a recession.

What's worse than a recession? That would be a depression. The poll asked Americans how likely they thought it would be that the United States will be in an economic depression within the next two years, defining a depression as "an economic downturn that is much more severe than most recessions and would last several years."

How likely do you think it is that the United States will be in an economic depression within the next two years -- very likely, somewhat likely, not too likely, or not at all likely?

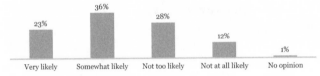

USA Today/Gallup, March 14-16, 2008

Just a little under a quarter of Americans say a depression is very likely, although another 36% say it is somewhat likely, yielding a total of almost 60% of Americans who believe a depression is at least somewhat likely.

Of note is the fact that almost half—46%—of Americans say they worry a great deal about the possibility of the U.S. economy going into a depression.

Regardless of how likely you think it is, how much does the possibility of the U.S. economy going into a depression worry you -- a great deal, a moderate amount, not much, or not at all?

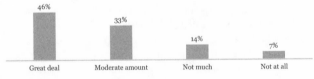

USA Today/Gallup, March 14-16, 2008

Implications

A great deal of survey data at this time demonstrate that the American public believes the country is in deep economic trouble. This latest poll shows that three-quarters believe the United States is in a recession, and a majority say it is at least somewhat likely that the country will slip into an economic depression.

The nation's political and economic leaders are aware of the economic challenges the country is facing and the decline in consumer confidence. In recent weeks, their actions to alleviate the situation have included the passing of the economic stimulus package in February, the Fed's decisions to lower interest rates, and government involvement to prevent the collapse of Bear Stearns.

The question is, of course, how long it will take before these and perhaps other measures begin to have an effect. One note of perhaps modest encouragement is that Americans were equally likely to pronounce that a recession was upon the country 16 years ago, and the country recovered, so that by the end of the 1990s, Gallup's economic rating measures were all in strongly positive territory.

Survey Methods

Results are based on telephone interviews with 1,025 national adults, aged 18 and older, conducted March 14-16, 2008. For results based on the total sample of national adults, one can say with 95% confidence that the maximum margin of sampling error is ±3 percentage points.

Interviews are conducted with respondents on land-line telephones (for respondents with a land-line telephone) and cellular phones (for respondents who are cell-phone only).

In addition to sampling error, question wording and practical difficulties in conducting surveys can introduce error or bias into the findings of public opinion polls.

March 20, 2008
MANY AMERICANS SAY HISTORY WILL JUDGE IRAQ WAR A "FAILURE"
Majority skeptical that United States had sufficient justification to attack Iraq

by Lydia Saad, Gallup Poll Senior Editor

Five years after the United States launched major air strikes on Iraq to remove Saddam Hussein from power, 42% of Americans believe history will judge the conflict a success, while 54% predict it will be remembered as a failure.

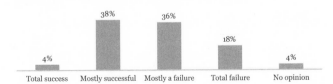

In the long run, how do you think history will judge the U.S. invasion and subsequent involvement in Iraq ?

USA Today/Gallup, Feb. 21-24, 2008

This generally negative indictment of the Iraq war is similar to the view 59% of Americans now hold that sending U.S. troops to Iraq in the first place was "a mistake." Only 42% of Americans con-

sidered sending troops to be a mistake shortly after the first anniversary of the invasion that began on March 19, 2003, but by 2005, the figure was regularly 50% or more, and it has approached 60% for about the past year.

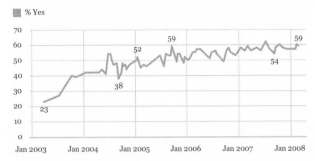

In view of the developments since we first sent our troops to Iraq, do you think the United States made a mistake in sending troops to Iraq, or not?

Public opposition to the Iraq war does not appear to be based on perceptions that the Iraqi people have suffered from the conflict. As troubled as Iraq is today by sectarian violence and damage to the nation's infrastructure from the war, two-thirds of Americans (67%) believe Iraq will be better off in the long run than it was before the U.S. and British invasion.

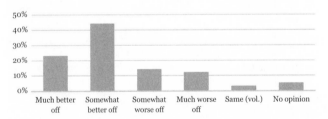

In your opinion, in the long run, will Iraq be much better off, somewhat better off, somewhat worse off, or much worse off than before the U.S. and British invasion?

USA Today/Gallup, Feb. 21-24, 2008

Rather, five years after President Bush directed the U.S. military to launch major air strikes on Iraq to drive Saddam Hussein out of power, a majority of Americans believe he overstated the dangers of that regime. More specifically, 53% agree with the statement that "the Bush administration deliberately misled the American public about whether Iraq had weapons of mass destruction," while 42% disagree.

A majority of Americans came to this damning conclusion about Bush in 2005, and have since maintained it.

Aside from whether Americans believe the administration lied about the threat Iraq posed, many Americans simply believe the threat didn't exist. More than half of those who consider the war a mistake (representing 32% of Americans) say they hold that view because they believe the United States lacked sufficient justification to invade Iraq in the first place. Significantly fewer (18% of Americans) cite mishandling of the war effort as the main reason they consider it to have been a mistake. Another 8% say both reasons are equally important to their criticism of the invasion.

Implications

In a special one-night reaction poll conducted March 20, 2003, Gallup found 76% of Americans saying they approved of the United

Do you think the Bush administration deliberately misled the American public about whether Iraq had weapons of mass destruction, or not?

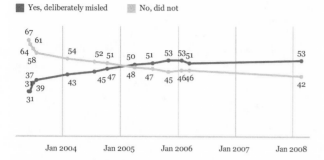

■ Yes, deliberately misled   ■ No, did not

How high do you think the price of a gallon of gasoline will go in the area where you live this year?

USA Today/Gallup, March 14-16, 2008

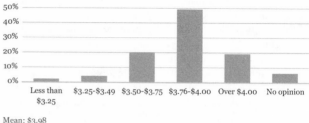

Mean: $3.98
Median: $4.00

States' decision to go to war with Iraq, including 60% who strongly approved. Only 8% predicted the conflict would last more than a year, and only 11% thought more than 1,000 troops would be killed. A majority of Americans at that time said that simply removing Saddam Hussein from power—even if he escaped capture—would qualify as "success."

Five years and roughly 4,000 U.S. deaths later, Americans got more than they bargained for, and it shows in diminished support for the war.

Survey Methods

Results are based on telephone interviews with 2,021 national adults, aged 18 and older, conducted Feb. 21-24, 2008. For results based on the total sample of national adults, one can say with 95% confidence that the maximum margin of sampling error is ±3 percentage points.

Interviews are conducted with respondents on land-line telephones (for respondents with a land-line telephone) and cellular phones (for respondents who are cell-phone only).

In addition to sampling error, question wording and practical difficulties in conducting surveys can introduce error or bias into the findings of public opinion polls.

March 24, 2008
AMERICANS EXPECT GAS PRICES TO INCREASE BY 21% THIS YEAR
Sixty-three percent say gas prices have already caused them financial hardship

by Dennis Jacobe, Gallup Chief Economist

Americans predict gas prices in their area will hit $3.98 a gallon this year.

Gas Prices Are Creating Financial Hardship

A new *USA Today*/Gallup Poll, conducted March 14-16, 2008, shows increasing gas prices are creating financial hardship for nearly two in three American families. However, the poll also suggests that the current degree of financial hardship has yet to reach post-Katrina levels.

As Hurricane Katrina was devastating New Orleans and parts of the Gulf Coast in August 2005, Americans reported paying an average of $2.65 for a gallon of gas. The percentage of Americans saying they were experiencing financial hardship as a result of

increasing gas prices surged from 59% in May 2005 to 69% in late August 2005, and then to 72% in mid-September 2005. While Americans report paying a much higher $3.30 on average for a gallon of gas in March 2008, 63% say they are currently experiencing financial hardship as a result of increasing gas prices.

So why are fewer Americans reporting that gas prices are causing them financial hardship today compared to late August and mid-September 2005, when the gas prices Americans currently report paying are about 25% higher than they reported then? In part, consumers may be adjusting somewhat, at least psychologically, to today's much higher gas prices. Of course, it is possible that some Americans have also adjusted their lifestyles to lessen the impact of higher gas prices on them and their families.

Another reason may involve future price expectations for gas. Following Katrina, gas prices soared and no one seemed to know how high they might go. By now, however, consumers have seen gas prices surge on several occasions. This year, they appear to have developed the expectation, on average, that pump prices are likely to reach $3.98 a gallon, a 21% increase over what they currently report paying. Only 19% of Americans think gas prices will exceed $4 a gallon this year. So while that price represents a huge increase, it may generate less consumer anxiety than a similar increase at a time when the future seemed more uncertain.

Summary: Expected Increase in Gas Prices per Gallon

	2008 Mar 14-16	2006 Apr 28-30
	%	%
Current price is the high for the year	2	4
Increase of $0.01 to less than $0.25	9	18
Increase of $0.25 to less than $0.50	17	20
Increase of $0.50 to less than $0.75	30	19
Increase of $0.75 or more	35	34
No opinion	7	6
Mean increase	+$0.67	+$0.65
Median increase	+$0.65	+$0.53

Financial Turmoil

While Gallup's polling shows that many factors affect the current consumer psychology as well as consumers' disposable incomes, it seems clear that higher gas prices are causing significant financial hardship. Given expectations that pump prices may well reach $4 a gallon this summer, the current degree of financial hardship is likely to increase in the months ahead.

Have recent price increases in gasoline caused any financial hardship for you or your household?

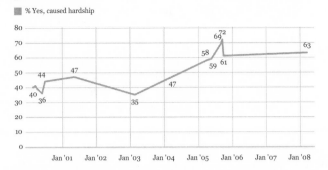

The Federal Reserve may be able to improve consumer psychology, at least on the margin, by lowering interest rates and making funds more readily available to the mortgage market. Congress and the Treasury may also help to some degree as they send out tax rebates to consumers. However, these efforts seem likely to pale in significance for most consumers when compared to another surge in gas prices in the months ahead. Perhaps once the Treasury and the Congress get finished bailing out the financial sector, they will turn their attention to one of the most regressive taxes being levied on Americans today—surging gas prices at the pump.

Survey Methods

Results are based on telephone interviews with 1,025 national adults, aged 18 and older, conducted March 14-16, 2008. For results based on the total sample of national adults, one can say with 95% confidence that the maximum margin of sampling error is ±3 percentage points.

In addition to sampling error, question wording and practical difficulties in conducting surveys can introduce error or bias into the findings of public opinion polls.

March 24, 2008
CLINTON, OBAMA CLOSELY MATCHED AMONG JEWISH DEMOCRATS
Clinton running strongly among Catholics

by Jeffrey M. Jones, Gallup Poll Managing Editor

Jewish Democratic voters show a slight preference for Hillary Clinton (48%) over Barack Obama (43%) for the party's 2008 presidential nomination. The five-point Clinton advantage is within the margin of error for this sample of Jewish Democrats.

The data are based on interviews with 348 Jewish Democratic voters conducted in Gallup Poll Daily tracking in March. So far this month, all Democratic voters regardless of religious affiliation are equally divided (46% each) in their nomination preferences between Clinton and Obama.

Obama's ability to win votes in the U.S. Jewish community has been questioned, given suggestions that he does not support Israel as strongly as other candidates. Some of Obama's supporters (including the Rev. Jeremiah Wright, former pastor of Obama's church) and foreign policy advisers are regarded as anti-Israel. Obama has met with Jewish leaders to reassure them of his commitment to Israel.

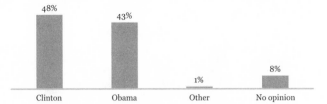

Democratic Nomination Preferences Among Jewish Democratic Voters

Based on March 1-22 Gallup Poll Daily tracking data

While the candidates run about evenly among Jewish Democrats, Clinton does better among Catholic Democratic voters, leading Obama by nearly 20 percentage points, 56% to 37%, in the March data among this group. Clinton outpolls Obama among both white Catholics (57% to 34%) and nonwhite Catholics (53% to 42%). The latter group largely comprises Hispanics, a core Clinton support group.

Democratic Nomination Preferences Among Catholic Democratic Voters

■ Clinton   ■ Obama

	All Catholics	White Catholics	Nonwhite Catholics
Clinton	56%	57%	53%
Obama	37%	34%	42%

Based on March 1-22 Gallup Poll Daily tracking data

Democratic voters who are Protestant (including those who say they are "Christian" but provide no specific denomination) divide about equally between Obama (47%) and Clinton (44%). But the overall Protestant numbers hide a deep racial gap, with Clinton leading by more than 20 points among white Protestant Democratic voters (56% to 34%) and Obama holding an even larger 45-point lead among nonwhite Protestant Democratic voters (70% to 25%).

Democratic Nomination Preferences Among Protestant Democratic Voters

■ Clinton   ■ Obama

	All Protestants	White Protestants	Nonwhite Protestants
Clinton	44%	56%	25%
Obama	47%	34%	70%

Based on March 1-22 Gallup Poll Daily tracking data

With Jewish and Protestant Democrats basically split in their preferences, and Catholics strongly in Clinton's corner, Obama is able to make up the difference by running better than she does among Democrats with no religious preference (54% to 40%) and among those who practice non-Christian religions (61% to 32%).

Survey Methods

Results are based on telephone interviews with 9,204 Democratic voters, aged 18 and older, in Gallup Daily tracking polling conducted

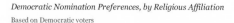

Democratic Nomination Preferences, by Religious Affiliation

Based on Democratic voters

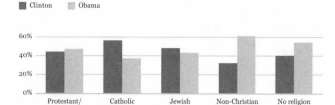

Based on March 1-22 Gallup Poll Daily tracking data

Do you think George W. Bush is -- or is not -- doing enough to find a peaceful solution to the conflict between the Israelis and Palestinians?

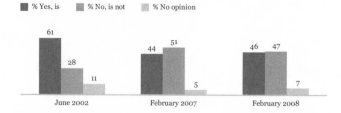

March 1-22, 2008. For results based on the total sample of national adults, one can say with 95% confidence that the maximum margin of sampling error is ±2 percentage points.

For results based on the sample of 368 Jewish Democratic voters, the maximum margin of sampling error is ±6 percentage points.

For results based on the sample of 2,375 Catholic Democratic voters, the maximum margin of sampling error is ±2 percentage points.

For results based on the sample of 4,449 Protestant and "Christian" Democratic voters, the maximum margin of sampling error is ±2 percentage points.

For results based on the sample of 468 non-Christian/non-Jewish Democratic voters, the maximum margin of sampling error is ±5 percentage points.

For results based on the sample of 1,340 Democratic voters with no religious affiliation, the maximum margin of sampling error is ±3 percentage points.

Interviews are conducted with respondents on land-line telephones (for respondents with a land-line telephone) and cellular phones (for respondents who are cell-phone only).

In addition to sampling error, question wording and practical difficulties in conducting surveys can introduce error or bias into the findings of public opinion polls.

March 25, 2008
MIXED REVIEWS FOR BUSH ADMINISTRATION'S MIDEAST PEACE PUSH
Majority still sympathizes with the Israelis rather than the Palestinians

by Lydia Saad, Gallup Poll Senior Editor

Only 46% of Americans believe President Bush is "doing enough" to help bring about a peaceful solution to the Israeli-Palestinian conflict, a figure similar to a year ago.

The Bush administration has arguably done more in the past year to further a Palestinian-Israeli peace accord than it did in the previous six years. It sponsored a peace summit in Annapolis, Md., last fall, and has followed up with several high-level visits to Israel and the Palestinian territories. Vice President Dick Cheney was in Israel and the Palestinian territories earlier this week, meeting with leaders, reiterating U.S. support for a two-state solution, and offering verbal encouragement that hard work and "painful concessions" at the negotiating table can pay off.

Yet as of Gallup's annual World Affairs survey, updated Feb. 11-14, Bush appeared to be getting little to no credit for these efforts with the U.S. public. As noted, there has been no increase since last February in Americans' belief that the administration is doing enough to bring about peace. At that time, 44% held this view.

Americans are slightly more upbeat than they were in February and November 2007 about the possibility that peace will eventually be achieved between Israel and the Arab nations, but the 39% currently optimistic (up from 34% in 2007) is still well below earlier high points on this measure. A majority of Americans (59%) believe Israel and her Arab neighbors will never "settle their differences and live in peace."

Do you think there will or will not come a time when Israel and the Arab nations will be able to settle their differences and live in peace?

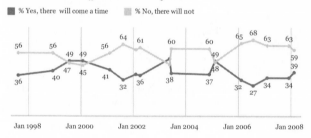

More generally, 59% of Americans sympathize more with the Israelis in the Middle East situation; only 17% say their sympathies lie more with the Palestinians. Gallup found a similar breakdown in each of the past two years.

In the Middle East situation, are your sympathies more with the Israelis or more with the Palestinians?

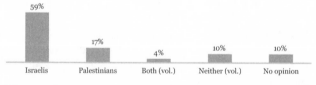

Feb. 11-14, 2008

In the same vein, Americans are more likely to want the United States to put greater pressure on the Palestinians than on the Israelis to "make the necessary compromises" to end the conflict. However, with only 38% calling for more pressure on the Palestinians and 25% calling for more pressure on the Israelis, both of these attitudes are minority points of view. An additional 15% of Americans think the United States should put more pressure on both sides; 10% say it should not increase the pressure on either side; and 11% have no opinion.

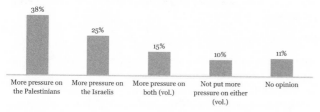

In order to resolve the Palestinian-Israeli conflict, do you think the United States should -- [put more pressure on the Palestinians to make the necessary compromises (or) put more pressure on the Israelis to make the necessary compromises]?

Feb. 11-14, 2008

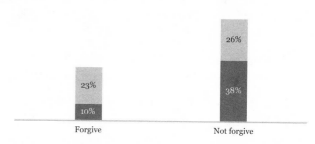

Would you definitely forgive, probably forgive, probably not forgive, or definitely not forgive your spouse if you found out [he/she] was having a sexual affair with another [woman/man]?

USA Today/Gallup, March 14-16, 2008

Bottom Line

Without a major breakthrough in the Palestinian-Israeli conflict, Americans seem set in their belief that the Bush administration is doing less than it could be doing to broker a Middle East peace agreement. They are as negative on this question today as they were a year ago—well before Bush and his diplomatic team rolled up their sleeves on the issue—and most are pessimistic about the long-term chances for peace.

To the extent the United States does get more involved, it is unclear what Americans would want their government to do. While the plurality say the United States should increase pressure on the Palestinians (38%), this is not substantially higher than the 25% wanting more pressure on Israel. Another 25% favor no change in the relative pressure being exerted, including 15% saying more pressure should be exerted on both sides, and 10% saying the United States should not put additional pressure on either.

Survey Methods

Results are based on telephone interviews with 1,007 national adults, aged 18 and older, conducted Feb. 11-14, 2008. For results based on the total sample of national adults, one can say with 95% confidence that the maximum margin of sampling error is ±3 percentage points.

Interviews are conducted with respondents on land-line telephones (for respondents with a land-line telephone) and cellular phones (for respondents who are cell-phone only).

In addition to sampling error, question wording and practical difficulties in conducting surveys can introduce error or bias into the findings of public opinion polls.

March 25, 2008
MOST AMERICANS NOT WILLING TO FORGIVE UNFAITHFUL SPOUSE
Six in 10 would tell unfaithful political spouse to face media alone

by Jeffrey M. Jones, Gallup Poll Managing Editor

Only about one in three Americans say they would forgive their spouse for marital infidelity, including just 10% who say they would definitely forgive him or her.

In recent weeks, the list of prominent politicians who have admitted having sexual relations outside their marriages has grown,

with revelations about former New York Gov. Eliot Spitzer, current New York Gov. David Paterson, and Detroit Mayor Kwame Kilpatrick coming to light. Unfaithfulness is certainly not confined to the political world—54% of Americans say they know someone who has an unfaithful spouse, according to the March 14-16 *USA Today*/Gallup poll.

The poll also finds—based on responses to several different questions—that just under two-thirds of Americans would not be willing to forgive their spouse for an extramarital affair. Specifically:

- As shown above, 64% of Americans say they would not forgive their spouse for having an extramarital affair, including 38% who say they would definitely not do so.
- Sixty-two percent say they would leave their spouse and get a divorce if they found out their spouse was having an affair; 31% would not.
- Hypothetically, only 36% say they would publicly stand by their spouse at the podium if that spouse were an elected official who had to face the media to answer questions about an affair, as the former New York and New Jersey first ladies have done when their husbands' affairs were brought to light. Sixty-one percent of Americans would tell their elected-official spouse to face the media alone.

On all but the latter count, Americans who are currently married appear to be somewhat more willing to forgive an unfaithful spouse than are those not currently married, particularly when it comes to the decision to divorce.

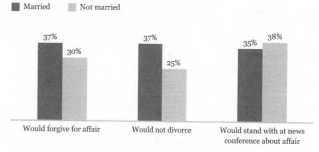

Forgive Spouse for Infidelity, by Current Marital Status

USA Today/Gallup, March 14-16, 2008

There are not meaningful differences by gender on these three forgiveness questions.

Is One Type of Marital Infidelity Worse Than Another?

While both the current and the previous New York governor admitted to marital infidelity, the details of the two cases differ. Former Gov. Spitzer had sex with prostitutes, and in the end was forced out of office because he reportedly broke other laws in order to carry on those trysts. On the day he was inaugurated to replace Spitzer, Gov. Paterson admitted having extramarital affairs with several women he knew.

The poll sought to assess whether the American public thinks one type of infidelity is worse than another. In general, the verdict is a split decision—35% say it is worse for a husband to pay to have sex with prostitutes and 34% say it is worse for a husband to carry on a romantic extramarital affair. Twenty-seven percent volunteer that both are equally bad.

Men and women differ in their views as to which is worse—women tend to believe sex with prostitutes is a greater betrayal, while men say a romantic extramarital affair is.

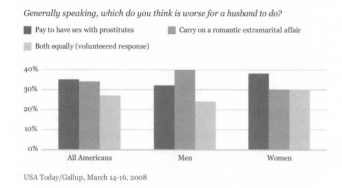

Generally speaking, which do you think is worse for a husband to do?

USA Today/Gallup, March 14-16, 2008

Married and unmarried respondents show minor, and not statistically meaningful, differences on this question.

Survey Methods

Results are based on telephone interviews with 1,025 national adults, aged 18 and older, conducted March 14-16, 2008. For results based on the total sample of national adults, one can say with 95% confidence that the maximum margin of sampling error is ±3 percentage points.

For results based on the sample of 557 respondents who are currently married, the maximum margin of sampling error is ±5 percentage points.

For results based on the sample of 444 respondents who are currently married, the maximum margin of sampling error is ±5 percentage points.

For results based on the sample of 505 men, the maximum margin of sampling error is ±5 percentage points.

For results based on the sample of 520 women, the maximum margin of sampling error is ±5 percentage points.

Interviews are conducted with respondents on land-line telephones (for respondents with a land-line telephone) and cellular phones (for respondents who are cell-phone only).

In addition to sampling error, question wording and practical difficulties in conducting surveys can introduce error or bias into the findings of public opinion polls.

March 26, 2008

HALF OF PUBLIC FAVORS THE ENVIRONMENT OVER GROWTH

Six in 10 Americans favor more conservation over more energy production

by Dennis Jacobe, Gallup Chief Economist

Although a recession is looming, Americans continue to favor protecting the environment even at the risk of curbing economic growth in a new Gallup Poll, conducted March 6-9.

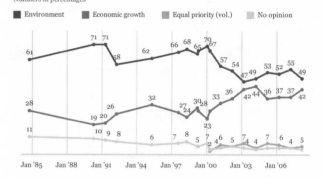

With which one of these statements about the environment and the economy do you most agree -- [ROTATED: protection of the environment should be given priority, even at the risk of curbing economic growth (or) economic growth should be given priority, even if the environment suffers to some extent]?

Numbers in percentages

Protecting the Environment Over Energy Production

The price of a gallon of regular gas nationwide hit $3.26 this week—up 65 cents from a year ago. Given such record prices and the general perception that the U.S. economy is experiencing a recession, it is somewhat surprising that Americans continue to say (by a seven percentage-point margin, 49% to 42%) protection of the environment should be given priority even at the risk of curbing economic growth. Still, this is down from the 18-point margin of a year ago, when 55% said they would prioritize the environment over economic growth. Further, the 49% of Americans currently favoring the environment over growth is only two points above the historical low over the past couple of decades.

Similarly, 50% of Americans say protection of the environment should be given priority even at the risk of limiting the amount of energy supplies such as oil, gas, and coal that the United States produces, while 41% hold the reverse position, saying energy production should be the priority. However, this 9-point margin is down from 24 points last year, when Americans favored prioritizing the environment by 58% to 34%. In this same vein, just over half of Americans continue to oppose opening up the Arctic National Wildlife Refuge in Alaska for oil exploration.

Americans Favor More Energy Conservation

Ninety-five percent of Americans believe the current U.S. energy situation is very (46%) or fairly serious (49%). Further, 62% think the United States is likely to face a critical energy shortage during the next five years.

What approach do Americans think the United States should follow right now to solve the nation's energy problems? By a margin of 61% to 29%, Americans favor emphasizing more consumer conservation of existing energy supplies, rather than emphasizing the

With which one of these statements about the environment and energy production do you most agree -- [ROTATED: protection of the environment should be given priority, even at the risk of limiting the amount of energy supplies -- such as oil, gas and coal -- which the United States produces (or) development of U.S. energy supplies -- such as oil, gas and coal -- should be given priority, even if the environment suffers to some extent]?

Numbers in percentages

■ Environment ■ Development of U.S. energy supplies
■ Both/Equally (volunteered response) ■ Neither/Other (volunteered response)
■ No opinion

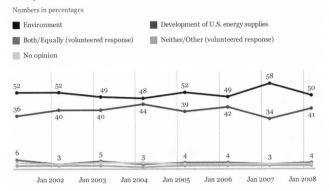

Which of the following approaches to solving the nation's energy problems do you think the U.S. should follow right now -- [ROTATED: emphasize production of more oil, gas and coal supplies (or) emphasize more conservation by consumers of existing energy supplies]?

Numbers in percentages

■ More production ■ More conservation
■ Both/Equally (volunteered response) ■ Neither/Other (volunteered response)
■ No opinion

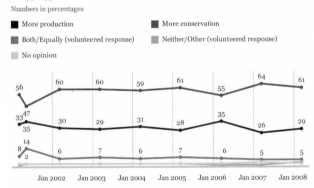

Americans May Get Their Conservation Wish

Gallup's polling shows why it has been so difficult for the United States to adopt an effective new energy policy. The public is almost equally divided between prioritizing the environment and prioritizing economic growth or developing new energy supplies. Given such a split in public opinion, it should not be surprising that the political response has been inaction, as politicians attempt to avoid alienating either side of the energy-versus-environment debate.

On the other hand, many Americans seem to agree that the best approach right now is increased energy conservation. These Americans are likely to get their wish because surging energy prices are a very effective "free market" way to encourage energy conservation. For example, at an emergency meeting last week, the South Korean army decided that it would ask its soldiers to make do with one bath a week in order to conserve energy and reduce its fuel use because of soaring energy costs. Perhaps energy prices won't rise so much that U.S. consumers are forced to take similarly drastic actions to conserve energy in the months ahead.

Survey Methods

Results are based on telephone interviews with 1,012 national adults, aged 18 and older, conducted March 6-9, 2008. For results based on the total sample of national adults, one can say with 95% confidence that the margin of sampling error is ±3 percentage points.

Interviews are conducted with respondents on land-line telephones (for respondents with a land-line telephone) and cellular phones (for respondents who are cell-phone only).

In addition to sampling error, question wording and practical difficulties in conducting surveys can introduce error or bias into the findings of public opinion polls.

March 26, 2008
IF MCCAIN VS. OBAMA, 28% OF CLINTON BACKERS GO FOR MCCAIN
If McCain vs. Clinton, 19% of Obama backers go for McCain

by Frank Newport, Gallup Poll Editor in Chief

A sizable proportion of Democrats would vote for John McCain next November if he is matched against the candidate they do not support for the Democratic nomination. This is particularly true for Hillary Clinton supporters, more than a quarter of whom currently say they would vote for McCain if Barack Obama is the Democratic nominee.

General Election Voting Among Democrats

Gallup Poll Daily tracking, March 7-22

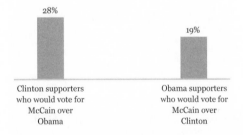

These conclusions are based on an analysis of Democratic voters' responses to separate voting questions in March 7-22 Gallup Poll Daily election tracking. In each day's survey, respondents are asked for their general election preferences in McCain-Clinton and McCain-Obama pairings. Democratic voters are then asked whom they support for their party's nomination.

The accompanying graph displays the results of the relationship between support for the Democratic Party's nomination and the general election vote between Obama and McCain.

As would be expected, almost all Democratic voters who say they support Obama for their party's nomination also say they would vote for him in a general election matchup against McCain. But only 59% of Democratic voters who support Clinton say they would vote for Obama against McCain, while 28% say they would vote for the Republican McCain. This suggests that some Clinton supporters are so strongly opposed to Obama (or so loyal to Clinton) that they would go so far as to vote for the "other" party's candidate next November if Obama is the Democratic nominee.

production of more oil, gas, and coal supplies. This is down from the 64% to 26% margin of a year ago. Still, despite their fears of a future energy shortage and in the face of record gas prices, Americans continue to favor a conservation approach by a margin similar to that seen in most Gallup Polls since 2001.

If Barack Obama were the Democratic Party's candidate and John McCain were the Republican Party's candidate, who would you be more likely to vote for -- [ROTATED: Barack Obama, the Democrat (or) John McCain, the Republican]?

Based on Democratic nomination preference

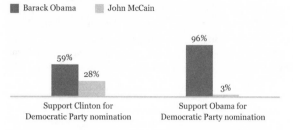

Gallup Poll Daily tracking, March 7-22, 2008

The results follow the same pattern, but not to quite the same extent, when the relationship between Democratic support and a general election matchup between Clinton and McCain is examined.

If Hillary Clinton were the Democratic Party's candidate and John McCain were the Republican Party's candidate, who would you be more likely to vote for -- [ROTATED: Hillary Clinton, the Democrat (or) John McCain, the Republican]?

Based on Democratic nomination preference

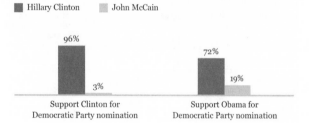

Gallup Poll Daily tracking, March 7-22, 2008

Here again, as expected, almost all of those who support Clinton for the Democratic Party's nomination say they would vote for her against McCain. Seventy-two percent of those who support Obama for the party's nomination would vote for Clinton against McCain, while 19% would desert and vote for the Republican.

Implications

The data suggest that the continuing and sometimes fractious Democratic nomination fight could have a negative impact for the Democratic Party in next November's election. A not insignificant percentage of both Obama and Clinton supporters currently say they would vote for McCain if he ends up running against the candidate they do not support.

Clinton supporters appear to be somewhat more reactive than Obama supporters. Twenty-eight percent of the former indicate that if Clinton is not the nominee—and Obama is—they would support McCain. That compares to 19% of Obama supporters who would support McCain if Obama is not the nominee—and Clinton is.

It is unknown how many Democrats would actually carry through and vote for a Republican next fall if their preferred candidate does not become the Democratic nominee. The Democratic campaign is in the heat of battle at the moment, but by November,

there will have been several months of attempts to build party unity around the eventual nominee—and a focus on reasons why the Republican nominee needs to be defeated.

Additionally, some threat of deserting the party always takes place as party nomination battles are waged, and this threat can dissipate. For example, in answer to a recent Gallup question, 11% of Republicans said they would vote for the Democratic candidate or a third-party candidate next fall if McCain does not choose a vice president who is considerably more conservative than he is. (And another 9% said they just wouldn't vote.) These results suggest that it may be normal for some voters to claim early on in the process—perhaps out of frustration—that they will desert their party if certain things do not happen to their liking. And it may be equally likely that they fall back into line by the time of the general election. It is worth noting that in Gallup's historical final pre-election polls from 1992 to 2004, 10% or less of Republicans and Democrats typically vote for the other party's presidential candidate.

Still, when almost 3 out of 10 Clinton supporters say they would vote for McCain over Obama, it suggests that divisions are running deep within the Democratic Party. If the fight for the party's nomination were to continue until the Denver convention in late August, the Democratic Party could suffer some damage as it tries to regroup for the November general election.

Survey Methods

Results are based on telephone interviews with 6,657 national Democratic voters, aged 18 and older, conducted March 7-22, 2008. For results based on the total sample of national adults, one can say with 95% confidence that the maximum margin of sampling error is ±2 percentage points.

Interviews are conducted with respondents on land-line telephones (for respondents with a land-line telephone) and cellular phones (for respondents who are cell-phone only).

In addition to sampling error, question wording and practical difficulties in conducting surveys can introduce error or bias into the findings of public opinion polls.

March 27, 2008
DEMOCRATIC GROUPS MOST AT RISK OF DESERTING
Independents, conservatives likeliest to vote for McCain

by Frank Newport, Gallup Poll Editor in Chief

Democrats are at most risk of losing the support of independents, conservative Democrats, and, among Hillary Clinton supporters, less well-educated Democrats if those voters' preferred candidate—Clinton or Barack Obama—does not win the party's nomination. Black Democrats appear loyal to the party regardless of who wins the nomination.

The finding that sizable percentages of Democrats say they would vote for Republican John McCain next November if the Democratic nominee is not their preferred candidate raises interesting questions about exactly whom the Democrats are most at risk of losing in the general election.

To answer those questions, Gallup analyzed the basic relationship between Democratic candidate support and the current general election vote within various subgroups of the population.

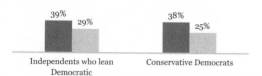

Vote for John McCain Among Democrats in General Election, if Preferred Candidate Loses Nomination

■ Clinton supporters (if Obama is nominee)

□ Obama supporters (if Clinton is nominee)

Clinton Nomination Supporters

The accompanying table displays the percentage of Clinton supporters who say they would vote for McCain if the general election matchup were McCain versus Obama.

Vote for John McCain if the General Election Ticket Were McCain vs. Barack Obama

Democrats who support Hillary Clinton for the Democratic nomination, March 7-22, 2008, Gallup Poll Daily tracking

	% Vote for John McCain
Independents/Lean Democratic	39
Conservative Democrats	38
High school or less	30
Moderate Democrats	30
Men	30
Non-Hispanic whites	29
White Hispanics	29
18-34	28
35-54	28
Some college	27
55+	27
Women	26
College graduate	25
Democratic identifiers	24
Postgraduate	21
Liberal Democrats	18
Non-Hispanic blacks	15

There are clear differences by subgroup in self-reported vote for McCain under an Obama-wins-the-nomination scenario. In other words, it appears that if Obama is on the ticket, some groups of Clinton-supporting Democrats are more susceptible to bolting the party and voting for the Republican nominee next fall than are others.

The average "defection rate" of Clinton-supporting Democrats away from Obama and to McCain in the general-election matchup is 28%. The two groups of Clinton-supporting Democrats who are significantly above this average in defection to McCain are independents who lean Democratic and conservative Democrats.

The groups that are below average in potential defection to McCain if Obama were running against him are blacks, liberal Democrats, those with postgraduate educations, and core Democrats (i.e., those who identify as Democrats when asked their party identification).

Clinton-supporting Democrats with the most education are the least likely to say they would vote for McCain if he were matched against Obama next fall. Those with less formal education are most likely to vote for McCain.

Among Clinton supporters, there are only small differences by gender in voting for McCain if Obama is on the ticket. There are no significant age differences.

Obama Nomination Supporters

The percentages of Democratic voters who support Obama for the nomination but who would vote for McCain if Clinton is the nominee are lower across most subgroups than is the case for Clinton supporters (in reference to a McCain-Obama race, as reviewed above). This is a reflection of the basic finding that Obama supporters are less likely to abandon their preferred party and vote for McCain—even if their candidate does not get the Democratic nomination—than is the case for Clinton supporters in the reverse scenario (19% of Obama supporters would vote for McCain if Clinton is the nominee, compared to 28% of Clinton supporters who would vote for McCain if Obama is the nominee).

But there are differences across subgroups of Obama supporters in their intentions to vote for McCain.

Vote for John McCain if the General Election Contest Were McCain vs. Hillary Clinton

Based on Democrats who support Barack Obama for the Democratic nomination, March 7-22, 2008, Gallup Poll Daily tracking

	% Vote for John McCain
Independents/Lean Democratic	29
Conservative Democrats	25
Moderate Democrats	25
Non-Hispanic whites	24
White Hispanics	21
Men	21
College graduate	20
35-54	20
High school or less	19
Postgraduate	19
18-34	19
55+	19
Some college	18
Women	18
Democratic identifiers	15
Liberal Democrats	11
Non-Hispanic blacks	10

Obama supporters who would be most likely to support McCain in a McCain-Clinton race are independents who lean Democratic, conservative Democrats, moderate Democrats, and non-Hispanic whites.

Those least likely to bolt the party and vote for McCain are blacks, liberal Democrats, and core Democrats.

There are no significant age differences.

Discussion

Across the board, the data show that Democratic support in the general election is more at risk among some subgroups of voters than among others. In particular, independent voters who lean Democratic are more likely than any other subgroup tested to say they would vote for McCain if their candidate does not gain the nomination. Additionally, conservative Democrats appear to be less attached to the party than are liberal Democrats, and more willing to say they would vote for McCain if their candidate is not the nominee.

Almost 4 out of 10 voters in these two groups who support Clinton say they would vote for McCain if Obama is the nominee. The percentages are still high, but about 10 points lower, for voters in these groups who support Obama when asked about a McCain-Clinton contest.

These findings are not necessarily surprising, but underscore Democrats' vulnerability with voters who are positioned somewhat more in the middle of the political or ideological spectrum. This may also reflect McCain's strong appeal to independent voters, who may not need much nudging to shift their vote from a Democratic candidate to McCain.

Black Democratic voters, regardless of whom they support, seem prepared to remain quite loyal to the Democratic Party. Fifteen percent of blacks who support Clinton would vote for McCain if Obama is the nominee, and only 10% of blacks who support Obama would vote for McCain if Clinton is the nominee. In other words, there is little apparent risk of losing a substantial proportion of black voters regardless of who the nominee is.

This last finding is significant. Obama has the overwhelming support of black Democratic voters at this point, and there has been discussion of the backlash that could occur if Obama were to lose the nomination to Clinton. But these data suggest that Clinton could still expect to receive the vote of most black Obama supporters were she to win and face McCain in the fall. (The data do not address the issue of motivation or turnout, which could be lower among blacks if Obama is not the nominee, nor do the data address the implications of the precise way in which Clinton might win the nomination. If Clinton were to win by the vote of super-delegates, for example, the blowback from black Obama supporters might be greater than if she were to win by gaining the highest percentage of the popular vote cast in primaries and caucuses.)

The data show an inverse relationship between education and Clinton voters defecting to McCain if Obama is the nominee. Thus, an Obama win of the Democratic nomination runs a risk of the Democratic Party losing the November support from less well-educated Democrats who support Clinton.

There is no significant gender difference evident in the data. Both men and women tend to mirror the overall sample patterns in terms of projected vote for McCain, with only minor differences. This may be surprising to some who might expect that women who support Clinton (who would be the first female president in U.S. history if she is nominated and wins the election) would be less loyal to the party if their candidate did not win the nomination. But this is not the case.

Although there are no significant differences in willingness to vote for McCain across age groups, a more detailed analysis suggests a greater hesitation to vote for the Democratic candidate as age increases—in a situation in which the voter's candidate is not the nominee. This occurs because the "undecided" vote goes up with age. Older Democrats are no more likely to vote for McCain if their candidate does not win than are those who are younger, as noted in the previous sections of this analysis. However, it appears that older voters *are* less likely to vote for the Democratic candidate when he or she is not the one they support. In other words, instead of declaring a vote for McCain in these situations, these older voters are more likely to be undecided.

The basic difference between Clinton and Obama supporters is observed across all three age groups. In each instance, Clinton supporters are less likely to support Obama against McCain than are Obama supporters to support Clinton against McCain.

Survey Methods

Results are based on telephone interviews with 6,657 national adults, aged 18 and older, conducted March 7-22, 2008. For results based on the total sample of national adults, one can say with 95% confidence that the maximum margin of sampling error is ±2 percentage points.

Interviews are conducted with respondents on land-line telephones (for respondents with a land-line telephone) and cellular phones (for respondents who are cell-phone only).

In addition to sampling error, question wording and practical difficulties in conducting surveys can introduce error or bias into the findings of public opinion polls.

March 27, 2008

PUBLIC BELIEVES AMERICANS HAVE RIGHT TO OWN GUNS
Nearly three in four say Second Amendment guarantees this right

by Jeffrey M. Jones, Gallup Poll Managing Editor

A solid majority of the U.S. public, 73%, believes the Second Amendment to the Constitution guarantees the rights of Americans to own guns. Twenty percent believe the amendment only guarantees the rights of state militia members to own guns.

Do you believe the Second Amendment to the U.S. Constitution guarantees the rights of Americans to own guns, or do you believe it only guarantees members of state militias such as National Guard units the right to own guns?

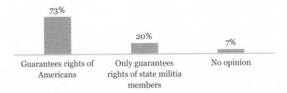

USA Today/Gallup, Feb. 8-10, 2008

The Supreme Court will soon weigh in on this issue, after recently hearing the arguments in the case of *District of Columbia v. Heller*, in which the Washington, D.C., ban on handgun ownership by city residents is facing a Second Amendment challenge.

The precise language of the Second Amendment reads:

A well regulated militia, being necessary to the security of a free state, the right of the people to keep and bear arms, shall not be infringed.

The often fierce debate over the Second Amendment has centered on whether it was intended to protect the rights of all Americans to own guns, or only those who are members of state militia groups.

The poll makes it clear which side Americans come down on. Gun owners (roughly one-third of the U.S. adult population) are nearly universal in endorsing the view that the Second Amendment guarantees their right to own guns. Non-owners are less likely to view the amendment this way, but a majority still does.

Do you believe the Second Amendment to the U.S. constitution guarantees the rights of Americans to own guns, or do you believe it only guarantees members of state militias such as National Guard units the right to own guns?

Results by gun ownership

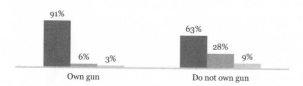

■ Guarantees rights of Americans to own guns

■ Only guarantees rights of state militia members to own guns

■ No opinion

USA Today/Gallup, Feb. 8-10, 2008

While the American public backs the view that gun ownership is a constitutional right, Americans favor having legal restrictions on it. In the same poll, 49% favor stricter gun laws than exist now and 38% would like to see gun laws remain as they are. Just 11% advocate gun laws that are less strict.

Would you like to see gun laws in this country made more strict, less strict, or remain as they are?

■ % More strict   ■ % Less strict   ■ % Remain the same

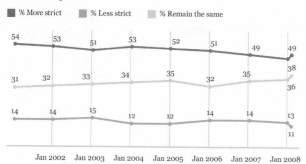

USA Today/Gallup, Feb. 8-10, 2008

The practical outcome of the case will be whether the Washington, D.C., handgun ban will be allowed to stand. In general, the public opposes sweeping bans on handguns. In the most recent Gallup Crime Poll, conducted last October, Americans opposed a law that would ban possession of handguns except by police and other authorized persons by 68% to 30%.

Implications

The Second Amendment case may well be the most significant Supreme Court ruling this year and arguably the most significant one in Court history on gun ownership. Reports suggest the Court was sympathetic to the notion that the Second Amendment does confer a right to own guns on Americans during the oral arguments in the case, in line with what most Americans think. While the Supreme Court is not supposed to be swayed by public opinion, Americans appear inclined to react favorably to a rul-

ing that affirms the right to own guns and unfavorably to one that does not.

Survey Methods

Results are based on telephone interviews with 1,016 national adults, aged 18 and older, conducted Feb. 8-10, 2008. For results based on the total sample of national adults, one can say with 95% confidence that the maximum margin of sampling error is ±3 percentage points.

For results based on the sample of 373 gun owners, the maximum margin of sampling error is ±6 percentage points.

For results based on the sample of 630 gun non-owners, the maximum margin of sampling error is ±4 percentage points.

Interviews are conducted with respondents on land-line telephones (for respondents with a land-line telephone) and cellular phones (for respondents who are cell-phone only).

In addition to sampling error, question wording and practical difficulties in conducting surveys can introduce error or bias into the findings of public opinion polls.

March 28, 2008

ECONOMIC ANXIETY SURGES IN PAST YEAR
Economy ties healthcare as Americans' top issue concern

by Lydia Saad, Gallup Poll Senior Editor

The percentage of Americans saying they worry "a great deal" about the economy has surged by more than 20 points over the past year, moving the issue from 6th on the list of 12 national issues measured in 2007 to tied for first today with healthcare.

Next, I'm going to read a list of problems facing the country. For each one, please tell me if you personally worry about this problem a great deal, a fair amount, only a little, or not at all?

The economy

■ % A great deal

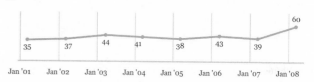

Gallup updates public concern about major issues confronting the country each March as part of its annual Environment survey. The only other issue for which Americans' level of concern increased a significant amount since 2007 is unemployment, a major economic sub-issue. Concern about the remaining 10 issues either held steady (as did energy, the environment, and race relations, among others) or declined slightly (healthcare, illegal immigration, and hunger/homelessness).

Aside from the economy's ascension to the top of this year's list, the 2008 ranking of issues is similar to that of 2007. Healthcare remains a dominant concern. Last year it was ranked No. 1, with 63% worried a great deal, far ahead of Social Security, in second place with 49%. This year, healthcare ties the economy for first, with only a two-point difference in the percentage worried about each: 60% for the economy and 58% for healthcare.

	March 2007	March 2008	Change
	%	%	pct. pts.
The economy	39	60	21
Unemployment	25	36	11
Energy	43	47	4
Crime and violence	48	49	1
Possible terrorism against the U.S.	41	40	-1
Race relations	19	18	-1
Drug use	45	43	-2
Social Security	49	46	-3
The environment	43	40	-3
Healthcare	63	58	-5
Illegal immigration	45	40	-5
Hunger/Homelessness	43	38	-5

Several issues are clustered in the 40% to 49% range as secondary concerns to the economy and healthcare this year. These are crime, energy, Social Security, drug use, the environment, illegal immigration, and possible terrorism against the United States.

Slightly fewer than 40% of Americans say they worry a great deal about hunger and homelessness or unemployment.

Only 18% rate race relations as a major concern. Race relations is the only issue about which the majority of Americans say they worry only a little or not at all.

Percentage Worried a "Great Deal" About Each Issue

	March 2008
	%
The economy	60
Healthcare	58
Crime and violence	49
Energy	47
Social Security	46
Drug use	43
The environment	40
Illegal immigration	40
Possible terrorism against the U.S.	40
Hunger/Homelessness	38
Unemployment	36
Race relations	18

Economic anxiety has grown fairly uniformly across various segments of the American public. In March 2007, fewer than half of men and women, as well as adults in all major age groups, and Republicans as well as Democrats were worried a great deal about the economy. Today, half or more in each of these demographic categories say they worry a great deal about it.

For each of the past two years, women have been more likely than men to say they worry about the economy (64% vs. 57% in 2008), and Democrats have been much more likely than Republicans to be worried (72% vs. 52%).

Other areas for which Gallup finds significant gender differences—all with women more concerned than men—include healthcare, crime, the environment, drug use, the possibility of terrorist attacks, unemployment, and hunger/homelessness.

The worry ratings for most issues are characterized by significant partisan differences, including seven (in addition to the economy) for which Democrats express more concern than Republicans:

healthcare, energy, Social Security, the environment, hunger/homelessness, unemployment, and race relations. Republicans express more concern than Democrats about only two issues: illegal immigration and the possibility of future terrorism against the United States. Republicans and Democrats express about equal levels of concern on the issues of crime and drug use.

Survey Methods

Results are based on telephone interviews with 1,012 national adults, aged 18 and older, conducted March 6-9, 2008. For results based on the total sample of national adults, one can say with 95% confidence that the maximum margin of sampling error is ±3 percentage points.

Interviews are conducted with respondents on land-line telephones (for respondents with a land-line telephone) and cellular phones (for respondents who are cell-phone only).

In addition to sampling error, question wording and practical difficulties in conducting surveys can introduce error or bias into the findings of public opinion polls.

March 28, 2008

NORTH KOREA DROPS OUT OF TOP THREE U.S. "ENEMIES"
Iran and Iraq lead the list, followed by China

by Lydia Saad, Gallup Poll Senior Editor

With the United States and North Korea reaching some major diplomatic agreements over North Korea's nuclear program in the past year, the percentage of Americans citing that country as the United States' greatest enemy has dropped by half, from 18% in February 2007 to 9% today. Iran and Iraq continue to lead the list, while China has moved into third.

What one country anywhere in the world do you consider to be the United States' greatest enemy today?

	Feb. 11-14, 2008
	%
Iran	25
Iraq	22
China	14
North Korea/Korea	9
United States itself	3
Afghanistan	3
Pakistan	2
Russia	2
Saudi Arabia	1
Venezuela	1
Other	6
None (vol.)	2
No opinion	8

No more than 3% of Americans name any other country as the United States' top enemy. The few others mentioned by at least 1%

include Afghanistan (3%), Pakistan (2%), Russia (2%), Saudi Arabia (1%), and Venezuela (1%). An additional 3% say the United States is its own greatest enemy.

Trends in Perceived Enemies

Gallup first asked this "greatest enemy" question in the pre-9/11, pre-Iraq war environment at the outset of George W. Bush's presidency in February 2001, at which time Iraq was the clear leader, followed by China and then Iran. Since then, the biggest changes have been a decline in the proportion of Americans naming Iraq, and big increases (at least through 2007) in the percentages naming Iran and North Korea.

Trend in Perceptions of United States' Greatest Enemy

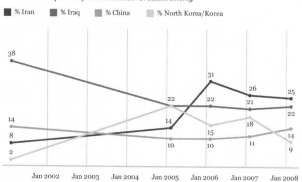

The percentage naming Iraq fell from 38% in 2001 to 22% in February 2005, and has remained at about that level in each subsequent year. No doubt the sectarian violence in Iraq and the ongoing U.S. military engagement there has kept Iraq in the top tier of countries Americans perceive as the greatest enemy, although the new Iraqi government is ostensibly an ally of the United States, supporting the U.S. military presence in Iraq.

Mentions of Iran and North Korea were only 8% and 2%, respectively, in February 2001. However, with President Bush defining both countries in his 2002 State of the Union address as part of an "axis of evil, arming to threaten the peace of the world," more Americans have given each country the top enemy designation. North Korea took a big jump to 22% by February 2005 while mentions of Iran expanded to 31% by February 2006.

All along, between 10% and 14% of Americans have named China, placing it either third or fourth on the list each time. It is unclear whether perceptions of China as an enemy are in the traditional political and military framework, or in economic terms. The same poll finds more Americans naming China rather than the United States as the world's leading economic power, so there is certainly the potential that some Americans view China's economic strength as a hostile threat.

In line with President Bush's current foreign policy worldview, Republicans are most likely to name Iran as the United States' top enemy (39%)—more than twice the percentage among Democrats (16%). Democrats are more likely than Republicans to mention Iraq (27% vs. 16%), while differences are not as pronounced in mentions of China and North Korea.

Identification of Iraq as the United States' top enemy today—arguably a misperception held over from attitudes formed during the regime of Saddam Hussein—is strongly associated with Americans' age and the related factor of self-reported attention to world affairs.

Country Designated the United States' Greatest Enemy Today

By Party I.D.

	Iran	Iraq	China	North Korea
	%	%	%	%
Republicans	39	16	19	7
Independents	24	22	14	8
Democrats	16	27	12	13

Feb. 11-14, 2008

Older Americans, and, correspondingly, those who closely follow news about foreign countries, are much less likely to designate Iraq as the United States' top enemy than are younger adults and those who are less attentive to international news.

Country Designated the United States' Greatest Enemy Today

By Age and Attention to News about Foreign Countries

	Iran	Iraq	China	North Korea
	%	%	%	%
18-34 years	17	30	11	15
35-54 years	30	23	13	9
55 years and older	25	15	19	6
Attention to World News				
Very close	28	12	20	9
Somewhat close	26	23	13	10
Not close	18	30	13	8

Feb. 11-14, 2008

Survey Methods

Results are based on telephone interviews with 1,007 national adults, aged 18 and older, conducted Feb. 11-14, 2008. For results based on the total sample of national adults, one can say with 95% confidence that the maximum margin of sampling error is ±3 percentage points.

Interviews are conducted with respondents on land-line telephones (for respondents with a land-line telephone) and cellular phones (for respondents who are cell-phone only).

In addition to sampling error, question wording and practical difficulties in conducting surveys can introduce error or bias into the findings of public opinion polls.

March 31, 2008
DEMOCRATS, REPUBLICANS AGREE:
OBAMA TOUGHER OPPONENT FOR MCCAIN
Perceived as having better chance than Clinton of winning in November

by Jeffrey M. Jones, Gallup Poll Managing Editor

A new Gallup Panel survey finds a majority of both Republicans and Democrats saying Barack Obama has a better chance than Hillary Clinton of defeating Republican John McCain in the November presidential election.

In your view, would Hillary Clinton or Barack Obama have a better chance of defeating John McCain in the presidential election in November?

Asked of Democrats and Democratic-leaning independents

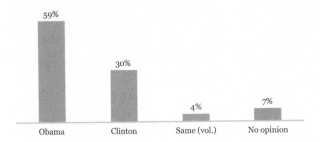

March 24-27, 2008
(vol.) = Volunteered response

In your view, would John McCain have a better chance of defeating Hillary Clinton or Barack Obama in the presidential election in November?

Asked of Republicans and Republican-leaning independents

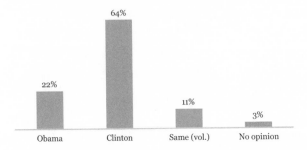

March 24-27, 2008

The survey was conducted March 24-27, interviewing a nationally representative sample of 1,005 Gallup Panel members. Democrats were asked whether Clinton or Obama has the better chance of defeating McCain in November: 59% say Obama does; 30% say Clinton. Republicans were asked whether McCain has a better chance of defeating Clinton or Obama on Election Day. Sixty-four percent say McCain has a better chance of beating Clinton, compared with only 22% choosing Obama, meaning Republicans view Obama as the more formidable candidate.

Gallup polling has recently shown some positive momentum for Obama in the Democratic nomination battle—he has moved into the lead over Clinton in the preferences of Democratic voters nationwide. Both candidates are competitive with McCain in Gallup's latest polling on registered voters' general election preferences, though Obama has tended to do marginally better than Clinton in the more recent updates.

Last Friday, Vermont Sen. Patrick Leahy became the most prominent Democrat to call on Clinton to drop out of the race. Democratic National Committee Chairman Howard Dean did not go that far, but urged the Democratic super-delegates to decide by July 1 so the nominee is known well before the late August convention. Tennessee Gov. Phil Bredesen has made a pitch for super-delegates to hold their own mini-convention in June to determine the nominee.

Those calls have been made out of concern that the increasingly contentious nomination battle will hurt the party's chances in November. Most rank-and-file Democrats seem to agree, according to the Gallup Panel survey results. When asked about the effects of the continuing Democratic nomination campaign on the party's general election chances, 56% of Democrats say it is doing "more harm than good," while 35% think it is doing "more good than harm."

As would be expected, most Democrats who favor Obama for the nomination believe the ongoing campaign is doing more to hurt (61%) than to aid (32%) the party's chances of winning in November. But Clinton supporters also tend to believe this—48% say the continuing campaign is doing more harm than good, while 40% say it is doing more good than harm.

Implications

Clearly at this point, the party rank-and-file thinks Obama would present a stronger challenge to McCain in the fall than Clinton would. Those attitudes could certainly change over the remainder of the campaign, but it is notable that Obama maintains a wide lead in these perceptions shortly after the Jeremiah Wright controversy knocked his campaign off stride.

Also, the poll shows there is a fairly widely held belief among party supporters—including a plurality of Clinton supporters—that the ongoing campaign is hurting their chances of winning in November. It seems unlikely those attitudes would improve much going forward, particularly if the tone of the Democratic campaign remains negative. If so, then it is likely there would be further calls for Clinton to drop out of the race, and that would put more pressure on her to do well in the Pennsylvania primary on April 22 and all the contests that follow.

Survey Methods

Results for this Gallup Panel study are based on telephone interviews with 1,005 national adults, aged 18 and older, conducted March 24-27, 2008. Gallup Panel members are recruited through random selection methods. The panel is weighted so that it is demographically representative of the U.S. adult population. For results based on this sample, one can say with 95% confidence that the maximum margin of sampling error is ±4 percentage points. In addition to sampling error, question wording and practical difficulties in conducting surveys can introduce error or bias into the findings of public opinion polls.

For results based on the sample of 502 Democrats and Democratic-leaning independents, the maximum margin of sampling error is ±5 percentage points.

For results based on the sample of 453 Republicans and Republican-leaning independents, the maximum margin of sampling error is ±6 percentage points.

Interviews are conducted with respondents on land-line telephones (for respondents with a land-line telephone) and cellular phones (for respondents who are cell-phone only).

In addition to sampling error, question wording and practical difficulties in conducting surveys can introduce error or bias into the findings of public opinion polls.

March 31, 2008

NET NEW HIRING ACTIVITY DIPS SLIGHTLY IN MARCH

Gallup daily surveys show declines in East and South, mostly offset by gains in Midwest

by Dennis Jacobe, Gallup Chief Economist

An analysis of daily Gallup polling shows a drop of 0.3 percentage points in net new hiring activity in the U.S. economy from February to March 2008.

Change in Net New Hiring Activity From February to March 2008, by Region
In percentage points

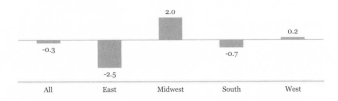

| All | East | Midwest | South | West |

Survey Data Continue to Suggest Weak Job Growth

Given the weaker-than-expected economic reports last week, all eyes on Wall Street are likely to be focused on Friday's Bureau of Labor Statistics (BLS) release of the jobs numbers for March. And while the ADP employment survey has not always been an accurate predictor of future job growth, the markets are likely to look to ADP's estimates for private company hiring in the United States on Wednesday as a possible indicator of what the BLS will report two days later.

Gallup's net new hiring activity measure is an effort to assess U.S. job creation or elimination based on a survey of individual workers. In order to calculate this measure, Gallup asks current full-time employees whether their employers are hiring new people and expanding the size of their workforces, not changing the size of their workforces, or letting people go and reducing the size of their workforces. Net new hiring activity is computed by subtracting the "reducing" percentage from the "expanding" percentage. The measure is based on samples of more than 8,000 employees per month.

February's results for the measure (a 2.1-point drop from January) suggested a decline in the number of jobs being created. In contrast, the slight March drop of 0.3 points suggests that hiring activity was essentially unchanged in the past month. On the other hand, Gallup's net new hiring activity measure is not seasonally adjusted and one would normally expect a pick-up in job growth from February to March. This tends to reinforce the idea that Gallup's data suggest—that seasonally adjusted job growth was flat at best in March and could have declined slightly.

While Gallup's net new hiring activity measure is only three months old, its regional results do seem to provide a degree of face-validity. The biggest drop in reported hiring activity was in the East, where the financial crisis has already begun to have a significant impact on employment. This was mostly offset by an increase of 2.0 points in the Midwest—part of which could be something of a bounce back from its big drop of 4.4 points last month; part could also be because of the apparent continued strength in the exports and agricultural sectors. Smaller changes in net new hiring activity took place in the South (-0.7 points) and the West (+0.2 points).

Net Hiring Expectations by Region
% Hiring new people minus % letting people go

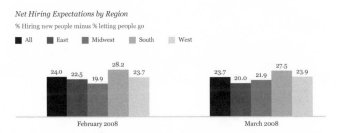

Is the U.S. Economy Creating New Jobs?

On Friday morning, the BLS will issue a new jobs report. Given all the bad economic news of the past month, many people may be expecting another decline in U.S. jobs. Of course, the government's unemployment rate and the new job growth numbers reported by the BLS tend to be volatile and subject to substantial revisions over time. Given those facts, however, Gallup's daily monitoring of the U.S. jobs situation suggests that the number of new jobs created will be essentially zero or perhaps slightly to the down side.

If this turns out to be the case, it will be further confirmation that last quarter's economic slowdown is morphing into a full-fledged recession. At the same time, however, if the jobs number is flat or shows a modest decline, it may be seen as good news relative to Wall Street's dismal expectations.

Survey Methods

Gallup is interviewing no fewer than 1,000 U.S. adults nationwide each day during 2008. The economic questions analyzed in this report are asked of a random half-sample of respondents each day. The results reported here are based on combined data of more than 8,000 interviews in January, February, and March. For results based on these samples, the maximum margin of sampling error is ±1 percentage point.

In addition to sampling error, question wording and practical difficulties in conducting surveys can introduce error or bias into the findings of public opinion polls.

ther before turning around. The poll finds that most Americans do not believe the bottom of the economic downturn has been reached—just 19% say the economy is now as bad as it will get. The vast majority—79%—expect it will get worse before it starts to recover, with 46% saying it will get "a little worse" and 33% saying it will get "a lot worse."

Do you think the U.S. economy is now as bad as it will get before it starts to recover, or do you think it will get worse before it starts to recover? Do you think it will get a lot worse, or only a little worse?

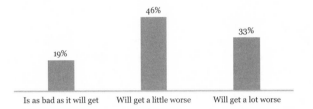

March 24-27 Gallup Panel survey

April 01, 2008
AMERICANS NOT EXPECTING QUICK ECONOMIC TURNAROUND
Majority do not expect recovery to begin for two or more years

by Jeffrey M. Jones, Gallup Poll Managing Editor

A majority of Americans, 55%, think it will be two or more years before the U.S. economy starts to recover.

Gallup asked a nationally representative sample of Americans drawn from its household panel how long they think it will be before the economy starts to recover. The question was asked in an open-ended fashion, so respondents could give any time estimate they chose.

Only about one in five think the economy will begin to recover quickly—within the next 12 months. An additional 20% think it will be at least a year before it starts to recover. The majority, though, expects a longer period of tough economic times, lasting two years or more in duration. That includes 20% who expect that it will be five years or longer before improvement is seen.

The median—or typical—expectation is that it will be two years before the economy turns around. The average estimate is 5.9 years, in part because some very pessimistic respondents essentially believe the economy will not get better for several generations.

Republicans are much more optimistic than Democrats or independents about the prospects for economic recovery. Whereas 63% of Democrats and 60% of independents expect the bad times to last for two or more years, only 41% of Republicans do.

Has the Bottom Been Reached?

Not only do Americans believe it will be years before the economy starts to get better, they also think it is in fact likely to deteriorate fur-

Even a majority of Republicans, 65%, expect the economy to deteriorate further. Many more independents (85%) and Democrats (87%) believe the bottom has not yet been reached.

Economy Surpasses Iraq as Top Priority for Government

In recent months, the economy has surpassed the Iraq war as the most important problem facing the country in Americans' eyes. The panel survey shows it has also passed Iraq as the public's top priority for the president and Congress to deal with at this time.

Forty-eight percent of Americans rate the economy in general terms as the government's top priority. That figure does not include more specific mentions of economic problems such as unemployment, inflation, or recession, to name a few, which would push economic concerns above the majority level. Forty-two percent rate the Iraq war as the top government priority. Healthcare is a distant third at 21%, with fuel prices and energy (10%) and immigration (8%) rounding out the top five issues.

In December, when the question was last asked, 55% said the war should be the government's top issue and 22% the economy. The Iraq war had topped the list every time Gallup asked this question, beginning in April 2006.

Just your best guess, how long do you think it will be before the economy starts to recover? [OPEN-ENDED]

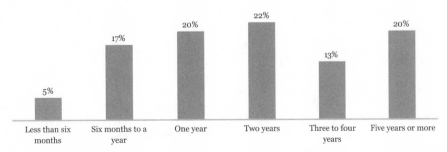

March 24-27 Gallup Panel survey

In your view, what one or two issues should be the top priorities for the president and Congress to deal with at this time? [OPEN-ENDED]

	Mar 24-27, 2008
	%
Economy in general	48
Situation in Iraq/War	42
Poor healthcare/hospitals; high cost of healthcare	21
Fuel/Oil prices/Lack of energy sources/The energy crisis	10
Immigration/Illegal aliens	8
National security	4
Social Security	4
Education/Poor education/Access to education	3
Unemployment/Jobs	3
High cost of living/Inflation	3
Terrorism	3
Environment/Pollution	2
Federal budget deficit/Federal debt	2
Taxes	2
Foreign aid/Focus overseas	1
Lack of money	1
International issues/problems	1
Poverty/Hunger/Homelessness	1
Poor leadership/Corruption/Dissatisfaction with government/Congress/politicians/candidates	1
Medicare	1
Recession	1

March 24-27 Gallup Panel survey

Survey Methods

Results for this Gallup Panel study are based on telephone interviews with 1,005 national adults, aged 18 and older, conducted March 24-27, 2008. Gallup Panel members are recruited through random selection methods. The panel is weighted so that it is demographically representative of the U.S. adult population. For results based on this sample, one can say with 95% confidence that the maximum margin of sampling error is ±4 percentage points. In addition to sampling error, question wording and practical difficulties in conducting surveys can introduce error or bias into the findings of public opinion polls.

Interviews are conducted with respondents on land-line telephones (for respondents with a land-line telephone) and cellular phones (for respondents who are cell-phone only).

In addition to sampling error, question wording and practical difficulties in conducting surveys can introduce error or bias into the findings of public opinion polls.

April 01, 2008
CLINTON LESS APPEALING THAN OBAMA AS POTENTIAL V.P.

Clinton backers favor an Obama-Clinton ticket; Obama backers do not

by Lydia Saad, Gallup Poll Senior Editor

Only 42% of Democrats nationwide want Hillary Clinton to be the Democratic vice presidential nominee if Barack Obama wins the

presidential nomination, while 55% think he should pick someone else. By contrast, the majority of Democrats—58%—would like to see Obama nominated as vice president if Clinton heads the ticket.

Democrats' Vice Presidential Preferences

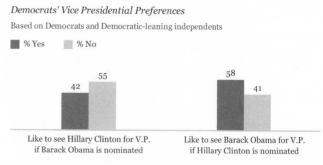

Based on Democrats and Democratic-leaning independents

March 24-27, 2008

Thus, if the Democratic electorate has its way, Obama will be on the Democratic presidential ticket this fall, as either president or vice president. Clinton's chances of being on the ticket seem more likely to end if she loses the nomination—at least according to Democrats' weak support for an Obama-Clinton unity ticket.

Lopsided Willingness to Embrace the Opponent

The reason for the disparity is that a relatively small number of Obama supporters—just 29% —favor Obama choosing Clinton as a possible running mate. Seventy percent say they'd rather he choose someone else. In contrast, a majority of Clinton supporters—53%— would want Clinton to choose Obama for vice president if she is nominated.

Similar percentages (a majority of both Clinton supporters and Obama supporters) say they would want their own candidate selected for vice president should the other candidate win the Democratic nomination for president.

Democrats' Support for Hillary Clinton and Barack Obama as the Vice Presidential Nominee -- Two Scenarios

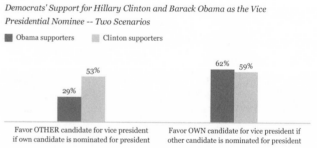

March 24-27, 2008

Bottom Line

Former New York Gov. Mario Cuomo, among other Democratic Party elders, has recently argued that the only way for Democratic voters to come together in the fall will be for the two candidates to come together on the Democratic ticket.

Last week, Gallup reported that Obama supporters are more likely to remain loyal to the Democratic ticket in the fall than are Clinton supporters if their respective candidates aren't nominated for president.

However, according to the vice presidential preferences reported here, party loyalty and party unity are not one and the same. Most

Obama supporters may be willing to bury the hatchet and vote for Clinton for president, but they don't seem eager to embrace Clinton as Obama's running mate for the sake of party unity.

Survey Methods

Results are based on telephone interviews with 1,005 national adults, aged 18 and older, conducted March 24-27, 2008. Respondents were randomly drawn from Gallup's nationally representative household panel, which was originally recruited through random selection methods. The final sample is weighted so it is representative of U.S. adults nationwide.

For results based on the total sample of national adults, one can say with 95% confidence that the margin of sampling error is ± 4 percentage points.

For results based on the sample of 502 Democrats and Democratic-leaning independents, the maximum margin of sampling error is ±5 percentage points.

In addition to sampling error, question wording and practical difficulties in conducting surveys can introduce error or bias into the findings of public opinion polls.

April 02, 2008

OBAMA, CLINTON LEVERAGE DIFFERENT GROUPS VS. MCCAIN

Obama has strength among independents, Clinton among core Democrats

by Frank Newport, Gallup Poll Editor in Chief

Gallup Poll Daily tracking results for the general election have shown that both Barack Obama and Hillary Clinton are essentially tied with John McCain among registered voters nationwide.

Overall Ballot for March 7 Through March 29

Registered voters

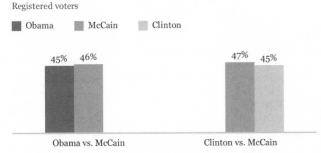

At this point, then, there would appear not to be a major difference in the overall strength that either Democratic candidate would bring to bear in the general election against McCain.

But an analysis of the vote patterns within segments of the voting population shows that the way in which the two Democratic candidates arrive at that parity with McCain is quite different.

A new Gallup analysis of 19,076 interviews conducted between March 7 and March 29 segments the registered voters into a number of groups, based on partisan identification and ideology.

The basic relationship between these two variables and the general election vote is displayed in the accompanying tables.

General Election Ballots for March 7-March 29

Registered voters

	% Obama	% McCain
Liberal Democrats	85	8
Moderate Democrats	72	18
Conservative Democrats	61	28
Pure Independents	29	42
Moderate Liberal Republicans	18	75
Conservative Republicans	6	90

General Election Ballots for March 7-March 29

Registered voters

	% Clinton	% McCain
Liberal Democrats	86	8
Moderate Democrats	77	16
Conservative Democrats	73	21
Pure Independents	23	48
Moderate Liberal Republicans	14	81
Conservative Republicans	4	92

In a broad sense, the difference in voting patterns for both Democratic candidates by partisan/ideological group follows a predictable pattern. The two candidates do best among liberal Democrats, and then progressively worse among moderate Democrats, conservative Democrats, "pure" independents (who do not lean toward one party or the other), and moderate/liberal Republicans. They do worst among conservative Republicans.

The analysis can be continued with a more detailed examination of the electorate, separating voters into three groups based on race and ethnicity. Given the dominant percentage of non-Hispanic whites in the sample, the accompanying table displays the vote of non-Hispanic whites broken into partisan and ideological categories, along with the voting patterns of white Hispanics and non-Hispanic blacks.

General Election Ballots for March 7-March 29

Registered voters

	% Obama	% McCain
Blacks	90	5
Non Hispanic white	37	53
Lib Dem	82	10
Mod Dem	66	22
Cons Dem	50	35
Pure Ind	25	47
Mod Lib Rep	17	77
Cons Rep	5	91
White Hispanic	54	37

General Election Ballots for March 7-March 29

Registered voters

	% Clinton	% McCain
Blacks	79	10
Non Hispanic white	40	53
Lib Dem	87	8
Mod Dem	75	18
Cons Dem	68	25
Pure Ind	20	52
Mod Lib Rep	13	82
Cons Rep	3	93
White Hispanic	59	36

Here, Obama's margin over McCain among non-Hispanic black registered voters is 85 points, while Clinton's margin is 69 points. In other words, while both Democrats dominate McCain among black voters, Obama has a significantly larger margin over McCain than does Clinton. (It appears that black voters are less likely to say they would vote for Clinton against McCain and more likely to say they don't have a preference between the two.)

Clinton does slightly better than Obama against McCain among Hispanics.

There are different, and interesting, patterns in the relative performances of Clinton and Obama against McCain among whites across party and ideological groups.

In general, Clinton does better among all three groups of white Democrats against McCain than does Obama. The difference between Obama and Clinton is largest among conservative white Democrats. In fact, among this group, Obama manages to get only 50% of the vote to McCain's 35%, while Clinton wins by a much larger 68% to 25% margin.

Obama makes up for this, however, with a stronger relative performance among independents and Republicans. While McCain outpolls both Clinton and Obama among "pure independents," Obama is somewhat more competitive with him among this group (trailing by 22 points, compared with 32 points for Clinton). McCain, of course, beats both candidates by significant margins among the two groups of Republicans used in this analysis. But again, Clinton loses by slightly larger margins than does Obama.

Implications

At this point in the election cycle, there are more Democrats and Democratic-leaning independents than there are Republicans and Republican-leaning independents. McCain has been able to hold his own against the two Democratic candidates in the general election trial heat ballots in the face of this disparity mostly because he does very well among conservative Republicans and wins among independents.

The two Democratic candidates offer different profiles of strengths and weaknesses when pitted against Republican McCain in the general election. Obama's strength is his appeal to black voters, and his somewhat greater appeal than Clinton's to independents and Republicans. On the other hand, although Clinton attracts the support of a lower percentage of blacks than Obama, she has a stronger appeal to white Democrats, particularly white conservative Democrats, only half of whom at this point say they would vote for

Obama if he were the nominee pitted against McCain. Clinton has a very slight advantage over Obama in the matchup with McCain among Hispanics.

When the votes of all registered voters are averaged, as noted previously, the two Democratic candidates end up performing about the same against McCain. Clinton appears better able to gain the support of the Democratic base, particularly Democrats more on the fringe of the party (conservatives), while Obama builds his coalition with a stronger appeal to independents, Republicans, and black voters.

Obama enjoys the traditionally high support from black Democrats that all recent Democratic nominees have received. However, Obama would have the challenge of shoring up support among white Democrats if he were the nominee, while Clinton would be faced with the prospect of expanding her support among independents and "soft" Republicans (while at the same time motivating black voters). Looking ahead to the fall election, it is not clear at this point if one of these profiles of support is better from a strategic campaign perspective than the other.

Survey Methods

Results are based on Gallup Poll Daily tracking interviews with 19,076 registered voters, aged 18 and older, conducted March 7-29, 2008. For results based on the total sample of registered voters, one can say with 95% confidence that the maximum margin of sampling error is ±1 percentage point.

Interviews are conducted with respondents on land-line telephones (for respondents with a land-line telephone) and cellular phones (for respondents who are cell-phone only).

In addition to sampling error, question wording and practical difficulties in conducting surveys can introduce error or bias into the findings of public opinion polls.

April 02, 2008
PRESIDENTIAL CANDIDATES' WEAKNESSES IN DEPTH
Clinton and Obama foes cite personal factors; McCain critics cite policy

by Lydia Saad, Gallup Poll Senior Editor

When Americans are asked which of the leading candidates left in the race for president they *least* want to see elected president this year, 40% name John McCain, 36% Hillary Clinton, and 20% Barack Obama.

Who do you LEAST want to see elected president this year -- [ROTATED: Hillary Clinton, John McCain, (or) Barack Obama]?

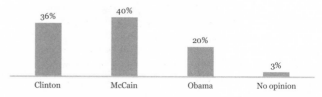

March 24-27, 2008

McCain leads this inauspicious list in part because he is the only Republican among the three candidates—meaning he is the primary focus of Democrats and independents who lean Democratic, while Republicans can split their choices between Obama and Clinton.

Seventy-one percent of Democrats name McCain. Republicans divide their answers between the two Democratic candidates, although they name Clinton by nearly 2-to-1 over Obama, 60% vs. 34%.

Who do you LEAST want to see elected president this year -- [ROTATED: Hillary Clinton, John McCain (or) Barack Obama]?

By party identification

■ McCain   ■ Clinton   ■ Obama

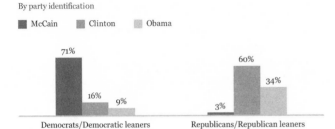

March 24-27, 2008

Why?

A follow-up question asking respondents for the reasons they least want to see their named candidate elected finds the overwhelming criticism of Obama is his lack of experience. The main rationale for spurning a Clinton presidency is the perception that she is untrustworthy, while the knocks against McCain are threefold: his associations with the Iraq war, with President George W. Bush, and with the Republican Party.

Obama: "Not Qualified"

Nearly 4 in 10 of those who least want to see Obama elected (39%) say they believe he is "inexperienced" or "not qualified" to be president. All other explanations are much less frequently mentioned. The reason cited second most frequently is trustworthiness, mentioned by 15% of those opposed to his becoming president. However, nearly as prevalent (12%) as an explanation for not wanting Obama elected is the belief that he is a Muslim. (Obama himself has said this is incorrect, and he is a member of the Chicago-based Trinity United Church of Christ.)

An additional 8% of Obama's detractors say they dislike his "religious affiliation," but it is unclear whether this is a reference to perceptions about Obama's connection to the Muslim religion, or to his ties to the Rev. Jeremiah Wright and Trinity United Church of Christ.

McCain: Iraq, Bush, and the GOP

Those who least want to see McCain elected president are most likely to cite his position on the Iraq war (27%), his similarity with President Bush (25%), or the fact that he is a Republican (23%). In line with these policy-oriented reasons for opposing him, an additional 8% say they "disagree with his views on most issues."

Although McCain's advanced age has been raised as a possible liability for his candidacy, only 7% of those most opposed to him say they think he's too old. Only 2% mention McCain's well-known temper management issues.

Can you tell me in your own words why you least want to see Barack Obama elected president? [OPEN-ENDED]

Based on 234 national adults who least want to see Obama elected; ±8 percentage points

	2008 Mar 24-27
	%
Inexperienced/Not qualified	39
Do not trust him	15
Muslim	12
Disagree with his views	11
Dislike his religious affiliation	8
Too liberal	6
Racist	5
His age/Too young	3
Do not like his attitude	3
Don't know enough about him	2
Scared of him	2
Lacks a platform	2
Other	10
No reason in particular (vol.)	1
No opinion	1

Percentages add to more than 100% due to multiple responses.

March 24-27, 2008
(vol.) = Volunteered response

Can you tell me in your own words why you least want to see John McCain elected president? [OPEN-ENDED]

Based on 379 national adults who least want to see McCain elected; ±6 percentage points

	2008 Mar 24-27
	%
Disagree with his position on the Iraq war	27
Too much like Bush/Need change	25
He is a Republican	23
Disagree with his views on most issues	8
Believe he is incompetent	8
His age/Too old	7
Do not trust him	4
Too conservative	3
Temper/Anger issues	2
Not well versed in politics	2
Inconsistent/Flip-flops	2
Other	4
No reason in particular (vol.)	1
No opinion	1

Percentages add to more than 100% due to multiple responses.

March 24-27, 2008
(vol.) = Volunteered response

Clinton: Don't Trust Her, Reservations About Bill, and Likability

The most prominent reason given by those opposed to Clinton being elected president is not trusting her—mentioned by 24%. However, the 18% saying they don't want Bill Clinton back in the White House and the 16% saying they don't like Hillary Clinton rank a fairly close second and third, respectively.

The 12% saying they think Clinton lacks the experience to be president is relatively small compared to the 39% saying this of Obama, but it is still more than a trivial issue for her. Half as many (6%) say the country is not ready for a woman to be president and only 2% cite her healthcare plan.

Bottom Line

The responses give an interesting initial indication of the potential vulnerabilities of these candidates in the general election. There is a notable difference in the negative perceptions of the candidates held

Can you tell me in your own words why you least want to see Hillary Clinton elected president? [OPEN-ENDED]

Based on 360 national adults who least want to see Clinton elected; ±6 percentage points

	2008 Mar 24-27
	%
Do not trust her	24
Do not want Bill Clinton back in White House	18
Do not like her	16
Is not qualified/Would do a bad job	12
Past baggage/Scandal	11
Do not agree with her views on politics	10
Too liberal	6
Not ready for a woman president	6
Dislike her attitude	3
Disagree with her healthcare plan	2
Too power-hungry	2
Other	3
No reason in particular (vol.)	2
No opinion	1

Percentages add to more than 100% due to multiple responses.

March 24-27, 2008
(vol.) = Volunteered response

by those most opposed to each one becoming president. The most prevalent criticisms leveled against Obama and Clinton are all personal in nature: trustworthiness, likability, experience, and family connections. By contrast, the top criticisms of McCain are all more policy oriented: Iraq, associations with Bush, and being a Republican.

Survey Methods

Results are based on telephone interviews with 1,005 national adults, aged 18 and older, conducted March 24-27, 2008. Respondents were randomly drawn from Gallup's nationally representative household panel, which was originally recruited through random selection methods. The final sample is weighted so it is representative of U.S. adults nationwide.

For results based on the total sample of national adults, one can say with 95% confidence that the maximum margin of sampling error is ±4 percentage points.

In addition to sampling error, question wording and practical difficulties in conducting surveys can introduce error or bias into the findings of public opinion polls.

April 03, 2008
AGE, VOTE MORE STRONGLY RELATED IN OBAMA-MCCAIN MATCHUP
Gender more strongly related in Clinton-McCain contest

by Jeffrey M. Jones, Gallup Poll Managing Editor

Republican John McCain and Democrat Barack Obama appeal to opposite ends of the age spectrum, with McCain faring better among older voters and Obama among younger voters. Hillary Clinton fares less well versus McCain than Obama does among younger voters, but she does better than Obama among older voters.

These analyses are based on aggregated data from Gallup Poll Daily tracking conducted between March 7 and March 31. The results are based on interviews with more than 21,000 registered vot-

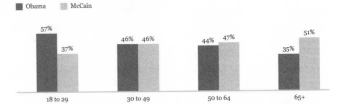

General Election Vote Preference by Age, Obama vs. McCain
Based on registered voters

March 7-31 Gallup Poll Daily tracking

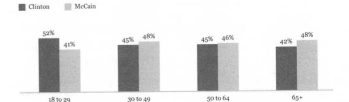

General Election Vote Preference by Age, Clinton vs. McCain
Based on registered voters

March 7-31 Gallup Poll Daily tracking

ers. Overall, both hypothetical general-election contests are close, with McCain holding a one percentage point advantage over both Obama and Clinton.

Obama's strength in a general-election matchup against McCain would be his appeal to young voters. Obama maintains a 20-point lead over McCain among 18- to 29-year-old registered voters, 57% to 37%, while McCain has nearly as large a lead among those 65 and older, 51% to 35%. The two are closely matched among the two middle age groups.

The general pattern of Democrat/Republican candidate support is the same in a Clinton-McCain contest, but Clinton's lead of 11 points over McCain among the youngest voters is only about half the lead Obama enjoys among this group. But she offsets her weaker performance among younger voters by doing better among older voters, trailing McCain by 6 points among senior citizens, compared to Obama's 16-point deficit versus McCain among older voters.

The analysis also affirms a significant gender gap in general-election voting preferences, as has been the case for the last several presidential elections. Female voters are once again aligning themselves with the Democratic candidate and male voters with the Republican. But here again, the sizes of the gender gaps differ, depending on whether Clinton or Obama is pitted against McCain. McCain has a 9-point advantage over Obama among male voters while Obama leads him by 5 points among women, for a total gender gap of 14 points. But if Clinton is the Democratic nominee, the gender gap expands to 22 points, with men going for McCain by 52% to 40% and women for Clinton by 51% to 41%.

Looking at the interaction between age and gender, a Clinton-McCain contest would primarily divide Americans according to gender, with age having far less of an impact. McCain currently leads Clinton among younger (under age 50) and older (aged 50+) men, and by a similar margin in each case. Meanwhile, Clinton leads among both groups of women, but runs stronger among younger than among older women.

The age and gender relationships are a little less cut and dried with regard to Obama-McCain preferences, in part because the normal patterns of candidate support by gender and age can sometimes

General Election Vote Preference by Gender, Obama vs. McCain
Based on registered voters

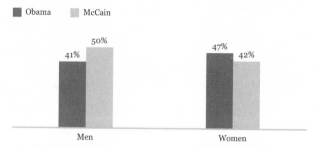

March 7-31 Gallup Poll Daily tracking

General Election Vote Preference by Gender, Clinton vs. McCain
Based on registered voters

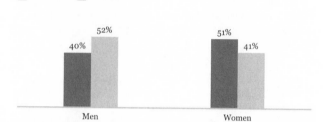

March 7-31 Gallup Poll Daily tracking

General Election Vote Preference by Gender and Age, Clinton vs. McCain
Based on registered voters

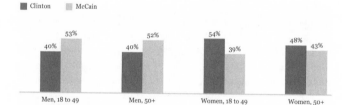

March 7-31 Gallup Poll Daily tracking

General Election Vote Preference by Gender and Age, Obama vs. McCain
Based on registered voters

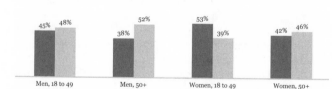

March 7-31 Gallup Poll Daily tracking

be at odds. Obama's strength among women and younger voters results in 18- to 49-year-old women breaking heavily in his direction in an Obama-McCain matchup, 53% to 39%. Conversely, McCain's relative strength with men and older voters results in men 50 years and older breaking heavily for him versus Obama: 52% to 38%. The other two gender/age groups—older women and younger men—represent conflicting political tendencies, and thus break about evenly for Obama and McCain, with McCain holding a slight edge in both cases.

Implications

Gallup found similar differences by age and gender in an analysis of February data. Given the usual relationships between age and gender and the vote in presidential elections, one would expect these patterns to persist throughout the election year. But the analysis does suggest there will be some key groups to track over the course of the election, including middle-aged voters (between 30 and 64), who currently equally divide between McCain and either Clinton or Obama.

Depending on who the Democratic candidate is, other groups may be important to deciding the outcome, including older women (in a McCain-Clinton contest) or younger men and older women (in an Obama-McCain election).

Survey Methods

Results are based on telephone interviews with 21,082 registered voters, aged 18 and older, conducted March 7-31, 2008. For results based on the total sample of national adults, one can say with 95% confidence that the maximum margin of sampling error is ±1 percentage point.

For results based on the sample of 10,341 male registered voters, the maximum margin of sampling error is ±1 percentage point.

For results based on the sample of 10,741 female registered voters, the maximum margin of sampling error is ±1 percentage point.

For results based on the sample of 1,545 registered voters age 18-29, the maximum margin of sampling error is ±3 percentage points.

For results based on the sample of 6,149 registered voters age 30-49, the maximum margin of sampling error is ±1 percentage point.

For results based on the sample of 7,086 registered voters age 50-64, the maximum margin of sampling error is ±1 percentage point.

For results based on the sample of 6,149 registered voters age 65 and older, the maximum margin of sampling error is ±1 percentage point.

Interviews are conducted with respondents on land-line telephones (for respondents with a land-line telephone) and cellular phones (for respondents who are cell-phone only).

In addition to sampling error, question wording and practical difficulties in conducting surveys can introduce error or bias into the findings of public opinion polls.

April 03, 2008
SIX IN 10 OPPOSE WALL STREET BAILOUTS
But majority of Americans support the government helping people stay in their homes

by Dennis Jacobe, Gallup Chief Economist

A new Gallup Poll, conducted March 24-27, shows that 6 in 10 Americans oppose the federal government taking steps to help prevent major Wall Street investment companies from failing.

Widespread Opposition to Helping Bear Stearns

On March 13, Bear Stearns told the Federal Reserve it would file for bankruptcy the next day and as a result, the Fed voted on March 14 to

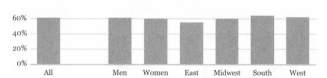

Democrats overwhelmingly (by a 71% to 27% margin) favor the federal government acting to help homeowners. Independents are also in favor, but by a slimmer margin of 55% to 43%. In contrast, Republicans oppose such efforts, with only 40% in favor compared to 58% opposed.

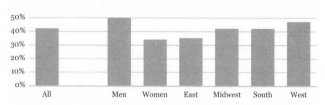

extend the investment company emergency credit to keep it from failing. On Sunday, March 16, the Fed, with the support of the U.S. Treasury, extended a $29 billion loan against Bear Stearns assets to facilitate its merger with JP Morgan.

On Wednesday, Fed Chairman Ben Bernanke defended this highly unusual emergency action by stating, "Given the current exceptional pressures on the global economy and financial system, the damage caused by a default by Bear Stearns could have been severe and extremely difficult to contain." He went on to explain essentially why the Fed felt Bear Stearns was too big to fail in terms of its role within the global financial system. He continued his explanation Thursday before the Senate Banking Committee.

While the Fed's effort to maintain financial stability is clearly justified when viewed in economic terms, it is opposed by a surprisingly uniform 6 in 10 Americans across a wide variety of demographic groups: men (61%) and women (60%); those in the East (55%), Midwest (60%), South (64%), and West (62%); those with annual incomes of less than $35,000 (61%), of $35,000 to $74,999 (59%), and of $75,000 or more (62%); and even those affiliated with political parties (or with no party): Republicans (61%), independents (64%), and Democrats (57%).

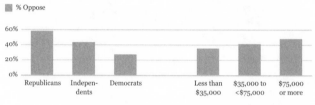

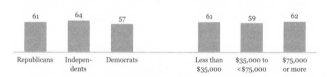

Differing Degrees of Support for Helping Homeowners

In sharp contrast to their opposition to helping Wall Street investment companies, Americans—by a margin of 56% to 42%—support having the federal government take steps to help prevent people from losing their homes because they can't pay their mortgages. More importantly, support for such federal efforts varies significantly across demographic groups. While women favor the government helping homeowners by 63% to 34%, men are evenly split, with 50% in opposition compared to 48% in favor.

People in the East favor the government helping homeowners, by a 63% to 35% margin, while those in the West are split (50% in favor, 47% opposed). Those making less than $35,000 a year (63% to 35%) and those making $35,000 to $74,999 (57% to 41%) tend to favor government help, while those making $75,000 or more are divided (51% in favor, 48% opposed).

Are Wall Street Firms "Too Big to Fail"?

For decades, observers of the financial markets have argued about the idea that some financial firms may simply be too big to fail. The nation's largest financial companies do business on a daily basis with other financial firms and individuals (counterparties) around the globe. These transactions are conducted based on a high degree of confidence that no one involved needs to worry that the very large financial companies they are dealing with might default on their obligations. The "too big to fail" concept suggests that the failure of a large financial services company not only might mean widespread losses for the stockholders and others doing business with the company, but would also severely shake the confidence of everyone in the financial system that the nation's largest financial services firms will always meet their financial obligations. Hard as it may be to believe, if confidence in the financial sector is shaken badly enough, the system could actually collapse, re-creating conditions similar to those of the Great Depression.

Most likely, Americans aren't highly cognizant of the actual possibility that there could be a global financial collapse. However, if the keepers of the financial system—the Fed and the Treasury—show fear that the system might lose its stability, they could shake the very confidence they are acting to preserve.

On the other hand, it is relatively easy for the average American to identify with a family that buys a house and gets a mortgage loan but finds it cannot make rising mortgage payments. By contrast with the financial services crisis, no one is particularly worried about pointing out the distress such mortgage situations are causing millions of American families.

While federal officials, the president, and the Congress may act against public opinion to preserve global financial stability, it seems hard to believe they will not also respond to help American home-owners. In fact, swooping in to rescue struggling homeowners could be crucial in offsetting consumer resentment toward the Fed over its Wall Street bailout.

Survey Methods

Results for this panel study are based on telephone interviews with 1,005 national adults, aged 18 and older, conducted March 24-27, 2008. Respondents were drawn from Gallup's household panel, which was originally recruited through random selection methods. The final sample is weighted so it is representative of U.S. adults nationwide. For results based on the total sample of national adults, one can say with 95% confidence that the maximum margin of sampling error is ±4 percentage points.

In addition to sampling error, question wording and practical difficulties in conducting surveys can introduce error or bias into the findings of public opinion polls.

April 04, 2008
WIVES STILL DO LAUNDRY, MEN DO YARD WORK
Husbands and wives view the household division of labor differently

by Frank Newport, Gallup Poll Editor in Chief

Married couples in America today maintain a strong and traditional division of labor, with 68% of married adults saying the wife does the laundry, and 57% saying the husband does the yard work.

Who is most likely to do each of the following in your household?
Based on married adults

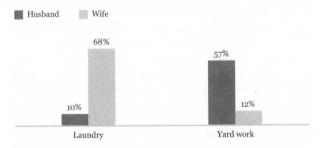

Dec. 6-9, 2007, GPSS Lifestyle Poll

Gallup's annual Social Series Lifestyle poll, conducted in December 2007, reveals that women continue to be much more likely than their husbands to perform a wide number of household duties, with men being reported as primarily responsible for only two. The survey asked all married respondents to indicate whether they or their spouse was "most likely" to do each of 10 chores, with those who said they had a child under the age of 18 also asked about child care.

Over half of married respondents say the wife is most likely to do six household chores: laundry, cleaning the house, making decisions about furniture and decoration, preparing meals, caring for the children (for couples with children under 18), and doing the grocery shopping. Respondents are also significantly more likely to say the wife, rather than the husband, washes dishes and pays the household bills.

Who is most likely to do each of the following in your household?
Dec 6-9, 2007, GPSS Lifestyle Poll
Based on 594 adults who are currently married

	Husband	Wife
	%	%
Keep the car in good condition	69	13
Do yard work	57	12
Make decisions about savings or investments	35	18
Pay bills	34	48
Wash dishes	16	48
Do grocery shopping	16	53
Prepare meals	14	58
Do laundry	10	68
Caring for the children on a daily basis (asked of parents with children under 18)	9	54
Clean the house	6	61
Make decisions about furniture and decoration	6	60

On the other hand, over half of married couples say the husband keeps the car in good condition and does yard work.

There is a little more equal distribution of labor on the one remaining chore included in the list—investments. Although 35% of married respondents say the husband makes decisions about savings and investments, compared to 18% saying the wife does this, almost half of respondents in the poll say these are shared equally.

Husbands and Wives Report Division of Labor Differently

These reports on who does what within the household are highly colored by the gender of the married partner who is doing the reporting. In other words, married men report what goes on in their household differently than married women.

Who is most likely to do each of the following in your household?
Dec. 6-9, 2007, GPSS Lifestyle Poll
Based on 594 adults who are currently married

	Reported by husband	Reported by husband	Reported by wife	Reported by wife
	% Saying husband does chore	% Saying wife does chore	% Saying husband does chore	% Saying wife does chore
Keep the car in good condition	79	6	58	20
Do yard work	63	8	51	17
Make decisions about savings or investments	49	11	21	25
Pay bills	46	37	21	61
Wash dishes	21	38	10	60
Do grocery shopping	20	44	12	63
Prepare meals	18	49	10	67
Do laundry	12	62	8	75
Caring for children on a daily basis	12	45	5	64
Clean the house	8	56	4	67
Make decisions about furniture and decoration	9	60	3	60

Generally, husbands are more likely than wives to say they are responsible for a given chore, and vice versa. Husbands and wives often appear to perceive who does what in the household differently.

The differences in some instances are substantial.

• One of the biggest discrepancies comes in reports of who pays the household bills. Men are more likely to report that they—the husbands—pay the bills, while women are strongly likely to claim that they—the wives—pay the bills.

- Six out of 10 women report that they are more likely to wash the dishes, while men are more likely than women to say the dishes are done equally.
- Two-thirds of women say they are more likely to prepare meals. A much smaller percentage of husbands say their wives prepare the meals.
- Although women are more likely to say their husbands, rather than they themselves, keep the cars in good condition and do yard work, the percentages are much lower than those reported by husbands, who overwhelmingly say they are responsible for these chores.
- Half of men say they are responsible for investments and savings, and only 11% of men say their wives are responsible. Women, however, are much more likely to say there is equal responsibility.

Trends Over Time

Married Americans were asked about this same list of chores (with the exception of child care) in a 1996 Gallup Poll. For the most part, there has been only slight change in the distribution of household labor over the last 11 years.

Who is most likely to do each of the following in your household ?
Gallup GPSS Lifestyle Poll

	Sep 3-5, 1996	Dec 6-9, 2007
	% Husband/% wife	% Husband/% wife
Keep the car in good condition	75/10	69/13
Do yard work	55/10	57/12
Make decisions about savings or investments	26/16	35/18
Pay bills	30/47	34/48
Wash dishes	13/53	16/48
Do grocery shopping	10/59	16/53
Prepare meals	9/63	14/58
Do laundry	8/70	10/68
Caring for children on a daily basis	-	9/54
Clean the house	6/60	6/61
Make decisions about furniture and decoration	5/57	6/60

Married adults are slightly more likely now than in 1996 to report that husbands are primarily responsible for a number of the items on the list, but in all instances, these changes are small.

Few Age Differences

Differences might be expected in these patterns of household labor distribution by age: younger married couples might be thought more likely to share chores equally or to establish responsibilities for the husband that have traditionally been more of the wife's domain.

But that does not appear to be the case. Husbands and wives over 50 report a distribution of these chores that differs little from that of husbands and wives under 50.

Implications

There continues to be a significant division of labor by gender within American married households. Women appear to be more likely than men to do a number of chores within the home. There has been little change in this pattern compared to Gallup's previous survey in 1996.

Who is most likely to do each of the following in your household ?
Dec 6-9, 2007 Gallup GPSS Lifestyle Poll

	18-49 years old	50+ years old
	% Husband/% wife	% Husband/% wife
Keep the car in good condition	67/13	72/13
Do yard work	55/13	59/12
Make decisions about savings or investments	35/19	35/17
Pay bills	33/48	35/47
Wash dishes	16/49	16/48
Do grocery shopping	14/56	20/49
Prepare meals	14/54	14/63
Do laundry	10/69	11/67
Caring for children on a daily basis	7/55	*
Clean the house	6/84	7/58
Make decisions about furniture and decoration	7/59	4/61

* Less than 0.5%.

Whether this state of affairs is good or bad, of course, is highly dependent on one's perspective. A division of labor in any social unit is often the most effective way to achieve goals and maintain orderly daily progress. Throughout history, certain household jobs have traditionally been considered more within the wife's domain, and others (fewer in number) within the husband's domain. That pattern appears to persist, even in an era in which wives are more likely to work outside the home than was the case in the past, and in which there has been much more of a focus on equality between the sexes.

The poll did not ask married respondents whether they thought the division of responsibility as reported was a positive or a negative. Such questioning might be of value in future surveys.

And there is the interesting dimension of the reporting party within each marriage. Husbands and wives view the household domain differently. The survey did not include a mechanism by which each married partner could be interviewed separately. But the analysis suggests that partners are generally more likely than their spouses to believe they are responsible for a given chore.

Survey Methods

Results are based on telephone interviews with 1,027 national adults, aged 18 and older, conducted Dec. 6-9, 2007. For results based on the total sample of national adults, one can say with 95% confidence that the maximum margin of sampling error is ±3 percentage points.

For results based on the sample of 594 adults who are currently married, the maximum margin of sampling error is ±4 percentage points.

In addition to sampling error, question wording and practical difficulties in conducting surveys can introduce error or bias into the findings of public opinion polls.

April 08, 2008
IRAQ WAR ATTITUDES POLITICALLY POLARIZED
Republicans generally favor the war; Democrats oppose it

by Jeffrey M. Jones, Gallup Poll Managing Editor

Republicans reject the idea of a timetable for withdrawing U.S. troops from Iraq, by a better than 2-to-1 margin, 65% to 32%. Democrats show an even greater margin in favor of a timetable, with 81% in favor and 15% opposed.

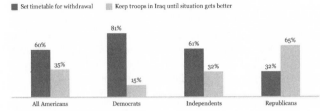

If you had to choose, which do you think is better for the U.S. -- [ROTATED: to keep a significant number of troops in Iraq until the situation there gets better, even if that takes many years, or to set a timetable for removing troops from Iraq and to stick to that timetable regardless of what is going on in Iraq]?

■ Set timetable for withdrawal　▢ Keep troops in Iraq until situation gets better

Feb. 21-24 USA Today/Gallup poll

Political divisions on the war have long been evident in Gallup polling data on Iraq, and those divisions continue today. Three national elections since the war began—the 2004 and 2008 presidential elections and the 2006 midterm elections—have shone a bright spotlight on those differences. In general, Republicans tend to support the war and oppose plans to end it before the situation is stabilized, while Democrats oppose it and seek an end to U.S. involvement.

This political divide on Iraq will be in clear public view on Tuesday when Gen. David Petraeus, commander of U.S. forces in Iraq, testifies before Congress. Among his questioners will be the three leading presidential candidates, Republican Sen. John McCain and Democratic Sens. Hillary Clinton and Barack Obama. The candidates' views on the war are in line with the rank-and-file of their parties.

In addition to the desirability of a troop withdrawal timetable, partisans have differing views on how successful the surge of U.S. troops in Iraq has been. Most Republicans, 70%, believe it is making the situation in Iraq better. In contrast, only 21% of Democrats say it is improving the situation, with nearly half (47%) saying it is not making much difference, and 31% saying the surge is making matters worse. Independents are about evenly divided in their views as to whether the surge is making the situation better (37%) or not making much difference (40%).

Based on what you have heard or read about the surge of U.S. troops in Iraq that began last year, do you think the increase in the number of U.S. troops in Iraq is -- [ROTATED: making the situation there better, not making much difference, (or is it) making the situation there worse]?

■ % Making the situation better　■ % No difference　▢ % Making the situation worse

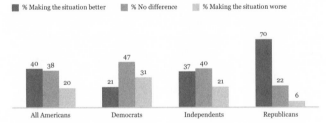

Feb. 21-24 USA Today/Gallup poll

Views of a withdrawal timetable and the progress of the surge are just two of a number of examples of wide political gaps in opinions about the war. The accompanying table shows some of the other polarized views on Iraq by party. The largest difference is evident in basic support for the war (whether the United States made a mistake in sending troops); there is a smaller gap on whether the United States has an obligation to establish security in Iraq.

As a whole, Democrats are opposed to the war, and their attitudes differ little by their political ideology. But Republicans of different ideological stripes differ on several Iraq issue dimensions. For

Opinions on the War in Iraq, by Political Party

	All Americans	Democrats	Independents	Republicans
Does U.S. have obligation to establish security in Iraq				
Yes, does	65%	54%	62%	83%
No, does not	32%	43%	34%	16%
Will Iraq be better off in long run than before war				
Yes, better off	67%	58%	62%	84%
No, worse off	26%	35%	29%	11%
Did U.S. make a mistake in sending troops to Iraq				
Yes, made a mistake	59%	82%	63%	24%
No, did not	39%	16%	34%	74%

Feb. 21-24 USA Today/Gallup poll

example, liberal or moderate Republicans are divided as to whether the United States should set a timetable for withdrawing from Iraq, while conservative Republicans overwhelmingly oppose a timetable.

Opinions About Iraq War Timetable, by Political Ideology, Among Republicans

■ Favor timetable for withdrawal　▢ Oppose timetable

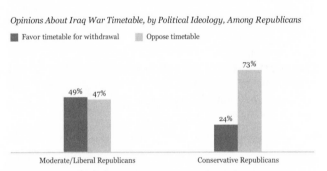

Feb. 21-24 USA Today/Gallup poll

Moderate and liberal Republicans (40%) are also twice as likely as conservative Republicans (19%) to say the United States made a mistake in getting involved in Iraq, and are somewhat less optimistic that the surge is making things better (52%) than are conservative Republicans (78%).

On the Iraq issue, McCain is closely aligned with the conservative wing of the party. That is notable given that conservative leaders have criticized McCain's positions on a number of issues, including immigration, taxes, and campaign finance.

Implications

The 2008 presidential election will present voters with a clear choice on Iraq, with Republicans putting forth one of the Senate's fiercest supporters of the war and Democrats choosing one of two leading Senate opponents, including Obama, who has made his opposition to the war from the beginning a major focus of his campaign. If McCain is elected, U.S. policy on Iraq will likely continue as it has under the Bush administration, with slower troop draw-downs tied to progress in establishing security in Iraq. If Obama or Clinton is elected, finding a quick end to the war will likely be the new president's top priority.

In general, the public tends to side with the Democrats from the standpoint of favoring a timetable, but relatively few advocate a quick withdrawal. And most seem sympathetic to the Republican argument about the United States needing to establish a certain level of security before leaving Iraq.

Results are based on telephone interviews with 2,021 national adults, aged 18 and older, conducted Feb. 21-24, 2008. For results based on the total sample of national adults, one can say with 95% confidence that the maximum margin of sampling error is ±2 percentage points.

For results based on the sample of 692 Democrats, the maximum margin of sampling error is ±4 percentage points.

For results based on the sample of 695 independents, the maximum margin of sampling error is ±4 percentage points.

For results based on the sample of 627 Republicans, the maximum margin of sampling error is ±4 percentage points.

Interviews are conducted with respondents on land-line telephones (for respondents with a land-line telephone) and cellular phones (for respondents who are cell-phone only).

In addition to sampling error, question wording and practical difficulties in conducting surveys can introduce error or bias into the findings of public opinion polls.

April 10, 2008

CONSUMER MOOD NEGATIVE BUT STEADY COMPARED TO MARCH

Confidence from April 1-8 still well below January and February averages

by Lydia Saad, Gallup Poll Senior Editor

Gallup's measure of Americans' positive economic mood stands at a gloomy 29.2 in Gallup Poll Daily tracking interviewing from April 1-8, 2008, similar to the 29.0 reading for all of March.

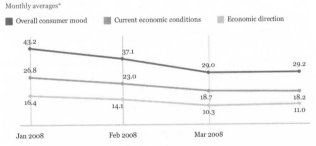

Gallup Poll Daily Consumer Mood Trends

Monthly averages*

* April 2008 results are based on Gallup Poll Daily tracking from April 1-8, 2008

The measure—reflecting Americans' positive perceptions of the U.S. economy—was 37.1 in February and 43.2 in January.

This measure is one way to summarize Gallup's daily tracking of the public's economic mood, which relies on two questions about the U.S. economy: 1) rating current economic conditions and 2) perceptions of whether the economy is getting better or worse. It indicates that the downward trend in consumer attitudes since January has leveled off (albeit at very negative levels).

The overall consumer mood rating is based on the sum of the positive answers to these two economic questions. The rating has a maximum possible score of 200 (under the ideal conditions that 100% of Americans rate the economy "excellent" or "good" and, separately, that 100% say it is "getting better"). The highest recorded

score in Gallup trends for these positive measures since the component questions were established in 1992 is 140 in January 2000.

There has been a generally strong correspondence between the direction of Gallup's economic mood measures and the monthly Reuters/University of Michigan Index of Consumer Sentiment. Thus, given the results of Gallup's roughly 4,000 interviews conducted thus far in April, it would be unusual if the preliminary April consumer sentiment figures being released to Reuters/University of Michigan subscribers on Friday, April 11, show either a major improvement or a deterioration in consumer attitudes since March.

Gallup Poll Consumer Mood vs. Reuters/University of Michigan Index of Consumer Sentiment -- January 2007-April 2008

* Results for 2007 are based on Gallup Poll monthly surveys; results for 2008 are based on monthly averages of Gallup Poll Daily tracking. April 2008 results are preliminary.

Since the start of Gallup Poll Daily tracking on Jan. 2, 2008, Gallup has released daily updates on consumer confidence based on three-day rolling averages. The averages reported for January through April obscure some important shifts that are evident in the detailed trend. Among these are the findings that consumer confidence fell sharply for the first three weeks of January, after which it regained nearly half its losses in the last week of January. Confidence slid again at the beginning of February, but then held steady through the remainder of the month, only to descend in the first half of March to the lowest level seen for the year. Confidence again rebounded somewhat toward the end of March and remained at that slightly improved level through early April.

Gallup Poll Daily Consumer Mood Index -- Jan. 2-April 8, 2008

Based on three-day rolling averages

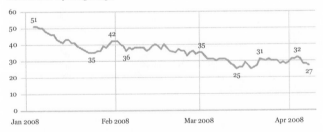

Confidence has softened slightly in the past few days (since April 6), although it is yet unclear whether this is a minor dip or the beginning of another substantial slide. While the average Gallup consumer mood score from April 1-8 (29.2) is similar to the 29.0 for all of March, consumers are a bit more negative about the economy at the start of April than they were at the start of March. This establishes the possibility that—if current attitudes persist or descend any further—April could produce the lowest consumer confidence scores of the year thus far.

Survey Methods

Approximately 1,000 national adults are interviewed each night for Gallup Poll Daily tracking (including weekdays and weekends, but not major holidays), of which a random half-sample of approximately 500 national adults are asked for their economic views. The results are reported in continuous three-day rolling averages.

The aggregate of Gallup Poll Daily tracking interviews from April 1-8 reported here is based on interviews with 3,979 national adults. For results based on this sample, the maximum margin of sampling error is ±2 percentage points. The January, February, and March monthly averages reported here each include interviews with at least 14,000 national adults. For results based on samples of this size, the maximum margin of sampling error is ±1 percentage point.

George W. Bush's Yearly Job Approval Averages

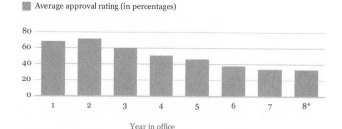

George W. Bush Approval by Political Party

Apr 6-9, 2008

April 11, 2008

BUSH JOB APPROVAL AT 28%, LOWEST OF HIS ADMINISTRATION

Only Nixon and Truman have had lower job approval ratings

by Frank Newport, Gallup Poll Editor in Chief

President George W. Bush's job approval rating has dropped to 28%, the lowest of his administration. Bush's approval is lower than that of any president since World War II, with the exceptions of Jimmy Carter (who had a low point of 28% in 1979), and Richard Nixon and Harry Truman, who suffered ratings in the low- to mid-20% range in the last years of their administrations.

George W. Bush Job Approval, January to April 2008

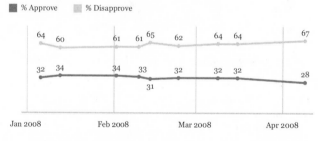

Bush's lowest job approval rating had been 29%, reached in a July 2007 Gallup Poll. Since that time, Bush's approval ratings have been generally in the low 30% range, averaging 32.5% across the eight polls conducted this year before the most recent poll, conducted April 6-9.

Bush's average for his first seven years in office was 52%, a tenure marked by a slide from high ratings in his first two years to the very low ratings in his sixth and seventh years, and in the first months of 2008. Bush's highest job approval rating is 90%, recorded in September 2001, just after the Sept. 11 terrorist attacks, and is the highest job approval rating in Gallup history.

On a year-by-year basis, Bush's ratings have gone from 68% and 71% averages in his first two years to 33% in his seventh year.

Bush's low rating in the current poll is the result of an extraordinarily low average approval rating from Democrats, a low level of support from independents, and support from just two-thirds of his base of Republicans.

When Bush received a 29% rating in Gallup's July 6-8, 2007, poll, the party approval ratings were similar to today's: 68% approval among Republicans, 21% among independents, and 7% among Democrats.

Historical Comparisons

Bush's current 28% job approval rating is at the very low end of the spectrum of approval ratings Gallup has recorded across the 11 presidents in office since World War II. The average presidential job approval rating during that time has been 55%. The highest reading, as noted, is the 90% for the current President Bush in September 2001; the lowest is the 22% for Truman in February 1952.

Presidential Approval

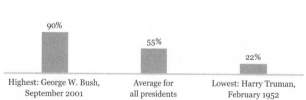

Only three presidents in Gallup's history have received job approval ratings of 28% or lower:

- Carter's low point of 28% was measured in late June and early July 1979, as the country underwent significant gas shortages and amid perceptions of a failing economy.
- Nixon had a number of readings below 28% in 1973 and 1974 prior to his leaving office as a result of the Watergate scandal.
- Truman recorded a number of readings below 28% in 1951 and 1952 as his administration was beset, similar to the current situation for Bush, with problems relating to the economy and an unpopular war (in Korea).

Of note is the fact that George W. Bush has now descended below the low point of his father's (George H.W. Bush's) administration. The senior Bush had a reading of 29% in July and August

1992. The former president also recorded a high point of 89%, the highest on record until his son's 90% in September 2001. Both Bushes, in short, have undergone radical 60-point drops in job approval in the course of their administrations.

Implications

Presidents who receive job approval ratings in the 20% range are generally beset by economic concerns, wars, or scandals. Truman, who has the dubious distinction of obtaining the lowest job approval rating in Gallup Poll history, had the triple whammy of a bad economy, an unpopular war, and hints of scandal in the last years of his administration. Nixon, of course, was primarily laid low by Watergate, although he had been the steward of an unpopular war for most of the years after he took office in January 1969. Carter was in the middle of a bad economy and sharply rising gas prices when he suffered a 28% job approval rating in the summer of 1979.

Now, Bush, the current president, has obtained a 28% job approval rating at a time when Americans are extraordinarily worried about the economy, when gas prices have risen to historical high points, in the middle of a war that the majority of Americans say was a mistake, and at a time when only 15% of Americans say they are satisfied with the way things are going in the United States.

Survey Methods

Results are based on telephone interviews with 1,021 national adults, aged 18 and older, conducted April 6-9, 2008. For results based on the total sample of national adults, one can say with 95% confidence that the maximum margin of sampling error is ±3 percentage points.

Interviews are conducted with respondents on land-line telephones (for respondents with a land-line telephone) and cellular phones (for respondents who are cell-phone only).

In addition to sampling error, question wording and practical difficulties in conducting surveys can introduce error or bias into the findings of public opinion polls.

April 11, 2008
GOOD JOBS ARE GETTING SCARCE
Only one in five Americans say now is a good time to find a quality job

by Dennis Jacobe, Gallup Chief Economist

The percentage of Americans saying now is a good time to find a quality job fell six percentage points to 20% in April from 26% in March and now stands at less than half its April 2007 reading of 46%.

Lower-Income Americans See Biggest Drop in Job Outlook

Earlier this month, the Labor Department reported that the United States lost 80,000 jobs in March. That was the third straight monthly job loss, and the unemployment rate has now increased to 5.1%. On Thursday, initial jobless claims fell by a more-than-expected 53,000, but the less volatile four-week moving average increased to 378,250, which represents the highest level since late 2005.

Gallup's monthly job measure shows a similarly dismal picture for early April, with just 20% of Americans saying now is a good

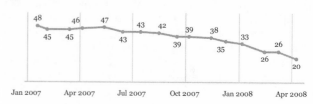

Is Now a Good Time or a Bad Time to Find a Quality Job?
January 2007 to April 2008

time to find a quality job. This is down from 26% in March and 46% in April of last year. It is also the lowest percentage for this measure since the 19% recorded in September 2003, and not much better than the record low of 16% of March 2003. The high since Gallup began tracking the measure in 2001 is 48% in January 2007.

The April decline in consumer perceptions of the job market differed significantly across income groups. Among those making less than $30,000 a year, positive perceptions of the job market fell by nearly half, from 23% in March to 12% in April. They fell more modestly, from 26% to 21%, among those making $30,000 but less than $75,000. However, job outlook perceptions were unchanged at 28% in April among those making $75,000 or more a year.

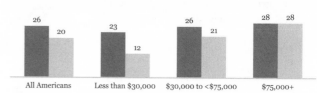

Is Now a Good Time or a Bad Time to Find a Quality Job?
By annual income

Many Americans Know Someone Who Lost His or Her Job

Fifty-four percent of Americans say they know someone who has been laid off or lost his or her job over the past six months. This percentage is up from the 50% who said they knew someone who had lost his or her job a year ago, but is still well below the 63% of April 2003.

The highest regional percentage for this question in the current poll is in the Midwest (62%); those in the West are next, at 55%, followed by 52% in the South and 47% in the East. The current high percentage in the Midwest is most likely explained by the continued decline in U.S. manufacturing during recent times. Of course, given the number of jobs currently being eliminated as a result of the credit crisis, the relative position of the East is likely to change significantly in the coming months.

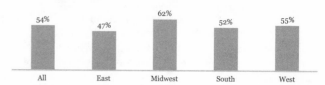

Do you, personally, know anyone who has been laid off or lost their job within the last six months, or not?
April 6-9, 2008

Underemployment Deserves Consideration

By historical standards, the current 5.1% unemployment rate would be considered close to full employment—not something associated with a recession. In part, today's relatively low unemployment rate may be because of the economic changes associated with globalization and the transformation of the United States into much more of a services economy. Whether these structural economic changes have reduced or just delayed the usual increase in the unemployment rate associated with a recession remains unclear. Regardless, the real job losses of the past three months in a row tend to confirm that the United States is already experiencing a recession.

Gallup's jobs question taps into not only Americans' perceptions of the unemployment rate, but also their sense of the availability of "quality" jobs. In this context, Gallup's jobs measure might be viewed, at least in part, as a reflection of "underemployment": that is, whether Americans are being forced to take jobs that do not fully make use of their talents, skills, and experience.

Survey Methods

Results are based on telephone interviews with 1,021 national adults, aged 18 and older, conducted April 6-9, 2008. For results based on the total sample of national adults, one can say with 95% confidence that the maximum margin of sampling error is ±3 percentage points.

Interviews are conducted with respondents on land-line telephones (for respondents with a land-line telephone) and cellular phones (for respondents who are cell-phone only).

In addition to sampling error, question wording and practical difficulties in conducting surveys can introduce error or bias into the findings of public opinion polls.

April 14, 2008

JUST HALF OF AMERICANS COMPLAIN TAX BILL IS TOO HIGH
Majority regard what they pay as "fair"

by Lydia Saad, Gallup Poll Senior Editor

It's tax time, and 52% of Americans complain that they pay too much in federal income taxes, but 42% say they pay the right amount, and a curious 2% say they pay too little.

Do you consider the amount of federal income tax you have to pay as too high, about right, or too low?

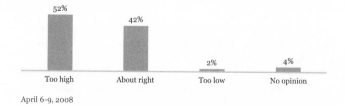

April 6-9, 2008

In fact, for all of the public's current dissatisfaction with the economy, with the direction of the United States, and with its leadership, Americans are fairly content with their federal tax obligation.

According to Gallup's 2008 Economy and Personal Finance survey, conducted in April, 60% regard the amount of income tax they have to pay this year as "fair." Only 35% say it's not fair.

Do you regard the income tax which you will have to pay this year as fair?

April 6-9, 2008

Additionally, more Americans believe "middle-income people"—a group most people are likely to associate themselves with—pay their "fair share" in federal taxes rather than "too much." By contrast, 51% believe lower-income Americans pay too much, while 63% believe upper-income people pay too little.

Interestingly, Americans' tax attitudes are almost entirely unrelated to personal income. Those living in households earning $75,000 or more annually are no more likely to believe they pay too much in taxes than are those earning less than $30,000. Similarly, Gallup finds no difference according to household income in perceptions of whether one's tax bill is fair or not.

Recent Contentment With Taxes

The public's attitudes about taxes have been fairly stable since at least 2003. Prior to that—particularly in the 1990s—Gallup found Americans holding much higher levels of dissatisfaction with federal taxes than are seen today.

Gallup's question on whether Americans feel their taxes are too high or too low originated in 1947. According to the recent trend, Americans are more content today with what they pay than they were from December 1994 through April 2001, when close to two-thirds typically said they paid too much.

Do you consider the amount of federal income tax you have to pay as too high, about right, or too low?

Notably, the 10-point rise in the percentage saying their taxes were too high from April 1994 (56%) to December 1994 (66%) coincided with the 1994 midterm congressional campaign and election, in which the Republican Party championed an anti-tax theme in its successful "Contract With America" strategy. Dissatisfaction with taxes remained high until January 2003—after the 9/11 terrorist attacks and just before the start of the Iraq war—when it dipped to 47%. It has continued to remain relatively low (with no more than 53% saying their taxes are too high) in each subsequent year. However, whether that is because of the impact on public attitudes of 9/11, of the U.S. involvement in Iraq, or of recent tax policies is unclear.

Similarly, the percentage of Americans saying the amount of taxes they will have to pay this year is "fair" has been at or above 60% since April 2003, but ranged from 45% to 58% from the late 1990s through 2002.

Even more dramatic is the shift in the percentage of Americans saying middle-income taxpayers pay their fair share. Since April 2003, no more than 47% of Americans have said that middle-income people pay too much in taxes. By contrast, from 1992 through 1999, a solid majority considered this group overtaxed.

How Much Are Middle-Income People Paying in Taxes?

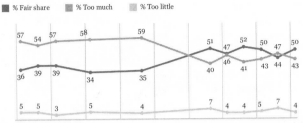

Survey Methods

Results are based on telephone interviews with 1,021 national adults, aged 18 and older, conducted April 6-9, 2008. For results based on the total sample of national adults, one can say with 95% confidence that the maximum margin of sampling error is ±3 percentage points.

Interviews are conducted with respondents on land-line telephones (for respondents with a land-line telephone) and cellular phones (for respondents who are cell-phone only).

In addition to sampling error, question wording and practical difficulties in conducting surveys can introduce error or bias into the findings of public opinion polls.

April 14, 2008
U.S. SATISFACTION AT 15%, LOWEST SINCE 1992
Economy remains most important problem

by Frank Newport, Gallup Poll Editor in Chief

The percentage of Americans who are satisfied with the way things are going in the United States is now at only 15%, according to the latest Gallup Poll update. This marks the lowest reading on this measure since June 1992, and the third lowest Gallup has recorded since 1979.

Satisfaction has been falling each month this year, beginning with an already-low 24% in January, dropping to 20% in February, 19% in March, and now this month's 15%.

Just before George W. Bush took office as president in January 2001, 56% of Americans were satisfied with the way things were going in the United States. That percentage soared to a near-record-high 70% in December 2001, a few months after the Sept. 11 terrorist attacks and the aggressive U.S. response in Afghanistan. (The record-high satisfaction rating across the 29 years in which Gallup

U.S. Satisfaction, Full Trend

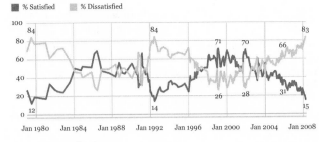

February 1979 to April 2008

has been using this measure is 71%, which came in February 1999 as President Bill Clinton was acquitted by the U.S. Senate on impeachment charges.) The average satisfaction rating for all of 2001 was 55%. Satisfaction for each year since then has declined, culminating in the 28% average for 2007 and the 20% average satisfaction in the first four months of this year.

Yearly Averages: "Satisfied With the Way Things Are Going in the United States"

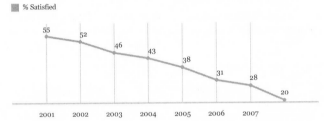

Gallup began asking this satisfaction question in February 1979, and by July of that year recorded what still stands as the all-time low on the measure, 12%, in the midst of worries about the economy and skyrocketing gas prices. The second-lowest measure of 14% came in June 1992, during the final year of the George H. W. Bush administration and another time of perceived economic recession.

What's Behind Low Satisfaction Levels?

One does not have to go much further than the daily newspaper headlines or the lead stories on cable news channels to discern proximate causes for the extraordinarily low levels of satisfaction with the way things are going in the United States today. But Gallup's monthly measure of what Americans themselves perceive to be the most important problem facing the country provides precise figures that help explain why the public is so negative about the current state of affairs in the United States.

There has been a steady rise in the percentage of Americans mentioning some aspect of the economy as the nation's top problem over the past six months, from 22% in October 2007 to 61% in this most recent April 2008 measure. About two-thirds of these are simply "the economy," with an additional 9% naming the price of gas, 6% unemployment, and 4% the high cost of living and inflation.

The second-most-commonly mentioned problem is Iraq, at 23%. The percentage mentioning Iraq as the nation's top problem has held fairly constant since last November, even as the percentage of Americans mentioning the economy has increased on a month-by-month basis.

Other problems mentioned by 5% or more of Americans include healthcare, dissatisfaction with government, and immigration.

"What do you think is the most important problem facing this country today?"

April 6-9, 2008

	%
Economy in general	41
Situation in Iraq/War	23
Fuel/Oil prices	9
Healthcare	8
Unemployment/Jobs	6
Dissatisfaction with government	6
Immigration/Illegal aliens	5
High cost of living/Inflation	4
Lack of money	3
Ethics/Morals/Religious/Family decline	3
Terrorism	3

Discussion

Gallup data—and a review of news headlines—suggest that the most important reason so many Americans are dissatisfied with the way things are going in the United States is the economy. The number of Americans mentioning some aspect of the economy as the nation's top problem has almost tripled in the last six months, and the economy now far eclipses the war in Iraq as the American public's dominant perceived problem. Additionally, Gallup's tracking measures of the economy continue to show consumer confidence at or near all-time lows.

Not surprisingly, the last two times satisfaction levels were lower than the current 15% were also times when the U.S. economy was perceived to be the dominant problem facing the nation—in 1992 and 1979.

The currently low satisfaction level is concurrent with President Bush's lowest job approval rating of his administration. Low satisfaction levels in 1992 and 1979 were major factors in both Jimmy Carter's and George H.W. Bush's failure to be re-elected to second terms as president. The current President Bush cannot run for re-election. It remains to be seen whether voters will take out their frustrations by electing a Democrat to the presidency, but if they are in the mood to punish Bush's party, it could make John McCain's presidential bid an uphill challenge (though he currently is highly competitive with the Democratic candidates in presidential election trial heats). Democrats currently control both houses of Congress, but Gallup's generic ballot tests of congressional election voting preferences suggest that voters still favor Democratic control of Congress and thus may not hold congressional Democrats accountable for the current situation.

Survey Methods

Results are based on telephone interviews with 1,021 national adults, aged 18 and older, conducted April 6-9, 2008. For results based on the total sample of national adults, one can say with 95% confidence that the maximum margin of sampling error is ±3 percentage points.

Interviews are conducted with respondents on land-line telephones (for respondents with a land-line telephone) and cellular phones (for respondents who are cell-phone only).

In addition to sampling error, question wording and practical difficulties in conducting surveys can introduce error or bias into the findings of public opinion polls.

April 15, 2008

AMERICANS HAVE NET-POSITIVE VIEW OF U.S. CATHOLICS

As pope visits, 45% of Americans view Catholics positively, 13% negatively

by Jeffrey M. Jones, Gallup Poll Managing Editor

As Pope Benedict XVI prepares to make his first U.S. visit as pope, a recent Gallup Panel survey finds Americans with a mostly positive view of U.S. Roman Catholics as a group.

Americans' Views of U.S. Catholics

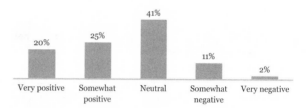

March 24-27, 2008, Gallup Panel survey

With 45% of Americans saying they have a positive view of U.S. Catholics and 13% reporting a negative opinion, the net positive score for Catholics is +32. A substantial proportion of Americans, 41%, say their view of Catholics is neutral.

These results are based on a March 24-27 Gallup Panel survey, which asked a representative sample of Americans whether they have a positive, negative, or neutral view of each of 10 spiritual or religious groups in the United States.

Pope Benedict will meet with President Bush, address the United Nations, meet with U.S. Catholic leaders, and celebrate public masses in New York and Washington, D.C., while in the United States.

Catholics are one of four U.S. religious groups tested in the survey with strongly positive ratings, along with Jews (+42) and two Protestant denominations, Methodists (+45) and Baptists (+35). The broader groups of "evangelical Christians" and "fundamentalist Christians" do not fare quite as well, but are still on balance rated more positively than negatively.

Americans are essentially split in their opinions of Latter-Day Saints or Mormons, with 24% viewing them positively and 26% negatively, for a net score of -2.

Three of the religious groups included in the survey are mostly viewed negatively, including Scientologists, atheists, and Muslims, with Scientologists having the lowest overall rating.

As the table makes clear, there is a considerable degree of ambivalence in ratings of religious groups, with substantial proportions of neutral ratings for each group, ranging from a low of 36% for evangelical and fundamentalist Christians to just under half of all ratings for Jews, Mormons, and Muslims.

Gallup first asked Americans to rate these religious groups in this fashion in an August 2006 panel survey, and since then, there have been declines in positive ratings for many of the more favorably viewed religious groups. For example, the net positive score for Catholics was +44 in the 2006 survey, compared to the current +32. But there were also declines in the net positive scores of Jews (from +54 to +42), Baptists (from +45 to +35), and Methodists (from +50 to +45).

Americans' Views of U.S. Religious and Spiritual Groups

	Total positive	Neutral	Total negative	Net positive
	%	%	%	Pct. pts.
Methodists	49	47	4	45
Jews	46	48	4	42
Baptists	45	44	10	35
Catholics	45	41	13	32
Evangelical Christians ^	39	36	23	16
Fundamentalist Christians ^	35	36	25	10
Latter-Day Saints, or Mormons	24	48	26	-2
Muslims	17	48	34	-17
Atheists	13	41	45	-32
Scientologists	7	37	52	-45

March 24-27, 2008, Gallup Panel survey
^ Asked of a half sample

It is unclear why the net positive ratings for most groups have declined, unless Americans are just less positive about religion overall today than they were two years ago. Groups such as atheists and Scientologists that rated negatively in 2006 are still rated negatively today, with similar scores over time in most cases. One exception concerns Muslims, who saw their net rating tumble from -4 in 2006 to -17 in the current survey.

Notably, the ratings of Mormons did not change since the last measurement, despite the presidential candidacy of Mitt Romney, whose campaign brought public attention to his Mormon faith. In 2006, the net score for Mormons was -1, compared with -2 today.

Implications

Certainly, one of the Pope's goals in visiting the United States will be to raise awareness and positive perceptions of the Catholic Church. Even though the church has been the subject of controversy in recent years—most visibly with revelations of sexual abuse by priests—Americans on balance view the church more positively than negatively.

Survey Methods

Results for this Gallup Panel study are based on telephone interviews with 1,005 national adults, aged 18 and older, conducted March 24-27, 2008. Gallup Panel members are recruited through random selection methods. The panel is weighted so that it is demographically representative of the U.S. adult population. For results based on this sample, one can say with 95% confidence that the maximum margin of sampling error is ±4 percentage points.

In addition to sampling error, question wording and practical difficulties in conducting surveys can introduce error or bias into the findings of public opinion polls.

April 15, 2008
MAJORITY OF AMERICANS STILL SEE BUYER'S MARKET FOR HOMES
Few expect local housing prices to increase over the next year

by Dennis Jacobe, Gallup Chief Economist

The percentage of Americans saying now is a good time for people in general to buy a house fell by only five percentage points over the past year, to 53% in April 2008 from 58% in April 2007, but is down significantly from 81% in 2003 and 71% in 2005.

For people in general, do you think that now is a GOOD time or a BAD time to buy a house?

% Good time

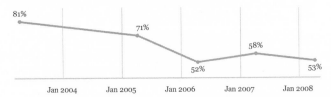

Upper-Income Americans See Good Time to Buy

Given all the doom and gloom in today's housing market, it may seem surprising that 53% of Americans say now is a good time to buy a house. Still, it is hard to argue with the idea that it is now a "buyer's market" in most of the nation's residential real estate markets for consumers who can get the financing they need to close a deal—although this is way down from the housing boom days of 2003 and 2005, when 81% and 71% of Americans, respectively, thought it was a good time to buy. So on an overall basis, most Americans still back a home purchase, but on a relative basis, they do not think it is as good a bet as it was three to five years ago.

While there are essentially no differences in how consumers view the opportunity to buy a house by region, there are differences by income. Only 34% of those making less than $30,000 a year see this as a good time to buy a house, compared with 56% of those making $30,000 but less than $75,000, and 69% of those making $75,000 or more. In part, this may be because lower-income households that once had access to housing financing using subprime loans are finding home loans harder to get.

For people in general, do you think that now is a GOOD time or a BAD time to buy a house?

By region and income

% Good time

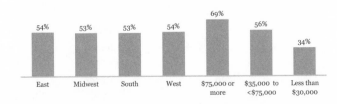

Far Fewer Expect Housing Prices to Increase

Housing price expectations have changed dramatically over the past few years. About three years ago, 7 in 10 Americans expected housing prices in their local areas to increase over the year ahead and only 1 in 20 thought they would decrease. In April 2006, 6 in 10 continued to expect house prices would increase, and, as recently as June 2007, about half felt this way. However, in the most recent poll, conducted April 6-9, only 3 in 10 expect their local housing prices to increase and about 4 in 10 expect prices to fall during the year ahead.

Over the next year, do you think that the average price of houses in your area will increase, stay the same, or decrease?

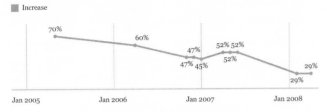

Twice as Many Say House Is Worth Less Than When They Bought It

Even with all the housing turmoil of recent years, around 9 in 10 homeowners maintained in 2006 and 2007 polling that their homes were worth more than when they bought them, and only 6% to 8% said this wasn't the case. This has changed in 2008, with 17% of homeowners—twice as many as in 2007—saying their homes are not worth more now than when they bought them. Still, the vast majority of homeowners believe their houses have gained value since they purchased them.

Is your home worth more than when you bought it, or not?

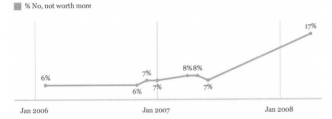

Housing as an Election-Year Issue

The Senate has passed housing legislation providing $24 billion focused largely on tax breaks for home builders. In sharp contrast, the House Ways and Means Committee approved temporary $7,500 tax credits to first-time home buyers that they would have to repay over a period of time. At the same time, all of the presidential candidates have proposed new efforts to help the housing market, although the program suggested by Republican John McCain is much more limited in scope than those proposed by his Democratic rivals Barack Obama and Hillary Clinton.

Of course, conditions in the housing market during the months ahead are important not only to buyers, sellers, lenders, and investors, but also to every homeowner. As a result, how the housing market reaches bottom, how the gains and losses are distributed, and how the recovery begins are likely to be major election-year issues.

Gallup's data suggest that many Americans recognize it is a good time to buy a house when there are relatively few buyers and lots of sellers. Although it sometimes seems heartless, free markets do provide opportunities for some, even as others experience the pain of financial loss. Most consumers also recognize that the home is the average American's basic source of wealth and will continue to be so once the current residential real estate debacle runs its course. Pol-

icymakers should keep in mind this essential willingness of Americans to continue investing in housing. It suggests that the solution to the current situation lies more in rebuilding the housing finance system than in propping up housing prices.

Survey Methods

Results are based on telephone interviews with 1,021 national adults, aged 18 and older, conducted April 6-9, 2008. For results based on the total sample of national adults, one can say with 95% confidence that the maximum margin of sampling error is ±3 percentage points.

For results based on the sample of 783 homeowners, the maximum margin of sampling error is ±4 percentage points.

Interviews are conducted with respondents on land-line telephones (for respondents with a land-line telephone) and cellular phones (for respondents who are cell-phone only).

In addition to sampling error, question wording and practical difficulties in conducting surveys can introduce error or bias into the findings of public opinion polls.

April 17, 2008
DEMOCRATS LEADING MCCAIN IN "PURPLE" STATES
Hold 47% to 43% leads in states decided by five points or less in 2004

by Jeffrey M. Jones, Gallup Poll Senior Editor

Democratic front-runner Barack Obama has a four-point advantage over presumptive Republican nominee John McCain among registered voters residing in states that were competitive in the 2004 election. Obama has a comfortable lead in states John Kerry won comfortably in 2004, as does McCain in states George W. Bush won easily.

2008 Presidential Election Preferences (Obama vs. McCain) Among Voters in Red, Blue, and "Purple" States

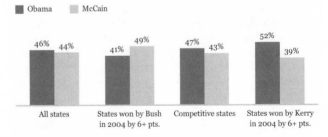

April 1-15 Gallup Poll Daily tracking

The analysis is based on aggregated data from Gallup Poll Daily tracking in April, consisting of interviews with more than 13,000 registered voters. Gallup considers states where Kerry won the 2004 presidential vote by six percentage points or more to be safe Democratic or "blue" states, and states where Bush won by six percentage points or more to be safe Republican or "red" states. The remaining states—in which the winning candidate prevailed by five percentage points or less—are considered competitive or "purple" states.

Based on this definition, the purple states include New Hampshire, Pennsylvania, Ohio, Michigan, Wisconsin, Minnesota, Iowa, Florida, Colorado, Nevada, New Mexico, and Oregon.

Hillary Clinton also leads McCain by the same 47% to 43% margin among purple-state voters. But she does not fare quite as well as Obama does in blue states, and she trails McCain by a slightly larger margin than Obama does in red states.

2008 Presidential Election Preferences (Clinton vs. McCain) Among Voters in Red, Blue, and "Purple" States

Based on registered voters

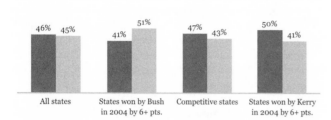

April 1-15 Gallup Poll Daily tracking

McCain and his supporters can take solace in that there are more red states, more voters, and thus, more electoral votes in those states. So even though he trails by four points in the most competitive states, he is down by only two points to Obama (46% to 44%), and is down by just one point to Clinton (46% to 45%), among registered voters when all states are combined.

According to 2004 election statistics, 36% of all voters in that election resided in red states, 33% lived in blue states, and 31% in purple states. So the Democratic candidate is starting out at a disadvantage, everything else being equal. Thus, in order to win the election, the Democratic candidate probably has to defeat the Republican by at least a couple of percentage points in the competitive states, assuming the vote distributions in the red and blue states stay relatively constant. The Republican can probably win by essentially breaking even in the competitive states, as Bush did in 2004. (While this analysis focuses on the popular vote, the electoral vote results should generally follow a similar pattern, in which the candidate who wins a greater share of the popular vote in the competitive states will probably also win a greater share of the electoral votes in those states.)

The final 2004 popular vote results were more polarized than the current poll data suggest is the case now. McCain is not faring as well as Bush did in 2004 in red states, where Bush defeated Kerry 59% to 40%. And Obama only matches the 13-point advantage Kerry had in blue states (56% to 43%). The two candidates essentially split the vote in the most competitive states in 2004, with Bush winning 50% and Kerry 49%.

One reason for the difference is that the 2004 data are based on actual voters, while the current data are based on registered voters. Registered voters may not be as firmly attached to their party affiliations as are actual voters. It's also possible that the vote will correlate more highly with party support once the general-election phase of the presidential campaign gets fully under way.

Implications

It's likely that the 2008 election will be fought in the battleground states, just as in prior elections. Gallup's election polling to date suggests that the presidential election could be very close, because nei-

2004 Presidential Election Vote (Kerry vs. Bush) Among Voters in Red, Blue, and "Purple" States

Based on final 2004 election statistics

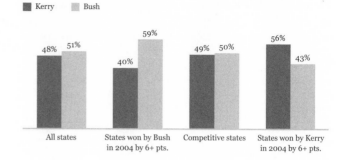

ther McCain nor his Democratic rivals have maintained much of a lead in recent weeks.

The analysis of competitive states adds insight into how the candidates are doing beyond the overall vote figures. A candidate must do reasonably well in those states to have a chance at winning. For example, McCain could open up a significant lead in the national vote based on a very strong performance in the red states, but that would not mean he was better positioned to win than if he were not doing as well in the red states but doing better in the more competitive states.

As of now, Obama and Clinton have an advantage over McCain among voters in the competitive states. Given that more states fall into the Republican column than into the Democratic column, the Democratic nominee probably needs to maintain that advantage in order to prevail in enough purple states to gain the electoral vote advantage in November.

Survey Methods

Results are based on aggregated telephone interviews with 13,217 registered voters, aged 18 and older, conducted April 1-15, 2008, as part of Gallup Poll Daily tracking. For results based on the total sample of registered voters, one can say with 95% confidence that the maximum margin of sampling error is ±1 percentage point.

For results based on the sample of 4,894 registered voters residing in states that George W. Bush won the 2004 presidential voting by 6 or more percentage points, the maximum margin of sampling error is ±2 percentage points.

For results based on the sample of 4,375 registered voters residing in states that John Kerry won the 2004 presidential voting by 6 or more percentage points, the maximum margin of sampling error is ±2 percentage points.

For results based on the sample of 3,948 registered voters residing in states where the margin of victory for the winning candidate in the 2004 presidential voting was 5 percentage points or less, the maximum margin of sampling error is ±2 percentage points.

Interviews are conducted with respondents on land-line telephones (for respondents with a land-line telephone) and cellular phones (for respondents who are cell-phone only).

In addition to sampling error, question wording and practical difficulties in conducting surveys can introduce error or bias into the findings of public opinion polls.

April 17, 2008

MOST AMERICANS SAY NOW IS BAD
TIME TO SPEND

Almost half say their finances are "getting worse"—the most this decade

by Dennis Jacobe, Gallup Chief Economist

Forty-nine percent of consumers say their financial situations are "getting worse" and only 32% say they are "getting better"—the worst consumer assessment of personal financial trends this decade.

Right now, do you think that your financial situation as a whole is getting better or getting worse?
Selected trend

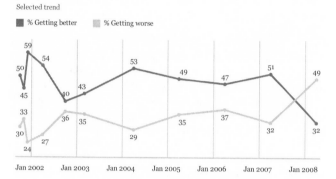

Consumers' Expectations for Their Finances Are Worst of Decade

American consumers tend to be optimistic about their own financial future, particularly in comparison to their attitudes about the national economy. For example, immediately after the 9/11 terrorist attacks, in October and November 2001, the percentage of consumers saying their financial situations were getting better ranged between 45% and 50%. The previous low this decade for such an optimistic view was 40% in October 2002, and 43% held this view in March 2003—just as the Iraq war was beginning. Given this context, the current percentage of consumers who say their finances are getting better (32%) and the percentage who say they are getting worse (49%) are not only a complete reversal of consumer perceptions from a year ago, but, more importantly, are the worst reading on the measure this decade. (Gallup first asked about personal finances using this question in 2001.)

Additionally, consumers' self-assessments of their current finances are more negative than at any time this decade. In the April poll, the percentage of consumers rating their financial situations as "poor" is 17%, while the percentage rating their situations as "excellent" or "good" is 45%.

Significantly, these are consumers' ratings of their own finances—something they know much more about and tend to relate more accurately than when they are asked to rate the national economy. As has generally been the case, consumers' perceptions of their own financial situations are considerably more positive than their ratings of the national economy (83% of Americans now say the U.S. economy is getting worse, and 46% rate the national economy as "poor").

Negative Implications for Consumer Spending

Consumers' perceptions of their current financial situations and their expectations for future improvement can have a major impact on

How would you rate your financial situation today -- as excellent, good, only fair, or poor?
Selected trend

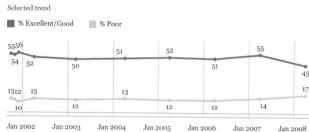

their spending intentions. When asked to consider their finances and assess their future spending, only 22% said they feel they are in a "good" position to buy some of the things they would like to have, while 74% said they feel it is a "bad" time to spend money. Gallup has asked this spending question only occasionally over the last 30 years, but the current readings are the worst of the six times it has been measured. More consumers feel now is a bad time to spend than the 53% who felt that way in September 2001 (just after 9/11) and the 67% holding that view during October 1991, just after the 1990-91 recession.

From another perspective, only 29% of consumers say they would feel comfortable making a major purchase such as a home, a car, major appliances, or other significant purchase in the next three months—down from 47% a year ago. Similarly, 37% of consumers say they are less comfortable making such purchases now than they were just three months ago.

Thinking of your own financial situation just now, do you feel you are in a GOOD position to buy some of the things you would like to have, or is now a rather BAD time for you to spend money?
Selected trend

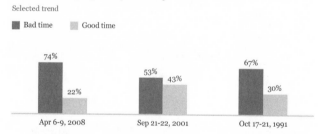

Could the Recession Be Worse Than Expected?

During recent months, fears of a financial crisis have dominated the business news, and the relief experienced as a result of the Federal Reserve's and the Treasury's aggressive response to assist the financial markets has been palpable. However, this improved perspective on the part of the credit markets may be hiding a rapidly deteriorating situation on Main Street.

Consumers are being squeezed not only in the credit markets, but also by record food and energy prices—not to mention a worsening jobs market. Gallup's new polling suggests that the current consumer squeeze is more intense than the situations consumers experienced following 9/11, the beginning of the Iraq war, and the aftermath of the 1990-91 recession. In turn, this implies that the weakened consumer spending levels that many retailers are already anticipating may turn out to be too optimistic. Consumers' perceptions and their spending intentions suggest this recession could be somewhat worse than the "mild" downturn of the consensus forecast, and that retailers may be wise to plan accordingly.

Results are based on telephone interviews with 1,021 national adults, aged 18 and older, conducted April 6-9, 2008. For results based on the total sample of national adults, one can say with 95% confidence that the maximum margin of sampling error is ±3 percentage points.

Interviews are conducted with respondents on land-line telephones (for respondents with a land-line telephone) and cellular phones (for respondents who are cell-phone only).

In addition to sampling error, question wording and practical difficulties in conducting surveys can introduce error or bias into the findings of public opinion polls.

April 18, 2008

IN THE U.S., 28% REPORT MAJOR CHANGES TO LIVE "GREEN"

Majority say they have made "minor changes"

by Jeffrey M. Jones, Gallup Poll Managing Editor

Even though there has been an increased focus on global warming and a growing market of environmentally friendly products, Gallup's annual Environment poll finds just 28% of Americans reporting they have made "major changes" in their lifestyles to protect the environment. Fifty-five percent have made "minor changes."

Thinking about your own shopping and living habits over the last five years, would you say you have made major changes, minor changes, or no changes to help protect the environment?

March 6-9, 2008

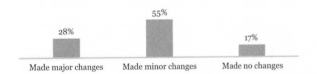

That is in keeping with the public's view about government's role in protecting the planet, with most believing that some additional actions need to be taken, but with Americans stopping short of calling for "immediate and drastic" action.

Furthermore, the environment ranks only in the middle of a list of "problems facing the country" that Americans worry about. Forty percent say they worry "a great deal" about "the quality of the environment," ranking far below the 60% who worry about the economy and the 58% who worry about the availability and affordability of healthcare.

Thus, Americans seem willing to play a small part in helping to protect the environment, but so far, most have not made substantial changes to their shopping and living habits.

Gallup has asked Americans about lifestyle changes to protect the environment twice before (in 2000 and 2003), and, contrary to what one might expect, there has not been a significant increase in the proportion who report making environmentally friendly lifestyle changes over time.

Among most major demographic subgroups, roughly 8 in 10 say they have made at least minor changes in their way of living to help

Thinking about your own shopping and living habits over the last five years, would you say you have made major changes, minor changes, or no changes to help protect the environment?

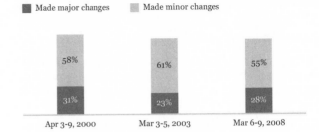

the environment. There are some variations in the percentages of different subgroups who report making "major changes," however.

For example, 34% of women but only 21% of men say they have made major changes in their lifestyles. Also, 32% of Democrats and 31% of independents have altered their habits in an environmentally friendly manner, but only 20% of Republicans have.

It stands to reason that those who express concern about the quality of the environment, about global warming, or the energy situation are more likely to say they have made major changes in their lifestyles than those who are not concerned about these issues.

A majority, 54%, of those who consider themselves "active participants in the environmental movement" have significantly adjusted their lifestyle habits to aid the environment, more than double the percentage of those who do not consider themselves active environmentalists.

This year's poll probed respondents who indicated they have made changes in their lifestyles about the specific changes they have made.

- The most common response is recycling—or recycling more than in the past—mentioned by 39%.
- Roughly one in four have taken steps to conserve fuel, including 17% who say they have cut back on driving, and 9% who report driving a more fuel-efficient car.
- About the same proportion have taken steps to conserve energy in the home, including using less electricity (10%), buying energy-saving light bulbs (7%), upgrading to energy-saving appliances (4%), and making their homes more energy efficient overall (2%)—such as by installing new windows or adding insulation.

Those who say they have made major changes in their habits do not differ much from those who have made minor changes in the types of activities they report doing on behalf of the environment.

Implications

Because those who are more concerned about the environment are more likely to live a "green" lifestyle, there may not be a notable increase in "green living" in the United States until there is a growth in concern about the environment. Environmental concern has been relatively flat in recent years, and since environmental concern often declines when the economy is struggling, a near-term increase in environmentally friendly living does not seem very likely.

Survey Methods

Results are based on telephone interviews with 1,012 national adults, aged 18 and older, conducted March 6-9, 2008. For results based on the total sample of national adults, one can say with 95% confidence that the maximum margin of sampling error is ±3 percentage points.

Asked of those who report making major or minor changes in their shopping and living habits to help protect the environment

	% Mentioning
Recycle/Recycle more	39
Drive less/Consolidate trips/Carpool	17
Buy biodegradable products	14
Use less electricity/Conserve energy	10
Drive more fuel-efficient car/Maintain car	9
Buy/Use more "green" products	7
Use energy-saving light bulbs	7
Eat more organic/home-grown foods	5
Conserve water	5
Upgrade to energy-saving appliances in home	4
Don't litter	3
Make home more energy efficient -- install new windows, insulation, solar panels, etc.	2
Other	7
None/Nothing	2
No opinion	12

Note: Responses total more than 100% due to multiple responses.

Interviews are conducted with respondents on land-line telephones (for respondents with a land-line telephone) and cellular phones (for respondents who are cell-phone only).

In addition to sampling error, question wording and practical difficulties in conducting surveys can introduce error or bias into the findings of public opinion polls.

April 21, 2008

LITTLE INCREASE IN AMERICANS' GLOBAL WARMING WORRIES

Public just can't seem to get worked up about it

by Frank Newport, Gallup Poll Editor in Chief

While 61% of Americans say the effects of global warming have already begun, just a little more than a third say they worry about it a great deal, a percentage that is roughly the same as the one Gallup measured 19 years ago.

I'm going to read you a list of environmental problems. As I read each one, please tell me if you personally worry about this problem a great deal, a fair amount, only a little, or not at all. First, how much do you personally worry about the "greenhouse effect?"

■ % Great deal

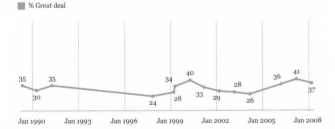

Despite the enormous attention paid to global warming over the past several years, the average American is in some ways no more worried about it than in years past. Americans do appear to have become more likely to believe global warming's effects are already taking place and that it could represent a threat to their way of life during their lifetimes. But the American public is more worried about a series of other environmental concerns than about global warming, and there has been no consistent upward trend on worry about global warming going back for two decades. Additionally, only a little more than a third of Americans say that immediate, drastic action is needed in order to maintain life as we know it on the planet.

These results are from Gallup's annual Environment poll, conducted March 6-9, 2008.

Understanding Global Warming

Eighty percent of Americans say they understand the issue of global warming, a percentage that is up significantly from 16 years ago, when only 53% said they understood the issue.

Next, thinking about the issue of global warming, sometimes called the "greenhouse effect," how well do you feel you understand this issue -- would you say very well, fairly well, not very well, or not at all?

	% Very well	% Fairly well	% Not very/not at all well
2008 Mar 6-9	21	59	20
2007 Mar 11-14	22	54	23
2006 Mar 13-16	21	53	26
2005 Mar 7-10	16	54	30
2004 Mar 8-11	18	50	32
2003 Mar 3-5	15	53	32
2002 Mar 4-7	17	52	31
2001 Mar 5-7	15	54	30
1997 Nov 6-9	16	45	38
1992 Jan	11	42	44

Self-reported understanding of global warming has increased slightly throughout this decade, as measured in Gallup's annual Environment study, from 69% who said they understood global warming very or fairly well in March 2001 to today's 80%. The percentage of Americans who understand global warming "very well" has been steady at a relatively low 21% to 22% for the last three years.

Effects of Global Warming Already Beginning?

Slightly less than half of Americans in 1997 said the effects of global warming had already begun to happen. That number has risen, particularly in the past two years, to the point where today 61% say the effects have already begun to happen at this point in time. About one out of four Americans, however, continue to say the effects of global warming will not happen in their lifetimes, if ever.

Threat?

There has also been an uptick in the percentage of Americans who say global warming will pose a serious threat to them in their lifetimes, from 25% in 1997 to 40% today.

Even with this increase over the last 11 years, the fact remains that still less than a majority of Americans, at this point, believe global warming will pose a serious threat to them in their lifetimes.

Worry?

The fact that a majority of Americans don't believe global warming will pose a threat to them in their lifetimes makes it perhaps less surprising to find that significantly less than a majority of Americans say they worry a great deal about it. In fact, worry about global

Which of the following statements reflects your view of when the effects of global warming will begin to happen: they have already begun to happen, they will start happening within a few years, they will start happening within your lifetime, they will not happen within your lifetime, but they will affect future generations, or they will never happen?

	% Already begun	% Within a few years/within your lifetime	% Not within lifetime, but affect future	% Will never happen
2008 Mar 6-9	61	14	13	11
2007 Mar 23-25	60	11	15	11
2007 Mar 11-14	59	11	19	8
2006 Mar 13-16	58	15	15	8
2005 Mar 7-10	54	15	19	9
2004 Mar 8-11	51	17	18	11
2003 Mar 3-5	51	18	17	10
2002 Mar 4-7	53	18	17	9
2001 Mar 5-7	54	17	18	7
1997 Nov 6-9	48	17	19	9

Do you think that global warming will pose a serious threat to you or your way of life in your lifetime?

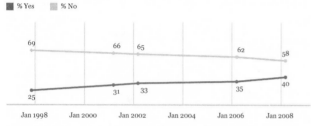

"No opinion" not shown

warming is low on a list of 12 environmental problems that Gallup asks about in the Environment surveys.

I'm going to read you a list of environmental problems. As I read each one, please tell me if you personally worry about this problem a great deal, a fair amount, only a little, or not at all.

March 6-9, 2008 (sorted by "great deal")

	% Worry a great deal	% Worry a fair amount	% Worry only a little/not at all
Pollution of drinking water	53	28	19
Pollution of rivers, lakes, and reservoirs	50	34	16
Contamination of soil and water by toxic waste	50	30	20
Maintenance of the nation's supply of fresh water for household needs	48	31	20
The loss of natural habitat for wildlife	44	33	23
Air pollution	43	35	23
The loss of tropical rain forests	40	29	31
Damage to the earth's ozone layer	39	29	31
Extinction of plant and animal species	37	31	31
The "greenhouse effect" or global warming	37	29	33

There is, in fact, little more evidence of worry about global warming now than there was when this question was first asked in 1989.

Since that time, there has been change, with the worry a "great deal" percentage rising to 40% in 2000, before dropping back from

2002 to 2004, and now increasing some over the last three years. This year's "great deal" worry number is slightly lower than last year's high to date of 41%.

This is not to say that Americans totally dismiss global warming. About two-thirds say they worry a great deal or a fair amount about it, and only 17% say they don't worry at all about it.

Still, the trend data suggest that despite the growing attention to and emphasis on global warming in recent years, there has been no consistent increase in worry about it since Gallup began asking the question way back in 1989.

Drastic Action Needed for Environment?

A Gallup Poll question asks Americans whether "additional, immediate, and drastic action" is necessary concerning the environment, and in this year's update, about a third answer "yes."

That number is down slightly from last year and, stretching back in time, is roughly the same as was measured in a 1995 poll. The only other three years in which Gallup has measured this variable were from 2001 to 2003, when a slightly lower percentage of Americans advocated drastic action.

All in all, which of the following best describes how you feel about the environmental problems facing the earth -- life on earth will continue without major environmental disruptions only if we take additional, immediate, and drastic action concerning the environment, we should take some additional actions concerning the environment, or, we should take just the same actions we have been taking on the environment?

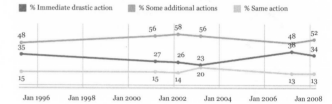

Implications

From a broad perspective, Gallup's data tracking Americans' perceptions of the environment are somewhat mixed. On some dimensions, Americans clearly demonstrate a reaction to the growing discussion and emphasis on global warming in the media and indeed as part of the popular culture. Americans now are more likely than they have been in the past to claim understanding of global warming, to recognize that global warming could be a threat in their lifetimes, and to say the effects of global warming have already begun.

At the same time, however, Gallup's broad measure of worry about environmental issues does not show a concomitant increase in concern. Although there have been fluctuations on this measure of worry over the years, the percentage of Americans who worry a great deal about global warming is no higher now than it was 19 years ago. And the percentage who do worry a great deal—37%—is still well less than a majority, and in fact lower than the percentage who worry a great deal about such environmental issues as pollution of drinking water, pollution of lakes and reservoirs, and toxic waste in the soil.

Survey Methods

Results are based on telephone interviews with 1,012 national adults, aged 18 and older, conducted March 6-9, 2008. For results based on the total sample of national adults, one can say with 95% confidence that the maximum margin of sampling error is ±3 percentage points.

Interviews are conducted with respondents on land-line telephones (for respondents with a land-line telephone) and cellular phones (for respondents who are cell-phone only).

In addition to sampling error, question wording and practical difficulties in conducting surveys can introduce error or bias into the findings of public opinion polls.

April 22, 2008

BUSH'S 69% JOB DISAPPROVAL RATING HIGHEST IN GALLUP HISTORY
Truman had 67% in 1952

by Frank Newport, Gallup Poll Editor in Chief

President George W. Bush's disapproval rating is at 69%—which is not only the highest of the Bush administration, but the highest disapproval rating in Gallup Poll history.

Lowest Five Disapproval Ratings in Gallup History

President	Date of Poll	% Disapproval Rating
George W. Bush	Apr 18-20, 2008	69
Harry Truman	Jan 6-11, 1952	67
George W. Bush	Apr 6-9, 2008	67
Richard Nixon	August 2-5, 1974	66
George W. Bush	July 6-8, 2007	66

President Bush's approval rating now is at 28%, which ties for the lowest of his administration, but is not the lowest in Gallup Poll history. Harry Truman reached a 22% approval rating in 1952, and Richard Nixon had two 24% job approval scores in 1974.

In other words, although Bush's disapproval rating is the highest in Gallup history, his approval rating is not the lowest. This seeming anomaly is mostly because of differences over the years in the percentage of respondents who say "don't know/no opinion" when asked to rate a president.

Harry Truman's 22% approval rating was accompanied by a 64% disapproval rating, leaving 14% of those interviewed who did not offer an opinion about his job performance. Richard Nixon's two 24% job approval ratings in 1974 were paired with 63% and 66% disapproval ratings, leaving 13% and 10% with no opinion.

In the most recent poll for Bush, his approval rating is 28% while his disapproval rating is 69%, leaving only 3.5% (rounded to 4%) who don't have an opinion.

Truman, Nixon, and Bush Job Performance Ratings

President	Dates of Gallup Poll	% Approve	% Disapprove	% No opinion
George W. Bush	Apr 18-20, 2008	28	69	4
Richard Nixon	Jul 12-15, 1974	24	63	13
Richard Nixon	Aug 2-5, 1974	24	66	10
Harry Truman	Feb 9-14, 1952	22	64	14

There is no single explanation for why the percentage who decline to give an opinion of the president's job performance is lower now than in the past. However, one hypothesis is as follows. When Gallup polled in the Truman and Nixon years, respondents may have been more likely to say they didn't have an opinion in lieu of saying they disapproved of the president. In other words, respondents who did not approve of the president's performance—rather than flat-out saying they disapproved—may have simply told interviewers they didn't have an opinion.

Today, as the percentage of "no opinion" responses to the presidential job approval question has declined, Americans appear to be more willing to give a negative response, resulting in the situation in which Bush's disapproval rating is at a record high while his approval rating is not at a record low.

Interviewing in the Truman and Nixon years was conducted in respondents' homes rather than by telephone, which may be related to some differences in the percentages of respondents who gave "no opinion" answers to the job approval question. But an interesting contrast is provided by polling conducted in the administration of the current president's father, George H.W. Bush, who in one poll in 1992 had a 29% approval rating—only one point higher than his son's current approval rating. In that 1992 poll, the senior Bush had only a 60% disapproval rating, leaving 11% with no opinion, similar to the "no opinion" percentages in the Truman and Nixon polls. Yet the 1992 poll was conducted by telephone in similar fashion to polling today, suggesting that the mode of interviewing per se is perhaps not the sole explanation for the differences over the years.

It may well be that the current president Bush is simply a more polarizing figure, one who generates strong opinions in the negative direction and therefore fewer ambivalent, no-opinion responses than was the case for George H.W. Bush, Truman, or Nixon at the nadirs of their administrations.

The bottom line remains that—perhaps for several reasons—the 69% disapproval rating generated by the current president is the highest such rating recorded over the years in which Gallup has been measuring the public's approval and disapproval of each president's job performance.

Survey Methods

Results for the current poll, including the latest George W. Bush approval ratings, are based on telephone interviews with 1,016 national adults, aged 18 and older, conducted April 18-20, 2008. For results based on the total sample of national adults, one can say with 95% confidence that the maximum margin of sampling error is ±3 percentage points.

Interviews are conducted with respondents on land-line telephones (for respondents with a land-line telephone) and cellular phones (for respondents who are cell-phone only).

In addition to sampling error, question wording and practical difficulties in conducting surveys can introduce error or bias into the findings of public opinion polls.

DEMOCRATS SPLIT ON WHETHER CAMPAIGN IS HURTING THE PARTY

Obama and Clinton supporters diverge

by Frank Newport , Gallup Poll Editor in Chief

Democrats are split right down the middle on whether the protracted campaign for the Democratic nomination is hurting the Democratic Party. Forty-eight percent say it's hurting the party, and 48% say it is not.

Is the Democratic Campaign Hurting the Party or Not?

Based on Democratic and Democratic-leaning voters
April 18-20, 2008

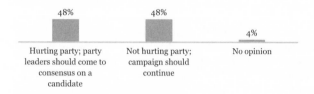

48%	48%	4%
Hurting party; party leaders should come to consensus on a candidate	Not hurting party; campaign should continue	No opinion

The reason for these split sentiments on the impact of the campaign is clear when the views of Obama supporters and Clinton supporters are separated from one another.

Is the Democratic Campaign Hurting the Party or Not?

Based on Democratic and Democratic-leaning voters
April 18-20, 2008

■ Hurting party   ▢ Not hurting party

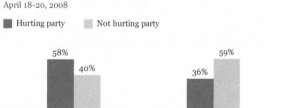

Obama supporters	Clinton supporters
58% / 40%	36% / 59%

A majority of Obama supporters say the campaign is hurting the party and that party leaders should get together to back one of the candidates. A majority of Clinton supporters, on the other hand, say the continuing campaign is not hurting the party and should continue. Since Obama leads in terms of earned delegates, popular vote, and national polling at the moment, it is perhaps not surprising that his supporters would be happy to see the race come to a close, presumably under the assumption that he would be declared the winner. Clinton supporters, it can be assumed, like the idea of continuing the campaign in the hope that Obama will stumble, leaving an opening or a rationale for super-delegates to support Clinton.

Democrats were also asked if the campaign for their party's nomination is too negative, with evenly divided results. Forty-seven percent of Democrats say it is, while 49% say it is not.

But there are again big differences within Democrats based on candidate support. Obama supporters by a 3-to-2 margin agree that the campaign is too negative, while Clinton supporters just as strongly believe the campaign has not become too negative.

Many observers have commented that *both* campaigns have been negative in the days leading into Tuesday's Pennsylvania primary. But Obama supporters who say things are too negative widely

Is the Democratic Campaign for President Too Negative or Not Too Negative?

Based on Democratic and Democratic-leaning voters
April 18-20, 2008

■ Too negative   ▢ Not too negative

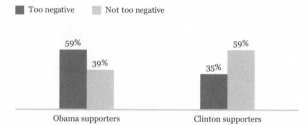

Obama supporters	Clinton supporters
59% / 39%	35% / 59%

say Clinton is mostly to blame. Clinton supporters who say things are too negative, on the other hand, blame both campaigns.

Implications

All in all, Democrats are divided on the impact of the continuing and protracted campaign for the Democratic nomination. The reasons for this division are clear. Clinton supporters, apparently realizing that their candidate's best hope of winning is to continue to campaign and hope something happens to give her a break, are fine with a continuing campaign, are not worried about its negativity, and do not think it is bad for their party. Given the fact that Obama is ahead in the race for the nomination at the moment, it is not surprising that his supporters would like to have the race wrapped up and believe that its protracted length is hurting the party overall.

Thus, it would appear difficult at this time for Democrats nationally to come to a consensus on ending the Democratic race. As long as Clinton can maintain a substantial base of support, her supporters will likely advocate continuing the race, to keep open the possibility that she can win the nomination.

Survey Methods

Results are based on telephone interviews with 1,016 national adults, aged 18 and older, conducted April 18-20, 2008. For results based on the total sample of national adults, one can say with 95% confidence that the maximum margin of sampling error is ±3 percentage points.

NEW LOW IN BUSH QUARTERLY AVERAGE APPROVAL RATING

Averaged 31% in most recent quarter in office

by Jeffrey M. Jones, Gallup Poll Managing Editor

George W. Bush averaged a 31.3% approval rating in his most recent quarter in office (spanning Jan. 20-April 19), a new low for his presidency.

The quarter included the new-low individual Bush approval ratings, 28% in the April 6-9 and April 18-20 polls, the latter of which was accompanied by a Gallup Poll-high 69% disapproval rating.

Although this is the worst quarterly average so far in Bush's presidency, it is not the worst in Gallup's history. Gallup has com-

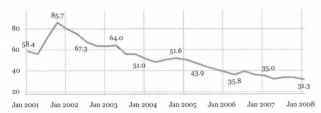

George W. Bush Quarterly Job Approval Averages

puted quarterly averages for all presidents since the Harry Truman administration, a total of 250 quarters. Bush's current average ranks No. 239, with Truman and Richard Nixon receiving most of the worst averages in the latter parts of their presidencies, and the remaining one belonging to Jimmy Carter during the gas crisis in 1979.

Fifteen Lowest Quarterly Approval Averages, Gallup Polls, 1945-2008

Rank	President	Dates	Quarter in office	Average rating	# of polls
250	Truman	Oct 20, 1951-Jan 19, 1952	27	23.0	2
249	Nixon	Jul 20-Aug 9, 1974	23	24.0	1
248	Truman	Jan 20-Apr 19, 1952	28	25.0	3
247	Nixon	Apr 20-Jul 19, 1974	22	26.0	7
246	Truman	Apr 20-Jul 19, 1951	25	26.0	3
245	Nixon	Jan 20-Apr 19, 1974	21	26.1	7
244	Truman	Jan 20-Apr 19, 1951	24	26.3	4
243	Nixon	Oct 20, 1973-Jan 19, 1974	20	28.0	5
242	Truman	Apr 20-Jul 19, 1952	29	29.8	4
241	Carter	Apr 20-Jul 19, 1979	10	30.7	6
240	Truman	Jul 20-Oct 19, 1951	26	30.7	3
239	G.W. Bush	Jan 20-Apr 19, 2008	29	31.3	8
238	Carter	Jul 20-Oct 19, 1979	11	31.4	7
237	G.W. Bush	Apr 20-Jul 19, 2007	26	31.8	6
236	Nixon	Jul 20-Oct 19, 1973	19	31.8	6

Bush is now dealing with record-high gas prices—one possible reason his already-low approval ratings have shown further decline in recent weeks. He has not had an approval rating at or above 40% since September 2006, and has not been at or above 50% since very early in his second term (May 2005).

The trend in Bush's approval ratings shares similarities with that of Truman's ratings. Both had record-high approval ratings early in their first terms following major rally events—with Truman receiving an 87% rating after the U.S. victory in Europe in World War II (shortly after Truman took office upon Franklin Roosevelt's death) and Bush earning an all-time high 90% approval rating following the Sept. 11 terrorist attacks. After winning hard-fought re-election battles, both presidents had low approval ratings throughout most of their second terms, with Truman averaging below 40% approval during the final three years of his presidency and Bush on his way to matching that.

The most recent quarter was Bush's 29th in office, a tenure achieved by only five post-World War II presidents. Dwight Eisenhower and Bill Clinton were relatively popular in that late stage of their presidencies, with average approval ratings above 60%. Bush and Truman were highly unpopular, with approval ratings around 30%. Ronald Reagan ranked in the middle, with an average 50% approval rating.

Presidents' 29th Quarter Approval Averages, Gallup Polls, 1945-2008

President	Dates of 29th quarter	Average approval rating	# of polls
Truman	Apr 20-Jul 19, 1952	29.8%	4
Eisenhower	Jan 20-Apr 19, 1960	64.3%	3
Reagan	Jan 20-Apr 19, 1988	50.0%	4
Clinton	Jan 20-Apr 19, 2000	61.0%	7
G.W. Bush	Jan 20-Apr 19, 2008	31.3%	8

Bush's current 28% approval rating ranks among the lowest in Gallup's polling history. The worst from an individual poll was Truman's 22% in February 1952, and Gallup recorded several measurements between 23% and 27% for Nixon and Truman. The looming threat of even higher gas prices in an already-struggling economy—in an environment where highly visible Democratic presidential candidates attempt to remind voters of the nation's struggles—suggests the potential for further decline in Bush's approval rating in the coming months.

Survey Methods

Results are based on averages of eight Gallup Polls, each consisting of telephone interviews with approximately 1,000 national adults, aged 18 and older, conducted between Jan. 20 and April 19, 2008. For each poll, one can say with 95% confidence that the maximum margin of sampling error is ±3 percentage points.

Interviews are conducted with respondents on land-line telephones (for respondents with a land-line telephone) and cellular phones (for respondents who are cell-phone only).

In addition to sampling error, question wording and practical difficulties in conducting surveys can introduce error or bias into the findings of public opinion polls.

April 24, 2008
OPPOSITION TO IRAQ WAR REACHES NEW HIGH
Sixty-three percent say U.S. made mistake in sending troops

by Jeffrey M. Jones, Gallup Poll Managing Editor

The most recent *USA Today/*Gallup poll finds 63% of Americans saying the United States made a mistake in sending troops to Iraq, a new high mark by one percentage point.

The new high in Iraq war opposition is also notable because it is the highest "mistake" percentage Gallup has ever measured for an active war involving the United States—surpassing by two points the 61% who said the Vietnam War was a mistake in May 1971. At that time, however, Gallup found greater uncertainty (11% no opinion) and lower outright support for the Vietnam War (28% said it was *not* a mistake) than it does for the Iraq war today (36%), so it is not clear-cut as to which war was less popular with the American public.

When Gallup has asked about Vietnam retrospectively over the years since the war ended, as many as 74% of Americans (in 1990) said it was a mistake.

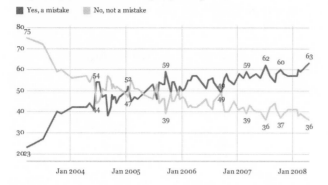

In February and March 1952, a majority of Americans also said the United States made a mistake in sending troops to Korea, the only other U.S. intervention since 1950 that has registered majority opposition.

Last summer, just 25% said the United States made a mistake in sending troops to Afghanistan. Opposition to the first Persian Gulf War reached only as high as 30%, in January 1991 (before actual fighting began; after fighting commenced, the high was just 21%).

By now, public opposition to the war is pretty well-established. Gallup has found at least half of Americans calling the war a mistake in all but one survey since December 2005. The average percentage saying the war is a mistake has increased every year of the conflict, and is nearly twice as high thus far in 2008 (the sixth year of the conflict) as it was in the initial year.

Mistake for U.S. to Send Troops to Iraq -- Yearly Averages

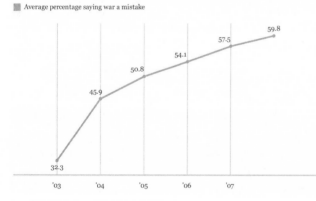

Implications

Even though majority opposition to the Iraq war is basically cemented, other Gallup polling has found that the public does not necessarily advocate a quick end to the war. While a majority now favors a timetable for withdrawing troops, only about one in five Americans think the withdrawal should begin immediately and be completed as soon as possible.

The public will implicitly choose one path on Iraq this fall, given its choice between Republican presidential candidate John McCain (who favors the war and argues the consequences of withdrawal would be severe) and either Democratic presidential candidate, Hillary Clinton or Barack Obama (both of whom oppose the war and want to end it as quickly as they deem prudent).

Survey Methods

Results are based on telephone interviews with 1,016 national adults, aged 18 and older, conducted April 18-20, 2008. For results based on the total sample of national adults, one can say with 95% confidence that the maximum margin of sampling error is ±3 percentage points.

Interviews are conducted with respondents on land-line telephones (for respondents with a land-line telephone) and cellular phones (for respondents who are cell-phone only).

In addition to sampling error, question wording and practical difficulties in conducting surveys can introduce error or bias into the findings of public opinion polls.

April 25, 2008

IN U.S., RECORD WORRY ABOUT MAINTAINING STANDARD OF LIVING

Fifty-five percent fear they won't be able to continue their current lifestyles

by Dennis Jacobe, Gallup Chief Economist

The percentage of Americans worried that they will not be able to maintain their standard of living increased by 14 points compared to last year, and now stands at 55%—exceeding the previous high of 49% reached two years ago, and the highest level since Gallup began asking this question in 2001.

Next, please tell me how concerned you are right now about each of the following financial matters, based on your current financial situation -- are you very worried, moderately worried, not too worried, or not worried at all?

Not being able to maintain the standard of living you enjoy

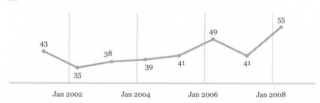

Many See Their Standard of Living Threatened

Presidential candidates and the popular press have made much of the current economic downturn/recession, and the current data make it clear that a fundamental economic worry bothering the majority of Americans is the threat that they will not be able to maintain their current standard of living. Surging food and gas prices have combined with a slowing economy and a lack of income growth to make more than half (55%) of all Americans fear that they may end up with a lower standard of living than they've enjoyed in the past.

While such fears permeate much of U.S. society, they are most pronounced among lower-income Americans. Among those earning less than $30,000 a year, 72% say they are very or moderately worried that they will not be able to maintain the standard of living they enjoy, compared to 58% of those making $30,000 to $74,999, and 41% of those making $75,000 or more.

Intensity of Worry About Not Being Able to Maintain Standard of Living, by Annual Income

% Very/Moderately worried

| All Americans | $75,000 or more | $30,000 to <$75,000 | Less than $30,000 |

Many Worry About Making Their Monthly Payments

One reason so many Americans feel their current standard of living is threatened may have to do with their worries about not having enough money to pay their normal monthly bills. This is a concern felt by 44% of those interviewed in the current poll, a new high. About a third of Americans had such fears when Gallup began asking this question in April 2001; the previous high was 38% in April 2006.

Not surprisingly, consumers' worries that they won't be able to make their normal monthly payments show a distribution by income similar to that of their fears about maintaining their standard of living. Seven in 10 of those earning less than $30,000 a year say they are worried that they will not have enough money to make their normal monthly payments, compared to 42% of those making $30,000 to $74,999, and 26% of those making $75,000 or more.

Intensity of Worry About Not Being Able to Pay Normal Monthly Bills, by Annual Income

% Very/Moderately worried

| All Americans | $75,000 or more | $30,000 to <$75,000 | Less than $30,000 |

Commentary

For several years, economists have debated whether globalization has had a significant depressing effect on average American income levels. What Americans are experiencing now with food and energy prices may be another aspect of globalization. As incomes have increased in many nations around the world, the demand for the essentials of everyday life has increased. Although speculators and other international distortions may have accelerated and intensified the potential impact of this aspect of globalization, one result for many Americans may be a reduction in their ability to maintain their current standard of living.

Gallup's data suggest that many Americans are now facing a significant decline in their living standards—they simply are having difficulty paying their current monthly bills given the current squeeze on their disposable incomes. This has been, and will continue to be, a significant issue in the current presidential campaign, as the remaining candidates battle to see who can put forth the most compelling ideas about how this new economic reality might be addressed.

Survey Methods

Results are based on telephone interviews with 1,021 national adults, aged 18 and older, conducted April 6-9, 2008. For results based on

the total sample of national adults, one can say with 95% confidence that the maximum margin of sampling error is ±3 percentage points.

Interviews are conducted with respondents on land-line telephones (for respondents with a land-line telephone) and cellular phones (for respondents who are cell-phone only).

In addition to sampling error, question wording and practical difficulties in conducting surveys can introduce error or bias into the findings of public opinion polls.

April 25, 2008

MANY AMERICANS OK WITH INCREASING TAXES ON RICH

Most say upper-income households pay too little in taxes

by Frank Newport, Gallup Poll Editor in Chief

Slightly over half of Americans believe the government should redistribute wealth by heavy taxes on the rich.

Do you think our government should or should not redistribute wealth by heavy taxes on the rich?

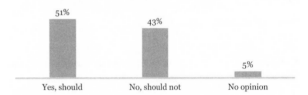

| Yes, should | No, should not | No opinion |

Economy and Personal Finance Poll Apr 6-9, 2008

The percentage holding this view, similar to that found in Gallup polling last year, is up from 1998 and in particular is higher than was found in a Roper poll conducted for *Fortune Magazine* back in 1939. Although the methods and sampling of polling done in the 1930s may differ significantly from those of today, the rough comparison suggests that Americans appear to have become even more "redistributionist" in their views than they were at the tail end of the Depression.

Other recent Gallup Poll questions underscore the finding that Americans are generally open to the idea of some type of effort to distribute wealth more evenly.

Asked if the distribution of money and wealth in this country is fair or if they need to be distributed more evenly, about two-thirds of Americans agree with the latter response. This is up slightly from last year and, by two points, is the highest "more evenly distributed" response to this question that Gallup has found over the eight times it has been asked since 1984.

The results of another question Gallup asks each April find 63% of Americans saying upper-income Americans pay "too little" in taxes (although this percentage is down slightly from previous polling).

One reason it may be easy for Americans to readily agree with wealth redistribution and increased taxes on the rich is that most Americans do not perceive themselves to be rich and therefore presumably assume they have nothing to fear—financially—from such new policies.

Do you feel that the distribution of money and wealth in this country today is fair, or do you feel that the money and wealth in this country should be more evenly distributed among a larger percentage of the people?

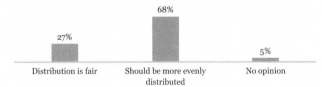

Distribution is fair — 27%
Should be more evenly distributed — 68%
No opinion — 5%

Economy and Personal Finance poll
April 6-9, 2008

As I read off some different groups, please tell me if you think they are paying their FAIR share in federal taxes, paying too MUCH or paying too LITTLE.

Upper-income people

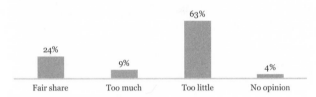

Fair share — 24%
Too much — 9%
Too little — 63%
No opinion — 4%

Economy and Personal Finance poll
April 6-9, 2008

Analysis of the responses to these two questions by income shows that there are some differences by respondents' income, but these differences are not large.

Do you feel that the distribution of money and wealth in this country today is fair, or do you feel that the money and wealth in this country should be more evenly distributed among a larger percentage of the people?

Based on annual income

	Distribution is fair	Should be more evenly distributed
	%	%
Less than $30,000	19	78
$30,000 to $74,999	26	70
$75,000+	35	63

Economy and Personal Finance poll
April 6-9, 2008

Do you think our government should or should not redistribute wealth by heavy taxes on the rich?

Based on annual income

	Yes, should redistribute	No, should not redistribute
	%	%
Less than $30,000	56	38
$30,000 to $74,999	54	41
$75,000+	46	52

Economy and Personal Finance poll
April 6-9, 2008

One issue here is that the top income category Gallup uses is $75,000 and higher, representing a little more than a quarter of the population. Clearly, results might have been different had it been possible to isolate a sample of those making, for example, $200,000 a year or more.

Implications

The possibility of some type of political policy that would institute higher tax rates on high-income households was discussed in the recent Philadelphia debate between the two Democratic contenders, and both Hillary Clinton and Barack Obama appeared to agree with some variant of this type of policy (although both are multimillion-aires, according to their recently released tax statements). The public opinion data reviewed here suggest a majority of Americans would be receptive to such a possibility.

Survey Methods

Results are based on telephone interviews with 1,021 national adults, aged 18 and older, conducted April 6-9, 2008. For results based on the total sample of national adults, one can say with 95% confidence that the maximum margin of sampling error is ±3 percentage points.

Interviews are conducted with respondents on land-line telephones (for respondents with a land-line telephone) and cellular phones (for respondents who are cell-phone only).

In addition to sampling error, question wording and practical difficulties in conducting surveys can introduce error or bias into the findings of public opinion polls.

April 28, 2008
MCCAIN WIDELY RECOGNIZED AS A "WAR HERO"
Nearly 4 in 10 are attracted by his Vietnam record to his candidacy

by Lydia Saad, Gallup Poll Senior Editor

The 5½ years John McCain spent as a prisoner of war in Vietnam, enduring solitary confinement and torture, and at one point refusing to be sent home ahead of other POWs, have earned him the mantle of "war hero" in the eyes of 66% of Americans.

Based on what you have heard or read about John McCain's military service, do you, personally, consider him to be a war hero, or not?

Asked of 506 national adults in Form A half sample

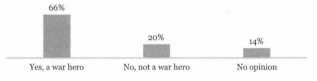

Yes, a war hero — 66%
No, not a war hero — 20%
No opinion — 14%

USA Today/Gallup, April 18-20, 2008

This is according to a *USA Today*/Gallup poll of the nation's adults, conducted April 18-20.

In contrast to the situation regarding the previous Vietnam War veteran to seek the presidency—Democratic Sen. John Kerry—there is bipartisan public agreement that McCain deserves this acclaim. Whereas nearly 6 in 10 Democrats (58%) currently say McCain is a war hero, in September 2004 only 29% of Republicans called Kerry a hero. There is also more universal agreement among Republicans today about McCain's war service than there was among Democrats four years ago about Kerry's. (As a result, fewer than half of Americans, overall, in 2004—48%—considered Kerry a war hero.)

Percentage Considering Each Man to Be a "War Hero," by Party ID

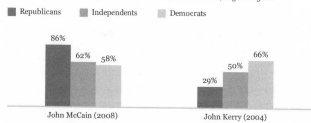

Kerry data from a Newsweek poll conducted by Princeton Survey Research Associates, Sept. 2-3, 2004

Indeed, McCain's broad-based reputation as a war hero may be a factor in his current success in going toe-to-toe with his likely Democratic opponents in Gallup Poll Daily trial heats for the fall election. McCain's relatively strong showing comes at a time when the Republican Party he's attached to is facing its worst image crisis in a decade, President George W. Bush's approval ratings are near the record lows for any president in over a half century, Americans' ratings of the Republican Party are near the lowest seen in the past decade, and the administration is fighting an unpopular war in Iraq that McCain supports.

When asked specifically how McCain's military service affects their vote for president, a fairly substantial 38% of Americans say it makes them more likely to vote for him, including 15% who say his service is a "major factor" in their vote decision. About a quarter of Republicans say it is a major factor, as do 14% of independents and 10% of Democrats. If sustained, this could be a critical advantage for McCain in attracting swing voters in a close election.

Impact of John McCain's Military Service on Supporting Him for President

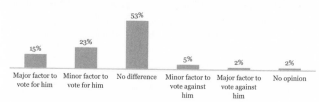

USA Today/Gallup, April 18-20, 2008

Basic Favorability

Another significant factor explaining why McCain is competitive with the Democrats for president at the moment is, no doubt, his general popularity as a public figure. Sixty percent of Americans have a favorable view of him; only 33% hold an unfavorable view. This immediately distinguishes McCain from President Bush, who is currently viewed much more unfavorably (66%) than favorably (32%).

Not only is McCain's favorable rating from Americans nearly twice as high as Bush's, but a majority of independents (62%) as well as more than a third of Democrats (36%) view him positively.

Percentage With Favorable Opinion of Each, by Party ID

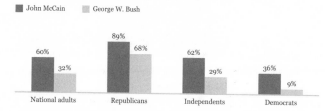

USA Today/Gallup, April 18-20, 2008

McCain's favorability is critical for his candidacy because both of his Democratic opponents are also well-liked by Americans. McCain and Obama are tied in favorability, each with a 60% favorable rating, including relatively high ratings from independents and members of the opposing party. Clinton has lower appeal among independents (only 48% have a favorable view of her); nevertheless, she is viewed favorably by 53% of all Americans.

Percentage With Favorable Opinion of Each, by Party ID

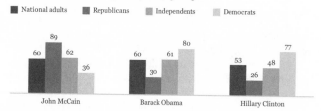

USA Today/Gallup, April 18-20, 2008

A Maverick?

In addition to his military experience, another reason McCain may be excelling in the popularity arena is his well-established reputation inside the nation's capital as a political maverick—someone who has bucked the Republican Party on such issues as the 2001 Bush tax cuts and regulation of the tobacco industry, and has forged alliances with Democrats on climate change legislation, judicial nominations, and campaign finance reform. However, it is not clear how much this aspect of his career is helping to differentiate him from the troubled Republican Party.

In answer to a question designed to determine whether the public perceives McCain to be a maverick, only 45% of Americans say he is "a different kind of Republican." Slightly more, 48%, say he is "basically the same as most other Republicans."

In your opinion, is John McCain a different kind of Republican, or is he basically the same as most other Republicans?

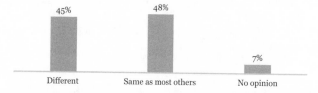

USA Today/Gallup, April 18-20, 2008

Sixty percent of Republicans consider McCain a different kind of Republican, compared with just under half of independents (46%) and only a third of Democrats (34%). Thus, in contrast to the bipartisan view that McCain is a war hero, his maverick image is more a matter of political debate.

Bottom Line

On paper, 2008 is a formidable year for a Republican to be seeking the presidency. Yet, since January, McCain has been roughly tied with both Clinton and Obama in trial heats for the fall election.

Two prominent theories as to why McCain has been able to rise above his party's image problems are that he has established himself as a political maverick who can work with Democrats, and his heroism in Vietnam. According to the new poll, it appears the latter may be the more influential of the two factors. While his war image may not directly translate into votes for his candidacy, it may help explain why the same Gallup Poll finds two-thirds of Americans calling McCain "honest and trustworthy," and about half saying he is someone who "cares about the needs of people like you," and "is someone you would be proud to have as president."

All of those perceptions likely contribute to McCain's overall favorability with the American public, and that, in turn, makes him a competitive candidate.

Survey Methods

Results are based on telephone interviews with 1,016 national adults, aged 18 and older, conducted April 18-20, 2008. For results based on the total sample of national adults, one can say with 95% confidence that the maximum margin of sampling error is ±3 percentage points.

For results based on the 506 national adults in the Form A half-sample and 510 national adults in the Form B half-sample, the maximum margins of sampling error are ±5 percentage points.

Interviews are conducted with respondents on land-line telephones (for respondents with a land-line telephone) and cellular phones (for respondents who are cell-phone only).

In addition to sampling error, question wording and practical difficulties in conducting surveys can introduce error or bias into the findings of public opinion polls.

April 28, 2008
ONLY 33% SAY MCCAIN HAS CLEAR PLAN TO SOLVE U.S. PROBLEMS
Further erosion in Clinton's honesty numbers also evident

by Jeffrey M. Jones, Gallup Poll Managing Editor

The latest *USA Today/*Gallup update on the presidential candidates' personal characteristics finds a significant decline since March in the percentage of Americans who believe John McCain "has a clear plan for solving the country's problems." Only 33% currently say this, compared with 42% in March.

This dimension is clearly a weakness for McCain. It rates as his lowest score among the eight qualities tested in the April 18-20 poll, well behind "shares your values" at 47%. But he also scores signifi-

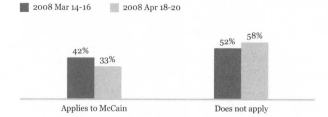

John McCain: Has a Clear Plan for Solving the Country's Problems

■ 2008 Mar 14-16   ▨ 2008 Apr 18-20

USA Today/Gallup polls

cantly worse on the "clear plan" dimension than his Democratic presidential rivals Hillary Clinton (47%) and Barack Obama (40%).

McCain may score lower on the "clear plan" dimension given his admitted weaknesses on economic matters, which Americans regard as the most important problem facing the country. In recent weeks, McCain has attempted to bolster his economic credentials by unveiling his economic plan, and revising his earlier plans for helping distressed homeowners.

McCain's strengths lie in perceptions of his leadership (66% describe him as a "strong and decisive leader") and honesty (65% say he is "honest and trustworthy").

Character Ratings of John McCain

	Applies to McCain	Does not apply
	%	%
Is a strong and decisive leader	66	28
Is honest and trustworthy	65	27
Can manage the government effectively	55	37
Cares about the needs of people like you	52	41
Is someone you would be proud to have as president	51	44
Understands the problems Americans face in their daily lives	50	43
Shares your values	47	47
Has a clear plan for solving the country's problems	33	58

April 18-20 USA Today/Gallup poll

In addition to the nine-point drop on the "clear plan" dimension, McCain's ratings on managing the government effectively and understanding the problems people face in their daily lives have both dropped five points since March.

The April poll also finds a decline in perceptions that Clinton is honest, with only 37% describing her in those terms, down from 44% in March. As recently as 2005, a majority of Americans thought Clinton was honest and trustworthy.

Ratings of Hillary Clinton as Honest and Trustworthy

Numbers in percentages

■ Applies to Clinton

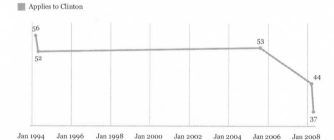

On the honesty dimension, Clinton now ranks even further behind Obama and McCain, both of whose ratings are in the 60% range.

Honesty was the only one of the eight dimensions that showed significant movement for Clinton in the past month, though the poll was conducted before her impressive Pennsylvania primary victory, so it is unclear whether any of these perceptions would have changed in the meantime. The poll finds that leadership, understanding the problems Americans face, and caring about people's needs rank as Clinton's strongest qualities in the eyes of the public.

Character Ratings of Hillary Clinton

	Applies to Clinton	Does not apply
Is a strong and decisive leader	62	35
Understands the problems Americans face in their daily lives	60	37
Cares about the needs of people like you	57	40
Can manage the government effectively	54	42
Is someone you would be proud to have as president	48	48
Has a clear plan for solving the country's problems	47	48
Shares your values	46	49
Is honest and trustworthy	37	58

April 18-20 USA Today/Gallup poll

Obama's comments about "bitter" voters sparked media discussion about whether he is an elitist. But his comments did not seem to affect Americans' view that he is a compassionate person, with 6 in 10 Americans saying that he both "understands the problems Americans face in their daily lives" and "cares about the needs of people like you."

Those were his strongest qualities before the comments, and they remain so after, though at slightly lower levels (each declined four points from the March poll).

Aside from those relatively small declines, ratings of Obama on the character dimensions are largely unchanged from March. He is widely viewed as being honest and trustworthy (60%), but like McCain has an apparent weakness in terms of having a clear plan for solving the country's problems.

Character Ratings of Barack Obama

	Applies to Obama	Does not apply
Understands the problems Americans face in their daily lives	63	34
Cares about the needs of people like you	62	33
Is honest and trustworthy	60	32
Is a strong and decisive leader	55	39
Is someone you would be proud to have as president	55	41
Shares your values	51	44
Can manage the government effectively	48	45
Has a clear plan for solving the country's problems	40	53

April 18-20 USA Today/Gallup poll

Implications

Clinton and McCain each have obvious weaknesses in the public's eyes at this point, honesty being Clinton's and having a clear plan McCain's. Clinton need only look to her husband for an example of a candidate who won the presidential election despite not being viewed as honest. And while McCain trails the other candidates in terms of being viewed as having a clear plan, none of the three score particularly well on that dimension.

That is not to say character weaknesses do not matter. Ultimately, voters will elect the candidate who best fits what they are looking for in the next president, and character evaluations clearly enter into that equation.

Survey Methods

Results are based on telephone interviews with 1,016 national adults, aged 18 and older, conducted April 18-20, 2008. For results based on the total sample of national adults, one can say with 95% confidence that the maximum margin of sampling error is ±3 percentage points.

Interviews are conducted with respondents on land-line telephones (for respondents with a land-line telephone) and cellular phones (for respondents who are cell-phone only).

In addition to sampling error, question wording and practical difficulties in conducting surveys can introduce error or bias into the findings of public opinion polls.

April 29, 2008

ONE IN FIVE AMERICANS EXPECT GAS TO HIT $5 PER GALLON
Nearly three in four say gas prices are causing hardship or changes in spending

by Dennis Jacobe, Gallup Chief Economist

While 9 in 10 Americans expect gas prices at the pump to hit $4 a gallon in their local areas this summer, one in five expect them to hit $5 a gallon, and 1 in 20 are looking for gas prices to reach $6 a gallon.

Do you think the price of gasoline in your local area will or will not reach -- [ITEMS READ IN ORDER] -- this summer?

Gallup Poll, April 25-27, 2008

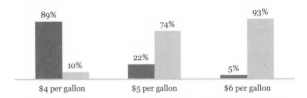

Surging Gas Prices Having Significant Impact on Three in Four Americans

On Monday in the nation's capital, American truckers protested high fuel prices. But the squeeze people find themselves in at the moment is not limited to those who drive the big rigs. Nearly three in four Americans say today's record gas prices are creating a hardship for them personally (20%) or have caused them to adjust their usual spending and saving habits in significant ways (52%).

Growing Political Issue

When asked in an open-ended format which one or two issues should be the top priorities for the president and Congress to deal with at this time, 22% of Americans say gas and energy prices. That is twice the level of a month ago and is well above mentions of any other specific economic issue, including healthcare (at 16%). (The top overall issue is general mentions of the economy, at 48%.)

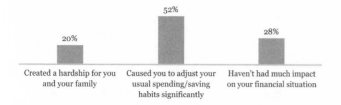

How have gas prices affected you personally?
Gallup Poll, April 25-27, 2008

20% — Created a hardship for you and your family

52% — Caused you to adjust your usual spending/saving habits significantly

28% — Haven't had much impact on your financial situation

While in reality, most government efforts to deal with the current gas-price crisis may do more harm than good, doing nothing as gas prices significantly disrupt the living standards of most Americans is likely to be unacceptable, particularly in an election year.

Survey Methods

Results for this Gallup Panel study are based on telephone interviews with 1,008 national adults, aged 18 and older, conducted April 25-27, 2008. Gallup Panel members are recruited through random selection methods. The panel is weighted so that it is demographically representative of the U.S. adult population. For results based on this sample, one can say with 95% confidence that the maximum margin of sampling error is ±4 percentage points.

In addition to sampling error, question wording and practical difficulties in conducting surveys can introduce error or bias into the findings of public opinion polls.

Vote in General Election Between Hillary Clinton and John McCain
Preferences by Key Demographic Groups
Based on registered voters

	Clinton	McCain	Net Clinton
	%	%	Pct. pts.
Registered voters	47	45	+2
Democrats	82	11	+71
Blacks	78	12	+66
Hispanics	63	30	+33
Monthly income less than $2,000	62	32	+30
18 to 29 years	58	35	+23
Unmarried	56	35	+21
Attend church seldom/never	54	36	+18
East	53	38	+15
Women	52	40	+12
Monthly income $2,000 to $4,999	50	43	+7
Catholics	50	43	+7
No college education	49	42	+7
65 years and older	45	45	0
Independents	42	46	-4
South	44	49	-5
Monthly income $7,500 or more	44	52	-8

April 21-27, 2008

May 01, 2008
CLINTON'S VS. OBAMA'S STRENGTHS IN THE GENERAL ELECTION
Clinton stronger than Obama among most core Democratic constituencies

by Lydia Saad , Gallup Poll Senior Editor

Gallup Poll Daily tracking over the past month indicates that the 2008 presidential election could be another nail-biter of the sorts seen in 2000 and, to a lesser extent, 2004. Both Democratic contenders are closely matched against John McCain in trial heats for the general election.

While the broad outlines of voter support for Hillary Clinton and Barack Obama are highly similar—both candidates attract traditional Democratic constituencies—there are some differences that could be important in assessing which of the two has the better chance of beating McCain.

A Mostly Traditional Democratic Coalition for Clinton

According to an aggregate of Gallup Poll Daily tracking from April 21-27, including interviews with more than 6,000 registered voters, a Clinton-McCain race looks highly typical of recent elections, with the Democrat widely favored by women, blacks, adults under 30 years of age, Easterners, low socioeconomic Americans (those with low incomes and low education), Catholics, Hispanics, secular Americans, unmarried adults, and Democrats.

Two important differences from recent general elections are Clinton's especially strong performance among women, and her relatively weak performance among black Americans. Her 12-point advantage among women over McCain (52% vs. 40%) contrasts with single-digit advantages among women for John Kerry, Al Gore, and Bill Clinton in the previous three presidential elections. And her 78% level of support from blacks contrasts with more than 90% support among blacks for those candidates. The latter clearly highlights the risk the Democratic Party faces with blacks (the overwhelming majority of whom are Democrats and who support Obama for the Democratic nomination) should Clinton win the nomination on the basis of the super-delegates or some other means that Obama's supporters perceive as unfair or undemocratic.

Also, only 82% of Democrats currently say they would vote for Clinton in the fall, whereas recent Democratic presidential candidates have received no less than 89% of the vote from their party.

Obama Charting a Different Course

An Obama-McCain race differs from a Clinton-McCain race mainly in terms of degrees of support for the Democrat. Obama beats McCain among nearly all of the aforementioned core Democratic constituencies. But his margin of support is lower among women, Easterners, low-income Americans, Catholics, Hispanics, and self-identified Democrats. (Obama also does less well than Clinton in the South, although both lose to McCain in that region.)

Obama largely offsets these losses by doing better than Clinton among blacks and high-income Americans. He also does slightly better among the one-third or so of voters who consider themselves political independents. Obama's near-universal support among blacks is the more typical pattern for a Democratic presidential candidate than is the lower support Clinton receives.

Vote in General Election Between Barack Obama and John McCain
Preferences by Key Demographic Groups
Based on registered voters

	Obama	McCain	Net Obama
	%	%	Pct. pts.
Registered voters	45	45	0
Blacks	91	4	+87
Democrats	74	17	+57
Hispanics	57	33	+24
18 to 29 years	57	35	+22
Unmarried	54	36	+18
Attend church seldom/never	51	37	+14
Monthly income less than $2,000	51	38	+13
East	49	41	+8
Women	47	42	+5
Monthly income $7,500 or more	49	47	+2
Catholics	46	44	+2
Monthly income $2,000 to $4,999	46	46	0
Independents	43	44	-1
No college education	40	47	-7
65 years and older	37	49	-12
South	39	52	-13

April 21-27, 2008

The accompanying table summarizes the differences in support for Clinton and Obama among these groups, highlighting that Clinton performs especially well relative to Obama among Americans of lower and lower-middle incomes, lower education (no college experience), and among Democrats, seniors, and Hispanics. Obama's distinguishing strengths are his stronger performance among blacks and higher-income Americans, although he also performs slightly better among independents.

The most recent weekly aggregate of Gallup Poll Daily tracking finds Clinton doing just as well as Obama among voters aged 18 to 29. However, this is a sharp reversal for Clinton, who had been trailing Obama among young voters for most of March and April, so it is not clear whether the current data are an anomaly or a dramatic shift in younger voters' preferences.

Difference Between Support for Clinton vs. Obama in Trial Heats Against McCain Among Key Demographic Groups

Based on registered voters

	Advantage
Monthly income less than $2,000	Clinton +17
No college education	Clinton +14
Democrats	Clinton +14
65 years and older	Clinton +12
Hispanics	Clinton +9
South	Clinton +8
Women	Clinton +7
East	Clinton +7
Monthly income $2,000 to $4,999	Clinton +7
Catholics	Clinton +5
Attend church seldom/never	Clinton+ 4
Unmarried	Clinton +3
18 to 29 years	Clinton +1
Independents	Obama +3
Monthly income $7,500 or more	Obama +10
Blacks	Obama +21

April 21-27, 2008

Obama Falls Short Among Conservative Democrats

Given the apparent willingness of many blacks to forsake Clinton in November if she is the Democratic Party's nominee—either by voting for McCain or not voting at all—it may seem surprising that Clinton still outperforms Obama among Democrats (82% vs. 74%). The reason for this is Obama's relatively poor performance among conservative Democrats.

Only 62% of Democrats who describe their political views as "conservative" choose Obama in a race between Obama and McCain. By contrast, 74% of conservative Democrats would vote for Clinton in a Clinton vs. McCain race. Obama does just as well as Clinton among liberal Democrats, and nearly as well among moderate Democrats. His great weakness is, and has been since early March, among conservative Democrats.

Bottom Line

These observations are made as the protracted battle for the Democratic nomination gets increasingly contentious, and before the eventual nominee has had the opportunity to heal party wounds. Much could change. At present, it seems both Clinton and Obama would win the support of traditional Democratic constituencies in the fall election if they are nominated for president. However, compared with previous Democratic nominees, Clinton seems poised to do historically well among women and less well among blacks. Obama could have trouble holding blue-collar and conservative Democrats, but

Percentage Voting for Obama/Clinton Against McCain in Fall Election

Based on registered voters

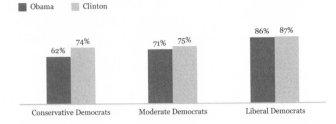

April 21-27, 2008

could make that up if he maintains his strong appeal to blacks and upper-income Americans, and continues to go toe-to-toe with McCain among political independents.

Survey Methods

Results are based on telephone interviews with 6,117 registered voters, aged 18 and older, conducted April 21-27, 2008. For results based on the total sample of registered voters, one can say with 95% confidence that the maximum margin of sampling error is ±1 percentage point.

Interviews are conducted with respondents on land-line telephones (for respondents with a land-line telephone) and cellular phones (for respondents who are cell-phone only).

In addition to sampling error, question wording and practical difficulties in conducting surveys can introduce error or bias into the findings of public opinion polls.

May 02, 2008

IS ONGOING DEMOCRATIC CAMPAIGN GOOD OR BAD FOR THE PARTY?

Significantly different views between Obama supporters and Clinton supporters

by Frank Newport, Gallup Poll Editor in Chief

Six out of 10 Democrats say the continuing campaign for the Democratic presidential nomination is doing more harm than good for the Democratic Party, up slightly from the percentage who felt this way last month.

Do you think the fact that Hillary Clinton and Barack Obama are still campaigning for the Democratic presidential nomination while the Republican nomination is settled is doing -- [ROTATED: more good than harm or more harm than good] -- to the Democratic Party's chances of winning the presidential election in November?

Asked of Democrats and Democratic-leaning independents

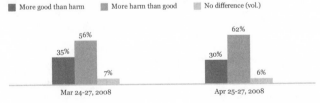

(vol.) = Volunteered response

This overall negative view of the impact of the continuing campaign among Democrats masks significant variations in attitudes based on candidate support.

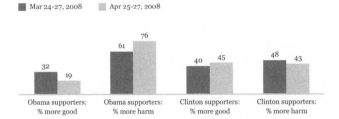

Do you think the fact that Hillary Clinton and Barack Obama are still campaigning for the Democratic presidential nomination while the Republican nomination is settled is doing: more good than harm or more harm than good to the Democratic Party's chances of winning the presidential election in November?

Asked of Democrats and Democratic-leaning independents

■ Mar 24-27, 2008   ■ Apr 25-27, 2008

Democrats who support Barack Obama are well above the overall Democratic average in their beliefs that the continuing campaign is doing harm. This is no doubt because Obama is the current leader in both the popular vote (excluding Florida and Michigan) and the overall delegate count. Continuing to campaign has very little upside potential for Obama and a lot of downside potential—as may be occurring now, with Obama having to deal with continuing controversies surrounding his relationship with the Rev. Jeremiah Wright.

The recent events probably contribute to Obama supporters' even greater likelihood to view the continuing campaign as harmful than was the case a month ago.

On the other hand, Democrats who support Hillary Clinton have much more mixed views. A slight plurality of 45% say the continuing campaign is doing more good than harm, while 43% agree that it is harmful. Again, given that Clinton's only realistic chance of winning the nomination is to continue to campaign and hope events will help convince super-delegates to switch and vote for her, this pattern is not surprising.

And, in the opposite reaction to that measured among Obama supporters, Clinton supporters have become slightly more positive about the impact of the continuing campaign than they were a month ago.

Implications

These data reinforce the degree to which the two groups of Democrats, as defined by the candidate they support, view the campaign world from significantly different perspectives. On average, Democrats appear to agree that the continuing campaign is harming their party's chances of winning in November. Obama supporters have become even more hardened in this view over the past month as they have watched the negative news that has surrounded their candidate. In contrast, Clinton supporters have become a little more likely to believe that the continuing campaign may not be so harmful after all.

Survey Methods

Results for this Gallup Panel study are based on telephone interviews with 1,008 national adults, aged 18 and older, conducted April 25-27, 2008. Gallup Panel members are recruited through random selection methods. The panel is weighted so that it is demographically representative of the U.S. adult population. For results based on this sample, one can say with 95% confidence that the maximum margin of sampling error is ±4 percentage points.

In addition to sampling error, question wording and practical difficulties in conducting surveys can introduce error or bias into the findings of public opinion polls.

May 05, 2008
CLINTON SUPPORTERS BELIEVE WRIGHT IS RELEVANT TO CAMPAIGN
Obama supporters reject it out of hand as a legitimate campaign topic

by Frank Newport, Gallup Poll Editor in Chief

Democrats nationally who have followed the controversy surrounding the relationship between Barack Obama and his former minister, the Rev. Jeremiah Wright, say by a 2-to-1 margin that Obama's association with Wright is not meaningful and should not be discussed in the campaign, while a majority of Republicans disagree.

Is Barack Obama's association with Jeremiah Wright a meaningful reflection on Obama's character and judgment that should be discussed in the campaign?

Asked of those who are following the Jeremiah Wright controversy

■ Meaningful, should be discussed

■ Not meaningful, should not be discussed

■ No opinion

USA Today/Gallup, May 1-3, 2008

About three-quarters of Democrats who are Hillary Clinton supporters and 8 out of 10 Obama supporters say they have followed the Jeremiah Wright controversy. Perhaps not surprisingly, there is a significant difference in the way Democrats view this matter based on the candidate they support. Clinton supporters who have followed the controversy believe, by a slight majority, that the story should be discussed in the campaign because it is a meaningful reflection on Obama's character (and in this way, they agree with Republicans). Even though Obama himself admitted on NBC's *Meet the Press* Sunday that his relationship to Wright is a legitimate campaign topic, Obama supporters overwhelmingly say it should not be discussed in the campaign.

The major short-term focus of the Wright controversy has been its potential impact on the race for the Democratic nomination. It is clear from the *USA Today*/Gallup poll data that it could be having some impact because Clinton supporters appear to be at least somewhat prone to take the controversy into account in assessing Obama—certainly more so than are Obama's own supporters.

Almost 3 out of 10 Clinton supporters who have followed the controversy say Obama agrees with the more controversial comments Wright has made. The vast majority of Obama supporters, almost 9 out of 10, believe that Obama disagrees with Wright's more controversial statements.

Is Barack Obama's association with Jeremiah Wright a meaningful reflection on Obama's character and judgment that should be discussed in the campaign?

Asked of those who are following the Jeremiah Wright controversy

■ Meaningful, should be discussed

■ Not meaningful, should not be discussed

▨ No opinion

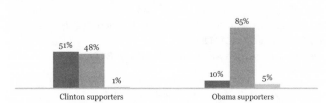

USA Today/Gallup, May 1-3, 2008

Just your best guess, do you think in general Barack Obama [ROTATED: strongly agrees, agrees, disagrees, or strongly disagrees] with the more controversial comments Jeremiah Wright has made?

Asked of those who are following the Jeremiah Wright controversy

■ Total agree   ■ Total disagree   ▨ No opinion

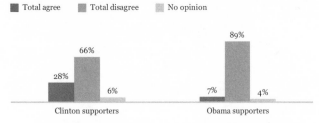

USA Today/Gallup, May 1-3, 2008

Additionally, 9 out of 10 Obama supporters believe Obama has handled the controversy well, a sentiment that a lower percentage—albeit still a majority—of 66% of Clinton supporters agree with.

Regardless of whether you think Obama agrees with Jeremiah Wright's statements, how do you think Obama has handled the controversy?

Asked of those who are following the Jeremiah Wright controversy

■ Total handled well   ■ Total handled poorly   ▨ No opinion

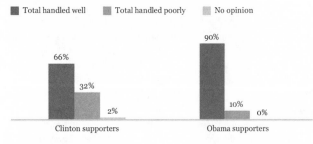

USA Today/Gallup, May 1-3, 2008

Asked directly whether Obama's association with Wright has made them more likely or less likely to vote for Obama, or whether it does not affect their vote, Obama supporters overwhelmingly say it makes no difference to them. On the other hand, a little less than a third of Clinton supporters say the association between Wright and Obama has made them less likely to vote for Obama. (These answers are among all Clinton and Obama supporters, regardless of how closely they have been following the controversy.)

Does Barack Obama's association with Rev. Jeremiah Wright make you more likely to vote for Obama, does it not affect your vote either way, or make you less likely to vote for Obama?

Total respondents

■ More likely to vote for Obama   ■ Does not affect vote either way

▨ Less likely to vote for Obama   ▨ No opinion

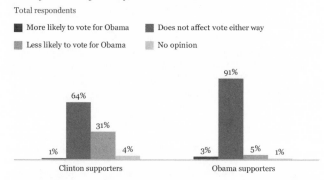

USA Today/Gallup, May 1-3, 2008

The Thursday through Saturday poll shows that Obama's unfavorable rating is up slightly from last month among Democrats.

Do you have a favorable or unfavorable opinion of Barack Obama?

Asked of Democrats and Democratic leaners

■ Favorable   ■ Unfavorable   ▨ No opinion

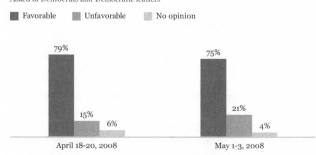

A detailed look at the trends on Obama's favorables by nomination support, show that Obama became slightly less popular among Clinton supporters, while his almost universally favorable rating among his own supporters stayed the same.

Do you have a favorable or unfavorable opinion of Barack Obama?

■ Favorable   ▨ Unfavorable

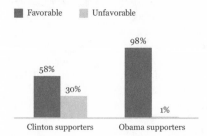

USA Today/Gallup, April 18-20, 2008

Bottom Line

It is sometimes difficult to tease out the specific impact of a high-profile news event on the fortunes of candidates in the middle of a heated presidential campaign. The data reviewed above indicate that

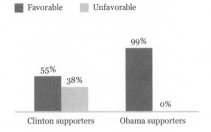

Do you have a favorable or unfavorable opinion of Barack Obama?

■ Favorable   ▨ Unfavorable

USA Today/Gallup, May 1-3, 2008

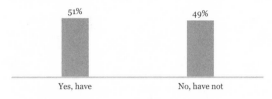

Have you and your family had to cut back significantly on your spending recently, or not?

Gallup Poll, April 25-27, 2008

the Wright controversy certainly seems to have had at least some impact on Democrats who support Clinton and who have followed the controversy. These voters say by a slight majority that the controversy is a legitimate topic for news media to discuss, and a not insignificant minority say Obama agrees with Wright's more controversial statements. About a third of all Clinton supporters say the relationship has made them less likely to vote for Obama. Additionally, Clinton supporters in this latest poll have a slightly less favorable view of Obama than they did two weeks ago.

Of course, it is not known whether the Wright controversy has actually caused some Obama supporters to defect and move into Clinton's camp, or whether it has simply reinforced Clinton supporters' pre-existing attitudes. Whether the controversy will affect the results of Tuesday's Indiana and North Carolina primaries remains to be seen, assuming that a question about it is included in the exit polls from those two states.

Survey Methods

Results are based on telephone interviews with 1,019 national adults, aged 18 and older, conducted May 1-3, 2008. For results based on the total sample of national adults, one can say with 95% confidence that the maximum margin of sampling error is ±3 percentage points.

Interviews are conducted with respondents on land-line telephones (for respondents with a land-line telephone) and cellular phones (for respondents who are cell-phone only).

In addition to sampling error, question wording and practical difficulties in conducting surveys can introduce error or bias into the findings of public opinion polls.

May 05, 2008
HALF OF AMERICANS SAY THEY'RE REINING IN SPENDING
Reducing driving and gas usage ranks as top savings strategy

by Lydia Saad, Gallup Poll Senior Editor

Americans can be divided about evenly into two financial camps: the 51% who say they have had to significantly cut back on their spending recently, and the 49% who say they haven't.

Rising gas and grocery store prices are two obvious sources of financial strain for American households, but pressure is also coming from other directions. Credit markets are tight, more Americans are out of work than a year ago, and, according to a recent Commerce

Department report, although wages are up, earnings are not keeping pace with inflation.

The effects of this squeeze are most evident among lower-income Americans. According to a recent Gallup Panel survey, not only are the vast majority of lower-income Americans having to cut back on spending, but they are largely cutting back on basics such as food and gas.

Seven in 10 Americans living in households earning less than $35,000 a year say they have had to cut back on their spending recently. Even half of those earning $35,000 to $74,999 per year are in this position. By contrast, most of those earning $75,000 or more per year have yet to feel enough of a financial pinch to force them to scale back their spending. Only 36% say they have.

Cutting Back on Spending, by Annual Household Income

■ Yes   ▨ No

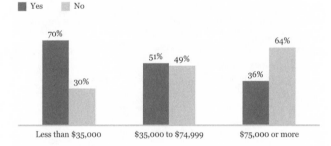

Gallup Poll, April 25-27, 2008

Specific Cuts

With a follow-up question asking those who have cut back on their spending to name the specific things they and their families are doing without, Gallup finds Americans cutting back on a range of items.

The No. 1 savings strategy, mentioned by 36% of Americans, concerns the use of gas for driving, including driving less, buying less gas, and buying cheaper grades of gas.

The No. 2 strategy is highly related to the first: cutting back on travel and vacations. This is named by 26% of Americans, and when combined with driving and gas, suggests that more than half of Americans are focused on transportation costs as the best way to save money right now.

The next-most-commonly cited area for cost cutting is food and groceries, mentioned by 25% of Americans. Entertainment and eating out are each mentioned by about one in five Americans.

Eleven percent of Americans say they are in a no-frills spending mode right now, buying only the essentials. Six percent say they are seeking to reduce their home energy bills, while 4% each are cutting back on luxury items and clothing.

What are the specific things that you and your family are cutting back on these days? [OPEN-ENDED]

Based on 510 national adults who have had to cut back on spending; ±5 pct. pts.

	Apr 25-27, 2008
	%
Driving/Gas	36
Travel/Vacations	26
Food/Groceries	25
Entertainment	21
Eating out	20
Only buying necessities/basics	11
Energy/Utilities	6
Luxury items (nonspecific)	4
Clothing	4
Other	5
Everything (vol.)	3
Nothing (vol.)	1
No opinion	*

(vol.) = Volunteered response
* Less than 0.5%

Different Perspectives on Sacrifice

Even though more than a third of upper-income Americans report having had to cut back on their spending recently, the types of sacrifices they are making may not be on par with those of lower-income Americans.

Among those earning less than $35,000 a year, the top three areas where they are spending less are driving and gas, food and groceries, and travel. Among those earning $75,000 or more per year, the top three areas of cuts are eating out, entertainment, and travel.

Cutting Back on Spending, by Household Income

	Less than $35,000	$35,000 to $74,999	$75,000 or more
	%	%	%
Gas/Driving	34	44	26
Food/Groceries	32	24	20
Travel/Vacations	29	23	30
Entertainment	16	20	32
Only buying necessities/basics	12	12	9
Eating out	10	20	37

Gallup Poll, April 25-27, 2008

Survey Methods

Results for this Gallup Panel study are based on telephone interviews with 1,008 national adults, aged 18 and older, conducted April 25-27, 2008. Gallup Panel members are recruited through random selection methods. The panel is weighted so that it is demographically representative of the U.S. adult population. For results based on this sample, one can say with 95% confidence that the maximum margin of sampling error is ±4 percentage points.

In addition to sampling error, question wording and practical difficulties in conducting surveys can introduce error or bias into the findings of public opinion polls.

May 06, 2008

FEWER AMERICANS EXPECT A COMFORTABLE RETIREMENT

Fifty-five percent fear they won't be able to continue their current lifestyles

by Dennis Jacobe, Gallup Chief Economist

Sixty-nine percent of Americans say they are living comfortably right now—down four percentage points from last year and six points from 2002. However, the percentage of those yet to retire who think they'll be able to live comfortably in retirement fell even more precipitously, dropping to only 46% from 53% a year ago and 59% in 2002.

Percentage Living Comfortably Now Versus Percentage Expecting to Live Comfortably in Retirement

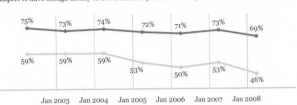

Many Worried About Having Enough Money for Retirement

When asked about their financial worries in Gallup's April 6-9 Economy and Personal Finance poll, 63% of Americans say they are worried they will not have enough money for retirement—exceeding the 56% who are worried about not being able to pay the medical costs associated with a serious illness or accident and the 55% who are afraid they will not be able to maintain the standard of living they now enjoy. Even as Americans are bombarded by a wide range of immediate-term economic concerns ranging from surging gas, food, and healthcare costs to a decline in jobs and a debacle in housing, their most prevalent fear seems to be centered on not being able to achieve a comfortable retirement.

In part, this may be an often-unnoticed result of today's economic turmoil. Not surprisingly given the soaring cost of everyday essentials, the percentage of Americans saying they have enough money to live comfortably right now is 69%, down from the 75% of 2002 as well as the 73% of last year. With incomes stagnating and prices surging, fewer Americans have enough income to live comfortably.

In this context, it seems reasonable for fewer Americans to feel confident they will have enough money to live comfortably in retirement, when their incomes are not only generally lower but also relatively fixed. Add in today's comparatively low interest rates, and one might argue that many of the 46% of Americans who think they'll be able to live comfortably in retirement are being somewhat optimistic. Of course, this does represent a 13-point drop from the percentage of Americans holding this view in April 2002 and a seven-point decline from just last year. Note also that the gap between the percentage of Americans feeling they have enough money to live comfortably now compared to those having similar expectations for when they retire has increased from 16 points in 2002 to 23 points today.

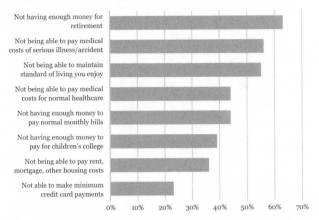

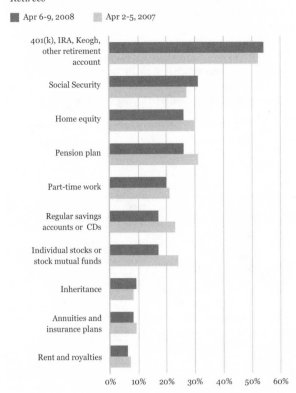

Expected Major Sources of Future Retiree Income Among Non-Retirees

■ Apr 6-9, 2008   ▢ Apr 2-5, 2007

Economy Affecting Retirement Income Expectations

Fifty-four percent of those who have yet to retire say they expect their 401(k), IRA, Keogh, or other retirement savings accounts to be a major source of income for them in retirement. This is up two points over the past year, despite the losses some people have experienced in their tax-favored accounts during the recent past. Social Security is mentioned second most frequently, with 31% seeing it as an expected major source of retirement income—up from 27% a year ago—and not necessarily good news given the current condition of the Social Security system.

One reason more future retirees fear they will not be able to live comfortably in retirement may have to do with the impact of recent economic trends on their financial well-being. For example, only 17% of future retirees expect individual stocks or mutual funds to be a major source of their retirement income, down by nearly one-third from the 24% who thought these investments would be a major source for them a year ago. There has been a similar six-point drop, from 23% to 17%, in the percentage expecting their regular savings accounts or CDs to fill this role. At the same time, the percentage of those looking to a work-sponsored pension plan as a major source of retirement income has fallen five points, from 31% last year to 26% this year, while those looking to the equity in their homes is down four points, and is now also at 26%.

Commentary

Today's economic stagflation has one in four Americans "very worried" that they will not be able to maintain the living standard they now enjoy. But with many baby boomers approaching retirement age, the full impact of today's economic woes may not be fully realized for several years.

For example, the home has traditionally been the average American's primary source of wealth. However, the current residential real estate debacle now threatens the value of that asset for many. Not only are many Americans experiencing foreclosure, but their neighbors are seeing their housing values plunge as potential purchasers hesitate to buy and as foreclosed properties drive down the value of nearby properties.

At the same time that their real estate values are declining, Americans see the interest rates on their savings deposits at low levels while the risks in the equity markets seem high. And while one in five Americans who have not yet retired now say they expect a part-time job to be a major source of their retirement income—dou-

ble the level of 2001—this number could grow as an increasing number of baby boomers find that today's economy will make it hard to retire comfortably.

Survey Methods

Results are based on telephone interviews with 1,021 national adults, aged 18 and older, conducted April 6-9, 2008. For results based on the total sample of national adults, one can say with 95% confidence that the maximum margin of sampling error is ±3 percentage points.

For results based on the sample of 310 retirees, the maximum margin of sampling error is ±6 percentage points.

For results based on the sample of 711 non-retirees, the maximum margin of sampling error is ±4 percentage points.

Interviews are conducted with respondents on land-line telephones (for respondents with a land-line telephone) and cellular phones (for respondents who are cell-phone only).

In addition to sampling error, question wording and practical difficulties in conducting surveys can introduce error or bias into the findings of public opinion polls.

May 07, 2008
OBAMA BEATS MCCAIN AMONG JEWISH VOTERS
Trails Clinton by slim margin among Jewish Democrats for the nomination

by Lydia Saad, Gallup Poll Senior Editor

Barack Obama is faring better than might be expected among Jewish voters, beating John McCain in Gallup Poll Daily general-election matchups and trailing Hillary Clinton only slightly in Jewish Democrats' preferences for the Democratic nomination.

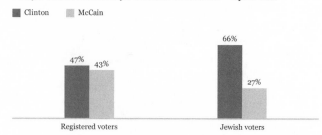

Vote for Clinton vs. McCain for President in November -- April 2008

Clinton   McCain

Preference for 2008 Democratic Presidential Nomination -- April 2008
Based on Democratic voters (including independents who lean Democratic)

Clinton   Obama

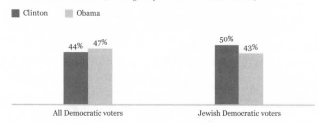

This is according to an aggregate of Gallup Poll Daily tracking from April 1-30, including interviews with close to 800 Jewish voters, and nearly 600 Jewish Democratic voters.

Furthermore, Gallup Poll Daily tracking finds no recent decline in the percentage of Jewish Democrats favoring Obama for the Democratic presidential nomination. Jewish Democrats continue to favor Clinton, but by only a slim margin over Obama—50% to 43% in April, compared with 51% to 41% in March.

In terms of the general election, Jewish voters nationwide are nearly as likely to say they would vote for Obama if he were the Democratic nominee running against the Republican McCain (61%), as to say they would vote for Clinton (66%).

Vote for Obama vs. McCain for President in November -- April 2008

Obama   McCain

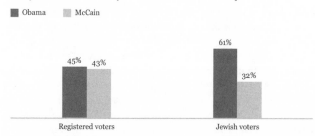

According to Gallup's aggregated tracking data for all of April, 61% of Jewish voters would vote for Obama, much higher than the national average of 45% of all registered voters.

Rather than declining between March and April, support for Obama versus McCain among Jewish voters has increased slightly, from a 23-point margin in favor of Obama (58% to 35%) to a 29-point margin (61% to 32%).

The results are similar for Clinton, who received 66% of the vote from Jewish Democrats in April, compared with 27% for McCain—a 39-point lead. Clinton led McCain by 29 points in March, 61% to 32%.

Bottom Line

Evidence of Obama's concern about Jewish support for his candidacy stretches back to at least January, when he first publicly refuted

Web-fueled rumors that he is or has been a Muslim—the implication of the rumors being that he would be sympathetic to Muslim political concerns and anti-Israel in his worldview. At the same time, he also disassociated himself from the anti-Semitic remarks of black activist Louis Farrakhan, and has recently disassociated himself from his former pastor, the Rev. Jeremiah Wright.

Thus, any damage to Jews' perceptions of Obama as someone who would be sympathetic and fair to their interests could have occurred much earlier in the campaign. However, in terms of recent events—particularly the ongoing controversy about why Obama would have belonged to a church led by someone with Wright's anti-Israel views (among other criticisms of Wright)—Gallup trends suggest Obama's Jewish support is holding up.

Survey Methods

These results are based on monthly aggregates of Gallup Poll Daily tracking interviews for March 2008 and April 2008.

The March 2008 aggregate is based on interviews conducted March 1-31, 2008. It includes interviews with 24,290 voters, 632 Jewish voters, 12,045 Democratic voters, and 449 Jewish Democratic voters.

The April 2008 aggregate is based on interviews conducted April 1-30, 2008. It includes interviews with 30,311 voters, 790 Jewish voters, 14,989 Democratic voters, and 588 Jewish Democratic voters.

In addition to sampling error, question wording and practical difficulties in conducting surveys can introduce error or bias into the findings of public opinion polls.

May 07, 2008
OBAMA'S SUPPORT SIMILAR TO KERRY'S IN 2004
Similar levels of support exist across white, black, blue-collar voters

by Frank Newport, Gallup Poll Editor in Chief

Barack Obama's current level of support among white voters in a head-to-head matchup against John McCain is no worse than John Kerry's margin of support among whites against George W. Bush in the 2004 presidential election.

Much of the talk following Tuesday's Indiana and North Carolina primaries has focused on just how electable Obama—now the highly probable nominee—will be in the general election. The Clinton campaign has argued that Obama's weaknesses among white voters and blue-collar voters will hurt him against McCain in the fall.

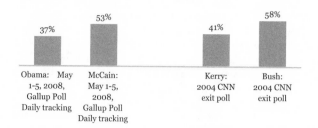

37% 53%   41% 58%

| Obama: May 1-5, 2008, Gallup Poll Daily tracking | McCain: May 1-5, 2008, Gallup Poll Daily tracking | Kerry: 2004 CNN exit poll | Bush: 2004 CNN exit poll |

But it appears that the way Obama stacks up against McCain at this point is similar to the way in which Kerry performed against Bush in 2004 within several key racial, educational, religious, and gender subgroups. That is, the basic underlying structure of the general-election campaign this year does not appear to be markedly different from that of the 2004 election. This conclusion is based on an analysis of exit-poll data from 2004 compared to the Obama-McCain matchup in 4,000 Gallup Poll Daily tracking interviews conducted during the first five days of May.

Comparison of Non College Grad Support for Candidates - 2008 and 2004

	Gallup Poll Tracking May 1-5, 2008	Gallup Poll Tracking May 1-5, 2008	CNN Exit Polls 2004 Election	CNN Exit Polls 2004 Election
	Obama	McCain	Kerry	Bush
White	37	53	41	58
Black	91	5	88	11
Hispanic	51	41	53	44
Non college grad	43	47	47	53
College grad	50	44	49	49
Post grad	57	38	55	41
Attend church weekly	36	55	39	61
Occasionally	43	49	53	47
Never	54	36	61	36
Men	44	49	44	55
Women	47	43	51	48

Kerry, the Democratic nominee in 2004, lost to the Republican Bush by a 51% to 48% margin in the popular vote. In Gallup Poll Daily tracking data from May 1-5, Obama is losing to McCain among registered voters by a 46% to 45% margin. Although there is a sizable component of "undecideds" in the Gallup Poll tracking data (and obviously no "undecideds" in the 2004 exit-poll data), the margins in these two races are quite similar, with Kerry losing by three points, and Obama by one point.

This overall comparison, in and of itself, suggests that Obama, assuming he captures the Democratic nomination, begins the general-election contest in roughly the same position in which Kerry ended his unsuccessful quest in 2004—that is, with the prospect of a very close race.

The more specific comparison of Obama's positioning versus Kerry's among various subgroups of the electorate suggests that the basic dynamic of the general presidential election is fairly predictable, based on past patterns. Regardless of Obama's specific characteristics, or the specific environment in which this year's election will take place, Obama will inherit a fairly structured general election environment.

Obama would be the first black candidate to receive a major party nomination in United States history. This could have racial implications in the voting. Some observers have argued that Obama has a particular liability among white voters, whom exit polls showed voted for Clinton in both North Carolina and Indiana.

The general-election exit poll in 2004 showed that Kerry lost the white vote to Bush by a 17-point, 58% to 41%, margin. At the moment, in Gallup's tracking of the general election across the first five days of May (with a sample of more than 4,000 registered voters), Obama is losing the white vote to McCain by a 53% to 37% margin, or 16 points. In short, Obama's relative performance among white voters—at least at the moment—is similar to Kerry's in 2004.

Democratic candidates at the presidential level have traditionally received the overwhelming majority of black votes. In 2004, Kerry won over Bush among blacks by 88% to 11%. At this point, Obama is winning over McCain by a 91% to 5% margin. So, there is little difference in how Obama fares among blacks compared to how Kerry did in 2004, in part a result of the already very high, "preexisting" Democratic tilt of black voters as seen in previous presidential elections.

Another issue that has arisen in the course of the Democratic nomination campaign this year is the so called blue-collar vote. Clearly in the primary campaigns, Obama has done better among those with a college degree than has Clinton, and worse among those without a college degree. But a comparison of Obama's performance against McCain among educational subgroups compared to Kerry's against Bush suggests that Obama is not at an unusual deficit among those with lower levels of education.

Obama loses by a four-point, 47% to 43%, margin among those with no college. Kerry lost to Bush among those with no college by a similar six-point, 53% to 47%, margin.

Kerry and Bush tied among college graduates in 2004. In Gallup Poll Daily tracking, Obama wins by 50% to 44% among college graduates. Among those with postgraduate educations, Kerry won over Bush by 55% to 44%, or 11 points. Obama is beating McCain by 57% to 38%, or 19 points among this group. The comparative data certainly suggest that Obama actually has a relative strength among well-educated voters.

So at the moment, it would appear that Obama's problems with less well-educated voters—emphasized heavily by the Clinton campaign—are no worse than were Kerry's in 2004, and are more than made up for by Obama's strength among those with college degrees.

There has been a significant gender gap in presidential voting for at least three decades. As would be predicted, Obama wins among women by four points, 47% to 43%, in the Gallup Poll tracking data. This is very close to the three-point margin by which Kerry beat Bush among women in 2004. Obama loses among men by five points, while Kerry lost among men in 2004 by 11 points. In other words, the gender swing for Obama now is nine points, while Kerry's swing was a slightly larger 14 points.

One of the fundamental verities of American political life is the significant religion gap in party identification and in presidential voting. Republicans typically do much better among those with high self-reported church attendance. In 2004, Bush beat Kerry by 61% to 39% among those who attend church weekly. McCain is beating Obama by 55% to 36% among this group. Among those who never attend church, Kerry won big in 2004, 61% to 36%. Obama wins among this group, 54% to 36%. It appears that the religion gap is slightly more muted this year than it was in 2004.

Implications

Each presidential campaign takes place in a new and different environment, with a new cast of characters and issues. If, as expected, Obama wins the Democratic nomination this year, the campaign will have an even more distinctive newness to it, as Obama would represent the first black major-party candidate in the country's history.

Still, the analysis reviewed here suggests that the basic structure of an Obama-McCain campaign is in many ways quite similar to that of the 2004 race between Kerry and Bush.

At the moment, Gallup Poll Daily tracking indicates that this November's election could be close, as has been the popular vote in 2000 and 2004. In other words, just as 2004 was in many ways a replay of 2000, this year's election could be a replay of 2004 with minor changes around the edges.

Certainly the current data show that the patterns of support for Obama when he is pitted against McCain—among various key racial, educational, religious, and gender groups—do not look like they have changed dramatically from the 2004 contest between Kerry and Bush.

Survey Methods

Results are based on telephone interviews with 4,536 national adults, aged 18 and older, conducted May 1–5, 2008. For results based on the total sample of national adults, one can say with 95% confidence that the maximum margin of sampling error is ±2 percentage points.

Interviews are conducted with respondents on land-line telephones (for respondents with a land-line telephone) and cellular phones (for respondents who are cell-phone only).

In addition to sampling error, question wording and practical difficulties in conducting surveys can introduce error or bias into the findings of public opinion polls.

May 08, 2008
BUSH APPROVAL RATING DOWN TO 60% AMONG REPUBLICANS
New low for his administration

by Jeffrey M. Jones, Gallup Poll Managing Editor

At a time when George W. Bush's job approval rating has fallen to 28%, just 6 in 10 Republicans approve of the job he is doing, the lowest of his administration.

George W. Bush Job Approval Among Republicans, 2001-2008 Gallup Polls
Percentage who approve

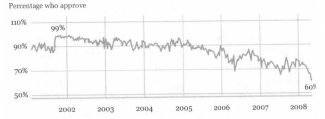

Bush has had a 28% overall job approval rating in each of the last three Gallup Polls, the worst of his administration, and the worst

for any president since Jimmy Carter's 28% approval rating in 1979. In the most recent poll, conducted May 1–3, Bush's approval rating among his own party's supporters has dropped to 60%.

Throughout his presidency, Bush has averaged 85% approval among Republicans, including a robust 92% his first term and 77% thus far in his second term. So the current figures among the GOP faithful represent a significant departure from the norm for the Bush presidency.

Lower support among Republicans is the primary mover behind the erosion in Bush's overall job approval rating in recent weeks. His approval ratings among Democrats and independents are already at low levels, and do not seem to be deteriorating much further.

George W. Bush Job Approval, Overall and by Party, Recent Gallup Polls
Numbers in percentages

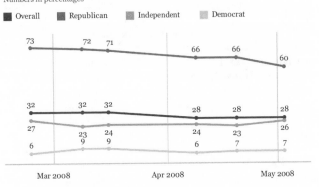

While discouraging for Bush, his 60% approval rating among his natural political base is similar to the low points for several recent presidents, including Bill Clinton, George H.W. Bush, and Gerald Ford. Dwight Eisenhower and John F. Kennedy never had very low overall approval ratings, so even their lowest ratings among their own party were still quite high (above 70%). While Ronald Reagan's job approval rating among all Americans did fall as low as 35% overall, Republicans' approval of him never fell below 67%.

Carter is the president with the dubious distinction of having the lowest job approval rating from his own party since 1953, when Gallup began to compile presidential approval ratings by party affiliation. Only 34% of Democrats approved of Carter in a pair of 1979 Gallup Polls. Carter's overall ratings at that time were similar to Bush's current overall ratings, but his ratings were not nearly as polarized along party lines as Bush's are: He did much better among Republicans than Bush is doing now among Democrats, while doing slightly better among independents than Bush is currently doing.

Lyndon Johnson and Richard Nixon also had troubled presidencies and are the only other presidents whose approval among their party's supporters fell below 50%.

Implications

George W. Bush's overall job approval rating had been running about 33% for quite a while, but has now fallen below 30% as some Republicans have stopped backing him. The most likely explanation for this loss in support could be rising gas prices, which historically have proven to act as a lead weight on presidential approval ratings.

Bush's job approval rating remains six percentage points above Harry Truman's all-time low, and if it falls below that, it will most likely do so as a result of further losses in support from his GOP base.

Lowest Approval Ratings by Own Political Party in Gallup Polls for Presidents, From Eisenhower to Bush

President	Party	Low approval by own party	Dates	Overall approval rating in poll
Eisenhower	R	79%	Mar 6-11, 1958 May 28-Jun 2, 1958 Jul 16-21, 1960	51% 54% 49%*
Kennedy	D	71%	Sep 12-17, 1963	56%*
Johnson	D	48%	Aug 7-12, 1968	35%*
Nixon	R	48%	May 10-13, 1974 Jun 21-24, 1974	25% 26%
Ford	R	57%	Jan 10-13, 1975	37%*
Carter	D	34%	Jun 29-Jul 2, 1979 Oct 5-8, 1979	28%* 29%
Reagan	R	67%	Jan 21-24, 1983	37%
G.H.W. Bush	R	57%	Jul 31-Aug 2, 1992	29%*
Clinton	D	63%	Jun 5-6, 1993	37%*
G.W. Bush	R	60%	May 1-3, 2008	28%*

*Lowest approval rating while president

Survey Methods

Results are based on telephone interviews with 1,019 national adults, aged 18 and older, conducted May 1-3, 2008. For results based on the total sample of national adults, one can say with 95% confidence that the maximum margin of sampling error is ±3 percentage points.

For results based on the sample of 287 Republicans, the maximum margin of sampling error is ±6 percentage points.

Interviews are conducted with respondents on land-line telephones (for respondents with a land-line telephone) and cellular phones (for respondents who are cell-phone only).

In addition to sampling error, question wording and practical difficulties in conducting surveys can introduce error or bias into the findings of public opinion polls.

May 09, 2008
AMERICANS CONVINCED RISE IN GAS PRICES IS PERMANENT
Seven in 10 say gas prices causing financial hardship

by Frank Newport, Gallup Poll Editor in Chief

Over three-quarters of Americans are now convinced that the rise in the price of gas is permanent, the highest such reading since Gallup began asking about gas prices in this way in 2000.

Thinking about the cost of gasoline, do you think the current rise in gas prices represents a temporary fluctuation in prices, or a more permanent change in prices?

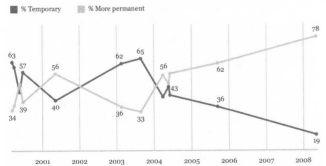

Gallup has asked this question during this decade at various times when the price of gas has gone up, and there has been considerable fluctuation in the responses. The lowest "permanent" response, 33%, was in August 2003, and the highest is the current 78%. At the moment, only 19% of Americans interviewed in the May 2-4 *USA Today*/Gallup poll believe the increase in prices is temporary. The previous "permanent" high point of 62% came in September 2005, shortly after Hurricane Katrina caused a spike in gas prices.

Underscoring this pessimism, the poll shows that over half of Americans believe the price of gasoline will reach $6 a gallon at some point over the next five years, although only 19% believe the price will reach as high as $10 a gallon.

Just your best guess, do you think the price of gasoline will reach $6 per gallon/$10 per gallon at some point over the next five years, or will the price not get that high?

Asked of half samples, May 2-4, 2008

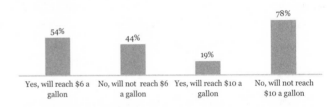

The negative impact of the rise in gas prices on Americans' daily lives is made clear in the responses to a Gallup Poll trend question that asks about financial hardship.

Have recent price increases in gasoline caused any financial hardship for you or your household?

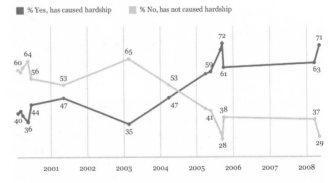

Although Americans' self-reported hardship caused by rising gas prices is very high at 71%, this is not the highest such report this question has engendered over the years Gallup has asked it. In the September 2005 post-Katrina poll, 72% of those interviewed said the increase in prices was causing hardship. That is the case even though inflation-adjusted gas prices are now the highest in history. One explanation for the lack of an increase in perceptions of hardship over the last several years may be that Americans have become habituated to the ever-rising price of gas, and perceptions of hardship may thus be leveling off as the public takes it into account in its household budgeting.

A follow-up question asked those who said gas prices have caused a hardship to indicate whether such hardship was moderate or severe.

The data show that only about 35% of those who say gas prices have caused a hardship say the hardship has been severe, meaning

(Asked of those who say gas prices have caused a hardship for them) Is that a severe hardship that affects your ability to maintain your current standard of living, or is it a moderate hardship that affects you somewhat but does not jeopardize your current standard of living?

Combined results

	Severe hardship	Moderate hardship	No hardship	No opinion
	%	%	%	%
2008 May 2-4	25	46	29	*
2008 Mar 14-16	19	44	37	*
2005 Sep 26-28	16	45	38	1
2005 Sep 12-15 ^	21	51	28	*
2005 Aug 28-30	18	51	31	*
2005 Apr 1-2	15	43	42	*

^ Asked of a half sample
* Less than 0.5%

that just 25% of the entire population says high gas prices are causing them severe financial hardship. Still, this is the highest such percentage in the six times this follow-up question has been asked.

Implications

The American public appears to be settling into the belief that the most recent run-up in gas prices is permanent, not temporary, and over half believe the price could be as high as $6 a gallon within a few years.

More than 7 out of 10 Americans say gas prices are causing them financial hardship, although the majority of these say such hardship is moderate rather than severe. The level of this self-reported increase in hardship is no higher now than it was in 2005, however, suggesting that Americans may be adjusting to or taking into account high gas prices in their daily financial dealings.

Survey Methods

Results are based on telephone interviews with 1,017 national adults, aged 18 and older, conducted May 2-4, 2008. For results based on the total sample of national adults, one can say with 95% confidence that the maximum margin of sampling error is ±3 percentage points.

For results based on the 505 national adults in the Form A half-sample and 512 national adults in the Form B half-sample, the maximum margins of sampling error are ±3 percentage points.

Interviews are conducted with respondents on land-line telephones (for respondents with a land-line telephone) and cellular phones (for respondents who are cell-phone only).

In addition to sampling error, question wording and practical difficulties in conducting surveys can introduce error or bias into the findings of public opinion polls.

May 09, 2008
MAJORITY NOW CUTTING BACK ELSEWHERE TO AFFORD GAS
Appeal of fuel-efficient cars is surging among Americans

by Lydia Saad, Gallup Poll Senior Editor

A full 60% of Americans now say they are cutting back significantly on their household spending to compensate for higher gas

prices; only 38% said this when gas prices were shooting up three years ago.

As a result of the recent rise in gas prices, would you say you have -- or have not -- done each of the following? How about -- ?

A. Cut back significantly on your household spending because of the higher gas prices

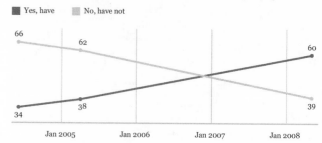

The same *USA Today*/Gallup poll, conducted May 2-4, 2008, finds more than 7 in 10 Americans saying they have seriously considered getting a more fuel-efficient car for their next vehicle. Closer to half of Americans were contemplating this at times of rising gas prices in 2004 and 2005.

As a result of the recent rise in gas prices, would you say you have -- or have not -- done each of the following? How about -- ?

B. Seriously considered getting a more fuel-efficient car the next time you buy a vehicle

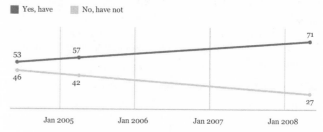

These are 2 of 10 different approaches for handling the record-high price of gas Americans were asked about in the new poll. In fact, most of the strategies have been embraced by at least half of Americans, with the most prevalent being cutting back on daily driving (mentioned by 84%) and making an effort to drive the most fuel-efficient car they own whenever possible (81%).

Additionally, at least 7 in 10 Americans say they have taken steps to increase the gas mileage of the car they already drive, have made a greater effort to find the cheapest gas they can, and have seriously considered buying a more fuel-efficient car for their next vehicle.

At least half of Americans cite carpooling, forgoing customary road trips, and cutting back on their household spending as things they are doing to deal with the rise in gas prices.

Only two approaches—switching to a lower grade of gasoline and using mass transportation or other alternate modes of travel—have been embraced by fewer than half of Americans.

The "Haves" vs. "Have-Nots" Divide

As might be expected, the prevalence of finding creative ways (like those tested in the poll) to compensate for the higher price of gas is inversely correlated with income—generally, the higher the income, the less likely Americans are to be using these strategies. However, even most high-income Americans (those with $75,000 or more in annual income) say they are trying to be more efficient with their

As a result of the recent rise in gas prices, would you say you have -- or have not -- done each of the following? How about -- [RANDOM ORDER]?

USA Today/Gallup poll, May 2-4, 2008

	Yes, have	No, have not
	%	%
Consolidated errands or taken other steps in order to cut back on your daily driving	84	16
Driven the most fuel efficient car you currently own whenever possible	81	17
Taken steps to increase the gas mileage of the car you drive, such as by driving slower, getting a tune-up, or using the air conditioning less often	76	23
Made more of an effort to find the gas station with the cheapest gas in your area	74	25
Seriously considered getting more fuel-efficient car the next time you buy a vehicle	71	27
Shared rides with friends or neighbors when you were going to the same place	62	38
Cut back significantly on your household spending because of the higher gas prices	60	39
Decided not to take a trip that you have taken regularly in previous years	51	48
Switched to using a lower grade of gasoline, such as from premium to regular	34	63
Used alternative means of travel, such as bus, subway, bicycle or walking	31	68

errands, have taken steps to increase the gas mileage of their car, are opting to drive their most fuel-efficient car when they can, and are shopping for the cheapest gas.

In a sign that expanding environmentalism in recent years may be converging with today's economic realities to redefine consumer desires, high-income Americans are actually as likely as middle- and low-income Americans (those earning less than $20,000 per year) to be considering a more fuel-efficient car for their next vehicle.

By contrast, there are substantial income gaps between high- and low-income Americans in the percentages saying they are switching to cheaper grades of gas for their car and finding alternate modes of travel.

However, two approaches for handling gas costs most strongly differentiate the economic "haves" from the "have-nots" in this time of skyrocketing fuel costs.

- Three-quarters of low-income Americans and nearly two-thirds of middle-income Americans say gas prices have compelled them to cut back on their household spending. In contrast, fewer than half of upper-income Americans say they have done this.
- Also, those in higher-income households are much less likely than middle- and low-income earners to have opted against taking a trip they would have ordinarily taken.

Bottom Line

The impact of today's high gas prices—record high in inflation-adjusted dollars—on consumers appears to be qualitatively different

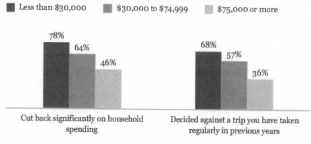

Steps Americans Have Taken as a Result of the Recent Rise in Gas Prices, by Annual Household Income

■ Less than $30,000   ■ $30,000 to $74,999   ▪ $75,000 or more

Cut back significantly on household spending: 78%, 64%, 46%

Decided against a trip you have taken regularly in previous years: 68%, 57%, 36%

USA Today/Gallup poll, May 2-4, 2008

from the impact of previous surges at the pump. It seems a tipping point has been reached.

Although the percentage of Americans saying prices are causing them severe financial hardship is not substantially higher than it has been in recent years, a much higher proportion of Americans today than in either 2004 or 2005 say they are cutting back on their household spending as a result. The same financial pressure may be boosting the mass appeal of fuel-efficient cars in the United States.

Americans of all financial means are striving to economize on their gas usage and purchases, but gas costs are having a particularly negative effect on the finances of low- and middle-income Americans. However, prices have yet to reach the point at which a majority of upper-income Americans are making significant sacrifices in their lives, such as by cutting back on household spending or canceling routine trips.

Survey Methods

Results are based on telephone interviews with 1,017 national adults, aged 18 and older, conducted May 2-4, 2008. For results based on the total sample of national adults, one can say with 95% confidence that the maximum margin of sampling error is ±3 percentage points.

Interviews are conducted with respondents on land-line telephones (for respondents with a land-line telephone) and cellular phones (for respondents who are cell-phone only).

In addition to sampling error, question wording and practical difficulties in conducting surveys can introduce error or bias into the findings of public opinion polls.

May 12, 2008

BUSH MAY BE AS HARMFUL TO MCCAIN AS WRIGHT IS TO OBAMA

One-third of likely voters say they are less likely to vote for McCain because of Bush

by Jeffrey M. Jones, Gallup Poll Managing Editor

George W. Bush may do as much damage to John McCain's chances of being elected as Jeremiah Wright does to Barack Obama's, according to results of a recent *USA Today*/Gallup poll.

The May 1-3 poll finds 38% of likely voters saying McCain's association with Bush makes them less likely to vote for McCain, while 33% say Obama's association with Wright diminishes their likelihood of voting for Obama. The Bush-McCain relationship does have more upside than the Obama-Wright association, though, as 7% say they are more likely to vote for McCain because of his association with Bush, while only 1% say they are more likely to vote for Obama because of his association with Wright.

Importantly, a majority of voters in both questions say the personal association will not affect their vote either way.

The nature of the relationships is clearly different—Wright was Obama's former pastor, while Bush and McCain were rivals for the 2000 presidential nomination but Bush has endorsed McCain in the 2008 election. But both present problems for the candidates—Wright

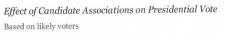

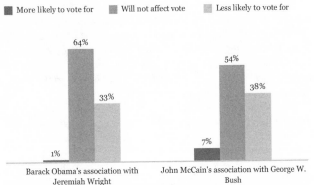

May 1-3 USA Today/Gallup poll

for his incendiary sermons and controversial remarks that have raised questions about Obama's beliefs and his personal judgment, and Bush for his low approval ratings that hurt the GOP in the 2006 elections and may well do so again in 2008.

The poll also asked how Bill Clinton might affect voters' propensity to vote for Hillary Clinton. While the 33% who say it makes them less likely to cast a ballot for Hillary for president rivals the percentages found for the McCain-Bush and Obama-Wright associations, the 18% who say it makes them more likely to vote for Hillary means Bill also helps to attract support for his wife. Just under half say the Clintons' association would not affect their vote.

Effect of Candidate Associations on Presidential Vote

Based on likely voters

Hillary Clinton's association with Bill Clinton

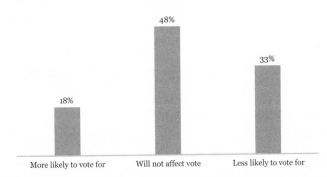

May 1-3 USA Today/Gallup poll

The percentages of voters saying they are less likely to vote for a candidate because of one of their personal associations probably overstates the true negative impact for the candidates, mainly because voters who might not seriously consider voting for a candidate in the first place (e.g., Democrats for McCain or Republicans for Obama) often respond that they are "less likely" to vote for that candidate. So it is instructive to see how the results compare among voters who are generally inclined to support a candidate—the rank-and-file of the candidate's party.

From this perspective, the data suggest that Wright may be more detrimental to Obama's candidacy than Bush is to McCain's. Nearly one-fifth of Democrats, 19%, say they are less likely to vote for Obama because of his ties to Wright (only 2% say the Wright-Obama

connection increases their odds of voting for Obama). Meanwhile, just 10% of Republicans say they are less likely to vote for McCain because of his association with Bush; about the same percentage (12%) say this relationship makes them more likely to vote for McCain.

Effect of Candidate Associations on Presidential Vote, by Political Affiliation

Based on likely voters

	More likely to vote for	Will not affect vote	Less likely to vote for
	%	%	%
Barack Obama's association with Jeremiah Wright			
Democrats/Democratic leaners	2	77	19
Republicans/Republican leaners	1	47	50
John McCain's association with George W. Bush			
Democrats/Democratic leaners	2	33	64
Republicans/Republican leaners	12	77	10
Hillary Clinton's association with Bill Clinton			
Democrats/Democratic leaners	29	54	16
Republicans/Republican leaners	5	41	53

May 1-3 USA Today/Gallup poll

It is important to note that the question asks about likelihood of voting for a candidate, so individual respondents may say that Obama's association with Wright makes them less likely to vote for Obama, but they still might vote for Obama. So in addition to measuring vote intention, the question probably also picks up some measure of enthusiasm for the candidates. As such, the actual percentages may best be thought of as a rough gauge of the risks that each of the controversial personalities poses to the respective candidate.

Implications

In general, the results are mixed as to whether Wright or Bush is a greater threat to his associate's presidential ambitions. Among the entire electorate, the two appear to be about equally damaging. In particular, Bush could hinder McCain's ability to attract independent and Democratic voters.

However, the poll suggests Obama may have a harder time holding his natural base of support given his association with Wright, and, as such, that may make Wright a greater threat to Obama than Bush is to McCain.

Survey Methods

Results are based on telephone interviews with 803 likely voters, aged 18 and older, conducted May 1-3, 2008. For results based on the total sample of national adults, one can say with 95% confidence that the maximum margin of sampling error is ±4 percentage points.

Interviews are conducted with respondents on land-line telephones (for respondents with a land-line telephone) and cellular phones (for respondents who are cell-phone only).

In addition to sampling error, question wording and practical difficulties in conducting surveys can introduce error or bias into the findings of public opinion polls.

May 13, 2008

POST-IN/NC, DEMOCRATS STILL OK WITH CONTINUING CAMPAIGN

Majority of Democrats favor Obama selecting Clinton as running mate

by Frank Newport, Gallup Poll Editor in Chief

A new *USA Today*/Gallup poll shows that 55% of Democrats say both Hillary Clinton and Barack Obama should continue campaigning for the Democratic presidential nomination, while 35% say Clinton should drop out.

In your view, what should happen now in the Democratic presidential nomination campaign?

Asked of Democrats and Democratic leaners

■ Clinton should drop out   ■ Both should continue to campaign
□ Obama should drop out

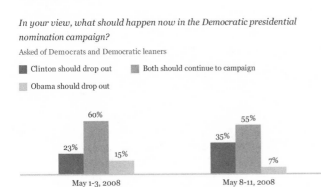

The new poll that included the update on this question was conducted May 8-11, after the North Carolina and Indiana primaries and amid much discussion in the news media about the inevitability of Obama being the nominee, given his current delegate and popular-vote count.

Compared to a May 1-3 poll conducted prior to last week's primaries, there has been a rise in the percentage of Democrats who say Clinton should drop out, and a drop in the already-small percentage who say Obama should drop out. Still, the overall structure of Democratic views has remained the same, with a majority in both of the May polls willing to sanction a continuation of the campaign.

There is—not surprisingly—a major difference in views on this issue between supporters of the two candidates. Three-quarters of Clinton supporters say she should stay in the race and that the campaign should continue (and only 14% say Obama should drop out). Six out of 10 Obama supporters, on the other hand, say Clinton should drop out, although this still leaves 39% who favor a continuation of the campaign.

In your view, what should happen now in the Democratic presidential nomination campaign?

Asked of Democrats and Democratic leaners

■ Clinton should drop out   ■ Both should continue to campaign
□ Obama should drop out

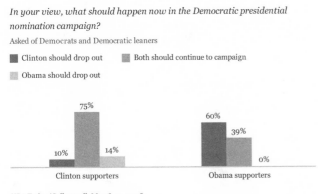

USA Today/Gallup poll, May 8-11, 2008

On the issue of whether Obama, if he wins the nomination, should choose Clinton as his running mate, a slight majority of Democrats say "yes."

If Barack Obama is the Democratic presidential nominee, would you like to see him choose Hillary Clinton as his vice presidential running mate, or would you rather he choose someone else?

Asked of Democrats and Democratic leaners

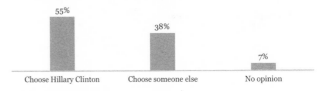

USA Today/Gallup poll, May 8-11, 2008

Fifty-five percent of Democrats say this would be a good idea, compared to 38% who think Obama should choose someone else.

There are again big differences in views on this issue between Obama supporters and Clinton supporters.

If Barack Obama is the Democratic presidential nominee, would you like to see him choose Hillary Clinton as his vice presidential running mate, or would you rather he choose someone else?

Asked of Democrats and Democratic leaners

■ Choose Hillary Clinton   □ Choose someone else   ■ No opinion

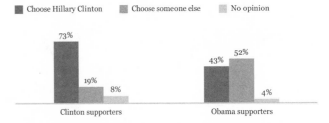

USA Today/Gallup poll, May 8-11, 2008

Clinton supporters appear enthusiastic about the idea of such an Obama-Clinton "dream ticket," with 73% saying they favor the idea. Just 19% of her supporters reject it.

Obama supporters, on the other hand, are much less enthusiastic—although a sizable 43% say they would favor it, while 52% say they would not.

Bottom Line

Despite the sense of inevitability that has settled over the assumption that Obama will be the Democratic Party's presidential nominee, and the discussion of the possible negative implications of Clinton's continuing campaign, a slight majority of Democrats continue to say both candidates should keep campaigning. About a third—most of them Obama supporters—say Clinton should drop out.

There is also strong support among Clinton supporters for her to be chosen as Obama's running mate, should he win the nomination. The data show that Obama supporters at the moment tend to reject that idea, but their opposition is not overwhelming.

Survey Methods

Results are based on telephone interviews with 1,017 national adults, aged 18 and older, conducted May 8-11, 2008. For results based on the total sample of national adults, one can say with 95% confidence that the maximum margin of sampling error is ±3 percentage points.

For results based on the sample of 537 Democrats or Democratic leaners, the maximum margin of sampling error is ±5 percentage points.

Interviews are conducted with respondents on land-line telephones (for respondents with a land-line telephone) and cellular phones (for respondents who are cell-phone only).

In addition to sampling error, question wording and practical difficulties in conducting surveys can introduce error or bias into the findings of public opinion polls.

May 13, 2008
U.S. SATISFACTION DOWN TO 14%, JUST SHY OF ALL-TIME LOW
Economy remains top problem in Americans' eyes

by Jeffrey M. Jones, Gallup Poll Managing Editor

A new Gallup Poll finds just 14% of Americans saying they are satisfied with the way things are going in the United States, two percentage points higher than the 1979 low and tied with a June 1992 rating for the second-lowest reading.

In general, are you satisfied or dissatisfied with the way things are going in the United States at this time?

■ % Satisfied

The latest results are based on a May 8-11 survey, and mark the third consecutive month that less than 20% of Americans have been satisfied with the direction of the nation. Since 1979, when Gallup first asked this question, sub-20% satisfaction levels have been rare, occurring twice in 1979, once in 1981, and four times in 1992.

The current poll finds 85% of Americans saying they are dissatisfied with the course of the nation, surpassing the previous high dissatisfaction readings from July 1979 and June 1992 by one point.

The high point in satisfaction was 71% in February 1999.

Only 6% of Democrats say they are currently satisfied with the nation's course. Twelve percent of independents and 26% of Republicans are also satisfied. Generally speaking, supporters of the president's party tend to express higher levels of satisfaction.

Economy Remains Top Problem

In addition to monthly updates on national satisfaction, each month Gallup also asks Americans to name "the most important problem facing this country" in their own words. For the fourth consecutive month, the economy in general terms tops the list, mentioned by 35% of Americans.

There were two notable movements in this month's results. The percentage of Americans naming fuel or oil prices has nearly doubled, from 9% in April to 17% in the latest poll. That does not include an additional 3% who mention the energy crisis, which effectively makes gas prices the No. 2 issue behind the economy.

Meanwhile, mentions of the Iraq war tumbled, from 23% in April to 15% this month. The percentage mentioning the war as the nation's most important problem has not been in this range since September 2005, when 16% mentioned it in the aftermath of Hurricane Katrina, and has not been lower since March 2004, when 11% did. Beginning in April 2004, Iraq ranked as the top problem (or tied for the top) each month through January 2008. The economy surpassed it in February.

Other issues that register notable public concern include healthcare (7%), unemployment (5%), dissatisfaction with government and politicians (5%), immigration (4%), and inflation (4%).

From a broad perspective, 61% of Americans mention something about the economy in any of their responses to this question, matching last month's "net economy" figure and roughly twice the percentage who did so as recently as December.

Survey Methods

Results are based on telephone interviews with 1,017 national adults, aged 18 and older, conducted May 8-11, 2008. For results based on the total sample of national adults, one can say with 95% confidence that the maximum margin of sampling error is ±3 percentage points.

Interviews are conducted with respondents on land-line telephones (for respondents with a land-line telephone) and cellular phones (for respondents who are cell-phone only).

In addition to sampling error, question wording and practical difficulties in conducting surveys can introduce error or bias into the findings of public opinion polls.

May 14, 2008
CONGRESS' APPROVAL RATING TIES LOWEST IN GALLUP RECORDS
Bush approval remains near record low

by Lydia Saad, Gallup Poll Senior Editor

Approval of Congress has dipped below 20% for only the fourth time in the 34 years Gallup has asked Americans to rate the job Congress is doing. Today's 18% score, based on a May 8-11 Gallup Poll, matches the record lows Gallup recorded in August 2007 and March 1992.

Do you approve or disapprove of the way Congress is handling its job?

■ % Approve

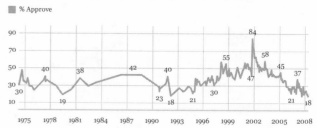

Congressional approval started off the year at a depressed 23%, then dipped to 21% in March and 20% in April, before reaching the current record-tying low. The 76% currently disapproving of Congress is just shy of the record-high 78% in March 1992.

Democrats Not Backing Congress

One reason Congress is doing so poorly in the court of public opinion is that rank-and-file Democrats are providing no support cushion for the Democratic-controlled institution. In fact, Democrats are about as likely to approve of Congress as are Republicans: 20% of Republicans approve, versus 16% of Democrats.

Not only is that true today, but it has been the pattern in Gallup's monthly approval ratings of Congress since December 2007. Prior to that—for the first 10 months of the new Democratic majority in Congress—Democrats tended to express slightly higher approval than Republicans, averaging seven points higher. However, by contrast, during most of the Republican-led Congress from 2000 to 2006, Republicans' approval of Congress was substantially higher than Democrats'.

Congressional Approval, by Party ID
May 2000-May 2008
Percentage who approve

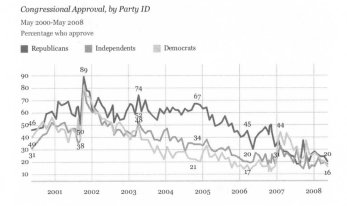

Bush Approval Now 29%

The partisan picture is quite different with respect to public approval of President George W. Bush.

The same poll finds President Bush's approval rating at 29%, only a shade above his personal worst approval score of 28%, first reached in April and repeated earlier in May. However, his rating would be even lower if not for the support of most Republicans.

Current Republican approval of Bush is much lower than it was early on in his presidency; however, it remains far better than approval from Democrats. Two-thirds of Republicans (66%) approve of Bush's job performance today, compared with only 7% of Democrats.

Bottom Line

Americans' ratings of Congress are almost always lower than their ratings of the sitting president. With Bush in a period of extremely low approval, and both houses of Congress controlled by the Democratic Party, one might expect that gap to be closer today. And, in fact, it was for a short period after the Democrats first returned to power in Congress at the start of 2007. However, that honeymoon quickly ended (about last August) and since then, Congress has lagged behind the president in approval.

Survey Methods

Results are based on telephone interviews with 1,017 national adults, aged 18 and older, conducted May 8-11, 2008. For results based on

Indicators of Americans' Mood
January 2006-May 2008
Numbers in percentages

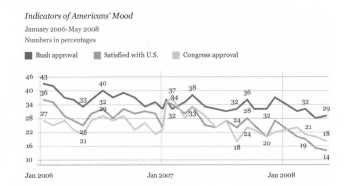

the total sample of national adults, one can say with 95% confidence that the maximum margin of sampling error is ±3 percentage points.

Interviews are conducted with respondents on land-line telephones (for respondents with a land-line telephone) and cellular phones (for respondents who are cell-phone only).

In addition to sampling error, question wording and practical difficulties in conducting surveys can introduce error or bias into the findings of public opinion polls.

May 15, 2008
CA RULING ON SAME-SEX MARRIAGE BUCKS MAJORITY VIEW
Nationally, 56% oppose legalizing same-sex marriage, but views differ regionally

by Lydia Saad, Gallup Poll Senior Editor

Even as a majority of Americans believe homosexuality ought to be an "acceptable alternative lifestyle," only 40% currently say marriage between same-sex couples should be legal; 56% disagree.

Do you think marriages between same-sex couples should or should not be recognized by the law as valid, with the same rights as traditional marriages?

Based on Form A half sample

Gallup Poll, May 8-11, 2008

The issue has been brought to the fore by Thursday's California Supreme Court decision to overturn a state ban on gay marriage, making California only the second state in the nation to legally recognize such marriages. Massachusetts blazed this trail with passage of a gay marriage act in 2004.

Public support for legalizing gay marriage is somewhat higher today than what Gallup found at the outset of polling on the subject 12 years ago. In 1996, about one in four Americans thought marriages between homosexuals should be recognized by the law as valid. That increased to 35% in 1999 and to 42% in 2004. However, for the past four years, public support has failed to grow in a linear fashion; rather, it has fluctuated between 37% and 46%.

Do you think marriages between same-sex couples should or should not be recognized by the law as valid, with the same rights as traditional marriages?

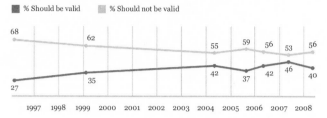

While the California and Massachusetts laws are out of step with national cultural norms on gay marriage, these states represent the two regions of the country—the West and East—that show the greatest support for legalizing gay marriage. Solid majorities of residents of the Midwest and South oppose it.

Support for Recognizing Same-Sex Marriages as Legally Valid, by Region

Gallup Poll, May 8-11, 2008

Split Decision on a Constitutional Ban

The Massachusetts gay marriage law was met by a call for a constitutional amendment in that state to define marriage as between a man and woman—something President Bush has advocated at the national level as well. There is already an initiative underway in California to put such an amendment to the state constitution on the ballot this fall.

The effort to constitutionally limit marriage to heterosexual couples failed in the Massachusetts legislature last June, but on a national basis, Gallup finds Americans evenly divided. About half (49%) favor a constitutional amendment to prevent gay marriage, while 48% are opposed.

Would you favor or oppose a constitutional amendment that would define marriage as being between a man and a woman, thus barring marriages between gay or lesbian couples?

Based on Form B half sample

Gallup Poll, May 8-11, 2008

Twenty-Six Percent vs. 2% at the Ballot Box

At the same time, politically, it seems that the anti-gay marriage faction has the advantage, benefiting from much greater intensity of feeling on the part of its supporters. One in four of those who are opposed to legal recognition of same-sex marriages (26%) say they will vote only for candidates for major office who share their view on the issue. By contrast, only 2% of those who favor making same-sex marriage legal define themselves as one-issue voters on the subject.

Would you only vote for a candidate who shares your views on gay marriage, consider a candidate's position on gay marriage as just one of many important factors when voting, or would you not see gay marriage as a major issue?

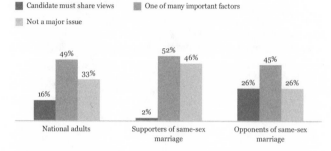

Gallup Poll, May 8-11, 2008

Tolerance for Gays

While gays battle for the right to marry, they enjoy near-universal support for equal job rights.

In general, do you think homosexuals should or should not have equal rights in terms of job opportunities?

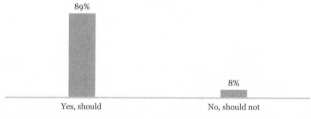

Gallup Poll, May 8-11, 2008

Also, basic acceptance of homosexuality as an alternative lifestyle has expanded over the years, after registering only 34% in 1982. Today, 57% of Americans agree that homosexuality should be considered acceptable, matching last year's record high.

Survey Methods

Results are based on telephone interviews with 1,017 national adults, aged 18 and older, conducted May 8-11, 2008. For results based on the total sample of national adults, one can say with 95% confidence that the maximum margin of sampling error is ±3 percentage points.

For results based on the 513 national adults in the Form A half-sample and 504 national adults in the Form B half-sample, the maximum margins of sampling error are ±5 percentage points.

Interviews are conducted with respondents on land-line telephones (for respondents with a land-line telephone) and cellular phones (for respondents who are cell-phone only).

Do you feel that homosexuality should be considered an acceptable alternative lifestyle or not?

■ % Acceptable　　■ % Not acceptable

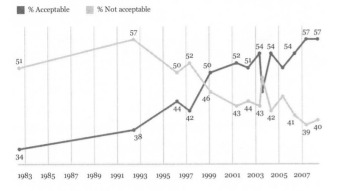

In addition to sampling error, question wording and practical difficulties in conducting surveys can introduce error or bias into the findings of public opinion polls.

May 16, 2008
U.S. JOB-MARKET PERCEPTIONS DIFFER BY POLITICAL PARTY
Nationally, 73% say now is a "bad time" to find a quality job

by Dennis Jacobe, Gallup Chief Economist

Seventy-three percent of Americans say now is a "bad time" to find a quality job—slightly better than the 75% who felt this way in April, which was the highest level since September 2003.

Is Now a Good Time or a Bad Time to Find a Quality Job?

■ % Good time　　■ % Bad time

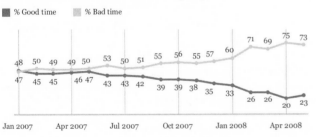

Job-Market Conditions Are Not Good

Over the first four months of this year, the U.S. economy lost more than a quarter of a million jobs. But the April jobs decline totaled only 20,000—smaller than was generally expected. In turn, some observers have interpreted this to suggest that while the labor market is weak, it is not as weak as in other economic downturns.

However, the reality is that Americans' perceptions of the job market are currently just about as bad as they've been at this time of year since Gallup began monitoring the issue in late 2001. Today's 73% of Americans rating now as a bad time to find a quality job far exceeds the 50% and 52% who felt this way in May 2007 and May 2006, respectively. In fact, it reflects the highest level of pessimism about the job market during this time of year since May 2003, when 75% held a similar opinion after the beginning of the war in Iraq.

Sixty-seven percent felt it was a bad time to find a quality job in May 2002, while just after Sept. 11, 71% felt this way in October and 75% in November 2001.

Is Now a Good Time or a Bad Time to Find a Quality Job?

■ % Good time　　■ % Bad time

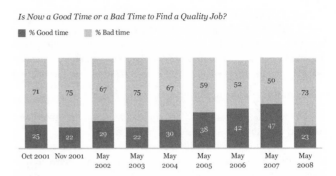

Republicans Much Less Pessimistic Than Democrats

Given the decline in manufacturing activity as reflected by the larger-than-expected 0.7% drop in U.S. industrial production, it is not surprising that job-market perceptions are worse in the Midwest (78%) and the East (76%) than in the South (72%) and the West (68%). Similarly, more lower-income (74%) and middle-income (79%) Americans rate this as a bad time to find a quality job than do those with higher incomes (68%).

However, the largest differences in job-market perceptions appear by political affiliation. Republicans are least pessimistic about current labor-market conditions, with 57% saying it is a bad time to find a quality job. A much-higher 86% of Democrats feel this way, along with 72% of independents.

Is Now a Good Time or a Bad Time to Find a Quality Job?

■ % Good time　　■ % Bad time

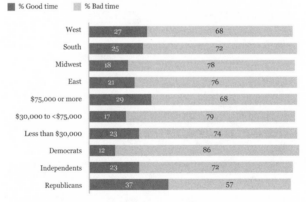

Gallup Poll, May 8-11, 2008

Commentary

While most Americans have concluded that the U.S. economy is already experiencing a recession, economists continue to debate the issue. Those who do not believe the United States is in a recession point to, among other things, the job market. For example, they see that initial jobless claims rose last week to 371,000, while the four-week moving average fell by 1,000 to 365,750, and they say job losses simply aren't at recessionary levels.

On the other side of the argument are those who suggest that today's job losses are different from past losses. Many companies appear to have entered this economic slowdown operating with much leaner staffing levels than in the past. In part, this may be because of increased globalization and job outsourcing that have allowed firms to grow while adding fewer employees. In turn, this seems to have made it easier for many companies to reduce their staffing through normal attrition as opposed to layoffs.

Whatever the reasons, Gallup's measurement of Americans' job-market perceptions tends to support the idea that current labor-market conditions are just about as bad as they've been at any time this decade. The only possible exception would be in 2003, before and after the beginning of the Iraq war, when the percentage of Americans saying it was a bad time to find a quality job actually hit 81% on two occasions. But even in May of that year, 75% of Americans held the view that it was not a good time to find a quality job.

At this point, the sharp disagreement in job-market perceptions among Republicans as opposed to Democrats is likely to make jobs an election-year issue. Whether federal rebate checks will improve current job-market conditions and ameliorate the issue, even temporarily, is yet to be seen. On the other hand, if the job situation continues to deteriorate, jobs are likely to become a much bigger election-year issue. Then, economists who currently doubt whether a recession is underway may find they agree with the majority of Americans who think the only real issue is how severe the current recession will be.

Survey Methods

Results are based on telephone interviews with 1,017 national adults, aged 18 and older, conducted May 8-11, 2008. For results based on the total sample of national adults, one can say with 95% confidence that the maximum margin of sampling error is ±3 percentage points.

Interviews are conducted with respondents on land-line telephones (for respondents with a land-line telephone) and cellular phones (for respondents who are cell-phone only).

In addition to sampling error, question wording and practical difficulties in conducting surveys can introduce error or bias into the findings of public opinion polls.

May 19, 2008
CULTURAL TOLERANCE FOR DIVORCE GROWS TO 70%
Along with polygamy, extramarital affairs are one of the least accepted acts

by Lydia Saad, Gallup Poll Senior Editor

More Americans than ever believe divorce is morally acceptable, with the percentage who say this jumping to 70% in Gallup's 2008 Values and Beliefs survey, up from 59% in 2001, and breaking the previous high of 67% in 2006.

Notably, while divorce tops Gallup's 2008 list of 16 ethical issues rated for moral acceptability, one of the main reasons many couples seek divorce—because one or both spouses have had an extramarital affair—is at the bottom.

Tolerance for divorce is comparable to public acceptance of gambling, the death penalty, embryonic stem-cell research, and premarital sex. However, married men and women having an affair is tied with polygamy in last place, and ranks just slightly below cloning humans and suicide in perceived moral acceptability.

Opinion of Divorce

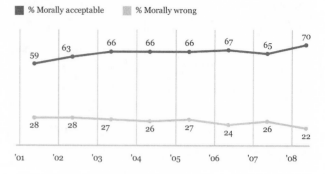

Next, I'm going to read you a list of issues. Regardless of whether or not you think it should be legal, for each one, please tell me whether you personally believe that in general it is morally acceptable or morally wrong.

	Morally acceptable	Morally wrong
	%	%
Divorce	70	22
Gambling	63	32
The death penalty	62	30
Medical research using stem cells obtained from human embryos	62	30
Sex between an unmarried man and woman	61	36
Medical testing on animals	56	38
Having a baby outside of marriage	55	41
Buying and wearing clothing made of animal fur	54	39
Doctor-assisted suicide	51	44
Homosexual relations	48	48
Abortion	40	48
Cloning animals	33	61
Suicide	15	78
Cloning humans	11	85
Polygamy, when one husband has more than one wife at the same time	8	90
Married men and women having an affair	7	91

Gallup Poll, May 8-11, 2008

Trend in Acceptance of Divorce

Since 2001, acceptance of divorce has risen across society, and, as a result, it is now considered morally acceptable by a majority of nearly every major demographic category of Americans. This is a shift from 2001, when fewer than half of adults aged 65 and older, Republicans, self-described political "conservatives," and highly religious Americans thought divorce was acceptable.

Tolerance of divorce continues to be higher among younger adults compared with those 65 and older. Also, conservatives show far less support than do self-described moderates and liberals. And barely half of Americans who say religion is very important in their lives believe divorce is morally acceptable, compared with virtually all non-religious Americans.

Other Findings

Divorce is the only issue measured in Gallup's 2008 Values and Beliefs survey for which U.S. public opinion has changed to a significant degree over the past year. However, compared with 2001, Americans have also become more accepting of sex between unmarried men and women, and homosexual relations. (Changes of fewer than five percentage points are not statistically significant.) They have become less accepting of medical testing on animals, and the use of animal fur for clothing—although the majority still support both.

Percentage Calling Divorce "Morally Acceptable"

	May 2001	May 2008	Change
	%	%	Pct. pts.
Men	63	70	+7
Women	56	69	+13
18 to 29	61	71	+10
30 to 49	65	74	+9
50 to 64	58	71	+13
65 and older	43	57	+14
East	63	68	+5
Midwest	63	71	+8
South	54	69	+15
West	57	72	+15
Republican	48	61	+13
Independent	69	74	+5
Democrat	59	72	+13
Conservative	49	57	+8
Moderate	63	72	+9
Liberal	72	87	+15
Protestant	53	65	+12
Catholic	60	75	+15
Importance of Religion			
Very important	47	55	+8
Fairly important	74	83	+9
Not very important	79	91	+12

Percentage Calling Each Issue "Morally Acceptable"

Based on national adults

	May 2001	May 2008	Change
	%	%	Pct. pts.
Divorce	59	70	+11
Sex between an unmarried man and woman	53	61	+8
Homosexual relations	40	48	+8
Cloning humans	7	11	+4
Doctor-assisted suicide	49	51	+2
Cloning animals	31	33	+2
Suicide	13	15	+2
Married men and women having an affair	7	7	0
Death penalty	63	62	-1
Abortion	42	40	-2
Buying and wearing clothing made of animal fur	60	54	-6
Medical testing on animals	65	56	-9

Only items measured in both May 2001 and May 2008 are shown

Bottom Line

People going through divorce often deal with a range of difficult emotions, including anger, sadness, trepidation, remorse, and a sense of failure. One issue becoming less and less a factor in that gut-wrenching mix is the sting of moral condemnation.

Survey Methods

Results are based on telephone interviews with 1,017 national adults, aged 18 and older, conducted May 8-11, 2008. For results based on the total sample of national adults, one can say with 95% confidence that the maximum margin of sampling error is ±3 percentage points.

Interviews are conducted with respondents on land-line telephones (for respondents with a land-line telephone) and cellular phones (for respondents who are cell-phone only).

In addition to sampling error, question wording and practical difficulties in conducting surveys can introduce error or bias into the findings of public opinion polls.

May 20, 2008
KEY CLINTON CONSTITUENCIES MOVING TOWARD OBAMA
Obama now competitive among women, whites, and the less educated

by Lydia Saad, Gallup Poll Senior Editor

Gallup Poll Daily tracking has documented a surge in Democratic voters' support for Barack Obama over Hillary Clinton in recent days, swelling from a four percentage-point lead for Obama during the first part of May to a record 16-point lead for him in polling from May 16-18.

2008 Democratic Presidential Nomination Preferences

Based on Democratic voters and voters who lean Democratic

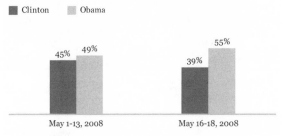

Gallup Poll Daily tracking

Prior to now, Obama's largest lead over Clinton was 11 percentage points, achieved briefly in mid-April. However, for most of the past month, Clinton and Obama have been fairly closely matched, with neither sustaining a significant lead for more than a few days. It thus remains to be seen whether this improvement in Obama's standing is a variation of the same pattern, or represents a turning point in the race.

Obama Swamps Clinton Among Young Voters and Others

The broadening of Obama's appeal for the nomination seen in Gallup's May 16-18 polling is fairly widespread, with the percentage favoring him increasing among most demographic categories of Democratic voters. However, as a result, certain groups that were already highly supportive of Obama for the nomination—men, 18-to 29-year-olds, postgrads, and upper-income Democrats—are now overwhelmingly in his camp. Obama is currently favored among these groups by a 2-to-1 margin, or better, over Clinton.

At the same time, support for Clinton among some of her traditionally stalwart support groups—women, Easterners, whites, adults with no college education, and Hispanics—has fallen below 50%.

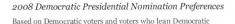

2008 Democratic Presidential Nomination Preferences

Based on Democratic voters and voters who lean Democratic

■ Clinton   ■ Obama

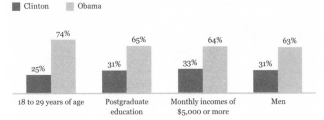

| 18 to 29 years of age | Postgraduate education | Monthly incomes of $5,000 or more | Men |

Gallup Poll Daily tracking, May 16-18, 2008

2008 Democratic Presidential Nomination Preferences

Based on Democratic voters and voters who lean Democratic

■ Clinton   ■ Obama

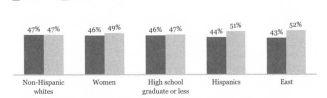

| Non-Hispanic whites | Women | High school graduate or less | Hispanics | East |

Gallup Poll Daily tracking, May 16-18, 2008

The only major demographic group still supporting Clinton to the tune of 51% or more is women aged 50 and older. This group's preferences have changed little during May, at the same time that Clinton's support among younger men (those 18 to 49) has declined by nearly 10 points.

Percentage Favoring Hillary Clinton for 2008 Democratic Presidential Nomination

Based on Democratic voters and voters who lean Democratic

■ May 1-13, 2008   ■ May 16-18, 2008

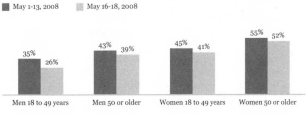

| Men 18 to 49 years | Men 50 or older | Women 18 to 49 years | Women 50 or older |

Gallup Poll Daily tracking

Bottom Line

After nearly 20 grueling weeks on the campaign trail since he shook up the Democratic primary race by winning the Iowa caucuses, Obama has finally stretched his lead over his chief rival into the teens.

Having previously captured nearly the maximum level of support from black voters, Obama's latest gains have come from a broad spectrum of rank-and-file Democrats. At least for now, he has expanded his position as the preferred candidate of men, young adults, and highly educated Democrats, and has erased Clinton's advantages with most of her prior core constituency groups, including women, the less well-educated, and whites.

Survey Methods

For the Gallup Poll Daily tracking survey, Gallup is interviewing no fewer than 1,000 U.S. adults nationwide each day during 2008.

The Democratic nomination results for May 1-13, 2008, are based on interviews with 5,474 Democratic and Democratic-leaning voters. The maximum margin of sampling error for samples of this size is ±1 percentage point.

The Democratic nomination results for May 16-18, 2008, are based on interviews with 1,261 Democratic and Democratic-leaning voters. The maximum margin of sampling error for samples of this size is ±3 percentage points.

May 21, 2008
OBAMA FACES UPHILL CLIMB VS. MCCAIN AMONG WHITE VOTERS
Among white women, Obama in tougher position than Clinton would be

by Frank Newport, Gallup Poll Editor in Chief

Barack Obama, the presumed Democratic nominee, will likely enter the general election with more of a handicap among white voters than would have been the case if Hillary Clinton had been the nominee, based mainly on Clinton's stronger performance among white women.

Who would you support if Barack Obama were the Democratic candidate and John McCain the Republican?

Who would you support if Hillary Clinton were the Democratic candidate and John McCain the Republican?

Among non-Hispanic whites

■ Barack Obama   ■ John McCain   ■ Hillary Clinton

| Obama vs. McCain | McCain vs. Clinton |

Based on registered voters
Gallup Poll Daily tracking, May 1-17, 2008

A new Gallup Poll analysis of Daily tracking data collected between May 1 and May 17 shows that Clinton's edge among white voters is not, as some have hypothesized, based on Obama's problems among blue-collar white men, but reflects more the fact of Clinton's strength among white women.

White Male Voters

In general, Obama and Clinton perform exactly the same among non-Hispanic white men when pitted against presumptive Republican nominee John McCain. Both Obama and Clinton lose to McCain among this group by 21-point margins, 36% to 57%.

There has been discussion of Obama's presumed problem among blue-collar white males should he win the Democratic nomination. The current analysis shows that relative to Clinton, however, Obama does not suffer from a large "blue-collar male" deficit as has been hypothesized. Obama loses to McCain in a hypothetical

Who would you support if Barack Obama were the Democratic candidate and John McCain the Republican?

Who would you support if Hillary Clinton were the Democratic candidate and John McCain the Republican?

Among non-Hispanic white men

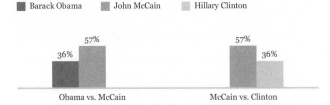

Based on registered voters
Gallup Poll Daily tracking, May 1-17, 2008

matchup among non-college-educated white men by 25 points, while Clinton loses by 20 points.

Who would you support if Barack Obama were the Democratic candidate and John McCain the Republican?

Who would you support if Hillary Clinton were the Democratic candidate and John McCain the Republican?

Among non-Hispanic white men -- no college education

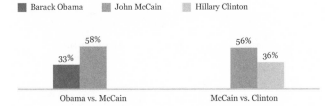

Based on registered voters
Gallup Poll Daily tracking, May 1-17, 2008

Additionally, Obama has a compensatory strength among white-collar men, defined here as those with a college education. Among this group, Obama loses to McCain by 13 points while Clinton loses by 22 points.

Who would you support if Barack Obama were the Democratic candidate and John McCain the Republican?

Who would you support if Hillary Clinton were the Democratic candidate and John McCain the Republican?

Among non-Hispanic white men -- college-educated

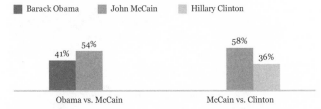

Based on registered voters
Gallup Poll Daily tracking, May 1-17, 2008

All in all, these data suggest that the Democrats' probable nomination of Obama rather than Clinton does not mean Democrats will enter the general election with a bigger deficit among white men than they would have if Clinton were the nominee. The data from May suggest that Clinton may have done only slightly better than Obama against McCain among blue-collar white men, and that this slight advantage likely would have been offset by Obama's slight advantage among college-educated men.

White Female Voters

Among non-Hispanic white women, however, there is a significant difference in the way the two Democratic candidates perform against McCain.

Who would you support if Barack Obama were the Democratic candidate and John McCain the Republican?

Who would you support if Hillary Clinton were the Democratic candidate and John McCain the Republican?

Among non-Hispanic white women

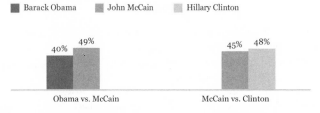

Based on registered voters
Gallup Poll Daily tracking, May 1-17, 2008

Both Obama and Clinton do better among white women than among white men vs. McCain—a typical pattern for Democratic presidential candidates. But there are differences between the two Democratic candidates. While Obama loses to McCain by a nine-point margin among white women, Clinton wins by a three-point margin.

This difference persists when white women are segmented into two groups by education.

Who would you support if Barack Obama were the Democratic candidate and John McCain the Republican?

Who would you support if Hillary Clinton were the Democratic candidate and John McCain the Republican?

Among non-Hispanic white women -- no college education

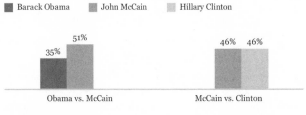

Based on registered voters
Gallup Poll Daily tracking, May 1-17, 2008

While Obama loses to McCain by 16 points among non-Hispanic white women with no college, Clinton ties McCain. And while

Obama does manage to squeak out a four-point advantage over McCain among college-educated white women, Clinton has an 11-point margin.

Who would you support if Barack Obama were the Democratic candidate and John McCain the Republican?

Who would you support if Hillary Clinton were the Democratic candidate and John McCain the Republican?

Among non-Hispanic white women -- college-educated

Based on registered voters
Gallup Poll Daily tracking, May 1-17, 2008

Implications

Although there has been a great deal of discussion of the problems that await Obama among white men should he win the Democratic nomination, this analysis suggests that while McCain certainly has a strength among this group, it is no more of a strength against Obama than it would be against Clinton. Clinton's slight advantage among blue-collar white men is offset by Obama's advantage among white-collar white men.

The bigger issue appears to be Obama's problems among white women, when compared to how Clinton would perform among this group. Obama loses to McCain by nine points among white women, while Clinton wins by three points. Clinton does better than Obama among both blue-collar and white-collar white women.

All in all, although both Democrats are to a degree handicapped against McCain among white voters, Clinton would perform better than Obama in a general-election matchup among non-Hispanic whites. Combining white voters of both genders, the current analysis shows that McCain wins over Obama among whites, 53% to 38%, and beats Clinton by a considerably smaller 51% to 42% margin.

It is important to note that Obama runs about as well vs. McCain as Clinton does, and both Democrats currently maintain a slight advantage over McCain in general-election trial heats. So any weaker relative performance for Obama vs. McCain among a demographic group (such as white women or lower-educated voters) is made up for by a stronger relative performance among another group (such as blacks or higher-educated voters).

Survey Methods

Results are based on telephone interviews with 14,755 national adults who report being registered to vote, aged 18 and older, conducted May 1-17, 2008, as part of the Gallup Poll Daily tracking program. For results based on the total sample of national adults, one can say with 95% confidence that the maximum margin of sampling error is ±1 percentage point.

Interviews are conducted with respondents on land-line telephones (for respondents with a land-line telephone) and cellular phones (for respondents who are cell-phone only).

In addition to sampling error, question wording and practical difficulties in conducting surveys can introduce error or bias into the findings of public opinion polls.

May 21, 2008
U.S. HIRING SLIPS FURTHER, SUGGESTS MORE JOB LOSSES AHEAD
Gallup Poll Daily surveys indicate that May could show the fourth consecutive monthly decline

by Dennis Jacobe, Gallup Chief Economist

Gallup's "Net New Hiring Activity" measure fell 1.1 percentage points from March to April, followed by a 3.6-point decline between April and the week of May 12-18—continuing the trend of steady declines since the beginning of the year.

Change in Net New Hiring Activity

In percentage points

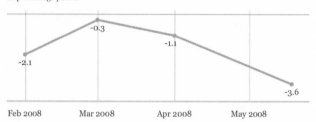

Job Growth Declining in April and Early May

Economic activity may be slowing more significantly than generally expected, based on Gallup's Net New Hiring Activity measures for April and May, with both months showing substantial declines. Gallup's Net New Hiring Activity measure is an effort to assess U.S. job creation or elimination based on a survey of more than 8,000 individual workers each month. In order to calculate this measure, Gallup asks current full-time employees whether their employers are hiring new people and expanding the size of their workforces, not changing the size of their workforces, or letting people go and reducing the size of their workforces. Net new hiring activity is computed by subtracting the "letting go and reducing" percentage from the "hiring and expanding" percentage.

Over the first four months of this year, the percentage of employees saying their companies are hiring has fallen from 39.8% in January to 38.1% in April. At the same time, the percentage of employees reporting that their firms are letting people go has increased from 13.7% to 15.5%. Although Gallup's weekly measurements (based on interviews with roughly 2,000 employees) tend to show more fluctuation than the monthly measurements, results for the week of May 12-18 show another sharp drop in net new hiring activity, with the percentage of companies hiring falling to 36.6% and the percentage letting people go increasing to 17.6%. The resulting drop in net new hiring activity of 3.6 points is greater than the large decline that took place between January and February.

Net New Hiring Activity by Region

On a regional basis, the East has suffered the most from the recent financial crisis, with many financial services firms announcing lay-

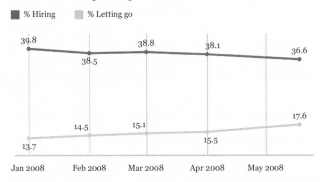

U.S. Net New Hiring Activity

■ % Hiring   ▨ % Letting go

offs. The 4.8 percentage-point decline in net new hiring activity between January and April reflects the significant impact on employment that has taken place. In fact, the added 2.2-point decline for mid-May suggests that while the credit markets may be stabilizing, the fallout from the credit crisis on employment is continuing.

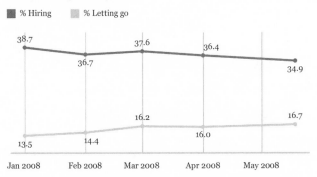

Net New Hiring Activity, East

■ % Hiring   ▨ % Letting go

Net new hiring activity in the Midwest has fluctuated somewhat more than in other regions. Between January and February, net new hiring activity fell by 4.4 percentage points, reflecting the continued job stress in this region of the country. Job activity seemed to stabilize and even improve in April, perhaps in response to increasing export activity, but has fallen to its lowest level of the year in mid-May. The May decline seems consistent with a lagging response to the larger-than-expected 0.7% drop in industrial production in April announced by the Federal Reserve Board last week.

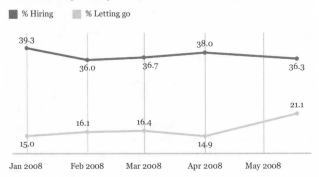

Net New Hiring Activity, Midwest

■ % Hiring   ▨ % Letting go

Net new hiring activity has fallen steadily in the South; this trend has continued in April. May results show a much bigger drop of 8.3

points in net new hiring activity—this is something that will need to be watched for further confirmation in the next few months.

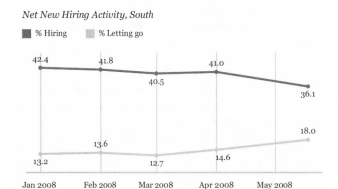

Net New Hiring Activity, South

■ % Hiring   ▨ % Letting go

Net new hiring activity in the West had fallen between January and March, although more moderately than in the other regions of the country. In April, job-market activity seemed to drop sharply, but May results actually show an improvement that more than offset the April decline as opposed to confirming it. Given these fluctuations, future results will need to clarify the actual trend in job activity in the West.

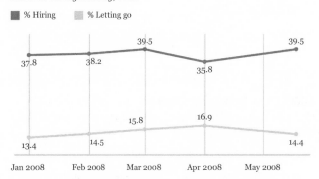

Net New Hiring Activity, West

■ % Hiring   ▨ % Letting go

Jobs Losses Will Add to Consumer Woes

On Monday, the National Association for Business Economics reported that 56% of the economists surveyed say the United States is in or will have a recession this year, suggesting they are less convinced than the general public that the current economic downturn has reached recessionary levels. The survey also suggested that the U.S. economy will be out of recession by September, with growth picking up to 2.1% in the second half of this year.

While employment measures tend to be trailing economic indicators, reflecting past levels of economic performance, Gallup's Net New Hiring Activity measure suggests that many consumers are just now beginning to feel the cumulative effects of the current economic downturn in terms of the job market. In fact, the mid-May results may mean the job losses associated with slowing economic activity may simply be lagging behind as opposed to structurally different from those of the past. Further, Gallup's Net New Hiring Activity measure is not seasonally adjusted, so the decline in job market activity it reflects may actually be more severe than when seasonal hiring needs are taken into account.

Right now, Gallup's consumer confidence measures reflect the fact that the consumer faces numerous significant economic headwinds, ranging from surging food and energy prices to falling real estate values and tightening credit-market conditions. Add a significant decline in May job growth as suggested by Gallup's Net New Hiring Activity measure and even today's reduced expectations for consumer spending in the months ahead may turn out to be optimistic.

Survey Methods

Gallup is interviewing no fewer than 1,000 U.S. adults nationwide each day during 2008. The economic questions analyzed in this report are asked of a random half-sample of respondents each day. The results reported here are based on combined data of more than 8,000 interviews each in January, February, March, and April 2008. For results based on these samples, the maximum margin of sampling error is ±1 percentage point.

Results based on the sample of 2,136 national adults for the week of May 12-18, 2008, have a maximum margin of error of ±2 percentage points.

Margins of error for the regional breaks are higher.

Interviews are conducted with respondents on land-line telephones (for respondents with a land-line telephone) and cellular phones (for respondents who are cell-phone only).

In addition to sampling error, question wording and practical difficulties in conducting surveys can introduce error or bias into the findings of public opinion polls.

May 22, 2008
ABORTION ISSUE LAYING LOW IN 2008 CAMPAIGN
Few Americans say candidates' abortion views are critical to their vote

by Lydia Saad, Gallup Poll Senior Editor

Once the 2008 presidential race shifts from the nomination phase to the general election, the differences between John McCain and the Democrats on abortion will likely come into better focus for most voters. Currently, just 13% of Americans say they will vote only for a candidate who shares their views on abortion, while another 49% say it will be just one of many important factors.

Thinking about how the abortion issue might affect your vote for major offices, would you -- [only vote for a candidate who shares your views on abortion (or) consider a candidate's position on abortion as just one of many important factors (or) not see abortion as a major issue]?

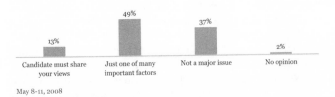

May 8-11, 2008

Single-issue abortion voters are in scarce supply, particularly compared with May 2001, when 20% identified themselves as such. But today's 13% is not atypical of results found in the first half of previous presidential election years. In May 2004, only 14% of Ameri-

cans said a candidate must share their views on abortion; that rose to 17% by October 2004. In March 2000, the figure was only 15%.

Impact of Abortion Issue on Voting for Major Offices

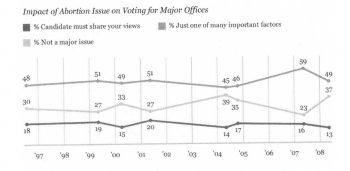

According to Gallup's annual Values and Beliefs survey, updated May 8-11, Americans as a whole are slightly more likely to call themselves "pro-choice" on abortion than "pro-life," 50% to 44%. This is nearly identical to where Americans stood on the issue a year ago, and is similar to the close division seen since 1998. Prior to that (from about 1995 to 1997) Gallup found a stronger pro-choice tilt.

Trend in Pro-Choice/Pro-Life Abortion Views

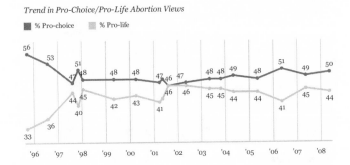

The current poll finds no difference between men and women in the percentages calling themselves pro-choice and pro-life. Americans 55 and older are a bit more "pro-life" than those aged 18 to 34 and 35 to 54. Much greater differences are seen by personal ideology and party affiliation. Three-quarters of liberals and 6 in 10 Democrats call themselves pro-choice, compared with only about 30% of Republicans and conservatives. Independents and moderates fall closer to the Democrats in their views.

As to how the issue will play in regional campaigning, a majority of residents of the East and West are pro-choice, while residents of the South are mostly pro-life and those in the Midwest are evenly split.

Calculating the Abortion Factor

Traditionally, Gallup has found more pro-life than pro-choice adherents saying a candidate must share their abortion views. The gaps were particularly wide in July 1996 and October 2004. In those two cases, only about 10% of pro-choice Americans, but more than 20% of pro-life persons, said a candidate must share their views.

This conforms with historical exit-poll information about the influence of the abortion issue on voters. From 1984 through 2000, the presidential exit polls asked voters to name the most important issues to their vote. As the accompanying table shows, for all five presidential elections in this period, the majority of voters citing abor-

Position on Abortion

	"Pro-choice"	"Pro-life"
	%	%
Men	49	46
Women	50	43
18 to 34	53	43
35 to 54	53	42
55+	44	48
Republican	30	66
Independent	54	38
Democrat	59	35
Conservative	29	66
Moderate	55	38
Liberal	75	20
East	54	41
Midwest	48	46
South	42	52
West	59	35

May 8-11, 2008

Abortion as Voting Issue Based on Abortion Position

	Jul 1996	Mar 2000	May 2004	Oct 2004	May 2008
	%	%	%	%	%
"PRO-CHOICE"					
Must share views	12	13	11	10	11
One of many important issues	52	50	45	49	49
Not a major issue	34	36	43	41	39
"PRO-LIFE"					
Must share views	22	18	17	28	15
One of many important issues	53	54	47	45	53
Not a major issue	21	26	35	25	31

May 8-11, 2008

tion said they were supporting the Republican candidate for president. Thus, while the overall percentage of voters mentioning abortion in each case was small, the issue netted the Republican Party's candidate two to three points in the election. (No comparable exit-poll data are available for 2004.)

Presidential Vote Choice Among Those Citing Abortion as One of Most Important Issues to Their Vote

Based on presidential election exit-poll surveys*

	Voters naming abortion as top voting issue	Voted for the Republican	Voted for the Democrat	Net voters for the Republican
	%	%	%	pct. pts.
2000	14	58	41	+2.4
1996	9	60	34	+2.3
1992	12	55	36	+2.3
1988	7	65	33	+2.2
1984	8	71	28	+3.4

* 1984 and 1988 are from CBS/New York Times Exit Poll surveys; 1992 is from Voter Research and Surveys Exit Poll; 1996 and 2000 are from Los Angeles Times Exit Poll surveys.

Today, pro-choice and pro-life Americans are fairly similar in their responses to Gallup's voting question. Only when factoring in

the percentage saying abortion is one of many important issues they consider do pro-life persons register as more activated to vote on abortion (68% vs. 60%).

Bottom Line

Abortion has been an important element in the Republican campaign playbook going back to Ronald Reagan's 1980 presidential campaign. Exit polls and Gallup data since 1984 indicate the issue has attracted more voters to the "pro-life" candidate (i.e., the Republicans) than it pushed away, and it has possibly helped drive up Republican turnout. However, at this point in the 2008 campaign, the issue appears to be of relatively low salience to Americans, and it is giving pro-life candidates only a slight advantage, at best.

Survey Methods

Results are based on telephone interviews with 1,017 national adults, aged 18 and older, conducted May 8-11, 2008. For results based on the total sample of national adults, one can say with 95% confidence that the maximum margin of sampling error is ±3 percentage points.

Interviews are conducted with respondents on land-line telephones (for respondents with a land-line telephone) and cellular phones (for respondents who are cell-phone only).

In addition to sampling error, question wording and practical difficulties in conducting surveys can introduce error or bias into the findings of public opinion polls.

May 23, 2008
TYPICAL MARRIAGE GAP EVIDENT IN EARLY 2008 VOTE
Clinton competitive with McCain for married women's votes

by Jeffrey M. Jones, Gallup Poll Managing Editor

The Democratic candidates lead Republican John McCain among unmarried voters, while McCain bests both Barack Obama and Hillary Clinton among married voters.

General Election Vote Preference by Marital Status, Obama vs. McCain

Based on registered voters

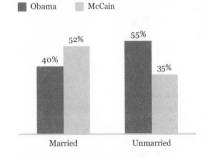

Gallup Poll Daily tracking, May 1-21, 2008

These results, based on interviews with more than 18,000 registered voters from Gallup Poll Daily tracking in May, are similar to what Gallup has observed in recent presidential elections.

Marital Status, Clinton vs. McCain

Based on registered voters

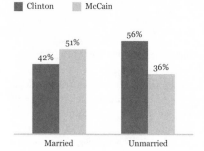

■ Clinton ▨ McCain

42% 51% 56% 36%

Married   Unmarried

Gallup Poll Daily tracking, May 1-21, 2008

General Election Vote Preference by Marital Status and Gender, Clinton vs. McCain

Based on registered voters

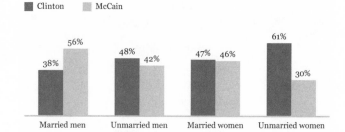

■ Clinton ▨ McCain

38% 56% 48% 42% 47% 46% 61% 30%

Married men   Unmarried men   Married women   Unmarried women

Gallup Poll Daily tracking, May 1-21, 2008

In the last three presidential elections, the Republican candidate has fared better among married voters of either gender—winning all of the marriage-by-gender groups except married women in 1996, which Bob Dole lost narrowly to Bill Clinton. Meanwhile, the Democratic candidate has won among unmarried voters of both genders in all three elections since 1996. (Gallup does not have data for the vote by marital status prior to the 1996 election.)

Usually, of the four marriage-by-gender groups, married men show the greatest support for the Republican candidate and unmarried women most strongly back the Democratic candidate. The degree to which those relationships hold in 2008 depends in part on which candidate the Democrats eventually nominate.

If, as seems likely, Obama is the Democratic nominee, he would enter the general-election phase of the campaign with commanding leads among both unmarried men and unmarried women. He leads McCain by 23 percentage points among unmarried women and by 16 points among unmarried men.

In turn, McCain outpolls Obama by a wide 17-point margin among married men, but holds a smaller 6-point advantage among married women.

General Election Vote Preference by Marital Status and Gender, Obama vs. McCain

Based on registered voters

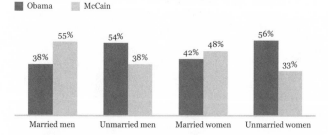

■ Obama ▨ McCain

38% 55% 54% 38% 42% 48% 56% 33%

Married men   Unmarried men   Married women   Unmarried women

Gallup Poll Daily tracking, May 1-21, 2008

The picture would look somewhat different if Clinton were the Democratic nominee. She would, like Obama, lead McCain among both unmarried groups, but by a larger margin among unmarried women (31 points) and by a smaller margin among unmarried men (6 points). McCain would fare just as well among married men vs. Clinton as he does against Obama, but these data suggest Clinton and McCain would be highly competitive for the votes of married women.

No doubt these relationships reflect Clinton's appeal to female voters, who have been among her most reliable supporters in the Democratic primaries. It is unclear whether Obama would be able to increase his standing among female voters if he were the Democratic nominee. But any disadvantage he has among female voters he has tended to make up for with greater support among blacks and young people.

Implications

These results suggest that the marriage gap evident in the past few elections will likely persist in 2008 as well, with McCain typically leading among married voters and the Democratic candidate leading among unmarried voters. Of the four marriage-by-gender groups, married women seem to be the most competitive, with Clinton and McCain essentially running even and McCain holding only a modest lead versus Obama among this group.

Survey Methods

Results are based on telephone interviews with 18,462 registered voters nationwide, aged 18 and older, conducted May 1-21, 2008, as part of Gallup's daily tracking survey. For results based on the total sample of national adults, one can say with 95% confidence that the maximum margin of sampling error is ±1 percentage point.

For results based on the sample of 6,085 registered voters who are married men, the maximum margin of sampling error is ±1 percentage point.

For results based on the sample of 2,965 registered voters who are unmarried men, the maximum margin of sampling error is ±2 percentage points.

For results based on the sample of 4,539 registered voters who are married women, the maximum margin of sampling error is ±2 percentage points.

For results based on the sample of 4,762 registered voters who are unmarried women, the maximum margin of sampling error is ±2 percentage points.

Interviews are conducted with respondents on land-line telephones (for respondents with a land-line telephone) and cellular phones (for respondents who are cell-phone only).

In addition to sampling error, question wording and practical difficulties in conducting surveys can introduce error or bias into the findings of public opinion polls.

May 27, 2008

SIX IN 10 DEMOCRATS CONFIDENT OF VICTORY IN 2008 ELECTION

Only 39% of Republicans are confident the GOP will win

by Jeffrey M. Jones, Gallup Poll Managing Editor

Democrats are much more confident that their party will win the November presidential election than are Republicans.

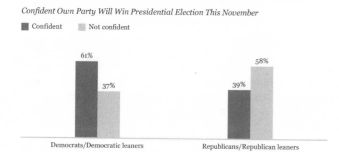

Confident Own Party Will Win Presidential Election This November

■ Confident   ■ Not confident

Gallup Poll, May 19-21, 2008

A new Gallup Panel survey, conducted May 19-21, finds 61% of Democrats saying they are confident their party will win the election, including 35% who are "very confident." Meanwhile, only 39% of Republicans are confident, with only 13% saying they are very confident.

Thus, rank-and-file Republicans are aware the party faces an uphill battle in retaining the White House given the problems in the economy, an ongoing and unpopular war, and an incumbent Republican president with some of the lowest job approval ratings in Gallup Poll history.

While Republicans generally agree that their odds of winning are long, a majority (58%) believe that likely presidential nominee John McCain gives the GOP the best chance of any of this year's Republican candidates of winning the election. Thirty-seven percent believe another candidate would have increased the party's odds of winning, with Mitt Romney and Mike Huckabee mentioned most often, by 16% and 9% of Republicans, respectively.

Democrats are likewise secure in the belief that their likely candidate, Barack Obama, gives the party the best chance of winning the presidential election. Sixty-two percent of Democrats say this. However, 34% disagree, and the vast majority of these Democrats believe Hillary Clinton would give the party a better chance of winning.

Clinton herself has raised doubts about Obama's ability to deliver the White House to the Democrats in the fall, citing her success in the primaries in large swing states such as Ohio and Pennsylvania, and her greater appeal to blue-collar voters, a key Democratic constituency.

Notably, Democrats who prefer Obama for the nomination are much more confident in the party's chances of winning the November presidential election than are Clinton supporters, 70% to 49%. Also, as would be expected, a majority of Clinton supporters believe Clinton would give the party the best chance of winning in November; only 22% of Clinton supporters believe Obama gives the Democrats the best chance of victory.

Implications

Rank-and-file Democrats are optimistic that the current political environment, which is favorable to them, will allow them to win the presidency, in the same way it allowed them to take control of Congress

Thinking about all the candidates who ran for the Republican nomination in this election, do you think John McCain gives the Republican Party the best chance of winning the election this fall, or do you think one of the other Republican candidates would have had a better chance?

Which other candidate do you think would have given the Republicans a better chance of winning the election this fall? [OPEN-ENDED]

Based on Republicans and Republican-leaning independents

	%
McCain gives Republicans best chance of winning	58
Other candidate would give Republicans better chance	37
(Mitt Romney)	(16)
(Mike Huckabee)	(9)
(Rudy Giuliani)	(3)
(Fred Thompson)	(3)
(Other specific candidate)	(2)
(Unspecified)	(4)
No opinion	5

Gallup Poll, May 19-21, 2008

Thinking about all the candidates who ran for the Democratic nomination in this election, do you think Barack Obama gives the Democratic Party the best chance of winning the election this fall, or do you think one of the other Democratic candidates would have had a better chance?

Which other candidate do you think would have given the Democrats a better chance of winning the election this fall? [OPEN-ENDED]

Based on Democrats and Democratic-leaning independents

	%
Obama gives Democrats best chance of winning	62
Other candidate would give Democrats better chance	34
(Hillary Clinton)	(26)
(John Edwards)	(6)
(Other specific candidate)	(1)
(Unspecified)	(1)
No opinion	3

Gallup Poll, May 19-21, 2008

following the 2006 midterm elections. A number of important political indicators underscore the Democratic advantage heading into the 2008 election, including party identification, favorable ratings of the two political parties, and party members' enthusiasm about voting in the fall election. Turnout in the Democratic primaries this year has dwarfed that in the Republican primaries, even in the early months when both contests were competitive.

Republican Party leaders are hoping that their supporters' pessimism does not result in depressed turnout on Election Day. Perhaps GOP leaders can take some solace in the fact that the rank-and-file believe the party will nominate the candidate who gives their party the best chance of winning, however long the odds may be.

Survey Methods

Results for this Gallup Panel study are based on telephone interviews with 1,013 national adults, aged 18 and older, conducted May 19-21,

2008. Gallup Panel members are recruited through random selection methods. The panel is weighted so that it is demographically representative of the U.S. adult population. For results based on this sample, one can say with 95% confidence that the maximum margin of sampling error is ±4 percentage points.

For results based on the sample of 523 Democrats and Democratic leaners, the maximum margin of sampling error is ±5 percentage points.

For results based on the sample of 438 Republicans and Republican leaners, the maximum margin of sampling error is ±5 percentage points.

In addition to sampling error, question wording and practical difficulties in conducting surveys can introduce error or bias into the findings of public opinion polls.

May 29, 2008
PUBLIC SAYS MEDIA HARDER ON CLINTON THAN OBAMA, MCCAIN
Close to half think coverage of three major candidates has been about right

by Jeffrey M. Jones, Gallup Poll Managing Editor

Although Americans in general think that news media coverage of the three major presidential candidates has been "about right," they are more inclined to say the media have been "too hard" on Hillary Clinton and "too easy" on Barack Obama and John McCain.

Do you think the news media has been too easy, about right or too hard on the presidential candidates?

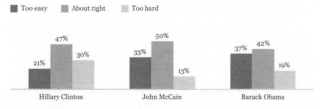

Gallup Panel Survey May 19-21, 2008

These results are based on the latest Gallup Panel survey, conducted May 19-21.

Bill and Hillary Clinton are two of the most prominent people to suggest that the news media have been unfairly critical of her and her campaign. The overall sentiment of the American public seems to tilt in agreement, with significantly more Americans saying the media have been too hard on Clinton than say that about either Obama or McCain.

Clinton's supporters generally share this negative view of her treatment by the media—a majority (56%) of Democrats who support Clinton for the presidential nomination say the media have been too hard on her. That is nearly double the percentage of Obama supporters who say this about Clinton.

Some—including the Clintons—have also argued the media were not taking a critical enough look at Obama, though that talk has subsided to some degree given the controversy over his association with the Rev. Jeremiah Wright and his remarks about "bitter" rural

Do you think the news media has been too easy, about right or too hard on Hillary Clinton?

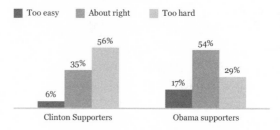

Gallup Panel Survey May 19-21, 2008

voters. Most Obama supporters seem satisfied with the coverage of their candidate—53% say it has been about right while 33% say it has been too harsh. On the other hand, Clinton supporters are twice as likely to say media coverage has been too easy on Obama as to say it has been too hard on him.

Do you think the news media has been too easy, about right or too hard on Barack Obama?

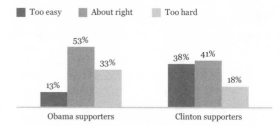

Gallup Panel Survey May 19-21, 2008

In addition to assessing the coverage of the presidential candidates, the poll asked Americans for their views on news coverage of the political parties during the campaign. The public is slightly more inclined to think the Democratic Party has gotten more favorable coverage, as 23% say the media have been too hard on the Republican Party, compared with 16% who say this about the Democratic Party.

Do you think the news media has been too easy, about right or too hard on the Democratic Party or the Republican Party?

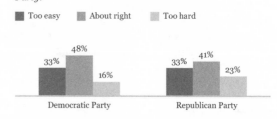

Gallup Panel Survey May 19-21, 2008

More generally, Americans are roughly divided as to whether they approve (47%) or disapprove (52%) of the job the news media are doing in covering the election. When those who disapprove were asked to explain why, their comments focused more on general criticisms than on treatment of specific candidates.

The most common responses involve general accusations of bias and not being completely truthful. Other criticisms include coverage being too "shallow" and not covering important issues, focusing too much on negative stories, and too much coverage of politics in general. Just 5% say the media have been too favorable to Obama, and only 3% say the media have been too negative toward Clinton.

Why would you say you disapprove of the news media coverage of the election?

Based on those who disapprove of media coverage of election

	% Mentions
Too biased (non specific)	24
Not completely truthful/slant facts	20
Do not cover important issues/shallow coverage	17
Too focused on negative	12
Too favorable to /too much focus on Democrats	11
Too much political coverage/overkill	10
Too favorable to/too focused on Barack Obama	5
Unfair to/not enough coverage of Hillary Clinton	3
Other	2
No reason/no opinion	2

Gallup Panel Survey May 19-21, 2008

Republicans who disapprove of media coverage are most likely to say it is because the coverage is biased or too focused on the Democrats. Democrats, on the other hand, tend to disapprove because the media coverage is too shallow and does not cover important issues, and because there is too much focus on the negative.

Implications

Although slightly more Americans disapprove than approve of media coverage of the election, the plurality of respondents say the coverage of each presidential candidate and both political parties has been "about right."

Americans have not always been very charitable in their ratings of the media, so while not overly positive, the current ratings are not necessarily bad when put into that context. The media to some extent are saddled with the perception that they do not treat a person's preferred candidate as well as they treat other candidates. This is apparent in the ratings of Clinton's and Obama's media treatment by their supporters, but also applies to ratings of McCain's media coverage by Republicans.

Survey Methods

Results for this Gallup Panel study are based on telephone interviews with 1,013 national adults, aged 18 and older, conducted May 19-21, 2008. Gallup Panel members are recruited through random selection methods. The panel is weighted so that it is demographically representative of the U.S. adult population. For results based on this sample, one can say with 95% confidence that the maximum margin of sampling error is ±4 percentage points.

In addition to sampling error, question wording and practical difficulties in conducting surveys can introduce error or bias into the findings of public opinion polls.

May 30, 2008

THE PEOPLE'S PRIORITIES: ECONOMY, IRAQ, GAS PRICES

Economy top priority for Democrats, gas prices for Republicans

by Jeffrey M. Jones, Gallup Poll Managing Editor

The latest Gallup Panel survey finds three issues—the economy, the war in Iraq, and gas prices—far and away rate as the public's top priorities for the president and Congress to deal with at this time.

In your view, what one or two issues should be the top priorities for the president and Congress to deal with at this time?

Open-ended question

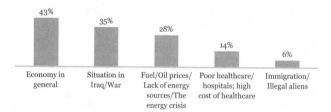

May 19-21, 2008

In the May 19-21 survey, 43% of Americans mention the economy, 35% the war in Iraq, and 28% gas prices or energy as the No. 1 government priority. Mentions of gas prices are up slightly from last month (22%) and are substantially higher than in March (10%).

Meanwhile, fewer mention the economy in general terms than did so in April (48%), but a significant number of respondents cite more specific aspects of the economy, including inflation, unemployment, recession, and taxes, as well as gas prices. All told, 67% of Americans mention some economic issue, which is the same percentage who did so in April.

The next-most-frequently mentioned issues after the "big three" are healthcare (14%) and immigration (6%). No other issue is mentioned by more than 3% of respondents.

Rank-ordering of the top three issues varies by party affiliation. A majority of Democrats mention the economy as the government's top priority (51%), putting it slightly ahead of the Iraq war (44%) and well ahead of gas prices (21%).

In contrast, gas prices rank as the most commonly mentioned issue among Republicans at 37%, compared with 32% who mention the economy and 27% who cite the Iraq war.

The rank ordering of political independents is similar to that of Democrats, though there is a larger gap between the No. 1 issue of the economy (46%) and the No. 2 issue of the war (31%). Twenty-four percent of independents believe gas prices and energy should be the top priority for the federal government.

Implications

While Americans' priorities for their elected representatives are fairly clear, the question is how government will respond. The president and Congress have already passed an economic stimulus package to help boost the economy, and are considering additional measures. Congress recently passed measures to address the energy situation, including halting future deposits in the government's Strategic Petroleum Reserve, though it is unclear that any government action could provide immediate relief on gas prices. The Bush administration continues to set the course on policy in Iraq, largely on the advice of

In your view, what one or two issues should be the top priorities for the president and Congress to deal with at this time?

Open ended question

	May 19-21, 2008 %	April 25-27, 2008 %	March 24-27, 2008 %
Economy in general	43	48	48
Situation in Iraq/war	35	38	42
Fuel/oil prices/lack of energy sources/the energy crisis	28	22	10
Poor health care/ hospitals; high cost of health care	14	16	21
Immigration/illegal aliens	6	7	8
High cost of living/inflation	3	4	3
Unemployment/jobs	3	3	3
Environment/ pollution	2	4	2
National security	2	3	4
Education/poor education/access to education	2	4	3
Foreign aid/focus overseas	2	1	1
Terrorism	2	2	3
Federal budget deficit/federal debt	2	2	2
Social Security	1	2	4
Taxes	1	2	2
Abortion	1	*	*
Poor leadership/corruption /dissatisfaction with government/ Congress/ politicians/candidates	1	1	1
Lack of money	1	*	1
Poverty/ hunger/ homelessness	1	1	1
International issues/ problems	1	1	1
War/conflict in the Middle East	1	1	*
Judicial system/courts/laws	1	1	*
Ethics/moral/religiou s/family decline; dishonesty; lack of integrity	1	*	*
Recession	1	*	1
Medicare	1	1	1

* Less than 0.5%

Gen. David Petraeus, while congressional Democrats have unsuccessfully tried to push for a quicker end to the war.

Survey Methods

Results for this Gallup Panel study are based on telephone interviews with 1,013 national adults, aged 18 and older, conducted May 19-21, 2008. Gallup Panel members are recruited through random selection methods. The panel is weighted so that it is demographically representative of the U.S. adult population. For results based on this sample, one can say with 95% confidence that the maximum margin of sampling error is ±4 percentage points.

For results based on the sample of 523 Democrats and Democratic leaners, the maximum margin of sampling error is ±4 percentage points.

For results based on the sample of 438 Republicans and Republican leaners, the maximum margin of sampling error is ±4 percentage points.

In addition to sampling error, question wording and practical difficulties in conducting surveys can introduce error or bias into the findings of public opinion polls.

June 02, 2008
AMERICANS FAVOR PRESIDENT MEETING WITH U.S. ENEMIES
Six in 10 think it's a good idea to meet with president of Iran

by Lydia Saad, Gallup Poll Senior Editor

Large majorities of Democrats and independents, and even about half of Republicans, believe the president of the United States should meet with the leaders of countries that are considered enemies of the United States. Overall, 67% of Americans say this kind of diplomacy is a good idea.

Americans' Views on the U.S. President Meeting With Leaders of Foreign Countries Considered Enemies of the United States

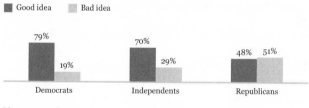

May 19-21, 2008

This is according to a Gallup Panel survey of a representative national sample of 1,013 Americans, conducted May 19-21.

Although separate Gallup polling shows that few Americans view Iran favorably, and that Iran leads Americans' list of top U.S. enemies in the world, the new Gallup survey also finds high public support for presidential-level meetings between the United States and Iran, specifically.

About 6 in 10 Americans (59%) think it would be a good idea for the president of the United States to meet with the president of Iran. This includes about half of Republicans, a majority of independents, and most Democrats.

Americans' Views on the U.S. President Meeting With the President of Iran

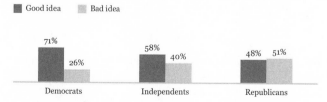

May 19-21, 2008

Both positions enjoy broad popular appeal, with majorities of men, women, younger and older Americans, and those from different regions of the country all saying direct presidential-level talks with Iran and other enemies are a good idea.

The issue of using presidential diplomacy with U.S. enemies distinguishes Barack Obama from the presumptive Republican presidential nominee, John McCain, and even from his opponent for the Democratic nomination, Hillary Clinton.

Obama is the only one of the three who has said he would personally meet with the leaders of countries like Iran, Syria, Cuba, and Venezuela as president, and he recently defended his position by saying "strong countries and strong presidents talk to their adversaries." Clinton has criticized Obama's approach as "naïve," and McCain has been unrelenting in his attacks on the issue, accusing Obama of being dangerously inexperienced and having "reckless judgment."

Bottom Line

McCain may eventually persuade more Americans that there is nothing for the president of the United States to discuss with hostile foreign leaders like Iranian President Mahmoud Ahmadinejad, and that to do so only undermines U.S. efforts to destabilize such regimes.

However, for now, whether it's the leader of an "enemy" country, generally, or the president of Iran, specifically, Americans think it's a good idea for the president of the United States to meet directly with the nation's adversaries.

Survey Methods

Results for this Gallup Panel study are based on telephone interviews with 1,013 national adults, aged 18 and older, conducted May 19-21, 2008. Gallup Panel members are recruited through random selection methods. The panel is weighted so that it is demographically representative of the U.S. adult population. For results based on this sample, one can say with 95% confidence that the maximum margin of sampling error is ±4 percentage points.

For results based on the 529 national adults in the Form A half-sample and 484 national adults in the Form B half-sample, the maximum margins of sampling error are ±5 percentage points.

In addition to sampling error, question wording and practical difficulties in conducting surveys can introduce error or bias into the findings of public opinion polls.

June 02, 2008
BUSH JOB APPROVAL AT 28%, TIED FOR LOWEST OF ADMINISTRATION
President's approval numbers static for the last two months

by Frank Newport, Gallup Poll Editor in Chief

President George W. Bush's job approval rating in the latest *USA Today*/Gallup poll, conducted May 30-June 1, is at 28%, essentially where it has been for the last two months, and tied for the lowest of his administration. Bush's disapproval rating is at 68%, one point off the highest such reading in Gallup history.

Bush's job approval ratings, already low as the year began, have been in a slight decline since January. Bush averaged 33% in three

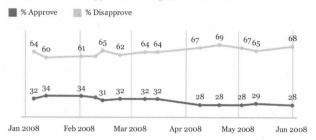

George W. Bush Job Approval, January 4 to June 1, 2008

■ % Approve　　% Disapprove

64　60　　61　65　62　　64　64　　　67　69　　67 65　　68

32　34　　34　31　32　　32　32　　　28　28　　28　29　　28

Jan 2008　Feb 2008　Mar 2008　Apr 2008　May 2008　Jun 2008

Gallup Index of Investor Optimism, January 2007 to May 2008

103　90　78　74　95　89　87　73　68　70　44　50　22　15

Jan '07　Mar '07　May '07　Jul '07　Sep '07　Nov '07　Jan '08　Mar '08　May '08

polls conducted in January, but in the five latest polls conducted in April and May, he has received four 28% ratings and one 29%.

The lowest job approval rating in Gallup's history is 22%, recorded by Harry Truman in 1952. The only other president to score lower than 28% was Richard Nixon in 1973 and 1974 (although Jimmy Carter also received a 28% rating in 1979).

A little less than seven years ago, in September 2001, Bush's job approval rating was 90%, the highest in Gallup Poll history. The 62-point swing between Bush's high point and his low point is reminiscent of the drop suffered by Truman, who received an 87% approval rating in 1945 shortly after he took office after Franklin Roosevelt's death, and by Bush's father, George H.W. Bush, whose approval rating dropped from 89% in February and March 1991 to 29% by the summer of 1992.

Survey Methods

Results are based on telephone interviews with 1,012 national adults, aged 18 and older, conducted May 30-June 1, 2008. For results based on the total sample of national adults, one can say with 95% confidence that the maximum margin of sampling error is ±3 percentage points.

Interviews are conducted with respondents on land-line telephones (for respondents with a land-line telephone) and cellular phones (for respondents who are cell-phone only).

In addition to sampling error, question wording and practical difficulties in conducting surveys can introduce error or bias into the findings of public opinion polls.

However, the Index remains slightly above its March 2003 low point of 5. The Index hit its all-time high of 178 in January 2000.

Gallup Index of Investor Optimism -- May Readings, 1999 to 2008

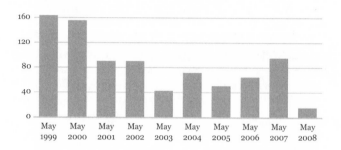

May 1999　May 2000　May 2001　May 2002　May 2003　May 2004　May 2005　May 2006　May 2007　May 2008

Investors remain pessimistic about the economic outlook for the year ahead, with the Economic Dimension of the Index at -31. This reflects less investor economic pessimism than the -40 of early March, which might be expected because the March measurement took place prior to the Bear Stearns bailout. Investors are currently as pessimistic about the economic outlook as they were in March 2003, at the outset of the Iraq war, when the Economic Dimension was at -30.

Economic Dimension -- May Readings, 1999 to 2008

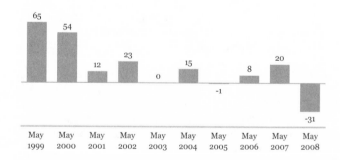

65　54　12　23　0　15　-1　8　20　-31

May 1999　May 2000　May 2001　May 2002　May 2003　May 2004　May 2005　May 2006　May 2007　May 2008

Investors' optimism about their portfolio investments over the next 12 months has also decreased. The Personal Dimension of the Index is at 46 in May—down from 62 in March and 75 in May a year ago, and the lowest point for this dimension of the Index since May 2003, when it was at 42.

Commentary

Gallup's Index of Investor Optimism suggests that the average American investor is a lot less optimistic than the professionals on Wall Street about the current investment outlook. In particular, average investors remain pessimistic about the prospects for the U.S. economy—not as pessimistic as they were when the Bear

June 02, 2008
U.S. INVESTOR OPTIMISM AT LOWEST POINT IN FIVE YEARS
Investors remain pessimistic about the outlook for the U.S. economy in the months ahead

by Dennis Jacobe, Gallup Chief Economist

Investor optimism tumbled to its lowest level since the beginning of the Iraq war, as the Gallup Index of Investor Optimism fell to 15 in May—down from 22 in March, 95 in May 2007, and 103 in January 2007.

Investors Pessimistic About the Economic Outlook

The May Index reading of 15 is far below the 95 of a year ago, and is the Index's lowest level for May since its inception in October 1996.

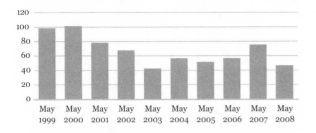

Stearns financial crisis was developing, but still at their pre-2008 pessimistic high.

Nothing indicates the divide between Wall Street and the average U.S. investor more than the way many of those on the Street are cheering the recent uptick in interest rates and the speculation that the Fed could actually increase interest rates later this year. Right now, the American consumer faces major challenges ranging from surging food and energy prices to plunging housing prices and a lack of job growth. The last thing Main Street needs is higher interest rates.

It is true that the global financial markets are highly emotional and it is argued that they tend to look past short-term economic events and focus on the 6 to 12 months ahead. Many on Wall Street seem to feel the U.S. economy will perform much better in the second half of 2008 and into early 2009. Gallup's Index of Investor Optimism suggests that the average U.S. investor is not nearly so confident that such will be the case.

Survey Methods

Results for this Gallup Panel study are based on telephone interviews with 576 investors, aged 18 and older, with at least $10,000 in investable assets, conducted May 19-21, 2008. Gallup Panel members are recruited through random selection methods. The panel is weighted so that it is demographically representative of the U.S. adult population. For results based on this sample, one can say with 95% confidence that the maximum margin of sampling error is ±5 percentage points.

Results for March are based on Gallup Poll Daily interviews conducted Feb. 28-March 2, 2008, with 1,947 investors with at least $10,000 in investable assets. For results based on this sample, the maximum margin of sampling error is ±2 percentage points.

For investor results prior to 2008, telephone interviews were conducted with at least 800 investors, aged 18 and older, with at least $10,000 of investable assets. For the total sample of investors in each of these surveys, the maximum margin of sampling error is ±4 percentage points.

In addition to sampling error, question wording and practical difficulties in conducting surveys can introduce error or bias into the findings of public opinion polls.

June 03, 2008

RECORD-HIGH 55% OF AMERICANS "FINANCIALLY WORSE OFF"
First time in Gallup history a majority see their financial situations as worse than the year before

by Frank Newport, Gallup Poll Editor in Chief

A majority of Americans say they are worse off financially than a year ago, marking the first time in Gallup's 32-year history of asking the question that more than half of Americans give this pessimistic assessment.

Would you say that you are financially better off now than you were a year ago, or are you financially worse off now?

Trend from September 1976 to June 2008

The previous high on this "worse off than a year ago" measure was back in 1982, in the first years of the Reagan administration, when 47% of those interviewed said they were worse off. When Gallup last asked this question in late January/early February of this year, 44% said they were worse off.

Only 26% of Americans now say they are *better* off financially than a year ago. This is one point shy of the all-time low reading on this measure, 25%, recorded several times from 1982 to 1990.

At the same time, Americans remain on a relative basis at least somewhat optimistic about the future. Fifty-two percent believe they will be better off financially a year from now than they are now, while just 31% say they will be worse off.

Looking ahead, do you expect that at this time next year you will be financially better off than now, or worse off than now?

Trend from August 1977 to June 2008

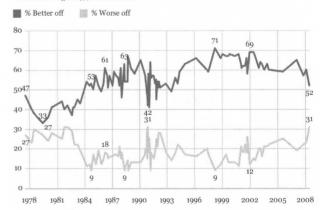

This "optimism" measure is actually quite a bit more positive than it has been at other times. The lowest reading on the "will be better off" measure is 33%, recorded in 1979, and the readings have been below 50% at several other points since then. The highest optimism reading occurred in March 1998, when 71% said they anticipated being better off in a year than they were at the moment.

Implications

The bad news from these data is clear: A record number of Americans have become convinced that their personal financial situations have deteriorated over the last year. Perhaps the high price of gasoline and the impact it is having on Americans' budgets is a major factor in these perceptions (although it should be noted that the negative read on the measure is worse than at other times when there was a sudden run-up in the price of gas). Because Americans are usually more positive about their personal situations than the situation "out there" more broadly, the record-high negative reading when the public is asked about its own financial situations suggests that the current economic downturn is having a significant personal impact.

The good news is that Americans have not lost their typical pattern of optimism: a little more than half retain some optimism that their financial situations will get better in the year ahead. In fact, a review of the history of asking these two questions shows that optimism is certainly the rule. There has never been a time when Americans have been more pessimistic than optimistic about their finances; and despite the sharp uptick in negative mood, that generally more optimistic attitude continues today.

Survey Methods

Results are based on telephone interviews with 1,012 national adults, aged 18 and older, conducted May 30-June 1, 2008. For results based on the total sample of national adults, one can say with 95% confidence that the maximum margin of sampling error is ±3 percentage points.

Interviews are conducted with respondents on land-line telephones (for respondents with a land-line telephone) and cellular phones (for respondents who are cell-phone only).

In addition to sampling error, question wording and practical difficulties in conducting surveys can introduce error or bias into the findings of public opinion polls.

June 04, 2008

AS PRIMARY CAMPAIGN ENDS, CLINTON'S IMAGE MOSTLY INTACT

Seventy-four percent of Democrats still view her favorably; same as Obama

by Lydia Saad, Gallup Poll Senior Editor

Hillary Clinton is emerging from the bitterly contested Democratic primary campaign with her public image among Democrats largely intact. More than three-quarters of Democrats (74%) still view her favorably, identical to national Democratic views of Barack Obama.

For most of 2007, 80% or more of national Democrats said they had a favorable view of Clinton. Positive views of her dipped below 80% in January and February of this year, rebounded to 85% in

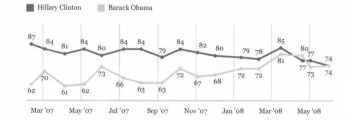

Percentage Who View Each Candidate Favorably -- Among Democrats
Trend from February 2007 to May/June 2008

March, but have since been in the mid- to high 70s. Over the same period, Obama's favorability rose by 12 points, from 62% last February to 74% today. This was as Obama became better known nationally, and more people were able to rate him.

While Clinton's favorable rating among Democrats is slightly lower today than it once was, it has remained nearly flat among political independents. Also, after about a year of receiving minimal favorable ratings from Republicans (ranging from 12% to 19%), she is now viewed favorably by a slightly more robust 24% of Republicans, similar to the 21% to 28% seen in February and March 2007.

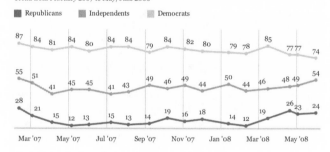

Percentage With "Favorable" Opinions of Hillary Clinton, by Party ID
Trend from February 2007 to May/June 2008

Bottom Line

2008 was supposed to be the year of complaining that the front-loaded primary schedule allowed the party front-runners to sew up their respective nominations too early. While they lasted, these critiques focused on the disproportionate influence of Iowa and New Hampshire compared with the more populous and nationally representative states that would hold their elections as "late" as March or April.

Instead, it has become the year of examining how Clinton, a candidate with a substantial lead in national Democratic preferences heading into the primaries and overwhelming advantages in party support, could lose the elected delegate war.

One thing is clear: Clinton did not lose on the basis of greatly diminished popular appeal—within her party, among political independents, or among registered voters for the fall election. She still has considerable strengths in those areas.

Survey Methods

The most recent results are based on telephone interviews with 1,012 national adults, aged 18 and older, conducted May 30-June 1, 2008. For results based on the total sample of national adults, one can say with 95% confidence that the maximum margin of sampling error is ±3 percentage points.

Interviews are conducted with respondents on land-line telephones (for respondents with a land-line telephone) and cellular phones (for respondents who are cell-phone only).

In addition to sampling error, question wording and practical difficulties in conducting surveys can introduce error or bias into the findings of public opinion polls.

Gallup Poll Daily Tracking Results for the Presidential General Election, by Age
May 1-31, 2008

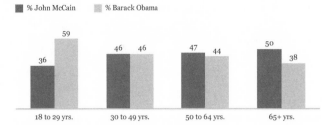

June 05, 2008

AN EARLY GALLUP ROAD MAP TO THE MCCAIN-OBAMA MATCHUP

Obama's appeal to young, highly educated apparent in general election

by Jeffrey M. Jones, Gallup Poll Managing Editor

As the general election campaign between Barack Obama and John McCain unofficially gets underway, many of the typical Democratic-Republican divides in the electorate—such as those by religion, gender, marital status, and income—already appear to be in place. Additionally, some of the special appeals each candidate had with voters in the nomination phase of the election (on the basis of age, education, race, and political affiliation) seem to be carrying over into the general election.

These findings are based on aggregated data from Gallup Poll Daily tracking in May, consisting of more than 25,000 total interviews with registered voters nationwide. Obama (supported by an average of 45.6% of national registered voters) and McCain (favored by 45.4%) were essentially tied in the full May dataset.

Gender

As is typically the case in U.S. presidential elections, the Republican candidate is running better among male voters, while the Democrat fares better among women. The data show McCain with a six-point advantage over Obama among men, and Obama leading McCain by the same margin among women.

Gallup Poll Daily Tracking Results for the Presidential General Election, by Gender
May 1-31, 2008

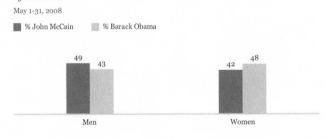

Age

Perhaps one of the greatest divides in the 2008 election will be along age lines, with Obama demonstrating great appeal to younger voters, but not faring as well among senior citizens. Obama leads McCain by 23 points among voters aged 18 to 29, while trailing McCain by 12 points among those 65 and older. The two run about evenly among the two middle age groups.

Race

It's no secret that Obama owes his nomination in large part to overwhelming support among blacks, and that high level of support will likely be evident in the general election. Roughly 9 in 10 blacks say they would vote for Obama if the election were held today, while McCain's support among blacks is in the low single digits. Blacks are typically a strong Democratic constituency, so the impact of the first black presidential candidate on a major-party ticket may be more evident in terms of motivating high black turnout than in overwhelming support for the Democrat.

Obama did not fare well against Hillary Clinton among Hispanics in the 2008 primaries, but the early indications are that he will do well among this increasingly Democratic group in the general election. The May data show Obama with a 62% to 29% advantage over McCain among Hispanics.

McCain currently maintains a strong advantage over Obama among non-Hispanic white voters, 53% to 38%.

Gallup Poll Daily Tracking Results for the Presidential General Election, by Race/Ethnicity
May 1-31, 2008

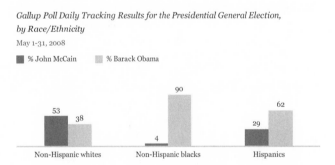

Education

Highly educated voters were another key group helping to propel Obama to the Democratic nomination. The two candidates run about evenly among all education groups except those with postgraduate educations, among whom Obama currently leads by a significant margin. It is notable that McCain runs competitively with Obama among voters with a high-school education or less, which is normally a solid Democratic group. Obama offsets that by running evenly with McCain in a usually strong Republican group—voters with a four-year degree but no postgraduate education.

Income

While Obama does not fare as well among the traditional Democratic group of lower-education voters, he does do well among the usually Democratic group of lower-income voters, beating McCain by double digits among this group. The two are competitive among middle- and

*Gallup Poll Daily Tracking Results for the Presidential General Election,
by Education*

May 1-31, 2008

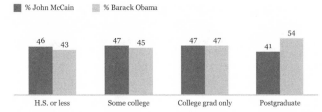

■ % John McCain   ▦ % Barack Obama

	H.S. or less	Some college	College grad only	Postgraduate
% John McCain	46	47	47	41
% Barack Obama	43	45	47	54

upper-income voters, with McCain doing slightly better among wealthier voters.

*Gallup Poll Daily Tracking Results for the Presidential General Election,
by Monthly Income*

May 1-31, 2008

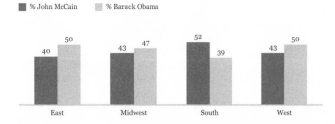

■ % John McCain   ▦ % Barack Obama

	Under $2,000	$2,000 to $4,999	$5,000 to $7,499	$7,500 or more
% John McCain	36	46	50	49
% Barack Obama	53	46	44	45

Region

McCain—like Republican candidates before him—is the heavy favorite in the South. Obama leads McCain in the East and West. The Midwest may be the most competitive region this election, with Obama currently maintaining a slight advantage in his home region.

Gallup Poll Daily Tracking Results for the Presidential General Election, by Region

May 1-31, 2008

■ % John McCain   ▦ % Barack Obama

	East	Midwest	South	West
% John McCain	40	43	52	43
% Barack Obama	50	47	39	50

Party Identification

Both McCain and Obama can thank independents for helping them gain their respective parties' presidential nomination. And the two candidates are closely matched among independents for the general election.

In terms of the two major political party groups, McCain is securing greater party loyalty at the moment, holding 85% of his fellow Republicans compared with 76% support for Obama among Democrats. But because at this point in the campaign, more Americans identify themselves as Democrats than as Republicans, it is more critical to McCain's fortunes to hold his base than it is for Obama.

Ideology

Liberals overwhelmingly support Obama, with 8 in 10 saying they would vote for him. McCain gets the support of 69% of conserva-

*Gallup Poll Daily Tracking Results for the Presidential General Election,
by Party ID*

May 1-31, 2008

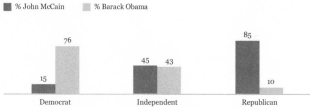

■ % John McCain   ▦ % Barack Obama

	Democrat	Independent	Republican
% John McCain	15	45	85
% Barack Obama	76	43	10

tives. Again, because more Americans identify themselves as conservatives than as liberals, Obama needs to keep his fellow ideologues in the fold more than McCain does. Obama leads McCain among political moderates, 50% to 38%.

*Gallup Poll Daily Tracking Results for the Presidential General Election,
by Ideology*

May 1-31, 2008

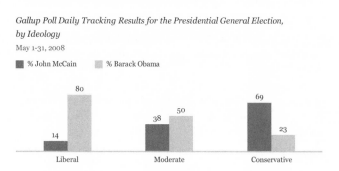

■ % John McCain   ▦ % Barack Obama

	Liberal	Moderate	Conservative
% John McCain	14	38	69
% Barack Obama	80	50	23

Religiosity

Religious commitment has proven to be one of the greatest dividing lines in U.S. politics, with highly religious voters aligning themselves with the Republican Party and nonreligious voters tending to vote Democratic. Those patterns are apparent in the 2008 campaign, with McCain holding a 19-point lead among voters who attend religious services weekly, and Obama leading by 16 points among those who rarely or never attend church. The two candidates are evenly matched among the middle group that attends church on an irregular basis.

*Gallup Poll Daily Tracking Results for the Presidential General Election,
by Church Attendance*

May 1-31, 2008

■ % John McCain   ▦ % Barack Obama

	Weekly	Nearly weekly/Monthly	Seldom/Never
% John McCain	55	46	37
% Barack Obama	36	46	53

Religious Preference

McCain leads Obama by 10 points among Protestants and other non-Catholic Christians, the largest religious group in the United States. McCain's lead would be even larger except for the facts that blacks are most likely to be Protestant and overwhelmingly support Obama. Catholics are a traditional swing group, and McCain and Obama are evenly matched among them at this point. Obama has a significant lead among two reliably Democratic groups—Jewish voters and voters with no religious affiliation.

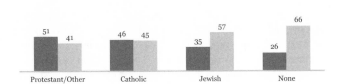

Gallup Poll Daily Tracking Results for the Presidential General Election, by Religious Preference

May 1-31, 2008

■ % John McCain   ▫ % Barack Obama

	Protestant/Other Christian	Catholic	Jewish	None
McCain	51	46	35	26
Obama	41	45	57	66

Marital Status

In recent presidential elections, married voters have tended to vote Republican, and unmarried voters Democratic. That relationship appears as if it will hold in 2008, with McCain up by 13 points over Obama among those currently married, while Obama has a 20-point lead among those who are not married.

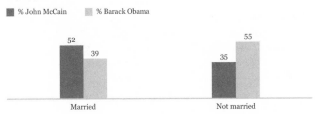

Gallup Poll Daily Tracking Results for the Presidential General Election, by Marital Status

May 1-31, 2008

■ % John McCain   ▫ % Barack Obama

	Married	Not married
McCain	52	35
Obama	39	55

Red vs. Blue States

The candidates will likely use the electoral map of 2004 as a starting point to plan their campaign strategies for 2008. As of now, both candidates are running strongly among voters in states their respective parties won by comfortable margins in 2004. Obama currently holds a slim advantage among voters in the swing states—those where the winning candidate won a narrow victory of five percentage points or less.

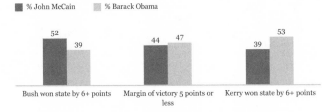

Gallup Poll Daily Tracking Results for the Presidential General Election, by 2004 Election Results

May 1-31, 2008

■ % John McCain   ▫ % Barack Obama

	Bush won state by 6+ points	Margin of victory 5 points or less	Kerry won state by 6+ points
McCain	52	44	39
Obama	39	47	53

Survey Methods

Results are based on telephone interviews with 25,512 registered voters, aged 18 and older, conducted May 1-31, 2008, as part of Gallup Poll Daily tracking. For results based on the total sample of registered voters, one can say with 95% confidence that the maximum margin of sampling error is ±1 percentage point.

Margins of error for subgroups are larger.

Interviews are conducted with respondents on land-line telephones (for respondents with a land-line telephone) and cellular phones (for respondents who are cell-phone only).

In addition to sampling error, question wording and practical difficulties in conducting surveys can introduce error or bias into the findings of public opinion polls.

June 05, 2008

NET NEW HIRING ACTIVITY SUGGESTS U.S. LOST JOBS IN MAY

Gallup Poll Daily May surveys show employer hiring declined while layoffs increased

by Dennis Jacobe, Gallup Chief Economist

Gallup's Net New Hiring Activity measure fell by 2.2 percentage points in May after a 1.1-point drop from March to April, matching the 2.1-point drop between January and February—the largest previous decline this year.

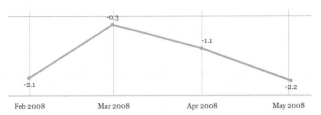

Month-to-Month Change in Net New Hiring Activity

% Whose employers are "Hiring new people" minus % whose employers are "Letting people go" In percentage points

Feb 2008	Mar 2008	Apr 2008	May 2008
-2.1	-0.3	-1.1	-2.2

More Job Losses in May

Wednesday morning, Challenger, Gray & Christmas—a private placement firm that monitors and reports on layoff activity each month—reported that firings announced by U.S. companies totaled 103,522 in May—the highest number of layoffs in more than two years. Just 45 minutes later, ADP reported that the private sector added 40,000 jobs in May, up from 13,000 jobs in April. The Bureau of Labor Statistics has reported that the U.S. lost 260,000 private- and public-sector jobs during the first four months of this year and is due to report its results for May on Friday.

Gallup's Net New Hiring Activity declined markedly from April to May, suggesting that the U.S. economy suffered significant job losses last month. At the same time, the current decline is less pronounced than the 3.6-point decline indicated by the preliminary Net New Hiring Activity estimate Gallup released a couple of weeks ago based on results for the first two weeks of the month. The data still indicate there were job losses in May, but these will not be as pronounced as seems to have been the case just a couple of weeks ago.

Gallup's Net New Hiring Activity measure was initiated in January 2008. It is an effort to assess U.S. job creation or elimination based on the self-reports of more than 8,000 individual employees each month about hiring and firing activity at their workplaces. In order to calculate this measure, Gallup asks current full-time employees whether their employers are hiring new people and expanding the size of their workforces, not changing the size of their workforces, or letting people go and reducing the size of their workforces. Net new hiring activity is computed by subtracting the "letting go and reducing" percentage from the "hiring and expanding" percentage. The assumption is that employees across the country have a good feel for what's happening in their companies, and that these insider perceptions can yield a useful summary indication of the nation's job situation.

Over the first five months of this year, the percentage of employees saying their companies are hiring has fallen from 39.8% in January to 38.1% in April and 36.8% in May. At the same time, the percentage of employees reporting that their firms are letting people go increased from 13.7% in January to 15.5% in April and 16.4% in May. The April to May drop in net new hiring activity of 2.2 points is essentially the same as the large decline that took place between January and February.

Percentage of Employers Expanding and Reducing Their Workforces, Nationwide

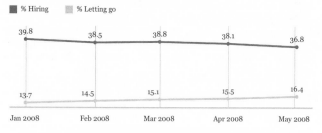

Does Bernanke Know Something Consumers Don't?

On Tuesday, Federal Reserve Board Chairman Ben Bernanke told an economics conference in Spain by way of satellite that the Fed is concerned about the declining value of the U.S. dollar and its potential impact on inflation and inflationary expectations. Many on Wall Street interpreted his comments as a signal that the Fed will not be cutting interest rates further this year, and may end up increasing them later as the year's end approaches.

It may be that a strong Fed stance in support of the U.S. dollar, particularly if fully supported by the Treasury, would help lower commodity prices in general, and oil prices in particular. This would be good news for the consumer and the U.S. economy. An effort to bolster the U.S. dollar and even higher interest rates would also make sense, assuming the economy is going to strengthen as the year progresses.

Right now, however, such an optimistic scenario for the second half of 2008 is hard to envision. The consumer is being squeezed not only by gas prices—up 27% from this time a year ago—but also by surging food prices, falling housing prices, and an underwriting-driven credit crunch. If Friday's jobs report shows continuing job losses for the U.S. economy, as Gallup's Net New Hiring Activity measure suggests, it is hard to see how the economy could strengthen in the near term.

On the other hand, perhaps Chairman Bernanke has some special insights into the labor market and is anticipating a stronger-than-expected growth of jobs in May. While that would not comport with the Gallup and Challenger measurements—or with current low consumer confidence levels or the seeming lack of a significant consumer spending boost because of the federal tax rebates that just over 30% of consumers report having received—it would certainly help bolster the case that the economy is stronger than many Americans currently perceive. Of course, whether such a surprisingly strong

government report on the jobs market, if it happens, would be more illusory than real might end up being worthy of debate.

Survey Methods

Gallup is interviewing no fewer than 1,000 U.S. adults nationwide each day during 2008. The economic questions analyzed in this report are asked of a random half-sample of respondents each day. The results reported here are based on combined data of more than 8,000 interviews each in January, February, March, April, and May. For results based on these samples, the maximum margin of sampling error is ±1 percentage point.

Interviews are conducted with respondents on land-line telephones (for respondents with a land-line telephone) and cellular phones (for respondents who are cell-phone only).

In addition to sampling error, question wording and practical difficulties in conducting surveys can introduce error or bias into the findings of public opinion polls.

June 06, 2008

AMONG BLACKS, HILLARY CLINTON'S IMAGE SINKS OVER LAST YEAR
McCain's image also deteriorates, while Obama's improves among blacks

by Frank Newport, Gallup Poll Editor in Chief

In an election year in which race is front and center, American blacks have grown more negative toward Hillary Clinton, with her favorable image sinking from 84% to 58% over the last year, while blacks' favorable opinions of Barack Obama have soared from 68% to 86%. Blacks have also become more negative toward John McCain.

Favorability Ratings for Clinton, Obama, and McCain

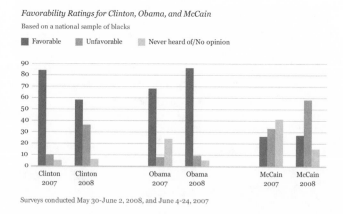

Surveys conducted May 30-June 2, 2008, and June 4-24, 2007

A new *USA Today*/Gallup survey, conducted May 30-June 2, 2008, shows that American blacks are significantly more likely now than they were a year ago to have an unfavorable opinion of Clinton. While in June of last year, an overwhelming 84% of blacks said their opinion of Clinton was favorable, that has dropped to 58% today. Unfavorable opinions of Clinton among blacks have jumped from 10% last June to 36% today.

The last year, of course, witnessed the rise of Obama from a little-known Illinois senator to his now being poised to be the first

Opinion of Hillary Clinton

Based on a national sample of blacks

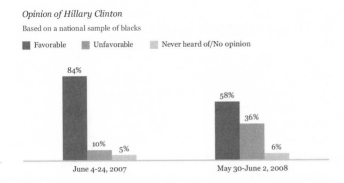

Opinion of John McCain

Based on a national sample of blacks

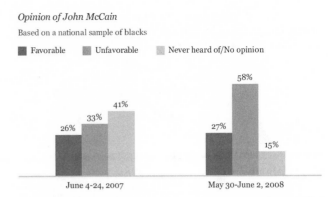

black candidate to win a major party's nomination for president in U.S. history. During that time, Clinton, formerly part of a political power couple with very strong ties to the black community, became Obama's opponent, and it appears that a perhaps inevitable fallout from that occurrence was a drop in her standing in the eyes of blacks across the country.

Indeed, blacks' opinions of presumptive Democratic nominee Obama have become more positive as he has become better known over the past year. Obama's image among blacks was an already very positive 68% favorable and 8% unfavorable last year at this time; now it's 86% favorable and 9% unfavorable. (Separately, year-to-year data show that among black Democrats, Clinton went from being competitive with Obama as first choice for the Democratic Party's nominee last year—42% for Obama, 43% for Clinton—to the point where an overwhelming majority of 82% of black Democrats favor Obama in the current survey, compared to 15% for Clinton.)

Opinion of Barack Obama

Based on a national sample of blacks

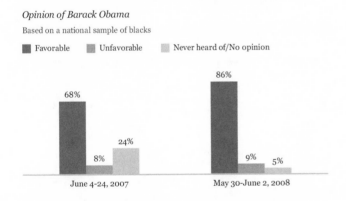

Clinton can perhaps take some comfort in the fact that the presumptive Republican nominee, McCain, has also seen his image become more negative in the eyes of black Americans over the last year. In June 2007, McCain's image among blacks was 26% favorable and 33% unfavorable, with 41% saying they either didn't have an opinion or had never heard of McCain. Now, as he has become better known, blacks' opinions of McCain have moved decidedly into the negative column: 58% are now unfavorable, while 27% are favorable.

A good deal of news coverage has been given to Obama's former minister, the Rev. Jeremiah Wright, over the past several months. Wright, for many years the minister of Trinity United Church of Christ in Chicago, was vaulted into the national spotlight when video excerpts of his sermons surfaced on the Internet. His image became even more controversial after a fiery speech at the National Press Club in Washington. The new *USA Today*/Gallup survey suggests that Wright certainly cannot claim to have the alle-

giance of the majority of blacks in this country: 54% of blacks say they have an unfavorable opinion of the controversial minister, while only 18% say their opinion is favorable.

Opinion of the Rev. Jeremiah Wright

Based on a national sample of blacks

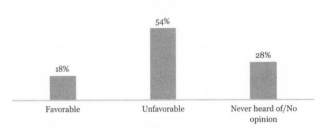

May 30-June 2, 2008

By contrast, blacks' opinions of another controversial minister, the Rev. Al Sharpton, are significantly more positive.

Opinion of the Rev. Al Sharpton

Based on a national sample of blacks

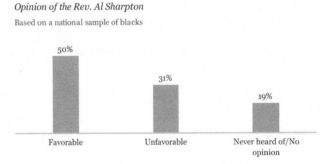

May 30-June 2, 2008

Survey Methods

Results are based on telephone interviews with 250 blacks, aged 18 and older, conducted May 30-June 2, 2008, some of which were drawn from Gallup's May 30-June 1 national sample and some of which were drawn from a special black oversample conducted May 30-June 2. The combined sample of blacks is weighted to be representative of U.S. blacks. For results based on the total sample, one can say with 95% confidence that the maximum margin of sampling error is ±7 percentage points.

Interviews are conducted with respondents on land-line telephones (for respondents with a land-line telephone) and cellular phones (for respondents who are cell-phone only).

In addition to sampling error, question wording and practical difficulties in conducting surveys can introduce error or bias into the findings of public opinion polls.

June 09, 2008

FOUR IN 10 AMERICANS SEE THEIR STANDARD OF LIVING DECLINING

Nearly as many say their standard of living has gotten worse as say it is better

by Jeffrey M. Jones, Gallup Poll Managing Editor

Forty-three percent of Americans say their standard of living is worse now than it was five years ago, nearly matching the percentage (45%) who say their standard of living has gotten better during that time.

Would you say your standard of living is better or worse now than it was five years ago?

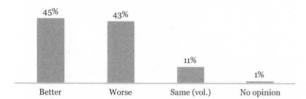

45%   43%   11%   1%
Better   Worse   Same (vol.)   No opinion

May 30-June 1, 2008, USA Today/Gallup poll
(vol.) = Volunteered response

These results are based on a May 30-June 1 *USA Today*/Gallup poll. In the same poll, Gallup for the first time found a majority of Americans saying their personal finances are worse now than a year ago.

Lower-income Americans, those aged 50 and older, and those without college educations are among the subgroups who are most likely to believe their standard of living has deteriorated during the past five years.

Would you say your standard of living is better or worse now than it was five years ago?

By selected subgroup

	Better	Worse	Same (vol.)
Age	%	%	%
18 to 29 years	52	41	6
30 to 49 years	54	37	9
50 years and older	34	50	15
Annual Household Income			
Less than $30,000	28	63	9
$30,000 to <$75,000	42	47	11
$75,000 or more	61	27	11
Education Level			
High school or less	38	51	11
Some college	47	43	9
College graduate only	48	36	14
Postgraduate	48	36	15

May 30-June 1, 2008, USA Today/Gallup poll
(vol.) = Volunteered response

Politics apparently color one's views on this matter, as a majority of Democrats and liberals, compared with fewer than half of Republicans and conservatives, report a diminished standard of living even as a Republican occupies the White House.

Would you say your standard of living is better or worse now than it was five years ago?

By political affiliation

	Better	Worse	Same (vol.)
Party Identification	%	%	%
Democrat	34	57	9
Independent	45	44	9
Republican	59	23	17
Political Ideology			
Liberal	37	53	8
Moderate	41	47	12
Conservative	55	32	12

May 30-June 1, 2008, USA Today/Gallup poll
(vol.) = Volunteered response

Typically, Americans are optimistic about how things will be in the future, and that applies in this case. When asked to project five years into the future, 62% say they expect their standard of living to be better; only 25% think it will be worse.

There is little variation on future expectations by demographic subgroup. One notable exception concerns age. Senior citizens, many of whom live on fixed incomes in retirement, are not optimistic about the future, with just 35% expecting an improved standard of living and 39% a worse one.

Five years from now, do you think your standard of living will be better or worse than it is now?

By age

■ % Better   ■ % Worse   ■ % Same (vol.)

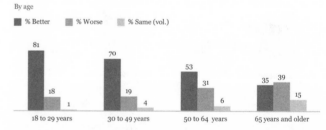

	18 to 29 years	30 to 49 years	50 to 64 years	65 years and older
Better	81	70	53	35
Worse	18	19	31	39
Same	1	4	6	15

May 30-June 1, 2008, USA Today/Gallup poll
(vol.) = Volunteered response

In addition to comparing their own standard of living to the recent past and near future, the poll asked Americans to compare where they are now to where their parents were at the same age, and where their children will be.

Sixty-three percent of Americans report that their current standard of living is better than their parents' at the same age, including 38% who say theirs is much better than their parents'. Only 18% say their standard of living is worse than that of their parents.

Americans are not quite as optimistic that their children will have a better quality of life than they do—45% expect their children's standard of living to be better than theirs is, 20% say it will be the same, and 28% believe it will be worse.

Younger adults are among the most optimistic about their children's economic situations, with 60% of 18- to 29-year-olds expecting their children to have a better standard of living than they do at the same age. That compares with just 38% of those aged 50 and older expecting a more comfortable financial situation for their children.

Implications

The problems in the economy are taking their toll on American consumers, with about as many now reporting a diminished standard of living as an improved one. Nevertheless, by and large, Americans still expect things to improve over the next five years.

Survey Methods

Results are based on telephone interviews with 1,012 national adults, aged 18 and older, conducted May 30-June 1, 2008. For results based on the total sample of national adults, one can say with 95% confidence that the maximum margin of sampling error is ±3 percentage points.

Interviews are conducted with respondents on land-line telephones (for respondents with a land-line telephone) and cellular phones (for respondents who are cell-phone only).

In addition to sampling error, question wording and practical difficulties in conducting surveys can introduce error or bias into the findings of public opinion polls.

June 09, 2008
MOST SAY RACE WILL NOT BE A FACTOR IN THEIR PRESIDENTIAL VOTE
But many think the campaigns will use race as an issue this year

by Frank Newport, Gallup Poll Editor in Chief

A large majority of blacks, 78%, and an even larger majority of whites, 88%, say the fact that Barack Obama is black makes no difference in terms of their likelihood of voting for him for president.

Does the fact that Barack Obama is black make you -- [ROTATED] much more likely to vote for him for president, somewhat more likely, does it make no difference, does it make you somewhat less likely, or much less likely to vote for him for president?

May 30-June 2, 2008

■ % Blacks   ▓ % Whites

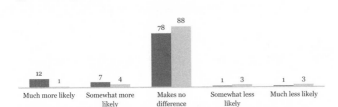

This may appear to be an unusually high percentage of blacks saying Obama's race makes no difference, given that his nomination will mark a historic moment in American political history—the first black candidate to capture a major party's nomination.

Without question, blacks are going to vote for Obama in overwhelming numbers; the latest Gallup tracking shows that Obama gets 93% of the black vote when pitted against Republican John McCain in a hypothetical trial heat.

So on the one hand, black voters say Obama's race makes no difference to them, and on the other hand, about 9 out of 10 blacks say they will vote for Obama. But the high percentage of the black vote going to Obama is not unusual. Gallup polling estimated that John Kerry received 93% of the black vote in 2004, and Al Gore received 95% in 2000. So it may be that black voters are making the (correct) self-observation that they would be voting for the Democratic candidate regardless of his or her race, meaning that Obama's particular race is not a deciding factor for them.

Whites are even less likely than blacks to say Obama's race would be a factor in their vote. Eighty-eight percent of non-Hispanic whites say his race makes no difference. Six percent of whites say they are less likely to vote for Obama because of his race; 5% say they are more likely to vote for him. There has been discussion this year of a "hidden" race factor in which certain groups of white voters will end up not voting for Obama because he is a black candidate. What these data show is that more than 9 in 10 whites, when asked about Obama's race directly, deny that it will be a negative factor in their vote.

A separate poll question measured the perceived impact of Obama's race by asking respondents to speculate about the impact of race on the election more generally.

Suppose Barack Obama is the Democratic candidate for president in the November election. Just your best guess, do you think in general, the fact that Barack Obama is black would -- [ROTATED] gain him more votes than it would cost him, or would it cost him more votes than it would gain him?

May 30-June 2, 2008

■ % Blacks   ▓ % Whites

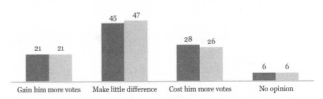

In this case, there is more variation in opinions, among both blacks and whites.

Blacks are quite divided in their responses to this question. A little more than a quarter, 28%, say Obama's race will cost him more than it will gain him in the election. But 21% of blacks give the opposite response and say Obama's race will be a net plus for his candidacy. The rest, 45%, say it will make little difference.

The responses among whites to this question are remarkably similar to the responses among blacks, differing by just a few percentage points.

A third set of questions asked about the potential use of race (the "race card" one hears so much about in campaign coverage) by the two political parties.

Blacks appear to believe race will be a factor in the way the election campaign is run by both Republicans and Democrats, but more so for the former than the latter.

Forty-eight percent of blacks say the Democrats' campaign will make race a factor this year, while 70% say Republicans will use race as an issue. Whites are much more uniform in their responses to this question: About half say each party will use race as an issue in the campaign.

The question did not ask respondents specific follow-up questions about how race would be used in the campaign, so it is unclear whether respondents who believe race will be made an issue think

If Barack Obama is the Democratic candidate for president, how likely do you think the Democratic Party is to use race as an issue in the campaign?

May 30-June 2, 2008

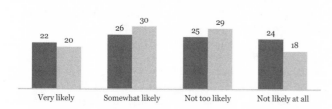

| Very likely | Somewhat likely | Not too likely | Not likely at all |

If Barack Obama is the Democratic candidate for president, how likely do you think the Republican Party is to use race as an issue in the campaign?

May 30-June 2, 2008

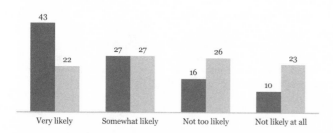

this is good or bad. Most blacks identify themselves as Democrats, making the precise meaning of the fact that half of blacks interviewed think the Democratic Party will use race as a factor in the campaign even less clear. It can be hypothesized that the strong majority of blacks who say Republicans will use race as an issue view that possibility in a more negative light.

Implications

Blacks overwhelmingly have favored the Democratic candidate in past elections, while the Republican candidate has typically won the majority of the white vote. General-election voting data so far in this campaign show that this pattern is continuing this year. Race is a strong factor in projected voting for Obama against McCain (as it was in Obama's Democratic primary race against Hillary Clinton). Blacks are overwhelmingly likely to vote for Obama, while the majority of non-Hispanic whites indicate that they will vote for McCain.

The analytic question becomes one of ascertaining whether the historic nature of Obama's nomination as a major-party black candidate will have an impact above and beyond the usual patterns of racial differences in voting.

The data reviewed here suggest that while most voters deny that Obama's race affects them personally, many do think it will have an effect on the race overall—either helping Obama or hurting him. Still, there is no consensus on the part of the average voter on whether Obama's race will be a net plus or a net minus.

Thus, there is little guidance from the voters themselves in the attempt to answer the question about the ultimate impact of Obama's race on the campaign this year.

Survey Methods

Results are based on telephone interviews with 1,012 national adults, aged 18 and older, conducted May 30-June 1, 2008. For results based on the total sample of national adults, one can say with 95% confidence that the maximum margin of sampling error is ±3 percentage points.

Results for the sample of 780 non-Hispanic whites, aged 18 and older, are based on telephone interviews drawn from the national sample poll. For results based on the total sample, one can say with 95% confidence that the maximum margin of sampling error is ±4 percentage points.

Results for blacks are based on telephone interviews with 250 blacks, aged 18 and older, conducted May 30-June 2, 2008, some of which were drawn from Gallup's May 30-June 1 national sample and some of which were drawn from a special black oversample conducted May 30-June 2. The combined sample of blacks is weighted to be representative of U.S. blacks. For results based on the total sample, one can say with 95% confidence that the maximum margin of sampling error is ±7 percentage points.

Interviews are conducted with respondents on land-line telephones (for respondents with a land-line telephone) and cellular phones (for respondents who are cell-phone only).

In addition to sampling error, question wording and practical difficulties in conducting surveys can introduce error or bias into the findings of public opinion polls.

June 10, 2008
AMERICANS HAVE POSITIVE VIEWS OF COUNTRIES BUSH WILL VISIT
Opinions of France, Germany have recovered since Iraq war run-up

by Lydia Saad, Gallup Poll Senior Editor and Jeffrey M. Jones, Managing Editor

President Bush's diplomatic tour through Europe this week will include visits to three countries Americans feel largely favorably toward, and whose U.S. images now stand close to what they were just prior to the acrimonious run-up to the Iraq war five years ago.

What is your overall opinion of the following countries?

Feb. 11-14, 2008

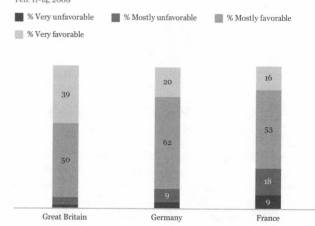

According to Gallup's annual World Affairs survey, conducted Feb. 11-14, 2008, Americans have particularly strong affection for Great Britain, with nearly 4 in 10 saying they have a very favorable view of the country, and a combined 9 in 10 having either a very or mostly favorable view of it.

Still, today's level of favorability toward Great Britain is a bit lower than it was from February 2005 to February 2007, when Great Britain, then led by Prime Minister Tony Blair, figured as one of President Bush's strongest allies in the Iraq war. While overall favorable views of Great Britain remain close to 90% today, the percentage having a very favorable view (now 39%) has dropped below 40% for the first time since 2000 (although it is similar to the 40% recorded in 2004).

What is your overall opinion of Great Britain?

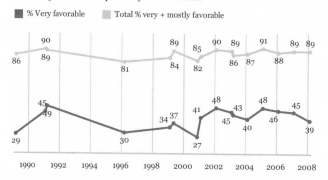

Germany also enjoys widespread popularity in the United States today, and is significantly better reviewed than in 2003, when—with Germany a leading adversary of the United States over the decision to go to war with Iraq—only 49% of Americans viewed it favorably. U.S. attitudes toward Germany rebounded to 83% last year—matching the highest reading since Gallup began asking this question in 1991—and remain at about that level today. Still, only about half as many Americans view Germany *very* favorably as feel this way about Great Britain (20% vs. 39%).

What is your overall opinion of Germany?

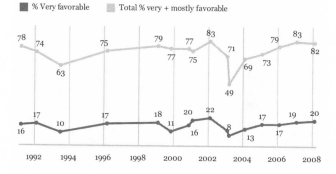

With 69% of Americans viewing France very or mostly favorably, this country—whose then-President Jacques Chirac leveled fierce criticism at the U.S. decision to go to war in Iraq in 2003—registers somewhat lower in U.S. public esteem than does either Great Britain or Germany. Furthermore, while neither Great Britain nor Germany attracts more than a smattering of "very unfavorable" mentions from the public, more Americans have a very or mostly unfavorable view than a very favorable view of France.

Country Favorability Comparison

Feb. 11-14, 2008

	% Very favorable	Total % very + mostly unfavorable
Great Britain	39	7
Germany	20	13
France	16	27

Current perceptions of France are markedly improved over 2003, at the height of the clash between France and the United States over Iraq policy, when barely one-third of Americans felt favorably toward France. This may reflect a change in French leadership to the more U.S.-friendly president Nicolas Sarkozy.

What is your overall opinion of France?

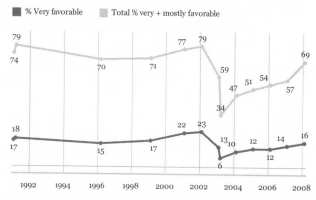

In addition to these three economic powerhouses, Bush will be visiting Italy and Vatican City in the coming week. Although Gallup has not asked Americans their views of Italy since 2003, it has generally received positive reviews, averaging 79% favorable ratings.

Also, a recent rating of Pope Benedict XVI shows him to be broadly popular in the United States. Nearly two-thirds of Americans polled April 18-20 have a favorable view of him and only 15% an unfavorable view, with 22% offering no opinion. That poll was conducted as the pope was wrapping up his widely praised visit to the United States.

Do you have a favorable or unfavorable opinion of Pope Benedict XVI?

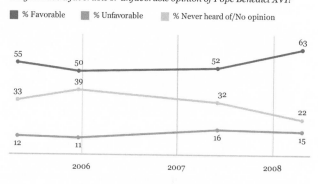

Bottom Line

Bush is taking what some observers have described as a "farewell tour" of Europe, where he will attempt to strengthen U.S.-European relations by focusing on Iran, Middle East peace, and other issues the Western allies can agree on.

It may be too little, too late for a president whose foreign policy ratings from the American people are dismally low. As of February 2008, only 32% of Americans said they approved of the job Bush was doing on foreign affairs and only 24% felt that leaders of other countries respect Bush. Still, perhaps by conferring with countries and leaders that Americans feel warmly toward, and engaging in positive dialogue with the new heads of Germany and France, who are eager to restore good relations across the Atlantic, Bush may restore some of his once-stellar image as a global leader.

Survey Methods

Results are based on telephone interviews with 1,007 national adults, aged 18 and older, conducted Feb. 11-14, 2008. For results based on the total sample of national adults, one can say with 95% confidence that the maximum margin of sampling error is ±3 percentage points.

Interviews are conducted with respondents on land-line telephones (for respondents with a land-line telephone) and cellular phones (for respondents who are cell-phone only).

In addition to sampling error, question wording and practical difficulties in conducting surveys can introduce error or bias into the findings of public opinion polls.

June 11, 2008
OBAMA GAINS AMONG WOMEN AFTER CLINTON EXIT
Now running as strongly vs. McCain among women as Clinton did

by Jeffrey M. Jones, Gallup Poll Managing Editor

Since Hillary Clinton decided to concede the Democratic nomination to Barack Obama last week, Obama has established a lead over Republican John McCain in general-election polling. Obama's gains have come more from women than men, though he has picked up among both groups in recent days.

Vote Preference in the General Presidential Election, Among Men

Based on registered voters

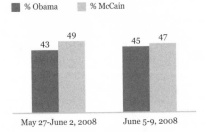

Based on aggregated Gallup Poll Daily tracking data

Obama's lead among women has now expanded from five percentage points to 13, while his deficit among men has shrunk from six points to two.

These figures are based on aggregated Gallup Poll Daily tracking interviews with national registered voters conducted May 27-June 2 (the week immediately before Obama clinched the nomination on June 3), which showed Obama and McCain tied at 46%, and June

Vote Preference in the General Presidential Election, Among Women

Based on registered voters

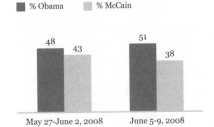

Based on aggregated Gallup Poll Daily tracking data

5-9 (the five days since it was reported that Clinton would suspend her campaign), which show Obama ahead, 48% to 42%. Obama clinched the nomination on the evening of June 3, and the news media reported Clinton would suspend her campaign on the evening of June 4. Thus, the data give a clear picture of voter support before and after Clinton's exit.

While campaigning for president, Clinton demonstrated an especially strong appeal to women. She led McCain by 52% to 40% in her final full week as a candidate, exactly equal to the average since mid-March. By comparison, Obama held only an average 47% to 42% lead over McCain among women during the same time span. At least for now, he seems to be matching Clinton's performance among women versus McCain, given his current 13-point lead among female voters.

One of Clinton's core groups of supporters during the nomination phase of the campaign was older women. During the last few days of her active candidacy, Clinton led McCain by 51% to 41% among women aged 50 and older, while Obama *trailed* McCain among this group, 46% to 43%.

Since Clinton suspended her campaign, older women's vote preferences have shifted toward Obama, so that he now enjoys a six-point advantage over McCain.

Vote Preference in the General Presidential Election, Among Women 50 and Older

Based on registered voters

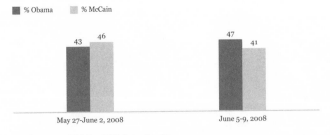

Based on aggregated Gallup Poll Daily tracking data

Obama had always run much better among younger women, in large part because of his strong appeal to younger voters. But his support has also risen among women aged 18 to 49 in the past few days, further expanding his already formidable 52% to 40% lead over McCain to 56% to 35%.

Obama has made major gains in the past few days among married women, erasing McCain's former 52% to 40% lead and pulling into a 45% to 45% tie. Meanwhile, the vote preferences among married men (a solid McCain group) and unmarried men and women (solid Obama groups) have changed little since Clinton decided to end her White House bid.

Vote Preference in the General Presidential Election,
by Gender and Marital Status

Based on registered voters

	May 27-June 2, 2008	June 5-9, 2008
Married men	McCain, 55%-38%	McCain, 53%-39%
Married women	McCain, 52%-40%	Tied, 45%-45%
Unmarried men	Obama, 54%-39%	Obama, 57%-35%
Unmarried women	Obama, 57%-32%	Obama, 57%-31%

Based on aggregated Gallup Poll Daily tracking data

Obama has also seen his support among non-Hispanic white women increase modestly, though McCain still holds a slim 46% to 43% advantage among this group. Prior to Clinton's departure, McCain led Obama by 50% to 41% among white women.

Interestingly, while white women were a major part of Clinton's primary constituency, she maintained only a slim (if any) advantage in general-election trial heats versus McCain among this group. In the last week of her campaign, she only tied McCain among white women, at 47%. Thus, her strong performance against McCain among all female voters in presidential trial heats was primarily because of strong support from minority women.

Implications

Obama's recent gains in the polls have been greatly aided by increased support from female voters. Now that Clinton is no longer campaigning and the focus of voters' decision-making is a choice between Obama and McCain, female voters may be taking a second look at Obama. Indeed, his current 13-point advantage over McCain is essentially the same advantage that Clinton held over McCain throughout her active candidacy.

Obama's challenge in the general-election campaign will be to bring core Democratic groups that did not strongly support him in the primaries—women, voters with less formal education, and conservative Democrats—back into the fold. He appears to be already doing that among women. However, it is not clear whether this is just a temporary rally in support for him upon clinching the nomination, or whether he will be able to sustain a high level of support from female voters for the duration of the campaign.

Survey Methods

Results are based on telephone interviews with 5,270 registered voters, aged 18 and older, conducted May 27-June 2, and 4,390 registered voters, aged 18 and older, conducted June 5-9 as part of Gallup's daily election tracking polling. For results based on the total sample of national adults, one can say with 95% confidence that the maximum margin of sampling error is ±2 percentage points.

For results based on the sample of 2,669 female registered voters in the May 27-June 2 sample and 2,263 female registered voters in the June 5-9 sample, the maximum margins of sampling error are ±2 percentage points.

Interviews are conducted with respondents on land-line telephones (for respondents with a land-line telephone) and cellular phones (for respondents who are cell-phone only).

In addition to sampling error, question wording and practical difficulties in conducting surveys can introduce error or bias into the findings of public opinion polls.

June 12, 2008

LARGE DEMOCRATIC BASE PROVIDES BIG ADVANTAGE FOR OBAMA

Over half of Americans identify as or lean toward being Democratic

by Frank Newport, Gallup Poll Editor in Chief

The current political landscape, with the percentage of those identifying themselves as Democrats outnumbering those who identify as Republicans by a 37% to 28% margin, provides a significant advantage for Barack Obama's presidential chances.

Party Identification

June 5-10, 2008

Among registered voters

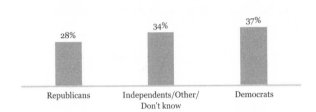

These data are based on 5,299 interviews with registered voters conducted as part of Gallup Poll Daily tracking during the six-day period of June 5-10, representing the period since the general-election matchup of Obama versus John McCain became definite. Thirty-seven percent of Americans identify themselves as Democrats, compared to 28% who identify as Republicans. Another 34% say they are independents and don't choose (in response to this initial question) to identify with either party.

Following very well-established patterns in American presidential elections, voter identification as a Republican or Democrat is strongly—but not totally—correlated with support for the two parties' candidates.

Presidential General Election, by Party ID

June 5-10, 2008

Among registered voters

■ John McCain   ▢ Barack Obama

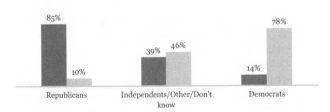

Those who identify as Republicans at this juncture appear to be a bit more loyal to their party's candidate, with 85% supporting McCain, compared to the 78% of those who identify as Democrats supporting Obama. Looked at differently, Democrats have a slightly higher defection rate—at this point—than do Republicans. (Although these data were collected after Hillary Clinton's announcement that she was suspending her campaign, it is possible that the Democratic defection rate represents some residual anger among Clinton-supporting Democrats, anger that may dissipate between now and November.)

Independents—who initially do not identify with either party—break toward Obama by a 46% to 39% margin. (McCain and Obama have been competitive for the independent vote since March.)

When all of these data for June 5-10 are put together, the overall vote pattern for this period among registered voters is a six-point margin for Obama over McCain, 48% to 42%. The margin is in Obama's favor in part because there are more Democrats than Republicans in the sample, which helps compensate for the fact that Democrats are slightly less loyal to Obama than are Republicans to McCain. Obama's margin is also based on Obama's ability to swing independents slightly in his direction.

Hypothetically speaking, if there were no independents in the race, Obama would still win by a five-point margin, 49% to 44%—reflecting the higher percentage of Democratic identifiers in the voting population.

All in all, for McCain to win the popular vote in November, some combination of the following would need to occur:

1. An increase in the percentage of the voting population who identify as Republicans
2. An increase in the percentage of Republicans who support McCain
3. An increase in the percentage of the vote McCain receives from those who identify as Democrats
4. An increase in the support McCain receives among independents
5. A much higher turnout rate for McCain supporters than for Obama supporters

It appears that McCain's chances of increasing his support among independents may not be extremely high. The accompanying table shows the split when the 34% who are independents are asked if they "lean" one way or the other.

Party Identification, Including Leaners
June 5-10, 2008
Among registered voters

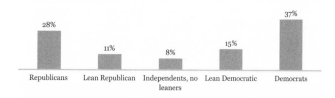

This more detailed analysis provides a better understanding of why Obama is leading among independents. When pressed to say which way they lean, independents tilt toward identifying with the Democratic Party by a significant margin. The 34% independent segment breaks down into 15% who lean Democratic, 11% who lean Republican, and 8% who remain "pure" independents and refuse to indicate which way they lean. Looked at differently, 44% of the initial independent segment leans Democratic, compared to just 33% who lean Republican.

These "leaners" are essentially as loyal to their party's candidate as are those who initially identified with a party without being prompted.

Eighty-one percent of independents who lean Republican support McCain, while 83% of those who lean Democratic support Obama.

Thus, all in all, this profile of the relationship between party identification with leaners allocated and vote choice reveals a situation similar to the situation before leaners are allocated. McCain gets

Presidential General Election, by Party ID (Including Leaners)
June 5-10, 2008
Among registered voters

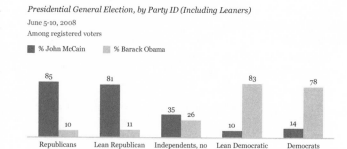

Presidential General Election by Party ID, With Leaners Allocated
June 5-10, 2008
Among registered voters

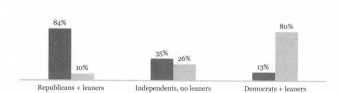

a slightly higher 84% of Republicans with leaners than Obama's 80% of Democrats with leaners, but the significantly higher percentage of Democrats in the electorate gives Obama his overall edge.

What about the small sliver of "pure independents" who refuse to admit that they lean toward one party or the other? This group constitutes only 8% of the voting electorate, and is largely an apolitical group. They are much more likely to be undecided than other voters, but the basic tilt is 35% to 26% for McCain over Obama. This, of course, is not nearly enough to compensate for the large number of Democratic identifiers.

Implications

At this point, Obama's lead in the general-election popular vote is correlated with the fact that there are more American voters who identify themselves as Democrats than as Republicans. This allows Obama to compensate for the slightly smaller percentage of those identifying as Democrats who support him than is the case for Republicans who support McCain. Obama is further helped by the fact that voters who initially identify as independents are more likely to lean toward identifying as Democrats than to lean toward the Republican Party. McCain does have a slight edge among pure independents, but this is not enough to compensate for these other dynamics.

Survey Methods

Results are based on telephone interviews with 5,299 registered voters, aged 18 and older, conducted June 5-10, 2008. For results based on the total sample of national adults, one can say with 95% confidence that the maximum margin of sampling error is ±2 percentage points.

Interviews are conducted with respondents on land-line telephones (for respondents with a land-line telephone) and cellular phones (for respondents who are cell-phone only).

In addition to sampling error, question wording and practical difficulties in conducting surveys can introduce error or bias into the findings of public opinion polls.

June 12, 2008

REPUBLICANS SOUR ON NATION'S MORAL CLIMATE

In contrast to Democrats, majority now say moral values are "poor"

by Lydia Saad, Gallup Poll Senior Editor

Republicans have grown more critical of the state of moral values in the United States, with the percentage rating present moral conditions "poor" rising from 36% in 2006 to 51% in 2007, and remaining at that level today. No comparable change is seen among independents or Democrats.

How would you rate the overall state of moral values in this country today -- as excellent, good, only fair, or poor?

% "Poor"

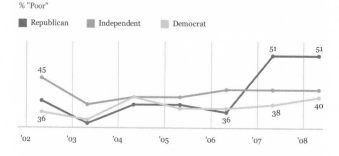

As a result, Republicans are now significantly more negative about moral values than independents or Democrats, marking a change from the recent past.

These findings come from Gallup's annual Values and Beliefs survey, updated May 8-11, 2008.

The overall results to the question about the state of moral values show that, as has been the case consistently throughout the decade, few Americans give the country's moral climate high marks. Only 15% consider moral values to be "excellent" or "good" while 41% call them "only fair" and 44% consider them to be "poor."

How would you rate the overall state of moral values in this country today -- as excellent, good, only fair, or poor?

May 8-11, 2008

A follow-up question asks Americans whether moral values are getting better or getting worse, and yields an equally negative answer. Only 11% of Americans perceive that values are improving, while 81% say things are getting worse.

It is unclear why Republicans' views about the state of the nation's current moral values would have soured sometime between the May 2006 and May 2007 Gallup surveys while those of Democrats and independents did not. However, since 2002, in response to the second question about moral values, all three partisan groups have grown increasingly pessimistic about the direction in which moral values are headed.

Right now, do you think the state of moral values in the country as a whole is getting better or getting worse?

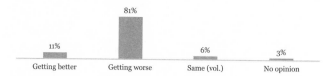

May 8-11, 2008

(vol.) = Volunteered response

Bottom Line

Americans are reliably negative when it comes to rating moral values in the country. Since 2002, a majority of Americans have consistently said the state of moral values is less than good and getting worse.

Apart from this general pattern, Republicans' disaffection with the nation's moral climate (but not Democrats' or independents') has been elevated over the past two years, A number of "values" issues have been in the news in recent years, including gay marriage, popstar misbehavior, and reports of high-profile elected officials involved in sex-related scandals, but it is unclear that any of these are responsible for the pattern in the data.

Whatever the cause, this may signal that Republicans will be particularly anxious to elect a new president this November who will help to uphold or restore the values they now find lacking in the country.

Survey Methods

Results are based on telephone interviews with 1,017 national adults, aged 18 and older, conducted May 8-11, 2008. For results based on the total sample of national adults, one can say with 95% confidence that the maximum margin of sampling error is ±3 percentage points.

Interviews are conducted with respondents on land-line telephones (for respondents with a land-line telephone) and cellular phones (for respondents who are cell-phone only).

In addition to sampling error, question wording and practical difficulties in conducting surveys can introduce error or bias into the findings of public opinion polls.

June 13, 2008

PUBLIC FAULTS BUSH FOR LACK OF ACTION ON ENERGY

Only 17% believe he is doing enough to solve the country's energy problems

by Jeffrey M. Jones, Gallup Poll Managing Editor

In the midst of record high gas prices, just 17% of Americans say President Bush is doing enough to solve the country's energy problems, a significant decline from already low figures in 2006.

Additionally, nearly half of Americans, 49%, say the Bush administration deserves a great deal of blame for the country's energy problems, up from 38% in 2006 and just 20% in May 2001, when rolling blackouts in California focused national attention on the issue.

Overall, do you think President Bush is or is not doing enough to solve the country's energy problems?

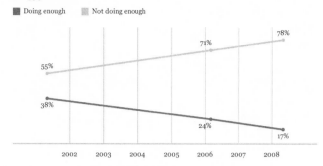

Do you think the following deserve a great deal of blame, some blame, not much blame, or no blame at all for the country's current energy problems?

Percentage point increase change in "great deal" of blame since March 2006

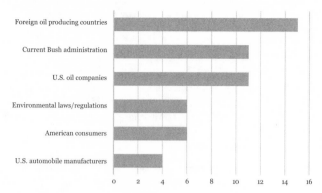

May 30-June 1, 2008

Of the seven government and business institutions tested in the poll, the Bush administration ranks second on the blame list, behind U.S. oil companies (60%). Oil companies have topped the list each time Gallup has asked the question, and—like Bush—are blamed more now than they were in 2006.

Do you think the following deserve a great deal of blame, some blame, not much blame, or no blame at all for the country's current energy problems?

% Blame a great deal

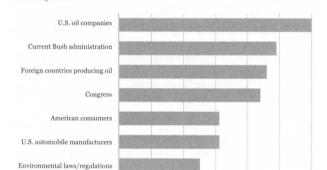

May 30-June 1, 2008

Who do you think should have the primary responsibility for spending money to develop alternative sources of energy to gasoline?

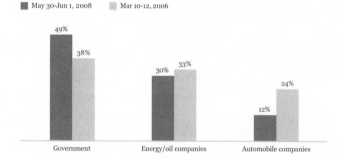

Implications

The Bush administration and Congress have taken action on energy in recent years, but those steps were largely targeted toward energy usage in the future and did little to address the more immediate concern of high gas prices. Bush himself has said there is no "magic wand" he can wave to cut gas prices. Though Americans may be more aware of the complex reasons for high gas prices, they still hold their elected officials accountable. That may be why the already low approval ratings of Bush and Congress have eroded further in recent months.

Survey Methods

Results are based on telephone interviews with 1,012 national adults, aged 18 and older, conducted May 30-June 1, 2008. For results based on the total sample of national adults, one can say with 95% confidence that the maximum margin of sampling error is ±3 percentage points.

Interviews are conducted with respondents on land-line telephones (for respondents with a land-line telephone) and cellular phones (for respondents who are cell-phone only).

In addition to sampling error, question wording and practical difficulties in conducting surveys can introduce error or bias into the findings of public opinion polls.

Even though these results find oil companies being blamed to a greater degree than in 2006, results of a recent Gallup Panel survey suggests that Americans are becoming more aware that high gas prices are a result of many factors beyond simple oil company greed. While "oil company greed" remains the most commonly mentioned reason for high gas prices, the percentage saying this has dropped significantly in the past year. Rather, Americans were more likely to cite a variety of other factors—such as greater demand for oil, the declining value of the U.S. dollar, and market speculators—as reasons for high gas prices.

This increase in blame for "big oil" from 49% to 60% may also reflect a more general pattern of the public assigning greater responsibility to all government and business institutions for the country's energy problems. All six institutions tested in the 2006 and 2008 Gallup Polls showed higher levels of blame this year.

Over the past two years, the public has increasingly looked to government to solve the nation's energy problems. Forty-nine percent of Americans now say the government should have the primary responsibility to develop alternative sources of energy to gasoline, up from 38% in 2006. Currently, 30% say oil and energy companies have the main responsibility, nearly the same as in 2006. Fewer now believe that automobile companies are largely responsible (12%) than did so in 2006 (24%).

June 13, 2008

RELIGIOUS AMERICANS PREFER MCCAIN OVER OBAMA

Preference is especially strong among religious white Americans

by Frank Newport, Gallup Poll Editor in Chief

John McCain beats Barack Obama in a general-election trial heat by a 47% to 42% margin among voters who say religion is an important part of their daily lives, while Obama wins by an overwhelming 58% to 33% margin among voters who say religion is not an important part of their lives.

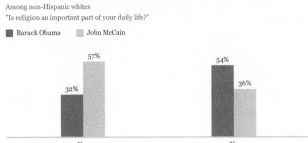

Presidential Trial Heat, by Importance of Religion in Respondents' Daily Lives

Among non-Hispanic whites
"Is religion an important part of your daily life?"

■ Barack Obama ■ John McCain

June 5-10, 2008

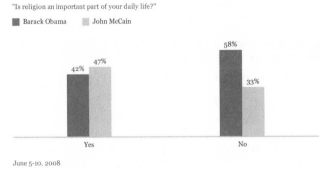

Presidential Trial Heat, by Importance of Religion in Respondents' Daily Lives

"Is religion an important part of your daily life?"

■ Barack Obama ■ John McCain

June 5-10, 2008

This analysis is based on a sample of more than 5,000 registered voters interviewed between June 5 and June 10, all interviews completed since Obama's status as the Democratic nominee became a near certainty after the final Democratic primaries. The data show that Americans' self-reports of the importance of religion in their lives are powerfully predictive of voting preferences in the coming general election.

Thirty-five percent of Americans at this time say religion is *not* an important part of their daily lives. Among this group, support for Obama's candidacy is 10 points higher than for the sample as a whole (Obama leads McCain overall by a 48% to 42% margin during this period), and support for McCain is nine points lower. This results in a swing from a six-point overall lead for Obama among all voters to a lead of 25 points among less religious voters. Among the group of Americans for whom religion is important—64% of the sample—the swing is from the Obama six-point lead to a McCain lead of five points.

This relationship, powerful as it is, is mitigated by the fact that the black Americans included in the sample are both highly religious and highly likely to support Obama. It therefore follows that the relationship between self-reported importance of religion and general-election vote is stronger when the sample is restricted only to whites.

McCain wins overall among non-Hispanic whites by a 49% to 40% margin, a common pattern for Republican candidates in recent presidential races. But among whites, as is true for the overall sample, religion remains a very strong dividing variable.

Among white voters for whom religion is an important part of their daily lives, McCain's margin stretches to a very large 25 points, 57% to 32%. Among white voters for whom religion is not an important part of their daily lives, about 37% of all white voters, Obama wins by an 18-point margin, 54% to 36%. This is a shift in the margin of an extraordinary 43 points between whites who are religious and those who are not. In short, this one dichotomous question about the importance of religion is by itself a potent predictor of white voters' presidential vote intentions.

The reasons for this relationship are complex. Self-reported importance of religion is itself highly related to a number of other demographic variables, which in turn are related to political orientation. Younger voters, for example, are less likely than those who are older to say religion is important in their lives, and younger voters are among Obama's largest support groups. Unmarried voters are less likely to say religion is important in their lives and more likely to support Obama. Highly educated voters are less likely to say religion is important in their lives (although they attend church with equal frequency to those with less education) and highly educated voters constitute a strong voter bloc for Obama.

At the same time, importance of religion is related to a number of social and values attitudes that are themselves related to political orientation.

Thus, it is difficult to pinpoint exactly what is driving the religion-vote relationship. It may be that religion per se is less important than some underlying causal factor—either demographic or attitudinal—that is correlated with both religion and voting propensity. Still, the fact remains that at the overarching level, a simple answer to a question about the importance of religion in a person's life is a strongly suggestive clue as to how that person will vote in the November general election.

Survey Methods

Results are based on telephone interviews with 5,299 registered voters, aged 18 and older, conducted June 5-10, 2008. For results based on the total sample of national adults, one can say with 95% confidence that the maximum margin of sampling error is ±2 percentage points.

Interviews are conducted with respondents on land-line telephones (for respondents with a land-line telephone) and cellular phones (for respondents who are cell-phone only).

In addition to sampling error, question wording and practical difficulties in conducting surveys can introduce error or bias into the findings of public opinion polls.

June 16, 2008

AMERICANS PREDICT OBAMA WILL BE NEXT U.S. PRESIDENT

A 52% majority thinks Obama Will Win, Versus 41% Choosing McCain

by Lydia Saad, Gallup Poll Senior Editor

Barack Obama and John McCain are now about tied in Gallup Poll Daily tracking of voter preferences for the general election; nevertheless, in a June 9-12 Gallup Poll, Obama leads McCain 52% to 41% in public perceptions of who will win in November.

Regardless of whom you support, and trying to be as objective as possible, who do you think will win the presidential election in November?

Rotated: Barack Obama or John McCain?

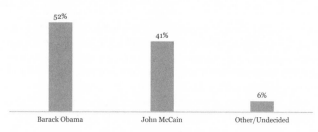

June 9-12, 2008

Democrats are slightly more confident that their presumptive nominee will prevail in November—76% say Obama will win—than Republicans are about McCain's chances (67%). What tips the balance of national opinion more strongly in favor of Obama is that, by a nine-percentage point margin, independents join Democrats in believing Obama is likely to win.

Presidential Election Prediction, by Party ID

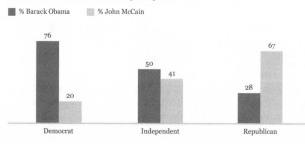

June 9-12, 2008

Bottom Line

They say perception becomes reality. At this early stage of the general election campaign, perceptions of who can win are working in Obama's favor, even among older generations of Americans and Southerners who are more likely to back McCain for the presidency.

Survey Methods

Results are based on telephone interviews with 822 national adults, aged 18 and older, conducted June 9-12, 2008. For results based on the total sample of national adults, one can say with 95% confidence that the maximum margin of sampling error is ±4 percentage points.

Gallup Poll Daily tracking results on the Obama-McCain race are based on telephone interviews with 2,536 registered voters interviewed June 9-10 and June 12, 2008.

Interviews are conducted with respondents on land-line telephones (for respondents with a land-line telephone) and cellular phones (for respondents who are cell-phone only).

In addition to sampling error, question wording and practical difficulties in conducting surveys can introduce error or bias into the findings of public opinion polls.

June 16, 2008

BUSH, CONGRESS, SUPREME COURT NEAR HISTORICAL LOW APPROVAL

Thirty percent approve of job Bush is doing as president

by Jeffrey M. Jones, Gallup Poll Managing Editor

Less than a majority of Americans approve of the job performance of each of the three branches of the federal government, with the Supreme Court rated most positively and Congress least positively. The ratings for all three branches approach the lowest Gallup has measured historically.

Do you approve or disapprove of the way the president, the members of Congress, and the Supreme Court are handling their jobs?

June 9-12, 2008

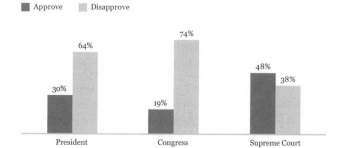

According to the June 9-12 Gallup Poll, 30% of Americans approve of the job George W. Bush is doing as president. That figure is two percentage points better than his personal low rating of 28%, which he has received four times in the past two months. The all-time low approval rating for any president in Gallup annals is 22% for Harry Truman in 1952.

The current poll marks Bush's first approval rating at 30% or above since March 2008. He has not had an approval rating at 40% or above since September 2006 and has not had one at 50% since May 2005.

Congress' 19% approval rating is one point better than last month's 18%, which matched August 2007 and March 1992 readings as the worst Gallup has measured since it began tracking Congressional job approval in 1974.

Congress typically receives the lowest approval ratings of the three branches. Since the beginning of Bush's presidency, Congress has averaged 39% approval, compared with 51% for Bush and 55% for the Supreme Court. The general pattern has held prior to Bush's presidency as well.

Do you approve or disapprove of the way George W. Bush is handling his job as president?

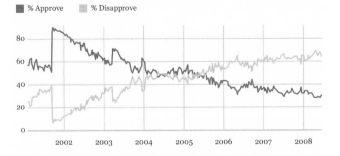

Do you approve or disapprove of the way Congress is handling its job?

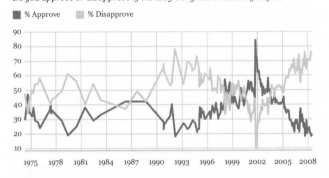

Currently, 48% of Americans approve of the job the Supreme Court is doing. Gallup does not have the same long track record of measuring approval of the Supreme Court (first asked in 2000) that it does for the president and Congress. But it has only measured a lower approval rating once before, in June 2005 when 42% approved of the Court following a controversial decision that allowed government greater power to seize private property for public purposes. That marked the only time more Americans disapproved than approved of the Court, even though it has made a number of controversial rulings in recent years concerning the disputed 2000 election outcome, affirmative action, and homosexual relations to name a few.

Do you approve or disapprove of the way the Supreme Court is handling its job?

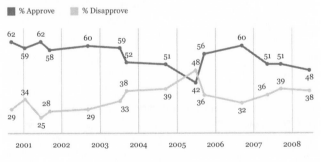

Survey Methods

Results are based on telephone interviews with 822 national adults, aged 18 and older, conducted June 9-12, 2008. For results based on the total sample of national adults, one can say with 95% confidence that the maximum margin of sampling error is ±4 percentage points.

Interviews are conducted with respondents on land-line telephones (for respondents with a land-line telephone) and cellular phones (for respondents who are cell-phone only).

In addition to sampling error, question wording and practical difficulties in conducting surveys can introduce error or bias into the findings of public opinion polls.

June 17, 2008
FUEL PRICES NOW CLEARLY AMERICANS' NO. 2 CONCERN
The economy/jobs still the top-mentioned problem facing America

by Lydia Saad, Gallup Poll Senior Editor

The high cost of fuel has eclipsed Iraq as the second highest ranking issue on Gallup's monthly "Most Important Problem" list, after roughly tying Iraq at No. 2 in May, and ranking third prior to that. The 25% citing fuel and energy prices in June as the nation's top problem is up from 17% in May and 6% in January.

Top Three Issues Named "Most Important Problem"

According to the June 9-12 Gallup Poll, the economy/jobs retains its position as No. 1, with the percentage of Americans citing the overall economic climate exceeding 40% for the fifth straight month. Top-of-mind concern about the Iraq conflict, now 20%, is down slightly from the start of the year, and is much lower than it was a year ago.

Long-Term Trends in Most Important Problem

Total economic mentions are about as high today as they have been at any time since the start of George W. Bush's presidency in January 2001.

The highest proportion citing the economy as the most important problem in the Bush era was 48% in May 2003 and April 2008. However, on a longer-term basis, Americans' current level of economic concern—based on their "most important problem" response—still lags behind what Gallup found at times between 1982 and early 1984, and from 1991 to 1992 (as well as in 1945). This may reflect the fact that there are other substantial issues of concern to the public right now (Iraq and gas prices) that compete with the economy for the public's focus, which may not have been the case at other times.

The contrast between Americans' focus on problems today versus in the past is even more striking in terms of fuel prices and other cost-of-living issues. Currently 25% of Americans mention fuel prices, specifically, and an additional 6% mention the related issue of inflation or the high cost of living generally as the nation's top

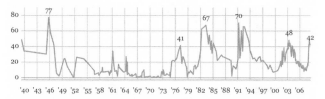

Long-Term Trend in Mentions of The Economy/Jobs as Most Important Problem in the United States Today*

April 1939 - June 2008

* Figures are based on sum of total mentions for each category, and thus may include duplication among respondents. The economy includes those citing "recession."

problem. That falls well below the 50% or more of Americans citing these issues at multiple times between 1973 and 1981. In October 1978 a remarkable 83% of Americans cited inflation or fuel prices as the nation's top problem.

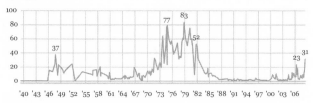

Long-Term Trend in Mentions of Fuel Prices/Inflation as Most Important Problem in the United States Today*

April 1939 - June 2008

* Figures are based on sum of total mentions for each category, and thus may include some duplication among respondents.

U.S. Satisfaction Hovering Near Rock Bottom

The same poll finds only 14% of Americans saying they are satisfied with the way things are going in the United States today, only two percentage points off the record low reported by Gallup in 1979. This month's satisfaction figure is identical to last month's, but is down from 24% in January.

The last time a majority of Americans were satisfied with the direction of the country was in January 2004. Except for a few brief rebounds, Americans' satisfaction with the way things are going in the country has essentially been in decline since early 2002.

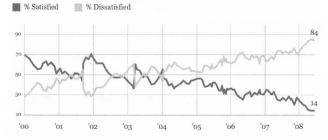

In general, are you satisfied or dissatisfied with the way things are going in the United States at this time?

January 2000 - June 2008

■ % Satisfied ▨ % Dissatisfied

Most of the recent decline in U.S. satisfaction can be attributed to Republicans who, after maintaining a relatively high level of satisfaction in 2007, finally succumbed to a more negative perspective in 2008. Currently, 26% of Republicans say they are satisfied with the direction of the country, compared with 8% of Democrats and

9% of independents. Thus, the only way satisfaction could drop much further is if Republicans become even more discouraged about the nation—unlikely with a Republican still in the White House.

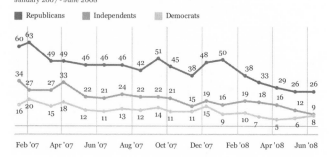

Percentage Satisfied with United States Direction, by Party I.D.

January 2007 - June 2008

■ Republicans ▨ Independents ▨ Democrats

Bottom Line

Americans' satisfaction with the country is about depleted, their focus on energy costs as the nation's top problem appears to be rising, and their concerns about the economy, generally, and the Iraq situation are not going away.

Still, as Gallup records show, Americans' economic anxiety (as expressed by their naming economic issues as the worst problems facing the country) has been much higher, historically. Americans' economic mood looks bad now, but it appears that it could be even worse.

Survey Methods

Results are based on telephone interviews with 822 national adults, aged 18 and older, conducted June 9-12, 2008. For results based on the total sample of national adults, one can say with 95% confidence that the maximum margin of sampling error is ±4 percentage points.

Interviews are conducted with respondents on land-line telephones (for respondents with a land-line telephone) and cellular phones (for respondents who are cell-phone only).

In addition to sampling error, question wording and practical difficulties in conducting surveys can introduce error or bias into the findings of public opinion polls.

June 18, 2008
AMERICANS EVENLY DIVIDED ON MORALITY OF HOMOSEXUALITY
However, majority supports legality and acceptance of gay relations

by Lydia Saad, Gallup Poll Senior Editor

Americans interviewed in Gallup's 2008 Values and Beliefs poll are evenly divided over the morality of homosexual relations, with 48% considering them morally acceptable and 48% saying they are morally wrong.

While similar to last year's results, current attitudes are more affirming of gays than what Gallup found at the start of the decade when the majority said such relations were morally wrong.

Perceptions of the Morality of Homosexual Relations

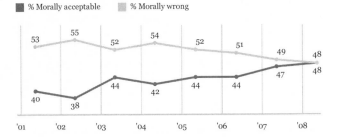

■ % Morally acceptable   ▨ % Morally wrong

Do you think homosexual relations between consenting adults should or should not be legal?

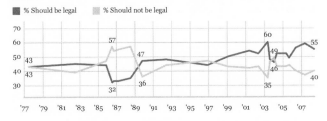

■ % Should be legal   ▨ % Should not be legal

Still, homosexuality emerges as the most divisive of 16 major social and cultural issues measured in the May 8-11, 2008 survey. Only doctor-assisted suicide and abortion come close to it in splitting public opinion.

All other issues have either higher majority agreement (including divorce, gambling, the death penalty, medical testing on animals, out-of-wedlock births, and several other issues) or majority disagreement (including cloning animals or humans, suicide, polygamy, and extramarital affairs).

Next, I'm going to read you a list of issues. Regardless of whether or not you think it should be legal, for each one, please tell me whether you personally believe that in general it is morally acceptable or morally wrong.

	Morally acceptable	Morally wrong
	%	%
Divorce	70	22
Gambling	63	32
The death penalty	62	30
Medical research using stem cells obtained from human embryos	62	30
Sex between an unmarried man and woman	61	36
Medical testing on animals	56	38
Having a baby outside of marriage	55	41
Buying and wearing clothing made of animal fur	54	39
Doctor assisted suicide	51	44
HOMOSEXUAL RELATIONS	48	48
Abortion	40	48
Cloning animals	33	61
Suicide	15	78
Cloning humans	11	85
Polygamy, when one husband has more than one wife at the same time	8	90
Married men and women having an affair	7	91

May 8-11, 2008

Despite Americans' divided reaction to homosexuality on a moral basis, the majority believes homosexual relations should be legal (55%) and accepted as an alternative lifestyle (57%).

Support for the legality of homosexual relations has advanced and receded over the years, beginning at 43% when Gallup first asked about it in 1977. Support then dipped in the 1980s to the low 30s, but gradually increased through the 1990s and reached 60% in May 2003.

In July 2003 (shortly after a U.S. Supreme Court decision striking down a Texas sodomy law) it fell to 50% and remained at about that level through 2005. However, in May 2006 it jumped to 56%, and since then a clear majority has agreed that homosexual relations should be legal.

Agreement that homosexuality should be considered an "acceptable alternative lifestyle" (a wording Gallup began using in 1982)

has followed a more linear path (though it, too, dipped after the Supreme Court ruling in the summer of 2003), increasing from 34% in 1982 to 44% in 1996, to 54% in 2003, and 57% in 2007, where it remains today.

Do you feel that homosexuality should be considered an acceptable alternative lifestyle or not?

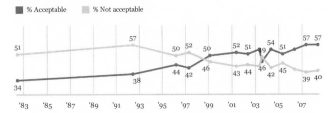

■ % Acceptable   ▨ % Not acceptable

Even in the 1970s, the majority of Americans believed homosexuals should have equal rights in terms of job opportunities. But support for this principle has become nearly universal in recent years, reaching 89% in 2004 and is still 89% today.

As you may know, there has been considerable discussion in the news regarding the rights of homosexual men and women. In general, do you think homosexuals should or should not have equal rights in terms of job opportunities?

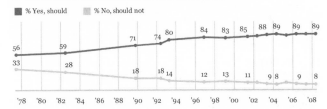

■ % Yes, should   ▨ % No, should not

The critical issue for the gay rights movement today is same-sex marriage. The latest poll shows there is still considerable public resistance to giving the same legal sanction to same-sex couples as the law does to traditional marriages. As Gallup reported on May 15, 2008, only 40% of Americans say such marriages should be legally valid—as they now are in Massachusetts and California—while 56% disagree.

Americans are more supportive of gay marriage today than they were when Gallup initiated this measure in 1996, but attitudes have changed little since about 2004 when 42% said they should be valid.

Bottom Line

Gallup polling chronicles important changes in public attitudes about homosexuality and gay rights over the past quarter century. Americans have shifted from frowning on homosexuality as an alternative lifestyle and being divided over whether it should be legal, to now supporting gay rights on both fronts. At the same time, the country

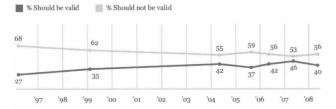

Do you think marriages between same-sex couples should or should not be recognized by the law as valid, with the same rights as traditional marriages?

■ % Should be valid   ■ % Should not be valid

remains highly ambivalent about the morality of homosexual relations, and as a result, support for legalizing gay marriage lags far behind the less culturally sensitive matter of gays having equal job rights.

Americans have generally grown more supportive of gay rights since 2001, reaching record high support on most measures in 2007; however, there has been no further increase in support over the past year.

Survey Methods

Results are based on telephone interviews with 1,017 national adults, aged 18 and older, conducted May 8-11, 2008. For results based on the total sample of national adults, one can say with 95% confidence that the maximum margin of sampling error is ±3 percentage points.

Interviews are conducted with respondents on land-line telephones (for respondents with a land-line telephone) and cellular phones (for respondents who are cell-phone only).

In addition to sampling error, question wording and practical difficulties in conducting surveys can introduce error or bias into the findings of public opinion polls.

June 19, 2008
ABOUT HALF OF AMERICANS REPORT RECEIVING STIMULUS REBATE
Little apparent impact of rebate on economic attitudes

by Frank Newport, Gallup Poll Editor in Chief and Dennis Jacobe, Gallup Chief Economist

Gallup Poll tracking shows that 45% of Americans are now reporting that they have received their tax rebate, but finds little apparent effect of these rebates on consumer attitudes.

Percent Reporting They Received A Tax Rebate

■ Percent Receiving Tax Rebate

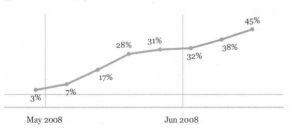

In late April, the IRS began sending out tax rebates to an estimated 130 million American families and households. Gallup Poll tracking data document the degree to which the rebates have made their way into Americans' bank accounts or mailboxes, with the percent reporting having received their rebate jumping from a minimal 3% in late April to the current 45%. The last checks are scheduled to be distributed on July 11.

Consumer Confidence and Tax Rebates

The main purpose of the stimulus legislation was to help the economy by "stimulating" consumer spending. Although reports indicate that May retail spending did increase, the day-by-day analysis of Gallup's tracking data (displayed above) shows that rebate penetration was quite low as May began and had only reached about a third of all adults by the time May ended. Furthermore, an analysis of rebate data shows that there is very little relationship between an individual having received the rebate and a positive change in his or her economic attitude.

As an example, and consistent with an earlier Gallup analysis of rebate data, the billions of dollars in tax rebates that have already been distributed to millions of Americans has apparently done nothing to improve overall consumer confidence in the U.S. economy. When asked to rate current economic conditions, 43% of those who have already received their tax rebates rate the U.S. economy as "poor" and 16% rate it as "excellent" or "good," while 44% of those who have not received a rebate rate the economy as "poor" and 16% rate it as "excellent" or "good."

Tax Rebate Impact on Consumer Ratings of Current Economic Conditions

■ Received Tax Rebate   ■ Not Received Tax Rebate

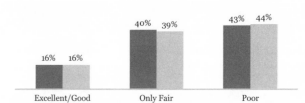

Similarly, 88% of those who have already received a rebate say economic conditions in the country as a whole are getting worse, not better, while 86% of those who have not received a rebate agree things are getting worse—meaning both groups essentially hold the same view.

Tax Rebate Impact on Consumer Expectations for the Economy

■ Received Tax Rebate   ■ Not Received Tax Rebate

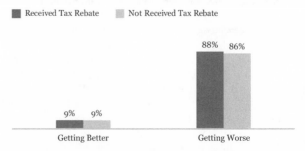

Worried About Money and Tax Rebates

There is a slight difference in consumers' worries about their own financial situations based on their rebate status, although this impact appears to be minimal at best in this area. When asked if they "worried about money yesterday," 34% of those who have already received their rebates stated that they worried. Among those who had not received a rebate, the results were slightly less positive with 36% saying they worried.

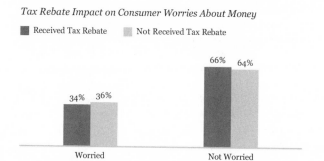

Tax Rebate Impact on Consumer Worries About Money

Commentary

Gallup's survey results suggest that much of the impact of the special tax rebates this year may have already been, or will soon be, realized. More than half of those in the $24,000 to $90,000 a year, middle-income group have already received their rebates. Importantly, the IRS will end the first mailings of the tax rebates by July 11, and the program was designed so that not everyone will receive a rebate.

Further, the stimulating effect of the tax rebates may be limited to its direct spending aspects, at best. There seems to be little likelihood that the tax rebates will stimulate additional non-rebate related consumer spending since they have done little, if anything, to improve consumer confidence.

Survey Methods

Gallup is interviewing no fewer than 1,000 U.S. adults nationwide each day during 2008. The rebate and economic questions analyzed in this report are based on combined data of more than 20,000 interviews in April, May and June. For results based on this sample, the maximum margin of sampling error is ±1 percentage point. The questions for June 10-16 are based on combined data of more than 3,000 interviews. For results based on this sample, the maximum margin of sampling error is ±2 percentage points.

In addition to sampling error, question wording and practical difficulties in conducting surveys can introduce error or bias into the findings of public opinion polls.

June 19, 2008
MAJORITY OF AMERICANS SUPPORT DRILLING IN OFF-LIMITS AREAS
Republicans much more in favor than Democrats

by Frank Newport, Gallup Poll Editor in Chief

A majority of Americans (57%) interviewed in a mid-May Gallup Panel survey approve of expanding drilling for oil in offshore and wilderness areas considered to be off-limits.

Please say whether you would favor or oppose taking each of the following steps to attempt to reduce the price of gasoline. How about: Allowing oil drilling in U.S. coastal and wilderness areas now off-limits to oil exploration?
May 19-21, 2008

This poll result suggests that President Bush's proposals this week to end bans on drilling for oil in areas held as off-limits and for opening up leases for oil shale production in federal lands may be generally in sync with majority American public opinion.

This question about drilling in off-limits areas was asked in this fashion for the first time in mid-May and was not part of a long-standing Gallup trend. Thus, while we do not have a good indication of whether or not these particular attitudes have changed recently as a result of the rapid rise in the price of gasoline, they suggest a broad approval at this time on the part of Americans for expanding oil production in off-limits areas.

The current May poll result does, however, show a somewhat different attitude than Gallup has measured over the years in specific reference to opening up the Arctic National Wildlife Refuge in Alaska for oil exploration. A Gallup trend question about ANWR was last updated in March of this year.

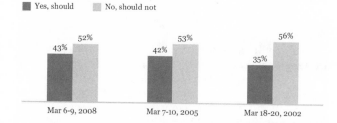

Do you think the Arctic National Wildlife Refuge in Alaska should or should not be opened up for oil exploration?

The responses to this question show that a slight majority of Americans oppose such oil exploration.

The differences in the responses to the broad May question and the earlier question focused specifically on ANWR could reflect the difference in the wording and could also reflect the difference in time frame. The May question asked about "coastal and wilderness areas now off-limits to oil exploration" while the March question was more specifically targeted to ANWR. Furthermore, there is a two-month difference in the timing of the questions. The price of gas has risen in a seemingly inexorable fashion even in this short time period, suggesting the possibility that attitudes may have changed concomitantly.

A recent NBC News/*Wall Street Journal* poll question gave respondents no less than five choices for dealing with the rise in energy and gas prices and asked them to choose the single one they most supported. The responses to this type of question do not provide information about the relative acceptability of the idea of each of the alternative proposals taken separately, but rather more simply reflect a forced-choice preference.

Still, the results show that the alternative "Open up protected areas in Alaska for oil and gas exploration" was the second most frequently chosen alternative, just behind "Encourage the development of wind and solar power."

Partisan Differences

There are perhaps predictable partisan differences in responses to the May Gallup question about the acceptability of the idea of opening up offshore and wilderness areas off-limits to oil exploration.

Please say whether you would favor or oppose taking each of the following steps to attempt to reduce the price of gasoline. How about: Allowing oil drilling in U.S. coastal and wilderness areas now off-limits to oil exploration?

May 19-21, 2008

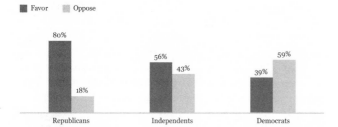

The differences are very large. Eighty percent of Republicans favor this approach, as do 56% of independents, but only 39% of Democrats agreed. These data suggest that wrangling between Democratic leaders in Congress and President Bush on the issue of lifting drilling bans may in fact reflect the strong differences of opinion among partisan groups of rank-and-file Americans on issues relating to drilling and more broadly on issues relating to the trade-off between economic development and environmental protection.

Implications

There are not yet any new survey data which speak directly to President Bush's proposal this week to end bans on drilling for oil in off-limits areas offshore and on federal lands. Although a majority of Americans in general have been opposed to drilling in the Arctic National Wildlife Refuge area over the last several years, a Gallup question included in a mid-May poll suggests that at this juncture in time Bush's proposals may well reflect majority public opinion. It is, of course, even possible that given the continuing increase in the price of gas in the weeks since the May poll was conducted, sentiment may have moved even more in favor of such policy changes.

Survey Methods

Results for the Gallup Panel study are based on telephone interviews with 1,013 national adults, aged 18 and older, conducted May 19-21, 2008. Gallup Panel members are recruited through random selection methods. The panel is weighted so that it is demographically representative of the U.S. adult population. For results based on this sample, one can say with 95% confidence that the maximum margin of sampling error is ±4 percentage points.

In addition to sampling error, question wording and practical difficulties in conducting surveys can introduce error or bias into the findings of public opinion polls.

June 20, 2008

CONFIDENCE IN CONGRESS: LOWEST EVER FOR ANY U.S. INSTITUTION
Just 12% of Americans express confidence in Congress

by Jeffrey M. Jones, Gallup Poll Managing Editor

Gallup's annual update on confidence in institutions finds just 12% of Americans expressing confidence in Congress, the lowest of the 16 institutions tested this year, and the worst rating Gallup has measured for any institution in the 35-year history of this question.

I am going to read you a list of institutions in American society. Please tell me how much confidence you, yourself, have in each one -- a great deal, quite a lot, some or very little?

June 9-12, 2008

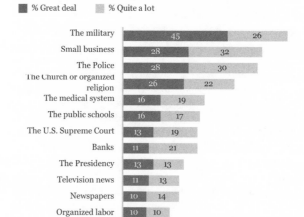

Gallup first asked about confidence in institutions in 1973, repeating the question biannually through 1983, and obtaining annual updates since then. This year's update comes from a June 9-12 Gallup Poll.

In the latest update, Congress ranks just below HMOs, for whom 13% of Americans express "a great deal" or "quite a lot" of confidence. Big business, the criminal justice system, organized labor, newspapers, television news, and the presidency all receive relatively low confidence ratings.

In contrast, Americans express the most confidence in the military, as they have each year since 1988 (with the exception of 1997, when small business edged it out). Small business ranks second in the current poll, just ahead of the police. These are the only three institutions that for whom a majority of Americans express a high degree of confidence.

From 1973 through 1985, organized religion was the top rated institution. Today, just 48% of Americans are confident in organized religion, one of its lowest ratings ever. The lowest score for religion to date was 45% in 2002 at the height of the Catholic Church's priest sex abuse scandal.

Crisis of Confidence?

Prior to this year's 12% confidence rating for Congress, HMOs had the registered the lowest historical score, of 13% in 2002. This rat-

Confidence in the Church or Organized Religion, 1973-2008

 % Great Deal/Quite a lot

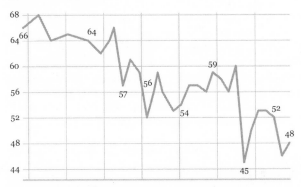

Jan 1974   Jan 1979   Jan 1984   Jan 1989   Jan 1994   Jan 1999   Jan 2004

ing does not include the 45% of Americans who now say they have "some" confidence in Congress; a nearly equal proportion—41%— say they have "little" or "no" confidence in Congress.

Even though the Supreme Court (32% "great deal" or "quite a lot" of confidence) and presidency (26%) are rated more positively than Congress, all institutions are at or near their lowest ratings to date. The rating for the presidency is just one percentage point above its worst rating of 25% from 2007, while the Supreme Court's rating is its worst.

Confidence in the Government Institutions, 1973-2008

Percentage with "a great deal" or "quite a lot of confidence"

■ Supreme Court   ■ Congress   ■ Presidency

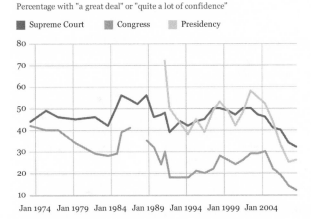

Jan 1974   Jan 1979   Jan 1984   Jan 1989   Jan 1994   Jan 1999   Jan 2004

Government institutions are not alone in experiencing a decline in public confidence. While only one institution (banks) has seen a significant decline in confidence over the past year, all have dropped compared with 2004, the last presidential election year. The three government institutions and banks have had the greatest drops in confidence over that time, while the military and big business have seen the least change.

Long-term changes as above are usually more evident in these confidence measures than year-to-year changes. The current data are no exception—there has been little change from the 2007 ratings, aside from a 9-point drop in confidence for banks (from 41% to 32%). Beyond that, the only other significant changes are modest increases in reported confidence for the police (58% up from 54%) and the medical system (35% up from 31%), but both cases mainly reflect a rebound to 2006 levels after experiencing declines in 2007.

Change in Confidence in Institutions, 2004-2008

Percentage with "a great deal" or "quite a lot of confidence"

	2004	2008	Change
The Presidency	52	26	-26
Banks	53	32	-21
Congress	30	12	-18
The U.S. Supreme Court	46	32	-14
The criminal justice system	34	20	-14
Organized labor	31	20	-11
The Medical system	44	35	-9
The public schools	41	33	-8
Newspapers	30	24	-6
Television news	30	24	-6
The police	64	58	-6
The church or organized religion	53	48	-5
Health Maintenance Organizations (HMOs)	18	13	-5
The Military	75	71	-4
Big business	24	20	-4

Implications

The poor economy and lack of effective government action on important issues such as gas prices, the Iraq War, and immigration help contribute to the erosion of trust and confidence in government institutions. Earlier this week, Gallup reported historically low job approval ratings for the three branches of the federal government. These confidence in institutions ratings underscore the public's frustration and signal an electorate that may be hungry for change in Washington come the fall's elections.

Survey Methods

Results are based on telephone interviews with 822 national adults, aged 18 and older, conducted June 9-12, 2008. For results based on the total sample of national adults, one can say with 95% confidence that the maximum margin of sampling error is ±4 percentage points.

Interviews are conducted with respondents on land-line telephones (for respondents with a land-line telephone) and cellular phones (for respondents who are cell-phone only).

In addition to sampling error, question wording and practical difficulties in conducting surveys can introduce error or bias into the findings of public opinion polls.

June 20, 2008
REPUBLICANS, DEMOCRATS DIFFER ON CREATIONISM
Republicans much more likely than Democrats to believe humans created as-is 10,000 years ago

by Frank Newport, Gallup Poll Editor in Chief

There is a significant political divide in beliefs about the origin of human beings, with 60% of Republicans saying humans were created in their present form by God 10,000 years ago, a belief shared by only 40% of independents and 38% of Democrats.

Which comes closest to your views: 1) Humans developed over millions of years, God guided, 2) Humans developed over millions of years, God had no part, 3) God created humans as is within the last 10,000 years

By party ID

■ % Evolved, God guided   ■ % Evolved, God had no part

■ % God created as is, 10,000 years ago

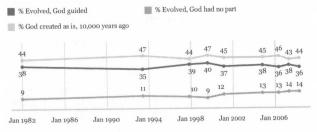

Gallup has been asking this three-part question about the origin of humans since 1982. Perhaps surprisingly to some, the results for the broad sample of adult Americans show very little change over the years.

Which comes closest to your views: 1) Humans developed over millions of years, God guided, 2) Humans developed over millions of years, God had no part, 3) God created humans as is within the last 10,000 years

■ % Evolved, God guided   ■ % Evolved, God had no part

■ % God created as is, 10,000 years ago

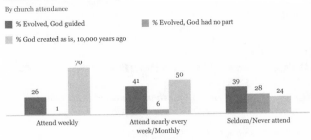

Between 43% and 47% of Americans have agreed during this 26-year time period with the creationist view that God created human beings pretty much in their present form at one time within the last 10,000 years or so. Between 35% and 40% have agreed with the alternative explanation that humans evolved, but with God guiding the process, while 9% to 14% have chosen a pure secularist evolution perspective that humans evolved with no guidance by God.

The significantly higher percentage of Republicans who select the creationist view reflects in part the strong relationship between religion and views on the origin of humans. Republicans are significantly more likely to attend church weekly than are others, and Americans who attend church weekly are highly likely to select the creationist alternative for the origin of humans.

Which comes closest to your views: 1) Humans developed over millions of years, God guided, 2) Humans developed over millions of years, God had no part, 3) God created humans as is within last 10,000 years

By church attendance

■ % Evolved, God guided   ■ % Evolved, God had no part

■ % God created as is, 10,000 years ago

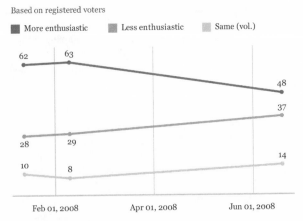

Implications

Although it is not a front-burner issue (particularly in light of the economy and the price of gasoline) the issue of teaching evolution in schools came up on the campaign trail last year, and could resurface in one way or the other between now and the November election.

Presumptive Republican nominee John McCain is facing the challenge of gaining the confidence and enthusiasm of conservative Republicans. Turnout among this group could be an important factor in determining the final vote outcome in a number of key swing states. As seen here, Republicans are in general sympathetic to the creationist explanation of the origin of humans, and if the issue of what is taught in schools relating to evolution and creationism surfaces as a campaign issue, McCain's response could turn out to be quite important.

Survey Methods

Results are based on telephone interviews with 1,017 national adults, aged 18 and older, conducted May 8-11, 2008. For results based on the total sample of national adults, one can say with 95% confidence that the maximum margin of sampling error is ±3 percentage points.

Interviews are conducted with respondents on land-line telephones (for respondents with a land-line telephone) and cellular phones (for respondents who are cell-phone only).

In addition to sampling error, question wording and practical difficulties in conducting surveys can introduce error or bias into the findings of public opinion polls.

June 23, 2008
ELECTION ENTHUSIASM DIPS AFTER PRIMARIES
Democrats maintain an edge over Republicans

by Jeffrey M. Jones, Gallup Poll Managing Editor

A new *USA Today*/Gallup poll finds a sharp drop in voter enthusiasm—48% of registered voters say they are "more enthusiastic than usual about voting," compared with 63% who said this in a poll conducted just after the Super Tuesday presidential primaries and caucuses in early February.

Compared to previous elections, are you more enthusiastic than usual about voting, or less enthusiastic?

Based on registered voters

■ More enthusiastic   ■ Less enthusiastic   ■ Same (vol.)

(vol.) = Volunteered response

The drop has occurred among both Republicans and Democrats, though the decline has been greater among Democrats, in large part because Republican enthusiasm was relatively low to begin with. Democrats continue to hold a wide advantage (61% to 35%) on this measure.

More Enthusiastic About Voting, by Party Affiliation

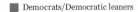
Democrats/Democratic leaners

Republicans/Republican leaners

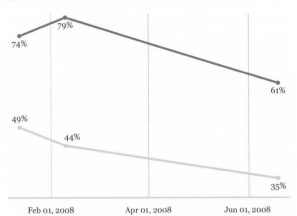

A post-primary voter hangover is not unprecedented, but Gallup did not observe as large a decline in enthusiasm in 2000 or in 2004 after the presidential nominees were largely decided.

Between January 2000 and March 2000, enthusiasm about voting dropped by six percentage points among both Republicans (from 51% to 45%) and Democrats (from 39% to 33%). In 2004, Democrats' enthusiasm dropped from late January to March (59% to 51%), while Republicans' enthusiasm basically stayed the same (53% to 52%). The lack of change in Republican enthusiasm in 2004 could have resulted from the fact that George W. Bush was running unopposed for the party's nomination.

The poll does not provide many clues as to why the drop may have been greater this year than in prior election years. For example, although polls have shown that the majority of Republicans and Democrats are satisfied with their parties' chosen nominees, it is possible those who strongly supported one of their challengers (such as Hillary Clinton or Mitt Romney) may be disappointed in the outcome and thus less excited about voting in November than if their chosen candidate had won the nomination. If that is the case, however, it is not apparent from the candidates' favorable ratings—both John McCain and Barack Obama are viewed more favorably by those who identify with their party now than they were in February.

It is important to note that the overall drop in enthusiasm from February does not mean Americans are any less engaged in the campaign. In the new poll, 75% say they have given "quite a lot of thought" to the election, essentially the same as the 76% from February. At least 7 in 10 Americans have reported giving this high degree of thought to the election since late January.

In fact, the current "thought" levels are significantly higher than they were in June 2004 (an average of 67%) and especially in June 2000 (an average of 45%).

Enthusiasm in a Historical Context

At 35%, the percentage of Republicans who say they are more enthusiastic than usual about voting is the lowest Gallup has measured for

Percentage of Americans Giving "Quite a Lot" of Thought to the Presidential Election, 2008

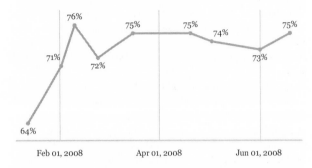

Republicans at any time during the last three presidential election years. (It is just two points higher than the low for either party, 33% for Democrats in March 2000.) The prior GOP low was in the post-Super Tuesday poll earlier this year. Republicans were much more enthusiastic about voting in 2004 when George W. Bush was seeking re-election.

More/Less Enthusiastic About Voting Than Usual, Republicans and Republican Leaners, Historical Trend

	% More enthusiastic	% Less enthusiastic	% Same (vol.)
2008 Jun 15-19	35	51	13
2008 Feb 8-10	44	48	8
2008 Jan 10-13^	49	37	12
2004 Oct 14-16^	68	19	12
2004 Sep 3-5^	69	18	13
2004 Aug 23-25^	60	30	9
2004 Jul 30-Aug 1^	62	27	11
2004 Jul 19-21^	51	32	15
2004 Mar 26-28	52	27	20
2004 Jan 29-Feb 1	53	31	15
2000 Mar 10-12	45	32	22
2000 Jan 7-10	51	32	16

^ Asked of a half sample
(vol.) = Volunteered response

In February, a record 79% of Democrats said they were more enthusiastic about voting. Even with the decline to 61%, Democratic enthusiasm remains relatively high from a historical perspective.

More/Less Enthusiastic About Voting Than Usual, Democrats and Democratic Leaners, Historical Trend

	% More enthusiastic	% Less enthusiastic	% Same (vol.)
2008 Jun 15-19	61	25	13
2008 Feb 8-10	79	15	6
2008 Jan 10-13^	74	19	6
2004 Oct 14-16^	67	23	10
2004 Sep 3-5^	62	29	7
2004 Aug 23-25^	60	30	10
2004 Jul 30-Aug 1^	73	21	6
2004 Jul 19-21^	68	20	12
2004 Mar 26-28	51	35	13
2004 Jan 29-Feb 1	59	34	6
2000 Mar 10-12	33	47	19
2000 Jan 7-10	39	42	17

^ Asked of a half sample
(vol.) = Volunteered response

Implications

Though the public is still highly engaged in the election, that engagement is apparently more subdued than it was earlier this year, given the drop in the percentage of registered voters who report being more enthusiastic about voting than usual. Voter enthusiasm may well pick up again as the campaign moves closer to Election Day—as occurred in 2004.

Gallup's long history of relating Americans' "thought" given to the election and turnout suggests 2008 will be another high-turnout election year.

Gallup has less historical data on the "more enthusiastic than usual about voting" question, and thus far, it has not established a strong link between enthusiasm and voter turnout. However, it generally has been the case in presidential and midterm election years that the party with the relative advantage on enthusiasm does better in the elections.

So even if Democratic enthusiasm has dropped since Obama clinched the party's presidential nomination, the fact that Democrats maintain a wide lead in enthusiasm over Republicans is a positive sign for the Democratic Party.

Survey Methods

Results are based on telephone interviews with 1,625 national adults, aged 18 and older, conducted June 15-19, 2008. For results based on the total sample of national adults, one can say with 95% confidence that the maximum margin of sampling error is ±3 percentage points.

For results based on the sample of 1,460 registered voters, the maximum margin of sampling error is ±3 percentage points.

Interviews are conducted with respondents on land-line telephones (for respondents with a land-line telephone) and cellular phones (for respondents who are cell-phone only).

In addition to sampling error, question wording and practical difficulties in conducting surveys can introduce error or bias into the findings of public opinion polls.

June 24, 2008
OBAMA HAS EDGE ON KEY ELECTION ISSUES
Better positioned than McCain on top two issues—gas prices and economy

by Frank Newport, Gallup Poll Editor in Chief

Americans see Barack Obama as better able than John McCain to handle energy issues and the economy, the two most important election issues in the public's eyes, according to a recent Gallup survey. Six other issues were tested in the poll, with the two candidates positioned roughly evenly on Iraq, moral values, and illegal immigration, while Obama has an edge on healthcare and taxes. McCain's only advantage is on terrorism.

The June 15-19 *USA Today*/Gallup poll asked Americans to rate the importance of the presidential candidates' positions on eight policy issues. The poll then asked respondents questions designed to measure the degree to which they perceive Obama and McCain as comparatively able to handle each of the eight issues.

A majority of Americans believe that the candidates' positions on all issues tested will be either "extremely" or "very important" to

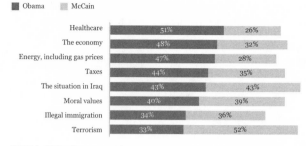

If you had to choose, who do you think would do a better job on [issue], [ROTATED] Barack Obama or John McCain?

USA Today/Gallup, June 15-19, 2008

their vote, not a surprising finding given that each issue included in the list was one that has received attention and focus in the campaign this year. The proportion of Americans who rate each issue as "extremely" important, perhaps a better test of each issue's impact this fall, ranges from 27% to 51%.

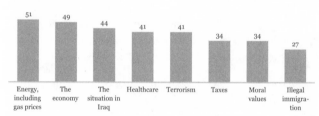

How important will the candidates' positions on these issues be in influencing your vote for president -- extremely important, very important, somewhat important, or not important?

USA Today/Gallup, June 15-19, 2008

Two issues top the list, based on the percentage rating each as extremely important in choosing between candidates: energy/gas prices and the economy. (Energy has spiked in its importance to voters in recent months as gas prices have risen to the $4-per-gallon level.)

Obama has a clear advantage over McCain on both of these top two issues. Americans give Obama a 19-point edge over McCain as best able to deal with energy, with 47% choosing Obama and 28% McCain. On the economy, Obama has a 16-point margin over McCain, 48% to 32%.

The next tier of issues—Iraq, healthcare, and terrorism—receive "extremely important" ratings from 41% to 44% of Americans. The positioning of the candidates on these three issues is mixed. Obama and McCain are tied as to who would be best able to handle Iraq; Obama wins by a substantial 25-point margin on healthcare; and McCain wins over Obama on terrorism by 19 points. (Terrorism is the only issue of the eight tested on which McCain has a significant margin over Obama.)

The bottom tier of issues is seen as extremely important by no more than a third of Americans: taxes, moral values, and illegal immigration. On two of these issues—moral values and illegal immigration—Obama and McCain are tied. Obama has a smaller, nine-point lead over McCain on taxes.

Summary

Obama is leading McCain by six points among registered voters in the head-to-head matchup included in the current *USA Today*/Gallup poll, and there are significantly more Americans at the moment who identify themselves as Democrats than as Republicans. So it may not be surprising that Obama is rated as better able to handle more of the tested issues than is McCain.

Regardless of the cause, the finding that Obama has significant strength on domestic issues is potentially quite meaningful in this year's election, given that gas prices and the economy are the two issues the public is most likely to see as important in choosing between presidential candidates. In fact, further analysis of the poll results shows that less than half of Americans believe McCain would be able to do a good job of handling either gas prices or the economy, while 59% say Obama would be able to do a good job on both of these issues.

Now, please think for a moment about the way in which Barack Obama and John McCain would handle important issues as president. When it comes to handling -- [RANDOM ORDER], please tell me if you think -- [ROTATED: both Obama and McCain would do a good job, neither would do a good job, only Obama would do a good job, (or) only McCain would do a good job]?

2008 Jun 15-19 (sorted by "both")	Both	Neither	Only Obama	Only McCain	No opinion
	%	%	%	%	%
Moral values	38	9	22	26	5
Terrorism	30	8	19	40	3
Illegal immigration	27	19	22	25	7
The economy	23	13	36	23	5
Energy, including gas prices	23	17	36	19	5
Healthcare	22	15	40	18	5
Taxes	21	15	33	27	4
The situation in Iraq	15	9	36	37	3

Iraq, on which the two candidates have sharply divergent positions, is not too far behind energy/gas prices and the economy in terms of imputed importance. At the moment, Americans are equally likely to choose Obama as positioned to do the better job on Iraq as they are to choose McCain.

The poll points to one undisputed strength for McCain: terrorism. Slightly less than half of Americans say Obama would do a good job of handling terrorism, while 70% say that about McCain. But terrorism is slightly less important as a voting issue in Americans' eyes than are economic issues, gas prices, and Iraq. shows that given a choice, Americans would rather have a president whose greatest strength is fixing the economy rather than one whose greatest strength is fighting terrorism.

These data would suggest that from a campaign perspective, Obama would be advised to play off his domestic strengths, particularly in terms of the economy, to attempt to neutralize McCain's strength on terrorism, and to increase his (Obama's) perceived strength on Iraq. McCain, on the other hand, has a clear base of strength on national security, but needs to move into a more competitive position with Obama in terms of critical domestic issues relating to the economy and gas prices.

Survey Methods

Results are based on telephone interviews with 1,625 national adults, aged 18 and older, conducted June 15-19, 2008. For results based on the total sample of national adults, one can say with 95% confidence that the maximum margin of sampling error is ±3 percentage points.

Interviews are conducted with respondents on land-line telephones (for respondents with a land-line telephone) and cellular phones (for respondents who are cell-phone only).

In addition to sampling error, question wording and practical difficulties in conducting surveys can introduce error or bias into the findings of public opinion polls.

June 25, 2008

MCCAIN VS. OBAMA AS COMMANDER IN CHIEF
McCain gets high marks, but Obama passes 50% threshold

by Lydia Saad, Gallup Poll Senior Editor

John McCain's life experience has earned him a solid national reputation as someone who can serve as the nation's commander in chief, with 80% saying he can handle the responsibilities of this important role. Barack Obama lags well behind on the same measure, but does pass the 50% public confidence threshold.

Do you think -- [John McCain/Barack Obama] -- can -- or cannot -- handle the responsibilities of commander in chief of the military?

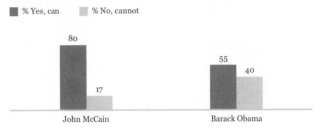

USA Today/Gallup, June 15-19, 2008

Whereas McCain is viewed as qualified to be commander in chief by large majorities of Republicans (94%), independents (79%), and Democrats (71%), perceptions of Obama as commander in chief are more divided along partisan lines.

Most Democrats and a solid majority of independents say Obama can handle the responsibilities of commander in chief of the nation's military. Most Republicans, however, say he is not qualified.

Can Barack Obama Handle the Responsibilities of Commander in Chief, by Party ID

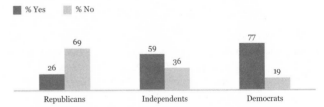

USA Today/Gallup, June 15-19, 2008

The same June 15-19 *USA Today*/Gallup poll finds much smaller advantages for McCain over Obama on the narrower questions of which candidate Americans trust more to make decisions about sending U.S. troops into combat generally, and into Iran specifically.

McCain leads Obama by 53% to 40% as the candidate more Americans say they would trust if a situation arose that required the president to make a decision about sending U.S. troops into combat.

The overwhelming majority of Republicans choose McCain, as do over half of independents and nearly a quarter of Democrats.

Whom Would You Trust More to Decide Whether to Send U.S. Troops Into Combat, Barack Obama or John McCain?

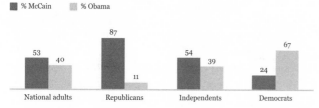

USA Today/Gallup, June 15-19, 2008

In terms of Iran specifically, however, Obama and McCain are nearly tied in public trust ratings. McCain's five percentage-point lead on this measure, 48% to 43%, is not statistically significant.

Nearly as many Republicans and Democrats choose McCain for sending troops into Iran as do so for the general sending troops into combat measure, but he has less support from independents. Whereas 54% of independents choose McCain as the candidate they trust more to make decisions about sending troops into combat generally, only 44% trust him more relative to sending troops to Iran.

Whom Would You Trust More to Decide Whether to Send U.S. Troops to Iran, Barack Obama or John McCain?

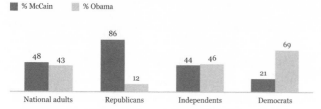

USA Today/Gallup, June 15-19, 2008

This could reflect Americans' general agreement with Obama about U.S. diplomacy with Iran. As Gallup reported on June 2, about 6 in 10 Americans (59%) think it would be a good idea for the president of the United States to meet with the president of Iran—a position Obama has espoused and McCain has roundly criticized.

Bottom Line

McCain clearly enjoys a more broad-based positive reputation with Americans for military matters than does Obama, but it is unclear how this will benefit him in the election.

McCain gets significantly more crossover acclaim from Democrats for being able to fulfill the duties of commander in chief than Obama does from Republicans, but this is unlikely to win him many crossover votes.

More importantly, independents express greater confidence in McCain than in Obama as a commander in chief; still, more than half do have confidence in Obama. And although more independents choose McCain as the candidate they trust to send U.S. troops into combat, generally, they are divided between McCain and Obama when it comes to sending troops into Iran.

In short, while defense issues are potentially one of McCain's strong suits, the more the issue is framed in terms of sending U.S.

troops into combat, and particularly into Iran, the less helpful it may be to his candidacy.

Survey Methods

Results are based on telephone interviews with 1,625 national adults, aged 18 and older, conducted June 15-19, 2008. For results based on the total sample of national adults, one can say with 95% confidence that the maximum margin of sampling error is ±3 percentage points.

For results based on the 781 national adults in the Form A half-sample and 844 national adults in the Form B half-sample, the maximum margins of sampling error are ±4 percentage points.

Interviews are conducted with respondents on land-line telephones (for respondents with a land-line telephone) and cellular phones (for respondents who are cell-phone only).

In addition to sampling error, question wording and practical difficulties in conducting surveys can introduce error or bias into the findings of public opinion polls.

June 26, 2008
AMERICANS IN AGREEMENT WITH SUPREME COURT ON GUN RIGHTS
Nearly three in four say Second Amendment guarantees right of Americans to own guns

by Jeffrey M. Jones, Gallup Poll Managing Editor

The Supreme Court's ruling on Thursday that a District of Columbia ban on handgun ownership is unconstitutional appears to be solidly in step with public opinion. A clear majority of the U.S. public—73%—believes the Second Amendment to the Constitution guarantees the rights of Americans to own guns. And almost 7 out of 10 Americans are opposed to a law that would make the possession of a handgun illegal, except by the police.

Do you believe the Second Amendment to the U.S. Constitution guarantees the rights of Americans to own guns, or do you believe it only guarantees members of state militias such as National Guard units the right to own guns?

USA Today/Gallup, Feb. 8-10, 2008

The practical outcome of the case was to overturn a Washington, D.C., handgun ban. In general, the public opposes sweeping bans on handguns. In the most recent Gallup Crime Poll, conducted last October, Americans opposed a law that would ban possession of handguns except by police and other authorized persons, by 68% to 30%.

The larger issue in the case centered on whether the Second Amendment to the Constitution was intended to protect the rights of individual Americans to own guns, or only those who are members of state militia groups.

The precise language of the Second Amendment reads:

A well regulated militia, being necessary to the security of a free state, the right of the people to keep and bear arms, shall not be infringed.

The Supreme Court's ruling today takes the view that the Second Amendment does confer on Americans who are not members of militias the right to own guns.

Gun owners (the roughly one-third of the U.S. adult population who say they personally own a gun) are nearly universal in endorsing the view that the Second Amendment guarantees their right to own guns. Non-owners are less likely to view the amendment this way, but a majority still do.

Do you believe the Second Amendment to the U.S. constitution guarantees the rights of Americans to own guns, or do you believe it only guarantees members of state militias such as National Guard units the right to own guns?

Results by gun ownership

■ Guarantees rights of Americans to own guns
■ Only guarantees rights of state militia members to own guns
■ No opinion

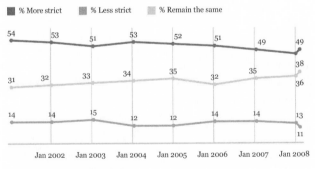

USA Today/Gallup, Feb. 8-10, 2008

While the American public backs the view that gun ownership is a constitutional right, Americans favor having legal restrictions on it. In the same poll, 49% favor stricter gun laws than exist now and 38% would like to see gun laws remain as they are. Just 11% advocate gun laws that are less strict.

Would you like to see gun laws in this country made more strict, less strict, or remain as they are?

■ % More strict ■ % Less strict ■ % Remain the same

USA Today/Gallup, Feb. 8-10, 2008

Survey Methods

Results are based on telephone interviews with 1,016 national adults, aged 18 and older, conducted Feb. 8-10, 2008. For results based on the total sample of national adults, one can say with 95% confidence that the maximum margin of sampling error is ±3 percentage points.

For results based on the sample of 373 gun owners, the maximum margin of sampling error is ±6 percentage points.

For results based on the sample of 630 gun non-owners, the maximum margin of sampling error is ±4 percentage points.

Other results are based on telephone interviews with 1,010 national adults, aged 18 and older, conducted Oct. 4-7, 2007. For results based on this sample, one can say with 95% confidence that the maximum margin of sampling error is ±3 percentage points.

Interviews are conducted with respondents on land-line telephones (for respondents with a land-line telephone) and cellular phones (for respondents who are cell-phone only).

In addition to sampling error, question wording and practical difficulties in conducting surveys can introduce error or bias into the findings of public opinion polls.

June 27, 2008

OBAMA BEATS MCCAIN ON MOST CHARACTER RATINGS
Obama leads on 7 of 10 characteristics, but McCain wins on leadership

by Lydia Saad, Gallup Poll Senior Editor

In the June 15-19 *USA Today*/Gallup poll, Barack Obama leads John McCain among registered voters in a presidential preference test, 48% to 42%. The same poll finds Obama swamping McCain in Americans' perceptions of who has the better grasp of the problems Americans face, while McCain leads Obama by a slight margin as a "strong and decisive leader."

Thinking about the following characteristics and qualities, please say whether you think each one applies more to Barack Obama or more to John McCain.

■ Obama ■ McCain

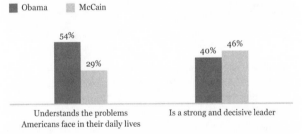

USA Today/Gallup, June 15-19, 2008

More generally, Obama is the more highly regarded of the two candidates on a number of positive personal and leadership characteristics, ranging from his empathy for average Americans, to his political independence, to his ability to solve the nation's problems. He leads McCain by a significant margin on 7 of 10 characteristics tested in the recent poll; he roughly ties McCain on two, and trails McCain on only one.

Empathy, Independence, and Effectiveness

The two dimensions on which Obama does best relative to McCain—understanding the problems Americans face in their daily lives and caring about "the needs of people like you"—both concern his perceived empathy for average Americans. He outscores McCain by more than 20 percentage points on both of these.

Barack Obama vs. John McCain on Empathy Characteristics

	Obama	McCain	Net for Obama
	%	%	pct. pts.
Understands the problems Americans face in their daily lives	54	29	+25
Cares about the needs of people like you	52	30	+22

USA Today/Gallup, June 15-19, 2008

Obama also leads by double digits on two dimensions that tap Americans' perceptions of the candidates' political independence: being independent in his thoughts and actions, and standing up to special interests.

Barack Obama vs. John McCain on Independent-Minded Characteristics

	Obama	McCain	Net for Obama
	%	%	pct. pts.
Is independent in his thoughts and actions	52	36	+16
Would stand up to special interests, including those aligned with his party	48	34	+14

USA Today/Gallup, June 15-19, 2008

Obama performs well on two dimensions related to his effectiveness in achieving public policy objectives: working well with both parties to get things done, and having a clear plan for solving the country's problems (though on this latter dimension, a substantial 28% do not express a preference for either candidate).

Barack Obama vs. John McCain on Effectiveness Characteristics

	Obama	McCain	Net for Obama
	%	%	pct. pts.
Would work well with both parties to get things done in Washington	48	35	+13
Has a clear plan for solving the country's problems	41	31	+10

USA Today/Gallup, June 15-19, 2008

Obama and McCain are more closely matched when it comes to their personal ethics or values. Obama leads McCain, but only slightly, on the "shares your values" dimension, while the two are nearly tied in perceptions of who is more "honest and trustworthy." Again, many Americans do not see either candidate as superior on the honesty dimension—something both candidates score well on when rated individually.

Barack Obama vs. John McCain on Values/Moral Characteristics

	Obama	McCain	Net for Obama
	%	%	pct. pts.
Shares your values	47	39	+8
Is honest and trustworthy	39	35	+4

USA Today/Gallup, June 15-19, 2008

A Competent Chief Executive

McCain is slightly more likely than Obama to be credited as a "strong and decisive leader." He also ties Obama in perceptions of which candidate can better manage the government effectively.

While neither dimension is a strong advantage for McCain, his relatively good performance on them signals that Americans see him as someone who can lead people and government agencies. These are core responsibilities of the presidency, and ones on which he at least measures up to Obama.

Barack Obama vs. John McCain on Leadership/Competence Characteristics

	Obama	McCain	Net for Obama
	%	%	pct. pts.
Can manage the government effectively	42	42	0
Is a strong and decisive leader	40	46	-6

USA Today/Gallup, June 15-19, 2008

Implications

Obama clearly wins Gallup's character ratings by volume; the question is whether he wins by a large enough margin on the dimensions that are most important to Americans when electing a president. Obama's six-point lead in the horse race in the same poll is an important summary indicator suggesting that he does.

Survey Methods

Results are based on telephone interviews with 1,625 national adults, aged 18 and older, conducted June 15-19, 2008. For results based on the total sample of national adults, one can say with 95% confidence that the maximum margin of sampling error is ±3 percentage points.

For results based on the 781 national adults in the Form A half sample and the 844 national adults in the Form B half sample, the maximum margins of error are ±4 percentage points.

Interviews are conducted with respondents on land-line telephones (for respondents with a land-line telephone) and cellular phones (for respondents who are cell-phone only).

In addition to sampling error, question wording and practical difficulties in conducting surveys can introduce error or bias into the findings of public opinion polls.

June 30, 2008
ABOUT ONE IN FOUR VOTERS ARE "SWING VOTERS"
Higher proportion than in 2004

by Jeffrey M. Jones, Gallup Poll Managing Editor

According to the most recent *USA Today*/Gallup survey, 23% of likely voters can be considered "swing voters"—including 6% who do not have a preference between Barack Obama and John McCain for president, and 17% who currently support either McCain or Obama but say they could change their minds between now and Election Day.

Obama's seven-point advantage over McCain among voters who have made up their minds (42% to 35%) is similar to the six-point advantage (50% to 44%) he enjoys among all likely voters in the June 15-19 poll.

This is Gallup's first measurement of swing voters in the U.S. electorate this election cycle. At no point in 2004—a year when swing voters were somewhat scarce from a historical perspective—

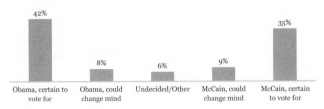

June 15-19 USA Today/Gallup Poll

did Gallup find as high a proportion of swing voters as it finds today. The high mark in swing voters in 2004 was just 18% in May, and in the final pre-election poll, only 9% of likely voters had not made a firm candidate choice.

Who Are the Swing Voters?

In a typical election year, political independents and moderates are among those most likely to fall into the swing voter group. And that is the case as well this year.

Percentage of Swing Voters, by Political Party
Based on likely voters

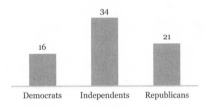

June 15-19 USA Today/Gallup Poll

Percentage of Swing Voters, by Political Ideology
Based on likely voters

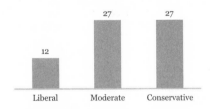

June 15-19 USA Today/Gallup Poll

In this year's election, it appears that swing voters are less likely to come from subgroups that show strong support for Obama, which is a positive sign for Obama. As shown in the accompanying graphs, liberals are the least likely of the ideological groups, and Democrats of the party affiliation groups, to fall into the swing voter group.

Additionally, only 12% of voters under age 30 are swing voters, compared with roughly a quarter of those aged 30 or older. Throughout the campaign, young adults have supported Obama overwhelmingly.

Also, white voters (26%) are more likely than nonwhites (18%) to be uncommitted at this point. Obama has typically held the support of more than 90% of blacks and 60% of Hispanics.

Swing Voters Tend to Like Both McCain and Obama

In general, swing voters seem to be positively disposed toward both candidates—50% have a favorable opinion of both McCain and Obama; only 11% view both negatively. By comparison, just one-quarter of committed voters have a positive opinion of both candidates.

Views of Barack Obama and John McCain, Swing Voters and Committed Voters
Based on likely voters

■ View both favorably
■ View Obama favorably, McCain unfavorably
■ View McCain favorably, Obama unfavorably
■ View both unfavorably

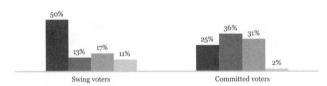

June 15-19 USA Today/Gallup Poll

In July 2004, just 25% of swing voters viewed both John Kerry and George W. Bush favorably, while 13% had negative opinions of both.

That indicates that in this election, swing voters are much more likely to choose between two appealing options rather than trying to pick "the lesser of two evils."

Implications

With a greater proportion of swing voters available in this year's presidential election than in 2004, the campaigns may not wish to follow the famous Bush 2004 strategy of concentrating resources on mobilizing existing supporters instead of persuading undecided voters.

If the campaigns choose to devote a substantial share of resources to winning over uncommitted voters, they may find a receptive audience. Half of swing voters have a positive opinion of both Obama and McCain, far more than had a favorable image of both Bush and Kerry in 2004. The candidates' messages, choices of vice presidential running mates, and performance in the fall debates all have the potential to bring voters into their camps.

Survey Methods

Results are based on telephone interviews with 1,310 likely voters, aged 18 and older, conducted June 15-19, 2008. For results based on the total sample of national adults, one can say with 95% confidence that the maximum margin of sampling error is ±3 percentage points.

Interviews are conducted with respondents on land-line telephones (for respondents with a land-line telephone) and cellular phones (for respondents who are cell-phone only).

In addition to sampling error, question wording and practical difficulties in conducting surveys can introduce error or bias into the findings of public opinion polls.

June 30, 2008

DEMOCRATS FAVORED TO RETAIN HOUSE IN NOVEMBER

Lead among registered voters matches 2006 final pre-election result

by Lydia Saad, Gallup Poll Senior Editor

The Democratic Party is in a good position to retain its majority status in Congress this November. Democrats lead the Republicans by 51% to 40% in the party preferences for Congress among all registered voters, and by 52% to 42% among likely voters.

If the elections for Congress were being held today, which party's candidate would you vote for in your congressional district -- [the Democratic Party's candidate or the Republican Party's candidate]?

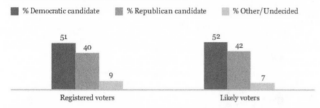

USA Today/Gallup, June 15-19, 2008

This is according to Gallup's "generic ballot" question, asking Americans which party's candidate they would vote for in their congressional district if the election were held today. The *USA Today*/Gallup survey was conducted June 15-19, 2008.

The Democrats' 11-point advantage among registered voters is slightly less than what Gallup found in mid-February—at that time, the Democrats led by 55% to 40%—however, it still puts them in a comfortable position heading into the fall.

The current registered-voter results are identical to those from Gallup's final pre-election survey in 2006. In that election, the Democrats wrested majority control of Congress from the Republicans, winning 53% of all votes cast nationally for congressional candidates, to the Republicans' 45%. The implication of this, of course, is that the Democrats are on track to hold on to their U.S. House seat majority in the 2008 elections.

Voter turnout typically helps the Republicans narrow any Democratic advantage seen in pre-election polls based on all registered voters. That was the case in 2004, when the Republicans trailed the Democrats by four percentage points among registered voters in Gallup's final pre-election survey, 45% to 49%, but the Republicans went on to win 47% of the national popular vote, and a 30-seat majority in Congress.

Since the 2004 election, however, the Republicans have generally trailed the Democrats on the generic ballot by a much larger margin. The 11-point gap Gallup now sees in the Democrats' favor is very close to the average Democratic lead for all of 2006.

Generic Ballot Trends for 2004, 2006, and 2008 Congressional Elections
Based on registered voters

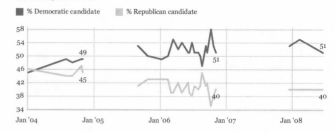

Although the balance of power in the U.S. House of Representatives will be determined by 435 individual congressional elections, Gallup's generic-ballot measure of national support for the two major parties—more specifically, the final pre-election generic ballot based on likely voters—has proven to be a strong predictor of the actual percentage of votes cast nationally for all Republican and Democratic candidates. This, in turn, bears a close relationship to the number of seats won by each party.

Survey Methods

Results are based on telephone interviews with 1,625 national adults, aged 18 and older, conducted June 15-19, 2008. For results based on the total sample of national adults, one can say with 95% confidence that the maximum margin of sampling error is ±3 percentage points.

For results based on the sample of 1,460 registered voters, the maximum margin of sampling error is ±3 percentage points.

Results for likely voters are based on the subsample of 1,310 survey respondents deemed most likely to vote in the November 2008 general election, according to a series of questions measuring current voting intentions and past voting behavior. For results based on the total sample of likely voters, one can say with 95% confidence that the maximum margin of sampling error is ±3 percentage points. The likely voter model assumes a turnout of 60% of national adults. The likely voter sample is weighted to match this assumption, so the weighted sample size is 974.

Interviews are conducted with respondents on land-line telephones (for respondents with a land-line telephone) and cellular phones (for respondents who are cell-phone only).

In addition to sampling error, question wording and practical difficulties in conducting surveys can introduce error or bias into the findings of public opinion polls.

Concern That McCain's Policies Will Be Too Similar to Bush's, by Party Affiliation

Asked of a half sample of national adults

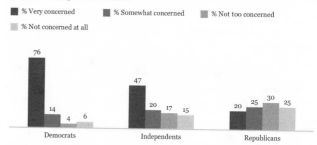

June 15-19, 2008, USA Today/Gallup poll

July 01, 2008

AMERICANS WORRY MCCAIN WOULD BE TOO SIMILAR TO BUSH

About half are concerned Obama would go too far in changing Bush policies

by Jeffrey M. Jones, Gallup Poll Managing Editor

A recent *USA Today*/Gallup poll finds about two in three Americans concerned that John McCain would pursue policies as president that are too similar to what George W. Bush has pursued. Nearly half—49%—say they are "very concerned" about this.

How concerned are you that, as president, John McCain would pursue policies that are too similar to what George W. Bush has pursued -- very concerned, somewhat concerned, not too concerned, or not concerned at all?

Asked of a half sample of national adults

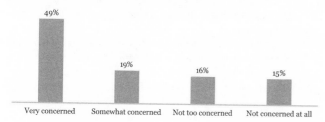

June 15-19, 2008, USA Today/Gallup poll

McCain faces a challenge in trying to convince voters to allow him to follow an unpopular president of the same party. Democratic candidate Barack Obama has attempted to link McCain to Bush by saying that electing McCain would effectively lead to a "third Bush term." Although McCain remains competitive in head-to-head matchups with Obama, the poll suggests that McCain may have more work to do to distance himself from Bush.

It is clearly a delicate balancing act for McCain, as Bush remains relatively popular with the Republican base. While only 28% of Americans approve of the job Bush is doing as president, a majority of Republicans (60%) still do. Bush's approval rating among current McCain supporters is slightly lower, at 55%.

Bush is deeply unpopular with Democrats (only 6% approve), and 9 in 10 Democrats say they are concerned that McCain's policies would be too similar to those of Bush. But among independents—a group to which McCain has demonstrated appeal—most are concerned about McCain-Bush similarities, including nearly half who are very concerned. Even one in five Republicans are very concerned about the similarities.

A recent CBS News poll asked registered voters what they thought McCain would do—continue Bush's policies, change to more conservative policies, or change to less conservative policies. A plurality of 43% believe he would continue Bush's policies, but more expect some change—either more conservative (21%) or less conservative (28%) policies. Thus, while most voters express concern about McCain being too much like Bush, most do not necessarily expect this to happen.

While most Democrats (65%) believe that McCain would generally continue Bush's policies, only 34% of independents and 20% of Republicans do. Independents are about evenly divided as to whether McCain would be more conservative or less conservative than Bush, while nearly half of Republicans think he would be less conservative.

Obama and "Change"

Obama is running as the "change" candidate, and while that would seem to be the advantageous positioning in an election to replace an unpopular incumbent, there is risk in advocating more change than perhaps Americans would be comfortable with. To the extent that McCain and the Republican Party can paint Obama as looking to make too great a departure from the status quo, they can make McCain seem like a safe alternative.

The *USA Today*/Gallup poll asked Americans how concerned they are that Obama would go too far in changing policies that Bush has pursued. About half say they are concerned, including 30% who are very concerned. One in three Americans—predominantly Democrats—are not concerned at all.

How concerned are you that, as president, Barack Obama would go too far in changing the policies that George W. Bush pursued -- very concerned, somewhat concerned, not too concerned, or not concerned at all?

Asked of a half sample of national adults

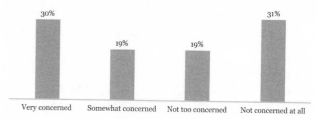

June 15-19, 2008, USA Today/Gallup poll

Most Republicans—who likely will vote for McCain anyway—are concerned about Obama making too much of a departure from Bush. Less than half of independents are, including only 22% who say they are very concerned (compared with 47% of independents who are very concerned about McCain being too similar to Bush).

Concern That Obama's Policies Will Go Too Far in Changing Bush's Policies, by Party Affiliation

Asked of a half sample of national adults

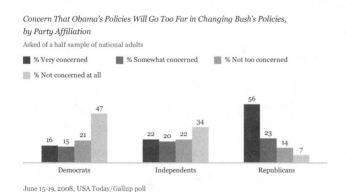

June 15-19, 2008, USA Today/Gallup poll

Implications

At this point, Americans seem more concerned about not getting enough change than about getting too much with the next president, which works to Obama's benefit. But the campaign has barely begun and Republicans will do their best to make the case that Obama is too inexperienced and too liberal to be trusted (Obama had the highest liberal voting score of any senator in 2007, according to the *National Journal*'s annual report).

McCain does have enough disagreements with Bush to perhaps make the argument that he will not represent a third Bush term seem credible. At the same time, on the major issues such as the economy and Iraq, McCain's and Bush's positions are essentially the same.

Survey Methods

Results are based on telephone interviews with 1,625 national adults, aged 18 and older, conducted June 15-19, 2008. For results based on the total sample of national adults, one can say with 95% confidence that the maximum margin of sampling error is ±3 percentage points.

The questions reported here are based on randomly selected half samples of the entire sample, and have a margin of sampling error of ±4 percentage points.

Interviews are conducted with respondents on land-line telephones (for respondents with a land-line telephone) and cellular phones (for respondents who are cell-phone only).

In addition to sampling error, question wording and practical difficulties in conducting surveys can introduce error or bias into the findings of public opinion polls.

July 02, 2008
HISPANIC VOTERS SOLIDLY BEHIND OBAMA
Few demographic differences evident among Hispanics

by Jeffrey M. Jones, Gallup Poll Managing Editor

Hispanic registered voters' support for Barack Obama for president remained consistent and strong in June, with Obama leading John McCain by 59% to 29% among this group.

While Hispanics generally preferred Hillary Clinton to Obama for the Democratic presidential nomination, a solid majority of His-

Presidential Election Preference, Among Hispanics

Based on registered voters

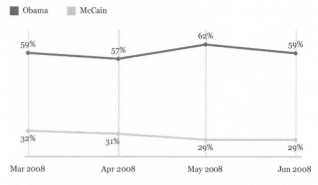

Based on aggregated Gallup Poll Daily tracking data, March-June 2008

panics have consistently backed Obama against McCain in general-election trial heats. Obama has led McCain by about a 2-to-1 margin since Gallup began tracking general-election voting preferences in early March.

Gallup has interviewed more than 4,000 Hispanic registered voters during this time period. An analysis of candidate support by subgroup within the U.S. Hispanic electorate reveals that many of the well-established divisions in this year's campaign—such as the gender gap and the marriage gap—are weak or nonexistent among Hispanic voters.

Rather, Hispanics of differing demographic backgrounds all tend to solidly support Obama. It thus appears that there isn't much beyond a shared Hispanic ethnicity or identity that explains Hispanic voting patterns.

Perhaps the only exceptions to this general pattern come among the minority of Hispanic voters who identify themselves as Republicans (18%) or who say they have conservative political views (36%). McCain leads Obama among Hispanic Republicans, and is about even with him among Hispanic conservatives.

Presidential Preference by Party Identification, Among Hispanics

Based on registered voters

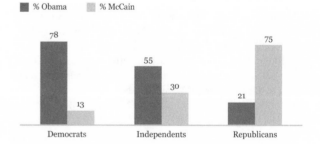

Based on aggregated Gallup Poll Daily tracking data, March-June 2008

In an election pitting one of the younger recent presidential candidates against one of the older ones, candidate preferences by age group have varied. Differences in the Hispanic vote by age, however, are fairly small. While younger Hispanic voters show greater support for Obama than for McCain, support for McCain increases only slightly among older Hispanics.

The accompanying table shows how McCain and Obama compare within various subgroups of Hispanics.

Presidential Preference by Ideology, Among Hispanics

Based on registered voters

■ % Obama   ▨ % McCain

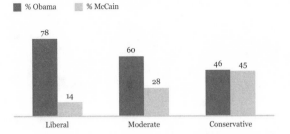

Based on aggregated Gallup Poll Daily tracking data, March-June 2008

Presidential Vote Preference by Age, Among Hispanics

Based on registered voters

■ % Obama   ▨ % McCain

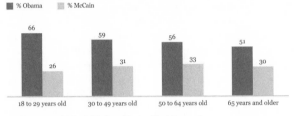

Based on aggregated Gallup Poll Daily tracking data, March-June 2008

Presidential Vote Preference by Demographic Subgroup, Among Hispanics

Based on registered voters

	% Obama	% McCain
Men	60	32
Women	59	29
College graduate	60	32
College non-graduate	59	29
Married	55	35
Not married	63	25
Attend church weekly	54	34
Attend church monthly	61	30
Seldom/Never attend	63	27
East	64	25
Midwest	63	25
South	52	36
West	62	29
Monthly income of <$2,000	62	23
Monthly income of $2,000 to <$5,000	60	31
Monthly income of $5,000 to <$7,500	58	34
Monthly income of $7,500 or more	54	39

Based on aggregated Gallup Poll Daily tracking data, March-June 2008

Implications

Some political experts assumed Obama's struggle to attract widespread Hispanic support in the primaries would carry over into the general-election campaign against the Republican candidate. But Hispanics have become a reliable Democratic voting bloc, and have so far shown little difficulty in transferring their loyalties from Clinton to Obama. Obama continues to lead McCain by about a 2-to-1 margin among Hispanic voters, as he has since March. Hispanic voters could be crucial in key swing states such as New Mexico, Colorado, and Florida.

While George W. Bush made a strong push for the Hispanic vote in the 2000 and 2004 elections, McCain faces an uphill climb to attract Hispanics' support, given their consistent and solid support for Obama in recent months.

Survey Methods

Results are based on telephone interviews with 4,604 Hispanic registered voters, aged 18 and older, conducted March 7-June 30, 2008, as part of Gallup Poll Daily tracking. For results based on the total sample of national adults, one can say with 95% confidence that the maximum margin of sampling error is ±2 percentage points.

For the sample of 1,123 Hispanic registered voters interviewed in June 2008, the maximum margin of sampling error is ±3 percentage points.

Interviews are conducted with respondents on land-line telephones (for respondents with a land-line telephone) and cellular phones (for respondents who are cell-phone only).

In addition to sampling error, question wording and practical difficulties in conducting surveys can introduce error or bias into the findings of public opinion polls.

July 03, 2008

NEARLY ALL AMERICANS CONSIDER MILITARY SERVICE "PATRIOTIC"

Symbolic gestures valued more highly by older Americans and the less educated

by Lymari Morales, Gallup Poll Staff Writer

Nearly two-thirds of Americans (62%) say serving in the U.S. military reveals "a great deal" about one's patriotism, ranking it second only to voting in elections among six items rated in a recent *USA Today*/Gallup poll. More than half of Americans (53%) say the same about reciting the pledge of allegiance, and far fewer about wearing an American flag pin.

How much does each act indicate that a person is patriotic -- a great deal, a moderate amount, not much, or not at all?

■ % Great deal   ▨ % Moderate amount

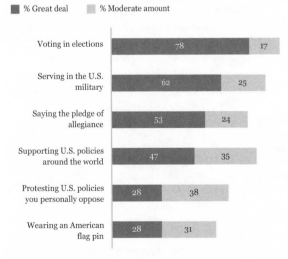

USA Today/Gallup, June 15-19, 2008

Democratic presidential candidate Barack Obama spent much of this Independence Day week trying to assure voters of his patriotism, having been faulted during the Democratic primary season for at times not wearing an American flag pin, and for not placing his hand over his heart during the national anthem on at least one occasion. Obama's speech on Monday, entitled "The America We Love," included praise for Republican rival John McCain's service to his country in Vietnam, in response to retired Gen. Wesley Clark's statement that McCain's experience as a Navy pilot and prisoner of war does not necessarily qualify him to be commander in chief.

McCain's service in Vietnam is generally considered an advantage in this wartime election against Obama, who has never served in the military, and a key reason 80% of Americans see McCain as capable of handling the responsibilities of commander in chief. The Gallup data reveal that Americans do in fact consider military service in general to be a sign of patriotism. While Republicans are among the most likely of all groups to say serving in the military reveals a great deal about one's patriotism, more than half of both Democrats and independents agree. Republicans also tend to place more value on saying the pledge of allegiance and wearing an American flag pin, while independents align more closely with Democrats, who are generally less likely to place a high value on each action.

How Much Do Various Actions Indicate That Someone Is "Patriotic"?
% "A great deal," by political party

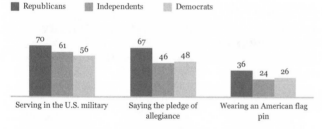

USA Today/Gallup, June 15-19, 2008

The high value Americans place on serving in the military holds fairly constant among most demographic groups. But interestingly, key subgroups with which Obama is seeking inroads in the presidential campaign are among those who place a greater value on the smaller, more symbolic expressions of patriotism. Older Americans, among whom Obama does less well compared to McCain in terms of projected voting, are more likely than younger Americans to place a high value on saying the pledge of allegiance and wearing an American flag pin.

How Much Do Various Actions Indicate That Someone Is "Patriotic"?
% "A great deal," by age

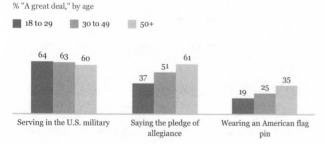

USA Today/Gallup, June 15-19, 2008

The same goes for the least educated Americans in comparison to the most highly educated Americans.

How Much Do Various Actions Indicate That Someone Is "Patriotic"?
% "A great deal," by education

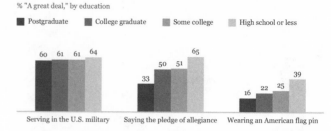

USA Today/Gallup, June 15-19, 2008

Implications

Gen. Clark has defended his comments about McCain's military record, saying they were meant to question McCain's leadership qualifications rather than his patriotism. The fact that Americans do consider serving in the U.S. military highly patriotic makes it difficult for the Obama campaign to criticize McCain on that score. Americans' views on patriotism suggest that it would be of greater benefit for Obama to reinforce his own patriotism through other acts Americans value. While it is clear that a small symbolic act like wearing a flag pin is not nearly as significant a sign of patriotism as acts such as voting and serving in the military, the fact that about 6 in 10 Americans say wearing such a pin is at least a moderate sign of patriotism suggests it certainly can't hurt.

Survey Methods

Results are based on telephone interviews with 781 national adults in the Form A half sample, aged 18 and older, conducted June 15-19, 2008. For results based this sample, one can say with 95% confidence that the maximum margin of sampling error is ±4 percentage points.

Interviews are conducted with respondents on land-line telephones (for respondents with a land-line telephone) and cellular phones (for respondents who are cell-phone only).

In addition to sampling error, question wording and practical difficulties in conducting surveys can introduce error or bias into the findings of public opinion polls.

July 07, 2008
PUBLIC WANTS CONGRESS TO APPROVE MILITARY ACTION, BOMBINGS
As was the case in 1973, Americans want president to get congressional approval

by Frank Newport, Gallup Poll Editor in Chief

An overwhelming 79% majority of Americans believe the president should get the approval of Congress before sending U.S. armed forces into action outside the United States, and 70% believe congressional approval should be required before the president decides to bomb suspected terrorists.

According to Gallup trends, there has been little change over the last 35 years in the basic sentiment that the president needs congressional approval before sending U.S. troops into combat overseas.

Do you think the president should or should not be required to get the approval of Congress before sending United States armed forces into action outside the United States?

How about using Air Force or Navy planes to bomb suspected terrorists?

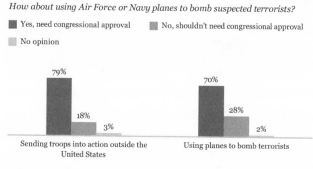

Gallup Poll, May 8-11, 2008

Do you think the president should or should not be required to get the approval of Congress before sending United States armed forces into action outside the United States?

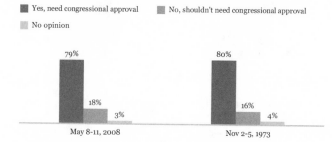

The year 1973 was significant in the history of debate over presidential war powers. That year, U.S. involvement in the Vietnam War was drawing to a close and Congress acted in an attempt to bring clarity to the war powers issue—enacting over President Nixon's veto the War Powers Act of 1973, which said, in part: "The President, in every possible instance, shall consult with Congress before introducing United States Armed Forces into hostilities or into situations where imminent involvement in hostilities is clearly indicated by the circumstances, and after every such introduction shall consult regularly with the Congress until United States Armed Forces are no longer engaged in hostilities or have been removed from such situations."

At that time, Congress was clearly reflecting the will of the people. Eighty percent of Americans in a November 1973 Gallup Poll agreed that Congress needed to give its stamp of approval before the president committed U.S. troops into action on foreign soil.

Now, some 35 years later, as the United States is involved in another drawn-out war, the percentage of Americans agreeing with this sentiment is almost exactly the same, at 79%.

What the U.S. Constitution's framers intended in terms of the war powers of the governmental branches and how exactly the nation should react in today's changed and fast-moving international environment continue to be a matter of dispute. This complexity led to the formation of a National War Powers Commission in 2007, created to review relevant legal and historical issues and, ultimately, to make a recommendation on how the executive and legislative branches should approach war situations. (The commission, headed by two former secretaries of state, James Baker and Warren Christopher, is set to make its final report Tuesday.)

The recent Gallup Poll shows that while there is some difference of opinion by partisanship on the idea that the president be required

to get congressional approval, a majority of every political group agrees.

Do you think the president should or should not be required to get the approval of Congress before sending United States armed forces into action outside the United States?

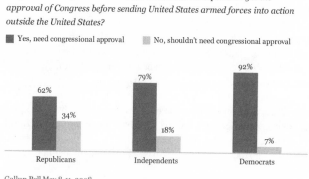

Gallup Poll May 8-11, 2008

Survey Methods

Results are based on telephone interviews with 1,017 national adults, aged 18 and older, conducted May 8-11, 2008. For results based on the total sample of national adults, one can say with 95% confidence that the maximum margin of sampling error is ±3 percentage points.

Interviews are conducted with respondents on land-line telephones (for respondents with a land-line telephone) and cellular phones (for respondents who are cell-phone only).

In addition to sampling error, question wording and practical difficulties in conducting surveys can introduce error or bias into the findings of public opinion polls.

July 08, 2008
RELIGIOUS INTENSITY PREDICTS SUPPORT FOR MCCAIN
Hispanic Catholics and black Protestants provide notable exceptions

by Frank Newport, Gallup Poll Editor in Chief

Americans who say religion is an important part of their daily lives support John McCain over Barack Obama for president, 50% to 40%, while their less religious counterparts support Obama over McCain, 55% to 36%.

Is religion important in your life?
Who do you support in the presidential election?

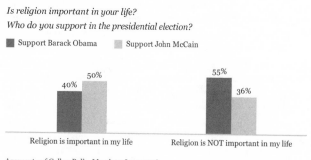

Aggregate of Gallup Polls, March to June 2008

These conclusions are based on an analysis of the relationship between presidential vote choice and responses to the question "Is religion an important part of your daily life?" among almost 95,000 registered voters interviewed as part of Gallup Poll Daily tracking, from March through June of this year. (About two-thirds of American registered voters respond in the affirmative when asked whether religion is important to them.)

The finding that the Republican candidate does better among more religious Americans is not a new one. White evangelical Christian voters, for example, have traditionally been among the most reliable Republican voters. The current analysis shows that the divide in vote preferences based on religiosity is not confined to white Protestants, but also occurs among non-Hispanic white Catholics. Indeed, the relationship between religiosity and vote choice is apparent among other groups that may not have been thought of in this regard traditionally, including in particular American Jews and, to a slight degree, those who identify with non-Christian and non-Jewish religions.

There are exceptions to the correlation between religiosity and likelihood to vote Republican. The strong support for Obama among Hispanic Catholics, black non-Catholic Christians, and those who do not have a specific religious identity appears to be little affected by self-reported importance of religion.

The relationship of religion to vote choice is most clearly seen in the large segment of Americans who are white and identify themselves as either Protestant or some other non-Catholic Christian religion. Among those in this group who say religion is important in their daily lives, McCain beats Obama by a 36-point margin, 63% to 27%. Among those in this group who say religion is not important, McCain and Obama are essentially tied, at 46% for McCain and 45% for Obama.

Is religion important in your life?
Who do you support in the presidential election?
Among non-Hispanic whites who are Protestants/non-Catholic Christians

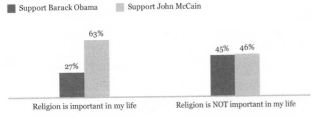

Aggregate of Gallup Polls, March to June 2008

The same pattern, although not quite as dramatic, is seen among non-Hispanic white Catholics. Those in this group for whom religion is important prefer McCain to Obama by a 16-point margin. Non-Hispanic white Catholics for whom religion is not important give Obama a slight, two-point margin over McCain, 47% to 45%.

These patterns, so starkly evident among white Christians, essentially disappear among Catholics who are Hispanic, and non-Catholic Christians who are black. Cultural considerations deriving from ethnicity and race among these groups are likely the dominant factors influencing their vote decision. The differential impact of personal intensity of religion within these groups, it appears to follow, is much less important than it is among other groups examined in this analysis.

Only 39% of U.S. Jews report that religion is important in their daily lives, well below the overall national average. Among this smaller group of religious Jews, however, Obama and McCain break even, 45% to 45%. This compares to Obama's 68% to 26% lead among the majority of Jews for whom religion is not important.

Is religion important in your life?
Who do you support in the presidential election?
Among non-Hispanic white Catholics

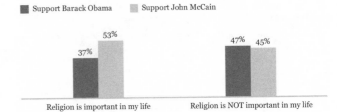

Aggregate of Gallup Polls, March to June 2008

Is religion important in your life?
Who do you support in the presidential election?
Among white Hispanic Catholics

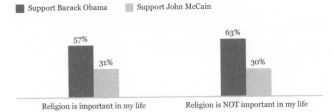

Aggregate of Gallup Polls, March to June 2008

Is religion important in your life?
Who do you support in the presidential election?
Among black non-Catholic Christians

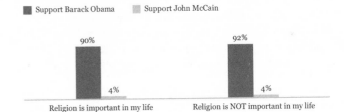

Aggregate of Gallup Polls, March to June 2008

Is religion important in your life?
Who do you support in the presidential election?
Among Jewish Americans

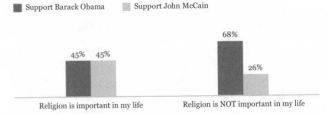

Aggregate of Gallup Polls, March to June 2008

There is a modest impact of the importance of religion among Americans who report identification with non-Christian, non-Jewish religions. Obama wins by a significant margin among these individuals regardless of whether they report religion to be important in their daily lives, but the Obama over McCain gap is larger among those for whom religion is not important (a 45-point margin versus a 30-point margin.)

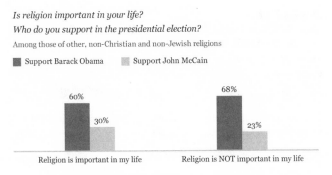

Is religion important in your life?
Who do you support in the presidential election?

Among those of other, non-Christian and non-Jewish religions

■ Support Barack Obama   ▪ Support John McCain

60%   30%   68%   23%

Religion is important in my life   Religion is NOT important in my life

Aggregate of Gallup Polls, March to June 2008

Finally, there is the group of about 12% of Americans who say that they have no specific religious identity or religious affiliation. This group taken as a whole is strongly likely to support Obama. There is no substantive difference in the pattern of support for Obama over McCain among the small group of 11% of this voter segment who—somewhat anomalously—say religion is important in their daily lives.

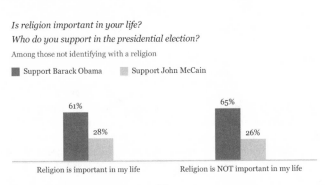

Is religion important in your life?
Who do you support in the presidential election?

Among those not identifying with a religion

■ Support Barack Obama   ▪ Support John McCain

61%   28%   65%   26%

Religion is important in my life   Religion is NOT important in my life

Aggregate of Gallup Polls, March to June 2008

Implications

It has been well established from an analysis of previous survey data that certain groups of highly religious Christians—usually defined as "evangelicals"—are reliably Republican in their presidential vote preferences. The current analysis expands the exploration of this relationship between religiosity and vote choice, taking advantage of a large sample of almost 95,000 interviews conducted as part of the Gallup Poll Daily tracking program from March through June.

The data confirm that among non-Hispanic white Christians—Catholics and non-Catholics alike—those who report that religion is important in their daily lives are significantly more likely to report voting for McCain over Obama than are those who say religion is not important.

Importantly, the analysis suggests that the presence of this relationship between religious intensity and presidential vote choice can be extended to include Jews and to some degree those who identify with a non-Christian, non-Jewish religion. In both of these groups, those who say religion is important are more likely to support McCain than are those who say religion is not important in their daily lives.

At the same time, the data show that for two voter groups, Hispanic Catholics and black non-Catholic Christians, there is little evidence of a relationship between the importance of religion and the vote. These two groups of voters appear to be strong Obama sup-

porters regardless of whether they report being personally religious. And, among the small segment of Americans who do not report identification with any religion, support for Obama is also strong and relatively unaffected by the self-reported importance of religion.

Survey Methods

Results are based on telephone interviews with 94,872 registered voters, aged 18 and older, conducted March-June 2008. For results based on the total sample of national adults, one can say with 95% confidence that the maximum margin of sampling error is ±1 percentage point for the entire sample. Sampling error for subgroups will vary.

Interviews are conducted with respondents on land-line telephones (for respondents with a land-line telephone) and cellular phones (for respondents who are cell-phone only).

In addition to sampling error, question wording and practical difficulties in conducting surveys can introduce error or bias into the findings of public opinion polls.

July 08, 2008
U.S. CONSUMER ECONOMIC RATINGS DOWN AGAIN IN EARLY JULY
Fifty percent of Americans rate current economy as "poor"

by Dennis Jacobe, Gallup Chief Economist

During early July, new Gallup polling shows that the percentage of Americans rating current economic conditions as "poor" averaged 50%—up from 47% in June, and 43% in April and May.

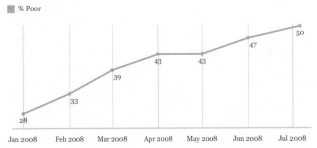

How would you rate economic conditions in this country today -- as excellent, good, only fair, or poor?

■ % Poor

28   33   39   43   43   47   50

Jan 2008   Feb 2008   Mar 2008   Apr 2008   May 2008   Jun 2008   Jul 2008

Consumer Perceptions Decline Across Income Distribution

On Friday, the Reuters/University of Michigan preliminary Index of Consumer Sentiment will be announced. Gallup's survey of more than 3,000 consumers (conducted June 30-July 6) suggests that consumer perceptions of the current economy continued to plunge in early July. In turn, this implies that other measures of consumer attitudes toward the current economy conducted in early July should also show a decline. (Gallup's and others' estimates also include measures of the economy's direction. Gallup's measure of the economy's direction was essentially unchanged in early July.)

Gallup's daily tracking of consumer perceptions of the current economy shows that the percentage of consumers rating current economic conditions as "poor" continued to increase in early July, averaging 50%, which essentially matches the highest level recorded since Gallup began asking the question in 1992. Significantly, the continuing decline in consumer ratings of current economic conditions took place across the income spectrum. The percentage of lower-income Americans (those making less than $24,000 a year) who rate current economic conditions as "poor" increased from 56% in June to 60% in early July. "Poor" ratings also increased among those making at least $90,000 a year (from 38% in June to 45% in early July) and $60,000 to less than $90,000 (from 39% to 46%). Only among those making $24,000 to less than $60,000 were "poor" ratings basically unchanged (from 49% to 50%).

Percentage Rating Economy as Poor, by Income

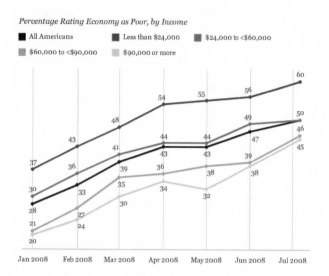

Survey Methods

Gallup is interviewing no fewer than 1,000 U.S. adults nationwide each day during 2008. The economic questions analyzed in this report are asked of a random half-sample of respondents each day. The results reported here are based on combined data of more than 8,000 interviews in January, February, March, April, May, and June. For results based on this sample, the maximum margin of sampling error is ±1 percentage point.

The questions for the first week of July are based on combined data of more than 3,000 interviews conducted June 30 to July 6, 2008. For results based on this sample, the maximum margin of sampling error is ±2 percentage points.

Interviews are conducted with respondents on land-line telephones (for respondents with a land-line telephone) and cellular phones (for respondents who are cell-phone only).

In addition to sampling error, question wording and practical difficulties in conducting surveys can introduce error or bias into the findings of public opinion polls.

July 09, 2008

MCCAIN'S AGE SEEN AS MORE OF A PROBLEM THAN OBAMA'S RACE

Majority, however, see neither as an obstacle to effective governing

by Frank Newport, Gallup Poll Editor in Chief

Twenty-three percent of Americans say John McCain's age would make him a less effective president were he to win in November, while only 8% say Barack Obama's race would make him less effective.

Everything else being equal, do you think the fact that Barack Obama is black/John McCain would be 72 years old when elected president would make him a more effective president, would not make any difference, or would make him a less effective president?

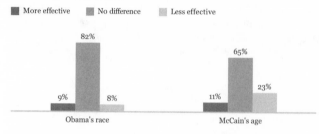

USA Today/Gallup, June 15-19, 2008

These results emanate from two questions included in a July 15-19 *USA Today*/Gallup poll. One question asked respondents whether Obama's race would make him more effective, would make him less effective, or would make no difference if he were to be elected president. A parallel question asked about the perceived impact of the fact that McCain would be 72 when inaugurated next January, were he to win.

More than 8 out of 10 Americans say Obama's race would make no difference in terms of his effectiveness in the White House. Of the rest, just as many say his being black would make him more effective as president as say it would make him less effective. Thus, as far the public is concerned, Obama's race appears to be a wash in terms of perceptions about his ability to serve effectively as president.

There is more expressed concerned about McCain's age. As is the case with Obama's race, the majority of Americans say that McCain's being 72 next January would not make any difference in terms of his effectiveness in the White House. But 23% say McCain would be less effective as a result of his age, while 11% say he would be more effective. The net result is a slightly negative view of the impact of McCain's advanced age.

Over a third of Obama voters in the poll's sample say McCain's age would make him a less effective president, although that leaves a majority who still say it would make no difference. On the other hand, just 19% of McCain's own supporters say his age would make him more effective (only 8% say less effective).

Exactly the same percentage—82%—of both Obama voters and McCain voters say Obama's being black would make no difference in terms of his effectiveness as a president. But, importantly, only 14% of McCain voters have a negative view of the impact of Obama's race (compared with the 37% of Obama voters who view the impact of McCain's age negatively).

There is a slight tendency for Obama voters to say Obama's being black would be a plus, while McCain voters are slightly

Everything else being equal, do you think the fact that John McCain would be 72 years old when elected president would make him a more effective president, would not make any difference, or would make him a less effective president?

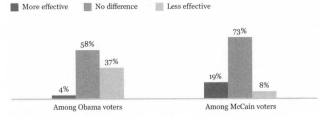

USA Today/Gallup, June 15-19, 2008

Everything else being equal, do you think the fact that Barack Obama is black would make him a more effective president, would not make any difference, or would make him a less effective president?

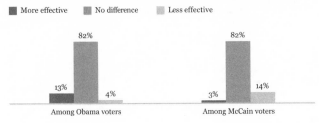

USA Today/Gallup, June 15-19, 2008

more likely to say it would be a negative, but these are not major differences.

Independents, the key group that both campaigns are heavily targeting, basically reflect the opinions of the overall average in their views of the impact of Obama's race and McCain's age.

Everything else being equal, do you think the fact that Barack Obama is black would make him a more effective president, would not make any difference, or would make him a less effective president?

	More effective	No difference	Less effective
Republicans	6%	80%	12%
Independents	8%	84%	7%
Democrats	11%	83%	6%

USA Today/Gallup, June 15-19, 2008

Everything else being equal, do you think the fact that John McCain would be 72 years old when elected president would make him a more effective president, would not make any difference, or would make him a less effective president?

	More effective	No difference	Less effective
Republicans	19%	69%	11%
Independents	9%	66%	25%
Democrats	5%	60%	34%

USA Today/Gallup, June 15-19, 2008

The Views of Older Americans and Black Americans

One might expect that older Americans would be more likely than younger Americans to be positive about the impact of McCain's age, but the differences by age group are slight.

Everything else being equal, do you think the fact that John McCain would be 72 years old when elected president would make him a more effective president, would not make any difference, or would make him a less effective president?

	More effective	No difference	Less effective
	%	%	%
18 to 29 yrs. old	11	62	26
30 to 49 yrs. old	9	67	23
50 to 64 yrs .old	9	64	26
65+ yrs. old	14	64	21

USA Today/Gallup, June 15-19, 2008

Even among the group of Americans 65 and older, McCain's age is seen as a net negative, with 21% saying it will make him less effective, and only 14% saying it will make him more effective. These views are only slightly different from those of the younger age groups. By the same token, young Americans, aged 18 to 29, are basically no more negative about McCain's age than are those in older age groups.

A separate analysis looked just at respondents who themselves are aged 72 or older, the group obviously most likely to be aware of the implications of McCain's age on his ability to govern as president.

Everything else being equal, do you think the fact that John McCain would be 72 years old when elected president would make him a more effective president, would not make any difference, or would make him a less effective president?
By respondent age

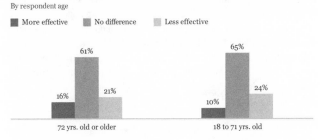

USA Today/Gallup, June 15-19, 2008

Among this group, there is a little more sentiment that McCain's age would make him less effective than there is that his age would make him more effective, while 6 out of 10 say it would make no difference.

Black Americans are little different from whites in their views of the impact of Obama's race.

Everything else being equal, do you think the fact that Barack Obama is black would make him a more effective president, would not make any difference, or would make him a less effective president?

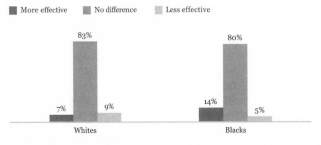

USA Today/Gallup, June 15-19, 2008

Blacks are slightly more likely than whites to perceive that Obama's race would be a net plus for his effectiveness as president, but the difference, as noted, is not large at all. Eight out of 10 or more of both whites and blacks perceive that Obama's race would make no difference.

Implications

The majority of Americans appear to believe that neither McCain's age nor Obama's race will make a difference in terms of either candidate's effectiveness as president should he be elected this November. Among those who do think these factors would make a difference, however, there is somewhat more concern about McCain's age than there is about Obama's race. This is fueled in part by the views of Obama's current supporters, more than a third of whom say McCain's age will make him less effective.

McCain, who has often referred to the health and vitality of his elderly mother as an indication of the fact that older people can be alert and effective, may be discouraged to find that he gets no strong endorsement of the positive impact of age from older Americans who are at least the age he will be in January. A majority of those who themselves are 72 and up say McCain's age will make no difference to his presidency. But among those who do have an opinion, slightly more still say it will make him less effective than say it will make him more effective as president.

It might be hypothesized that black Americans would see Obama's race as a plus for his effectiveness in the White House, for example in terms of his ability to reach across racial lines in addressing race problems in the country. But there is little evidence of such attitudes in these data. Black Americans are as likely as white Americans to say Obama's race will make no difference, and only a small 14% of blacks say Obama would be more effective as a result of his race. At the same time, an even smaller 5% of blacks say Obama's race would make him less effective, suggesting little concern that he might face resistance to his presidency as a result of his race.

Survey Methods

Results are based on telephone interviews with 1,625 national adults, aged 18 and older, conducted June 15-19, 2008. For results based on the total sample of national adults, one can say with 95% confidence that the maximum margin of sampling error is ±3 percentage points.

Interviews are conducted with respondents on land-line telephones (for respondents with a land-line telephone) and cellular phones (for respondents who are cell-phone only).

In addition to sampling error, question wording and practical difficulties in conducting surveys can introduce error or bias into the findings of public opinion polls.

July 10, 2008
FEWER AMERICANS FAVOR CUTTING BACK IMMIGRATION
Public as likely to favor status quo as to favor decreased immigration

by Jeffrey M. Jones, Gallup Poll Managing Editor

A new Gallup Poll finds 39% of Americans in favor of reductions in immigration, down from 45% a year ago. Currently, the public is just as likely to favor maintaining the status quo on immigration as it is to favor a decrease. Only a relatively small minority of 18% of Americans believe immigration levels should be increased.

In your view, should immigration be kept at its present level, increased, or decreased? (Trend since 1986)

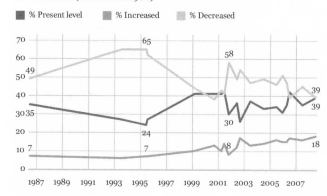

These results are based on Gallup's annual Minority Rights and Relations survey, conducted June 5-July 6 of this year, and consisting of interviews with more than 1,900 adults nationwide, including large samples of U.S. blacks and Hispanics. The poll sample is weighted to be representative of the entire U.S. adult population.

During much of this decade, a plurality if not a majority of Americans have favored cutbacks in immigration, reaching as high as 58% shortly after the Sept. 11 terrorist attacks. But the current percentage in favor of reduced immigration levels is within a percentage point of the lowest Gallup has measured in the last 20 years or so (a 38% reading in 2000; the all-time low was 33% way back in 1965). In 2006, 39% also favored decreased immigration.

The post-9/11 reading was not the historical high point in calls for reduced immigration—in the mid-1990s, roughly two in three Americans wanted to see less immigration during a backlash against immigrants symbolized by California's Proposition 187, which denied government benefits to illegal immigrants.

The apparent softening on immigration is also evident in the fact that 64% of Americans now say immigration is a good thing for the country today, up from 60% last year, and the second highest reading in the now eight-year history of the Minority Rights and Relations survey.

One reason anti-immigration opinion has diminished somewhat may be that immigration has receded as an issue this year as Americans have focused on the struggling economy and record-high gas prices. In a June Gallup Poll, just 4% named immigration as the most important problem facing the country, down from 11% at the beginning of the year. Also, in June, just 27% of Americans said illegal immigration would be an extremely important issue to their vote for president this year, ranking it dead last of eight issues tested.

On the whole, do you think immigration is a good thing or a bad thing for this country today?

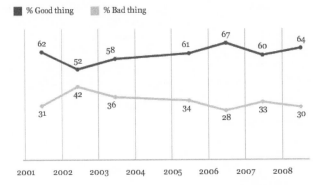

■ % Good thing   ▒ % Bad thing

62 · 52 · 58 · 61 · 67 · 60 · 64
31 · 42 · 36 · 34 · 28 · 33 · 30

2001 2002 2003 2004 2005 2006 2007 2008

President Bush and Congress failed in their attempt to pass comprehensive immigration reform last year, and the issue has been put on the shelf during this presidential election year.

Immigration and the Economy

The poll finds that Americans have mixed views on some of the precise effects of immigration on the economy. On the one hand, by a 2-to-1 margin, the public says immigrants cost taxpayers too much by using government services as opposed to becoming productive citizens who pay their fair share of taxes. Those views are essentially unchanged from 2006.

Which comes closer to your point of view -- [ROTATED: illegal immigrants in the long run become productive citizens and pay their fair share of taxes, (or) illegal immigrants cost the taxpayers too much by using government services like public education and medical services?]

■ % Pay fair share of taxes   ▒ % Cost taxpayers too much

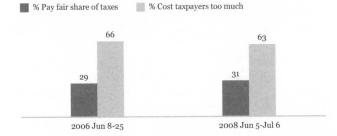

66 · 63
29 · 31

2006 Jun 8-25   2008 Jun 5-Jul 6

But, on the other hand, Americans by an even wider margin see some economic benefit from the standpoint that illegal immigrants tend to take low-paying jobs that Americans don't want (79%) as opposed to taking away jobs that would otherwise go to Americans (15%). Again, these sentiments have not changed materially since 2006.

Implications

As the illegal immigration issue has faded from the public consciousness, Americans have become somewhat less likely to take anti-immigration stances. It is unclear at this point whether that means the public is coming to terms with the immigration issue and the complexities in dealing with illegal immigrants living in the United States, or whether the public might become somewhat less tolerant of it should the public's elected leaders take up the issue again.

Which comes closer to your view -- [ROTATED: illegal immigrants mostly take jobs that American workers want, (or) illegal immigrants mostly take low-paying jobs Americans don't want]?

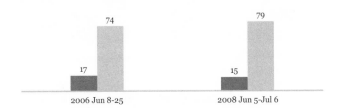

■ % Take jobs American workers want

▒ % Take low-paying jobs Americans don't want

17 · 74
15 · 79

2006 Jun 8-25   2008 Jun 5-Jul 6

Survey Methods

Results are based on telephone interviews with 1,935 national adults, aged 18 and older, conducted June 5-July 6, 2008. For results based on the total sample of national adults, one can say with 95% confidence that the maximum margin of sampling error is ±4 percentage points.

For results based on the sample of 702 non-Hispanic whites, the maximum margin of sampling error is ±5 percentage points.

For results based on the sample of 608 non-Hispanic blacks, the maximum margin of sampling error is ±5 percentage points.

For results based on the sample of 502 Hispanics, the maximum margin of sampling error is ±6 percentage points (120 of the 502 interviews with Hispanics were conducted in Spanish).

Interviews are conducted with respondents on land-line telephones (for respondents with a land-line telephone) and cellular phones (for respondents who are cell-phone only).

In addition to sampling error, question wording and practical difficulties in conducting surveys can introduce error or bias into the findings of public opinion polls.

July 11, 2008
FEWER AMERICANS SEE MCCAIN, OBAMA VIEWS AS "ABOUT RIGHT"

by Lymari Morales, Gallup Poll Staff Writer

Americans are less likely now than they were during the primary season to see presidential contenders John McCain and Barack Obama as having political views that are "about right," while they are notably more likely to see McCain as "too conservative."

Both McCain and Obama face the challenge of modifying their primary platforms for the general election, and both have been accused of "flip-flopping" on their viewpoints to achieve the gains they seek. At the same time, some Americans may be getting to know the candidates better, or for the first time. Yet, compared to the days immediately following Super Tuesday, a *USA Today*/Gallup poll finds both candidates losing, rather than gaining, fans of their political views.

This shift appears to be worse for McCain than Obama, notably among independents, who are at once more likely than they were in February to see McCain's political views as "too conservative" and less likely to see his views as "about right."

Do you think John McCain's political views are too conservative, about right, or too liberal?

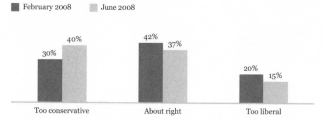

USA Today/Gallup polls, June 15-19, 2008, and Feb. 8-10, 2008

Do you think Barack Obama's political views are too conservative, about right, or too liberal?

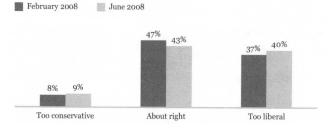

USA Today/Gallup polls, June 15-19, 2008, and Feb. 8-10, 2008

McCain: "Too Conservative"

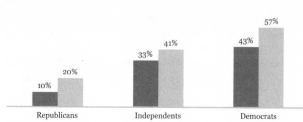

USA Today/Gallup polls, June 15-19, 2008, and Feb. 8-10, 2008

McCain: "About Right"

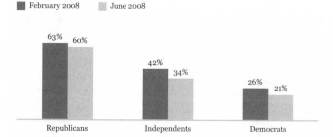

USA Today/Gallup polls, June 15-19, 2008, and Feb. 8-10, 2008

McCain's shift toward the right on offshore drilling, taxes, immigration, and other issues does not appear to be paying off among Republicans as of yet. Republicans overall have become no more likely to consider McCain's views "about right." At the same time, Republicans have grown twice as likely to consider him "too conservative" (which could be a negative among moderate or liberal Republicans). Although McCain was once lauded for his bipartisan views, the percentage of Democrats who see him as "too conservative" has jumped by 14 points to become a majority.

Since the February poll, Obama endured several more months of campaigning against Hillary Clinton, and since he secured the nomination, some observers have characterized him as shifting toward more middle-of-the-road positions on gun ownership, late-term abortions, foreign intelligence surveillance, and Iraq. But Gallup finds Obama gaining positioning strength among Democrats, who are more likely now than in February to consider his positions "about right." Republicans, on the other hand, are now even less approving of Obama's views than before.

Obama: "Too Liberal"

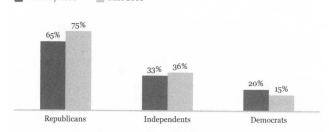

USA Today/Gallup polls, June 15-19, 2008, and Feb. 8-10, 2008

Obama: "About Right"

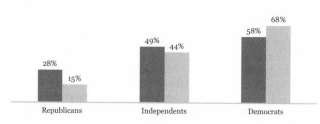

USA Today/Gallup polls, June 15-19, 2008, and Feb. 8-10, 2008

Too Radical?

While fewer Americans currently say McCain's views are "about right" than say that about Obama's, the presumptive Democratic nominee has his own vulnerability in that more than half of Americans (52%) say they are very or somewhat concerned that Obama has aligned himself with people who hold radical views. Only 42% of Americans say the same about McCain.

How concerned are you that John McCain/Barack Obama may be too closely aligned with people who hold radical political views?
Numbers in percentages

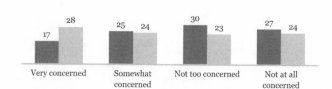

USA Today/Gallup poll, June 15-19, 2008

In Obama's case, the data may suggest continuing fallout from comments made by his former pastor, the Rev. Jeremiah Wright, or perhaps his association with former political radical William Ayers.

McCain is not without some uncomfortable associations of his own, most notably for first seeking but ultimately rejecting the endorsement of the Rev. John Hagee, who made controversial statements about Catholics and Jews. The fact that McCain's associations are less likely to generate concern, however, might be a result of the fact that some notable conservatives, whom some liberals might perceive as "radical," have been critical of McCain, including Rush Limbaugh and Ann Coulter.

Bottom Line

Together, these findings underscore the challenge the candidates face in repositioning themselves for November. Both McCain and Obama are walking the traditional fine line between attempting to attract new support and at the same time being careful not to lose traction among their existing backers. Now, both campaigns must contend with the finding that fewer voters now than earlier this year see their candidate's political views as "about right."

Survey Methods

Results are based on telephone interviews with 1,625 national adults, aged 18 and older, conducted June 15-19, 2008. For results based on the total sample of national adults, one can say with 95% confidence that the maximum margin of sampling error is ±3 percentage points.

Interviews are conducted with respondents on land-line telephones (for respondents with a land-line telephone) and cellular phones (for respondents who are cell-phone only).

In addition to sampling error, question wording and practical difficulties in conducting surveys can introduce error or bias into the findings of public opinion polls.

July 11, 2008
MORE AMERICANS SAY U.S. A NATION OF HAVES AND HAVE-NOTS
Half now say it is, up from 37% four years ago

by Lydia Saad, Gallup Poll Senior Editor

Along with their mounting concerns about national economic conditions in recent years, Americans have grown more likely to perceive structural economic inequality in the country. Nearly half of Americans, 49%, now say the nation is divided into two groups: the "haves" and the "have-nots." This is up from 45% two years ago, and from 37% in June 2004.

The perception of an unequal society has risen at an especially sharp rate among blacks and Hispanics, although non-Hispanic whites are also more likely to perceive a haves/have-nots division today than they were four years ago. Nearly three-quarters of blacks (72%) and close to half of Hispanics (49%) and whites (45%) now believe the nation is divided along have/have-not lines.

These results are from Gallup's annual Minority Rights and Relations survey, conducted each June. The 2008 survey includes nationally representative interviews with 1,935 adults, including more than 700 non-Hispanic whites, more than 600 blacks, and more

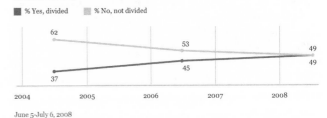

Some people think of American society as divided into two groups -- the "haves" and "have-nots," while others think it's incorrect to think of America that way. Do you, yourself, think of America as divided into haves and have-nots, or don't you think of America that way?

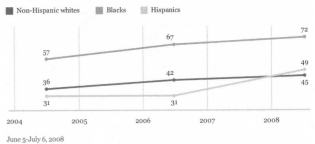

June 5-July 6, 2008

Percentage Perceiving U.S. as Divided Into "Haves" and "Have-Nots"
by Race/Ethnicity

June 5-July 6, 2008

than 500 Hispanics, all weighted to represent their correct proportions in the population.

At the same time that more Americans see an economic class divide in the country, the percentage of Americans holding a profoundly negative view of the U.S. economy has jumped sharply, from 41% in June 2004 to 55% in June 2006 to 84% in June 2008.

Majority Still Identify Themselves as "Haves"

Despite their heightened sense that America is a land of the haves and have-nots, Americans have not changed the way they categorize themselves along the same lines. Since 2004, the percentage of Americans identifying themselves as a member of the "haves" in Gallup polling has registered just under 60%, while about a third have consistently considered themselves "have-nots." (An additional 8% to 12% don't put themselves in either group.)

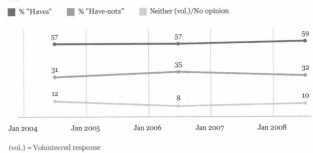

If you had to choose, which of these groups are you in, the haves or the have-nots?

(vol.) = Volunteered response

Implications

The fact that recent economic events—such as the mortgage crisis, surging energy prices, and rising food costs—are hitting some Americans harder than others may partly explain why more Americans in

2008 than four years ago believe the nation is divided into the haves and the have-nots.

But economics may not tell the whole story. Blacks and Hispanics—even those living in high-income households—lag significantly behind whites in believing they are among the nation's "haves." Beyond financial issues, these groups may be more likely today than four years ago to perceive that certain obstacles stand in the way of members of their own racial and ethnic groups' ability to break into the advantaged class.

Survey Methods

Results are based on telephone interviews with 1,935 national adults, aged 18 and older, conducted June 5-July 6, 2008, including over-samples of blacks and Hispanics that are weighted to reflect their proportions in the general population. For results based on the total sample of national adults, one can say with 95% confidence that the maximum margin of sampling error is ±4 percentage points.

For results based on the sample of 702 non-Hispanic whites, the maximum margin of sampling error is ±5 percentage points.

For results based on the sample of 608 non-Hispanic blacks, the maximum margin of sampling error is ±5 percentage points.

For results based on the sample of 502 Hispanics, the maximum margin of sampling error is ±6 percentage points (120 out of the 502 interviews with Hispanics were conducted in Spanish).

Interviews are conducted with respondents on land-line telephones (for respondents with a land-line telephone) and cellular phones (for respondents who are cell-phone only).

In addition to sampling error, question wording and practical difficulties in conducting surveys can introduce error or bias into the findings of public opinion polls.

July 14, 2008
"BLACK SPOKESMAN" TITLE STILL UP FOR GRABS
But blacks generally optimistic an Obama presidency would be helpful

by Lydia Saad, Gallup Poll Senior Editor

Twenty-nine percent of black Americans name Barack Obama as the individual or leader in the United States whom they would choose as their spokesman for race issues, but 49% name someone else and nearly a quarter produce no name.

The issue came up last week over controversial remarks the Rev. Jesse Jackson made about Obama. Jackson criticized Obama's campaign messages of personal responsibility for blacks as "talking down to black people." Jackson claimed that Obama has not adequately emphasized the need for the government to take more responsibility and action to help blacks.

The poll, conducted before the Jackson controversy erupted, finds that Obama is clearly the most dominant individual blacks think of in terms of representing their views on racial matters. He far outpaces the Rev. Al Sharpton, mentioned by 6%; Jackson (with 4%); Bill and Hillary Clinton, each with 3%; and an array of academic, political, and entertainment icons of the black community. However, consistent with Obama's efforts to downplay the racial symbolism of his candidacy, most blacks don't think of Obama as their racial

If you had to name one individual or leader in the U.S. to speak for you on issues of race, who would that be?

	Blacks
	%
Barack Obama	29
Al Sharpton	6
Jesse Jackson	4
Bill Clinton	3
Hillary Clinton	3
Oprah Winfrey	2
Maya Angelou	1
Colin Powell	1
Louis Farrakhan	1
Bill Cosby	1
Tavis Smiley	1
Cornel West	1
My minister/pastor	1
Me/Myself	6
Other	18
No one (vol.)	7
No opinion	16
Total	101%

June 5-July 6, 2008
(vol.) = Volunteered response

spokesman. A total of 49% cite someone else (including 6% who name themselves).

These results are from Gallup's annual Minority Rights and Relations survey, conducted each June. The 2008 survey consists of nationally representative interviews with 1,935 adults, including more than 700 non-Hispanic whites, more than 600 blacks, and more than 500 Hispanics, all weighted to represent their correct proportions in the population.

This is not to say that black Democrats are not excited about Obama's candidacy or that they don't hold out high hopes for what an Obama victory could achieve for black Americans. A remarkable 90% of black Democrats—compared with 64% of non-Hispanic white Democrats and 36% of all Republicans—say they are "more enthusiastic" about voting than usual this year.

Additionally, the Minority Rights and Relations survey shows that a 59% majority of blacks say they would view Obama's winning the presidency as one of the most important advances of the past century for blacks. This contrasts with a slightly smaller 48% of non-Hispanic white Americans who view the prospect of putting the first black American in the White House as a key civil rights milestone.

An overwhelming majority of whites (73%) and blacks (85%) believe an Obama win would be a sign of progress toward racial equality in the United States. Most whites and blacks also believe it would open up national political opportunities for other blacks, and majorities think it would make it easier for blacks to advance their own careers.

Now that Obama has become the first African-American to be a major party's presumptive nominee for president, one might ask how black America will react if he doesn't win. Only a third of blacks (34%) predict that race relations in the country would worsen (either a little or a lot) if Obama loses. While only 18% say relations would improve, the plurality, 45%, say they would not change.

If Barack Obama is elected president, how will you view it in terms of progress for blacks in the United States -- [as one of the two or three most important advances for blacks in the past one hundred years, as important, but not one of the two or three most important advances for blacks, (or would you view it as) not that important]?

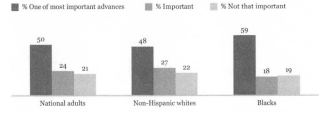

June 5-July 6, 2008

If Barack Obama is elected president, do you think it will or will not -- (Rotate A-C)?
% Yes shown

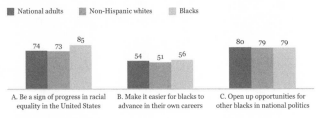

June 5-July 6, 2008

Whites generally agree, with a slim majority saying race relations will not change if Obama loses, but with more saying they will get worse than get better.

If Barack Obama LOSES the presidential election, do you think race relations in this country will -- [get a lot better, get a little better, not change, get a little worse, (or) get a lot worse]?

	Get a lot better	Get a little better	Not change	Get a little worse	Get a lot worse
	%	%	%	%	%
National adults	3	12	53	22	8
Non-Hispanic whites	2	11	54	25	6
Blacks	5	13	45	16	18

June 5-July 6, 2008

At the same time, blacks have muted expectations for how much an Obama win would improve race relations. Although the vast majority of blacks think it would improve race relations to some degree, only 23% say race relations would "get a lot better."

If Barack Obama WINS the presidential election, do you think race relations in this country will -- [get a lot better, get a little better, not change, get a little worse, (or) get a lot worse]?

	Get a lot better	Get a little better	Not change	Get a little worse	Get a lot worse
	%	%	%	%	%
National adults	16	40	23	9	9
Non-Hispanic whites	13	41	25	9	11
Blacks	23	42	16	10	6

June 5-July 6, 2008

Bottom Line

Twenty-nine percent of blacks name Obama as the individual or leader in the United States whom they would choose as their

spokesman for race issues, far more than name any other individual, including the 4% who mention Jackson. This suggests a passing of the baton for the political leadership of black Americans, which some have suggested may be what is troubling Jackson.

In discussing Jackson's controversial remarks about Obama recently, Sharpton said, "Sen. Obama is running for president of all Americans, not just African-Americans." To the extent that's true, it is not curtailing black Americans' willingness to support Obama for president. According to Gallup Poll Daily tracking in the first week of July, 90% of black registered voters say they are voting for him, compared with only 4% backing McCain. And, as noted, blacks are almost universally enthusiastic about the election.

However, the poll does suggest that black Americans see beyond race when thinking about Obama. By not heavily associating Obama with the "black spokesman" role (49% name someone else and nearly a quarter name no one), and by holding somewhat muted expectations for his ability to improve race relations, blacks seem to agree with the essence of Sharpton's commentary: Obama is more than "the black candidate for president"; he's a candidate for president who happens to be black.

Survey Methods

Results are based on telephone interviews with 1,935 national adults, aged 18 and older, conducted June 5-July 6, 2008, including over-samples of blacks and Hispanics that are weighted to reflect their proportions in the general population. For results based on the total sample of national adults, one can say with 95% confidence that the maximum margin of sampling error is ±4 percentage points.

For results based on the sample of 702 non-Hispanic whites, the maximum margin of sampling error is ±5 percentage points.

For results based on the sample of 608 non-Hispanic blacks, the maximum margin of sampling error is ±5 percentage points.

For results based on the sample of 502 Hispanics, the maximum margin of sampling error is ±6 percentage points (120 out of the 502 interviews with Hispanics were conducted in Spanish).

Interviews are conducted with respondents on land-line telephones (for respondents with a land-line telephone) and cellular phones (for respondents who are cell-phone only).

In addition to sampling error, question wording and practical difficulties in conducting surveys can introduce error or bias into the findings of public opinion polls.

July 14, 2008
WIDE GULF IN PERSONAL VS. NATIONAL SATISFACTION
Only 15% satisfied with national conditions, 86% with personal lives

by Jeffrey M. Jones, Gallup Poll Managing Editor

A recent Gallup Poll finds a major gap between Americans' satisfaction with the way things are going in the country and their satisfaction with their personal lives, with whites, blacks, and Hispanics all showing the same pattern.

These results are based on Gallup's annual Minority Rights and Relations survey, conducted June 5-July 6. The survey of 1,935 U.S.

Personal vs. National Satisfaction, Among U.S. Adults and Racial/Ethnic Groups

■ % Satisfied, national conditions   ■ % Satisfied, personal lives

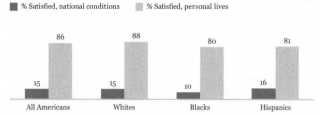

June 5-July 6 Gallup Minority Rights and Relations Poll

adults included interviews with more than 500 Hispanics and more than 600 blacks, weighted to their proper proportion in the overall population.

Over the eight-year history of the Minority Rights and Relations poll, Americans have consistently expressed much greater satisfaction with their personal lives than with national conditions, but this is easily the largest gulf between the two since 2001.

While Americans have become increasingly less satisfied with the way things are going nationally as the decade has progressed—the percentage satisfied has dropped from 51% to 15% since 2001—their personal satisfaction was essentially unchanged from 2001 through 2007, varying only from 88% to 91%.

This year's decline in personal satisfaction to 86% is the first statistically significant change in that measure seen since 2001. But the decline in U.S. satisfaction from 29% to 15% over the past year is much greater, resulting in the largest gap to date between the satisfaction measures.

Personal vs. National Satisfaction, Among U.S. Adults, 2001-2008
Minority Rights and Relations Polls

■ % Satisfied, national conditions   ■ % Satisfied, personal lives

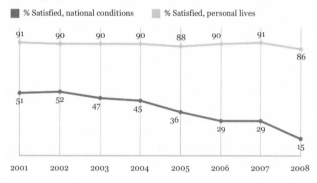

The decline in national satisfaction over the past year has come primarily among whites and Hispanics. Blacks' reported satisfaction levels were already quite low in 2007, and have remained so. In prior years, whites and Hispanics were much more likely than blacks to say they were satisfied with the state of the nation, but now, the three groups give similarly low ratings.

Personal Satisfaction Dips

Even though Americans' reported personal satisfaction is still relatively high at 86%, it is the lowest reading Gallup has measured in the eight Minority Relations polls. Typically, 90% or more of Americans are satisfied with their personal lives.

Moreover, just 46% of Americans now say they are "very satisfied" with their personal lives, down 11 percentage points from a year ago, and the first time this percentage has fallen below the majority level.

National Satisfaction, Among Racial and Ethnic Groups, 2001-2008
Minority Rights and Relations Polls

■ % Whites satisfied   ■ % Blacks satisfied   ■ % Hispanics satisfied

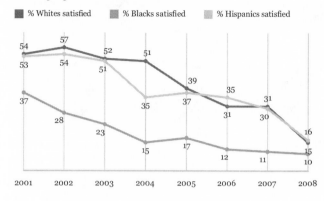

Percentage of Americans "Very Satisfied" With Personal Lives, 2001-2008
Minority Rights and Relations Polls

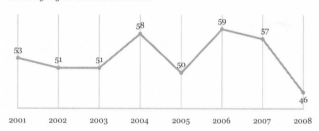

As is the case with national satisfaction, the decline in high personal satisfaction ratings has come chiefly among whites and Hispanics, with black satisfaction holding steady at the previous low level. Typically, whites have been most likely to say they are very satisfied with their personal lives, with blacks the least likely to do so, and Hispanics in the middle.

Very Satisfied With Personal Lives, Among Racial and Ethnic Groups, 2001-2008
Minority Rights and Relations Polls

■ % Whites very satisfied   ■ % Blacks very satisfied   ■ % Hispanics very satisfied

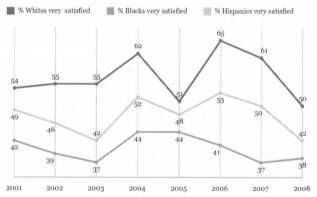

Implications

Even though the decline in national satisfaction compared to 2007 is much greater than the decline in personal satisfaction, the latter change may in some ways be more notable because those numbers had been highly stable prior to this year. This clearly suggests that the economic troubles are affecting not only how Americans view national conditions, but also to a degree how they assess their own situations. And this re-assessment is taking place among members of most racial, ethnic, and income groups.

Survey Methods

Results are based on telephone interviews with 1,935 national adults, aged 18 and older, conducted June 5-July 6, 2008. For results based on the total sample of national adults, one can say with 95% confidence that the maximum margin of sampling error is ±4 percentage points.

For results based on the sample of 702 non-Hispanic whites, the maximum margin of sampling error is ±5 percentage points.

For results based on the sample of 608 non-Hispanic blacks, the maximum margin of sampling error is ±5 percentage points.

For results based on the sample of 502 Hispanics, the maximum margin of sampling error is ±6 percentage points (120 of the 502 interviews with Hispanics were conducted in Spanish).

Interviews are conducted with respondents on land-line telephones (for respondents with a land-line telephone) and cellular phones (for respondents who are cell-phone only).

In addition to sampling error, question wording and practical difficulties in conducting surveys can introduce error or bias into the findings of public opinion polls.

July 15, 2008

NO DEEPENING OF U.S. CONSUMER CONFIDENCE CRISIS—YET

Eighty-seven percent of Americans say economy is "getting worse"

by Dennis Jacobe, Gallup Chief Economist

During the first two weeks of July, new Gallup polling shows 87% of Americans saying economic conditions are "getting worse"—the same as the 87% of June, and not much different from the 86% of May and the 85% of April.

Right now, do you think that economic conditions in the country as a whole are getting better or getting worse?

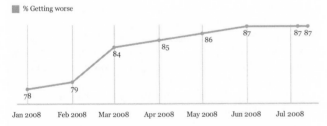

Consumer Expectations Highly Negative but Stable

Over the weekend, the Federal Reserve and the Treasury developed a plan to support Fannie Mae and Freddie Mac—the two quasi-federal agencies that account for about 70% of the mortgage market. This is the second major public policy milestone in the current financial crisis, following the Bear Stearns bailout that took place in mid-March.

Despite this unfolding of another stage in the credit crisis, consumer expectations have remained stable, although highly negative, over the second quarter and the first two weeks of July. Significantly, this has been the case for Americans regardless of their income group during recent weeks.

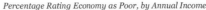

Percentage Rating Economy as Poor, by Annual Income

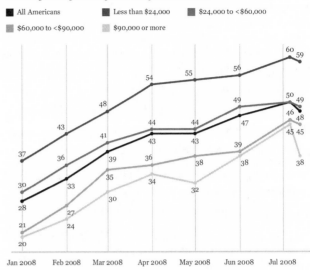

Consumer Ratings of the Economy
Negative but Stable

The percentage of consumers giving the economy a "poor" rating averaged 47% in June, ticked up to 50% in the first week of July, and fell back to 48% in the second week of July. The percentage of lower-income Americans (those making less than $24,000 a year) rating current economic conditions as "poor" increased from 56% in June to 60% in the first week of July and 59% in the second week of the month. "Poor" ratings among upper-income Americans (those making at least $90,000 a year) increased from 38% in June to 45% in the first week of July, before going back to 38% in the second week. Among those making $60,000 to less than $90,000, the percentage went from 39% to 46% and then to 45% during the same time, while among those making $24,000 to less than $60,000, the "poor" ratings remained basically unchanged, going from 49% in June to 50% in the first week and 49% in the second week of July.

Percentage Saying Economy Is Getting Worse, by Annual Income

	Jan '08	Feb '08	Mar '08	Apr '08	May '08	Jun '08	Jun 30- Jul 6, '08	Jul 7-13, '08
All Americans	78	79	84	85	86	87	87	87
Less than $24,000	77	79	85	85	88	88	89	86
$24,000 to <$60,000	81	81	87	87	89	90	89	86
$60,000 to <$90,000	76	81	84	88	88	88	86	88
$90,000 or more	78	79	84	84	83	85	86	87

Survey Methods

Gallup is interviewing no fewer than 1,000 U.S. adults nationwide each day during 2008. The economic questions analyzed in this report are asked of a random half-sample of respondents each day. The results reported here are based on combined data of more than 8,000 interviews in January, February, March, April, May, and June. For results based on this sample, the maximum margin of sampling error is ±1 percentage point.

The questions for the first and second week of July are based on combined data of more than 3,000 interviews conducted June 30-July 6 and July 7-13, 2008. For results based on this sample, the maximum margin of sampling error is ±2 percentage points.

Interviews are conducted with respondents on land-line telephones (for respondents with a land-line telephone) and cellular phones (for respondents who are cell-phone only).

In addition to sampling error, question wording and practical difficulties in conducting surveys can introduce error or bias into the findings of public opinion polls.

Approval of Congress, by Party ID

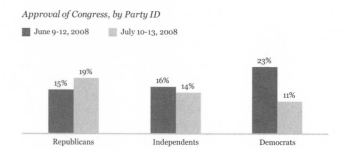

July 16, 2008
CONGRESSIONAL APPROVAL HITS RECORD-LOW 14%
Democrats less positive than Republicans about Congress

by Lydia Saad, Gallup Poll Senior Editor

Congress' job approval rating has dropped five percentage points over the past month, from 19% in June to 14% in July, making the current reading the lowest congressional job approval rating in the 34-year Gallup Poll history of asking the question. The previous low was 18%, last reached in May.

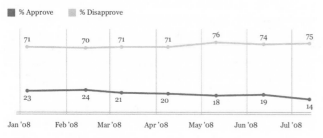

The 75% currently disapproving of Congress is just shy of the record-high 78% in March 1992.

These results, from a July 10-13 Gallup Poll, follow 18 months of dismal job approval ratings for Congress, during which approval has usually registered below 30%, and has averaged only 25%.

Still, the 14% approval rating is extraordinary. Approval of Congress has fallen below 20% only six times in the 34 years Gallup has measured it. Including the latest reading, four of those have come in the past year: in July, June, and May 2008, and in August 2007. The two additional readings were from March 1992 (in the midst of the House bank check-kiting scandal) and June 1979 (during an energy crisis that resulted in surging gas prices and long gas lines), when either 18% or 19% of Americans approved of the job Congress was doing.

The most recent decline comes almost exclusively from Democrats, whose approval of Congress fell from 23% in June to 11% in July, while independents' and Republicans' views of Congress did not change much. As a result, Republicans are now slightly more likely than Democrats to approve of the job the Democratic-controlled Congress is doing (19% vs. 11%).

The 11% of Democrats now approving of Congress is slightly lower than Gallup found in 2006, toward the end of the Republican-led 109th Congress. Democratic approval of Congress initially surged after the Democratic takeover of the U.S. House and Senate, from 16% in December 2006 to 44% in February 2007, but by August 2007 it had fallen to 21%. Democrats' approval of Congress

rebounded to 37% later that year, but has since been in a nearly continuous decline.

Republicans' approval of Congress dipped at the point of transition from Republican to Democratic control after the 2006 midterm elections, from 50% in November 2006 to 31% in February 2007—and has continued to trend downward except for a brief spike last fall after Gen. Petraeus' testimony before Congress.

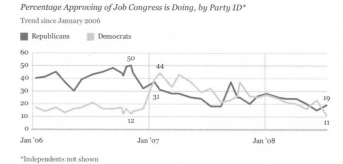

Percentage Approving of Job Congress is Doing, by Party ID*
Trend since January 2006

Bottom Line

Gallup's latest monthly update of public approval of Congress leads to several observations:

1. As economic conditions in the country are worsening, Congress is taking the brunt of it. Since the start of the year, public approval of Congress has fallen from 23% to 14%, while approval of President George W. Bush has been more stable: 32% approved of the job he was doing in early January versus 31% today, with a range of just 28% to 34%.

2. One reason for the growing congressional/Bush approval gap is that Bush benefits from a core group of Republicans nationally who continue to stick by him (67% of whom approve in the latest poll), and who, at this point, are likely to remain supportive of him through the close of his term. This contrasts with the paltry 11% of Democrats who currently approve of the job Congress is doing. By its nature, Congress may simply be less able to engender this kind of political loyalty—it typically trails the sitting president in approval—and thus, the current Democratic Congress lacks a reliable pool of Democratic support to keep its approval ratings afloat.

3. Still, the Democratic Congress has received much less intra-party support for its leadership of the kind that the Republican Congress enjoyed from Republicans in 2006. The mild honeymoon the current Congress enjoyed with its own party at the start of last year quickly faded as Democrats grew upset with congressional inaction on Iraq and immigration reform.

4. Finally, 2008 now looks an awful lot like 1979, and for some of the same reasons: mounting inflation, record-high gas prices,

and a looming recession. Public approval of President Jimmy Carter in mid-July 1979 was 29%, very similar to Bush's current 31%. And approval of Congress was also comparable: 19% in June 1979 vs. 14% today.

Survey Methods

Results are based on telephone interviews with 1,016 national adults, aged 18 and older, conducted July 10-13, 2008. For results based on the total sample of national adults, one can say with 95% confidence that the maximum margin of sampling error is ±3 percentage points.

Interviews are conducted with respondents on land-line telephones (for respondents with a land-line telephone) and cellular phones (for respondents who are cell-phone only).

In addition to sampling error, question wording and practical difficulties in conducting surveys can introduce error or bias into the findings of public opinion polls.

July 17, 2008
BUSH QUARTERLY AVERAGE ESTABLISHES NEW LOW: 29%
Ranks as one of 10 worst since 1945

by Jeffrey M. Jones, Gallup Poll Managing Editor

George W. Bush will end his 30th quarter in the White House with just a 29% average approval rating for the last three months, the worst of his presidency.

George W. Bush Quarterly Job Approval Averages

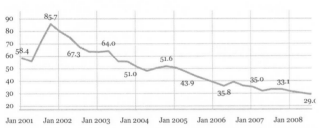

Bush's previous low quarterly average was 31.3% in the prior (29th) quarter. During his 30th quarter (spanning April 20 through July 19), Bush's six individual Gallup Poll approval ratings ranged between 28% and 31%. The 31% reading is from the most recent update, based on a July 10-13 Gallup Poll.

High gas prices, numerous economic troubles, and ongoing U.S. military action in Iraq and Afghanistan all contributed to Bush's recent low ratings, which rank among the lowest Gallup has measured historically. The lowest single rating for any president is Harry Truman's 22% job approval rating in February 1952. Bush has achieved a personal low of 28% five times, three of which occurred in his most recent quarter in office.

Bush spent a good part of 2001 and 2002 at the opposite end of the spectrum, registering some of the highest approval ratings in Gallup's polling history, including a record-high 90% from a poll conducted shortly after the Sept. 11 terrorist attacks. Since then, Bush's approval rating has steadily declined.

Gallup has measured only eight presidential quarterly averages lower than Bush's current 29% since it regularly began tracking presidential approval ratings in 1945—all by Truman in 1951 and 1952 or Richard Nixon in 1973 and 1974. Jimmy Carter joins Bush, Truman, and Nixon as presidents with the 15 worst quarterly averages.

Fifteen Lowest Quarterly Approval Averages, Gallup Polls, 1945-2008

Rank	President	Dates	Quarter in office	Average rating	# of polls
251	Truman	Oct 20, 1951-Jan 19, 1952	27	23.0	2
250	Nixon	Jul 20-Aug 9, 1974	23	24.0	1
249	Truman	Jan 20-Apr 19, 1952	28	25.0	3
247 (tie)	Nixon	Apr 20-Jul 19, 1974	22	26.0	7
247 (tie)	Truman	Apr 20-Jul 19, 1951	25	26.0	3
246	Nixon	Jan 20-Apr 19, 1974	21	26.1	7
245	Truman	Jan 20-Apr 19, 1951	24	26.3	4
244	Nixon	Oct 20, 1973-Jan 19, 1974	20	28.0	5
243	G.W. Bush	Apr 20-Jul 19, 2008	30	29.0	6
242	Truman	Apr 20-Jul 19, 1952	29	29.8	4
240 (tie)	Carter	Apr 20-Jul 19, 1979	10	30.7	6
240 (tie)	Truman	Jul 20-Oct 19, 1951	26	30.7	3
239	G.W. Bush	Jan 20-Apr 19, 2008	29	31.3	8
238	Carter	Jul 20-Oct 19, 1979	11	31.4	7
236 (tie)	G.W. Bush	Apr 20-Jul 19, 2007	26	31.8	6
236 (tie)	Nixon	Jul 20-Oct 19, 1973	19	31.8	6

Bush is only the fifth president since World War II to have served a 30th quarter in office, and he now rates as the president with the worst approval average during this time of his presidency. Truman previously had the lowest 30th quarter average, at 32%, while Dwight Eisenhower, Ronald Reagan, and Bill Clinton all averaged above 50%.

Presidents' 30th Quarter Approval Averages, Gallup Polls, 1945-2008

President	Dates of 30th quarter	Average approval rating	# of polls
Truman	Jul 20-Oct 19, 1952	32.0%	3
Eisenhower	Apr 20-Jul 19, 1960	58.8%	5
Reagan	Apr 20-Jul 19, 1988	50.3%	6
Clinton	Apr 20-Jul 19, 2000	58.0%	7
G.W. Bush	Apr 20-Jul 19, 2008	29.0%	6

Implications

Bush is clearly limping toward the finish line, with just eight months and two quarters left in his presidency, and unless national conditions improve significantly, he will likely leave office with low ratings (even if he gets a post-election bounce, as outgoing presidents typically do).

His historically low approval ratings are a challenge for John McCain and for the Republican Party's hopes of retaining the presidency. The closest historical parallel to the current situation is the 1952 election, when Democratic candidate Adlai Stevenson unsuccessfully sought to succeed the unpopular Harry Truman as president. But the outgoing president's approval ratings are not very predictive of the outcome of the presidential election. Among the more popular presidents in the late stages of their terms, only Reagan was succeeded as president by a member of his party.

Survey Methods

Results are based on averages of six Gallup Polls, each consisting of telephone interviews with approximately 1,000 national adults, aged 18 and older, conducted between April 20 and July 19, 2008. For each poll, one can say with 95% confidence that the maximum margin of sampling error is ±3 percentage points.

The most recent results are based on telephone interviews with 1,016 national adults, aged 18 and older, conducted July 10-13, 2008. For results based on the total sample of national adults, one can say with 95% confidence that the maximum margin of sampling error is ±3 percentage points.

Interviews are conducted with respondents on land-line telephones (for respondents with a land-line telephone) and cellular phones (for respondents who are cell-phone only).

In addition to sampling error, question wording and practical difficulties in conducting surveys can introduce error or bias into the findings of public opinion polls.

July 17, 2008

WHITES MAY EXAGGERATE BLACK-HISPANIC TENSIONS

Most blacks and Hispanics say relations between the two groups are good

by Lydia Saad, Gallup Poll Senior Editor

Fewer than half of white adults in the United States—contrasted with 60% of Hispanics and two-thirds of blacks—believe good relations exist between U.S. blacks and Hispanics.

Perceived Quality of Relations Between Blacks and Hispanics in the United States
by Racial/Ethnic group

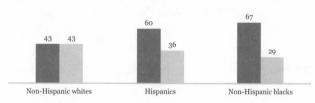

June 5-July 6, 2008

Blacks are clearly the most upbeat of the three groups about the state of black-Hispanic relations, as only 29% of blacks, compared with 36% of Hispanics and 43% of whites, say relations are bad. But Hispanics are significantly more positive than whites.

These findings are from the 2008 installment of Gallup's Minority Rights and Relations survey, conducted each June since 2001. This year's survey, fielded June 5 to July 6, includes interviews with 608 blacks and 502 Hispanics, and includes Spanish-language interviewing with nearly a quarter of the Hispanic sample. The black and Hispanic samples are weighted so they are correctly represented in the national totals.

The 2008 Gallup results are not new. For each of the past eight years, whites have had a substantially worse opinion than have blacks of black-Hispanic relations. And for most of this period, whites have had a more negative view than Hispanics.

Trend in Percentage Rating Relations Between Blacks and Hispanics as "Good"
By Racial/Ethnic group

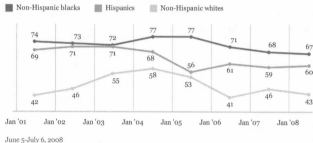

June 5-July 6, 2008

Gallup's race-relations question asks all Americans to rate relations between blacks and Hispanics as either "very good," "somewhat good," "somewhat bad," or "very bad." Because of the relatively less positive perspective of whites, just 49% of Americans as a whole believe these relations are good, while 40% perceive them to be bad. This makes black-Hispanic relations the worst rated of the four racial/ethnic pairings measured in the survey.

Eighty-one percent of Americans see whites and Asians as getting along well, while about two-thirds of Americans consider both white-black and white-Hispanic relations positive.

Next, we'd like to know how you would rate relations between various groups in the United States these days. Would you say relations between -- [RANDOM ORDER] -- are very good, somewhat good, somewhat bad, or very bad?

	National adults	Non-Hispanic whites	Non-Hispanic blacks	Hispanics
	%	%	%	%
Whites and Asians	81	83	73	71
Whites and blacks	68	70	61	57
Whites and Hispanics	65	65	58	71
Blacks and Hispanics	49	43	67	60

% = Percent resonding either "very good" or "somewhat good."

June 5 - July 6, 2008

The issue has obvious importance this election year, with Barack Obama soon to become the nation's first black on the ballot as a major-party candidate for president. Obama had difficulty carrying the Hispanic vote in the Democratic primaries earlier this year—something that led to considerable media speculation about black-Hispanic animosity as the cause—but Gallup polling has shown him solidly beating Republican John McCain among Hispanics throughout the campaign.

Just focusing on Hispanic Democrats (who favored Hillary Clinton over Obama, 52% to 44% for the nomination in Gallup Poll Daily tracking throughout May), 84% in May said they would vote for Clinton in a Clinton vs. McCain matchup in November, compared with 80% who said they would vote for Obama if the choice were Obama vs. McCain.

Hispanics preferred Clinton over Obama for the Democratic nomination, but they were not so opposed to Obama (or the idea of electing a black president) that they were willing to vote for McCain in the general election.

Bottom Line

The generally positive review of black-Hispanic relations in Gallup polling among members of the two leading U.S. minority groups contrasts with considerable media speculation about the impact of Hispanic animosity toward blacks in this year's primary elections.

Some of that commentary has speculated that the trend is getting worse as the Hispanic population grows and starts to outnumber blacks in some neighborhoods and entire cities. Others posit that older Hispanics are more likely than the younger generation to harbor biases and resentments against blacks.

In a January 2008 *New York Times* article titled, "In Obama's Pursuit of Latinos, Race Plays Role," the authors write, "Mr. Obama confronts a history of often uneasy and competitive relations between blacks and Hispanics, particularly as they have jockeyed for influence in cities like Chicago, Los Angeles, and New York. 'Many Latinos are not ready for a person of color,' Natasha Carrillo, 20, of East Los Angeles, said. 'I don't think many Latinos will vote for Obama. There's always been tension in the black and Latino communities. There's still that strong ethnic division. I helped organize citizenship drives, and those who I've talked to support Clinton.'"

While black-Hispanic animosity may exist and could even have been a factor in some state caucuses or primaries, the Gallup data indicate it is not overwhelmingly obvious to members of either group. Whites are much more likely to believe the two are in conflict.

Survey Methods

Results are based on telephone interviews with 1,935 national adults, aged 18 and older, conducted June 5-July 6, 2008, including over-samples of blacks and Hispanics that are weighted to reflect their proportions in the general population. For results based on the total sample of national adults, one can say with 95% confidence that the maximum margin of sampling error is ±4 percentage points.

For results based on the sample of 702 non-Hispanic whites, the maximum margin of sampling error is ±5 percentage points.

For results based on the sample of 608 non-Hispanic blacks, the maximum margin of sampling error is ±5 percentage points.

For results based on the sample of 502 Hispanics, the maximum margin of sampling error is ±6 percentage points (120 out of the 502 interviews with Hispanics were conducted in Spanish).

Interviews are conducted with respondents on land-line telephones (for respondents with a land-line telephone) and cellular phones (for respondents who are cell-phone only).

In addition to sampling error, question wording and practical difficulties in conducting surveys can introduce error or bias into the findings of public opinion polls.

July 18, 2008
SURGING PRICES CHANGING U.S. CONSUMER BEHAVIOR
Eight in 10 Americans have made more of an effort to find the cheapest prices for products

by Dennis Jacobe, Gallup Chief Economist

When asked to name the most important financial problem facing their families today, nearly half of Americans point to energy and gas prices (29%) or to the high cost of living and inflation (18%). Fourteen percent say a lack of money and low wages, and 9% each say healthcare costs or the cost of owning or renting a home.

What is the most important financial problem facing your family today?

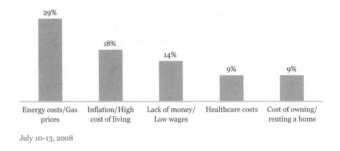

Energy costs/Gas prices	Inflation/High cost of living	Lack of money/ Low wages	Healthcare costs	Cost of owning/ renting a home
29%	18%	14%	9%	9%

July 10-13, 2008

Consumer Behaviors Are Changing

No one needs to tell the average American that prices are increasing, but the Labor Department confirmed Wednesday that consumer prices rose 5% over the past 12 months—the most rapid rate of increase since May 1991. This follows the previous day's report that wholesale prices increased 9.2% over the past year—the biggest jump since 1981. It is thus not surprising to find that the top two categories of personal financial problems named by Americans relate to rising costs.

It follows that surging consumer prices are creating financial problems for many families. And Americans are responding by changing their behavior as consumers. A recent Gallup Poll asked Americans to react to eight possible ways in which families could in theory cope with rising prices. In response, an overwhelming 81% reported that they have made more of an effort to find the cheapest prices for the products they buy. Three in four say they have cut back on spending on entertainment, recreation, or eating out, while two-thirds have made a greater effort to keep track of family spending, such as a monthly budget. Nearly half have bought cheaper, lower-quality goods (49%) or have shopped more often at discount stores (46%).

Change in Consumer Behaviors in Response to Increasing Prices

	% Yes
Made more of an effort to find the cheapest price for the products you buy	81
Cut back on spending on entertainment, recreation, or eating out	73
Made a greater effort to keep track of family's spending, such as a monthly budget	65
Put off purchases otherwise planned	61
Cut back on the amount of money you save	50
Switched to buying cheaper but lower quality goods	49
Shopped more often at discount stores	46
Working a second job or more hours	30

July 10-13, 2008

Commentary

Increasing prices are not a new challenge for consumers, despite what economists might say regarding the changes in the consumer price index and so-called core inflation—a price measure that excludes food and energy prices. Still, it appears that consumer perceptions of price inflation have intensified. Compared with April, roughly twice as many consumers volunteer that energy costs or inflation is the most important financial problem facing their families.

More importantly, inflation seems to be having a major impact on consumer buying behaviors. Consumers are not only cutting back on their entertainment spending and deferring some purchases they previously intended to make, but they are also shopping differently. While it is not surprising that they are more price conscious and looking for sales, it may be somewhat less well recognized that so many—about half—also admit to buying lower-quality items and shopping more at discounters because of price.

Assuming this change in consumer purchasing behaviors continues even if the cost of gas at the pump declines from its recent record levels, the change itself suggests that discounters like Wal-Mart will continue to benefit at the expense of department stores and the top-quality brands they sell. In this regard, the real question going forward may be whether this consumer spending shift to low-cost-provider companies and brands is large enough to offset the overall decline in consumer purchasing activities—making today's low-cost providers actual winners in terms of sales growth, as opposed to being "lesser losers." Low-cost providers may be getting a larger piece of the consumer-purchases pie, but the size of that pie is shrinking.

Survey Methods

Results are based on telephone interviews with 1,016 national adults, aged 18 and older, conducted July 10-13, 2008. For results based on the total sample of national adults, one can say with 95% confidence that the maximum margin of sampling error is ±3 percentage points.

Interviews are conducted with respondents on land-line telephones (for respondents with a land-line telephone) and cellular phones (for respondents who are cell-phone only).

In addition to sampling error, question wording and practical difficulties in conducting surveys can introduce error or bias into the findings of public opinion polls.

July 18, 2008
UNFAIR CAMPAIGNING? IT DEPENDS ON WHOM YOU ASK
Solid majorities of Americans believe McCain, Obama will not use personal attacks in campaign

by Dr. Deborah Jordan Brooks, Gallup Guest Scholar, Dartmouth College

Presidential candidates Barack Obama and John McCain have both claimed that they will not engage in below-the-belt attacks during this race. And while the candidates have made some pointed comments regarding their issue differences, they have largely refrained from intense personal attacks to this point. History has shown, however, that campaigns tend to get considerably more negative as Election Day approaches, so it is an open ques-

tion as to whether the candidates will keep their promises for the duration of the campaign.

A recent *USA Today*/Gallup survey shows that most Americans are at least somewhat optimistic that one or both candidates will follow through on that promise. But a variety of data show that many people view the tone of a race from a partisan perspective. As a result, there is likely to be little agreement about what constitutes fair or unfair attacks on the campaign trail once the general-election advertising season begins in earnest.

In the June 15-19 *USA Today*/Gallup poll, Americans were asked about the likelihood that the presidential candidates would keep their promises to refrain from personal attacks. Specifically, respondents were asked "Both John McCain and Barack Obama have said they want to conduct a presidential campaign based only on the issues and not based on personal attacks. How likely do you think (John McCain/Barack Obama) is to conduct a campaign based only on the issues?"

How likely is Barack Obama/John McCain to conduct a campaign based only on the issues?

Numbers in percentages

USA Today/Gallup poll, June 15-19, 2008

Thirty-six percent of respondents agree that Obama is "very likely" to do so, compared with 27% who say the same about McCain. Combining the "somewhat likely" and "very likely" responses yields a solid 73% and 68%, respectively, who think it is likely that the candidates will refrain from personal attacks. In other words, more than two in three Americans think there is a reasonable chance that each candidate will run a campaign focused on the issues.

A look at the results for the two candidates in tandem shows that only a modest 13% of Americans think *both* Obama and McCain are "very likely" to stay focused on the issues. Just over half (53%) think both Obama and McCain are at least somewhat likely to do so. The composite numbers are lower than the numbers for each candidate alone largely because optimism about the ability of the candidates to stay positive is not uniformly distributed across the public. Partisanship plays a very strong role.

More than twice as many Republicans (40%) as Democrats (19%) think McCain is "very likely" to conduct a campaign based only on the issues (along with 24% of independents). And while half (50%) of Democrats think Obama is "very likely" to focus only on the issues, only 17% of Republicans agree, with independents falling in the middle at 38%.

The partisan tilt of these results is consistent with data from past elections. In a Sept. 24-26, 2004, poll, Gallup asked "In your view, which [2004 presidential election] campaign ads have been more unfair—the campaign ads that have been attacking John Kerry, or the campaign ads that have been attacking George W. Bush?" Sixty percent of Democrats felt the ads attacking Kerry were more unfair, while only 13% of Democrats felt the ads attacking Bush were more unfair (the balance volunteered "Both equally," "Neither," or "Don't know"). Similarly, 55% of Republicans rallied to Bush's defense and

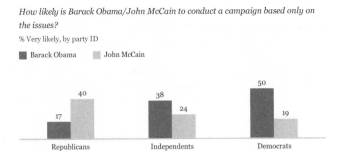

How likely is Barack Obama/John McCain to conduct a campaign based only on the issues?

% Very likely, by party ID

■ Barack Obama ▨ John McCain

USA Today/Gallup poll, June 15-19, 2008

said the ads attacking Bush were more unfair, while just 10% of Republicans said the ads attacking Kerry were more unfair.

For a different look at the question, I conducted an Internet experiment using a nationally representative sample of 425 American adults in November 2006. All respondents viewed the same 30-second attack advertisement against a fictional State Assembly candidate. The ad consisted of fairly standard negative advertising fare: ominous music and sound effects; a strong, deep voiceover; and black-and-white video footage. It included accusations of absenteeism while in office, investigations into tax evasion within a family business, and accusations of bad debts and campaign violations. Respondents were randomly assigned to one of two ads: one where the sponsoring candidate was a Republican and the target was a Democrat; and the other, the same ad with the partisanship of the candidates reversed. When asked whether the advertisement was "fair," people who shared the partisanship of the sponsoring candidate were far more likely to think the ad was fair (3.3 on a 7-point scale, where 1 was "Strongly disagree" and 7 was "Strongly agree") than were respondents who shared the partisanship of the target of the ad (with a lower fairness assessment of just 2.5). In other words, simply switching the partisanship of the candidates significantly changed perceptions of the fairness of two otherwise identical advertisements.

So will the public believe that the candidates are upholding their promises to refrain from personal attacks as the election season continues? The data suggest that the answer will depend, in part, on whom one asks.

Survey Methods

Results are based on telephone interviews with 1,625 national adults, aged 18 and older, conducted June 15-19, 2008. For results based on the total sample of national adults, one can say with 95% confidence that the maximum margin of sampling error is ±3 percentage points.

Interviews are conducted with respondents on land-line telephones (for respondents with a land-line telephone) and cellular phones (for respondents who are cell-phone only).

In addition to sampling error, question wording and practical difficulties in conducting surveys can introduce error or bias into the findings of public opinion polls.

July 21, 2008
DESPITE SALMONELLA CASES, AMERICANS CONFIDENT IN FOOD SAFETY
Confidence in grocery stores, restaurants steady compared to one year ago

by Lymari Morales, Gallup Staff Writer

Even before the Food and Drug Administration lifted its warning on raw tomatoes—because of the salmonella outbreak now considered the most widespread for a food-borne illness in the United States in more than a decade—Americans remained as confident as they were a year ago that the food available in grocery stores is safe to eat.

Do you feel confident or not confident that the food available at most grocery stores is safe to eat?

■ % Confident   ▨ % Not confident

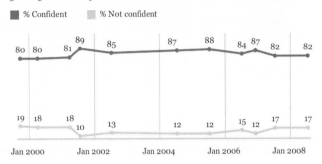

Federal officials still can't say for sure what made more than 1,100 sick across 42 states and the District of Columbia since April. Although the FDA first warned against certain types of tomatoes, it now says the salmonella may have come from jalapeno peppers, serrano peppers, or fresh cilantro. Yet, despite extensive media coverage and at least 220 cases involving hospitalization, Gallup finds average Americans no more worried about food safety than they were a year ago, but still slightly less confident than at other times in the past decade. Overall, it seems confidence has yet to recover from two high-profile outbreaks in 2006—one involving E. coli in bagged spinach and the other involving salmonella in peanut butter—and several high-profile food recalls in 2007.

While many restaurants have had to change their offerings or take extra precautions because of this year's salmonella outbreak, Americans are only slightly less confident in restaurant food than they were a year ago. Although Americans are usually less confident in restaurants than in grocery stores, this measure has seen a modest downward trend since 2001.

Do you feel confident or not confident that the food served at most restaurants is safe to eat?

■ % Confident   ▨ % Not confident

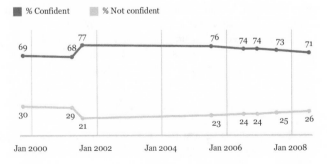

About two-thirds of Americans (60%) do report avoiding certain foods or brands as a result of a government food safety advisory or a product recall, and this number remains stable compared to a year ago. Fewer Americans say they threw food away or returned it to the store (33%), or worried about having eaten something contaminated (25%).

Have you, personally, done any of the following in the past year as a direct result of a government food safety advisory or a product recall, or not?

% Yes, have

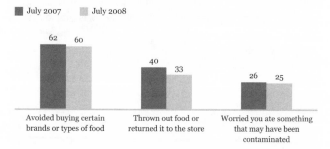

Gallup Polls, July 12-15, 2007, and July 10-13, 2008

While some have expressed frustration in the U.S. government's inability to pinpoint the source of the salmonella, Americans place no less confidence in the government to ensure the safety of the nation's food supply than they did a year ago. Still, confidence remains at a Gallup low and shows no improvement since the FDA added a new "food safety czar" in May 2007.

How much confidence do you have in the federal government to ensure the safety of the food supply in the U.S.?

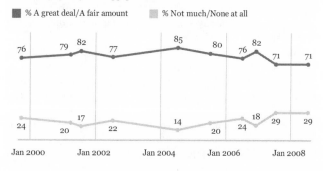

Bottom Line

Despite the widespread and perplexing nature of this year's salmonella outbreak in the United States, Americans are not expressing any heightened sense of worry about the food they buy at grocery stories and in restaurants. Beyond avoiding certain foods that they are warned about, consumers appear generally unfazed, though this could be in some part because they are unaware of the outbreak or its relatively limited agricultural scope. Nonetheless, confidence in the U.S. government to ensure the safety of the food supply remains lower than at times over the past decade, suggesting some room for improvement.

Survey Methods

Results are based on telephone interviews with 1,016 national adults, aged 18 and older, conducted July 10-13, 2008. For results based on

the total sample of national adults, one can say with 95% confidence that the maximum margin of sampling error is ±3 percentage points.

Interviews are conducted with respondents on land-line telephones (for respondents with a land-line telephone) and cellular phones (for respondents who are cell-phone only).

In addition to sampling error, question wording and practical difficulties in conducting surveys can introduce error or bias into the findings of public opinion polls.

July 21, 2008
IMPACT OF SMOKING, BEING OVERWEIGHT ON A PERSON'S IMAGE
Majority of Americans say neither affects their opinion

by Frank Newport, Gallup Poll Editor in Chief

The majority of Americans say the fact that a person smokes or is significantly overweight does not affect their opinion of that person, although 40% say they have a more negative opinion of smokers, and 29% have a more negative opinion of someone who is significantly overweight.

Everything else being equal, please tell me whether each of the following makes you [ROTATED: view a person more positively, does not affect your opinion, or makes you view a person more negatively]?

A. If a person smokes

B. If a person is significantly overweight

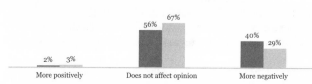

Gallup Poll Social Series Consumption Poll, July 10-13, 2008

The impact of a person's habits or external appearance on his or her image is a significant factor in today's society, given that groups of people claim they are unfairly discriminated against because of these types of personal characteristics. Smokers have often complained about societal discrimination, and, in recent years, some U.S. states and municipalities have included or are considering including weight in broad laws banning discrimination on the basis of such fundamental personal characteristics as race, gender, or age.

The July Gallup Poll Social Series Consumption Poll probed Americans' images of people who smoke and of those who are significantly overweight. The interpretation of the data (presented in the accompanying graph) depends on one's vantage point. Fifty-six percent of Americans say the fact that a person smokes makes no difference in their opinion of that person, and an even higher 67% say the fact that a person is significantly overweight doesn't affect their opinion. Still, that leaves substantial minorities who say these characteristics do make them think more negatively of a person.

Perhaps not surprisingly, most smokers themselves say the fact that a person smokes doesn't affect their opinion of that person. But almost half of nonsmokers say they feel more negatively about a person if that person smokes. This suggests that smokers should realize that one out of two nonsmokers they come in contact with will think less of them simply because of their tobacco habit.

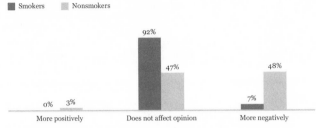

How do you view a person who smokes?

■ Smokers ■ Nonsmokers

- More positively: 0% / 3%
- Does not affect opinion: 92% / 47%
- More negatively: 7% / 48%

Gallup Poll Social Series Consumption Poll, July 10-13, 2008
NOTE: The percentage "more positively" for smokers is <0.5%.

On the other hand, there is more self-flagellation among those who say they are overweight (42% of respondents in the July survey). Twenty-five percent of these self-described overweight adults say they think more negatively of a person who is significantly overweight. Among those who say their weight is "about right," 33% hold negative perceptions of the significantly overweight.

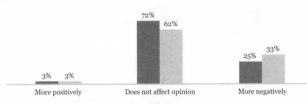

How do you view a person who is significantly overweight?

■ Overweight respondents (self-reported)

■ Respondents whose weight is "about right" (self-reported)

- More positively: 3% / 3%
- Does not affect opinion: 72% / 62%
- More negatively: 25% / 33%

Gallup Poll Social Series Consumption Poll, July 10-13, 2008

Despite the fact that a majority of Americans do not think more negatively of those who are significantly overweight, the poll finds most Americans believing that being overweight is a result of personal lifestyle choices rather than representing a biological or genetic factor.

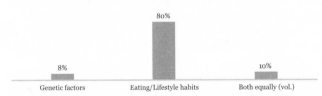

Thinking about the reasons why some people are significantly overweight or obese, do you think it is due more to: [ROTATED: genetic factors a person is born with or eating and lifestyle habits]?

- Genetic factors: 8%
- Eating/Lifestyle habits: 80%
- Both equally (vol.): 10%

Gallup Poll Social Series Consumption Poll, July 10-13, 2008
(vol.) = Volunteered response

This does not vary by self-reported weight status. Eighty percent of both those who describe themselves as overweight and those who describe their weight as about right say being significantly overweight is the result of eating and lifestyle habits rather than genetic factors.

Survey Methods

Results are based on telephone interviews with 1,016 national adults, aged 18 and older, conducted July 10-13, 2008. For results based on the total sample of national adults, one can say with 95% confidence that the maximum margin of sampling error is ±3 percentage points.

Interviews are conducted with respondents on land-line telephones (for respondents with a land-line telephone) and cellular phones (for respondents who are cell-phone only).

In addition to sampling error, question wording and practical difficulties in conducting surveys can introduce error or bias into the findings of public opinion polls.

July 22, 2008
CONDITIONS RIPE FOR A MIDSUMMER NIGHT'S HEADACHE
Eight in 10 Americans dissatisfied with the way things are going in U.S.

by Lydia Saad, Gallup Poll Senior Editor

The country's current state of affairs may not be the most restful topic to contemplate when drifting off to sleep this summer; instead, it could call for two aspirin. Just 17% of Americans are now satisfied with the way things are going in the country—only marginally better than the 14% who were satisfied in June—while 81% are dissatisfied.

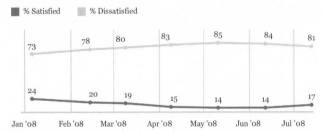

In general, are you satisfied or dissatisfied with the way things are going in the United States at this time?

Recent trend

■ % Satisfied ■ % Dissatisfied

	Jan '08	Feb '08	Mar '08	Apr '08	May '08	Jun '08	Jul '08
Dissatisfied	73	78	80	83	85	84	81
Satisfied	24	20	19	15	14	14	17

The latest results, from a July 10-13, 2008, Gallup Poll, represent the fifth straight month that dissatisfaction with the country has registered 80% or above, including the record-high 85% in May.

Gallup's long-term trend on this measure of national mood, instituted in 1979, shows only a few other times when public dissatisfaction with the country rose as high as it is today. It registered 84% in July 1979 and June 1992, and 80% in March, April, and July 1992.

Broad dissatisfaction with the country is found throughout society, although it is particularly high among women and Democrats, and is more pronounced among seniors than among young adults.

Nation's "Most Important Problem"

The former Sen. Phil Gramm, who is now former co-chairman of John McCain's presidential campaign, recently described this sort of public disaffection with the country as "whining" (a sentiment McCain strongly disavowed).

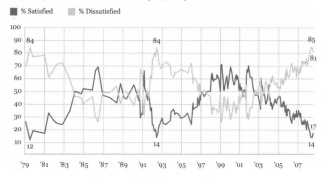

U.S. Satisfaction Among Demographic Groups

	Satisfied	Dissatisfied
	%	%
Men	20	77
Women	14	84
18 to 29	25	73
30 to 49	16	82
50 to 64	16	81
65+	11	86
Republicans	29	69
Independents	16	82
Democrats	8	90

July 10-13, 2008

The why behind the "whine" is evident in Americans' answers to Gallup's monthly measure of the "most important problem" facing the country. In July, the economy, gas prices, and the situation in Iraq are the clear leaders.

Other economic issues registering at least 5% include the high cost of living, generally, and unemployment. Other domestic issues in this league include dissatisfaction with government leaders, lack of energy sources, concern about morality in the country, and problems with the healthcare system.

Most Important Problem Facing the Country -- Top Responses

Responses mentioned by at least 5% of Americans

	July 10-13, 2008
	%
Economy in general	35
Fuel/Oil prices	23
Situation in Iraq/War	18
Dissatisfaction with government/Congress/politicians; poor leadership; corruption; abuse of power	9
Lack of energy sources; the energy crisis	6
Ethics/Moral/Religious/Family decline; dishonesty; lack of integrity	6
Poor healthcare/hospitals; high cost of healthcare	6
Unemployment/Jobs	5
High cost of living/Inflation	5

Gallup's monthly updates on this measure show no major shifts since May in the public's focus on the economy and Iraq (though the percentage citing Iraq has declined from earlier this year). After ris-

ing between April and June, mentions of gas and other fuel prices have leveled off at about 25%.

Most Important Problem -- 2008 Trend in Top Problems

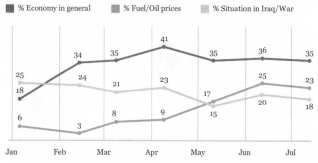

Survey Methods

Results are based on telephone interviews with 1,016 national adults, aged 18 and older, conducted July 10-13, 2008. For results based on the total sample of national adults, one can say with 95% confidence that the maximum margin of sampling error is ±3 percentage points.

Interviews are conducted with respondents on land-line telephones (for respondents with a land-line telephone) and cellular phones (for respondents who are cell-phone only).

In addition to sampling error, question wording and practical difficulties in conducting surveys can introduce error or bias into the findings of public opinion polls.

July 23, 2008
OBAMA GAINS OVER MCCAIN IN SWING STATES SINCE JUNE
Gap has moved at least 3 points in his favor in all state groups since June

by Jeffrey M. Jones, Gallup Poll Managing Editor

Since Barack Obama clinched the Democratic nomination and moved into a front-running position for the general presidential election in early June, he has seen his standing versus John McCain improve among voters in red states, blue states, and competitive (or purple) states. Obama has gained at least 3 points in the Obama-McCain gap in all three state groupings compared with voter sentiments in March through May.

Prior to Obama's securing the Democratic nomination in early June, he and McCain were running even nationally, with each averaging 45% of the total vote in Gallup Poll Daily tracking from March through May. Since then, Obama has gained a slight upper hand, averaging a 3 percentage-point national advantage over McCain (46% to 43%) in June and July interviewing.

These results are based on data from tens of thousands of interviews with registered voters in all 50 states plus the District of Columbia, so the changes—despite their relatively small size—are statistically meaningful.

Obama's gains have come across the political and geographic spectrum, as he has improved his relative positioning versus McCain

Change in Gap in Barack Obama-John McCain Vote Preference in Red, Blue, and Purple States

Based on Gallup Poll Daily tracking

■ March-May   ■ June-July

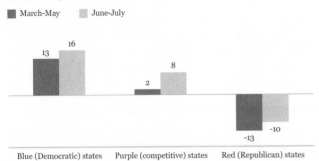

Note: Positive numbers represent an Obama advantage; negative numbers represent a McCain advantage

Barack Obama-John McCain Vote in Purple States

Based on Gallup Poll Daily tracking

■ % Vote for Obama   ■ % Vote for McCain

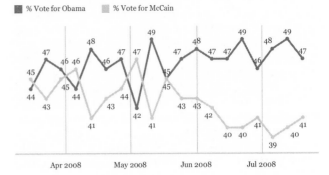

in "red states" (defined as those Republican George W. Bush won by 6 percentage points or more in 2004), "blue states" (those Democrat John Kerry won by 6 percentage points or more in 2004), and "purple states" (those in which the margin of victory for the winning candidate was less than 6 points).

While Obama has gained slightly in each of these state groupings, he has gained somewhat more in the most competitive states, seeing his lead expand in these by 6 points, as opposed to 3-point gains in the Obama-McCain gap in red and blue states. Since early June, he has averaged a 16-point lead over McCain in blue states and an 8-point lead in purple states, while trailing McCain by an average of 10 points in red states (McCain trails by only 3 points overall given the greater number of voters in red states).

Barack Obama-John McCain Vote Preference in Red, Blue and Purple States

Based on Gallup Poll Daily tracking

	March-May	June-July	Change
Blue (Democratic) states			
Obama	52%	53%	+1
McCain	39%	37%	-2
Obama-McCain gap	+13	+16	+3
Purple (competitive) states			
Obama	46%	48%	+2
McCain	44%	40%	-4
Obama-McCain gap	+2	+8	+6
Red (Republican) states			
Obama	39%	40%	+1
McCain	52%	50%	-2
Obama-McCain gap	-13	-10	+3

Note: Positive numbers represent an Obama advantage; negative numbers represent a McCain advantage

And while the changes in voter preferences have not been great, Obama has clearly established himself as the consistent leader in purple states since late May, whereas the two candidates were more competitive in these states prior to that.

Meanwhile, McCain has always enjoyed a comfortable lead in red states while Obama has done the same in blue states.

Despite his growing deficit in the competitive states, McCain

Barack Obama-John McCain Vote in Blue States

Based on Gallup Poll Daily tracking

■ % Vote for Obama   ■ % Vote for McCain

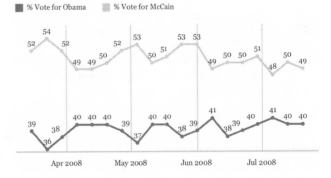

Barack Obama-John McCain Vote in Red States

Based on Gallup Poll Daily tracking

■ % Vote for Obama   ■ % Vote for McCain

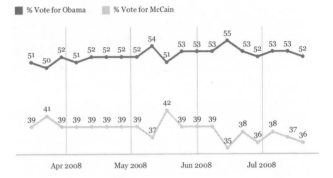

has been able to remain close to Obama on the national level given that more voters reside in red states (40%) than in blue states (31%). Thus, while McCain would merely need to break even with Obama in the most competitive states in order to win (he could win even if he trails Obama by a couple of points in those states), Obama needs to have at least a modest advantage in purple states in order to win the popular vote. Thus, the key to watch over the remainder of the campaign is not *whether* Obama has the lead over McCain in these states, but *by how much*.

Of course, the winner of the actual election is determined by electoral votes. This analysis groups all competitive states together and assumes the better Obama does in the popular vote in these states, the better his chances of winning a greater share of these states and their electoral votes.

Survey Methods

For the Gallup Poll Daily tracking survey, Gallup is interviewing no fewer than 1,000 U.S. adults nationwide each day during 2008.

Results for March 7 through June 1 are based on telephone interviews with 71,175 national registered voters, aged 18 and older, including interviews with 26,229 registered voters in red states, 23,873 in blue states, and 21,078 in purple states. For results based on the total sample of national adults, one can say with 95% confidence that the maximum margin of sampling error is ±1 percentage point.

Results for June 2 through July 20 are based on telephone interviews with 39,603 national registered voters, aged 18 and older, including interviews with 14,548 registered voters in red states, 13,311 in blue states, and 11,744 in purple states. For results based on the total sample of national adults, one can say with 95% confidence that the maximum margin of sampling error is ±1 percentage point.

Interviews are conducted with respondents on land-line telephones (for respondents with a land-line telephone) and cellular phones (for respondents who are cell-phone only).

In addition to sampling error, question wording and practical difficulties in conducting surveys can introduce error or bias into the findings of public opinion polls.

July 23, 2008
SLIM HOPE FOR BACK-TO-SCHOOL SALES
Half of all Americans rate the current economy as "poor"

by Dennis Jacobe, Gallup Chief Economist

With the critical back-to-school season approaching, the nation's retailers are hoping consumer sentiment will improve and consumer spending will follow. But new Gallup polling shows 49% of consumers rating the economy as "poor" in the third week of July, not much different from June and early July readings—and not good news for the nation's retailers.

How would you rate economic conditions in this country today -- as excellent, good, only fair, or poor?

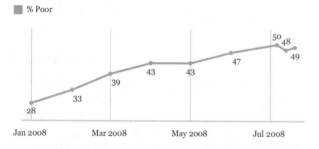

■ % Poor

Consumer Ratings of the Economy Remain Negative

Last week started with talk of the Fannie Mae and Freddie Mac bailout—an effort to save these two so-called government-sponsored enterprises that form the core of today's mortgage finance system. However, by midweek, oil prices were plunging and the stock market was surging, led by an improvement in financial-sector stocks

as investors became increasingly familiar with the "too-big-to-fail" concept.

Gallup's continuous measurement of consumer economic perceptions showed little response last week, as the financial sector experienced the onset of the Fannie/Freddie crisis that seemed to match in intensity the stress the Bear Stearns debacle placed on the financial sector. While the daily variations in ratings do suggest some consumer response within the week to last week's events, consumer perceptions for the week were just about as bleak as those for the previous week.

The percentage of lower-income Americans rating current economic conditions as "poor" was 56% in June, and after flirting with 60% during the first two weeks of July, it fell back to 56% in the third week of the month. At the same time, "poor" ratings among higher-income Americans that were at 38% in June have bounced around during the first two weeks of the month before settling at 44% during the most recent week. The increasing number of higher-income consumers holding a negative view of the economy should be of particular concern to high-end retailers.

Percentage Rating Economy as Poor, by Annual Income

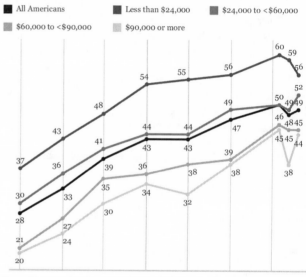

Consumer Expectations
Remain Highly Negative

Similarly, consumer expectations for the future course of the economy have remained highly negative, with 87% of Americans saying economic conditions are "getting worse" during each of the first three weeks of July—the same as the June reading, and little different from the 86% of May and the 85% of April. And, these negative expectations have remained high across different income groups.

Survey Methods

Gallup is interviewing no fewer than 1,000 U.S. adults nationwide each day during 2008. The economic questions analyzed in this report are asked of a random half-sample of respondents each day. The results reported here are based on combined data of more than 8,000 interviews in January, February, March, April, May, and June. For results based on this sample, the maximum margin of sampling error is ±1 percentage point.

Percentage Saying Economy Is Getting Worse, by Annual Income

	Jan '08	Feb '08	Mar '08	Apr '08	May '08	Jun '08	Jun 30-Jul 6, '08	Jul 7-13, '08	Jul 14-20, '08
	%	%	%	%	%	%	%	%	%
All Americans	78	79	84	85	86	87	87	87	87
Less than $24,000	77	79	85	85	88	88	89	86	90
$24,000 to <$60,000	81	81	87	87	89	90	89	86	89
$60,000 to <$90,000	76	81	84	88	88	88	86	88	86
$90,000 or more	78	79	84	84	83	85	86	87	86

The questions for the first and second week of July are based on combined data of more than 3,000 interviews conducted June 30 to July 6, July 7-13, and July 14-20, 2008. For results based on this sample, the maximum margin of sampling error is ±2 percentage points.

Interviews are conducted with respondents on land-line telephones (for respondents with a land-line telephone) and cellular phones (for respondents who are cell-phone only).

In addition to sampling error, question wording and practical difficulties in conducting surveys can introduce error or bias into the findings of public opinion polls.

July 24, 2008
U.S. SMOKING RATE STILL COMING DOWN
About one in five American adults now smoke

by Lydia Saad, Gallup Poll Senior Editor

The percentage of U.S. adults saying they smoked cigarettes in the past week, now 21%, is similar to what Gallup found in 2007. However, it represents a decline from earlier this decade, when between 22% and 28% said they smoked, and is among the lowest figures Gallup has recorded in more than six decades of polling on tobacco use in America.

Have you, yourself, smoked any cigarettes in the past week?
Recent trend: 2000-2008

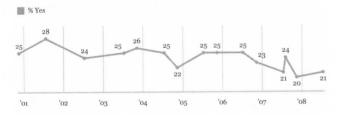

More specifically, in three of the past four Gallup smoking measurements (conducted between July 2007 and today), only 20% or 21% of American adults have said they smoked cigarettes in the past week. Compared with the average of 25% who said they smoked from 2000 through 2006, this suggests a recent decline in U.S. smoking. (For the full trend, see the table elsewhere in this report.)

The latest result comes from Gallup's annual Consumption Habits survey, conducted July 10-13, 2008.

Self-reported adult smoking peaked in 1954 at 45%, and remained at 40% or more through the early 1970s, but has since gradually declined. The average rate of smoking across the decades fell from 40% in the 1970s to 32% in the 1980s, 26% in the 1990s, and 24% since 2000.

Cigarette Smoking, by Decade

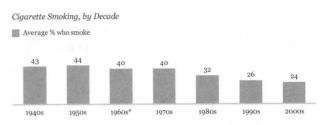

* 1960s includes only one measurement

A Youthful Habit

Cigarette smoking is more prevalent among younger adults (18 to 49 years) than among older adults and seniors, something Gallup has seen consistently over the years. Thirty percent of 18- to 29-year-olds and 26% of those 30 to 49 say they had a cigarette in the past week. This contrasts with only 17% of those 50 to 64 and 9% of those 65 and older.

Current Cigarette Smoker, by Age

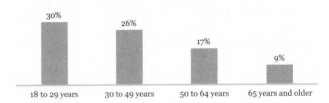

July 10-13, 2008

A major reason for the difference in smoking rates by age is that many older Americans have quit the habit. For nearly every current smoker in the 30- to 49-year age bracket, there is another who says he or she used to smoke. Among those 50 to 64, the ratio of former smokers to current smokers is nearly 2-to-1, while among those 65 and older it swells to more than 5-to-1.

As a result, a greater proportion of seniors have "ever" smoked (56%), compared with young adults (42%).

Lifetime Smoking Status, by Age

	18 to 29 years	30 to 49 years	50 to 64 years	65 years and older
	%	%	%	%
Current smoker	30	26	17	9
Former smoker	12	23	33	47
Total ever smoked	42	49	50	56
Never smoked	58	51	49	44

July 10-13, 2008

Presumably, the older age brackets would include even more current and former smokers relative to the younger age brackets, if not for the disproportionately higher rate of deaths among older Americans because of tobacco use.

Never Too Young to Quit?

The difficulty of quitting smoking is evident in the finding that two in three current smokers consider themselves "addicted" to cigarettes. An even greater number—74%—say they would like to give up smoking, but have not.

Do you consider yourself addicted to cigarettes or not?
All things considered, would you like to give up smoking, or not?
Based on smokers

July 10-13, 2008

Young smokers could find quitting easier now than when they are older. According to Gallup smoking trends since 2005, while 18- to 29-year-olds are about as likely as those 30 to 64 to say they would like to give up smoking (and more likely than those 65 and older), younger smokers are much less likely than older generations of smokers to consider themselves addicted (58% vs. 78% to 79%).

Perceptions of Addiction to Cigarettes, by Age
Based on smokers

% Yes, addicted

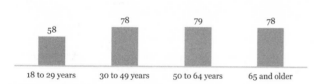

Based on combined 2005-2008 Gallup Polls

Additionally, young adults smoke an average of 11 cigarettes a day, or about half a pack. This rises to about 15 cigarettes a day among those 30 and older—a potentially important difference.

Bottom Line

Smoking rates have been coming down for about the past quarter century, and recent Gallup polling suggests they have continued to drop in just the past few years. About one in five Americans today say they smoke cigarettes, down from about one in four at the start of the decade.

Although most smokers feel they are addicted to cigarettes, that fact that so many older adults have reportedly succeeded in quitting should give young smokers who want to quit the encouragement to try.

Survey Methods

Results are based on telephone interviews with 1,016 national adults, aged 18 and older, conducted July 10-13, 2008. For results based on the total sample of national adults, one can say with 95% confidence that the maximum margin of sampling error is ±3 percentage points.

For results based on the sample of 184 smokers, the maximum margin of sampling error is ±8 percentage points.

For results based on the sample of 832 nonsmokers, the maximum margin of sampling error is ±4 percentage points.

Results based on the aggregate of 2005 to 2008 polls include interviews with 982 adults who say they smoked cigarettes in the past week, including 117 respondents aged 18 to 29, 293 aged 30 to 49, 256 aged 50 to 64, and 103 aged 65 and older. The polls combined for this aggregate were conducted July 10-13, 2008; July 12-15, 2007; July 6-9, 2006; and July 7-10, 2005.

Interviews are conducted with respondents on land-line telephones (for respondents with a land-line telephone) and cellular phones (for respondents who are cell-phone only).

In addition to sampling error, question wording and practical difficulties in conducting surveys can introduce error or bias into the findings of public opinion polls.

July 25, 2008
BEER BACK TO DOUBLE-DIGIT LEAD OVER WINE AS FAVORED DRINK
Shift back to beer most evident among 30- to 49-year-olds

by Jeffrey M. Jones, Gallup Poll Managing Editor

Beer has regained a comfortable margin over wine when U.S. drinkers are asked to name which alcoholic beverage they most often drink. In recent years, wine had narrowed the gap, including pulling slightly ahead in 2005 (though not by a significant margin), but for the first time since 2002, beer enjoys a better-than-double-digit advantage over wine.

Do you most often drink liquor, wine, or beer?
Based on U.S. adults who drink alcoholic beverages

% Beer   % Wine   % Liquor

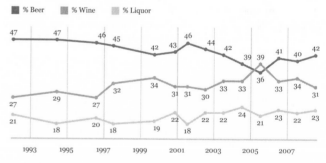

These results are based on Gallup's annual Consumption Habits poll, conducted July 10-13 of this year.

As the graph shows, beer still is not as widely preferred today as it was in the early 1990s, when close to half of Americans said it was their alcoholic drink of choice. Preferences for wine have fallen back from their 2005 high (39%) to 31%.

The shift back to beer from wine in recent years has occurred mostly among Americans between the ages of 30 and 49. In combined data from the 2004 and 2005 Consumption surveys, drinkers between 30 and 49 were about as likely to prefer wine as beer. Now, drinkers in this age bracket have shifted back to beer, with an average of 47% in the combined 2007-2008 data saying they most often drink beer.

Preferred Alcoholic Beverage, Among Drinkers Aged 30 to 49

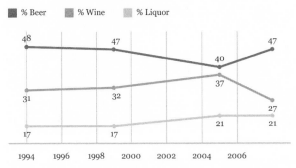

*Data are based on two-year averages -- 1992/1994, 1997/1999, 2004/2005, and 2007/2008

Drinking preferences of younger adults have remained stable in recent years, with 18- to 29-year-olds still showing a wide preference for beer, though nowhere near as large as it was in the 1992-1994 data. Younger adults are more likely to say they drink liquor most often than to say they drink wine.

Preferred Alcoholic Beverage, Among Drinkers Aged 18 to 29

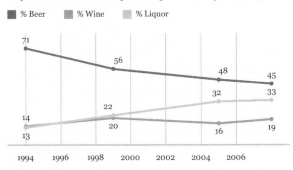

*Data are based on two-year averages -- 1992/1994, 1997/1999, 2004/2005, and 2007/2008

In contrast, wine is the preferred beverage of older drinkers, and has been since the early 1990s. Drinkers aged 50 and older have also had stable preferences in recent years.

Preferred Alcoholic Beverage, Among Drinkers Aged 50+

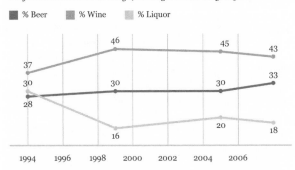

*Data are based on two-year averages -- 1992/1994, 1997/1999, 2004/2005, and 2007/2008

This year's consumption poll also finds:
- Sixty-two percent of Americans say they drink alcohol, a percentage that has varied little in the last 10 years.

- The average drinker reports having consumed 3.8 alcoholic drinks in the past week. This is the first time the average has dropped below 4 drinks since 2001. It had been as high as 5.1 in 2003.
- Continuing a recent trend, Gallup finds a higher proportion of drinkers claiming to have had an alcoholic beverage in the last 24 hours. Exactly 36% of Americans have reported drinking alcohol in the last 24 hours in each of the last four Gallup consumption polls. This compares to an average of 30% from 2000-2004.
- "Daily drinking" is more common among Americans of higher socioeconomic status. Over the past four years, an average of 42% of college graduates report having had a drink in the last 24 hours, compared with 32% of those who have not graduated from college.
- Similarly, 41% of drinkers with incomes of $75,000 or greater say they have had a drink in the past 24 hours, compared with 36% of middle-income respondents (those with household incomes between $30,000 and $74,999) and just 23% of those residing in lower-income households (with incomes of less than $30,000).
- Men are more likely than women to have had a drink during the previous day, 43% to 28%.
- Older drinkers are more likely than younger drinkers to have consumed alcohol in the previous 24 hours—39% of those aged 50 and older say they drank in the last 24 hours, compared with 35% of those aged 30 to 49 and just 28% of those below 30.

Survey Methods

Results are based on telephone interviews with 1,016 national adults, aged 18 and older, conducted July 10-13, 2008. For results based on the total sample of national adults, one can say with 95% confidence that the maximum margin of sampling error is ±3 percentage points.

For results based on the sample of 625 adults who drink alcoholic beverages, the maximum margin of sampling error is ±4 percentage points.

Interviews are conducted with respondents on land-line telephones (for respondents with a land-line telephone) and cellular phones (for respondents who are cell-phone only).

In addition to sampling error, question wording and practical difficulties in conducting surveys can introduce error or bias into the findings of public opinion polls.

July 28, 2008
BELIEF IN GOD FAR LOWER IN WESTERN U.S.
Overall, 78% believe in God, 15% in a higher spirit

by Frank Newport, Gallup Poll Editor in Chief

Americans who live in the Western part of the United States are much less likely to believe in God than are those living elsewhere, particularly in the South, where belief in God is highest.

There are a number of ways to ask about belief in God. Gallup's annual Values and Beliefs poll, conducted May 8-11, used a question structure that gave Americans three choices concerning their belief: a) You believe in God, b) You don't believe in God, but you

Which of the following statements comes closest to your belief about God -- you believe in God, you don't believe in God, but you do believe in a universal spirit or higher power, or you don't believe in either?

By region of the country

■ % Believe in God   ■ % Believe in universal spirit   ▦ % Don't believe in either

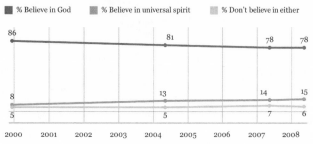

Gallup Poll Social Series: Values and Beliefs, May 8-11, 2008

do believe in a universal spirit or higher power, or c) You don't believe in either. The inclusion of the middle alternative has the overall impact of lowering the percentage of those interviewed who say straight-out that they believe in God.

Gallup has asked this question only four times. The trend shows a decrease in the percentage choosing the "belief in God" alternative compared to the initial asking in December 1999. The fact that this baseline reading was obtained in the weeks before Christmas may partially explain why the reading was higher that year than in 2004, 2007, and this year.

Which of the following statements comes closest to your belief about God -- you believe in God, you don't believe in God, but you do believe in a universal spirit or higher power, or you don't believe in either?

■ % Believe in God   ■ % Believe in universal spirit   ▦ % Don't believe in either

Gallup Poll Social Series: Values and Beliefs, May 8-11, 2008

Clearly, as seen previously, Americans living in the West are significantly less likely to choose the first "belief in God" alternative than are those living in any of the other three regions of the country. Westerners are much more inclined to believe in a universal spirit or higher power than are Americans from the East, Midwest, or South. One out of 10 Westerners say they don't believe in either.

By age, the major differentiation in belief in God is between seniors and those younger than 65. Eighty-eight percent of the older group professes belief in God, compared to percentages between 74% and 77% for those in the three younger age groups. It is well-known that older Americans are the most religious. The interesting fact here, though, is the relatively high percentage of belief in God among those 18 to 29—usually the least religious group.

The major difference by educational level is between those with a high school diploma or less and those with higher education levels. While 88% of Americans with a high school education or less profess a belief in God, just more than 7 out of 10 Americans with postgraduate degrees believe in God. Another 19% of this highly educated group professes belief in a universal spirit or higher power.

It is well-known that Republicans are more religious than are Democrats (or independents). These data confirm that finding.

Which of the following statements comes closest to your belief about God?

By age

■ % Believe in God

■ % Don't believe in God, but believe in universal spirit/higher power

▦ % Don't believe in either

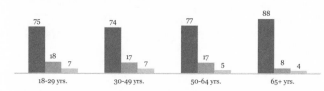

Gallup Poll Social Series: Values and Beliefs, May 8-11, 2008

Which of the following statements comes closest to your belief about God?

By education

■ % Believe in God

■ % Don't believe in God, but believe in universal spirit/higher power

▦ % Don't believe in either

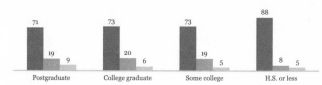

Gallup Poll Social Series: Values and Beliefs, May 8-11, 2008

Eighty-nine percent of Republicans believe in God, compared to 77% of Democrats and an even lower 70% of independents.

Which of the following statements comes closest to your belief about God?

By political party

■ % Believe in God

■ % Don't believe in God, but believe in universal spirit/higher power

▦ % Don't believe in either

Gallup Poll Social Series: Values and Beliefs, May 8-11, 2008

Even among Americans who say they have no religious identity (that is, have no religion or denomination with which they identify), only 30% say they do not believe in either God or a universal spirit/higher power. The majority say they believe in the latter, with just 15% believing in God. Protestants and other non-Catholic Christians have a slightly higher percentage of belief in God than do Catholics, and for both groups, the percentage is much higher than for those who profess to identify with a non-Christian religion.

Summary

Overall, just fewer than 8 out of 10 Americans profess belief in God, while the majority of the rest say they do not believe in God but do believe in a higher spirit or universal power. Only 6% of Americans say they simply do not believe in either. The fact that, compared with other regions, those from the Western United States have the lowest likelihood of believing in God does not come as a total surprise given

Which of the following statements comes closest to your belief about God?

By religious affiliation

■ % Believe in God

■ % Don't believe in God, but believe in universal spirit/higher power

░ % Don't believe in either

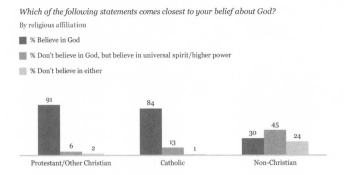

Gallup Poll Social Series: Values and Beliefs, May 8-11, 2008

In general, how harmful do you feel smoking is to adults who smoke?

■ % Very harmful ░ % Somewhat harmful ░ % Not too/Not at all harmful

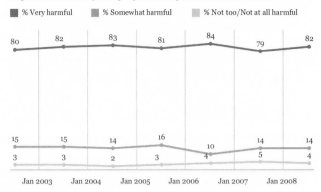

In general, how harmful do you feel secondhand smoke is to adults?

■ % Very harmful ░ % Somewhat harmful ░ % Not too/Not at all harmful

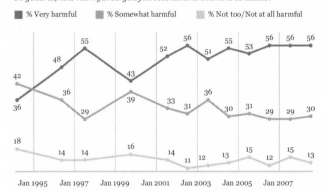

other data showing that the West has a lower level of religiosity overall. Still, the contrast between Westerners and those from other regions reflected in these data is fairly substantial.

The differences in belief in God by education and age confirm findings relating to these demographic variables and church attendance and the importance of religion. Generally, however, belief in God is at the 70% or higher level among even the traditionally least religious subgroups, such as those younger than 30.

Survey Methods

Results are based on telephone interviews with 1,017 national adults, aged 18 and older, conducted May 8-11, 2008. For results based on the total sample of national adults, one can say with 95% confidence that the maximum margin of sampling error is ±3 percentage points.

Interviews are conducted with respondents on land-line telephones (for respondents with a land-line telephone) and cellular phones (for respondents who are cell-phone only).

In addition to sampling error, question wording and practical difficulties in conducting surveys can introduce error or bias into the findings of public opinion polls.

July 28, 2008
MOST AMERICANS CONSIDER SMOKING VERY HARMFUL
Majority blame smokers, rather than tobacco companies, for smokers' health problems

by Lymari Morales, Gallup Staff Writer

As multibillionaires Bill Gates and Michael Bloomberg team up to reduce smoking worldwide, a Gallup Poll finds that most Americans would likely agree in principle with the thrust of the initiative, as 82% consider smoking very harmful, up slightly from last year and on par with what Gallup has measured during this decade.

A smaller percentage, but still a majority of Americans (56%), also believe smoking is very harmful to secondhand smokers, a number that has remained at a Gallup high for three consecutive years.

Microsoft's founder and New York City's mayor last week pledged a total of $500 million to reduce smoking around the world. In the United States, smoking has been trending downward over the last half century—this year, 21% of Americans tell Gallup they smoke, down from 28% as recently as 2001. Around the world, a median of 22% surveyed by Gallup say the same, ranging by country

from 6% in Nigeria to 40% in Cuba, with no clear relationship between GDP and likelihood of smoking.

To achieve what two hugely successful multibillionaires themselves admit is a difficult and ambitious goal, Gates and Bloomberg say they plan to target governments, companies, and individuals alike. Over four years, they hope to encourage higher tobacco taxes, outlaw smoking in public places, ban advertising targeted toward children, and to help people avoid or quit the habit.

Gallup Polls in the United States suggest that while raising individuals' awareness of the harmful effects of smoking in other countries is an essential first step in helping to lower smoking rates, the kinds of policies Gates and Bloomberg are pursuing to make smoking more difficult for people are also an important part of any winning strategy. When in the 1960s, the U.S. surgeon general first warned about the dangers of smoking and the U.S. Congress began to require warning labels on cigarette packs, Gallup found a sharp increase in public perceptions of smoking risks, but no immediate decline in the smoking rate. It was not until the 1970s that the rate of smoking dropped below 40% (possibly reflecting a lag in full public acceptance of the risks) and not until 1989 (well into the period of government regulation of smoking in public) that it fell below 30%.

When Americans today are asked whether the blame for smokers' health problems lies with tobacco companies or smokers themselves, a near-record-high 66% say smokers are responsible.

These data suggest at least some support for an awareness campaign emphasizing the role of individual choice and personal responsibility in efforts to stop smoking.

Bottom Line

Most Americans recognize the harmful effects of smoking, and tend to blame smokers, rather than tobacco companies, for the health

Relationship Between the Smoking Rate and Perceptions That Smoking Causes Lung Cancer

Gallup Polls, 1954-1999

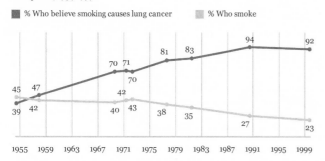

Who's to blame for the health problems faced by smokers in this country?

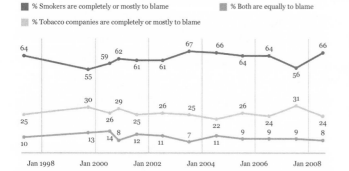

problems associated with the habit. While raising awareness of the harmful effects of smoking is part of the battle, Gallup Polls conducted in the United States, where such awareness is already high, suggest that Gates and Bloomberg will also need to depend on both policies and patience to achieve their goals.

Survey Methods

Results are based on telephone interviews with 1,016 national adults, aged 18 and older, conducted July 10-13, 2008. For results based on the total sample of national adults, one can say with 95% confidence that the maximum margin of sampling error is ±3 percentage points.

Interviews are conducted with respondents on land-line telephones (for respondents with a land-line telephone) and cellular phones (for respondents who are cell-phone only).

In addition to sampling error, question wording and practical difficulties in conducting surveys can introduce error or bias into the findings of public opinion polls.

July 29, 2008
ASSESSING THE IMPACT OF OBAMA'S TRIP
Americans, especially Republicans, critical of media's coverage of candidates

by Frank Newport, Gallup Poll Editor in Chief and Jeffrey M. Jones, Managing Editor

Could John McCain benefit from Barack Obama's much-publicized foreign trip? Several observations from the just-completed *USA Today*/Gallup poll suggest that this is a possibility.

Americans' overall reaction to the trip was muted, as shown in the accompanying results.

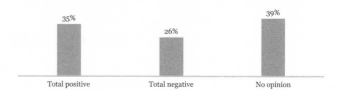

As you may know, Barack Obama is concluding his overseas trip to Afghanistan, Iraq, the Middle East and Europe. Would you say you have a -- [ROTATED: very positive, positive, negative, (or) very negative] opinion of this trip, or don't you know enough to say?

July 25-27, 2008, USA Today/Gallup poll

Thirty-five percent had a positive opinion, while 26% had a negative opinion, with the rest—more than a third—saying they didn't know enough about the trip to be able to say.

Not surprisingly, there were highly partisan reactions to the trip. Notably, Democrats are slightly less likely than Republicans to have an opinion on the trip at all.

View of Obama Overseas Trip, by Party Affiliation

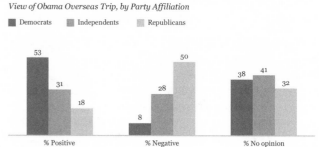

July 25-27, 2008, USA Today/Gallup poll

The slightly higher degree of attention Republicans paid to the trip could in part reflect the fact that Republican leaders—including McCain himself and, in particular, conservative commentators—were highly vocal in their efforts to blunt the impact of the trip and were quick to criticize and politicize it, finding fault with Obama for a number of reasons at almost every stop.

The heavy coverage of the trip may have fueled speculation (or reinforced pre-existing attitudes) about news media bias in Obama's favor. A separate set of questions in the weekend poll asked Americans about their views of the news media's coverage of the two major-party candidates. Americans are more than twice as likely to say media coverage of Obama is unfairly positive as to say it is unfairly negative. For McCain, the opposite is true, with many more seeing coverage of him as unfairly negative than as unfairly positive.

The differences in views of the media are enormous between those who are voting for McCain and those voting for Obama. In general, McCain voters largely believe their candidate is being treated unfairly while Obama is getting overly friendly media coverage. In turn, Obama voters tend to view the media coverage of both candidates as even-handed.

Since the previous *USA Today*/Gallup poll, Obama's image has suffered to some degree, while McCain's has slightly improved. In the June 15-19 poll, 64% of Americans had a positive view of

Opinion of News Media Coverage of the Candidates

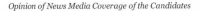

■ Unfairly positive   ■ Unfairly negative   ▨ About right

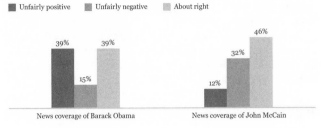

News coverage of Barack Obama   News coverage of John McCain

July 25-27, 2008, USA Today/Gallup poll

Opinion of News Media Coverage of the Candidates

	Unfairly positive	Unfairly negative	About right
McCain voters			
Coverage of Obama	61%	9%	24%
Coverage of McCain	5%	49%	40%
Obama voters			
Coverage of Obama	21%	21%	53%
Coverage of McCain	18%	18%	55%

July 25-27, 2008, USA Today/Gallup poll

Obama, compared with 61% today. McCain's favorable rating has increased from 59% to 62%.

While those changes are not large, the most interesting finding is that the change in opinions of Obama has come only among Republicans and independents; Democrats' views of Obama (and of McCain, for that matter) have not changed.

Favorable Ratings of Barack Obama and John McCain, by Party

	Favorable/ Unfavorable among Democrats	Favorable/ Unfavorable among independents	Favorable/ Unfavorable among Republicans
Barack Obama			
July 25-27, 2008	86% / 11%	61% / 33%	31% / 67%
June 15-19, 2008	85% / 12%	66% / 27%	37% / 59%
John McCain			
July 25-27, 2008	35% / 59%	67% / 27%	92% / 5%
June 15-19, 2008	37% / 58%	57% / 34%	89% / 9%

July 25-27, 2008, USA Today/Gallup poll

These changes, which are all relatively slight, may reflect the type of normal fluctuation one sees in election seasons, or perhaps emerging negative reactions over his recent trip.

The trip may also be responsible for the finding of a difference in the preferences of likely versus registered voters in the new *USA Today*/Gallup poll. McCain gains among likely voters compared to registered voters in this poll, something he has not done in previous *USA Today*/Gallup polls this year.

The reasons for the shift between registered and likely voters in this poll compared to previous polls is not entirely clear, but the data show that in this poll, Republicans have become slightly more likely to say they are giving quite a lot of thought to the election, while independents and Democrats are giving less thought—compared to what has been the case throughout this year. In other words, Republicans have become more attentive to the election on a relative basis, which increases their percentage of the likely voter pool. A Democratic advantage in thought given to the election (and indeed in qual-

USA Today/Gallup Polls, Registered Voters and Likely Voters

	Registered voters		Likely voters	
	Obama	**McCain**	**Obama**	**McCain**
	%	%	%	%
2008 Jul 25-27	47	44	45	49
2008 Jun 15-19	48	42	50	44
2008 May 30-Jun 1	47	44	49	44
2008 May 1-3	45	47	47	48
2008 Apr 18-20	47	44	49	44
2008 Mar 14-16	48	47	49	47
2008 Feb 21-24	49	45	47	48
2008 Feb 8-10	49	46	50	46
2008 Jan 10-13	44	50	45	50

July 25-27, 2008, USA Today/Gallup poll

ifying as a likely voter, according to Gallup's model) is not the norm historically, so in some ways, after the excitement of the Democratic nomination campaign has subsided, the current poll may suggest that the electorate is returning to a more normal state of affairs.

Implications

It is difficult to pinpoint the exact causes of any of these changes. But the available data show that Republicans are strongly convinced that the media are much too positive in their coverage of Obama and too negative in their coverage of McCain. The media's coverage of Obama's foreign trip, coupled with a strong reaction from McCain and other conservatives, may have created the seemingly paradoxical effect of increasing Republicans' energy and excitement about voting for McCain. If this is the case, the degree to which this is short-term versus long-term is still not clear.

Survey Methods

Results are based on telephone interviews with 1,007 national adults, aged 18 and older, conducted July 25-27, 2008. For results based on the total sample of national adults, one can say with 95% confidence that the maximum margin of sampling error is ±3 percentage points.

Interviews are conducted with respondents on land-line telephones (for respondents with a land-line telephone) and cellular phones (for respondents who are cell-phone only).

In addition to sampling error, question wording and practical difficulties in conducting surveys can introduce error or bias into the findings of public opinion polls.

July 30, 2008
AFGHAN WAR EDGES OUT IRAQ AS MOST IMPORTANT FOR U.S.
Two-thirds say U.S. involvement in Afghanistan not a mistake

by Frank Newport, Gallup Poll Editor in Chief

By a slim margin, Americans say the war in Afghanistan is more important for the United States than is the conflict in Iraq.

This question was asked for the first time in the July 25-27 *USA Today*/Gallup poll, so there is no historical record of changes over

If you had to choose, which is the more important war for the United States: the war in Iraq or the war in Afghanistan?

USA Today/Gallup poll, July 25-27, 2008
(vol.) = Volunteered response

time—if any—in the public's views of the relative importance of these two wars.

President George W. Bush in essence began both wars, sending U.S. troops into Afghanistan in the fall of 2001, and into Iraq in March 2003. Faced with this choice between the two, however, Republicans tilt toward saying the Iraq conflict is more important. Independents and Democrats say the Afghan war is more important.

If you had to choose, which is the more important war for the United States: the war in Iraq or the war in Afghanistan?
By political party

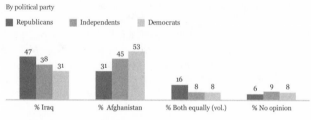

USA Today/Gallup poll, July 25-27, 2008
(vol.) = Volunteered response

These results reinforce the conclusion that the Iraq war has been the more politicized (and controversial) of the two wars.

Support for the War in Afghanistan

Americans appear to strongly support the initial decision to go to war in Afghanistan, based on responses to Gallup's classic "mistake" question (which has been asked about U.S. conflicts since the Korean War in the early 1950s). Two-thirds (68%) affirm the basis for sending military forces to Afghanistan, saying it was not a mistake.

Do you think the United States made a mistake in sending military forces to Afghanistan, or not?

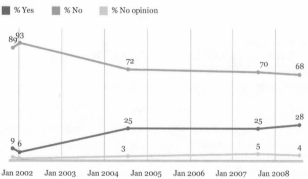

Support for U.S. military involvement in Afghanistan decreased between 2002 and 2004, but has remained fairly constant since that point.

The poll showing two-thirds of Americans who say the war in Afghanistan was *not* a mistake can be contrasted to polling in recent years showing that the majority of Americans have consistently said the war in Iraq *was* a mistake.

There is a significant difference in the way the three partisan groups respond to this question, although less than half of any group says the Afghanistan intervention was a mistake.

Do you think the United States made a mistake in sending military forces to Afghanistan, or not?
By political party

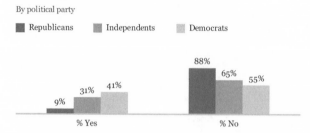

USA Today/Gallup poll, July 25-27, 2008

There has been a good deal of negative publicity about the way things are going for the United States in Afghanistan in recent months, but the current poll shows only a slight increase in the percentage of Americans who say things are going badly there. In general, views of the way the war is going are split.

In general, how would you say things are going for the U.S. in Afghanistan -- very well, moderately well, moderately badly, (or) very badly?

	Very well	Moderately well	Moderately badly	Very badly	No opinion	Total well	Total badly
2008 Jul 25-27	5	41	33	18	3	46	51
2006 Sep 15-17	6	43	30	16	5	49	46

Survey Methods

Results are based on telephone interviews with 1,007 national adults, aged 18 and older, conducted July 25-27, 2008. For results based on the total sample of national adults, one can say with 95% confidence that the maximum margin of sampling error is ±3 percentage points.

For results based on the 506 national adults in the Form A half-sample and 501 national adults in the Form B half-sample, the maximum margins of sampling error are ±5 percentage points.

Interviews are conducted with respondents on land-line telephones (for respondents with a land-line telephone) and cellular phones (for respondents who are cell-phone only).

In addition to sampling error, question wording and practical difficulties in conducting surveys can introduce error or bias into the findings of public opinion polls.

July 30, 2008

OBAMA RETAINS STRENGTH AMONG HIGHLY EDUCATED

McCain does best among those with college degrees but no further education

by Frank Newport, Gallup Poll Editor in Chief

Barack Obama has by far his greatest strength among voters with postgraduate education, while John McCain has his highest level of support among voters who have a college degree but no postgraduate education.

Preference for the General Election, by Education

■ % Obama ■ % McCain

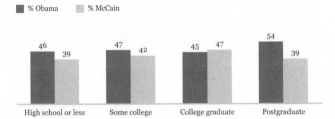

Weekly aggregate of registered voters, July 21-27, 2008

This analysis is based on Gallup's detailed weekly assessment of the vote within subgroups.

The latest weekly update, consisting of more than 6,000 interviews conducted July 21-27, shows that the relationship between education and the Obama versus McCain margin in the presidential vote is a U-shaped curve of sorts. Presumptive Democratic nominee Obama does well compared to McCain among those without a college degree, and among those with postgraduate education. McCain's support increases on a relative basis among those with a college degree.

Preference for the General Election, by Education

Obama-McCain gap in support, in percentage points

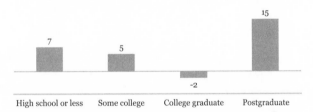

Weekly aggregate of registered voters, July 21-27, 2008

There is also an interesting trend in the percentage of each educational group that is undecided. The percentage of undecided voters is highest among those with the least formal education, and shrinks among groups with higher average educational attainment. The data indicate that McCain's strength among college graduates, compared to his position among those with less than a college education, is based on his gain as the percentage of undecideds decreases. Obama's percentage of the vote is relatively constant across all three groups of those with college educations or less.

Whites

Obama wins overwhelmingly among blacks across all educational levels. An analysis of the vote by education among whites (with

Preference for the General Election, by Education

Among registered voters

	% Barack Obama	% John McCain	% Other	% Neither/ Undecided
High school or less	46	39	1	14
Some college	47	42	1	10
College graduate	45	47	1	8
Postgraduate education	54	39	*	7

* Less than 0.5%

Gallup Poll Daily tracking, July 21-27, 2008

blacks and Hispanics taken out of the equation), however, shows the same basic pattern as is the case among all voters.

Overall, as has been well-established, McCain does much better against Obama among whites in general than he does among non-whites. The presumptive Republican nominee in fact "wins" in each educational group of whites except those with postgraduate education. But, as is the case for all voters, McCain's relative advantage is greatest among college graduates, and the data to a degree reflect the same U-shaped curve evident among all voters.

Preference for the General Election, by Education

Obama-McCain gap in support among non-Hispanic whites, in percentage points

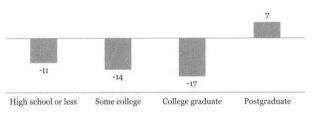

Weekly aggregate of registered voters, July 21-27, 2008

Preference for the General Election, by Education

Among non-Hispanic white registered voters

	% Barack Obama	% John McCain	% Other	% Neither/ Undecided
High school or less	36	47	1	16
Some college	37	51	1	11
College graduate	38	55	1	7
Postgraduate education	50	43	*	6

* Less than 0.5%

Gallup Poll Daily tracking, July 21-27, 2008

The accompanying chart displays the trend in the Obama-McCain gap over the summer months on a weekly basis.

There has been some weekly variation, as can be seen. In every week, however, Obama has had his greatest margin over McCain among those with postgraduate education.

McCain's margin over Obama among the college graduate group has been a little more consistent over the last three weeks. At several points in June, Obama beat McCain among this group.

Still, there does not appear to be a meaningful pattern in this trend so far this summer. The relative appeal of Obama and McCain, whose standing in the Gallup Poll Daily tracking has remained roughly the same all summer on an averaged basis, does not appear to have shifted much within specific educational categories.

Preference for the General Election, by Education

Obama-McCain gap, among registered voters

	% High school or less	% Some college	% College graduate	% Postgraduate
Jul 21-27, 2008	7	5	-2	15
Jul 14-20, 2008	0	0	-1	22
Jul 7-13, 2008	3	0	-1	18
Jun 30-Jul 6, 2008	1	6	0	13
Jun 23-29, 2008	0	4	1	7
Jun 16-22, 2008	-4	0	7	20
Jun 9-15, 2008	5	2	-5	16
Jun 2-8, 2008	1	1	3	11

Weekly aggregate of Gallup Poll Daily Tracking

Implications

The overall pattern of the vote by education this summer is roughly consistent with that of the last election in 2004, although the margins within each group vary across elections. In 2004, Gallup's final analysis of the vote showed John Kerry winning among voters with high school educations or less, and winning among those with post-graduate education—similar to Obama's edge in these groups today. Bush won among those with college degrees (but no postgraduate education) in 2004, as does McCain today (but by a slimmer margin). The biggest difference between the two years: Bush won strongly among those with some college in 2004, whereas Obama leads among that group at this point this year.

Survey Methods

Results for the week of July 21-27 are based on telephone interviews with 6,248 registered voters, aged 18 and older, conducted July 21-27, 2008. For results based on the total sample of registered voters, one can say with 95% confidence that the maximum margin of sampling error is ±2 percentage points.

Results for non-Hispanic whites for the week of July 21-27 are based on telephone interviews with 5,202 registered voters who are non-Hispanic whites, aged 18 and older, conducted July 21-27, 2008. For results based on the total sample of these registered voters, one can say with 95% confidence that the maximum margin of sampling error is ±2 percentage points.

Interviews are conducted with respondents on land-line telephones (for respondents with a land-line telephone) and cellular phones (for respondents who are cell-phone only).

In addition to sampling error, question wording and practical difficulties in conducting surveys can introduce error or bias into the findings of public opinion polls.

July 31, 2008

NEARLY HALF OF U.S. ADULTS NOW APPLAUD THE IRAQ SURGE

No change, however, in lack of support for the war

by Lydia Saad, Gallup Poll Senior Editor

A new *USA Today*/Gallup poll finds nearly half of Americans saying the U.S. troop surge in Iraq, now over, has made the situation there better, up from 40% in February and just 22% a year ago.

Accordingly, the percentage believing the surge "is not making much difference" has declined from 51% a year ago, and 38% in February, to just 32%.

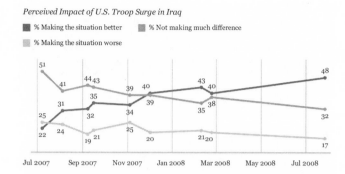

Perceived Impact of U.S. Troop Surge in Iraq

■ % Making the situation better   ■ % Not making much difference
▨ % Making the situation worse

The net result is that, for the first time, Americans are about evenly divided in their overall assessments of the surge: 48% say it is making the situation better while a combined 49% indicate it is not.

Although this balance of views is still not highly positive, it is more of an endorsement of the surge than what Gallup has previously found. The very first reading, from July 2007, was the most negative, when half of Americans (51%) believed the surge was having no impact and as many said it was making matters worse as said it was improving things.

Since then, the percentage crediting the surge with making things better has gradually come up and the percentage saying it is having no impact has gone down. There has been less change in the percentage blaming the surge for creating more problems, varying within an 8-point range from 25% to 17%.

Americans' views about the surge have been, and remain, highly politicized. However, all three partisan groups—Republicans, independents, and Democrats—have grown more likely since February to believe the surge is helping.

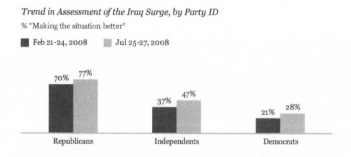

Trend in Assessment of the Iraq Surge, by Party ID

% "Making the situation better"

■ Feb 21-24, 2008   ▨ Jul 25-27, 2008

No Ripple Effect on War Views

Americans' growing confidence in the surge does not appear to be softening their broader criticism of the Iraq war. Although close to half of Americans now believe the surge is helping the situation in Iraq, the majority continue to say that sending troops to Iraq was a "mistake," and that things there are going "badly" for the United States.

Neither of these views has changed much in recent months.

The 56% saying the war is a mistake in the July 25-27 poll is similar to the 60% of last month and 59% in February. In fact, despite some fluctuation, views on this question have not changed substantively for the past 18 months.

In view of the developments since we first sent our troops to Iraq, do you think the United States made a mistake in sending troops to Iraq, or not?

Recent trend: January 2007–July 2008

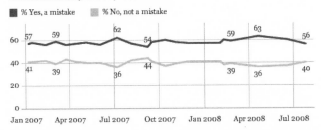

Gallup now finds 46% of Americans saying things are going very or moderately well for the United States in Iraq, while 51% say things are going moderately or very badly. Compared to the current poll, the last time this question was asked, in November/December 2007, a similar number (43%) said things were going well, while slightly more (56%) said they were going badly. However, today's results are not much different from those recorded in January 2006.

In general, how would you say things are going for the U.S. in Iraq --
[ROTATED: very well, moderately well, moderately badly, (or) very badly]?

Recent trend: January 2006–July 2008

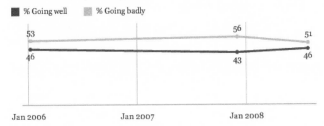

Bottom Line

In what could be Gallup's final assessment of the U.S. troop surge in Iraq that started in 2007 and ended earlier this month, Americans credit the surge with bringing about some progress in Iraq—but not enough to convince them that the war is going well for the United States, or that sending troops there initially was the right course of action.

Survey Methods

Results are based on telephone interviews with 1,007 national adults, aged 18 and older, conducted July 25-27, 2008. For results based on the total sample of national adults, one can say with 95% confidence that the maximum margin of sampling error is ±3 percentage points.

Interviews are conducted with respondents on land-line telephones (for respondents with a land-line telephone) and cellular phones (for respondents who are cell-phone only).

In addition to sampling error, question wording and practical difficulties in conducting surveys can introduce error or bias into the findings of public opinion polls.

Given the lack of positive momentum in perceptions that Obama can handle the military or key international issues, Republican presidential candidate John McCain still retains a wide advantage over Obama in terms of being commander in chief and dealing with terrorism. This is not unexpected, based on the extensive foreign policy and military experience McCain has accrued while serving in Congress for more than two decades and in the U.S. Navy for most of the rest of his adult life. Obama did not serve in the U.S. military and has been in the U.S. Senate for only four years, though he does hold a position on the prestigious Senate Foreign Relations Committee.

Comparison of Barack Obama and John McCain on Foreign Policy Matters

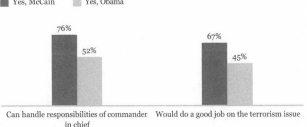

July 25-27, 2008, USA Today/Gallup poll

The two candidates are more evenly matched on the Iraq war issue, even as McCain continues to criticize Obama for not backing the surge of U.S. troops to Iraq, which by most accounts appears to have worked. At least on this issue, Obama is able to offset McCain's experience in foreign policy matters because of Obama's long-held opposition to the war, which appeals to the majority of Americans who consider the war "a mistake."

Comparison of Barack Obama and John McCain on Handling the Situation in Iraq

July 25-27, 2008, USA Today/Gallup poll

One area of international relations in which Obama appears to have an advantage over McCain is diplomacy. When asked to rate how each candidate would handle "relations with other countries," a total of 62% say Obama would do a good job while 55% say McCain would. But when respondents are asked to choose which of the two would do a better job in this area, Obama wins by a comfortable 52% to 37% margin. This particular item was not asked prior to the Obama trip, so it is unclear whether his standing is any better or worse than it was before his overseas tour. Many of the images of Obama's trip showed him meeting with foreign leaders, so it would not be surprising if the trip did help him somewhat in this regard.

In addition to assessing the candidates' perceived performance on foreign policy matters, the poll asked for Americans' judgments

---

August 01, 2008
VIEWS OF OBAMA ON INTERNATIONAL MATTERS LITTLE CHANGED
Public gives Obama the edge over McCain in handling relations with other countries

by Jeffrey M. Jones, Gallup Poll Managing Editor

A clear aim of Barack Obama's overseas trip was to demonstrate to Americans who questioned his foreign policy credentials that he is up to the job of commander in chief of the military and can handle key matters of foreign policy. However, at least in the short term, the trip does not appear to have accomplished that goal—just 52% say Obama can handle the job of commander in chief of the military, compared with a 55% reading before the trip.

Do you think Barack Obama can -- or cannot -- handle the responsibilities of commander in chief of the military?

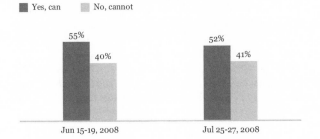

Additionally, Americans are no more likely now than before Obama visited Europe, Afghanistan, and Iraq and other Middle Eastern countries to believe he would do a good job of handling the terrorism and Iraq war issues as president.

Think Barack Obama Would Do a Good Job of Handling the Issue

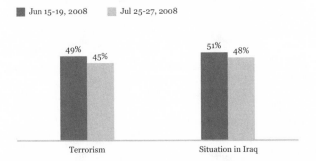

These findings are based on the July 25-27 *USA Today*/Gallup poll, conducted just as Obama was wrapping up his trip abroad.

about the candidates' ability to handle two major domestic issues—the economy and energy. On both of these domestic issues, more Americans say Obama would do a good job than say McCain would.

Comparison of Barack Obama and John McCain on Domestic Policy Matters

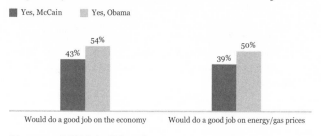

July 25-27, 2008, USA Today/Gallup poll

Implications

Clearly, Obama still has some work to do to convince Americans he can handle some of the international responsibilities of the presidency. While he already is viewed as being better than McCain at handling "relations with other countries," McCain has wide advantages over Obama in perceptions that he would be able to handle the job of commander in chief and to do a good job of handling the terrorism issue.

Even though fewer Americans say Obama is able to handle the role of commander in chief than say this about McCain, it is important to note that a majority of Americans think the Illinois senator is up to the task. In some ways, it may not be as important for Obama to close this perceptual gap with McCain as it is to keep his own percentage above the majority level. That may especially be true in an election year when Americans rate domestic issues like the economy and energy as the top issues that will affect their vote. Thus, Obama could in theory win the election on the basis of his perceived strengths on domestic issues, so long as Americans don't disqualify him for perceived weaknesses on military and defense issues.

Survey Methods

Results are based on telephone interviews with 1,007 national adults, aged 18 and older, conducted July 25-27, 2008. For results based on the total sample of national adults, one can say with 95% confidence that the maximum margin of sampling error is ±3 percentage points.

Interviews are conducted with respondents on land-line telephones (for respondents with a land-line telephone) and cellular phones (for respondents who are cell-phone only).

In addition to sampling error, question wording and practical difficulties in conducting surveys can introduce error or bias into the findings of public opinion polls.

August 04, 2008
MAJORITY OF AMERICANS SAY RACISM AGAINST BLACKS WIDESPREAD
More than three-quarters of blacks say racism against blacks is widespread

by Jeffrey M. Jones, Gallup Poll Managing Editor

A recent *USA Today*/Gallup poll finds most Americans saying racism is widespread against blacks in the United States. This includes a slim majority of whites (51%), a slightly higher 59% of Hispanics, and the vast majority of blacks (78%).

Do you think racism against blacks is or is not widespread in the U.S.?

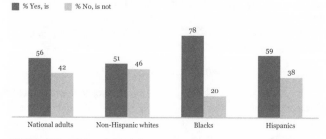

USA Today/Gallup poll, June 5-July 6, 2008

These results are based on a national sample of 1,935 U.S. adults, including large samples of more than 600 blacks and 500 Hispanics, weighted to represent their correct proportions in the U.S. population.

Americans also see racial discrimination as a major or minor factor in four specific problems facing the black community—lower average education levels for U.S. blacks, lower average income levels for U.S. blacks, lower average life expectancies for blacks, and a higher percentage of blacks serving time in U.S. prisons.

Racism is most widely believed to be a major reason for the higher percentage of blacks in U.S. prisons, and least likely to be seen as a primary factor in blacks' lower average life expectancies.

Do you think racial discrimination against blacks is a major factor, a minor factor, or not a factor in [RANDOM ORDER] ... ?
Based on national adults

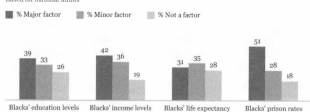

USA Today/Gallup poll, June 5-July 6, 2008

On all four issues, blacks are more likely than whites and Hispanics to see racial discrimination as a major factor. In fact, a majority of blacks say racial discrimination is a major reason each problem is occurring.

Whites are more inclined to view racial discrimination as a minor reason in three of the four areas, but a plurality of 44% of whites believe it is a major factor in higher prison rates for blacks.

Hispanics are more likely to see racism as a major rather than a minor reason why blacks have had worse experiences in these four areas. This includes a majority of Hispanics who view anti-black

Do you think racial discrimination against blacks is a major factor, a minor factor, or not a factor in [RANDOM ORDER] ... ?

Based on blacks

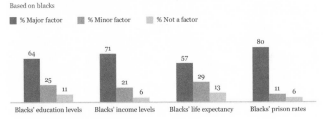

USA Today/Gallup poll, June 5-July 6, 2008

Do you think racial discrimination against blacks is a major factor, a minor factor, or not a factor in [RANDOM ORDER] ... ?

Based on non-Hispanic whites

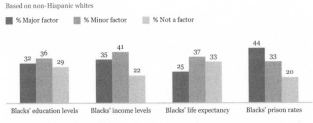

USA Today/Gallup poll, June 5-July 6, 2008

discrimination as a major factor in the higher prison rates among blacks.

Do you think racial discrimination against blacks is a major factor, a minor factor, or not a factor in [RANDOM ORDER] ... ?

Based on Hispanics

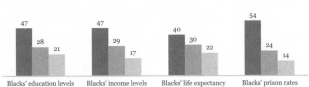

USA Today/Gallup poll, June 5-July 6, 2008

Racism Against Whites?

Generally speaking, racism in the United States is thought of as a problem that victimizes blacks and members of other racial or ethnic minority groups. But that does not preclude the possibility that members of minority groups could themselves harbor ill will against members of the majority racial group. Some could also label the result of affirmative-action policies as racism against whites if in fact minorities are given preferential treatment for jobs or other valued positions. The poll sought to find out whether Americans believe there is racism against whites. In general, Americans reject the notion of anti-white racism, but not overwhelmingly. While a majority of adults think such racism is not widespread, 41% think it is. This includes roughly 4 in 10 whites, blacks, and Hispanics.

Implications

The majority of Americans believe racism against blacks is common in the United States, particularly with respect to the fact that blacks are more likely to occupy U.S. prisons on a proportional basis. Although less than half of Americans see racism against whites as very common, roughly 4 in 10 believe it is.

Do you think racism against whites is or is not widespread in the U.S.?

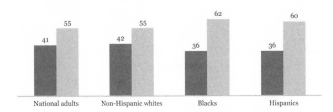

USA Today/Gallup poll, June 5-July 6, 2008

As on most issues involving race in the United States, blacks are much more likely to see racism as a problem than are whites. However, other questions in the poll showed that Americans remain optimistic that race relations could improve, if Americans could hold an open national dialogue on race and if Barack Obama were elected as the first black president.

Survey Methods

Results are based on telephone interviews with 1,935 national adults, aged 18 and older, conducted June 5-July 6, 2008. For results based on the total sample of national adults, one can say with 95% confidence that the maximum margin of sampling error is ±4 percentage points. For results based on the sample of 702 non-Hispanic whites, the maximum margin of sampling error is ±5 percentage points.

For results based on the sample of 608 non-Hispanic blacks, the maximum margin of sampling error is ±5 percentage points.

For results based on the sample of 502 Hispanics, the maximum margin of sampling error is ±6 percentage points (120 of the 502 interviews with Hispanics were conducted in Spanish).

August 05, 2008
EXPLORING THE IRAQ TIMETABLE ISSUE
Public split if assured that withdrawal is a given

by Frank Newport, Gallup Poll Editor in Chief

The results of a July 25-27 *USA Today*/Gallup poll suggest that Americans split down the middle on the complex issue of whether the United States should set an explicit timetable or target date for the removal of U.S. troops from Iraq—when it is made clear that withdrawal is a given in either circumstance.

The question wording from this poll was developed to reflect as well as possible the positions of the two major-party presidential candidates on Iraq.

Both candidates have indicated in their policy positions that they favor the ultimate withdrawal of troops from Iraq, but they differ in terms of specifying a timetable for that withdrawal.

- Barack Obama's official Web site says: "Obama will give his Secretary of Defense and military commanders a new mission in Iraq: ending the war. The removal of our troops will be responsible and phased, directed by military commanders on the ground and done in consultation with the Iraqi government. Military experts believe we can safely redeploy combat brigades

If you had to choose, which do you think is better for the U.S.: to plan for the withdrawal of U.S. troops from Iraq but NOT set a timetable or target date when most U.S. troops would be out or to plan for the withdrawal of U.S. troops with a projected timetable or target date when most U.S. troops would be out?

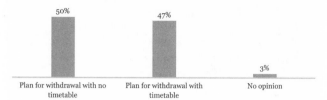

USA Today/Gallup poll, July 25-27, 2008

from Iraq at a pace of one to two brigades a month that would remove them in 16 months."

- John McCain's Web site says: "I do not want to keep our troops in Iraq a minute longer than necessary to secure our interests there. Our goal is an Iraq that can stand on its own as a democratic ally and a responsible force for peace in its neighborhood. Our goal is an Iraq that no longer needs American troops. And I believe we can achieve that goal, perhaps sooner than many imagine. But I do not believe that anyone should make promises as a candidate for president that they cannot keep if elected. To promise a withdrawal of our forces from Iraq, regardless of the calamitous consequences to the Iraqi people, our most vital interests, and the future of the Middle East, is the height of irresponsibility. It is a failure of leadership."

The differences in the two candidates' positions focus on the explicitness with which a timetable for withdrawal should be announced and planned for ahead of time. Obama's statement specifies a timetable and target date, while McCain's specifically cautions against setting a date or timetable.

Thus, the question wording used in the *USA Today*/Gallup poll outlined two positions on the issue (without any reference to specific candidates or others who might support that position) and explicitly told respondents that *both* positions were based on an assumption of a withdrawal of troops. The difference in the two positions as read to respondents was the issue of whether there was a "timetable or target date when most U.S. troops would be out."

The results, as noted, show an almost even split, with 50% choosing the "no timetable" alternative and 47% choosing the "timetable" alternative.

Even though no candidate names are mentioned in the question wording, there are predictable and very large differences in response by partisanship.

If you had to choose, which do you think is better for the U.S.: to plan for the withdrawal of U.S. troops from Iraq but NOT set a timetable or target date when most U.S. troops would be out or to plan for the withdrawal of U.S. troops with a projected timetable or target date when most U.S. troops would be out?

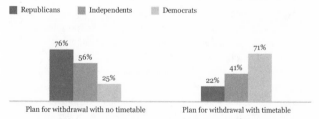

USA Today/Gallup poll, July 25-27, 2008

The slight overall 3-point edge in support for withdrawal without a timetable is a result of the slightly stronger Republican feelings on this question (compared to those of Democrats), and the tendency of independents to tilt in the "no timetable" direction—despite the fact that at this point, self-identified Democrats outnumber Republicans in the American populace.

Implications

The review of these questions concerning a timetable for Iraq suggests that American attitudes on the topic depend to a degree on the way in which the alternatives are presented to them. As has been witnessed in the arguments on a timetable going back and forth between the Obama and McCain campaigns, it is not a simple issue. While all concerned may assume that most American troops will eventually leave Iraq, just when and under what circumstances that will occur is a murky issue.

The public opinion data show that:

1. Given a basic choice between a timetable and no timetable, the majority of Americans favor the timetable. This may reflect the concern or assumption that the "no timetable" option implies that troops will remain indefinitely.
2. Citing the fact that the Iraqi president wants U.S. troops to withdraw, with a timetable, results in majority support for the idea.
3. Reminding respondents that Obama has taken a "timetable" position and McCain has taken a "no timetable" position yields a split in results similar to the split in candidate support.
4. Stipulating withdrawal as a given, with the only difference being a timetable versus no timetable for that withdrawal—a phrasing that mirrors the presidential candidates' positions—shows a split right down the middle in attitudes.

Survey Methods

Results are based on telephone interviews with 1,007 national adults, aged 18 and older, conducted July 25-27, 2008. For results based on the total sample of national adults, one can say with 95% confidence that the maximum margin of sampling error is ±3 percentage points.

Interviews are conducted with respondents on land-line telephones (for respondents with a land-line telephone) and cellular phones (for respondents who are cell-phone only).

In addition to sampling error, question wording and practical difficulties in conducting surveys can introduce error or bias into the findings of public opinion polls.

August 05, 2008
VOTERS NOT STRONGLY BACKING INCUMBENTS FOR CONGRESS
Percentage backing re-election for their member and most members near all-time lows

by Jeffrey M. Jones, Gallup Poll Managing Editor

In a year when approval of Congress has reached a new low, just 36% of U.S. registered voters say most members of Congress deserve re-election. This is among the lowest ratings Gallup has measured in a recent presidential or congressional election year.

Please tell me whether you think each of the following political officeholders deserves to be re-elected, or not. How about -- [most members of Congress]?

Based on registered voters

■ % Yes, deserves

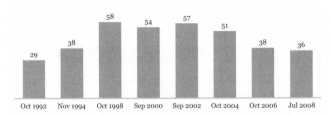

These results are based on a July 25-27 *USA Today*/Gallup poll of 900 registered voters nationwide. The poll was conducted before Congress began a month-long recess late last week. Gallup has found ratings in the neighborhood of the current 36% in three other election years—1992, 1994, and 2006. All of these years brought about significant change in the membership of Congress.

In the 1994 and 2006 midterm election years, when 38% of registered voters said most members of Congress were deserving of another term, enough seats switched party hands that control of Congress switched from one party to the other—from the Democrats to the Republicans in 1994 and from the Republicans to the Democrats in 2006.

In 1992, as few as 29% of registered voters said most members deserved re-election. Congress did experience a great deal of turnover that year, though Democrats retained party control and the actual change in the party composition of Congress was much less than in 1994 or 2006. That could be because a large number of incumbent members retired rather than run for re-election in 1992. But it also could be the fact that the congressional elections were overshadowed by the presidential election that year.

Does Your Member Deserve to Be Re-Elected?

Voters are usually much more charitable when asked whether their own member of Congress deserves to be re-elected (as opposed to most members), and that is also the case in the latest poll. Fifty-seven percent of registered voters say the U.S. representative from their own congressional district deserves to be re-elected. That, too, is on the low end of what Gallup has measured historically for one's own member, slightly higher than the 1994 (54%) and 2006 (54%) readings, and somewhat better still than the all-time low of 48% in 1992.

Please tell me whether you think each of the following political officeholders deserves to be re-elected, or not. How about -- [the U.S. representative in your congressional district]?

Based on registered voters

■ % Yes, deserves

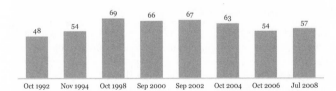

Both items (most members and your member) seem to show similar changes from one poll to another, and low ratings tend to presage significant turnover in Congress. Thus, congressional incumbents may be in for a bumpy ride during this fall's campaign, as many try to hold on to their seats in a year when voters are looking to change the government.

On a variety of measures, 2008 looks like a better year for Democrats than for Republicans. But at the same time, Democrats hold party control of the House (as well as the Senate). So it is not immediately clear which party's incumbents might be more vulnerable if voters want to change Congress. The poll sought to get some traction on the issue by asking voters to report whether their member of Congress is a Republican or a Democrat. That gives a sense of whom voters have in mind when they say their member of Congress does or does not deserve re-election.

A fairly large proportion of voters (35%) are unsure whether their member of Congress is a Democrat or a Republican. But among those who are aware, the data suggest that Democratic members might be a little safer this year than Republicans.

Among voters who report that their member of Congress is a Democrat, 64% say he or she deserves re-election. That compares to the 57% who say their (Republican) representative deserves another term. Among the roughly one in three voters who are unsure whether a Republican or a Democrat represents their district, barely half (51%) say their member deserves to be re-elected.

Representative Deserves Re-Election, Based on Party of Member of Congress

Based on registered voters

■ % Yes, deserves re-election   ■ % No, does not

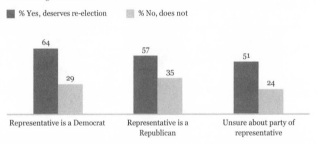

USA Today/Gallup poll, July 25-27, 2008

Implications

One major theme of the 2008 election thus far has been "change." Most of the presidential candidates sounded that theme during their campaigns, but voters apparently are in the mood to change Congress as well. Typically, when lower percentages of voters say their member of Congress and most members of Congress deserve re-election, the membership of Congress is shaken up on Election Day.

There are, however, countervailing forces that make the direction of the change somewhat unpredictable this year—the Democrats hold the majority of seats in Congress in a year when Congress is historically unpopular, but the political environment in 2008 seems to favor the Democrats. These data suggest the favorable political environment may be the stronger force at work, given that voters with a Democrat representing them are more likely to say that representative deserves another term than are voters with a Republican representing them.

Survey Methods

Results are based on telephone interviews with 900 registered voters, aged 18 and older, conducted July 25-27, 2008. For results based on the total sample of registered voters, one can say with 95% confidence that the maximum margin of sampling error is ±4 percentage points.

Interviews are conducted with respondents on land-line telephones (for respondents with a land-line telephone) and cellular phones (for respondents who are cell-phone only).

In addition to sampling error, question wording and practical difficulties in conducting surveys can introduce error or bias into the findings of public opinion polls.

August 06, 2008

U.S. CONGRESS, GOUGING BLAMED EQUALLY FOR GAS PRICES

The recent plunge in oil prices might simply reinforce these negative consumer perceptions

by Dennis Jacobe, Gallup Poll Chief Economist

Americans rate price gouging by the oil companies, price gouging by foreign oil producers, and a lack of effective action by Congress as the most important reasons why the price of gasoline is so high—essentially equating congressional inaction with price gouging.

Top Reasons Why the Price of Gasoline Is So High

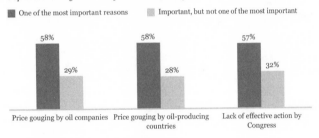

USA Today/Gallup poll, July 25-27, 2008

Lots of Blame to Go Around

Last week as Congress adjourned for its August recess, House Republicans began a mini-demonstration on the House floor, protesting the unwillingness of the congressional leadership to vote on various proposed energy issues—including offshore oil drilling. Recent Gallup polling, conducted before Congress recessed, suggests the Republicans may be on to something politically, with Americans rating a lack of congressional action as one of the most important reasons for today's high gas prices.

However, people obviously feel there is a lot of blame to go around, with 52% pointing to speculation by oil/commodity investors and 51% to a lack of effective action by the Bush administration. Nearly as many—48%—blame American consumers in general for a lack of energy conservation while 46% say increased demand from China, India, and other developing countries deserves a significant part of the blame.

Survey Methods

Results are based on telephone interviews with 1,007 national adults, aged 18 and older, conducted July 25-27, 2008. For results based on the total sample of national adults, one can say with 95% confidence that the maximum margin of sampling error is ±3 percentage points.

Do you think each of the following is one of the most important reasons why the price of gasoline is so high, an important reason, but not one of the most important reasons, or not an important reason?

% One of most important reasons

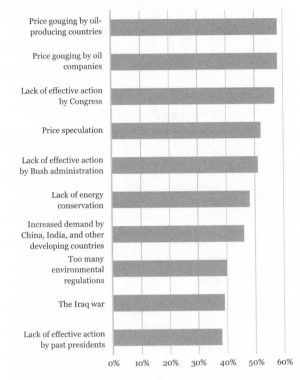

USA Today/Gallup poll, July 25-27, 2008

Interviews are conducted with respondents on land-line telephones (for respondents with a land-line telephone) and cellular phones (for respondents who are cell-phone only).

In addition to sampling error, question wording and practical difficulties in conducting surveys can introduce error or bias into the findings of public opinion polls.

August 07, 2008

NUCLEAR POWER LESS POPULAR THAN OTHER ENERGY STRATEGIES

Conservation-oriented proposals draw widest support

by Lydia Saad, Gallup Poll Senior Editor

John McCain has ramped up his longstanding call for building more nuclear power plants—45 new ones by 2030—drawing the sharpest distinction between himself and Barack Obama on energy policy, but also, to some degree, throwing the political dice.

According to a July *USA Today*/Gallup poll, the impact of a candidate's favoring greater use of nuclear power is mixed. Forty-seven percent of Americans say they are more likely to back a candidate who favors expanding nuclear power, while 41% say they are less likely to back such a candidate. But on a relative basis, the nuclear option is near the bottom of a list of possible solutions to the energy situation.

Would you be more likely or less likely to vote for a candidate who supported building more nuclear power plants?

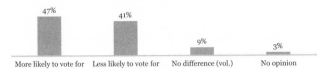

47% More likely to vote for
41% Less likely to vote for
9%   No difference (vol.)
3%   No opinion

USA Today/Gallup poll, July 25-27, 2008
(vol.) = Volunteered response

Despite the fact that a plurality of Americans favor a pro-nuclear-energy candidate, more say they would shun a candidate who wants to build nuclear power plants than say this about any of nine other energy reform positions.

Americans seem more prepared to reward candidates who focus on encouraging energy conservation by consumers, raising fuel efficiency standards for vehicles, raising government spending on alternative fuels, establishing price controls on gasoline, imposing a windfall profits tax on oil companies, and easing restrictions on off-shore drilling. At least 57% of Americans say they would be more likely to vote for candidates taking each of these positions.

Thinking now about some of the solutions offered to address the energy situation in the United States, please say whether you would be more likely or less likely to vote for a candidate who supported -- [RANDOM ORDER]?

	More likely to vote for	Less likely to vote for
	%	%
Establishing tax incentives to encourage energy conservation	69	20
Raising fuel mileage standards on vehicles	68	20
Authorizing a $150 billion investment by the federal government in research on bio-fuels and clean energy source	64	25
Establishing price controls on gasoline	62	28
Imposing a windfall profits tax on oil companies	58	31
Easing restrictions on offshore domestic drilling	57	31
Releasing up to 10% of the U.S. strategic petroleum reserve	53	33
Offering a $300 million government prize for the development of an electric car with a long-lasting battery	50	34
Building more nuclear power plants	47	41
Suspending the federal gasoline tax for several months	46	39

USA Today/Gallup poll, July 25-27, 2008

Two positions that generate a positive reaction from about half of Americans, but that could turn off as much as a third, are:

- releasing 10% of the nation's U.S. Strategic Petroleum Reserve (something Obama has called for)
- McCain's proposal for establishing a $300 million government reward for inventing a fully electric car with a long-lasting battery

The only issue besides nuclear power to draw opposition from about 4 in 10 Americans is suspending the federal gasoline tax for several months—the so-called gas-tax holiday that McCain has proposed and Obama has opposed. Thirty-nine percent of Americans say they would be less likely to support a candidate who wants to suspend the gas tax—perhaps because it isn't a long-term solution.

Bottom Line

Four-dollar-a-gallon gas prices have put the nation's energy woes at the center of the 2008 presidential campaign, renewing discussion of options like oil drilling and nuclear power production that have long been pushed aside in Washington.

Whichever candidate is seen as the more serious in addressing the problem could ultimately benefit. That may be just what McCain is banking on. However, when it comes to specifics, Obama's approach of focusing on energy conservation and the development of fossil-fuel alternatives seems highly safe. Large majorities of Americans have a positive reaction to the various proposals that fall within this realm.

Oil drilling is also a winning issue, and one that could work in McCain's favor. However, his close association with a bold proposal to expand nuclear power usage could be somewhat more risky. While close to half of Americans say they would be more likely to support a candidate who proposes this, 4 in 10 political independents—a group McCain can't afford to scare off—downgrade their chances of voting for such a candidate.

Survey Methods

Results are based on telephone interviews with 1,007 national adults, aged 18 and older, conducted July 25-27, 2008. For results based on the total sample of national adults, one can say with 95% confidence that the maximum margin of sampling error is ±3 percentage points.

Interviews are conducted with respondents on land-line telephones (for respondents with a land-line telephone) and cellular phones (for respondents who are cell-phone only).

In addition to sampling error, question wording and practical difficulties in conducting surveys can introduce error or bias into the findings of public opinion polls.

August 07, 2008
SWIMMING TOPS TRACK AS PUBLIC'S FAVORITE OLYMPIC EVENT
Fifty-six percent of Americans plan to watch a great deal or fair amount of Olympics

by Jeffrey M. Jones, Gallup Poll Managing Editor

A recent *USA Today*/Gallup poll finds 27% of Americans naming swimming as their favorite summer Olympic event, making it the clear leader after vying with track and field for the top spot in 2000 and 2004.

The percentage of Americans naming gymnastics as their favorite sport tumbled from 17% in the last two Summer Olympic years to 12% today. Basketball (5%) and diving (4%) round out the top five.

Women have propelled swimming to its status as the favored Olympic event in 2008. Thirty-five percent of women name swimming as their favorite sport, well ahead of gymnastics (19%) and track and field (8%). When Gallup asked the same question in 2004, women were equally likely to mention swimming (25%) and gymnastics (25%) as their favorite event. It is unclear why the shift has occurred—one explanation could be that swimming has received more media attention leading up to the games, most

What is your favorite Summer Olympic event? [open-ended]

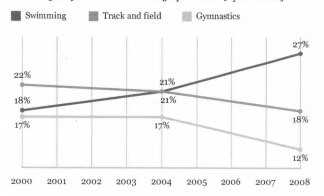

Favorite Summer Olympic Event, Among Women

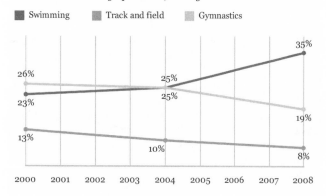

Men slightly prefer track and field (24%) to swimming (18%), with basketball third (9%). Their preferences are similar to what they were in 2004, though men have become more likely to mention swimming than they were eight years ago.

Favorite Summer Olympic Event, Among Men

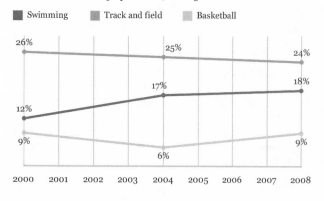

Interest in the Games

Americans' interest in this year's games is similar to interest levels measured at similar points prior to the beginning of previous Olympics. Fifty-six percent say they plan to watch a "great deal" or "fair amount" of the Olympics, compared with 59% readings in both 2000 and 2004.

notably 41-year-old swimmer Dara Torres' improbable victory at the U.S. Olympic Trials.

How much of the Olympics do you intend to watch?

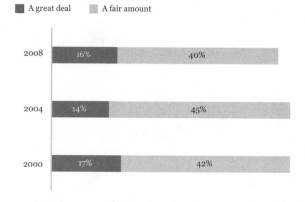

Plans for watching the Olympics do not vary much among different subgroups of Americans. For example, men (56%) and women (56%) are equally likely to say they plan to watch a great deal or fair amount of the Olympics. There are modest differences by age, with younger adults between the ages of 18 and 29 (49%) somewhat less likely to say they will watch at least a fair amount of the Olympics than are those aged 30 and older (57%).

For the first time, fans of the Olympics can watch almost any event they choose live via streaming video over the Internet. Given the time difference between the United States and China, this might seem an attractive option for the most fervent Olympics fans who prefer to see the events unfold live. According to the poll, about half of Americans who plan to watch the Olympics will watch some of the coverage on the Internet—just 48% say they will watch only the TV coverage. However, in addition to the 48% who will watch the games only on television, another 41% say they will watch the Olympics mostly on television, so clearly, television will be the dominant medium by which Americans view the Olympics. Just 9% say they will watch both TV and Internet about equally, and only 2% will do all or most of their viewing online.

While Americans' interest in this year's games is no higher than in the past, Americans' knowledge of where the Olympics are taking place compares favorably to past Summer Olympics games. In the summer of five past Olympic years, Gallup has asked Americans if they knew where that year's summer games were being held. This year, 79% of Americans correctly identify Beijing or China as the 2008 location, the highest Gallup has measured for an Olympiad thus far (notably, this excludes any Olympics held on U.S. soil).

The greater awareness of Beijing and China as the host city and nation may result from the media spotlight focused on China leading up to the games, first by the worldwide protests against China during the Olympic torch relay earlier this year, by controversy over world leaders' decisions to attend the games, and by some of the problems China has had in its preparation for the games, especially in trying to deal with air pollution in Beijing.

Clearly, Americans are much more aware of where Olympics are being held than they were in the 1940s and 1950s. This could reflect the fact that the Olympics were not televised until 1960, and thus Americans may not have had the immediate connection to the games that they have had in recent years.

Survey Methods

Results are based on telephone interviews with 1,007 national adults, aged 18 and older, conducted July 25-27, 2008. For results based on

Do you by chance know where the Summer Olympics are being held?

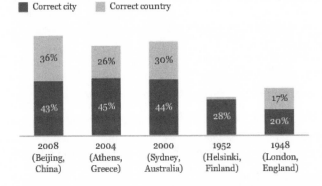

■ Correct city ▨ Correct country

36%	26%	30%		17%
43%	45%	44%	28%	20%
2008 (Beijing, China)	2004 (Athens, Greece)	2000 (Sydney, Australia)	1952 (Helsinki, Finland)	1948 (London, England)

the total sample of national adults, one can say with 95% confidence that the maximum margin of sampling error is ±3 percentage points.

Interviews are conducted with respondents on land-line telephones (for respondents with a land-line telephone) and cellular phones (for respondents who are cell-phone only).

In addition to sampling error, question wording and practical difficulties in conducting surveys can introduce error or bias into the findings of public opinion polls.

August 08, 2008
CAN FALLING GAS PRICES SAVE BACK-TO-SCHOOL?
Over the past few weeks, consumers have become less gloomy as pump prices have declined

by Dennis Jacobe, Gallup Poll Chief Economist

As gas prices have tumbled during the past few weeks, the percentage of Americans saying economic conditions are "getting worse" has also declined, although the overall level of pessimism—like pump prices—remains high.

Change in Energy Measures

■ % Change in gas prices

▨ Change in % saying economic conditions are "getting worse" (in pct. pts.)

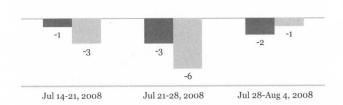

Jul 14-21, 2008	Jul 21-28, 2008	Jul 28-Aug 4, 2008

Consumers Getting a Little Less Gloomy

Plunging oil prices globally have been reflected in U.S. gas prices at the pump over the past several weeks, with the average retail price for a gallon of regular gasoline now at $3.88 nationwide—down 7.5 cents over the past week and 23.4 cents since prices peaked on July 7 but still $1.04 above prices of a year ago. The week gas prices

peaked (July 7-13) and the week that followed, 87% of Americans said current economic conditions were getting worse, not better. During the most recent two weeks, the percentage of Americans expressing this sentiment has declined to 84% and then to 81%.

Consumer expectations for the future course of the economy have improved across income levels during the past two weeks. And the impact has been fairly uniform, with those in the lowest income grouping showing an improvement of 8 percentage points and those in the highest income group an improvement of 6 points.

Percentage Saying Economy Is Getting Worse, by Annual Income

	Feb '08	Mar '08	Apr '08	May '08	Jun '08	Jun 30-Jul 6, '08	Jul 7-13, '08	Jul 14-20, '08	Jul 21-27, '08	Jul 28-Aug 3, '08
	%	%	%	%	%	%	%	%	%	%
National adults	79	84	85	86	87	87	87	87	84	81
Less than $24,000	79	85	85	88	88	89	86	90	87	82
$24,000 to $59,999	81	87	87	89	90	89	86	89	84	82
$60,000 to $89,999	81	84	88	88	88	86	88	86	87	80
$90,000 or more	79	84	84	83	85	86	87	86	79	80

Commentary

Gallup Poll Daily tracking suggests that consumers are reacting positively to the decline in gas prices—something that may not be fully apparent in the monthly consumer confidence and consumer sentiment numbers for July. Of course, this small improvement continues to leave consumer confidence at extremely weak levels, particularly since consumers continue to rate current economic conditions no better than they did in June. Still, any improvement in consumer attitudes is welcome as retailers enter the important back-to-school season.

In this regard, it is doubtful that recent gas price declines have been steep enough or long-lasting enough to save the current sales season for most retailers. And at this point, it doesn't appear as though there will be a delayed spending of the tax rebates. As the nation's biggest retailers asserted Thursday, prospects for the back-to-school season are not good and a need for added promotions will not help margins or earnings.

Still, if gas prices show some more declines, consumers will have a little more money to spend on things other than gas at the pump. In addition, there could be further improvements in consumer attitudes reflected in Gallup's daily monitoring of consumer perceptions in the days and weeks ahead. More money in consumers' pockets and a little less gloom may not be enough to save the back-to-school sales season, but they might provide retailers with at least some hope that things could get better in time for Christmas.

Survey Methods

Gallup is interviewing no fewer than 1,000 U.S. adults nationwide each day during 2008. The economic questions analyzed in this report are asked of a random half-sample of respondents each day. The results reported here are based on combined data of more than 8,000 interviews in January, February, March, April, May, and June. For results based on this sample, the maximum margin of sampling error is ±1 percentage point.

The questions for July are based on combined data of more than 3,000 interviews conducted each week: June 30-July 6, July 7-13,

Perceptions of U.S. Economic Conditions
Weekly averages from June 2, 2008, through Aug. 3, 2008

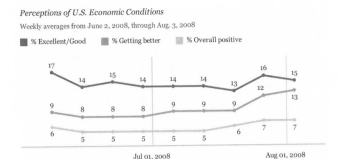

■ % Excellent/Good   ■ % Getting better   ■ % Overall positive

July 14-20, July 21-27, and July 28-Aug. 3, 2008. For results based on these samples, the maximum margin of sampling error is ±2 percentage points.

Interviews are conducted with respondents on land-line telephones (for respondents with a land-line telephone) and cellular phones (for respondents who are cell-phone only).

In addition to sampling error, question wording and practical difficulties in conducting surveys can introduce error or bias into the findings of public opinion polls.

August 11, 2008
BY AGE 24, MARRIAGE WINS OUT
At age 24, 30% are married while 20% are living together with someone

by Lydia Saad, Gallup Poll Senior Editor

Cohabitation is more prevalent than marriage among very young couples in the United States—those in which at least one partner is 18 to 20 years of age. However, by age 21, marriage is just as common, and by age 24, young adults are more likely to be married than "living together."

Marital Status, by Age (From 18 to 29)

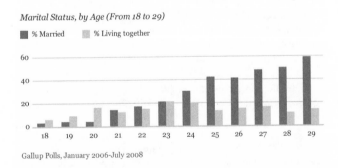

■ % Married   ■ % Living together

Gallup Polls, January 2006-July 2008

These findings are based on combined data from 59 separate Gallup Poll surveys conducted since January 2006, including nearly 60,000 U.S. adults. This affords an ample number of cases to review the marital status of adults of every age from 18 through 90.

According to this immense dataset, the practice of living together rises sharply between the ages of 18 and 20, while the rate of marriage is fairly minimal, in the 3% to 4% range. The pattern changes at age 21, when the percentage who are married jumps to 14%, roughly equaling the percentage living together with a partner.

The percentages married and cohabiting are about the same through age 23. But at age 24, the percentage married takes another

big jump to 30%, overtaking cohabitation, which is at 20%. The rate of marriage continues to escalate through age 29, when it reaches 59%, while cohabitation gradually falls back to 14%. (The proportion who are married is at its peak among Americans aged 30 to 49: an average of 64% of U.S. adults in this age range are married.)

Rate of Living Together Adds Up Over Time

Although the overall percentage of American adults living together outside of marriage is fairly small—averaging just 6% to 7% each year since 1999—Gallup polling has found that a large segment of currently married couples have lived together before marriage. According to a 2002 Gallup survey, this included more than half of married adults under age 50.

Lived Together With Spouse Before Marriage
Based on married U.S. adults

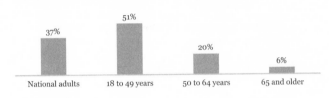

July 22-24, 2002

A Trial Period (but No Money-Back Guarantee)

The bigger picture, then, is that most couples use cohabiting not so much as an alternative to marriage, but as a trial period. And if that trial succeeds, they generally marry.

What is society's reaction to this practice? Do Americans believe that couples who live together before they walk down the aisle have better marriages? In a recent *USA Today*/Gallup poll, about half (49%) of U.S. adults say partners who live together first are less likely to get divorced after they marry. However, nearly as many either believe such couples are more likely to get divorced (31%) or say it makes no difference whether a couple has lived together (13%). Thus, overall public opinion is mixed, though more positive than negative.

Do you think couples that live together before marriage are more likely or less likely to get divorced than couples that do not live together before marriage?

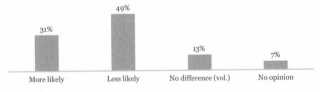

USA Today/Gallup poll, July 25-27, 2008
(vol.)=volunteered response

Societal perceptions about how living together affects children are also mixed, but more negative than positive. About half of Americans believe that having a household led by an unmarried couple has no effect on the children. The other half are much more likely to believe it has a negative than a positive effect: 38% vs. 12%.

Suppose an unmarried couple lives together with children in the household. Do you think that has a -- [ROTATED: positive effect on the children, does it not make a difference, (or does it have a) negative effect on the children]?

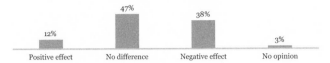

Positive effect 12% · No difference 47% · Negative effect 38% · No opinion 3%

USA Today/Gallup poll, July 25-27, 2008

A Serious Relationship?

More generally, 57% of Americans believe that two people who have lived together for five years are just as committed in their relationship as a couple that has been married for five years.

In general, do you think that an unmarried couple that has lived together for five years is just as committed in their relationship as a couple that has been married for five years, or not?

Yes, just as committed 57% · No, not as committed 40% · No opinion 3%

USA Today/Gallup poll, July 25-27, 2008
Based on Form B half sample

By contrast, only 42% of Americans believe that unmarried couples who have lived together for just one year are just as committed as those who have been married for one year; the slim majority are skeptical.

In general, do you think that an unmarried couple that has lived together for one year is just as committed in their relationship as a couple that has been married for one year, or not?

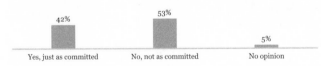

Yes, just as committed 42% · No, not as committed 53% · No opinion 5%

USA Today/Gallup poll, July 25-27, 2008
Based on Form A half sample

Generation Gaps

Not only is there a big gap between younger adults and seniors in terms of their lifestyle histories, but the two groups have very different views about the impact that living together has on couples and children.

When it comes to successful marriages, most adults aged 18 to 29 and 30 to 49 believe that living together before marriage reduces the chance of divorce. They see it as a positive. Older adults (those 50 to 64) are more likely to see cohabiting as a positive than a negative, while seniors are about equally divided.

In terms of children living in unmarried households, the majority of 18- to 29-year-olds say the arrangement has no impact on the children, as do about half of those 30 to 49 and 50 to 64. Relatively few in any of these age categories see it as a positive, while somewhat more see it as a negative. However, the majority of those 65 and older believe living together has a negative effect on the children involved.

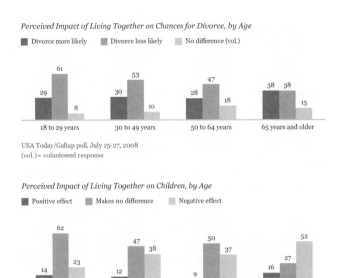

Perceived Impact of Living Together on Chances for Divorce, by Age

■ Divorce more likely   ■ Divorce less likely   ▨ No difference (vol.)

18 to 29 years: 29, 61, 8
30 to 49 years: 30, 53, 10
50 to 64 years: 28, 47, 18
65 years and older: 38, 38, 15

USA Today/Gallup poll, July 25-27, 2008
(vol.)= volunteered response

Perceived Impact of Living Together on Children, by Age

■ Positive effect   ■ Makes no difference   ▨ Negative effect

18 to 29 years: 14, 62, 23
30 to 49 years: 12, 47, 38
50 to 64 years: 9, 50, 37
65+ years: 16, 27, 52

USA Today/Gallup poll, July 25-27, 2008

Bottom Line

With at least half of U.S. adults under 50 having spent some time living together with their spouse before marriage, cohabitation holds possibly important implications for the future of marriage and child rearing.

However, unlike certain parts of Europe where marriage may be going out of style, in the United States, marriage still seems to be the favored long-term living arrangement for couples, even very young couples.

Survey Methods

The marital status results are based on 59 Gallup Poll surveys conducted by telephone between January 2006 and July 2008. The aggregated dataset includes interviews with 59,512 national adults, aged 18 and older. For results based on the total sample, one can say with 95% confidence that the maximum margin of sampling error is ±1/2 of 1 percentage point.

The results for attitudinal questions about living together before marriage are based on a *USA Today*/Gallup poll conducted by telephone July 25-27, 2008. For results based on the total sample of 1,007 national adults, one can say with 95% confidence that the maximum margin of sampling error is ±3 percentage points.

Interviews were conducted with respondents on land-line telephones (for respondents with a land-line telephone) and cellular phones (for respondents who are cell-phone only).

In addition to sampling error, question wording and practical difficulties in conducting surveys can introduce error or bias into the findings of public opinion polls.

August 12, 2008

AMERICANS BECOME MORE OPTIMISTIC ABOUT GAS PRICES

More positive attitudes could affect consumer spending

by Frank Newport, Gallup Poll Editor in Chief

There's been a wholesale turnaround in Americans' expectations about the direction of gas prices between now and the end of the year. Last month, nearly 9 in 10 Americans said gas prices in their local areas would be even higher by the end of the year; now, with the price of gas at the pump dropping on a weekly basis, that percentage has dropped by more than half.

Between now and the end of the year, do you think gas prices in your local area will [ROTATED: increase a lot, increase a little, stay about the same, decrease a little, or decrease a lot]?

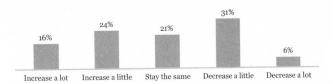

Gallup Poll Social Series, Aug. 7-10, 2008

It's uncommon to see the type of change evident in responses to this type of question in as little as one month. While last month, only 5% of Americans said gas prices would decrease, that number is up to 37% now, and there's been a jump from 6% to 21% in the percentage who say gas prices will stay the same. Importantly, only 16% of Americans now say gas prices will increase by "a lot" by the end of the year, compared to 52% last month.

All in all, a majority of Americans in Gallup's Aug. 7-10 poll optimistically say gas prices will stay the same or decrease by the end of the year, with just 40% hanging on to the belief that they will go higher.

The cause for this turnaround in attitudes is almost certainly the self-evident fact that gas prices have declined significantly in the time between the July and August surveys.

Republicans are a little more positive about gas prices than are Democrats and independents.

Between now and the end of the year, do you think gas prices in your local area will [ROTATED: increase a lot, increase a little, stay about the same, decrease a little, or decrease a lot]?

By political party

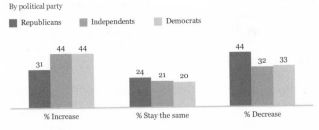

Gallup Poll Social Series, Aug. 7-10, 2008

On average, Republicans are more likely to say gas prices will decrease than to say they will increase, while independents and Democrats tilt in the opposite direction.

Gallup analysis has shown repeatedly that Republicans are generally more positive about the economy than are independents and Democrats, most likely reflecting attitudinal loyalty to the Republican administration in the White House.

Implications

Gallup Poll Daily tracking of economic attitudes has shown that Americans' views of the U.S. economy have been a little less negative of late.

Americans' Views of U.S. Economic Conditions

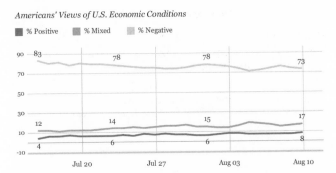

Classifications into Positive, Mixed, and Negative groups based on Americans' assessments of current economic conditions and outlook on the direction of economic conditions going forward.

The percentage of Americans classified as "negative" about the economy—those who rate current conditions as only fair or poor and think the economy is getting worse or staying the same—is 73% in Gallup's Aug. 8-10 Daily tracking average, compared to 83% who were negative in the average for July 14-16, a little less than a month ago.

Although there is no direct evidence proving that this decrease in economic negativity is a result of the drop in gas prices, such a causal connection is certainly a reasonable explanation. The current data showing that a majority of Americans project static or lower gas prices by the end of the year presumably suggest the possibility of an even more positive consumer outlook—which in turn could have a salutary effect on consumer spending.

Survey Methods

Results are based on telephone interviews with 1,009 national adults, aged 18 and older, conducted Aug. 7-10, 2008. For results based on the total sample of national adults, one can say with 95% confidence that the maximum margin of sampling error is ±3 percentage points.

Interviews are conducted with respondents on land-line telephones (for respondents with a land-line telephone) and cellular phones (for respondents who are cell-phone only).

In addition to sampling error, question wording and practical difficulties in conducting surveys can introduce error or bias into the findings of public opinion polls.

August 12, 2008

SUPPORT FOR THIRD-PARTY CANDIDATES APPEARS LIMITED THUS FAR

Just 2% say they will vote for a third-party candidate this fall

by Jeffrey M. Jones, Gallup Poll Managing Editor

A new Gallup Poll finds only 2% of registered voters naming a third-party candidate when asked in an open-ended fashion whom they will vote for this fall.

Now, thinking about the upcoming presidential election, which one of the candidates running for president do you plan to vote for in November? (OPEN ENDED)

Based on registered voters

Candidate	%
Barack Obama (Democrat)	45
John McCain (Republican)	38
Bob Barr (Libertarian Party)	1
Ralph Nader (Independent)	1
Cynthia McKinney (Green Party)	*
Hillary Clinton	1
Other	1
None	5
Won't vote (vol.)	2
No opinion	6

Gallup Poll, Aug. 7-10, 2008

* Less than 0.5%

(vol.) = Volunteered response

The question, part of an Aug. 7-10 Gallup Poll, allowed respondents to name any candidate or political party, without prompting of specific names from Gallup interviewers. This is a different approach than Gallup takes in its Daily tracking polling and *USA Today*/Gallup polls, in which voters are asked whether they would vote for Barack Obama or John McCain for president if the election were held today.

With the unaided question used in the new poll, 83% of registered voters named either Obama (45%) or McCain (38%) as their preferred candidate. Obama's 7-point advantage over McCain on the open-ended ballot is similar to the 5-point lead he currently holds in Gallup's Daily tracking poll.

Another 1% of voters mentioned Hillary Clinton, who conceded the Democratic nomination to Obama in early June after a long and intense campaign, but who retains a loyal following. An additional 1% mentioned one of several other candidates (mainly Republicans) who are ineligible to run (George W. Bush) or have long since ended their campaigns (Mitt Romney, Mike Huckabee, and Ron Paul) and will not appear on the ballot this fall.

Thirteen percent of registered voters are either undecided (6%) or say they do not plan to vote (7%).

That leaves only about 2% who say they plan to vote for a third-party candidate in November—not much different from the 1% in Gallup Poll Daily tracking who typically volunteer that they will vote for someone other than Obama or McCain. On the open-ended question, 1% specifically name Libertarian Party candidate Bob Barr and 1% name Ralph Nader, who is running as an independent this year after unsuccessful presidential bids in 1996, 2000, and 2004. Less than 1% mention the name of Cynthia McKinney, the Green Party's

nominee. No other organized third parties running a presidential candidate were named by poll respondents.

It is important to note that Gallup interviewers accepted the actual name of the candidate *or* the candidate's party affiliation as a valid response. So, for example, if a supporter of the Libertarian Party was not aware that Barr was the party's candidate, his or her response would still be registered as a Libertarian vote.

Implications

While it is not out of the question that third-party voting could be higher this year than it has been in most recent elections, the new Gallup Poll clearly suggests there is no unmeasured groundswell of support for any of the minor-party candidates running at this point in the campaign.

Survey Methods

Results are based on telephone interviews with 903 registered voters, aged 18 and older, conducted Aug. 7-10, 2008. For results based on the total sample of national adults, one can say with 95% confidence that the maximum margin of sampling error is ±4 percentage points.

Interviews are conducted with respondents on land-line telephones (for respondents with a land-line telephone) and cellular phones (for respondents who are cell-phone only).

In addition to sampling error, question wording and practical difficulties in conducting surveys can introduce error or bias into the findings of public opinion polls.

August 13, 2008

GENDER GAP AMONG WHITE VOTERS BIGGER NOW THAN IN 2004

Obama loses to McCain among white men, ties him among white women

by Frank Newport, Gallup Poll Editor in Chief

John McCain continues to have a significant advantage over Barack Obama among non-Hispanic white males while doing much less well among white females—winning among the former by a 20-point margin, while only tying Obama among the latter.

Gender Gap Among Non-Hispanic Whites (2008)

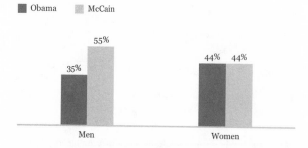

Aggregate of Gallup Poll Daily tracking, Aug. 1-11, 2008

This finding, based on Gallup Poll Daily tracking interviews with more than 8,200 non-Hispanic white registered voters conducted between Aug. 1 and Aug. 11, shows that McCain now does slightly better among white men compared to George W. Bush's final position against John Kerry in the 2004 election. But McCain is doing worse among white women. The net effect of this expanded gender gap is to give Obama a slightly better position among whites than was the case for Kerry in 2004.

The Gender Gap Among Whites in Historical Perspective

Democratic presidential candidates have generally done less well among white men than among white women in recent elections. But the gap between the two genders among whites is significantly larger this year than it was in 2004. In Gallup's final poll of registered voters in late October 2004, Kerry trailed Bush by 9 points among non-Hispanic white women and by 16 points among non-Hispanic white men. That produced a 7-point gender gap, about one-third the size of this year's 20-point gap.

Gender Gap Among Non-Hispanic Whites, 2004 Presidential Election

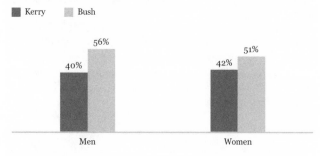

CNN/USA Today/Gallup poll, Oct. 29-31, 2004

McCain's relative advantage among men is slightly better this year than was Bush's in 2004. But McCain has lost ground to Obama among white women; Bush's 9-point lead over Kerry among this group four years ago has evaporated.

The larger gender gap overall is giving Obama a modest boost compared to the final positioning of the 2004 candidates. In Gallup's late October 2004 poll, Kerry was behind Bush by 12 points among non-Hispanic white registered voters. This year, Obama is down to McCain by a modestly smaller 9-point margin. Obama's gains among white women more than compensate for his slight loss of positioning among white men.

Education

The impact of education in patterns of support for Obama and McCain plays out differently between white men and white women.

Gender Gap Among Non-Hispanic Whites, by Education

Aggregate of Gallup Poll Daily tracking, Aug. 1-11, 2008

	% Men for Obama	% Men for McCain	% Women for Obama	% Women for McCain
High school or less	37	53	39	46
Some college	30	59	42	47
College graduate	33	59	48	44
Postgraduate	44	50	58	33

Among men, McCain leads regardless of education. He does particularly well among white men with some college and those who

are college graduates, slightly less well among those who have high school educations or less, and least well among white men with postgraduate educations (among whom he wins by just 6 points).

The pattern is somewhat different among non-Hispanic white women. Obama trails McCain by 7 points among white women with high school educations or less, and then does progressively better among those with higher levels of formal education. Obama beats McCain by a slight margin among white women who are college graduates. Remarkably, Obama has a very large 25-point margin among white women with postgraduate degrees.

Implications

The slightly weaker position for McCain vis-à-vis Obama among whites is not a major shift, but does represent a loss for McCain compared to his fellow Republican's performance among whites in 2004.

The data reviewed here show that the explanation lies with Obama's stronger showing among white women. Whereas Bush led Kerry by 9 points among white women in 2004, McCain and Obama are now tied among this group. This gain by Obama is partially mitigated by the fact that he does slightly less well among white men than did Kerry, but the net impact of the widening gender gap overall is a gain for Obama among whites.

There has been much talk about Obama's relative problems this year in reaching white men, particularly those with less than a college education. The data reviewed here from early August show that Obama in general does indeed trail McCain significantly among white men, particularly those who have a college degree or less. This white male deficit appears to be slightly larger than it was for Kerry in 2004. But Obama's relative strength among white women, particularly those with postgraduate educations, has to this point more than made up for his deficit among white men.

Survey Methods

Results are based on telephone interviews with 9,817 registered voters, aged 18 and older, conducted Aug. 1-11, 2008, and 8,208 registered voters who are non-Hispanic whites. For results based on both of these samples, one can say with 95% confidence that the maximum margin of sampling error is ±1 percentage point, with larger margins of sampling error among subgroups.

Interviews are conducted with respondents on land-line telephones (for respondents with a land-line telephone) and cellular phones (for respondents who are cell-phone only).

In addition to sampling error, question wording and practical difficulties in conducting surveys can introduce error or bias into the findings of public opinion polls.

August 13, 2008
U.S. SATISFACTION STEADY AT A DISMAL 17%
Dissatisfaction registers 80% or more for sixth straight month

by Lydia Saad, Gallup Poll Senior Editor

Americans' views of national circumstances haven't deteriorated in the past month, but they also haven't improved. Just 17% of Americans whom Gallup interviewed Aug. 7-10 say they are satisfied with the way things are going in the United States, the same as in July.

In general, are you satisfied or dissatisfied with the way things are going in the United States at this time?

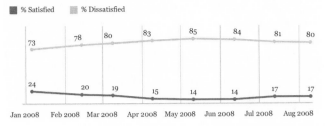

■ % Satisfied ■ % Dissatisfied

	Jan 2008	Feb 2008	Mar 2008	Apr 2008	May 2008	Jun 2008	Jul 2008	Aug 2008
Dissatisfied	73	78	80	83	85	84	81	80
Satisfied	24	20	19	15	14	14	17	17

This is the sixth straight month the percentage of Americans "dissatisfied" with the country has registered at least 80%, including the record-high 85% recorded in May. Since the establishment of this Gallup trend in 1979, there has been only one other period of similarly prolonged public dissatisfaction. That was in 1992, when dissatisfaction was 80% or higher for four out of five months from March to July, before dropping back to 73% in late August and early September.

U.S. Satisfaction, Full Trend Since February 1979

■ % Satisfied ■ % Dissatisfied

Economy the Most Important Problem

The economy remains the most common answer to Gallup's open-ended question asking Americans to name "the most important problem facing this country today." Thirty-eight percent name the economy in the new August poll, similar to the 34% to 41% citing it each month since February.

It appears that Americans' near-term concerns about fuel prices have ebbed slightly, as the percentage mentioning the issue fell from 23% in July to 15% today. This is most likely a direct reflection of the roughly 20-cent decline in average gas prices nationwide between the two polling periods. At the same time, Americans' underlying concerns about the nation's energy supply—what respondents term the "energy crisis"—rose slightly, from 6% to 9%.

At 19%, the percentage mentioning the Iraq war as the nation's top problem has not changed much since July. However, as a result of the decline in mentions of gas prices since July, Iraq now ranks No. 2 on the list of problems, replacing fuel prices, which fell to No. 3.

Today's order of perceived problems is quite different from that of January 2008, when Iraq ranked No.1, mentioned by 25%; the economy ranked No. 2, with 18%; and healthcare (13%) and immigration (11%) both surpassed fuel prices (6%). Despite recent political and media attention to the U.S. military challenges in Afghanistan, this conflict has yet to register on the list of most important problems with as much as 1% of Americans mentioning it.

Bottom Line

Public opinion about the country is in a negative rut if there ever was one. The six-month run of 80% or higher dissatisfaction ratings fol-

What do you think is the most important problem facing this country today?
Recent trend in top mentions

	Aug 7-10, 2008	Jul 10-13, 2008	Jun 9-12, 2008
	%	%	%
Economy in general	38	35	36
Situation in Iraq/War	19	18	20
Fuel/Oil prices	15	23	25
Dissatisfaction with government/Congress/politicians	9	9	6
Lack of energy sources; the energy crisis	9	6	7
Unemployment/Jobs	6	5	5
Poor healthcare/hospitals; healthcare costs	6	6	4
High cost of living/Inflation	5	5	6

lows 11 months of 70% or higher dissatisfaction, and consistently high readings of 60% or more stretching back to late 2005. The last time a majority of Americans were satisfied with the direction of the country was January 2004—four and a half years ago.

The reason for this rut has shifted over time, from a clear emphasis on the Iraq war between 2005 and 2007 to a clear emphasis on the economy today. High energy prices have only added fuel to the fire of public discontentment with the economy in 2008; but even as gas prices are receding from record highs, the economy remains the top perceived problem facing the country and, rolling into the election, dissatisfaction with the country abounds.

Survey Methods

Results are based on telephone interviews with 1,009 national adults, aged 18 and older, conducted Aug. 7-10, 2008. For results based on the total sample of national adults, one can say with 95% confidence that the maximum margin of sampling error is ±3 percentage points.

Interviews are conducted with respondents on land-line telephones (for respondents with a land-line telephone) and cellular phones (for respondents who are cell-phone only).

In addition to sampling error, question wording and practical difficulties in conducting surveys can introduce error or bias into the findings of public opinion polls.

August 14, 2008
SEVERAL INDUSTRIES TAKE BIG IMAGE HIT THIS YEAR
Real estate shows biggest one-year decline for an industry

by Jeffrey M. Jones, Gallup Poll Managing Editor

Rising prices, a sagging housing market, and the mortgage crisis are likely behind sharp drops in Americans' positive ratings of the real estate, banking, restaurant, grocery, airline, and retail industries compared to last year.

In fact, ratings of all 25 business sectors included in the Gallup ratings except for the sports industry are lower now than last year, though only drops of 6 points or more should be considered statistically meaningful.

These results are based on data from Gallup's annual Work and Education poll, conducted Aug. 7-10. Each year, Gallup asks Americans to rate each of 25 different business and industry sectors as positive, neutral, or negative.

Change in Positive Ratings of Business and Industry Sectors, 2007 to 2008

	% Positive, 2007	% Positive, 2008	Change in positive ratings
Real estate industry	34	16	-18
Grocery industry	53	36	-17
Banking	50	36	-14
Restaurant industry	63	51	-12
Retail industry	51	39	-12
Airline industry	30	18	-12
Automobile industry	38	29	-9
Travel industry	42	34	-8
Advertising and public relations industry	35	27	-8
Publishing industry	43	36	-7
Telephone industry	46	39	-7
Education	47	41	-6
Internet industry	54	49	-5
The legal field	31	26	-5
Accounting	40	36	-4
Television and radio industry	41	37	-4
Electric and gas utilities	31	27	-4
Oil and gas industry	19	15	-4
The federal government	21	18	-3
Pharmaceutical industry	33	31	-2
Computer industry	61	60	-1
Farming and agriculture	51	50	-1
Movie industry	36	35	-1
Healthcare industry	28	27	-1
Sports industry	35	36	1

Gallup Poll, Aug. 7-10, 2008

This year's poll was conducted at a time when Americans were in a sour mood about the economy given high gas prices, the rising price of food, and ongoing problems in banking and the housing market.

Since Gallup began tracking opinion of business and industry in 2001, one-year declines of 10 points or more in positive ratings have been rare. But this year, six different industries have lost 10 points or more, and another (the automobile industry, with a 9-point drop) comes close.

One industry whose image didn't worsen much this year is the oil and gas industry (down just 4 points), but that is because its ratings have been low and at the bottom of the list for several years. However, the oil and gas industry's current 15% positive rating is notable in that it is the lowest such score for any industry in the eight years Gallup has conducted this poll.

Record Declines

The 18-point decline in Americans' positive ratings of the real estate industry is the largest one-year change Gallup has measured for any industry. That clearly results from the subprime mortgage crisis, which has led to large numbers of foreclosures and falling home values. The 17-point drop in positive ratings of the grocery industry this year also surpasses the previous high.

Prior to this year, the largest one-year decline Gallup had measured for an industry was a 16-point drop in positive ratings of accounting from 2001 (47%) to 2002 (31%), after reports that large corporations like Enron and Tyco had been filing false financial reports with the knowledge of their accounting firms.

Overall Ratings of Industries

As a result of the decline in ratings of the real estate industry (now just 16% rate it positively), it ranks with the oil and gas industry (15%) as having the lowest percentage of favorable reviews. How-

ever, even though the two industries have similarly low positive ratings, many more Americans have a neutral opinion of real estate and a negative opinion of the oil and gas industry. When a net positive score is computed by subtracting negative ratings from positive ones, oil and gas (-61) scores much worse than real estate (-40).

Joining oil and gas and real estate as the most negatively rated industries and sectors are the federal government (-42 net positive rating), airline industry (-34), healthcare industry (-30), and electric and gas utilities (-25).

At the other end of the spectrum, the most positively rated industries are computers (+50), restaurants (+39, even with the large decline in positive ratings this year), farming and agriculture (+31), Internet (+31), and accounting (+24).

Net Positive Ratings of Business and Industry Sectors, 2008

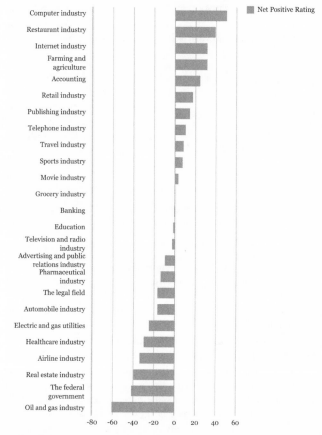

Gallup Poll, Aug. 7-10, 2008

Americans have typically rated the grocery and banking industries more positively than negatively, but now about as many rate these two industries negatively as rate them positively. In addition to the restaurant industry, the retail sector remains in positive territory even with the declines this year.

Implications

Clearly, the issues plaguing the economy are affecting the way Americans view a variety of industries, in particular the ones most closely associated with rising prices (grocery, restaurant, and retail) and the mortgage crisis (banking and real estate).

Historically, Gallup has not seen many similarly steep declines in ratings of an industry from one year to the next, but the few historical examples show that an industry's ratings are about as likely to improve the year after a sharp decline as to stay the same or go down further. The example of the accounting industry is illustrative. After suffering a large one-year decline in ratings in 2002, its image has improved, though it remains below where it was before the scandal.

Just as the ratings of many industries have declined in the current negative economic climate, one might expect a sort of "rising tide" effect when the economy improves, which would lift the ratings of these industries.

Survey Methods

Results are based on telephone interviews with 510 national adults, aged 18 and older, conducted Aug. 7-10, 2008. For results based on the total sample of national adults, one can say with 95% confidence that the maximum margin of sampling error is ±5 percentage points.

Interviews are conducted with respondents on land-line telephones (for respondents with a land-line telephone) and cellular phones (for respondents who are cell-phone only).

In addition to sampling error, question wording and practical difficulties in conducting surveys can introduce error or bias into the findings of public opinion polls.

August 15, 2008
BUSH'S JOB APPROVAL INCHES UP TO 33%
Highest score since February

by Jeffrey M. Jones, Gallup Poll Managing Editor

While George W. Bush's 33% job approval rating is still low from a historical perspective, it is an improvement from the 28% readings he received in April, May, and June, and is his best rating since February.

George W. Bush's Presidential Job Approval Ratings, 2008

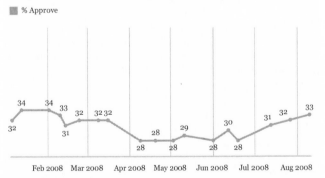

Bush's already-low job approval ratings dipped below 30% through much of the spring and early summer amid rising gas prices. But Gallup's last three measurements have all been above the 30% mark.

Most of the recent improvement in his ratings has come among Republicans. In the current poll, 71% of Republicans approve of Bush, compared with an average of 64% in April through June. Twenty-five percent of independents now give Bush a positive review (compared with 23% between April and June) as do just 7% of Democrats (compared with 6% in the April-June period).

Overall approval ratings in the 30s are well below average. The historical average job approval rating for all presidents in Gallup Polls is 55%. Bush has not had an approval rating in the 50s since May 2005, and it's been nearly two years since he registered an approval rating of 40% or above.

In the near future, there may be some movement in Bush's job approval rating. It is not uncommon for incumbent presidents' approval ratings to decline after the opposing party holds its presidential nominating convention.

In all but one case (of the six years for which Gallup has approval ratings before and shortly after the opposing party's convention), the president's approval rating declined, showing a statistically significant drop in three of these. That includes 5-point drops for Lyndon Johnson in 1968 and Bill Clinton in 1996, and a 6-point drop for George H.W. Bush in 1992.

Presidential Job Approval Ratings Before and After Opposing Party's Convention

President	Year	Approval rating before opposing party's convention	Approval rating after opposing party's convention	Change
Johnson	1968	40%	35%	-5
Reagan	1984	55%	52%	-3
Bush	1992	38%	32%	-6
Clinton	1996	57%	52%	-5
Clinton	2000	57%	57%	0
Bush	2004	49%	48%	-1

But usually, any losses after the opposition's convention are made up after the party of the president holds its convention. In fact, each sitting president has received an increase in support after his own party's convention, and in all but two cases, the increase has been statistically significant.

Presidential Job Approval Ratings Before and After Own Party's Convention

President	Year	Approval rating before own party's convention	Approval rating after own party's convention	Change
Johnson	1968	35%	42%	7
Reagan	1984	54%	57%	3
Bush	1992	35%	40%	5
Clinton	1996	53%	60%	7
Clinton	2000	58%	62%	4
Bush	2004	49%	52%	3

Thus, Americans will likely more critically evaluate Bush during the week of the Democratic convention, Aug. 25-28, as the Democrats seek to make their case for electing Barack Obama for president in part by emphasizing the shortcomings of the Bush administration and its approach to governing. But Bush will probably get a more favorable review from the public the following week, when it's the Republicans' turn to tout John McCain as the next president. Given the short time between the conventions this year, the polls may not pick up any short-term movement in Bush's approval rating tied to the conventions.

Survey Methods

Results are based on telephone interviews with 1,009 national adults, aged 18 and older, conducted Aug. 7-10, 2008. For results based on the total sample of national adults, one can say with 95% confidence that the maximum margin of sampling error is ±3 percentage points.

Interviews are conducted with respondents on land-line telephones (for respondents with a land-line telephone) and cellular phones (for respondents who are cell-phone only).

In addition to sampling error, question wording and practical difficulties in conducting surveys can introduce error or bias into the findings of public opinion polls.

August 15, 2008

CONSUMER CONFIDENCE EDGES UP AS GAS PRICES GO DOWN

Some measures as positive as they have been since early this year

by Frank Newport, Gallup Poll Editor in Chief

Gallup Poll Daily Tracking data continue to show an upward tick in Americans' positive views of the U.S. economy. Although economic views overall are still pessimistic, the percentage of Americans Gallup classifies as having a negative view of the economy is now as low as it has been since February, dropping in recent weeks in close correspondence to the drop in gas prices.

The change in consumer confidence is not a major shift. From a big-picture perspective, Americans remain very much on the negative side of the ledger when asked to rate their views of the economy.

Still, there is little question that there has been a swing in the trajectory of Americans' confidence in the economy, and after reaching an extraordinary low point in mid-July, attitudes are showing signs of increased optimism.

Gallup's overall summary measure of consumer confidence now pegs 9% of Americans as positive, 19% as mixed, and 70% as negative. Although this certainly does not represent a cheerily upbeat public, the numbers have not been this positive since February. And they certainly represent an improvement from Gallup's July 14-16 data, when Gallup classified 83% of Americans as having negative economic outlooks.

Americans' Views of U.S. Economic Conditions

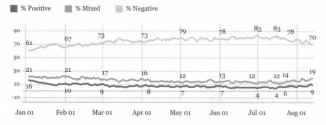

Classifications into Positive, Mixed, and Negative groups based on Americans' assessments of current economic conditions and outlook on the direction of economic conditions going forward.

The turnaround in consumer attitudes is no doubt to a significant degree the result of declining gas prices. The downward swing in the percentage of Americans with a negative economic mood in recent weeks has closely matched the downward swing in gas prices.

On a more specific measure, 19% of Americans say the U.S. economy is getting better, while 76% say it is getting worse.

U.S. Economy -- Getting Better or Getting Worse?

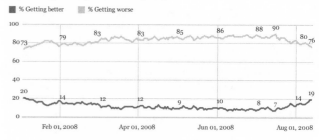

These are still fairly dismal readings, but nowhere near as negative as about one month ago, when Gallup's July 14-16 report found only 7% saying the economy was getting better and 90% saying it was getting worse. Furthermore, the last time as few as 76% said the economy was getting worse was late January of this year, and one has to go back to early January to find a time when the optimistic percentage was as high as 19%.

Ratings of Current U.S. Economic Conditions

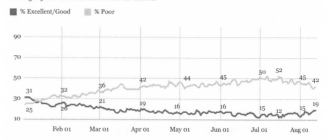

Survey Methods

For the Gallup Poll Daily tracking survey, Gallup is interviewing no fewer than 1,000 U.S. adults nationwide each day during 2008. Each day's report of Americans' economic mood is based on combined data from three days of interviewing, with the questions asked of a half sample each day. For results based on these sample sizes of approximately 1,500 national adults, the maximum margin of sampling error is ±2 percentage points.

Interviews are conducted with respondents on land-line telephones (for respondents with a land-line telephone) and cellular phones (for respondents who are cell-phone only).

In addition to sampling error, question wording and practical difficulties in conducting surveys can introduce error or bias into the findings of public opinion polls.

August 18, 2008

HALF OF AMERICANS SAY THEY ARE UNDERPAID

Middle- and lower-income Americans more likely to say so

by Dennis Jacobe, Gallup Poll Chief Economist

When asked to say in all honesty how they personally feel about their pay, 51% of Americans feel they are underpaid for the work they do, 46% feel they are paid about the right amount, and 3% feel they are overpaid.

In all honesty, do you think you, personally, are -- [ROTATED: underpaid for the work you do, paid about the right amount, (or are you) overpaid for the work you do]?

Based on 557 adults employed full- or part-time

Margin of error: ±5 percentage points

More Middle- and Lower-Income Americans Feel Underpaid

Some groups of Americans are more likely than others to say they are underpaid. Only 38% of those making $75,000 or more a year say they are underpaid, compared to 62% of those making less than $75,000. Somewhat surprisingly, the difference between men and women on this measure is much smaller, with 47% of men and 55% of women saying they are underpaid. Similarly, 59% of Democrats say they are underpaid, compared to 49% of independents and 44% of Republicans.

Percentage Who Think They Are Underpaid, by Annual Income and Gender

Based on adults who are employed full- or part-time

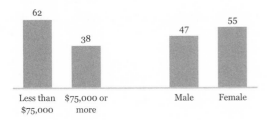

Gallup Poll, Aug. 7-10, 2008

Percentage Who Think They Are Underpaid, by Party ID

Adults who are employed full-/part-time

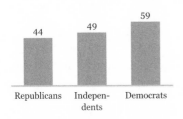

Gallup Poll, Aug. 7-10, 2008

Little Difference by Race or Education

There is little difference by race or by education in perceptions of being underpaid. Fifty-one percent of both whites and nonwhites say they feel underpaid. Similarly, 49% of those with high school edu-

cations or less say they are underpaid, compared to 52% of those with at least some college education.

In all honesty, do you think you, personally, are?

Percent Saying Underpaid

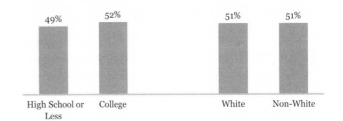

Survey Methods

Results are based on telephone interviews with 557 national adults, aged 18 and older and employed full- or part-time, conducted Aug. 7-10, 2008. For results based on the sample of employed adults, one can say with 95% confidence that the maximum margin of sampling error is ±5 percentage points.

Interviews are conducted with respondents on land-line telephones (for respondents with a land-line telephone) and cellular phones (for respondents who are cell-phone only).

In addition to sampling error, question wording and practical difficulties in conducting surveys can introduce error or bias into the findings of public opinion polls.

August 18, 2008
U.S. EMPLOYEE-REPORTED LAYOFFS HIGHEST IN FIVE YEARS
Three in four say now is a "bad time" to find a quality job

by Dennis Jacobe, Gallup Poll Chief Economist

Thirty percent of Americans report that their employers have laid off employees during the past six months—up from 22% a year ago, and the highest level since August 2003, when 34% of employees said this was the case.

Percent of Workers Saying Their Companies Have Laid Off Employees During the Past Six Months

Percent Reporting Layoffs

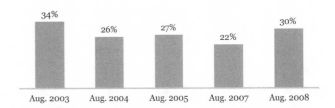

The percentage of Americans reporting job layoffs at their companies does not vary significantly by income. However, perceptions of layoffs over the past six months are greatest in the West, with 40% of employees reporting this—more than in any other region.

As far as you know, in the past six months, has your employer laid off any employees, or not?

By annual household income and region

■ % Yes, has

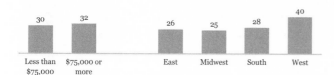

Gallup Poll, Aug. 7-10, 2008

Bad Time to Find a Quality Job

Additionally, 75% of Americans believe now is a bad time to find a quality job—a percentage that has remained essentially unchanged since April. The last few months have seen the highest level of job market pessimism since 2003.

Thinking about the job situation in America today, would you say that it is now a good time or a bad time to find a quality job?

Selected trend from August polls

■ % Good time   ■ % Bad time

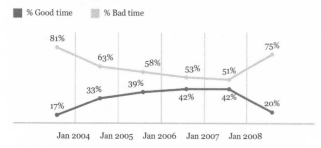

Employees' Personal Job Worries Have Not Increased

While Americans' perceptions of employer layoffs and their ability to find a quality job are at five-year lows, working Americans' worries that their wages will be reduced, that they personally will be laid off, or that their companies will move jobs overseas are not much different than they have been in recent years. Lower- and middle-income Americans are somewhat more worried than upper-income Americans that their benefits will be reduced and that their work hours will be cut.

Next, please indicate whether you are worried or not worried about each of the following happening to you, personally, in the near future. How about --

% Worried, by annual household income

■ $75,000 or more   ■ Less than $75,000

Gallup poll, Aug. 7-10, 2008

Commentary

Last week, the government's four-week moving average of first-time claims for unemployment increased to its highest level since April 2002. This suggests that job market conditions are likely to continue to deteriorate in the months ahead. Employers are unlikely to build their employee workforces given the slowing economy, the end of the tax rebates, and all of the factors potentially affecting consumer spending in a negative way—including energy prices, housing, and the consumer credit crunch. As a result, employed Americans' worries about their personal job situations may tend to increase as the remainder of this year unfolds.

On the other hand, the sharp drop in oil and gas prices over the past 30 days has had a positive impact on consumer confidence. As a result, the real question for the economy looking ahead—including the all-important Christmas shopping season—seems to be whether declining gas prices, even though they remain far above year-ago levels, will be enough not only to offset further deterioration in the jobs market but also to increase consumers' real disposable incomes enough to significantly stimulate consumer spending. At this point, it appears the downward momentum in the jobs market may be hard to reverse in time for the Christmas holidays.

Survey Methods

Results based on telephone interviews with 1,009 national adults, aged 18 and older, conducted Aug. 7-10, 2008. For results based on the full sample of national adults, one can say with 95% confidence that the maximum margin of sampling error is ±3 percentage points.

For results based on interviews conducted with 557 adults employed full or part-time, one can say with 95% confidence that the maximum margin of sampling error is ±5 percentage points.

Interviews are conducted with respondents on land-line telephones (for respondents with a land-line telephone) and cellular phones (for respondents who are cell-phone only).

In addition to sampling error, question wording and practical difficulties in conducting surveys can introduce error or bias into the findings of public opinion polls.

August 19, 2008

VETERANS SOLIDLY BACK MCCAIN

Prefer McCain to Obama by 56% to 34%

by Jeffrey M. Jones, Gallup Poll Managing Editor

With both presidential candidates addressing the Veterans of Foreign Wars convention this week (John McCain on Monday and Barack Obama on Tuesday), Gallup finds that registered voters who have served in the U.S. military solidly back McCain over Obama, 56% to 34%.

This is based on aggregated data from Aug. 5-17 Gallup Poll Daily tracking, involving interviews with more than 11,000 registered voters, including 2,238 military veterans. Veterans are defined as those who are or have been members of the U.S. military. Obama leads McCain 46% to 43% among all registered voters during this time.

The veteran vote is of some interest this year given McCain's notable service in the U.S. Navy, including several years as a pris-

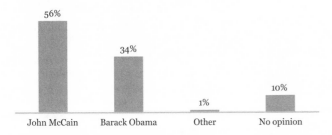

Aug. 5-17 Gallup Poll Daily tracking

oner of war in North Vietnam. Obama did not serve in the U.S. military.

But even without the distinction provided this year by McCain's well-known military service, veterans tend to be Republican in their political orientation, and Republican candidates generally fare better than Democratic candidates among this voting group. For example, in Gallup's final pre-election poll in 2004, 55% of registered voters who had served in the military backed George W. Bush, compared with 39% who supported John Kerry.

It is notable, then, that McCain is doing only about as well among military veterans as Bush did in 2004, despite the two Republican candidates' varying military backgrounds. (Bush was in the Texas Air National Guard, but did not serve overseas.)

Veterans' affinity for the Republican Party is confirmed by the finding that 47% of those who have served in the military currently identify with or lean to the Republican Party while 39% identify with or lean to the Democratic Party. By comparison, 48% of all U.S. adults are Democratic in their party orientation and 37% are Republican.

Party Affiliation

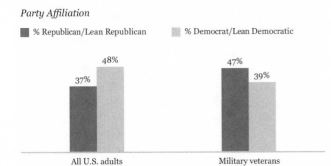

Aug. 5-17 Gallup Poll Daily tracking

Even if it wasn't for their shared military service, veterans' alignment with McCain would not be surprising given the demographic composition of the group. Veterans are overwhelmingly male (91% of the veterans in the sample are men) and tend to be older (the majority are aged 50 or above). Those also happen to be two of McCain's stronger voting constituencies in this campaign.

Implications

McCain clearly holds an advantage over Obama among veterans, but that is probably due more to the fact that veterans tend to be Republicans than to the fact that McCain himself served in the mil-

itary and is regarded by some as a war hero. Veterans showed similarly strong support for Bush in the 2004 presidential election. The data suggest there still is an effect of military service on candidate preference, but it is rather small and is overwhelmed by the effects of party affiliation.

Survey Methods

Results are based on telephone interviews with 11,593 registered voters, aged 18 and older, conducted Aug. 5-17, 2008, as part of Gallup Poll Daily tracking. For results based on the total sample of national adults, one can say with 95% confidence that the maximum margin of sampling error is ±1 percentage point.

For results based on the sample of 2,238 military veterans who are registered to vote, the maximum margin of sampling error is ±3 percentage points.

Interviews are conducted with respondents on land-line telephones (for respondents with a land-line telephone) and cellular phones (for respondents who are cell-phone only).

In addition to sampling error, question wording and practical difficulties in conducting surveys can introduce error or bias into the findings of public opinion polls.

August 20, 2008

MCCAIN STILL DOMINANT AMONG THE HIGHLY RELIGIOUS

Key question is strength of McCain's support, turnout

by Frank Newport, Gallup Poll Editor in Chief

John McCain continues to dominate Barack Obama among religious Americans, winning among those who attend worship services weekly by a 53% to 37% margin, and losing to Obama among those who seldom or never attend church by 54% to 34%.

Support for Presidential Nomination Candidates, by Church Attendance

Weekly aggregate based on registered voters, Aug. 11-17, 2008

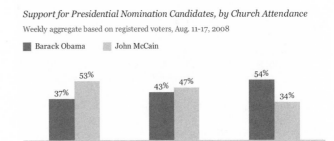

Both presidential candidates appeared this past weekend at a "Civil Forum on the Presidency" at Saddleback Church in California, moderated by the church's pastor, Rick Warren. The candidates answered questions about their faith and other campaign and policy issues.

The Gallup data reviewed here (from a Gallup aggregate of interviews conducted Aug. 11-17) show that in terms of those in attendance at the church, McCain was likely more well-appreciated than Obama, as he no doubt was to religious voters around the country watching at home on television. Not only does McCain do much better against Obama among those who attend church frequently, but he also beats Obama by an 8-point margin among Americans who say religion is important in their lives, while Obama wins by a 22-point margin among those for whom religion is not important.

Support for Presidential Nomination Candidates, by Importance of Religion in Respondents' Lives

Weekly aggregate based on registered voters, Aug. 11-17, 2008

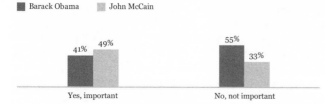

This strong relationship between religiosity and vote behavior is not new. In 2004, Gallup data from late October showed that George W. Bush was ahead of John Kerry by a 19-point margin among registered voters who were weekly church attenders, while Kerry was ahead by a 24-point margin among registered voters who seldom or never attended church.

Black Americans are both highly religious and highly likely to vote Democratic in presidential contests. Thus, when the data are restricted just to whites, the relationship between religion and the vote is even more pronounced.

Support for Presidential Nomination Candidates, by Church Attendance, Among Non-Hispanic Whites

Weekly aggregate based on registered voters, Aug. 11-17, 2008

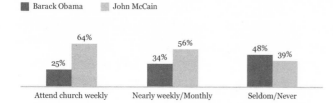

Among whites, McCain has a very large 39-point margin among those who attend church weekly, while Obama still manages to win among whites who seldom or never attend church, albeit by a more modest 9-point margin. (In this same weekly aggregate, McCain beats Obama overall among whites by a 51% to 37% margin.)

Implications

The relationship between religiosity and identifying with the Republican Party has been so strong in recent years that there is little question McCain will do well among this group in November. The interesting question is more about the degree to which highly religious white Americans are excited by the McCain candidacy and therefore willing to work for his election and to turn out on Election Day. At this point, the estimate is that McCain is doing about as well among registered voters who are weekly church attenders as did Bush in 2004.

Survey Methods

Results are based on telephone interviews with 6,228 registered voters, aged 18 and older, and 5,202 non-Hispanic white registered voters, aged 18 and older, conducted Aug. 11-17, 2008. For results

based on both of these samples, one can say with 95% confidence that the maximum margin of sampling error is ±2 percentage points.

Interviews are conducted with respondents on land-line telephones (for respondents with a land-line telephone) and cellular phones (for respondents who are cell-phone only).

In addition to sampling error, question wording and practical difficulties in conducting surveys can introduce error or bias into the findings of public opinion polls.

August 21, 2008

THE MARRIAGE GAP IN SUPPORT FOR MCCAIN, OBAMA

Marriage gap reflects underlying differences in composition of the parties

by Frank Newport, Gallup Poll Editor in Chief

Among American registered voters who are married and whom Gallup interviewed Aug. 1-19, John McCain is leading Barack Obama by 13 points; among unmarried American voters, Obama has a 22-point margin.

Preference for the General Election, by Marital Status

Among registered voters

Gallup Poll Daily tracking, Aug. 1-19, 2008

A large part of the explanation for this marriage gap resides in the basic fact that the two major political parties are fundamentally divided by marital status. Almost two-thirds of Americans who identify with the Republican Party are married, while a majority of Democrats are unmarried.

Marital Status, by Political Party

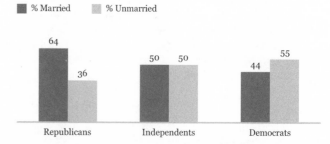

Gallup Poll Daily tracking, Aug. 1-19, 2008

Demographic Differences

This marriage gap is one of several such demographic gaps in support for the two major-party candidates. There is, for example, a significant gender gap (Obama does better among women; McCain, among men) and a significant age gap (Obama does better among younger Americans).

Since men are significantly more likely than women to be married in America today, and since those under age 35 are significantly more likely to be unmarried than are those who are older, could it be that the marriage gap is merely a reflection of these other two basic demographic characteristics?

An analysis of Gallup's August data would answer "no" to that question. The differences in support by marital status persist across gender and age groups.

Although women are in general somewhat stronger in their support for Obama, married women tilt more toward McCain (by 46% to 42%) while unmarried women favor Obama. The same pattern holds for men.

Preference for the General Election, by Gender and Marital Status
Among registered voters

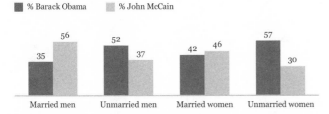

Gallup Poll Daily tracking, Aug. 1-19, 2008

Younger Americans in general are among Obama's strongest supporters. Yet among those 18 to 34 who are married, McCain manages to best Obama by 4 points (47% to 43%), while among 18- to 34-year-olds who are unmarried, Obama wins by an overwhelming 36-point margin (63% to 27%). The same pattern holds among those who are older. Among both 35- to 54-year-olds and those 55 and older, those who are married skew toward McCain while those who are not married skew toward Obama.

Preference for the General Election

By marital status and age

	Barack Obama	John McCain
	%	%
18 to 34 married	43	47
18 to 34 unmarried	63	27
35 to 54 married	38	52
35 to 54 unmarried	56	33
55+ married	36	52
55+ unmarried	48	38

Gallup Poll Daily tracking, Aug. 1-19, 2008

Survey Methods

Results are based on telephone interviews with 16,941 registered voters, aged 18 and older, conducted Aug. 1-19, 2008. For results based on the total sample of national adults, one can say with 95% confidence that the maximum margin of sampling error is ±1 percentage point.

Interviews are conducted with respondents on land-line telephones (for respondents with a land-line telephone) and cellular phones (for respondents who are cell-phone only).

In addition to sampling error, question wording and practical difficulties in conducting surveys can introduce error or bias into the findings of public opinion polls.

August 21, 2008
U.S. WORKERS' JOB SATISFACTION IS RELATIVELY HIGH
Older employees are more upbeat than younger workers

by Lydia Saad, Gallup Poll Senior Editor

At a time when Americans' ratings of the country and of the nation's economy are near record lows, the percentage of U.S. workers feeling "completely satisfied" with their jobs—now 48%—is at the high end of the range seen in the past eight years.

How satisfied or dissatisfied are you with your job? Would you say you are -- completely satisfied, somewhat satisfied, somewhat dissatisfied, or completely dissatisfied with your job?

Based on 557 adults employed full or part-time; ±5 percentage points.

Another 42% of part-time and full-time workers in the United States say they are "somewhat satisfied," resulting in most workers' being generally upbeat about their employment. Only 9% are dissatisfied to any degree.

Overall Job Satisfaction of U.S. Workers
Based on 557 full-time and part-time employees; ±5 percentage points

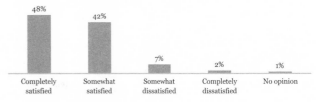

Gallup Poll, Aug. 7-10, 2008

This year's Gallup Poll Social Series Work and Education poll, conducted Aug. 7-10, shows little difference between men and women, and even between upper- and middle-income workers, in overall job satisfaction. The more notable differences are by age, with the oldest category of workers (aged 55 and older) much more likely to be "completely satisfied" than are those still building their careers (18 to 34): 57% vs. 42%.

Overall Job Satisfaction of U.S. Workers, by Age

Based on full-time and part-time employees

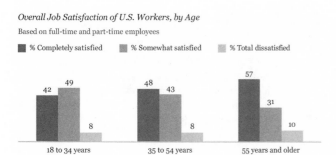

Gallup Poll, Aug. 7-10, 2008

Bottom Line

Worker satisfaction is refreshingly positive to see amid otherwise gloomy public attitudes about the country. To some extent, this may reflect a heightened appreciation on the part of some workers for having a job at a time when they realize good jobs are hard to come by, and when being out of work is no picnic. (It also reflects the basic reality that dissatisfied workers—like unhappy spouses—don't stay put for long, so the percentage of workers who are dissatisfied should never be overly high.)

Although workers clearly think their pay, benefits, promotion opportunities, and stress could all be better, generally high satisfaction with their coworkers and boss, flexibility in their hours, and job security seem to largely offset those negatives.

Survey Methods

Results are based on telephone interviews with 1,009 national adults, aged 18 and older, conducted Aug. 7-10, 2008. For results based on the total sample of national adults, one can say with 95% confidence that the maximum margin of sampling error is ±3 percentage points.

For results based on the sample of 557 adults employed full or part-time, the maximum margin of sampling error is ±5 percentage points.

Interviews are conducted with respondents on land-line telephones (for respondents with a land-line telephone) and cellular phones (for respondents who are cell-phone only).

In addition to sampling error, question wording and practical difficulties in conducting surveys can introduce error or bias into the findings of public opinion polls.

August 22, 2008

OBAMA LAGS IN DEMOCRATIC SUPPORT

Democrats' lead on party ID greater than Obama's lead over McCain

by Lydia Saad, Gallup Poll Senior Editor and Jeffrey M. Jones, Gallup Poll Managing Editor

As the national political conventions are poised to start, the party orientation of U.S. voters clearly favors the Democratic Party, similar to the pattern seen for the past five months. Among all national registered voters interviewed thus far in August for the Gallup Poll Daily tracking survey, 35% identify as Democrats compared with 28% who identify as Republicans. An additional 36% are independents.

Party Identification of U.S. Registered Voters -- Recent Trend

Percentage of independents not shown

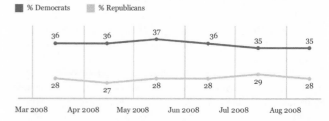

The current 7-point Democratic advantage in party ID expands to 10 points when the party leanings of independents are taken into account. Fifty percent of U.S. registered voters identify with or lean to the Democratic Party and 40% are Republican or lean Republican.

Party Identification of U.S. Registered Voters -- Including Independent Leaners

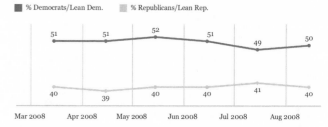

This Democratic advantage contrasts with the close nature of the presidential contest between Democrat Barack Obama and Republican John McCain in monthly averages of the Obama vs. McCain horse race since March.

Although Obama has led by as many as 9 percentage points over McCain in Gallup Poll Daily tracking three-day rolling averages, the results on a monthly basis show Obama averaging no better than a 3-point lead among registered voters in any month. This includes August (according to interviews from Aug. 1-19), during which Obama has led 46% to 43% (though in the past week, Obama has averaged just a 1-point advantage).

Preference for Obama vs. McCain -- Monthly Averages*

Based on registered voters

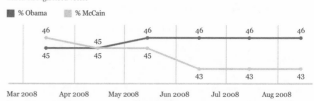

* Data are from Gallup Poll Daily tracking; August result includes Aug. 1-19, 2008.

Gallup's most recent weekly aggregate, based on Aug. 11-17 data, found Obama up by an average of only 2 points over McCain, 45% to 43%. At the same time, voters' party preferences broke 35% Democratic and 28% Republican (with a 50% to 40% Democratic advantage on party identification, including leaners).

The reasons this is not translating into a stronger lead for Obama are twofold:

1. Although Democrats outnumber Republicans in the electorate, McCain receives the support of a greater share of his party base than does Obama.

Whereas 84% of Republicans polled from Aug. 11-17 say they will vote for McCain in November, only 79% of Democrats say they will vote for Obama. A similar gap in party loyalty has been seen each week since Obama clinched the Democratic nomination in early June. Over this period, Obama's Democratic support has ranged from 78% to 82% while McCain's Republican support has ranged from 83% to 85%.

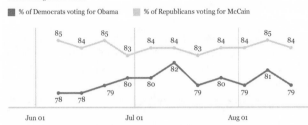

Support for Obama and McCain From Members of Their Respective Parties
Based on registered voters

■ % of Democrats voting for Obama   ░ % of Republicans voting for McCain

Data are from Gallup Poll Daily tracking; weekly averages (through Aug. 17)

2. The race has been extremely close among the roughly 36% of voters who call themselves political independents.

Since early June, Obama and McCain have swapped the lead among independents, with neither ever achieving a very large lead. Overall, Obama has averaged just a 1-point lead over McCain among independents, and in interviews conducted Aug. 11-17, the two were tied at 42%.

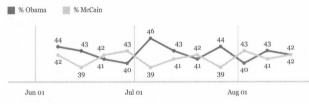

Support for Obama vs. McCain Among Independents
Based on registered voters

■ % Obama   ░ % McCain

Data are from Gallup Poll Daily tracking; weekly averages (through Aug. 17)

Given the stability in support for Obama and McCain among their respective party regulars, and the underlying stability in the party identification of voters, nearly all of the movement in the overall horse race since early June—ranging from a tie to a 9-point lead for Obama—can be explained by shifts in support for the candidates among political independents.

Bottom Line

More voters this year have aligned themselves with the Democratic Party than the Republican Party. The Democrats have a 7-point advantage in terms of core partisans, and a 10-point advantage when factoring in the leanings of political independents.

If each candidate were supported equally by his partisans, and independents split equally, that would translate into a 7- to 10-point lead for Obama over McCain in the race for president. But the race has been closer than that, primarily because a greater proportion of Republicans than Democrats are backing their own party's candidate for president.

Going into the convention period, it thus appears that a crucial test for Obama will be winning over heretofore reluctant Democrats

to his candidacy, and the challenge for McCain will be retaining his Republican base. The vice presidential selections could be key factors in both cases. At the same time, both candidates will face the challenge of attracting more independents to their candidacies. In a close race, even a slight swing in the preferences of this group could be decisive.

Survey Methods

For the Gallup Poll Daily tracking survey, Gallup interviews no fewer than 1,000 U.S. adults nationwide each day, generally including approximately 880 registered voters.

The average weekly results reported here are based on combined data from approximately 6,200 registered voters interviewed each week from Monday through Sunday. For results based on samples of this size, the maximum margin of sampling error is ±1 percentage point. For results based on subgroups of registered voters, the margins of sampling error are higher.

The average monthly results reported here are based on combined data from at least 21,000 registered voters for each month from March through July, and 13,198 registered voters for the partial month of August (Aug. 1-19). For results based on samples of this size, the maximum margin of sampling error is ±1 percentage point. For results based on subgroups of registered voters, the margins of sampling error are higher.

Interviews are conducted with respondents on land-line telephones (for respondents with a land-line telephone) and cellular phones (for respondents who are cell-phone only).

In addition to sampling error, question wording and practical difficulties in conducting surveys can introduce error or bias into the findings of public opinion polls.

August 23, 2008
BIDEN DOES NO HARM, BUT MAY NOT HELP MUCH
Seen as qualified, but less than half call him an excellent or pretty good choice

by Lydia Saad, Gallup Poll Senior Editor

Barack Obama's selection of U.S. Sen. and former presidential candidate Joe Biden as his running mate is not generating a momentous immediate reaction from the nation's voters. Just 14% of registered voters interviewed in a new *USA Today*/Gallup poll say Biden makes them more likely to vote for Obama in November and 7% say less likely while 72% say he will not have much effect on their vote.

This results in Biden potentially having a net positive impact on voter support for the Democratic ticket of +7 percentage points—small by comparison with other recent vice presidential selections.

- A net 17% of nationwide registered voters said they were more likely to vote for John Kerry in 2004 on the basis of his selection of John Edwards as his running mate (24% more likely and 7% less likely).
- A net 12% of voters reported being more likely to vote for Al Gore in 2000 on account of his choosing Joe Lieberman (16% more likely and 4% less likely).
- A net 18% of voters indicated they were more likely to vote for Bob Dole in 1996 on the basis of his choice of Jack Kemp to complete the ticket (26% more likely and 8% less likely).

Does having Joe Biden as his running mate make you more likely to vote for Barack Obama in November, less likely, or will it not have much effect on your vote?

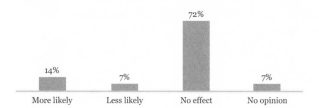

USA Today/Gallup poll, Aug. 23, 2008
Based on registered voters

- A net 25% of voters were more likely to vote for Bill Clinton in 1992 on account of Al Gore (33% more likely and 8% less likely).

The only recent vice presidential choices to spark less voter reaction than Biden were Dick Cheney in 2000 (net 4%, with 14% more likely and 10% less likely) and Dan Quayle in 1988 (net score of 0, with 10% more likely and 10% less likely).

It should be noted that all of these poll figures represent initial public reaction to new vice presidential selections. Voters' reactions to Biden could well change as the campaign progresses.

The only vice presidential nominee who appeared to be an actual drag on a presidential ticket around convention time was Quayle in August 1992 (then the sitting vice president), when 6% of voters said they were more likely to vote for Bush because of Quayle and 25% were less likely—a 19-point *negative* differential.

Biden Not Widely Known

One possible reason for Biden's minimal impact on voter support for Obama today is that more than half of U.S. voters have no views of the veteran U.S. senator from Delaware, either not knowing enough about him to express an opinion or saying they have never heard of him. On this basis, Biden looks very much like Lieberman in 2000.

Favorability Ratings of Joe Biden Today vs. Joe Lieberman in 2000

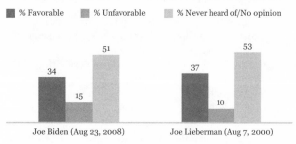

Based on registered voters

Biden Is Seen as "Qualified"

Biden does pass a basic public opinion hurdle in terms of being seen as qualified to serve as president. His 57% "qualified" score is similar to the vice presidential choices from the last three elections, and clearly separates him from the dreaded category occupied by Dan Quayle, the only recent vice presidential selection whom a majority of Americans said was "not qualified."

Perceptions of Vice Presidential Candidates' Ability to Serve as President if It Becomes Necessary

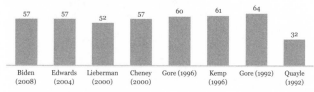

Based on registered voters

More generally, 16% of voters consider Biden an "excellent" choice for vice president, 31% a "pretty good" choice, 21% "only fair," and 12% "poor." The total of 47% viewing him as excellent or pretty good is lower than the immediate post-vice-presidential-announcement ratings of Edwards in 2004, and Lieberman and Cheney in 2000—in part because of the high percentage (20%) with no opinion of the Biden choice.

Ratings of Vice-Presidential Selections as Excellent or Pretty Good

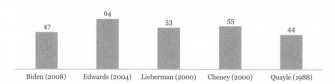

Based on registered voters

With Obama consistently getting a lower share of support from Democrats than John McCain gets from Republicans, Biden's contribution to the ticket might be most important in terms of his ability to bring in more of the traditional Democratic base.

Democrats' initial reaction to Biden is positive, but not extraordinarily so. Half of Democrats say they have a favorable view of Biden (with nearly half having no opinion), 64% think he is an excellent or pretty good choice for vice president, and 70% think he is qualified to be president. Perhaps most importantly, 21% say they are more likely to vote for Obama as a result of Biden's presence on the ticket, and only 2% say less likely. Is that enough to elevate Obama's numbers within the party? It's unclear, but it compares with a net 34% of Democrats more likely to vote for Kerry on the basis of Edwards' being selected in 2004, and a net 23% of Democrats more likely to vote for Gore because of Lieberman.

Bottom Line

One approach to picking a vice president is to "do no harm." Perhaps with Quayle's and his father's unsuccessful 1992 re-election campaign in mind, George W. Bush was quoted in 2000 as saying, "You want ... somebody who's not going to hurt you."

Obama's own campaign manager recently echoed this sentiment, saying, "Whether someone helps win you an election, I think, is kind of a side benefit. You certainly want to pick someone who doesn't hurt you."

The initial evidence is that Biden won't hurt Obama in the election, but with only 14% of voters saying they are more likely to vote for the ticket with Biden on it, and 7% less likely, he is not positioned at this point to help Obama much either.

Survey Methods

Results are based on telephone interviews with 876 registered voters, aged 18 and older, conducted Aug. 23, 2008. For results based on the total sample of national adults, one can say with 95% confidence that the maximum margin of sampling error is ±4 percentage points.

Interviews are conducted with respondents on land-line telephones (for respondents with a land-line telephone) and cellular phones (for respondents who are cell-phone only).

Polls conducted entirely in one day, such as this one, are subject to additional error or bias not found in polls conducted over several days.

In addition to sampling error, question wording and practical difficulties in conducting surveys can introduce error or bias into the findings of public opinion polls.

August 25, 2008

OBAMA HOLDS LEAD OVER MCCAIN ON TOP ISSUE OF ECONOMY

Voters give McCain edge on international issues

by Jeffrey M. Jones, Gallup Poll Managing Editor

As the Democratic National Convention gets underway, voters, by a 52% to 40% margin, believe Barack Obama is better able than John McCain to handle the economy. The economy easily tops the list when voters are asked which of five issues will be most important to their vote for president.

If you had to choose, which of the following issues will be most important to your vote for president -- [ROTATED: the economy, terrorism, the situation in Iraq, health care, energy, including gas prices], or some other issue?

Based on registered voters

■ % Choosing as most important issue

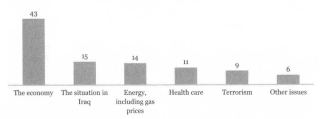

Aug 21-23 USA Today/Gallup Poll

Obama's 12 percentage point advantage over McCain on the economy marks a significant improvement from early February, when Gallup last asked this question. At that time, his advantage was 46% to 43%. More recently, Gallup asked slightly different questions about the candidates' economic aptitude, and found Obama faring significantly better than McCain in those polls as well.

At a broad level, voters clearly see the candidates as having opposing areas of strength. They give Obama the advantage on each of the four domestic issues tested in the poll, and McCain the advantage on all three international issues.

Obama's biggest issue advantage versus McCain comes with regard to health care policy (56% to 34%), a traditionally strong issue for the Democratic Party.

The candidates have spent much time on the campaign trail discussing the nation's energy challenges and their ideas for solving them, and so far registered voters rate Obama as better able to handle the issue, 51% to 40%.

Obama only holds a slight edge on taxes, 47% to 44%.

Regardless of which presidential candidate you support, please tell me if you think Barack Obama or John McCain would better handle each of the following issues. How about -- [RANDOM ORDER]?

Based on registered voters

■ % Obama   ▪ % McCain

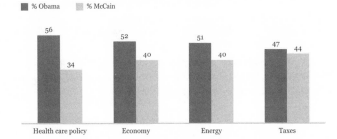

Aug 21-23 USA Today/Gallup Poll

McCain leads Obama by double-digits on the three international issues tested, with the largest margin a 24-point advantage in reference to terrorism.

The presumptive Republican nominee also outpolls Obama on U.S. policy toward Russia, 52% to 35%. This issue has emerged in the campaign given Russia's recent invasion of U.S. ally and former Soviet republic Georgia, a move the United States government strongly opposed. This international flare up may be one reason that McCain has pulled closer to Obama in presidential trial heat polls in recent days.

Regardless of which presidential candidate you support, please tell me if you think Barack Obama or John McCain would better handle each of the following issues. How about -- [RANDOM ORDER]?

Based on registered voters

■ % Obama   ▪ % McCain

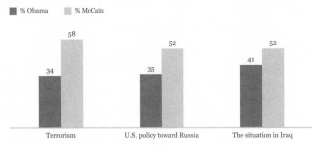

Aug 21-23 USA Today/Gallup Poll

Despite giving McCain a clear advantage on international issues, a slim majority of voters, 53%, say Obama can handle the responsibilities of commander in chief. That pales in comparison to the 80% who believe McCain is up to the role, but is an important threshold for Obama given his relatively thin experience in dealing with international issues. Even if voters believe Obama is better able to address the economy, they could conceivably disqualify him for the job if they do not believe he is capable of handling the president's international responsibilities. Obama's selection of Sen. Joe Biden as his vice presidential running mate adds significant expertise on foreign policy and national defense to the Democratic ticket.

Obama's perceptual advantage over McCain in terms of handling the economy is a major plus for the Democrat's campaign. However, even with that advantage the overall presidential race remains close, which could reflect McCain's superior performance on international issues and concerns about Obama's lack of experience.

Obama may never overtake McCain in terms of being perceived as better able to handle international issues, so the Illinois senator's test may be in convincing voters he is competent to deal with such issues. Currently, a slim majority of voters believe he is, and a key goal for his acceptance speech on Thursday will be to maintain or expand that level while retaining his perceptual advantage over McCain on voters' top issue of the economy.

Meanwhile, McCain may not need to burnish his international credentials during the Republican convention, but a key for him is to convince voters he can do as well or better than Obama on the economy.

Survey Methods

Results are based on telephone interviews with 923 registered voters, aged 18 and older, conducted Aug. 21-23, 2008. For results based on the total sample of national adults, one can say with 95% confidence that the maximum margin of sampling error is ±4 percentage points.

Interviews are conducted with respondents on land-line telephones (for respondents with a land-line telephone) and cellular phones (for respondents who are cell-phone only).

In addition to sampling error, question wording and practical difficulties in conducting surveys can introduce error or bias into the findings of public opinion polls.

Although Americans are more likely to say Obama, rather than McCain, will raise their taxes, they favor Obama as the candidate better able to handle taxes by 48% to 43%. In part, this may be because a majority of Americans see Obama's policies as benefiting the middle class and the poor the most, while a majority see McCain's policies as benefiting the wealthy. In turn, this could work against Mitt Romney, who has a Wall Street background, in the vice presidential stakes since McCain may want to avoid reinforcing this "favoring the wealthy" perception.

It is also possible that McCain's record of voting against the Bush tax cuts (although he now supports extending them) and his reputation as a "maverick" have some Americans believing—contrary to what might be expected with a Republican in the White House—he will raise federal income taxes if elected. In this regard, the fact that about one in three independents see a tax increase in a McCain presidency is something that might be of concern to the Republicans in the weeks ahead. In fact, how the candidates handle the tax issue in a time of recession may give voters significant insight into the fundamental economic policies of each candidate.

Survey Methods

Results are based on telephone interviews with 1,023 national adults, aged 18 and older and employed full- or part-time, conducted Aug. 21-23, 2008. For results based on the sample of employed adults, one can say with 95% confidence that the maximum margin of sampling error is ±3 percentage points.

Interviews are conducted with respondents on land-line telephones (for respondents with a land-line telephone) and cellular phones (for respondents who are cell-phone only).

In addition to sampling error, question wording and practical difficulties in conducting surveys can introduce error or bias into the findings of public opinion polls.

August 26, 2008

HALF OF AMERICANS EXPECT OBAMA TO RAISE THEIR TAXES

One-third expect a federal income tax increase in a McCain presidency

by Dennis Jacobe, Gallup Poll Chief Economist

Fifty-three percent of Americans expect their federal income taxes to increase if Barack Obama is elected president, while 34% think they would increase if John McCain gets the job—both of which are higher than expectations were for their counterparts in the 2004 election.

If [Barack Obama/John McCain] is elected president, do you think your federal income taxes would increase, decrease, or remain the same?

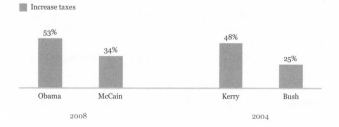

August 26, 2008

HILLARY'S STOCK STILL HIGH AMONG DEMOCRATS

Eighty percent have favorable opinion of her

by Jeffrey M. Jones, Gallup Poll Managing Editor

The intense battle for the Democratic nomination between Hillary Clinton and Barack Obama seems to have done little to diminish Democrats' affinity for the New York senator. Eighty percent of Democrats have a favorable opinion of her, compared to 74% just before Obama clinched the presidential nomination in early June and 82% before the primaries began, when she still rated as a strong front-runner for the nomination. Her favorable rating among all Americans is 54%, the most positive since just after she officially announced her candidacy in early 2007.

Obama rates above Clinton on basic favorability—among both the general public (63%) and the Democratic rank-and-file (86%). Obama has typically rated higher than Clinton among the general public since the presidential primaries got under way in January.

But his higher favorable rating among Democrats is a more recent development. Clinton typically had higher favorable ratings than Obama throughout this presidential campaign season, but that to a large degree

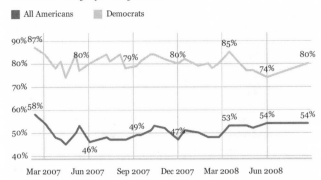

Favorable Ratings of Hillary Clinton

■ All Americans   ■ Democrats

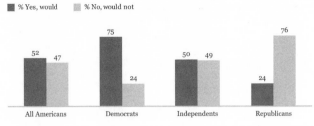

Would you like to see Hillary Clinton run for president again someday, or not?

■ % Yes, would   ■ % No, would not

USA Today/Gallup poll, Aug. 21-23, 2008

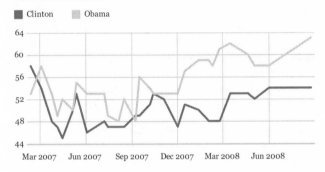

Favorable Ratings of Hillary Clinton and Barack Obama

Based on national adults

■ Clinton   ■ Obama

reflected Democrats' greater familiarity with Clinton than Obama (until recently, a substantial minority of Democrats did not have an opinion of Obama), rather than a more negative evaluation of Obama.

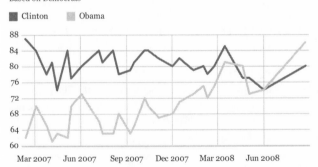

Favorable Ratings of Hillary Clinton and Barack Obama

Based on Democrats

■ Clinton   ■ Obama

In any case, Democrats still see a future for Clinton in the Democratic Party. Seventy-nine percent want her to be a major national spokesperson for the party over the next four years as she completes her second term in the U.S. Senate. Just 18% of Democrats would prefer she have a less prominent role within the party.

Additionally, 75% of Democrats say they would like to see Clinton run for president again someday. Overall, Americans are not as high on a second Clinton presidential bid, with 52% in favor. That includes 50% of independents and only 24% of Republicans.

Implications

Obama and Clinton are doing their best to heal any remaining wounds within the Democratic Party from their protracted nomina-

tion battle. In general, Democrats still view Clinton positively, and welcome a prominent role for her within the party in the future.

While some Clinton supporters have yet to fall in line and support Obama for president, for the most part they have a positive opinion of Obama (as well as a largely negative view of McCain). So it is still not out of the question that they will come home by Election Day. But it is important to note that unifying the party is not a challenge unique to the Democratic Party, as many Republican supporters who are not enthusiastic about McCain have yet to return to the GOP fold.

Survey Methods

Results are based on telephone interviews with 1,023 national adults, aged 18 and older, conducted Aug. 21-23, 2008. For results based on the total sample of national adults, one can say with 95% confidence that the maximum margin of sampling error is ±3 percentage points.

For results based on the sample of 341 Democrats, the maximum margin of sampling error is ±6 percentage points.

Interviews are conducted with respondents on land-line telephones (for respondents with a land-line telephone) and cellular phones (for respondents who are cell-phone only).

In addition to sampling error, question wording and practical difficulties in conducting surveys can introduce error or bias into the findings of public opinion polls.

August 27, 2008
BILL CLINTON'S IMAGE HAS TAKEN HIT; LEGACY LARGELY INTACT
Roughly half say he will go down in history as above-average president

by Jeffrey M. Jones, Gallup Poll Managing Editor

Former President Bill Clinton's controversial remarks against Barack Obama earlier this year were a major part of the 2008 campaign narrative. Some political observers wondered whether Clinton was harming his legacy while campaigning on his wife's behalf. The latest *USA Today/*Gallup poll suggests that is not the case. Nearly half of Americans believe history will regard Clinton as an outstanding or an above-average president, little changed from the last pre-campaign rating and his most positive review to date.

Clinton will address the Democratic National Convention Wednesday night. He and Obama have had an uneasy relationship, in part because of remarks Clinton made against the Illinois senator while campaigning for Hillary Clinton. This included using the word

How do you think Bill Clinton will go down in history -- as an outstanding president, above average, average, below average, or poor president?

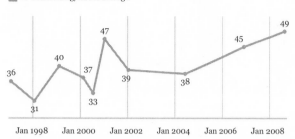

■ % Outstanding/Above average

"fairy tale" in reference to Obama's campaign and apparently dismissing Obama's South Carolina primary victory by reminding people that Jesse Jackson had also won the state's primary in 1984 and 1988.

In the last pre-campaign reading, from December 2006, 45% of Americans said Clinton would go down in history as an outstanding or above-average president; with 49% saying that today, the public does not believe his legacy has been damaged.

Notably, Obama supporters are largely positive when assessing Bill Clinton's historical significance. Among Democrats and Democratic-leaning independents who say they supported Obama in the primaries, 60% say Clinton will be regarded as an outstanding or above-average president. That pales in comparison to the 80% above-average or better ratings from Democrats who supported Hilary Clinton during the primaries, but is little different from the 65% of all Democrats in 2006 who said Bill Clinton would get a favorable historical review.

Even though perceptions of his historical legacy have not suffered, there has been some short-term damage to the former president's image during the last several months. Currently, 52% of Americans say they have a favorable opinion of him. He has averaged just a 51% favorable rating in four 2008 readings, all of which were taken after Clinton's most controversial remarks. That compares with an average 60% favorable score last year.

Bill Clinton Favorable Ratings, 2007-2008

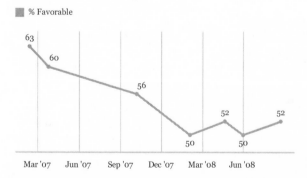

■ % Favorable

The poll provides some suggestive evidence that the decline may chiefly result from more negative assessments from Obama supporters. In the October 2007 poll—the last reading before the primaries began—87% of all Democrats and 24% of all Republicans rated Clinton favorably. In the latest poll, Clinton's favorable rating remains 24% among Republicans but has declined to 74% among Democrats.

Bill Clinton Favorable Ratings, by Political Party

■ % Favorable, Oct 2007   ■ % Favorable, Aug 2008

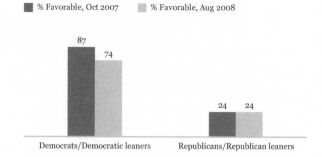

But when Democrats in the current poll are subdivided as to their candidate of choice in the primaries, Obama backers give Bill Clinton an average 64% favorable score, compared with 90% among Hillary Clinton supporters.

Survey Methods

Results are based on telephone interviews with 1,023 national adults, aged 18 and older, conducted Aug. 21-23, 2008. For results based on the total sample of national adults, one can say with 95% confidence that the maximum margin of sampling error is ±3 percentage points.

Interviews are conducted with respondents on land-line telephones (for respondents with a land-line telephone) and cellular phones (for respondents who are cell-phone only).

In addition to sampling error, question wording and practical difficulties in conducting surveys can introduce error or bias into the findings of public opinion polls.

August 28, 2008

HILLARY CLINTON'S SPEECH WELL-RECEIVED
More than half of Americans rate it as excellent or good

by Jeffrey M. Jones, Gallup Poll Managing Editor

Fifty-two percent of Americans—and 83% of those who tuned in—give Hillary Clinton's Tuesday night speech at the Democratic National Convention a positive review.

From what you have heard or read, how would you rate Hillary Clinton's speech at the Democratic Convention on Tuesday night, as -- excellent, good, just okay, poor, or terrible?

■ % Excellent/Good   ■ % Just OK   ■ % Poor/Terrible   ■ % Did not see/No opinion

USA Today/Gallup poll, Aug. 27, 2008

These results are based on a *USA Today*/Gallup poll conducted Wednesday, Aug. 27, the day after Clinton's prime-time speech.

The speech was one of many attempts by the Clinton and Obama campaigns to unite the Democratic Party behind Obama's presidential candidacy after the long and sometimes acrimonious nomination campaign between the junior senators from Illinois and New York.

Hillary Clinton's speech scored better than the speech Bill Clinton gave at the 2000 Democratic National Convention several months before he would complete his presidential term. Forty-four percent of Americans rated that speech either excellent or good. The former president spoke again Wednesday night at this year's Democratic Convention, too late to be evaluated in interviewing conducted the same night.

As would be expected, Democrats were especially positive about Hillary Clinton's Tuesday night address, with 69% rating it positively. But close to half of Republicans, 45%, also rated it positively.

The high 83% positive rating of the speech among those who watched it is in part due to the partisan nature of the audience. The poll estimates that 49% of those who watched the Clinton speech were Democrats, 22% were Republicans, and the remaining 28% were independents. Ninety-four percent of Democrats who watched the speech rated it positively, as did solid majorities of the Republicans and independents who tuned in.

Survey Methods

Results are based on telephone interviews with 1,023 national adults, aged 18 and older, conducted Aug. 27, 2008. For results based on the total sample of national adults, one can say with 95% confidence that the maximum margin of sampling error is ±3 percentage points.

Interviews are conducted with respondents on land-line telephones (for respondents with a land-line telephone) and cellular phones (for respondents who are cell-phone only).

In addition to sampling error, question wording and practical difficulties in conducting surveys can introduce error or bias into the findings of public opinion polls.

Polls conducted entirely in one day, such as this one, are subject to additional error or bias not found in polls conducted over several days.

August 28, 2008
OBAMA STILL LAGS MCCAIN AS LEADER, COMMANDER IN CHIEF
Obama's strengths lie in domestic, softer issues

by Frank Newport, Gallup Poll Editor in Chief

John McCain has an edge over Barack Obama in the public's eyes as a strong and decisive leader, and McCain is also significantly more likely to be viewed as able to handle the job of commander in chief. These facts underscore an area of weakness for Obama that McCain has attempted to exploit in recent campaign ads, and that Obama could in theory fruitfully address in his high-visibility acceptance speech at the Democratic National Convention Thursday night.

The latest *USA Today*/Gallup poll, conducted Aug. 21-23, asked Americans to indicate whether a list of characteristics and qualities best fit Obama or McCain.

Obama beats McCain by a 7-point or larger margin on four dimensions: caring about people's needs, the ability to work well with both parties to get things done, being independent, and sharing

Next, thinking about the following characteristics and qualities, please say whether you think each one applies more to Barack Obama or more to John McCain. How about -- ?

USA Today/Gallup poll, Aug. 21-23, 2008

	% Obama	% McCain	Advantage (pct. pts.)
Cares about the needs of people like you	53	33	Obama +20
Would work well with both parties to get things done in Washington	51	38	Obama +13
Is independent in his thoughts and actions	50	37	Obama +13
Shares your values	47	40	Obama +7
Puts the country's interests ahead of his own political interests	44	42	Obama +2
Is honest and trustworthy	39	39	EVEN
Can manage the government effectively	43	44	McCain +1
Is a strong and decisive leader	40	48	McCain +8

respondents' values. The two are essentially tied in perceptions that they put the country's interests ahead of their own, that they are honest, and that they are able to manage government effectively.

McCain is significantly ahead on a single, but important, dimension: "is a strong and decisive leader." Not coincidentally, this has been a key focus in recent McCain attack ads against Obama. (Despite the ads, there has been almost no change since mid-June in perceptions of who is the better leader.)

A separate set of questions included in the recent poll asked respondents to indicate whether they believe Obama and McCain could "handle the responsibilities of commander in chief of the military."

Do you think -- [Barack Obama/John McCain] -- can -- or cannot -- handle the responsibilities of commander in chief of the military?

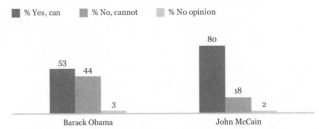

USA Today/Gallup poll, Aug. 21-23, 2008

Obama clearly operates at a decided perceptual deficit compared to McCain on this dimension. Eighty percent of Americans say McCain can handle the responsibilities of being commander in chief, compared to 53% for Obama. These views have not changed throughout the summer.

McCain's edge almost certainly reflects in part that he was a graduate of the U.S. Naval Academy and an officer in the U.S. Navy for decades, while Obama did not serve in the military. It may also reflect the fact that McCain is older, has more experience in the U.S. Senate and federal government, and has taken a leading role in the Senate in many foreign policy issues, most notably the Iraq war. If these are the major underlying facts informing Americans' opinions about the candidates, then it is unclear to what extent Obama's rhetoric or McCain's campaign ads could change the existing perceptions.

But the trend lines from four years ago suggest that the views of the public on this dimension can change. George W. Bush and John Kerry scored similarly on the commander-in-chief item in two polls conducted in June and late July/early August 2004. But from September on, after the two conventions and particularly the now-famous

"Swift Boat" attacks on Kerry, Bush had a significant advantage on the commander-in-chief dimension.

Implications

A previous Gallup analysis reviewed data showing that Obama has the edge over McCain in the eyes of Americans on domestic issues such as the economy, healthcare, and energy, while McCain does better on international issues such as terrorism, the situation in Russia, and Iraq.

Coupled with the data reviewed here on personal characteristics and qualities, it is clear that Obama has a cluster of strengths relating to "soft" dimensions such as caring and values, and domestic issues. McCain has a "harder" image, with credit for being a strong leader and potential commander in chief, and being able to handle international issues. This positioning of the two candidates is not unusual in a broad sense, and reflects broad Republican versus Democratic strengths in recent elections (although as noted, Kerry for a period of time early in the 2004 campaign was able to tie Bush on the commander-in-chief dimension).

There are as many theories about what Obama "needs to do" in his acceptance speech Thursday night at Denver's Invesco Field at Mile High as there are pundits or observers' opinions. Obama's speech will no doubt end up touching on a wide variety of issues, themes, and positions. If the speech does not focus on changing some Americans' minds on Obama's leadership and commander in chief abilities, however, McCain will continue to have the opportunity to exploit a perceived weakness on Obama's part between now and Nov. 4.

Survey Methods

Results are based on telephone interviews with 1,023 national adults, aged 18 and older, conducted Aug 21-23, 2008. For results based on the total sample of national adults, one can say with 95% confidence that the maximum margin of sampling error is ±3 percentage points.

Interviews are conducted with respondents on land-line telephones (for respondents with a land-line telephone) and cellular phones (for respondents who are cell-phone only).

In addition to sampling error, question wording and practical difficulties in conducting surveys can introduce error or bias into the findings of public opinion polls.

August 29, 2008

CAN SARAH PALIN APPEAL TO WHITE, FEMALE INDEPENDENTS?

Biggest gender gap is among those who are white and independent

by Frank Newport, Gallup Poll Editor in Chief

John McCain's surprise selection of Alaska Gov. Sarah Palin as his vice presidential running mate raises again the issue of gender in presidential politics. McCain, as is typical of Republican presidential candidates, does significantly less well among women than among men, and an analysis of more than 25,000 Gallup Poll Daily tracking interviews in August shows that the biggest gender gap is among whites who are independents.

Here are the key points relating to gender and presidential politics:

1. Among all registered voters Gallup has interviewed in August (through Aug. 28), McCain wins over Obama by a 6-point, 48% to 42% margin among men, while Obama wins among women by a 10-point, 49% to 39% margin. The swing in the margin of support for the two candidates between genders is thus 16 points.

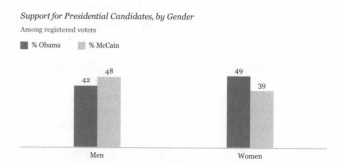

Support for Presidential Candidates, by Gender
Among registered voters

2. Most of this gender gap is evident among whites; there is little difference by gender in candidate support among blacks or Hispanics.

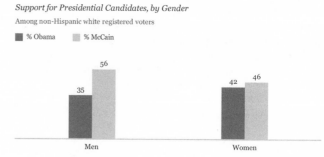

Support for Presidential Candidates, by Gender
Among non-Hispanic white registered voters

Black registered voters very strongly support Obama over McCain regardless of gender. Hispanics also support Obama, although at a lower level, but there is also little meaningful difference by gender. Among (non-Hispanic) whites, however, it's a different story. White men favor McCain by 21 points, while white women support McCain by a much smaller 4 points. In other words, there is a 17-point swing by gender in candidate support among whites.

3. Among whites, most of the gender difference can be narrowed down to differences within independents.

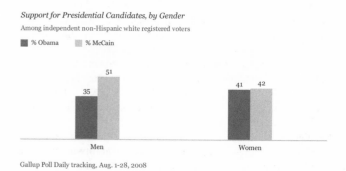

Support for Presidential Candidates, by Gender
Among independent non-Hispanic white registered voters

White Republicans overwhelmingly support McCain over Obama, and that doesn't differ meaningfully by gender. White Democrats overwhelmingly support Obama, and that too doesn't vary by gender. But there is a big swing in support by gender among independents—individuals who in response to an initial party identification question say they do not identify with either party. White male independents go strongly for McCain, by a 16-point margin, while white female independents are evenly divided, 41% for Obama and 42% for McCain. This represents a 15-point swing by gender in candidate support.

Implications

There is a significant gender gap in American presidential politics today, but it is confined for the most part to white voters who are politically independent. There is very little difference in presidential vote choice by gender among blacks and Hispanics, and among whites who are Republican or Democratic in their political identification.

Many assume that McCain's choice of a female running mate could increase his chances among female voters. If that is the case, it would appear that white independent women—who are currently split almost down the middle in terms of their candidate support—would be most susceptible to changing sides, given the strongly skewed (and gender-neutral) existing vote choice among blacks, Hispanics, and loyal partisans.

Additionally, of course, McCain's selection may have been designed as much to help reinforce loyalty from his conservative Republican base as it was to change voters' minds. If that was the case, it would be Gov. Palin's conservative positions on issues—including abortion, same-sex marriage, gun control, and taxes—more than her gender that would be the operative factor.

Survey Methods

Results are based on telephone interviews with 25,007 registered voters, aged 18 and older, conducted Aug. 1-28, 2008 as part of the Gallup Poll Daily tracking program. For results based on the total sample of national adults, one can say with 95% confidence that the maximum margin of sampling error is ±1 percentage point.

Interviews are conducted with respondents on land-line telephones (for respondents with a land-line telephone) and cellular phones (for respondents who are cell-phone only).

In addition to sampling error, question wording and practical difficulties in conducting surveys can introduce error or bias into the findings of public opinion polls.

August 29, 2008

U.S. CONSUMER PESSIMISM MODERATING IN BATTLEGROUND STATES

But 79% of "purple state" consumers still believe the economy is getting worse

by Dennis Jacobe, Gallup Poll Chief Economist

Consumer pessimism moderated in August in the key battleground or "purple" states, as well as in "red" and "blue" states. The percentage of consumers saying the economy is "getting worse"

declined by 7 to 8 points from July in each of these groupings of states, and now essentially matches where things were in January.

Percentage Saying Economy Is Getting Worse

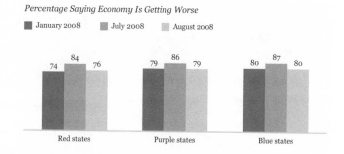

Consumer Pessimism Moderating Across the Political Landscape

On Tuesday, the Conference Board surprised many economists by announcing that consumer confidence improved more than economists had anticipated during August. As Gallup has been reporting over the past several weeks, consumer pessimism has moderated in response to the decline in gas prices since mid-July. Significantly, this easing in the degree of consumer pessimism has taken place across the political landscape.

As the percentage of consumers saying the economy is getting worse has declined in the purple, red, and blue states since July, so has the percentage rating the economy "poor." In the battleground states, the percentage of consumers rating the economy "poor" fell to 42% in August from 50% in July, but remains significantly higher than the 30% who provided this rating in January. Although consumers in red states are least likely—and those in the blue states are most likely—to rate the economy as poor, once again, the overall pattern is essentially the same as the "getting worse" ratings: the August numbers for all three state groups show a decrease from July (though they are up from January's readings).

Percent Rating Economy Poor

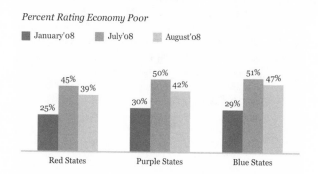

Commentary

On Wednesday, the Commerce Department reported that the U.S. economy grew at a 3.3% annual rate during the second quarter—far above the 1.9% originally estimated, and largely the result of stronger U.S. exports creating a smaller trade deficit. This was in addition to a surprisingly good durable goods report the same day. Add in the increase in consumer confidence, and the bulls on Wall Street began to repeat their assertions that the U.S. economy isn't really that bad.

Before the Republicans jump on this bandwagon politically, they would do well to consider consumers' views of the economy, particularly in the battleground states. The percentage of purple-state consumers thinking the economy is getting worse may be down 7 percentage points from July, but even after this improvement, essentially 8 in 10 consumers in those states are pessimistic about the direction of the economy.

Even more importantly, a similar decline of 8 points in the number of consumers rating the economy "poor" in the battleground states leaves 42% of purple-state consumers giving this rating—12 points higher than the 30% who held this view in January. And, while a higher percentage of blue-state consumers (47%) give the economy poor ratings, even in the red states, 39% of consumers share this view.

With a Republican in the White House, the party and its presidential candidate may be tempted to use the recent rays of sunshine in the economic data to argue that wise international free-trade policies are keeping the U.S. economy much stronger than is generally perceived. And, of course, voter perceptions of the economy may improve even more between now and November. But, as George H.W. Bush's campaign learned in 1992, there can be problems with such an approach. Even if McCain ends up being prescient by saying the economy has turned a corner and is getting better, he risks appearing out of touch with Main Street if his campaign attempts to paint too rosy an economic picture even as the overwhelming majority of Americans still believe the economy is getting worse.

In politics as well as economics, perceptions are often reality. In this case, the reality is that most battleground consumers continue to see the economy going in the wrong direction and are looking for leadership to alter that course. For McCain's sake, they had better not perceive that "he doesn't get it."

Survey Methods

Gallup is interviewing no fewer than 1,000 U.S. adults nationwide each day during 2008. The economic questions analyzed in this report are asked of a random half-sample of respondents each day. The results reported here are based on combined data of more than 8,000 interviews in January, July, and August. For results based on these samples, the maximum margin of sampling error is ±1 percentage point. The margins of error for subgroups are higher.

Interviews are conducted with respondents on land-line telephones (for respondents with a land-line telephone) and cellular phones (for respondents who are cell-phone only).

In addition to sampling error, question wording and practical difficulties in conducting surveys can introduce error or bias into the findings of public opinion polls.

August 30, 2008
OBAMA ACCEPTANCE SPEECH GETS HIGH MARKS FROM PUBLIC
Overall reaction to Denver convention is typical, but doesn't match 1992

by Jeffrey M. Jones, Gallup Poll Managing Editor

Fifty-eight percent of Americans give Barack Obama's speech a positive review, including 35% who describe it as "excellent." Both marks surpass those given to the 2000 and 2004 presidential candidates, with the excellent ratings for Obama's speech 10 percentage points higher than any other recent candidate has received.

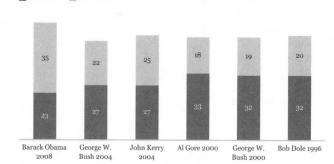

From what you have heard or read, how would you rate Barack Obama's acceptance speech at the Democratic Convention on Thursday night, as -- excellent, good, just okay, poor, or terrible?

■ % Good   ■ % Excellent

Barack Obama 2008	George W. Bush 2004	John Kerry 2004	Al Gore 2000	George W. Bush 2000	Bob Dole 1996
35	22	25	18	19	20
23	27	27	33	32	32

Note: Gallup did not measure reaction to Bill Clinton's 1996 convention speech

These results are based on a one-night *USA Today*/Gallup poll conducted Aug. 29, the night following Obama's acceptance speech.

Obama is widely praised for his rhetorical skills, so perhaps his positive reviews are not surprising. His speech was rated more positively by Americans than Hillary Clinton's Tuesday night convention speech, which also was highly regarded by the public.

Democrats give Obama's speech rave reviews, with 62% saying it was an excellent speech and another 21% describing it as good. A majority of independents rate Obama's speech as either excellent (27%) or good (25%), but Republicans were less impressed (12% excellent and 25% good).

In addition to measuring reaction to Obama's speech, the poll attempted to assess the impact of the convention more broadly on the public. Forty-three percent of Americans say they are more likely to vote for Obama as a result of what they saw or read about the convention; 29% say they are less likely.

Those ratings are typical of what Gallup has measured for most conventions since 1984. The 1992 Democratic convention stands out above all others with 60% saying that convention made them more likely to vote for Bill Clinton. The 1988 Democratic convention that nominated Michael Dukakis also got above-average ratings.

Does what you saw or read of this week's Democratic National Convention in Denver make you more likely or less likely to vote for Barack Obama?

	More likely	Less likely	No difference (vol.)	No opinion
2008 Aug 29	43	29	19	8
Prior conventions				
Post-GOP 2004	41	38	15	6
Post-Dem. 2004	44	30	18	8
Post-Dem. 2000	43	28	19	10
Post-GOP 2000	44	27	15	14
Post-Dem. 1996	44	29	19	8
Post-GOP 1996	45	34	13	8
Post-Dem. 1992	60	15	17	8
Post-GOP 1988	43	27	16	14
Post-Dem. 1988	56	21	9	14
Post-Dem. 1984	45	29	12	14

Note: Gallup did not measure reaction to the 1984 and 1992 GOP conventions

Obama's speech produced record TV ratings. More generally, six in 10 Americans say they watched a "great deal" or "some" of the convention. That is similar to reports from the 2004 conventions, but higher than what Gallup found for prior conventions.

How much, if any, of the Democratic convention did you watch on T.V. this week -- none of it, very little, some of it, or a great deal?

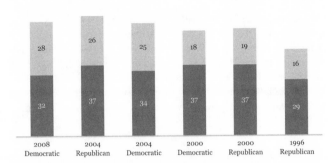

Note: Gallup did not measure viewership of the 1996 Democratic convention

Does having Sarah Palin as his running mate make you more likely to vote for John McCain in November, less likely, or will it not have much effect on your vote?

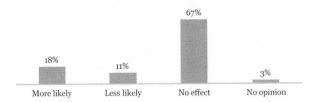

USA Today/Gallup poll, Aug. 29, 2008
Based on registered voters

Perceptions of Vice Presidential Candidates' Ability to Serve as President if It Becomes Necessary

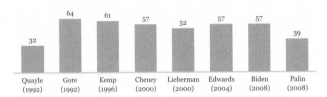

Based on registered voters

Survey Methods

Results are based on telephone interviews with 1,016 national adults, aged 18 and older, conducted Aug. 29, 2008. For results based on the total sample of national adults, one can say with 95% confidence that the maximum margin of sampling error is ±3 percentage points.

Polls conducted entirely in one day, such as this one, are subject to additional error or bias not found in polls conducted over several days.

Interviews are conducted with respondents on land-line telephones (for respondents with a land-line telephone) and cellular phones (for respondents who are cell-phone only).

In addition to sampling error, question wording and practical difficulties in conducting surveys can introduce error or bias into the findings of public opinion polls.

August 30, 2008
PALIN UNKNOWN TO MOST AMERICANS
Immediate reaction on par with reaction to Biden

by Frank Newport, Gallup Poll Editor in Chief

The initial reaction of the American public to John McCain's surprise selection of Alaska Gov. Sarah Palin as his running mate is muted, similar to the reaction of Joe Biden being named Barack Obama's running mate.

Perhaps the most significant finding about Palin in the Aug. 29 *USA Today*/Gallup poll is that she is largely unknown to most Americans. A substantial majority of Americans don't know enough about her yet to have an opinion, and her name identification is lower than that of any other recent vice presidential candidate when measured immediately after selection. Among those who do know her, her image is significantly more positive than negative, and her 3-to-1 positive-to-negative ratio is better than the 2-to-1 ratio measured for Biden a week ago.

A large majority say that at this point her selection will not have an impact on their presidential vote either way. However, almost as many Americans say that she is not qualified to serve as president as say she is qualified, giving her a more negative reading on this measure than most other recent vice presidential selectees, with the exception of Dan Quayle.

The sections that follow outline the data measured in *USA Today*/Gallup interviewing conducted Friday, August 29.

1. Overall Reaction to Palin's Selection Similar to Biden Selection

Americans' overall reaction to the McCain selection of Sarah Palin as his vice presidential running mate is very similar to last week's reaction to Obama's selection of Biden.

A little less than half of Americans rate the selection of Palin as excellent or pretty good, while 37% rate it as only fair or poor (the rest have no opinion). Gallup's measure of reaction to Biden's selection on August 23 was only slightly different, even though many more Americans were familiar with the Delaware senator when he was named.

In turn, the Palin and Biden assessments are well below the positive reaction the public had to John Kerry's selection of John Edwards in 2004, and slightly less positive than Al Gore's selection of Joe Lieberman and George W. Bush's selection of Dick Cheney in 2000. All recent VP selections are more positive compared to George H. W. Bush's selection of Quayle in 1988, the only selection to be reviewed more negatively than positively by the public.

As was the case for Biden a week ago and all vice presidential selections of the last two decades, the substantial majority of Americans say that the selection of Palin will not have much impact on their vote for president this year.

Of those who do have a reaction, the impact is more positive than negative for both Palin and Biden, though the reaction to Palin's selection is the more positive of the two, by a modest margin.

These reactions to the 2008 vice presidential running mates are similar to those that greeted both 2000 vice presidential selections, but slightly less positive than other recent selections such as Edwards in 2004, Jack Kemp in 1996, Gore in 1992, and Lloyd Bentsen in 1988.

How would you rate [John McCain's] choice of [Sarah Palin] for vice president?

Based on registered voters

	Interview dates	Excellent/ Pretty good	Only fair/ Poor	No opinion
		%	%	%
2008				
McCain-Palin	Aug 29, 2008	46	37	17
Obama-Biden	Aug 23, 2008	47	33	20
2004				
Kerry-Edwards	Jul 6, 2004	64	28	8
2000				
Gore-Lieberman	Aug 7, 2000	53	28	19
Bush-Cheney	Jul 24, 2000	55	34	11
1988				
Bush-Quayle	Aug 19-21, 1988*	44	52	4

* Poll of likely voters by Louis Harris and Associates

Does having [Sarah Palin] as his running mate make you more likely to vote for [John McCain] in November, less likely, or will it not have much effect on your vote?

Based on registered voters

	Interview dates	More likely	Less likely	No effect/ No opinion
		%	%	%
2008				
McCain-Palin	Aug 29, 2008	18	11	70
Obama-Biden	Aug 23, 2008	14	7	79
2004				
Kerry-Edwards	Jul 6, 2004	24	7	69
2000				
Gore-Lieberman	Aug 7, 2000	16	4	80
Bush-Cheney	Jul 24, 2000	14	10	76
1996				
Dole-Kemp	Aug 11, 1996	26	8	66
1992				
Clinton-Gore	Jul 9, 1992*	33	8	59
Bush-Quayle	Aug 10-12, 1992	6	25	69
1988				
Bush-Quayle	Aug 17-18, 1988**	10	10	80
Dukakis-Bentsen	Aug 1988*	26	9	65

* Source: Time/CNN poll
** Source: USA Today poll

Even among Republicans, the reaction is muted. Thirty percent of Republicans say that Palin's selection makes them more likely to vote for McCain, while just 5% say they are less likely to vote for McCain, leaving the rest saying that her selection, at least so far, has no impact on their vote. Still, this is a slightly stronger partisan reaction than Democrats had to Biden, as just 21% of Democrats said they were more likely to vote for Obama because Biden was his running mate.

Among the crucial bloc of independents, the impact of Palin's selection is mixed, with the majority saying "no impact," and about as many of the rest saying that it made them less likely to want to vote for her as more likely to vote for her.

Importantly, there is no sign yet of a vehemently negative reaction from Democrats. Just 14% say they are less likely to vote for

McCain as a result of the Palin selection, while 6% say they are more likely to vote for McCain.

2. Palin a Mystery to Majority of Americans

One reason for the lack of a self-reported impact of Palin's selection may be the fact that she is a mystery to many Americans at this early point. More than 7 out of 10 Americans interviewed on Friday night said they had never heard of Palin, or didn't know enough about her to have an opinion. This is a much higher "don't know" than measured by Gallup immediately after the initial vice presidential announcement of Biden a week ago, or Edwards, Lieberman, Cheney, Kemp, or Gore in previous years' elections.

Favorable Ratings of Vice Presidential Candidates

Based on registered voters

	Interview dates	Favorable	Unfavorable	Never heard of/ No opinion
		%	%	%
Sarah Palin	Aug 29, 2008	22	7	71
Joe Biden	Aug 23, 2008	34	15	51
John Edwards	Jul 6, 2004	54	16	30
Joe Lieberman	Aug 7, 2000	37	10	53
Dick Cheney	Jul 24, 2000	51	11	38
Jack Kemp	Aug 11, 1996	56	14	30
Al Gore	Jul 23-24, 1992	59	13	28

This finding is not surprising. The other vice presidential picks in recent years have actively sought their party's presidential nomination in the year they were selected or in previous years, or had well-established careers in Congress or the federal government. Palin has been governor of a small state for less than two years and has no national political experience.

Of interest is the fact that almost 6 out of 10 Republicans say they have never heard of Palin or don't know enough to have an opinion about her. These data underscore that the degree to which Palin is featured at the Republican convention in St. Paul, Minn., next week will be critical in the establishment of her overall image in the minds of many members of her own party, as well as independents and other potential swing voters.

Even at this point, however, Palin has a positive image among those who know enough to have an opinion of her, with more than a 3-to-1 ratio of favorable to unfavorable ratings, more positive than Biden's ratio measured last weekend.

Latest Favorability Ratings of 2008 Vice Presidential Selections

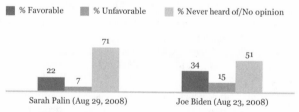

Based on registered voters

By comparison, Edwards, Lieberman, Cheney, Kemp, and Gore all had much more positive favorable-to-unfavorable ratios than either of this year's vice presidential selections. All in all, Gallup's initial reads of the recognition and image of both Biden and Palin after their selections this year are more muted than has been the case for other recent vice presidential selections.

3. Potential Problem for Palin: Perceived Qualifications to Serve as President

Palin rates substantially below other recent vice presidential selectees in terms of perceptions that she is qualified to serve as president. Asked if from what they know about Sarah Palin, they believe she is "qualified to serve as president if it becomes necessary," only 39% of Americans say yes, while almost as many, 33%, say no.

These results are highly partisan in nature—63% of Republicans say she is qualified, but 53% of Democrats say she is not. Independents are more likely to say she is qualified (41%) than not (31%).

Taken as a whole, the reaction of Americans to Palin's qualifications is much more negative than was given to Biden a week ago after his selection by Obama, when 57% said Biden was qualified to serve, and only 18% said he was not.

In terms of the ratio of "yes" to "no" responses, the perception of Palin's qualifications is more negative than the "qualification" affirmations given to any other recent selection with the exception of Quayle in 1992. The rating of Quayle's qualifications, however, was at a time in which he had already served for four years as vice president, and thus not directly comparable to these initial reactions to the other selectees.

Based on what you know about [Sarah Palin], do you think she is qualified to serve as president if it becomes necessary, or not?

Based on registered voters

	Interview dates	Yes, qualified	No, not qualified	No opinion
		%	%	%
2008				
Palin	Aug 29, 2008	39	33	29
Biden	Aug 23, 2008	57	18	26
2004				
Edwards	Jul 6, 2004	57	29	14
2000				
Lieberman	Aug 7, 2000	52	13	35
Cheney	Jul 24, 2000	57	18	25
1996				
Gore	Aug 11, 1996	60	34	6
Kemp	Aug 11, 1996	61	16	23
1992				
Gore	Jul 24-26, 1992	64	19	17
Quayle	Jul 24-26, 1992	32	62	6

Bottom Line

The initial reaction of the American public to McCain's surprise selection of Palin as his vice presidential running mate is muted. A substantial majority of Americans don't know enough about her yet to have an opinion, and a large majority says that at this point her selection will not have an impact on their presidential vote either way.

The good news for McCain and Palin is that among those who do know her, her image is significantly more positive than negative, and in fact more positive on a ratio basis than the image of Biden when his was measured a week ago.

On the negative side of the ledger for the Republicans is that almost as many Americans say she is not qualified to serve as president as say she is qualified, giving her a more negative reading on this measure than any other recent vice presidential selection with the exception of Quayle in 1992.

Given the fact that so many Americans profess at this point to know nothing about Palin, the next several weeks may be critical to her success as a vice presidential nominee as her image is shaped and formed in the harsh spotlight of national media attention. The data suggest that one major task of the Republican convention in particular will be to convince a skeptical public that she would be able to serve as president if needed.

Survey Methods

Results are based on telephone interviews with 898 registered voters, aged 18 and older, conducted August 29, 2008. For results based on the total sample of registered voters, one can say with 95% confidence that the maximum margin of sampling error is ±3 percentage points.

Polls conducted entirely in one day, such as this one, are subject to additional error or bias not found in polls conducted over several days.

Interviews are conducted with respondents on land-line telephones (for respondents with a land-line telephone) and cellular phones (for respondents who are cell-phone only).

In addition to sampling error, question wording and practical difficulties in conducting surveys can introduce error or bias into the findings of public opinion polls.

September 02, 2008
OBAMA GAINS AMONG FORMER CLINTON SUPPORTERS

Obama gains on other dimensions, including terrorism and leadership

by Frank Newport, Gallup Poll Editor in Chief

The Democratic convention appears to have helped solidify support for Barack Obama among former Hillary Clinton supporters, with the percent saying they will vote for Obama in November moving from 70% pre-convention to 81% after the convention, and the percent certain to vote for Obama jumping from 47% to 65%.

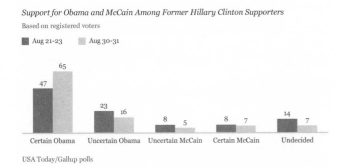

Support for Obama and McCain Among Former Hillary Clinton Supporters
Based on registered voters

■ Aug 21-23   ■ Aug 30-31

USA Today/Gallup polls

Other pre and post comparisons show that Obama gained modestly in his positioning against John McCain on several dimensions, including the perception that he is better able to handle terrorism and the situation in Iraq, and that he is a strong and decisive leader.

Pre- and Post-Convention Surveys

The analysis reported here compares interviews conducted Aug. 21-23, prior to the beginning of the Democratic National Convention, to interviews conducted Aug. 30-31, days after the conclusion of the convention.

The main purpose of the comparisons is to provide an initial measurement of the impact of the convention on the images of the two candidates (and the two parties) coincident with the convention. This year's timeline provides a challenge of interpretation. In addition to the Democratic convention, the time period between the two surveys being compared here also encompassed McCain's surprise announcement of Alaska Gov. Sarah Palin as his vice presidential running mate on Friday, and the intensifying news coverage of the approach of Hurricane Gustav throughout the rest of the weekend. Nevertheless, the comparisons give us a basic indication of the overall impact of the convention.

Tracking Hillary Clinton Voters

The Democratic convention appears to have increased certainty of support for Obama among Democratic voters, including in particular among the critical group of Democrats who earlier this year supported Hillary Clinton in the Democratic primaries (see graph above).

Much attention was given to the fact that only 47% of former Clinton supporters said they were certain to vote for Obama in the pre-convention *USA Today*/Gallup poll, and that 16% of these voters said they were going to vote for McCain, with another 14% undecided.

The new polling shows that many of these disaffected Clinton voters have now returned to the loyal Democratic fold. The percentage of former Clinton voters who say they are certain to vote for Obama has now jumped to 65%. Although 12% of former Clinton voters persist in saying that they are going to vote for McCain, that's down from 16%, and the percentage who are undecided has dropped in half.

Overall, support for Obama among this group has moved from 70% pre-convention to 81% post-convention.

To be sure, former Clinton supporters are still less enthusiastic than former Obama supporters in the post-convention poll. And, the fact that 12% still say they are going to vote for McCain is no doubt troubling to the Obama camp. But it appears that, from a broad perspective, the concentrated effort by Obama's campaign managers to feature both Hillary and Bill Clinton in prominent roles, and efforts by Hillary Clinton to emphasize her support for Obama going into the November election, may have paid off.

Finally, certainty to vote for Obama also moved up from 80% to 87% among voters who previously supported Obama in the Democratic primaries, further suggesting that the Democratic convention had the effect of solidifying party support for the Obama candidacy.

Favorable Ratings of the Two Candidates

There was only slight change in the basic images of the two major party candidates in the time period between these two polls. The basic expectation would ordinarily be that Obama's image would become more positive while McCain's would become more negative as a result of the Democratic convention. The data show that Barack Obama's favorable rating actually dropped very slightly by two percentage points, while McCain's favorable rating dropped by a larger 5-point margin, the latter more in line with expectations.

All in all, Obama now has a 7-point higher favorable percentage than McCain, only slightly more positive for Obama than the 4-point margin he held over McCain pre-convention.

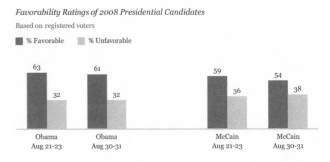

Favorability Ratings of 2008 Presidential Candidates
Based on registered voters

■ % Favorable   ■ % Unfavorable

Obama Aug 21-23	Obama Aug 30-31	McCain Aug 21-23	McCain Aug 30-31
63 / 32	61 / 32	59 / 36	54 / 38

Implications

All in all, the Democratic convention appears to have accomplished—at least to a modest degree—some of the objectives Democratic leaders were probably hoping for. A healthy percentage of former supporters of Hillary Clinton, many of whom were public in their disaffection for Obama before the convention, appear to have returned to the fold and now say they are certain to vote for the Democratic nominee. This no doubt reflects the fact that Hillary (and Bill) Clinton were accorded an extraordinary amount of attention during the convention, and that Hillary Clinton was very vocal in declaring her loyalty and support for Obama.

Still, 19% of former Clinton supporters continue to say they are either going to vote for McCain or are currently undecided, indicating that there may be some residual anger which has not yet been dissipated by Obama's efforts, and that there is still work to do for the Democrats to bring the remaining Clinton supporters into the Obama camp.

The convention also appears to have improved Obama's image on several dimensions, including several which have been McCain's heretofore strengths: handling terrorism and being perceived as a strong leader, in particular.

The focus now will be on the extent to which the GOP convention in St. Paul will reverse Obama's recent gains in favor of McCain on these image dimensions—something which will not be discernible until polling conducted this weekend after the convention ends.

Survey Methods

Results are based on telephone interviews with 1,835 registered voters, aged 18 and older, conducted Aug. 30-31, 2008. For results based on the total sample of national adults, one can say with 95% confidence that the maximum margin of sampling error is ±2 percentage points.

Interviews are conducted with respondents on land-line telephones (for respondents with a land-line telephone) and cellular phones (for respondents who are cell-phone only).

In addition to sampling error, question wording and practical difficulties in conducting surveys can introduce error or bias into the findings of public opinion polls.

September 02, 2008
U.S. EDUCATION SYSTEM GARNERS SPLIT REVIEWS
Grade school earns best parent ratings

by Lydia Saad, Gallup Poll Senior Editor

As the nation's schoolchildren dig out and dust off their backpacks, only 44% of U.S. adults are satisfied with the quality of primary and secondary education in the country, contrasted with 77% of parents of school-aged youth saying they are satisfied with their own children's education. Gallup has recorded a similar perception gap for the past decade.

The corollary findings, from Gallup's Aug. 7-10 Work and Education survey, are that 53% of Americans are dissatisfied with the quality of education in the country and 20% of parents are dissatisfied with their oldest child's schooling. (Parents with more than one child were asked to rate the education their oldest child is receiving.)

Since 1999, public satisfaction with the quality of education in kindergarten through grade 12 has generally fallen near the average 46% level seen across this period. One exception is August 2000,

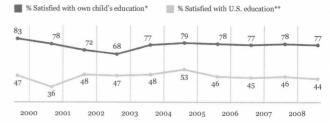

Satisfaction With K-12 Education in the United States
■ % Satisfied with own child's education*   ■ % Satisfied with U.S. education**

* Based on parents of children attending K-12 this fall; ** Based on national adults
Gallup Poll, Aug. 7-10, 2008

when only 36% of Americans were satisfied. Diminished satisfaction with the quality of education in that survey could have reflected public reaction to George W. Bush's focus on problems in education and the need for standards-based reform in his 2000 presidential campaign—a focus that ultimately led to the passage of the No Child Left Behind Act of 2001.

Barely a Third of Parents "Completely Satisfied"

While parents are generally satisfied with their own children's schooling, there is ample room for improvement in those attitudes. Overall, just 35% of all K-12 parents say they are "completely satisfied." The figure is even lower (28%) among the subset of parents whose children attend public schools.

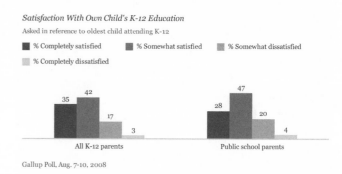

Satisfaction With Own Child's K-12 Education
Asked in reference to oldest child attending K-12
■ % Completely satisfied   ■ % Somewhat satisfied   ■ % Somewhat dissatisfied
■ % Completely dissatisfied

Gallup Poll, Aug. 7-10, 2008

The greatest work in addressing parents' concerns needs to be done at the upper grade levels. Only 28% of parents of children attending grades 7 through 12 are "completely satisfied" with their children's education, compared with 43% of parents of kindergartners through sixth graders.

Parents' Satisfaction With Oldest Child's Education According to That Child's Grade in School
■ % Completely satisfied   ■ % Somewhat satisfied   ■ % Total dissatisfied

Gallup Poll, Aug. 7-10, 2008

Bottom Line

Parents of school-aged children are feeling pretty good about the education their oldest child will receive this fall. That's the good news out of Gallup's annual update on attitudes toward education in the United States. The troublesome news is that, despite several years of No Child Left Behind changes operating in the nation's schools, Americans are no more confident about the quality of education being delivered than they were in 1999, before Bush formally proposed the reforms.

Survey Methods

Results are based on telephone interviews with 1,009 national adults, aged 18 and older, conducted Aug. 7-10, 2008. For results based on the total sample of national adults, one can say with 95% confidence that the maximum margin of sampling error is ±3 percentage points.For results based on the sample of 253 parents with children in kindergarten through grade 12, the maximum margin of sampling error is ±7 percentage points.

Interviews are conducted with respondents on land-line telephones (for respondents with a land-line telephone) and cellular phones (for respondents who are cell-phone only).

In addition to sampling error, question wording and practical difficulties in conducting surveys can introduce error or bias into the findings of public opinion polls.

September 03, 2008
OBAMA GAINS OVERALL, MCCAIN AMONG GOP WOMEN

McCain manages to increase support among women of his own party

by Frank Newport, Gallup Poll Editor in Chief

An update on gender differences in white voters' presidential vote shows that Barack Obama's gains vis-à-vis John McCain in the days since the Democratic National Convention have come among independents and Democrats of both genders, but that McCain has actually gained slightly among Republican women. The preferences of Republican men have not changed. The net effect of these patterns: Obama has registered significant overall gains among white men, but there has been no net change in his support among white women.

Support for Presidential Candidates, by Gender
Among non-Hispanic white registered voters

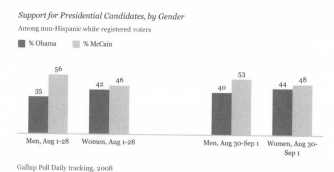

Gallup Poll Daily tracking, 2008

In August, McCain led Obama among non-Hispanic white men by 21 points; his lead is now 13 points. Among white women, McCain led Obama by 4 points, and McCain leads by the same amount today. This means that McCain's *relative* position among

women has improved. (Gallup's previous analysis shows that Obama has a huge lead among both black men and black women, and that he also leads among Hispanics, regardless of gender. The only racial or ethnic group among which there is a notable gender gap is non-Hispanic whites.)

Partisan Groups

One gains a better understanding of these gender differences among white voters by breaking the data into partisan groups.

Overall, this analysis shows that Obama's gains over the last week among white men are fairly straightforward. They occurred among both independent and Democratic men. There has been no change among Republican white men.

On the other hand, Obama's gains among independent and Democratic women appear to have been mostly offset by McCain's gains among Republican women.

Support for Presidential Candidates, by Party and Gender
Among non-Hispanic white registered voters

	Aug 1-28 % Obama	Aug 1-28 % McCain	Aug 30-Sep 1 % Obama	Aug 30-Sep 1 % McCain
Republicans				
Men	7	89	6	90
Women	8	85	7	90
Independents				
Men	35	51	42	47
Women	41	42	46	39
Democrats				
Men	74	18	82	13
Women	74	15	82	13

Gallup Poll Daily tracking, 2008

Previous Gallup analysis has suggested that McCain's selection of a woman as his vice-presidential running mate might have the most impact on independent white women, who before the Democratic Convention were essentially split down the middle in terms of candidate support. These data show, however, that at least initially, McCain has lost ground among both white independent women and white independent men (and among Democrats of both genders) since the convention and his vice-presidential selection.

Instead, the data suggest that McCain has in essence fought a rear-guard action of sorts among white women of his own GOP base, building their support to a degree even as he was losing support among independents and Democrats of both genders.

It is possible, but not provable with these data, that McCain's selection of a woman, Gov. Sarah Palin of Alaska, as his vice-presidential running mate may have had the effect of solidifying support among women of his own party.

The Republicans no doubt hope that this week's convention, and in particular Palin's address on Wednesday, will help them make inroads not only among white Republican women, but also among independent (and perhaps Democratic) women.

Survey Methods

Results for Aug. 1-28 are based on telephone interviews with 25,007 registered voters, aged 18 and older, conducted Aug. 1-28, 2008, as part of Gallup Poll Daily tracking. For results based on this total sample of registered voters, one can say with 95% confidence that the maximum margin of sampling error is ±1 percentage point. Results for Aug. 30-Sept. 1 are based on a sample of 2,772 registered voters, for which the maximum margin of sampling error is ±2 percentage points.

Interviews are conducted with respondents on land-line telephones (for respondents with a land-line telephone) and cellular phones (for respondents who are cell-phone only).

In addition to sampling error, question wording and practical difficulties in conducting surveys can introduce error or bias into the findings of public opinion polls.

September 03, 2008
WILL THE ABORTION ISSUE HELP OR HURT MCCAIN?

Women divide 50% pro-choice, 43% pro-life

by Lydia Saad, Gallup Poll Senior Editor

By tapping Alaska Gov. Sarah Palin to be his running mate, John McCain is in part gambling that putting a female reform-minded governor (who happens to be staunchly pro-life) on the Republican ticket will help to cut into Obama's substantial lead among female voters. Obama is now countering that strategy by running ads in swing states highlighting McCain's and Palin's opposition to abortion.

Who stands to gain? To start with, female voters as a whole tilt pro-choice over pro-life in how they describe their abortion stances, 50% to 43%. Among the independent and Democratic women who are the primary focus of this battle, the balance of opinion is a bit more strongly pro-choice.

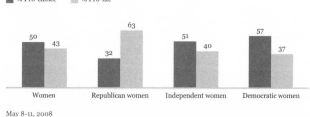

Abortion Stance Among Women, by Party ID
■ % Pro-choice　　■ % Pro-life

May 8-11, 2008

However, as Gallup polling in 2008 and all recent past elections shows, only a small fraction of Americans are highly activated on the abortion issue. Most Americans downgrade the importance of abortion to their vote, saying either that it's not a major issue for them (37%), or that it's just one of many important issues they consider (49%). Only 13% of Americans told Gallup in May 2008 that they vote only for candidates for major offices who share their views on abortion.

That may largely explain why 32% of Republican women call themselves pro-choice, yet only 7% of Republican women are voting for Obama. Similarly, in contrast to the 37% of Democratic women who say they are pro-life, only 9% are voting for McCain. Abortion is simply not a pivotal issue for these voters.

Although a third of Republican women are pro-choice, McCain's selection of Palin last Friday already appears to have helped him with his female Republican base. Republican women

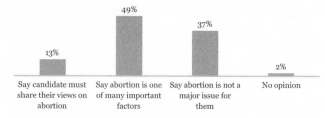

Effect of Abortion Issue on Americans' Vote for Major Offices

May 8-11, 2008

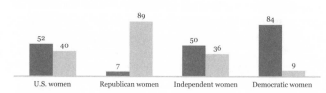

Presidential Preference Among Women, by Party ID
Based on registered voters

■ % Obama　　■ % McCain

Gallup Poll Daily tracking, Aug. 31-Sept. 2, 2008

grew more likely to support McCain, not less likely, in polling from Saturday to Monday.

There is something closer to a 1-to-1 correspondence between abortion views and presidential preferences among independent women, at least numerically. Independent women split 51% vs. 40% pro-choice over pro-life in May. Today they are voting for Obama over McCain by 50% to 36%.

But the abortion issue appears to be even less of a factor for independent women than it is for their partisan counterparts. According to Gallup's May 2008 Values and Beliefs survey, 20% of Republican women said they vote only for candidates who share their views on abortion, as did 14% of Democratic women but only 8% of independent women.

Abortion as Voting Issue Among Women, by Party ID
■ % Say candidate must share abortion views　　■ % Say abortion just one of many issues
■ % Say abortion not important

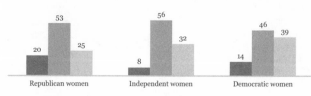

May 8-11, 2008

Bottom Line

The 2008 Republican and Democratic presidential candidates present a sharp contrast on abortion policy, and that contrast is now bursting into the open with the emerging battle for female voters.

Whether the selection of Palin as his running mate helps or hurts McCain with independent and Democratic women going forward will only partially depend on how Obama and McCain play the abortion issue. Relatively few Democratic women and even fewer independent women say abortion is the most important issue they consider. Palin's story as a working mother may prove more compelling to women attracted to the idea of breaking the presidential glass ceiling. If, however, Obama and McCain both take the gloves off and seek to paint each other, respectively, as a dangerous opponent of a woman's choice versus a radical proponent of late-term abortions, the issue could resonate with more than the few female voters who typically care. Many women are cross-pressured in their political views (pro-choice Republicans and pro-life Democrats) so there is significant room for changing voter preferences on the issue on both sides. And if the arguments cut deeply enough, they could also be influential with independents.

Survey Methods

The latest abortion public opinion results are based on telephone interviews with 1,017 national adults, aged 18 and older, conducted May 8-11, 2008. For results based on the total sample of national adults, one can say with 95% confidence that the maximum margin of sampling error is ±3 percentage points.

Interviews are conducted with respondents on land-line telephones (for respondents with a land-line telephone) and cellular phones (for respondents who are cell-phone only).

In addition to sampling error, question wording and practical difficulties in conducting surveys can introduce error or bias into the findings of public opinion polls.

September 04, 2008
INTENSE POLITICAL WEEK BRINGS DECLINE IN SWING VOTERS
Uncommitted voters down from 30% to 21% in past week

by Jeffrey M. Jones, Gallup Poll Managing Editor

The percentage of voters who are "up for grabs" has declined sharply in the past week, from 30% to 21%, according to the latest *USA Today*/Gallup poll.

Swing Voters in the 2008 Presidential Election
Based on registered voters

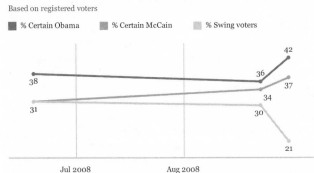

Note: Swing voters are defined as those who do not currently have a candidate preference or have a candidate preference but are not certain to vote for that candidate.

The decline in the proportion of voters classified as swing voters is coincident with two major political events that took place over the past seven days—the Democratic National Convention and John McCain's announcement of Sarah Palin as his vice-presidential run-

ning mate. Each event certainly had the potential to ease particular voter concerns, such as Obama's readiness to be president and McCain's commitment to core Republican principles.

At this point, 42% of registered voters say they are certain to vote for Obama, up from 36% immediately before the convention. Thirty-seven percent are now committed to McCain, up slightly from 34%. Thus, with 79% of voters committed to one candidate or the other, 21% are "swing voters" who could vote for either candidate or for a third-party candidate.

Historically, the proportion of swing voters tends to decline as Election Day approaches. However, there have been examples of temporary expansions in the pool of uncommitted voters in response to high-profile campaign events such as debates. So it is unclear what impact the Republican National Convention will have on the electorate in the coming days.

Implications

The percentage of voters who have yet to commit to a candidate has declined sharply in the past week, and now is similar to what Gallup measured between conventions in 2004. Earlier this year, there was a higher proportion of uncommitted voters than at a comparable time in 2004. And while the Republican Convention and upcoming debates could help voters make up their minds, these events also have the potential to make voters less certain about their choice, at least in the short run.

To some degree, it appears as if swing voters are uncommitted this year because they still have doubts about Obama's and McCain's ability to handle issues that are not their known areas of strength, namely, the economy for McCain and foreign affairs (especially terrorism) for Obama. Thus, both candidates stand to gain support if they can address voters' concerns in these areas between now and Election Day.

Survey Methods

Results are based on telephone interviews with 1,835 registered voters, aged 18 and older, conducted Aug. 30-31, 2008. For results based on the total sample of national adults, one can say with 95% confidence that the maximum margin of sampling error is ±3 percentage points.

For results based on the sample of 401 swing voters, the maximum margin of sampling error is ±5 percentage points.

For results based on the sample of 1,434 committed voters, the maximum margin of sampling error is ±3 percentage points.

Interviews are conducted with respondents on land-line telephones (for respondents with a land-line telephone) and cellular phones (for respondents who are cell-phone only).

In addition to sampling error, question wording and practical difficulties in conducting surveys can introduce error or bias into the findings of public opinion polls.

September 04, 2008

JOB MARKET WORSENING AS ELECTION APPROACHES

Gallup's Net New Hiring Activity measure shows further deterioration in job-market perceptions

by Dennis Jacobe, Gallup Poll Chief Economist

Gallup's Net New Hiring Activity measure shows that U.S. workers' perceptions of the job market have been bad in recent months—and they became distinctly worse in August.

Month-to-Month Change in Net New Hiring Activity, Nationwide, 2008

Percentage of employees who say their employers are hiring minus percentage who say their employers are letting people go

Numbers in percentage points

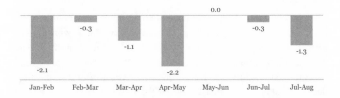

Eighth Straight Month of Job Losses in August

With the presidential election approaching at a dizzying pace, job losses may soon be vying with gas prices as the major economic issue facing the nation and the presidential candidates. According to government figures, payroll employment has declined by 463,000 jobs over the first seven months of this year. Over the past 12 months, the number of unemployed persons has increased by 1.6 million and the unemployment rate has increased by 1 full percentage point to 5.7%.

Gallup's Net New Hiring Activity measure, based on interviews with more than 8,000 employees in August, suggests the bad jobs situation of July deteriorated significantly in August. The percentage of employees saying their companies are hiring was essentially unchanged last month while the percentage saying their companies are letting people go increased by 1.6 points—the biggest increase this year—and consistent with Gallup's layoff report last month.

In turn, this suggests that jobs probably declined for the eighth month in a row in August and by more than the 75,000 decline economists predict, according to Bloomberg. More importantly, it also implies that the unemployment rate did not remain at 5.7% as expected, but increased to at least 5.8% in August. Whatever numbers the Bureau of Labor Statistics reports on Friday morning, these Gallup job findings, combined with declining oil and gas prices, suggest jobs and the need to address the lack of job creation in this country will become an increasingly important election issue over the coming weeks.

Percentage of Employers Expanding and Reducing Their Workforces, Nationwide

■ % Hiring   ▪ % Letting go

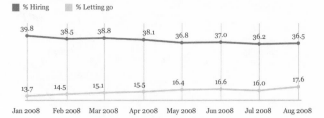

Job-Related Recession

So far this year, the U.S. economy has been slowed by surging oil and gas prices combined with a housing and financial sector debacle. As a result, the economic fallout has been spreading slowly across the economy as consumers pull back on their spending, and job-market conditions deteriorate.

However, the August Net New Hiring Activity results suggest that the economic downturn may be reaching critical mass—at least as far as job-market conditions are concerned. The rate of job losses looks like it may increase to the six-digit range and the unemployment rate could soon reach 6%. As job losses escalate, they will tend to have their traditional impact on consumer confidence and consumer spending. In turn, the U.S. economy could go into a more traditional jobs-related recession on top of the economic slowdown already underway.

If this turns out to be the case and a traditional recession begins to take hold, it will present some significant challenges to the presidential candidates now and after the election. At this point, the Federal Reserve has done just about all it can with monetary policy. It will do well to continue to safeguard the financial system as the oil and commodities bubble bursts, and hedge funds and financial services firms experience additional losses.

Declining gas prices will help by providing consumers with more disposable income. But the continuing credit crunch, financial sector deleveraging, and increasing job losses will likely require the federal government to act to help create the necessary conditions for a solid economic recovery in 2009. The team of candidates that can best convince Americans over the next two months that they not only understand the current economic situation and identify with the pain, but also can provide a viable economic solution, may have the inside track for the November election.

Survey Methods

Gallup's Net New Hiring Activity measure was initiated in January 2008. It is an effort to assess U.S. job creation or elimination based on the self-reports of more than 8,000 individual employees each month about hiring and firing activity at their workplaces. In order to calculate this measure, Gallup asks current full-time employees whether their employers are hiring new people and expanding the size of their workforces, not changing the size of their workforces, or letting people go and reducing the size of their workforces. Net new hiring activity is computed by subtracting the "letting go and reducing" percentage from the "hiring and expanding" percentage. The assumption is that employees across the country have a good feel for what's happening in their companies, and that these insider perceptions can yield a useful summary indication of the nation's job situation.

Gallup is interviewing no fewer than 1,000 U.S. adults nationwide each day during 2008. The economic questions analyzed in this report are asked of a random half-sample of respondents each day. The results reported here are based on combined data of more than 8,000 interviews in January, February, March, April, May, June, July, and August. For results based on these samples, the maximum margin of sampling error is ±1 percentage point.

Interviews are conducted with respondents on land-line telephones (for respondents with a land-line telephone) and cellular phones (for respondents who are cell-phone only).

In addition to sampling error, question wording and practical difficulties in conducting surveys can introduce error or bias into the findings of public opinion polls.

September 05, 2008
RELIGION REMAINS MAJOR DIVIDING FACTOR AMONG WHITE VOTERS
Patterns are similar to 2004

by Frank Newport, Gallup Poll Editor in Chief

John McCain has led Barack Obama all summer among highly religious white voters and continues to do so in the first three days of September, with no sign of change coincident with the selection of Alaska Gov. Sarah Palin as his vice-presidential running mate.

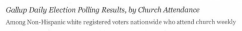

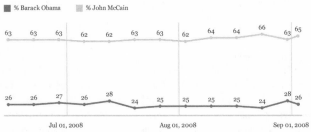

Gallup Daily Election Polling Results, by Church Attendance
Among Non-Hispanic white registered voters nationwide who attend church weekly

Based on weekly averages of Gallup Poll Daily tracking except for Sept. 1-3

About 33% of non-Hispanic white registered voters are weekly church attenders, and the data make it clear that this group forms one of Republican McCain's key constituencies.

The more than 2-to-1 support levels for McCain among this group have been remarkably consistent all summer. Much attention was paid to the possibility that the choice of Palin would help boost McCain's support even further among this group. That may happen in the days to come, but interviewing conducted during the first three days of the Republican National Convention—Monday through Wednesday—suggests little change in support patterns among highly religious white voters compared to previous weeks. These religious voters remain about as supportive of McCain as they have been. (These data were mostly collected before Palin's speech on Wednesday night; any impact from that speech will not be apparent for several days.)

McCain also has the support of the smaller group of about 19% of white registered voters who attend church nearly weekly or monthly, but by a somewhat smaller margin. There has been a little more variation in support levels among this group as the summer has progressed, including a slight shift toward Obama in the Sept. 1-3 data.

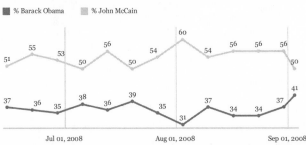

Gallup Daily Election Polling Results, by Church Attendance
Among Non-Hispanic white registered voters nationwide who attend church nearly weekly/monthly

Based on weekly averages of Gallup Poll Daily tracking, except for Sept. 1-3

Finally, there is a distinctly different pattern of candidate support evident among white voters who report seldom or never attending church.

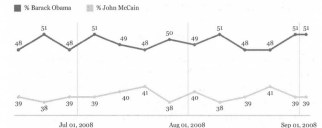

Gallup Daily Election Polling Results, by Church Attendance
Among Non-Hispanic white registered voters nationwide who attend church seldom/never

Based on weekly averages of Gallup Poll Daily tracking except for Sept. 1-3

This large group—about 47% of the white registered voter population—skews toward Obama by a 12-point margin in the last week of August and in the first three days of September. Again, there has been little substantive change in these voter support patterns all summer.

2004 Comparison

Indeed, this same pattern of candidate support by religiosity among whites has not only remained fairly constant this year, but is very close to where things stood four years ago, just before the 2004 election.

Gallup Daily Election Polling Results, by Church Attendance

Among non-Hispanic white registered voters nationwide

Sep 1-3, 2008*	Barack Obama	John McCain
Attend church weekly	26%	65%
Attend almost weekly/monthly	41%	50%
Attend seldom/never	51%	39%

Oct 29-31, 2004**	John Kerry	George W. Bush
Attend church weekly	27%	66%
Attend almost weekly/monthly	36%	62%
Attend seldom/never	53%	40%

* Gallup Poll Daily tracking
** CNN/USA Today/Gallup poll

George W. Bush led John Kerry on the eve of the 2004 election by 66% to 27% among white registered voters who attended church weekly, almost identical to where McCain and Obama stand today. Bush did a little better than McCain is doing now among white voters who attend almost weekly/monthly, but the Kerry margin over Bush among infrequent church attenders and non-attenders in 2004 was very close to Obama's margin over McCain among this same group now.

Bigger Picture

Overall, in the first three days of September, McCain is winning over Obama among all non-Hispanic white registered voters by a 49% to 41% margin. This lead is based on the fact that his margin among the slightly more than half of all whites who attend church at least monthly is more than enough to compensate for his deficit among those who seldom or never attend church. From a larger perspective, Obama has an overall lead of 7 points over McCain for Sept. 1-3. The Democratic nominee's support among nonwhites (including blacks, Hispanics, and Asians) is so strong that when averaged in with white voters, he comes out on top.

Implications

McCain has seen no immediate increase in support among highly religious white voters after his selection of Palin as his vice-presidential running mate. McCain has been ahead of Obama by better than a 2-to-1 margin among this group all summer, and that margin continues more or less unchanged in the first three days of September through Wednesday night. Meanwhile, Obama continues to dominate McCain among white voters who seldom or never attend church.

It should be reiterated that the data reviewed here do not yet reflect any possible impact of Palin's widely discussed acceptance speech on Wednesday night at the GOP Convention. Even if McCain does gain ground in the next several days as part of a positive reaction to Palin or the usual convention "bounce," it will be important to see whether he gains equally across all groups of white voters regardless of religion, or whether his gains are particularly concentrated in the highly religious group to which observers believe Palin may have a particularly strong appeal. Also, the selection of Palin may serve the function of manifesting a change in enthusiasm and turnout propensity among various subgroups of voters. That is, highly religious white voters could now become more motivated than they have been in their support for the GOP ticket, and could therefore increase McCain's overall total vote count on Election Day. By the same token, the selection of Palin may generate increased enthusiasm among Obama's less religious supporters who likely disagree with her conservative views on social issues. All of this will be sorted out as Gallup continues to analyze data over the next several days.

Survey Methods

The general-election results are based on combined data from Sept. 1-3, 2008. For results based on this sample of 2,771 registered voters, the maximum margin of sampling error is ±2 percentage points.

Interviews are conducted with respondents on land-line telephones (for respondents with a land-line telephone) and cellular phones (for respondents who are cell-phone only).

In addition to sampling error, question wording and practical difficulties in conducting surveys can introduce error or bias into the findings of public opinion polls.

September 08, 2008
REPUBLICANS' ENTHUSIASM JUMPS AFTER CONVENTION
McCain edges ahead; Palin speech may be a factor

by Frank Newport, Gallup Poll Editor in Chief

As the remarkable two-week stretch of back-to-back presidential nomination conventions ends, a weekend *USA Today*/Gallup Poll finds that the John McCain-Sarah Palin ticket has more than matched the Barack Obama-Joe Biden ticket's convention bounce of last week with a "rebound" bounce, and in the immediate aftermath of the GOP convention McCain and Palin now have a slight edge over their opponents.

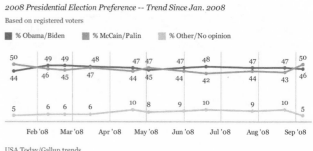

2008 Presidential Election Preference -- Trend Since Jan. 2008
Based on registered voters

USA Today/Gallup trends

The presidential race was dead even at 45% to 45% among registered voters in Gallup tracking conducted prior to the Democratic convention. Then, by the *USA Today*/Gallup Poll conducted in the first few days after the Democratic convention (and also after McCain had made his announcement of Sarah Palin as his running mate), Obama had moved ahead by a 47% to 43% margin. (In Gallup Poll Daily tracking extending into the beginning of last week, Obama reached a point where he had 50% of the vote and an eight percentage point lead.) Obama's lead has now disappeared totally, and McCain sits on a 4-point advantage among registered voters in the Friday through Sunday poll. That's the largest advantage for McCain in either *USA Today*/Gallup Polls or Gallup Poll Daily tracking since May.

The convention and/or McCain's selection of Sarah Palin as his vice presidential running mate not only had the effect of moving the horserace needle in McCain's direction, but also increased several measures of enthusiasm for the GOP.

There has been a very substantial jump in the percentage of Republicans saying they are more enthusiastic about voting in this election, from 42% a week ago (after the Democratic convention, but before the Republican convention) to 60% today. Democrats still retain a slight lead on this measure, having increased their enthusiasm slightly this last week as well. But the enthusiasm gap, which has been so much a part of the story of the presidential election so far this year, has dwindled from 19 points in the Democrats' favor a week ago to only seven points today.

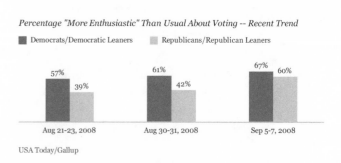

Percentage "More Enthusiastic" Than Usual About Voting -- Recent Trend

USA Today/Gallup

Likely Voters

The gap between registered voters and likely voters has once again enlarged in the McCain-Palin ticket's favor in this poll. While the Republican ticket leads by 50% to 46% among registered voters, that lead stretches to a 54% to 44% lead among those Gallup sees as most likely to actually turn out and vote.

Presidential Preference Comparison -- Registered Voters vs. Likely Voters

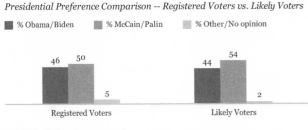

USA Today/Gallup, Sept. 5-7, 2008

This difference between likely voters and registered voters indicates that *if the election were held today*, McCain would benefit from a differential advantage over the Democrats in terms of those voters actually likely to turn out and vote—as has often been typical of recent presidential elections.

McCain also had a similar likely voter advantage in the *USA Today*/Gallup Poll conducted in the immediate aftermath of Barack Obama's foreign tour, July 25-27, interpreted at the time as a significant partisan reaction to the visibility given Obama by that tour. That advantage for the GOP did not appear in the *USA Today*/Gallup Poll conducted about a month later as the conventions began, but has appeared again in this poll.

Thus, these trends suggest that the Republican ticket has the *potential* for a significant turnout advantage on Election Day, but that it appears to be very dependent on the election environment and is by no means certain.

The Palin Factor

Candidates typically receive a bounce in their standing in the polls after their party's convention, so McCain moving into a lead over Barack Obama by a slim margin is not unexpected. Obama received a bounce from his convention, and now McCain has received a bounce from his own. One of the most remarkable things that occurred during the last week, of course, was McCain's highly unexpected selection of Alaska Gov. Sarah Palin on Aug. 29 as his vice presidential running mate. That selection, and Palin's speech on Wednesday night at the convention (coupled with her appearance on a number of different national magazine covers in the days that followed) certainly could be hypothesized to have added a little extra energy to standard convention bounce.

The weekend poll included a number of questions addressing the Palin factor.

The conclusion? Sarah Palin certainly appears to have made a strong impression with her convention speech, but other indications in the data show that her selection has engendered an overall polarizing effect—with both high positives and high negatives.

Here are some of the key points:

1. Sarah Palin's speech Wednesday night was clearly a success. Her speech was very positively received and reaction to it overwhelmed the tepid response to John McCain's speech on Thursday night.

Barack Obama's speech before 80,000 people in the football stadium at the Democratic convention a week and a half ago was not rated in this most recent weekend poll, but was rated in a one-night poll on the evening of Aug. 29, the day after his speech. Obama's speech received very positive ratings, but slightly lower than Palin did in this weekend's poll.

Rating of Sarah Palin's and John McCain's Acceptance Speeches

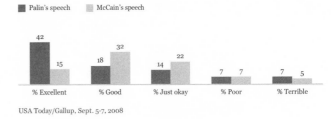

USA Today/Gallup, Sept. 5-7, 2008

2. Other measures included in the weekend poll show a positive rating for aspects of Palin's selection, as well as a pattern of responses that reinforces the conclusion that McCain's choice may have been risky in some respects.

The 36% of voters who said McCain's selection of Palin was "excellent" was higher than was measured in reaction to Obama's selection of Biden. But, and this is a big caveat, at the same time the percent of voters who rated McCain's selection of Palin as "poor"— 24%—is also high. Compared to a one-night poll conducted Aug. 29, the percentage of Americans rating the selection of Palin as excellent has risen, as has, to a lesser degree, the percentage who rated it poor.

3. The important question of asking voters whether McCain's selection of Palin influenced their vote in either direction showed a similarly polarizing pattern of responses, with relatively high positives, but also high negatives.

Does having Sarah Palin as his running mate make you more likely to vote for John McCain in November, less likely, or will it not have much effect on your vote?

Based on registered voters

■ % More likely ■ % Less likely ■ % No effect □ % No opinion

	Aug 29, 2008	Sep 5-7, 2008
% More likely	18	29
% Less likely	11	21
% No effect	67	49
% No opinion	3	1

USA Today/Gallup

Gallup asked Americans about the selection of Palin in a one-day poll on Aug. 29, and since that time voters have both become more positive about the impact of the selection on their vote, and also more negative. The "net" difference between the two reactions has remained almost exactly the same over the last week.

4. Voters have also—on balance—not changed their views of Palin's qualifications to be president. These views remain decidedly mixed.

In Gallup's Aug. 29 poll, the spread between those saying that Palin was qualified and those saying she was not qualified was six points. Now, in the weekend poll, although both percentages have risen, the spread is almost identical at four points.

5. A question asking about the implications of the choice of Palin on McCain's ability to make important presidential decisions shows that while 55% of voters say it reflects favorably on his ability to make important decisions, 40% say it reflects unfavorably.

Implications

At least in the short-term, McCain appears to have used the Republican convention to neutralize the bounce Obama received following the Democratic convention, to the point where McCain now has a

Based on what you know about Sarah Palin, do you think she is qualified to serve as president if it becomes necessary, or not?

Based on registered voters

■ % Yes, qualified   ■ % No, not qualified   ▦ % No opinion

```
                    48  44
         39  33                    8
              29
      Aug 29, 2008        Sep 5-7, 2008
```

USA Today/Gallup

slight advantage over Obama among registered voters and a larger advantage among likely voters. It remains to be seen whether or not McCain can hold on to his advantage in the days ahead as news coverage continues to shift from the conventions to the race itself.

The Republican convention certainly appears to have energized the Republican voting base, visible not only in the data showing a major 18-point jump in enthusiasm among Republicans, but also from the fact that McCain's advantage over Obama increases in this poll when just likely voters are taken into consideration. Again, the issue is whether or not this advantage can be sustained.

Republican vice presidential nominee Palin's speech at the Republican convention on Wednesday night received a highly positive response, significantly more so than her running mate McCain received for his speech. Other indicators suggest that the selection of Palin was a polarizing move by McCain, generating significant positives and negatives. Thus, it is reasonable to expect that the long-term impact of the Palin selection may not be fully understood until her visibility increases further, including the important planned debate with Joe Biden in early October in St. Louis.

Survey Methods

Results are based on telephone interviews with 1,022 national adults, aged 18 and older, conducted Sept. 5-7, 2008. For results based on the total sample of national adults, one can say with 95% confidence that the maximum margin of sampling error is ±3 percentage points.

Interviews are conducted with respondents on land-line telephones (for respondents with a land-line telephone) and cellular phones (for respondents who are cell-phone only).

In addition to sampling error, question wording and practical difficulties in conducting surveys can introduce error or bias into the findings of public opinion polls.

September 09, 2008
MCCAIN NOW WINNING MAJORITY OF INDEPENDENTS
Majority of independents now prefer him over Obama, 52% to 37%

by Lydia Saad., Gallup Poll Senior Editor

John McCain's 6 percentage-point bounce in voter support spanning the Republican National Convention is largely explained by politi-

cal independents shifting to him in fairly big numbers, from 40% pre-convention to 52% post-convention in Gallup Poll Daily tracking.

Support for John McCain by Party ID -- Pre- and Post-GOP Convention

Based on registered voters

■ Pre-convention (Aug 29-31)   ▦ Post-convention (Sep 5-7)

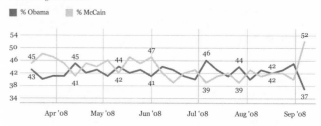

```
   90%  89%
                    40%  52%
                                   9%  14%
   Republicans    Independents    Democrats
```

Gallup Poll Daily tracking

By contrast, Democrats' support for McCain rose 5 percentage points over the GOP convention period, from 9% to 14%, while Republicans' already-high support stayed about the same.

The surge in political independents who favor McCain for president marks the first time since Gallup began tracking voters' general-election preferences in March that a majority of independents have sided with either of the two major-party candidates. Prior to now, McCain had received no better than 48% of the independent vote and Obama no better than 46%, making the race for the political middle highly competitive.

Trend in Presidential Preferences of Independents

Based on registered voters

■ % Obama   ▦ % McCain

```
54                                                    52
50
46  45      45      44      47      46    44    42
42  43       41      42      41             39   42    37
38                                    39   39
34
   Apr '08  May '08  Jun '08  Jul '08  Aug '08  Sep '08
```

Source: Gallup Poll Daily tracking weekly aggregates from March 10-16, 2008, through Aug. 18-24, 2008; most recent results based on Aug. 29-31, 2008, and Sept. 5-7, 2008, Gallup Poll Daily tracking results.

Layering voters' political ideology over their party identification provides the additional finding that the slim group of "pure independents"—those with no political leanings to either major party—grew more favorable to McCain by an even larger amount over the past week or so. McCain was preferred over Obama by 20% of pure independents in Gallup Poll Daily tracking from Aug. 29-31. In the latest three-day rolling average, from Sept. 5-7, he is favored by 39% of non-leaning independents, a 19-point increase. (Nearly 40% of pure independents remain undecided.)

The more modest expansion of McCain's support among Democrats has come mainly from the right wing of that party, with 25% of conservative Democrats now favoring him over Obama, compared with 15% just before the Republican gathering. Moderate and liberal Democrats show only slightly more support for McCain than they did prior to the GOP convention.

There has been no change in the presidential preferences of either conservative Republicans or moderate-to-liberal Republicans.

Final Points

The events on the Republican stage in St. Paul, Minn., from Sept. 2-4 appear to have provided two important boosts to the McCain-Palin ticket.

Support for John McCain by Party/Ideology -- Pre- and Post-GOP Convention
Based on registered voters

	Pre-convention (Aug 29-31, 2008)	Post-convention (Sep 5-7, 2008)
	%	%
Liberal Democrats	2	4
Moderate Democrats	11	16
Conservative Democrats	15	25
Pure independents	20	39
Moderate/Liberal Republicans	81	80
Conservative Republicans	95	95

Gallup Poll Daily tracking

First, according to the latest *USA Today*/Gallup poll, conducted Sept. 5-7, McCain has energized his Republican base and, as a result, has potentially strengthened his positioning on Election Day with "likely voters." Second, as the Gallup Poll Daily trends discussed here show, voter movement toward McCain since the Republican convention occurred mainly with independents, thus broadening McCain's appeal beyond the party.

Republicans had already lined up for McCain before the convention started. Now, they are excited, and are joined by more independents than at any other time in the campaign. Those gains may not last—"bounces" rarely do—but they enable McCain to launch the next phase of the campaign with the knowledge of what his winning coalition might look like.

Survey Methods

Gallup Poll Daily tracking results from Sept. 5-7, 2008, and Aug. 29-31, 2008, are each based on interviews with 2,733 registered voters. For results based on these samples, the maximum margin of sampling error is ±2 percentage points.

Weekly averages of Gallup Poll Daily tracking from March 10-16, 2008, through Aug. 18-24, 2008, are generally based on interviews with more than 6,000 registered voters. For results based on this samples of this size, the maximum margin of sampling error is ±1 percentage points. Results based on various subgroups of voters are associated with larger margins of sampling error.

Interviews are conducted with respondents on land-line telephones (for respondents with a land-line telephone) and cellular phones (for respondents who are cell-phone only).

In addition to sampling error, question wording and practical difficulties in conducting surveys can introduce error or bias into the findings of public opinion polls.

September 09, 2008
MCCAIN REGAINS UPPER HAND ON LEADERSHIP DIMENSION
Obama had erased McCain advantage after Democratic convention

by Jeffrey M. Jones, Gallup Poll Managing Editor

After a Republican National Convention that saw him take the lead over Barack Obama in national trial-heat polls, John McCain is once again perceived as superior to Obama in terms of being a strong and decisive leader.

Next, thinking about the following characteristics and qualities, please say whether you think each one applies more to Barack Obama or more to John McCain. How about -- Is a strong and decisive leader?

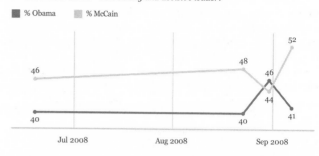

Obama had erased McCain's former advantage on the leadership dimension after the Democratic National Convention, but now McCain has regained the advantage. McCain has a larger advantage over Obama on leadership than on any of the other eight character dimensions tested in the Sept. 5-7 *USA Today*/Gallup poll. He also leads Obama in terms of being honest and trustworthy, putting the country's interests ahead of his own political interests, being able to manage the government effectively, and being able to work with both parties to get things done in Washington.

Ratings of McCain and Obama on Character Dimensions

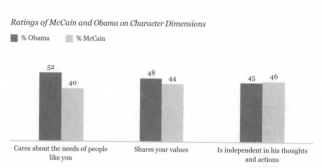

USA Today/Gallup poll, Sept. 5-7, 2008

Obama's strengths compared with McCain's this year have been on matters dealing with empathy—the public gives the Democratic nominee the edge when asked which presidential candidate "cares about the needs of people like you" and "shares your values." The public is evenly divided as to which candidate is more "independent in his thoughts and actions," something McCain tried to emphasize during his acceptance speech.

Ratings of McCain and Obama on Character Dimensions

USA Today/Gallup poll, Sept. 5-7, 2008

Obama has led McCain throughout the campaign on the two caring dimensions, but his margin on both was reduced after the GOP convention, from a 20-point advantage on "cares about the needs of people like you" to 12 points, and from a 13-point advantage on "shares your values" down to 4 points.

It is not unusual for the public's perceptions of the candidates to shift after each is cast in a warm glow at his party's nominating convention. John Kerry gained on George W. Bush on each of eight comparative character ratings asked before and after the 2004 Democratic convention, while Bush gained on five of six dimensions asked before and after the 2004 Republican convention. Bush also saw gains an all nine quality ratings asked after the 2000 Republican convention, while Al Gore's ratings improved on the same nine ratings after the 2000 Democratic convention. In fact, in that year, the public rated Bush as better than Gore on all nine dimensions after the Republican convention, but then shifted to rate Gore as better than Bush on eight of the nine dimensions after the Democratic convention.

Usually, the public's assessments return to more typical levels once the campaign moves forward from the conventions. Thus, McCain's stronger positioning on these dimensions in the current poll is likely to recede in the coming weeks.

Notwithstanding any short-term movement tied to the party conventions, there seem to be well-established party stereotypes influencing how voters rate the candidates on these comparative character items. The most common are to rate the Democratic candidate as better on caring about people's needs, and the Republican candidate as superior on leadership. Democrats Bill Clinton (1996), Gore (2000), Kerry (2004), and Obama have all been viewed as better than their respective Republican opponents on caring about people for most of their presidential campaigns, while Republicans George W. Bush (2000 and 2004) and McCain have usually been perceived as stronger leaders than their Democratic rivals. Thus, Obama's advantage on empathy and McCain's on leadership may reflect party stereotypes in addition to a basic assessment of each individual's relative merits on each dimension.

Survey Methods

Results are based on telephone interviews with 1,022 national adults, aged 18 and older, conducted Sept. 5-7, 2008. For results based on the total sample of national adults, one can say with 95% confidence that the maximum margin of sampling error is ±3 percentage points.

Interviews are conducted with respondents on land-line telephones (for respondents with a land-line telephone) and cellular phones (for respondents who are cell-phone only).

In addition to sampling error, question wording and practical difficulties in conducting surveys can introduce error or bias into the findings of public opinion polls.

September 10, 2008
MAJORITY OF AMERICANS NOT FEARFUL OF TERRORIST ATTACK
A slim majority (52%) are satisfied with U.S. progress in the war on terrorism

by Lymari Morales, Gallup Poll Staff Writer

While a new bipartisan report concludes that the United States remains "dangerously vulnerable" to terrorist attacks, most Americans do not fear being directly affected. Only 38% are very or some-

what worried that they or a family member will become a victim of terrorism. This is down from 47% last July, and from a high of 59% in October 2001, but is still short of a post-9/11 low of 28% in January 2004.

How worried are you that you or someone in your family will become a victim of terrorism?
Trend since Sept. 11, 2001

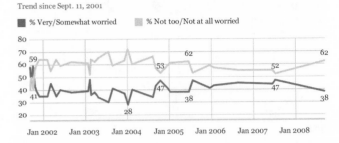

The report from the Partnership for a Secure America comes on the eve of the seventh anniversary of the terrorist attacks of Sept. 11, 2001, and less than eight weeks before Americans elect a new leader who will continue the nation's fight against terrorism. The report gives the U.S. government a "C" grade on how it has managed the terrorist threat, and urges the country's next president to improve counterproliferation efforts.

Americans are roughly split on how things are going for the United States in the war on terrorism, with 52% saying they are very or somewhat satisfied and 47% saying they are not too or not at all satisfied. Satisfaction on this measure peaked at 75% during the first year of the war in Afghanistan, subsequently dipping below 60% in 2004, and leveling off in the current range since then.

How satisfied are you with the way things are going for the U.S. in the war on terrorism?

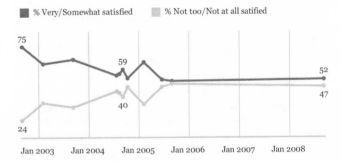

Currently, terrorism does not appear to factor high in Americans' choice for a new president, as only 12% consider terrorism the most important factor in their vote. Earlier this year, when given a choice, a majority of Americans said they would prefer a presidential candidate whose greatest strength is fixing the economy rather than one whose greatest strength is protecting the country from terrorism. This may reflect the huge volume of negative economic news on the airwaves, compared to the more muted discussion of the ongoing global terrorist threat. In August of this year, only 2% of Americans mentioned terrorism when asked to name the most important problem facing the country, down from 46% in October 2001.

Any increased attention to the issue of terrorism is most likely to benefit Republican presidential nominee John McCain, as he has consistently outperformed Democratic rival Barack Obama on this

What do you think is the most important problem facing this country today?
[OPEN-ENDED]

Trend, October 2001-August 2008

■ % "Terrorism"

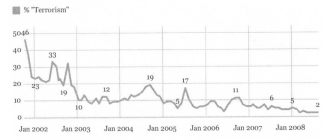

issue throughout this election year, most recently by 17 percentage points.

Regardless of which presidential candidate you support, please tell me if you think Barack Obama or John McCain would better handle the issue of terrorism?

■ % Obama   ■ % McCain

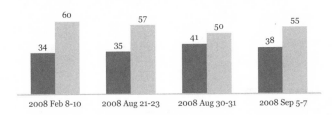

Bottom Line

Seven years after the terrorist attacks of Sept. 11, 2001, Americans appear to have mixed feelings about the progress the U.S. government has made to protect them from future attacks. While a majority of Americans express little worry about being directly affected by a terrorist attack, only a slim majority are satisfied with how the United States is handling the war on terrorism overall. Although a new report concludes that the next U.S. president will have much work to do on the counterterrorism front, up to now, Americans have not been making the terrorism issue a top priority in the ongoing presidential campaign. A majority say that a president's being able to handle the economy is more important to their vote than his ability to handle terrorism. It is of course possible that the bipartisan report or a terrorism-related news event could change attitudes or bring this issue back to the forefront.

Survey Methods

Results are based on telephone interviews with 1,022 national adults, aged 18 and older, conducted Sept. 5-7, 2008. For results based on the total sample of national adults, one can say with 95% confidence that the maximum margin of sampling error is ±3 percentage points. For results based on the half sample of 465 adults in Form B, the maximum margin of sampling error is ±5 percentage points.

Interviews are conducted with respondents on land-line telephones (for respondents with a land-line telephone) and cellular phones (for respondents who are cell-phone only).

In addition to sampling error, question wording and practical difficulties in conducting surveys can introduce error or bias into the findings of public opinion polls.

September 10, 2008
ON ECONOMY, MCCAIN GAINS GROUND ON OBAMA
Obama has advantage on education, healthcare

by Frank Newport, Gallup Poll Editor in Chief

In the Sept. 5-7 *USA Today*/Gallup poll, 48% of Americans say Barack Obama can better handle the economy, while 45% choose John McCain. This marks a significant gain by McCain; just before the Democratic National Convention in late August, Obama had a 16-point margin over McCain on the economy.

Regardless of which candidate you support, please tell me if you think Barack Obama or John McCain would better handle the ECONOMY?

■ % Obama   ■ % McCain

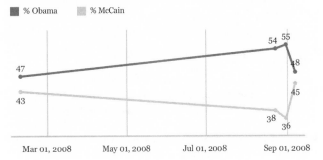

This type of improved positioning on McCain's part is not unexpected. Candidates generally enjoy an overall "bounce" in the horse race after their conventions, and concomitantly gain ground on specific issues and characteristics as well.

It's fair to say both candidates will continue to focus heavily on the economy between now and the election. That, coupled with the possibility that some of McCain's convention-related gains will dissipate, suggests there could be further change in this measure in the weeks ahead.

It's a critically important issue. In this poll, voters overwhelmingly choose the economy as the most important issue they will take into account in their vote for president.

If you had to choose, which of the following issues will be most important to your vote for president -- [ROTATED: the economy, terrorism, the situation in Iraq, healthcare, energy, including gas prices], or some other issue?

	2008 Aug 21-23	2008 Sep 5-7
	%	%
The economy	43	42
The situation in Iraq	15	13
Energy, including gas prices	14	13
Healthcare	11	13
Terrorism	9	12
Illegal immigration (vol.)	1	1
Abortion (vol.)	1	1
Education (vol.)	*	1
Environment (vol.)	*	*
Other	4	4
No opinion	3	1

* Less than 0.5%

(vol.) = Volunteered response

The positioning of the candidates on 10 other issues tested in the Sept. 5-7 poll is displayed on the accompanying chart.

Regardless of which presidential candidate you support, please tell me if you think Barack Obama or John McCain would better handle each of the following issues.

	Obama	McCain
	%	%
Education	53	36
Healthcare policy	52	40
Abortion	47	42
The economy	48	45
Energy	46	46
Taxes	43	49
Illegal immigration	38	47
The situation in Iraq	42	52
Foreign trade	38	51
Gun policy	37	51
Terrorism	38	55

USA Today/Gallup poll, Sept. 5-7, 2008

Obama has significant strength on two domestic issues: education and healthcare policy. McCain, on the other hand, has significant strength on five issues, mostly dealing with international matters: terrorism, gun policy, foreign trade, the situation in Iraq, and illegal immigration.

These strengths are generally representative of Obama's and McCain's positioning throughout the campaign, and to a degree are similar to broad Democratic versus Republican strengths in previous elections. Democrats typically have the advantage on domestic issues, while Republicans do better on international issues, and, in particular since 9/11, on the issue of terrorism.

Gallup has not previously asked Americans to choose between the two candidates on gun policy. In this poll, at any rate, McCain wins big on the issue. As has become widely known, Sarah Palin, McCain's vice-presidential nominee, is a hunter and a member of the National Rifle Association. Whether this has affected the public's views of the candidates on this issue is unknown.

Similarly, this is the first time respondents have been asked to choose between the two candidates on abortion. Obama has a slight edge on the issue, as seen in the accompanying table. Palin's strong pro-life position has become widely known since her selection by McCain, particularly in light of the fact that she recently gave birth to a Down syndrome baby (whose condition Palin knew during her pregnancy) and that her daughter is pregnant and electing to have the baby (and to marry the father). Americans at this point in time tilt pro-choice in their orientation, so Obama's slight advantage on abortion is perhaps not surprising. But again, it is not possible to determine what impact, if any, McCain's selection of Palin as his running mate may have had on these perceptions.

Survey Methods

Results are based on telephone interviews with 1,022 national adults, aged 18 and older, conducted Sept. 5-7, 2008. For results based on the total sample of national adults, one can say with 95% confidence that the maximum margin of sampling error is ±3 percentage points.

Interviews are conducted with respondents on land-line telephones (for respondents with a land-line telephone) and cellular phones (for respondents who are cell-phone only).

In addition to sampling error, question wording and practical difficulties in conducting surveys can introduce error or bias into the findings of public opinion polls.

September 11, 2008

NO DISPROPORTIONATE SHIFT IN WHITE WOMEN'S PREFERENCES
4-Point shift toward McCain appears about average

by Frank Newport, Jeffrey M. Jones, and Lydia Saad, Gallup Poll Editor

An analysis of Gallup Poll Daily tracking interviewing conducted before and after the two major-party conventions shows that the impact of the conventions was not materially different for white women than it was for white men, and neither group's shifts were substantially different than the changes among the overall electorate.

Gallup Poll Daily Tracking: Changes in Candidate Support Through Convention Period

	Pre-Biden	Biden/ DNC	Post-DNC	RNC	Post-RNC
	Aug 20-22	Aug 23-28	Aug 29-31	Sep 1-4	Sep 5-8
	%	%	%	%	%
All registered voters					
Obama	46	47	49	48	44
McCain	44	43	43	43	49
Sample size	2655	5411	2733	3716	3638
White reg. voters					
Obama	38	39	42	40	37
McCain	51	51	51	51	55
Sample size	2244	4519	2326	3105	3049
White Men (RV)					
Obama	36	37	40	36	34
McCain	56	55	53	56	59
Sample size	1131	2234	1150	1553	1512
White Women (RV)					
Obama	40	41	43	44	40
McCain	47	47	49	46	51
Sample size	1113	2285	1176	1552	1537

Gallup Poll Daily Tracking

These conclusions are based on comparisons of very large samples of Gallup Poll Daily tracking interviews conducted at intervals before, during, and after the two conventions. In general, the comparison shows only a modest change in vote patterns, with white women shifting in the same broad ways as the overall sample average.

Just before the Democratic National Convention (in Gallup Poll Daily tracking interviewing from Aug. 20-22), white women broke 47% to 40% in favor of McCain over Obama. In interviewing from Sept. 5-8, after both conventions were completed, white women's margin of support for McCain over Obama edged up modestly to 51% to 40%. This represents a gain of four percentage points for McCain among white women and no change in their support for Obama.

Among white men, the change in preference for McCain was very similar to the change among white women, coupled with a slight loss of support for Obama. White men went from 56% to 36% support for McCain over Obama to a 59% to 34% split now.

More generally, the data show that McCain gained four points among all white voters (both men and women), and Obama lost one point.

(For all voters, regardless of race or gender, the race shifted from a 46% to 44% advantage for Obama in Aug. 20-22 polling to a 49% to 44% advantage for McCain after the conventions. That's a gain of five points for McCain and a loss of two for Obama.)

In short, it appears that the impact of the two conventions was not materially different for white women than it was for white men, and neither group's shifts were substantially different than the changes among the overall electorate. Among all groups, McCain gained during the time period encompassing the two conventions, and Obama was roughly stable.

Despite the intense focus on the potential impact on white women of McCain's selection of Sarah Palin as his vice presidential running mate, the Gallup data do not show that to this point white women have been significantly different in their response to the convention period than has the average voter.

Survey Methods

Results are based on telephone interviews conducted between August 20 and September 8, 2008, as part of the Gallup Poll Daily Tracking Survey, for which Gallup is interviewing no fewer than 1,000 U.S. adults nationwide each day during 2008.

Interviews reported here are based on registered voters, aged 18 and older. The sample sizes for each time period analyzed in this analysis are displayed in the table above. The margin of sample error varies for each of these groups, but in all cases, one can say with 95% confidence that the maximum margin of sampling error is ±3 percentage points or less.

Interviews are conducted with respondents on land-line telephones (for respondents with a land-line telephone) and cellular phones (for respondents who are cell-phone only).

In addition to sampling error, question wording and practical difficulties in conducting surveys can introduce error or bias into the findings of public opinion polls.

September 12, 2008

BATTLE FOR CONGRESS SUDDENLY LOOKS COMPETITIVE

Democrats' double-digit lead on the "generic ballot" slips to 3 points

by Lydia Saad, Gallup Poll Senior Editor

A potential shift in fortunes for the Republicans in Congress is seen in the latest *USA Today*/Gallup survey, with the Democrats now leading the Republicans by just 3 percentage points, 48% to 45%, in voters' "generic ballot" preferences for Congress. This is down from consistent double-digit Democratic leads seen on this measure over the past year.

As is true for the current structure of voting preferences for president, Democratic voters are nearly uniform in their support for the Democratic candidate in their congressional districts (92%), Republican voters are nearly uniform in their support for the Republican candidate (94%), and independents are closely split, with 44% backing the Democrat and 40% the Republican.

The new results come from a Sept. 5-7 survey conducted immediately after the Republican National Convention and mirror the resulting enhanced position of the Republican Party seen in several other indicators. These range from John McCain's improved standing against Barack Obama in the presidential race to improved favorability ratings of the Republicans, to Republican gains in party iden-

If the elections for Congress were being held today, which party's candidate would you vote for in your congressional district -- (the Democratic Party's candidate or the Republican Party's candidate)?

Based on registered voters

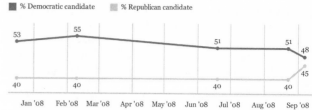

tification. The sustainability of all of these findings is an open question that polling will answer over the next few weeks.

The positive impact of the GOP convention on polling indicators of Republican strength is further seen in the operation of Gallup's "likely voter" model in this survey. Republicans, who are now much more enthused about the 2008 election than they were prior to the convention, show heightened interest in voting, and thus outscore Democrats in apparent likelihood to vote in November. As a result, Republican candidates now lead Democratic candidates among likely voters by 5 percentage points, 50% to 45%.

Generic Ballot Comparison

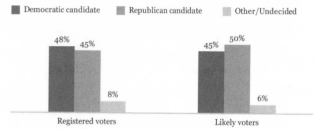

USA Today/Gallup poll, Sept. 5-7, 2008

If these numbers are sustained through Election Day—a big if—Republicans could be expected to regain control of the U.S. House of Representatives.

As Gallup's long-term "generic ballot" trend shows, the Democrats held a sizable lead on this measure from the time they won back control of Congress in the fall of 2006 through last month. If the current closer positioning of the parties holds, the structure of congressional preferences will be similar to most of the period from 1994 through 2005, when Republicans won and maintained control of Congress.

Generic Ballot -- Trend Since 1992

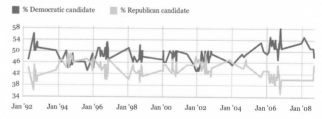

Congressional Approval Also Troubling for Democrats

With only 18% of Americans in August saying they approve of the job Congress is doing, similar to the average 20% approval rating for

Congress all year, the Democrats in Congress have additional cause for concern. This scant level of approval could signal that voters are in the mood for change, disproportionately hurting Democratic incumbents.

The last time the yearly average for approval of Congress approached this low a level was in 2006, when the Republicans lost majority control of Congress after 12 years in power. The previous occasion was in 1994, when the Republicans wrested control from the Democrats. In both of these midterm election years, the average congressional approval score was 25%. However, with an 18% approval rating for Congress in 1992, the Democrats succeeded in holding their majority in Congress. That was a presidential year in which the Democratic candidate, Bill Clinton, won.

Average Annual Approval Ratings for U.S. Congress

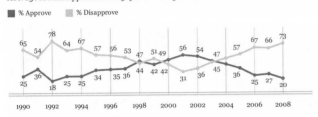

Note: 2008 ratings are for January through August

The issues raised by today's low approval ratings of Congress are reinforced by recent Gallup Poll findings that relatively few voters generally believe "most members" of Congress deserve re-election. That figure was only 36% in July, much lower than the 51% or better reading found in recent election years when the party of the sitting majority in Congress maintained power.

Bottom Line

The new *USA Today*/Gallup measurement of generic ballot preferences for Congress casts some doubt on the previously assumed inevitability of the Democrats' maintaining control of Congress. Until now, the dark shadow cast by George W. Bush's widespread unpopularity has suppressed Republican Party identification nationwide, as well as voters' willingness to support the Republican candidate running for Congress in their district.

Now that the symbolic leadership of the party is shifting away from Bush and toward the suddenly popular Republican presidential ticket of John McCain and Sarah Palin, things may be changing. This shrinks Bush's shadow over the Republicans, revealing more of the Democrats' own shadow stemming from high disapproval of Congress. The key question is how much of this is temporary because of the tremendous bounce in support for the Republicans on many dimensions coming right off of their convention. The degree to which the Republican bounce is sustained, rather than dissipates, in the weeks ahead will determine whether the 2008 race for Congress could in fact be highly competitive, rather than a Democratic sweep.

Survey Methods

Results are based on telephone interviews with 1,022 national adults, aged 18 and older, conducted Sept. 5-7, 2008. For results based on the total sample of national adults, one can say with 95% confidence that the maximum margin of sampling error is ±3 percentage points. For results based on the sample of 959 registered voters, the maximum margin of sampling error is ±3 percentage points.

Results for likely voters are based on the subsample of 823 survey respondents deemed most likely to vote in the November 2008 general election, according to a series of questions measuring current voting intentions and past voting behavior. For results based on the total sample of likely voters, one can say with 95% confidence that the maximum margin of sampling error is ±4 percentage points. The "likely voter" model assumes a turnout of 60% of national adults. The likely voter sample is weighted to match this assumption, so the weighted sample size is 613.

Interviews are conducted with respondents on land-line telephones (for respondents with a land-line telephone) and cellular phones (for respondents who are cell-phone only).

In addition to sampling error, question wording and practical difficulties in conducting surveys can introduce error or bias into the findings of public opinion polls.

September 15, 2008
REPUBLICANS CRY FOUL OVER MEDIA COVERAGE OF PALIN
Majority say coverage of Palin, and of McCain, has been unfairly negative

by Lydia Saad, Gallup Poll Senior Editor

The pundit-fueled firestorm around media coverage of John McCain's running mate Sarah Palin is evident in Americans' highly mixed views on the subject. About the same proportion of Americans say media coverage of Palin has been unfairly negative (33%) as say it has been about right (36%). An additional 21% say coverage of her has been unfairly positive.

In your view, has the news media's coverage of Sarah Palin during the presidential campaign been -- [ROTATED: unfairly positive, about right, or unfairly negative]?

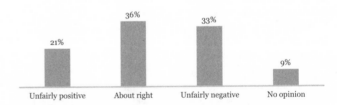

Gallup Poll, Sept. 8-11, 2008

These views—taken from a Sept. 8-11 Gallup Poll conducted mostly before the airing of Palin's interview with ABC News' Charlie Gibson—are sharply partisan. A majority of Republicans (54%), compared with only 29% of independents and 18% of Democrats, think Palin is getting a raw deal from the press. Three times as many Democrats as Republicans (34% vs. 11%) think coverage of her has been too positive.

By contrast, a majority of Americans say media treatment of McCain has been about right (53%). However, among the remainder, the balance tilts more than 2-to-1 toward saying coverage of him has been unfairly negative: 30% vs. 13%. Republicans are closely divided on this, with the slight majority (51%) saying coverage of McCain has been too negative and close to half (43%) saying it has been about right.

Americans' Evaluation of Media Coverage of Sarah Palin

	Unfairly positive	About right	Unfairly negative	No opinion
	%	%	%	%
National adults	21	36	33	9
Republicans	11	31	54	4
Independents	18	38	29	15
Democrats	34	39	18	8

Gallup Poll, Sept. 8-11, 2008

These perceptions haven't changed much since they were previously measured, in late July. The view that coverage of McCain is about right has increased slightly (from 46% to 53%), as the percentage with no opinion on the issue has declined. But there has been no meaningful change in perceptions that he is getting either unfair positive treatment or unfair negative treatment.

Americans' Evaluation of Media Coverage of John McCain

	Unfairly positive	About right	Unfairly negative	No opinion
	%	%	%	%
2008 Sep 8-11*	13	53	30	4
Republicans	5	43	51	1
Independents	12	58	22	9
Democrats	23	57	16	3
2008 Jul 25-27*	12	46	32	10

* Among national adults

Close to half of Americans—including most Democrats—believe media treatment of Obama is about right. This is a slight increase from late July, when only 39% took this view. At the same time, the perception that media treatment of Obama is unfairly positive has fallen from 39% to 32%. However, twice as many Americans still hold this view as say coverage of him is unfairly negative. Six in 10 Republicans think Obama has received overly favorable press coverage.

Americans' Evaluation of Media Coverage of Barack Obama

	Unfairly positive	About right	Unfairly negative	No opinion
	%	%	%	%
2008 Sep 8-11*	32	47	16	5
Republicans	60	32	6	3
Independents	24	50	18	8
Democrats	16	58	23	2
2008 Jul 25-27*	39	39	15	7

* Among national adults

Americans broadly view the media's treatment thus far of Joe Biden as fair. Nearly 6 in 10 (59%) say coverage of Obama's running mate has been about right, while much smaller proportions believe it has been either unfairly positive (15%) or unfairly negative (11%).

Americans' Evaluation of Media Coverage of Joe Biden

	Unfairly positive	About right	Unfairly negative	No opinion
	%	%	%	%
National adults	15	59	11	16
Republicans	24	53	7	16
Independents	12	56	9	23
Democrats	9	66	16	9

Gallup Poll, Sept. 8-11, 2008

Men and women have nearly identical views of how Palin, Biden, and McCain are being treated in the media. However, men are slightly more likely than women (36% vs. 29%) to say the media's coverage of Obama has been unfairly positive.

Media Ratings Turn More Negative

Republicans' criticism of how the media is treating their party's presidential and vice-presidential candidates may be taking a toll on broader public confidence in the mass media.

The percentage of Americans saying they have a great deal or fair amount of confidence in the media when it comes to fairness and accuracy is now just 43%, the lowest level seen over the past decade (in 2004, it was a similar 44%). At 21%, the percentage of Americans saying they have no confidence at all in the media is a record high.

In general, how much trust and confidence do you have in the mass media -- such as newspapers, TV, and radio -- when it comes to reporting the news fully, accurately, and fairly -- a great deal, a fair amount, not very much, or none at all?

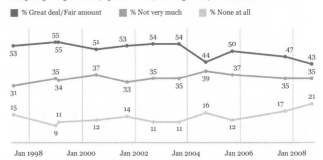

The increase since 2007, from 17% to 21%, in those saying they have no confidence in the media is mostly because of worsening attitudes among Republicans.

In general, how much trust and confidence do you have in the mass media?
% None at all, by party ID

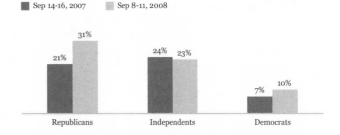

Bottom Line

During the Democratic primary season, Hillary Clinton's campaign representatives issued steady complaints that their candidate wasn't getting the same favorable treatment that Obama was receiving from the media. That charge seemed to filter into public opinion in July, when Gallup found as many Americans saying media coverage of Obama was too positive as said it was about right. This included 60% of Republicans and 22% of Democrats.

That sentiment has simmered down somewhat, although there is a persistent tilt toward believing Obama is getting a break from the media.

Today, there is much more controversy among Americans about the media's coverage of Palin. More than half are dissatisfied with the nature of coverage of her, saying it is either too positive or too negative. This seems to reflect the raging political pundit debate over whether the media's commentary on Palin's governmental qualifications and personal life has gone too far. Whether valid, or merely a political tactic, the election-year shots at the media for biased coverage seem to be eroding public confidence in the entire news media as a reputable institution.

Survey Methods

Results are based on telephone interviews with 1,007 national adults, aged 18 and older, conducted Sept. 8-11, 2008. For results based on the total sample of national adults, one can say with 95% confidence that the maximum margin of sampling error is ±3 percentage points.

Interviews are conducted with respondents on land-line telephones (for respondents with a land-line telephone) and cellular phones (for respondents who are cell-phone only).

In addition to sampling error, question wording and practical difficulties in conducting surveys can introduce error or bias into the findings of public opinion polls.

(Asked of those with a candidate preference) What would you say are the one or two most important reasons why you would vote for [preferred candidate]? [OPEN-ENDED]

(Asked of those with a candidate leaning) What would you say are the one or two most important reasons why you lean toward voting for [preferred candidate]?

Based on 944 adults with a candidate preference or leaning; ±4 pct. pts.

2008 Sep 8-11	National adults	Obama voters ^	McCain voters †
	%	%	%
Want change/Fresh approach	21	37	3
Experienced/Qualified	12	2	27
Always support that party	11	12	10
Economy/His economic plan	11	16	6
Honest/Has integrity/Good character	11	9	12
Agree with his values/views (nonspecific)	10	13	7
National security/Terrorism issue	9	2	18
Iraq war/plans for handling it	6	9	4
For the working/middle class	6	10	1
Like his choice of running mate	5	1	10
Trustworthy/Trust him	5	4	6
Military background/Service to country	5	1	9
Smart/Intelligent/Knowledgeable	4	7	2
International affairs/Foreign policy	3	3	4
Favors smaller government	3	2	4
Independent/Goes against party/A maverick	3	1	4
Conservative/More conservative candidate	3	1	6
Healthcare reform	2	4	1
Energy/His energy plan	2	2	1
Taxes/His tax plan	2	*	4
Education/His education plan	1	2	*
Environment/Global warming	1	2	--
Other	4	4	4
No reason in particular (vol.)	2	1	2
No opinion	1	1	--

* Less than 0.5%
(vol.) = Volunteered response
^ Based on 448 Obama voters, ±5 pct. pts.
† Based on 446 McCain voters, ±5 pct. pts.

September 16, 2008

FOR OBAMA'S VOTERS, IT'S CHANGE; FOR MCCAIN'S, EXPERIENCE

Only 3% of McCain supporters volunteer "change" as reason for their vote

by Frank Newport, Gallup Poll Editor in Chief

Despite John McCain's recent efforts to adopt the "change" positioning that has been central to Barack Obama's campaign strategy for much of the year, new Gallup Poll data show only 3% of McCain supporters volunteering that they are voting for the Republican nominee because of his ability to bring about change. Thirty-seven percent of Obama's supporters give "change" as the reason for their support. McCain supporters are most likely to explain their vote with references to McCain's experience and qualifications.

In a Sept. 8-11 poll, Gallup asked voters to cite the main reasons they support their preferred presidential candidate. The open-ended question, asked as a follow-up to the basic ballot question, reads: "What would you say are the one or two most important reasons why you would vote for (John McCain/Barack Obama)?"

It is clear that the "change" mantra has resonated with Obama supporters. Thirty-seven percent of his supporters cite "change" as

the reason for their support, by far the largest single response category for his voters.

Other reasons given by those supporting Obama include his economic plan/ability to handle the economy, general agreement with his values or issues, the respondent's propensity to vote Democratic, Obama's support for the working and middle classes, his plan for the Iraq war, and his honesty.

These themes in general appear to reflect the dominant thrusts of the Obama campaign: change, fixing the economy, helping the working and middle classes, and Iraq.

Only 3% of McCain's supporters say they are supporting him because of his ability to bring about change. (Another 4% mention that McCain is a maverick and goes against his own party.) The current data were collected Monday through Thursday, Sept. 8-11, well after the Republican National Convention, at which McCain emphasized change, including his acceptance speech statement that "We need to change the way government does almost everything." In fact, 10% of McCain's supporters in this poll say they are planning on voting for McCain because of his selection of Alaska Gov. Sarah Palin as his running mate, suggesting that events occurring in and around the convention in general are reflected in voters' views in the current poll. Yet, there is little indication that McCain's supporters have adopted the change theme as their stated reason for supporting him.

Instead, the dominant reasons given by McCain's supporters focus first and foremost on the experience dimension, named by 27%. That's followed by 18% who mention McCain's ability to handle terrorism and national security. Other categories of reasons for supporting McCain include his honesty, his choice of a vice-presidential running mate (as noted above), the fact that the respondent always votes Republican, and McCain's military background and service to his country.

These themes, as is the case for Obama, echo McCain's general campaign positioning this year—with the exception of the McCain campaign's recent emphasis on change.

Conclusions

1. Not surprisingly, when asked why they are supporting a candidate, supporters tend to feed back the basic positioning themes that the candidates' campaigns have developed and that the candidates have delivered in interviews, speeches, and campaign commercials throughout the year.
2. But McCain's recent emphasis on change as one of his dominant campaign positions has not yet been reflected to any substantial degree in the reasons McCain's supporters give for voting for him.
3. McCain's surprise selection of Palin as his vice-presidential running mate has apparently had a direct impact on some of his supporters, 1 out of 10 of whom volunteer his choice of her as their reason for supporting him. By way of contrast, only a small fraction of Obama supporters mention the choice of Joe Biden as their reason for supporting Obama.
4. In a broad sense, the explanations given for voting for the two candidates reflect the domestic (Democratic)/international (Republicans) divide seen in recent years in the positioning of the two parties in Americans' eyes, although some Obama supporters do say their reason for voting for Obama results from his position on the Iraq war.

Survey Methods

Results are based on telephone interviews with 1,007 national adults, aged 18 and older, conducted Sept. 8-11, 2008. For results based on the total sample of national adults, one can say with 95% confidence that the maximum margin of sampling error is ±3 percentage points.

Interviews are conducted with respondents on land-line telephones (for respondents with a land-line telephone) and cellular phones (for respondents who are cell-phone only).

In addition to sampling error, question wording and practical difficulties in conducting surveys can introduce error or bias into the findings of public opinion polls.

September 18, 2008
OBAMA'S VOTERS MORE NEGATIVE ON ECONOMY THAN MCCAIN'S
Obama's voters mostly perceive grave problems; McCain's more upbeat

by Lydia Saad, Gallup Poll Senior Editor

Supporters of Barack Obama for president have views about the nation's economy that differ strongly from those of John McCain supporters, with Obama's supporters describing it in much more grave terms. According to a Sept. 15-16 *USA Today*/Gallup poll, most Obama voters (73%), contrasted with less than half of McCain voters (45%), believe the economy is in either a "recession" or a "depression."

Right now, do you think the U.S. economy is growing, slowing down, in a recession, or in an economic depression?

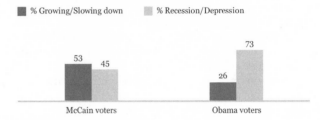

USA Today/Gallup, Sept. 15-16, 2008

In sync with McCain's often-stated view that the fundamentals of the economy are strong, voters who plan to back McCain in November are more likely to think the economy is at worst slowing down. A combined 53% of McCain supporters say the economy is either slowing down or, in fact, growing. Only a quarter of Obama's voters (26%) agree.

These voter differences in economic perceptions are similar to those seen between Republicans and Democrats, more broadly. Importantly, political independents (who represent the swing voting group potentially most influenced by the candidates' stances on the issue) are much more similar to Democrats than to Republicans on this question.

Perceived State of U.S. Economy -- by Party ID

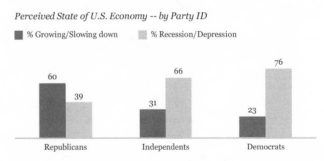

USA Today/Gallup, Sept. 15-16, 2008

As a result, a majority of Americans overall—61%—now believe the U.S. economy is experiencing either a recession or a depression, up from 45% holding one of these views in January. Few Americans surveyed at either point have said the economy is growing, but in January the slight majority (53%) said it was either growing or slowing down. Today, only 37% hold either of those more positive views.

Perceived State of U.S. Economy -- Trend

■ Jan 30-Feb 2, 2008   ■ Sep 15-16, 2008

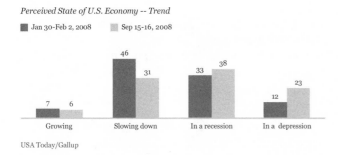

USA Today/Gallup

Although the United States is technically not in a "depression," the current problems on Wall Street are being widely described as the "deepest crisis since the Depression." This could be contributing to the near-doubling since January of public perceptions that the economy is in a depression, from 12% to 23%. Slightly more Americans today also believe that the economy is in a recession—something many economists have already pronounced is underway. This is up five percentage points since January, from 33% to 38%.

The expansion since January in perceptions that the economy is in a recession or depression coincides with the decline in Americans' more basic consumer confidence over the same period. Gallup Poll Daily tracking from Jan.30-Feb. 1 found 66% of Americans classified as negative in their economic views and 11% positive. Today, those figures are 78% negative and 7% positive.

Better Days to Come

The consumer confidence picture is not entirely bleak, however. In contrast to Americans' grave views of current economic conditions, they are markedly upbeat about where the economy will be a year from now. Nearly half believe the economy will be growing at that point. Only 28% believe it will be in a recession or depression.

This outlook is not much different from that measured in January, when Americans' underlying perceptions of current economic conditions were much more positive than they are today.

A year from now, do you think the U.S. economy will be growing, slowing down, in a recession, or in an economic depression?

■ Jan 30-Feb 2, 2008   ■ Sep 15-16 , 2008

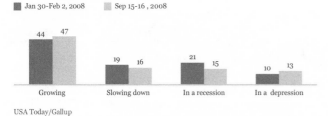

USA Today/Gallup

Bottom Line

Americans as a whole have grown substantially more negative in their characterization of the U.S. economy than they were at the outset of 2008. While Republicans (and McCain supporters) view the current situation in less dire terms than do Democrats (and Obama supporters), most political independents share most Democrats' view that the economy is in either a recession or a depression.

From the standpoint of the election, it is clearly important, therefore, that the candidates demonstrate concern and competency on the issue. At the same time, the fact that most Americans think the situation will improve markedly by this time next year suggests they

have enough confidence left in the economy to believe it can recover fairly quickly. That could have important implications for how Obama and McCain frame the current economic problems, and their proposed solutions.

Survey Methods

Results are based on telephone interviews with 1,015 national adults, aged 18 and older, conducted Sept. 15-16, 2008. For results based on the total sample of national adults, one can say with 95% confidence that the maximum margin of sampling error is ±3 percentage points.

Interviews are conducted with respondents on land-line telephones (for respondents with a land-line telephone) and cellular phones (for respondents who are cell-phone only).

In addition to sampling error, question wording and practical difficulties in conducting surveys can introduce error or bias into the findings of public opinion polls.

September 18, 2008
TRUST IN GOVERNMENT REMAINS LOW
Only 26% are satisfied with way nation is being governed

by Jeffrey M. Jones, Gallup Poll Managing Editor

Gallup's annual Governance poll finds a continued deterioration in public confidence in U.S. government institutions. Just 26% of Americans say they are satisfied with the way the nation is being governed, the lowest in the eight-year history of the Governance poll and tying a 1973 Gallup reading as the lowest ever.

On the whole, would you say you are satisfied or dissatisfied with the way the nation is being governed?

■ Satisfied

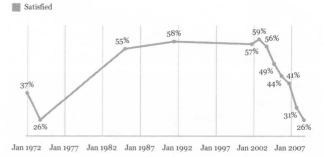

The percentage of Americans satisfied with the way the nation is being governed has declined each year since 2002, when a high of 59% were satisfied.

The low levels of satisfaction with the government measured in this year's poll, conducted Sept. 8-11, seem to derive from highly negative evaluations of the jobs President Bush (31% approve) and Congress (18% approve) are doing. Fifty percent approve of the Supreme Court. Another indication of Americans' disappointment with Bush and Congress is the historically low levels of trust the public has in the executive and legislative branches of the federal government. The poll finds trust in the executive branch, headed by the president, near the record low from the Watergate era. Just 42% of Americans say they have a great deal or fair amount of trust in the executive branch, similar to last year's 43%, but the lowest since a 40% reading in April 1974. Trust in the executive branch has been below 50% each of the last three years. That coincides with the roughly two-year trend in sub-40% job approval ratings for Bush.

Amount of Trust and Confidence in the Executive Branch Headed by the President

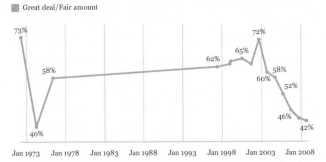

The poll finds just 48% of Americans saying they have a great deal or fair amount of trust in the government's ability to handle domestic problems, essentially the same as last year's all-time low of 47%.

Amount of Trust and Confidence in Federal Government to Handle Domestic Problems

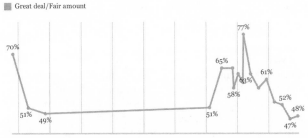

Trust in the legislative branch is only slightly better than trust in the executive branch, with 47% saying they have a great deal or fair amount of trust in Congress. But this marks a new low for Congress, as trust in the legislative branch has dropped below 50% for the first time in 15 measurements Gallup has taken since 1972.

Amount of Trust and Confidence in the Legislative Branch Consisting of the U.S. Senate and House of Representatives

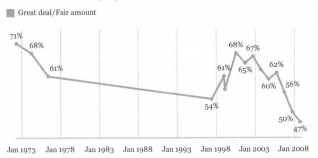

At 69%, Americans' level of trust in the judicial branch of the federal government remains strong, and is virtually unchanged from where it has been each of the last four years.

Amount of Trust and Confidence in the Judicial Branch Headed by the U.S. Supreme Court

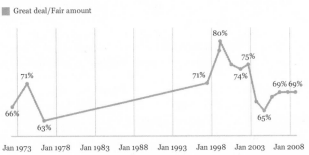

While public frustration with the government seems directed more at Congress and the president than the Supreme Court, it also appears to have to do more with the government's performance on domestic rather than international matters.

At the same time, a majority of 56% trusts the government's ability to handle international problems. This is a rare area where public attitudes about government have actually improved. Last year, 51% were satisfied with the federal government's handling of international matters, which was an all-time low. The greater trust may result from U.S. progress in the Iraq war over the last 12 months.

Amount of Trust and Confidence in Federal Government to Handle International Problems

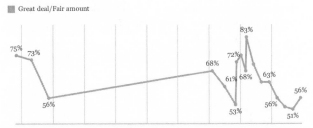

Partisan Differences

While no demographic or political subgroup of Americans shows a high level of satisfaction with the way the nation is being governed, Republicans (48%) are much more likely to do so than are independents (23%) or Democrats (9%).

Republicans also express greater trust in the executive and judicial branches, as well as in the government's ability to handle international and domestic problems, than do Democrats and independents. On the other hand, Democrats are more trusting than other party groups in the legislative branch, currently controlled by the Democratic Party. Thus, trust to a large degree is influenced by which party controls the various branches of government.

Implications

The public is clearly frustrated with the government's performance; thus, the presidential candidates' competition to be viewed as the "candidate of change" makes sense. It is unclear how much a change in leadership by itself will necessarily improve public trust. Gallup has only limited evidence in this regard, having asked about trust in the government's ability to deal with domestic and international issues around the last administration change in 2001. The public expressed

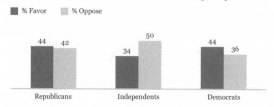

	Democrat	Independent	Republican
Federal gov't., domestic problems	35%	39%	69%
Federal gov't., international problems	39%	50%	83%
Executive	14%	33%	83%
Legislative	61%	44%	36%
Judicial	59%	62%	86%

Sept. 8-11 Gallup Poll

slightly more trust in the government to deal with both domains in February 2001 compared with July 2000—suggesting a modest "honeymoon" period in public trust for the new administration.

But ratings of government institutions are to a large degree influenced by assessments of conditions for the United States both domestically (especially in terms of the economy) and internationally. Historically, these assessments have been slow to recover when at similarly low levels.

Survey Methods

Results are based on telephone interviews with 1,007 national adults, aged 18 and older, conducted Sept. 8-11, 2008. For results based on the total sample of national adults, one can say with 95% confidence that the maximum margin of sampling error is ±3 percentage points.

Interviews are conducted with respondents on land-line telephones (for respondents with a land-line telephone) and cellular phones (for respondents who are cell-phone only).

In addition to sampling error, question wording and practical difficulties in conducting surveys can introduce error or bias into the findings of public opinion polls.

September 19, 2008
AMERICANS SPLIT ON AIG BAILOUT
There is no consensus about who is "too big to fail"

by Dennis Jacobe, Gallup Poll Chief Economist

While there seems to be widespread support for the recent bailout of AIG in Washington, D.C., and the financial markets, the results of a new *USA Today*/Gallup poll show Americans evenly split on whether the federal government should have loaned money to the insurance company.

Americans' Opinions on the Federal Government's Loan to AIG

Favor	Oppose
40%	42%

USA Today/Gallup poll, Sept. 17, 2008

Independents Most Widely Opposed to the Bailout

As the financial crisis has unfolded during recent weeks, the Treasury Department and the Federal Reserve Board of Governors have acted to preserve financial stability by helping a number of individual financial companies deemed "too big to fail" to avoid going into bankruptcy. While leaders of both political parties and many on Wall Street have supported these "bailouts," the general public is essentially split over the wisdom of the most recent effort to assist AIG.

Significantly, members of both parties are split on this issue: 44% of Republicans are in favor while 42% are opposed, and 44% of Democrats are in favor with 36% opposed. However, independents oppose the government's loan to AIG by a 50% to 34% margin. Men oppose the AIG loan by 49% to 38% while women support it by 42% to 36%. Whites and nonwhites are also evenly split on this issue.

Opinions on the Federal Government's Loan to AIG, by Party ID

■ % Favor   ▨ % Oppose

	Republicans	Independents	Democrats
% Favor	44	34	44
% Oppose	42	50	36

USA Today/Gallup poll, Sept. 17, 2008

Opinions on the Federal Government's Loan to AIG, by Gender and Race

■ % Favor   ▨ % Oppose

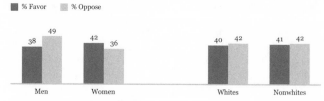

	Men	Women	Whites	Nonwhites
% Favor	38	42	40	41
% Oppose	49	36	42	42

USA Today/Gallup poll, Sept. 17, 2008

Commentary

Many of the actions taken by the Treasury and the Fed during the current financial crisis are unprecedented. The concept that a financial company could become "too big to fail"—meaning if it went into bankruptcy, the repercussions for the entire financial system would be so great as to threaten the system's collapse—has been around for a long time. While it has been debated, no one has ever really defined how it might be measured or which financial companies might be so large that they qualify for such a special status.

Many on Wall Street, in the banking business, and in the nation's capital seem to believe that the public sees risk to the financial system in the same way they do. However, as this new *USA Today*/Gallup poll shows, that is not necessarily the case. Many Americans feel this "bailout" process is unfair and that those who profit from our free-market system should pay the consequences when they fail.

Over the last few weeks, there have been a series of major financial-firm bailouts and one notable exception: Lehman Brothers. To this point, all of these actions seem justified based upon the risk assessments made by numerous public officials. Going forward, however, those at the Fed and the Treasury should keep in mind that there is no public consensus on the "too big to fail" idea. If they don't, they may join Securities and Exchange Commission Chairman Christopher Cox in the ranks of those who have been called on to resign in the face of the current financial debacle.

Further, this opposition to taxpayer bailouts also suggests that the rumored "New Resolution Trust Corporation" that sent stocks surging Thursday may not have smooth sailing with the American people or the Congress. In fact, it may well become an election issue, particularly if such a new entity is widely seen as simply a way to bail out Wall Street and the banking industry.

Survey Methods

The results reported here are based on 1,056 interviews completed Sept. 17, 2008. For results based on this sample, the maximum margin of sampling error is ±4 percentage points.

Interviews are conducted with respondents on land-line telephones (for respondents with a land-line telephone) and cellular phones (for respondents who are cell-phone only).

Polls conducted entirely in one day, such as this one, are subject to additional error or bias not found in polls conducted over several days.

In addition to sampling error, question wording and practical difficulties in conducting surveys can introduce error or bias into the findings of public opinion polls.

September 19, 2008
WALL STREET CRISIS MAY GIVE OBAMA SLIGHT POLITICAL BENEFIT
Even though public is divided over who would better handle the crisis

by Jeffrey M. Jones, Gallup Poll Managing Editor

When asked how the Wall Street crisis might affect their presidential vote, slightly more registered voters say it increases their chances of voting for Barack Obama (29%) than say this about John McCain (23%), with roughly 4 in 10 saying it will have no impact on their decision.

Do the current problems on Wall Street make you -- [ROTATED: more likely to vote for John McCain, more likely to vote for Barack Obama], or will they not affect your vote?

Based on registered voters

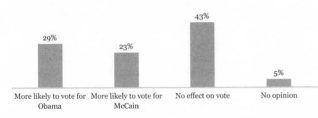

USA Today/Gallup poll, Sept. 17, 2008

This is based on a one-night Sept. 17 *USA Today/*Gallup poll measuring public reaction to the Wall Street crisis more generally, and the government bailout of AIG in particular.

In general, it appears that the crisis may just be reinforcing existing preferences. Most Obama voters say the crisis makes them more likely to vote for him, and about half of McCain voters say the Wall Street crisis increases their chances of supporting McCain.

Effect of Wall Street Crisis on Presidential Vote, based on Current Voting Intention
Based on registered voters

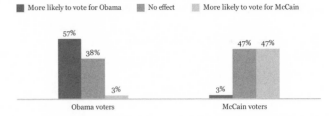

USA Today/Gallup poll, Sept. 17, 2008

However, there has been a definite shift toward Obama in Gallup Poll Daily tracking since Monday, when the crisis began to dominate the headlines. McCain, who had held an advantage ever since the Republican National Convention, now finds himself trailing Obama by 5 percentage points in the latest Gallup Poll Daily tracking update.

Gallup Daily Election Polling Results for the Presidential General Election
Obama vs. McCain, trend since Sept. 5-7, 2008
Based on registered voters

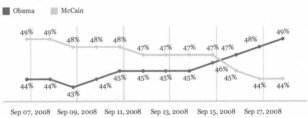

Despite the political advantage that may be accruing to Obama as a result of the Wall Street problems, Americans give neither candidate an edge when asked directly which would do a better job of handling the crisis.

Which presidential candidate do you think can do a better job of handling the current problems on Wall Street -- [ROTATED: Barack Obama (or) John McCain]?

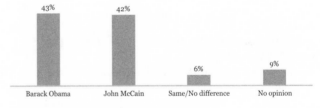

USA Today/Gallup poll, Sept. 17, 2008

The candidates have spent much of their time on the campaign trail this week discussing the financial crisis, which has in large part overshadowed the presidential election in the news. And while McCain in particular has struggled to reconcile his anti-regulation philosophy with the government's actions to bolster AIG, Fannie Mae, and Freddie Mac, at least as of Wednesday night, the public did not give either candidate an edge in terms of his ability to deal with the issue.

This is the case even though Obama has more consistently supported increased government regulation of Wall Street, which 59% of Americans say they favor in the poll.

Americans' assessments of which candidate would better handle the issue are strongly aligned with their party affiliation, with

Republicans overwhelmingly giving McCain the advantage, Democrats doing the same for Obama, and independents roughly equally divided between the two.

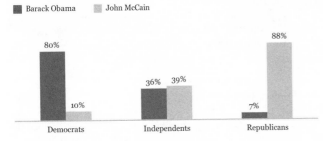

Candidate Who Can Do a Better Job of Handling the Current Problems on Wall Street, by Party Affiliation

USA Today/Gallup poll, Sept. 17, 2008

Survey Methods

Results are based on telephone interviews with 1,056 national adults, aged 18 and older, conducted Sept. 17, 2008. For results based on the total sample of national adults, one can say with 95% confidence that the maximum margin of sampling error is ±3 percentage points. For results based on the sample of 959 registered voters, the maximum margin of sampling error is ±3 percentage points.

Interviews are conducted with respondents on land-line telephones (for respondents with a land-line telephone) and cellular phones (for respondents who are cell-phone only).

In addition to sampling error, question wording and practical difficulties in conducting surveys can introduce error or bias into the findings of public opinion polls.

Polls conducted entirely in one day, such as this one, are subject to additional error or bias not found in polls conducted over several days.

September 22, 2008
AMERICANS MORE TUNED IN THAN EVER TO POLITICAL NEWS
Record interest in political news coincides with record distrust in media

by Lymari Morales, Gallup Poll Staff Writer

A record-high 43% of Americans say they follow news about national politics very closely, up from 30% at this time last year and 36% during the last presidential election.

In the Sept. 8-11 Gallup Poll, an additional 44% say they follow political news "somewhat closely," meaning nearly 9 in 10 Americans (87%) are tuned in to the national political dialogue. This significantly exceeds anything Gallup has measured since it began asking this question in 1995. While it is common for attention to political news to increase in presidential election years, this month's 43% easily surpasses the 36% who in September 2004 said they were very closely following news about national politics.

The unprecedented upswing in interest in political news comes during a presidential election that, still more than six weeks from

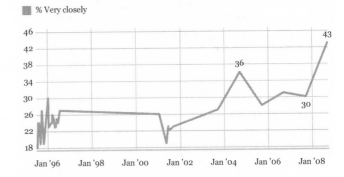

How closely do you follow news about national politics?

% Very closely

Election Day, is already historic many times over. Not only did election primaries and caucuses start earlier than ever, triggering a record early interest in the election, but they stayed competitive longer than they ever have, because of the extended Democratic primary battle between Hillary Clinton and Barack Obama. Add in the back-and-forth nature of the horse race between Obama and Republican nominee John McCain, the historical firsts for Obama (as an African-American) and vice presidential nominee Sarah Palin (as a Republican woman) and the promise that one of them will further make history by being elected, and Americans have more than enough reasons to pay attention.

Americans' hyper-vigilance also comes at a time when they have more news sources than ever to choose from. In particular, the Internet and blogs have become a major source of election news—so much so that a study released earlier this month by Northwestern University's Media Management Center found young adults to be "overwhelmed" by the amount of election news available online. Nonetheless, voters aged 18 to 29 are more interested than they have been in the past, with 31% saying they are following national political news very closely, up from 18% at this time during the last presidential election. Yet, because other age groups are paying about the same or more attention, younger voters remain the least engaged overall.

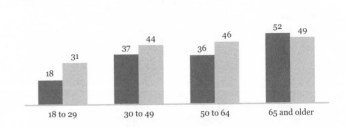

How closely do you follow news about national politics?

% Very closely, by age

Skeptical Audience

In an interesting paradox, Americans' record-high interest in political news coincides with their continued distrust in the news media, specifically newspapers, television, and radio. A record-low 43% of Americans say they place a great deal or fair amount of trust in such media outlets to report the news "fully, accurately, and fairly," down from 47% last year and similar to the 44% who said this during the last presidential election.

The distrust expressed in the 2004 and 2008 election seasons likely reflects the perception that the media have become increas-

How much trust and confidence do you have in the mass media -- such as newspapers, T.V., and radio -- when it comes to reporting the news fully, accurately, and fairly ?

■ % Great deal/Fair amount

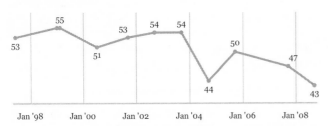

ingly partisan. In fact, Gallup finds Republicans particularly critical of the mass media and of its 2008 presidential election coverage. But interestingly, concern about media bias has been fairly constant over the years. This year, 47% perceive the news media to be too liberal and 13% perceive them to be too conservative, with only 36% seeing media coverage as "about right."

In general, do you think the news media are --
[ROTATED: too liberal, just about right, or too conservative]?

■ % Too liberal   ■ % Just about right   ■ % Too conservative

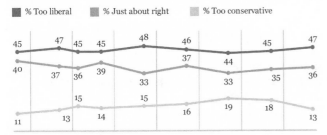

Bottom Line

This historic presidential campaign has inspired a level of interest in national politics unseen in recent years. Nearly 9 in 10 Americans (87%) are following national political news at least somewhat closely, with a record-high 43% following it very closely. While Americans place increasingly less trust and confidence in the mass media in general, their views about partisan bias have remained fairly steady over the past decade. Taken together, it might be fair to conclude that it's the content of the news—not the sources that provide it—that has Americans captivated.

Survey Methods

Results are based on telephone interviews with 1,007 national adults, aged 18 and older, conducted Sept. 8-11, 2008. For results based on the total sample of national adults, one can say with 95% confidence that the maximum margin of sampling error is ±3 percentage points.

Interviews are conducted with respondents on land-line telephones (for respondents with a land-line telephone) and cellular phones (for respondents who are cell-phone only).

In addition to sampling error, question wording and practical difficulties in conducting surveys can introduce error or bias into the findings of public opinion polls.

September 23, 2008
BEFORE RECENT CRISIS, PUBLIC WARY OF ACTIVE FEDERAL GOV'T.
Americans have become less accepting of a government role in promoting morality

by Jeffrey M. Jones, Gallup Poll Managing Editor

An early September Gallup Poll showed that Americans continue to believe the government is doing "too many things that should be left to individuals and businesses," rather than preferring an expanded government role to deal with the country's problems.

Some people think the government is trying to do too many things that should be left to individuals and businesses. Others think that government should do more to solve our country's problems. Which comes closer to your own view?

■ % Gov't. doing too many things   ■ % Gov't. should do more

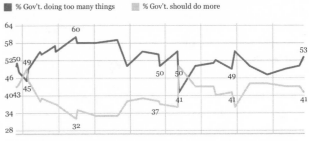

These results are based on Gallup's annual Governance poll, conducted Sept. 8-11 this year, and show 53% believing the government is doing too many things that individuals and businesses should be doing, a slight increase from prior years. These data are helpful in understanding the public-opinion environment in which the federal government's massive financial bailout plan is being played out.

It is too early yet to measure the public's reaction to that plan, the details of which the Bush administration and Congress are still working out. However, a *USA Today*/Gallup poll last week found a majority of Americans in favor of increased regulation of Wall Street, but divided on the specific proposal to loan up to $85 billion to troubled insurance conglomerate AIG. These two findings suggest that it is unclear whether the public will end up supporting the broader government intervention being considered this week.

Since 1992, Gallup has frequently asked Americans about their preferences for government's role in solving the nation's problems. Only twice during that time have more Americans expressed a preference for more government action rather than less—in March 1993, during the early months of the Clinton presidency, and shortly after the Sept. 11, 2001, terrorist attacks.

In this year's poll, as is typical, these preferences reflect the dominant political philosophies in the United States, with Republicans favoring a lesser role for the government in solving economic problems and Democrats a more active one. Independents also tend to favor a less active government role.

In addition to asking about the government's role in solving economic problems, the poll also measures public preferences for what the government should do in regard to moral values. For the first time since 1993, Americans are evenly divided about what its role should be, with 48% saying it should promote traditional values, and 48% saying it should not favor any set of values. A majority had favored government's promoting traditional values from 1993-2006, before falling below that level in 2007. Last year, however,

Views of Government Involvement to Solve Nation's Problems, by Party Affiliation

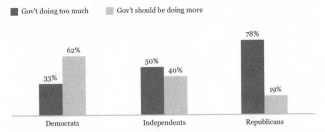

Gallup Poll, Sept. 8-11, 2008

more Americans still favored government's promoting traditional values than not promoting them.

Some people think the government should promote traditional values in our society. Others think the government should not favor any particular set of values. Which comes closer to your own view?

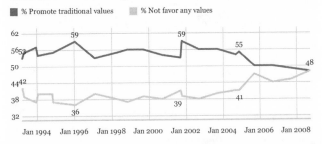

Consistent with the respective party platforms, Republicans tend to favor a more active role for government in this area, while Democrats tend to believe the government should not be heavily involved. Independents' preferences are similar to those of Democrats.

Views of Government Role in Promoting Traditional Values, by Party Affiliation

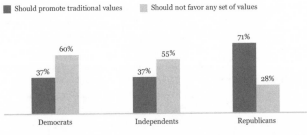

Gallup Poll, Sept. 8-11, 2008

Implications

At least as of early September, it seemed like Americans' preferences more closely aligned with those of the Republican Party and John McCain in terms of what the government's role should be in solving the country's problems. However, since that time, the Republican presidential administration has intervened to develop a government program to help keep major financial institutions from collapsing under the weight of bad loans they have made in recent years. Initial public reaction to the events from early last week gives no strong indication on whether the public will support or oppose this more comprehensive proposal.

It's possible that the developments on Wall Street have shifted Americans' preferences on government intervention in the economy,

though the direction of that shift is unclear. Both candidates have publicly endorsed the government's approach with some reservations, though McCain's position evolved from a more anti-regulation stance taken earlier in the week.

In some ways, the public's preferred government role in addressing economic problems in the wake of the Wall Street crisis may hold the key to the election outcome, since Americans are evenly divided as to what role the government should take with regard to morality.

Survey Methods

Results are based on telephone interviews with 1,007 national adults, aged 18 and older, conducted Sept. 8-11, 2008. For results based on the total sample of national adults, one can say with 95% confidence that the maximum margin of sampling error is ±3 percentage points.

Interviews are conducted with respondents on land-line telephones (for respondents with a land-line telephone) and cellular phones (for respondents who are cell-phone only).

In addition to sampling error, question wording and practical difficulties in conducting surveys can introduce error or bias into the findings of public opinion polls.

September 23, 2008
DEMOCRATS RE-ESTABLISH DOUBLE-DIGIT LEAD IN PARTY AFFILIATION
Gap had closed after the Republican National Convention

by Jeffrey M. Jones, Gallup Poll Managing Editor

Democrats have re-established a double-digit advantage over Republicans in party affiliation, with 49% of Americans identifying themselves as Democrats or leaning to the Democratic Party, and 39% identifying as Republicans or leaning to the Republican Party. This is a shift from immediately after the Republican National Convention, when Democrats enjoyed their smallest advantage of the year, leading only 47% to 42%.

Leaned Party Identification, Recent Gallup Poll Daily Tracking

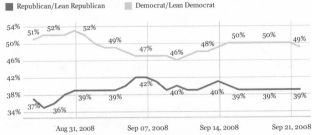

For 2008 to date (based on more than 250,000 Gallup Poll Daily tracking interviews), an average of 50% of Americans have identified themselves as Democrats or have initially identified as independents but said they leaned to the Democratic Party, while 37% have aligned themselves with the Republican Party, a 13-point average advantage for the Democrats. So, with roughly half the country supporting it, 2008 has clearly been a favorable political year for the Democratic Party.

Republicans cut into that advantage in the wake of their party's convention, reducing their partisan deficit to single digits from Sept. 3-5 polling through Sept. 12-14 polling, when the averages were 47% Democratic and 40% Republican (according to the more than 9,000 interviews conducted during that time period). But in the last week, with the Wall Street financial crisis dominating the news, Democrats have regained a double-digit advantage. It is unclear whether the recent movement in partisanship reflects public reaction to the crisis, or perhaps just a return to a more normal state as the effects of the Republican convention fade. During this past week, Democratic presidential nominee Barack Obama has also re-established an advantage over Republican John McCain in Gallup's presidential election trial heat. Obama had led by a slight margin most of the summer after clinching the Democratic nomination, but McCain emerged from the Republican convention with the lead and continued to have at least a slim advantage as recently as Sept. 13-15 polling.

The Democratic advantage in party affiliation is slightly smaller when the partisan leaners from each party group are excluded. In the Sept. 20-22 tracking data, 35% of Americans identify as Democrats, 26% Republicans, and 33% as independents, resulting in a 9-point Democratic advantage.

For the year, an average of 34% of Americans have identified as Democrats and 26% as Republicans, for an 8-point average Democratic lead.

Implications

Any momentum the Republican Party had coming out of its convention has been halted in the past week, and the Democrats have essentially re-established their dominant political positioning.

Even so, the presidential election remains close, in part because McCain has been able to command greater party loyalty than Obama. In the past week, 89% of Republican supporters said they would vote for McCain, compared with 86% of Democratic supporters favoring Obama. Additionally, the Democratic advantage in party affiliation is not as large among registered voters (51% to 42%) as it is in the total adult population (49% to 39%).

While the Democratic Party certainly is in a more advantageous position than the Republican Party to win the election, the Democrats' ability to do so will depend on their maintaining an advantage in party support over Republicans between now and Election Day, and on ensuring that their supporters remain mostly loyal to Obama and turn out to vote on Nov. 4. So far, the lesser Democratic voting loyalty to their nominee has not hurt the party because of the significant Democratic advantage in partisanship. To the extent the partisanship gap narrows (as it did the week after the Republican convention), Democratic loyalty and turnout will become more critical.

Survey Methods

Results are based on telephone interviews with 3,042 national adults, aged 18 and older, conducted Sept. 20-22, 2008, as part of Gallup Poll Daily tracking. For results based on the total sample of national adults, one can say with 95% confidence that the maximum margin of sampling error is ±2 percentage points.

Interviews are conducted with respondents on land-line telephones (for respondents with a land-line telephone) and cellular phones (for respondents who are cell-phone only).

In addition to sampling error, question wording and practical difficulties in conducting surveys can introduce error or bias into the findings of public opinion polls.

September 24, 2008
DID PALIN HELP MCCAIN AMONG WHITE WOMEN?
Obama's problem with white men much bigger than that among white women

by Frank Newport, Gallup Poll Editor in Chief

Did John McCain's selection of Sarah Palin as his vice presidential running mate lead to significant gains for McCain among white women? While this hypothesis fits easily into the media's coverage and the excitement around Palin's historic status as the first female Republican vice presidential candidate, continuing analysis of large Gallup Poll Daily tracking samples from recent weeks do not provide evidence to support it.

Gallup Daily tracking has shown some variation in support levels for the two candidates—McCain and Barack Obama—across the last month and a half, but the shifts in candidate preferences of white women do not appear to have been much different from those of all voters.

Preferences for the General Election

Weekly aggregate of registered voters
Gallup Poll Daily tracking

	% Obama, among white women	% McCain, among white women	% Obama, among all registered voters	% McCain, among all registered voters
Sep 15-21, 2008	45	47	49	44
Sep 8-14, 2008	40	51	45	47
Sep 1-7, 2008	42	49	47	45
Aug 25-31, 2008	43	47	48	42
Aug 18-24, 2008	39	48	45	45

When Obama gained among all voters, he gained among white women. And when McCain gained among all voters—in the week of Sept. 8-14 in particular—he gained among white women as well. White women appear to have been lifted and set down by the same tidal patterns that affected all voters.

By the week of Sept. 15-21, a rising tide for Obama had in general lifted his strength among white women as much as it did among everyone else. Obama ended last week in a slightly stronger position among white women than was the case as the political conventions began—in fact, coming within 2 points of McCain.

White Men More of a Problem for Obama Than White Women

From a more general perspective, Obama continues to do less well among white women than he does among women of other racial or ethnic backgrounds.

An aggregate of more than 23,000 interviews Gallup conducted with female registered voters between Aug. 1 and Sept. 21 shows McCain leading Obama by 47% to 42% among all white women, while McCain loses significantly among black, Hispanic, and Asian women.

Preference for the General Election, Among Women

Aggregate of registered voters, Aug. 1-Sept. 21, 2008

Gallup Poll Daily tracking

	% Barack Obama	% John McCain
Non-Hispanic white women	42	47
Non-Hispanic black women	91	3
Hispanic white women	53	35
Asian women	60	28

So, in this regard, Obama has a problem among white women, regardless of whether it was exacerbated by McCain's selection of Palin as his vice presidential running mate. But, from a different perspective, and reflecting the fairly normal gender-gap pattern of recent years, Obama's position among white women is much better than his position among white men, among whom he trails McCain by a large 56% to 35% margin.

Thus, although Obama has a problem among all white voters, in the sense that he loses among them to McCain, his relative standing among white women is certainly better than it is among white men.

Discussion

It has been well-established that Obama does not do as well among white women as he does among Hispanic, black, and Asian women.

This fact, however, predates McCain's selection of Palin as his running mate. The data reviewed here suggest that Palin's presence on the GOP ticket did not appear to shift white women disproportionately toward McCain, nor did it appear to engender more loyalty to McCain among white women over the past week when the general trend was toward Obama. As is true for the entire electorate, McCain now is doing slightly less well among this group than he did before the two conventions began.

More generally, commentators who opine that Obama has a problem among white women are correct as far as that goes. Obama does less well among whites in general and less well among white women than among women of other racial and ethnic backgrounds.

However, commentators would be perhaps more on target by pointing out Obama's larger problem among white men, among whom he is losing by 35% to McCain's 56%.

And, of course, white women are not a monolithic voting group. There are big differences in the level of support given to both candidates within subgroups of the white female population. For example, data show that Obama has significant problems among white women who are not college graduates—among whom he has been losing to McCain by a 50% to 37% margin over the last month and a half—and among married white women, among whom McCain has been winning by a 17-point margin, 54% to 37%.

Survey Methods

Results are based on telephone interviews with 47,087 registered voters, aged 18 and older, conducted Aug. 1-Sept. 21, 2008. For results based on the total sample of registered voters, one can say with 95% confidence that the maximum margin of sampling error is ±1 percentage point. Margins of sampling errors vary for individual subsamples.

Interviews are conducted with respondents on land-line telephones (for respondents with a land-line telephone) and cellular phones (for respondents who are cell-phone only).

In addition to sampling error, question wording and practical difficulties in conducting surveys can introduce error or bias into the findings of public opinion polls.

September 26, 2008

AMERICANS FAVOR CONGRESSIONAL ACTION ON CRISIS

Four out of 10 say this is biggest financial crisis of their lifetimes

by Frank Newport, Gallup Poll Editor in Chief

Americans overwhelmingly favor Congress' passing a plan that would help fix the current Wall Street economic crisis, but a Wednesday night *USA Today*/Gallup poll (conducted before Thursday's high-level negotiations between President Bush and congressional leaders on a new plan) shows that by more than a 2-to-1 ratio, Americans would like to see Congress pass a different plan rather than the $700 billion plan proposed by the Bush administration.

As you may know, the Bush administration has proposed a plan that would allow the Treasury Department to buy and re-sell up to $700 billion of distressed assets from financial companies. What would you like to see Congress do?

Based on national adults

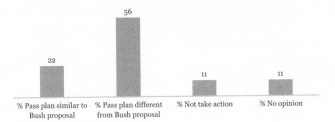

USA Today/Gallup poll, Sept. 24, 2008

This key question was asked of more than 1,000 Americans on Wednesday night (Sept. 24), and described the Bush administration's plan as allowing "the Treasury Department to buy and re-sell up to $700 billion of distressed assets from financial companies." With this description, and given three choices of their preferred action (pass a plan similar to the Bush plan, pass a plan different from the Bush proposal, or not take any action at all), the majority of Americans opted for the middle alternative, with smaller percentages opting for either passing the Bush plan or not taking any action.

These data suggest that Americans should in broad terms favor the type of plan Congress was working on Thursday, but may have some disagreements as the precise details become known, particularly if it is viewed as being similar to the original Bush administration proposal.

Eight out of 10 Americans say they are following news of the financial problems on Wall Street and the Bush administration's proposals very or somewhat closely, with 43% "very" closely. This ranks in the upper tier of what Gallup has measured historically for news topics.

How closely are you following the news about the financial problems on Wall Street and the Bush administration's proposals to address the problems?

Based on national adults

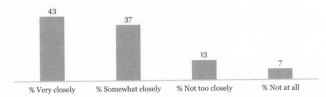

USA Today/Gallup poll, Sept. 24, 2008

All discussions of the current financial crisis and proposals to resolve it are highly complex, even for professionals in the financial field. One can assume that Americans who are following the news very closely are more knowledgeable than others, but the views of the closely attentive group toward the plan are little different from those of the total sample: 24% of the attentive group favors the Bush proposal, 58% a plan different from the Bush proposal, and 12% no action at all.

One reason a high percentage of Americans feel some type of plan should be passed is evident from the fact that 74% of Americans believe the U.S. economy would get worse if Congress does not act at this time.

Suppose Congress takes no action on this issue. Over the next few years, do you think the U.S. economy would -- [ROTATED: get better, not be affected much, or get worse]?

Based on national adults

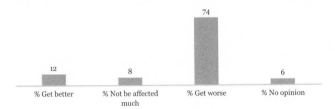

USA Today/Gallup poll, Sept. 24, 2008

Moreover, 4 out of 10 Americans describe the current situation as the "biggest financial crisis" in their lifetimes.

Which of the following would you say best describes the current situation?

Based on national adults

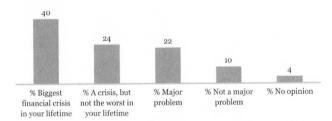

USA Today/Gallup poll, Sept. 24, 2008

The biggest variation in responses to this question by age is among those who are 18 to 34. This group—despite having had fewer years to be exposed to other financial crises in their lifetimes—is actually less likely than those who are older to say this is the biggest financial crisis of their lifetimes. Americans 55 and older, some of whom may have been exposed to the Great Depression of the 1930s, are little different from the overall sample average in their views that this is the biggest financial crisis of their lifetimes.

The bailout plan is still being worked out, but almost two-thirds of Americans say it would be very important to include in any government plan limits on compensation for executives at corporations that participate in the plan. About half say it is very important to include provisions to help homeowners who cannot pay their mortgages.

Survey Methods

Results are based on telephone interviews with 1,019 national adults, aged 18 and older, conducted Sept. 24, 2008. For results based on

Which of the following would you say best describes the current situation?

Based on national adults, by age

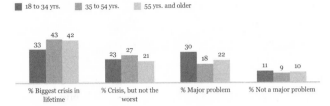

USA Today/Gallup poll, Sept. 24, 2008

How important is it to you that any government plan to deal with the financial problems ...

A. Set limits on compensation for executives at corporations that participate in the plan

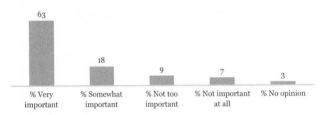

USA Today/Gallup poll, Sept. 24, 2008

How important is it to you that any government plan to deal with the financial problems ...

B. Include provisions to help homeowners who cannot pay their mortgages

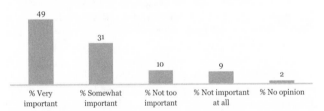

USA Today/Gallup poll, Sept. 24, 2008

the total sample of national adults, one can say with 95% confidence that the maximum margin of sampling error is ±3 percentage points.

Interviews are conducted with respondents on land-line telephones (for respondents with a land-line telephone) and cellular phones (for respondents who are cell-phone only).

In addition to sampling error, question wording and practical difficulties in conducting surveys can introduce error or bias into the findings of public opinion polls. Polls conducted entirely in one day, such as this one, are subject to additional error or bias not found in polls conducted over several days.

September 26, 2008
PUBLIC DIVIDED ON NEED FOR THIRD PARTY
Republicans, Democrats think major parties adequately represent Americans

by Jeffrey M. Jones, Gallup Poll Managing Editor

Americans divide evenly in a recent Gallup Poll on whether the two major political parties are adequately representing the public, or whether a third party is needed. That represents a shift from 2007, when a majority said the Democrats and Republicans were doing "such a poor job that a third major party is needed."

In your view, do the Republican and Democratic parties do an adequate job of representing the American people, or do they do such a poor job that a third major party is needed?

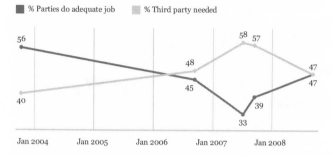

Gallup has asked this question since 2003, and over that time, the public's views on this matter have not been consistent. The first time it was asked, in October 2003, a majority opposed the idea of a third major party. Two separate polls from last year showed most Americans in favor of another party. This year's results are similar to what Gallup found in September 2006.

Not surprisingly, political independents are most likely to favor the emergence of a third major party, with 63% holding this view. In contrast, a majority of Democrats (56%) and Republicans (55%) think the two major parties are doing an adequate job and thus there is no need for another party that can compete with them.

Opinions on Need for Third Party, by Party Affiliation

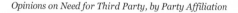
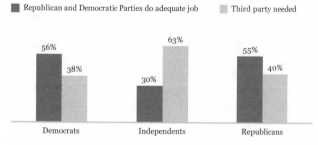

Gallup Poll, Sept. 8-11, 2008

The change in the balance of opinion since 2007 from favoring a third major party to dividing evenly on this question is largely because of a shift in Democrats' attitudes. Last September, Democrats favored a third party by 53% to 43%—nearly the mirror image of this year's result, which finds just 38% in favor and 56% opposed. It is not clear why the shift has occurred, but throughout this presidential election year, Gallup polling has found Democrats highly engaged in the election and expressing heightened enthusiasm about voting.

Republicans' attitudes are virtually unchanged from September of last year, when 57% supported the current party structure and 40% wanted a third option. Independents are slightly less likely to favor a third party this year (63%) than they were last year (72%).

Beyond the political differences seen by party affiliation in attitudes toward a third party, there are fairly consistent differences by political ideology that help reveal what sort of third party Americans would most like to see.

Gallup has typically found self-identified liberals to be the most likely ideological group to say a third party is needed. Even in 2003, when close to 6 in 10 Americans thought the Democratic and Republican Parties were doing an adequate job of representing Americans, a majority of liberals disagreed. Liberal support for a third party climbed to 66% in 2007, ironically shortly after the Democratic Party had assumed control of Congress for the first time since 1994. This year, with Barack Obama heading the Democratic ticket, marks the low point in liberal support for a third party, at 51%, but it is still above the majority level.

This year's drop in liberal support for a third party may suggest that liberals' penchant for favoring a third major party reflects a desire for a party that more closely reflects their political views, and perhaps they see Barack Obama as doing that better than Democratic leaders who have come before him.

Views of Need for a Third Party, Among Political Liberals

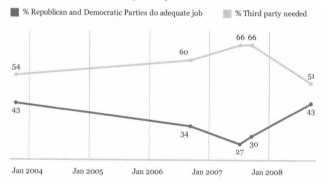

Those who identify as political moderates, a disproportionate percentage of whom also are independent in their partisan orientation, have generally preferred that there be a third party to help represent the opinions of Americans.

Views of Need for a Third Party, Among Political Moderates

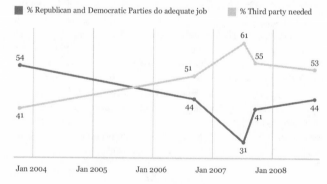

Conservatives, who in general tend to favor the status quo, have usually expressed satisfaction with the two-party system.

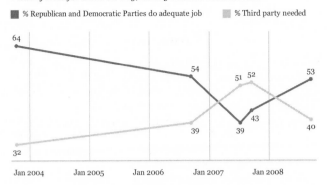

Views of Need for a Third Party, Among Political Conservatives

■ % Republican and Democratic Parties do adequate job   ▨ % Third party needed

64 — 54 — 51 — 52 — 53

32 — 39 — 39 — 39 — 43 — 40

Jan 2004   Jan 2005   Jan 2006   Jan 2007   Jan 2008

Implications

Americans' views on the need for a third political party have varied in recent years, and in this presidential election year the public is divided down the middle. That could reflect general satisfaction with the major parties' presidential candidates, both of whom enjoy favorable ratings near 60%. This question was not asked in 1992, when independent candidate Ross Perot had the best showing for a third-party candidate in recent memory.

The lower desire for a major third party does not bode well for the third-party candidacies of Ralph Nader, Bob Barr, and Cynthia McKinney, who have registered only minimal support when included in presidential election polls this year, and who have struggled to attract campaign dollars that have flowed rather freely to Obama and McCain.

Survey Methods

Results are based on telephone interviews with 1,007 national adults, aged 18 and older, conducted Sept. 8-11, 2008. For results based on the total sample of national adults, one can say with 95% confidence that the maximum margin of sampling error is ±3 percentage points.

Interviews are conducted with respondents on land-line telephones (for respondents with a land-line telephone) and cellular phones (for respondents who are cell-phone only).

In addition to sampling error, question wording and practical difficulties in conducting surveys can introduce error or bias into the findings of public opinion polls.

September 28, 2008
DEBATE WATCHERS GIVE OBAMA EDGE OVER MCCAIN
Obama seen as improving his standing on the economy

by Frank Newport, Gallup Poll Editor in Chief

Americans who watched the first presidential debate on Sept. 26 gave Barack Obama the edge over John McCain as having done the better job in the debate, by a 46% to 34% margin. These results are based on a special *USA Today*/Gallup poll conducted on Saturday, Sept. 27, the first day after the debate.

The questions about the debate were asked of a random sample of 1,005 national adults as part of the Gallup Poll Daily tracking pro-

Regardless of which candidate you happen to support, who do you think did a better job in last night's debate?

■ Sep 27, 2008

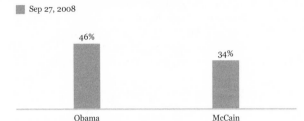

gram on Saturday. Of the total sample of adults, 63% said they had watched the debate. Another 12% said that they had seen, heard, or read news coverage of the debate, and the rest said they had neither seen the debate nor news coverage thereof.

Did you happen to watch or listen to the nationally televised presidential debate or see, hear, or read any news coverage of the debate?

	%
Yes	63
No	37
Saw news coverage	12
Did not see news coverage	25

The data show a predictable pattern of response from Republicans and Democrats. Seventy-two percent of the former and 74% of the latter said that their party's candidate did the better job in the debate. This reinforces the conventional wisdom that many viewers watch a debate through their preexisting perceptual framework and end up with nothing more than reinforcement for what they believed before the debate began. But among the crucial group of independents who watched the debate—those most likely to actually be swayed by what transpired, Obama won by 10 points, 43% to 33%.

Not only did Obama win the debate among debate watchers, they say that their attitudes towards the Democratic candidate also improved as a result. Thirty percent of debate watchers said they came away with a more favorable image of Barack Obama, while just 14% said they had a less favorable image. On the other hand, John McCain did not fare as well. Just as many watchers said that they developed a less favorable image of John McCain—21%—as said they gained a more favorable image of McCain as a result of the debate.

How has your opinion of the candidates been affected by the debate?

■ More favorable   ■ Less favorable   ▨ Not changed much
▨ No opinion

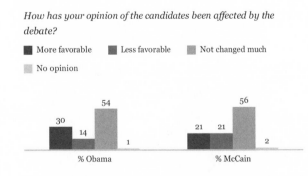

Although the debate was supposed to deal with foreign policy, the first portion of the questions asked by moderator Jim Lehrer focused on the economy and the financial bailout plan being negotiated by Congress. This economic focus appears to have been positive for Obama; debate watchers ended up with more confidence in Obama's ability to deal with the economic problems facing the country, rather than less confidence as a result of the debate. By contrast, 37% of debate watchers said that the debate gave them less confidence in John McCain on economic matters rather than more.

Do you now have more confidence, less confidence or the same amount of confidence in the candidate's ability to deal with the economic problems facing the country?

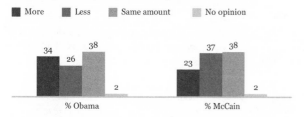

Debate watchers saw little difference between the two candidates on national defense and foreign policy as a result of the debate; both Obama and McCain appeared to have come away with slightly improved images on foreign policy.

Do you now have more confidence, less confidence or the same amount of confidence in the candidate's ability to deal with matters of national defense and foreign policy?

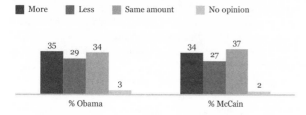

Finally, by a fairly substantial margin, debate watchers said that Obama was the candidate who offered the best proposals for change in the debate, by a 17 percentage point margin over McCain.

Based on what you saw or read about the debate, which candidate offered the best proposals for change to solve the country's problems?

	%
Obama	52
McCain	35
Neither	8
No Opinion	5

Implications

History shows that "winning" the first presidential debate does not necessarily translate into winning the election. Ross Perot, Al Gore, and John Kerry are among those who were seen by debate watchers in quick reaction polls as having done the better job in the first debate of their campaign year, and all eventually lost their elections. There are two presidential (and one vice presidential) debates yet to come, and much can change. The most important indicator of the impact of

the debate may be trends in overall candidate support, where, at the moment, Obama leads McCain.

Survey Methods

Results are based on telephone interviews with 1,005 national adults, aged 18 and older, and 701 people who watched the Sept. 26 presidential debate, conducted Sept. 27, 2008. For results based on the total sample of national adults, one can say with 95% confidence that the maximum margin of sampling error is ±3 percentage points, and for the sample of registered voters, one can say with 95% confidence that the maximum margin of sampling error is ±4% percentage points.

Interviews are conducted with respondents on land-line telephones (for respondents with a land-line telephone) and cellular phones (for respondents who are cell-phone only).

In addition to sampling error, question wording and practical difficulties in conducting surveys can introduce error or bias into the findings of public opinion polls. Polls conducted entirely in one day, such as this one, are subject to additional error or bias not found in polls conducted over several days.

September 29, 2008
PERSONAL FINANCIAL ASSESSMENTS REMAIN AT 32-YEAR LOW
Majority, however, say they will be better off next year at this time

by Frank Newport, Gallup Poll Editor in Chief

Over half of Americans say they are worse off financially now than they were a year ago, tied for the most negative reading in Gallup's 32-year history of asking this question. Still, close to 6 in 10 say they hope to be better off at this time next year. And despite the recent financial crisis, these results are no worse than those of four months ago, at the beginning of the summer.

Would you say that you are financially better off now than you were a year ago, or are you financially worse off now?

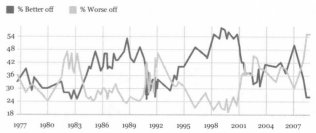

Americans are as likely to say they are worse off financially compared to a year ago as they have been at any time since 1976, when Gallup first asked the question. About a quarter of Americans are holding on to a more positive mental attitude, and say they are better off than a year ago. Of interest is that Americans were identical in their negativity in late May/early June of this year (matching the current reading as the most negative in Gallup's history), well before the current Wall Street and financial crisis. This is an important reminder that Americans' gloomy financial outlook did not begin

Looking ahead, do you expect that at this time next year you will be financially better off than now, or worse off than now?

■ % Better off   ▨ % Worse off

just over the last several weeks, but has been in place for a while now amid rising gas prices, inflation worries, and rising joblessness.

On the other hand, in terms of predicting their financial future, Americans—as is typical—are relatively rosy.

The 58% who say they will be better off in a year is certainly more positive than many previous readings on this measure over the years, including the late 1970s and early 1980s, when well under half of Americans said they would be better off financially in a year. The highest reading for "better off in a year" came in March 1998, when 71% gave this positive response.

The current "better off in a year" reading is up slightly from late May/early June of this year. This suggests, but of course does not prove, that there may be some slight benefit from last week's attempts to pass legislation designed to improve the financial future. Or it could reflect the relative stabilization of gas prices. (The current data were collected through Saturday of this past weekend and do not reflect the events of Monday relating to possible congressional legislation and the drop in the stock market.)

The weekend *USA Today*/Gallup poll also asked Americans how worried they were about a list of five financial concerns. Based on a rank ordering of those who are "very" and "moderately" worried, Americans are most concerned about not having enough money for retirement and not being able to maintain the standard of living they enjoy. On a relative basis, Americans are least worried that they will not be able to make the minimum payments on their credit cards.

Next, please tell me how concerned you are right now about each of the following financial matters, based on your current financial situation.

	% Very worried	% Moderately worried	Total % worried	Total % not worried
Not having enough money for retirement	33	31	64	31
Not being able to maintain the standard of living you enjoy	24	32	56	43
Not having enough to pay your normal monthly bills	20	24	44	54
Not being able to get a loan for a home, car, tuition, or business	20	15	35	55
Not being able to make the minimum payments on your credit cards	13	12	25	58

The trend data on these measures suggest that worry has increased as of April of this year, but has not increased since then.

For example, the accompanying graph displays the trend on the percentage "very worried" about "not being able to maintain the standard of living you enjoy" and "not having enough to pay your normal monthly bills." Worry on these measures edged up in April to new highs, but is essentially the same now. The bottom line here: The recent problems on Wall Street have seemed not to make consumers' perceptions about their own finances any worse than they already were earlier this year.

How worried are you about not having enough money for retirement?

▨ Total % worried

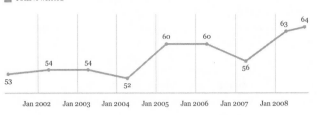

How worried you are about not being able to maintain the standard of living you enjoy?

▨ Total % worried

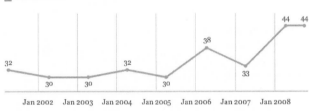

How worried are you about not having enough to pay your normal monthly bills?

▨ Total % worried

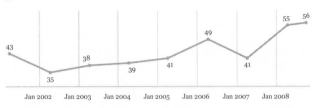

How worried are you about not being able to make the minimum payments on your credit cards?

▨ Total % worried

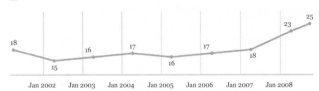

Survey Methods

Results are based on telephone interviews with 1,011 national adults, aged 18 and older, conducted Sept. 26-27, 2008. For results based on the total sample of national adults, one can say with 95% confidence that the maximum margin of sampling error is ±3 percentage points.

Interviews are conducted with respondents on land-line telephones (for respondents with a land-line telephone) and cellular phones (for respondents who are cell-phone only).

In addition to sampling error, question wording and practical difficulties in conducting surveys can introduce error or bias into the findings of public opinion polls.

September 29, 2008

U.S. LEADERS NOT GETTING HIGH MARKS ON CREDIT CRISIS

None receives majority approval, but Obama comes closest

by Lydia Saad, Gallup Poll Senior Editor

A *USA Today*/Gallup poll conducted Friday and Saturday finds more Americans disapproving than approving of how most of the major national political players have handled the recent problems on Wall Street. Only Barack Obama squeaks by with more Americans approving than disapproving of his performance on the issue, 46% to 43%.

Next, please say whether you approve or disapprove of the way each of the following has responded to the problems on Wall Street.

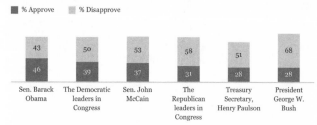

USA Today/Gallup poll, Sept. 26-27, 2008

The Sept. 26-27 poll was conducted before Sunday morning's announcement that congressional leaders and the Bush administration had reached agreement on a $700 billion bailout plan. It includes interviews before, during, and after the first presidential debate between Obama and John McCain on Friday night.

Both Obama and McCain are rated more favorably for their responses to the Wall Street mess than are their respective parties in Congress. Obama wins the approval of 46% of Americans, compared with 39% approving of the Democratic leaders in Congress more generally. Similarly, 37% of Americans approve of how McCain has responded, compared with 31% approving of the Republican leaders in Congress.

Democrats Kinder to Their Leadership on the Issue

The higher scores of Obama and the Democrats in Congress relative to McCain and the Republicans in Congress are mainly owing to differences in intraparty support for each side. Nearly 8 in 10 Democrats approve of the way Obama has responded to the Wall Street crisis, compared with only 7 in 10 Republicans approving of McCain. Similarly, 65% of Democrats approve of the Democratic leaders in Congress, in contrast to 55% of Republicans approving of the Republican leaders in Congress.

Importantly, Obama and McCain receive similar ratings on the Wall Street issue from political independents, with only about a third of this group approving of each.

The worst-rated political players on the Wall Street issue both come from the Bush administration—Treasury Secretary Henry Paulson, one of the chief authors of the original bailout plan, and President George W. Bush himself. Only 28% of Americans approve of how each has responded to the recent financial problems. Of the two, however, Bush has a net score that is significantly worse, as 68% disapprove of his performance, compared with 51% disapproving of Paulson's. A much greater number have no opinion of Paulson's performance than of Bush's (21% vs. 5%).

Rating How Political Players Have Responded to Wall Street Crisis, by Party ID
Percentage approving of the way each has responded

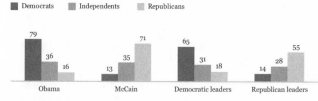

USA Today/Gallup poll, Sept. 26-27, 2008

Next, please say whether you approve or disapprove of the way each of the following has responded to the problems on Wall Street. [RANDOM ORDER]

	Approve	Disapprove	No opinion
	%	%	%
Sen. Barack Obama	46	43	11
The Democratic leaders in Congress	39	50	11
Sen. John McCain	37	53	10
The Republican leaders in Congress	31	58	11
Treasury Secretary, Henry Paulson	28	51	21
President George W. Bush	28	68	5

USA Today/Gallup poll, Sept. 26-27, 2008

Bottom Line

Though Obama and McCain have offered prescriptions for the Wall Street crisis, and McCain attempted to demonstrate his commitment to solving it by dramatically suspending his campaign last week and returning to Washington, neither candidate has won majority public approval on the issue. Obama outscores McCain in approval on the issue 46% to 37%, mostly because his fellow Democrats rate his response more highly than Republicans rate McCain's.

In terms of winning over the political center where most swing voters reside, however, the jury still seems to be out. Obama and McCain receive nearly identical ratings from political independents for their handling of the Wall Street crisis, and they're not positive. Only about a third of independents approve of the way each candidate has responded.

As Americans take a few days to digest Friday night's debate and Sunday's compromise bailout plan, their reviews of the political players' performances on the issue could change. The initial finding, however, is that with the near-Wall Street collapse putting U.S. credit and housing markets in serious jeopardy, and setting up worrisome forecasts for wages and jobs, Americans may be in no mood to dole out praise on the issue.

Survey Methods

Results are based on telephone interviews with 1,011 national adults, aged 18 and older, conducted Sept. 26-27, 2008. For results based on the total sample of national adults, one can say with 95% confidence that the maximum margin of sampling error is ±3 percentage points.

Interviews are conducted with respondents on land-line telephones (for respondents with a land-line telephone) and cellular phones (for respondents who are cell-phone only).

In addition to sampling error, question wording and practical difficulties in conducting surveys can introduce error or bias into the findings of public opinion polls.

September 30, 2008

BUSH'S APPROVAL RATING DROPS TO NEW LOW OF 27%

Decline of 4 points since financial crisis intensified

by Jeffrey M. Jones, Gallup Poll Managing Editor

According to a Sept. 26-27 *USA Today*/Gallup poll, just 27% of Americans approve of the job George W. Bush is doing as president, the lowest rating of his presidency.

George W. Bush's Job Approval Ratings Trend (2001-Present)

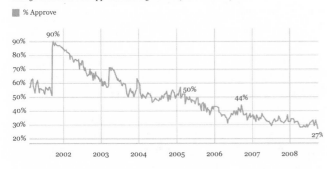

The new personal low rating for Bush comes amid the financial crisis that has rocked Wall Street in recent weeks. Bush's approval rating has declined from 31% in the previous Gallup Poll, conducted before the crisis intensified with the bankruptcy of Lehman Brothers, the near-collapse of Merrill Lynch, and the federal government bailout of AIG. It is down 6 points from 33% just after the Republican National Convention early this month. Bush's previous low had been 28%, measured at several points earlier this year. (The most recent poll was conducted before the House of Representatives voted down a bill to address the problems on Monday.)

The timing of the decline strongly suggests that it is because of the financial crisis, and the government's largely unpopular response to it. In a separate question in the Sept. 26-27 poll, only 28% of Americans approved and 68% disapproved of Bush's response to the financial crisis—the worst of six government leaders tested in the poll (although no leader received a majority positive response). While most Americans agreed that some type of government action is necessary to address the crisis, last week only a small minority seemed to favor passing a bill similar to the Bush administration's original proposal.

Republicans are mostly responsible for the further erosion in Bush's job rating. Sixty-four percent of Republicans approve of Bush, down from 71% in the prior poll. Independents' and Democrats' ratings are essentially the same as two weeks ago.

Bush Approval Rating, by Party Affiliation, Recent Gallup Polls

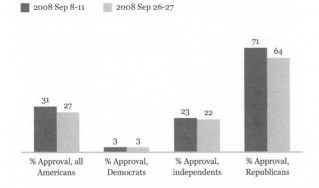

There has been an even sharper drop in Bush's ratings among self-identified conservatives, from 59% to 47%, likely reflecting opposition to the expansion of government involvement in the economy that the Bush administration proposed.

Bush's Long Losing Streak Continues

Low approval ratings have become routine for Bush. He has not had an approval rating above 40% for over two years, and only a handful of ratings at or above 50% his entire second term in office. The low ratings throughout much of his second term have arguably been because of the unpopular war in Iraq. But as conditions for the United States in Iraq have improved in the past year, the economy has gotten much worse and has served as an anchor on Bush's ratings. Bush has registered 28% approval ratings several times this year, in the spring and summer months as gas prices rose. His high rating for the year is only 34%.

The all-time low rating for any president is 22%, for Harry Truman in February 1952. Bush now joins Truman and Richard Nixon as the only presidents who have had approval ratings of 27% or lower in Gallup Polls.

Bush, like Truman, has the distinction of having some of the highest individual approval ratings in Gallup polling history and some of the lowest. That includes a record-high 90% approval rating for Bush just after the Sept. 11 terrorist attacks. Truman recorded an 87% approval in 1945 just after V-E Day.

Survey Methods

Results are based on telephone interviews with 1,011 national adults, aged 18 and older, conducted Sept. 26-27, 2008. For results based on the total sample of national adults, one can say with 95% confidence that the maximum margin of sampling error is ±3 percentage points.

Interviews are conducted with respondents on land-line telephones (for respondents with a land-line telephone) and cellular phones (for respondents who are cell-phone only).

In addition to sampling error, question wording and practical difficulties in conducting surveys can introduce error or bias into the findings of public opinion polls.

September 30, 2008

LATE SEPTEMBER RATINGS DRAG DOWN CONSUMER CONFIDENCE

by Lydia Saad, Gallup Poll Senior Editor

Americans' confidence in the U.S. economy was better in the first half of September than in August, but that's ancient history now. Consumer attitudes took a sharp turn for the worse after Sept. 15, when Wall Street fell into a worrisome tailspin over the collapse of Lehman Brothers and the bailout of AIG, and remain highly negative at the month's end.

Gallup Poll Daily tracking underscores the degree to which economic attitudes can change quickly, making it essential to monitor consumer confidence on an ongoing basis rather than taking periodic measurements, or reporting monthly averages.

The percentage of Americans Gallup classifies as "negative" about the economy, now 81% according to Gallup's daily tracking

Gallup Daily: Consumer Confidence

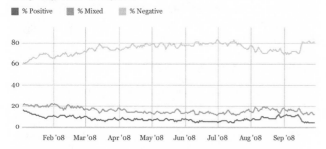

Americans classified as "positive" rate current economic conditions "excellent" or "good" and think the economy is getting better or staying the same. Americans classified as "negative" rate current economic conditions "only fair" or "poor" and think the economy is getting worse or staying the same. Americans classified as "mixed" give a combination of positive and negative responses.

from Sept. 27-29, nearly ties the record high of 83% seen at three points in July. The minuscule 4% currently classified as "positive" ties the lowest scores seen all year. Attitudes had improved to as much as 12% of Americans feeling positive about the economy and only 70% negative in Gallup tracking conducted Sept. 12-14.

These findings differ sharply from Tuesday's Conference Board report on consumer confidence, which stated that confidence improved slightly in September. That poll, based on a mail survey of U.S. households that are members of a consumer panel, had a reported cutoff date of Sept. 23, meaning most of its returns were probably received in the first half of the month, when confidence was indeed up over August.

Gallup Poll Daily Recent Weekly Averages

The weekly averages of consumer confidence in September help to underscore the degree to which consumer confidence changed in the middle of the month. Whereas a slightly improved 11% of Americans felt positively about the economy in each of the first two weeks of September, up from 9% in August, this fell to 6% from Sept. 15-21, and to 4% from Sept. 22-28 as President Bush and congressional leaders began negotiations over a $700 billion financial rescue package.

Gallup Daily: Consumer Confidence -- Recent 2008 Trends

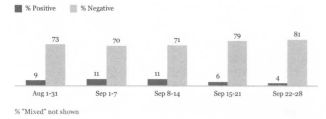

% "Mixed" not shown

Gallup's consumer mood summary is a composite of Americans' answers to two questions about the economy: one asking for their ratings of current economic conditions, and the other asking about their perceptions of whether conditions are getting better or

worse. Since mid-September, attitudes have grown more negative on both dimensions.

Ratings of Current Economic Conditions -- Recent 2008 Trends

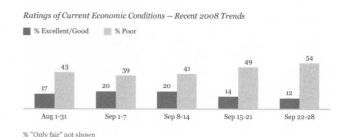

% "Only fair" not shown

Perceptions of Economic Momentum -- Recent 2008 Trends

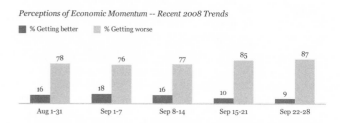

No Immediate "Plunge" Effect

The stock market showed its displeasure with Congress' failure to pass a bailout bill on Monday, Sept. 29, with the Dow Jones tumbling more than 700 points. Gallup polling that night showed no immediate effect on consumers' already-grim attitudes. As noted, the most recent three-day rolling average, from Sept. 27-29, shows 4% of Americans positive and 81% negative about the economy. This is identical to the reading from Sept. 26-28.

Survey Methods

For the Gallup Poll Daily tracking survey, Gallup is interviewing no fewer than 1,000 U.S. adults nationwide each day during 2008. The economic questions analyzed in this report are asked of a random half-sample of respondents.

The Sept. 27-29 results reported here are based on combined data from 1,549 telephone interviews. For results based on this sample, the maximum margin of sampling error is ±3 percentage points. Results based on weekly averages include interviews with more than 3,500 national adults, and have a margin of sampling error of ±2 percentage points. Results for the month of August are based on interviews with 15,796 national adults, and have a margin of sampling error of less than ±1 percentage point.

Interviews are conducted with respondents on land-line telephones (for respondents with a land-line telephone) and cellular phones (for respondents who are cell-phone only).

In addition to sampling error, question wording and practical difficulties in conducting surveys can introduce error or bias into the findings of public opinion polls.

absence of a financial rescue plan, while another 22% believe there would be a "depression." Thirty-one percent believe the country would suffer major problems, but not a severe recession, while 5% expect no major problems would result.

What do you think will happen to the U.S. economy if Congress does not pass legislation to address the financial events of the last two weeks ... ?

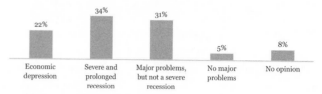

22%	34%	31%	5%	8%
Economic depression	Severe and prolonged recession	Major problems, but not a severe recession	No major problems	No opinion

USA Today/Gallup poll, Sept. 30, 2008

Democrats are more pessimistic about the economic future if no plan is passed than are either independents or Republicans. Republicans tend to be the most optimistic.

Economic Predictions if Congress Does Not Address Financial Events, by Party ID

■ % Depression   ■ % Severe recession   ■ % Major problems   ░ % No problems

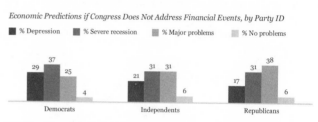

USA Today/Gallup poll, Sept. 30, 2008

The members of Congress who voted against the original $700 billion rescue bill may enjoy some political benefit from their constituents come November. More Americans say they approve of those members than say they disapprove, by a 10-point margin, 47% to 37%. That's better than the mixed ratings seen for the Democratic leaders in Congress and the net negative ratings for the Republican leaders in Congress, both of whom pushed for passage of the plan.

At the same time, the most positive reviews go to Barack Obama, with 51% of Americans saying they approve of his handling of the financial rescue bill process. That's 9 points better than the 42% approving of John McCain.

As was seen in a *USA Today*/Gallup poll from late last week, President George W. Bush receives the worst ratings of all the major political players involved for his handling of the issue.

Next, please say whether you strongly approve, approve, disapprove, or strongly disapprove of the way each of the following handled their role in the efforts to pass that bill.

	Total approve	Total disapprove	No opinion
	%	%	%
Sen. Barack Obama	51	32	17
Members of Congress who voted against bill	47	37	16
Sen. John McCain	42	41	16
The Democratic leaders in Congress	40	43	16
The Republican leaders in Congress	38	45	18
President George W. Bush	31	57	12

USA Today/Gallup poll, Sept. 30, 2008

October 01, 2008

AMERICANS TO CONGRESS: START FROM SCRATCH

Support for financial rescue is high, but not for something similar to Monday's failed bill

by Lydia Saad, Gallup Poll Senior Editor

A majority of Americans—57%—want Congress to start from scratch in devising a plan to deal with the Wall Street financial crisis, rather than pass a bill akin to the $700 billion plan that was defeated on Monday.

As you may know, the House of Representatives on Monday voted against a proposed $700 billion bill to deal with the current financial crisis. What do you think Congress should do now ... ?

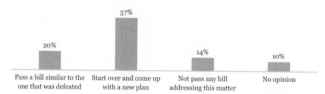

20%	57%	14%	10%
Pass a bill similar to the one that was defeated	Start over and come up with a new plan	Not pass any bill addressing this matter	No opinion

USA Today/Gallup poll, Sept. 30, 2008

More broadly, the latest *USA Today*/Gallup poll, conducted Sept. 30, finds most Americans in favor of Congress' taking some sort of legislative action to deal with the financial crisis. Only 14% think it should not pass any bill.

The poll finds little difference in attitudes on this question between Republicans and Democrats. Political independents are a bit more likely than either partisan group to say Congress should not pass any bill. But the majority of all three groups want to see Congress start over and come up with a new plan.

Preferred Approach to Handling Financial Rescue Package, by Party ID

■ % Pass bill similar to failed bill   ■ % Come up with new plan   ░ % Not pass any bill

USA Today/Gallup, Sept. 30, 2008

The perceived outlook for the U.S. economy if Congress fails to act is generally bleak. Roughly a third of Americans—34%—believe the country would suffer a severe and lengthy recession in the

Bottom Line

Congress is representing the public's wishes this week by intervening legislatively in the Wall Street financial crisis. The vast majority of Americans want some sort of bill passed addressing it. However, by only tinkering around the edges of the original $700 billion plan that failed in the U.S. House of Representatives on Monday, the U.S. Senate—now taking the lead on the bill—may not be going far enough in satisfying Americans' desire for a completely different approach.

Survey Methods

Results are based on telephone interviews with 1,021 national adults, aged 18 and older, conducted Sept. 30, 2008. For results based on the total sample of national adults, one can say with 95% confidence that the maximum margin of sampling error is ±3 percentage points.

Interviews are conducted with respondents on land-line telephones (for respondents with a land-line telephone) and cellular phones (for respondents who are cell-phone only).

In addition to sampling error, question wording and practical difficulties in conducting surveys can introduce error or bias into the findings of public opinion polls. Polls conducted entirely in one day, such as this one, are subject to additional error or bias not found in polls conducted over several days.

October 02, 2008
MAJORITY OF AMERICANS ANGRY ABOUT FINANCIAL CRISIS
Most expect their own finances to be harmed in the long term

by Jeffrey M. Jones, Gallup Poll Managing Editor

A *USA Today*/Gallup poll finds 53% of Americans describing themselves as "angry" about the financial crisis that has gripped the nation the past two weeks. Fewer Americans, but still a substantial 41%, say the recent events have made them feel "afraid."

Emotional Responses to the Financial Crisis Over the Past Two Weeks

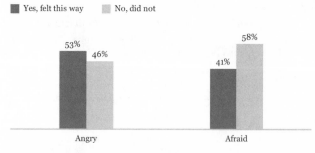

USA Today/Gallup poll, Sept. 30, 2008

These results are based on a one-night *USA Today*/Gallup reaction poll conducted Sept. 30, the night after the U.S. House rejected the proposed $700 billion plan to deal with the growing financial crisis.

Feelings of anger are more prevalent among Americans of higher socioeconomic status—63% of college graduates say they

have felt anger over the recent events in the financial world, compared with 50% of non-graduates (and only 43% of those who have not attended college).

Similarly, 62% of respondents in upper-income households (with annual incomes of $60,000 or more) have been angry, compared with 50% of those in lower-income households.

Fear has not been as common an emotion as anger in response to the financial crisis, and subgroup differences in expressed fear tend to be rather modest. For example, 46% of college graduates say they have felt afraid because of the recent economic problems, compared with 39% of non-graduates.

The poll does find that women (49%) are significantly more likely than men (32%) to say they have felt afraid as a result of the economic problems, but it is unclear whether this reflects a real difference in response to the events or a typical pattern in poll results by which men appear more reluctant than women to express fear.

Anger and fear are not surprising reactions given that most Americans already report some harm to their own finances, and an even higher number expect their finances to be affected in the long term.

According to the poll, 56% of Americans say their finances have already been harmed "a great deal" (20%) or "a moderate amount" (36%) by the events of the last two weeks. Only 16% say their own financial situations have not been harmed at all.

How much do you think your own financial situation has been harmed by the events of the last two weeks -- a great deal, a moderate amount, not much, or not at all?

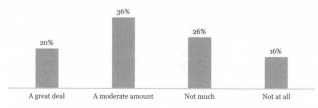

USA Today/Gallup poll, Sept. 30, 2008

Looking long-term, an even higher 69% of Americans expect their finances to be harmed by the recent events, as well as any future problems that result from them. Only 7% expect to totally avoid any repercussions.

Now, I'd like you to think about the events of the last two weeks and any future problems that might result from them. How much do you think your own financial situation will be harmed in the long run -- a great deal, a moderate amount, not much, or not at all?

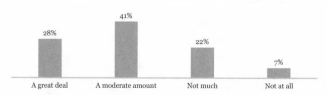

USA Today/Gallup poll, Sept. 30, 2008

Upper-income Americans (56%) are only slightly more likely than lower-income Americans (52%) to say their finances have already been harmed by the recent events on Wall Street. And while both groups are more likely to expect harm to their financial situations in the long run than in the short term, they are about equally likely to do so (70% of upper-income Americans and 69% of lower-income Americans).

Thus far, 63% of college graduates say their finances have been harmed by the events of the last two weeks, compared with 52% of non-graduates. But both groups are about equally likely to expect harm in the long run (71% and 67%, respectively).

Survey Methods

Results are based on telephone interviews with 1,021 national adults, aged 18 and older, conducted Sept. 30, 2008. For results based on the total sample of national adults, one can say with 95% confidence that the maximum margin of sampling error is ±3 percentage points.

Interviews are conducted with respondents on land-line telephones (for respondents with a land-line telephone) and cellular phones (for respondents who are cell-phone only).

In addition to sampling error, question wording and practical difficulties in conducting surveys can introduce error or bias into the findings of public opinion polls. Polls conducted entirely in one day, such as this one, are subject to additional error or bias not found in polls conducted over several days.

October 02, 2008

SHRINKING JOB MARKET: THE NEXT CRISIS?

Gallup's Net New Hiring Activity measure shows sharp deterioration in job-market perceptions

by Dennis Jacobe, Gallup Poll Chief Economist

Gallup's Net New Hiring Activity measure shows that U.S. workers' perceptions of the job market at their places of employment—already down significantly in August—became much worse in September.

Month-to-Month Change in Net New Hiring Activity, Nationwide, 2008
Percentage of employees who say their employers are hiring minus percentage who say their employers are letting people go

Numbers in percentage points

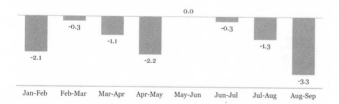

Job Losses Reaching Crisis Proportions

With the presidential election weeks away, the financial crisis and the Treasury bailout are dominating the headlines. Still, once Congress acts to shore up the U.S. banking system, the focus of most Americans may immediately turn to the Main Street economy and the accelerating pace of job losses taking place across the nation—something the financial crisis has only made worse during recent weeks.

Gallup's Net New Hiring Activity measure, based on interviews with more than 9,000 employees in September, suggests the jobs sit-

uation that worsened significantly during August deteriorated even more significantly during September. The percentage of employees saying their companies are hiring fell to 34.8%, the lowest level of the year, while the percentage saying their companies are letting people go increased to 19.2%—the highest.

In turn, this suggests that the number of jobs not only declined again in September (for the ninth consecutive month), but probably did so by substantially more than the 100,000 jobs decline generally expected. More importantly, the unemployment rate may actually surge past last month's 6.1%. A number of variables make it hard to predict exactly what job numbers the Bureau of Labor Statistics will report on Friday morning. Regardless, these Gallup jobs findings suggest the next crisis facing the American people—and just possibly the key issue of the last few weeks before the election—may be jobs.

Percentage of Employers Expanding and Reducing Their Workforces, Nationwide

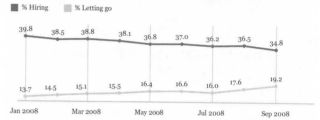

Jobs Crisis

While everyone's attention is focused on the financial crisis, the Main Street economy is deteriorating rapidly. Gallup's consumer confidence measures show a sharp decline beginning in mid-September. Add in the accelerating decline in job-market conditions and the further tightening of consumer credit, together with the fear created by debate surrounding the Treasury's "rescue" plan, and consumer perceptions are likely to continue plummeting in the weeks ahead.

The coming elections are not likely to help. Each political party is likely to try to escape blame for the economic policies of the past and to blame the other party instead. But the decline of the jobs market and the deepening recession on Main Street may have many Americans looking for solutions to the deepening economic downturn—not just a villain to blame. Providing those solutions and turning around the increasing pessimism among consumers may be the key to winning for the presidential candidates in the few weeks remaining before the election.

Survey Methods

Gallup's Net New Hiring Activity measure was initiated in January 2008. It is an effort to assess U.S. job creation or elimination based on the self-reports of more than 8,000 individual employees each month about hiring and firing activity at their workplaces. In order to calculate this measure, Gallup asks current full-time employees whether their employers are hiring new people and expanding the size of their workforces, not changing the size of their workforces, or letting people go and reducing the size of their workforces. Net new hiring activity is computed by subtracting the "letting go and reducing" percentage from the "hiring and expanding" percentage. The assumption is that employees across the country have a good feel for what's happening in their companies, and that these insider perceptions can yield a useful summary indication of the nation's job situation.

Gallup is interviewing no fewer than 1,000 U.S. adults nationwide each day during 2008. The economic questions analyzed in this report are asked of a random half-sample of respondents each day. The results reported here are based on combined data of more than 8,000 interviews in each month, January through September. For results based on these samples, the maximum margin of sampling error is ±1 percentage point.

Interviews are conducted with respondents on land-line telephones (for respondents with a land-line telephone) and cellular phones (for respondents who are cell-phone only).

In addition to sampling error, question wording and practical difficulties in conducting surveys can introduce error or bias into the findings of public opinion polls.

October 03, 2008
PUBLIC GIVES SUPREME COURT PASSING GRADE
50% approve of the job it is doing

by Jeffrey M. Jones, Gallup Poll Managing Editor

As the Supreme Court begins a new term Monday, 50% of Americans say they approve of the job the Supreme Court is doing, similar to the ratings from last year. Thirty-nine percent disapprove.

Do you approve or disapprove of the way the Supreme Court is handling its job?

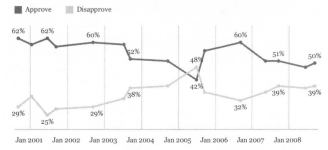

Americans had rated the Supreme Court higher earlier this decade, with close to 6 in 10 approving from 2000-2002. Approval dropped in subsequent years following controversial decisions on gay rights and the government's ability to seize private property. After a brief recovery in 2006, the ratings have declined again. The recent lower ratings for the Supreme Court may simply reflect greater frustration with government in general, as evidenced by President Bush's job approval ratings near 30% and Congress' near 20%.

Republicans (65%) are more likely than Democrats (38%) and independents (47%) to approve of the Supreme Court, according to the Sept. 8-11 Gallup Poll. This has typically been the case since 2000, when Gallup first began tracking Supreme Court approval.

However, the gap between Republicans and Democrats has widened in recent years after President Bush appointed two conservative-leaning jurists (John Roberts and Samuel Alito) to the court.

Since 1993, the plurality of Americans has expressed satisfaction with the Supreme Court's ideological orientation. In the poll, 43% of Americans say the Supreme Court is "about right," with slightly more saying it is too conservative (30%) than too liberal (21%).

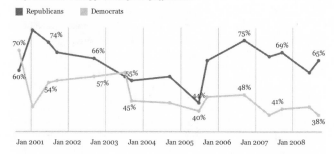

Supreme Court Job Approval, by Party Affiliation

Americans have been more likely to say that the Supreme Court is too conservative than too liberal since Roberts and Alito joined the court. Prior to that, Americans were either more likely to see the court as too liberal than as too conservative, or about equally divided between the two opinions.

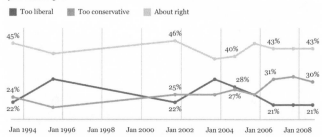

In general, do you think the current Supreme Court is too liberal, too conservative, or just about right?

Currently, a majority of Republicans, and the plurality of independents, say the Supreme Court's ideology is about right. Half of Democrats, however, believe it is too conservative. Interestingly, Republicans are much more likely to believe the Supreme Court is too liberal (35%) than conservative (8%).

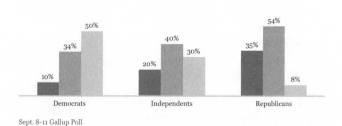

View of Supreme Court Ideology, by Party Affiliation

Sept. 8-11 Gallup Poll

Survey Methods

Results are based on telephone interviews with 1,007 national adults, aged 18 and older, conducted Sept. 8-11, 2008. For results based on the total sample of national adults, one can say with 95% confidence that the maximum margin of sampling error is ±3 percentage points.

Interviews are conducted with respondents on land-line telephones (for respondents with a land-line telephone) and cellular phones (for respondents who are cell-phone only).

In addition to sampling error, question wording and practical difficulties in conducting surveys can introduce error or bias into the findings of public opinion polls.

October 03, 2008
WOMEN WHO ARE POLITICALLY INDEPENDENT: UP FOR GRABS?

Independent women who are Catholic, middle aged, middle-income split in their votes

by Frank Newport, Gallup Poll Editor in Chief

Independent women who are Catholic, middle aged, not college graduates, of average religiosity, and of mid-range incomes are most evenly split in their presidential candidate choices, and thus may be most "up for grabs" in the remaining weeks of the campaign.

The importance of the female vote has been underscored by the selection of Sarah Palin as John McCain's vice-presidential running mate. The reaction of women to Thursday night's debate between Palin and Joe Biden—which will not be fully evident until the days to come—will thus be carefully watched.

Taken as a whole, women who are registered voters tilt in their candidate preferences toward the Democrat Barack Obama, reflecting the usual gender gap that affects national politics today. But since over half of all voters in the United States are women, this broad-brush look at their preferences is only the beginning point.

Most importantly, about two-thirds of women today identify themselves as either Democrats or Republicans, and are highly likely to be voting for their party's candidate. A special Gallup analysis of more than 26,000 interviews conducted in September confirms that Democratic women overwhelmingly support Obama, and Republican women overwhelmingly prefer McCain. This leaves independent women, who are much more even in their vote-choice distribution.

Gallup Daily Election Polling Results for the Presidential General Election
Barack Obama vs. John McCain

Among national female registered voters -- Sept. 1-29, 2008

■ % Obama   ▨ % McCain

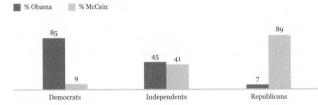

Based on Gallup Poll Daily tracking

It's a reasonable assumption that changing minds among partisan Democratic and Republican women will be difficult, although these groups remain highly important in terms of turnout. Indeed, motivating the "base" is a key dictum of modern-day politics. It has been argued that one motivation behind McCain's choice of Palin as his vice-presidential running mate may have been to increase enthusiasm among Republican women.

But it is the group of independent women who—based on the fact that they are currently about evenly divided between the two candidates—were perhaps the most important viewers of Thursday's debate, at least in terms of the possibility that their voting preferences will change. Assuming that independent female registered voters are a key "swing" group in the campaign, it is useful to delve further into the ways in which they subdivide in terms of candidate preferences. Gallup's large sample of September interviews allows for a careful analysis of the vote patterns of demographic subgroups *within* the larger group of independent women. The accompanying table displays candidate choices among a number of these different subgroups of independent women.

Preference for the General Election Among Independent Female Voters

Aggregate registered voters, Sept. 1-29, 2008
Gallup Poll Daily tracking

	% Obama	% McCain
Married	40	48
Not married	50	34
Have children under 18	48	40
No children under 18	43	42
Attend church weekly	35	50
Attend church almost weekly/monthly	47	41
Attend church seldom/never	52	33
18 to 34	57	30
35 to 54	45	43
55+	38	44
College	54	37
No college	41	43
Protestant	40	44
Catholic	43	43
No religion	66	24
<$2,000 per month	46	36
$2,000 to <$5,000 per month	45	43
$5,000 to <$7,500 per month	50	44
$7,500 or more per month	49	42

Most of these patterns are microcosms of the divisions evident in the overall voting population this year—e.g., younger Americans, regardless of their other characteristics, are more likely to support Obama than are those who are older.

All in all, the segments of independent women who are strongest in their support of Obama—and thus who were presumably most sympathetic to Biden in Thursday's debate—include:

- those with no religious identification
- those aged 18 to 34
- those with college educations
- those who seldom or never attend church

The segments of independent women who are most likely to support McCain and thus may have been sympathetic to Palin Thursday night include:

- those who attend church weekly
- those who are married
- those aged 55 or older

Finally, the following groups of independent women are most closely divided in their candidate preferences, and—it could be assumed—were the most likely to be swayed one way or the other by the debate (and indeed the events of the final few weeks of the campaign):

- Catholics
- those who do not have a college degree
- those with no children under 18
- the middle aged, 35 to 54
- those making between $12,000 and $60,000 a year in household income
- those mid-range in religiosity, attending church almost every week or monthly

Implications

In theory, because of a lack of a strong partisan attachment, independent women are more susceptible to changing their vote preference than are women who identify as Republicans or Democrats. Within the group of independent women, subgroups that are currently most evenly divided in their existing vote between the two major-party candidates may be in turn the most amenable to changing their vote preferences as a result of the campaign. For example, the finding that independent women who are Catholic were exactly split between Obama and McCain (in September interviewing) suggests that there is no strong tendency among this group taken as a whole to go for one candidate or the other. The individuals who make up the group may be less rigid in their support patterns, and thus more open to shifting.

Thus, if the McCain-Palin ticket is to pick up steam either as a result of Thursday night's debate or forthcoming campaigning, one logical place to look for that process to occur is among independent women who are Catholic, middle aged, not college graduates, of average religiosity, and of mid-range incomes.

Survey Methods

Results are based on telephone interviews with 26,620 registered voters, aged 18 and older, conducted Sept. 1-29, 2008. For results based on the total sample of national adults, one can say with 95% confidence that the maximum margin of sampling error is ±1 percentage point. The maximum margin of sampling error for results based on interviews conducted with 13,362 female registered voters is also ±1 percentage point.

Interviews are conducted with respondents on land-line telephones (for respondents with a land-line telephone) and cellular phones (for respondents who are cell-phone only).

In addition to sampling error, question wording and practical difficulties in conducting surveys can introduce error or bias into the findings of public opinion polls.

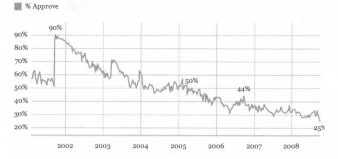

George W. Bush's Job Approval Ratings Trend (2001-Present)

% Approve

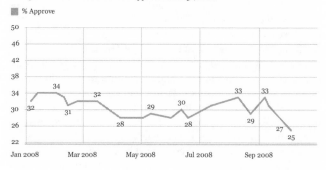

George W. Bush's Presidential Job Approval Ratings, 2008

% Approve

Nixon's lowest job approval rating of 24% measured in the summer of 1974, and it is just three points higher than Harry Truman's all-time Gallup low job approval rating of 22% measured in 1952. No other presidents have had job approval ratings of 27% or lower in Gallup Poll history.

The current poll recording Bush's low job approval rating was conducted after Congress passed the economic rescue bill on Oct. 3. Americans recognize the economy as the nation's top problem, but apparently, the passage of this bill—which the Bush administration had heavily advocated—did nothing to affect Bush's approval ratings. Indeed, only 55% of members of Bush's own party approve of him in the poll, perhaps a reflection of some pushback from conservatives who do not strongly support the economic bill. Nineteen percent of independents and 5% of Democrats approve of the way Bush is handling his job as president.

October 6, 2008

BUSH JOB APPROVAL AT 25%, HIS LOWEST YET

Only 3 points above the lowest in Gallup Poll history

by Frank Newport, Gallup Poll Editor in Chief

President Bush's job approval rating is at 25% in the latest Oct. 3-5 Gallup Poll, the lowest of the Bush administration, and only three percentage points above the lowest presidential approval rating in Gallup Poll history.

Bush's previous low point was 27%, measured about a week ago. The 25% approval rating is one point higher than Richard

---

October 06, 2008

U.S. FINANCIAL RESCUE PLAN WINS SLIM PUBLIC SUPPORT

Republicans and Democrats mostly agree passage was a good thing

by Lydia Saad, Gallup Poll Senior Editor

More Americans consider it a "good thing" that Congress passed a financial rescue package for U.S. financial institutions last week than call it a "bad thing," but only by a narrow 9 percentage-point margin, 50% to 41%. Another 9% have no opinion about it.

According to the Oct. 3-5 Gallup Poll, Republicans are nearly as supportive of the financial rescue as are Democrats: 54% of

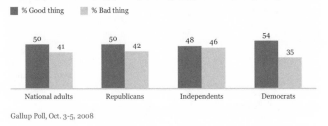

Gallup Poll, Oct. 3-5, 2008

Democrats and 50% of Republicans say it's a good thing the plan passed.

Both Barack Obama and John McCain voted for the plan last week, and the new poll shows that about equal levels of Obama and McCain supporters are positive about the plan. However, McCain supporters are slightly more likely than those backing Obama to say it's a bad thing the plan passed. More Obama voters than McCain voters are unsure.

Reaction to Financial Rescue, by Presidential Preference
Based on national adults

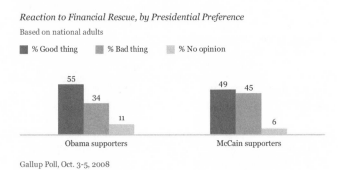

Gallup Poll, Oct. 3-5, 2008

The $700 billion Wall Street bailout bill easily passed in the U.S. House of Representatives on a 263-171 vote on Friday, but not without the continued opposition from a majority of House Republicans, who had helped to kill an earlier version of the bill. Their resistance drew on traditional conservative free-market themes.

Along the same lines, the highest level of opposition Gallup finds to the bill among political subgroups is from political "conservatives." Half of self-described conservatives say it's a bad thing the plan passed. This contrasts with only 36% of "moderates" and a third of "liberals."

Reaction to Financial Rescue, by Political Ideology
Based on national adults

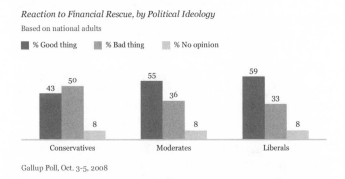

Gallup Poll, Oct. 3-5, 2008

Some variation in support for the financial package is also seen by household income. A solid majority of upper-income Americans

(57%) are glad the bill passed, compared with only 44% of those making less than $30,000. However, an equal number of both groups—about 40%—say it's a bad thing. Many more lower-income households have no opinion about the bill.

Reaction to Financial Rescue, by Annual Household Income
Based on national adults

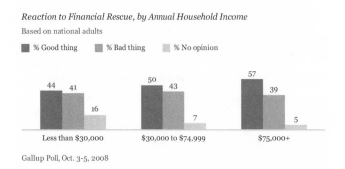

Gallup Poll, Oct. 3-5, 2008

Bottom Line

Last week, as Congress was debating the details of a financial rescue package after the first deal fell short of the necessary votes in the U.S. House of Representatives, Americans expressed greater support for Congress' starting over with a new plan than merely revising the one that failed. Now that Congress has done just that—passed a retooled version of the original failed bill—Americans seem more likely than not to accept it, albeit by a slim margin. There is, however, relatively little partisan friction in the mix.

Survey Methods

Results are based on telephone interviews with 1,011 national adults, aged 18 and older, conducted Oct. 3-5, 2008. For results based on the total sample of national adults, one can say with 95% confidence that the maximum margin of sampling error is ±3 percentage points.

Interviews are conducted with respondents on land-line telephones (for respondents with a land-line telephone) and cellular phones (for respondents who are cell-phone only).

In addition to sampling error, question wording and practical difficulties in conducting surveys can introduce error or bias into the findings of public opinion polls.

October 06, 2008
YOUNG VOTERS '08: PRO-OBAMA AND MINDFUL OF OUTCOME
Majority of 18- to 29-year-olds perceive a direct impact of president on their lives

by Lymari Morales, Gallup Poll Staff Writer

America's youngest voters are mindful of history and the impact on their own lives as they prepare to cast ballots on Nov. 4. Among 18- to 29-year-old registered voters surveyed for a *USA Today*/MTV/ Gallup poll, 61% support the Obama-Biden ticket, versus 32% who prefer the McCain-Palin ticket, with Obama's voters being far more likely to be certain about their vote than McCain's.

Obama's strong appeal to younger voters is apparent in that he outperforms McCain by double digits on every single character

If the presidential election were being held today... Would you vote for [ROTATED: Barack Obama and Joe Biden, the Democrats (or) John McCain and Sarah Palin, the Republicans]? Are you certain or do you think you may change your mind between now and the November election?

Among 18- to 29-year-old registered voters

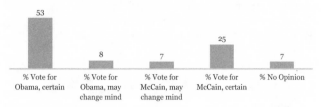

USA Today/MTV/Gallup Poll

dimension tested in the poll of more than 900 18- to 29-year-olds nationwide, conducted by Gallup for *USA Today* and MTV Sept. 18-28, 2008. The 47-year-old Obama swamps 72-year-old McCain, 71% to 12%, on understanding the "problems of people your age" and even wins on what is a McCain strength among the broader electorate, being a "strong and decisive leader," 46% to 36%.

Thinking about the following characteristics and qualities, please say whether you think each one applies more to Barack Obama or more to John McCain. How about – [RANDOM ORDER]?

Among 18- to 29-year-olds

	Obama	McCain
Understands the problems of people your age	71%	12%
Is inspiring	67%	18%
Has a sense of humor	58%	17%
Is optimistic about the country's future	55%	23%
Is independent in his thoughts and actions	55%	28%
Will unite the country and not divide it	55%	25%
Shows good judgment	54%	29%
Puts the country's interests ahead of his own political interests	53%	29%
Is a strong and decisive leader	46%	36%

USA Today/MTV/Gallup Poll

While only a minority (37%) of young adults have qualms about McCain's age, a majority (55%) do have concerns about his running mate Sarah Palin's qualifications to step in as president if necessary. In contrast, a majority are satisfied with both Obama's experience and running mate Joe Biden's qualifications. (The poll was conducted before the Oct. 2 vice presidential debate.)

On Experience, Age & their VP Picks

Among 18- to 29-year-olds

	Yes	No
Does Obama have enough experience to be president?	57%	36%
Is McCain too old to be president?	37%	59%
Is Joe Biden qualified to serve as president if necessary?	59%	19%
Is Sarah Palin qualified to serve as president if necessary?	32%	55%

USA Today/MTV/Gallup Poll

Obama also beats McCain on several lighter dimensions tested in the poll. A majority of 18- to 29-year-olds would choose Obama over McCain as a teacher, boss, drinking buddy, or advisor. McCain's only appeal on this level with young adults appears to be

his personal life story as young adults are more likely to be interested in reading McCain's private diary than Obama's. While such items may seem trivial, basic likeability can be a key indicator of a presidential candidate's ability to win votes.

Which presidential candidate would you most want to...?

Among 18- to 29-year-olds

	Obama	McCain
Have as a teacher in a class	65%	27%
Have as your boss	63%	28%
Have a beer with	52%	27%
Ask for advice	51%	36%
Read his private diary	39%	43%

USA Today/MTV/Gallup Poll

When asked in an open-ended fashion to name the single most important issue affecting their vote for president this year, 18- to 29-year-old registered voters most often cite the economy (30%), followed by the war in Iraq (13%), healthcare (5%), energy and gas prices (4%), and international issues (4%). These issues are, in a broad sense, little different from those listed by all voters, regardless of age. Asked which candidate they think would do a better job on their top-priority issue, 58% say Obama versus 27% who say McCain, again echoing their basic candidate choice.

On the Outcome

The poll results make it clear that young Americans perceive that the outcome of the election really does matter, both to the country and to their own lives. Nearly-two thirds (64%) of 18- to 29-year-olds surveyed say they have already given the election a lot of thought. Nearly half (44%) consider this election to be the most important of the last 50 years, and another 37% consider it more important than other elections.

When asked about the consequences of the two possible election outcomes, 84% say an Obama victory would have a great deal (47%) or moderate amount (37%) of impact on their lives and 72% say the same about McCain (36% great deal, 36% moderate amount).

Going a step further, the survey asked those who said an Obama or McCain victory would impact them "a great deal" or "not at all" to explain in their own words why they feel that way. In Obama's case, nearly one in four (24%) volunteered that good or positive changes would take place, while in McCain's case, the most common responses were negative or pertained to the War in Iraq.

Asked in a separate question how a McCain administration might compare to the Bush administration, 55% said they would view a McCain victory as "four more years of the Bush administration" versus 37% who said they would view it as "real change from the Bush administration."

The two tickets this year also carry the distinction of the first major party black nominee in U.S. history, and only the second major party female vice presidential nominee. In the eyes of young voters, victory for the Obama-Biden ticket would be much more of an historical event than victory for the McCain-Palin ticket. A majority (53%) agree that if Barack Obama is elected president, it would be one of the most important advances in racial equality over the past 100 years. By contrast, only one-third (32%) agree that if Sarah Palin becomes vice president, it will be one of the most important advances in gender equality in the past 100 years.

Of those who say Obama's election will have "a great deal" of impact or "none at all" on their lives -- Why do you say that? [OPEN-ENDED]

Among 18- to 29-year-olds

	%
Good/Positive changes would take place	24
Views/policies (non-specific)	8
First black president/Historic election	8
Dislike him/Don't trust him	7
Economy would improve	6
For the middle class	6
Taxes	6
Military/defense issues	4
Healthcare	4
War in Iraq	3
Jobs/Employment	2
Views on social issues	2
Education	2
Other	5
No reason in particular (vol.)	8
No opinion	5

USA Today/MTV/Gallup Poll

Of those who say McCain's election will have "a great deal" of impact or "none at all" on their lives -- Why do you say that? [OPEN-ENDED]

Among 18- to 29-year-olds

	%
Would not help economy/Would get worse	15
War in Iraq	15
No changes would be made	14
Like him/Would do a good job	9
Dislike him	9
Disagree with his views	7
Taxes	2
Healthcare	2
Other	7
No reason in particular (vol.)	13
No opinion	7

USA Today/MTV/Gallup Poll

Bottom Line

A majority of 18- to 29-year-olds are registered to vote in this election and have given it a lot of thought. They prefer Barack Obama, both as an alternative to John McCain, but also as the candidate who is the most likely to understand their problems and to bring positive change to their own lives. Casting a ballot for Obama also carries the excitement of making history. Nearly 8 in 10 consider this election to be more important than other elections, if not the most important in the past 50 years. What remains to be seen is how many of this highly sought-after demographic will in fact turn out and vote on Election Day, and thus help to determine the winner.

Survey Methods

Results are based on telephone interviews conducted September 18-28, 2008, with 903 U.S. adults between the ages of 18 and 29, 633 respondents of whom were randomly selected from a national sample of land-line and cellular telephone numbers, and 270 respondents of whom had participated in earlier national Gallup polls and agreed to be re-interviewed for a future poll. For results based on the total sample, which is weighted for demographic information to be representative of 18- to 29-year-olds nationwide, one can say with 95% confidence that the maximum margin of sampling error is ±4 percentage points. For results based on the sample of 742 registered voters, the maximum margin of sampling error is ±5 percentage points.

In addition to sampling error, question wording and practical difficulties in conducting surveys can introduce error or bias into the findings of public opinion polls.

October 07, 2008
RECORD-HIGH 82% SAY NOW IS A BAD TIME TO FIND A JOB
Stealth issue is beginning to reveal itself to American voters

by Dennis Jacobe, Gallup Poll Chief Economist

The percentage of Americans saying now is a "bad time" to find a quality job is up 26 percentage points from a year ago and now stands at 82%—the highest level since Gallup began asking this question in October 2001.

Thinking about the job situation in America today, would you say that it is now a good time or a bad time to find a quality job?

■ % Bad time, October trend

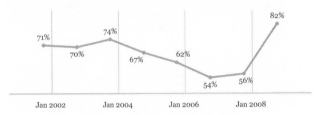

Job-Market Conditions Are Not Good

Over the first three quarters of this year, the U.S. economy lost more than three-quarters of a million jobs—giving up many of the 1.1 million jobs created in 2007. In early October, Americans' perceptions of the job market are worse than they've been at this time of year since Gallup began monitoring the issue in late 2001.

Today's 82% of Americans rating now as a bad time to find a quality job far exceeds the 56% and 54% who felt this way in October 2007 and October 2006, respectively. In fact, the current degree of pessimism about the job market is the highest level Gallup has recorded at any time over the past seven years—the previous high was 81%, reached around the beginning of the war with Iraq, in March and August 2003.

This degree of pessimism is shared broadly across demographic groups, with 80% of men and 85% of women holding this view of the job market. And 80% or more of Americans in each region of the country have a similar job-market perspective.

Percentage Saying Now Is a Bad Time to Find a Quality Job
By gender and region

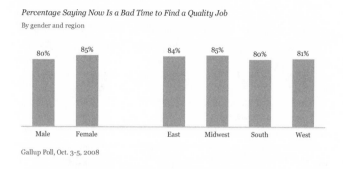

Gallup Poll, Oct. 3-5, 2008

Huge Increase in Republican Pessimism About Jobs

In May of this year, the largest differences in job-market perceptions were by political affiliation. Republicans were least pessimistic about current labor-market conditions, with a relatively low 57% saying it was a bad time to find a quality job. In contrast, 86% of Democrats felt this way, along with 72% of independents. By October, the party differences remained but the percentage of Republicans pessimistic about the jobs outlook surged 17 points to 74%; the percentage of Democrats increased 5 points to 91%; and the percentage of independents increased 8 points to 80%.

Percentage Saying Now Is a Bad Time to Find a Quality Job
By party ID

■ May 2008   ■ October 2008

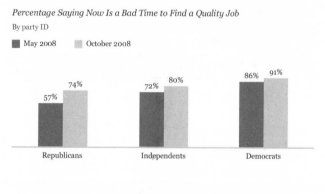

Commentary

Earlier this year, far fewer Republicans than either Democrats or independents were pessimistic about the job-market outlook. Although differences in perspective remain, nine consecutive months of job losses and the financial crises of the past several weeks have significantly closed this gap in perceptions, with pessimism now dominating the outlook.

Further, the impact of the crisis in confidence that Gallup began detecting around mid-September is yet to be fully reflected in today's job-market perceptions.

The current lack of confidence on top of the many other challenges to the U.S. economy is creating what appears to be a traditional and fairly severe recession. In turn, this suggests that the jobs situation will continue to worsen before it begins to get better.

Although the next government report on jobs won't be released until after the November elections, the presidential candidates would do well to have a plan to deal with the potential of a sharply deteriorating post-election job market. Congress left town without addressing this seeming stealth issue, as it failed to extend unemployment

insurance benefits. It would seem unwise for the candidates to avoid the issue in Tuesday night's debate.

Survey Methods

Results are based on telephone interviews with 1,011 national adults, aged 18 and older, conducted Oct. 3-5, 2008. For results based on the total sample of national adults, one can say with 95% confidence that the maximum margin of sampling error is ±3 percentage points.

Interviews are conducted with respondents on land-line telephones (for respondents with a land-line telephone) and cellular phones (for respondents who are cell-phone only).

In addition to sampling error, question wording and practical difficulties in conducting surveys can introduce error or bias into the findings of public opinion polls.

October 08, 2008
VOTERS SEE ECONOMIC PLANS AS NET PLUS FOR OBAMA
McCain economic plan more likely to repel than attract voters

by Jeffrey M. Jones, Gallup Poll Managing Editor

Forty-three percent of voters say Barack Obama's economic and tax plans make them more likely to vote for him, compared with 30% who say this about John McCain and his plans. In fact, more voters say McCain's plan for the economy and taxes makes them less likely to vote for him.

Effect of Candidates' Economic and Tax Plans on Vote
Based on registered voters

■ More likely to vote for   ■ No difference   ■ Less likely to vote for

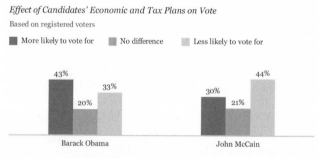

Gallup Poll, Oct. 3-5, 2008

In its Oct. 3-5 poll, Gallup asked a random sample of registered voters nationwide whether each of eight factors—spanning many of the candidates' important policy differences and background characteristics—made them more likely or less likely to vote for Obama, or made no difference to their vote. The same eight factors were asked separately in regard to McCain.

Most voters say the candidates' past positions on the Iraq war will influence their vote. In general, voters tend to view Obama's past Iraq war opposition as a plus—43% say it makes them more likely to vote for him, tying his economic plan as the voting factor making the biggest positive contribution to the Obama candidacy. With this positive endorsement of Obama's war opposition, it is thus not surprising that McCain's support for the decision to go to war in 2003 is viewed as more of a drawback in voters' minds.

Effect of Candidates' Positions on Iraq War on Vote

Based on registered voters

■ More likely to vote for   ■ No difference   ■ Less likely to vote for

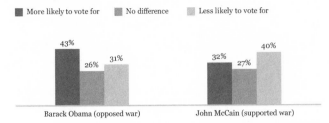

Barack Obama (opposed war)   John McCain (supported war)

Gallup Poll, Oct. 3-5, 2008

However, the candidates' differing positions on the U.S. troop surge in Iraq work to McCain's benefit. Thirty-eight percent say McCain's support of the 2007 troop surge makes them more likely to vote for him; only 32% cite Obama's opposition to the surge as something that increases their likelihood of voting for him.

Effect of Candidates' Positions on Iraq War Surge on Vote

Based on registered voters

■ More likely to vote for   ■ No difference   ■ Less likely to vote for

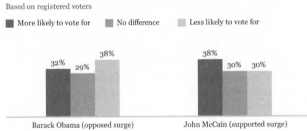

Barack Obama (opposed surge)   John McCain (supported surge)

Gallup Poll, Oct. 3-5, 2008

In fact, this is the only one of the eight items tested in the poll that appears to be a disadvantage for Obama. On the seven others, more voters say it makes them more likely to vote for the Democratic nominee than say it makes them less likely to do so. This could largely reflect Obama's leading position in the polls at this stage of the campaign.

Race and Age

Both candidates would make history if elected in November, with Obama seeking to become the first black president and McCain the oldest elected to a first term. Voters may not necessarily consider either factor a plus—lingering racism could cause some voters to cast a ballot against Obama solely on the basis of his race, and some voters may be uncomfortable electing a president as old as McCain to such a demanding job.

The poll finds that age appears to be a much more relevant factor in the vote this year than is race—at least based on these self-reports.

Relatively few voters say race will be a factor in their vote—at least 85% say it will make no difference in their decision to support either candidate. The impact of Obama's race has been the focus of much discussion in this campaign. According to what voters say in this poll, his race is actually a net plus. Of the small number of voters who say Obama's race will affect their vote, a slightly higher percentage say his race will make them more likely (9%) rather than less likely (6%) to vote for him. Interestingly, these responses are not sig-

Factors Affecting Vote for President

Based on registered voters

	More likely to vote for	No difference	Less likely to vote for	More likely minus less likely
	%	%	%	Pct. pts.
Barack Obama				
His economic and tax plans	43	20	33	10
That he opposed the war in Iraq in 2003	43	26	31	12
His pro-choice position on abortion	39	28	32	7
His choice of Joe Biden as his vice presidential running mate	37	43	19	18
That he opposed the surge of U.S. troops in Iraq in 2007	32	29	38	-6
That he is a Democrat	29	50	20	9
His age	24	67	9	15
His race	9	85	6	3
John McCain				
That he supported the surge of U.S. troops in Iraq in 2007	38	30	30	8
His pro-life position on abortion	35	27	36	-1
His choice of Sarah Palin as his vice presidential running mate	33	26	41	-8
That he supported the war in Iraq in 2003	32	27	40	-8
His economic and tax plans	30	21	44	-14
That he is a Republican	23	49	29	-6
His age	7	55	38	-31
His race	7	87	6	1

Gallup Poll, Oct. 3-5, 2008

nificantly different from the percentages who say McCain's race will affect their vote.

Effect of Candidates' Races on Vote

Based on registered voters

■ More likely to vote for   ■ No difference   ■ Less likely to vote for

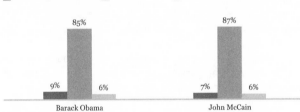

Barack Obama   John McCain

Gallup Poll, Oct. 3-5, 2008

Voters are somewhat more likely to factor the candidates' ages into their voting calculus, but in each case a majority say this will not affect their vote (although fewer say it makes no difference in their decision to vote for McCain than in their decision to vote for Obama).

On balance, age is clearly a negative factor for McCain, and a positive one for Obama. Thirty-eight percent of voters say McCain's age makes them less likely to vote for him; only 7% say it makes them more likely. Meanwhile, 24% say Obama's age increases their odds of voting for him, while 9% say it decreases those odds.

That more negative assessment of McCain's age is in large part because of the opinions of Democrats—a majority of whom say it makes them less likely to support the GOP nominee. Most independents and Republicans say his age makes no difference to their vote.

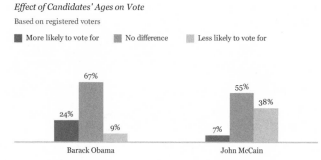

Effect of Candidates' Ages on Vote

Based on registered voters

■ More likely to vote for   ■ No difference   ■ Less likely to vote for

Barack Obama: 24%, 67%, 9%
John McCain: 7%, 55%, 38%

Gallup Poll, Oct. 3-5, 2008

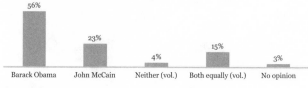

Regardless of which candidate you happen to support, who do you think did the better job in last night's debate -- [ROTATED: John McCain (or) Barack Obama]?

Based on national adults who watched the Oct. 7 presidential debate

Barack Obama: 56%
John McCain: 23%
Neither (vol.): 4%
Both equally (vol.): 15%
No opinion: 3%

USA Today/Gallup poll, Oct. 8, 2008
(vol.) = Volunteered response

The Running Mates

The poll suggests that, overall, Joe Biden does more to help the Democratic ticket than Sarah Palin does the Republican ticket. Thirty-seven percent of voters say Obama's selection of Biden as his vice-presidential running mate makes them more likely to vote for the Democratic candidate, compared with 19% who say it makes them less likely to do so. By 41% to 33%, voters say McCain's choice of Palin makes them *less* likely to vote for the Republicans in November.

Even so, Palin appears to be doing more to fire up her party's natural supporters than Biden is doing to motivate the Democratic base. Sixty-five percent of Republicans say Palin's presence on the ticket makes them more likely to vote for McCain, compared with 57% of Democrats who say Obama's choice of Biden makes them more likely to vote for Obama.

Survey Methods

Results are based on telephone interviews with 926 registered voters, aged 18 and older, conducted Oct. 3-5, 2008. For results based on the total sample of national adults, one can say with 95% confidence that the maximum margin of sampling error is ±4 percentage points.

Interviews are conducted with respondents on land-line telephones (for respondents with a land-line telephone) and cellular phones (for respondents who are cell-phone only).

In addition to sampling error, question wording and practical difficulties in conducting surveys can introduce error or bias into the findings of public opinion polls.

October 09, 2008
OBAMA RATED AS WINNER OF SECOND PRESIDENTIAL DEBATE
Debate watchers say Obama won by 56% to 23%

by Jeffrey M. Jones, Gallup Poll Managing Editor

A one-night *USA Today*/Gallup reaction poll finds a random sample of debate watchers saying Barack Obama (56%) did a better job than John McCain (23%) in Tuesday's town hall debate.

The poll was conducted Oct. 8, the night after the debate at Belmont University in Nashville, in which Obama and McCain answered questions posed by a group of uncommitted voters. Sixty-six percent of Americans reported watching the debate, up from 63% for the first debate on Sept. 26.

Obama also was rated as the winner of the first presidential debate, though by a lesser margin (46% to 34%) than for the second presidential debate.

Gallup has measured public reaction to most presidential debates since 1960—either on the same night immediately after the debate or (as is true for the current results) in the first day(s) after the debate. More often than not, those who have watched the debate have rated the Democratic candidate as the winner, so Obama's perceived victories are not unusual from a historical perspective. However, his 56% to 23% victory for the most recent debate is one of the more decisive Gallup has measured, similar to Bill Clinton's wins in the 1992 town hall debate versus George H.W. Bush and Ross Perot, and in both 1996 debates versus Bob Dole.

While most who watched the debate say their opinions of Obama and McCain have not changed much, the movement that did occur tended to be in the positive direction for Obama and the negative direction for McCain.

How has your opinion of the candidates been affected by the debate? Is your opinion of -- [RANDOM ORDER] -- more favorable, less favorable, or has it not changed much?

Based on national adults who watched the Oct. 7 presidential debate

■ More favorable   ■ Not changed   ■ Less favorable

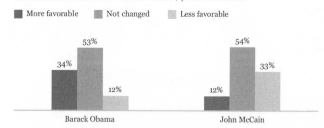

Barack Obama: 34%, 53%, 12%
John McCain: 12%, 54%, 33%

USA Today/Gallup poll, Oct. 8, 2008

The results for Obama are similar to what Gallup measured for him after the first debate (30% more favorable, 14% less favorable, 54% no change). But opinions of McCain seem to have deteriorated more after the second debate than after the first (21% more favorable, 21% less favorable, 56% no change).

Survey Methods

Results are based on telephone interviews with 1,004 national adults, aged 18 and older, conducted Oct. 8, 2008. For results based on the total sample of national adults, one can say with 95% confidence that the maximum margin of sampling error is ±3 percentage points.

For results based on the sample of 735 national adults who watched the Oct. 7 presidential debate, the maximum margin of sampling error is ±4 percentage points.

Interviews are conducted with respondents on land-line telephones (for respondents with a land-line telephone) and cellular phones (for respondents who are cell-phone only).

In addition to sampling error, question wording and practical difficulties in conducting surveys can introduce error or bias into the findings of public opinion polls.

Polls conducted entirely in one day, such as this one, are subject to additional error or bias not found in polls conducted over several days.

October 09, 2008
OBAMA'S RACE MAY BE AS MUCH A PLUS AS A MINUS
Not much different from the impact of McCain's race

by Frank Newport, Gallup Poll Editor in Chief

While 6% of voters say they are less likely to vote for Barack Obama because of his race, 9% say they are more likely to vote for him, making the impact of his race a neutral to slightly positive factor when all voters' self-reported attitudes are taken into account.

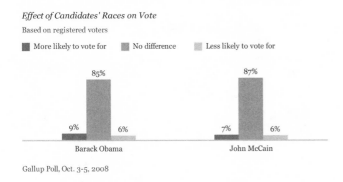

Effect of Candidates' Races on Vote
Based on registered voters

Gallup Poll, Oct. 3-5, 2008

At the same time, 6% of voters say John McCain's race will make them less likely to vote for him, with 7% saying it makes them more likely to vote for him, leading to the same basic conclusion: McCain's race, like Obama's, is on balance neither a plus nor a minus.

These conclusions are based on eight dimensions potentially affecting the vote for both candidates. The dimensions were included in Gallup's Oct. 3-5 poll, and analyzed overall by Gallup's Jeff Jones.

One of the dimensions tested for each candidate was "his race." More specifically, as was true for each of the other seven dimensions, respondents were asked to indicate whether each candidate's race made them more likely, or less likely, to vote for him for president. The data are presented in the charts here.

Eighty-five percent of voters say Obama's race makes no difference, and 87% say McCain's race makes no difference. This makes race the single dimension out of the eight tested that is the least likely to have an impact on the vote.

As noted above, the self-reported impact of race for both Obama and McCain is mixed, with about as many respondents saying race

will make them more likely to vote for each candidate as say race will make them less likely to vote for each.

The potential impact of Obama's race on the election has been the more scrutinized this year. These data, taken at face value, show that if anything, his race could be a net plus, in the sense that it makes slightly more voters want to vote for him than not want to vote for him.

There is, as expected, a difference by the race of the respondent in answers to this question.

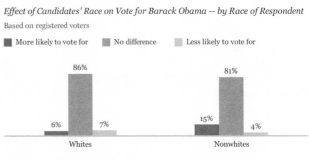

Effect of Candidates' Race on Vote for Barack Obama -- by Race of Respondent
Based on registered voters

Gallup Poll, Oct. 3-5, 2008

Among nonwhites in the sample, there is a net difference of 11 percentage points in Obama's favor in terms of the likelihood to vote for him because of his race. Among non-Hispanic whites in the sample, there is a slight net negative for Obama of -1 point.

The impact of McCain's race among nonwhites, on the other hand, is -8 points. Among whites it is +4.

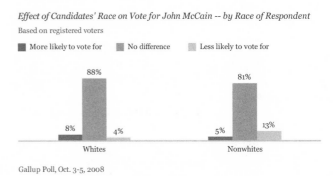

Effect of Candidates' Race on Vote for John McCain -- by Race of Respondent
Based on registered voters

Gallup Poll, Oct. 3-5, 2008

Implications

Much has been written about the impact of race in this year's election, a not surprising fact given that Obama is the first black major-party candidate in U.S. presidential history to gain his party's nomination.

The data analyzed here—based on voters' self-reports—show that the impact of Obama's and McCain's races appears to cut both ways. Enough voters, particularly nonwhites, say they are more likely to vote for Obama because of his race to offset the small percentage who say they are less likely to vote for him because of his race. And the same is true in reverse for McCain: the impact of nonwhites' saying his race is a negative is offset by those who say it is a positive. More specifically, to review perhaps the most important finding in these data, 7% of white voters say Obama's race makes them less likely to vote for him. But 6% of white voters say Obama's race makes them *more* likely to vote for him. And among nonwhite voters, Obama's race is a significant net plus.

It is important to note that these data are based on self-reports of survey respondents, and may not reflect the unconscious impact of race and/or the willingness of respondents to admit that the race of a candidate affects their voting behavior. But the racial data discussed here were collected in a grid of eight different dimensions, which may have had the impact of downplaying any particular significance to race as a concept that respondents focused on.

In the final reality, it may be impossible to tell exactly what impact the fact that Obama is black and McCain white may have on the outcome of the Nov. 4 election. These results suggest that the large majority of American voters at this point say neither man's race will be a factor in their vote decision. Certainly it's true that a small percentage of white voters say Obama's race will be a negative to them, and a small percentage of nonwhite voters say McCain's race will be a negative. These results are offset by the fact that each man's race is a plus to other voters. Perhaps more importantly, in the context of other candidate dimensions tested in the recent research, race is actually the least important factor tested.

Survey Methods

Results are based on telephone interviews with 926 registered voters, aged 18 and older, conducted Oct. 3-5, 2008. For results based on the total sample of national adults, one can say with 95% confidence that the maximum margin of sampling error is ±4 percentage points.

Interviews are conducted with respondents on land-line telephones (for respondents with a land-line telephone) and cellular phones (for respondents who are cell-phone only).

In addition to sampling error, question wording and practical difficulties in conducting surveys can introduce error or bias into the findings of public opinion polls.

October 10, 2008

MCCAIN'S VALUES/VIEWS A GROWING FACTOR FOR HIS VOTERS

Little change in Obama voters' reasons for their vote over past month

by Lydia Saad, Gallup Poll Senior Editor

More of John McCain's voters cite his "values" or "views" as one of the main reasons they are supporting him for president today than did so a month ago: 20%, up from 7% in early September. McCain's values and views now compete with his experience and qualifications (26%) as the top draw for his voters.

Key Trends in Reasons for Supporting John McCain

Based on McCain supporters

Numbers in percentages

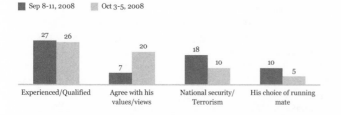

According to the new Gallup Poll, conducted Oct. 3-5, slightly fewer McCain voters today than a month ago mention either national security concerns or Alaska Gov. Sarah Palin's presence on the ticket as the main reason they are supporting McCain.

Gallup's initial measure of voters' reasons for choosing their candidate was conducted Sept. 8-11, shortly after the Republican National Convention, when McCain was slightly ahead in the race. Gallup Poll Daily tracking from Sept. 8-10 showed him leading Obama by 48% to 44%. The new Oct. 3-5 poll is contemporaneous with Gallup Poll Daily tracking showing Obama with an 8-point lead, 50% to 42%.

In the period between surveys, the nation became embroiled in a major economic crisis, and also had the chance to see the candidates face off in a presidential debate. Both of these factors could explain the shifts in what McCain voters say compels them to back him for president, particularly in terms of the increase in those citing his values and views. However, there has been no real change in the small number specifically mentioning the economy or McCain's economic views (now 4%, versus 6% in September).

Despite the significant increase in voter support for Obama since Sept. 8-11, Gallup finds little change in the voting mindset of his supporters. The dominant rationale they give for favoring Obama—mentioned by 40% of his supporters in Gallup's Oct. 3-5 survey—is that he represents change or a "fresh approach." Lower-ranked factors, mentioned by at least 10% of his voters, include his economic proposals (13%), his plans for handling the Iraq war (10%), and his views more generally (12%).

Key Trends in Reasons for Supporting Barack Obama

Based on Obama supporters

Numbers in percentages

As with McCain's voters, Obama's voters are no more likely to mention the economy today than they were in September.

Aside from the factors already mentioned, supporters of both major-party candidates mention a variety of other candidate positions and traits. Small percentages of Obama's voters (fewer than 10%) cite his intelligence (8%), support for the working/middle class (7%), honesty (5%), and position on healthcare reform (4%). Fewer than 10% of McCain's voters cite his honesty (8%), his military background (6%), and his conservative views (5%).

In early September, McCain's voters were 10 times more likely than Obama's voters to cite their candidate's running mate as the primary reason they were voting for their chosen candidate, 10% vs. 1%. Today, McCain's voters are only about twice as likely to do this, 5% vs. 2%.

Bottom Line

Obama's voters see him primarily as an agent of change. Relatively few of his supporters mention other specific issues associated with him, including the economy. This hasn't changed over the past month, despite the enormous changes in the economic landscape, which have largely benefited Obama's candidacy in Gallup's pre-election polling.

McCain's image has sharpened somewhat over the past month. In early September, five different factors emerged as important to at least 10% of his supporters: his experience, national security, his honesty and integrity, his being a Republican, and his choice of a running mate. Today, there are only three: his experience, his values and views, and national security.

There is little overlap in the top factors identified by each set of voters: In sharp contrast to the 40% of Obama's voters citing change, only 1% of McCain's voters mention this. Similarly, whereas 26% of McCain's voters mention McCain's experience and qualifications, only 3% of Obama's voters say the same about Obama.

Survey Methods

Results are based on telephone interviews with 1,011 national adults, aged 18 and older, conducted Oct. 3-5, 2008. For results based on the total sample of national adults, one can say with 95% confidence that the maximum margin of sampling error is ±3 percentage points.

Interviews are conducted with respondents on land-line telephones (for respondents with a land-line telephone) and cellular phones (for respondents who are cell-phone only).

In addition to sampling error, question wording and practical difficulties in conducting surveys can introduce error or bias into the findings of public opinion polls.

October 10, 2008
RECORD CRISIS OF CONFIDENCE ON MAIN STREET
Gallup's Daily documents increasing crisis despite bailout and global interest-rate reduction

by Dennis Jacobe, Gallup Poll Chief Economist

Despite passage of the Treasury bailout and a global reduction in interest rates, consumer pessimism hit a new record high early this week, with the percentage of Americans rating the economy as "poor" increasing by 21 percentage points from a month ago and the percentage saying the economy is "getting worse" increasing by 12 points.

Consumer Ratings of the Economy
Gallup Poll Daily tracking

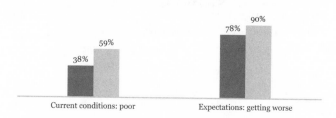

Percentage Rating Economy "Poor" Continues to Increase

Pointing to a variety of anecdotal evidence, many observers have noted that consumer spending seemed to hit a wall around mid-Sep-

tember. Gallup's daily measurement of consumer confidence tends to confirm these general perceptions. A month ago, around the time of the Fannie Mae/Freddie Mac bailout, 38% of consumers rated current economic conditions "poor." By the time of the Treasury's bailout proposal in mid-September, the percentage rating the economy poor had increased 15 points to 53%. Even with the congressional passage and president's signing of the Treasury proposal, consumer pessimism has continued to increase. Early this week, the percentage of Americans rating the economy "poor" hit a record new high of 59%—up 21 points from the same time a month ago.

Consumer Ratings of the Economy: Current Conditions
Selected trend, Sept. 6-8 through Oct. 6-8, 2008

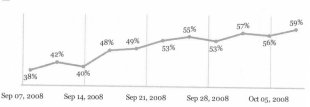

Gallup Poll Daily tracking

Percentage Saying Economy Is "Getting Worse" Continues to Increase

A month ago, 78% of Americans said current economic conditions were "getting worse," rather than better. By the time of the Treasury's proposal, 87% of Americans felt this way. Even with the president's signing of the Treasury's requested new emergency legislation, a record 90% of Americans now say the economy is "getting worse."

Consumer Ratings of the Economy: Expectations
Selected trend, Sept. 6-8 through Oct. 6-8, 2008

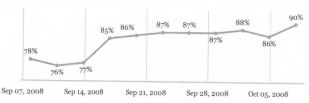

Gallup Poll Daily tracking

Commentary

The way the stock market has plunged this week, it appears investors share the growing consumer pessimism reflected in Gallup's daily polls.

The problem seems to be that the freeze-up of the credit markets and the debate over the Treasury bailout may have taken the crisis of confidence in the banking sector and on Wall Street to Main Street. And, as the Dow Jones Industrial Average plummets, Americans see their financial assets disappearing, on top of the losses they have already taken on the value of their homes.

It appears that passage of the Treasury's bailout proposal may have had at least a temporary positive effect on how much consumers are currently worrying about money. However, even the combined efforts of the Treasury, the Federal Reserve Board of Governors, and the Congress have, at least to this point, not been enough to shore up consumer confidence in the U.S. economy. In turn, plunging stocks and ever-increasing pessimism may mean that any reduction in money worries associated with adoption of this new legislation is short-lived at best. Consumer psychology is much more fragile than many people tend to realize. Behavioral economics suggests that this is particularly the case when long-held assumptions about the safety of consumers' investments—their overall perceptions of risk—turn out to be wrong.

Gallup's polling suggests that consumer confidence is reaching historic lows. In turn, this suggests that consumers may pull back from spending, to a degree not seen in many decades. And unemployment is likely to increase sharply.

Given the current financial crisis and associated recession, it is likely to take some dramatic efforts to turn consumer confidence around. In a sense, the country may be lucky that the presidential election is only weeks away. No matter who is elected, the new president and Congress are likely to have an important opportunity to reinvigorate consumer confidence.

Survey Methods

Gallup is interviewing no fewer than 1,000 U.S. adults nationwide each day during 2008. The economic questions analyzed in this report are asked of a random half-sample of respondents each day. The results reported here are based on combined data from approximately 1,500 interviews for each three-day period of polling, conducted from Sept. 6-8 to Oct. 6-8, 2008. For results based on these samples, the maximum margin of sampling error is ±3 percentage points.

Interviews are conducted with respondents on land-line telephones (for respondents with a land-line telephone) and cellular phones (for respondents who are cell-phone only).

In addition to sampling error, question wording and practical difficulties in conducting surveys can introduce error or bias into the findings of public opinion polls.

October 10, 2008

THIRD-PARTY CANDIDATES RECEIVING ONLY MINIMAL SUPPORT

Nader is tops with 2% of the vote

by Frank Newport, Gallup Poll Editor in Chief

A recent Gallup Poll in which four third-party candidates were explicitly listed for voters along with the two major-party candidates found only minimal support for any candidate other than John McCain or Barack Obama.

Ralph Nader (independent candidate) received 2% of voter choices, Bob Barr (Libertarian Party) and Cynthia McKinney (Green Party) 1%, and Chuck Baldwin (Constitution Party) received less than 1%. The two major-party candidates, Obama and McCain, combined to receive 90% of registered voters' choices.

The percentage of voters choosing Nader has declined from 4% in a similar poll a month ago. Gallup's usual presidential ballot in which third-party candidates are not read, but in which respondents are given the choice of naming any candidate they

Next, I'm going to read a list of six candidates for president who may appear on the ballot in a significant number of states this November. Supposing that all of these candidates were on the ballot in your state, which one would you be most likely to vote for -- [ROTATED]?

Among registered voters

	Oct 3-5, 2008	Sep 8-11, 2008
	%	%
Barack Obama (Democrat)	48	47
John McCain (Republican)	42	44
Ralph Nader (Independent)	2	4
Bob Barr (Libertarian Party)	1	1
Cynthia McKinney (Green Party)	1	1
Chuck Baldwin (Constitution Party)	*	*
Other	2	1
Won't vote (vol.)	3	1
No opinion	1	1

* Less than 0.5%
(vol.) = Volunteered response

choose, finds about 1% who mention candidates other than McCain and Obama.

Gallup also monitors interest in third-party candidates by asking an open-ended question in which no candidate names are read for respondents. In an Aug. 7-10 poll, the results showed that only 1% volunteered the name of Nader and 1% Barr, with no other candidates getting enough supporters to round to 1%. Again, Obama and McCain received almost all mentions of candidates in this open-ended format.

Survey Methods

Results are based on telephone interviews with 926 registered voters, aged 18 and older, conducted Oct. 3-5, 2008. For results based on the total sample of voters, one can say with 95% confidence that the maximum margin of sampling error is ±4 percentage points.

Interviews are conducted with respondents on land-line telephones (for respondents with a land-line telephone) and cellular phones (for respondents who are cell-phone only).

In addition to sampling error, question wording and practical difficulties in conducting surveys can introduce error or bias into the findings of public opinion polls.

October 13, 2008

AMERICANS' FINANCIAL WORRIES BECOMING MORE WIDE-RANGING

Energy/Gas costs still the top problem, but to lesser degree overall

by Lymari Morales, Gallup Poll Staff Writer

A Gallup Poll update on Americans' personal financial problems shows that the public has shifted away from a hyperfocus on gas and energy prices and has started to voice increasing concerns about a wider range of money issues, including debt.

In July, Americans' worries about three day-to-day pocketbook issues—energy costs, an overall lack of money, and the high cost of living—easily trumped anything else they could think of when asked

What is the most important financial problem facing your family today? [OPEN-ENDED]

	Oct 3-5, 2008	Jul 10-13, 2008
Energy costs/Oil and gas prices	12	29
Lack of money/Low wages	11	14
High cost of living/Inflation	10	18
Healthcare costs	9	9
Too much debt/Not enough money to pay debts	9	3
Retirement savings	7	4
Cost of owning/renting a home	7	9
College expenses	6	5
Unemployment/Loss of job	4	4
Taxes	3	2
Stock market/Investments	3	2
State of the economy	2	2
Lack of savings	1	2
Transportation/Commuting costs	1	1
Controlling spending	1	--
Social Security	*	1
Interest rates	--	1

* Less than 0.5%
Percentages add to more than 100% due to multiple responses.

to name the most important financial problem facing their families. But a Gallup Poll conducted Oct. 3-5 reflects a more broad-ranging picture today.

The percentage of Americans who single out energy costs in this open-ended question has decreased considerably, from 29% to 12%, coincident with a drop in gas prices. Now, it is one of several issues mentioned by about 1 in 10 Americans as their most pressing financial concern, along with lack of money, inflation, healthcare costs, and too much debt. There has been a modest increase since July in the percentage of Americans citing retirement savings, from 4% to 7%. However, the October poll was conducted before this past week's series of stock market losses, so it is possible that concerns about retirement have since increased.

Despite considerable demographic differences between Americans who support Barack Obama and those who support John McCain, there is not a great deal of difference in the financial concerns voiced by these two groups.

What is the most important financial problem facing your family today? [OPEN-ENDED]
By candidate support

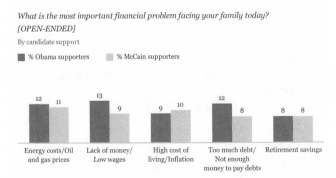

Gallup Poll, Oct. 3-5, 2008

Americans' financial concerns do, however, vary across income groups. Those with lower incomes are most likely to be worried about not having enough money, while those with higher incomes are most likely to mention retirement.

What is the most important financial problem facing your family today? [OPEN-ENDED]
By annual household income

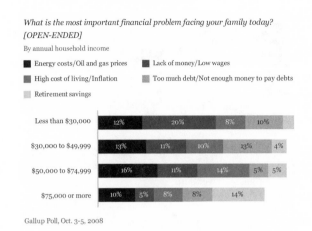

Gallup Poll, Oct. 3-5, 2008

With Gallup Polls indicating record levels of concern on the part of Americans about the U.S. economy and increasing signs of worry about personal financial situations, these data reveal that these signs of real economic anxiety are not driven by any paramount financial issue in Americans' eyes, but rather by a whole host of concerns. This in many ways echoes the financial crisis itself, which each day seems to touch more industries, companies, countries, and individuals.

Survey Methods

Results are based on telephone interviews with 1,011 national adults, aged 18 and older, conducted Oct. 3-5, 2008. For results based on the total sample of national adults, one can say with 95% confidence that the maximum margin of sampling error is ±3 percentage points.

Interviews are conducted with respondents on land-line telephones (for respondents with a land-line telephone) and cellular phones (for respondents who are cell-phone only).

In addition to sampling error, question wording and practical difficulties in conducting surveys can introduce error or bias into the findings of public opinion polls.

October 13, 2008
DEMOCRATS' ELECTION ENTHUSIASM FAR OUTWEIGHS REPUBLICANS'
Different pattern than occurred in 2004

by Frank Newport, Gallup Poll Editor in Chief

Only 51% of Republicans say they are more enthusiastic about voting than in previous years, compared to 71% of Democrats, marking a shift from October 2004, when enthusiasm was about the same for both partisan groups.

This disproportionate enthusiasm, measured in a *USA Today*/Gallup poll conducted over the weekend, is not a new phenomenon this year. Democrats have reported a higher "more enthusiastic" reading each of the seven times Gallup has asked the

Compared to previous elections, are you more enthusiastic than usual about voting, or less enthusiastic?

% More enthusiastic

■ Republicans ▨ Democrats

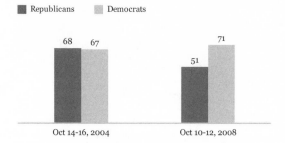

question in 2008. The smallest gap was a 7-point Democratic advantage in the Sept. 5-7 *USA Today*/Gallup poll, conducted just after the Republican National Convention.

Compared to previous elections, are you more enthusiastic than usual about voting, or less enthusiastic?

% More enthusiastic

■ Republicans ▨ Democrats

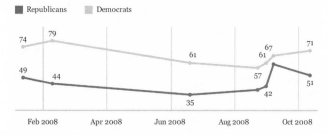

The largest partisan discrepancy came in February, in the middle of the heated Democratic primaries, when 79% of Democrats said they were more enthusiastic about voting this year, compared to just 44% of Republicans.

Compared to previous elections, are you more enthusiastic than usual about voting, or less enthusiastic?

% More enthusiastic

■ Republicans ▨ Democrats

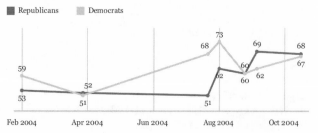

Enthusiasm was much more equal between Republicans and Democrats prior to the 2004 election. In Gallup's Oct. 14-16 poll that year, 68% of Republicans and 67% of Democrats said they were more enthusiastic about voting, and in a Sept. 3-5, 2004, poll, conducted shortly after the conclusion of the Republican convention, Republicans held a 7-point advantage over Democrats.

As a result of the relatively low enthusiasm levels evinced by Republicans this year, the overall percentage of voters who say they are more enthusiastic about voting is slightly lower than it was in 2004 at about this time.

Obama Voters vs. McCain Voters

As would be expected given the significant partisan enthusiasm gap, there is a major difference in enthusiasm between Obama voters and McCain voters.

Compared to previous elections, are you more enthusiastic than usual about voting, or less enthusiastic?

USA Today/Gallup poll, Oct. 10-12, 2008

■ % More enthusiastic ▨ % Less enthusiastic

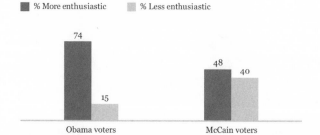

Seventy-four percent of Obama voters say they are more enthusiastic about voting compared to previous elections, with just 15% saying they are less enthusiastic. That yields an extraordinarily high +59-point "more enthusiastic" margin for Obama voters. Among McCain voters, it's a substantially different picture: The net "more enthusiastic" margin is just 8 points, with 48% saying they are more enthusiastic and 40% less enthusiastic about voting this year.

Survey Methods

Results are based on telephone interviews with 1,269 national adults, aged 18 and older, conducted Oct. 10-12, 2008. For results based on the total sample of national adults, one can say with 95% confidence that the maximum margin of sampling error is ±3 percentage points. For results based on the sample of 1,201 registered voters, the maximum margin of sampling error is ±3 percentage points.

For results based on the sample of 626 Democrats and Democratic leaners, the maximum margin of sampling error is ±4 percentage points. For results based on the sample of 558 Republicans and Republican leaners, the maximum margin of sampling error is ±4 percentage points.

Interviews are conducted with respondents on land-line telephones (for respondents with a land-line telephone) and cellular phones (for respondents who are cell-phone only).

In addition to sampling error, question wording and practical difficulties in conducting surveys can introduce error or bias into the findings of public opinion polls.

October 14, 2008
OBAMA WINS ON THE ECONOMY, MCCAIN ON TERRORISM
Independents give Obama his solid advantage over McCain on the economy

by Lydia Saad, Gallup Poll Senior Editor

Barack Obama enjoys a solid advantage over John McCain—53% to 39%—in U.S. public perceptions of which of the two candidates would better handle the economy as president.

Would Barack Obama or John McCain Better Handle the Economy?

Based on national adults

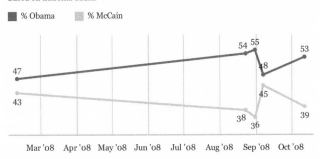

Regardless of which presidential candidate you support, please tell me if you think Barack Obama or John McCain would better handle each of the following issues. How about -- [RANDOM ORDER]?

Based on national adults

	Obama	McCain	Advantage
	%	%	
Healthcare policy	61	32	O, +29
The economy	53	39	O, +14
Energy, including gas prices	52	40	O, +12
Taxes	52	40	O, +12
The situation in Iraq	46	50	M, +4
Gun policy	38	50	M, +12
Terrorism	39	55	M, +16

USA Today/Gallup poll, Oct. 10-12, 2008

Obama's current 14-point lead on the economy is better than the 3-point edge he held right after the Republican National Convention in early September (48% to 45%), but is not quite as great as his 19-point margin after the Democratic convention in late August. At that time, 55% preferred him on the issue, compared to 36% choosing McCain.

According to the new *USA Today*/Gallup poll, conducted Oct. 10-12, most Republicans and Democrats consider their own party's candidate to be more capable of handling the economy than his opponent. The main problem, electorally, for McCain is that a majority of political independents favor Obama on the issue, while only 32% name McCain.

Candidate Preference for Handling the Economy, by Party ID

Based on national adults

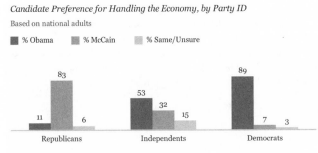

USA Today/Gallup poll, Oct. 10-12, 2008

Wednesday night's presidential debate at Hofstra University on Long Island, N.Y., gives McCain a major opportunity to reverse this deficit, as, by prior agreement between the campaigns, the questions to be asked by moderator Bob Schieffer will deal primarily with the economy and domestic policy issues.

The weekend poll shows, additionally, that Obama is preferred over McCain by 12-point margins on the issues of taxes and energy. Obama's lead on these issues is particularly notable because McCain and his running mate, Sarah Palin, have strived to capture the political upper hand on both issues. The Democratic nominee has an even bigger advantage on healthcare, on which 61% of Americans say Obama would do the better job, and just 32% name McCain.

On the other hand, McCain is not entirely without his own perceptual strengths on the issues, but they are ones unlikely to surface as major issues in the upcoming debate. McCain has a strong advantage over Obama—55% to 39%—on the issue of terrorism, and also leads by 50% to 38% on gun policy. He has a slight advantage on the situation in Iraq, although his 4-point edge, 50% to 46%, is not statistically significant. (Earlier this year, McCain led Obama by larger margins on the Iraq issue.)

Bottom Line

Americans recognize important strengths in both of the major-party nominees for president, but the potential impact of these on the election could partly be a matter of timing.

Seven years ago, nothing was more important to Americans than terrorism. Just a year ago, the U.S. war in Iraq was a paramount public concern. McCain might have been better positioned to run for president at either of these times than he is today, given Americans' relative confidence in him on those issues. Instead, with the ailing economy swamping all other national concerns, and Obama beating McCain by double digits in public preferences on the issue, McCain is running uphill against steady headwinds in trying to convince a majority of voters—and particularly independents—that he's the right man for the times.

Survey Methods

Results are based on telephone interviews with 1,269 national adults, aged 18 and older, conducted Oct. 10-12, 2008. For results based on the total sample of national adults, one can say with 95% confidence that the maximum margin of sampling error is ±3 percentage points.

Interviews are conducted with respondents on land-line telephones (for respondents with a land-line telephone) and cellular phones (for respondents who are cell-phone only).

In addition to sampling error, question wording and practical difficulties in conducting surveys can introduce error or bias into the findings of public opinion polls.

October 14, 2008
SEVEN IN 10 SAY OBAMA UNDERSTANDS AMERICANS' PROBLEMS
Public also more likely to think Obama has plan to solve problems

by Jeffrey M. Jones, Gallup Poll Managing Editor

Americans are much more likely to believe that Barack Obama understands the problems Americans face in their daily lives than to believe John McCain does.

Applies to McCain/Obama: Understands the Problems Americans Face in Their Daily Lives

■ Yes, applies　■ No, does not

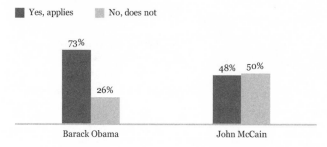

USA Today/Gallup poll, Oct. 10-12, 2008

These results, based on an Oct. 10-12 *USA Today*/Gallup poll, suggest Obama has a significant perceptual advantage in a presidential election campaign in which Americans overwhelmingly name the economy as the most important problem facing the country.

Throughout the campaign, Obama has been viewed as a candidate who understands the public's problems, but the 73% who say this about him in the current poll is the high for the year. Meanwhile, Americans are somewhat less convinced today than they were in March that McCain understands Americans' problems.

Applies to McCain/Obama: Understands the Problems Americans Face in Their Daily Lives

■ Obama　■ McCain

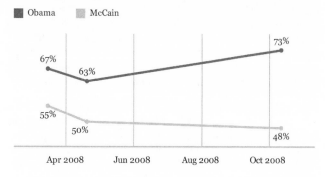

The public not only gives Obama credit for understanding its problems, but also for having a plan to solve them. While neither candidate scores particularly well when the public is asked whether the candidates have "a clear plan for solving the country's problems," Americans are much more likely to say Obama does (51%) than to say this about McCain (35%).

Americans have become increasingly likely to think Obama has a plan to solve the country's problems since this was last measured in the spring.

Much of this increase is because of changes in the views of Democrats, who were divided into Hillary Clinton and Obama camps in the spring, but now are mostly united behind Obama. In March, just 59% of Democrats thought Obama had a clear plan for solving the nation's problems, while 82% do now.

McCain is more competitive with Obama on the other three character dimensions tested in the poll.

McCain and Obama are viewed similarly in terms of their leadership and ability to manage the government. Sixty-three percent say McCain is a strong and decisive leader, while 61% say this about Obama. The two are now essentially tied on this measure, which had been an advantage for McCain earlier this year.

Applies to McCain/Obama: Has a Clear Plan for Solving the Country's Problems

■ Obama　■ McCain

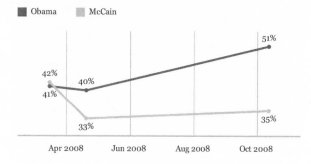

Applies to McCain/Obama: Is a Strong and Decisive Leader

■ Obama　■ McCain

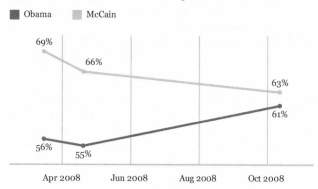

Exactly 55% of Americans say each candidate can manage the government effectively, which is an improvement for Obama since the spring (when 48% said he could). Views of McCain's management ability have not changed since April, when the question was last asked, but are down slightly from a 60% reading in March.

At least half of Americans say each candidate shares their values, although more say this about Obama (58%) than McCain (50%). Both candidates now score slightly more highly on this dimension than they did in the spring.

Applies to McCain/Obama: Shares Your Values

■ Obama　■ McCain

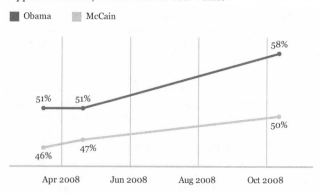

Implications

In an election in which the economy is the top issue on voters' minds, Obama is already seen as the candidate who can better handle the issue. During the campaign, Obama has been able to convince a growing number of Americans that he understands Americans' problems and has a clear plan for solving them, and now many more believe that he exhibits these qualities than does McCain—a major plus for Obama's electoral prospects given voter anxiety about the economy. Also, Obama has been able to largely erase the advantage McCain had over him on perceptions of their leadership ability. That doesn't leave much important territory where Americans believe that McCain is superior to Obama on character or issues, aside from McCain's continued advantage for handling matters of international policy. Thus, in order for McCain to prevail, in the remaining weeks he will either have to convince voters that he is as good as or better than Obama on the economy, or try to shift the agenda so that international matters carry greater weight in voters' minds.

Survey Methods

Results are based on telephone interviews with 1,269 national adults, aged 18 and older, conducted Oct. 10-12, 2008. For results based on the total sample of national adults, one can say with 95% confidence that the maximum margin of sampling error is ±3 percentage points.

Interviews are conducted with respondents on land-line telephones (for respondents with a land-line telephone) and cellular phones (for respondents who are cell-phone only).

In addition to sampling error, question wording and practical difficulties in conducting surveys can introduce error or bias into the findings of public opinion polls.

October 15, 2008
AMERICANS' SATISFACTION AT NEW ALL-TIME LOW OF 7%
President George W. Bush's disapproval rating of 71% sets Gallup record again

by Elizabeth Mendes, Gallup Poll Staff Writer

A mere 7% of Americans say they are satisfied with the way things are going in the United States, the lowest satisfaction reading in Gallup history. This finding, from a weekend *USA Today*/Gallup poll conducted Oct. 10-12 after a week of devastating losses on Wall Street, is down 2 points from the previous record low of 9% recorded just over a week ago. Prior to this month, Gallup's lowest satisfaction reading had been 12%, measured in 1979.

In general, are you satisfied or dissatisfied with the way things are going in the United States at this time?

At the same time that a record-low number of Americans say they are satisfied with the state of the country, a record-high number, 71%, say they disapprove of the job President George W. Bush is doing. This is an increase over the then-record 70% disapproval rating Bush received in an Oct. 3-5 poll.

George W. Bush's Presidential Job Approval, 2008

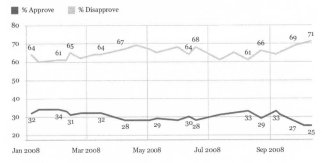

George W. Bush's Job Approval Ratings Trend (2001-Present)

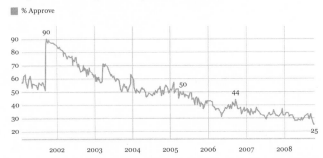

At 25%, President Bush's approval rating ties the lowest of his administration, and is just 3 points above the all-time low of 22% for Harry Truman, recorded in 1952.

Lowest Presidential Job Approval Ratings

President	Dates of Gallup Poll	% Approve	% Disapprove	% No opinion
George W. Bush	Oct 3-5, 2008	25	70	6
George W. Bush	Oct 10-12, 2008	25	71	4
Richard Nixon	Jul 12-15, 1974	24	63	13
Richard Nixon	Aug 2-5, 1974	24	66	10
Harry Truman	Feb 9-14, 1952	22	64	14

Survey Methods

Results are based on telephone interviews with 1,269 national adults, aged 18 and older, conducted Oct. 10-12, 2008. For results based on the total sample of national adults, one can say with 95% confidence that the maximum margin of sampling error is ±3 percentage points.

Interviews are conducted with respondents on land-line telephones (for respondents with a land-line telephone) and cellular phones (for respondents who are cell-phone only).

In addition to sampling error, question wording and practical difficulties in conducting surveys can introduce error or bias into the findings of public opinion polls.

October 15, 2008

TWO-THIRDS OF AMERICANS FINANCIALLY HURT BY CRISIS

Seventy percent say their financial situations will be harmed in the long run

by Dennis Jacobe, Gallup Poll Chief Economist

Americans of all incomes and party affiliations report that the banking crisis of the past month has harmed their personal financial situations.

Now, I'd like you to think about the events of the last two weeks and any future problems that might result from them. How much do you think your own financial situation will be harmed in the long run -- a great deal, a moderate amount, not much, or not at all?

By party ID and annual household income

■ % Great deal/Moderate amount

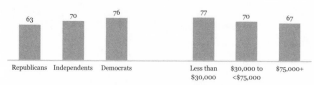

USA Today/Gallup poll, Oct. 10-12, 2008

Most Americans Say They Will Be Hurt in Long Run

Given the banking crisis, the credit freeze, the various taxpayer bailouts, and the historic decline in the equity markets last week, it is not surprising that so many Americans believe the economic events over the past month have harmed their personal financial situations. Nor is it unexpected that the percentage saying they have been harmed "a great deal" or "a moderate amount" has increased from 56% at the end of September to 66% two weeks later.

How much do you think your own financial situation has been harmed by the events of the last month -- a great deal, a moderate amount, not much, or not at all?

■ Great deal ■ Moderate amount ■ Not much ■ Not at all

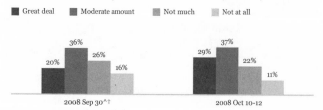

^ USA Today/Gallup poll asked on Gallup tracking survey
† WORDING: harmed by the events of the last two weeks

On the other hand, some might think that the impact of the financial crisis will be disproportionately high on upper-income Americans since the latter tend to have more investable assets and therefore potentially more losses. However, the sharp reduction in credit availability tends to have a disproportionately negative impact on middle-income Americans. And job losses will affect everyone.

Probably of even greater economic concern is the generally held perception that the financial damage done by the chaos of the past two weeks will do long-term harm. The percentage of Americans holding this view ranges from 63% to 77% across income groups and party affiliations.

Now, I'd like you to think about the events of the last two weeks and any future problems that might result from them. How much do you think your own financial situation will be harmed in the long run -- a great deal, a moderate amount, not much, not at all?

By party ID and annual household income

■ % Great deal/Moderate amount

USA Today/Gallup poll, Oct. 10-12, 2008

Commentary

There is no doubt that the current financial crisis and related credit freeze have done real damage not only in terms of Americans' assets and investments, but also to overall economic activity. For example, retail sales fell 1.2% in September—the biggest drop in three years—and those data don't reflect events of the past couple of weeks.

While the plunge in retail sales may be only the "tip of the iceberg" in terms of the immediate-term fallout from the financial crisis, of even greater concern is the potential longer-term impact. If all of the recent efforts to get the banking system working are successful and free up the credit markets in the near-term, some might hope that the long-term fallout from the recent financial chaos would be sharply negative, but brief—something like the post-9/11 economy. When asked in the poll to guess the effects of the recent problems on the overall health of the economy, 47% said they expect it will involve only a temporary downturn from which the economy will soon recover.

On the other hand, 49% of Americans believe that the recent financial crisis reflects something of a more permanent change in the economy and that it will not recover for a long time. This may be somewhat prescient on the part of many Americans because no matter what is done, it is unlikely that either Wall Street or Main Street will soon return to the easy credit and high-risk excesses of the past several years.

The Great Depression of the 1930s had a profound psychological effect on the way everyone from financial advisers, bankers, and business executives to average Americans viewed credit, savings, risk, and homeownership, among many other things. It appears that about half of all Americans already perceive that the current financial debacle—as the worst financial crisis since the Great Depression—may have a similarly profound impact on their financial perspectives for years to come.

Survey Methods

Results are based on telephone interviews with 1,269 national adults, aged 18 and older, conducted Oct. 10-12, 2008. For results based on the total sample of national adults, one can say with 95% confidence that the maximum margin of sampling error is ±3 percentage points.

Interviews are conducted with respondents on land-line telephones (for respondents with a land-line telephone) and cellular phones (for respondents who are cell-phone only).

In addition to sampling error, question wording and practical difficulties in conducting surveys can introduce error or bias into the findings of public opinion polls.

October 16, 2008

AMERICANS SEE SERIOUS CHALLENGES AHEAD FOR NEW PRESIDENT

Obama and McCain supporters agree economy should be top priority

by Lymari Morales, Gallup Poll Staff Writer

An overwhelming majority of Americans (84%) believe the next U.S. president will face challenges that are more serious than what other new presidents have faced, though Barack Obama supporters are slightly more likely to say this than are John McCain supporters.

Thinking now about the challenges facing the next president, do you think these will be -- [ROTATED: more serious, about the same, (or) less serious] -- than what other new presidents have faced?

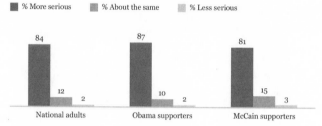

USA Today/Gallup poll, Oct. 10-12, 2008

When a follow-up question is asked of those who say the challenges will be "more serious," the combined results of the two questions show nearly half of Americans (44%) going so far as to see the next president's challenges as the most serious in half a century. While it's clear that all Americans, no matter their candidate preference, see significant challenges ahead for the new president, far more Obama supporters (52%) than McCain supporters (34%) choose the most serious option.

Do you think the challenges facing the next president will be more serious than any new president has faced in the last 50 years, much more serious than usual, but not the most serious of the last 50 years, or only somewhat more serious than what new presidents have faced?

Among national adults

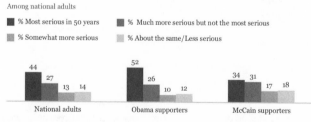

USA Today/Gallup poll, Oct. 10-12, 2008
NOTE: Question asked of those saying next president will face "more serious" challenges than other new presidents have faced; results here are combined with "about the same" and "less serious" responses from that question

While one might presume that different challenges come to mind for Obama supporters and McCain supporters, the *USA Today*/Gallup poll conducted Oct. 10-12 finds both camps in agreement as to what the new president's top priority should be when he takes office in January. Two out of three in each group think the new president should focus first on stabilizing the U.S. economy, outnumbering by roughly 6 to 1 those who would like the new president to prioritize managing the nation's ongoing wars or developing new sources of energy.

Which of these issues should be the top priority for the new president when he takes office next January -- [RANDOM ORDER: stabilizing the U.S. economy, managing the wars in Iraq and Afghanistan, reforming the healthcare system, developing new sources of energy for the United States], or something else?

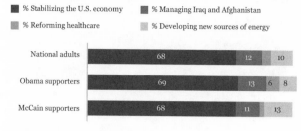

USA Today/Gallup poll, Oct. 10-12, 2008

Bottom Line

Most Americans, no matter whom they would like to see elected president, agree that their new leader will face more serious challenges than other new presidents have, and nearly half believe these will be the most serious a president has faced in the last 50 years. While Obama voters are more likely than McCain voters to see those challenges as the most serious in half a century, supporters of both candidates are united in their view that stabilizing the U.S. economy should be the new president's top priority. Together, these data suggest that even after a long and contentious presidential campaign, the importance of the work ahead has not been lost on Americans, and that the public is ready to send a clear mandate to the next president on what he should tackle first.

Survey Methods

Results are based on telephone interviews with 1,269 national adults, aged 18 and older, conducted Oct. 10-12, 2008. For results based on the total sample of national adults, one can say with 95% confidence that the maximum margin of sampling error is ±3 percentage points.

Interviews are conducted with respondents on land-line telephones (for respondents with a land-line telephone) and cellular phones (for respondents who are cell-phone only).

In addition to sampling error, question wording and practical difficulties in conducting surveys can introduce error or bias into the findings of public opinion polls.

October 17, 2008

DEMOCRATS LEAD IN CONGRESSIONAL RACES
Generic ballot shows Democrats with a 51% to 45% edge

by Jeffrey M. Jones, Gallup Poll Managing Editor

A mid-October *USA Today*/Gallup poll finds the Democrats leading the race to control the U.S. House of Representatives. Gallup's generic congressional ballot finds likely voters preferring the Democratic candidate in their district to the Republican by 51% to 45%, regardless of the likely voter model used.

These results represent an improved positioning for the Democratic Party compared to the previous reading on congressional voting intention, taken right after the Republican convention. At that time, Republicans led 50% to 45% among likely voters using

If the elections for Congress were being held today, which party's candidate would you vote for in your congressional district -- [ROTATE: the Democratic Party's candidate or the Republican Party's candidate]?

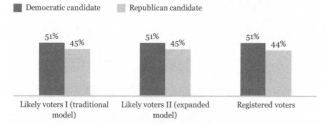

USA Today/Gallup poll, Oct. 10-12, 2008

Gallup's traditional likely voter model, which assesses likelihood to vote based on current voting intentions and past voting behavior. But that was a temporary boost for the Republicans, and inconsistent with earlier polls that showed Democrats leading.

Congressional Election Voting Preference, 2008 Election Campaign
Based on likely voters, using traditional Gallup likely voter model

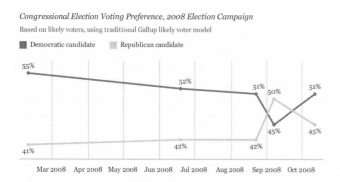

A second, "expanded" likely voter model, which assesses likelihood to vote based only on current voting intentions and would reflect increased turnout by groups that have not voted in past elections, also indicates a stronger showing for the Democrats compared with just after the GOP convention. Using this model, Democrats currently lead 51% to 45% in congressional voting, as opposed to a 48% to 47% Republican advantage in early September. Democrats led in an Aug. 21-23 poll conducted before both parties' conventions took place.

Congressional Election Voting Preference, 2008 Election Campaign
Based on likely voters, using expanded Gallup likely voter model

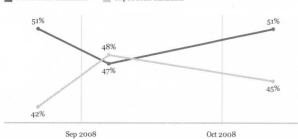

The generic congressional ballot has proven to be an accurate predictor of the overall vote for the House of Representatives historically, and is correlated with the number of seats a party can expect to win. These results indicate that if the election were held

today, the Democratic Party would probably retain control of the House. However, it is unclear whether the Democrats would be able to increase their majority much, since the current likely voter results are similar to Gallup's 2006 House vote estimate of 51% to 44% and the actual vote for the House that year, 53% to 45%.

Party loyalty is high in congressional voting, with 95% of Republicans saying they will vote for the Republican candidate in their district and 93% of Democrats intending to vote for the Democrat. Independents help swing the pendulum in the Democrats' direction, preferring the Democratic candidate to the Republican by 49% to 40%.

Congressional Election Voting Preference, by Party Affiliation
Based on likely voters, using traditional Gallup likely voter model

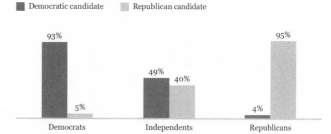

USA Today/Gallup poll, Oct. 10-12, 2008

In the post-GOP convention poll, independents were evenly divided in their vote, and Democrats were less likely than Republicans to exhibit party loyalty.

Congressional Election Voting Preference, by Party Affiliation
Based on likely voters, using traditional Gallup likely voter model

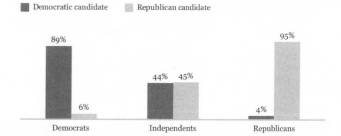

USA Today/Gallup poll, Sept. 5-7, 2008

Survey Methods

Results are based on telephone interviews with 1,201 registered voters, aged 18 and older, conducted Oct. 10-12, 2008. For results based on the total sample of registered voters, one can say with 95% confidence that the maximum margin of sampling error is ±3 percentage points.

For results based on the 825 survey respondents deemed most likely to vote according to the traditional Gallup likely voter model (based on past voting behavior and current voting intention), the maximum margin of sampling error is ±4 percentage points.

For results based on the 1,030 survey respondents deemed most likely to vote according to the expanded Gallup likely voter model (based on current voting intention only), the maximum margin of sampling error is ±3 percentage points.

Interviews are conducted with respondents on land-line telephones (for respondents with a land-line telephone) and cellular phones (for respondents who are cell-phone only).

In addition to sampling error, question wording and practical difficulties in conducting surveys can introduce error or bias into the findings of public opinion polls.

October 17, 2008
OBAMA VIEWED AS WINNER OF THIRD DEBATE
Completes "sweep" of three debates for Obama

by Jeffrey M. Jones, Gallup Poll Managing Editor

Round three of the presidential debates went to Barack Obama, according to a one-night *USA Today*/Gallup poll of debate watchers conducted Oct. 16, completing a sweep of the three debates for Obama.

Regardless of which candidate you happen to support, who do you think did the better job in last night's debate -- [ROTATED: John McCain (or) Barack Obama]?
Based on debate watchers

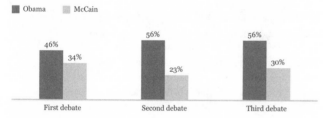

Based on USA Today/Gallup polls conducted the night after each debate

Debate watchers were more likely to say McCain did a better job than Obama in the third debate than in the second debate (30% to 23%), but McCain's best showing in the eyes of the viewing public was the first debate, when 34% said he did the better job. Still, Obama won each debate by a convincing margin.

Obama's debate wins generally keep tradition with what Gallup has found historically. Gallup polls seeking reaction to past presidential debates as early as 1960—conducted either immediately after each debate concluded or in the succeeding days—have most often shown that the Democratic candidate has been viewed as the winner over the Republican candidate. Gallup has found that, despite all the attention paid to the debates, they generally do little to transform the presidential race. For example, John Kerry was viewed as the winner of all three presidential debates in 2004 but still lost the election to George W. Bush.

Opinions of Candidates

In each of the three debate-reaction polls *USA Today* and Gallup conducted this year, roughly half of the viewers said their opinions of each candidate were not affected by the debate. But the debates apparently did more to enhance Obama's image than McCain's. After each of the three debates, more debate watchers said their opinion of Obama was more favorable than said it was less favorable.

In contrast, those whose opinion of McCain was influenced by the debates tended to come away with a less positive view of the Republican nominee.

How has your opinion of the candidates been affected by the debate? Is your opinion of Barack Obama more favorable, less favorable, or has it not changed much?
Based on debate watchers

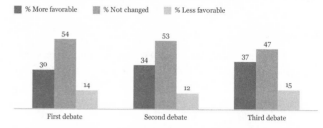

Based on USA Today/Gallup polls conducted the night after each debate

How has your opinion of the candidates been affected by the debate? Is your opinion of John McCain more favorable, less favorable, or has it not changed much?
Based on debate watchers

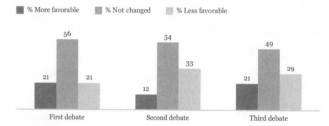

Based on USA Today/Gallup polls conducted the night after each debate

The Debate Audience

Roughly two-thirds of Americans reported tuning in to each of the three presidential debates, including 63% for the Sept. 26 debate largely focused on foreign policy, 66% for the Oct. 7 town-hall-style debate, and 65% for the most recent debate, which concentrated on domestic policy.

Seventy-three percent of self-identified Democrats, 68% of Republicans, and 55% of independents reported watching Wednesday night's debate.

Survey Methods

Results are based on telephone interviews with 1,015 national adults, aged 18 and older, conducted Oct. 16, 2008. For results based on the total sample of national adults, one can say with 95% confidence that the maximum margin of sampling error is ±3 percentage points.

For results based on the sample of 729 national adults who watched the Oct. 15 debate, the maximum margin of sampling error is ±4 percentage points.

Interviews are conducted with respondents on land-line telephones (for respondents with a land-line telephone) and cellular phones (for respondents who are cell-phone only).

In addition to sampling error, question wording and practical difficulties in conducting surveys can introduce error or bias into the findings of public opinion polls.

Polls conducted entirely in one day, such as this one, are subject to additional error or bias not found in polls conducted over several days.

October 20, 2008

A BLEAK FIRST LOOK AT CHRISTMAS SPENDING

Record-high number predict their spending will be lower than last year's

by Lydia Saad, Gallup Poll Senior Editor

A record-high 35% of Americans say they will spend less on Christmas gifts this year than what they spent in 2007. Only 9% plan to spend more.

Amount You Intend to Spend on Gifts This Year: More or Less Than You Spent Last Year?

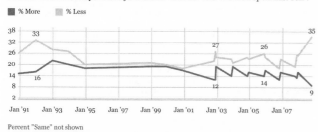

Percent "Same" not shown

This is based on a Gallup Poll conducted Oct. 3-5. That survey started on the day the U.S. House of Representatives passed, and President Bush signed into law, a $700 billion plan to rescue distressed financial institutions, and before much of the slide in the U.S. stock market seen this month, but at a time when general consumer confidence was similar to what it is today.

Gallup trends on this question since 1990 show that Americans are typically conservative in their spending plans, with more saying they will spend less money on Christmas gifts than the year before, rather than more money. (The majority tend to say they will spend the same amount, as do 54% this year.) However, this year's more-spending-to-less-spending ratio is by far the most inauspicious Gallup has seen for the nation's retailers.

Until now, the worst Christmas spending outlook in Gallup records was in late November/early December 1991 (the first Christmas season after the 1990-1991 recession), when 33% of Americans said they would spend less on gifts than the year before and only 16% said they would spend more.

More recently, a November 2002 Gallup Poll found 27% of Americans saying they would spend less on gifts, and only 12% saying they would spend more. That year, December consumer retail spending rose by a mere 1.4% over December of the previous year—one of the worst holiday retail seasons on record in the past 15 years. (According to the Census Bureau's "GAFO" measure of department store-type retail sales for December of each year since 1993, an annual increase of 5% in spending is about the norm.)

All of this suggests that the disappointingly weak holiday retail sales seen in 2007—with a mere 1.7% annual increase in retail spending for December 2007—could be even worse in 2008.

Spending Forecast

Another sign that consumers will temper their usual holiday spending comes from Americans' estimates of the total amount of money they will spend on Christmas gifts this year. According to the Oct. 3-5 poll, the average amount Americans think they will spend this year is now $801, roughly $100 lower than the average amount Americans estimated last October that they would spend in 2007.

The current figure is higher than the average $695 estimated in October 2002, but in inflation-adjusted dollars, the $695 in 2002 would be $845 today. Thus, today's spending projection of $801 is slightly lower than what Gallup found in 2002, itself a highly anemic holiday retail season.

Americans' estimate of the total amount they will spend on gifts often changes as the holiday season progresses. In each of the past two years, the average estimate Gallup recorded in mid-October fell by mid-November; in other years, consumers' average estimate of what they would spend increased closer to the holiday.

Average Anticipated Spending on Christmas Gifts

	October	Early/Mid-November	Late November/Early December
2008	$801		
2007	$909	$866	$833
2006	$907	$826	--
2005	--	$763	$840
2004	--	$730	$862
2003	--	$734	$776
2002	$695	$690	$753
2001	--	--	$794
2000	--	$817	--
1999	--	$857	--

Bottom Line

As of early October, a time of extraordinarily weak consumer confidence and economic uncertainty, Americans were already exhibiting much caution in their holiday spending plans. A mid-October Gallup survey found two-thirds of Americans saying their personal financial situations had been harmed by the banking crisis—a figure not likely to have been much better at the start of the month.

The degree to which the U.S. economy is perceived as either improving or falling further off the tracks in the next two months will be an important factor in how Americans perceive their own financial situations, and in how the holiday retail season ultimately plays out.

Gallup will update Americans' Christmas spending intentions in November, and again in early December.

Survey Methods

Results are based on telephone interviews with 1,011 national adults, aged 18 and older, conducted Oct. 3-5, 2008. For results based on the total sample of national adults, one can say with 95% confidence that the maximum margin of sampling error is ±3 percentage points.

Interviews are conducted with respondents on land-line telephones (for respondents with a land-line telephone) and cellular phones (for respondents who are cell-phone only).

In addition to sampling error, question wording and practical difficulties in conducting surveys can introduce error or bias into the findings of public opinion polls.

October 21, 2008
AS THE ECONOMY GOES, SO GOES THE VOTE
View of economy strong predictor of vote

by Frank Newport, Gallup Poll Editor in Chief

A new Gallup analysis of more than 40,000 interviews conducted over the last month and a half shows a strong correlation between trends in voters' candidate preferences in the election and consumer views of the U.S. economy. Barack Obama's margin of support over John McCain has risen proportionately when the percentage of Americans who are negative about the U.S. economy increases. Obama's front-runner margin has fallen when economic negativity decreases. As is seen in the accompanying graph, the relative rise or fall in the Obama-McCain margin generally tracks the ups and downs in Americans' views of the economy. In particular, as Americans became more negative about the economy coincident with the onset of the Wall Street crisis in mid-September, Obama gained against McCain. Then, beginning around Oct. 13, Americans became somewhat less negative about the economy, and McCain gained back some lost ground. By the end of that week, as the stock market lost much of what it had gained earlier in the week, economic negativity began to rise again, and McCain's relative support dropped. This relationship is ecological, in the sense that it is based on the relationship between two aggregate-level population-level measurements. But when data for October are put together into one large data set and examined cross-sectionally at the individual level, the relationship between the two variables becomes very clear. Americans who see the economy as negative are much more likely to say they would vote for Obama than are those who see it as either mixed or positive.

Views of the Economy, by Support for Presidential Candidates

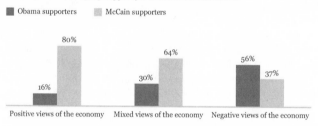

■ Obama supporters   ▨ McCain supporters

Positive views of the economy: 16% / 80%
Mixed views of the economy: 30% / 64%
Negative views of the economy: 56% / 37%

Gallup Poll Daily tracking, Oct. 1-18, 2008

In the Gallup Poll tracking survey, the vote-choice questions are asked first. It is only later in the survey that respondents are asked for their views about the economy. Thus, respondents are not "primed" to think about the economy when indicating their vote choice in the survey context. These data suggest that one of McCain's best hopes of improving his positioning against Obama in the remaining two weeks of the presidential campaign would be for a sharp drop to take place in the percentage of Americans holding negative views of the U.S. economy. Although McCain has been roundly castigated by his opponent for his September comment that the "fundamentals" of the U.S. economy are strong, these data would suggest that the statement was not necessarily an illogical effort on McCain's part, for it appears that if Americans come to believe things are not as bleak as they may seem, he gains.

Survey Methods

Presidential election results are based on telephone interviews with 43,217 registered voters, aged 18 and older, interviewed in September and October 2008. For results based on the total sample of registered voters, one can say with 95% confidence that the maximum margin of sampling error is ±2 percentage points. Economic outlook results are based on telephone interviews with 23,867 adults, aged 18 and older, interviewed in October 2008. For results based on the total sample of national adults, one can say with 95% confidence that the maximum margin of sampling error is ±2 percentage points.

Interviews are conducted with respondents on land-line telephones (for respondents with a land-line telephone) and cellular phones (for respondents who are cell-phone only).

In addition to sampling error, question wording and practical difficulties in conducting surveys can introduce error or bias into the findings of public opinion polls.

October 21, 2008
HISPANIC VOTERS DIVIDED BY RELIGION
Catholics and those who attend church less often are most supportive of Obama

by Frank Newport, Gallup Poll Editor in Chief

Taken as a group, Hispanic voters solidly support Barack Obama over John McCain for president, but there is a significant difference in the Hispanic vote by religion. Catholic Hispanics support Obama by a 39-point margin, while Hispanics who are Protestant or who identify with some other non-Catholic Christian faith support Obama by a much smaller 10-point margin.

Hispanic Support for Presidential Candidates, by Religion

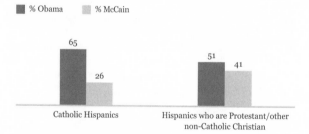

■ % Obama   ▨ % McCain

Catholic Hispanics: 65 / 26
Hispanics who are Protestant/other non-Catholic Christian: 51 / 41

Gallup Poll Daily tracking, Oct. 1-19, 2008

An examination of interviews with registered voters conducted between Oct. 1 and Oct. 19 shows Obama leading among all Hispanic registered voters by a 62% to 30% margin. (For purposes of this analysis, Hispanics are those who say "yes" when asked "Are you, yourself, of Hispanic origin or descent such as Mexican, Puerto Rican, Cuban, or some other Spanish background?")

Catholic Hispanics, who make up 50% of all Hispanic registered voters in this October sample, support Obama by a substantial 65% to 26% margin. But the one-third of Hispanics who identify their religion as Protestant or another non-Catholic Christian faith support Obama by only 51% to 41%.

There is also a significant difference in presidential candidate choice among Hispanics by religiosity. Hispanic voters who attend church weekly support Obama by a 51% to 40% margin, compared to a 57% to 33% margin among those who attend nearly every week or monthly, and an overwhelming 72% to 21% margin among those who seldom or never attend church.

Hispanic Support for Presidential Candidates, by Religiosity

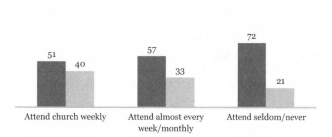

Gallup Poll Daily tracking, Oct. 1-19, 2008

These patterns of candidate support by religious identity and religious service attendance reflect the same patterns evident in the general population. Among all voters, Protestants and non-Catholic Christians are more likely than Catholics to support McCain over Obama, as are voters who attend church most frequently.

Bottom Line

Hispanic voters in the United States today represent a diverse group of individuals who share a common, although in some instances distant, Spanish heritage. Not only are there geographic differences and distinctions based on country of origin within the Hispanic electorate, but there are differences based on religion as well. Among Hispanic registered voters Gallup has interviewed in October, about half are Catholic, with a third being some other non-Catholic Christian religion (and the rest either having no religious identity or identifying with a non-Christian religion). This religious identity makes a difference. Catholic Hispanics are more supportive of Obama, while non-Catholic Christians are much more symmetrical in their support patterns, although still tilting toward Obama. Additionally, as is true in the general population, Hispanics who are most religious are most supportive of McCain, while Obama garners his greatest support among Hispanics who attend church services least often.

Survey Methods

Results are based on telephone interviews with 836 Hispanic registered voters, aged 18 and older, conducted Oct. 1-19, 2008. For results based on the total sample of national adults, one can say with 95% confidence that the maximum margin of sampling error is ±4 percentage points.

Interviews are conducted with respondents on land-line telephones (for respondents with a land-line telephone) and cellular phones (for respondents who are cell-phone only).

In addition to sampling error, question wording and practical difficulties in conducting surveys can introduce error or bias into the findings of public opinion polls.

October 22, 2008

EIGHT OUT OF 10 VOTERS AWARE OF POWELL ENDORSEMENT

But only 12% of this group say it makes them more likely to vote for Obama

by Frank Newport, Gallup Poll Editor in Chief

While 80% of registered voters are aware of former Secretary of State Colin Powell's endorsement of Barack Obama for president, only 12% of this attentive group say the endorsement makes them more likely to vote for Obama, while 4% say it makes them less likely to vote for the Democratic nominee.

Do You Know Who Colin Powell Endorsed for President?
Among registered voters

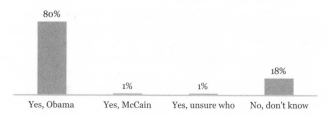

Gallup Poll, Oct. 21, 2008

Powell's announcement of his endorsement of Obama on Sunday's "Meet the Press" program received a considerable amount of press coverage. This may help account for the fact that 80% of registered voters interviewed Tuesday night were able to correctly identify not only that Powell had made an endorsement, but also that the recipient of that endorsement was Obama. (Eighteen percent of registered voters were unaware of the endorsement, and another 2% either misidentified or were unable to identify the person Powell endorsed.)

But only a relatively small 12% of those aware of the Powell endorsement indicated in the survey that Powell's gesture makes them more likely to vote for Obama. (This means only 10% of the entire registered-voter population is both aware of the endorsement and report that it makes them more likely to vote for Obama.) An even smaller group of 4% of those aware of the endorsement (or 3% of all voters) say it makes them less likely to vote for Obama.

How Will Colin Powell's Endorsement Affect Your Vote?
Among registered voters who knew that Powell endorsed Obama

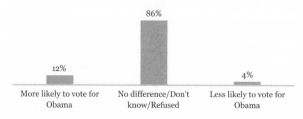

Gallup Poll, Oct. 21, 2008

It might be expected that Obama supporters would be more aware of Powell's endorsement of their candidate, but the results show no difference in awareness between current supporters of Obama and current supporters of John McCain.

Do You Know Who Colin Powell Endorsed for President?

Among registered voters

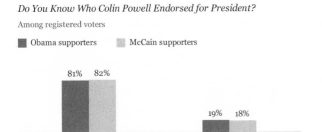

Gallup Poll, Oct. 21, 2008

The Obama campaign may have hoped that the endorsement would move McCain supporters into the Obama camp. However, its exact impact is difficult to pinpoint, because some voters who are currently for Obama, for example, may have been McCain supporters before the endorsement. Having said that, the Tuesday night data show that 20% of current Obama supporters (a group that could in theory include voters who are recent converts to Obama as well as longtime Obama voters) say the endorsement makes them more likely to vote for Obama. And only 9% of current McCain supporters (a group that could include defectors from Obama since the endorsement) say it makes them *less* likely to vote for Obama.

Impact of Powell's Endorsement of Obama

Registered voters who were aware of the endorsement

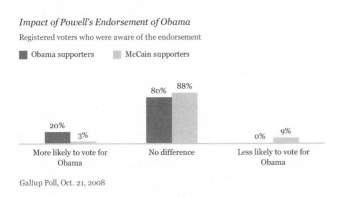

Gallup Poll, Oct. 21, 2008

Bottom Line

These data suggest that the high-profile Powell endorsement of Obama has had fairly minimal direct impact. A high percentage of voters are aware of the endorsement, but only 12% of those aware and 8% of the total population of registered voters say it makes them more likely to vote for Obama. The endorsement produced a small backlash against Obama, all from current McCain voters, many of whom were not going to vote for Obama anyway.

There has been little major change in the structure of the presidential race coincident with Sunday's endorsement: Obama was ahead before the endorsement and remains ahead in the latest Gallup Poll Daily tracking results. The significant majority of both candidates' current supporters say the endorsement did not affect their vote choice. So it's difficult to prove the endorsement has had a major impact on the status of the two candidates in the presidential race—which has, in recent weeks, of course, been moving in Obama's favor anyway.

Given that most of the "more likely to vote for Obama" sentiment comes from current Obama supporters themselves, one effect of Powell's gesture may have been to shore up support among the Democratic base—and thus to increase Democrats' motivation and potentially their turnout on Election Day. It is also possible that the

endorsement had a more subtle effect on voters' perceptions of Obama—one that has not yet translated into a change in vote choice, but could be a building block that would have this effect before the voter casts his or her ballot.

Survey Methods

Results are based on telephone interviews with 845 registered voters, aged 18 and older, conducted Oct. 21, 2008. For results based on the total sample of national adults, one can say with 95% confidence that the maximum margin of sampling error is ±4 percentage points.

Interviews are conducted with respondents on land-line telephones (for respondents with a land-line telephone) and cellular phones (for respondents who are cell-phone only).

Polls conducted entirely in one day, such as this one, are subject to additional error or bias not found in polls conducted over several days.

In addition to sampling error, question wording and practical difficulties in conducting surveys can introduce error or bias into the findings of public opinion polls.

October 22, 2008

YOUNG VOTERS FAVOR OBAMA, BUT HOW MANY WILL VOTE?

Still lag behind older voters on key turnout indicators

by Frank Newport, Gallup Poll Editor in Chief and Jeffrey M. Jones, Managing Editor

Although Barack Obama leads John McCain by almost 30 percentage points among 18- to 29-year-old registered voters, these younger voters are still less likely than older voters to report being registered to vote, paying attention to the election, or planning to vote this year.

Obama is clearly the favored candidate among young voters, while Obama and McCain are much more competitive among the older age groups.

Presidential Vote Preference, by Age

Based on registered voters

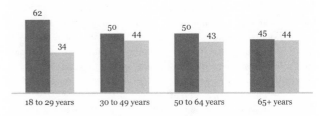

Gallup Poll Daily tracking, Oct. 1-20, 2008

Obama leads McCain by 62% to 34% among registered voters 18 to 29 years of age, based on Gallup Poll Daily tracking interviewing conducted Oct. 1-20. That's a much larger margin than in any other age group. Among those aged 30 to 49, Obama maintains a 6-point margin. His lead is similar among voters between the ages of 50 and 64 (7 points). The two candidates are essentially tied among senior citizens. (Over this same period, Obama is leading McCain among all registered voters by 9 points, 51% to 42%.)

This strength of support for a Democratic presidential nominee among the youth is not a new phenomenon. In Gallup's final poll before the 2004 election, the Democratic nominee John Kerry received 59% of the support of 18- to 29-year-old registered voters, while the Republican George W. Bush received 36% support. That compared to the overall sample of registered voters in which Kerry was leading Bush by 2 points, 48% to 46%. (Bush led Kerry among likely voters by 49% to 47%.)

Despite the skew among 18- to 29-year-old voters toward Obama, it's important to note that their vote is not monolithically for the Democratic nominee. A general increase in voting among younger voters will bring one McCain voter to the polls for every two Obama voters. Thus, a general increased turnout among the under-30 voting group will increase Obama's overall percentage of the vote, but most likely not as dramatically as would, for example, increased turnout among black voters, of whom 9 out of 10 prefer Obama.

There is evidence of an increase in new-voter registration and potentially higher participation among young voters given Obama's appeal. But to what extent can Gallup's large daily tracking samples provide insight into whether younger voters will in fact vote at high rates? Based on Oct. 14-20 tracking data, which include interviews with more than 6,500 registered voters, 18- to 29-year-olds still lag well behind older voters on key predictors of turnout.

At the most basic level, younger voters are significantly less likely than those who are older to report that they are registered to vote.

Self-Reported Voter Registration, by Age
Based on national adults

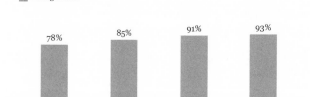

Gallup Poll Daily tracking, Oct. 14-20, 2008

This is not a surprising finding. Young people are more mobile, less likely to have a permanent residence, and in general less plugged in to the political system. This year, there has been discussion about efforts to register young people (on college campuses, for example), but these data suggest that those in the under-30 group have a way to go before they are registered at the same rates as those who are older, particularly those aged 50 and above.

The data also show that younger voters, despite the sense that they are deeply involved in the political process this year, are less likely than those who are older to say they have given quite a lot of thought to the election.

Perhaps most importantly, younger voters are much less likely to self-report that they are likely to vote. One of Gallup's series of likely voter questions asks respondents to place themselves on a 1 to 10 scale, where 10 means they will definitely vote and 1 means they definitely will not vote. The results show that those under 30 are signif-

Giving "Quite a Lot of Thought" to the 2008 Presidential Election, by Age
Based on national adults

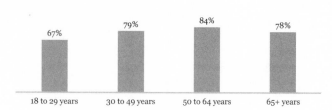

Gallup Poll Daily tracking, Oct. 14-20, 2008

icantly less likely to put themselves in the 9 or 10 position (definitely or almost definitely likely to vote) than is the case among their elders.

Rate Chances of Voting as "9" or "10" on 10-Point Scale, by Age
Based on national adults

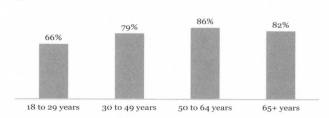

Gallup Poll Daily tracking, Oct. 14-20, 2008

Gallup has found similar patterns by age in past elections, and the current data suggest younger voters still have a way to go to match the levels of registration, interest, and intention to vote of older Americans. That is not to rule out the possibility that young voters' propensity to vote could increase in the final two weeks of the campaign, or that massive Democratic "get out the vote" efforts on Election Day could motivate many latent Obama supporters to officially register that preference in the voting booth.

Bottom Line

Gallup Poll daily tracking suggests that 18- to 29-year-olds are not nearly as likely as older voters to be registered to vote, to say they are thinking about the election, or to express strong intentions to vote. Thus, as of mid-October, there is not convincing evidence in the Gallup data that young voters will in fact vote at higher rates than in past elections. But even if things change over the next two weeks and many more young adults do become motivated to vote, turnout alone would do little to change the candidates' overall support, according to Gallup's likely voter models.

Gallup will continue to monitor the responses of 18- to 29-year-olds to the likely voter questions between now and Election Day to see whether the current situation changes.

Survey Methods

Results are based on telephone interviews with 7,063 national adults, aged 18 and older, which were conducted Oct. 14-20 as part of Gallup Poll Daily tracking. For results based on the total sample of national adults, one can say with 95% confidence that the maximum margin of sampling error is ±1 percentage point.

For results based on the sample of 604 adults aged 18 to 29, the maximum margin of sampling error is ±4 percentage points.

For results based on the sample of 6,508 registered voters, the maximum margin of sampling error is ±1 percentage point.

For results based on the sample of 484 registered voters aged 18 to 29, the maximum margin of sampling error is ±5 percentage points.

Interviews are conducted with respondents on land-line telephones (for respondents with a land-line telephone) and cellular phones (for respondents who are cell-phone only).

In addition to sampling error, question wording and practical difficulties in conducting surveys can introduce error or bias into the findings of public opinion polls.

October 23, 2008

OBAMA WINNING OVER THE JEWISH VOTE

Three-quarters of U.S. Jewish voters now plan to back Obama for president

by Lydia Saad, Gallup Poll Senior Editor

Jewish voters nationwide have grown increasingly comfortable with voting for Barack Obama for president since the Illinois senator secured the Democratic nomination in June. They now favor Obama over John McCain by more than 3 to 1, 74% to 22%.

*Presidential Preferences of Jewish Voters -- Monthly Averages^*
Based on Gallup Poll Daily tracking

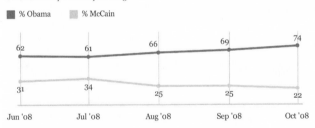

^ October data based on interviews conducted Oct. 1-21, 2008

This is based on monthly averages of Gallup Poll Daily tracking results, including interviews with more than 500 Jewish registered voters each month.

Support for Obama among all registered voters was fairly stable from June through September, but then rose sharply in October—in apparent reaction to the U.S. economic crisis. By contrast, support for Obama among Jewish voters has expanded more gradually, from the low 60% range in June and July to 66% in August, 69% in September, and 74% today.

The current proportion of U.S. Jews backing Obama is identical to the level of support the Democratic ticket of John Kerry and John Edwards received in the 2004 presidential election (74%). It is only slightly lower than what Al Gore and Joe Lieberman received in 2000 (80%)—when the first Jewish American appeared on the presidential ticket of a major party.

Recent support for Obama is a bit higher among older Jews than among Jews younger than 55. According to combined Gallup Poll Daily tracking data from Sept. 1 through Oct. 21, an average of 74% of Jews aged 55 and older supported Obama for president

*Percentage of Registered Voters Supporting Barack Obama for President -- Monthly Averages Since June^*
Based on Gallup Poll Daily tracking

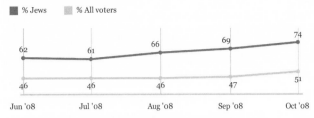

^ October data based on interviews conducted Oct. 1-21, 2008

across this period, compared with about two-thirds of younger Jews.

*Jewish Voters' Presidential Preferences, by Age^*
Based on Gallup Poll Daily tracking

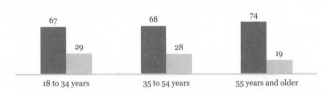

^ Data include interviews conducted from Sept. 1-Oct. 21, 2008

The slightly more pro-McCain orientation of the youngest category of Jewish voters (those 18 to 34) could be related to the fact that they are more apt than older Jewish voters to consider themselves political conservatives (29% vs. 16%). However, ideology does not appear to explain the gap between middle-aged and older Jewish voters. Whereas those 35 to 54 are more likely to support McCain, they are no more likely than older Jewish voters to describe their political views as conservative.

*Jewish Voters' Political Ideology, by Age^*
Based on Gallup Poll Daily tracking

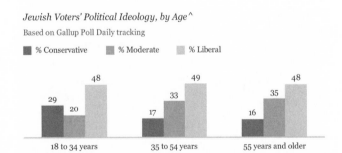

^ Data include interviews conducted from Sept. 1-Oct. 21, 2008

There is little difference among Jewish voters by age in their basic party identification. Between 55% and 57% of all three age groups are Democratic, 28% to 30% are independent, and only 13% to 17% are Republican.

Bottom Line

The Obama/Biden ticket is poised to perform about on par with other recent Democratic presidential tickets when it comes to support from American Jewish voters.

Survey Methods

The monthly averages of Gallup Poll Daily tracking reported here span from June 1, 2008, through Oct. 21, 2008. Monthly results based on all registered voters are generally based on more than 23,000 interviews conducted in each full month, and 19,400 interviews conducted in the partial month of October. For results based on samples of this size, the maximum margin of sampling error is ±1 percentage point.

The monthly results of Jewish registered voters are generally based on more than 650 interviews conducted in each full month, and 564 interviews conducted in the partial month of October.

Interviews are conducted with respondents on land-line telephones (for respondents with a land-line telephone) and cellular phones (for respondents who are cell-phone only).

In addition to sampling error, question wording and practical difficulties in conducting surveys can introduce error or bias into the findings of public opinion polls.

October 24, 2008
OBAMA, MCCAIN TWO OF THE BEST-LIKED CANDIDATES
Favorable ratings near 60% among best for recent presidential hopefuls

by Jeffrey M. Jones, Gallup Poll Managing Editor

Barack Obama (61%) and John McCain (57%) each received favorable ratings near 60% among likely voters in the most recent *USA Today*/Gallup poll. Both presidential candidates have been near that mark throughout 2008.

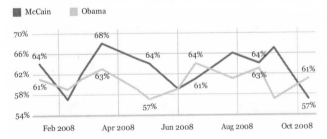

Favorable Ratings for Barack Obama and John McCain, 2008

Based on likely voters

Gallup has measured presidential candidate favorability in its current format for the last five election cycles, beginning with the 1992 election. Usually, by this late stage of the campaign, presidential candidates' ratings have settled in the 50% range. George W. Bush had the highest favorable rating at the end of the campaign for any president since 1992, at 58% just before the 2000 election.

Thus, if Obama and McCain can maintain their most recent favorable ratings, they would finish the 2008 campaign among the top three most positively rated presidential candidates in recent memory. Either could become the first with a rating of 60% or higher. Obama may be the better bet to achieve this, as his favorable rating

Favorable Ratings for Presidential Candidates in Gallup's Final Pre-Election Poll, 1992-2008

Based on likely voters

Candidate	Year	Favorable rating
George W. Bush	2000	58%
Bill Clinton	1996	56%
Al Gore	2000	55%
George W. Bush	2004	53%
Bill Clinton	1992	51%
Bob Dole	1996	51%
John Kerry	2004	51%
George H.W. Bush	1992	46%
Ross Perot	1992	46%

has been 60% or higher since he clinched the Democratic nomination in June, apart from a slight dip to 57% immediately after the Republican National Convention in early September.

Whether McCain and Obama can maintain their lofty scores between now and Nov. 4 is unclear. Historically, candidates' ratings have not varied much from their October average to the final poll before the election. Any variation that has occurred in the final weeks of the campaign has been inconsistent—some have shown a decline, and others, an increase.

For example, Bush's high 58% rating at the end of the 2000 campaign represented a drop from what he had been averaging in October 2000 (62%). Bob Dole's favorable rating also declined slightly in the final weeks of the 1996 campaign. But some candidates, such as Bill Clinton and Ross Perot in 1992 and Al Gore in 2000, finished the campaign with a higher favorable rating than they had been getting in October.

Change in Favorable Ratings for Presidential Candidates in Final Weeks of Campaign, 1992-2008

Based on likely voters

Candidate	Year	Avg. favorable rating, October	Final rating	Change
George W. Bush	2004	54%	53%	-1
John Kerry	2004	52%	51%	-1
George W. Bush	2000	62%	58%	-4
Al Gore	2000	53%	55%	+2
Bill Clinton	1996	59%	56%	-3
Bob Dole	1996	53%	51%	-2
Bill Clinton	1992	49%	51%	+2
George H.W. Bush	1992	46%	46%	0
Ross Perot	1992	44%	46%	+2

Favorable Ratings as Predictors of the Election Outcome

A positive sign for Obama's prospects of becoming the 44th U.S. president is that the candidate who has had the higher favorable rating among likely voters at the end of the election has been elected president each time since 1992.

Given the positive public evaluations that McCain and Obama have received throughout 2008, it could be argued that Americans will be comfortable with either as the next commander in chief. While only one can be president, the loser of this year's election is poised to supplant Al Gore as the best-liked presidential candidate not to get elected.

Results are based on telephone interviews with 825 likely voters, aged 18 and older, conducted Oct. 10-12, 2008. For results based on the total sample of likely voters, one can say with 95% confidence that the maximum margin of sampling error is ±4 percentage points.

Interviews are conducted with respondents on land-line telephones (for respondents with a land-line telephone) and cellular phones (for respondents who are cell-phone only).

In addition to sampling error, question wording and practical difficulties in conducting surveys can introduce error or bias into the findings of public opinion polls.

October 27, 2008

MCCAIN RETAINS SUPPORT OF HIGHLY RELIGIOUS WHITE VOTERS

White weekly church attenders support McCain over Obama by 37-point margin

by Frank Newport, Gallup Poll Editor in Chief

A Gallup update based on more than 21,000 interviews conducted as part of Gallup Poll Daily tracking in October shows that registered voters' religious intensity continues to be a powerful predictor of their presidential vote choice. John McCain wins overwhelmingly among non-Hispanic whites who attend church weekly, while Barack Obama dominates among whites who seldom or never attend church.

Support for Candidates, by Race/Ethnicity and Church Attendance

			% Barack Obama	% John McCain
Non-Hispanic white	Attend church	Weekly	28	65
		Nearly weekly/ Monthly	41	53
		Seldom/ Never	56	37
	Total		44	49
Non-Hispanic black	Attend church	Weekly	89	5
		Nearly weekly/ Monthly	93	1
		Seldom/ Never	91	3
	Total		91	3
White Hispanic	Attend church	Weekly	43	46
		Nearly weekly/ Monthly	49	43
		Seldom/ Never	64	31
	Total		53	39

Gallup Poll Daily tracking from October 2008

The relationship between church attendance and voting has been well-established in previous presidential elections, and the analysis of Gallup data collected Oct. 1-26 suggests that this year is no different.

The swing in vote choice between groups of non-Hispanic white voters differentiated by their religious intensity (operationalized in this review as self-reported church attendance) is dramatic, ranging from a 37-point McCain advantage among whites who attend church weekly (about 32% of all non-Hispanic white registered voters) to a 19-point Obama advantage among those who seldom or never attend worship services (about 47% of white voters). The middle group of non-Hispanic whites who attend church nearly every week or monthly (20%) support McCain by a 12-point margin.

McCain's selection of Sarah Palin as his running mate just before the Republican National Convention might have been expected to bolster his standing among highly religious whites, given her credentials as a staunch conservative on moral or values issues.

However, a comparison of Gallup's October data to data collected in August—for the most part before McCain's selection of Palin as his running mate—shows that McCain's strength among highly religious white voters has not changed substantially over that time period. In August, McCain was beating Obama among weekly church-attending white voters by a 64% to 25% margin, or 39 points, compared to a similar 37 points today. Importantly, McCain was doing better in August among whites than he has been in October, winning in August by a 51% to 39% margin, compared to a narrower margin of 49% to 44% in the Oct. 1-26 data. The fact that support for McCain did not slip among highly religious whites, while slipping overall among whites, could be in part attributable to Palin's presence on the GOP ticket, although the precise impact of her selection is not clear. (Among those who seldom or never attend church, McCain was losing by 11 points in August, and is losing by 19 points today.)

Support for Candidates, by Church Attendance
Among Non-Hispanic whites

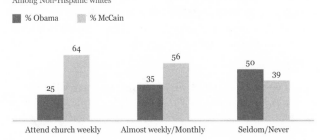

Gallup Poll Daily tracking from August 2008

Black voters overwhelmingly support Obama regardless of their relative level of religiosity. But highly religious blacks who attend church weekly (39% of non-Hispanic black voters) give Obama an 84-point margin, slightly lower than the 92- and 88-point margins for Obama among blacks who attend almost every week/monthly (33%) and those who seldom/never attend (26%), respectively.

Among Hispanics, the biggest difference in vote choice by religion is between those who attend monthly or more frequently, and those who seldom or never attend church. Hispanics who attend church weekly (36% of non-white Hispanic registered voters) favor McCain by a very narrow 3-point margin, and those who attend almost every week or monthly (23%) favor Obama by a similarly narrow 6-point margin. But among Hispanics who seldom or never attend church (40%), the margin for Obama swings to a highly significant 33 points.

Bottom Line

A positive correlation between religious intensity and voting for the Republican candidate for president has been a part of the American political landscape for a number of years.

Early in this election cycle, there was discussion that McCain was perhaps not the favorite candidate of highly religious whites, and indeed former Arkansas Gov. Mike Huckabee (a former Southern Baptist seminarian and preacher) did well among religious whites in some GOP primaries.

But McCain appears to have had little problem in gaining the vote of religious whites. The data reviewed here show that McCain was doing very well among highly religious whites in August, and continues to do so in October, despite the fact that his overall standing has slipped some among whites.

Survey Methods

Results are based on telephone interviews with 23,111 registered voters, aged 18 and older, conducted Oct. 1-26, 2008. For results based on the total sample of national adults, one can say with 95% confidence that the maximum margin of sampling error is ±2 percentage points.

Interviews are conducted with respondents on land-line telephones (for respondents with a land-line telephone) and cellular phones (for respondents who are cell-phone only).

In addition to sampling error, question wording and practical difficulties in conducting surveys can introduce error or bias into the findings of public opinion polls.

October 28, 2008
POLL: 7 IN 10 AMERICANS SAY OBAMA WILL WIN
Even McCain supporters slightly more likely to say Obama, rather than McCain, will win

by Frank Newport, Gallup Poll Editor in Chief

By a 71% to 23% margin, Americans expect that Barack Obama will be elected president in next Tuesday's election, including a 49% to 46% ratio of John McCain's own supporters who say Obama, rather than their own candidate, will win.

Regardless of whom you support, and trying to be as objective as possible, who do you think will win the presidential election in November?

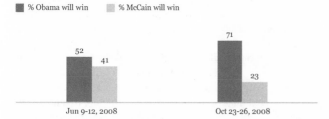

Jun 9-12, 2008   Oct 23-26, 2008

Belief that Obama will win has increased significantly from last June, when Americans viewed his victory as probable by a narrower 52% to 41% margin.

As is often the case for candidates who are down in the polls in the last weeks of a campaign, McCain has incorporated into his speech a statement to the effect that despite polls showing him losing to Obama, he will ultimately win.

The current Gallup Poll data, from Oct. 23-26, suggest that McCain's own supporters have not yet come to the point where they agree with their candidate that he will be able to pull off a victory in the election. By a 49% to 46% margin, McCain voters say Obama will win. On the other hand, perhaps not surprisingly, Obama voters overwhelmingly believe that their candidate will win, by a 94% to 2% margin.

Regardless of whom you support, and trying to be as objective as possible, who do you think will win the presidential election in November?

Gallup Poll, Oct. 23-26, 2008

The implications of this belief structure on the actual vote next Tuesday are unclear, as are the implications on the vote of those who have already voted via absentee ballot or early voting. Some may argue that Obama might be hurt if his supporters become complacent and end up not voting (something Obama himself has warned against on the campaign trail).

Others may argue that McCain supporters might "give up" and not vote if they feel their candidate does not have a chance of winning. But the weekend poll shows that Republicans (the vast majority of whom say they will vote for McCain) have actually gained significantly on enthusiasm about voting since Gallup's Oct. 10-12 poll, despite their pessimism about their candidate's chances of winning. In mid-October, 51% of Republicans were more enthusiastic about voting this year than in previous elections; now that number is 65%. (Republicans still lag behind Democrats on this enthusiasm measure, however; 76% of Democrats are more enthusiastic than usual about voting.)

Whatever the implications, the data certainly indicate that Obama is winning the expectations game at this point in the campaign, with the substantial majority of Americans holding the opinion that Sen. Obama will be their next president.

Survey Methods

Results are based on telephone interviews with 1,010 national adults, aged 18 and older, conducted Oct. 23-26, 2008. For results based on the total sample of national adults, one can say with 95% confidence that the maximum margin of sampling error is ±3 percentage points.

Interviews are conducted with respondents on land-line telephones (for respondents with a land-line telephone) and cellular phones (for respondents who are cell-phone only).

In addition to sampling error, question wording and practical difficulties in conducting surveys can introduce error or bias into the findings of public opinion polls.

October 28, 2008
VOTERS NOT EAGER FOR ONE-PARTY CONTROL OF GOVERNMENT
Divide as to which party should control Congress if Obama is elected

by Jeffrey M. Jones, Gallup Poll Managing Editor

Registered voters appear cautious about giving one party control of the federal government in this election. Most would prefer that the Democrats control Congress if John McCain is elected, but they divide evenly as to which party should control Congress if Barack Obama becomes the next president.

If [ROTATED: John McCain/Barack Obama] is elected president in November, which party would you prefer to have in control of Congress -- [ROTATED: the Republican Party, or the Democratic Party]?

Based on registered voters

Gallup Poll, Oct. 23-26, 2008

These results are based on an Oct. 23-26 Gallup Poll. They come as McCain has tried to remind voters that electing Obama as president to go along with a Democratically controlled Congress would give the Democratic Party control of the federal government.

That argument appears to resonate, as voters appear reluctant to want to give one party full control of the government regardless of who is elected president.

Relation of Vote Choice to Divided-Government Preference

It is unclear to what extent voters who prefer divided government would split their own votes for president and Congress in a deliberate attempt to promote divided party control of the two branches. In fact, this sort of ticket-splitting is fairly rare among voters, at least in terms of their votes for president and Congress. In the last two Gallup Polls that asked about both presidential and congressional vote choices, only 9% of voters indicated they would vote for a president of one party and member of Congress of the other.

Moreover, a preference for divided control may be only one of many factors influencing their congressional vote, including their opinions of their local incumbent member of Congress. Indeed, despite record-low approval ratings for Congress this year, most voters (59%) continue to say that their own member of Congress deserves to be re-elected. And with Democrats currently in control of Congress, high incumbent re-election rates would help Democrats maintain control.

Gallup measures congressional voting intentions directly using a generic ballot, which asks respondents whether they would vote for the Republican candidate or the Democratic candidate in their district. The generic ballot has proven to be an accurate predictor of the congressional vote. As of mid-October—and indeed through much of the campaign—the Democrats lead on the generic ballot.

Congressional Election Voting Preference, 2008 Election Campaign
Based on likely voters, using traditional Gallup likely voter model

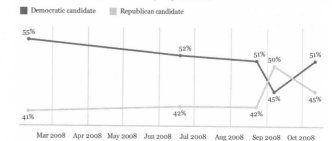

Perhaps the most likely outcome of the 2008 election may be unified Democratic control, given the Democratic lead in the generic ballot and Obama's lead in the polls for much of the fall, though the potential for change in the final week of the campaign still exists. Obama himself is being careful to warn his supporters not to take the outcome for granted.

While voters do not express a clear preference for one-party control, they seem to be more amenable to full Democratic control than full Republican control. In both 2004 and 2008, more voters said they'd like to see the Democrats control Congress if the Republican presidential candidate won than said they'd like to see the Republicans control Congress if the Democratic presidential candidate prevailed. In neither case was there majority support for one-party government. Of course, voters did elect George W. Bush and a Republican Congress in the 2004 election, so their actual voting choices on Election Day may not necessarily reflect nor replicate their preferences for one-party versus divided government.

The possibility of full Republican control in 2008 seems remote at this point, given the available polling data to date, and Republicans' best chance of sharing power with the Democrats may rest in McCain's pulling off a comeback win.

Survey Methods

Results are based on telephone interviews with 957 registered voters, aged 18 and older, conducted Oct. 23-26, 2008. For results based on the total sample of national adults, one can say with 95% confidence that the maximum margin of sampling error is ±3 percentage points.

Interviews are conducted with respondents on land-line telephones (for respondents with a land-line telephone) and cellular phones (for respondents who are cell-phone only).

In addition to sampling error, question wording and practical difficulties in conducting surveys can introduce error or bias into the findings of public opinion polls.

October 29, 2008
ECONOMY REIGNS SUPREME FOR VOTERS
More than half rate it "extremely important" to their vote for president

by Lydia Saad, Gallup Poll Senior Editor

As John McCain and Barack Obama figuratively round the bend into the final stretch of the 2008 presidential race, a new Gallup Poll identifies the economy as the runaway top election issue for Americans.

The 55% of Americans now naming the economy as "extremely important" to their vote for president outranks the situation in Iraq—which received the highest score in February—and energy, which had topped the list in June.

Trends in Importance of Key Election Issues
Percentage of national adults rating each "extremely important" to their vote for president

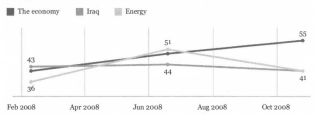

This finding is from an Oct. 23-26 Gallup Poll in which Americans were asked to rate the importance of 12 policy issues to their vote for president.

Six issues cluster in second place behind the economy, all considered extremely important by between 40% and 44% of Americans: the federal budget deficit (44%), terrorism (42%), energy/gas prices (41%), the situation in Iraq (41%), healthcare (41%), and taxes (40%). Education (39%), moral values (39%), and the situation in Afghanistan (37%) fall right below these six in the October ranking. The environment (26%) and illegal immigration (25%) are positioned to be the least influential issues of the 12 tested.

Now I am going to read a list of some of the issues that have been discussed in this year's presidential election campaign. As I read each one, please tell me how important the candidates' positions on that issue have been in influencing your vote for president -- extremely important, very important, somewhat important, or not important.

Based on national adults

	Extremely important	Very important	Somewhat/ Not important
	%	%	%
The economy	55	40	4
The federal budget deficit	44	38	18
Terrorism	42	38	20
Energy, including gas prices	41	44	15
The situation in Iraq	41	40	18
Healthcare	41	37	22
Taxes	40	41	19
Education	39	41	20
Moral values	39	34	25
The situation in Afghanistan	37	40	22
The environment	26	36	37
Illegal immigration	25	32	42

Gallup Poll, Oct. 23-26, 2008

In fact, not only is the economy perceived to be the most important issue in this election, the 55% who rate it as extremely important to their vote is the highest Gallup has found for any issue in the last four presidential election years (since 1996).

Republicans and Democrats have somewhat predictably different outlooks about which issues are most important to their vote. While the economy is the top-rated issue for both groups (as well as for political independents), it is rated extremely important by a higher proportion of Democrats than Republicans (63% vs. 52%). And whereas the economy is clearly the top-rated issue for Democrats, among Republicans the economy roughly ties with terrorism and moral values in perceived importance.

Top Five Election Issues, by Party Identification
Percentage rating each "extremely important" to their vote for president

	Republican national adults	Independent national adults	Democratic national adults
1.	Economy – 52%	Economy – 50%	Economy – 63%
2.	(2. tie) Terrorism – 51%	Federal budget deficit – 39%	Healthcare – 57%
3.	(2. tie) Moral values – 51%	(3. tie) Terrorism – 37%	Federal budget deficit – 54%
4.	Taxes – 47%	(3. tie) Iraq – 37%	Education – 53%
5.	Energy – 39%	(5. tie) Education – 34%	Energy – 49%
		(5. tie) Energy – 34%	

Oct. 23-26, 2008

Healthcare ranks second among Democrats, but doesn't appear in the top five issues of Republicans or independents. The corresponding issues for Republicans are moral values and taxes: these issues rank tied for second and fourth, respectively, for Republicans, but don't register in the top five for independents or Democrats.

Aside from the economy, energy is the only other election issue that ranks among the top five for all three political groups.

Bottom Line

In February, it appeared that the situation in Iraq would be on par with the economy in its importance to voters in choosing the next president. By June, the energy issue had emerged as at least as important as the economy, and had displaced Iraq at the top of the rankings. Today, the economy has no peer among the issues Americans say they will consider in the polling booth next Tuesday. It is the undisputed top concern of independents and Democrats and ties for first among Republicans.

Survey Methods

Results are based on telephone interviews with 1,010 national adults, aged 18 and older, conducted Oct. 23-26, 2008. For results based on the total sample of national adults, one can say with 95% confidence that the maximum margin of sampling error is ±3 percentage points.

Interviews are conducted with respondents on land-line telephones (for respondents with a land-line telephone) and cellular phones (for respondents who are cell-phone only).

In addition to sampling error, question wording and practical difficulties in conducting surveys can introduce error or bias into the findings of public opinion polls.

October 29, 2008
OBAMA BEATING MCCAIN ON VOTER OUTREACH
Majority of swing-state voters have heard from Obama's campaign

by Lydia Saad, Gallup Poll Senior Editor

More U.S. voters say the Obama campaign has contacted them at some point in the last few weeks than say the McCain campaign has done so, 38% vs. 30%.

In the last few weeks, have you, personally been contacted about your vote for president by the [Barack Obama/John McCain] campaign -- including by e-mail, phone, in person, mail, or in some other way?

■ Contacted by Obama campaign   ■ Contacted by McCain campaign

34% 28%   38% 30%

All Americans   Registered voters

Oct. 27-28, 2008

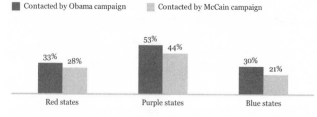
*Campaign Contact According to State Political Category^*

Based on registered voters

■ Contacted by Obama campaign   ■ Contacted by McCain campaign

33% 28%   53% 44%   30% 21%

Red states   Purple states   Blue states

Oct. 27-28, 2008

^Red states are those George W. Bush won in 2004 by 6 or more points; Blue states are those John Kerry won in 2004 by 6 or more points; Purple states are those where the victory margin for either candidate was less than 6 points. See the complete list at the end of the story.

Both presidential campaigns appear to be focusing their voter outreach efforts on those who already support their own candidate—suggesting that "get out the vote" activity is the primary game being played "on the ground" at this late stage of the campaign. Many more Obama voters say they have been contacted by the Obama campaign than by the McCain campaign: 46% and 30%, respectively. Likewise, more McCain voters have heard from the McCain campaign than from the Obama campaign: 39% vs. 24%.

However, even on this basis, Obama holds an advantage. Restated, nearly half of Obama voters (46%) say the Obama campaign has contacted them in recent weeks, compared with 39% of McCain voters whom the McCain campaign has contacted.

Fueled by a record-setting campaign war chest—he is on track to raise nearly three-quarters of a billion dollars, including $150 million in September alone—Obama has also made greater inroads into the undecided bloc. A third of this group nationwide say they have been contacted by Obama's campaign, compared with 21% who have been contacted by McCain's.

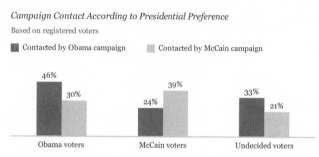
Campaign Contact According to Presidential Preference

Based on registered voters

■ Contacted by Obama campaign   ■ Contacted by McCain campaign

46% 30%   24% 39%   33% 21%

Obama voters   McCain voters   Undecided voters

Oct. 27-28, 2008

The intensity of the so-called campaign "ground war" in the battleground states such as Florida, Ohio, Pennsylvania, Colorado, and New Hampshire is clear from a regional breakdown of the voter contact question. More than half of voters living in "purple states" (53%)—those where the margin of victory for either George W. Bush or John Kerry in 2004 was less than 6 points—say they have been contacted by Obama's campaign. Somewhat fewer, but still close to half (44%), have been contacted by McCain's.

Both campaigns appear to be putting far less effort into reaching voters in the red and blue states, although whereas about equal proportions of voters in each of these regions say Obama's campaign has contacted them, more red-state than blue-state voters say McCain's campaign has contacted them.

Survey Methods

Results are based on telephone interviews with 2,014 national adults, aged 18 and older, conducted Oct. 27-28, 2008, as part of the Gallup Poll Daily tracking survey. For results based on the total sample of national adults, one can say with 95% confidence that the maximum margin of sampling error is ±2 percentage points. For results based on the subsample of 1,858 registered voters, one can say with 95% confidence that the maximum margin of sampling error is ±3 percentage points.

Interviews are conducted with respondents on land-line telephones (for respondents with a land-line telephone) and cellular phones (for respondents who are cell-phone only).

In addition to sampling error, question wording and practical difficulties in conducting surveys can introduce error or bias into the findings of public opinion polls.

Red states: Alabama, Alaska, Arizona, Arkansas, Georgia, Idaho, Indiana, Kansas, Kentucky, Louisiana, Mississippi, Missouri, Montana, Nebraska, North Carolina, North Dakota, Oklahoma, South Carolina, South Dakota, Tennessee, Texas, Utah, Virginia, West Virginia, Wyoming

Purple states: Colorado, Florida, Iowa, Michigan, Minnesota, Nevada, New Hampshire, New Mexico, Ohio, Oregon, Pennsylvania, Wisconsin

Blue states: California, Connecticut, Delaware, District of Columbia, Hawaii, Illinois, Maine, Maryland, Massachusetts, New Jersey, New York, Rhode Island, Vermont, Washington

October 30, 2008

AMERICANS SPLIT ON REDISTRIBUTING WEALTH BY TAXING THE RICH

Majority do say money and wealth should be more evenly distributed

by Frank Newport, Gallup Poll Editor in Chief

A majority of Americans (58%) say money and wealth should be more evenly distributed among a larger percentage of the people, although slightly less than half (46%) go so far as to say that the government should redistribute wealth by "heavy taxes on the rich."

Do you feel that the distribution of money and wealth in this country today is fair, or do you feel that the money and wealth in this country should be more evenly distributed among a larger percentage of the people?

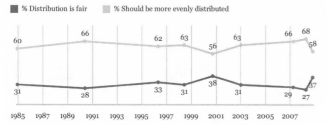

■ % Distribution is fair   ■ % Should be more evenly distributed

Gallup has been asking Americans periodically for over 20 years whether the distribution of money and wealth in this country is "fair," or whether they should be "more evenly distributed among a larger percentage of the people." (The question wording does not include a reference to exactly how they would be more evenly distributed and does not mention the government.) Across the nine times the question has been asked, a majority of Americans have agreed with the thought that money and wealth should be more evenly distributed. The current 58% who agree is one of the two lowest percentages Gallup has measured (along with a 56% reading in September 2000). Sixty-eight percent agreed in April of this year and 66% in April 2007.

The responses to this question are extraordinarily differentiated by partisan orientation, reflecting a fundamental fissure in Americans' views on this money/wealth distribution concept.

Do you feel that the distribution of money and wealth in this country today is fair, or do you feel that the money and wealth in this country should be more evenly distributed among a larger percentage of the people?

By party ID

■ % Distribution is fair   ■ % Should be more evenly distributed

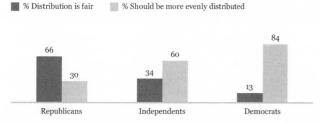

Gallup Poll, Oct. 23-26, 2008

Just 30% of Republicans say there should be a more even distribution of money and wealth, compared to 60% of independents and an overwhelming majority of 84% of Democrats.

The sentiment that money and wealth should be more evenly distributed does not address the issue of exactly how this objective would be achieved. One of the more contentious points on the presidential campaign trail in recent weeks has been John McCain's continuing assertion that Barack Obama's tax plan, which would involve higher taxes for high-income families, is "redistributionist," with some McCain supporters going so far as to argue that Obama's tax plans would be "socialist." These disputes focus on the longtime argument in economic and political philosophy over government's ideal role, if any, in attempting to redistribute money and wealth through the use of taxes.

Gallup has from time to time asked a question that addresses this issue in part—a question that Roper first asked in a *Fortune Magazine* survey conducted in March 1939, near the end of the Depres-

sion. The question is phrased as follows: "People feel differently about how far a government should go. Here is a phrase which some people believe in and some don't. Do you think our government should or should not redistribute wealth by heavy taxes on the rich?"

Do you think our government should or should not redistribute wealth by heavy taxes on the rich?

■ % Yes, should   ■ % No, should not

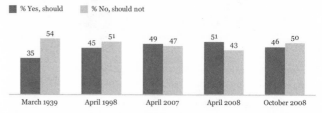

This question is notable because it directly invokes the idea that government should intervene and redistribute wealth through taxes on the rich. The question phrase "heavy taxes on the rich" is certainly not one the Obama campaign would choose to describe its plan, which Obama repeatedly says would return high income tax rates only back to where they were under Bill Clinton in the 1990s, before the Bush administration tax cuts. Still, the question generally addresses the basic issue of taxing high-income individuals to transfer wealth in a society.

Gallup has asked this question only four times over the last decade, and, in a broad sense, sentiment has been split every time. In 1998, there was a slight tilt toward the negative response; in 2007, sentiment was split almost equally; in April of this year, there was a slight tilt toward the positive response; and in the current poll, sentiment is more evenly split, with a slight tilt back toward the negative.

Still, in each of the four times Gallup has asked this question in recent years, between 45% and 51% of Americans have gone so far as to agree with the fairly harsh-sounding policy of "redistribut[ing] wealth by heavy taxes on the rich." Although the survey methods used now certainly differ in a number of ways from those for surveys conducted in 1939, the trend lines at least suggest that Americans are currently as willing as, if not more willing than, they were during the Depression to sanction the use of taxes on the rich as a mechanism for redistributing wealth.

Again, there are big differences by partisan orientation in response to this question.

Do you think our government should or should not redistribute wealth by heavy taxes on the rich?

By party ID

■ % Yes should   ■ % No, should not

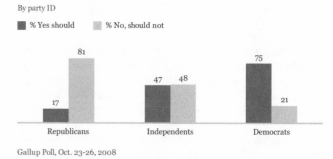

Gallup Poll, Oct. 23-26, 2008

Republicans overwhelmingly reject the concept, independents are split down the middle, and Democrats strongly support it.

Implications

Perhaps the most important implication of these data is the extraordinary partisan differences found in responses to both questions dealing with money and wealth distribution in this country. Democrats believe that wealth should be more evenly distributed, and that this redistribution should be accomplished by heavy taxes on the rich. Although Obama has not advocated what he would call "heavy" taxes on the rich, the general sentiment that taxes on high-income families should be increased in order to help provide tax relief for those making less money is a part of his campaign platform.

Republicans fairly strongly reject both the concept that the current distribution of money and wealth is unfair and the idea of imposing heavy taxes on the rich. In this, they certainly reflect the campaign statements and platform of McCain.

Independents, the most crucial group in a close election, are more ambivalent—as one would expect. Independents swing to the Democratic side in their majority (60%) belief that the distribution of money and wealth is not fair and should be more even, but split almost exactly evenly on the concept of heavy taxes on the rich.

Survey Methods

Results are based on telephone interviews with 1,010 national adults, aged 18 and older, conducted Oct. 23-26, 2008. For results based on the total sample of national adults, one can say with 95% confidence that the maximum margin of sampling error is ±3 percentage points.

For results based on the 511 national adults in the Form A half-sample and 499 national adults in the Form B half-sample, the maximum margins of sampling error are ±5 percentage points.

For results based on the sample of 957 registered voters, the maximum margin of sampling error is ±3 percentage points.

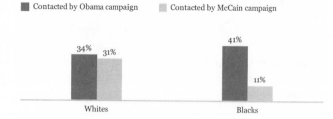

In the last few weeks, have you, personally been contacted about your vote for president by the [Barack Obama/John McCain] campaign -- including by e-mail, phone, in person, mail, or in some other way?

■ Contacted by Obama campaign   ■ Contacted by McCain campaign

This high level of contact almost certainly reflects an effort by the Obama campaign to help encourage a record-high turnout of black voters—more than 9 out of 10 of whom, based on Gallup data, will pull the lever for Obama if they vote.

In fact, Gallup analysis shows that blacks this year are just as likely as whites to report being registered to vote, and match the high levels of interest in the campaign and self-reported intention to vote seen among whites. The increase since 2004 on the latter two measures among blacks most likely reflects black voters' reaction to the candidacy of the first major-party black presidential nominee in U.S. history.

Turnout Indicators by Race, October 2004 and October 2008 Gallup Polls

Based on national adults

	Whites	Blacks
	%	%
Registered to vote, 2008	94	93
Registered to vote, 2004	92	91
Giving quite a lot of thought to election, 2008	88	85
Giving quite a lot of thought to election, 2004	85	81
Rate chances of voting 9 or 10, 2008	88	91
Rate chances of voting 9 or 10, 2004	88	84

October 31, 2008
BLACKS APPEAR POISED FOR HIGH TURNOUT
Constitute 11% of both of Gallup's likely voter groups, up from 8% in 2004

by Jeffrey M. Jones, Lydia Saad, and Frank Newport, Gallup Poll Editors

Black voters are scoring highly this election season on several election interest and voting measures, and thus constitute a higher percentage of Gallup's projected likely voter pool than in previous elections. Additionally, blacks report having received election-related contact from the Obama campaign at a higher rate than do whites, although many fewer blacks have been contacted by the McCain campaign.

Campaign Contact

As is the case among 18- to 29-year-old voters, blacks report having been contacted in disproportionately higher numbers by the Obama campaign than by the McCain campaign. While rates of contact by the Obama and McCain campaigns are similar among whites, blacks are almost four times as likely to report having been contacted by the Obama campaign as by the McCain campaign.

Blacks now make up a greater share of Gallup's likely voter pool (using the traditional model that takes into account past voting behavior) than they did in 2004. In Gallup's most recent update on likely voters, blacks constitute 11% of both the expanded and traditional likely voter group, higher than the 8% representation in Gallup's final estimate of voters from 2004. If these trends continue through the election next Tuesday, black turnout rates this year may approach or match turnout rates among whites.

Survey Methods

Results are based on telephone interviews with 2,279 national adults, aged 18 and older, conducted Oct. 10-12 and Oct. 23-26, 2008. For results based on the total sample of national adults, one can say with 95% confidence that the maximum margin of sampling error is ±2 percentage points.

For results based on the sample of 203 black respondents, the maximum margin of sampling error is ±7 percentage points.

Interviews are conducted with respondents on land-line telephones (for respondents with a land-line telephone) and cellular phones (for respondents who are cell-phone only).

In addition to sampling error, question wording and practical difficulties in conducting surveys can introduce error or bias into the findings of public opinion polls.

October 31, 2008

INTEREST HIGH: ONE IN FIVE HAVE ALREADY VOTED

Voter mobilization efforts well underway

by Frank Newport, Gallup Poll Editor in Chief and Jeffrey M. Jones, Managing Editor

At this stage in the election process, some four days before Nov. 4, Gallup reviews and updates several key indicators relating to voter turnout in this year's election.

1. Attention Being Paid to the Election

A Gallup Poll conducted Oct. 23-26 found 92% of registered voters saying they had given quite a lot or some thought to the election. This is a classic measure of interest in the election that Gallup has been tracking for decades, and the current reading is one of the highest such percentages found prior to an election in recent Gallup history.

There were similarly high attention levels in 1992 and 2004, which turned out to be higher-turnout elections. The campaigns of 1996 and 2000 captured significantly lower levels of voter attention, and were also lower-turnout elections. The high reading on this measure in 2008, perhaps not surprisingly, suggests a high-turnout election again this year.

Thought Given to the Election, Recent Presidential Elections

Based on registered voters

% Quite a lot of/Some thought

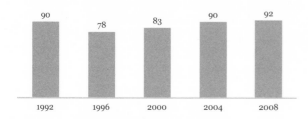

2. Early Voting

Gallup's latest update—based on interviewing conducted through Wednesday, Oct. 29—shows that 21% of registered voters who plan to vote say they have already voted early or by absentee ballot. This percentage has been increasing steadily over the last two weeks. Another 12% of registered voters say they still plan on voting early, leaving about two-thirds of those who plan on voting who indicate they will actually vote on Election Day itself, next Tuesday.

Early Voting in the 2008 Election

Based on registered voters who plan to vote in the election

% Already voted   % Plan to vote before Election Day

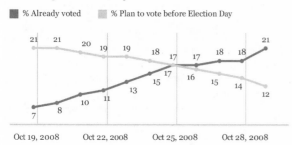

These early voters are more likely to say they have voted for Barack Obama than for John McCain, by a 55% to 40% margin. Among those who plan to vote on Election Day, the spread is much closer—only a 48% to 45% Obama advantage.

Despite some perceptions that there may be disproportionate early voting among blacks, Gallup's data show that black voters and white voters are roughly proportionate in their reports of already having voted.

There does, however, continue to be a significant age skew in the early voting patterns, such that older voters are significantly more likely than those who are younger to report having already voted.

3. First-Time Voters

Eleven percent of registered voters interviewed by Gallup this week claim to be first-time voters, which is similar to the percentage recorded in 2004 (13%). Most of these voters are under age 30, and, as is the case for this demographic group in general, they tend to be strongly oriented toward voting for Obama, according to their self-reported vote intentions.

But an important question is how many of these first-time voters will actually end up voting? Gallup's traditional likely voter model estimates that 8% of the electorate will be first-time voters (even though this model is based partly on past voting behavior, first-time voters are not penalized if they were too young to vote in past elections, and if they report already having voted, they also qualify as likely voters). In an expanded model, which does not rely on past voting experience to predict turnout in the coming election, they represent a slightly higher 10% of the electorate.

4. Voter Mobilization Efforts

Gallup has been asking Americans whether they have been contacted by the Obama campaign and by the McCain campaign. Thus far, the Obama campaign appears to have a modest edge in terms of voter contact and get-out-the-vote efforts. Gallup's updated estimate is that about 37% of registered voters say the Obama campaign has contacted them, while 30% say the McCain campaign has done so. Both numbers are likely to grow in the coming few days, as much of the mobilization is likely to occur in the final weekend and final days of the election.

The contact rates have tended to be higher for those residing in battleground states.

Survey Methods

Results for thought given to the election are based on telephone interviews with 1,010 national adults, aged 18 and older, conducted Oct. 23-26, 2008. For results based on the total sample of national adults, one can say with 95% confidence that the maximum margin of sampling error is ±3 percentage points.

Results for the other questions are based on interviews drawn from Gallup Poll daily tracking, consisting of approximately 3,000 or more interviews each. These results have a maximum margin of sampling error of ±2 percentage points.

Interviews are conducted with respondents on land-line telephones (for respondents with a land-line telephone) and cellular phones (for respondents who are cell-phone only).

In addition to sampling error, question wording and practical difficulties in conducting surveys can introduce error or bias into the findings of public opinion polls.

October 31, 2008

OBAMA RETAINS SLIGHT EDGE OVER MCCAIN ON TAXES

Americans still more likely to say Obama will increase taxes

by Elizabeth Mendes, Gallup Poll Staff Writer

A new Gallup Poll, conducted Oct. 23-26, finds Americans still favoring Barack Obama over John McCain as the candidate better able to handle taxes, 50% to 44%, but to a slightly lesser extent than earlier this month. The positioning of the two candidates on the tax issue has taken on increased importance in the last several weeks as McCain in particular has been focusing heavily on the differences between his approach and Obama's approach to taxes.

Would Barack Obama or John McCain Better Handle Taxes?

Based on national adults

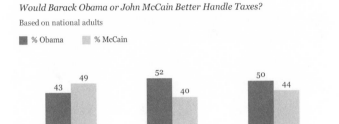

The most recent poll continues to reflect a somewhat higher percentage of Americans believing that Obama would raise taxes compared to the percentage who believe this about McCain. The results come at a time when Obama has been emphasizing his pledge to cut taxes for "95% of working families," while McCain claims he wants to make permanent the Bush tax cuts, which include cuts for higher-income Americans.

Thirty-six percent now say McCain will *increase* taxes, compared to 32% in early September. In the same period, the percentage of Americans who think Obama will increase their taxes has gone down by five points.

If [Barack Obama/John McCain] is elected president, do you think your federal income taxes would increase, decrease, or remain the same?

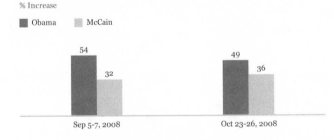

Assessing the Bush Tax Cuts

McCain has been emphasizing his proposal to make the Bush tax cuts permanent for all Americans while Obama wants to roll back the Bush tax cuts for those making over $250,000, raising the question of how Americans have reacted to the Bush tax cuts over the years since they were enacted.

A review of past Gallup Polls shows that support for the tax cuts ushered in by President George W. Bush after he took office was ini-

tially fairly high, but support for making the tax cuts permanent eroded somewhat during his first term. In a CNN/*USA Today*/Gallup poll, conducted Jan. 5-7, 2001, before Bush took office and before Congress began debating Bush's proposed $1.3 trillion tax cut, over half (52%) of Americans favored Bush's tax cuts. When it came to making the Bush tax cuts permanent, support dropped from 64% in November 2002 to 52% in December 2004, with opposition rising from 29% to 40% during that period.

Views on Making Bush Tax Cuts Permanent

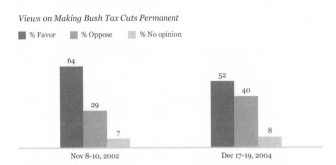

Separate Gallup polling conducted in October 2004 showed that 35% of Americans said the Bush tax cuts had mostly hurt the U.S. economy and just 39% said they had mostly helped.

Around the same time, a December 2004 poll found Americans generally favoring significant reforms to the federal income tax system, with a majority (59%) saying it either needed to be completely overhauled or needed major changes.

Which of the following statements best represents what you feel about the federal income tax system ... ?

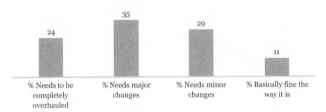

CNN/USA Today/Gallup poll, Dec. 17-19, 2004

"Haves" and "Have-Nots"

At the root of the tax issue is the subject of who benefits most from specific tax policies. Both candidates claim that their tax policy will benefit middle-class Americans. These appeals to middle-class sentiment may be resonating with a public that increasingly sees the United States as a nation divided into "haves" and "have-nots." In July of this year, almost half of Americans, 49%, said the United States is divided into two groups: the "haves" and the "have-nots." This was up from 45% two years ago, and from 37% in June 2004.

Additionally, in Gallup's annual Economy and Personal Finance poll, a large majority (63%) of Americans (though one of the lowest readings in the last two decades) said that upper-income people pay too little in taxes, while just 4% said the same about middle-income people. A large percentage of Americans (73%) also said corporations pay too little in taxes.

Further, in an Aug. 21-23 *USA Today*/Gallup poll, more than half of Americans (55%) said they believed that if Obama becomes president, his policies would benefit the middle class (33%) and the

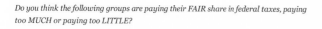

Do you think the following groups are paying their FAIR share in federal taxes, paying too MUCH or paying too LITTLE?

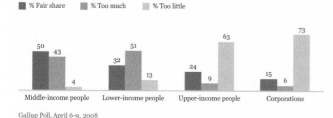

Gallup Poll, April 6-9, 2008

poor (22%) the most. However, if McCain were to be elected, 53% believed his policies would benefit the wealthy the most.

If [Barack Obama/John McCain] is elected president, who do you think his policies would benefit the most -- [ROTATED: the wealthy, the middle class, the poor], or all about equally?

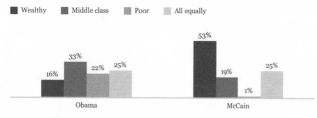

USA Today/Gallup poll, Aug. 21-23, 2008

Bottom Line

Outside of the context of the current presidential election, Americans have voiced frustration with tax policies that benefit the wealthy. Currently, Americans are more likely to see Obama than McCain as the candidate whose policies would benefit the middle class and the poor the most. This could be a benefit to Obama at a time when about half of the public sees American society as divided into "haves" and "have-nots."

Both candidates have used the Bush tax cuts as a reference point, with McCain vowing to continue them while Obama says he will rescind them for upper-income Americans. Although Gallup has not measured attitudes toward the Bush tax cuts in recent years, by 2004 they had become less favorably received. The fact that Obama has an edge, though it is small, over McCain on taxes at this time may point to an American public that is ready for a change from the fiscal policy of the Bush years.

Survey Methods

Results are based on telephone interviews with 1,010 national adults, aged 18 and older, conducted Oct. 23-26, 2008. For results based on the total sample of national adults, one can say with 95% confidence that the maximum margin of sampling error is ±3 percentage points.

Interviews are conducted with respondents on land-line telephones (for respondents with a land-line telephone) and cellular phones (for respondents who are cell-phone only).

In addition to sampling error, question wording and practical difficulties in conducting surveys can introduce error or bias into the findings of public opinion polls.

October 31, 2008
UPDATE: LITTLE EVIDENCE OF SURGE IN YOUTH VOTE
Obama campaign has contacted about one in three 18- to 29-year-olds

by Jeffrey M. Jones, Frank Newport, and Lydia Saad, Gallup Poll Editors

Gallup polling in October finds little evidence of a surge in young voter turnout beyond what it was in 2004. While young voter registration may be up slightly over 2004, the reported level of interest in the election and intention to vote among those under 30 are no higher than they were that year.

Turnout Indicators Among 18- to 29-Year-Olds, 2004 vs. 2008 Elections
Based on national adults aged 18 to 29

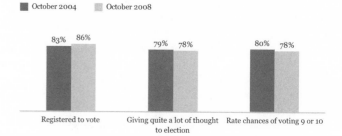

What's more, 18- to 29-year-olds continue to lag behind Americans aged 30 and older on these important turnout indicators.

Turnout Indicators by Age, October 2008 Gallup Polls
Based on national adults

Age	Registered to vote	Giving quite a lot of thought to election	Rate chances of voting 9 or 10
	%	%	%
18 to 29	86	78	78
30 to 49	92	85	87
50 to 64	97	94	92
65+	96	87	96

As a result, 18- to 29-year-olds now constitute 12% of Gallup's traditional likely voter sample, basically the same as the estimate in the final 2004 pre-election poll (13%). Gallup's expanded likely voter model, which defines likely voters differently (on the basis of current voting intentions only), estimates a slightly higher proportion of young voters in the electorate (14%). However, even if the share of the youth vote were adjusted upward, doing so has little or no impact on the overall Obama-McCain horse-race numbers using either likely voter model.

It is possible that the 18- to 29-year-old share of the likely voter electorate will grow in the final days of the election. Although interest in the election and voting intentions usually increase as Election Day grows nearer, Gallup did not observe much of an increase from mid- to late October 2004, because interest was already at high levels (as it is this year).

A second possibility for heightened youth turnout would be voter mobilization efforts. Such efforts can convince people with little motivation or interest in the campaign to actually vote on Election Day. Gallup has been measuring voter contact in its daily tracking poll this week in an effort to gain a better understanding of this important component of the "ground game" in the final days of the campaign.

As of Oct. 27-29 polling, 39% of 18- to 29-year-olds had been contacted by either the Obama or McCain campaigns. That is the same contact rate seen among 30- to 49-year-olds, but is well below that of Americans 50 and older. So thus far, in a general sense, mobilization efforts have not reached the young voters to the same extent that they have older voters.

Contacted by McCain or Obama Campaigns in Recent Weeks, by Age
Based on national adults

■ % Contacted by either campaign

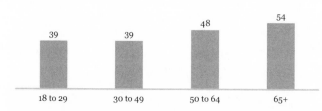

Gallup Poll Daily tracking, Oct. 27-29, 2008

The overall contact rates by age hide a significant disparity in contact by the two campaigns. Americans under 30 are about twice as likely to report having been contacted by the Obama campaign as by the McCain campaign. Thirty-one percent of 18- to 29-year-olds have been contacted by the Obama campaign, compared to just 16% who say the McCain campaign has contacted them.

The rate of Obama campaign contact of young adults compared to those who are older is similar, ranging from 31% among younger Americans to 40% for those 65 and older. On the other hand, there is a much larger age skew in reported contact by the McCain campaign, ranging from just 16% for the younger group to 38% for those 65 and older.

Contacted by McCain or Obama Campaigns in Recent Weeks, by Age
Based on national adults

■ % Contacted by Obama campaign   ▨ % Contacted by McCain campaign

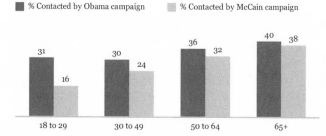

Gallup Poll Daily tracking, Oct. 27-29, 2008

The higher contact rates for Obama among the younger group reflect his greater level of support among this group than among the general population, a fact that has been well-documented. These contact levels for younger voters no doubt reflect that each candidate's campaign this year appears to be targeting its contact toward its known supporters—reflecting the strategic decision that voter contact best serves to reinforce the base and get out the vote rather than to attempt to change voters' minds. Plus, given the historic fact that younger voters are less likely to turn out at the polls and vote, it may be that the Obama campaign sees a fertile opportunity among this group for increased votes.

The graph also makes clear that the Obama campaign has been more successful in reaching voters, regardless of their age.

Implications

While Gallup data do suggest that voter turnout among young people will be high this year (as it was in 2004) compared to historical turnout rates, the data do not suggest that it will be appreciably higher than in 2004. Even if more young voters are registered this year, they do not appear to be any more interested in the campaign or in voting in the election than they were in 2004.

Unless turnout rates among older age groups drop substantially from what they were in 2004, young voters should represent about the same share of the electorate as in the last presidential election. And Gallup's data suggest interest in the campaign and voting are the same or higher among older voters compared to what they were in 2004.

Gallup will continue to monitor campaign contact between now and the end of its pre-election polling, to see whether that could be a factor in promoting higher turnout among voters this year.

Survey Methods

Results are based on telephone interviews with 2,279 national adults, aged 18 and older, conducted Oct. 10-12 and Oct. 23-26, 2008. For results based on the total sample of national adults, one can say with 95% confidence that the maximum margin of sampling error is ±2 percentage points.

For results based on the sample of 237 18- to 29-year-olds, the maximum margin of sampling error is ±7 percentage points.

Interviews are conducted with respondents on land-line telephones (for respondents with a land-line telephone) and cellular phones (for respondents who are cell-phone only).

In addition to sampling error, question wording and practical difficulties in conducting surveys can introduce error or bias into the findings of public opinion polls.

November 03, 2008

OBAMA'S SUPPORT BUILT ON CHANGE, MCCAIN'S ON EXPERIENCE

Reasons given for support echo findings from earlier this year

by Frank Newport, Gallup Poll Editor in Chief

As voters prepare to go to the polls on Nov. 4, a new Gallup Poll panel survey shows that Barack Obama voters say they are motivated to vote for their candidate because he would bring about change and provide a fresh approach to governing, while John McCain voters are supporting their candidate both because of his experience, and because they agree with his views on issues.

These results are based on 1,942 interviews conducted with members of the Gallup Panel during Oct. 27-30 who have a candidate preference. Gallup Panel members are recruited using the same random sampling techniques used for all Gallup national polls.

Previous polls asking a similar question found that Obama voters are consistently likely to mention their desire for change as the rationale for their vote choice, a finding which either precedes or echoes the major theme of the Obama campaign. Over a third of his supporters spontaneously mentioned change in this survey.

Other key points derived from an examination of the volunteered reasons given by Obama voters for supporting their candidate include:

- After the change dimension, Obama voters are most likely to give generic reasons for their support: they agree with his views, or have the perception that he is the best man for the job.
- Obama voters also mention a number of specific dimensions as reasons why they support him, including his plans for dealing with the economy, the fact that he would work for the working/middle class, and his approach to health care.
- Six percent of Obama voters say they are supporting him because they dislike his opponent (McCain).

McCain's supporters don't coalesce around any one rationale for their support the way Obama supporters do. As noted, the most frequently given responses by McCain supporters are that he is experienced (which has been an often given response by McCain supporters in previous research), and that they agree with his views.

Other key points:

- McCain supporters are slightly more likely than Obama supporters to say they are voting for McCain because they dislike his opponent. An additional 5% specifically mention that they are voting for McCain because his opponent is too liberal or a socialist. These responses almost certainly reflect the McCain campaign's focus in recent weeks on reinforcing negative perceptions of Obama.
- Other specifics given by McCain supporters include the fact that he is conservative, his approach to taxes, and his honesty and integrity.
- McCain's pro-life stance on abortion is, apparently, a significant draw to his candidacy, as 5% of his supporters say they are voting for him because of the abortion issue.

Survey Methods

Results for this panel study are based on telephone interviews with 2,021 national adults, aged 18+, conducted Oct. 27-30, 2008. Respondents were

Please tell me in your own words why you are supporting Barack Obama or John McCain?

	National adults	Obama voters	McCain voters
Want change/Fresh approach	20	35	2
Agree with his values/views (non-specific)	17	17	18
Best man for the job	14	16	11
Experienced/Qualified	10	2	20
Dislike opponent	8	6	10
Economy/His economic plan	7	8	6
Always support that party	7	7	7
Honest/Has integrity/Good character	5	4	6
Taxes/His tax plan	5	4	7
Conservative/More conservative candidate	4	1	8
Like his choice of running mate	3	3	3
For the working/middle class	3	5	1
Health care reform	3	4	1
Smart/Intelligent/Knowledgeable	3	4	1
Abortion issue	3	1	5
Lesser of two evils	2	1	4
Opponent too liberal/A socialist	2	*	5
Trustworthy/Trust him	2	1	4
Iraq War/Plans for handling it	2	3	1
Military background/Service to country	2	*	4
International affairs/Foreign policy	2	2	2
National security/Terrorism issue	1	*	2
Education/His education plan	1	2	*
Favors smaller government	1	*	1
Liberal/The more liberal candidate	1	*	1
Independent/Goes against party/A maverick	*	*	1
Energy/His energy plan	*	*	*
Environment/Global warming	*	*	*
Other	2	2	1
No reason in particular (vol.)	1	1	1
No opinion	1	1	2

Based on adults with a candidate preference or leaning, Oct. 27-30, 2008

drawn from Gallup's household panel, which was originally recruited through random selection methods. The final sample is weighted so it is representative of U.S. adults nationwide. For results based on the total sample of National Adults, one can say with 95% confidence that the maximum margin of sampling error is ±3 percentage points.

For results based on the 1,942 registered voters who have a candidate preference, the maximum margins of sampling error is ±3 percentage points.

In addition to sampling error, question wording and practical difficulties in conducting surveys can introduce error or bias into the findings of public opinion polls.

November 04, 2008

VOTERS HAVE HIGH PERSONAL INVESTMENT IN ELECTION OUTCOME

Three-quarters say outcome matters more than in prior elections

by Jeffrey M. Jones, Gallup Poll Managing Editor

A recent Gallup Poll finds 74% of Americans saying the outcome of this year's presidential election matters more to them than in previous years—slightly more than said this about the 2004 election, and well above the figures from the 1996 and 2000 elections.

Does the outcome of this year's presidential election matter to you more than in previous years, less than in previous years, or about the same?

Based on registered voters

■ % Matters more

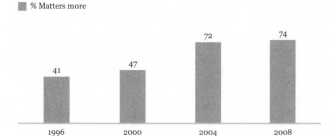

The results suggest that Americans have come to view the outcome of elections as increasingly important. While at least 7 in 10 said the election mattered more to them in both 2004 and 2008, fewer than half said this about the 1996 or 2000 elections.

The increased importance attributed to the election outcomes helps explain the surge in voter turnout in 2004, which experts predict could be eclipsed in this year's election. Gallup has found an extraordinarily high level of interest in the election throughout this year, and its data also suggest turnout will exceed what it was in 2004.

Democrats (80%) are slightly more likely than Republicans (74%) to attribute greater importance to the 2008 election outcome. That is a similar pattern to what Gallup showed for the 2004 election. In 2000, Republicans were slightly more likely to view the outcome as more important than prior elections, and in 1996, Republicans and Democrats were about equal in their perceptions.

Percentage Saying the Outcome of the Election Matters More Than in Previous Years, by Party Affiliation

Based on registered voters

	Democrats	Independents	Republicans
2008	80%	68%	74%
2004	77%	73%	69%
2000	45%	43%	52%
1996	45%	34%	47%

Stakes Viewed as Higher

Voters' personal investment in the outcome is further underscored by the poll finding that 92% of registered voters agree with the statement that "the stakes in this presidential election are higher than in previous years," including 76% who strongly agree. The percentage strongly agreeing exceeds the percentage who said this about the 2004 election, and is more than twice what Gallup measured for the 1996 election.

Agree or Disagree: The stakes in this presidential election are higher than in previous years

Based on registered voters

■ % Strongly agree ■ % Somewhat agree ■ % Somewhat disagree
■ % Strongly disagree

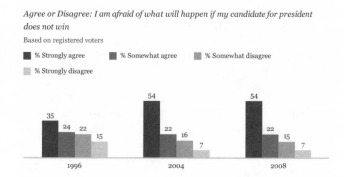

All party groups overwhelmingly agree that the stakes in the 2008 election are higher than in prior years, but Democrats (84%) are slightly more likely to say they strongly agree than are Republicans (76%) or independents (68%).

Voters go so far as to express trepidation about the election going against their wishes. Fifty-four percent of voters say they strongly agree that they are "afraid of what will happen if [their] candidate for president does not win." Another 22% agree somewhat.

These figures exactly duplicate what Gallup measured in 2004. U.S. voters were far less likely to say they were fearful about how the 1996 election would be decided.

Agree or Disagree: I am afraid of what will happen if my candidate for president does not win

Based on registered voters

■ % Strongly agree ■ % Somewhat agree ■ % Somewhat disagree
■ % Strongly disagree

Republicans (59%) and Democrats (58%) are about equally likely to say they strongly agree with this statement, while independents (46%) are less likely to.

Implications

It would appear that U.S. voters as a whole view the outcome of presidential elections as more consequential than they did in the recent past. This has fueled a surge in turnout in the 2004 election, which is likely to be repeated again this Election Day. It is possible that the contested election outcome in 2000—when Al Gore won the popular vote but lost to George W. Bush in the Electoral College on the basis of the disputed Florida vote—has caused more voters to realize that their vote can make a difference in the outcome, and can greatly affect the course of the nation over the subsequent four years.

Survey Methods

Results are based on telephone interviews with 957 registered voters, aged 18 and older, conducted Oct. 23-26, 2008. For results based on the total sample of registered voters, one can say with 95% confidence that the maximum margin of sampling error is ±3 percentage point.

Interviews are conducted with respondents on land-line telephones (for respondents with a land-line telephone) and cellular phones (for respondents who are cell-phone only).

In addition to sampling error, question wording and practical difficulties in conducting surveys can introduce error or bias into the findings of public opinion polls.

November 05, 2008

OBAMA'S ROAD TO THE WHITE HOUSE: A GALLUP REVIEW

Race was tight until convention period followed by economic crisis

by Lydia Saad, Jeffrey M. Jones, and Frank Newport, Gallup Poll Editors

Barack Obama's victory over John McCain in the 2008 presidential election concludes a race that was highly competitive for much of the year.

2008 Presidential Preferences for Obama vs. McCain

Based on registered voters

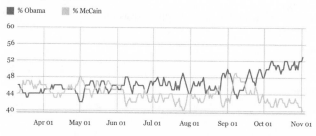

Gallup Poll Daily tracking, March 7-11 through Oct. 31-Nov. 2, 2008

The two were essentially tied during the primary election season, from March through May. Obama moved slightly ahead of McCain once he clinched the Democratic nomination in early June. McCain then succeeded in overtaking Obama after the Republican National Convention in September. But the economic events that followed helped shift voters back into Obama's column, and appear to have been a turning point in the campaign. The presidential debates during the fall may have further strengthened Obama's position, buoying him to double-digit leads among registered voters nationwide in the last few weeks of the campaign.

A Competitive Start

Obama's road to the White House was far from assured during the 2008 primary season when he ran nip and tuck with McCain in early Gallup Poll trial heats for the general election. There were 85 Gallup Poll Daily tracking reports published between March 12 and June 7. McCain was ahead of Obama by one or more percentage points in 39 of those reports, Obama was ahead by one or more points in 31, and they were exactly tied in the remaining 15. The only candidate of the pair to achieve a statistically significant lead during this phase of the campaign was McCain, advancing to five- and six-point leads for a brief period in late April/early May. At that point, the Obama campaign was fighting off a hornet's nest of adverse publicity surrounding Obama's former pastor, the Rev. Jeremiah Wright, as well

as Obama's comments about "bitter" voters in Pennsylvania, and his recent primary loss to Clinton in that state.

Presidential Preferences During Primary Election Season, Obama vs. McCain

Based on registered voters

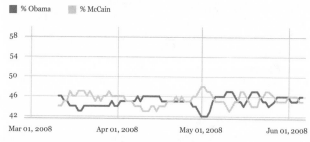

Gallup Poll Daily tracking, March 7-11 through June 2-6, 2008

The closeness of the race in the primary campaign phase of the election year likely can be credited to the then-ongoing Democratic nomination fight, which helped depress Obama's support among Democrats who favored Hillary Clinton for the nomination. Obama's support among Democrats averaged just 75% from March through May, compared with 90% in the final week of the general-election campaign.

By comparison, McCain averaged 86% Republican support from March through May, and finished the campaign at 87% among Republican registered voters.

Summer Winning Streak

After Obama secured the Democratic nomination in early June (Clinton conceded to Obama on June 7), support for him immediately expanded somewhat, resulting in a 75-day stretch (through late August) when he continuously led or tied McCain.

Obama's average lead over McCain during this period was only three percentage points, but it reached as much as nine points in late July after his widely covered trip to parts of Europe and the Middle East.

Presidential Preferences During Summer Period, Obama vs. McCain

Based on registered voters

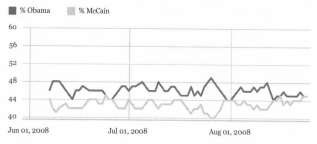

Gallup Poll Daily tracking, June 3-7 through Aug. 22-24, 2008

The Convention Period

Obama's fortunes turned, temporarily, on Aug. 26, when Gallup reported him to be trailing McCain by two percentage points. The Aug. 23-25 interviews on which that report was based represented the first three days of tracking after Obama's announcement of Joe Biden as his running mate. The immediate implication was that his vice-presidential pick, at best, delivered no bounce in support for Obama and, at worst, possibly hurt the ticket. The subsequent Democratic National

Convention enabled Obama to turn things back around in his favor. He took the lead again and attained an eight-point advantage over McCain toward the end of the convention.

With the conventions held back-to-back spanning the Labor Day weekend, public preferences seesawed and McCain quickly reversed the Obama tide in early September. McCain moved into the lead immediately after the end of the Republican National Convention, after McCain's, and his vice-presidential running mate Sarah Palin's, highly acclaimed acceptance speeches.

At this point, McCain experienced his longest front-runner stretch of the general-election phase of the campaign: 10 days from Sept. 7 to Sept. 16.

Presidential Preferences During Convention Period, Obama vs. McCain
Based on registered voters

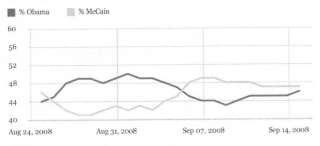

Gallup Poll Daily tracking, Aug. 23-25 through Sept. 13-15, 2008

The Economic Game-Changer

McCain's lead came to an abrupt halt with the onset of the Wall Street crisis in mid-September. By Sept. 17, the Republican nominee again trailed Obama by a few percentage points, and while the race briefly closed to a tie later in the month, McCain never regained the lead.

McCain attempted a bold move by suspending his campaign in late September to return to Washington to focus on legislation to address the financial crisis, but he resumed his campaign in time to debate Obama on Sept. 26 even though Congress had not formulated a legislative plan. The debates were perhaps McCain's best opportunity to reverse Obama's growing momentum, but he was unable to do so. *USA Today*/Gallup polls found that Americans rated Obama the winner of all three debates, and these may have helped him solidify his gains. October proved to be Obama's best month of the campaign, as he averaged a nine-point lead among registered voters over McCain in Gallup Poll Daily tracking.

Presidential Preferences During Post-Convention Period, Obama vs. McCain
Based on registered voters

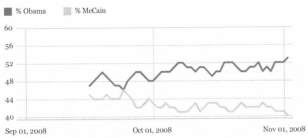

Gallup Poll Daily tracking, Sept. 14-16 through Oct. 31-Nov. 2, 2008

Bottom Line

Obama and McCain ran essentially neck and neck for much of the presidential campaign—from March through early September. Obama enjoyed the slight upper hand once he secured the nomination in early June. But as many observers commented, for a long time he failed to "close the sale" with voters by stretching his lead over McCain to 10 or more points, or by surpassing the 50% support threshold. (He finally reached both of these targets in October.)

Still, as close as the race was, Obama technically held the advantage for much of the year. In 230 Gallup Poll Daily tracking reports from March through Nov. 2, Obama was ahead of McCain in 155 of these (67%), including by a significant margin in 66. McCain had an advantage in only 50 of these reports (22%), and a statistically significant lead in only 6.

McCain pulled ahead briefly after the Republican National Convention. But the economic crisis struck and he failed to "win" any of the three presidential debates in the eyes of Americans. Obama—who had struck the right chord with voters on the economy and met or exceeded expectations in the debates—thus ended the campaign running at his strongest level of the entire race.

Survey Methods

Results are based on telephone interviews with 900+ registered voters, aged 18 and older, conducted each day from March 7 through Nov. 2, 2008. The three-day rolling averages of registered voters' preferences have a maximum margin of sampling error of ±2 percentage points.

Interviews are conducted with respondents on land-line telephones (for respondents with a land-line telephone) and cellular phones (for respondents who are cell-phone only).

In addition to sampling error, question wording and practical difficulties in conducting surveys can introduce error or bias into the findings of public opinion polls.

November 06, 2008
BLACKS, POSTGRADS, YOUNG ADULTS HELP OBAMA PREVAIL
Women, non-churchgoers also provide strong backing

by Lydia Saad, Gallup Poll Senior Editor

The final pre-election Gallup Poll Daily tracking survey of nearly 2,500 likely voters shows that Barack Obama won the 2008 presidential election with practically total support from black Americans, and heavy backing from those with postgraduate educations, young adults (male and female alike), and non-churchgoers. At least 6 in 10 voters in all of these categories cast their votes for Obama.

Additionally, across Gallup's Oct. 31-Nov. 2 final pre-election tracking, Obama won majority support nationwide from women, middle-aged adults (30 to 49 and 50 to 64 years of age), and Catholics.

These findings are aside from the typical political support patterns whereby Democrats and liberals are reliably strong supporters of the Democratic presidential candidate, and Republicans and conservatives are strong supporters of the Republican.

2008 Presidential Preferences

Groups Showing Supermajority Support for Barack Obama

Based on likely voters

	Obama	McCain
	%	%
Blacks	99	1
Postgraduates	64	36
18 to 29 years	61	39
Seldom/Never attend church	61	39

USA Today/Gallup, Oct. 31-Nov. 2, 2008

2008 Presidential Preferences

Groups Showing Modest Majority Support for Barack Obama

Based on likely voters

	Obama	McCain
	%	%
Women	56	44
50 to 64 years	54	46
30 to 49 years	53	47
Catholics	53	47

USA Today/Gallup, Oct. 31-Nov. 2, 2008

Among likely voters, 93% of each partisan group supported their own party's candidate for president and 7% of each supported the opposing party's candidate. Political independents were evenly divided at 50%. The advantage for Obama came from the fact that many more voters who participated in the 2008 election were Democratic in their party orientation than were Republican (39% vs. 29%).

2008 Presidential Preferences, by Party ID

Based on likely voters

■ % Obama ▨ % McCain

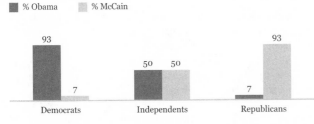

USA Today/Gallup, Oct. 31-Nov. 2, 2008

Additionally, certain groups historically aligned with each party showed predictably high support for that party's candidate. Most voters living in households with at least one union member backed Obama, while veterans and gun owners were solidly behind McCain.

McCain's Hobbled Coalition

John McCain's principal electoral strengths on Tuesday were with frequent churchgoers, whites, seniors, Protestants, and men. However, for all except Protestants, the extent of support he received from these groups was not as great as Obama's support from their counterparts (non-churchgoers, blacks, young voters, Catholics, and women).

2008 Presidential Preferences Among Traditionally Partisan Groups

Based on likely voters

■ % Obama ▨ % McCain

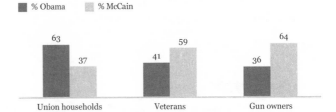

USA Today/Gallup, Oct. 31-Nov. 2, 2008

2008 Presidential Preferences

Groups Showing Modest Majority Support for John McCain

Based on likely voters

	Obama	McCain
	%	%
Attend church weekly	44	56
Non-Hispanic whites	44	56
65 years and older	46	54
Protestants	47	53
Men	49	51

USA Today/Gallup, Oct. 31-Nov. 2, 2008

What Changed Since 2004?

Gallup's preliminary analysis of the trends in voting among various subgroups suggests that Obama outperformed other recent Democratic nominees in attracting the near-universal support of blacks. Black support for the Democratic candidate is always high, but their 99% support for Obama exceeded the 93% received by John Kerry in 2004, the 88% support for Bill Clinton in 1992, and the 88% support for Mike Dukakis in 1988. Clinton approached universal support from blacks with his 96% backing in 1996, as did Gore in 2000 with 95%.

There was virtually no change in the percentage of white voters supporting the Democratic candidate in each of the last four presidential elections, ranging from 43% to 46%, with Obama's 45% about average.

Percentage Supporting Democratic Presidential Candidate, by Race
1988-2008 Final Gallup Pre-Election Polls

Based on likely voters

■ Blacks ▨ Whites^

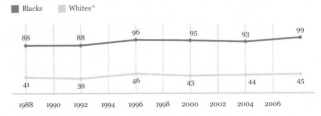

^ Whites include Hispanic and non-Hispanic whites

Gallup's 2004 final pre-election polling showed young voters heavily favoring the Democratic nominee (Kerry), as they did in the 2008 election. What changed is that middle-aged voters moved from the Republican column into the Democratic column. This more than offset a modest shift of seniors from the Democratic to the Republican side.

Percentage Supporting Democratic Presidential Candidate, by Age
2004 and 2008 Final Gallup Pre-Election Polls
Based on likely voters

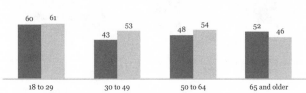

Another striking change between the 2004 and 2008 elections is the preferences of the most highly educated Americans. Obama attracted the highest level of support from postgraduate educated Americans (64%) of any recent Democratic candidate. Four years ago, 53% of this group backed Kerry, fairly typical of the historic pattern. Obama also made gains among college graduates and those with only some college. The only group to show a decline in support for the Democratic nominee in 2008 was those with no college education.

Percentage Supporting Democratic Presidential Candidate, by Education
2004 and 2008 Final Gallup Pre-Election Polls
Based on likely voters

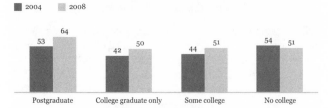

Where Did All the Republicans Go?

Obama and McCain fought hard during the campaign for the independent vote, and in the end it was a draw, with each getting 50% of the independent vote. However, that parity masks a more fundamental shift of voters away from the Republican Party over the past four years. In 2004, Republicans and Democrats were about equally represented in Gallup's final pre-election pool of likely voters: 39% were Republican, 37% Democratic, and 24% independent. This year, only 29% of likely voters were Republican and 39% Democratic, with 31% independent—a political balance much more favorable to Obama than what Kerry faced in 2004.

Bottom Line

Obama's victory is owed in part to extraordinarily high support from blacks. Not only did nearly all blacks who participated in the election vote for Obama, but blacks came out in record numbers—constituting 13% of Gallup's final likely voter pool, up from 8% in 2004.

Secondly, Obama achieved greater support than his Democratic predecessors from highly educated voters, and he attracted significant new support from middle-aged voters.

Thirdly, far fewer voters considered themselves Republican in this election than did so in 2004. Gallup polling has documented this decline over the past four years, along with a steep deterioration of President George W. Bush's approval rating. The resulting more pro-

Democratic political climate in the country may be the ultimate reason Obama won.

Survey Methods

Results are based on telephone interviews with 3,050 national adults, aged 18 and older, conducted Oct. 31-Nov. 2, 2008. For results based on the total sample of national adults, one can say with 95% confidence that the maximum margin of sampling error is ±2 percentage points. For results based on the sample of 2,824 registered voters, the maximum margin of sampling error is ±2 percentage points.

For results based on the sample of 2,472 likely voters (using Gallup's traditional likely voter model which identifies likely voters on the basis of current voting intention and past voting behavior), the maximum margin of sampling error is ±2 percentage points. The likely voter model assumes a turnout of 64% of national adults. The sample is weighted to reflect this assumption, so the weighted sample size of likely voters is 1,952.

Interviews are conducted with respondents on land-line telephones (for respondents with a land-line telephone) and cellular phones (for respondents who are cell-phone only).

In addition to sampling error, question wording and practical difficulties in conducting surveys can introduce error or bias into the findings of public opinion polls.

November 07, 2008
CONSUMER CONFIDENCE UP SLIGHTLY AFTER OBAMA'S ELECTION
Daily tracking shows perceptions improving over past couple of days

by Dennis Jacobe, Gallup Poll Chief Economist

President-elect Barack Obama on Friday signaled he will focus on the economy when he takes office in January. In electing Obama, Americans sought positive change on the economy, and since his election, Gallup Poll Daily tracking has documented a further uptick in U.S. consumer confidence, which has been improving since mid-October. The percentage of consumers saying the economy is "getting worse" is down four points and the percentage rating the economy "poor" is down three points in the past few days.

Percentage of Consumers Saying Economy Is Getting Worse
Weekly/Daily trend

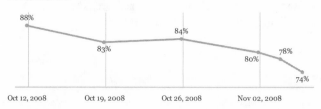

Slightly Fewer Saying Economy Is "Getting Worse"

During mid-October, the percentage of Americans saying the economy was getting worse reached a weekly high for the year of 88%. During the following few weeks, consumer pessimism eased steadily, as the percentage "getting worse" fell eight points to 80% for the week of Oct. 27-Nov. 2. Over the three days ending on Election Day, this measure of consumer expectations stood at 78%, and in the past three days (from Election Day to Thursday), it fell another four points to 74%.

Slightly Less Rating Economy "Poor"

In mid-October, the percentage of consumers rating current economic conditions "poor" also reached a weekly high of 60%. Pessimism eased a little in the following weeks, with the percentage "poor" declining to 56% for the week of Oct. 27-Nov. 2. Over the three days ending on Election Day, the percentage rating the economy "poor" remained at 56%, but in the three days since then, "poor" ratings have fallen another three points to 53%.

Percentage of Consumers Rating Economy "Poor"
Weekly/Daily trend

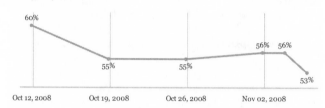

Survey Methods

Gallup is interviewing no fewer than 1,000 U.S. adults nationwide each day during 2008. The economic questions analyzed in this report are asked of a random half-sample of respondents each day.

The questions for individual weeks are based on combined data of approximately 3,000 interviews for individual weeks from Oct. 6-12 to Oct. 27-Nov. 2, 2008. For results based on these samples, the maximum margin of sampling error is ±2 percentage points.

The questions reported on a three-day rolling basis combine data of approximately 1,500 interviews from Nov. 2-4 and Nov. 4-6, 2008. For results based on these samples, the maximum margin of sampling error is ±3 percentage points.

Interviews are conducted with respondents on land-line telephones (for respondents with a land-line telephone) and cellular phones (for respondents who are cell-phone only).

In addition to sampling error, question wording and practical difficulties in conducting surveys can introduce error or bias into the findings of public opinion polls.

November 10, 2008
OBAMA AND BUSH: A CONTRAST IN POPULARITY
Transition marked by sharp divergence in leaders' ratings

by Lydia Saad, Gallup Poll Senior Editor

Monday's White House meeting between President George W. Bush and President-elect Barack Obama presents a remarkable contrast between one of the least popular two-term presidents in modern times at the close of his administration, and one of the most popular candidates to win the presidency.

According to Gallup Poll Daily tracking from Nov. 6-8, only 27% of Americans approve of the job Bush is doing as president. This contrasts with the 70% of Americans holding a favorable view of Obama.

Post-Election Ratings of President Bush and President-elect Obama

Gallup Poll Daily tracking, Nov. 6-8, 2008

Although this contrast between Obama and Bush is based on different measures—presidential job approval and general favorability—the ratings produced by the two typically track very closely for U.S. presidents, and thus provide a good indication of the vast popularity gap that exists between Bush and Obama.

Additionally, nearly two-thirds of Americans say they are confident in Obama's ability to be a good president, similar to his 70% favorable reading.

Are you confident or not confident in Barack Obama's ability to be a good president?

Gallup Poll Daily tracking, Nov. 6-8, 2008

Gallup will be tracking all three of these measures—Bush job approval, Obama favorability, and Obama confidence—for the entire presidential transition period, and reporting the results on the basis of three-day rolling averages, similar to Gallup's previous reporting of the presidential trial heats.

Obama's Historic Popularity

Obama's favorable ratings from the American people have increased since the election—rising to 70%, up from 61% in Gallup Poll Daily tracking from Nov. 1-3. But even the pre-election 61% reading broke records, marking the highest rating for any presidential candidate in the 1992-2008 period in which Gallup measured favorability using the current question.

Gallup also occasionally measures favorability using the "scalometer" format that it routinely employed between 1956 and 1992, in which respondents are asked to rate individuals on a 10-point scale, from "+5" at the high end to "-5" at the low end (with no zero midpoint).

In an Oct. 23-26 poll, Obama scored a 37% highly favorable rating on this measure (+4 and +5 on the scale), on par with several earlier popular presidential candidates, including Ronald Reagan in 1984, Jimmy Carter in 1976, Richard Nixon in 1968 and 1972, and

John Kennedy and Nixon in 1960. (Obama's +37 contrasts with McCain's +28.)

Bush's Unwelcome Distinction

With barely two months remaining in his second term, Bush could quite possibly finish with the lowest final job approval score of any president serving out his term in at least a half century. His current 27% job approval rating is below Harry Truman's final rating of 32% in December 1952, as well as Carter's 34% in December 1980. No other president since the advent of polling was rated below 49% as he was leaving office.

Final Presidential Job Approval Ratings, Presidents Who Served Out Their Terms in Office

Last Gallup Poll rating before end of last term in office

	Approve	Disapprove
	%	%
Harry Truman (Dec 11-16, 1952)	32	56
Dwight Eisenhower (Dec 8-13, 1960)	59	28
Lyndon Johnson (Jan 1-6, 1969)	49	37
Gerald Ford (Dec 10-13, 1976)	53	32
Jimmy Carter (Dec 5-8, 1980)	34	55
Ronald Reagan (Dec 27-29, 1988)	63	29
George H.W. Bush (Jan 8-11, 1993)	56	37
Bill Clinton (Jan 10-14, 2001)	66	29

As was recently reported by Gallup Poll Managing Editor Jeff Jones, the 29.4% average job approval rating for Bush in the third quarter of this year (from July 20-Oct. 19) was one of the worst Gallup has measured for any president in the last half century and, thus far, it appears his rating for the fourth quarter could be even worse.

Over the next two months, Gallup Poll Daily tracking will document whether Bush receives an "exit bounce" in job approval ratings similar to the one that occurred for his father in the three-month period between October 1992 and the time he left office in January 1993. The elder Bush's approval rating rose from 34% right before the 1992 election (which he lost to Bill Clinton) to 56% by the end of his term. Lesser exit bounces were seen for Clinton and Reagan, who each completed two terms in office.

Bottom Line

Presidential transitions are always fascinating spectacles, but Monday's White House encounter between Bush and Obama promises to be especially so because of the historic aspect of the nation's first black president-elect taking a step closer to assuming the highest office. It will also be fascinating because of the sharp contrast between Bush and Obama in popularity. At no time in a half century—and maybe more—has a president as beleaguered in public opinion as Bush been replaced by someone so highly esteemed. The transition from Truman to Dwight Eisenhower in 1953 may have approached this, but while Gallup documented Truman's final approval rating of 32% in December 1952, Gallup had not yet instituted favorability readings, and thus provided no measure of Eisenhower's popularity at that time. What the Bush vs. Obama contrast might mean for Obama's ability to enjoy an extended honeymoon with the American public after his inauguration on Jan. 20 remains to be seen.

Results are based on telephone interviews with 1,546 national adults, aged 18 and older, conducted Nov. 6-8, 2008. For results based on the total sample of national adults, one can say with 95% confidence that the maximum margin of sampling error is ±3 percentage points.

Interviews are conducted with respondents on land-line telephones (for respondents with a land-line telephone) and cellular phones (for respondents who are cell-phone only).

In addition to sampling error, question wording and practical difficulties in conducting surveys can introduce error or bias into the findings of public opinion polls.

November 11, 2008
AMERICANS WANT REGULATION MORE THAN RESCUE
Say tightening financial regulations on banks ought to come first

by Lydia Saad, Gallup Poll Senior Editor

On the all-important subject of the U.S. economy, Americans are much more interested in having Barack Obama tighten regulations on the nation's financial institutions when he becomes president than they are in having him provide corporate entities with additional bailout help.

Six in 10 Americans whom *USA Today*/Gallup surveyed from Nov. 7-9 say "passing new, stricter regulations on financial institutions" is critical or very important for Obama to do as president, while only about one in five say Obama should help bail out large financial institutions or provide financial assistance to the ailing automobile industry.

In terms of improving the economy, please say whether each of the following is critical for Barack Obama to do as president, very important but not critical, important, or not that important.

■ % Critical/Very important

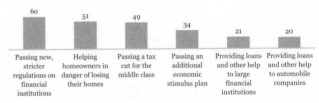

USA Today/Gallup, Nov. 7-9, 2008

Targeting Help to Ordinary Americans

In addition to the 60% of Americans who say regulating financial institutions should be a critical or high priority for the Obama administration, roughly half of Americans rate helping homeowners in danger of losing their homes (51%) and passing a tax cut for the middle class (49%) as either critical or very important economic goals for Obama to pursue. This suggests that, beyond preventing a repeat of the financial meltdown, Americans are primarily interested in economic steps that would immediately benefit average Americans.

While some of these proposals could be included in the second economic stimulus package that Obama says is essential to fixing the economy, the idea of an economic stimulus plan, per se, ranks further down Americans' economic priority list. Only 34% consider it critical or very important for Obama to pass such a plan as president.

A Hard Sell for the Auto Industry

The original economic stabilization act passed in October authorized the federal government to spend up to $700 billion to purchase distressed assets from financial institutions, with the goal of freeing up credit and restoring confidence in the credit markets. The U.S. auto industry, with the support of Democratic congressional leaders, is now pressuring the Bush administration to use some of that funding to help forestall its collapse.

While it is not clear whether Americans would support diverting bailout funds originally intended for banks to help the auto industry, the entire scheme of providing loans and financial help to corporate America is the lowest of Americans' economic priorities. Only about one in five say providing such financial aid to large financial institutions or to auto companies ought to be a critical or very important goal for Obama.

Economy Eclipses Other Issues

The general importance of the economy to Americans is clear in a separate question asking which of five major issues Obama should make his top priority as president. Nearly two-thirds of Americans choose the economy (64%), contrasted with only 11% choosing the situations in Iraq and Afghanistan, 7% the federal budget deficit, 6% energy, and 5% healthcare.

Which of the following should be Barack Obama's top priority as president --
[ROTATED: the economy, healthcare, the situations in Iraq and Afghanistan, energy, the federal budget deficit], or something else?

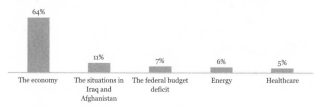

USA Today/Gallup, Nov. 7-9, 2008

Survey Methods

Results are based on telephone interviews with 1,010 national adults, aged 18 and older, conducted Nov. 7-9, 2008. For results based on the total sample of national adults, one can say with 95% confidence that the maximum margin of sampling error is ±3 percentage points.

Interviews are conducted with respondents on land-line telephones (for respondents with a land-line telephone) and cellular phones (for respondents who are cell-phone only).

In addition to sampling error, question wording and practical difficulties in conducting surveys can introduce error or bias into the findings of public opinion polls.

November 11, 2008
ELECTION LIFTS ECONOMIC SPIRITS FOR DEMOCRATS, INDEPENDENTS
More likely since election to say economic conditions are "getting better"

by Frank Newport, Gallup Poll Editor in Chief

The election of Barack Obama as the next U.S. president has been accompanied by a significant increase in optimism about the economy among Democrats and independents, even while Republicans have become somewhat more negative.

Right now, do you think that economic conditions in the country as a whole are getting better or getting worse?

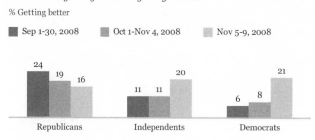

Gallup Poll Daily tracking

Gallup Poll Daily tracking of Americans' economic outlook clearly demonstrates how economic perceptions are bound up with politics. Republicans had been much more positive about the direction of the economy than were either independents or Democrats in September, and, to a slightly lesser degree, from October through Election Day, Nov. 4. This relative difference in optimism reflects a normal pattern by which those who identify with the party in the White House are generally more positive than those who are "on the outs."

But views on the direction of the economy shifted virtually overnight in the days after the election.

Republicans' views didn't change a lot, shifting slightly more toward the negative. But independents and Democrats' views shifted significantly in a positive direction. Independents' net optimism (the percentage saying the economy is "getting better" minus the percentage saying it is "getting worse") improved from -74 for Oct. 1 through Nov. 4 to -54 in the five days after the election (Nov. 5-9), while Democrats' net optimism improved even more dramatically, from -82 prior to the election to -52 in the days afterward.

These changes are, of course, relative. A majority of independents and Democrats did not suddenly become convinced that the economy was getting better. But the percentage "getting better" among Democrats jumped from 6% and 8% in September and October, respectively, to 21% in the days after the election, while the percentage saying the economy was getting worse dropped from 91% and 90%, respectively, to 73%. Independents saw a similar, though less dramatic, change.

Looked at differently, while Republicans were more positive about the economy than were independents and Democrats during September and from Oct. 1 through the election, in the days after the election, the last two groups have suddenly become the more optimistic.

(Of interest is that there has been little significant change in the three partisan groups' perceptions of current economic conditions—as opposed to changes in perceptions of the *direction* of the economy, as discussed above. The election of Obama, in other words,

Right now, do you think that economic conditions in the country as a whole are getting better or getting worse?

	% Getting better	% Getting worse	% Net
Total sample			
Sep 1-30	13	82	-69
Oct 1-Nov 4	12	84	-72
Nov 5-9	19	75	-56
Republicans			
Sep 1-30	24	68	-44
Oct 1-Nov 4	19	75	-56
Nov 5-9	16	77	-61
Independents			
Sep 1-30	11	83	-72
Oct 1-Nov 4	11	85	-74
Nov 5-9	20	74	-54
Democrats			
Sep 1-30	6	91	-85
Oct 1-Nov 4	8	90	-82
Nov 5-9	21	73	-52

Gallup Poll Daily tracking

has had much less effect on views of where the economy stands today.)

Implications

The uptick in positive views on the direction of the economy among independents and Democrats has moved average consumer confidence in this country to a somewhat more positive level since the Nov. 4 election. Net optimism across the American population was -69 in September and -72 from Oct. 1 to Nov. 4, but is now down to a somewhat less negative -56.

This finding underscores the degree to which consumer confidence can depend on intangibles rather than on consumers' hard-nosed assessments of real economic data. Obama's election and the pending arrival of a Democrat in the White House have already caused a mild shift toward the positive in consumer confidence.

There are two things to watch going forward. One, will this uptick in consumer confidence be short-lived, or can Obama sustain the more positive outlook as he makes appointments and outlines his economic plans between now and Jan. 20? Second, will this increase in consumer confidence translate into actual behavior and will consumers begin to spend more, particularly in the all-important Christmas shopping season? Gallup will be monitoring and reporting on these questions over the next few weeks and months.

Survey Methods

Results are based on telephone interviews with national adults, aged 18 and older, conducted as part of Gallup Poll Daily tracking, including 15,342 interviews conducted in September 2008; 17,585 interviews conducted between Oct. 1 and Nov. 4, 2008; and 2,530 interviews conducted Nov. 5-9, 2008. For results based on the sample of national adults interviewed in September and from Oct. 1-Nov. 4, one can say with 95% confidence that the maximum margin of sampling error is ±1 percentage point. For results based on the sam-

ple of national adults interviewed Nov. 5-9, the maximum margin of sampling error is ±2 percentage points.

Interviews are conducted with respondents on land-line telephones (for respondents with a land-line telephone) and cellular phones (for respondents who are cell-phone only).

In addition to sampling error, question wording and practical difficulties in conducting surveys can introduce error or bias into the findings of public opinion polls.

November 12, 2008
AMERICANS HOPEFUL OBAMA CAN ACCOMPLISH MOST KEY GOALS
Most hopeful about gains for minorities and the poor, U.S. respect abroad

by Jeffrey M. Jones, Gallup Poll Managing Editor

When asked whether the Obama administration would be able to accomplish each of 16 possible goals for its time in office, Americans are most likely to predict that it will improve conditions for minorities and the poor, and improve respect for the United States abroad, and are least likely to think the new government can avoid raising their taxes and control illegal immigration.

Regardless of which presidential candidate you preferred, do you think the Obama administration will or will not be able to do each of the following? How about -- [RANDOM ORDER]?

	% Yes, will	% No, will not
Improve conditions for minorities and the poor	80	19
Increase respect for the United States abroad	76	22
Improve education	71	27
Improve the quality of the environment	70	28
Reduce unemployment	67	32
Bring U.S. troops home from Iraq in a way that is not harmful to the U.S.	66	33
Improve the healthcare system	64	34
Create a strong economic recovery	64	34
Keep the U.S. safe from terrorism	62	36
Bring U.S. troops home from Afghanistan in a way that is not harmful to the U.S.	58	40
Reduce U.S. dependence on oil	57	41
Heal political divisions in this country	54	44
Control federal spending	52	46
Substantially reduce the federal budget deficit	42	56
Avoid raising your taxes	36	61
Control illegal immigration	35	62

Nov. 7-9 USA Today/Gallup poll

These results are based on a Nov. 7-9 *USA Today*/Gallup poll, which included a version of a question about incoming administrations after presidential elections. The question asks whether the new administration will or will not be able to accomplish a list of common presidential goals, though the specific goals asked for each president-elect have varied over the years.

In general, Americans are quite optimistic in the Obama administration's potential to achieve most of the goals tested in this year's survey. A majority believe the new administration will be able to accomplish 13 of the 16 goals. The three goals Americans express doubts about the Obama administration's ability to deliver on are controlling illegal immigration, reducing the federal budget deficit, and avoiding a tax increase.

Since he was elected last week, Barack Obama has made clear that improving the economy is his top priority when he takes office next January. And Americans are optimistic those efforts will pay off—64% believe his administration will be able to create a strong economic recovery, and 67% believe it will be able to reduce unemployment.

While John McCain was generally regarded as better able to handle international matters than Obama throughout the campaign, Americans generally agree that the Obama administration will also fare well in this area. In addition to the 76% who say the new administration will increase respect for the United States abroad, 62% believe it will be able to keep the country safe from terrorism, and majorities believe it will be able to bring U.S. troops home from Iraq (66%) and Afghanistan (58%) in ways that are "not harmful to the United States."

Comparison to Prior Presidents-Elect

The optimism Americans express about the Obama administration is not unusual compared to what Gallup has found for other incoming presidents. Gallup asked a similar question in November 1980 for the Ronald Reagan administration, in November and December 1988 for the George H.W. Bush administration, in November 1992 for the Bill Clinton administration, and in January 2001 for the George W. Bush administration. Typically, Americans are more likely to say the incoming president will be able to accomplish most of the items rated than to say he will not. And, for the most part, Obama scores well where other presidents-elect have scored well, and poorly where others have rated poorly.

For example, Americans have always believed the new president would make the economy better (when it was struggling) or keep it good when it was doing well.

Expectations for Presidents-Elect to Promote/Maintain a Good Economy

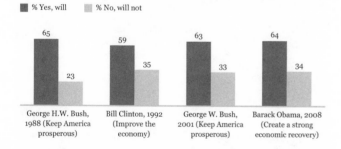

And when a president took office during difficult economic times, the public has generally been confident that he would be able to reduce unemployment.

On two of Obama's lowest-scoring items—reducing the budget deficit and avoiding raising Americans' taxes—other incoming presidents faced similar public doubts. (This is the first time Gallup has asked about a president's ability to control illegal immigration, so it is not clear whether other presidents would also have scored poorly on that item.)

But Obama does significantly exceed the expectations for his predecessors on improving conditions for minorities and the poor, and increasing respect for the United States abroad.

He also fares much better than George W. Bush did in expectations that he will be able to heal political divisions in this country.

Expectations for Presidents-Elect to Reduce Unemployment

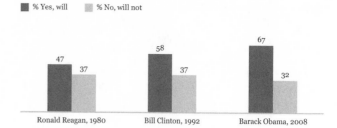

Expectations for Presidents-Elect to Reduce Federal Budget Deficit

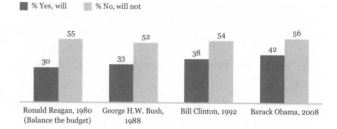

Expectations for Presidents-Elect to Avoid Raising Your Taxes

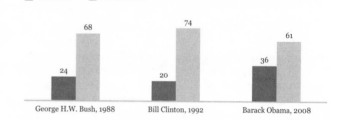

Expectations for Presidents-Elect to Improve Conditions for Minorities and the Poor

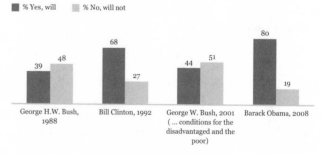

Expectations for Presidents-Elect to Increase Respect for the United States Abroad

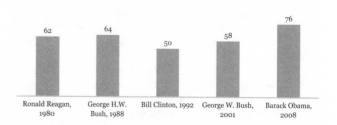

Expectations for Presidents-Elect to Heal Political Divisions in This Country

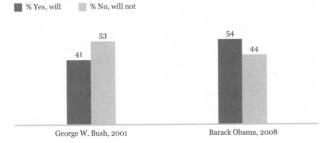

■ % Yes, will   ■ % No, will not

George W. Bush, 2001   Barack Obama, 2008

Confidence in Barack Obama's Ability to Be a Good President,
by Political Ideology

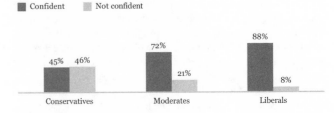

■ Confident   ■ Not confident

Conservatives   Moderates   Liberals

Gallup Poll Daily tracking, Nov. 9-11, 2008

Implications

Americans apparently have high hopes for the Obama administration, believing Obama will be able to accomplish most of a list of 16 goals presidents often hope to achieve. But the expectations for Obama are not universally greater or lower than what they were for prior incoming presidents. Americans generally have faith in new presidents to re-establish or maintain economic growth, and to reduce unemployment when it is high, as they do for Obama. And though the public is skeptical in Obama's ability to avoid raising taxes and to reduce the federal budget deficit, the public was also skeptical about prior presidents-elect in this regard.

Where Obama may stand apart from his predecessors is in the public's optimism that he can improve conditions for minorities and the poor, increase respect for the United States abroad, and heal political divisions in the country.

Survey Methods

Results are based on telephone interviews with 1,010 national adults, aged 18 and older, conducted Nov. 7-9, 2008. For results based on the total sample of national adults, one can say with 95% confidence that the maximum margin of sampling error is ±3 percentage points.

Interviews are conducted with respondents on land-line telephones (for respondents with a land-line telephone) and cellular phones (for respondents who are cell-phone only).

In addition to sampling error, question wording and practical difficulties in conducting surveys can introduce error or bias into the findings of public opinion polls.

November 12, 2008
NEARLY HALF OF CONSERVATIVES CONFIDENT IN OBAMA
Less surprising is that most liberals and moderates are also confident

by Lydia Saad, Gallup Poll Senior Editor

The extent to which Barack Obama is experiencing a post-election wave of good will from Americans is evident in the latest Gallup Poll Daily tracking results, from Nov. 9-11, in which close to half of political conservatives—45%—say they are "confident in his ability to be a good president." About the same percentage (46%) disagree.

Naturally, self-described liberals are overwhelmingly positive about the outlook for Obama's success (88% are confident), as are most political moderates (72%). These figures are roughly in line

with these groups' candidate preferences right before Election Day. According to Gallup's final pre-election polling from Oct. 31-Nov. 2, 94% of liberals and 62% of moderates supported Obama for president.

The surprise is that conservatives are evenly divided in their forecasts for Obama's presidency. The 45% who now say they are confident in Obama's ability to be a good president contrasts with the mere 23% of this group who supported him over John McCain in the election.

This relatively strong endorsement from conservatives boosts overall confidence in Obama well beyond the 53% of the national vote he received on Election Day. Overall, 65% of Americans now say they are confident Obama will be a good president, while only 27% are not confident and 8% are unsure.

Sentiments on this question haven't changed in the five days since the election, when Gallup began tracking them—not surprising, given the relatively low profile the president-elect has kept since winning the presidency. Gallup will continue to track this measure until Obama assumes the presidency in January.

Are you confident or not confident in Barack Obama's ability to be a good president?
Post-election trend

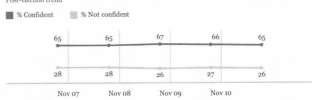

■ % Confident   ■ % Not confident

Nov 07   Nov 08   Nov 09   Nov 10

Gallup Poll Daily tracking

Forecasts for Obama's presidency diverge more on the basis of party affiliation. Democrats are nearly unanimous in their confidence that Obama will be a good president, whereas two-thirds of Republicans are not confident.

Confidence in Obama's Ability to Be a Good President, by Party ID

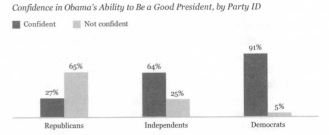

■ Confident   ■ Not confident

Republicans   Independents   Democrats

Gallup Poll Daily tracking, Nov. 9-11, 2008

One of the most optimistic groups in America today about the next administration is young adults. Three-quarters of those aged 18 to 29 predict Obama will be a good president. Adults 30 and older are also positive, only less so, with at least 6 in 10 in every older age group expressing confidence.

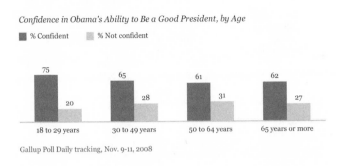

Confidence in Obama's Ability to Be a Good President, by Age

■ % Confident   ▨ % Not confident

Gallup Poll Daily tracking, Nov. 9-11, 2008

Nine in 10 blacks (92%), but also a majority of whites (58%), say they are confident in Obama's ability to be a good president. Obama overwhelmingly won the black vote on Election Day, but lost to McCain among whites.

Bottom Line

Gallup's post-election polling has documented an increase in Obama's already positive favorable ratings—from 61% immediately prior to the election to roughly 70% in recent days. Also, large majorities of Americans have said they are optimistic, excited, and proud about Obama's being elected.

The fact that nearly two-thirds of Americans—including a broad coalition of liberals, moderates, and conservatives—are also confident in Obama's ability to be a good president underscores the tremendous public backing he will have come January to advance his agenda, but also Americans' high expectations.

It will be important to see whether Obama's cabinet selections and policy statements between now and his inauguration on Jan. 20 alter the public's confidence in his ability to be a good president in any way. Gallup will be tracking this confidence measure until Jan. 20, after which it will be replaced by the traditional presidential job approval rating for Obama.

Survey Methods

Results are based on telephone interviews conducted as part of Gallup Poll Daily tracking with 1,539 national adults, aged 18 and older, conducted Nov. 9-11, 2008. For results based on the total sample of national adults, one can say with 95% confidence that the maximum margin of sampling error is ±3 percentage points.

Interviews are conducted with respondents on land-line telephones (for respondents with a land-line telephone) and cellular phones (for respondents who are cell-phone only).

In addition to sampling error, question wording and practical difficulties in conducting surveys can introduce error or bias into the findings of public opinion polls.

November 13, 2008
ECONOMIC CRISIS AFFECTING MOOD AS WELL AS WALLETS
Bad economic news triggered new lows in Americans' overall happiness

by Elizabeth Mendes, Gallup Poll Staff Writer

Although Americans continue to be emotionally affected by the nation's economic crisis, they seem to be slightly less affected than they were during the initial shockwaves in mid-September, when happiness and enjoyment without a lot of stress and worry consistently hit record lows for the year. During the period of Sept. 15 to Oct. 15, there were eight days on which Americans' collective level of happiness and enjoyment without a lot of stress and worry dipped below 40%. Since then, the same has only happened once, on Nov. 6.

Gallup Daily: Mood

Based on emotion experienced Sept. 1, 2008 - Nov. 10, 2008

■ % With a lot of happiness/enjoyment without a lot of stress/worry

▨ % With a lot of stress/worry without a lot of enjoyment/happiness

Gallup-Healthways Well-Being Index

The initial downswing in Americans' moods came as the full scope of the economic crisis began to unfold, with Americans' levels of happiness hitting lows of 37%, 38%, and 39% eight times throughout the last two weeks of September and first two weeks of October. Prior to that, happiness had been at higher levels, hitting at or above 40% every day from Sept. 1-14, with previous lows also coinciding with negative financial news.

The Gallup-Healthways mood measure, which asks Americans 18 and older to reflect on the level of happiness and stress they experienced the day before the survey, has shown consistent (and not surprising) upswings in mood on weekends and holidays for most Americans. Prior to September, Gallup found that 58% of Americans reported a lot of happiness and enjoyment without a lot of stress or worry on a typical Saturday or Sunday compared to 46% on a typical Monday. In contrast, the week that saw the collapse of Washington Mutual and intense strife on Capitol Hill over the proposed bailout plan, happiness sank to uncharacteristic weekend lows of 53% on both Saturday, Sept. 27, and Sunday, Sept. 28.

Starting the week of Oct. 13, Americans' moods began to pick back up, with happiness staying at 41% or above for six consecutive days and reaching a typical weekend level of 57% on Saturday, Oct. 18. Happiness remained above 40% during the rest of October, as enthusiasm for the election picked up toward the end of the month, turning attention away, slightly, from the fiscal crisis.

Immediate Reaction by Group

Looking more closely at the Gallup-Healthways data collected Sept. 15- Oct. 15, when happiness and enjoyment consistently hit record

Gallup Daily: Mood - A look at correspondence with major events

Based on emotion experienced the day of the event

	Event	% Happiness-Enjoyment
Nov. 6, 2008	--	38% *
Oct. 19, 2008 (Sunday)	--	54%
Oct. 18, 2008 (Saturday)	--	57%
Oct. 14, 2008	--	41%
Oct. 13, 2008	Stock market soars 11 percent	44%
Oct. 12, 2008 (Sunday)	World leaders pledge to help global financial system	57%
Oct. 9, 2008	Dow fell 679 points	38% *
Oct. 8, 2008	Fed cuts interest rate	44%
Oct. 7, 2008	Dow fell 508 points	39% *
Oct. 5, 2008 (Sunday)	--	55%
Oct. 4, 2008 (Saturday)	--	54%
Oct. 3, 2008	Pres. Bush signs the bailout bill into law	43%
Oct. 2, 2008	--	39% *
Oct. 1, 2008	Senate approves revised bailout bill	41%
Sept. 29, 2008	Bailout plan rejected; Dow fell 778 points	37% *
Sept. 28, 2008 (Sunday)	--	53%
Sept. 27, 2008 (Saturday)	--	53%
Sept. 25, 2008	Washington Mutual fails	39%
Sept. 24, 2008	John McCain announces he will suspend campaign	44%
Sept. 23, 2008	--	38% *
Sept. 18, 2008	Initial bailout plan announced	42%
Sept. 17, 2008	Dow fell 449 points	37% *
Sept. 15, 2008	Dow fell 504 points	39% *

Gallup-Healthways Well-Being Index

lows, reveals that Americans with more negative perceptions of the economy were far more likely to report lower levels of happiness and higher levels of stress, than those with a more positive economic outlook.

Gallup Daily: Mood - Economic Outlook

Based on an aggregate of Gallup Poll Daily tracking interviews conducted Sept. 15 - Oct. 15, 2008

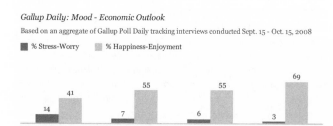

Gallup-Healthways Well-Being Index

The Gallup-Healthways data also reveals that Americans with an annual income of $36,000 or more per year were more likely to experience happiness during this time period than those making $35,999 per year or less.

Additionally, Americans with one or more children in their household also report lower levels of happiness, and those with six children or more experienced a much higher level of stress.

Together, it is clear that the effect of the economy on daily happiness-stress is likely compounded for people with less income and more children.

Gallup Daily: Mood - Annual Income

Based on an aggregate of Gallup Poll Daily tracking interviews conducted Sept. 15 - Oct. 15, 2008

Gallup-Healthways Well-Being Index

Gallup Daily: Mood - By number of children in household

Based on an aggregate of Gallup Poll Daily tracking interviews conducted Sept. 15 - Oct. 15, 2008

Gallup-Healthways Well-Being Index

Survey Methods

For the Gallup Poll Daily tracking survey, Gallup is interviewing no fewer than 1,000 U.S. adults nationwide each day during 2008.

The U.S. mood results are based on data from Sept. 15-Nov. 10, 2008. For results based on the total sample of registered voters, one can say with 95% confidence that the maximum margin of sampling error is ±2 percentage points.

Interviews are conducted with respondents on land-line telephones (for respondents with a land-line telephone) and cellular phones (for respondents who are cell-phone only).

In addition to sampling error, question wording and practical difficulties in conducting surveys can introduce error or bias into the findings of public opinion polls.

November 13, 2008
NO CLAMORING FOR PALIN TO BECOME A NATIONAL POLITICAL FIGURE
But she enjoys support of three-quarters of Republicans

by Frank Newport, Gallup Poll Editor in Chief

Just 45% of Americans would like to see Sarah Palin become a major national political figure for many years to come, while a slight majority of 52% say they would not. These sentiments are sharply divided along partisan political lines.

Over three-quarters of Republicans would like to see the former vice-presidential nominee and current governor of Alaska become a major national political figure in the years ahead, in sharp contrast to the 43% of independents and 20% of Democrats who share that attitude.

Palin has been much in evidence since the Republican ticket's defeat on Election Day, appearing in interviews on NBC's "Today" show, Fox News, and CNN. Palin is also slated to give a major address to the Republican Governors Association meetings in Miami Thursday, followed by a press conference.

Would you, personally, like to see Sarah Palin be a major national political figure for many years to come, or not?

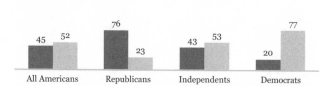

■ % Yes   ■ % No

USA Today/Gallup poll, Nov. 7-9, 2008

Palin's post-election media appearances certainly fuel speculation that she is interested in playing a major role on the national political scene in the years ahead, perhaps by running for the Republican presidential nomination in 2012 or 2016, or for the U.S. Senate from Alaska. The data reviewed above, from the Nov. 7-9 *USA Today*/Gallup poll, suggest that she has a way to go to convince the average American that her presence would be a positive addition to the crowded political landscape.

Certainly one of the most prevalent reactions to Palin's run as vice-presidential nominee was her appeal to base Republican voters, a conclusion that is reinforced by the current data showing that 76% of her fellow Republicans would like her to be on the national scene in the years ahead. The negative reaction from Democrats is not unexpected, but the tepid reaction from independent voters might give Palin pause as she contemplates her future.

In the same weekend poll, Palin's favorable ratings had climbed to the point where they were equal to her unfavorable ratings, a slightly more positive reaction than was generated in the final Gallup Poll conducted before the election.

Next, we'd like to get your overall opinion of some people in the news. As I read each name, please say if you have a favorable or unfavorable opinion of these people.

Sarah Palin

■ % Favorable   ■ % Unfavorable

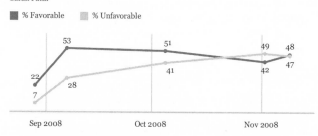

Gallup's initial read on Palin's image—taken on Aug. 29, the day John McCain announced that he was selecting her as his running mate—showed that more than 7 out of 10 Americans didn't know enough about her to have an opinion of her, but among the few who did, she had a 3-to-1 positive-to-negative ratio. She continued to be rated more positively than negatively after the Republican National Convention and her well-regarded acceptance speech, but after a series of widely panned interviews with network news anchors, her unfavorables climbed, and, by the time of the election, more Americans viewed her unfavorably than favorably.

While Palin's ratings have improved somewhat after the election, they remain significantly more negative than those of either her former running mate, McCain, or the two Democratic nominees—Barack Obama and Joe Biden.

Her favorable ratings by party group are sharply divided, reflecting the same basic pattern evident in reactions to the idea of her becoming a national political figure.

Next, we'd like to get your overall opinion of some people in the news. As I read each name, please say if you have a favorable or unfavorable opinion of these people.

Sarah Palin

■ % Favorable   ■ % Unfavorable

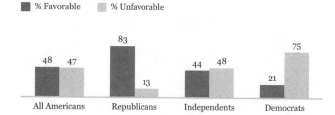

USA Today/Gallup poll, Nov. 7-9, 2008

Implications

Palin's recent actions—including granting a number of broadcast interviews, giving speeches, and holding press conferences—make it clear that she is interested in staying on the national political scene rather than retiring to her previous obscurity as governor of the remote state of Alaska.

The current data suggest that she may have some tough sledding ahead of her if that is indeed the case. Although Palin enjoyed a huge jump in name identification in the slightly more than two months between her selection as McCain's running mate and the Nov. 4 election, she emerged with the most negative ratings of any of the four major-party presidential and vice-presidential candidates. And a majority of Americans say they are not interested in her becoming a fixture on the national political scene in the years ahead.

Survey Methods

Results are based on telephone interviews with 1,010 national adults, aged 18 and older, conducted Nov. 7-9, 2008. For results based on the total sample of national adults, one can say with 95% confidence that the maximum margin of sampling error is ±3 percentage points.

Interviews are conducted with respondents on land-line telephones (for respondents with a land-line telephone) and cellular phones (for respondents who are cell-phone only).

In addition to sampling error, question wording and practical difficulties in conducting surveys can introduce error or bias into the findings of public opinion polls.

November 14, 2008
FEWER SEE COUNTRY DIVIDED THAN AFTER 2000, 2004 ELECTIONS
Majority believes Obama can heal political divisions in the country

by Jeffrey M. Jones, Gallup Poll Managing Editor

Although a majority of the public (57%) still views the country as more divided on the major issues than it has been in recent years,

Americans are less inclined to believe this than they were after the 2000 and 2004 elections.

Do you think the country is -- or is not -- more deeply divided this year on the major issues facing the country than it has been in the past several years?

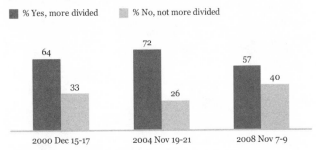

These results are based on a Nov. 7-9 *USA Today*/Gallup poll, which repeated a question first asked in December 2000—shortly after the Supreme Court ruled in George W. Bush's favor in the Florida election recount case—and asked again in November 2004, after Bush won a bitterly fought contest against John Kerry for a second term as president.

After this year's election, Republicans (73%) are more likely than Democrats (47%) to view the country as more deeply divided, with independents' (52%) views more similar to Democrats'. That is a reversal from 2004, when Democrats (87%) were more likely than Republicans (57%) to perceive the country as more divided. Democrats were also more likely than Republicans to view the country as divided in 2000, but by a smaller, 73% to 62%, margin.

Percentage Viewing Country as Being More Deeply Divided on Major Political Issues, by Party Affiliation, Recent Presidential Elections

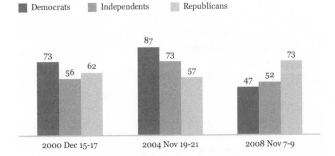

Though the data are somewhat limited—based on just three elections—they suggest that supporters of the party that won the election tend to view the country as being more unified, and supporters of the party that failed to win the White House see the country as being more divided.

Time to Heal?

To the extent that the country is divided, most Americans believe that the Obama administration can heal the political divisions in the country: 54% say it will be able to, and 44% say it will not. While not an overwhelming endorsement, it is a much more optimistic assessment than the public gave Bush after the 2000 (41%) and 2004 (33%) elections.

Regardless of which presidential candidate you preferred, do you think the [Obama/Bush] administration will or will not be able to heal political divisions in the country?

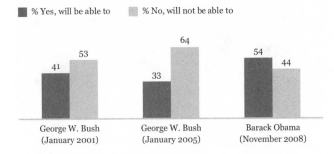

Those who believe the country is more divided than it has been in the past are only slightly less optimistic (48%) than the general public about the new administration's ability to heal political divisions.

Americans seem hopeful of an air of cooperation in Washington once Obama takes office. The poll finds 80% believing the new president "will make a sincere effort to work with the Republicans in Congress to find solutions that are acceptable to both parties" when trying to tackle the major issues facing the country. Fewer, but still a solid majority (62%), believe the Republicans in Congress will return the favor. About the same percentage (59%) expect the Democrats in Congress to make an attempt to work with the Republicans in Congress.

Implications

The decline in perceptions of the country's being divided, and expectations for sincere attempts at bipartisanship, may reflect the passing of the Bush era. Bush's approval ratings were the most polarized by party of any president in Gallup polling history, surpassing the highly polarized ratings of Bill Clinton.

It may also reflect the aftermath of a presidential contest between two relatively well-liked candidates—candidates who have reputations for working with members of the other party on legislative matters. Earlier in the year, Americans also perceived that Obama and McCain were more likely to unify than to divide the country.

Survey Methods

Results are based on telephone interviews with 1,010 national adults, aged 18 and older, conducted Nov. 7-9, 2008. For results based on the total sample of national adults, one can say with 95% confidence that the maximum margin of sampling error is ±3 percentage points.

Interviews are conducted with respondents on land-line telephones (for respondents with a land-line telephone) and cellular phones (for respondents who are cell-phone only).

In addition to sampling error, question wording and practical difficulties in conducting surveys can introduce error or bias into the findings of public opinion polls.

November 14, 2008
SHARP INCREASE IN AMERICANS' WORRY ABOUT MONEY
Worry has increased, although it is lower on weekends

by Frank Newport, Gallup Poll Editor in Chief

About 4 out of 10 Americans in recent weeks report that they worried about money "yesterday," a sentiment that increased sharply in mid-September, and that, despite having fluctuated somewhat since that point, remains higher now than it was earlier this year.

Did you worry about money yesterday?
Seven-day rolling averages

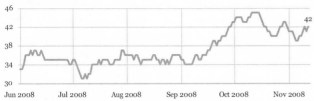

Gallup Poll Daily tracking, June 1-Nov. 12, 2008

The percentage of Americans who responded "yes" when asked if they worried about money the previous day as part of Gallup Poll Daily tracking was around the 35% level for most of the year leading up to mid-September. At that point, when the Wall Street financial crisis became front-page news, worry about money jumped to as high as 48% in early to mid-October. Since that time, worry has fluctuated, dropping to around the 40% level at several points, but increasing slightly in recent days. For the first 12 days of November, the average percentage worried has been 41%, while 59% of Americans on average have said they did not worry about money.

Did you worry about money yesterday?

Gallup Poll Daily tracking, Nov. 1-12, 2008

An analysis of responses to this question by day of interview (using data from Oct. 1 through Nov. 12 to provide a larger sample size) shows that worry is lowest when the day in question is Saturday or Sunday (in other words, when respondents are interviewed on Sunday and Monday and are asked about their worries "yesterday"), with higher numbers when the day in question is Monday through Friday.

Implications

It is not surprising to find that Americans are now more likely to say they worry about money than they were earlier this year. Perhaps it is most surprising to find that even in this time of economic turmoil, more than half of Americans on an average day say they did not worry about money.

Did you worry about money yesterday?
By day of interview
% Yes

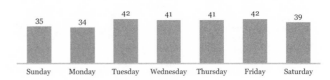

Gallup Poll Daily tracking, Oct. 1-Nov. 12, 2008

The weekend, it appears from these data, provides at least a little break from monetary concerns. Plus, it is clear from the data that there is the entirely predictable relationship between income and worry about money, with those who make the most worrying the least.

Older Americans, despite being on fixed incomes for the most part and to some degree at the mercy of market forces beyond their control, are least likely to have worried about money the previous day. It may be that they have fewer concerns about losing their jobs (since most are retired or not working), that they have fewer unexpected expenses, or that they have simply learned over the years not to let short-term worries concern them.

The big-picture implication of personal worry about money is that it translates into reduced consumer spending. Certainly from most news reports, retailers have been reporting downturns in their sales at the same time that these attitudinal data show an increase in monetary worries.

Survey Methods

Results are based on telephone interviews with 6,029 national adults, aged 18 and older, conducted Nov. 1-12, 2008, as part of Gallup Poll Daily tracking. For results based on the total sample of national adults, one can say with 95% confidence that the maximum margin of sampling error is ±2 percentage points.

Interviews are conducted with respondents on land-line telephones (for respondents with a land-line telephone) and cellular phones (for respondents who are cell-phone only).

In addition to sampling error, question wording and practical difficulties in conducting surveys can introduce error or bias into the findings of public opinion polls.

November 17, 2008
AMERICANS HOLD FIRM TO SUPPORT FOR DEATH PENALTY
Only 21% say it is applied too often

by Lydia Saad, Gallup Poll Senior Editor

Last week's recommendation by a Maryland commission that the state's death penalty law be repealed contrasts with broad U.S. public support for the punishment. According to Gallup's annual Crime survey in October, 64% of Americans favor the death penalty for someone convicted of murder, while just 30% oppose it.

Are you in favor of the death penalty for a person convicted of murder?

2001-2008 trends from Gallup Poll Crime Survey, conducted each October

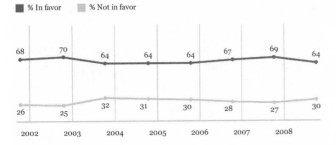

Generally speaking, do you believe the death penalty is applied fairly or unfairly in this country today?

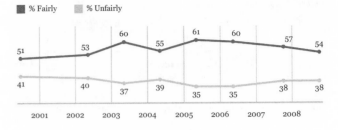

In addition to the majority of Americans who support the death penalty, nearly half (48%) believe it is not imposed often enough. Only 21% of Americans say it is imposed too often, with a nearly equal number, 23%, saying it is imposed about the right amount of time.

In your opinion, is the death penalty imposed -- [too often, about the right amount, or not often enough]?

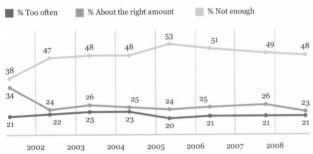

The death penalty is favored by most Republicans nationwide, but it also receives the general support of a solid majority of independents and more than half of Democrats.

Support for the Death Penalty, by Party ID

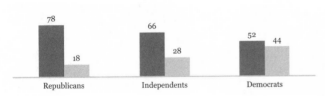

Oct. 3-5, 2008

In its preliminary report—the final report will be issued next month—the Maryland Commission on Capital Punishment cited evidence that the death penalty does not act as a deterrent to crime, and that it is racially biased in its application. Americans don't share the same view on at least one of these arguments. The slight majority of Americans in the Oct. 3-5, 2008, poll—54%—say they believe the death penalty is applied fairly in the country today—a rough indication that Americans don't perceive bias to be a major problem with the death penalty system.

On the other hand, previous Gallup research has found that most Americans believe the death penalty is not a deterrent to crime. According to a May 2006 Gallup Poll, only 34% said it was a deter-

rent, while 64% disagreed. Open-ended questions asked in previous years have shown that most Americans who favor the death penalty do so because they believe it provides an "eye for an eye" type of justice.

Long-Term Trend

Although the current 64% support for capital punishment is high, support is a bit lower than it has been at other times over the past decade, when 69% or 70% were in favor. Those readings, in turn, are lower than the ones from the 1980s and 1990s, when support averaged 75%. The highest individual measure of public support for the death penalty in Gallup's records is 80%, recorded 14 years ago in September 1994.

Death penalty support was substantially lower from the late 1950s through the early 1970s. As Gallup has previously reported, it appears that Supreme Court rulings on the death penalty in the 1970s may have sparked increased public support for the punishment, starting around 1976.

Are you in favor of the death penalty for a person convicted of murder?

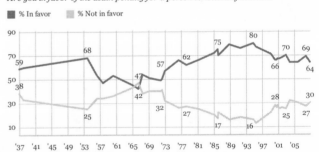

Death Penalty vs. Life in Prison

Over the years, Gallup has consistently found lower support for the death penalty when it is offered as an alternative to life imprisonment with no possibility of parole. Most recently, in May 2006, Gallup found 47% naming the death penalty as the better penalty for murder, versus 48% preferring life imprisonment.

Bottom Line

The majority of Americans continue to support the use of the death penalty as the punishment for murder. Most Americans (71%) also say the death penalty is used either about the right amount or not often enough.

While Americans generally agree that the death penalty is not a deterrent, and, as previous Gallup research has shown, widely acknowledge that some innocent people have been executed, most nevertheless support the death penalty as punishment for murder. The reason is very likely their concept of justice. According to a 2003 Gallup study, close to half of Americans who supported the death penalty cited some aspect of retribution for the crime as the reason.

Survey Methods

Results are based on telephone interviews with 1,011 national adults, aged 18 and older, conducted Oct. 3-5, 2008. For results based on the total sample of national adults, one can say with 95% confidence that the maximum margin of sampling error is ±3 percentage points.

Interviews are conducted with respondents on land-line telephones (for respondents with a land-line telephone) and cellular phones (for respondents who are cell-phone only).

In addition to sampling error, question wording and practical difficulties in conducting surveys can introduce error or bias into the findings of public opinion polls.

November 17, 2008

CONGRESS RETURNS TO MOSTLY DISAPPROVING CONSTITUENCY

Only 19% approve, slightly higher than all-time low of 14%

by Frank Newport, Gallup Poll Editor in Chief

As the 110th Congress returns for its final lame-duck session Monday, new Gallup polling shows that only 19% of Americans approve of the job Congress is doing, while about three-quarters disapprove.

Do you approve or disapprove of the way Congress is handling its job?

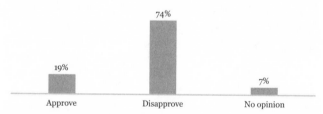

Gallup Poll, Nov. 13-16, 2008

The all-time low point for congressional job approval is 14%, measured in July of this year. Since that point, congressional job approval has "risen" to 18% in August, September, and October, and is now, as noted, at 19%.

After the 2006 midterm elections two years ago, congressional job approval was 26%. Previous low points for congressional job approval in Gallup's history have included a 19% reading in 1979 and an 18% reading in 1992. The highest Gallup Poll-measured congressional job-approval rating on record is 84%, measured in October 2001, a month after the Sept. 11 terrorist attacks.

Although Democrats currently control both houses of Congress and will have even stronger majority control after newly elected representatives and senators take their seats in January, there is little substantive difference in approval of Congress by partisan orientation at this time.

Republicans and independents give Congress identical 17% approval ratings, while Democrats are only slightly more positive, with a 22% approval rating.

Do you approve or disapprove of the way Congress is handling its job?

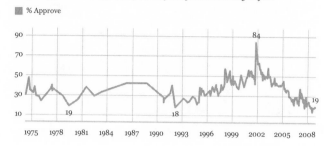

Do you approve or disapprove of the way Congress is handling its job?
By party ID

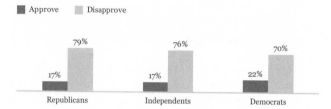

Gallup Poll, Nov. 13-16, 2008

Survey Methods

Results are based on telephone interviews with 1,009 national adults, aged 18 and older, conducted Nov. 13-16, 2008. For results based on the total sample of national adults, one can say with 95% confidence that the maximum margin of sampling error is ±3 percentage points.

Interviews are conducted with respondents on land-line telephones (for respondents with a land-line telephone) and cellular phones (for respondents who are cell-phone only).

In addition to sampling error, question wording and practical difficulties in conducting surveys can introduce error or bias into the findings of public opinion polls.

November 17, 2008

MAJORITY OF AMERICANS CUTTING BACK ON SPENDING

Including nearly two-thirds of families with children

by Lymari Morales, Gallup Poll Staff Writer

A majority of Americans (55%) are cutting back on household spending as a result of recent problems in the stock markets and the economy, with 30- to 49-year-olds and families with children among those feeling the pinch most strongly.

A *USA Today*/Gallup poll conducted Oct. 20 finds roughly two-thirds of Americans with children, whether married or not, say they are cutting back due to the country's economic problems. The same is true for Americans ages 30-49, who are at least 10 percentage points more likely than those in other age groups to say they are cutting back. Women are also more likely to be cutting back on spending than men, 61% to 48%, respectively.

The financial strain does not appear to be concentrated in certain parts of the country. In fact, Americans in all regions appear to

Have the recent problems in the stock markets and the economy caused you to cut back on household spending, or not?

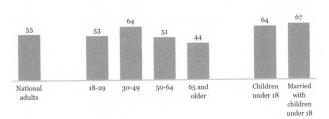

USA Today/Gallup Poll, Oct. 20, 2008

be cutting back at about equal rates: 52% in the Midwest, 55% in the East, and 56% in the South and West.

Examining the topic further, the poll asked Americans in which specific areas they were cutting back and found significant numbers of Americans saying they are cutting back on eating out at restaurants (44%), entertainment like movies and concerts (40%), and travel for the holidays (34%). Those numbers may not seem that high, but are noteworthy considering only 55% of Americans say they have cut back on spending at all. Among those who are cutting back, a large majority have made cuts in these areas.

Have the recent problems in the stock markets and the economy caused you to cut back on the following, or not?

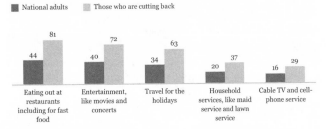

USA Today/Gallup Poll, Oct. 20, 2008

The findings could foretell tough times for the entertainment, hospitality, and travel sectors, as Americans cut back on more luxury spending to reserve more for basics. At the same time, it is important to note that the question did not ascertain if the respondent had previously spent or planned to spend in these areas, only if they were going to cut back on them. It is possible many Americans do not have household services such as maid or lawn service, or were not planning expensive holiday travel, thus explaining the relatively low percentages who say they are cutting back in these areas. Cable and cell phone service may be viewed as a utility for many Americans, who either already have just basic service in both areas, or for whom the possibility of cutting back is too daunting (and a proportion of Americans still do not have cable or cell phone service at all).

Christmas spending will, of course, provide a key measure of Americans' economic temperature. Overall, about the same percentage of Americans who, in this survey, said they are cutting back on household spending also say they will spend less than they had planned on Christmas gifts this year (56%), reinforcing the findings of a previous Gallup Poll, which pointed toward a tough holiday spending season ahead.

Survey Methods

Results are based on telephone interviews with 1,008 national adults, aged 18 and older, conducted Oct. 20, 2008. For results based on the total sample of national adults, one can say with 95% confidence that the maximum margin of sampling error is ±3 percentage points. For results based on the sample of 524 adults who are cutting back on spending as a result of the problems with the economy and stock market, the maximum margin of sampling error is ±5 percentage points.

Interviews are conducted with respondents on land-line telephones (for respondents with a land-line telephone) and cellular phones (for respondents who are cell-phone only).

In addition to sampling error, question wording and practical difficulties in conducting surveys can introduce error or bias into the findings of public opinion polls.

November 17, 2008
U.S. WORKERS CONTINUE TO SEE A DETERIORATING JOB MARKET
Hiring picture looking grimmer over last several months

by Frank Newport, Gallup Poll Editor in Chief

American workers continue to report a deteriorating job situation at the companies where they work, with Gallup's hiring measure for Nov. 14-16 showing that 26% of employees say their company is letting people go, 26% say that their company is hiring, and 43% say the hiring situation at their company has not changed.

Gallup Daily: U.S. Job Market
Each result is based on a three-day rolling average

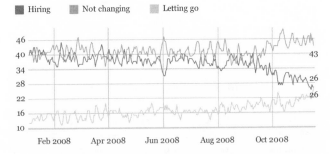

Gallup Poll Daily tracking (Jan. 2-Nov. 16, 2008)

Gallup's hiring measure asks a random sample of workers interviewed each day as part of the Gallup Poll Daily tracking program if their company is "hiring new people and expanding the size of its workforce", "not changing the size of its workforce", or "letting people go and reducing the size of its workforce". When the year began, 40% or more of workers routinely reported that their company was hiring; those saying their company was letting people go was routinely well under 20%. In recent months, however, the percent reporting that their company is hiring has fallen, with a gradual rise in the percent who say their company is letting people go.

There are day to day fluctuations in the Gallup Poll Daily tracking three-day rolling average reports of its hiring measure, and the

Nov. 14-16 average is not statistically different from previous days' reports. Still, the broad overall trend continues to be one in which the percentage of workers who say their company is letting people go is rising, while the percentage who say their company is hiring is declining. Today's results mark the first time this year that the percent "laying off" has been as high as the percent "hiring", providing further evidence about the degree to which the faltering economy is leading to workplace layoffs as companies attempt to adjust to today's economic realities.

Survey Methods

Results are based on telephone interviews with 891 national adults, aged 18 and older, conducted Nov. 14-16, 2008 as part of Gallup Poll Daily tracking. For results based on the total sample of national adults, one can say with 95% confidence that the maximum margin of sampling error is ±3 percentage points.

Interviews are conducted with respondents on land-line telephones (for respondents with a land-line telephone) and cellular phones (for respondents who are cell-phone only).

In addition to sampling error, question wording and practical difficulties in conducting surveys can introduce error or bias into the findings of public opinion polls.

November 18, 2008
AMERICANS DIVIDED ON AID TO BIG THREE AUTOMAKERS
Slim majority would favor aid if one or more U.S. auto companies were certain to fail

by Jeffrey M. Jones, Gallup Poll Managing Editor

The latest Gallup Poll suggests Americans are divided over the federal government's helping the "Big Three" U.S. auto companies stay afloat.

Would you favor or oppose the federal government giving major financial assistance to the Big Three U.S. automotive companies if they are close to going broke or declaring bankruptcy?

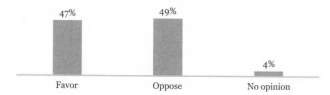

Gallup Poll, Nov. 13-16, 2008

Republicans and Democrats hold opposing views on the matter, with 60% of Democrats in favor of government assistance to the auto companies and 65% of Republicans opposed. Independents are more likely to oppose than to favor government assistance.

The vast majority of those who oppose government help for the auto companies—79% (equivalent to 39% of all Americans)—say in a follow-up question that they would be opposed to the aid even if one or more of the Big Three were certain to fail without it. But

Favor/Oppose Federal Government Assistance to U.S. Auto Companies, by Party Affiliation

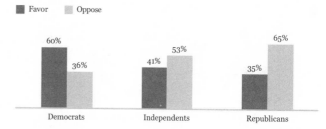

Gallup Poll, Nov. 13-16, 2008

18% (9% of all Americans) would favor assistance under those circumstances, bringing overall support for government aid to the majority level (56%)—assuming government assistance is the difference between the companies' surviving or going under.

Would you favor or oppose the federal government giving major financial assistance to the Big Three U.S. automotive companies if they are close to going broke or declaring bankruptcy?

(If opposed): Suppose one or more of the three major U.S. automotive companies was certain to fail unless the government provided assistance. In that case, would you favor or oppose the federal government providing assistance to the major U.S. automotive companies?

	National adults	Oppose assistance on initial question
Favor	47%	--
Oppose, but favor if one or more certain to fail	9%	18%
Oppose even if one or more certain to fail	39%	79%
No opinion	5%	2%

Gallup Poll, Nov. 13-16, 2008

Most key demographic and attitudinal subgroups show majority-level support for government assistance to spare one or more of the auto companies from certain demise, with between 50% and 60% of most groups in favor. Republicans (42%) and self-described conservatives (46%) are the two most notable groups that oppose government assistance even if that meant reducing the "Big Three" by one or more.

The poll was conducted in a political environment in which the government has already taken extraordinary steps to regulate economic activity. Most notably, Congress passed and President Bush signed legislation pledging up to $700 billion earlier this fall to help ease the credit crisis that was putting large U.S. financial institutions in peril. At the time, the public was hardly enthusiastic in its support for this measure, with 50% saying it was a good thing and 41% a bad thing. Now, that support has eroded slightly, with those describing the $700 billion "rescue bill" as a good thing (47%) barely outnumbering those who say it was a bad thing (45%).

So far, the Bush administration has resisted attempts to use some of that $700 billion to help the U.S. automotive companies. Congressional leaders are still trying to persuade the White House to change its mind, but Congress is also moving forward with plans to consider legislation this week to bring it up as a separate measure, though it is far from certain to pass.

Survey Methods

Results are based on telephone interviews with 1,009 national adults, aged 18 and older, conducted Nov. 13-16, 2008. For results based on

Views of Government Legislation to Provide up to $700 Billion to Address Problems Faced by U.S. Financial Institutions

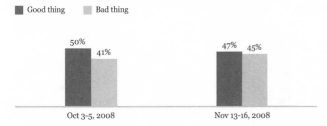

Oct 3-5, 2008 — Good thing 50%, Bad thing 41%
Nov 13-16, 2008 — Good thing 47%, Bad thing 45%

the total sample of national adults, one can say with 95% confidence that the maximum margin of sampling error is ±3 percentage points.

Interviews are conducted with respondents on land-line telephones (for respondents with a land-line telephone) and cellular phones (for respondents who are cell-phone only).

In addition to sampling error, question wording and practical difficulties in conducting surveys can introduce error or bias into the findings of public opinion polls.

November 18, 2008

MOST AMERICANS CLOSELY WATCHING OBAMA'S TRANSITION

Though not as many as followed the presidential election

by Lymari Morale, Gallup Poll Staff Writer

While Americans are not currently as engrossed in national politics as they were in the months and weeks leading up to the U.S. presidential election, 83% say they are following the news of Barack Obama's presidential transition at least somewhat closely. Nearly half (48%) of Americans are following the transition "very closely," compared to 68% who say they followed the election as intensely.

How closely did you follow the news about the 2008 presidential election in the months and weeks leading up to it?

How closely are you following the news about Barack Obama's presidential transition leading up to his inauguration on January 20th?

2008 presidential election   Barack Obama's presidential transition

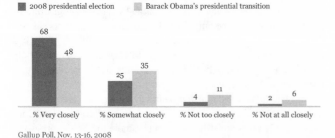

% Very closely — 68, 48
% Somewhat closely — 25, 35
% Not too closely — 4, 11
% Not at all closely — 2, 6

Gallup Poll, Nov. 13-16, 2008

Since the U.S. presidential election two weeks ago, nonstop election coverage has evolved into a nonstop presidential transition watch, with media outlets covering the president-elect's every move and constantly speculating about every possible staff and cabinet appointment. President-elect Obama has maintained a fairly low profile outside of his Nov. 7 press conference on the economy, his Nov.

10 visit to the White House, and an interview last Sunday night on "60 Minutes." The Nov. 13-16 Gallup Poll was conducted amid rampant speculation about Obama's possible appointment of former Democratic rival Hillary Clinton as his secretary of state and before his meeting with former Republican rival John McCain.

Not surprisingly, Democrats are more likely than Republicans to say they are paying very close attention to the presidential transition, 60% to 41%. Democrats are also more likely to say they paid very close attention to the election, reinforcing prior Gallup findings showing that Democrats were generally much more enthusiastic than Republicans about this year's election. Both groups have lost interest in the nation's leading domestic political story at roughly the same rate.

How closely did you follow the news about the 2008 presidential election in the months and weeks leading up to it?

How closely are you following the news about Barack Obama's presidential transition leading up to his inauguration on January 20th?

% Very closely

2008 presidential election   Barack Obama's presidential transition

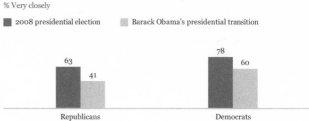

Republicans — 63, 41
Democrats — 78, 60

Gallup Poll, Nov. 13-16, 2008

Not since Bill Clinton's victory in 1992 have Americans had the opportunity to witness a presidential transition that extended from Election Day to Inauguration Day, as George W. Bush's 2000 transition was delayed for weeks by the Florida recount battle. Gallup is tracking daily President-elect Obama's favorability rating, as well as Americans' confidence in his ability to be a good president, as key measures that can gauge rapid public reaction to the decisions he makes during this critical transition time.

Survey Methods

Results are based on telephone interviews with 1,009 national adults, aged 18 and older, conducted Nov. 13-16, 2008. For results based on the total sample of national adults, one can say with 95% confidence that the maximum margin of sampling error is ±3 percentage points.

Interviews are conducted with respondents on land-line telephones (for respondents with a land-line telephone) and cellular phones (for respondents who are cell-phone only).

In addition to sampling error, question wording and practical difficulties in conducting surveys can introduce error or bias into the findings of public opinion polls.

November 19, 2008
CHRISTMAS SPENDING PROJECTION DROPS TO NEW LOW
Projected shopping at department stores takes biggest hit

by Frank Newport, Gallup Poll Editor in Chief

Americans' projected average Christmas spending this year, $616, is the lowest in Gallup's 10-year history of tracking this question in its current format, and provides further evidence of the heavy toll the current economic turmoil is taking on America's retailers.

Roughly how much money do you think you personally will spend on Christmas gifts this year?

Mean (with zero)

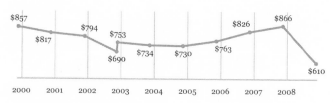

Gallup Poll Social Series Polls

Last year, at approximately this same time in November, Americans' average Christmas spending estimate was $866. The previous low point of the last 10 years came in November 2002 (the year of one of the worst holiday retail seasons in over a decade), when the estimate was $690.

Asked directly whether the amount they plan on spending on Christmas gifts this year is more than, less than, or the same as last Christmas, 46% of Americans say "less," the highest response in this negative category in almost two decades of asking this question.

Roughly how much money do you think you personally will spend on Christmas gifts this year?

Is that more, less, or about the same amount as you spent last Christmas?

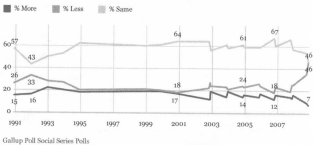

Gallup Poll Social Series Polls

Over the years, Americans have typically said they were going to spend the same amount on gifts as they did the previous year. But the 46% saying this today is low by historical standards, and is only the second time this measure has dropped below 50% in Gallup history.

Bottom Line

The drop in anticipated Christmas shopping this year comes as no surprise, given the grim reality of so much other negative consumer economic data Gallup has been measuring. According to Gallup Poll Daily tracking, 60% of Americans now rate the U.S. economy as "poor" and more than 8 out of 10 say it's getting worse, while perceptions of the job market are at an all-time Gallup low.

Still, this latest update of Gallup's venerable Christmas shopping trends reinforces just how vulnerable America's retailers may be this season as consumers pull way back on spending in the face of continuing economic turmoil.

Survey Methods

Results are based on telephone interviews with 1,009 national adults, aged 18 and older, conducted Nov. 13-16, 2008. For results based on the total sample of national adults, one can say with 95% confidence that the maximum margin of sampling error is ±3 percentage points.

Interviews are conducted with respondents on land-line telephones (for respondents with a land-line telephone) and cellular phones (for respondents who are cell-phone only).

In addition to sampling error, question wording and practical difficulties in conducting surveys can introduce error or bias into the findings of public opinion polls.

November 19, 2008
MOST AMERICANS BACK IDEA OF CLINTON AS SECRETARY OF STATE
Nearly 8 in 10 Democrats favor the possibility

by Jeffrey M. Jones, Gallup Poll Managing Editor

A new Gallup Poll finds a majority of Americans (57%) in favor of Barack Obama appointing Hillary Clinton as the secretary of state in his administration. Thirty percent oppose it.

Do you favor or oppose President-elect Barack Obama appointing Senator Hillary Clinton as his secretary of state?

Nov. 18, 2008

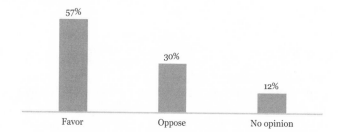

The poll, conducted Nov. 18, was taken as the political world buzzed with the possibility that Obama will bring his chief rival for the Democratic presidential nomination into his cabinet in a high-profile role. As secretary of state, Clinton would be the top U.S. official for conducting foreign policy.

Democrats strongly endorse the idea of Obama making this move, with 79% in favor of it. Most Republicans, not surprisingly, oppose the idea, while a majority of independents (57%) favor it.

Clinton would become the third woman to serve as secretary of state, following Madeleine Albright in Bill Clinton's administration and Condoleezza Rice in George W. Bush's administration. While Hillary Clinton has consistently demonstrated a strong appeal to women as first lady and as a presidential candidate, men (56%) and women (58%) are about equally likely to favor her becoming the next secretary of state.

Favor or oppose Barack Obama appointing Hillary Clinton as secretary of state, by party affiliation

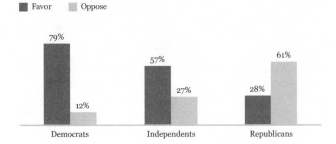

Clinton's appointment as the secretary of state is by no means certain as of now. In addition to news reports that the Obama transition team is still exploring what possible conflicts or problems former President Clinton's international business dealings might pose, it is unclear if Clinton would want to leave the U.S. Senate to serve the Obama administration. Nevertheless, these data do indicate the public would likely react favorably toward her appointment as secretary of state.

Survey Methods

Results are based on telephone interviews with 1,013 national adults, aged 18 and older, conducted Nov. 18, 2008. For results based on the total sample of national adults, one can say with 95% confidence that the maximum margin of sampling error is ±3 percentage points.

Interviews are conducted with respondents on land-line telephones (for respondents with a land-line telephone) and cellular phones (for respondents who are cell-phone only).

In addition to sampling error, question wording and practical difficulties in conducting surveys can introduce error or bias into the findings of public opinion polls.

Polls conducted entirely in one day, such as this one, are subject to additional error or bias not found in polls conducted over several days.

November 20, 2008
GOP TAKES ANOTHER IMAGE HIT POST-ELECTION
Republicans favor tacking right; independents offer mixed guidance

by Lydia Saad, Gallup Poll Senior Editor

The Republican Party's image has gone from bad to worse over the past month, as only 34% of Americans in a Nov. 13-16 Gallup Poll say they have a favorable view of the party, down from 40% in mid-October. The 61% now holding an unfavorable view of the GOP is the highest Gallup has recorded for that party since the measure was established in 1992.

By contrast, the public's views of the Democratic Party remain as positive after the election as they were just prior to it. More than half of Americans, 55%, currently hold a favorable view of the Democratic Party and only 39% an unfavorable view, highly typical of views toward the Democrats all year.

The Republican Party's image deficit began well before 2008. In December 2005, the Republicans and the Democrats were rated

Next, please tell me whether you have a favorable or unfavorable opinion of each of the following parties. How about ... The Republican Party?
2008 trend

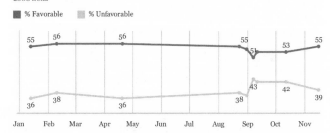

Next, please tell me whether you have a favorable or unfavorable opinion of each of the following parties. How about ... The Democratic Party?
2008 trend

about equally, with just under half of Americans viewing each party favorably. Shortly thereafter, the Republicans' favorable rating fell to 36%, and has since struggled to cross the 40% threshold. The Democrats' favorable rating gradually improved during 2006, and has not fallen below 51% since the spring of that year.

Favorable Ratings of the Two Major Political Parties -- January 2000-November 2008
% Having a favorable view of each party

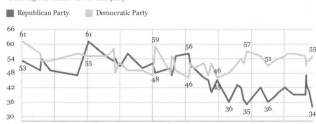

The Republican Party is notably less well reviewed by members of its own party than the Democratic Party is by its own: 78% of Republicans have a favorable view of the GOP, versus 91% of Democrats viewing their own party favorably. Fewer political independents rate the Republican Party (32%) than rate the Democratic Party (47%) favorably.

Where to Go From Here?

The Republican Party heads into the New Year with its brand tattered by the election after decisive losses in the 2008 presidential and congressional races. Such a defeat inevitably leads to introspection in party circles about its message going forward.

Gallup addressed this issue in the recent poll with a question asking, "Over the next few years, would you like to see the Republican Party and its candidates move in a more conservative direction, a less conservative direction, or stay about the same?"

Nov. 13-16, 2008

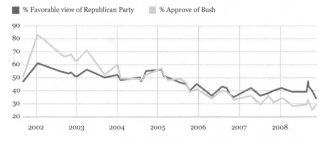

Most rank-and-file Republicans (59%) want to see the party move in a more conservative direction and another 28% want it to remain about the same. Only 12% would prefer to see the Republican Party become less conservative.

Neither party can win the presidency or majority power in Congress without attracting substantial support from political independents. But right now, independents are not offering any clear guidance about what they want from Republicans. About a third say the party should become more conservative, an equal percentage say it should become less conservative, and just under one-quarter say it should stay the same.

Democrats—whose views about the Republican Party are far less relevant to its future—are most likely to favor its moving in a less conservative direction.

Over the next few years, would you like to see the Republican Party and its candidates move in a more conservative direction, a less conservative direction, or stay about the same?

	More conservative	Less conservative	Stay about the same	No opinion
	%	%	%	%
National adults	37	37	20	6
Republicans	59	12	28	1
Independents	35	35	22	8
Democrats	25	56	13	6

Nov. 13-16, 2008

Bottom Line

The Democratic Party is enjoying an extended stretch of popularity with Americans that started in 2006, and is likely to continue as long as its new party leader, President-elect Barack Obama, continues to inspire high confidence ratings—and eventually job approval ratings—from the American people.

After suffering major blows in the election, the Republican Party is experiencing its worst image rating in at least a decade (similar to the public relations hit it took after the Republican-controlled House of Representatives impeached Bill Clinton in December 1998). Previous Gallup analysis linked the party's decline to the downward track of President George W. Bush's job approval ratings in 2005 and 2006. However, the latest drop in the Republican Party's favorable rating, from 40% to 34% (with much of that drop coming from Republicans), is not associated with a corresponding decline in Bush's job approval score; rather, it most likely reflects Americans' reaction to the Republicans' big losses on Election Day.

With Bush no longer around to symbolize the Republican Party, the GOP will soon have an opportunity to redefine itself. The initial guidance from rank-and-file Republicans is to tack to the right—

returning to core Republican principles, as many Republican thought leaders are currently advocating. However, with only about a third of independents wanting the party to be more conservative, it is unclear how much that approach might help to expand the Republican base.

Survey Methods

Results are based on telephone interviews with 1,009 national adults, aged 18 and older, conducted Nov. 13-16, 2008. For results based on the total sample of national adults, one can say with 95% confidence that the maximum margin of sampling error is ±3 percentage points.

Interviews are conducted with respondents on land-line telephones (for respondents with a land-line telephone) and cellular phones (for respondents who are cell-phone only).

In addition to sampling error, question wording and practical difficulties in conducting surveys can introduce error or bias into the findings of public opinion polls.

November 20, 2008
POST-ELECTION UPTICK IN CONSUMER CONFIDENCE SHORT-LIVED
Consumers were getting more pessimistic even before the current stock market plunge

by Dennis Jacobe, Gallup Poll Chief Economist

Consumer confidence, after improving slightly in late October and early November, has now returned to its mid-October level. The percentage of consumers rating current economic conditions "poor" reached a weekly high of 60% during the week ending Oct. 12; this highly negative sentiment moderated in the 55% range over the next four weeks, culminating in election week. However, consumer assessments of the economy deteriorated significantly once again last week, with 61% rating the economy poor—a new weekly high.

More Americans Rating Economy "Poor"

Immediately after the presidential election, it seemed as though plunging gas prices and stabilizing credit markets were combining with something of a President-elect Barack Obama "halo effect" to suggest consumer confidence was improving—at least on the margin. However, even as pump prices have continued to decline, it seems the positive impact of Obama's victory has been short-lived at best. The percentage of Americans rating the economy "poor" last week ranged from 57% in the Midwest to 65% in the East.

Percentage of Consumers Rating Current Economic Conditions "Poor"

Weekly trend

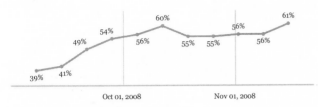

Percentage of Consumers Rating Economy Poor, by Region

Week of Nov. 10-16, 2008

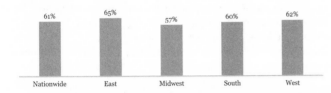

More Americans Saying Economy Is "Getting Worse"

The percentage of consumers saying the economy is "getting worse" peaked in mid-October at 88%, and seemed to be gaining positive momentum during the week of President-elect Obama's election victory as it hit 75%. However, it has since reversed course once more, rising to 80% last week. Essentially 8 in 10 Americans in each region of the country told Gallup last week that economic conditions are getting worse, rather than better.

Percentage of Consumers Saying Economy Is Getting Worse

Weekly trend

Percentage of Consumers Saying Economy Is Getting Worse, by Region

Week of Nov. 10-16, 2008

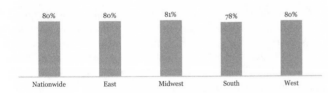

Survey Methods

Gallup is interviewing no fewer than 1,000 U.S. adults nationwide each day during 2008. The economic questions analyzed in this report are asked of a random half-sample of respondents each day. The results reported here are based on combined weekly data from 3,543 interviews, conducted Nov. 10-16, 2008. For results based on this sample, the maximum margin of sampling error is ±2 percentage points.

Interviews are conducted with respondents on land-line telephones (for respondents with a land-line telephone) and cellular phones (for respondents who are cell-phone only).

In addition to sampling error, question wording and practical difficulties in conducting surveys can introduce error or bias into the findings of public opinion polls.

November 21, 2008
GOP FAITHFUL LIKE PALIN, ROMNEY, HUCKABEE IN 2012
Palin leading contender among conservative Republicans

by Jeffrey M. Jones, Gallup Poll Managing Editor

Republicans and Republican-leaning independents are most interested in seeing Sarah Palin, Mitt Romney, and Mike Huckabee run for the party's presidential nomination in 2012. Those three received the highest scores among the 10 possible candidates evaluated in a recent Gallup Panel survey.

Now, thinking ahead to the 2012 presidential election, please say whether you would or would not like to see each of the following Republicans run for president in 2012.

Based on Republicans/Republican leaners

	Would like to see run	Would not like to see run	No opinion
	%	%	%
Sarah Palin	67	30	3
Mitt Romney	62	32	5
Mike Huckabee	61	33	6
David Petraeus	49	39	12
Rudy Giuliani	48	47	5
Newt Gingrich	47	48	5
Bobby Jindal	34	36	30
Jeb Bush	31	61	9
Charlie Crist	23	46	31
Lindsey Graham	21	53	25

Nov. 5-16 Gallup Panel survey

The Nov. 5-16 survey asked a nationally representative sample of Gallup panelists who identify themselves as Republicans or are political independents but "lean" to the Republican Party to say whether they "would or would not like to see" each of 10 Republicans "run for president in 2012."

Palin, Romney, and Huckabee—all of whom raised their national profiles during the 2008 campaign—top the list. Romney and Huckabee unsuccessfully sought the presidential nomination versus John McCain, and McCain tapped Palin as his vice-presidential running mate.

But not all 2008 GOP national candidates rated as highly in the survey. Republicans are evenly divided as to whether Rudy Giuliani should make another attempt at the White House. Giuliani was the early front-runner for the 2008 nomination, but performed poorly in the early primaries and caucuses before dropping out of the race.

The only other person evaluated who received a more positive than negative review is Gen. David Petraeus, head of the United States Central Command. It is unclear whether Petraeus would enter politics, but his growing acclaim owing to U.S. progress in Iraq could make him somewhat of a "dream" candidate for the GOP, similar to ruminations about Gen. Dwight Eisenhower in 1952 (who ran) and Gen. Colin Powell in 1996 (who did not).

Republicans are also evenly divided on potential candidacies from former Speaker of the House Newt Gingrich and Louisiana Gov. Bobby Jindal. Of the two, Gingrich is much better known, but the young governor was considered a potential McCain running mate and is thought to be a serious contender for national office in the future.

Republicans are decidedly unenthusiastic about possible White House bids from former Florida Gov. Jeb Bush, current Florida Gov. Charlie Crist, and South Carolina Sen. Lindsey Graham. Bush's prospects are obviously hurt by the dissatisfaction with his older brother's White House term and perhaps a lack of enthusiasm for a third member of the Bush family as president.

Crist and Graham were key McCain supporters early in the primaries, and helped him to critical primary wins in their home states. But the GOP rank-and-file apparently does not want these McCain loyalists to become presidential candidates themselves. It is unclear whether this has anything to do with their affiliation with McCain, although it should be pointed out that Republicans still regarded McCain quite positively after his election defeat.

Survey Methods

Results for this Gallup Panel study are based on telephone interviews with 799 Republicans and Republican-leaning independents, aged 18 and older, conducted Nov. 5-16, 2008. The survey was the post-election phase of a pre-/post-election survey of approximately 2,000 Gallup Panel members.

Gallup Panel members are recruited through random selection methods. The panel is weighted so that it is demographically representative of the U.S. adult population. For results based on this sample, one can say with 95% confidence that the maximum margin of sampling error is ±4 percentage points.

In addition to sampling error, question wording and practical difficulties in conducting surveys can introduce error or bias into the findings of public opinion polls.

November 24, 2008
NURSES SHINE, BANKERS SLUMP IN ETHICS RATINGS
Annual Honesty and Ethics poll rates nurses best of 21 professions

by Lydia Saad, Gallup Poll Senior Editor

For the seventh straight year, nurses enjoy top public accolades in Gallup's annual Honesty and Ethics of professions survey. Eighty-four percent of Americans call their honesty and ethical standards either "high" or "very high."

This year's results are based on a Nov. 7-9 *USA Today*/Gallup poll rating the honesty and ethics of workers in 21 different professions.

Nurses have topped Gallup's Honesty and Ethics ranking every year but one since they were added to the list in 1999. The exception is 2001, when firefighters were included on the list on a one-time basis, shortly after the Sept. 11 terrorist attacks. (Firefighters earned a record-high 90% honesty and ethics rating in that survey.)

Please tell me how you would rate the honesty and ethical standards of people in these different fields -- very high, high, average, low, or very low. How about ... Nurses?

Nov. 7-9, 2008
* Less than 0.5% gave this response

Bankers Take a Hit

The standing of most of the professions surveyed in 2008 is similar to that of a year ago. The only significant change is a 12 percentage-point decline in positive ratings for bankers, from 35% to 23%—not surprising given that the banking industry is at the center of the Wall Street meltdown currently gutting many Americans' investment accounts and destabilizing the U.S. economy. (Earlier this year, Gallup reported a similar decline in public confidence in banking as an institution.)

The 2008 Gallup Honesty and Ethics poll marks the first time since 1996 that the honesty and ethics of bankers has registered below 30%. The last time bankers took a hit of similar magnitude to their image was in 1988, when it fell from 38% to 26% during the savings and loan crisis. However, the 23% recorded today marks a record low for the field.

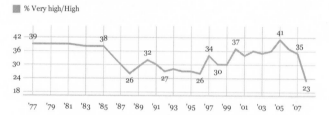

Honesty and Ethics of Bankers -- 1977-2008

% Very high/High

2008 Integrity Rankings

Nurses have no peer in the Gallup rankings today, but they are followed by pharmacists, high-school teachers, and medical doctors, all with close to two-thirds of Americans rating them highly. Just over half of Americans consider the honesty and ethics of clergy members and the police high or very high.

While fewer than half of Americans consider funeral directors or accountants to be highly ethical, these professions are much more likely to be viewed positively than negatively.

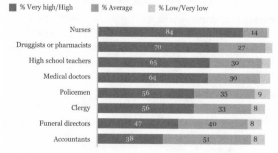

Top-Rated Professions for Honesty and Ethics -- 2008

% Very high/High   % Average   % Low/Very low

Nov. 7-9, 2008

Building contractors, bankers, journalists, and real estate agents each receive relatively neutral ratings. About as many Americans think each of these professions has low honesty and ethics as rate them highly, while the plurality or majority consider these professions of "average" integrity.

Neutrally Rated Professions for Honesty and Ethics -- 2008

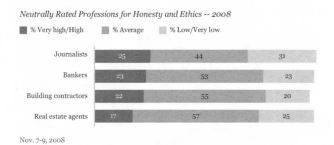

Nov. 7-9, 2008

While bankers could be faring much worse, a year ago they were in the top-rated category, with 35% rating their ethics high or very high and only 15% rating them low or very low.

Indeed, several professions suffer from a heavily negative tilt in their image ratings. The worst of these are lobbyists, telemarketers, and car salesmen, all of which are considered to have low or very low honesty and ethics by a majority of Americans.

Although several other professions—congressmen, stockbrokers, advertising practitioners, business executives, lawyers, and labor union leaders—are not as negatively viewed as the bottom three, the ratings for them skew negative by more than a 2-to-1 ratio. The 12% very high/high honesty and ethics ratings for business executives, although not appreciably different from the 14% recorded in 2007, is a record low for that profession. It had registered as high as 25% in 1990 and 2001.

Least Well-Rated Professions for Honesty and Ethics -- 2008

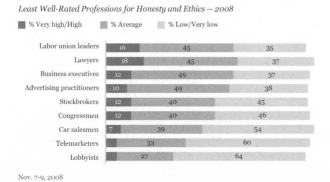

Nov. 7-9, 2008

Survey Methods

Results are based on telephone interviews with 1,010 national adults, aged 18 and older, conducted Nov. 7-9, 2008. For results based on the total sample of national adults, one can say with 95% confidence that the maximum margin of sampling error is ±3 percentage points.

Interviews are conducted with respondents on land-line telephones (for respondents with a land-line telephone) and cellular phones (for respondents who are cell-phone only).

In addition to sampling error, question wording and practical difficulties in conducting surveys can introduce error or bias into the findings of public opinion polls.

November 24, 2008
ONLY 12% BELIEVE NOW IS A GOOD TIME TO FIND A QUALITY JOB
Job-market evaluations worst in seven years

by Jeffrey M. Jones, Gallup Poll Managing Editor

A recent Gallup Poll found just 12% of Americans saying now is "a good time to find a quality job." This continues a steady deterioration of job market perceptions over the past two years.

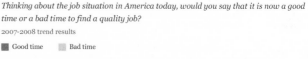

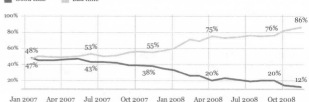

In fact, Americans' current evaluations of the job market are the worst Gallup has found since it began measuring this on a monthly basis in 2001. Prior to this year, the low point for ratings of the job market came in March 2003, just before the war with Iraq began, when just 16% of Americans said it was a good time to find a quality job.

The latest figures are based on a Nov. 13-16 Gallup Poll, which was conducted before new weekly unemployment claims hit a 16-year high. But Americans' opinions about the job market have been souring for quite some time. In the early months of 2007, Americans were about as likely to say it was a good time to find a quality job as to say it was a bad time. But by the summer of 2007—when Americans were beginning to feel the effects of rising gas prices and concerns about the housing market were growing—perceptions of the job market had begun to worsen.

In January and February of this year, concerns about a recession prompted the Bush administration and Congress to pass an economic stimulus package, and from January to February, the percentage of Americans describing the job market in positive terms fell from 33% to 26%. Gallup saw another notable drop this fall on the heels of the financial crisis that led to the government's $700 billion rescue bill.

Implications

Americans' perceptions of the job market and the overall economy are overwhelmingly gloomy and are among the worst Gallup has measured since it began measuring consumer economic perceptions on a regular basis in the early 1990s. This dour economic mood will almost certainly lead to a dismal holiday shopping season for retailers, and the lack of consumer confidence has no doubt been one major factor in President-elect Barack Obama's decision to act swiftly to pass an economic stimulus package once he takes office in January.

Survey Methods

Results are based on telephone interviews with 1,009 national adults, aged 18 and older, conducted Nov. 13-16, 2008. For results based on the total sample of national adults, one can say with 95% confidence that the maximum margin of sampling error is ±3 percentage points.

Interviews are conducted with respondents on land-line telephones (for respondents with a land-line telephone) and cellular phones (for respondents who are cell-phone only).

In addition to sampling error, question wording and practical difficulties in conducting surveys can introduce error or bias into the findings of public opinion polls.

November 25, 2008
AMERICANS REMAIN CONFIDENT IN OBAMA AS PRESIDENT
Roughly two-thirds say they are confident in Obama's ability to be a good president

by Frank Newport, Gallup Poll Editor in Chief

Between 63% and 67% of Americans have said they are confident in Barack Obama's ability to be a good president in the weeks since his election on Nov. 4, a sentiment that doesn't yet appear to have been affected, positively or negatively, by news coverage of the president-elect's staff and Cabinet appointments, or by reports of his economic and other policy plans.

Are you confident or not confident in Barack Obama's ability to be a good president?

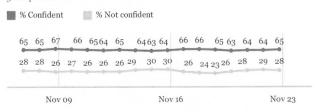

Gallup Poll Daily tracking

Gallup Poll Daily tracking has included the basic question, "Are you confident or not confident in Barack Obama's ability to be a good president?" every day since Nov. 5. The results have been remarkably consistent, as seen in the accompanying graph. Almost two-thirds of Americans have said they are confident in his ability to be president, with only minor day-to-day fluctuations, since Nov. 5.

The days since Obama's election have been filled with news reports of projected and actual staff choices, Cabinet member appointments, and his planned economic stimulus proposal, as well as his weekly radio addresses. Some of the news reports, including the probability that he will appoint former rival Hillary Clinton as secretary of state, have the potential to be controversial. Still, nothing Obama has done so far appears to have changed the basic—and generally positive—structure of American public opinion about his coming presidency.

Notably, the percentage of Americans who are confident in his ability to be a good president substantially exceeds his share of the vote (53%) in the November election.

As would be expected, there are highly significant differences in views on Obama's abilities among Republicans, independents, and Democrats.

Are you confident or not confident in Barack Obama's ability to be a good president?
By political party

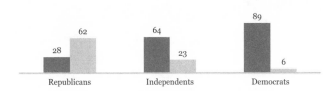

Gallup Poll Daily tracking, Nov. 17-23, 2008

Across seven days of interviewing last week (Nov. 17-23), 89% of Democrats said they were confident in Obama's ability to be a good president, along with 64% of independents and a much smaller 28% of Republicans. Given that an estimated 7% of Republicans and 51% of independents voted for Obama in the election, these numbers suggest that at least for the moment, a number of Americans who did not vote for Obama have given him the benefit of the doubt.

While partisan differences are by far the most important factor in predicting confidence in Obama, there are significant differences by age even while controlling for party. Americans between 18 and 34 express the most widespread confidence in Obama within the ranks of both Republicans and independents. There are only slight differences by age among Democrats.

Are you confident or not confident in Barack Obama's ability to be a good president?
% Confident by political party and age

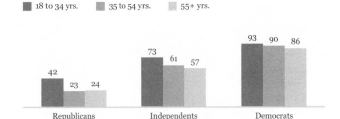

Gallup Poll Daily tracking, Nov. 17-23, 2008

The data show little variation in views of Obama according to gender or whether respondents have a college education.

Are you confident or not confident in Barack Obama's ability to be a good president?
% Confident by political party and gender

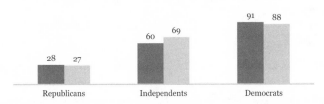

Gallup Poll Daily tracking, Nov. 17-23, 2008

Are you confident or not confident in Barack Obama's ability to be a good president?

% Confident by political party and education

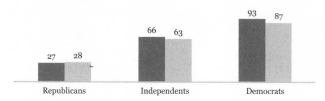

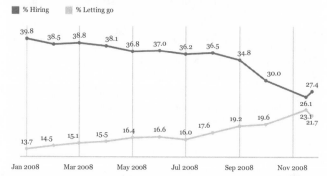

Gallup Poll Daily tracking, Nov. 17-23, 2008

Implications

Obama has apparently been given a honeymoon of sorts after his election, with a substantial majority of Americans (significantly higher than the percentage who voted for him) saying they are confident in his ability to be a good president. This positive sentiment has persisted to date even as reports of possible and actual Obama appointments have dominated news coverage of the nascent Obama administration.

Obama's challenge will be to continue this good will for the roughly two months left before his inauguration, and then to translate it into public support as he begins his duties as chief executive next Jan. 20. Gallup will continue to track and report Americans' views of their newly elected president between now and then.

Survey Methods

Gallup is interviewing no fewer than 1,000 U.S. adults nationwide each day during 2008. The trend results reported here are based on data collected between Nov. 5 and Nov. 23, and the analysis within subgroups based on combined weekly data from 3,559 interviews, conducted Nov. 17-23, 2008. For results based on the tracking samples, the maximum margin of sampling error is ±3 percentage points, while the results for the weekly aggregate have a maximum margin of sampling error of ±2 percentage points.

Interviews are conducted with respondents on land-line telephones (for respondents with a land-line telephone) and cellular phones (for respondents who are cell-phone only).

In addition to sampling error, question wording and practical difficulties in conducting surveys can introduce error or bias into the findings of public opinion polls.

November 25, 2008
HIRING MEASURE PROJECTS SLIGHTLY LOWER JOBLESS CLAIMS
Still, seasonally adjusted unemployment claims continued to surge last week

by Dennis Jacobe, Gallup Poll Chief Economist

U.S. employees' perceptions of the job situation at their companies got a little less grim as Gallup's Net New Hiring measure improved a little last week. Since Gallup's measure is inversely related to job-

less claims, this suggests better than 7-in-10 odds that Wednesday's Labor Department report of first-time jobless benefits claims for the week ending Nov. 22 increased less than the 542,000 reported last week, and probably less than the 537,000 consensus estimate.

Hiring and Letting Go

On Monday, President-elect Barack Obama warned that the United States faces the loss of millions of jobs next year. Gallup's hiring measure tends to confirm these expectations: the percentage of employees reporting their companies are letting people go increased from 19.6% in October to 21.7% in the week ending Nov. 23, while the percentage reporting that their companies are hiring decreased from 30% to 27.4%. The results for last week are slightly less gruesome than those for the week before, with net new hiring (the percentage hiring minus the percentage letting go) improving from 3.0 in the week ending Nov. 16 to 5.7 in the week ending Nov. 23—explaining the projection of slightly lower weekly jobless claims.

Percentage of Employers Expanding and Reducing Their Workforces, Nationwide

Anticipating Jobless Claims

Gallup's hiring measure is based on aggregated interviews with a nationally representative sample of more than 2,000 U.S. workers each week. Gallup asks current full- and part-time employees whether their employers are hiring new people and expanding the size of their workforces, not changing the size of their workforces, or letting people go and reducing the size of their workforces. Gallup's hiring measure is computed by subtracting the "letting go and reducing" percentage from the "hiring and expanding" percentage. The assumption is that employees across the country have a good feel for what's happening in their companies, and that these insider perceptions can yield a meaningful indication of the nation's job situation.

Using weekly results for 2008, Gallup's analysis suggests that its hiring measure has a better than 7-in-10 probability of correctly projecting the direction of weekly jobless claims. While a number of variables make it hard to predict the exact number of new unemployment claims the Labor Department will report on Wednesday morning, Gallup figures suggest jobless claims will be less than the 542,000 reported last week. At the same time, the seasonally adjusted four-week average of Gallup's hiring measure continued to decrease last week, suggesting an 8-in-10 probability that seasonally adjusted four-week average jobless claims continued to increase.

Surging Unemployment

The fallout from the way the U.S. economy hit a wall in mid-September is being transmitted to Main Street with amazing speed. In this regard, unemployment measures that have always been thought of as trailing measures of economic activity—simply confirming the strengthening or weakening of the U.S. economy—may now be morphing into leading indicators. In turn, this suggests that the overall level of economic activity is likely to continue to fall at a precipitous pace over the weeks ahead.

This week, in likely recognition of how fast the Main Street economy is deteriorating, President-elect Obama and his economic team seemed to step into the economic leadership vacuum that has been plaguing the markets. In response, global equity markets surged. And, in another positive sign, Treasury Secretary Paulson and Federal Reserve Board Chairman Bernanke announced new programs to help stimulate consumer credit.

Gallup's economic data suggest that all of these efforts most likely are going to be too late to save the Christmas sales season. They are also unlikely to prevent a surge in job losses in the months ahead. However, aggressive actions by the Congress and current/future economic policy-makers may be able to begin the process of rebuilding public confidence in the U.S. economy and its future direction. Gallup's Daily economic tracking will provide a continuous monitoring of the success of any such efforts.

Survey Methods

Gallup's Net New Hiring Activity measure was initiated in January 2008. It is an effort to assess U.S. job creation or elimination based on the self-reports of more than 2,000 individual employees aggregated each week about hiring and firing activity at their workplaces.

For results based on these samples, the maximum margin of sampling error is ±3 percentage points.

Interviews are conducted with respondents on land-line telephones (for respondents with a land-line telephone) and cellular phones (for respondents who are cell-phone only).

In addition to sampling error, question wording and practical difficulties in conducting surveys can introduce error or bias into the findings of public opinion polls.

November 25, 2008
STEEP RISE IN "STRUGGLING" AMERICANS IN EARLY NOVEMBER
The number of thriving Americans drops to lowest level all year

by Elizabeth Mendes, Gallup Poll Staff Writer

The Gallup-Healthways Well-Being Index finds that in the first two weeks of November, the average number of "struggling" Americans hit 60%, higher than weekly averages seen throughout September and October. At the same time, the weekly average number of Americans who were "thriving" hit a new low of 36%.

When the Gallup-Healthways Well-Being Index first started asking Americans about their well-being in the beginning of 2008, the number of Americans who were considered to be thriving consistently came in at roughly 50%. However, Gallup reported that beginning in April the number of struggling Americans outnumbered those who are thriving, a trend that has continued since.

The Gallup-Healthways Well-Bering Index asks at least 1,000 Americans each day to evaluate their current lives as well as their

Gallup Daily: U.S. Well-Being
Weekly aggregates since Sept. 1-7, 2008

expectations of where they will be in five years using a "ladder" scale with steps numbered from 0 to 10, where "0" indicates the worst possible life and "10" the best possible life. Americans classified as "thriving" say that they *presently stand on step 7 or higher of the ladder* and *expect to stand on step 8 or higher* about five years from now. "Suffering" Americans are those who say they *presently stand on steps 0 to 4 of the ladder* and *expect to stand on steps 0 to 4* five years from now. Americans that Gallup does not classify as thriving or suffering are considered to be "struggling."

Income

Americans making $24,000 or more per year showed an increase in struggling for several months, but struggling within these income groups reached new highs in early November. For the first time, a majority of Americans (57%) making $60,000 to $90,000 per year fell into the struggling category, and even those making $90,000 or more saw a significant increase in struggling. While the lowest-income Americans are still those most likely to be struggling, they did not see the stark increase in struggling in the first two weeks of November that those making over $24,000 did.

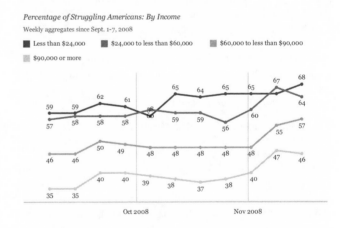

Percentage of Struggling Americans: By Income
Weekly aggregates since Sept. 1-7, 2008

A similar contrast can also be seen in the last two weeks of September, when the fiscal crisis accelerated and the stock market took big hits. At that time, more Americans making $60,000 or more moved into the struggling category, and the lower income groups stayed fairly level. One possible explanation is that higher income Americans are more likely to have savings in the stock market, which recorded sharp losses during that time.

The Job Market

Increased struggling among those with higher incomes, as well as the level seen among all Americans, coincides with increasingly negative news about the job market. Gallup's hiring measure tracks U.S. workers' perceptions of the job market and last week correctly projected higher than expected unemployment claims. Those working Americans who tell Gallup their employer is letting people go have, for the most part, also been significantly more likely to be "struggling." However, the overall increase in struggling Americans in early November is now almost equally distributed among those who say their employer is letting go and those who say their employer is hiring.

Percentage of Struggling Americans: By Views on Job Market
Weekly aggregates since Sept. 1-7, 2008

■ Among those who report that their company or employer is hiring new people

■ Among those who report that their company or employer is letting people go

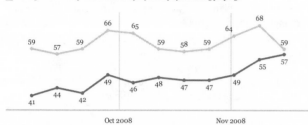

The increase in struggling Americans among those who say their employer is hiring might suggest that more Americans are aware of the deterioration in the job market even if their own employer is not letting go. It is interesting to note, however, the sudden decline in struggling among those who say their employer is letting people go in the Nov. 10-16 weekly aggregate when compared with prior aggregates for that group. Gallup Chief Scientist of Workplace Management and Well-Being, Dr. Jim Harter, says that one possible theory may be that "people who are employed in companies that are laying people off might appreciate that they still have a job."

Overall, these data suggest the economic crisis is taking a toll on the well-being of Americans on a much broader scale than even two months ago, and this deterioration of well-being is not necessarily insulated by a higher income or a relatively secure job.

About The Gallup-Healthways Well-Being Index

The Gallup-Healthways Well-Being Index is the first and largest survey of its kind, with 1,000 calls a day, seven days a week. It is designed to be the Dow Jones of health, giving a daily measure of people's well-being at the close of every day based on the World Health Organization (WHO) definition of health as not only the absence of infirmity and disease but also a state of physical, mental, and social well-being. The Well-Being Index will be a daily measure determining the correlation between the places where people work and the communities in which they live, and how that and other factors affect their well-being. Additionally, The Well-Being Index will increase the understanding of how those factors affect the financial health of corporations and communities. For additional information, go to www.well-beingindex.com.

Survey Methods

For the Gallup-Healthways Well-Being Index, Gallup is interviewing no fewer than 1,000 U.S. adults nationwide each day during 2008. For results based on these samples, the maximum margin of sampling error is ±2 percentage points.

Interviews are conducted with respondents on land-line telephones (for respondents with a land-line telephone) and cellular phones (for respondents who are cell-phone only).

In addition to sampling error, question wording and practical difficulties in conducting surveys can introduce error or bias into the findings of public opinion polls.

November 26, 2008
AMERICANS' WEIGHT ISSUES NOT GOING AWAY
Six in 10 want to lose weight, but only 30% are seriously trying to do so

by Lydia Saad, Gallup Poll Senior Editor

Just in time for the holiday feasting, a new Gallup Poll finds that nearly 6 in 10 Americans (59%) would like to lose weight. While this figure is unchanged from 2001, Americans report weighing an average of six pounds more today than they did seven years ago: 177 vs. 171 pounds.

On average, women now report weighing 160 pounds, up from 153 in 2001—a gain of nearly a pound per year. Men currently report weighing 194 pounds, up from 189.

What is your approximate current weight?
Average reported weight, in pounds

■ Men ■ Women

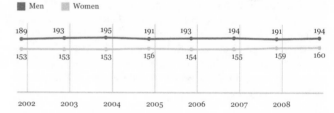

Trends are for November of each year from 2001 to 2008

Aside from some minor fluctuations from 2002 through today in men's average reported weight, most of the increase among men was observed earlier this decade. In contrast, most of the gain in women's average reported weight was seen in the past two years.

A Middle-Aged Dieting Bulge

According to the Nov. 13-16, 2008, Gallup Health and Healthcare Poll, 59% of Americans would like to lose weight, 34% want to remain at their present weight, and 7% (mostly younger men) want to gain weight.

However, the desire to lose weight is notably more prevalent among middle-aged Americans. Nearly two-thirds of those aged 30 to 49 and 50 to 64 say they would like to lose weight, compared with 55% of those 65 and older and only 41% of adults younger than 30.

Indeed, middle-aged adults are about twice as likely as those 18 to 29—and significantly more likely than those 65 and older—to say they are currently making a serious effort to lose weight.

Three in 10 Are Trying to Reduce

Overall, 30% of Americans say they are seriously trying to lose weight, up slightly—although not significantly—from the 28%

Personal Weight Preferences, by Age

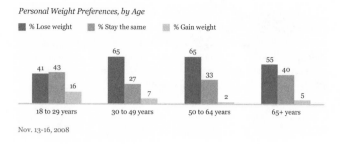

■ % Lose weight   ■ % Stay the same   ■ % Gain weight

18 to 29 years: 41, 43, 16
30 to 49 years: 65, 27, 7
50 to 64 years: 65, 33, 2
65+ years: 55, 40, 5

Nov. 13-16, 2008

Percentage Seriously Trying to Lose Weight, by Age

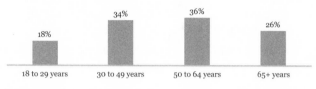

18 to 29 years: 18%
30 to 49 years: 34%
50 to 64 years: 36%
65+ years: 26%

Nov. 13-16, 2008

recorded each of the past two years. This includes 38% of women who are seriously trying to lose weight, up from 32% in 2007 and the highest level seen for women since the start of the decade. The 22% of men seriously trying to lose weight today is not much different from the levels men have reported in recent years, although it is slightly higher than in 2001 and 2002.

Percentage Seriously Trying to Lose Weight, by Gender, 2001-2008

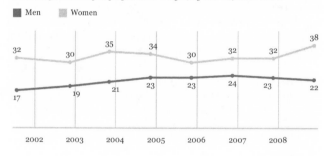

■ Men   ■ Women

Women: 32, 30, 35, 34, 30, 32, 32, 38
Men: 17, 19, 21, 23, 23, 24, 23, 22

2002 2003 2004 2005 2006 2007 2008

Notably, the percentage saying they are seriously trying to lose weight (30%) is only about half the percentage saying they would like to lose weight (59%).

Women Raise Their Ideal Weight Target

Women, in particular, may be helping themselves reach their weight goals by adjusting their target weight up a bit. Whereas from 2001 to 2007, the average answer women gave to a question asking for their "ideal body weight" ranged from 134 to 138 pounds, today that figure is 140. Thus, on average, women currently weigh about 20 pounds more than their ideal.

By contrast, the average 180-pound ideal weight now reported by men is consistent with the 177- to 181-pound range seen over the past eight years. Going by men's self-reported average weight of 194 pounds, men weigh about 14 pounds more, on average, than their ideal.

Summing Up

U.S. adults are heavy, and apparently getting heavier. Six in 10 Americans want to lose weight, and the average self-reported weight of U.S. adults has risen six pounds since 2001.

Average "Ideal Weight," by Gender, 2001-2008

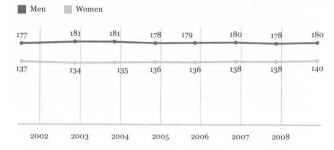

■ Men   ■ Women

Men: 177, 181, 181, 178, 179, 180, 178, 180
Women: 137, 134, 135, 136, 136, 138, 138, 140

2002 2003 2004 2005 2006 2007 2008

While no doubt distressing for overweight Americans, this can only be good news for the multibillion-dollar weight-loss industry as it seeks to meet the demands of those actively looking for diet aids. At least 30% of Americans, including a record-high 38% of women, tell Gallup they are currently trying to lose weight.

Survey Methods

Results are based on telephone interviews with 1,009 national adults, aged 18 and older, conducted Nov. 13-16, 2008. For results based on the total sample of national adults, one can say with 95% confidence that the maximum margin of sampling error is ±3 percentage points.

Interviews are conducted with respondents on land-line telephones (for respondents with a land-line telephone) and cellular phones (for respondents who are cell-phone only).

In addition to sampling error, question wording and practical difficulties in conducting surveys can introduce error or bias into the findings of public opinion polls.

November 28, 2008
AMERICANS IN NO MOOD TO SHOP
Variety of Gallup indicators suggest consumers will spend cautiously

by Lydia Saad, Gallup Poll Senior Editor

The suspense over whether U.S. consumers will shop 'til they drop or stay home on Black Friday could be a matter of survival for a great many retailers this year. From Americans' pessimistic views about their standard of living, to their frugal estimates of what they will spend on Christmas gifts this year, to their lack of confidence in the overall economy, consumers are sending a strong message that holiday sales will be light.

1. Consumers' Christmas Shopping Estimate

Gallup's most direct advance indicator of holiday retail sales comes from a question asking Americans to estimate the total amount they will spend on Christmas gifts each year.

Gallup's latest Christmas spending figure, from mid-November, found Americans, on average, planning to spend $616. Ominously, this is down 29% from the $866 recorded at a comparable point in November 2007. It is also the lowest holiday spending estimate Gallup has found in any year since it began tracking these trends on an annual basis in 1999.

Roughly how much money do you think you personally will spend on Christmas gifts this year?

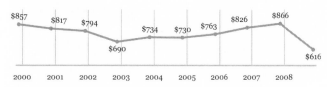

■ Mean estimate

$857 $817 $794 $690 $734 $730 $763 $826 $866 $616

2000 2001 2002 2003 2004 2005 2006 2007 2008

Trends are from November of each year

2. Plans to Increase or Decrease Christmas Budget

A related Gallup question asks consumers whether they plan to spend more, about the same, or less on Christmas gifts than they did the year before. Again, Americans' current answers point to weak holiday sales.

Only 7% of Americans surveyed Nov. 13-16 say they will spend more this year than they did in 2007, while 46% predict they will spend less. Historically, the percentage spending less and the percentage spending more have been more evenly balanced, with only a modest tilt toward less spending.

Furthermore, there is no sign that consumer caution is easing. In fact, in just the past month, the percentage saying they will spend less on gifts this year grew from 35% to 46%, shattering Gallup records maintained since 1990.

(Roughly how much money do you think you personally will spend on Christmas gifts this year?) Is that more, less, or about the same amount as you spent last Christmas?

■ % More   ■ % Less

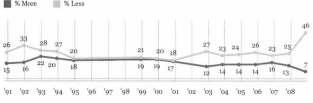

'91 '92 '93 '94 '95 '96 '97 '98 '99 '00 '01 '02 '03 '04 '05 '06 '07 '08

Selected dates for November or December of each year

3. Financial Comfort

A somewhat less direct measure of consumer willingness to part with cash or rack up credit-card bills this season comes from a question asking Americans about their standard of living. On balance, more Americans today say they feel their standard of living is getting worse, rather than getting better, 45% vs. 36%.

Not only are Americans feeling glum about their standard of living, but their current mood sharply contrasts with how they felt at the start of January, when 56% said their standard of living was improving and only 26% said it was declining.

2008 Gallup Poll Daily: Personal Standard of Living

Right now, do you feel your standard of living is getting better or getting worse?

■ % Getting Better   ■ % Getting Worse

Feb '08   Apr '08   Jun '08   Aug '08   Oct '08

Gallup Poll Daily tracking (Jan. 2 - Nov. 25, 2008)

The percentage of Americans worrying about money is also higher today than it was in January, although not dramatically so. A total of 40% currently say they worried about money "yesterday." This includes 14% saying they were very worried and 26% somewhat worried. At the start of the year, 31% were worried, including 7% very worried and 24% somewhat worried.

2008 Gallup Poll Daily: Personal Finances

Did you worry about money yesterday?

■ % Yes, worried   ■ % No, did not worry

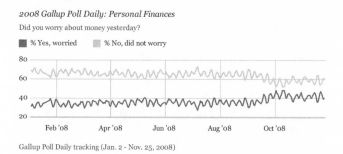

Feb '08   Apr '08   Jun '08   Aug '08   Oct '08

Gallup Poll Daily tracking (Jan. 2 - Nov. 25, 2008)

4. Economic Confidence

Beyond Americans' evaluations of their personal financial well-being, they are highly aware of the troubling economic news in the world around them, and that could have a real impact on their willingness to take financial risks.

Gallup tracks consumer confidence in the U.S. economy on a daily basis, reporting the results in ongoing three-day rolling averages. According to the latest results, from Nov. 23-25, nearly three-quarters of Americans (73%) have negative overall views of the national economy, while only 4% have positive views and 19% have mixed views. These summary evaluations come from the independent findings that 60% of Americans consider current economic conditions to be "poor," and that 76% perceive them to be getting worse.

The 2008 Gallup trend in public perceptions about current economic conditions clearly displays the dramatic change in economic mood that has taken place.

2008 Gallup Poll Daily Consumer Confidence Trend

How would you rate economic conditions in this country today -- as excellent, good, only fair, or poor?

■ % Excellent/Good   ■ % Poor

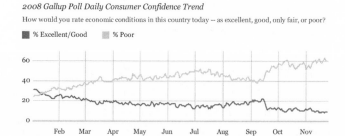

Feb   Mar   Apr   May   Jun   Jul   Aug   Sep   Oct   Nov

Additionally, the late October/November readings on this measure since 1992 punctuate just how negative consumer attitudes are today compared with past holiday retail seasons. Public confidence about the economy is more negative today than at any other time since the trend was established in 1992.

Bottom Line

Consumer confidence has undergone a dramatic decline over the past year, sinking this fall to a recent historical low. Americans' awareness of the sharp downturn is reflected in their own economic and financial mood. The question is whether consumers will heed that heightened sense of financial fear and stay home on the day they traditionally help retailers turn a profit, or toss

How would you rate economic conditions in this country today -- as excellent, good, only fair, or poor?

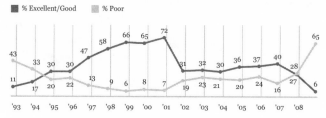

■ % Excellent/Good   ■ % Poor

Selected dates closest to mid-November of each year

their fear to the wind as they point their car toward the nearest mall.

After several months of lackluster retail sales, it's possible that the promise of heavily discounted prices—and descending gas prices—could unleash some of the pent-up demand for clothing, electronics, toys, and other traditional holiday purchases that may have been building up. At least that's what many retailers are hoping.

December 01, 2008
AMERICANS REMAIN BROADLY SUPPORTIVE OF LABOR UNIONS
Public divided as to whether their influence should increase, decrease, or stay the same

by Jeffrey M. Jones, Gallup Poll Managing Editor

Americans remain broadly supportive of labor unions, as they have been over the past seven decades, including a 59% approval rating for unions in Gallup's most recent update from August.

Do you approve or disapprove of labor unions?

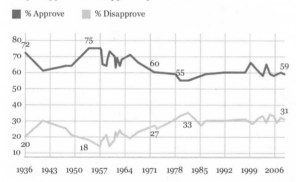

Organized labor unions played an important part in helping Democrat Barack Obama get elected president this year, by providing financial support and manpower for the campaign. Labor leaders now hope that the new administration and Congress will pass legislation favorable to their cause, including steps to make it easier for company workforces to unionize.

Labor unions have also received negative attention lately, with some blaming the financial woes of the Big Three U.S. automotive companies, in part, on generally higher-cost union labor. Leaders of the United Auto Workers have indicated they would be willing to make concessions to the companies to help the Big Three obtain financial assistance from the federal government.

Only about 1 in 10 Americans belong to a labor union, according to Gallup's recent estimates, and about one in six U.S. households include a union member.

While it is not clear to what degree the public's image of labor unions might have changed since the election or in light of the Big Three's financial crisis, Americans have generally held a favorable view of unions for decades—with no less than 55% of Americans saying they approve of labor unions in Gallup polls conducted from 1936 to 2008.

The public, however, does not have clear preferences as to whether unions should have more, less, or the same influence as they

have today. The Aug. 7-10 Gallup Poll finds 35% of Americans favoring greater influence for unions in the future, while 32% would rather unions have less influence, and 28% advocate no change in union strength.

Would you, personally, like to see labor unions in the United States have -- [ROTATED: more influence than they have today, the same amount as today, (or) less influence than they have today]?

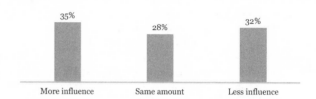

At a broad level, Americans have shown a divide on future union strength since Gallup first asked this question in 1999. However, in the last four years a slightly higher percentage have expressed a preference for increased union influence, with slightly less saying it should stay the same. The percentage that favors decreased union influence has stayed relatively flat over the years.

Would you, personally, like to see labor unions in the United States have -- [ROTATED: more influence than they have today, the same amount as today, (or) less influence than they have today]?

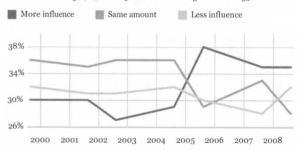

Apart from their preferences, Americans are inclined to expect that unions will become weaker in the future. The poll finds 41% holding this view, while 30% believe union strength will stay the same, and 22% think they will become stronger.

Thinking about the future, do you think labor unions in this country will become -- [ROTATED: stronger than they are today, the same as today, (or) weaker than they are today]?

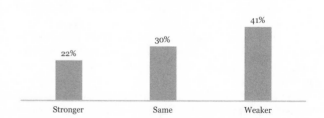

Implications

Americans have been consistently supportive of labor unions at a very general level for at least the past seven decades. Even so, there is not a public consensus to see labor unions increase their influence going forward, and the greatest percentage of Americans seems to see union strength as weakening.

Survey Methods

Results are based on telephone interviews with 1,009 national adults, aged 18 and older, conducted Aug. 7-10, 2008. For results based on the total sample of national adults, one can say with 95% confidence that the maximum margin of sampling error is ±3 percentage points.

Interviews are conducted with respondents on land-line telephones (for respondents with a land-line telephone) and cellular phones (for respondents who are cell-phone only).

In addition to sampling error, question wording and practical difficulties in conducting surveys can introduce error or bias into the findings of public opinion polls.

December 01, 2008
HEALTHCARE ACCESS, COST ARE TOP HEALTH CONCERNS
Majority mention either access to or cost of healthcare as most urgent health problem

by Jeffrey M. Jones, Gallup Poll Managing Editor

Americans' perceptions of the most urgent health problem facing the United States focus on systemic factors such as access to healthcare and the cost of it rather than specific medical conditions.

What would you say is the most urgent health problem facing this country at the present time?

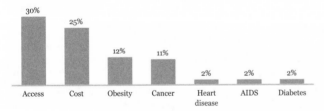

Nov. 13-16, 2008

These results are based on Gallup's annual Health and Healthcare Poll, conducted Nov. 13-16. Each year, Gallup asks Americans to name, without prompting, the "most urgent health problem facing this country at the present time."

For the last seven years—and eight of the last nine—either healthcare cost or access has topped the list, and these two issues have been first or second on the list for the last six years. Only in 2001, when the anthrax scare pushed bioterrorism to the top of the list, did some other health concern trump either cost or access as the most urgent health concern.

Prior to this decade, the public was most likely to mention a specific medical condition—AIDS—as the greatest health concern.

What would you say is the most urgent health problem facing this country at the present time?

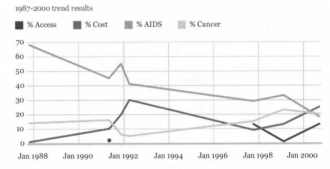

What would you say is the most urgent health problem facing this country at the present time?

After cost and access, obesity and cancer are the next most pressing health issues in the public's mind this year. Obesity has been more commonly mentioned in recent years, and the 12% who mention it in the current survey is the highest Gallup has found to date.

Concern about cancer has diminished slightly in recent years, since a high of 23% mentioned it in 1999.

But that decline pales in comparison to the steep drop in concern about AIDS, which had been the top concern from 1987 to 1999, but has registered in the single digits since 2001 and is mentioned by just 2% of Americans this year.

Percentage Mentioning AIDS as Most Urgent Health Problem, 1987-2008

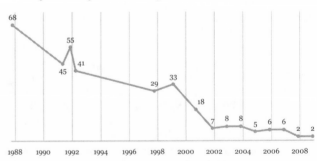

Survey Methods

Results are based on telephone interviews with 1,009 national adults, aged 18 and older, conducted Nov. 13-16, 2008. For results based on the total sample of national adults, one can say with 95% confidence that the maximum margin of sampling error is ±3 percentage points.

Interviews are conducted with respondents on land-line telephones (for respondents with a land-line telephone) and cellular phones (for respondents who are cell-phone only).

In addition to sampling error, question wording and practical difficulties in conducting surveys can introduce error or bias into the findings of public opinion polls.

December 02, 2008

OBAMA NATIONAL SECURITY PICKS GET HIGH MARKS

Sixty-nine percent approve of Obama choosing Hillary Clinton as secretary of state

by Jeffrey M. Jones, Gallup Poll Managing Editor

Americans widely approve of Barack Obama's decisions, announced on Monday, to name Hillary Clinton secretary of state and to ask Robert Gates to stay on as secretary of defense.

Approval of Barack Obama's National Security Appointments

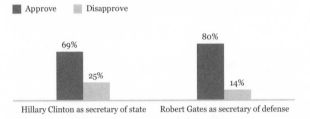

Dec. 1 USA Today/Gallup Poll

These results are based on a one-night *USA Today*/Gallup reaction poll conducted Dec. 1, just after Obama announced his national security team.

During the recent period of speculation that Obama would appoint his chief rival for the Democratic presidential nomination as his secretary of state, a Gallup poll conducted Nov. 18 found a majority of Americans (57%) in favor of him making that choice. Now that he has officially named Clinton as the nation's top diplomatic official, the percentage that supports the move has risen closer to 70%.

Support for the Gates appointment is higher than for the Clinton selection primarily because Republicans are much more likely to approve of Gates serving as secretary of defense than they are of Clinton as secretary of state. That, no doubt, reflects the fact that Gates has served under Republican presidents in the past, including both George W. Bush and George H.W. Bush. Democrats are slightly more likely to approve of the Clinton choice, but think highly of both choices.

Approval of Barack Obama's National Security Appointments, by Party Affiliation

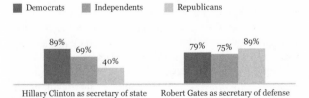

Dec. 1 USA Today/Gallup Poll

At a more basic level, 78% of Americans approve of the way Obama is handling his presidential transition, with only 13% disapproving. A majority of Democrats (94%), independents (79%), and Republicans (57%) say they approve.

That overall 78% approval rating compares favorably to the reaction Americans had to George W. Bush's transition, for which an average of 63% approved in January 2001, and Bill Clinton's transition, when an average of 66% approved from November 1992 through January 1993.

One of the most frequent criticisms of Obama's staff selections is that many held key roles in Bill Clinton's administration. To some, that does not reflect the "change" that Obama promised to deliver if elected. Nevertheless, Americans view the Obama-Clinton connection in positive terms, with a slim majority believing Obama's government will be "more effective" with the former Clinton officials in key positions. Only 14% say it will make his government "less effective," and 28% believe it will "not make much difference".

Democrats seem particularly unfazed by the number of former Clinton officials in the new administration, as only 3% say his government will be less effective as a result. The vast majority of Democrats say it will be more effective (77%). Republicans are most likely to believe Obama will be poorly served by the former Clinton staffers (28%), but the plurality of Republicans say it will not make much difference.

As you may know, Barack Obama has named several people who were in Bill Clinton's administration to key positions in the Obama administration. Do you think this will make the Obama administration – [ROTATED: more effective, will it not make much difference, (or will it make the Obama administration) less effective]?

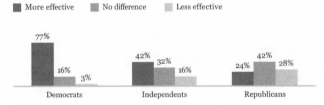

Dec. 1 USA Today/Gallup Poll

Majority Favors Obama Stimulus Package

Since Obama was elected, he has promised to make the economy his top priority, and has pledged to work with his economic advisers to come up with a proposal that Congress can vote on shortly after he takes office Jan. 20. This package is expected to be large and expensive, estimated by some to have a price tag of $500 billion to $700 billion. When asked whether they would favor such a measure, 58% of Americans say they would and 33% say they would oppose it.

While Democrats largely favor this planned economic stimulus package (77%), Republicans oppose it by about a 2-to-1 margin (32% in favor, 63% opposed).

Implications

It is common for presidents to enjoy a "honeymoon period" once they take office, but that era of good will seems to begin even before the president-elect takes office. To date, Americans have largely been supportive of Obama's appointments and actions to date, and initially seem to be in favor of what is likely to be his key policy initiative once he takes office—a large economic stimulus package.

Barack Obama says that once he takes office he will push Congress to pass a large spending package, estimated by others at $500 billion to $700 billion, to spur economic growth. Would you favor or oppose such a measure?

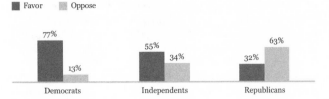

Dec. 1 USA Today/Gallup Poll

Survey Methods

Results are based on telephone interviews with 1,010 national adults, aged 18 and older, conducted Dec. 1, 2008. For results based on the total sample of national adults, one can say with 95% confidence that the maximum margin of sampling error is ±3 percentage points.

Interviews are conducted with respondents on land-line telephones (for respondents with a land-line telephone) and cellular phones (for respondents who are cell-phone only).

In addition to sampling error, question wording and practical difficulties in conducting surveys can introduce error or bias into the findings of public opinion polls.

Polls conducted entirely in one day, such as this one, are subject to additional error or bias not found in polls conducted over several days.

December 03, 2008
BLACKS AS CONSERVATIVE AS REPUBLICANS ON SOME MORAL ISSUES
One explanation: Black Democrats are much more religious than nonblack Democrats

by Frank Newport, Gallup Poll Editor in Chief

Only 31% of black Democrats in America say homosexual relations are morally acceptable, roughly the same as the 30% of Republicans who agree, while very much different from the 61% of nonblack Democrats who say homosexual relations are morally acceptable.

Next, I'm going to read you a list of issues. Regardless of whether or not you think it should be legal, for each one, please tell me whether you personally believe that in general it is morally acceptable or morally wrong. How about -- homosexual relations?

% Morally acceptable

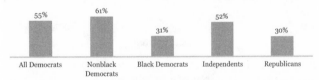

Aggregate of May 2006, May 2007, and May 2008 Gallup Polls

The fact that black Democrats are much closer to Republicans' than to nonblack Democrats' position on this issue is noteworthy given that blacks overwhelmingly identify themselves as Democrats (to be discussed in detail below). The issue of black views on family-related moral issues is also noteworthy given the recent vote in California to approve Proposition 8, which effectively amended the state constitution to define legal marriage as only between a man and a woman. Exit-poll results after that vote on Nov. 4 suggested that black California voters had overwhelmingly voted in favor of the amendment, while overall, Democrats in California overwhelmingly voted against it—essentially confirming the national attitude structure apparent from Gallup's analysis.

Gallup each year asks Americans to indicate whether they believe that each of a series of behaviors or actions is morally acceptable. The data reported in this article are based on an aggregated sample of the results from May 2006, May 2007, and May 2008, involving interviews with more than 3,000 Americans.

In this particular aggregate of data, 65% of blacks identify themselves as Democrats (and another 16% say they lean toward the Democratic Party). Only 5% identify as Republicans. Yet, as seen in the accompanying table, there are major gulfs between the attitudes of black Democrats and the attitudes of nonblack Democrats on a number of moral issues, and in most instances, blacks come much closer to the positions of Republicans than to those of Democrats.

Morally Acceptable or Morally Wrong, by Party ID
% Morally acceptable

	All Democrats	Nonblack Democrats	Black Democrats	Independents	Republicans
	%	%	%	%	%
Having baby outside of marriage	59	64	38	60	39
Homosexual relations	55	61	31	52	30
Abortion	51	54	37	44	25
Death penalty	57	59	47	65	80
Sex between an unmarried man and woman	64	68	46	66	46
Stem cell research using human embryos	72	76	56	63	48
Should marriages between same-sex couples be recognized by law as valid? (% Yes)	52	57	30	47	22

Aggregate of May 2006, May 2007, and May 2008 Gallup Polls

There is an exception to the basic conservatism of black Democrats on the issues listed in this table. Black Democrats are actually less likely to find the use of the death penalty morally acceptable than are nonblack Democrats (or Republicans). But on the other moral-based issues included, black Democrats are consistently much more conservative than nonblack Democrats.

Just 30% of black Democrats say they would agree that marriages between same-sex couples should be recognized by law as valid, compared to 57% of nonblack Democrats. Black Democrats are not quite as conservative on this policy issue as Republicans (among whom just 22% favor legalization of same-sex marriage), but are closer to Republican attitudes than to nonblack Democratic attitudes. And, as noted at the beginning of this story, black Democrats' views on the moral acceptability of homosexual relations are almost identical to those of Republicans, and the attitudes of both blacks and Republicans are significantly different from the attitudes of nonblack Democrats on this issue.

One of the underlying explanations for the divergence between the views of black and nonblack Democrats on these moral issues is religion. Black Democrats are much more religious than nonblack Democrats, and religion is highly related to views on homosexual relations.

Church Attendance, by Party ID and Race

Percentage who attend weekly/almost weekly/monthly

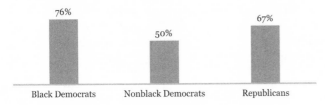

Aggregate of May 2006, May 2007, and May 2008 Gallup Polls

Moral Acceptability of Homosexual Relations, by Frequency of Church Attendance

% Morally acceptable

Aggregate of May 2006, May 2007, and May 2008 Gallup Polls

In general, it appears that black Americans may be conflicted in their attitudes toward certain values issues such as same-sex marriage and homosexual relations. Despite the liberal orientation of the Democratic Party toward moral issues, blacks, perhaps because of their high degree of religiosity, are pulled in the other, more conservative direction that is typical of Republicans. In the case of same-sex marriage, it appears that the power of religion in shaping black attitudes, coupled with the fact that black turnout in California was driven up in general because of the high-profile candidacy of Barack Obama for president, helped push Proposition 8 to victory.

Survey Methods

Results are based on telephone interviews with 3,022 national adults, aged 18 and older, conducted in May 2006, May 2007, and May 2008. For results based on the total sample of national adults, one can say with 95% confidence that the maximum margin of sampling error is ±2 percentage points.

Interviews are conducted with respondents on land-line telephones (for respondents with a land-line telephone) and cellular phones (for respondents who are cell-phone only).

In addition to sampling error, question wording and practical difficulties in conducting surveys can introduce error or bias into the findings of public opinion polls.

December 04, 2008
AMERICANS RATE NATIONAL AND PERSONAL HEALTHCARE DIFFERENTLY
Public thinks U.S. healthcare system has problems, but own coverage is fine

by Lydia Saad, Gallup Poll Senior Editor

Since earlier this decade, Americans have grown more receptive to the idea of replacing the current healthcare system based on private health insurance with a new government-run system. However, on balance, Americans still favor maintaining the current system, 49% to 41%.

Which of the following approaches for providing healthcare in the United States would you prefer -- [replacing the current healthcare system with a new government-run healthcare system, (or) maintaining the current system based mostly on private health insurance]?

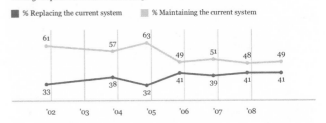

Gallup's annual healthcare trends, updated each November since 2001, show that public concern about U.S. healthcare centers on access and costs, not the quality of medical care. In fact, nearly 6 in 10 Americans (57%) interviewed Nov. 11-13, 2008, describe the quality of healthcare in the country as excellent or good. Attitudes on this have been stable in recent years.

Overall, how would you rate the quality of healthcare in this country -- as excellent, good, only fair, or poor?

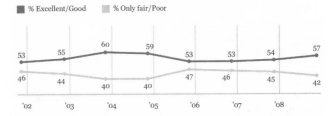

Americans' perceptions are much more negative when it comes to healthcare coverage. Only about one in four Americans currently believe healthcare coverage in the country is excellent or good.

Overall, how would you rate the healthcare coverage in this country -- as excellent, good, only fair, or poor?

Also, the overwhelming majority of Americans—79%—say they are dissatisfied with the total cost of healthcare in this country, a figure up slightly from the 71% found in 2001.

Are you generally satisfied or dissatisfied with the total cost of healthcare in this country?

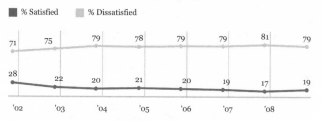

■ % Satisfied   ▨ % Dissatisfied

Perceptions That the System Is Broken

The net result of these observations about the way U.S. healthcare works is that Americans generally believe the system is highly troubled: 14% say it is "in a state of crisis" and 59% think it has "major problems." Only 26% believe it has minor problems and a slight 1% say it does not have any problems.

Which of these statements do you think best describes the U.S. healthcare system today -- it is in a state of crisis, it has major problems, it has minor problems, (or) it does not have any problems?

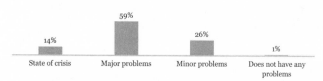

Nov. 13-16, 2008

Also, in line with Barack Obama's campaign promise to fill in the gaps in health insurance coverage for Americans, more than half of Americans believe it is the federal government's responsibility to make sure all Americans have access to healthcare coverage. The 54% currently saying this is the lowest recorded this decade, but still the dominant public view.

Do you think it is the responsibility of the federal government to make sure all Americans have healthcare coverage, or is that not the responsibility of the federal government?

■ % Yes, government's responsibility   ▨ % No, not government's responsibility

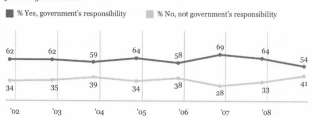

Bottom Line

As the incoming Obama administration considers how to tackle the nation's healthcare woes without producing the backlash that the Clinton administration faced in 1993-1994, it will be important for it to understand the sharp distinction between how Americans perceive national healthcare conditions and how the system is serving

Americans' own personal healthcare needs. Americans believe the system needs reform, particularly when it comes to healthcare coverage and costs. At the same time, they are pleased with the quality of medical treatment in the country, and are mostly satisfied with their own healthcare quality, coverage, and costs.

In short, the public seems to be calling for surgery on the current system—essentially to expand coverage to those who need it and to rein in costs—rather than an entire transplant operation.

Survey Methods

Results are based on telephone interviews with 1,009 national adults, aged 18 and older, conducted Nov. 13-16, 2008. For results based on the total sample of national adults, one can say with 95% confidence that the maximum margin of sampling error is ±3 percentage points.

Interviews are conducted with respondents on land-line telephones (for respondents with a land-line telephone) and cellular phones (for respondents who are cell-phone only).

In addition to sampling error, question wording and practical difficulties in conducting surveys can introduce error or bias into the findings of public opinion polls.

December 05, 2008
CABINET PICKS NOT AFFECTING OVERALL CONFIDENCE IN OBAMA
Throughout transition, two-thirds of Americans consistently confident

by Lymari Morales, Gallup Poll Staff Writer

Americans' positive reactions to President-elect Barack Obama's cabinet appointments this week have not yet translated into a more general boost in their already-high confidence in Obama to be a good president. Two-thirds of Americans (65%) in Dec. 1-3 interviewing remain confident in Obama, exactly matching Gallup's pre-Thanksgiving update on this measure.

Gallup Daily: Confidence in Obama

Are you confident or not confident in Barack Obama's ability to be a good president?

■ % Confident   ▨ % Not confident

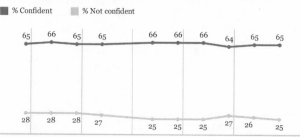

Gallup Poll Daily tracking reports since Nov. 23

Gallup has tracked Americans' confidence in Obama to be a good president since he was elected, finding Americans to be remarkably steadfast in their views. The first three days of interviewing, Nov. 5-7, also found exactly 65% confident in Obama. This week's official announcements that Obama would nominate Sen.

Hillary Clinton as secretary of state and keep Robert Gates as secretary of defense didn't affect Americans' overall views.

While observers have noted that Obama's picks of Clinton, Gates, and retired Marine Gen. James Jones as White House national security adviser represent more centrist and conservative positions than his own, Gallup Poll Daily tracking data find party loyalists neither rattled nor reassured. Republicans, independents, and Democrats remain as confident in Obama as they were before the announcements. This is the case even though Republicans were far less enthusiastic than independents or Democrats about the Clinton pick.

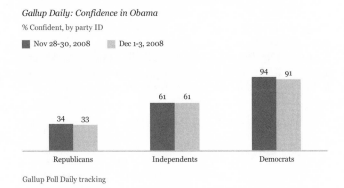

Gallup Daily: Confidence in Obama
% Confident, by party ID
■ Nov 28-30, 2008   ▨ Dec 1-3, 2008

Gallup Poll Daily tracking

Interestingly, liberals are one of the few groups showing a shift in their confidence in Obama since the announcements, from 91% to 84%, suggesting this group may have hoped for more of the "change" Obama promised on the campaign trail within his inner circle.

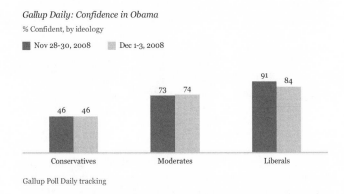

Gallup Daily: Confidence in Obama
% Confident, by ideology
■ Nov 28-30, 2008   ▨ Dec 1-3, 2008

Gallup Poll Daily tracking

Overall, the Gallup Daily tracking data find Americans holding firm to their general notion that Obama will make a good president, and little he has done throughout the transition period thus far has changed opinions for better or for worse. Gallup Daily tracking will continue to monitor confidence in Obama's ability to be a good president leading up to his inauguration on Jan. 20, 2009, at which time it will begin to track Obama's presidential job approval daily.

Survey Methods

Results are based on telephone interviews conducted as part of Gallup Poll Daily tracking. The most recent results are based on interviews conducted Dec. 1-3, 2008, with 1,564 national adults, aged 18 and older, and interviews conducted Nov. 28-30, 2008, with 1,514 national adults, aged 18 and older. For results based on these total samples of national adults, one can say with 95% confidence that the maximum margin of sampling error is ±2 percentage points.

Interviews are conducted with respondents on land-line telephones (for respondents with a land-line telephone) and cellular phones (for respondents who are cell-phone only).

In addition to sampling error, question wording and practical difficulties in conducting surveys can introduce error or bias into the findings of public opinion polls.

December 05, 2008
THREE IN 10 HOUSEHOLDS STILL DEFERRING MEDICAL CARE
Rate of deferring medical treatment has been stable for past four years

by Lydia Saad, Gallup Poll Senior Editor

Approximately 3 in 10 American adults (29%) say they or a family member put off medical treatment in the past 12 months because of what they'd have to pay. This prevalence of delaying treatment is similar to what Gallup has found each year since 2005, but higher than earlier this decade.

Within the last 12 months, have you or a member of your family put off any sort of medical treatment because of the cost you would have to pay?

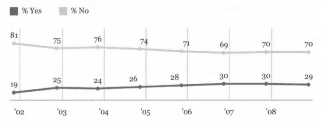

The latest finding comes from Gallup's annual polling on healthcare, conducted Nov. 13-16, 2008. Thus, even as economic conditions have deteriorated significantly over the last 12 months, Gallup finds no evidence that this is affecting people's ability or willingness to seek medical treatment.

A little more than half of those who report having put off treatment in the past year say it was for either a "very serious" or a "somewhat serious" medical condition or illness. The resulting picture is that 17% of households, overall, delayed treatment for a serious medical issue and 12% put off treatment for a non-serious issue, while 70% did not put off treatment.

When you put off this medical treatment, was it for a condition or illness that was very serious, somewhat serious, not very serious, or not at all serious?
Based on national adults

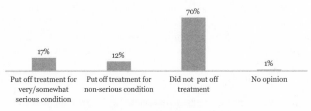

Nov. 13-16, 2008

According to combined data from Gallup's 2007 and 2008 healthcare surveys, the vast majority of people who say they or a family member put off medical treatment—77%—have health insurance, either in the form of Medicare or Medicaid, or private insurance. Only about a quarter—23%—have no health insurance.

However, these statistics largely reflect the fact that there are far more insured than uninsured Americans (89% vs. 11%). They also mask the important reality that delaying medical care is the norm for the uninsured.

Among the 11% of Americans with no health insurance, 61% tell Gallup they put off seeking medical treatment in the past year. This contrasts with 29% of those with private health insurance, and only 18% of those with Medicaid or Medicare coverage.

Percentage Saying Self or Family Member Put Off Medical Treatment, Based on Type of Health Insurance Coverage

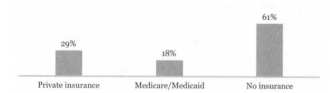

Based on combined November 2007/November 2008 data

Their high earnings don't completely shield upper-income Americans from the burden of healthcare costs. However, the aggregate healthcare data clearly indicate that putting off medical care is directly related to income, rising from 20% among those earning $75,000 or more annually to 39% among those earning less than $30,000.

Percentage Saying Self or Family Member Put Off Medical Treatment, by Income

Based on combined November 2007/November 2008 data

Bottom Line

Medical care can run the gamut from routine checkups and elective surgery, to visiting the doctor for flu symptoms, to lifesaving medical treatments and procedures. As the Gallup healthcare data show, many Americans say the medical attention they or a family member chose not to seek because of cost was for a less-than-serious condition. However, the 17% who say it was serious is nothing to sneeze at.

An important goal of healthcare reform will be to make sure this 17% of Americans receive proper medical care in the future. For some this would entail providing access to healthcare coverage. For most, however, it would involve making healthcare more affordable.

Survey Methods

Results are based on telephone interviews with 1,009 national adults, aged 18 and older, conducted Nov. 13-16, 2008. For results based on

the total sample of national adults, one can say with 95% confidence that the maximum margin of sampling error is ±3 percentage points.

Interviews are conducted with respondents on land-line telephones (for respondents with a land-line telephone) and cellular phones (for respondents who are cell-phone only).

In addition to sampling error, question wording and practical difficulties in conducting surveys can introduce error or bias into the findings of public opinion polls.

December 08, 2008
AMERICANS DON'T SEE ECONOMIC TURNAROUND ANYTIME SOON
Two-thirds expect it will be two years or more before recovery begins

by Lymari Morales, Gallup Poll Staff Writer

The news that the United States is already a year into an official recession hasn't dramatically altered Americans' views of how much longer the economic downturn will last. From a broad perspective, the view remains the same—that the United States is at least two years away from an economic turnaround.

Just your best guess, how long do you think it will be before the economy starts to recover? [OPEN-ENDED]

Numbers in percentages

■ Nov 13-16, 2008   ■ Dec 4-7, 2008

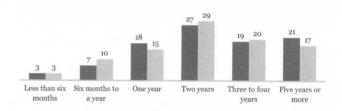

The Gallup Poll, conducted Dec. 4-7, 2008, followed a week of some of the worst economic news yet, including official reports determining that the United States has been in a recession since December 2007 and that the unemployment rate now stands at 6.7%. Nonetheless, Americans' views of the duration of the downturn fall almost exactly where they did three weeks ago: Two-thirds of Americans continue to say it will be two years or more before the economy starts to recover, while 28% expect it to be less.

Just your best guess, how long do you think it will be before the economy starts to recover? [OPEN-ENDED]

■ Nov 13-16, 2008   ■ Dec 4-7, 2008

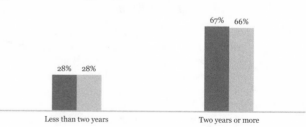

Because the United States is already a year into the current recession, if another two years pass before the start of a recovery, it would in fact constitute one of the worst economic downturns in the country's history. The 10 recessions since World War II lasted an average of 10.4 months, from 6 months in 1980 to 16 months in 1981-1982, while the Great Depression lasted 43 months. Economists tend to be more positive than the general public, with many suggesting that the current recession will continue for less than another full year. Nonetheless, the importance of Americans' views cannot be underestimated, as fears of a long recession are likely to affect consumer confidence and spending—risking the chance of a self-fulfilling prophecy.

Survey Methods

Results are based on telephone interviews with 1,009 national adults, aged 18 and older, conducted Dec. 4-7, 2008. For results based on the total sample of national adults, one can say with 95% confidence that the maximum margin of sampling error is ±3 percentage points.

Interviews are conducted with respondents on land-line telephones (for respondents with a land-line telephone) and cellular phones (for respondents who are cell-phone only).

In addition to sampling error, question wording and practical difficulties in conducting surveys can introduce error or bias into the findings of public opinion polls.

December 08, 2008
CONSUMER SPENDING REMAINS HIGHER SINCE THANKSGIVING
Daily spending $124 over the eight days from Black Friday through Dec. 5

by Frank Newport, Gallup Poll Editor in Chief

American consumer spending has picked up since Thanksgiving Day, as would be expected given the holiday shopping period. Average consumer spending from Friday, Nov. 28 through Friday, Dec. 5 is well above the average for November prior to Thanksgiving, and also above the average spending for all of 2008 so far.

Next, we'd like you to think about your spending yesterday. How much money did you spend or charge yesterday on all other types of purchases you may have made, such as at a store, restaurant, gas station, online, or elsewhere?

Gallup Poll Daily tracking

■ Average amount spent "yesterday"

Note: Does not include the purchase of a home, motor vehicle, or normal household bills

Gallup's daily spending measure asks Americans each day to report on how much money they spent "yesterday," excluding the purchase of a house, a motor vehicle, or normal household bills.

For the period from Nov. 1 through Nov. 25 (the Tuesday before Thanksgiving), average spending was $94. This total for the pre-Thanksgiving days of November was below the year-to-date average daily spending of $109, consistent with the general pullback in consumer spending Gallup has noted over the last several months.

Spending on Thanksgiving Day itself plunged to the lowest daily average of the year so far ($39), but on Black Friday, consumer spending zoomed to $177, among the top 10% of spending days so far this year.

Since Black Friday, daily spending has dropped back some, but has generally remained above both the yearly average as measured by Gallup, and the average for November through Thanksgiving.

Average daily spending for the period encompassing Friday, Nov. 28 through Friday, Dec. 5 is $124, a significant increase over the pre-Black Friday period in November. Average post-Thanksgiving spending is also above the year-to-date average for 2008 ($109), indicating not only an uptick from the very anemic pre-Thanksgiving spending patterns but also a lift from the year-to-date spending patterns.

Gallup began tracking consumer spending on Jan. 2 of this year, and therefore there are no comparable data from previous years against which to benchmark this year's daily spending in the crucial Christmas shopping period. Therefore, it is difficult to judge whether the increase in post-Thanksgiving spending is above, below, or about where it would be in a typical year.

(It should also be noted that the "how much did you spend yesterday" measure is not specific just to holiday shopping but encompasses spending for all reasons. It is a reasonable assumption, however, that changes in overall spending reflect at least in part added shopping relating to Christmas.)

Separately, Gallup's traditional direct measure of Christmas spending has shown that on a comparative basis, Americans report lower average anticipated spending on gifts this year than in any previous year in which this measure has been updated, and that a higher percentage of Americans have reported that they are spending less than usual.

Survey Methods

For the Gallup Poll Daily tracking survey, Gallup is interviewing no fewer than 1,000 U.S. adults nationwide each day during 2008. The consumer spending questions reviewed in this article are based on interviews with a random half-sample of approximately 500 adults each night. For results based on each night's sample, the maximum margin of sampling error is ±$43.

For results based on the sample of approximately 7,000 adults in the 14-day rolling average, the maximum margin of sampling error is ±$13.

Interviews are conducted with respondents on land-line telephones (for respondents with a land-line telephone) and cellular phones (for respondents who are cell-phone only).

In addition to sampling error, question wording and practical difficulties in conducting surveys can introduce error or bias into the findings of public opinion polls.

December 09, 2008
AMERICANS BLAME CAR COMPANY EXECS FOR U.S. AUTO CRISIS
Almost two-thirds say auto execs deserve a great deal of blame

by Frank Newport, Gallup Poll Editor in Chief

Americans place the blame for the current U.S. auto company crisis squarely on the backs of those companies' executives, with 65% of Americans saying the execs deserve a great deal of blame for the problems of the auto industry—a much higher percentage than blame labor unions, the current economic recession, government regulations, or the American consumer.

Please tell me whether you think each of the following deserves a great deal of blame, some blame, not much blame, or no blame at all for all the problems faced by the three major U.S. auto companies.

% Great deal of blame

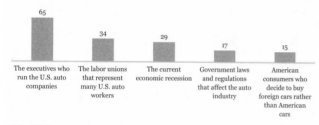

Gallup Poll, Dec. 4-7, 2008

Executives of the Big Three U.S. auto companies have been very much in evidence in recent weeks, traveling to Washington—first by corporate jet and then by private auto—to testify before Congress about the dire straits in which their industry finds itself. The executives have asked for a massive loan package from Congress with the stated or unstated premise that without such help in the near term, one or more of their companies would declare bankruptcy, possibly by the end of this year.

There is no doubt that the automobile industry's current problems are owing in part to the current economic recession—particularly the drying up of the credit markets, which makes it difficult for consumers to get financing for new cars.

But when given a list of five explanations or causes for the auto industry's slump today, Americans are overwhelmingly most likely to blame the auto executives themselves. Almost two-thirds of Americans say the executives should shoulder a great deal of blame, well above the 34% who feel that way about labor unions and the 29% who fault the recession. Even fewer Americans assign a great deal of blame to government regulations or American consumers who buy foreign rather than domestic cars.

There are some differences by partisan orientation in blame for the auto industry's problems.

- Democrats are more likely than Republicans to blame the auto company executives, but a majority of all three groups say these leaders deserve a great deal of blame.
- Republicans are nearly three times as likely as Democrats to blame the labor unions that represent U.S. autoworkers for the industry's problems. In fact, Republicans are only slightly less likely to blame the unions than the executives. Democrats are somewhat more likely than Republicans to blame the economic recession.

Implications

The average American is strongly likely to believe that auto company executives themselves should shoulder much of the blame

Great Deal of Blame for Problems Faced by the Three Major U.S. Auto Companies

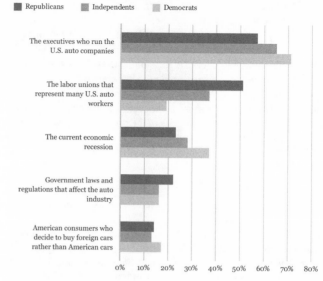

Gallup Poll, Dec. 4-7, 2008

when it comes to the current woes of the U.S. automobile industry. At least one senator (Christopher Dodd of Connecticut) has called for the resignation of General Motors Chairman Rick Wagoner as a requirement for federal bailout assistance, and the data reviewed here would suggest that the public would likely be sympathetic to this requirement.

Survey Methods

Results are based on telephone interviews with 1,009 national adults, aged 18 and older, conducted Dec. 4-7, 2008. For results based on the total sample of national adults, one can say with 95% confidence that the margin of sampling error is ±3 percentage points.

Interviews are conducted with respondents on landline telephones (for respondents with a landline telephone) and cellular phones (for respondents who are cell phone only).

In addition to sampling error, question wording and practical difficulties in conducting surveys can introduce error or bias into the findings of public opinion polls.

December 09, 2008
AMERICANS STILL NOT BUYING IN TO AUTO BAILOUT
No ringing endorsement of federal assistance

by Frank Newport, Gallup Poll Editor in Chief

A slight majority of 51% of Americans say they oppose the federal government's giving major financial assistance to the Big Three U.S. automotive companies, while 43% favor it—representing a slight decrease in support compared to three weeks ago. However, if it is stressed that one of the Big Three companies were certain to fail without government assistance, support rises to the majority level of 52% and opposition falls to 42%.

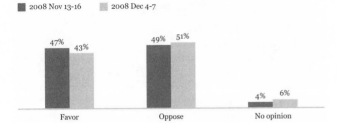

Would you favor or oppose the federal government giving major financial assistance to the Big Three U.S. automotive companies if they are close to going broke or declaring bankruptcy?

■ 2008 Nov 13-16   ■ 2008 Dec 4-7

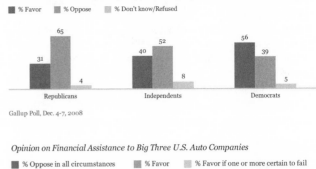

Would you favor or oppose the federal government giving major financial assistance to the Big Three U.S. automotive companies if they are close to going broke or declaring bankruptcy?

■ % Favor   ■ % Oppose   ■ % Don't know/Refused

Gallup Poll, Dec. 4-7, 2008

The responses to these questions, as was the case three weeks ago when they were first asked, show an American public essentially giving mixed signals on what Congress should do in regard to the auto industry crisis.

The basic question on the auto industry bailout is as follows:

Would you favor or oppose the federal government giving major financial assistance to the Big Three U.S. automotive companies if they are close to going broke or declaring bankruptcy?

The 43% of Americans who say they favor major assistance marks a slight decrease in support for the bailout from Gallup's Nov. 13-16 poll (47%). Meanwhile, there has been a slight, two-point increase in the percentage who are opposed, from 49% last month to 51% currently. This notable lack of movement to the more positive side of the ledger suggests that the recent testimony of auto executives on Capitol Hill and the case they made for needing assistance was not effective in moving public opinion.

Support for federal assistance rises when the respondents who say they are opposed are presented with a scenario under which one or more of the three major U.S. automotive companies were certain to fail without the assistance. Given this follow-up, 18% of those initially opposed shift their views to the "support" column, leaving the overall distribution of opinion showing a slight majority approval.

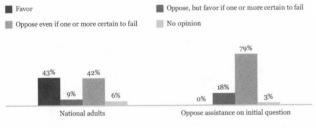

Would you favor or oppose the federal government giving major financial assistance to the Big Three U.S. automotive companies if they are close to going broke or declaring bankruptcy?

■ Favor   ■ Oppose, but favor if one or more certain to fail
■ Oppose even if one or more certain to fail   ■ No opinion

Gallup Poll, Dec. 4-7, 2008

There are differences—in fact, highly significant differences—in views of the bailout by the partisan orientation of respondents.

On the basic question of the bailout, almost two-thirds of Republicans are opposed, while 56% of Democrats are in favor. Independents tilt toward opposing the bailout.

Some Republicans who were initially opposed shift to the "favor" side of the ledger when probed for their views if one of the "Big Three" were certain to fail, but even with that, 55% of Republicans remain opposed.

(By way of comparison, a question asked in a Dec. 1-2 CNN/Opinion Research poll was phrased as follows: "The major U.S. auto companies have asked the government for a program that would provide them with several billion dollars in assistance. The auto companies say they may go into bankruptcy without that assistance. Based on what you have read or heard, do you favor or oppose this program?"

The results showed that 36% of Americans favored assistance, with 61% opposing it. This is a significantly more negative response than to either of the Gallup Poll surveys on the issue. The most likely explanation for the difference is question wording. The CNN/Opinion Research poll began by stating that the "major U.S. auto companies have asked the government for a program that would provide them with several billion dollars in assistance." The Gallup question more directly asks respondents if they favor or oppose "the federal government giving major financial assistance to the Big Three U.S. automotive companies." The CNN question mentioned "billions" while the Gallup question did not specify a dollar amount beyond "major financial assistance." Both questions did remind respondents that the companies were in danger of going into bankruptcy.)

Implications

There is no groundswell of support from the American people in favor of congressional approval of a massive loan or bailout for the automobile industry. If anything, support has dropped slightly over the last several weeks, even as automobile executives have been testifying on Capitol Hill, and Congress now seems close to voting on a scaled-down measure. If it is made clear that one or more of the auto companies would fail without government assistance, a bare majority of Americans would favor it, but this is hardly a ringing endorsement.

Because the decision on an auto industry bailout will ultimately be made in the context of a political congressional environment in Washington, it is important to note that bailout support is highly divided by partisanship across the country. Republicans oppose it, while Democrats favor it.

Survey Methods

Results are based on telephone interviews with 1,009 national adults, aged 18 and older, conducted Dec. 4-7, 2008. For results based on

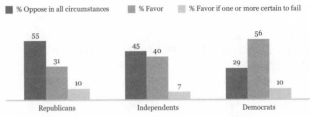

Opinion on Financial Assistance to Big Three U.S. Auto Companies

■ % Oppose in all circumstances   ■ % Favor   ■ % Favor if one or more certain to fail

Gallup Poll, Dec. 4-7, 2008

the total sample of national adults, one can say with 95% confidence that the margin of sampling error is ±3 percentage points.

Interviews are conducted with respondents on land-line telephones (for respondents with a land-line telephone) and cellular phones (for respondents who are cell-phone only).

In addition to sampling error, question wording and practical difficulties in conducting surveys can introduce error or bias into the findings of public opinion polls.

December 09, 2008
INITIAL BAILOUT FALLING OUT OF FAVOR WITH AMERICANS
More likely now than in October to see it as a "bad thing"

by Lymari Morales, Gallup Poll Staff Writer

With lawmakers weighing the prospect of a multi-billion dollar bailout for the U.S. auto industry, Gallup finds its $700 billion predecessor falling out of favor with Americans. Since October, Americans have flipped from being more positive than negative on the Wall Street bailout, 50% to 41%, to being slightly more negative than positive, 47% to 46%.

All in all, do you think it is a good thing or a bad thing that the government passed legislation to provide up to $700 billion of assistance to address the problems faced by U.S. financial institutions?

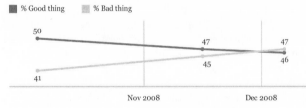

Gallup Polls conducted Oct. 3-5, Nov. 13-16, Dec. 4-7, 2008

The $700 billion package for U.S. financial institutions signed into law in early October was supposed to be the tourniquet to stop the bleeding of the U.S. economy. And while the United States has not seen further collapse of major financial institutions, the economy continues to struggle. Further, the Government Accountability Office last week reported that the legislation did not incorporate enough safeguards to oversee how financial institutions spent the money, prompting the Senate this week to appoint New York prosecutor Neil M. Barofsky to oversee the program.

Bottom Line

Considering the relatively low levels of support for an auto industry bailout and the falloff in support for the Wall Street bailout, lawmakers considering the legislation should be aware of the possibility that Americans will become more disapproving if they do not perceive swift benefits. Overall, the lack of a positive perception of the assistance package passed in October suggests that Americans don't necessarily see government money as the key to solving the country's economic problems. In fact, these recent poll results only bolster previous Gallup findings in which Americans signaled far greater sup-

port for policies that would increase government regulation over those that would provide financial assistance to struggling industries.

Survey Methods

Results from Dec. 4-7, 2008 are based on telephone interviews with 1,009 national adults, aged 18 and older. Results from Oct. 3-5, 2008 are based on telephone interviews with 1,011 national adults, aged 18 and older. For results based on each total sample of national adults, one can say with 95% confidence that the maximum margin of sampling error is ±3 percentage points.

Interviews are conducted with respondents on land-line telephones (for respondents with a land-line telephone) and cellular phones (for respondents who are cell-phone only).

In addition to sampling error, question wording and practical difficulties in conducting surveys can introduce error or bias into the findings of public opinion polls.

December 09, 2008
NEW SURGE IN WEEKLY JOBLESS CLAIMS LIKELY
Gallup's hiring measure projects jobless claims will exceed 525,000 consensus estimate

by Dennis Jacobe, Gallup Poll Chief Economist

Gallup's Net New Hiring Activity measure shows U.S. employees' perceptions of the job situation at their companies worsened considerably last week—more than reversing the slight improvement of the past two weeks. In turn, this suggests that Thursday's Labor Department report of first-time unemployment claims for the week ending Dec. 6 will not only exceed the 509,000 reported for the prior week, but actually surge past the 525,000 consensus estimate.

Relationship Between Weekly Initial Unemployment Claims and Gallup's Net New Hiring Measure

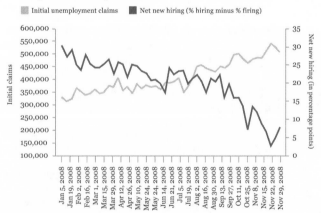

Job Losses Accelerating

Net new hiring (the percentage of employees saying their companies are hiring minus the percentage saying their companies are letting people go) fell from 6.9 points in the week ending Nov. 30 to 0.0 in the most recent week, ending Dec. 7. That is the worst reading thus far in 2008.

While a number of variables make it hard to predict the exact number of new unemployment claims the Labor Department will report on Thursday morning, Gallup figures suggest jobless claims will surge and are likely to hit a new high for the year—surpassing the seasonally adjusted 543,000 of the week ending Nov. 15. The seasonally adjusted four-week average of Gallup's hiring measure also shows that four-week average jobless claims continued to increase during the week ending Dec. 6.

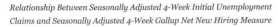

Relationship Between Seasonally Adjusted 4-Week Initial Unemployment Claims and Seasonally Adjusted 4-Week Gallup Net New Hiring Measure

Survey Methods

Using weekly results for 2008, Gallup's analysis suggests that its hiring measure has a better than 7-in-10 probability of correctly projecting the direction of weekly jobless claims and a better than 8-in-10 probability of predicting the direction of the 4-week average of jobless claims.

Gallup's hiring measure is based on aggregated interviews with a nationally representative sample of more than 2,000 U.S. workers each week. Gallup asks current full- and part-time employees whether their employers are hiring new people and expanding the size of their workforces, not changing the size of their workforces, or letting people go and reducing the size of their workforces. Gallup's hiring measure is computed by subtracting the "letting go and reducing" percentage from the "hiring and expanding" percentage. The assumption is that employees across the country have a good feel for what's happening in their companies, and that these insider perceptions can yield a meaningful indication of the nation's job situation.

Gallup's Net New Hiring Activity measure was initiated in January 2008. It is an effort to assess U.S. job creation or elimination based on the self-reports of more than 2,000 individual employees aggregated each week about hiring and firing activity at their workplaces.

For results based on these samples, the maximum margin of sampling error is ±3 percentage points.

Interviews are conducted with respondents on land-line telephones (for respondents with a land-line telephone) and cellular phones (for respondents who are cell-phone only).

In addition to sampling error, question wording and practical difficulties in conducting surveys can introduce error or bias into the findings of public opinion polls.

December 10, 2008

ECONOMY ENTRENCHED AS NATION'S MOST IMPORTANT PROBLEM

Majorities name economy as top problem in November and December

by Lydia Saad, Gallup Poll Senior Editor

The 55% of Americans naming the economy, generally, as the nation's top problem in December marks the second straight month that a majority of Americans have coalesced around the issue.

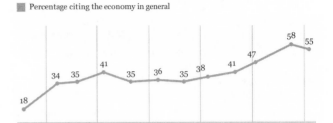

Economy as Nation's "Most Important Problem," 2008

According to the Dec. 4-7 poll, the combined percentage of Americans naming any aspect of the economy as the nation's top problem is 77%, identical to last month's figure. This includes unemployment, "lack of money," recession, taxes, and other specific issues, in addition to simply "the economy."

After registering in the mid-30s for most of the year, the percentage of Americans naming the economy in general as the most important problem rose to 41% in September and 47% in October, before surpassing the 50% mark in November with 58%. Prior to this year, the highest percentage mentioning the economy was 42%, in 1991.

Still, Gallup's long-term Most Important Problem trend includes several years when public concern about specific economic issues exceeded today's general concern about the economy.

- From 1978 to 1981—overlapping the start of the 1980 recession—more than half of Americans consistently mentioned inflation or the high cost of living as the nation's top problem. This included several readings above 60% and a remarkable 83% reading in October 1978.
- Between 1973 and 1975, spanning a recession of the same time frame, there were several instances when mentions of inflation and the high cost of living registered above 60% and even 70%.
- Unemployment was a dominant concern in 1945, when 77% cited the lack of jobs as the nation's top problem. The issue re-emerged in the early 1980s, with readings as high as 53%.

Gallup's first Most Important Problem measure was asked in April 1939, during the Great Depression. At that time, the most often-cited problem was unemployment/jobs, mentioned by 46%.

"Economy" Far Outpaces "Jobs"

Today's findings are unique in that most Americans perceive the entire economy—not just one aspect of it—to be the country's chief problem. While concern about unemployment is growing as job losses continue to mount, the percentage citing that specific issue remains fairly low at 12%. It was 8% in November and only 3% in October.

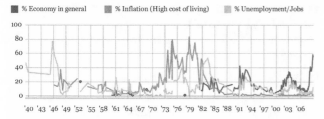

■ % Economy in general   ■ % Inflation (High cost of living)   % Unemployment/Jobs

In terms of other specific mentions, the situation in Iraq now ties dissatisfaction with government and "lack of money" as the third-highest-ranking public concern, each mentioned by 9%. Ethics/Moral decline and healthcare tie for fourth place, each cited by 5%. The last time Iraq was in the single digits on this measure was in August 2003.

No other issue is cited by more than 3% of Americans.

*Top Responses to "Most Important Problem"^*

Ranked according to Dec. 4-7, 2008, result

	Dec 4-7, 2008	Nov 13-16, 2008	Oct 3-5, 2008
	%	%	%
Economy in general	55	58	47
Unemployment/Jobs	12	8	3
Lack of money	9	9	12
Situation in Iraq/War	9	13	11
Dissatisfaction with government/Congress/ politicians; poor leadership; corruption; abuse of power	9	6	9
Ethics/Moral/Religious/Family decline; dishonesty	5	4	4
Poor healthcare/hospitals; high cost of healthcare	5	9	5

^Responses mentioned by at least 5% of national adults in December poll are shown

What a Difference a Year Makes

Today's order of perceived top problems is quite different from that of December 2007, when Iraq (with 29% mentions) ranked No. 1 and the economy (13%) No. 2. It is also starkly different from perceptions in June of this year, when a quarter of Americans mentioned fuel prices—nearly matching the economy, the top-ranked issue, with 36%. With fuel prices now well below $2 in most of the country, the cost of energy has virtually disappeared as a concern. Today, only 1% of Americans cite it as the top problem.

Recent Trend in Selected Issues as Most Important Problem, December 2007-December 2008

■ % Economy in general   ■ % Fuel/Oil prices   % Situation in Iraq/War

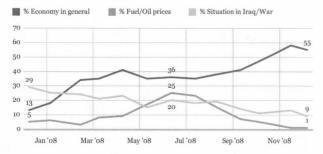

Bottom Line

The current economic recession, reportedly already a year in progress, may or may not be worse than what the country experi-

enced in the 1970s or early 1980s, but it certainly has a different flavor. Whereas those downturns were particularly challenging in one area, such as inflation or jobs, the current economic meltdown involves a dizzying cycle of bad economic news that encompasses the housing market, the job market, the stock markets, the credit markets, and the entire retail sector of the economy.

While over three-quarters of Americans name some aspect of the economy as the nation's most important problem, the increasing percentage of Americans, now 55%, who mention just "the economy," without further specification, underscores the broad scope of the current economic crisis in Americans' minds.

Survey Methods

Results are based on telephone interviews with 1,009 national adults, aged 18 and older, conducted Dec. 4-7, 2008. For results based on the total sample of national adults, one can say with 95% confidence that the maximum margin of sampling error is ±3 percentage points.

Interviews are conducted with respondents on land-line telephones (for respondents with a land-line telephone) and cellular phones (for respondents who are cell-phone only).

In addition to sampling error, question wording and practical difficulties in conducting surveys can introduce error or bias into the findings of public opinion polls.

December 10, 2008
PERSONAL SATISFACTION RATINGS DECLINE TO LOWEST SINCE 1992
Now less than half of Americans say they are very satisfied with their personal lives

by Jeffrey M. Jones, Gallup Poll Managing Editor

Though the significant majority of Americans say they are satisfied with the way things are going in their personal lives—as has been the case for decades—there has been a notable decline in reported satisfaction over the past 12 months to 80%, the lowest Gallup has measured since 1992.

In general, are you satisfied or dissatisfied with the way things are going in your personal life at this time?

■ % Satisfied

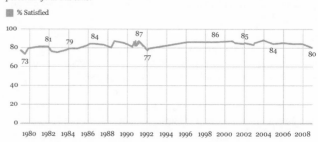

This is based on Gallup's annual Lifestyle Poll, conducted Dec. 4-7 this year. Personal life satisfaction ratings have been highly stable over the years. For example, over the past four years these have been either 84% or 85%. So while a drop of four percentage points is not large in an absolute sense, it is notable in light of the overall stability of this trend line.

Gallup first asked about personal satisfaction in this format in 1979, and has found ratings below 80% in only a limited number of polls, usually at times (like the present) when the economy was in poor shape, such as the late 1970s, the early 1980s, and in 1991-1992. Yet, a poor economy drags down Americans' personal life satisfaction only to a small degree because these ratings have never been below the 73% measured in July 1979.

The current decline comes in a year in which Gallup has found record-low ratings of satisfaction with the way things are going in the country and of economic conditions, as well as record or near-record lows in trust in government, and approval of Congress and the president.

Perhaps the more significant change in Americans' personal satisfaction comes in the results of the follow-up question—first asked in the 2001 Lifestyle survey—that asks Americans to say to what degree they are satisfied or dissatisfied. This year, just 47% of Americans say they are "very satisfied" with the way things are going in their personal lives, the first sub-50% measure over the past eight years. The current figure also represents a sharp drop from the 59% reporting a high degree of personal satisfaction at this time last year.

Are you very satisfied/dissatisfied, or just somewhat satisfied/dissatisfied (with the way things are going in your personal life at this time)?

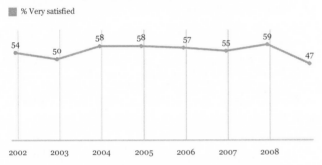

Survey Methods

Results are based on telephone interviews with 1,009 national adults, aged 18 and older, conducted Dec. 4-7, 2008. For results based on the total sample of national adults, one can say with 95% confidence that the maximum margin of sampling error is ±3 percentage points.

Interviews are conducted with respondents on land-line telephones (for respondents with a land-line telephone) and cellular phones (for respondents who are cell-phone only).

In addition to sampling error, question wording and practical difficulties in conducting surveys can introduce error or bias into the findings of public opinion polls.

December 11, 2008
BAILOUTS AREN'T INCREASING CONSUMER CONFIDENCE
Increasing number of Americans rate economy "poor," say conditions are getting worse

by Dennis Jacobe, Gallup Poll Chief Economist

Talk of the auto bailout and the Obama stimulus plan may have helped the stock market but is not doing the same for consumer con-

fidence. The percentage of consumers rating the economy "poor" increased from November's 58% to 60% during the week of Dec. 1-7 and 62% Dec. 8-10, continuing an ever-worsening trend since August.

Percentage of Consumers Rating Current Economic Conditions "Poor"
Monthly/Weekly trend

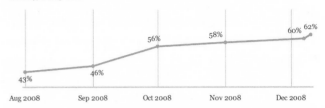

At the same time, the percentage of Americans saying economic conditions are "getting worse" increased from 78% in November to 81% during the first week of December and 82% over the last three days.

Percentage of Consumers Saying Economy Is Getting Worse
Monthly/Weekly trend

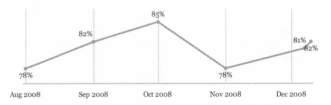

Commentary

At this point, it is not clear whether House passage of the auto bailout Wednesday night will help improve overall consumer confidence. Clearly, jobs continue to be a major issue. So far, Americans seem to be suffering from so-called "bailout fatigue," with majorities or pluralities now opposing not only the auto bailout, but also the original $700 billion financial institutions bailout.

On the other hand, another failure of the Congress to pass bailout legislation, as happened during the initial unsuccessful effort to rescue the financial institutions, could raise economic concerns even further. This is especially problematic given concerns about the current vacuum in economic leadership between now and President-elect Obama's inauguration. It seems instructive that consumer confidence did improve slightly during the week Obama held press conferences on three consecutive days to announce his new economic team. And while Jan. 20 is only weeks away, it can seem like a long time when the economy is losing more than 100,000 jobs a week.

Regardless, what has been happening in Washington, D.C., has seemed to do little to boost consumer confidence and may be doing just the opposite, as Gallup's consumer confidence measures suggest a slight further deterioration in early December. This is not good news for the nation's retailers hoping for a last-minute surge in holiday spending, or for the economy as a whole. Still, one can hope that Americans' optimism will be renewed—at least to some degree—simply by turning the calendar to a new year, in particular one that will bring new leadership to the country.

Survey Methods

Gallup is interviewing no fewer than 1,000 U.S. adults nationwide each day during 2008. The economic questions analyzed in this report are asked of a random half-sample of respondents each day. The monthly results reported here are based on combined data of more than 8,000 interviews each in August, September, October, and November 2008. For results based on these samples, the maximum margin of sampling error is ±1 percentage point.

Results for Dec. 1-7, 2008, are based on combined data of more than 3,000 interviews. For results based on this sample, the maximum margin of sampling error is ±2 percentage points. Results for Dec. 7-9, 2008, are based on combined data of more than 1,500 interviews. For results based on this sample, the maximum margin of sampling error is ±3 percentage points.

Interviews are conducted with respondents on land-line telephones (for respondents with a land-line telephone) and cellular phones (for respondents who are cell-phone only).

In addition to sampling error, question wording and practical difficulties in conducting surveys can introduce error or bias into the findings of public opinion polls.

December 11, 2008
CONSERVATIVE REPUBLICANS STILL WIDELY SUPPORT BUSH
Averaging just 29% job approval overall thus far in December

by Jeffrey M. Jones, Gallup Poll Managing Editor

George W. Bush remains popular among conservative Republicans (72% approve of him) despite his low overall approval rating. Meanwhile, moderate and liberal Republicans are as likely to disapprove as to approve of the job he is doing, and Democrats of all political orientations hold Bush in low regard.

Approval of George W. Bush, by Party Affiliation and Ideology

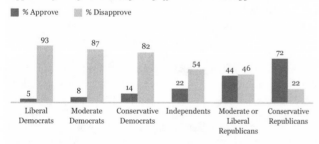

Dec. 1-9 Gallup Poll Daily tracking
Note: Independents who lean to a party are included with that party's supporters

These results are based on Gallup Poll Daily tracking conducted Dec. 1-9, including interviews with more than 9,000 U.S. adults.

During this time, Bush has averaged 29% job approval among all Americans—reflecting a slight improvement from the 25% approval rating he had at the time of the November election, yet still dismal by historical standards.

With such a low approval rating, it is hard to find many population subgroups that are favorable to Bush. A look at the groups giving Bush the 10 highest average approval ratings clearly shows how much one's opinion of the president is driven by political attitudes as opposed to demographic characteristics. Only four groups give Bush ratings in excess of 40% approval, and all are

defined by political points of view. But because membership in these four groups overlaps (e.g., Republicans and conservative Republicans), when they are subdivided into mutually exclusive groups (as in the first graph), it really is only Americans who are both Republicans *and* conservatives who hold Bush in high esteem.

Subgroups With Highest Average Approval Ratings of George W. Bush

	Approve	Disapprove
	%	%
Conservative Republicans	72	22
Republicans, including leaners	62	31
Conservatives	50	43
Moderate/Liberal Republicans	44	46
Attend church weekly	38	52
Married men	35	58
$7,500+ household income per month	35	60
Whites	34	60
South	34	57
Married	34	58
Protestants/Other Christians	34	58
Married with children	34	57

Dec. 1-9 Gallup Poll Daily tracking

Thus, it is not surprising that those at the other end of the political spectrum—Americans who are liberal Democrats—are least likely to approve of the job Bush is doing. The list of groups giving Bush his 10 lowest average approval ratings is dominated by left-leaning political groups.

Subgroups With Lowest Average Approval Ratings of George W. Bush

	Approve	Disapprove
	%	%
Liberal Democrats	5	93
Blacks	7	88
Democrats, including leaners	8	88
Moderate Democrats	8	87
Liberals	9	84
Conservative Democrats	14	82
No religion	14	80
Nonwhites	16	71
Moderates	19	72
Hispanics	19	60

Dec. 1-9 Gallup Poll Daily tracking

In contrast to the situation among Republicans of differing ideologies, there is not much separation in views of Bush among Democratic identifiers according to their ideological orientation. Basically all Democrats have a very low opinion of Bush, though conservative Democrats are somewhat more charitable in their ratings than are liberal or moderate Democrats.

Nonwhites—who traditionally align with the Democratic Party—also give Bush very low approval ratings. Just 16% of all nonwhites approve of Bush, including 7% of blacks and 19% of Hispanics. The finding for Hispanics is notable given Bush's efforts to court the Hispanic community while governor of Texas and while campaigning for president in 2000 and 2004.

Implications

As Bush serves his final weeks in office, he does so with the support of a small minority of Americans. Conservative Republicans essentially stand alone in their solid support of Bush. However, over the years, Bush has lost a significant number of supporters even among this core group, which formerly supported him at better than 90%.

Even so, Bush's approval rating has improved slightly in recent weeks—similar to what has occurred for prior lame-duck presidents—and further modest improvement is not out of the question.

Survey Methods

Results are based on telephone interviews with 9,000+ national adults, aged 18 and older, conducted Dec. 1-9, 2008, as part of Gallup Poll Daily tracking. For results based on the total sample of national adults, one can say with 95% confidence that the maximum margin of sampling error is ±1 percentage point.

Margins of error for subgroups will be higher.

Interviews are conducted with respondents on land-line telephones (for respondents with a land-line telephone) and cellular phones (for respondents who are cell-phone only).

In addition to sampling error, question wording and practical difficulties in conducting surveys can introduce error or bias into the findings of public opinion polls.

December 12, 2008

AMERICANS' CHRISTMAS BUDGET FALLS $200 BELOW LAST YEAR'S

Average anticipated spending is $639, down from $833 in December 2007

by Lydia Saad, Gallup Poll Senior Editor

Americans' forecast for what they will spend on Christmas gifts this season is as budget conscious as it was a month ago. The current $639 in anticipated spending, based on Dec. 4-7 Gallup polling, is statistically similar to the $616 in mid-November (the lowest in Gallup's records), but down from $833 last December.

Roughly how much money do you think you personally will spend on Christmas gifts this year?

Mean (including zero)

This decline is the result of far fewer Americans running up holiday bills of at least $1,000. Only 22% of national adults in the new survey said they would spend $1,000 or more this year on gifts, down from 33% in December 2007, and the lowest in any year since 1994. As spending contracts, the percentages of Americans falling into the

lower income categories have increased, particularly the $100 to $249 category.

Roughly how much money do you think you personally will spend on Christmas gifts this year?

	$1,000 or more	$500 to $999	$250 to $499	$100 to $249	Under $100
	%	%	%	%	%
2008 Dec 4-7	22	24	18	19	3
2007 Dec 6-9	33	22	15	15	4
2006 Nov 9-12	34	25	15	14	3
2005 Dec 5-8	33	27	14	12	3
2004 Dec 5-8	33	24	17	11	3
2003 Dec 11-14	31	28	18	13	3
2002 Nov 22-24	30	30	15	15	3
2001 Nov 26-27	32	30	15	13	2
2000 Nov 13-15	33	28	15	13	2
1999 Nov 18-21	35	27	14	13	6
1998 Dec 4-6	24	25	22	14	8
1994 Dec 2-5	22	20	23	19	9
1993 Dec 4-6	19	27	20	17	8
1992 Dec 12-18	19	24	20	18	10
1991 Dec 12-15	20	24	22	19	7
1990 Nov 29-Dec 2	17	25	23	19	7
1989 Oct 12-15	18	23	25	15	4

Final Gallup pre-Christmas measures for each year

Everyone's Cutting Back

Intended Christmas spending is down compared with December 2007 among all income categories, although the drop has been particularly steep among wealthy shoppers (those in households making $75,000 or more per year) and middle-income consumers (in households making $30,000 to $74,999 per year).

The December 2008 average estimated spending of $954 among adults in upper-income households is the first time since at least 2001 that spending among this group has averaged below $1,100. The average $625 estimate among middle-income adults marks the first time in the same period that this group has fallen below $750.

Estimated Christmas Spending by Income, 2001-2008

Mean dollar amount, including zero

■ $75,000+   ■ $30,000 to $74,999   ■ Less than $30,000

It is interesting to note that on a long-term basis, since 2001, spending has dropped most sharply among lower-income households, falling 38% from $531 to $331. By contrast, spending has fallen by 26% among those in middle-income households (from $850 to $625) and by only 20% (from $1,190 to $9,540) among higher-income earners.

Gallup's 2008 Christmas spending data suggest Americans are highly reluctant to part with their hard-earned dollars right now, and, short of possibly capitalizing on deep holiday discounts and promotions, they show relatively little enthusiasm for Christmas shopping.

In a good year, the retail industry hopes to beat the 10-year average of 4.4% growth in holiday sales. Last year it saw a below-average 3.0% rise in year-over-year sales for the months of November and December, making 2007 one of the worst holiday retail seasons in recent memory. But given the sharp decline in Americans' projected spending, this year's spending figures could easily wind up in negative territory, with November/December retail sales totaling less than they did a year ago.

Survey Methods

Results are based on telephone interviews with 1,009 national adults, aged 18 and older, conducted Dec. 4-7, 2008. For results based on the total sample of national adults, one can say with 95% confidence that the maximum margin of sampling error is ±3 percentage points.

Interviews are conducted with respondents on land-line telephones (for respondents with a land-line telephone) and cellular phones (for respondents who are cell-phone only).

In addition to sampling error, question wording and practical difficulties in conducting surveys can introduce error or bias into the findings of public opinion polls.

December 15, 2008

CABLE, INTERNET NEWS SOURCES GROWING IN POPULARITY

Local television news remains preferred daily source

by Lymari Morales, Gallup Poll Staff Writer

Amid announcements from the Tribune Company, National Public Radio, and *Newsweek* last week of cutbacks to deal with extreme economic pressures, Gallup's update on Americans' go-to news sources reveals little encouragement for these media. Among daily news sources, only cable and Internet news have shown significant gains in popularity since 2006, while all other media are stable or declining.

How often do you get your news from each of the following sources -- every day, several times a week, occasionally, or never. How about -- [RANDOM ORDER]?

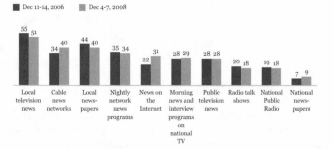

Local television news continues to be Americans' preferred source of daily news, with more than half of Americans (51%) say-

ing they turn to it daily. Cable news and local newspapers are everyday sources of news for 40% of Americans. And for the first time since Gallup began asking this question in 1995, significantly more Americans say they turn to cable news networks daily than say they turn to nightly network news programs, though it is worth noting that the popularity of the network news programs has remained fairly stable compared with recent years.

Please indicate how often you get your news from each of the following sources -- every day, several times a week, occasionally, or never. How about -- ?

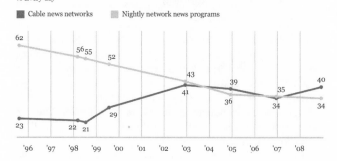

Not surprisingly, the Internet has shown the biggest increase in popularity as a news source, with 31% of Americans now saying it is a daily news source. This marks a nearly 50% increase since 2006 and a more than 100% increase from 2002. Use of the Internet as a news source has increased each time Gallup has asked about it, beginning in 1995.

Please indicate how often you get your news from each of the following sources -- every day, several times a week, occasionally, or never. How about -- ?

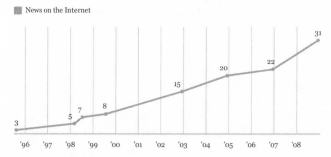

The bankruptcy filing last week by the Tribune Co.—which publishes the *Chicago Tribune*, the *Los Angeles Times*, *The Baltimore Sun* and other daily newspapers—is a sign of continuing distress for the nation's newspapers, which have in recent years struggled to stay afloat in the midst of declining readership and dwindling advertising dollars. Fewer Americans than at any time in a decade say they read a local newspaper daily, and fewer than 1 in 10 say they read a national newspaper like *The New York Times*, the *Wall Street Journal*, or *USA Today* each day. This year's slight uptick for the latter, from 7% to 9%, is within the survey's margin of error.

National Public Radio, which last week announced its first organization-wide layoffs in 25 years owing to a steep decline in underwriting, has actually maintained steady listenership over the years. The 18% of Americans this year who say they turn to National Public Radio daily is in fact exactly on par with the 18% who said the same in 1995.

Please indicate how often you get your news from each of the following sources --
every day, several times a week, occasionally, or never. How about -- ?

% Every day

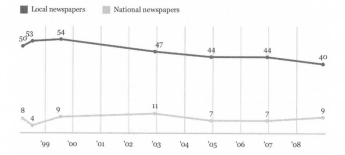

Among weekly news sources, Sunday morning television news programs are up ever so slightly in popularity and now are at their highest point ever. On the flip side, evening television newsmagazine shows are declining in popularity, as are weekly newsmagazines.

How often do you get your news from each of the following weekly sources of
news: every week, several times a month, occasionally, or never. How about --
[ITEMS READ IN ORDER]?

% Every week

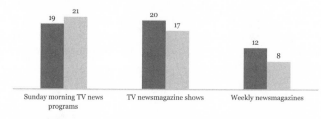

The decline in popularity for weekly magazines like *Newsweek*, which announced layoffs last week, marks a steep dropoff from 2006 and an all-time Gallup low.

How often do you get your news from each of the following weekly sources of
news: every week, several times a month, occasionally, or never. How about --
[ITEMS READ IN ORDER]?

% Every week

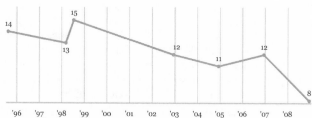

Because most news organizations rely on advertising as an important source of revenue, Americans in the critical 25 to 54 age demographic are the most sought after. This year's update reveals, for the most part, solid gains among young and middle-aged Americans for Internet news, cable news, and, interestingly, national newspapers. More generally, Americans 65 and older remain the most frequent consumers of all types of daily news.

Bottom Line

In already-tough times for the news organizations, there are few signs that things will get easier anytime soon. Only cable and Internet news sources appear to be growing their audiences in any measurable way. At the same time, most media are holding steady or slipping only slightly, which may come as good news for some. Together, these data suggest the audience may still be there for most traditional news sources, underscoring the need for media organizations to find new ways to turn eyeballs into revenue. For many, this may require discovering creative ways to capitalize on the growing thirst for Internet news.

Survey Methods

Results are based on telephone interviews with 1,009 national adults, aged 18 and older, conducted Dec 4-7, 2008. For results based on the total sample of national adults, one can say with 95% confidence that the maximum margin of sampling error is ±3 percentage points.

Interviews are conducted with respondents on land-line telephones (for respondents with a land-line telephone) and cellular phones (for respondents who are cell-phone only).

In addition to sampling error, question wording and practical difficulties in conducting surveys can introduce error or bias into the findings of public opinion polls.

December 16, 2008
REPUBLICANS IN CONGRESS LESS POPULAR THAN BUSH
Only one in four approve of the Republicans, their worst rating since 1999

by Jeffrey M. Jones, Gallup Poll Managing Editor

Just one in four Americans approve of the job the Republicans in Congress are doing, an approval rating just below that given to President Bush. Americans are somewhat more charitable in their ratings of the Democrats in Congress.

Latest Job Approval Ratings

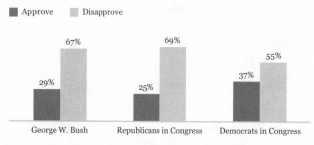

Dec. 12-14 USA Today/Gallup Poll

The 25% approval rating for the Republicans in Congress establishes a new Gallup Poll low, surpassing the 26% measured about this time last year. Gallup first began asking about approval of the Congressional parties in 1999.

Congressional Democrats' approval rating is also low from an historical perspective, but does represent a significant improvement from 30% measured a year ago, their lowest rating to date.

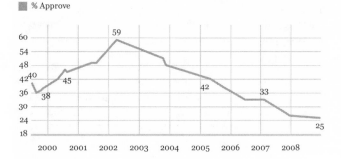

Approval Ratings of Republicans in Congress, 1999-2008 Gallup Polls

ever, Richard Nixon has the distinction for the lowest term average of 34.4% from the beginning of his second term to his resignation amidst the Watergate scandal.

Bolstered by very high ratings following the Sept. 11 terrorist attacks, Bush averaged 62% job approval his first term in office, one of the better term averages for a president.

The overall unpopularity of the current government incumbents stands in contrast to the high ratings given to president-elect Barack Obama. The Dec. 12-14 poll finds 75% approving of the way he is handling his presidential transition. Certainly, the decisions made during a presidential transition are not likely to be as controversial as those made while governing, and all president-elects and new presidents enjoy a bit of a "honeymoon period" with positive ratings. Indeed, both Bush and Bill Clinton received very high scores for the way they handled their transitions.

Even so, Obama has been rated significantly more positively than both Bush (who averaged 63% approval) and Clinton (66%) during their transitions.

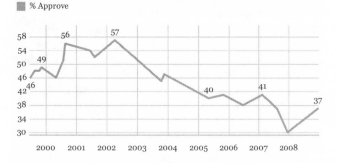

Approval Ratings of Democrats in Congress, 1999-2008 Gallup Polls

Survey Methods

Results are based on telephone interviews with 1,008 national adults, aged 18 and older, conducted Dec. 12-14, 2008. For results based on the total sample of national adults, one can say with 95% confidence that the maximum margin of sampling error is ±3 percentage points.

Interviews are conducted with respondents on land-line telephones (for respondents with a land-line telephone) and cellular phones (for respondents who are cell-phone only).

In addition to sampling error, question wording and practical difficulties in conducting surveys can introduce error or bias into the findings of public opinion polls.

Congress' overall approval rating—asked without reference to either party and measured in a Dec. 4-7 Gallup Poll—is just 20%. Typically, both Congressional parties receive higher approval ratings than the institution overall. Asking about the individual parties appears to cause respondents to answer in more partisan terms. In general, ratings of Congress overall do not vary much by party affiliation, but the approval ratings of the parties in Congress show large differences when looking at party affiliation.

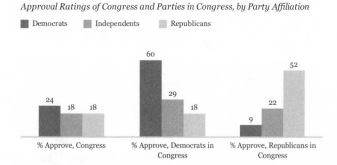

Approval Ratings of Congress and Parties in Congress, by Party Affiliation

Bush Job Approval Slump Continues

Bush's 29% job approval rating in the Dec. 12-14 *USA Today*/Gallup poll matches his average since Election Day. It remains slightly above the 25% rating he had in the final pre-election poll. However, it continues Bush's 27-month streak of approval ratings below 40%—his last approval rating above that mark came in September 2006.

Bush has now matched Harry Truman's string of sub-40% approval ratings which began in late October 1950 and continued through the end of his presidency. Bush will surpass Truman's record if his approval ratings remain below 40% for his last month in office.

In his second term in office to date, Bush has averaged 36.5% approval. That is the same as Truman's second-term average. How-

December 16, 2008

UNIONS SECOND TO AUTO EXECS IN BAILOUT BLAME GAME

Americans split evenly between wanting legislation to pass or fail

by Lydia Saad, Gallup Poll Senior Editor

Executives of the U.S. auto industry take the brunt of public criticism for the failure of Congress to pass an auto bailout package last week, with 64% of Americans saying the auto executives deserve a great deal of the blame. However, the unions representing U.S. autoworkers are next in line, faulted by 43% of Americans—more than the 35% who blame the Republicans in Congress.

Only 20% of Americans blame the failure of the auto bailout bill on the Democrats in Congress—most of whom voted for the $14 billion aid package for the Big Three U.S. auto manufacturers.

This is according to a Dec. 12-14 *USA Today*/Gallup poll, conducted in the first few days after an auto bailout agreement reached between congressional Democrats and the Bush administration fell apart on a procedural vote in the U.S. Senate on Dec. 11.

Split Decision on Bailout Vote

According to the same survey, Americans are about evenly divided over the merits of the failed bailout package: 47% say they would rather have seen the legislation pass, while 46% preferred that it fail.

As you may know, legislation to provide government financial assistance to the Big Three U.S. auto companies failed in Congress this past week. ...

How much do you blame each of the following for the failure of this legislation to pass -- a great deal, a moderate amount, not much, or not at all?

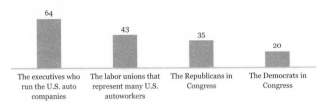

USA Today/Gallup, Dec. 12-14, 2008

Most Democrats support the auto bailout, while most Republicans and half of independents oppose it.

As you may know, legislation to provide government financial assistance to the Big Three U.S. auto companies failed in Congress this past week. Would you rather have seen this legislation pass or see this legislation fail?

USA Today/Gallup, Dec. 12-14, 2008

In a follow-up question, most of those who wanted the plan to fail—representing about a third of all Americans—said they oppose the government's providing any sort of bailout package for the auto companies. However, a smaller number, representing 14% of all Americans, say they support a bailout, just not the particular plan that came to a vote.

Would you rather have seen this legislation pass or see this legislation fail? (If fail: Is that mainly because -- [you would support a bailout plan but not the one that failed this week, (or mainly because) you oppose the idea of the government providing any bailout plan to the auto companies]?)

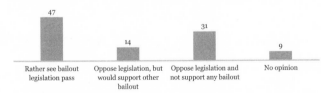

USA Today/Gallup, Dec. 12-14, 2008

Thus, in total, 61% of Americans favor some sort of government help for the auto industry.

Unions vs. the Republicans

That most Americans assign a high degree of blame to auto industry executives for the auto bailout's demise may not be surprising given the substantial negative publicity surrounding the way these execu-

tives handled their initial appearances before Congress leading up to the vote—both their arrival by private jet and their failure to have a business plan for using the bailout money. This seems to be reflected in the fact that large majorities of Republicans, independents, and Democrats fault the executives a great deal for the bill's failure.

Percentage Blaming U.S. Auto Executives "a Great Deal" for Failure of Bailout Legislation, by Party ID

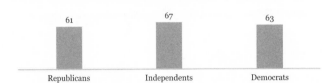

USA Today/Gallup, Dec. 12-14, 2008

It is somewhat more intriguing that Americans blame the autoworker unions to a greater extent than the Republicans in Congress, as the last-minute collapse of the bill was widely reported as occurring on the basis of the auto unions' failing to yield to Republican demands for more wage concessions.

Among the partisan groups, rank-and-file Republicans are the most critical of the auto unions, with 59% saying they bear a great deal of blame for the bailout's demise—similar to the degree to which they blame the auto executives. Only 23% of Republicans blame the Republicans in Congress. However, political independents are also much more likely to blame the auto unions than the Republicans, 41% to 29%. Democrats, by contrast, see things the other way, with more blaming the Republicans than the unions, 48% to 35%.

The Democrats in Congress receive little blame from all three parties.

How much do you blame each of the following for the failure of this legislation to pass -- a great deal, a moderate amount, not much, or not at all? How about [RANDOM ORDER]?

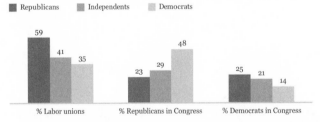

USA Today/Gallup, Dec. 12-14, 2008

Earlier this month, Gallup found less public criticism of the autoworker unions with respect to culpability for the financial problems that the three major U.S. auto companies face. In a Dec. 4-7 Gallup Poll, only 34% blamed the labor unions for the industry's problems, while 65% blamed the executives who run the auto companies.

Bottom Line

Americans are very clear in holding the U.S. auto executives responsible for the financial mess they find themselves in, with 65% saying they deserve a great deal of blame for the financial problems of their companies, and 64% assigning them great blame for the failure of bailout legislation. Americans are more likely to blame the autoworker unions than the Republicans for the auto bailout bill's failure to pass last week.

Still, it appears that as many as 6 in 10 Americans are in favor of the government's providing financial help to the Big Three—if not in the form of the specific package that failed, then something else. With a few weeks remaining before the new Congress is installed, the solvency of the U.S. auto industry may now depend on whether President Bush decides to provide it with funds from the $700 billion bailout of the financial industry, but it remains to be seen whether Americans would support that approach.

40. How much do you blame each of the following for the failure of this legislation to pass -- a great deal, a moderate amount, not much, or not at all? How about [RANDOM ORDER]?

	Great deal	Moderate amount	Not much	Not at all	No opinion
	%	%	%	%	%
The executives who run the U.S. auto companies	64	20	7	5	5
The labor unions that represent many U.S. auto workers	43	26	15	9	6
The Republicans in Congress	35	30	15	11	9
The Democrats in Congress	20	29	24	17	10

USA Today/Gallup, Dec. 12-14, 2008

Survey Methods

Results are based on telephone interviews with 1,008 national adults, aged 18 and older, conducted Dec. 12-14, 2008. For results based on the total sample of national adults, one can say with 95% confidence that the maximum margin of sampling error is ±3 percentage points.

Interviews are conducted with respondents on land-line telephones (for respondents with a land-line telephone) and cellular phones (for respondents who are cell-phone only).

In addition to sampling error, question wording and practical difficulties in conducting surveys can introduce error or bias into the findings of public opinion polls.

December 17, 2008
JOBLESS, BAILOUT NEWS TRIGGER UNHAPPIEST DAY SO FAR IN 2008
The five least happy days of 2008 in U.S. coincide with negative economic news

by Elizabeth Mendes, Gallup Poll Staff Writer

The percentage of Americans experiencing a lot of happiness or enjoyment without a lot of stress or worry fell to a new low of 35% on Thursday, Dec. 11, the same day the U.S. Labor Department announced that new jobless claims jumped to a 26-year high and the auto bailout bill failed in the Senate. The Gallup-Healthways mood measure, which consistently finds happiness higher on weekends and lower on weekdays, finds that thus far in 2008, the five days on which Americans experienced the lowest levels of happiness all coincided with highly negative economic news.

On two of those five days, Nov. 20 and Dec. 11, the Labor Department reported a steep rise in new jobless claims. The other

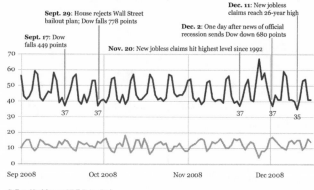

Gallup Daily: Mood
Based on emotion experienced Sept.1-Dec.16, 2008

■ % With a lot of happiness or enjoyment without a lot of stress or worry
▬ % With a lot of stress or worry without a lot of happiness or enjoyment

Gallup-Healthways Well-Being Index

three lows in happiness occurred the day of or the day after major drops in the Dow.

Gallup Daily: Mood -- Five Least Happy Days in 2008
Based on Gallup-Healthways Well-Being Index

	Event	% Happiness/ Enjoyment
Dec 11, 2008	New jobless claims reach 26-year high	35%
Dec 2, 2008	One day after news of official recession sends Dow down 680 points	37%
Nov 20, 2008	New jobless claims hit highest level since 1992	37%
Sep 29, 2008	House rejects Wall Street bailout plan; Dow falls 778 points	37%
Sep 17, 2008	Dow falls 449 points	37%

* Denotes a tie.

Exactly two weeks prior to the Dec. 11 low, happiness had hit an all-time high for the year of 67% on Thanksgiving Day. Including Thanksgiving, the four happiest days of the year have occurred on holidays, with New Year's Day, the day after Independence Day, and Father's Day tying for the fifth happiest.

Gallup Daily: Mood -- Five Happiest Days in 2008
Based on Gallup-Healthways Well-Being Index

	Event	% Happiness/ Enjoyment
Nov 27, 2008	Thanksgiving	67%
Mar 23, 2008	Easter	65%
Jul 4, 2008	Independence Day	64%
May 11, 2008	Mother's Day	63%
Jan 1, 2008*	New Year's	62%
Jul 5, 2008*	Day after Independence Day	62%
Jun 15, 2008*	Father's Day	62%

* Denotes a tie.

For a majority of Americans, holidays are an occasion when they can spend a larger-than-normal amount of time socializing with friends and family. The Gallup-Healthways mood measure has previously reported that the days of the year when the most Americans experience happiness or enjoyment also tend to be days they report spending more time with friends and family. On the other hand, throughout 2008, Gallup has found lows in happiness to be consistent with news of a faltering economy.

Prior to the worsening of the financial crisis in September, Gallup found that 58% of Americans reported a lot of happiness or enjoyment without a lot of stress or worry on a typical Saturday or Sunday, compared to 46% on a typical Monday. Since mid-September, weekend levels as well as weekday levels of happiness have frequently been lower than they were before the crisis.

Survey Methods

For the Gallup Poll Daily tracking survey, Gallup is interviewing no fewer than 1,000 U.S. adults nationwide each day during 2008. The U.S. mood results are based on data from Sept. 1-Dec. 16, 2008, and the maximum margin of sampling error is ±2 percentage points.

Interviews are conducted with respondents on land-line telephones (for respondents with a land-line telephone) and cellular phones (for respondents who are cell-phone only).

In addition to sampling error, question wording and practical difficulties in conducting surveys can introduce error or bias into the findings of public opinion polls.

December 17, 2008
NO EVIDENCE BAD TIMES ARE BOOSTING CHURCH ATTENDANCE
An average of 42% have attended regularly all year

by Frank Newport, Gallup Poll Editor in Chief

Despite some news reports to the contrary, a review of almost 300,000 interviews conducted by Gallup so far in 2008 shows no evidence that church attendance in America has been increasing late this year as a result of bad economic times. In September, October, November, and so far in December, about 42% of Americans reported that they attended church weekly or almost every week, exactly the same as the percentage who reported attending earlier in the year.

How often do you attend church, synagogue, or mosque -- at least once a week, almost every week, about once a month, seldom, or never?

% At least once a week/Almost every week, monthly averages

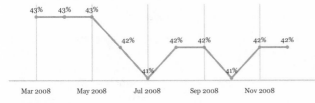

Gallup Poll Daily tracking

A recent story in the *New York Times*, written by Paul Vitello, was headlined "Bad Times Draw Bigger Crowds to Churches," and reported that evangelical churches in particular had enjoyed a "burst

of new interest" since September, but also that "a recent spot check of some large Roman Catholic parishes and mainline Protestant churches around the nation indicated attendance increases there, too." Producers for NBC's "Today" show picked up this *New York Times* story, and it became the basis for a similarly themed feature broadcast on that show on Dec. 16.

It may be true that some evangelical churches, such as those whose leaders were interviewed in the *New York Times* article, have enjoyed big increases in attendance this fall as the economic crisis has worsened. But a review of Gallup Poll Daily tracking data, in which 1,000 randomly selected people each day are asked how often they attend church, shows absolutely no change this year in the overall self-reported pattern of church attendance across the country as a whole. About 42% of American adults aged 18 and older have reported since mid-February that they attend church at least once a week or almost every week, and there has been no sign of any increase this fall. (There has also been no significant change in the percentage of Americans who say they attend church about once a month, seldom, or never.)

A separate Gallup Poll question asking about church attendance "in the last seven days" was updated in a Dec. 4-7 Gallup Poll, and also found no sign of an increase in church attendance. Thirty-nine percent of those interviewed in this poll said they had attended church or synagogue in the last seven days, unchanged from May of this year, and below the typical 40%+ estimates from prior years.

Did you, yourself, happen to attend church or synagogue in the last seven days, or not?

% Yes

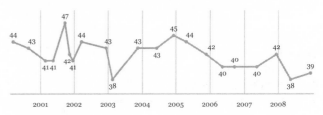

Gallup Poll Daily tracking

These Gallup figures are self-reports of church attendance, and do not represent actual attendance in terms of respondents' demonstrable, physical presence at a worship service.

It is possible that actual church attendance within any given week may be different from these self-reports. The question wording for Gallup's main church attendance question neither asks respondents to specify attendance in a recent time period (such as the last week) nor asks them for a generalized average. It simply says: "How often do you attend church, synagogue, or mosque?" Respondents may still average or generalize in their answers. If so, it is possible that short-term worship service attendance could increase while at the same time these types of self-reports of attendance remain constant. Still, it is a reasonable presumption that if real-world church attendance had gone up this fall in some type of meaningful way, this increase would be reflected in the response patterns to the church attendance question.

It is also possible that certain specific churches or even types of churches (such as the evangelical churches featured in the *New York Times* article) have seen an increase in attendance but that on a percentage basis, these represent such a tiny part of the universe of all churches that this increase is not reflected in broad, national church attendance percentages. Of course, this to some degree is the point the present analysis is making. If there has been some alteration in church attendance caused by the economic bad times, it does not appear to have been of sufficient magnitude or scope to have altered ongoing church attendance patterns in the overall U.S. population.

In summary, the available data on self-reported church attendance among American adults do not appear—as of mid-December—to support the hypothesis that on a society-wide basis, the current bad economic times have resulted in an increase in Americans' church-going behavior.

Survey Methods

For the Gallup Poll Daily tracking survey, Gallup is interviewing no fewer than 1,000 U.S. adults nationwide each day during 2008. For the monthly "How often do you attend church" results reviewed in this article, based on approximately 30,000 interviews, the maximum margin of sampling error is ±1 percentage point.

Results of the "Last seven days" question are based on telephone interviews with 1,009 national adults, aged 18 and older, conducted Dec. 4-7, 2008. For results based on this sample of national adults, one can say with 95% confidence that the maximum margin of sampling error is ±3 percentage points.

Interviews are conducted with respondents on land-line telephones (for respondents with a land-line telephone) and cellular phones (for respondents who are cell-phone only).

In addition to sampling error, question wording and practical difficulties in conducting surveys can introduce error or bias into the findings of public opinion polls.

December 18, 2008
AUTOMAKER WOES NOT A MAJOR FACTOR IN CAR-BUYING DECISIONS
Broader economic concerns more consequential

by Jeffrey M. Jones, Gallup Poll Managing Editor

A recent Gallup Poll found 24% of Americans saying they considered getting a new car in the past six months but decided against it. They were most likely to cite broad economic concerns—rather than the plight of the U.S. automakers—as reasons for their decision.

Would you say that each of the following is a major reason, a minor reason, or not a reason why you have put off looking for a car?

Based on those who have considered buying a car in the last six months but who decided not to

■ Minor reason   ▨ Major reason

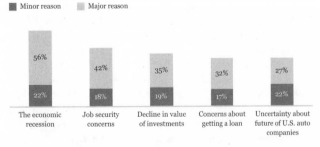

Gallup Poll, Dec. 4-7, 2008

Less than half of those who have dropped out of the car-buying market said uncertainty about the future of the "Big Three" U.S. auto companies was either a major (27%) or a minor (22%) factor in their

decision. A majority of these respondents cited the economic recession as a major reason.

The latest *USA Today*/Gallup poll also finds that the Big Three's current struggles are not yet acting as a major deterrent to those who in general would consider buying an American car. Just 7% say the possibility that one or more of the Big Three U.S. automakers will go bankrupt would make them "much less willing" to buy an American car. Another 18% say they would be "somewhat less willing," but the vast majority say it would not affect their decision.

Does the possibility that one or more of the three U.S. auto companies might go into bankruptcy make you much less willing to buy an American car, somewhat less willing, or would it not affect your decision about buying an American car?

Based on those who would consider buying an American car

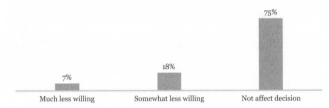

USA Today/Gallup poll, Dec. 12-14, 2008

While this suggests that most of the normal U.S. car market would still be in play for the Big Three even as they struggle to remain solvent, the 7% who are much less willing to buy from them at this time, though a small proportion of the total, represents potentially millions of buyers.

However, if one of the Big Three does in fact go into bankruptcy, that company's pool of potential buyers would be limited even further. Thirty percent of those who would consider buying an American car say they would definitely not buy from a company that is in bankruptcy, though the majority of 67% would still consider it.

Implications

These data suggest that the broader economic problems are contributing more to the slump in U.S. car sales than concerns about the health of the Big Three U.S. auto companies. But clearly, some proportion of buyers are concerned enough about the health of these companies that it is causing them to factor it into their decision-making, if not rule out U.S. cars altogether.

With the auto companies needing all the help they can get—and the federal government so far not stepping forward to provide any—this is not welcome news for the Big Three. However, the news could be a lot worse since most Americans still say they would consider buying American cars, with a significant proportion even willing to do so from a bankrupt automaker.

Survey Methods

Results are based on telephone interviews with 1,008 national adults, aged 18 and older, conducted Dec. 12-14, 2008. For results based on the total sample of national adults, one can say with 95% confidence that the maximum margin of sampling error is ±3 percentage points.

Interviews are conducted with respondents on land-line telephones (for respondents with a land-line telephone) and cellular phones (for respondents who are cell-phone only).

In addition to sampling error, question wording and practical difficulties in conducting surveys can introduce error or bias into the findings of public opinion polls.

December 19, 2008

ABOUT 40% OF AMERICANS WORRYING ABOUT MONEY

Percentage is higher than the average for the first eight months of 2008

by Frank Newport, Gallup Poll Editor in Chief

About 40% of Americans on average are currently worrying about money, sustaining a slight but significant increase in worry compared to readings before September of this year.

Gallup Daily: Personal Finance

% Who worried about money "yesterday"

 Seven-day rolling average

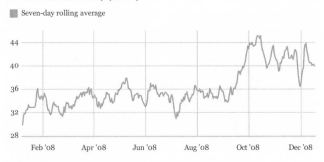

Gallup Poll Daily tracking

Gallup's personal finance measure reports the percentage of Americans who say they worried about money "yesterday." The results, although varying significantly by day of the week, are highly stable when aggregated on a rolling, seven-day basis, as reflected in the accompanying seven-day rolling average chart. (Gallup.com reports a three-day rolling average daily.)

Americans' self-reports that they worried about money began 2008 near 30% on average, and then rose to an average of about 35% through the end of the summer. Then, as was the case for other consumer economic measures Gallup tracks, financial worry begin to rise in mid- to late September, coincident with the highly publicized credit crisis. The average worry level peaked at about 45% in early October, and has fallen back slightly since, generally remaining above the 40% level. The notable exception was a drop in financial worry around the Thanksgiving holiday.

Thus, on average, there appears to have been about a five-point increase in the percentage of Americans who worry about money, when the current situation is compared to that which obtained for the first eight months of the year. The large sample sizes involved in this tracking—about 3,500 interviews per seven-day rolling average—underscore the conclusion that while the increase in worry is not large on an absolute basis, it is significant and meaningful.

At the same time, it is worth noting that fewer Americans report personally having worried about money than report a negative evaluation of the U.S. economy. The latter has been running at about a 75% to 80% negative rating in recent days, almost twice as high as the financial worry number. In other words, Americans are much more likely to report having a negative view of the overall economy than they are to say they personally worried about money. This is another indication that Americans remain personally resilient in the face of the highly negative economic news and environment that engulf the country at this time.

Not surprisingly, there are significant variations in worry by day of the week. An analysis of more than 150,000 interviews conducted since the beginning of the year shows that Americans are most likely to say they worried about money on the first four days of the work week, with a slight dropoff in worry on Friday, and then a bigger dropoff in financial worry on Saturday and Sunday.

Gallup Daily: Personal Finance

% Who worried about money, by day of the week they worried

2008 average for each day

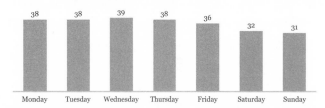

Gallup Poll Daily tracking

These results suggest that the weekend is a "time off" from financial worry for many Americans, even though for some, the weekend may be a time to focus on paying bills, household shopping, and other financial chores.

Implications

There is good news and bad news in a consideration of these "worry" data, which Gallup tracks on a daily basis. The good news is that the majority of Americans on a day-in, day-out basis say they did not worry about money "yesterday," a number that is far less negative than Americans' ratings of the economy and their ratings of how easy it is to find a quality job. The bad news is that this worry percentage has increased significantly since September, and shows no signs at the moment of dropping to the lower benchmark set in the first half of the year.

Survey Methods

For the Gallup Poll Daily tracking survey, Gallup is interviewing no fewer than 1,000 U.S. adults nationwide each day during 2008. The "did you worry about money yesterday" results are asked of a random half sample of each day's interviews, and for any given 7-day rolling average of results, consisting of approximately 3,500 interviews, the maximum margin of sampling error is ±2 percentage points.

Results of the "Did you worry about money yesterday" question aggregated by day of the week are based on approximately 21,500 interviews per weekday. For results based on this sample of national adults, one can say with 95% confidence that the maximum margin of sampling error is ±1 percentage point.

Interviews are conducted with respondents on land-line telephones (for respondents with a land-line telephone) and cellular phones (for respondents who are cell-phone only).

In addition to sampling error, question wording and practical difficulties in conducting surveys can introduce error or bias into the findings of public opinion polls.

December 19, 2008

DESPITE ECONOMY, CHARITABLE DONORS, VOLUNTEERS KEEP GIVING

Most Americans gave financial support to a charity in past year

by Lydia Saad, Gallup Poll Senior Editor

Despite the significant downturn in economic conditions in recent years, the percentage of U.S. adults opening their wallets to charitable organizations has hardly diminished. More than four in five Americans continue to say they donated money to a charitable cause or organization in the past 12 months—now 84%, compared with 87% in December 2005.

Total Percentage of Americans Donating Money to Charitable Organization/Cause in Past 12 Months

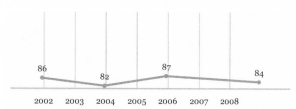

The latest results come from Gallup's 2008 Lifestyle Survey, conducted Dec. 4-7. The total number of charitable donors is based on separate measures asking Americans whether they financially support religious organizations and whether they support nonreligious organizations.

Gallup trends on these measures show virtually no change since 2005 in the percentage of Americans making donations to nonreligious causes (76% in 2005 vs. 75% today), but a slight dip, from 64% to 59%, in the percentage supporting religious entities.

Which of the following things, if any, have you, personally, done in the past 12 months?

■ % Donated money to a religious organization

▨ % Donated money to any other charitable cause

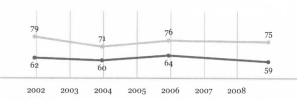

The survey asks only whether respondents donated or not, not how much they gave, and thus cannot quantify the extent to which the amount of charitable giving may, in fact, be down because of the recession.

Time Is Money—and Harder to Come By

Aside from cash donations, many charities rely heavily on the free labor volunteers provide to staff events, perform office duties, and run fundraisers, among countless other tasks.

According to the Gallup data, fewer Americans part with their time than their money on behalf of charity groups. Sixty-four percent of Americans currently say they have volunteered their time to a charity in the past 12 months, similar to the 62% recorded in 2005.

Total Percentage of Americans Volunteering Time to a Charitable Organization/Cause in Past 12 Months

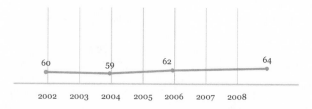

Gallup finds little difference between volunteerism on behalf of religious organizations and that for nonreligious organizations. Exactly half of all Americans in 2008 say they volunteered their time to a nonreligious charitable cause over the past year, while 43% say they volunteered with a religious group or organization, resulting in a modest seven-point gap between the two activities. This contrasts with the 16-point gap in religious vs. nonreligious financial giving: 59% vs. 75%.

Neither type of volunteering has changed appreciably over the past three years, although nonreligious volunteerism is up from 2003, when the figure was 43%.

Which of the following things, if any, have you, personally, done in the past 12 months?

■ % Volunteered your time to a religious organization

▨ % Volunteered your time to any other charitable cause

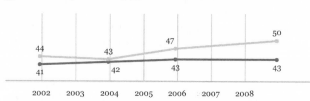

A special form of giving involves donating blood to a medical blood bank, such as the American Red Cross. The rate of Americans' provision of this important service has been stable at around 15% each year in the past several years. It was substantially higher when Gallup first measured it in December 2001, but that was just three months after the Sept. 11 terrorist attacks—an event that may have raised public awareness of the need for blood donations, or temporarily boosted Americans' willingness to make the effort to give.

Total Percentage of Americans Donating Blood in Past 12 Months

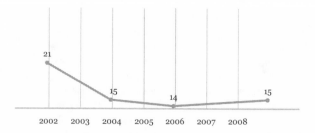

Protestants Lead in Religious Giving

Religious giving and volunteerism are naturally much higher among Americans who proclaim a religious affiliation than among those with no particular affiliation and the nonreligious. Among Christians, the prevalence of financial donors and volunteers to religious organizations is higher among Protestants than among Catholics.

By contrast, there is no difference among Protestants, Catholics, and the nonreligious in the percentage of each saying they contributed money to a nonreligious charity over the past year. There is also no appreciable difference in the percentages donating blood. (The number of respondents falling into other religious categories is too small to analyze.)

Charitable Activity, by Religion
% Who did each of the following in the past 12 months

	Protestants	Catholics	No religion
	%	%	%
Donated to nonreligious groups	77	74	74
Donated to religious groups	72	60	19
Volunteered for nonreligious groups	48	49	60
Volunteered for religious groups	51	38	17
Donated blood	15	14	17

Dec. 4-7, 2008

Bottom Line

Charitable giving is a way of life for Americans, most of whom (75%) have provided financial support to a nonreligious charity over the past year. Additionally, more than half (59%) have donated money to a religious organization—quite likely their own church or other house of worship.

The fact that the nation has been in recession for the past year may have cut into the amount of money Americans are able to contribute (the survey does not record the dollar value of donations); however, it has not had much impact on the total pool of givers. The percentage of Americans donating money to nonreligious charities is as high today as it was in 2005, and the percentage giving to religious groups is down only slightly.

Survey Methods

Results are based on telephone interviews with 1,009 national adults, aged 18 and older, conducted Dec. 4-7, 2008. For results based on the total sample of national adults, one can say with 95% confidence that the maximum margin of sampling error is ±3 percentage points.

Interviews are conducted with respondents on land-line telephones (for respondents with a land-line telephone) and cellular phones (for respondents who are cell-phone only).

In addition to sampling error, question wording and practical difficulties in conducting surveys can introduce error or bias into the findings of public opinion polls.

December 22, 2008
IDEA OF ECONOMIC DEPRESSION BECOMING LESS FAR-FETCHED
One-quarter now rule it out, vs. 40% in March

by Lydia Saad, Gallup Poll Senior Editor

Since March, the percentage of Americans largely ruling out the possibility of an economic depression in the next two years has shrunk

from 40% to 25%, while the percentage saying it is "very likely" has grown from 23% to 35%. Although Americans who predict the worst for the economy remain in the minority, another 39% think a depression is "somewhat likely" to occur.

Likelihood United States Will Be In an Economic Depression Within Next Two Years

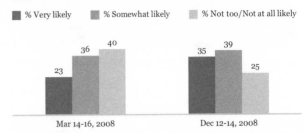

Even if they don't think a true economic depression—defined for respondents as a particularly severe recession lasting several years—is very likely, the majority of Americans consider the current economic situation in the United States to be the "biggest economic crisis" the country has faced in their lifetimes. Sixty percent hold this view, while another 16% call it a crisis, but not the worst in their lifetimes.

Which of the following would you say best describes the current economic situation in the United States -- the biggest economic crisis the U.S. has faced in your lifetime, a crisis but not the worst in your lifetime, a major problem, but not a crisis, or not a major problem?

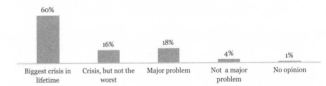

USA Today/Gallup, Dec. 12-14, 2008

Americans' generally bleak economic outlook is borne out in their prediction that it will be much more than another year or two before the economy starts to recover. The majority believe it will take three or more years for that to happen, with the average prediction falling at five years.

Estimated Time Before U.S. Economy Starts to Recover

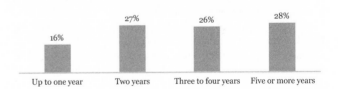

USA Today/Gallup, Dec. 12-14, 2008

Generational Differences in Perspective

One's assessment of how bad the economy is depends in part on whether one was alive during the Great Depression. Solid majorities of adults in the 18 to 34 and 35 to 64 age brackets perceive the current economy to be the worst of their lifetimes. By contrast, half of

Americans 65 and older (those old enough to have lived between 1929 and the early 1940s) do not.

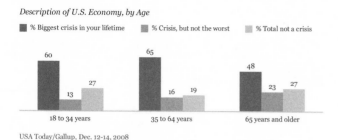

Description of U.S. Economy, by Age

■ % Biggest crisis in your lifetime ■ % Crisis, but not the worst □ % Total not a crisis

USA Today/Gallup, Dec. 12-14, 2008

In spite of being less likely than younger adults to perceive the current economy as the worst in their lifetimes, U.S. seniors are more likely than younger Americans to believe the United States could soon face another depression.

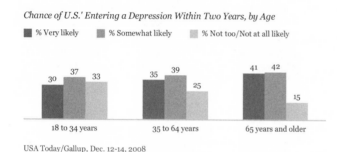

Chance of U.S.' Entering a Depression Within Two Years, by Age

■ % Very likely ■ % Somewhat likely □ % Not too/Not at all likely

USA Today/Gallup, Dec. 12-14, 2008

Bottom Line

Prior to 2008, the Great Depression had seemingly become a curiosity of American history, particularly for young and middle-aged adults who didn't live through it. Now, the idea that the country could slip into a depression lasting several years has expanded to a majority of Americans, with more than a third considering it very possible. Seniors, many of whom experienced the ravages of depression economics firsthand, are the most likely today to believe a depression is in the cards.

Survey Methods

Results are based on telephone interviews with 1,008 national adults, aged 18 and older, conducted Dec. 12-14, 2008. For results based on the total sample of national adults, one can say with 95% confidence that the maximum margin of sampling error is ±3 percentage points.

Interviews are conducted with respondents on land-line telephones (for respondents with a land-line telephone) and cellular phones (for respondents who are cell-phone only).

In addition to sampling error, question wording and practical difficulties in conducting surveys can introduce error or bias into the findings of public opinion polls.

December 22, 2008
U.S. INVESTORS OPTIMISTIC ABOUT LONGER TERM
Slightly optimistic about personal portfolios; highly pessimistic about economy

by Dennis Jacobe, Gallup Poll Chief Economist

Not surprisingly, American investors—defined as those having $10,000 or more of investable assets—remain highly pessimistic about the overall investment with the Gallup Index of Investor Optimism falling to -49 in a new Dec. 16-18 poll. This is down slightly from the already highly pessimistic rating of -47 in November.

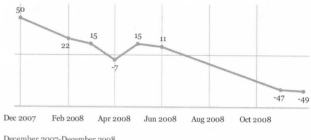

Gallup Index of Investor Optimism

December 2007-December 2008

Investors Highly Pessimistic About the Economic Outlook

A year ago in December 2007, investors were slightly pessimistic about the economic outlook for the next 12 months with the Economic Dimension of the Index at -7—a negative number reflects investors as a group turning pessimistic about the future direction of the economy. This turned out to be a prescient view, as we now know that the U.S. economy has been in recession since December of last year.

Earlier this year, investors turned even more pessimistic about the economic outlook as the Economic Dimension of the Index plunged to -40 in February, surpassing its previous low of -30 in March 2003 set at the outset of the Iraq war. By November, investor pessimism concerning the outlook for the economy over the next 12 months deepened with this dimension of the Index falling even further to -60 before its most recent decline to -64 this month.

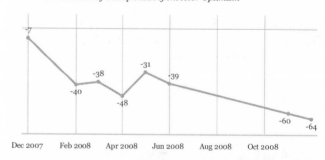

Economic Dimension of Gallup Index of Investor Optimism

Investors Slightly Optimistic About Their Own Portfolios

In sharp contrast to their expectations concerning the future direction of the economy, investors have been reasonably optimistic about their own investment portfolios. Last December, the Personal Dimension of the Index stood at +57. In February of this year, even as they became considerably more pessimistic about the economic outlook, investors remained fairly optimistic about their own portfolios as the Personal Dimension of the Index was at +62. Not surprisingly given the plunging equity markets and the global financial crisis, investor expectations concerning their own investment portfolios have fallen sharply. Nonetheless, in December of this year, investors remained slightly optimistic about their personal portfolios, with the Personal Dimension at +15—one of the lowest levels of personal financial optimism since inception of the Index in October 1996. Still, this positive number is somewhat amazing considering how much the investment climate has deteriorated since the equity markets peaked in October 2007.

Personal Dimension of Gallup Index of Investor Optimism

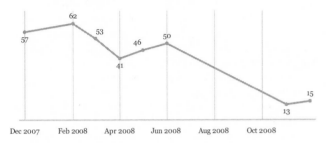

Investors Optimistic About Longer Term

One key source of investor optimism about their personal portfolios has to do with their view of the longer term. By a margin of 57% to 28%, investors say they are optimistic as opposed to pessimistic about their ability to achieve their investment goals over the next five years.

On the other hand, investors have more mixed views of the near term. In terms of their income, they are more optimistic (53%) than pessimistic (27%) about being able to maintain or increase their earnings over the next 12 months. However, in terms of being able to reach their investment targets over the next 12 months, they are more pessimistic (47%) than optimistic (33%).

Survey Methods

Gallup Poll Daily interviewing includes no fewer than 1,000 U.S. adults nationwide each day during 2008. The Index of Investor Optimism results are based on questions asked of 1,000 or more investors over a three-day period each month (Dec. 16-18, Nov. 24-26, June 3-6, April 25-28, March 28-31, and Feb. 28-March 2). For results based on this sample, the maximum margin of sampling error is ±3 percentage point.

Results for May are based on the Gallup Panel study and are based on telephone interviews with 576 national adults, aged 18 and older, conducted May 19-21, 2008. Gallup Panel members are recruited through random selection methods. The panel is weighted so that it is demographically representative of the U.S. adult population. For results based on this sample, one can say with 95% confidence that the maximum margin of sampling error is ±5 percentage points.

For investor results prior to 2008, telephone interviews were conducted with at least 800 investors, aged 18 and older, with at least $10,000 of investable assets. For the total sample of investors in these surveys, one can say with 95% confidence that the margin of sampling error is ±4 percentage points.

In addition to sampling error, question wording and practical difficulties in conducting surveys can introduce error or bias into the findings of public opinion polls.

December 23, 2008
AMERICANS BELIEVE RELIGION IS LOSING CLOUT
Percentage saying influence of religion is slipping at 14-year high

by Lydia Saad, Gallup Poll Senior Editor

Two-thirds of U.S. adults today perceive that the influence of religion in American life is waning, while just 27% believe it is rising. This represents a sharp decline in the image of religion compared with only three years ago, when 50% thought its influence was on an upswing, and marks one of the weakest readings on the influence of religion in Gallup's five-decade history of asking the question.

At the present time, do you think religion as a whole is increasing its influence on American life or losing its influence?

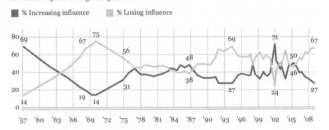

The percentage of Americans saying religion, as a whole, is increasing its influence on American life was 50% in April 2005, 39% in May 2006, 34% in May 2007, and 30% in May 2008. The 27% recorded in the new Dec. 4-7 Gallup Poll thus marks a continuation of the recent downward trend.

The current weak image of religion stands on par with the low ebb recorded in the first half of the Clinton administration in the mid 1990s, but is still not quite as low as it was during the late 1960s and Vietnam War. The record low came in a 1970 Gallup Poll when only 14% of Americans said religion was increasing in influence at that time, while 75% thought it was losing influence.

Indeed, this measure of public perceptions about religion has been quite volatile over the forty-plus years of its existence, with shifts in perception often corresponding to major political events.

The pinnacle for perceptions of religious clout came in Gallup's initial asking of the question in March 1957. At that time, 69% of Americans thought religion was gaining in societal influence while only 14% saw it declining—resulting in a net 55 percentage point advantage for those saying the influence of religion was increasing. This was nearly matched in a December 2001 Gallup Poll—just three months after the 9/11 terrorist attacks—in which 71% said religious influence was increasing and 24% decreasing—a net 47-point advantage to those saying religious influence was on the rise.

After a long period of doubt about the influence of religion during the Vietnam War era—from 1965 through 1975—a December 1976 Gallup Poll found nearly as many Americans saying religion was increasing in influence, as disagreed (44% vs. 45%). This relative high point for perceptions that religion was on the rise could have been associated with the election a month earlier of Jimmy Carter as president, an avowed born-again Christian.

Religion rose even higher in perceived prominence in the 1980s during the presidency of Ronald Reagan, when religious conservatism—also known as the "religious right"—was in ascendance as a potent political force. From 1983 to 1986, Gallup consistently recorded more Americans perceiving religion to be on the rise than in decline.

Given this historical context, it is possible that the recent decline in perceptions that religion is increasing in influence is partially a result of the decline of Republican political strength throughout President George W. Bush's second term, a trend that was punctuated by the election of Democrat Barack Obama last month.

Differences

Large majorities of all gender, age, and political groups perceive religion to be losing influence, but that view is higher among men than women (70% vs. 64%) and is particularly prevalent among regular attendees of their church or other place of worship.

Perceptions of Influence of Religion, Based on Frequency of Attending Religious Services

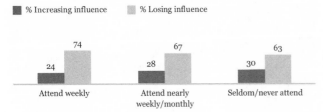

Dec. 4-7, 2008

Is Religion Old-Fashioned?

Public perceptions about the influence of religion have varied widely over the last half-century, and may be more a reflection of changing political realities than of personal beliefs about religion. However, the new poll also finds the percentage of Americans believing that religion can answer society's problems is at an all-time low. Although still a majority, just 53% of Americans say religion "can answer all or most of today's problems." While 28% say it is "largely old-fashioned and out of date."

Do you believe that religion can answer all or most of today's problems, or that religion is largely old-fashioned and out of date?

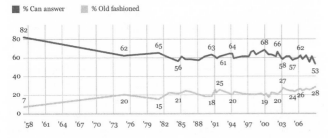

The current 53% affirming religion as a relevant tool for solving today's problems is not much different from the 55% recorded a year ago, but is below the 57% to 66% range seen earlier this decade. It comes at a time when the vast majority of Americans perceive the U.S. economy to be the nation's greatest challenge—and perhaps one that religion is not particularly well suited to address.

The vast majority of Americans who attend church or another worship service weekly (82%) say religion can answer today's problems, as do 59% of those attending at least monthly, but only 27% of those who rarely or never attend agreed.

Confidence in religion to solve problems increases with age, but even young adults (aged 18 to 34 years) are more likely to affirm the value of religion than reject it (44% vs. 36%).

Belief in Ability of Religion to Answer Today's Problems, Based on Age

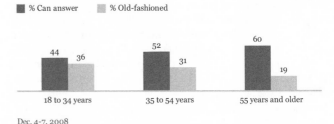

Dec. 4-7, 2008

Bottom Line

At the close of 2008, few Americans perceive that religion is thriving in U.S. society, and a relatively small majority believe religion is relevant to solving today's problems. These perceptions may stem in part from the political climate—characterized by a weakened Republican Party and the incoming Democratic administration—as well as from the overwhelming consensus that the main problems facing the country today are economic.

At the same time, a solid majority of Americans (56%), largely unchanged from recent years, say that religion plays a very important role in their own lives. Also, Gallup Poll Daily tracking data show no decline in the percent of Americans' self-reported church attendance this year.

Survey Methods

Results are based on telephone interviews with 1,009 national adults, aged 18 and older, conducted Dec. 4-7, 2008. For results based on the total sample of national adults, one can say with 95% confidence that the maximum margin of sampling error is ±3 percentage points.

Interviews are conducted with respondents on land-line telephones (for respondents with a land-line telephone) and cellular phones (for respondents who are cell-phone only).

In addition to sampling error, question wording and practical difficulties in conducting surveys can introduce error or bias into the findings of public opinion polls.

December 23, 2008
CONSUMER CONFIDENCE REMAINS NEAR LOW POINT FOR YEAR
Key will be trend in confidence as new year begins

by Frank Newport, Gallup Poll Editor in Chief

The latest update of Gallup's daily measure of consumer confidence, for Dec. 19-21, continues to show a very negative frame of mind on the part of the public. Seventy-eight percent of Americans can be classified as negative about the economy, and only 4% as positive, while the rest have consumer sentiments that can be classified as mixed. This yields a "net positive" value of -74 points.

Gallup's consumer confidence measure has been deeply underwater (i.e., the negative outweighing the positive) all year. The 2008 pattern has not been one relentless downward drift, but rather, a downturn, followed by an upturn, and then a crash back down. Unfortunately, after all has been said and done, Gallup's estimate of consumer confidence at this point remains near the low point for the year.

Gallup Daily: Consumer Confidence

Gallup Poll Daily tracking, Dec. 19-21, 2008

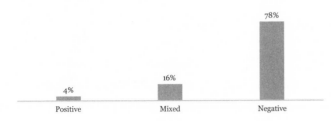

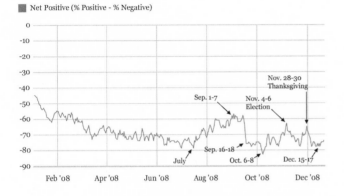

Gallup Poll Daily Tracking: Consumer Confidence

The consumer confidence measure began the year with a 61% negative rating, with another 16% positive and 21% mixed. That essentially marked the high point of 2008, with consumer confidence deteriorating steadily through the first six months of the year. Confidence then began to recover through August and into September.

But on the heels of the massive credit crisis that began to dominate the news in mid-September, consumer confidence took a major nosedive about Sept. 16. Confidence has stayed particularly low since that time, with two notable exceptions. Americans became more confident around the time of the Nov. 4 election, and again around Thanksgiving. These trends suggest that there is more to consumer confidence than a straightforward reflection of economic news and economic indicators. Holidays and other events can influence it.

Some of the uptick at Thanksgiving could be the result of a coincidental increase in the stock market that week. But the Thanksgiving "bump" could also indicate there will be a similar uptick in consumer confidence in the holiday period encompassing the last two weeks of December, the first vestiges of which may be happening now. But this uptick could be misleading if it is misinterpreted. If Thanksgiving is a guide, there is a good chance that any increase that occurs as a result of holiday periods will soon fall back down.

One obviously significant key will be the direction of consumer confidence after Jan 2. Will consumer confidence sag to new lows after the new year begins, or will it begin to recover? Any boost in confidence as a result of the holidays will be over. President-elect Barack Obama's inauguration will be in the near distance. At this point, there has been no apparent impact that can be directly attributed to Obama's efforts to focus on the economy—including cabinet picks, announcements of planned stimulus plans, and the like. It is possible, of course that any positive impact of the new administration will not be apparent until Obama actually takes office on Jan. 20. But so far, his election does not appear in and of itself to have wrought highly positive benefits.

Survey Methods

For the Gallup Poll Daily tracking survey, Gallup is interviewing no fewer than 1,000 U.S. adults nationwide each day during 2008. The consumer confidence questions are asked of a random half sample of each day's interviews, and for any given three-day rolling average of results, consisting of approximately 1,500 interviews, the maximum margin of sampling error is ±2 percentage points.

Interviews are conducted with respondents on land-line telephones (for respondents with a land-line telephone) and cellular phones (for respondents who are cell-phone only).

In addition to sampling error, question wording and practical difficulties in conducting surveys can introduce error or bias into the findings of public opinion polls.

December 24, 2008

IN THE U.S., CHRISTMAS NOT JUST FOR CHRISTIANS

While 81% identify themselves as Christians, 93% celebrate Christmas

by Frank Newport, Gallup Poll Editor in Chief

Despite the fact that only a little more than 80% of Americans identify with a Christian faith, 93% of those interviewed in a recent *USA Today*/Gallup poll indicate that they celebrate Christmas. Remarkably in this time of economic turmoil, slightly more Americans say this Christmas will be happier than in prior years than say it will be less happy.

Do you celebrate Christmas?

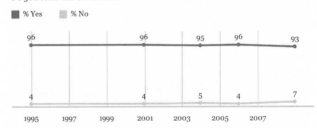

USA Today/Gallup, Dec. 12-14, 2008

These results are based on a *USA Today*/Gallup poll conducted Dec. 12-14. Respondents were asked simply: "Do you celebrate Christmas?" The 93% who responded "yes" is just slightly lower than what Gallup has found the four previous times it has asked this question since 1994. The results for Gallup's latest breakdown of religious identification, based on more than 21,000 interviews conducted during the first 21 days of December, are shown in the accompanying table.

All in all, 81% of Americans identify with some form of the Christian faith. Thus, the fact that 93% of Americans say they celebrate Christmas (the major Christian holiday) underscores that Christmas has ramifications for U.S. society beyond just the Christian segment of the population. One logical hypothesis is that some of the 15% of Americans who do not give a religious affiliation were raised as Christians or were previously Christians, and still celebrate

Americans' Religious Affiliation

Aggregated results, Gallup Poll Daily tracking, Dec. 1-21, 2008

Numbers in percentages

	Dec 1-21, 2008
Protestant/Other Christian	56%
Catholic	25
Jewish	2
Muslim	0.4
Other non-Christian religion	3
None/Atheist/Agnostic	13
No response	2

the holiday in some fashion despite not formally identifying with a Christian religion. Additionally, some of those who responded "yes" to the Christmas question but who do not identify with a Christian faith may celebrate in some secular fashion, such as exchanging gifts at school or the office.

Survey Methods

Results are based on telephone interviews with 1,008 national adults, aged 18 and older, conducted Dec. 12-14, 2008. For results based on the total sample of national adults, one can say with 95% confidence that the maximum margin of sampling error is ±3 percentage points.

Interviews are conducted with respondents on land-line telephones (for respondents with a land-line telephone) and cellular phones (for respondents who are cell-phone only).

In addition to sampling error, question wording and practical difficulties in conducting surveys can introduce error or bias into the findings of public opinion polls.

December 26, 2008

OBAMA, HILLARY CLINTON SHARE "MOST ADMIRED" BILLING

Palin makes impressive showing as second most admired woman

by Lydia Saad, Gallup Poll Senior Editor

A remarkable 32% of Americans choose Barack Obama as the man they most admire living anywhere in the world today, putting him in the No. 1 position on Gallup's annual Most Admired Man list. Hillary Clinton earns the top spot for Most Admired Woman, named by 20%.

No one comes close to matching Obama in percentage mentions on this year's list of most admired men, based on a Dec. 12-14 *USA Today*/Gallup poll. By contrast, Alaska Gov. Sarah Palin makes a strong showing in second place for Most Admired Woman, garnering 11% of all mentions.

Obama

The 32% of Americans naming Obama as the man they most admire is extraordinarily high, nearly matching the 39% of Americans who named George W. Bush in the immediate wake of the 9/11 attacks. At that time, Bush's presidential job approval rating was a soaring 86%. It is also higher than former presidents Bill Clinton and George

Most Admired Man, 2008

Ranked by number of responses

	%
1. Barack Obama	32
2. George W. Bush	5
3. John McCain	3
4. (tie) Pope Benedict XVI	2
4. (tie) Rev. Billy Graham	2
4. (tie) Bill Clinton	2
7. Colin Powell	2
8. Nelson Mandela	1
9. Bill Gates	1
10. The Dalai Lama	1

Dec. 12-14, 2008

Most Admired Woman, 2008

Ranked by number of responses

	%
1. Hillary Clinton	20
2. Sarah Palin	11
3. Oprah Winfrey	8
4. Condoleezza Rice	7
5. Michelle Obama	3
6. Margaret Thatcher	2
7. (tie) Laura Bush	2
7. (tie) Angelina Jolie	2
9. Barbara Bush	1
10. (tie) Madeleine Albright	1
10. (tie) Ellen DeGeneres	1

Dec. 12-14, 2008

H. W. Bush received in any of their appearances on Gallup's Most Admired Man list.

Obama is the first president-elect since Dwight Eisenhower in 1952 to top the list. And he has done it with a runaway high figure. For comparison, as president-elect in December 2000, George W. Bush was mentioned by just 5% of Americans, ranking him fourth. In December 1992, president-elect Bill Clinton ranked second behind outgoing president George H.W. Bush, with 15%. And in 1988, then president-elect Bush achieved third place, with 9%.

Most Admired Men

After Obama, President George W. Bush comes in second place on Gallup's Most Admired Man list, but is named by just 5% of Americans. The percentage naming Bush on this measure has steadily declined since 2003, consistent with his sinking job approval ratings. But 2008 marks the first year of his presidency that he did not earn the Most Admired Man distinction.

There have only been a few other instances in Gallup's history of asking this question since 1948 that the sitting president was not named Most Admired Man, and few when a sitting president received this low percentage of mentions. Those include Lyndon Johnson in 1967 and 1968 (when Eisenhower was chosen, instead), Jimmy Carter in 1980 (when Pope John Paul II was chosen), and Richard Nixon followed by Gerald Ford from 1973 through 1975 (when Henry Kissinger topped the list).

John McCain ranks third in this year's list with 3%, while Pope Benedict XVI, Rev. Billy Graham, Bill Clinton, and Colin Powell

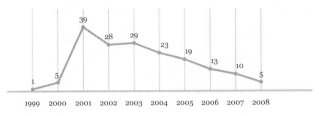

Percentage Naming George W. Bush as Most Admired Man

December of each year

are each mentioned by 2% of Americans. Nelson Mandela, Bill Gates, and the Dalai Lama round out the top ten, each named by 1%.

Most Admired Women

This is the seventh consecutive year that Hillary Clinton has secured top billing as Americans' Most Admired Woman—and the 13th year she has made the top ten since her first appearance on the list in 1993. The 20% naming Clinton this year is comparable to what she received in 2007 (18%), but falls short of the 28% naming her in 1998.

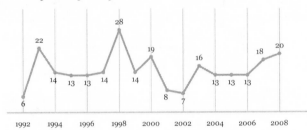

Percentage Naming Hillary Clinton as Most Admired Woman

December of each year

Palin, McCain's 2008 vice presidential pick and the first woman ever to run on a Republican presidential ticket, makes a strong second place debut, named by 11% of Americans. Her entrance on the list crowds Oprah Winfrey out of second place, a position she held each year from 2002 through 2007. Winfrey now ranks third, mentioned by 8% of Americans (down from 16%) a year ago.

Secretary of State Condoleezza Rice ranks fourth, with 7%, followed by a variety of other political figures and entertainment stars.

First lady Laura Bush has topped the list only once since her husband took office in 2001. First ladies are much less likely than presidents to win a top spot on Most Admired Woman, although Clinton did it six times in Bill Clinton's two terms as president, Nancy Reagan three times in Ronald Reagan's two terms, and Barbara Bush twice in her husband's one term. Even Rosalyn Carter, whose husband suffered from low approval ratings for much of his last two years in office, achieved the top spot three out of her four years in the White House.

Survey Methods

Results are based on telephone interviews with 1,008 national adults, aged 18 and older, conducted Dec. 12-14, 2008. For results based on the total sample of national adults, one can say with 95% confidence that the maximum margin of sampling error is ±3 percentage points.

Interviews are conducted with respondents on land-line telephones (for respondents with a land-line telephone) and cellular phones (for respondents who are cell-phone only).

In addition to sampling error, question wording and practical difficulties in conducting surveys can introduce error or bias into the findings of public opinion polls.

December 29, 2008

FOOTBALL REMAINS RUNAWAY LEADER AS FAVORITE SPORT
Basketball's popularity declining

by Jeffrey M. Jones, Gallup Poll Managing Editor

The holiday season brings a bevy of college bowl games and the final determination of the National Football League's playoff participants. That suits Americans just fine, because football is the runaway winner when Americans are asked to name their favorite sport to watch. Forty-one percent mention football, with baseball (10%) and basketball (9%) a distant second, and no other sport reaching the 5% level.

What Is Your Favorite Sport to Watch?

	% Mentioning
Football	41
Baseball	10
Basketball	9
Ice hockey	4
Soccer	3
Auto racing	3
Golf	2
Boxing	2
Tennis	1
Ice/Figure skating	1
Gymnastics	1
Volleyball	1
Other	7
None/No opinion	14

Gallup Poll, Dec. 4-7, 2008

These results are based on Gallup's annual Lifestyle poll, conducted Dec. 4-7 this year. Gallup first asked this open-ended "favorite sport" question in 1937, and has updated it on a regular basis since 1990. In the very early years, baseball was king, with football second by a considerable margin. But by 1972, football had overtaken baseball, and it has been the top sport ever since, surpassing 40% mentions in each of the last three years.

After showing a modest uptick in the 1990s and the early part of this decade, basketball has slipped in recent years. The 9% who consider basketball their favorite sport this year is the lowest Gallup has measured since 1981, when the sport was beginning a surge in popularity fueled by prominent star players such as Magic Johnson, Larry Bird, and, later, Michael Jordan.

Basketball's popularity reached as high as 17% in April 1997, though that estimate may have been slightly elevated given that the poll was conducted just after the NCAA tournament concluded and just as the NBA playoffs were getting underway. Still, even as recently as December 2003, a relatively high 14% of Americans rated basketball as their No. 1 sport to watch.

What Is Your Favorite Sport to Watch?

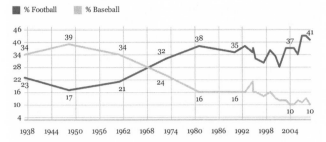

Percentage Mentioning Basketball as Favorite Sport

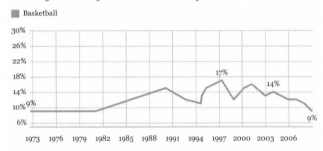

On a somewhat smaller scale, figure skating has also declined in popularity, peaking at a high of 6% in December 2003 and steadily declining since then to just 1% in the latest poll.

Football is the top sport among all key demographic groups, based on aggregated data from the last four times the question has been asked (each December since 2005). But there is some variation in the extent to which football is mentioned. For example, men are more likely than women, and younger Americans are more likely than older Americans, to name football as their top sport.

Favorite Sport, by Gender and Age

Based on aggregate of 2005-2008 data

	Football	Baseball	Basketball
	%	%	%
Men	49	11	9
Women	32	13	13
18 to 29 years old	46	6	16
30 to 49 years old	43	11	10
50 to 64 years old	37	14	10
65 years and older	33	17	11

As the table shows, on a relative basis, younger adults are more likely to rate basketball as their favorite sport and older adults are more likely to name baseball.

The subgroup most likely to name basketball as their favorite sport is blacks: 26% mention it, though football still rates as blacks' favorite (39%). Just 4% of blacks name baseball, putting it on par with boxing among blacks.

Survey Methods

Results are based on telephone interviews with 1,009 national adults, aged 18 and older, conducted Dec. 4-7, 2008. For results based on the total sample of national adults, one can say with 95% confidence that the maximum margin of sampling error is ±3 percentage points.

Interviews are conducted with respondents on land-line telephones (for respondents with a land-line telephone) and cellular phones (for respondents who are cell-phone only).

In addition to sampling error, question wording and practical difficulties in conducting surveys can introduce error or bias into the findings of public opinion polls.

December 30, 2008
DESPITE CHEAPER GAS, NEW DRIVING HABITS STICKING
Lower-income, younger Americans most likely to be among 12% reverting

by Dennis Jacobe, Gallup Poll Chief Economist

Nearly two in three Americans (64%) report adjusting their driving habits in significant ways in response to surging gas prices earlier this year, but only 12% have reverted to their old habits as prices at the pump have plunged. Even as the price of a gallon of gas has fallen below $2 in most areas, 52% of Americans say they have not gone back to their old driving habits.

U.S. Regular Retail Gasoline Prices, by Week

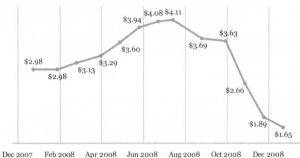

Source: U.S. Energy Information Administration

Upper-Income Americans Least Likely to Have Changed Driving Habits

Gas prices at the pump represent a smaller percentage of disposable income for upper-income Americans than for those making less. As a result, it is not surprising that lower- and middle-income respondents (those whose annual household income is less than $75,000) are more likely than upper-income respondents to say they have changed their driving habits in response to surging pump prices.

There is not much difference between age groups when it comes to adjusting driving habits: 61% of Americans aged 18 to 34 and 62% of Americans aged 55 and older say they changed their driving habits in significant ways. However, Americans aged 35 to 54 are slightly more likely, at 67%, to say they have changed their driving habits. Of course, this seems logical because at this stage of the life cycle these Americans are more likely to have to commute and to have children involved in many after-school activities.

Percentage of Americans Who Have Adjusted Their Driving Habits in Response to Higher Gas Prices Earlier This Year, by Annual Income and Age

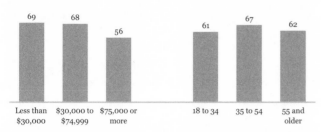

Dec. 12-14, 2008

Lower-Income and Younger Americans Most Likely to Return to Old Driving Habits

Necessity is more likely to force lower-income Americans to make significant changes in their driving habits than their upper-income counterparts. Therefore, as pump prices plunged, it should not be surprising that 19% of lower-income Americans say they have returned to their old driving habits compared with 11% of middle-income and 8% of upper-income Americans. Similarly, 19% of younger Americans say they have returned to their old driving habits compared with 12% of those aged 35 to 54 and only 6% of those aged 55 and older.

Percentage of Americans Who Have Gone Back to Their Old Driving Habits, by Annual Income and Age

Based on those who say they have adjusted their driving habits in response to higher gas prices

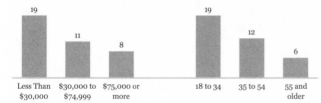

Dec. 12-14, 2008

Commentary

Americans stated responses to plunging pump prices might be instructive in several important ways. First, they reinforce the punitive nature of higher gas prices on lower-income and younger Americans. While welcomed by most Americans, today's sharply lower gas prices threaten to undo many of the efforts to develop alternative sources of energy—at least in the immediate term. In turn, this situation plus the need for added tax revenues could lead to new efforts to impose higher taxes on gas at the pump in the months ahead. The immense burden such taxes would place on lower-income and younger Americans needs to be considered in any such tax calculations.

Second, the plunge in gas prices is similar to distributing a huge tax rebate by how much individuals drive. Like the tax rebate from earlier this year, lower-income Americans tend to be most likely to spend the rebate, but *all* Americans are likely to save a large portion of any tax rebate. In part, it may be that most Americans have not gone back to their old driving habits for fear that pump prices will surge once more in the future. Just as likely, however, particularly for upper-income Americans, returning to old driving habits may be a lot like spending money—something left for better times.

As Congress begins deliberating on major fiscal stimulus plans next week, policy-makers should keep in mind that the real objective needs to be increasing consumer confidence in the U.S. economy and the job market so Americans will feel comfortable spending. One lesson to be learned from the plunge in prices at the pump is that you can push money into the hands of consumers, but you can't make them spend it. A major stimulus effort is essential, but the form it takes will be the key to determining whether it has the needed so-called multiplier effects or simply repeats the overall ineffectiveness of earlier stimulus efforts.

Survey Methods

Results are based on telephone interviews with 1,008 national adults, aged 18 and older, conducted Dec. 12-14, 2008. For results based on the total sample of national adults, one can say with 95% confidence that the maximum margin of sampling error is ±3 percentage points.

Interviews are conducted with respondents on land-line telephones (for respondents with a land-line telephone) and cellular phones (for respondents who are cell-phone only).

In addition to sampling error, question wording and practical difficulties in conducting surveys can introduce error or bias into the findings of public opinion polls.

Index

of Clinton, Bill, 288
of Clinton, Hillary Rodham, 97–98
of Congress, 10–12, 95, 166–167, 202–203, 236, 312, 395,
431–432
of Democratic Party, 431–432
of economy, 16–17, 137
of labor unions, 413
of McCain, John, 97–98, 147, 297, 305
of Obama, Barack, 97–98, 297, 383–384
of Palin, Sarah, 294, 305
of Republican Party, 431–432
of Supreme Court, 202–203, 336
of Wall Street bailouts, 123–125, 318–319, 398, 424
Arctic National Wildlife Refuge (ANWR), 207
armed forces. *See* military
Asian Americans
McCain, John, and, 324
Obama, Barack, and, 324
atheism, atheists
and candidate matchups, 225
Christmas and, 444
opinion of, 133–134
athletics. *See* sports
attentiveness
to elections, 22–23, 41–42, 372
to transition, 398
automobile(s)
dealers, honesty and ethical standards of, 404
fuel-efficient, consideration of, 162–163
have made changes to help protect environment,
138–139
put off looking for, reasons why, 436
racing, as favorite sport to watch, 445
upkeep on, gender and, 125
automobile industry
bailout for, 384, 397, 423, 432–433
and car purchase deferral, 436
energy and, 200
image of, 274
responsibility for auto crisis, 422

Baldwin, Chuck, 348
banker(s), honesty and ethical standards of, 403–404
banks and banking
confidence in, 208–209
image of, 274
regulation of, 384
Baptists, opinion of, 133–134
Barr, Bob, 348
baseball, as favorite sport to watch, 445–446
basketball
as favorite sport to watch, 445–446
as favorite Summer Olympic event, 266
Bear Stearns, 123–124
beer, 248–249, 340
Benedict XVI, 133
admiration of, 444
opinion of, 195
Bernanke, Ben, 16, 22, 28, 61, 124, 190

Biden, Joe
ability to serve as president, 293, 295, 340
approval ratings, 284, 294
effect on vote for Obama, 283–284, 343–344
likely to support, 5–6, 8
and media, 313
as qualified, 284
big business. *See* corporations
bill paying
gender and, 125
worry about, 145, 157, 329
bingo, 40
biodegradeable products, 138–139
bioterrorism, as most important issue, 414
bipartisanship
McCain, John, and, 99, 289, 307
Obama, Barack, and, 99, 289, 307, 386, 388, 392
blacks
Bush, George W., and, 428
and candidate matchups, 119–120, 151–152, 159, 187, 224,
365
civil rights progress and, 26–27
Clinton, Hillary, and, 190–191
Democratic Party and, 37–38
discrimination and, 260–261
economy and, 231
election of 2008 and, 371
enthusiasm for election and, 232
McCain, John, and, 191
morality and, 416–417
Obama, Barack, and, 17–18, 20, 48–49, 64, 82–83, 98–99,
109–110, 191, 227, 255, 381
race and, 193–194, 227–228
race relations and, 238–239
satisfaction of, 234
Sharpton, Al, and, 191
spokesperson of, 232–233
Wright, Jeremiah, and, 191
blood donation, 438
Bloomberg, Mike, 30, 251
blue states
and candidate matchups, 135–136, 189, 245
economy and, 291
voter outreach in, 369
bombing, Congress and, 223
boxing
as favorite sport to watch, 445
gambling on, 40
Brazil, GDP of, 67
Bredesen, Phil, 114
Brown, Jerry, support for, 56
Buchanan, Pat, support for, 56
budget, federal, and desire for change, 24
budget deficit, federal
as most important issue, 65–66, 93
Obama, Barack, and, 386–387
as priority, 118, 182, 385
as voting issue, 53–54, 368
building contractors, honesty and ethical standards of, 404

civil unions. *See* gay marriage
clergy, honesty and ethical standards of, 403
Clinton, Bill
    admiration of, 444
    approval ratings, 25, 161, 275, 384
        quarterly averages for, 143, 237
    bring back, 59–60
    and change, 23
    Clinton, Hillary, and, 121, 164
    expectations of, 387
    favorability ratings (as candidate), 364
    image of, 287–288
    legacy of, 287–288
    as spokesperson for blacks, 232
    support for, 56
Clinton, Hillary Rodham
    admiration of, 444–445
    age and, 74–75
    approval ratings, 97–98
    blacks and, 17
    in candidate matchups, 19–20, 52–53, 69–72, 113–114,
        119–120, 122–123, 151–152, 172–174
    change and, 26
    church attendance and, 68–69
    Clinton, Bill, and, 121, 164
    Democratic convention speech, 288–289
    as divisive candidate, 70–71
    education and, 47–48
    enthusiasm for, 40–41, 50–52
    experience and, 81–82
    gender and, 39–40, 47–49, 75
    geographic region and, 135–136
    has best chance of winning, 179
    Hispanics and, 37–38, 82–83
    honesty of, 99–100
    image of, 186, 190–192, 286–287
    Iowa caucuses and, 1–2
    Jews and, 103–104, 158
    likely to support, 5, 8
    likely to win nomination, 9
    marriage and, 177–178
    media and, 180
    and meeting with enemies, 183
    personal characteristics of, 7, 72–74, 148–149
    as secretary of state, 399–400, 415
    should run for president again someday, 287
    as spokesperson for blacks, 232
    superdelegates and, 89
    support for, 14–15, 20–22, 171–172
    weaknesses of, 120–122
Clinton administration, Obama, Barack, and, 415
Clinton supporters
    on campaign as hurting Democratic Party, 142, 152–153, 165
    dream ticket and, 87–88, 118–119, 165
    McCain, John, and, 107–109
    Obama, Barack, and, 297
    Wright, Jeremiah, and, 153–155
cloning, as morally acceptable, 170–171, 205
clothing, cutting back spending on, 156

cohabitation
    age and, 268–269
    with children, 269
    duration of, 269
college
    as most important issue, 349
    See also education
commuting costs, as most important issue, 349
computer industry, image of, 274
Congress
    approval ratings, 10–12, 95, 166–167, 202–203, 236, 312, 395
    confidence in, 208–209, 317
    economy and, 324–325, 333
    energy and, 200
    gasoline and, 264
    members of
        economy and, 333
        honesty and ethical standards of, 404
    military and, 222–223
    as most important issue, 93, 244, 273, 426
    priorities for, 117–118, 182
    as priority, 182
    responsibility for auto crisis, 433
Congressional elections, 58–59
    generic ballots, 218, 311, 356
    incumbents in, 262–263
    one-party control and, 367
conservatives
    abortion and, 177
    Bush, George W., and, 428
    and candidate matchups, 119, 152, 188
    divorce and, 171
    economy and, 43, 339
    Hispanics and, 221
    Iraq War and, 44, 127
    Jews and, 363
    McCain, John, and, 108–110
    Obama, Barack, and, 388, 419
    Republican Party and, 401
    standard of living and, 192
    swing voters and, 217
    third party and, 327
Constitution
    amendments to, on marriage, 168
    Second Amendment, 110–111, 214–215
    and war powers, 223
Constitution Party, 348
consumers
    behavior of, 239–240
    car purchase deferrals, 436
    confidence of, 28, 55–56, 95–96, 128–129, 206, 235, 246, 267,
        276, 291, 331–332, 347, 382–383, 402, 410–411, 427,
        442–443
    energy and, 200
    responsibility for auto crisis, 422
    spending and, 358, 396, 399, 409–410, 421
conventions, political
    bounce in polls after, 304
    Clinton, Hillary, and, 288–289

satisfaction of, 97, 166, 204, 244
standard of living and, 192
superdelegates and, 89
Supreme Court and, 336
swing voters and, 217
third party and, 326
unifying candidate and, 70–71
United Nations and, 84–85
U.S. global position and, 83
voting issues and, 53–54, 368
wealth distribution and, 370
Wright, Jeremiah, and, 153–155
Democrats in Congress
approval ratings, 431–432
economy and, 330, 333
election of 2008 and, 58–59, 311
incumbents, 263
responsibility for auto crisis, 433–434
depression (economic)
Congress and, 333
in next year, 100
outlook for, 45–46, 316, 439–440
worry about, 100–101
diabetes, as most important issue, 414
dining out, cutting back spending on, 156, 239
discount stores, 239
dishonesty
as most important issue, 244, 426
as priority, 182
dish washing, gender and, 125
divorce
cohabitation and, 268
as morally acceptable, 170–171, 205
doctor(s), honesty and ethical standards of, 403
doctor-assisted suicide, as morally acceptable, 170–171, 205
Dodd, Christopher, 5–6
Dole, Bob
age of, 74
favorability ratings, 364
support for, 56
domestic issues
and candidate matchups, 260
government and, confidence in, 317
drivers and driving
cutting back spending on, 156
gasoline prices and, 163, 447
have made changes to help protect environment, 138–139
druggists, honesty and ethical standards of, 403
drugs, worry about, 112
Dukakis, Michael, support for, 56

economic conditions
approval ratings, 16–17, 80–81, 137
as biggest crisis of lifetime, 325, 439
Bush, George W., and, 64–65
China and, 66–67
church attendance and, 435
closely follow news about, 324

confidence in, 28, 55–56, 95–96, 128–129, 225, 235, 246–247, 267–268, 270, 276, 291, 331–332, 347, 382–383, 402, 410–411, 427, 442–443
Congress and, 324–325
credit crunch, 46–47
as depression/recession, 45–46
desire for change and, 24
economic stimulus bill, 28, 42–44, 384, 415–416
election of 2008 and, 10, 380, 385–386
environment and, 106–107
feelings about, 334
financial rescue package, 333–334, 338–339
Gramm and, 243
as harmful, 354
as haves and have-nots, 231, 373–374
healthcare and, 419–420
immigrants and, 229
investors and, 184–185, 440–441
job creation, 86, 115
leadership and, 330
McCain, John, and, 73, 212, 285, 309–310, 315, 319, 328, 342–343, 351
mood and, 389–390, 434
as most important issue, 13–14, 65–66, 92–93, 132–133, 166, 203–204, 244, 273, 349, 425
Obama, Barack, and, 73, 212–213, 285, 309–310, 315, 319–320, 328, 342–343, 346, 351, 386, 415
outlook for, 117–118, 316, 325, 347, 386, 420, 427, 439
as priority, 117–118, 181, 355, 385
recession, 100–101
regulation and, 384
responsibility for auto crisis, 422
retirement and, 88–89
satisfaction with, 34–36
spending and, 137, 155–156
standard of living, 192–193
stimulus rebate, 206–207
too big to fail, 124–125, 318–319
as voting issue, 10, 53–54, 74, 212, 285, 309, 319, 342, 359, 368, 377
Wall Street bailouts, 123–125, 318–319, 398, 424
worry about, 111–112, 144–145, 207, 393
See also financial situation
personal; stock market
education
alcohol and, 249
and candidate matchups, 151–152, 159, 172–173, 187–188
Clinton, Hillary, and, 76
Democratic Party and, 47–48
economy and, 277
election of 2008 and, 337, 382
enthusiasm for elections and, 42
gambling and, 40
gender gap and, 272
image of, 274
McCain, John, and, 76, 109, 310
as most important issue, 66, 93
Obama, Barack, and, 64, 76, 255–256, 310, 381, 386, 406
patriotism and, 222

presidential candidates and, 73

    as priority, 182

    rate honesty and ethical standards of people in different fields [list], 403–404

    satisfaction with, 34, 37

    See also values

European Union, as economic leader, 66–67

euthanasia. *See* doctor-assisted suicide

evangelical Christianity, opinion of, 133–134

evolution, 209–210

experience

    McCain, John, and, 81–82, 314, 346

    Obama, Barack, and, 81–82

    as voting issue, 72–74, 76, 377

    youth and, 340

extinction, worry about, 91, 140

extramarital affairs, as morally acceptable, 170–171, 205

family(ies)

    division of labor in, 125–126

    as most important issue, 132–133, 244, 426

    as priority, 182

family values. *See* morality; values

farms, farming, image of, 274

Farrakhan, Louis, as spokesperson for blacks, 232

Father's Day, mood and, 434

federal government. *See* budget, federal; government

figure skating, as favorite sport to watch, 445

financial situation, personal

    approval ratings, 137, 354

    better off next year than now, 185, 329

    better off now than year ago, 185, 328

    better or worse today, 185

    crisis and, 334

    gas prices and, 102–103

    gender and, 125

    most important issue in, 239

    worry about, 32–33, 67–68, 144–145, 329, 410, 437

    See also income; money; spending

flag pin, as patriotic, 221–222

food

    avoided certain types, 242

    cutting back spending on, 156

    have made changes to help protect environment, 138–139

    safety of, 241–242

    thrown out/returned, 242

    worry about, 242

football, as favorite sport to watch, 445–446

Forbes, Steve, support for, 56

Ford, Gerald, approval ratings, 161, 384

foreign affairs/policy

    Bush, George W., and, 64–65

    desire for change and, 24

    government and, 317

    McCain, John, and, 259

    Obama, Barack, and, 259

    as priority, 182

    protesting, as patriotic, 221–222

    satisfaction with, 34, 36, 83–84

    support for, as patriotic, 221–222

    as voting issue, 315, 377

foreign aid

    as most important issue, 66, 93

    as priority, 118

Fourth of July, mood and, 434

France

    GDP of, 67

    opinion of, 79–80, 194–195

fuel, prices

    and desire for change, 24

    as most important issue, 65–66, 102–103, 166, 203–204, 244, 273, 426

    as priority, 181

    as voting issue, 54

funeral directors, honesty and ethical standards of, 403

furniture, gender and, 125

gambling

    as morally acceptable, 170, 205

    types, popularity of, 40

gasoline

    cutting back spending on, 156

    predictions for, 149–150

    prices, 446

        causing financial hardship, 102–103, 149, 161–162

        and consumer confidence, 267, 276

        and desire for change, 24

        McCain, John, and, 212–213, 351

        as most important issue, 65–66, 102–103, 239, 349

        Obama, Barack, and, 212–213, 351

        predictions for, 161–162, 270

        as priority, 149–150

        responsibility for, 264

        as voting issue, 54, 212, 285, 309, 368

    See also energy; oil

Gates, Bill, 251

    admiration of, 444

Gates, Robert, 60

    as secretary of defense, 415

gay marriage, 167–168, 205–206

    blacks and, 416

    See also homosexuals and homosexuality

gender

    abortion and, 177, 300

    alcohol and, 249

    and candidate matchups, 122–123, 152, 159, 172–174, 187, 281

    Democratic Party and, 47–48

    division of labor and, 125–126

    divorce and, 171

    economy and, 277

    election of 2008 and, 177–178, 337

    environment and, 138

    favorite sport and, 446

    gambling and, 40

    McCain, John, and, 109, 197, 299

    most important issue and, 112

    Obama, Barack, and, 63, 197, 299, 381, 405

    satisfaction with U.S. and, 244

high school teachers, honesty and ethical standards of, 403
Hispanics
    Bush, George W., and, 428
    and candidate matchups, 119–120, 151–152, 159, 172, 187, 224, 365
    Clinton, Hillary, and, 82–83
    Democratic Party and, 37–38, 48–49
    economy and, 231
    McCain, John, and, 109, 324
    Obama, Barack, and, 63, 98–99, 220–221, 238–239, 324
    race relations and, 238–239, 261
    religion and, 359
    satisfaction of, 234
hockey, as favorite sport to watch, 445
holidays, mood and, 434
homelessness
    as most important issue, 66, 93
    as priority, 118, 182
    satisfaction with, 34
    worry about, 112
home ownership, government and, 325, 384
homosexuals and homosexuality
    acceptability of, 417
    blacks and, 416–417
    gay marriage, 167–168, 205–206, 416
    as morally acceptable, 168–171, 204–206
    satisfaction with, 34, 37
    should be legal between consenting adults, 205
    should have equal rights in job opportunities, 168, 205
    as voting issue, 168
honesty
    Clinton, Hillary, and, 99–100, 148–149
    McCain, John, and, 148, 216, 289, 307, 315
    Obama, Barack, and, 149, 216, 289, 307, 315
    of presidential candidates, 99
    as voting issue, 377
    See also ethics
horse racing, 40
hospitals. *See* healthcare
household chores, gender and, 125–126
House of Representatives, 58–59
    projections for, 218
    See also Congress
housing
    government and, 124
    as most important issue, 239, 349
    prices, 49–50, 134–135
    value of, 135
    as voting issue, 135
    worry about, 157
Huckabee, Mike
    in candidate matchups, 19
    challenge for, 35–36
    as divisive candidate, 70–71
    has best chance of winning, 179
    Iraq War and, 45
    likely to support, 2, 6, 8–9, 14, 20
    likely to win nomination, 9
    personal characteristics of, 8

    religion and, 18–19
    would like to see run in 2012, 402
humans, cloning, as morally acceptable, 170–171
hunger
    as most important issue, 66, 93
    as priority, 118, 182
    worry about, 112
Hunter, Duncan, support for, 14, 21

ice hockey, as favorite sport to watch, 445
ice skating, as favorite sport to watch, 445
ideology
    abortion and, 177
    Bush, George W., and, 428
    and candidate matchups, 188
    economy and, 42–43, 339
    Hispanics and, 221
    Iraq War and, 44, 126–128
    Jews and, 363
    Obama, Barack, and, 388, 419
    standard of living and, 192
    Supreme Court and, 336
    swing voters and, 217
    third party and, 326–327
    as voting issue, 377
    See also political affiliation
"I Have a Dream" speech, familiarity with, 27
illegal immigration. *See* immigrants, immigration
immigrants, immigration
    as most important issue, 14, 65–66, 93, 132–133, 166
    desire for change and, 24
    satisfaction with, 34–35, 37
    as voting issue, 53–54, 74, 212, 309, 368
    Bush, George W., and, 64–65
    worry about, 112
    as priority, 118, 181
    McCain, John, and, 212–213, 310
    Obama, Barack, and, 212–213, 310, 386
    levels of, 228–229
imprisonment, 394
    race and, 260–261
income
    alcohol and, 249
    Bush, George W., and, 428
    and candidate matchups, 151–152, 187–188
    consumer confidence and, 55–56
    driving habits and, 447
    economy and, 42–43, 45–46, 65–66, 80–81, 96, 144–145, 155–156, 225–226, 235, 246–247, 277–278, 334, 339
    election of 2008 and, 337, 374
    employment and, 62
    enthusiasm for elections and, 42
    financial worry and, 32–33
    gambling and, 40
    gasoline and, 162–163
    healthcare and, 420
    housing and, 124, 134
    mood and, 390
    race and, 260–261

timeframe of, 60–61, 92, 126–128, 261–262

as voting issue, 53–54, 74, 212, 285, 309, 315, 343, 368, 377

withdrawal from, 94–95, 386

Islam. *See* Muslims

Israel

Bush, George W., and, 104–105

opinion of, 79–80

issues, most important, 13–14, 65–66, 92–93, 111–112, 132–133, 166, 244, 273, 425–426

economy and, 65–66, 92–93, 349

fuel prices as, 203–204

terrorism as, 309

Italy, GDP of, 67

Jackson, Jesse

as spokesperson for blacks, 232

support for, 56

Japan

as economic leader, 66–67

opinion of, 79

Jefferson, Thomas, bring back, 59

Jews

and candidate matchups, 103–104, 158, 188–189, 224

Christmas and, 444

Obama, Barack, and, 103–104, 158, 363

opinion of, 133–134

Jindal, Bobby, would like to see run in 2012, 402

jobs

and car purchase deferral, 436

employer has laid off employees in past six months, 277–278

homosexuals should have equal rights in job opportunities, 168

immigrants and, 229

as most important issue, 65–66, 93, 132–133, 203–204, 244, 273, 426

outlook, 22, 61–62, 85–86, 115, 130–131, 169–170, 174–176, 189–190, 277–278, 302, 335, 341–342, 396, 404, 406, 424–425

as priority, 118

satisfaction with, 276–277, 281–282

second, 239

well-being and, 408

worry about, 32–33, 62, 278

See also employment; unemployment

Johnson, Lyndon B., approval ratings, 160–161, 275, 384

Jolie, Angelina, admiration of, 444

Jones, James, 419

journalists

honesty and ethical standards of, 404

See also media; news

Judaism. *See* Jews

judicial branch

confidence in, 317

as most important issue, 66, 93

as priority, 182

See also criminal justice system; Supreme Court

Kemp, Jack

ability to serve as president, 293, 295

approval ratings, 294

Kennedy, John F.

approval ratings, 161

bring back, 59–60

Kenya, opinion of, 79–80

Kerry, John

favorability ratings, 364

personal qualities of, 147

support for, 56, 158–160

Keyes, Alan, support for, 14, 21

Kilpatrick, Kwame, 105

King, Martin Luther, Jr., 26–27

Kucinich, Dennis, likely to support, 5–6, 8, 15, 21

labor (organized; unions)

approval ratings, 413

confidence in, 208–209

election of 2008 and, 381

leaders of, honesty and ethical standards of, 404

opinions on, 413

predictions on, 413

responsibility for auto crisis, 422, 433–434

lakes, pollution of, worry about, 91, 140

Latinos/as. *See* Hispanics

laundry, gender and, 125

law enforcement. *See* police and police officers

laws

energy and, 200

as most important issue, 66, 93

as priority, 182

lawyer(s)

honesty and ethical standards of, 404

image of, 274

leadership

Clinton, Hillary, and, 149

credit crisis and, 330

McCain, John, and, 148, 215, 289, 307–308, 340, 352

as most important issue, 93, 244, 426

Obama, Barack, and, 149, 215, 289, 307–308, 340, 352

of presidential candidates, 73, 99

as priority, 118, 182

as voting issue, 73, 76, 82

Leahy, Patrick, 114

legislative branch, confidence in, 317

Lehrer, Jim, 327

liberals

abortion and, 177

Bush, George W., and, 428

and candidate matchups, 119, 152, 188

divorce and, 171

economy and, 43, 339

Hispanics and, 221

Iraq War and, 44, 127

Jews and, 363

McCain, John, and, 109

Obama, Barack, and, 388, 419

Republican Party and, 401

standard of living and, 192

swing voters and, 217

third party and, 326

media
- bias in, 321
- Biden, Joe, and, 313
- confidence in, 208–209, 313, 321
- election of 2008 and, 180–181, 252–253
- McCain, John, and, 313
- Obama, Barack, and, 313
- Palin, Sarah, and, 312–313
- and presidential candidates, 180–181
- *See also* news; *specific medium*

medical care
- confidence in, 208–209
- deferral of, 419–420
- *See also* healthcare

Medicare
- as priority, 118, 182
- satisfaction with, 34–35
- as voting issue, 53–54

men
- abortion and, 177
- admiration of, 444–445
- alcohol and, 249
- and candidate matchups, 122–123, 159, 172–173, 187, 290–291, 299
- Clinton, Hillary, and, 38, 47–48, 68, 75
- division of labor and, 125–126
- divorce and, 171
- economy and, 277
- election of 2008 and, 177–178, 381
- environment and, 138
- favorite sport and, 446
- gambling and, 40
- McCain, John, and, 75, 109, 196, 310, 323
- Obama, Barack, and, 38, 196, 271–272, 310, 323, 405
- satisfaction of, 244
- time pressures and, 3–4
- weight and, 408

Methodists, opinion of, 133–134

Mexico, opinion of, 79–80

Middle East
- Bush, George W., and, 104–105
- Iraq war and, 94
- as priority, 182
- *See also* Iraq War

military
- confidence in, 208–209
- Congress and, 222–223
- McCain, John, and, 147, 213–214, 259, 278–279, 289, 315
- Obama, Barack, and, 213–214, 259, 289, 315
- as patriotic, 221–222
- relatives of service members, on Iraq War, 12–13
- strength of, 86–87
- as voting issue, 377

ministers, as spokesperson for blacks, 232

minorities, racial. *See* Asian Americans; blacks; Hispanics; non-whites; race

moderates
- abortion and, 177
- Bush, George W., and, 428
- and candidate matchups, 119, 152, 188

divorce and, 171
- economy and, 339
- Hispanics and, 221
- Iraq War and, 44, 127
- Jews and, 363
- Obama, Barack, and, 388, 419
- Republican Party and, 401
- standard of living and, 192
- swing voters and, 217
- third party and, 326

Mondale, Walter, support for, 57

money
- distribution of, 370
- worry about, 393, 410, 437
- *See also* financial situation personal; income; wages

morality
- acceptability of various issues [list], 171, 205
- blacks and, 416–417
- desire for change and, 24
- as most important issue, 66, 93, 132–133, 244, 426
- as priority, 182
- Republican Party and, 199
- satisfaction with, 34, 37
- as voting issue, 53–54
- willingness to forgive unfaithful spouse, 105–106
- *See also* ethics; values

Mormonism, opinion of, 133–134

morning news programs, as news source, 430

Mother's Day, mood and, 434

movies, industry, overall view of, 274

Muslims
- Christmas and, 444
- opinion of, 133–134

Nader, Ralph, 348

national newspapers, as news source, 430–431

national pride. *See* patriotism

National Public Radio, as news source, 430

national security
- desire for change and, 24
- McCain, John, and, 346
- as most important issue, 66, 93
- Obama, Barack, and, 386, 415
- as priority, 118
- as voting issue, 315, 377

National War Powers Commission, 223

negative campaigning, likelihood candidates will engage in, 240

New Hampshire, 5–7

news
- economic, following, 324
- political, following, 320, 398
- presidential debates, saw coverage of, 327, 357
- sources for, 430–431

newsmagazines, as news source, 431

newspapers
- confidence in, 208–209
- as news source, 430–431
- *See also* media

New Year's Day, mood and, 434

nightly news programs, as news source, 430

Nixon, Richard, approval ratings, 25, 129, 141, 160–161, 353

    quarterly averages for, 143, 237

non-religious persons

    and candidate matchups, 225

    Christmas and, 444

    religion and, 250

nonwhites

    election of 2008 and, 345

    See also Asian Americans; blacks; Hispanics

North Korea, opinion of, 79–80, 112–113

nuclear power

    versus other energy sources, 264–265

    as voting issue, 265

nurses, honesty and ethical standards of, 403

Obama, Barack

    abortion and, 310

    acceptance speech, 292

    admiration of, 444

    age and, 74–75, 339–340, 344, 361

    appointees of, 415

    blacks and, 17–18, 37–38, 82–83

    Bush, George W., and, 219–220

    in candidate matchups, 19–20, 52–53, 69–70, 113–114,
        119–120, 122–123, 151–152, 172–174, 187–189

    change and, 23, 26, 314, 346

    church attendance and, 68–69

    Clinton supporters and, 297

    as commander in chief, 213–214, 259, 289

    confidence in, 383, 388–389, 405–406, 418–419

    debates and, 327–328, 344, 357

    defense and, 328

    Democratic Party and, 17–18, 37–38, 82–83, 197–198,
        282–283

    economy and, 285, 309–310, 319–320, 328, 330, 333, 342–343,
        351, 415

    education and, 47–48, 255–256, 310

    effects of election of, 233, 341, 373–374

    energy and, 310

    enthusiasm for, 40–41, 50–52

    expectations of, 386–387

    experience and, 81–82

    favorability ratings, 97–98, 253, 297, 364, 383–384

    foreign trade and, 310

    foreign trips and, 252–253

    gender and, 39–40, 47–49, 75, 196–197, 271–272, 299, 337

    geographic region and, 135–136

    gun policy and, 310

    has best chance of winning, 179

    has clear plan for solving country's problems, 328, 352

    healthcare and, 310

    Hispanics and, 220–221, 238–239

    ideology of, 229–231

    image of, 190–191, 287, 357

    immigration and, 310

    independents and, 283, 306

    Iraq War and, 310

    Jews and, 103–104, 158, 363

    leadership and, 149, 215, 289, 307–308, 340, 352

    likely to support, 1, 5–9, 21, 63–64

    likely to win, 202, 366

    likely to win nomination, 9, 71–72

    marriage and, 177–178, 280–281

    media and, 180, 313

    and meeting with enemies, 183

    military and, 278–279

    opinion of, 154–155, 186

    personal attacks and, 240

    personal characteristics of, 7–8, 72–74, 99, 149, 215–216,
        259–260, 289–290, 307, 340, 352

    Philadelphia speech, 98–99

    Powell, Colin, and, 360–361

    priorities for, 385

    race and, 17–18, 37–38, 48–49, 82–83, 193–194, 226, 345,
        359–360

    race relations and, 98–99

    religion and, 201, 223, 279–280, 303–304, 359–360

    as spokesperson for blacks, 232

    superdelegates and, 89

    support for, 14, 158–160, 171–172, 310, 319, 323–324, 365,
        377, 379–380

    swing states and, 245

    taxes and, 286, 310, 373

    terrorism and, 309–310

    transition, following, 398

    understands problems Americans face in daily lives, 149, 215,
        340, 352

    as unifying candidate, 70–71

    voter outreach and, 369, 371, 375

    voting issues and, 212, 343

    weaknesses of, 120–122

    Wright, Jeremiah, and, 154, 163–164

Obama, Michelle, admiration of, 444

Obama supporters

    on campaign as hurting Democratic Party, 142, 152–153, 165

    challenges for next president and, 355

    dream ticket and, 87–88, 118–119, 165

    economy and, 315, 339, 359

    enthusiasm for election and, 350

    McCain, John, and, 107–108

    Wright, Jeremiah, and, 153–155

obesity

    and image, 242

    as most important issue, 414

    See also weight

office pools, 40

oil

    desire for change and, 24

    favor drilling in off-limits areas, 207–208

    as most important issue, 66, 93, 132–133, 166

    Obama, Barack, and, 386

    prices

        as most important issue, 203–204, 244, 273, 349, 426

        as priority, 118, 181

    See also energy; fuel; gasoline

oil companies

    energy and, 200

    gasoline and, 264

    image of, 274

oil-producing countries
   energy and, 200
   gasoline and, 264
Olympic Games, summer
   intend to watch how much of, 266
   location of, 266–267
   your favorite event [list], 266
opportunities, satisfaction with, 33, 35
optimism, 31–32
   youth and, 340
organic foods, have made changes to help protect environment, 138–139
outsourcing, worry about, 278
ozone layer, worry about, 91, 140

Pakistan, opinion of, 80, 112
Palestinian Arabs, Bush, George W., and, 104–105
Palestinian Authority, opinion of, 79–80
Palin, Sarah, 290
   ability to serve as president, 293, 295, 306, 340
   acceptance speech, 305
   admiration of, 444
   effect on vote for McCain, 293–294, 305, 343–344, 346
   favorability ratings, 294, 305
   media and, 312–313
   support for, 391
   as vice-presidential candidate, 294
   would like to see run in 2012, 402
parents
   satisfaction with schools, 298
   and time pressures, 3–4
party identification, 197–198
   Bush, George W., and, 65
   and candidate matchups, 188
   Democratic Party and, 322–323
   election of 2008 and, 382
   marital status and, 57–58
   Obama, Barack, and, 63–64
   Republican Party and, 15–16
   standard of living and, 192
   See also political affiliation
Paterson, David, 105–106
patriotism, expressions of, 221–222
Paul, Ron
   Iraq War and, 44–45
   likely to support, 14, 21
   personal characteristics of, 8
Paulson, Henry, 330
Perot, Ross, favorability ratings, 364
Petraeus, David, 127
   would like to see run in 2012, 402
pharmaceutical industry, image of, 274
pharmacists, honesty and ethical standards of, 403
plant species, extinction of, worry about, 91, 140
pledge of allegiance, as patriotic, 221–222
police and police officers
   confidence in, 208–209
   honesty and ethical standards of, 403
political affiliation
   abortion and, 177, 300

Afghanistan and, 254
attentiveness to transition and, 398
auto crisis and, 422, 433
Bush, George W., and, 11, 428
and candidate associations, 164
and candidate matchups, 113–114
Clinton, Hillary, and, 186, 400
Congress and, 11, 236, 356, 395
creationism and, 209–210
death penalty and, 394
divorce and, 171
economy and, 42, 100, 277, 315, 320, 330, 333, 351, 385–386, 397, 416
election of 2008 and, 179, 202, 381
employment and, 169–170, 342
enemies and, 113
enthusiasm for elections and, 28–30, 211, 349–350
environment and, 138
experience and, 81–82
favored nations and, 79–80
gender and, 299
government and, 317, 322
housing and, 124
ideology and, 230
importance of election and, 378
Iraq War and, 44, 60, 126–128, 256, 262
marital status and, 280
McCain, John, and, 227
and meeting with enemies, 183
military and, 86–87, 213–214, 279
morality and, 199
most important issue and, 112
national security and, 415
Obama, Barack, and, 227, 252, 388, 405, 419
oil and, 208
optimism and, 32
Palin, Sarah, and, 391
patriotism and, 222
personal attacks and, 241
and president you would bring back, 59
religion and, 250
satisfaction by, 14, 97
satisfaction with U.S. and, 204, 244
Supreme Court and, 336
swing voters and, 217
third party and, 326
unifying candidate and, 70–71
United Nations and, 84–85
U.S. global position and, 83
as voting issue, 343, 377
voting issues and, 368
wealth distribution and, 370
   See also party identification; *specific party*
politicians
   adulterous, willingness to forgive, 105–106
   as most important issue, 166, 244, 273, 426
   as priority, 182
politics, closely follow news about, 320, 398
pollution
   as priority, 118

worry about, 91, 140

See also environment

polygamy, as morally acceptable, 170, 205

poor people. *See* poverty

poverty

desire for change and, 24

as most important issue, 66, 93

Obama, Barack, and, 386–387

as priority, 118, 182

satisfaction with, 34–35

Powell, Colin

admiration of, 444

Obama, Barack, and, 360–361

as spokesperson for blacks, 232

president/presidency

bring back, 59–60

challenges for, 355

confidence in, 208–209, 317

Congress and, 223

meeting with enemies, 183

priorities for, 182, 355, 385

presidential candidates

any candidate running who would make a good president, 30–31

enthusiasm for, 50–52

gender and, 39–40

Iowa caucuses and, 1–3

Iraq War and, 44

New Hampshire and, 14–15

personal characteristics of, 7–8, 99–100

talking about issues you care about, 30

unification and, 70–71

See also specific candidate

primary process

Democratic, 142, 152–153, 165, 171–172

dream ticket, 87–88, 118–119, 165

experience and, 72–74, 76, 81–82

front-loaded, 4–5, 22

gender gap and, 39–40

Indiana and, 165

Iowa caucuses and, 1–3

New Hampshire and, 5–7, 20–22

North Carolina and, 165

purple states and, 135–136

religion and, 18–19, 35–36, 68–69, 103–104

superdelegates and, 89, 114

Wright, Jeremiah, and, 153–155

Protestants, Protestantism

and candidate matchups, 188–189, 224

charitable activity and, 439

Christmas and, 444

divorce and, 171

election of 2008 and, 381

Hispanics and, 359

opinion of, 133–134

and presidential candidates, 103

religion and, 251

public schools

confidence in, 208–209

See also education

public television, as news source, 430

publishing industry, image of, 274

purple states

and candidate matchups, 135–136, 245

economy and, 291

voter outreach in, 369

quality of life, satisfaction with, 33

Quayle, Dan

ability to serve as president, 293, 295

as vice-presidential candidate, 284

race

Bush, George W., and, 428

and candidate matchups, 172, 187

Democratic Party and, 37–38

economy and, 277

election of 2008 and, 343, 345, 381

gender gap and, 272

morality and, 416–417

Obama, Barack, and, 64, 98–99, 226, 255, 345

as voting issue, 193–194

race relations

blacks and, 238–239

black spokesperson and, 232–233

Hispanics and, 238–239

Obama, Barack, and, 232–233, 386–387

progress in, 26–27

satisfaction with, 33, 37

whites and, 238–239

worry about, 112

racism, 260–261

radio

industry, image of, 274

as news source, 430

See also media

rain forests, loss of, worry about, 91, 140

Reagan, Ronald

approval ratings, 25, 161, 275, 384

quarterly averages for, 143, 237

bring back, 59–60

expectations of, 387

support for, 57

real estate

agents, honesty and ethical standards of, 404

industry, image of, 274

recession

auto crisis and, 422, 436

Congress and, 333

current, 45–46, 100–101

jobs and, 302

mood and, 434

as most important issue, 66, 93, 203

outlook for, 316

predictions for, 137

as priority, 118, 182

unemployment and, 175–176

recreation. *See* entertainment; sports

recycling, 138–139

red states

and candidate matchups, 135–136, 189, 245

economy and, 291

voter outreach in, 369

region. *See* geographic region

religion

believe in God or higher power, 249–251

Bush, George W., and, 428

can answer today's problems, 442

and candidate matchups, 188–189

charitable activity and, 439

charitable donations and, 438–439

Christmas and, 443–444

confidence in, 208–209

creationism and, 209–210

divorce and, 171

election of 2008 and, 18–19, 337

Hispanics and, 359

influence of, 441–442

McCain, John, and, 102–103, 201, 223–225, 279–280, 303–304, 365

as most important issue, 244, 426

Obama, Barack, and, 102–103, 201, 279–280, 303–304, 363, 365

satisfaction with, 33

religion gap, 159

Republican Party

abortion and, 177, 300

Afghanistan and, 254

attentiveness to elections and, 23

attentiveness to transition and, 398

auto crisis and, 422, 433

Bush, George W., and, 11, 65, 160–161, 167, 219, 428

and candidate associations, 164

and candidate matchups, 113–114, 119, 151, 188

change candidate and, 26

Clinton, Bill, and, 288

Clinton, Hillary, and, 70, 186, 287, 400

Congress and, 11, 167, 236, 356, 395

creationism and, 209–210

divorce and, 171

economy and, 42–43, 100, 277, 315, 320, 330, 333, 339, 351, 385–386, 397, 416

election of 2008 and, 179, 202, 218, 337, 357, 381

employment and, 169–170, 342

enemies and, 113

enthusiasm for election and, 28–30, 41–42, 50, 211, 304, 349–350

environment and, 138

experience and, 81–82

favored nations and, 79–80

gender and, 299

government and, 317–318, 322

Hispanics and, 220

housing and, 124

Huckabee and, 35–36

identification with, 15–16, 197–198, 282, 322, 382

ideology and, 230, 401

image of, 400

importance of election and, 378

Iowa caucuses and, 1–2

Iraq War and, 44, 60, 126–128, 256, 262

marital status and, 57–58, 280

McCain, John, and, 70, 74, 219, 227, 282–283

media and, 180, 313

and meeting with enemies, 183

military and, 86–87, 213–214, 279

morality and, 199

most important issue and, 112

national security and, 415

New Hampshire primary and, 6, 20–21

Obama, Barack, and, 70–72, 220, 227, 252, 388, 405, 419

oil and, 208

one-party control and, 367

optimism and, 32

Palin, Sarah, and, 294, 391

patriotism and, 222

personal attacks and, 241

president you would bring back, 59

projections for, 401

religion and, 18–19, 159, 250

satisfaction of, 97, 166, 204, 244

standard of living and, 192

Supreme Court and, 336

swing voters and, 217

third party and, 326

unifying candidate and, 70–71

United Nations and, 84–85

U.S. global position and, 83

voting issues and, 53–54, 368

wealth distribution and, 370

Wright, Jeremiah, and, 153–155

Republicans in Congress

approval ratings, 431–432

economy and, 330, 333

election of 2008 and, 58–59, 311

incumbents, 263

responsibility for auto crisis, 433–434

reservoirs, pollution of, worry about, 91, 140

respect, as most important issue, 66, 93

restaurants

image of, 274

safety of food served at, 241

retail industry, image of, 274

retirement

expectations of, 156–157

as most important issue, 349

small-business owners and, 88–89

worry about, 156–157, 329

See also Social Security

Rice, Condoleezza, admiration of, 444

Richardson, Bill, likely to support, 5–6, 8

rich people

election of 2008 and, 374

paying their fair share in federal taxes, 374

taxes on, 145–146

wealth distribution and, 370

rivers, pollution of, worry about, 91, 140

Roe v. Wade. See abortion

Romney, Mitt

in candidate matchups, 20

change and, 23

as priority, 182
rebates, 206–207
on rich, 145–146, 370
as voting issue, 53–54, 212, 285, 315, 342, 368, 377
See also income tax; tax cuts
teachers, honesty and ethical standards of, 403
telemarketers, honesty and ethical standards of, 404
telephone industry, image of, 274
television
confidence in, 208–209
industry, image of, 274
plan to watch Olympics on, 266
watched Democratic convention, 293
See also media
television news, as news source, 430
tennis, as favorite sport to watch, 445
terrorism
Bush, George W., and, 64–65
Iraq War and, 94
McCain, John, and, 212–213, 259, 309–310, 346, 351
as most important issue, 66, 93, 132–133, 309
Obama, Barack, and, 212–213, 259, 309–310, 351, 386
presidential candidates and, 73
as priority, 118
as voting issue, 53–54, 74, 212, 285, 309, 315, 368, 377
worry about, 112, 308
Thanksgiving, mood and, 434
Thatcher, Margaret, admiration of, 444
third-party candidacy, desire for, 30–31, 326–327, 348
Thompson, Fred
has best chance of winning, 179
likely to support, 9, 14, 20–21
likely to win nomination, 9
threats, most critical. *See* issues, most important
time
pressures, 3–4
volunteering, 438
tobacco companies, 252
toxic waste, worry about, 91
track and field, as favorite Summer Olympic event, 266
trade deficit, candidate matchups and, 310
traditional values. *See* values
transportation costs, as most important issue, 349
travel
alternative means of, 163
cutting back spending on, 156, 163
industry, image of, 274
tropical rain forests, loss of, worry about, 91, 140
Truman, Harry S., approval ratings, 25, 129, 141, 353, 384
quarterly averages for, 143, 237
trust, as voting issue, 377

understanding
Clinton, Hillary, and, 149
McCain, John, and, 148, 215, 340, 352
Obama, Barack, and, 149, 215, 340, 352
unemployment
mood and, 434
as most important issue, 65–66, 93, 132–133, 166, 244, 273, 349, 426

Obama, Barack, and, 386–387
outlook, 85–86, 335, 341–342, 424–425
as priority, 118
worry about, 112
See also employment; jobs
unification, presidential candidates and, 70–71
United Kingdom
GDP of, 67
opinion of, 79, 194–195
United Nations
opinion of, 84–85
role of in world affairs today, 84
United States
division in, 392
image of, Obama, Barack, and, 386–387
opinion of, 112
satisfaction with, 13–14, 31–37, 83–84, 96–97, 132–133, 166, 204, 233–234, 243–244, 272–273, 353
universal spirit, belief in, 249–251
utilities, cutting back spending on, 156

vacation, cutting back spending on, 156
values
acceptability of various issues [list], 171, 205
Clinton, Hillary, and, 73, 99, 149
government and, 322
McCain, John, and, 73, 99, 148, 212–213, 216, 289, 307, 315, 346, 352
Obama, Barack, and, 73, 99, 149, 212–213, 216, 289, 307, 315, 346, 352
as voting issue, 53–54, 212, 346, 368, 377
See also morality
Venezuela, opinion of, 79–80, 112
veterans
election of 2008 and, 381
McCain, John, and, 278–279
video poker, 40
Vietnam War, as mistake, 143
violence. *See* crime
vision
of presidential candidates, 73, 99
as voting issue, 76
volleyball, as favorite sport to watch, 445
volunteering, 438–439
voters
first-time, 372
likely, 305
outreach to, 369, 371, 375
registered, 305
registration of, age and, 362
turnout of, 371
age and, 362, 374–375
race and, 371
See also under election(s)
voting
early, 372
enthusiasm for, 28–30
factors affecting, 343
as patriotic, 221–222
See also under election(s)

wages

    as most important issue, 93, 349

    satisfaction with, 276–277

    See also income; money

war

    Congress and, 222–223

    as priority, 182

    See also Iraq War

War on Terrorism, satisfaction with, 308

Warren, Rick, 279

Washington, George, bring back, 59

water

    have made changes to help protect environment, 138–139

    pollution of, worry about, 140

    supply, worry about, 90–91

wealth, distribution of, 370

weapons of mass destruction, Bush administration and, 101–102

weight

    current, 408

    factors affecting, 243

    ideal, 408

    and image, 242

    trying to lose, 408–409

        seriously, 408

West, Cornel, as spokesperson for blacks, 232

whites

    and candidate matchups, 119–120, 159, 172–173, 187, 290, 365

    civil rights progress and, 26–27

    Clinton, Hillary, and, 68–69, 82–83

    Democratic Party and, 37–38, 48–49

    economy and, 231

    election of 2008 and, 381

    McCain, John, and, 109, 310, 323, 345

    Obama, Barack, and, 64, 98–99, 227, 255, 310, 323, 345

    on race as voting issue, 193–194

    race relations and, 238–239, 261

    satisfaction of, 234

    See also race relations

wildlife, worry about loss of habitat for, 140

wine, 248–249

Winfrey, Oprah

    admiration of, 444

    as spokesperson for blacks, 232

women

    abortion and, 177, 300

    admiration of, 444–445

    alcohol and, 249

    and candidate matchups, 122–123, 151–152, 159, 172–174, 187, 290–291, 299

    Clinton, Hillary, and, 38, 47–48, 68, 75

    division of labor and, 125–126

    divorce and, 171

    economy and, 277

    election of 2008 and, 177–178

    environment and, 138

    favorite sport and, 446

    gambling and, 40

    McCain, John, and, 109, 196–197, 310, 323, 337

    Obama, Barack, and, 38, 75, 196–197, 271–272, 310, 323, 337, 381, 405

    position of, satisfaction with, 33, 37

    satisfaction of, 244

    time pressures and, 3–4

    weight and, 408

world peace, and desire for change, 24

Wright, Jeremiah, 153–155, 163–164, 191

yard work, gender and, 125

youth

    Obama, Barack, and, 339–340

    turnout among, 362, 374–375